Human Rights and the Global Marketplace:

Economic, Social, and Cultural Dimensions

Jeanne M. Woods
Hope Lewis

 Transnational Publishers

Published and distributed by
Transnational Publishers, Inc.
410 Saw Mill River Road
Ardsley, NY 10502

Phone: 914-693-5100
Fax: 914-693-4430
E-mail: info@transnationalpubs.com
Web: www.transnationalpubs.com

Library of Congress Cataloging-in-Publication Data

Woods, Jeanne M.
　　Human rights and the global marketplace : economic, social, and cultural
dimensions / Jeanne M. Woods and Hope Lewis.
　　　　p. cm.
　　Includes bibliographical references and index.
　　ISBN 1-57105-274-7
　　　　1. Human rights.　2. Civil rights—United States.　I. Lewis, Hope.　II. Title.

K3240.W66 2004
343.7308'5—dc22

2004062066

Manufactured in the United States of America

TABLE OF CONTENTS

PART I: HUMAN RIGHTS AND THE GLOBAL MARKETPLACE: DISCURSIVE THEMES

Chapter 1: Global Narratives/Global Realities

Chapter 2: Theoretical Paradigms

PART II: INTERNATIONAL INSTRUMENTS AND THEIR IMPLEMENTATION

Chapter 3: International Treaties

Chapter 6: Self-Determination, Culture and Rights: Conflicts, Challenges and Possibilities

PART IV: COMPARATIVE APPROACHES

Chapter 7: India: The "Directive Principles" Approach

Chapter 8: South Africa: The Bill of Rights Approach

Chapter 9: The Council of Europe—A Blending of the Categories

Chapter 10: The United States of America: Federal Rejection, State Protection

PREFACE

This book project, *Human Rights & The Global Marketplace: Economic, Social and Cultural Dimensions*, was realized at a time of great change, turmoil and contradictions in international human rights law and politics. Contemporary globalization, with its worldwide influence on communications, trade, development and cultural values, seems, on the one hand, resistant to the application of international human rights protections, while at the same time to necessitate the guarantee of certain rights to promote neoliberal economic agendas. The end of the Cold War did not bring an end to the international trade in weapons, but instead signaled a disturbing resurgence of old and violent conflicts. The world watched helplessly as genocide raged in Rwanda and Eastern Europe. Following the attacks on the U.S. World Trade Center and the Pentagon on September 11, 2001, U.S.-led invasions brought war to Afghanistan and Iraq, and the seemingly endless, borderless "War on Terrorism." Commentators discuss a "clash of cultures" between North and South, and among religions. Many question whether the post-World War II international human rights framework is capable of responding to the new realities of the 21st century.

Meanwhile, the economic, social and cultural violence that has been an ongoing feature of the lives of millions of poor and marginalized people continues unabated. Even more alarmingly, it goes relatively unnoticed. Millions die from treatable diseases such as HIV/AIDS, malaria and tuberculosis. Millions lack clean water, the means to purchase food or adequate housing and the access to the land necessary for subsistence. Indigenous peoples see the loss of their land, their natural resources, their cultural objects and traditions, and even their genes to powerful international actors that are yet to be subjected to international human rights law.

As teachers of international law and as participants in struggles for human rights for many years, we seek to respond to the growing need for a classroom text that focuses squarely on economic, social and cultural rights—the neglected step-children of the human rights family—and that highlights their intimate inter-relationship to civil and political rights. Our work on this book has made the theoretical concept of "interdependency" a vibrant reality for us. We trust that students and instructors who explore these materials will have a similar experience.

As human rights norms proliferate, challenges in implementation seem daunting. Nevertheless, today we are witnessing a burgeoning of interest and new possibilities for rights-based approaches to economic, social and cultural justice. New questions arise. Globalization now requires human rights scholars and activists to analyze the impact of international trade agreements, the debt crisis and other economic policies. At the same time, resistance to the apparent globalization of certain aspects of Western culture has taken the form of a resurgence of strict cultural norms, giving new meaning to old debates about cultural relativism versus universalism.

Unlike previous U.S. human rights texts, *Human Rights and the Global Marketplace* makes economic, social and cultural themes central to an examination of the full range of international human rights. Jeanne M. Woods, the Henry F. Bonura, Jr. Distinguished

Professor of Law at Loyola, New Orleans School of Law, teaches International Law and Human Rights. She first envisioned this text in the summer of 1998, as she prepared materials for her innovative approach to "Law and Poverty," a required course at Loyola. Her initial goal was to approach the subject matter from an international and comparative perspective. This led inevitably to an exploration of a rights-based approach. For seven years, Professor Woods has treated her law and poverty students to an unexpected course in international human rights law. The materials have also been used in courses on Comparative Law and Human Rights. Through these interactions, she expanded and adapted the structure and content of the book. Hope Lewis is Professor of International Law at Northeastern University School of Law, and has taught courses in Human Rights and Development, Human Rights in the Global Economy, and Human Rights: Race, Gender, and Culture. Hope joined the project in 2002, enriching the scope of the book and taking it in many new and exciting directions. Our collaboration has been rewarding intellectually and personally.

We believe that students and instructors will find the results of our efforts both informative and provocative. We also hope that it will spark continuing interest and activism on these issues. We intend the text for use in law school, graduate and undergraduate survey courses as well as seminars on human rights. The book is useful for teachers using either international or comparative approaches, or both.

Instructors certainly should feel free to experiment with the order in which the materials are presented and to supplement as they see fit, but the following approach may be most effective. The book is divided into four major parts. We begin with Part I "Human Rights and the Global Marketplace: Discursive Themes," which introduces the nature and scope of human rights discourse. Chapter One, "Global Narratives/Global Realities," alerts students to the vast array of issues that now fall within the purview of "human rights." The chapter also provides a list of Web sites useful for additional research and topic ideas for student papers. Chapter Two, "Theoretical Paradigms," explores the historical and theoretical underpinnings of rights discourse in general and of economic and social rights in particular. It also includes critical analyses on rights discourse from Western, African, and Asian perspectives. These first two chapters give students grounding in the fundamental problems of human rights.

Depending on the nature and focus of the course, instructors may then choose to examine the issues in a variety of specific contexts, whether international, regional or comparative. For example, an instructor might choose to move directly to Part II, "International Instruments and Their Implementation," which takes students through an array of international and regional human rights treaties that address economic, social and cultural rights. In addition to excerpts of relevant treaties, each chapter also provides examples of how the implementing bodies associated with those treaties do their work. We decided not to place the international human rights instruments in an appendix or in an expensive document supplement where they might never be read. Rather, we hope that teachers and students will explore the specifics of treaty language to see how it enhances (or impedes) the fulfillment of these rights. Part II also challenges students to think about the application of human rights standards to the questions of discrimination and other identity issues raised by the Race Convention, the Women's Convention and the Children's Convention. The important roles played by regional organizations in advancing social welfare rights in the Americas, Europe and Africa are similarly discussed.

Some instructors might choose, instead, to follow Part I with the more theoretical and contextual analyses in Part III, "Power, Politics and Poverty: Structural Obstacles to the Realization of Economic, Social and Cultural Rights." Part III addresses major controversies in, and barriers to, the realization of socio-economic and cultural rights. For example, Chapter Five, "Human Development and Human Rights," places human rights in the context of the development process. "Development," broadly defined to include human and social development as well as economic growth, is discussed as both influencing the attainment of other human rights and as a right in itself. We also include a case study of the impact of underdevelopment as it applies to poor communities in the Global North. In addition, the chapter addresses the relationship of human rights and development to the globalization of trade, as well as to migration and trafficking of human beings.

Chapter Six, "Self-Determination, Culture and Rights: Conflicts, Challenges, Possibilities," grapples with the crucial issues for human rights that are associated with cultural and other forms of group identity. What rights do indigenous peoples have to ancestral lands, cultural objects, natural resources and state-sponsored economic and social benefits? What are the economic, social and cultural rights of peoples living under occupation? What roles do concepts of self-determination and sovereignty play relative to notions of individual human rights? As a related matter, the language rights of ethnic and religious minorities have been recognized even prior to the founding of the United Nations. What is the contemporary status of such rights in the Global North and the Global South? What impact is globalization having on such rights? Finally, a section on "the Exotic Other" discusses the complex, and seemingly intractable, issues raised by the intersection of gender, culture and religion.

Part IV, "Comparative Approaches" is valuable for international human rights, comparative law and comparative constitutional law courses. It gives students an introduction to the rapidly developing jurisprudence on economic, social and cultural rights in India, South Africa, Europe, and the United States. By doing so, we contradict the notion that economic, social and cultural rights are not justiciable in domestic or international courts. The examples provided demonstrate that leading courts are doing just that. Of course, fundamental questions continue as to the justiciability and status of such rights under particular domestic systems, the efficacy of different approaches to justiciability, and most importantly, whether judicial approaches actually result in the realization of such rights in the lives of people. We expect that these issues will lead to lively classroom discussions as well. Chapter Seven examines India's groundbreaking "Directive Principles" approach to constitutional social welfare rights. Chapter Eight discusses South Africa's inspiring and influential "Bill of Rights" approach. Chapter Nine discusses the interdependency paradigm that is emerging under the highly respected European human rights system. Finally, Chapter 10 examines the resistance to economic, social and cultural rights on the federal level in the United States, and the resort to state constitutions as a source of specified social welfare rights. The chapter ends with a discussion of the rapidly developing grassroots movement for the full panoply of human rights in the United States.

To facilitate further investigation into these areas, we have included appendices with a bibliography of texts and articles on the general subject of ESC rights and a selection of NGOs that focus on these issues. Throughout the book, we provide notes, questions, and "further reading" suggestions to stimulate classroom discussion, debate, and research. Readers should check for periodic updates at the Transnational Publishers website, http://www.transnationalpubs.com/ and they may contact Jeanne Woods at woods@loyno.edu and Hope Lewis at HRGMlewis@neu.edu with comments. We have omitted footnotes or endnotes from most excerpted items. Where footnotes are included, they have been renumbered consecutively. Omitted text is indicated by asterisks.

This project was both extremely challenging and exciting for the co-editors and for those who worked with us. We look forward to your comments and suggestions for future editions.

Jeanne M. Woods   Hope Lewis
New Orleans, Louisiana   Boston, Massachusetts

FOREWORD

Economic, Social and Cultural (ESC) rights have always been a part of modern international human rights law, as reflected by the far reaching provisions included within the Universal Declaration of Human Rights that deal with them. Despite this, ESC rights have been often regarded as somehow inferior, as second generation rights. Within the tradition of international human rights law, civil and political rights have been usually characterized as essential, as primary. ESC rights are taken to refer to a more complicated and problematic category of rights, if rights they are at all. As this comprehensive and illuminating textbook makes clear, however, the concerns that led the authors of the Universal Declaration of Human Rights to include ESC rights within that profoundly important document continue to be vitally relevant to the international community. Despite all the advances made over the last sixty or so years, the challenge remains of providing billions of people with a means of satisfying their most basic needs—for education, food, drinking water, health. What is especially disturbing is that deprivation and inequality continue to be such an entrenched characteristic of the international system at a time when the world enjoys unprecedented wealth—the information is provided in stark terms in UNDP and World Bank Reports that deal with these issues—and which are cited in this text. The achievement of "development" furthermore, continues to prove elusive as suggested by the numerous initiatives undertaken by the international community to bring about development—the most recent and prominent of these being the program establishing Millennium Development Goals.

The environment in which ESC rights must operate has changed dramatically since the time of their initial articulation, and one of the most valuable features of this book is its examination of this new international reality and the effect it has upon ESC rights. Globalization, the emergence of the World Trade Organization, and the prevalence of neo-liberal development policy, have all presented new challenges to the furtherance of ESC rights.

Equally significantly, new questions arise as to what is meant by "development" and whether in fact ESC rights are undermined rather than furthered by certain types of development policies. Further, it is not only the case that economic and social needs are not being fulfilled but rather, that various developments are threatening to cause further hardship and deprivation: these include the escalating problem of AIDS and initiatives to privatize water. And while the tendency to dismiss ESC as 'human rights' may not be as evident as was once the case, the whole discussion of ESC rights has acquired new and more complex dimensions—as a result of debates regarding, for example, cultural relativism and the Asian human rights debate, and the initiatives undertaken by the International Financial Institutions which proclaim that they intend on furthering social and economic welfare. Equally significantly, ESC rights have evolved in a manner such that they have been given shape and structure by a developing jurisprudence found in countries such as India and South Africa. In addition, this text shows the many ways in which ESC intersect with the concerns of women and those of indigenous people.

This book may be approached, then, as a conventional textbook that covers all the relevant materials. As a textbook, this volume is eminently successful: it provides a detailed and comprehensive treatment of all the areas that are traditionally encompassed by ESC rights; it examines the major debates regarding the theory of ESC; and, most importantly, it connects both the Third World and the First World, and demonstrates the fallacy of regarding ESC rights as being somehow relevant only to the Third World. Nor are principles that are often thought of as belonging to the category of civil and political rights excluded: several sections of the text deal with issues such as non-discrimination in ways that demonstrate the clear connections between the two sets of rights—and indeed, questions the validity of such a distinction.

Quite apart from the coverage this text provides, it seems to me that there is immense value in the approach taken by the authors, that of using ESC rights as the prism through which so many different aspects of the jurisprudence of international human rights law and international law may be viewed: globalization, the activities of international institutions, the ongoing question of reparations for colonial exploitation, the unique disadvantages suffered by women as a result of development policy, the ongoing struggles confronting indigenous peoples—all these issues can be instructively viewed through the lens of ESC rights. In addition, given all the challenges facing ESC rights, questions continue to arise as to what changes need to be made to ESC rights in order to bring about the changes in political, social and economic structures, both at the national and international level, that appear to be required if they are to be realized, and these issues too are covered with depth and insight.

Further, this book may be read as an argument as to why, in this time where issues of security and terror have overwhelmed international institutions and debate, ESC rights are more important than ever. The international system is, at the moment, preoccupied with assessing and addressing new threats and challenges presented by terrorism. Security, the various controversies regarding the use of force, all these issues continue to be the subject of intense debate. It is surely self-evident, however, that a world riven with intensifying inequalities will produce different forms of frustration that could more readily result in extremism. And while the tragic spread of AIDS presents a dramatically formidable challenge to the international community, we cannot ignore the more mundane, quotidian ways in which economic and social deprivations destroy communities and erode human dignity.

The two authors of this book have taught courses relating to the subject matter covered in this book for many years. And their knowledge and expertise is evident in the range, organization and selection of the materials they have presented, and the new lines of inquiry that they suggest. Equally importantly, they have brought to bear on this project a passion and commitment which is evident from even the most cursory examination of this pioneering book, and we are fortunate to be the beneficiaries of these labors.

Tony Anghie
S.J. Quinney School of Law
University of Utah
September 2004

ACKNOWLEDGMENTS

We have benefited from the perspectives and encouragement of numerous colleagues, students, and activists over the years, only some of whom are named below.

We wish to thank the many students at Loyola School of Law who assisted in the research on the rather expansive subject-matter examined between these covers, including Leah Cluchey, Johanna Lohrman, Johanna Lundgren, Aubrey Harris, Mia Martin, Holly Roberts, Jason Chambers, Steve Robinson, Clara Safir, and Tammy Thompson. Joseph Nwokoro and James M. Donovan worked closely with Professor Woods over extended periods of time, and must be singled out for their exceptional contributions. We are also indebted to the countless students who explored these materials with Professor Woods and provided feedback in courses at Loyola on Law and Poverty, International Human Rights, and Comparative Constitutional Law, as well as in a course in the University of Miami's London Summer Program entitled Economic Social and Cultural Rights: International and Comparative Perspectives.

This project could not have been completed without Janice Burke, on whose organizational skills we relied, and whose tireless work and cheerful, supportive spirit made even the mechanical work on the book a pleasure. Janice maintained the complete manuscript and managed long distance logistics with patience and efficiency. We would also like to thank International Law Librarian Nona Beisenherz for her generous assistance and constant support, as well as Library Director, P. Michael Whipple, and librarians Elizabeth Moore, Francis X. Norton, and Etheldra Scogin. You were all there when we needed you. I would like to thank my colleagues, Dominique Custos, for her feedback on European law and Luz Molina, for translations. Thanks to Jessica Howard for her assistance in the copyright permissions process.

At Northeastern University School of Law, we gratefully acknowledge Dean Emily Spieler for her support in the form of summer research stipends and, as part of the law school's Initiative on Economic, Social, and Cutlural Rights, a generous grant to assist in the completion of the project. Professor Lewis notes that her participation in this project would not have been possible without the hard work, patience, and friendship of Jan McNew, her administrative assistant at Northeastern University School of Law. Ms. McNew spent countless hours typing materials, inserting revision after revision, assisting with the copyright permissions process, and otherwise contributing to the project.

Many talented and energetic Northeastern law students worked on the book as research assistants, including, James Alexander, Ryan J. Borgen, Amy Bowden, Julie Bowden, Zachary R. Cincotta, Laura E. Collins, Maxwell O. Foster, Joanna Golding, Meaghan Maher, Nic Mazanec, Emie J. Michaud, Jody A. Reid, Ellen Scott, Trina M. Sears, Ellen B. Sullivan, and Monica Van Toch. We thank them for their tireless commitment and outstanding work. Professor Lewis would also like to thank the many law students who participated in her classes on International Law, Human Rights and Development, Human Rights: Race, Gender, Culture, and Human Rights in the Global Economy and those who worked with her as research assistants on other projects over the years. Their comments, observations, and optimism contributed to the book as well.

Professor Lewis' colleagues among the faculty, administrators, and staff at Northeastern provided various forms of personal and professional support for which she is deeply appreciative. Susan Zago and the library staff at Northeastern provided efficient, helpful assistance in a number of areas. She would also like to say a special word of thanks to her colleagues James Hackney, Margaret Woo, John Flym, David Hall, Margaret Burnham, Karl Klare, and Associate Dean James Rowan for their personal support. David Phillips and Stephen Subrin provided very useful insights on religious law. Roger Abrams and Stacey Dogan provided us with helpful insights on the publication process at critical times. Valerie Luyckx, M.D., and David M. Nathan, M.D., provided helpful technical information on access to health care.

Of course, we are inspired by the leadership shown by our colleagues at other institutions who have advanced scholarship, teaching, and activism in international human rights. We are equally influenced by the many human rights activists who work toward the realization of human rights despite personal or professional risk. They are too numerous to name individually, but such a project would not be possible without their commitment and leadership in this field.

Our editors at Transnational Publishers believed in the importance of the project from the beginning and demonstrated great patience as time passed. Thanks to John Berger, who, though no longer with Transnational, first recognized the valuable contribution such a book could make to the field of human rights law. Managing Editor Maria Angelini provided enthusiastic encouragement at critical junctures in the process.

Ibrahim Gassama, Professor of International Law at the University of Oregon School of Law, provided important insights and expertise on international trade and development issues. He also reminded us at crucial points about the significance and impact a text on this subject could have. We appreciate his friendship and the inspiration he has been to us as both a human rights activist and scholar.

Professor Antony Anghie of the Quinney School of Law, University of Utah, graciously and cogently framed the themes of the book in a Foreword.

We want to express our deepest appreciation to our family and friends who patiently supported and encouraged us during the long hours, nights, and weekends we spent on this project. Professor Woods would like to express her gratitude for the love and guidance of her late mother, Bernice Quezergue Woods. She would also like to thank her father and step-mother, Verdun and Vertner Woods, daughter, Imani Brown, and numerous siblings, aunts, uncles, cousins, nieces and nephews who expressed pride in her work and enthusiasm for the project. Professor Lewis would like to thank her father, Stuart Lewis, her sister, Hara Lewis, Cordia Beverley Lewis, and her uncles, aunts, cousins, friends, and the congregation of Bethel A.M.E. Church for their love. She has no words to fully describe her thanks for the wisdom, patience, and encouragement shown to her by her mother, Blossom Stephenson, and her late grandmother, Edith Louise Stephenson (who passed away at the age of 102 years and 10 months of age shortly before publication). Through their lives and work, each reminded her daily of why we work to make human rights a reality.

We have made every effort to contact copyright holders of the excerpted works for necessary permissions. For the sake of consistency, credit lines and copyright notices are listed below rather than with the text of each item. The following works appear through the gracious permission of the copyright holders. They are listed below in alphabetical order:

AFP (Agence France Presse) for permission to reprint material from *Amina Lawal in Court to Appeal Stoning Sentence*, AFP, June 2, 2003; *Death Toll in Bolivian Unrest Rises to 30*, AFP, Feb. 14, 2003. Reprinted with permission.

Dr. Paula W. Adams, *Disability Rights as Human Rights* (unpublished manuscript) (2004). Copyright © 2004, Dr. Paula W. Adams. Reprinted with permission.

Adeno Addis, *Cultural Integrity and Political Unity: The Politics of Language In Multilingual States*, 33 ARIZ. ST. L.J. 719 (2001). Reprinted with permission.

The Advocate for permission to reprint material from Doug Myers, *School Lawsuit Rejected; Appeal Court Says Louisiana Fulfills Its Funding Mandate*, THE ADVOCATE (Baton Rouge, LA.), June 30, 1998 at 1A. Reprinted with permission.

American Anthropological Association, *Statement On Human Rights*, AMERICAN ANTHROPOLOGIST NEW SERIES, Vol. 49, Oct.–Dec., 1947, No. 4 at 539.

The American Society of International Law, for permission to reprint material from the following works: S. James Anaya, *Superpower Attitudes Toward Indigenous Peoples and Group Rights*. Reprinted with permission from 93 AM. SOC'Y INT'L L. PROC. 251 (1999). Hilary Charlesworth, Christine Chinkin, & Shelley Wright, *Feminist Approaches To International Law*, 85 AM. J. INT'L L. 613 (1991). Reprinted with permission from 85 AJIL 613 (1991). Bilahari Kausikan (with remarks by Sharon Hom), *An Asian Approach To Human Rights*. Reprinted with permission from 89 AM. SOC'Y INT'L L. PROC. 146 (1995). Copyright © 1991, 1995, 1999, The American Society of International Law.

Amnesty International, for permission to reprint excerpts from the following report: AMNESTY INTERNATIONAL, ISRAEL AND THE OCCUPIED TERRITORIES: SURVIVING UNDER SIEGE: THE IMPACT OF MOVEMENT RESTRICTIONS ON THE RIGHT TO WORK (September 7, 2003). Copyright © Amnesty International.

Antony Anghie, *Time Present And Time Past: Globalization, International Financial Institutions, and the Third World*, 32 NYU J. INT'L L. & POL. 243 (2000). Reprinted with permission.

The Associated Press, for permission to reprint excerpts of the following articles: *Bomb Kills Girl At School Where Many Shun Veils*, ASSOCIATED PRESS, Dec. 23, 1996; *Palestinians 'Reduced To Begging,'* ASSOCIATED PRESS-GENEVA, July 19, 2003; *Texaco Under Fire In Ecuadorian Lawsuit* THE ASSOCIATED PRESS, Oct. 21, 2003; *U.S. To Spend $110m To Fight Trafficking*, ASSOCIATED PRESS, Feb. 17, 2004, Copyright © 2003 & 2004 by the Associated Press. Permissions conveyed through Valeo Intellectual Property,

The Atlanta Journal-Constitution, for permission to reprint material from Susan Ferriss, *Mexican Rebel Standoff Becomes a Way of Life*, THE ATLANTA JOURNAL-CONSTITUTION, Dec. 28, 2003, at 3C. Reprinted with permission; permission conveyed through Copyright Clearance Center, Inc.

BAOBAB for Women's Human Rights, for permission to reprint material from *Please Stop The International Amina Lawal Protest Letter Campaign*, May 2, 2003. Copyright © 2003 BAOBAB for Women's Human Rights. Reprinted with permission of BAOBAB for Women's Human Rights.

The Center for Economic and Social Rights, for permission to reprint excerpts from Center for Economic and Social Rights, *Economic, Social and Cultural Rights Organizations and Networks*. The Center assisted in the organization of a network of such organizations, the International Network on Economic, Social, and Cultural Rights, which is now located at http://www.escr-net.org/.

Christian Barry, *Dealing Justly With Debt*, INPRINT, Carnegie Council of Ethics and International Affairs Newsletter, Jan./Feb. 2003, *available at*

http://www.cceia.org/viewMedia.php/prmID/825. © Carnegie Council of Ethics and International Affairs, 2003. Reprinted with permission.

Upendra Baxi, *Judicial Discourse: Dialectics Of The Face And The Mask*, 35 J. INDIAN L. INST. 1 (1993). Necessary permission has been taken from the Indian Law Institute for reprinting.

Mohammed Bedjaoui, *The Right To Development in* INTERNATIONAL LAW: ACHIEVEMENTS AND PROSPECTS 1177 (MOHAMMED BEDJAOUI, ED.,1991). Copyright © UNESCO 1991. Reproduced by permission.

Eric Berger, *Note: The Right To Education Under The South African Constitution*, 103 COLUM. L. REV. 614 (2003). Reprinted with permission; permission conveyed through Copyright Clearance Center, Inc.

Jacqueline Bhabha, *Internationalist Gatekeepers?: The Tension Between Asylum Advocacy And Human Rights*, 15 HARV. HUM. RTS. J. 155 (2002). Copyright © 2002 by the President and Fellows of Harvard College and the Harvard Human Rights Journal. Reprinted with permission.

Raj Bhala, *Symposium: Globalization and Sovereignty: Theological Categories for Special and Differential Treatment*, 50 KAN. L. REV. 635 (2002). Reprinted with permission.

Isabella D. Bunn, *The Right To Development: Implications For International Economic Law*, 15 AM. U. INT'L L. REV. 1425 (2000). Reprinted with permission.

Cambridge University Press, for permission to reprint material from the following works: IMMANUEL KANT, *The Doctrine Of Virtue, in* THE METAPHYSICS OF MORALS (1797) (Mary J. Gregor, tr./ed.1991). Copyright © 1991 Mary J. Gregor. JOHN LOCKE, LOCKE: TWO TREATISES OF GOVERNMENT (1698) (Peter Laslett, ed., Cambridge University Press, 3rd/stdnt. ed. 1988) (Cambridge Texts in the History of Philosophy Series). Copyright © 1988 Cambridge University Press. Reprinted with the permission of Cambridge University Press.

David Copp, *Capitalism Versus Democracy: The Marketing of Votes and the Marketing of Political Power, in* ETHICS AND CAPITALISM 91 (JOHN DOUGLAS BISHOP, ED., 2000). Reprinted with permission of the publisher, University of Toronto Press.

Modhurima DasGupta, *Social Action for Women? Public Interest Litigation in India's Supreme Court*, LAW, SOCIAL JUSTICE & GLOBAL DEVELOPMENT JOURNAL 2002 (1) at 7–8, *available at:* http://elj.warwick.ac.uk/global/issue/2002-1/dasgupta.htm. Reprinted with permission.

James M. Donovan, *Same-sex Union Announcements: Whether Newspapers Must Publish Them, and Why We Should Care*, 68 BROOKLYN L. REV. 721 (2003). Reprinted with permission.

Dover Publications, Inc., for permission to reprint excerpts from ARISTOTLE, POLITICS (Benjamin Jowett, H.W.C. Davis, eds., Dover Publications ed. 2000). Reprinted with permission.

Asbjorn Eide, *Economic, Social And Cultural Rights as Human Rights in* ECONOMIC, SOCIAL AND CULTURAL RIGHTS: A TEXTBOOK 23–25 (A. EIDE, C. KRAUS, AND A. ROSAS, EDS.,2d rev.

ed. 2001). Copyright © by Asbjorn Eide and Brill Academic Publishers. Reprinted with permission of Brill Academic Publishers and Asbjorn Eide.

Karen Engle, *Culture and Human Rights: The Asian Values Debate in Context*, 32 N.Y.U. J. INT'L L. & POL. 291 (2000). Reprinted with permission.

William Finnegan, *Leasing the Rain*, THE NEW YORKER, Apr. 8, 2002, at 43. Copyright © 2002 William Finnegan. Reprinted with permission.

Eleanor M. Fox, *Globalization and Human Rights: Looking Out For The Welfare Of The Worst Off*, 35 N.Y.U. J. INT'L L. & POL. 201 (2002). Reprinted with permission.

Charles F. Furtado, Jr., *Guess Who's Coming To Dinner? Protection For National Minorities In Eastern and Central Europe Under the Council of Europe*, 34 COLUM. HUMAN RIGHTS L. REV. 333 (2003). Reprinted with permission; permission conveyed through Copyright Clearance Center, Inc.

Gale Group, for permission to reprint material from 5 ENCYCLOPAEDIA JUDAICA (Keter Publishing, 1971) 338 and 15 ENCYCLOPAEDIA JUDAICA (Keter Publishing, ed. 1971) 1156. Reprinted with permission of the Gale Group.

James Gathii, *Beyond Market-Based Conceptions Of Rights: Social and Economic Rights In Context*, (unpublished manuscript). Copyright © 2004 by James Gathii. Reprinted with permission.

James Thuo Gathii, *The Legal Status of the Doha Declaration on Trips and Public Health under the Vienna Convention On The Law Of Treaties*, 15 HARV. J. LAW & TEC 291 (2002). Copyright © 2002 by the President and Fellows of Harvard College and the Harvard Journal of Law and Technology. Reprinted with permission.

Mary Ann Glendon, *The Sources Of 'Rights Talk'*, COMMONWEAL, Vol. 28 No. 17 (October 13, 2001 at 11. Copyright © 2004 Commonweal Foundation. Reprinted with permission. For Subscriptions: www.commonwealmagazine.org.

Gertrude Schaffner Goldberg, *The Feminization Of Poverty* in THE FEMINIZATION OF POVERTY: ONLY IN AMERICA (GERTRUDE SHAFFNER GOLDBERG & ELEANOR KREMEN, EDS., 1990). Copyright © 1990 by Gertrude Schaffner Goldberg. Reproduced with permission of Greenwood Publishing Group, Inc. Westport, CT.

Carmen Gonzalez, *Institutionalizing Inequality: The WTO Agreement on Agriculture, Food, Security, and Developing Countries*, 27 COLUM. J. ENVT'L. L. 433 (2002). Reprinted with permission; permission conveyed through Copyright Clearance Center, Inc.

Julia Graff, *Corporate War Criminals and the International Criminal Court: Blood and Profits in the Democratic Republic of Congo*, 11 HUM. RTS. BR. (No. 2) 23 (2004). Reprinted with permission.

The Guardian, for permission to reprint an excerpt from Chris McGreal, *South Africans Vow To Grab The Land: Government Pulls Out The Stops To Prevent Brazilian-Style Seizures*, THE GUARDIAN (London), July 26, 2001 at 18. Copyright © 2001 Guardian. Reprinted with permission.

Isabelle R. Gunning, *Arrogant Perception, World-Traveling, And Multicultural Feminism: The Case Of Female Genital Surgeries*, 23 COLUM. HUM. RTS. L. REV. 189 (1991–1992). Reprinted with permission; permission conveyed through Copyright Clearance Center, Inc..

GUSTAVO GUTIERREZ, A THEOLOGY OF LIBERATION 45, 64–66 (1973). Second Edition, SCM Press 1988; Orbis Books edition 1988. Reprinted with permission of SCM-Canterbury Press Ltd. and Orbis Books.

Geri L. Haight, *Unfulfilled Obligations: The Situation Of The Ethnic Hungarian*, 4 ILSA JOURNAL OF INTERNATIONAL AND COMPARATIVE LAW 27 (1997). Reprinted with permission.

Danna Harman, *In Uganda, Disability is Less of a Burden*, CHRISTIAN SCIENCE MONITOR, April 9, 2001, at 7. Copyright © 2001, Danna Harman. Reprinted with permission.

Harvard University Press, for permission to reprint material from JOHN RAWLS, A THEORY OF JUSTICE (Cambridge, Mass.: The Belknap Press of Harvard University Press, Copyright © 1971, 1999 by the President and Fellows of Harvard College. Reprinted with permission of the publisher.

Philip Harvey, *Human Rights and Economic Policy Discourse: Taking Economic and Social Rights Seriously*, 33 COLUM. HUMAN RIGHTS L. REV. 363 (2002). Reprinted with permission; permission conveyed through Copyright Clearance Center, Inc.

Nicholas Haysom, *Constitutionalism, Majoritarian Democracy and Social-Economic Rights*, 8 S. AFR. J. HUM. RTS. 451 (1992). Reprinted with permission of the author and the South African Journal of Human Rights.

R. H. Helmholz, *Natural Human Rights: The Perspective of the Ius Commune*, 52 CATH. U.L. REV. 301 (2003). Reprinted with permission.

Louis Henkin, *Rights: Here And There*, 81 COLUM. L. REV. 1582 (1981). Reprinted with permission; permission conveyed through Copyright Clearance Center, Inc.

CARLOS HEREDIA AND MARY PURCELL, STRUCTURAL ADJUSTMENT IN MEXICO: THE ROOT OF THE CRISIS, The Development Group for Alternative Policies, Inc. (1995). Reprinted with permission of Development GAP.

Ellen T. Hoen, *TRIPS, Pharmaceutical Patents and Access to Essential Medicines: A Long Way from Seattle to Doha*, 3 CHI. J. INT'L L. 1, 30–31 (2002). Copyright 2002 by the Chicago Journal of International Law. Reprinted with permission.

Wesley Newcomb Hohfeld, *Some Fundamental Legal Conceptions As Applied In Judicial Reasoning*, 23 YALE L.J. 16 (1913). Reprinted with permission of the Yale Law Journal.

Rhoda E. Howard (now Howard-Hassmann), *Law and Economic Rights in Commonwealth Africa*, 15 CAL. WEST INT'L L.J. 607 (1985). Reprinted with permission; permission conveyed through Copyright Clearance Center, Inc.

Human Rights Watch, for permission to reprint excerpts from the following reports: HUMAN RIGHTS WATCH, FORGOTTEN SCHOOLS: RIGHT TO BASIC EDUCATION FOR CHILDREN ON FARMS IN SOUTH AFRICA (May, 2004) *available at*, http://hrw.org/reports/2004/southafrica0504/

and HUMAN RIGHTS WATCH, FRANCE: HEADSCARF BAN VIOLATES RELIGIOUS FREEDOM: BY DISPROPORTIONATELY AFFECTING MUSLIM GIRLS, PROPOSED LAW IS DISCRIMINATORY *available at*: http://hrw.org/english/docs/2004/02/26/france7666jxt.htm. Copyright © 2004. Reprinted with permission.

Duncan Innes, *Reparations Debate Puts Cart Before Horse*, SOUTH AFRICA MAIL & GUARDIAN, Apr. 18, 2003. Reprinted with permission.

The Irish Times, for permission to reprint excerpts from Lara Marlowe, *Debate on Islamic Veils Inflames Passions,* THE IRISH TIMES, Jan. 13, 1999, at 14. Reprinted with permission.

LUTHER D. IVORY, TOWARD A THEOLOGY OF RADICAL INVOLVEMENT: THE THEOLOGICAL LEGACY OF DR. MARTIN LUTHER KING, JR., 152–153 (1997). Used by permission of the author and the publisher, United Methodist Publishing House, . Abingdon Press.

Daisy M. Jenkins, *From Apartheid To Majority Rule: A Glimpse Into South Africa's Journey Towards Democracy,* 13 ARIZ. J. INT'L & COMP. L. 463 (1996). Reprinted with permission.

Robin Haas, *Uniting On The Domestic Front / Group Wins $ 50G Grant To Help In Its Fight For Fellow Workers' Rights,* NEWSDAY (N.Y.), Dec. 18, 2000 at A27. Copyright © 2000 by Robin Haas. Reprinted with permission.

The Johns Hopkins University Press, for permission to reprint excerpts from the following articles: Paolo G. Carozza, *From Conquest to Constitutions: Retrieving A Latin American Tradition of the Idea of Human Rights,* 25 HUM. RTS. Q. 281 (2003); William F. Felice, *The UN Committee on the Elimination of All Forms Of Racial Discrimination: Race and Economic and Social Human Rights,* 24 HUM. RTS. Q. 205 (2002); Cindy L. Holder & Jeff J. Corntassel, *Indigenous Peoples And Multicultural Citizenship: Bridging Collective and Individual Rights,* 24 HUM. RTS. Q. 126 (2002); Craig Scott, *Reaching Beyond (Without Abandoning) the Category of "Economic, Social and Cultural Rights,"* 21 HUM. RTS. Q. 633 (1999). Copyright © 1999, 2002, 2003 by The Johns Hopkins University Press. Reprinted with permission of the publisher, The Johns Hopkins University Press.

Ratna Kapur, *Un-Veiling Women's Rights In The "War On Terrorism",* 9 DUKE J. GENDER L. & POL'Y 211 (2002). Reprinted with permission.

Ratna Kapur, *The Tragedy Of Victimization Rhetoric: Resurrecting The "Native" Subject In International/Post-Colonial Feminist Legal Politics,* 15 HARV. HUM. RTS. J. 1 (2002). Copyright © 2002 by the President and Fellows of Harvard College and the Harvard Human Rights Journal.

Kenneth L. Karst, *Paths To Belonging: The Constitution and Cultural Identity,* 64 N.C. L. REV. 303 (1986). Reprinted with permission.

David Kennedy, *The International Human Rights Movement: Part of the Problem?,* 15 HARV. HUM. RTS. J 101 (2002). Copyright © 2002 by David Kennedy. Reprinted with permission.

Karl E. Klare, *A Brief Legal History of Santa Clara Pueblo, or, What Has U.S. Law Got to Do with it?, in* CRITICAL LEGAL THEORY (Karl E. Klare, ed. 2003) (unpublished teaching materials). Copyright © 2003 by Karl E. Klare. Reprinted with permission.

Karl E. Klare, *Legal Theory & Democratic Reconstruction: Reflections on 1989,* 26 UNIV. OF BRITISH COLUMBIA L. REV. 69 (1991). Reprinted with permission.

Hope Lewis, *Between* Irua *and "Female Genital Mutilation": Feminist Human Rights Discourse and the Cultural Divide,* 8 HARV. HUM. RTS. J. 1 (1995). Copyright © 1995 by the President and Fellows of Harvard College and the Harvard Human Rights Journal. Reprinted with permission.

Hope Lewis, *Global Intersections: Critical Race Feminist Human Rights And Inter/National Black Women,* 50 MAINE L. REV. 309 (1998). Reprinted with permission.

Hope Lewis, *Universal Mother: Transnational Migration and the Human Rights Of Black Women in the Americas,* 5 J. GENDER RACE & JUST. 197 (2001). Reprinted with permission.

Hope Lewis, *Women (Under) Development: The Relevance of "The Right to Development" to Poor Women of Color in the United States*, 18 L. & POL'Y (U.K.) 281 (1996). Reprinted with permission of the publisher, Blackwell Publishing.

The Los Angeles Times, for permission to reprint excerpts of Dexter Filkins, *Ending Centuries Of Illiteracy: A Social Revolution Is Sweeping India*, THE LOS ANGELES TIMES, Dec. 7, 1999 at A1. Reprinted with permission; permission conveyed through Copyright Clearance Center, Inc.

Gwendolyn Mikell, *African Structural Adjustment: Women and Legal Challenges*, 69 ST. JOHN'S L. REV. 7 (1995). Reprinted with permission.

Geetanijali Misra, Veronica Magar, and Susan Legro, *Poor Reproductive Health and Environmental Degradation: Outcomes Of Women's Low Status In India*, 6 COLO. J. INT'L ENVTL. L. & POL'Y 273 (1995). Reprinted with permission.

Makau Wa Mutua, *The Ideology Of Human Rights*, 36 VA. J. INT'L L. 589 (1996). Reprinted with permission.

Saraladevi Naicker, *End-Stage Renal Disease in Sub-Saharan and South Africa*, 63 KIDNEY INTERNATIONAL (Supp. 83) S119 (2003). Copyright © 2003 Blackwell Publishing. Reprinted with permission of the publisher, Blackwell Publishing.

E. Dana Neacsu, *The Draft of the EU Charter of Fundamental Rights: A Step in the Process of Legitimizing the EU as a Political Entity, and Economic-Social Rights as Fundamental Human Rights*, 7 COLUM. J. EUR. L. 141 (2001). Reprinted with permission; permission conveyed through Copyright Clearance Center, Inc.

Burt Neuborne, *Is Money Different?>*, 77 TEX. L. REV. 1609 (1999). Copyright © 1999 Texas Law Review Association. Reprinted with permission.

The New York Times Company, for permission to reprint excerpts from the following articles: *The Cancun Failure*, N.Y. TIMES (Editorial), Sept. 16, 2003 at A 24; *Modern-Day Slavery*, N.Y. TIMES (Editorial) Sept. 9, 2000 at A14; Lawrence K. Altman, *South Africa Says It Will Fight Aids With A Drug Plan*, N.Y. TIMES, Aug. 9, 2003, at A1; Youssef M. Ibrahim, *Bareheaded Women Slain In Algiers*, N.Y. TIMES, Mar. 31, 1994, at A3; Charlie Leduff, *For Migrants, Hard Work In Hostile Suburbs*, N.Y. TIMES, Sept. 24, 2000 at A1; Terry Pristin, *Civil Liberties: Behind the Legal and Private Worlds of the Veil*, N.Y. TIMES, Aug. 11, 2002, at 4; Susan Sachs, *A Nation Challenged: Islam; Where Muslim Traditions Meet Modernity Force Of Islam: A Woman's Place*, N.Y. TIMES, Dec. 17, 2001, at B1; Elaine Sciolino, *Hair as a Battlefield for the Soul*, N.Y. TIMES, Nov. 18, 2001, at Sec. 4, p. 5; Michael Specter, *Contraband Women—A Special Report: Traffickers' New Cargo: Naïve Slavic Women*, N.Y. TIMES, Jan. 11, 1998, at A1; Ginger Thompson, *Water Tap Often Shut To South Africa's Poor*, N.Y. TIMES, May 29, 2003, at A1. Copyright © 1998, 1999, 2000, 2001, 2002, 2003, 2004 by The New York Times Co. Reprinted with permission.

The New York Times Syndication Sales Corp. for permission to reprint excerpts from W.B. Rubenstein & R. Bradley Sears, *Toward More Perfect Unions*, (Opinion) N.Y. TIMES, Nov. 20, 2003, at 31. Copyright © 2003 by The New York Times Syndication Sales Corp. Reprinted with permission.

Newsday, for permission to reprint excerpts from Letta Tayler, *Nobody's Children*, NEWSDAY (N.Y.), Dec. 8, 2002 at A7. Copyright, 2002, Newsday. Distributed by Tribune Media Services.

Celestine Nyamu, *How Should Human Rights And Development Respond To Cultural Legitimization Of Gender Hierarchy In Developing Countries?*, 41 HARV. INT'L L.J. 381 (2000). Copyright © 2000 by The President and Fellows of Harvard College and the Harvard International Law Journal. Reprinted with permission.

L. Amede Obiora, *Bridges And Barricades: Rethinking Polemics And Intransigence In The Campaign Against Female Circumcision*, 47 CASE W. RES. L. REV. 275 (1997). Reprinted with permission; permission conveyed through Copyright Clearance Center, Inc.

Oxford University Press, for permission to reprint material from MARC L. MIRINGOFF, MARQUE-LUISA MIRINGOFF, & SUSAN OPDYCKE, THE SOCIAL HEALTH OF THE NATION: HOW AMERICA IS REALLY DOING (1999). Copyright © 1999 Oxford University Press. Reprinted with permission of the publisher, Oxford University Press.

Princeton University Press, for permission to reprint material from the following works: Azizah Y. Al-Hibri, *Is Western Patriarchal Feminism Good For Third World and Minority Women?, in* IS MULTICULTURALISM BAD FOR WOMEN? 41 (JOSHUA COHEN, ET AL, EDS., 1999); Abdullahi An-Na'im, *Promises We Should All Keep In Common Cause, in* IS MULTICULTURALISM BAD FOR WOMEN? 59 (JOSHUA COHEN, ET AL, EDS., 1999); Susan Moller Okin, *Is Multiculturalism Bad for Women?, in* IS MULTICULTURALISM BAD FOR WOMEN? 7 (JOSHUA COHEN, ET AL, EDS., 1999). Copyright © 1999 Princeton University Press. Reprinted with permission of the publisher.

Balakrishnan Rajagopal, *From Resistance To Renewal: The Third World, Social Movements, And The Expansion Of International Institutions*, 41 HARV. INT'L L.J. 529 (2000). Copyright © 2000 by the President and Fellows of Harvard College and the Harvard International Law Journal. Reprinted with permission.

Mart Rannut, *The Common Language Problem, in* LANGUAGE: A RIGHT AND A RESOURCE: APPROACHING LINGUISTIC HUMAN RIGHTS 99 (MIKLOS KONTRA, ED., 1999). Reprinted with permission of the Central European University Press.

RSiCopyright.com for permission to reprint material from the following Reuters articles: *African Nations Plan To Monitor One Another*, REUTERS, Feb. 15, 2004, ICopyright Clearance License 3.5398.2984736-88990; *Rich Nations Flunk In Educating Poor: U.S., Greece And New Zealand Languish At Bottom Of Class*, REUTERS, Nov. 18, 2003, ICopyright Clearance License 3.5398.2984736-87454; Mark Egan, *Wall Street Ups Opposition To IMF Bankruptcy Plan*, REUTERS, Dec. 17, 2002. ICopyright Clearance License 3.5398.2984736-88734. Reprinted with permission.

RANDALL ROBINSON, THE DEBT: WHAT AMERICA OWES TO BLACKS (2000). Copyright © 2000 by Randall Robinson. Used by permission of Dutton; a division of Penguin Group (USA) Inc.

Thomas Ross, *The Rhetoric Of Poverty: Their Immorality, Our Helplessness,* 79 GEORGETOWN L.J. 1499 (1991). Reprinted with permission of the publisher, Georgetown Law Journal © 1991.

Sherrie L. Russell-Brown, *Labor Rights As Human Rights: The Situation of Women Workers in Jamaica's Export Free Zones*, 24 BERKELEY J. EMP. & LAB. L. 179 (2003). Copyright © 2003 by the Regents of the University of California. Reprinted from the Berkeley Journal of Employment and Labor Law by permission of the Regents of the University of California.

Philippe Sands, *Human Rights, the Environment, and the Lopez-Ostra Case: Context and Consequences*, 6 EUR. HUM. RTS. L. REV. 597 (1996). Reprinted from the European Human Rights Law Review with the permission of the publisher, Sweet & Maxwell.

Saskia Sassen, *Toward A Feminist Analytics Of The Global Economy*, 4 INDIANA J. GLOBAL LEGAL STUD. 7 (1996). Reprinted with permission of the publisher, Indiana University Press.

Ben Saul, *In the Shadow of Human Rights: Human Duties, Obligations, and Responsibilities*, 32 COLUM. HUMAN RIGHTS L. REV. 565 (2001). Reprinted with permission; permission conveyed through Copyright Clearance Center, Inc.

Herman Schwartz, *Do Economic and Social Rights Belong in a Constitution?*, 10 AM. U.J. INT'L L. & POL'Y 1233 (1995). Reprinted with permission.

AMARTYA SEN, DEVELOPMENT AS FREEDOM (1999). Copyright © 1999 by Amartya Sen. Used by permission of Alfred A. Knopf, a division of Random House, Inc.

ISSA SHIVJI, *Human Rights Ideology: Philosophical Idealism and Political Nihilism, in* THE CONCEPT OF HUMAN RIGHTS IN AFRICA 45 (1989). Reprinted with permission of the publisher, Council for the Development of Social Science Research in Africa (CODESRIA).

The South China Morning Post, for permission to reprint an excerpt from S.N.M. Abdi, *Law To Encourage 2-Child Families*, SOUTH CHINA MORNING POST, July 18, 2003 at 11.

Emily A. Spieler, *The Case For Occupational Safety and Health as a Core Worker Right in* WORKERS RIGHTS AS HUMAN RIGHTS 78 (JAMES A. GROSS, ED., 2003). Copyright © 2003 by Cornell University. Used by permission of the publisher, Cornell University Press.

Barbara Stark, *Deconstructing The Framers' Right To Property: Liberty's Daughters and Economic Rights*, 28 HOFSTRA L. REV. 963 (2000). Reprinted with permission of the Hofstra Law Review Association.

Barbara Stark, *U.S. Ratification of the Other Half of the International Bill of Rights, in* THE UNITED STATES AND HUMAN RIGHTS 75 (David P. Forsythe, ed., 2000). Reprinted with the permission of the publisher, University of Nebraska Press.

Henry J. Steiner, *The Youth of Rights*, 104 HARV. L. REV. 917 (1991). Copyright © 1991, by the Harvard Law Review Association. Reprinted with permission.

JOSEPH STIGLITZ, GLOBALIZATION AND ITS DISCONTENTS 76 (W. W. Norton & Co. ed. 2003). Copyright © 2002 by Joseph E. Stiglitz. Reprinted with permission.

Sukhvinder Kaur Stubbs, *Fear and Loathing in the EU: Ethnic Minorities and Fundamental Rights, in* THE EU CHARTER OF FUNDAMENTAL RIGHTS: TEXT AND COMMENTARIES 207 (Kim Feus, ed., 2000). Reprinted with permission.

Ann R. Tickamyer, *Public Policy and Private Lives: Social and Spatial Dimensions of Women's Poverty and Welfare Policy in the United States*, 84 KY. L.J. 721 (1995/1996). Reprinted with permission.

Leti Volpp, *Feminism Versus Multiculturalism*, 101 COLUM. L. REV. 1181 (2001). Reprinted with permission.

The Wall Street Journal. for permission to reprint material from Peter Landers, *Who Gets Health Care? Rationing in an Age of Rising Costs Filtering Process: Longer Dialysis Offers New Hope But Poses Dilemma: Who Gets Costly Treatment? Personality, Persistence and Housekeeping Count*, THE WALL STREET JOURNAL, Oct. 2, 2003, at A1. Reprinted with permission of the publisher, Dow Jones, Inc.; permission conveyed through Copyright Clearance Center, Inc.

The Washington Post Writers' Group, for permission to reprint excerpts from the following articles: Darryl Fears, *Aging Sons Of Slaves Join Reparations Battle; Financial Corporations Targeted By Lawsuits*, WASH. POST, Sept. 30, 2002, at A3; Mary Jordan & Kevin Sullivan, *Trade Brings Riches, But Not To Mexico's Poor: Nafta's Critics Say Pact Has Failed To Improve Lives Of Impoverished*, WASH. POST, Mar. 22, 2003, at A10. Copyright © 2002 & 2003, The Washington Post. Reprinted with permission.

James Q. Wilson, *"Liberal Ghosts": A Review of* NEW DEAL LIBERALISM IN RECESSION AND WAR *by Alan Brinkley*, THE NEW REPUBLIC, May 22, 1995 at 31. Reprinted with permission.

Kwasi Wiredu, *An Akan Perspective on Human Rights, in* KWASI WIREDU, CULTURAL UNIVERSALS AND PARTICULARS: AN AFRICAN PERSPECTIVE 158 (Indiana Univ. Press ed. 1996). Originally published as Kwasi Wiredu, *An Akan Perspective on Human Rights, in* HUMAN RIGHTS IN AFRICA: CROSS-CULTURAL PERSPECTIVES (ABDULLAHI AN-NA'IM & FRANCIS DENG, EDS., 1990) at 243. Reprinted with permission of The Brookings Institution Press.

Margaret Y.K. Woo, *Biology And Equality: Challenge For Feminism In The Socialist And The Liberal State*, 42 EMORY L.J. 143 (1993). Reprinted with permission.

Jeanne M. Woods, *Reconciling Reconciliation*, Originally published in 3 UCLA J. INT'L L. & FOR. AFF. 81 (1998). Reprinted with permission.

Shelley Wright, *Women and the Global Economic Order: A Feminist Perspective*, 10 AM. U.J. INT'L L. & POL'Y 861 (1995). Reprinted with permission.

Alicia Ely Yamin, *Reflections on Defining, Understanding, and Measuring Poverty in Terms of Violations of Economic and Social Rights under International Law*, 4 GEO. J. ON FIGHTING POVERTY 273 (1997). Reprinted with permission of the publisher, Georgetown Journal on Poverty Law & Policy © 2003.

PART I

HUMAN RIGHTS AND THE GLOBAL MARKETPLACE: DISCURSIVE THEMES

Part I engages the philosophical, theoretical and historical discourses on economic, social and cultural rights, and the significant conceptual difficulty and practical challenge they pose to the prevailing construct of rights. We begin by introducing readers to the subject matter of second generation rights through narratives that portray the contemporary realities of life for most of the world's population. Those realities reflect vast disparities in the distribution of economic and social goods as well as the misappropriation of culture. These glimpses of daily life help delineate the major themes of economic, social and cultural rights discourse in an era defined by the acceleration of the process of globalization and the dominance of neoliberal market policies.

We then trace the historical roots of socio-economic rights concepts in both Western and non-Western traditions, as revealed in religious, philosophical, legal and political sources. We examine the rights paradigms of liberalism and its critics, and their implications for the normative standing and practical implementation of second generation rights. Finally, we consider the ubiquitous problems of justiciability and democratic accountability. The context and debates first encountered in Part I will be of continuing relevance as readers engage the approaches to implementation, political contestation, and comparative jurisprudence explored in the remainder of the book.

CHAPTER ONE

GLOBAL NARRATIVES/GLOBAL REALITIES

INTRODUCTION

The post-Cold War expansion of the global marketplace has brought economic, social and cultural rights to the forefront of human rights discourse. A recent search of the Web site of the U.N. Office of the High Commissioner for Human Rights, for example, includes on the list of human rights issues: homelessness and malnutrition; income distribution; the HIV/AIDS pandemic; racial and religious discrimination; trafficking of women and children; labor migration; the human rights roles of transnational corporations; and the impact of environmental degradation on the rights of indigenous peoples.[1] In theory, all human rights are "equal, interdependent, and indivisible." In practice, however, socio-economic rights are the normatively underdeveloped stepchildren of the human rights family. Our focus on these issues aims to affirm their intimate connection to classic civil and political rights, and thus to expand the theoretical and practical exploration of human rights in general.

What are economic, social and cultural rights? How should their normative content be formulated? How are they to be promoted and implemented? What priority should they have in a world of continuing, and widespread, violations of civil and political rights?

Our exploration of these questions begins with a survey of human rights-related events throughout the world. These materials, drawn primarily from popular press and U.N. sources, reflect the rich diversity of issues and challenges that fall within the scope of contemporary human rights discourse. The articles selected introduce major themes developed throughout the book: globalization; economic development as a human rights issue; women's rights; rights of racial, ethnic, and indigenous groups; the justiciability of economic, social and cultural rights; and the diversity of approaches to social issues among regional and domestic legal systems.

Consider the following questions as you read the materials in this chapter. You may wish to reevaluate your responses as you continue your journey through the book:

1. Why should any of these issues rise to the level of a human rights concern?

2. If the problems described are human rights violations, who are the respective rights-holders and duty-holders? What remedies would be appropriate?

3. How would you rank the issues in comparison to classic violations of civil and political rights, for example, reports of torture of political prisoners?

---

[1]   *See* Office of the High Commissioner for Human Rights, "Human Rights Issues" page, *available at* http://www.unhchr.ch/html/menu2/hrissues.htm (last visited Apr. 10, 2004).

4. Does "rights-talk" bring us any closer to resolving these problems? Does it obscure the need for more fundamental solutions (*e.g.*, political engagement)?

5. Is the current state-centered system (and the inter-governmental institutions it has spawned) capable of addressing these challenges?

6. What alternative approaches should be considered?

UNITED NATIONS DEVELOPMENT PROGRAMME: HUMAN DEVELOPMENT REPORT 9–13 (2001)

Human development challenges remain large in the new millennium. Across the world we see unacceptable levels of deprivation in people's lives. Of the 4.6 billion people in developing countries, more than 850 million are illiterate, nearly a billion lack access to improved water sources, and 2.4 billion lack access to basic sanitation. Nearly 325 million boys and girls are out of school. And 11 million children under age five die each year from preventable causes—equivalent to more than 30,000 a day. Around 1.2 billion people live on less than $1 day *** and 2.8 billion on less than $2 a day. Such deprivations are not limited to developing countries. In OECD countries more than 130 million people are income poor, 34 million are unemployed, and adult functional illiteracy rates average 15%.

South Asia and Sub-Saharan Africa lag far behind other regions.*** The adult literacy rate in South Asia is still 55% and in Sub-Saharan Africa 60%, well below the developing country average of 73%. Life expectancy at birth in Sub-Saharan Africa is still only 48.8 years, compared with more than 60 in all other regions. And the share of people living on less than $1 a day is as high as 46% in Sub-Saharan Africa and 40% in South Asia, compared with 15% in East Asia and the Pacific and in Latin America.***

At the end of 2000 about 36 million people were living with HIV/AIDS—95% of them in developing countries and 70% in Sub-Saharan Africa. More than 5 million became newly infected in 1999 alone. In Sub-Saharan Africa, mainly because of HIV/AIDS, more than 20 countries experienced drops in life expectancy between 1985–90 and 1995–2000. In six countries—Botswana, Burundi, Namibia, Rwanda, Zambia and Zimbabwe—life expectancy declined by more than seven years. The spread of HIV/AIDS has multiple consequences for development. It robs countries of people in their prime, and leaves children uncared for. By the end of 1999, 13 million children were AIDS orphans.

S.N.M. ABDI, LAW TO ENCOURAGE TWO-CHILD FAMILIES

SOUTH CHINA MORNING POST, July 18, 2003, at 11

CALCUTTA— The Indian government plans to enact a law barring people with more than two children from politics and government jobs.

Deputy Prime Minister Lal Krishna Advani said yesterday the proposed legislation prohibiting men and women with more than two children from contesting elections or holding government jobs was being discussed with opposition parties before it was tabled in parliament.

Table 1.1 Serious Deprivations in Many Aspects of Life
Developing countries
Health
968 million people without access to improved water sources (1998)
2.4 billion people without access to basic sanitation (1998)
34 million people living with HIV/AIDS (end of 2000)
2.2 million people dying annually from indoor air pollution (1996)
Education
854 million illiterate adults, 543 million of them women (2000)
325 million children out of school at the primary and secondary levels, 183 million of them girls (2000)
Income poverty
1.2 billion people living on less than $1 day (1993 PPP US$), 2.8 billion on less than $2 a day (1998)
Children
163 million underweight children under age five (1998)
11 million children under five dying annually from preventable causes (1998)
OECD Countries
15% of adults lacking functional literacy skills (1994–98)
130 million people in income poverty (with less than 50% of median income) (1999)
• 8 million undernourished people (1996–98)
• 1.5 million people living with HIV/AIDS (2000)
* *Source:* Smeeding 200lb; UNAIDS 2000a, 2000b, UNESCO 2000b; World Bank 2000d, 2001b, 2001c, 2001f, WHO 1997, 2000b; OECD and Statistics Canada 2000.

"A new law is badly needed to enforce the government's two-child policy as persuasive methods have miserably failed to curb the population explosion," he said ***

But Calcutta-based human rights activist Maitreyi Chatterjee has warned a coercive two-child policy will spur the abortion of female foetuses and murder of new-born girls, practices already rampant across India. "The gender ratio is badly disbalanced because of the mass murder of baby girls," Ms Chatterjee said."Enforcement of the new law will provoke more killings, worsening the man-woman ratio."

Last year, a proposal to deny free education and health care to a couple's third child enraged child rights activists, who accused the government of trying to penalise a child for the parents' "crime."

Successive governments in India—the world's most populous country after China—have experimented with various strategies to curb the country's billion-plus population and failed. They have tried desperately to control the baby boom through slogans, awareness campaigns and a brief period of forced sterilisations in the mid-1970s.

Experts say the answer to India's problem lies in popularising the oral contraceptive pill. According to the latest National Family Health Survey findings, only 29 per cent of the population uses the pill.

Leading demographers say at present rates, India's population will reach 1.25 billion by 2016 and could surpass China's by 2045.

Notes and Questions

1. Why did the Indian government institute a two-child policy? Should the government penalize parents who violate this policy? Does your answer depend on the degree of coercion? On the type of punishment?

2. Whose rights are affected by such a policy, if any? What is the nature of these rights?

LETTA TAYLER, NOBODY'S CHILDREN

NEWSDAY (New York) December 8, 2002, at A7

PORT-AU-PRINCE, Haiti—During his first few days as a live-in servant with an affluent family here, 11-year-old Dieusibon Delci thought he'd found paradise. Though he slept on the floor and worked from dawn to late evening, for the first time in his life he had enough to eat.

Then the matron of the house began striking him in the head with hot, cast-iron pans to make him work harder. When he nodded off one day while washing dishes, she slammed a gigantic pot filled with boiling oil on his left hand, smashing his fingers.

"She kept beating me and telling me to work more," whispered Dieusibon, whose left fingers are fused at the knuckles and whose temple is flat and shiny from repeated blows. After two years of abuse, Dieusibon ran away from his keepers. But nearly one in 10 children, most of them from impoverished families, continue to work for nothing but room and board in the homes of relatives or strangers.

Haitians call the children "restaveks," a Creole term from the French phrase "*rester avec*" ("to stay with"). Human rights and labor organizations call them slaves.

"At the least, most of these children don't receive the schooling or care that they should," said Merrie Archer, senior policy associate for the National Coalition for Haitian Rights, who recently co-authored a blistering report on the restavek phenomenon. "And many are subjected to physical, emotional and sexual abuse."

Haitians, particularly in the countryside, have sent their children to live and work with wealthier families since the 18th-century colonial era. But with four-fifths of the country's 8 million people struggling to survive on less than a dollar a day, the practice continues to flourish—a bitter irony to many observers, given that Haitian slaves two centuries ago ousted the French and established the world's first black republic.

"The very slaves who fought for independence wanted to live as their former masters had, so they took the children of those who were even poorer and enslaved them," said Jean-Robert Cadet, a teacher at the University of Cincinnati whose 1998 memoir, "Restavec: From Haitian Slave Child to Middle-Class American," helped focus attention on the issue.

As a restavek three decades ago, Cadet said, his masters beat him with the same kind of leather whip the French used on slaves. "To be a restavek is to be an untouchable, the ultimate have-not in a society of have-nots," Cadet said.

An estimated 300,000 children who are 14 or younger work as restaveks, and a fifth of those are younger than 12, according to the National Coalition on Haitian Rights. The group's report, like many studies, accuses Haitian authorities of doing little to combat the problem. Officials counter that they are doing the best they can with few resources in what is the hemisphere's poorest country.

Many restaveks work for Haitian families that aren't wealthy enough to pay for servants and who often aren't much better off than the children's parents. Still, many Haitians believe the children will fare better than at home.

"The lady who took them told me she'd treat them well," said Rosanna Saint-Hilaire, a widow who in the past six years sold two of her nine children to a restaurant owner here for the equivalent of $60 apiece. The children, both boys, were 11 and 8 years old when she sold them. "Anyway," she added, her lips tightening, "I had to sell them because otherwise, I had no way to feed the rest of my children."

Saint-Hilaire said she sold her older son for money to find a new home after her shack in Cite Soleil, one of the worst squatter slums of Port-au-Prince, burned down during a riot. She now lives in the worst part of another Port-au-Prince slum, Waph Jeremie, a mile from main roads along paths overflowing with sewage and next to a massive dump where naked children crawl through sooty garbage, scrounging for food.***

Restaveks' masters are almost never prosecuted for abuse, according to many children's advocates. "The laws are so weak and poorly enforced, they're useless," said Michael Brewer, the director of Haitian Street Kids.

Haitian President Jean-Bertrand Aristide, a former parish priest, last year called the restavek phenomenon "one of the cancers on our social body in Haiti that keep democracy from growing."

Still, Haitian law lets children work as domestics from age 12 and doesn't require them to be paid until they are 15. A government hotline to report abuses against restaveks and other children is understaffed, making follow-ups on complaints minimal.***

Government officials said they are working on education and rural development projects and also have started a program to help return restaveks to their families of origin.***

However, authorities claim their efforts are hamstrung by a U.S.-led blockade of about $500 million in foreign aid earmarked for Haiti—about 1 1/2 times the nation's annual budget. Western donors are withholding the funds to press Haitian political leaders to resolve a dispute over allegations that Aristide's Lavalas party rigged the legislative elections in 2000.***

Notes and Questions

1. This type of exploitation of children persists in various forms in many poor countries. In what ways are the rights of these children being violated? What role should governments play in addressing these violations? What alternatives exist to punitive measures?

2.   What economic factors contribute to the institutionalization of this practice? What historical factors? Do you feel comfortable judging the practice? If not, what concerns do you have about condemning such a practice?

The following articles discuss the commodification of women in the international sex trade:

MICHAEL SPECTER, CONTRABAND WOMEN—A SPECIAL REPORT: TRAFFICKERS' NEW CARGO: NAÏVE SLAVIC WOMEN

NEW YORK TIMES, January 11, 1998, at A1

RAMLE, Israel—Irina always assumed that her beauty would somehow rescue her from the poverty and hopelessness of village life. A few months ago, after answering a vague ad in a small Ukrainian newspaper, she slipped off a tour boat when it put in at Haifa, hoping to make bundle dancing naked on the tops of tables.

She was 21, self-assured and glad to be out of Ukraine. Israel offered a new world and for a week or two everything seemed possible. Then, one morning, she was driven to a brothel, where her boss burned her passport before her eyes.

"I own you," she recalled his saying. "You are my property and you will work until you earn your way out. Don't try to leave. You have no papers and you don't speak Hebrew. You will be arrested and deported. Then we will get you and bring you back."

It happens every single day. Not just in Israel, which has deported nearly 1,500 Russian and Ukrainian women like Irina in the past three years. But throughout the world, where selling naive and desperate young women into sexual bondage has become one of the fastest-growing criminal enterprises in the robust global economy.

The international bazaar for women is hardly new, of course. Asians have been its basic commodity for decades. But economic hopelessness in the Slavic world has opened what experts call the most lucrative market of all to criminal gangs that have flourished since the fall of Communism: white women with little to sustain them but their dreams. Pimps, law enforcement officials and relief groups all agree that Ukrainian and Russian women are now the most valuable in the trade.

Because their immigration is often illegal—and because some percentage of the women choose to work as prostitutes—statistics are difficult to assess. But the United Nations estimates that four million people throughout the world are trafficked each year—forced through lies and coercion to work against their will in many types of servitude. The International Organization for Migration has said that as many as 500,000 women are annually trafficked into Western Europe alone.

Many end up like Irina. Stunned and outraged by the sudden order to prostitute herself, she simply refused. She was beaten and raped before she succumbed. Finally she got a break. The brothel was raided and she was brought here to Neve Tirtsa in Ramle, the only women's prison in Israel. Now, like hundreds of Ukrainian and Russian women with no documents or obvious forgeries, she is waiting to be sent home.

"I don't think the man who ruined my life will even be fined," she said softly, slow tears filling her enormous green eyes. "You can call me a fool for coming here. That's my crime. I am stupid. A stupid girl from a little village. But can people really buy and sell women and get away with it? Sometimes I sit here and ask myself if that really happened to me, if it can really happen at all."***

The women are smuggled by car, bus, boat and plane. Handed off in the dead of night, many are told they will pick oranges, work as dancers or as waitresses. Others have decided to try their luck at prostitution, usually for what they assume will be a few lucrative months. They have no idea of the violence that awaits them.

The efficient, economically brutal routine—whether here in Israel, or in one of a dozen other countries—rarely varies. Women are held in apartments, bars and makeshift brothels; there they service, by their own count, as many as 15 clients a day. Often they sleep in shifts, four to a bed. The best that most hope for is to be deported after the police finally catch up with their captors.

Few ever testify. Those who do risk death. Last year in Istanbul, Turkey, according to Ukrainian police investigators, two women were thrown to their deaths from a balcony while six of their Russian friends watched. In Serbia, also last year, said a young Ukrainian woman who escaped in October, a woman who refused to work as a prostitute was beheaded in public.

In Milan a week before Christmas, the police broke up a ring that was holding auctions in which women abducted from the countries of the former Soviet Union were put on blocks, partially naked, and sold at an average price of just under $1,000.***

*** Ukraine—and to a lesser degree its Slavic neighbors Russia and Belarus—has replaced Thailand and the Philippines as the epicenter of the global business in trafficking women. The Ukrainian problem has been worsened by a ravaged economy, an atrophied system of law enforcement, and criminal gangs that grow more brazen each year. Young European women are in demand, and Ukraine, a country of 51 million people, has a seemingly endless supply. It is not that hard to see why.

Neither Russia nor Ukraine reports accurate unemployment statistics. But even partial numbers present a clear story of chaos and economic dislocation. Federal employment statistics in Ukraine indicate that more than two-thirds of the unemployed are women. The Government also keeps another statistic: employed but not working. Those are people who technically have jobs, and can use company amenities like day-care centers and hospitals. But they do not work or get paid. Three-quarters are women. And of those who have lost their jobs since the Soviet Union dissolved in 1991, more than 80 percent are women.

The average salary in Ukraine today is slightly less than $30 a month, but it is half that in the small towns that criminal gangs favor for recruiting women to work abroad. On average, there are 30 applicants for every job in most Ukrainian cities. There is no real hope; but there is freedom.***

Notes and Questions

1. Irina asks if people can "really buy and sell women and get away with it." How is this possible? Who is responsible for preventing this kind of trafficking?

2. If the "international bazaar for women is hardly new" and "Asians have been basic commodities for years," why is there increased attention to the issue now? Why has it taken so long to put effective protections in place?

MODERN-DAY SLAVERY

NEW YORK TIMES (EDITORIAL) September 9, 2000, at A14

By a conservative estimate, there are 27 million people working under various forms of slavery in the world today, and the number is growing. In contrast to the slavery America knew, today's slaveholders mainly exploit people of their own race. But as in the American past, they use violence and threats to force people to labor for no pay. Slavery is illegal everywhere, but it thrives because of the corruption of police and government authorities. Many people are unaware that modern slavery exists.

People held in some form of bondage pick sugar cane in the Dominican Republic, make the charcoal used in Brazil's steel industry and work as prostitutes in Thailand. In Mauritania and Sudan blacks are forced into domestic and agricultural slavery in Muslim households. Similar forms of oppression are not unknown in developed nations. The Central Intelligence Agency estimates that 45,000 women and children are smuggled into the United States each year with false promises of decent jobs. Instead, most find that their passports are stolen and they are forced to work as prostitutes or maids, on farms or in sweatshops.

But the majority of people who are treated like slaves, perhaps 20 million, according to the United Nations, are South Asians in debt bondage. The system is chillingly described in "Disposable People," a survey of contemporary forms of slavery by Kevin Bales, who teaches at the University of Surrey in England. Whole families, including children, are trapped into peonage to pay debts incurred by medical expenses, a funeral or crop failure. Their debts are inflated by outrageous prices for food and usurious interest rates. Families can essentially be enslaved for generations.

Slavery and related kinds of servitude are a growing business because the number of desperately poor people is increasing and globalization has disrupted rural communities. In many nations, children, mainly girls, must drop out of school to work. A girl in a northern Thai village can be sold into prostitution for $2,000—a huge sum there. A Thai survey found that many families knowingly sold daughters into prostitution because they felt pressure to buy consumer goods such as televisions. Girls stay until they contract AIDS, and are then sent back to their villages to die in disgrace.

While slavery is illegal, it is hard to eradicate. Even the United States lacks adequate criminal penalties for those who traffic in human beings. Moreover, the victims—the potential witnesses—are usually deported. This may change, however, as both houses of Congress recently passed a bill that would criminalize trafficking, end the rapid deportation of victims and provide help for them here and modest programs to prevent slavery abroad.

Slavery and forced labor are even more difficult to fight in nations where they draw support from traditional structures of power and corruption, the devaluation of women and, in India, the caste system. Educating the poor about how to avoid falling victim helps, as do small loans and skill training. India has an excellent program to pay off laborers' debts and give them training and land. But Dr. Bales argues that local officials and judges often sabotage it.

The first step in combating modern variations of slavery, however, is education. The developed world needs to realize that slavery exists, and that its victims may have helped produce the clothes, rugs and other goods we buy. It is especially important for people in nations where it is widespread not to accept it as a traditional practice but to see it as one of the most serious abuses of human rights.

U.S. TO SPEND $110M TO FIGHT TRAFFICKING

ASSOCIATED PRESS (Newsday), February 17, 2004

JAKARTA, Indonesia (AP)—The U.S. government said Tuesday that it will spend $100 million to eradicate human trafficking, which it described as a modern day form of slavery.

John Miller, director of the State Department's anti-people trafficking office, said in a statement that countries that qualify will get money for law enforcement training, education and assistance to victims, most of whom are women and children forced to work as prostitutes, laborers and maids.

"The U.S. government is increasing its commitments in the growing movement of governments, activists and law-abiding citizens worldwide to put an end to this modern-day form of slavery," Miller said. "The horrible practice of human trafficking exists in many forms, particularly sex and forced labor, and it reaches into almost every country."

Miller, on a regional tour of Asia that includes Indonesia, Japan, Singapore, Malaysia and Vietnam, said Monday he believed the world's largest Muslim country was making progress in the fight against trafficking but needed to do more.

On a visit to a Jakarta hospital which treats trafficking victims, Miller praised Indonesia for taking part in a recent U.S.-sponsored law enforcement training session on trafficking and setting up a special anti-trafficking unit within the national police department.

But he said the country should move to pass anti-trafficking legislation that has been pending since last year. "I hope the legislation is passed in the next few months. It will give additional tools to the police and provide tougher punishment for the traffickers," he said.

Notes and Questions

1. Are unilateral efforts to end trafficking likely to be successful? What are the possible drawbacks to such an approach?

2. Is education of "First-World" consumers important in combating slavery? Can consumers make a difference if they stop buying goods produced with slave labor? How much of a difference?

3. How does one distinguish between a traditional practice and a serious abuse of human rights? Are the two mutually exclusive?

MARY JORDAN AND KEVIN SULLIVAN, TRADE BRINGS RICHES, BUT NOT TO MEXICO'S POOR: NAFTA'S CRITICS SAY PACT HAS FAILED TO IMPROVE LIVES OF IMPOVERISHED

WASHINGTON POST, March 22, 2003, at A10

MEXICO CITY—Irma Osorio Soriano crouched on the muddy ground outside her shack washing dishes in soapless gray water. A dreamy look came into her eyes as she imagined the luxurious trappings she doubts she will ever afford: "A refrigerator and a TV," she said, scrubbing in hard circles. "And a big radio."

Osorio, 30, wanted to keep going to school after she turned 14, but she couldn't afford not to work. So she cleans offices. As she pockets $2.50 a day, her childhood hope of being a nurse has vanished into an adulthood of day-dreaming about unattainable appliances.

Osorio is in the majority in Mexico: she was born in poverty and she sees no way out. "Life is hard," she said. "There is no use hoping."

Despite the assurances of four presidents that Mexico was moving up from its Third World status and a landmark free trade agreement with the United States that was to have enriched the country, the number of people living in poverty has soared over the past two decades.

While the percentage of poor Mexicans is about the same now as it was in the early 1980s—a little more than 50 percent—the population has grown over the same period, from 70 million to 100 million.

That means about 19 million more Mexicans are living in poverty than 20 years ago, according to the Mexican government and international organizations. About 24 million—nearly one in every four Mexicans—are classified as extremely poor and unable to afford adequate food.

President Vicente Fox last week called poverty "the biggest problem confronting Mexico." His government estimates that a total of 54 million of the country's 100 million people live in poverty, unable to meet basic needs.

"Mexico is worse off today than it was 20 years ago in almost every way—except democracy," said Gabriel Guerra Castellanos, a political analyst, who called it "a disgrace" that so many Mexicans were still mired in poverty.

At the same time, Mexico has grown richer. Its $600 billion economy is now the world's ninth-largest. Trade volume has nearly tripled since the 1994 North American Free Trade Agreement (NAFTA), placing Mexico ahead of Britain, South Korea and Spain as a trading power.

Mexico's state-run oil monopoly, Pemex, is one of the world's largest oil companies. Beaches from Los Cabos to Cancun draw 20 million tourists a year, making the country one of the world's 10 premier vacation destinations.

The paradox haunts Mexico: With so many advantages, why are so many of its people still so poor?***

Starting with Miguel de la Madrid, president from 1982 to 1988, a succession of Ivy League-educated presidents bet on a formula intended to create prosperity for all. They advocated opening Mexico's markets, making government smaller, and decreasing its involvement in agriculture and industry.

"There was heavy reliance on a rising tide carrying all boats," said Guerra, who served as spokesman for two presidents in the 1990s. "Well, free-market policies have done nothing to alleviate poverty."

Instead, such policies have helped the upper classes and widened the divide between rich and poor. Studies show that the richest 10 percent now control about half of the country's financial and real estate assets.***

Angel and Francisca Martinez *** moved to Mexico City a month ago from a corn-farming village on the border between the states of Oaxaca and Veracruz. Now they and their girls, ages 2 and 4, wander through traffic downtown in plastic sandals, selling penny candy from plastic bags.

They earn about $100 in a good month. They rent a single room for $70 a month, which leaves them $30 to live on. There's never enough to eat, the children wear little more than rags, they get no government benefits. It's a hard life in the city, Angel said, but he'd never go back to his village.

"I live better now," he said.

Notes and Questions

1. Do you think the 24 million Mexicans unable to afford adequate food have had their rights violated? If so, who is/are the perpetrator(s) of the violations? Do national governments have a legal or moral obligation to work towards the eradication of poverty?

2. Is there a human right to trade? If a trade agreement is found to increase poverty, does it violate the rights of those adversely affected? Do those who benefit from the pact have a right to those benefits?

CHARLIE LEDUFF, FOR MIGRANTS, HARD WORK IN HOSTILE SUBURBS

NEW YORK TIMES, September 24, 2000, at A1

When dusk comes, the streets empty and the esquineros hurry to the homes they share with 15, 20 and sometimes 30 others to drink beer and eat supper.

The *esquineros*—the men of the corner—used to walk home alone from the corners where they gather each morning to be hired out for yardwork or other day jobs. Now they walk in groups. At one house, where the Guatemalans live, the door is punctured with bullet holes; a white man recently drove by and unloaded a pistol.

The next block over, there is a white man who put his house up for sale after 20 Mexicans moved in next door. As he pulled into his driveway, he stared at his unwanted neighbors. He is a tough-looking guy, and he did not turn his eyes away. One of the Mexicans wore a secondhand shirt that read, "We don't like you either."

Up until now, the culture divide of the suburbs has been more a cold war than a hot one, an uneasy peace with periodic clashes over public issues like limits on the number of boarders allowed in a house or a proposal in Suffolk County to sue the Immigration and Naturalization Service to more stringently enforce immigration laws.

But when two Hispanic immigrants seeking work were lured to an abandoned building on Sunday and attacked by two white men wielding a knife, a crowbar and a shovel, the assault was a sobering reminder of the lives of the unwanted strangers. The divide plays out in towns like Brewster, Mount Kisco and Yonkers, N.Y., and Freehold, N.J.

But the emotions are rawest in Farmingville, where it is estimated that in the summertime, one in 15 residents is a migrant worker. When October comes, a few men stay, but most follow their money home.

The violence last Sunday shocked some whites and even prompted the formation of a community group by politicians and church leaders looking for ways to ease the tensions. But if the violence was a revelation to many whites, the hostility behind it was hardly news to the brown men in the Goodwill T-shirts and muddy jeans who come to the corner each morning looking for work.***

There are plenty of jobs in this tree-lined hamlet in central Long Island that is home to 15,000 residents and acres of blacktop and strip malls. Mostly they are menial jobs like cleaning pools and landscaping, and like a quarter of all jobs in the United States, they pay about $8 an hour.

The Latinos have come in great numbers over the past four years to take the jobs locals are unwilling or unable to do. Most are here illegally, and it is their illegal status that most irritates local residents.

The people taunt each other. Some Americans picket the Latinos every Saturday as they stand on the corners waiting for work. The esquineros have become schooled in the ways of America. They picket back. And after the ambush of the two workers, more than 500 of the illegal immigrants took to the streets demanding their civil rights.***

Notes and Questions

1.   Is there a connection between the NAFTA-related economic conditions in Mexico and the influx of undocumented workers into the United States? Does the U.S. government or citizenry bear any responsibility for these conditions?

2.   The article notes that "there are plenty of jobs" in at least one of the affected communities. If that is so, why would white residents be upset by the presence of *esquineros*? Could their immigrant status or national backgrounds be a factor? If many of the immigrant workers are in the United States illegally, what limitations might they have in defending themselves against exploitation and violence by private actors?

3.   There seems to be an informal tolerance of undocumented immigration in some quarters in the United States. Yet these immigrants face formidable challenges to survive, and are not free to assert themselves politically. What are the human rights implications of this contingent informal acceptance and formal legal disenfranchisement? How might international human rights law intervene?

PALESTINIANS "REDUCED TO BEGGING"

ASSOCIATED PRESS (GENEVA), July 19, 2003

Palestinians in Gaza and the West Bank have been "reduced to begging" by Israeli military action, and Israel is breaching international law by failing to provide much-needed aid, a UN expert said yesterday.

"There is permanent, grave violation of the right to food by the occupying forces. There is a catastrophic humanitarian situation," said Jean Ziegler, UN special expert on the right to food.

Palestinian villages are encircled by troops, preventing food being delivered and farmers from reaching their fields, he said. Many villages had to buy their water because sources had been cut off.

Mr. Ziegler also cited the destruction or confiscation of fertile Palestinian land for military zones or Jewish colonies. "We saw thousands of olive trees destroyed by bull-dozers," he said.

Trucks of food sent to Palestinian villages either as aid or for sale are stopped at roadblocks and unloaded. Villagers must find another truck to load the food again after inspection and complete the journey, he said.

According to the World Bank, almost one child in 10 in Gaza and the West Bank is suffering from severe malnutrition.

Notes and Questions

1. The economic problems facing the Palestinians are inextricably connected with the larger political conflict. Do basic needs such as housing, land, water, education, and travel always have legal, moral, and political dimensions? How might a human rights perspective on these issues "change the dynamic that has come to be called the 'cycle of violence'?"

2. Do Palestinians have a right to cultivate the land they live on? To trade with each other? To build houses where they are? To have access to water? Where do these rights come from? Who is responsible for enforcing them?

ROBIN HAAS, UNITING ON THE DOMESTIC FRONT/GROUP WINS $50G GRANT TO HELP IN ITS FIGHT FOR FELLOW WORKERS' RIGHTS

NEWSDAY (New York), December 18, 2000, at A27

In the middle of the night, one live-in domestic worker was ordered to leave the home where she lived and worked.

She was fired on the spot when she finally spoke up against the exploitation of working 16-hour days, six or seven days a week with few breaks, no overtime and a salary well below the legal minimum wage.

That's just one of the harrowing experiences Workers' Awaaz is fighting to eradicate. Representing South Asian women who are employed as domestic workers, many of whom are from Queens, the Jackson Heights group recently was recognized with a $ 50,000 grant to continue its work.

Awaaz, which means "voice" in several South Asian languages, is made up of women from Queens who are employed as domestic workers or were at one time, and want to help ensure that others are treated fairly. The group operates on a shoestring budget out of one member's Jackson Heights home.

"You'd be surprised what people do and don't do for the people who live and work in their house," said Shahbano Aliani, a founder and a group spokeswoman. "There are very few protections and even those are not abided by."

Aliani said most domestic workers receive about $250 a week in salary plus room and board, but that often the room is a bed in the basement, next to the washing machine. They also frequently must abide by strict rules, such as being prohibited from eating the more expensive items in the refrigerator.***

To help draw attention to extreme cases, Awaaz has organized protest demonstrations in front of the offices it accuses of such violations. It also files lawsuits on behalf of victims.

The group's members raise public awareness with appearances on area radio and Indian-culture TV, and seek out domestic workers directly by staffing tables at community events and shopping areas.

The women provide counseling, resources, information and moral support. Awaaz hopes to find office space soon, enabling it to provide help for emergency walk-ins.

So far, the group has successfully secured payment of back wages, and, in one case, Aliani said, Awaaz was able to obtain a public apology from one employer and a promise to treat future domestic workers with respect.

The $50,000 grant came from the Union Square Awards, which are given to grass roots activists by the Fund for the City of New York. These annual awards go to people who, despite limited time and money, fight social injustice and do what they can to help make the city a better place to live.***

Notes and Questions

1.   Domestic workers in the United States are almost all women, almost all immigrants, and almost all poorly compensated. Why? How do these factors work against their ability to press for improved working conditions?

2.   How might the ability of domestic workers to assert their rights be affected by their work environment? Is it easier to assert your rights in a factory? In the service industry? As a private contractor?

SETH MYDANS, IN PAKISTAN, RAPE VICTIMS ARE THE "CRIMINALS"

New York Times, May 17, 2003, at A3

CHORLAKI, Pakistan—The evidence of guilt was there for all to see: a newborn baby in the arms of its mother, a village woman named Zafran Bibi.

Her crime: she had been raped. Her sentence: death by stoning.

Now Ms. Zafran, who is about 26, is in solitary confinement in a death-row cell in Kohat, a nearby town. The only visitor she is allowed is her baby daughter, now a year old and being cared for by a prison nurse.

In photographs, Ms. Zafran is a tall woman with striking green eyes—a peasant woman of the hot and barren hills of Pakistan's northwest frontier country. Unschooled and illiterate, like most other women here, she may have little understanding of what has happened to her. But her story is not uncommon under Pakistan's strict Islamic laws.

Thumping a fat red statute book, the white-bearded judge who convicted her, Anwar Ali Khan, said he had simply followed the letter of the Koran-based law, known as hudood, that mandates punishments.

"The illegitimate child is not disowned by her and therefore is proof of zina," he said, referring to laws that forbid any sexual contact outside marriage. Furthermore, he said, in accusing her brother-in-law of raping her, Ms. Zafran had confessed to her crime.

"The lady stated before this court that, yes, she had committed sexual intercourse, but with the brother of her husband," Judge Khan said. "This left no option to the court but to impose the highest penalty."

Although legal fine points do exist, little distinction is made in court between forced and consensual sex.

When hudood was enacted 23 years ago, the laws were formally described as measures to ban "all forms of adultery, whether the offense is committed with or without the consent of the parties." But it is almost always the women who are punished, whatever the facts.

The case of Ms. Zafran fits a familiar pattern. But it raised an outcry, even in Pakistan, because of the sentence of death by stoning, a punishment called for by hudood but never carried out here. The facts of her case have become the subject of editorials and news stories in Pakistan, bringing her some notoriety, and in early May, a higher court called for a review of Ms. Zafran's sentence.

But even if the case returns to a more typical course, she is likely to spend 10 to 15 years in prison as the result of her rape, said Rukhshanda Naz, who heads the local branch of a women's rights group called Aurat. As many as 80 percent of all women in Pakistani jails have been convicted under laws that ban extramarital sex, according to Aurat.

Ms. Zafran, whether she was angry or just naive, chose to point her finger at the man she said raped her. The assaults, she said, came sometimes on the hillside behind her house when she went to cut hay, sometimes at home when nobody was there to see.

Sardar Ali Khan, her lawyer, said that Ms. Zadran had told him she cried when she was raped and that she had cried again as she spoke to him about what happened.

Her husband, Niamat Khan, was serving a prison sentence for murder and in his absence, she had become the plaything of at least one of his brothers.

"She complained to her mother-in-law and her father-in-law," her lawyer said, "but they just turned away." It was her pregnancy that forced her accusations into the open and led to her conviction for zina.

Human rights groups say abuse of women is endemic in Pakistan. Often, they are locked inside their homes where they are subjected to beatings, acid attacks, burning and rape. Every year there are hundreds of "honor killings," in which a woman is murdered for perceived breaches of modesty.

For the most part, abuses like these are carried out with impunity, and often with the support of traditional communities.

Rape itself is a crime under hudood, but it is so difficult to prove that men are rarely convicted. On the other hand, human rights workers say, as many as half the women who report a rape are charged under zina laws with adultery.

"With the men, they apply the principle that you are innocent until proven guilty," said Asma Jahangir, an official of the independent Human Rights Commission of Pakistan and the author of a book on hudood. "With the women, they apply the principle that you are guilty until proven innocent."

The man Ms. Zafran accused, Jamal Khan, was set free without charges. A case against him would have been a waste of the court's time. Under the laws of zina, four male witnesses, all Muslims and all citizens of upright character, must testify to having seen a rape take place. The testimony of women or non-Muslims is not admissible. The victim's accusation also carries little weight; the only significant testimony she can give is an admission of guilt.

"The proof is totally impossible," said Ms. Naz. "If a woman brings a charge of rape, she puts herself in grave danger." If, on the other hand, the woman does not report the rape and becomes pregnant out of wedlock, her silence can be taken as proof of guilt.

It is not only women but also young girls who are at risk, Aurat says. If girls report a rape, they face the same prospects of punishment as women.

A man can deflect an accusation of rape by claiming that his victim, of any age, consented. If the victim has reached puberty, she is considered to be an adult and is then subject to prosecution for zina. As a result, the Aurat report says, girls as young as 12 or 13 have been convicted of having forbidden sexual relations and have been punished with imprisonment and a public whipping.

With no safe recourse, rights workers say, rape victims often flee to the protection of influential families, which may take them in as servants.

The harsh life of women like Ms. Zafran seems to blend with the harshness of the land on which they live. The dry, rocky hills along the frontier with Afghanistan, where only thorn bushes thrive, offer no hint to the people here that a gentler life is possible. Flat mud houses scattered like tiny forts across the landscape suggest that there is little companionship among the people who toil here.

When Ms. Zafran was given in marriage to Niamat Khan, his family took possession of her and she disappeared into their mud-walled compound a mile away. Her parents rarely saw her again; they are too poor even to have a photograph to remind them of her.

In this barren world, where people grow hard to survive, their tenderness for their daughter seems all the more painful. They sat silently one recent day on the string beds that are the only furnishings of their bare one-room home.

Ms. Zafran's father, Zaidan, an unsmiling, weatherbeaten man, spread his hands as if he had no words to offer.

"When we heard the sentence, we couldn't breathe," he said at last. "We couldn't think. For days we couldn't eat. There was nothing we could do for our daughter." He said he had sold his family's only possessions, two thin goats, to help pay for a lawyer.

His wife, Shiraka, whose beauty seems only to have been deepened by her difficult life, looked away. "I have been sucked dry by grief," she said.

DEXTER FILKINS, ENDING CENTURIES OF ILLITERACY: A SOCIAL REVOLUTION IS SWEEPING INDIA

Los Angeles Times, December 7, 1999, at A1

KHAJOURTOLA, India—The people in this hamlet of rice paddies and mud do not know what year it is, they cannot name the country they live in, and they are demanding an end to their ignorance.

In October, in a document scratched out by one of the village's only literate men and signed with residents' thumbprints, the villagers took up the unprecedented offer of the state's chief minister to provide a teacher and books within 90 days to any village that requested them.

"We are all waiting for our school," said Prem Singh, standing in the darkness with a lantern near his face. Singh and the villagers of Khajourtola are the latest enrollees in a social revolution that is sweeping the Indian countryside and bringing education to villages whose inhabitants have led lives of almost total isolation. Begun nearly three years ago here in Madhya Pradesh, a sprawling and impoverished state of 80 million people, the "education guarantee" program has created 21,000 schools—a pace of about 20 a day—in the most remote villages.

It's education at its most basic: Children study in mud huts, next to bean fields, under the open sky. The teachers, drawn from the villages, often have received little formal schooling themselves. Many students are the sons and daughters of the social pariahs in India known as the "untouchables." A large number are girls—historically deprived of education in India—going to school for the first time.

"I don't want to be a thumb-stamper," said Sunita Kumari, a 9-year-old girl in the remote low-caste village of Ganeshpura, using a term to describe people who cannot write their name. "I want to stay in school as long as I can."

Madhya Pradesh's village schools have spread so fast and created such a stir that two other states have decided to send an identical message to their illiterate villagers: Demand a school and we'll give you one. Rajasthan state has created 11,000 makeshift schools since April; Uttar Pradesh, population 140 million, is just getting started. The World Bank and European Union, encouraged by the effort's success, have agreed to help fund schools in the three states.

The small group of Indian bureaucrats and politicians that dreamed up the program believes that it has found a way to provide basic education to the villages of India, where the population of 350 million constitutes the world's largest pool of illiterate people.

The program's backers believe that the lack of universal education in India has been one of the main obstacles to the country's attempts to modernize. They say the goal is to break long-held traditions of caste and gender, which for centuries have made the schooling of girls and the impoverished among the lowest national priorities.***

India has a long history of neglecting primary education. Today, the country spends about 3.4% of its gross national product on public education, well below the world average. India stood still as many of the countries of East Asia invested heavily in primary education and now are approaching universal literacy.***

In Fakibiza, a remote village in Madhya Pradesh inhabited by the indigenous Baiga tribe, none of the adult women can read. But at the one-room school, begun two years ago under the education guarantee program, girls outnumber boys 23 to 11.

Dev Lal, a father with two young girls, said the family believes that it is even more important for girls to be educated than boys. When his daughters get married, they will probably go to a faraway village to a strange family that might not treat them well.

"After marriage, the girl belongs to the husband's family—she is their property, and I will have no rights," Lal said. "If the family tries to exploit one of my daughters, their ability to cope will be strengthened by education."

On the other side of the state, in the village of Pratapura, another school day came to an end. Like most of the villages in Madhya Pradesh, Pratapura is dominated by Hinduism, whose pantheon contains tens of thousands of gods. Drawing together in a small circle and joining hands, the 41 children began a prayer to Saraswati, the goddess of education.

"O Saraswati, give us knowledge," the children prayed. "For those who are able to read shall have many opportunities in life. And those who are not will toil in the fields forever."***

DOUG MYERS, SCHOOL LAWSUIT REJECTED; APPEAL COURT SAYS LOUISIANA FULFILLS ITS FUNDING MANDATE

THE ADVOCATE (Baton Rouge, LA.), June 30, 1998, at 1A

Louisiana's Constitution requires only "minimum," not "adequate," state aid to public schools, an appeals court ruled Monday as it dismissed a lawsuit alleging the state doesn't adequately or equitably fund the schools.

State government officials are meeting the constitutional requirement to provide Louisiana's 760,000 public school students a minimum education and have greatly increased spending on schools in recent years, a three-judge panel of the 1st Circuit Court of Appeal said.

The unanimous ruling reverses 19th Judicial District Judge Janice Clark, who ruled in favor of the school districts suing the state because they say they are unfairly underfunded.***

State government gives local school districts about $ 2.2 billion annually to help run Louisiana's 1,400 public schools. A coalition of school districts, parents and the American Civil Liberties Union had hoped the court would force the state to pump significantly more money into public education.***

[The 1st Circuit panel] said the Louisiana Constitution doesn't require that educational funding provided by the state be "adequate" or "sufficient," or that it achieve some measurable result for each pupil or each school district.

The constitution only requires that the Board of Elementary and Secondary Education annually develop and adopt a formula, and, "This is being done," the panel said.

The judges also said the Legislature must annually allot enough money to fund state government's share of the formula. The judges said the state, through its school spending formula, has appropriately taken steps to help poorer school districts catch up with more affluent systems that can't raise much money from local taxes.

The plaintiffs argue that insufficient funds have been provided to them, thereby violating the constitutional provision requiring the state to "insure a minimum foundation of education in all public elementary and secondary schools."

However, the three-judge panel said state funding for public schools has grown by 59.8 percent since 1987–88, while total state general funds available increased by only 40 percent. "These facts demonstrate that the state's commitment to public education has grown in real terms, and as a percentage of available funds," the panel said.

Notes and Questions

1.   Indian activists say the goal of their movement is to "break long-held traditions of caste and gender" through educational equality. How can education itself achieve such an ambitious goal? Might similar motivations underlie the efforts in Louisiana?

2.   Should governments be required to provide more than a minimal education? What is the purpose of public education? Who are its beneficiaries? How can educational inequality be reconciled with meritocratic norms?

RICH NATIONS FLUNK IN EDUCATING POOR: U.S., GREECE AND NEW ZEALAND LANGUISH AT BOTTOM OF CLASS

REUTERS, November 18, 2003

WASHINGTON (Reuters)—The Netherlands is top of the class and the United States third from last among rich nations that help educate the world's poor, a report by an alliance of development agencies found.

The report, released on Tuesday by the Global Campaign for Education, an international coalition of development agencies, teachers' unions and community groups, looked at 22 rich countries and how much of their aid budgets go toward boosting education in developing countries.

It said the report was a first look at how rich countries have performed on promises made during a conference in Dakar in 2000 to supply funds needed to give the world's children a basic education by the year 2015, under an "Education for All" initiative.

More than 100 million children around the world are not now attending school and another 150 million will not complete their basic education this year, the Global Campaign for Education estimated.

"The contrast between rhetoric and reality is staggering," the report said.

It gave the Netherlands, Norway and Sweden top marks in their support for education of the poor, followed by Ireland, Belgium, Luxembourg, Canada and Denmark.

Japan, Spain, Italy, Austria, the United States, Greece and New Zealand were the least supportive, it said.

It gave U.S. President George W. Bush 12 marks out of 100, just above the leaders of Greece and New Zealand, saying the United States was the least generous aid giver as a share of national income.

Development groups and the United Nations estimated that $5.6 billion in additional aid is needed to ensure that children in poor countries get a basic education, equating it with just three days of global military spending.

Rich countries now provide $1.4 billion annually toward aid for basic education in poor countries, the report said.

"The $5.6 billion extra needed to eduacate all children is one-fifth the amount Americans spend on pizza each year, and half of what Europeans spend on ice cream," said Oliver Buston, senior policy advisor for the development group Oxfam.

Notes and Questions

Why do rich countries contribute toward education in poorer countries? What role does education play in economic development? Is educational aid more or less important than other forms of aid?

W.B. RUBENSTEIN AND R. BRADLEY SEARS, TOWARD MORE PERFECT UNIONS

NEW YORK TIMES (EDITORIAL PAGE), November 20, 2003, at 31

LOS ANGELES—On Tuesday, the highest court in Massachusetts issued a path-breaking decision, making the state the first to extend to gay couples not just many of the rights and benefits of marriage but the right to marry itself. In another sense, however, the decision is simply one more in a series of steps that have already provided legal rights to tens of thousands of same-sex couples throughout America.

According to data from the 2000 United States census, about one in five people who identified themselves as living with an "unmarried partner" of the same sex now resides in a jurisdiction that grants some legal recognition to gay unions. While the census didn't count all same-sex couples—only those who identified themselves as such—it greatly advanced our knowledge about the prevalence and distribution of gay couples throughout the United States.

Counting Massachusetts, there are now four states that extend at least some of the rights of marriage to gay couples. Although their laws have no impact on federal rights or religious recognition of same-sex unions, these states have already begun the experiment of gay marriage.

The Hawaii legislature passed a law in 1997 that provides a range of marital benefits and responsibilities to same-sex couples. The Vermont legislature voted in 2000 to allow civil unions between gay couples. And in a series of laws passed in the last several years, California has extended benefits and responsibilities to same-sex couples nearly equivalent to those enjoyed by married couples.

All told, these four states have about 42 million residents, or about 15 percent of the United States population. They are also home to more than 113,000 gay couples, or 19 percent of the 600,000 or so same-sex couples the 2000 census identified in the

United States. If the entire gay population is distributed throughout the country in the same way that gay couples are, that would mean that about one in five gay Americans now lives in a jurisdiction that provides some significant legal recognition for his or her relationship.

Opponents of same-sex marriage argue that recognition of such unions undermines the sanctity of marriage, harms children and demoralizes society. There is no evidence of any of this—or of any other harmful impact—in Hawaii, Vermont or California. On the contrary, studies have shown that parents' sexual orientation doesn't hurt their children. As the census shows, gay people are already parents to hundreds of thousands of children. Aren't those children better off if their family's relationships are protected by law?***

Notes and Questions

1. Many of us think of marriage as a relationship between two people or two families. But in many countries, it is also a relationship between the couple and the state. Should the sex of the individuals involved in the relationship matter? Why or why not? How is culture or religion affected by changes in the legal structure of domestic relations?

2. Is there a human right to marry? Does a state's rejection of same-sex marriage constitute discrimination? If so, is it justifiable discrimination? Why or why not? Who should make this determination? Should domestic courts decide? Legislatures? What about international bodies?

LAWRENCE K. ALTMAN, SOUTH AFRICA SAYS IT WILL FIGHT AIDS WITH A DRUG PLAN

NEW YORK TIMES, August 9, 2003, at A1

Bowing to regional and international clamor for a more vigorous attack against the AIDS epidemic, the South African government yesterday changed its stand on providing drugs to combat the virus, saying it would develop a plan to offer them to infected people through its public health system by Oct. 1.

"Government shares the impatience of many South Africans on the need to strengthen the nation's armory in the fight against AIDS," the South African cabinet said in a statement after a special meeting to assess the financial costs of a national anti-H.I.V. drug plan and to explore options for treating those with the infection.

South Africa has the largest number of H.I.V.-infected people in the world, about 5 million, or over 11 percent of its population of 43.8 million, according to the United Nations AIDS program. The figures are more staggering for the 23.7 million people aged 15 to 49; about 20 percent of them are infected.

The epidemic poses a major threat to the future of South Africa's economy and security by primarily affecting young sexually active adults and incapacitating the traditional extended family system that cares for sick and orphaned relatives. So far, the epidemic has left 660,000 South African children as orphans.

Yet, for years, as the AIDS virus has spread, President Thabo Mbeki and his top aides have resisted national programs to provide anti-H.I.V. drugs, known as antiretrovirals, making him the target of intense criticism at home and abroad.

The South African government said that because not every infected person needed anti-H.I.V. drugs, its program would provide them initially to people with more advanced cases of AIDS. The drugs can extend life for many people but are not a cure. The government program is also expected to provide prevention programs aimed at the tens of millions of people who are not infected.

The change in policy comes in the same week that South Africa held its first AIDS conference, and just a month after President Bush pressed Mr. Mbeki during his visit to Africa to come up with a plan that included both a drug regimen and prevention efforts. Mr. Bush has pledged to provide $15 billion over five years in fighting global AIDS, although it remains uncertain whether Congress will appropriate that much.***

In the past, Mr. Mbeki and his aides have questioned the safety, effectiveness and costs of the drugs, as well as questioned the very connection between H.I.V. and AIDS. Mr. Mbeki has also emphasized the difficulties that many Africans experience in taking the complicated regimens of multiple drugs every day.

He has stressed the importance of reducing poverty, calling it a major factor in producing the AIDS epidemic, and urging improvement in the diets of poor people.***

Of the 42 million people living with AIDS in the world, an estimated 30 million, or 70 percent, are in sub-Saharan Africa, which has a population of 640 million. Women make up about 58 percent of them, the United Nations says.

Zachie Achmat, the chairman of one advocacy group, the Treatment Action Campaign, had led a growing grass-roots campaign to force the government to make the drugs widely and cheaply available and had become internationally known for refusing to take the drug cocktails himself until the government changed its policies.***

The availability of generic or cheaper anti-AIDS drugs has been a long-fought battle in developing countries. In April 2001, the pharmaceutical industry dropped its legal fight against South Africa, which the industry contended had been violating international trade agreements and patent restrictions through the government's efforts to buy brand-name drugs at the lowest rates available in the world.

Notes and Questions

1.   As this article indicates, more than 40 million people in the world are HIV-positive. Even though effective medical treatment exists, most of the afflicted do not have access to affordable medicine. Is this a human rights violation?

2.   Who is responsible for combating this pandemic? Is individual responsibility an effective approach? Should governments be required to support access to treatment? Should South Africa be required to develop an infrastructure for treating HIV-positive citizens? Do wealthy countries have any responsibility to ensure access? What about private corporations? Should pharmaceutical companies be required to share their drug patents with low-cost "generic" producers? Is there a role for the international community?

3.   In addition to access to medicines, how else does poverty affect the treatment of HIV/AIDS?

LARRY ROHTER, THE HOMES OF ARGENTINES ARE AT RISK IN I.M.F. TALKS

NEW YORK TIMES, June 23, 2003, at A6

BUENOS AIRES, June 22—After a decade as renters, Ariel and Norma Brofman were finally able to buy a small house here four years ago. But if the Argentine government yields to International Monetary Fund pressure to rescind emergency legislation meant to protect ordinary families like the Brofmans, the couple stand to lose their home and the $32,000 they have paid for it so far.

Like other middle-class Argentines, the Brofmans, whose household includes their two daughters, aged 9 and 13, and their widowed mothers, were severely battered by the collapse of the economy here last year. In just a few months, Mr. Brofman lost his job as an electronics technician, exhausted his scant savings and fell behind on the monthly $555 mortgage payment on their two-bedroom, 1,000-square-foot house.

"We did not create this situation," said Mr. Brofman, 38, who now tries to make ends meet by repairing cellular telephones. "The rules of the game were changed on us from one day to the next, and we were hoping the government would take steps to defend us until this country is back on its feet and we can begin paying again."

*** [N]early a year ago, at the peak of the crisis, the Argentine Congress approved a bill that suspended mortgage foreclosures for 90 days on homes that were a family's "sole and permanent residence." That law has since been renewed three times, but will expire in August unless Congress extends it again.

It has, however, brought the Argentine government into conflict with the I.M.F., whose managing director, Horst Kohler, is scheduled to arrive here Monday for a two-day visit. Though Argentina now has a budget surplus and has taken numerous other steps urged by the I.M.F., government officials say that the fund is insisting that the freeze on foreclosures be lifted as a pre-condition for any comprehensive agreement.

In January, the Fund agreed to reschedule payment of nearly $7 billion that it was owed by Argentina. But that accord expires in August, around the same time as the mortgage foreclosure bill. The new president here, Nestor Kirchner, who took office late last month, wants to negotiate a long-term agreement with the Fund that would restore credit lines and bring back the foreign investors who fled the country when the economy imploded.

Other issues are also on the table in the negotiations, including an even larger government budget surplus and the end of a freeze on utility rate increases. But the foreclosure issue is the most politically explosive for Mr. Kirchner and has come to symbolize for many Argentines what they consider to be the I.M.F.'s intrusive and callous attitude.

Most mortgages here were contracted in the 1990's, when the Argentine peso was linked to the American dollar at a value of one to one as part of a policy intended to end Argentina's chronic four-digit annual inflation rate and attract investment. But that system collapsed early last year after the I.M.F. suspended Argentina's credit line, complaining, among other things, that the country had not fulfilled agreements to slash government spending. The government then in power here defaulted on most of its $141 billion in public debt. Several months of financial chaos ensued.

Bank accounts, many of which were denominated in dollars, were frozen by government decree. For a time, banks suspended normal operations. As a result, many debtors did not have access to the money they needed to meet their obligations, and when the freeze was eased, they found that their dollar assets had been converted into pesos, which had lost more than 70 percent of their value against the dollar.

The Argentine Debtors' Association, a group that represents mortgage holders, calculates that as many as 40 percent of the estimated 5.5 million households with bank mortgage loans have fallen behind on their payments. That compares with just over 10 percent at the end of 2001, before the freeze on bank accounts and the crisis that shrank the economy by more than 10 percent last year.***

Notes and Questions

The IMF mandates that governments enforce a particular set of economic policies as a condition for receiving credit. Often these policies involve the use of a free-market "shock therapy" that leaves people like the Brofmans in financial crisis. Who is responsible for their hardship? Who can they hold accountable?

MARK EGAN, WALL STREET UPS OPPOSITION TO IMF BANKRUPTCY PLAN

REUTERS, December 17, 2002

A group of financial market associations strongly opposed on Tuesday the International Monetary Fund's plan to set up an international bankruptcy court for countries that default on their debts.

The IMF has proposed setting up a Sovereign Debt Restructuring Mechanism (SDRM) to allow for orderly defaults by nations unable to repay their debts. The plan would work in similar fashion to courts that allow companies to operate during bankruptcy. Wall Street has already expressed strong criticism of the plan, but upped the ante on Tuesday, issuing a paper that called the IMF's plan fundamentally flawed.***

After Argentina defaulted on much of its international debt in January, interest in creating a better way to deal with sovereign defaults has gathered steam. The IMF wants to set up the bankruptcy court. Others, including the U.S. Treasury and Wall Street, proposed using new language in bond contracts as a more market-based approach.

The Group of Seven industrialized nations—the United States, Japan, Britain, Germany, Canada, France and Italy—and IMF are now pursuing both options simultaneously. Concrete proposals are to be unveiled at the IMF's meetings in April.***

IMF spokesman Tom Dawson dismissed the report as, "old wine in a new bottle." "Their rejection of even being able to discuss this calls into question their good faith," Dawson said. "We have a mandate from 184 nations to continue this work and this statement does nothing to help the process along."

The analogy with private bankruptcy tribunals was "fundamentally flawed," [the Wall Street groups] said, since sovereign debtors would not be subject to the "appropriate checks and balances that legitimize and make such a bankruptcy regime fair and effective."***

Notes and Questions

Why would financial markets oppose an international bankruptcy court for nations? What role does bankruptcy play in a market economy? How might the Brofmans have benefited from such a court?

DEATH TOLL IN BOLIVIAN UNREST RISES TO 30

AGENCE FRANCE PRESSE (AFP), February 14, 2003

LA PAZ—The number of lives lost in the past two days during violent protests in Bolivia over a promised income tax hike has risen to 30, hospital officials said Friday.

"Many died in our hands with irreversible damage to the heart and lungs," said Juan Malaga, a doctor at one of three La Paz hospitals that reported a total of 25 dead.

"Others will be left maimed by the severity of their wounds," he added. Authorities estimated more than 100 people had been wounded in the bloody protests. The army hospital reported an additional four dead, and on Thursday a coca farmer died in Chapare,*** in clashes with the army as he tried to barricade a highway in protest.***

Riots rocked the capital Thursday as the political opposition and trade unions called on the president to resign, following a day of pitched battles between troops and police. Friday, mourners brought politics to the procession, chanting against Sanchez de Lozada as the coffins slowly passed. The angry crowd also shoved away four lawmakers, seen as unsympathetic, who tried to join the funeral procession.

Meanwhile, in the coca-producing Chapare region six army troops were injured Friday as they tried to take down a roadblock by demonstrators demanding the resignation of Sanchez de Lozada's government.

Bolivia's main labor federation joined the chamber of commerce in condemning the government's proposed tax hike, which had been aimed at reducing the nation's debt.

In 2002, the country's debt represented 8.6 percent of Bolivia's eight-billion-dollar gross domestic product. Sanchez de Lozada wants to reduce it to five percent.

A key party in the government alliance, the Revolutionary Movement of the Left (MIR), declared late Thursday it wanted changes in the neo-liberal economic model used in Bolivia since 1985.

Pope John Paul II has called on Bolivians to "avoid further outbreaks of violence," and Organization of American States chief Cesar Gaviria has urged Bolivians to address their differences peacefully and "within constitutional norms."

Sanchez de Lozada, 72, took office six months ago and has been attempting to open up the Bolivian economy as he did during his first 1993–1997 presidential term.

Notes and Questions

1. If the chamber of commerce, labor unions, and farmers in Bolivia all oppose the same economic policy, why would the government press forward with it? If a

democratically elected government spent its way into debt, are the country's people responsible for paying that debt? Would your answer change if the country is authoritarian?

2.   Coca farming is enormously important in Bolivia. Many people in the Andean region chew coca leaves for its medicinal properties and drink coca tea for pleasure. It is also processed into cocaine. Can a country like Bolivia develop a stable free market economy if its principal crop is considered contraband? If there is demand for coca, should farmers be punished for furnishing the supply? What policies should be adopted to address international demand?

TEXACO UNDER FIRE IN ECUADORIAN LAWSUIT

ASSOCIATED PRESS, October 21, 2003

LAGO AGRIO, Ecuador (AP)—A decade after Texaco pulled out of the Amazon jungle, the U.S. petroleum giant went on trial Tuesday in a lawsuit filed on behalf of 30,000 poor Ecuadoreans who say the company's 20 years of drilling poisoned their homeland.

The case is the first time a multinational oil company has been subjected to Ecuadorean jurisdiction for allegedly damaging the environment in this small Andean nation, which depends on oil for its development.

Former Ecuadorean Supreme Court Justice Alberto Wray, with the assistance of an American legal team, wants California-based ChevronTexaco to pay for cleanup and medical monitoring costs, which the plaintiffs say could reach $1 billion.

Judge Alberto Guerra rejected an opening challenge to the court's authority by the oil company's lawyers, who argued the judge did not have the authority to bring ChevronTexaco to trial for alleged damage caused by Texaco, which merged with the parent company in 2001.

ChevronTexaco "is not the successor to Texaco. Therefore it cannot be held responsible for anything," ChevronTexaco lawyer Adolfo Callejas said. Wray dismissed that argument, saying "we believe that ChevronTexaco assumed Texaco's obligations."

Some 300 people—including Indians in body paint and feathers—marched outside the courthouse in Lago Agrio, a ramshackle town about 110 miles northeast of Quito. Among the 30,000 plaintiffs are an estimated 5,000 Indians whose ancestral jungle homelands have allegedly been polluted.

The lawsuit alleges that Texaco took advantage of lax Ecuadorean environmental standards to cut costs by pouring wastewater brought to the surface by drilling into some 350 open pits instead of reinjecting it deep underground.

"We have water studies that show that people are drinking contaminated water caused by this pollution, caused by the oil, that they are drinking contaminants that are known to cause cancer," said Steve Donziger, a U.S. lawyer representing the Ecuadorean plaintiffs.

A ruling in favor of his clients would send "a powerful message to the oil industry that they have to adhere to the best technical practices when they drill in the Third World," Donziger said.

ChevronTexaco has denied the allegations, saying it followed Ecuadorean environmental laws and spent $40 million under a clean-up agreement with the Ecuadorean government in 1995. The government certified the clean-up three years later.

The plaintiffs' lawyers originally wanted the case tried in U.S. courts, arguing the Ecuadorean government's dependence on oil revenues would make the country's courts unlikely to deliver justice. Oil exports account for about 40 percent of Ecuador's revenue.

The case was sent to Ecuador in August 2002 when the 2nd U.S. Circuit Court of Appeals in New York ruled it should be heard where the damage allegedly occurred.

For settler Jose Aguilar, the legal arguments mean little, compared with damage to crops and farm animals and the health of the region's inhabitants. "It is irreparable damage," he said outside the courthouse as protesters read testimonials from cancer victims. "Everything has been damaged. People have died. Everything has been lost."

Swamps and streams are frequently covered with a thin layer of oil. The region's inhabitants complain of stomach cramps, sore throats and difficult-to-treat skin rashes, which they blame on the pollution.

Ricardo Beija, a vice president and legal adviser for the oil company, told reporters the damage caused by drilling was "minimal" and "normal for any operation."

"We have confidence in the Ecuadorean courts," he added.

In the company's opening arguments, Callejas also warned the case would scare away other multinational corporations considering investing in Ecuador.

Notes and Questions

1.   Suppose it is true that Texaco followed Ecuador's environmental laws as they understood them. Is it fair to hold the company to a higher standard based on the unfortunate consequences?

2.   Why would a developing country fear high environmental standards? What role could international law play in preventing a "race to the bottom?"

CHRIS MCGREAL, SOUTH AFRICANS VOW TO GRAB THE LAND: GOVERNMENT PULLS OUT THE STOPS TO PREVENT BRAZILIAN-STYLE SEIZURES

GUARDIAN (London), July 26, 2001, at 18

The South African government is wielding the courts, the police and a lot of invective to reassure the rest of the world that the country's blossoming land crisis is nothing like Zimbabwe's. But South Africa's difficult neighbour may not be the example it has to fear. That privilege will soon fall to Brazil.

The government has admitted that the invasion of a sprawling piece of neglected land on the outskirts of Johannesburg by 10,000 people prompted a "pivotal shift" in its land redistribution policy. Less than 2% has been transferred from white to black ownership since the African National Congress came to power in 1994.***

While the land grabs in Zimbabwe have been systematic and nationally coordinated, in South Africa they have been led by disparate local groups, whose actions have been easily contained. That is about to change, and the government is worried.

In the coming days an array of militant and increasingly popular land-rights groups throughout the country will launch an organisation to coordinate occupations. At the forefront of the group will be the National Land Committee (NLC).***

The National Landless Peoples Grouping, as the umbrella body is provisionally called, will [adopt land grab strategies based on the Brazilian experience].***

"The constitution in Brazil has a use it or lose it clause. You can't just own land, it has to be put to productive use. Landless people occupy land that is under-utilised and they force the government to implement the constitution," he said.

There is no shortage of potential targets in South Africa. For a start, the state owns about a quarter of all the land. Much of it, particularly property in the hands of the military, stands idle or is under-utilised.

Nor is there any shortage of people in search of land: the demand near the big cities, where there is a better chance of finding a job, is no less acute than it is in the country.

About 17 [million] people are still crowded into the old Bantustan, the homelands, with no legal title to the land they live on. Technically it is held in trust for them by the government, a legacy of the days when black people were not allowed to own land. But there are now too many people on too little territory.

Another 7 [million] black people, mostly workers and their families, live on white-owned farms. Although they have marginally more protection than they did during apartheid, escalating crime and violence and some farmers' fear of land claims has led to tens of thousands of black people being driven out of their homes.

The sense of crisis is heightened by a cycle of violence on the farms in which hundreds of white landowners and their workers die each year.

It is difficult to distinguish the killing of white farmers from other, unrelated deaths that burden South Africa with a dire murder rate, but there is little doubt that some of the murders are the direct consequence of the years of abuse suffered by farm workers, leaving them bitter and fearful of being thrown off their land.***

Notes and Questions

Do people who have been systematically excluded from land have a right to take it on their own initiative? Why or why not? Would the government have the right to redistribute the land? What rights do landowners have?

THE MILLENNIUM DEVELOPMENT COMPACT (UNITED NATIONS DEVELOPMENT PROGRAMME, HUMAN DEVELOPMENT REPORT 2003)

Available at http://www.undp.org/hdr2003/pdf/hdr03_MDC.pdf

In September 2000 the world's leaders adopted the UN Millennium Declaration, committing their nations to stronger global efforts to reduce poverty, improve health and promote peace, human rights and environmental sustainability. The millennium Development Goals that emerged from the Declaration are specific, measurable targets, including the one for reducing—by 2015—the extreme poverty that still grips more than 1 billion people of the world's people. These goals, and the commitment of rich and poor countries to achieve them were affirmed in the Monterrey Consensus that emerged from the March 2002 UN Financing for Development conference, the September 2002 world Summit on Sustainable Development and the launch of the Doha Round on international Trade.***

THE CANCUN FAILURE

NEW YORK TIMES (EDITORIAL), September 16, 2003, at A24

Cancun means "snakepit" in the local Mayan language, and it lived up to its name as the host of an important World Trade Organization meeting that began last week. Rather than tackling the problem of their high agricultural tariffs and lavish farm subsidies, which victimize farmers in poorer nations, a number of rich nations derailed the talks.

The failure by 146 trade delegates to reach an agreement in Mexico is a serious blow to the global economy. And contrary to the mindless cheering with which the breakdown was greeted by antiglobalization protesters at Cancun, the world's poorest and most vulnerable nations will suffer most. It is a bitter irony that the chief architects of this failure were nations like Japan, Korea and European Union members, themselves ads for the prosperity afforded by increased global trade.

The Cancun meeting came at the midpoint of the W.T.O.'s "development round" of trade liberalization talks, one that began two years ago with an eye toward extending the benefits of freer trade and markets to poorer countries. The principal demand of these developing nations, led at Cancun by Brazil, has been an end to high tariffs and agricultural subsidies in the developed world, and rightly so. Poor nations find it hard to compete against rich nations' farmers, who get more than $300 billion in government handouts each year.

The talks appeared to break down suddenly on the issue of whether the W.T.O. should extend its rule-making jurisdiction into such new areas as foreign investment. But in truth, there was nothing abrupt about the Cancun meltdown. The Japanese and Europeans had devised this demand for an unwieldy and unnecessary expansion of the W.T.O.'s mandate as a poison pill—to deflect any attempts to get them to turn their backs on their powerful farm lobbies. Their plan worked.

The American role at Cancun was disappointingly muted. The Bush administration had little interest in the proposal to expand the W.T.O.'s authority, but the American farm lobby is split between those who want to profit from greater access to foreign markets and less efficient sectors that demand continued coddling from Washington. That is one reason the United States made the unfortunate decision to side with the more protectionist Europeans in Cancun, a position that left American trade representatives playing defense on subsidies rather than taking a creative stance, alongside Brazil, on lowering trade barriers.

This was an unfortunate subject on which to show some rare trans-Atlantic solidarity. The resulting "coalition of the unwilling" lent the talks an unfortunate north-versus-south cast. Any hope that the United States would take the moral high ground at Cancun, and reclaim its historic leadership in pressing for freer trade, was further dashed by the disgraceful manner in which the American negotiators rebuffed the rightful demands of West African nations that the United States commit itself to a clear phasing out of its harmful cotton subsidies. American business and labor groups, not to mention taxpayers, should be enraged that the administration seems more solicitous of protecting the most indefensible segment of United States protectionism rather than of protecting the national interest by promoting economic growth through trade.

For struggling cotton farmers in sub-Saharan Africa, and for millions of others in the developing world whose lives would benefit from the further lowering of trade barriers, the failure of Cancun amounts to a crushing message from the developed world—one of callous indifference.***

Notes and Questions

1.   This article highlights the fact that rich countries have historically chosen to employ protectionist measures. The editorial assumes the moral high ground by claiming that all protectionism is bad, but especially from rich countries. Do you agree? Who are the primary beneficiaries of agricultural subsidies, the family farmer or agri-business?

2.   Do "Third World" producers have a right to sell freely in rich markets? Would the IMF tolerate American-style agricultural subsidies in a poor country?

AFRICAN NATIONS PLAN TO MONITOR ONE ANOTHER

REUTERS, February 15, 2004

IGALI, Rwanda, Feb. 14 (Reuters)—African leaders trying to fight poverty through better governance said Saturday that they planned "peer reviews" of 16 nations by March 2006 to try to improve the reputation of this continent, where much of the news has been about conflict and disease.

Peer scrutiny is a central part of Africa's rescue plan, the New Partnership for Africa's Development, promising improved political and economic management in return for increased foreign investment and trade for the poorest continent.

"Africa has appreciated that its fortune is in its own hands," President Olusegun Obasanjo of Nigeria said at the close of a summit meeting of 10 African heads of state in Rwanda. "We are not doing this just for the fun of it. We are doing it because we know it is in our best interests to do it."

Described by its architects as a long-term project, the effort is being watched by both Africans and international donors to gauge the continent's seriousness. Officials at the summit meeting, convened to establish the peer review program, said experts would start the process by traveling to the first nation to be reviewed, Ghana, in April, followed shortly afterward by trips to Rwanda, Kenya and Mauritius.

Next up for review, from 2005, are Mozambique, Nigeria, Senegal, South Africa, Ethiopia, Mali, Uganda, Burkina Faso, Algeria, Cameroon, Gabon, and the Congo Republic.

"The panel is keen to ensure that all 16 participating countries are reviewed by March 2006," said a document circulated at the meeting. "The rationale of this strategy is that all participating countries should be reviewed in a limited period" if it is to be an "effective learning process among participating countries."

The plan by African leaders to monitor one other's performance on human rights, corruption, and democracy is expected to have cost $13.8 million by 2006, with most financing coming from African countries, the documents show.

Notes and Questions

1.   Why would African countries monitor each other's performance on human rights, corruption and democracy? What are the advantages and disadvantages of this approach, as opposed to the usual monitoring by the U.S. State Department, U.N. agencies or international NGOs?

2.   The following article considers the role transnational corporate actors have played in violent conflict in Africa and elsewhere. Should corporations, or their representatives, be legally accountable for violations of human rights under international criminal law?

JULIA GRAFF, CORPORATE WAR CRIMINALS AND THE INTERNATIONAL CRIMINAL COURT: BLOOD AND PROFITS IN THE DEMOCRATIC REPUBLIC OF CONGO

11 HUM. RTS. BR. (No. 2) 23 (2004)

Human rights organizations have long criticized corporations operating in war-torn countries for maximizing profits at the expense of human rights. Shareholders' primary concern with the bottom line often leads corporate decision-makers to purchase raw materials in developing countries at the cheapest price, regardless of the human rights credentials of their suppliers. Some corporations, increasingly concerned by allegations of complicity in human rights abuses, are implementing stronger monitoring devices to ensure that they comply with international standards.

Other companies intentionally engage in illegal business ventures with armed groups in places where weak judiciaries are unlikely to prosecute much-needed investors for corporate malfeasance. In countries experiencing ongoing civil conflict, the systematic elimination of independent judges, prosecutors, and witnesses willing to testify reduces the likelihood of prosecution and weakens the rule of law. This article explores the possibility of holding corporate officers and managers criminally responsible before the International Criminal Court (ICC) for grave human rights violations committed by their agents, employees, or business partners, using the Democratic Republic of Congo (DRC) as a test case.***

Nearly two years after the Rome Statute entered into force, the ICC is now almost fully operational. The Court has jurisdiction over war crimes, crimes against humanity, and genocide committed after July 1, 2002. The Office of the Prosecutor (OTP) may receive referrals of cases from the UN Security Council, states, individuals, and non-governmental organizations, but the OTP may also act on its own initiative to investigate and prosecute cases, with authorization from the Pre-Trial Chambers. The ICC may try the nationals of states parties as well as the nationals of non-ratifying states if they commit certain crimes within the territory of a state party. Under the principle of complementarity embodied in the Statute, the Court only has jurisdiction when the relevant states are unable or unwilling to prosecute. Chief Prosecutor Luis Moreno Ocampo made clear in his September 2003 policy paper that the OTP intends to focus the Court's limited resources on those leaders who bear the most responsibility for crimes, "such as the leaders of the state or organisation allegedly responsible for those crimes."

The ICC can prosecute heads of state, political and military leaders, and the leaders of irregular warring factions, yet corporations are not subject to criminal liability before the ICC. Some delegations argued during the drafting stages of the Rome Statute that the inclusion of corporations within the Court's jurisdiction would facilitate victims' compensation. Others cautioned that the evidentiary challenges of prosecuting legal entities, and many national legal systems' rejection of the criminal liability of corporations, made the exclusion of corporations from ICC jurisdiction more appropriate. Following the philosophy of the Nuremberg Tribunal that "international crimes are committed by men, not by abstract entities," article 25(1) of the Rome Statute ultimately limited the Court's jurisdiction to "natural persons." The OTP may prosecute corporate officers, managers, and employees, but not the corporate entity itself.

*** From Nuremberg to the *ad hoc* tribunals for the former Yugoslavia and Rwanda, international courts have found individual corporate officers, managers, and employees criminally responsible for war crimes, crimes against humanity, and genocide. Moreno Ocampo has recently made several statements indicating the OTP's interest in investigating the financial links to crimes committed in the Democratic Republic of Congo (DRC). In the OTP policy paper, Moreno Ocampo stated that "financial transactions *** for the purchase of arms used in murder, may well provide evidence proving the commission of such atrocities."

At the September 2003 Assembly of States Parties, Moreno Ocampo announced that his office is closely following the situation in the Ituri district of the northeastern DRC, where massacres, rape, and forcible displacement routinely occur. While it is not certain that the first cases before the Court will be from the DRC, the chief prosecutor revealed that he is prepared to seek authorization from the PreTrial Chambers to begin an investigation of those responsible for the crimes committed there. He emphasized the possibility that those who direct operations in the extractive industries "may also be the authors of crimes, *even if they are based in other countries*" (emphasis added). Such statements, along with the broad prosecutorial discretion granted to the OTP, lead some to wonder how far the Court will go in pursuing military, political, and even corporate leaders.***

In June 2000, the Security Council established a Panel of Experts on the Illegal Exploitation of Natural Resources and Other Forms of Wealth in the Democratic Republic of Congo (Panel) to investigate the extent to which investment in the extractive industries fueled the war. In its October 2002 report, the Panel alleged that 85 companies were involved in business activities in the DRC that breached the Guidelines for Multinational Enterprises of the Organization for Economic Cooperation and Development (OECD). American, European, and South African corporations figure high on the list. The Panel also named specific Congolese and international businesspeople as well as high-ranking military officers and political officials from Uganda, the DRC, Zimbabwe, and Rwanda who were connected to illegal mining activities and arms trafficking. The violations include "theft, embezzlement, diversion of public funds, undervaluation of goods, smuggling, false invoicing, non-payment of taxes, kickbacks to public officials and bribery."

The Panel's 2002 report provoked strong reaction from the companies and countries it alleged were helping to perpetuate the war in the DRC. Western governments and business lobbies pressured the UN to excise a controversial section of the Panel's subsequent 2003 report that detailed the continued participation of military officials and businesses in the illegal export of minerals. The UN complied, voicing concerns that the information could endanger the DRC's transitional government. The 2003 report also states that cases against 48 of the companies have been resolved, while the rest of the cases are either pending or require further monitoring.

The 2002 report describes in great detail the way in which "elite networks" of political and military leaders, as well as businessmen and certain rebel leaders, cooperate to protect and exploit resources and generate revenue in areas controlled by the DRC government, Rwanda, and Uganda. By controlling the various armies and local security forces and carrying out select acts of violence, these elite networks monopolize the production, commerce, and financing involved in extracting diamonds, gold, copper, cobalt, and coltan. Rebel administrations in the occupied territories serve as fronts for these international operations, generating public revenue which is then diverted into network coffers.***

[Individuals associated with corporate misconduct] could thus be implicated in, and found criminally liable for, a number of violations of international criminal law committed in the DRC. Such violations include subjecting local populations, including children, to forced labor in the extraction of natural resources; the torture, rape, and murder of thousands of civilians during military operations to secure mineral-rich land; and the destruction of agricultural infrastructure to force peasant farmers to participate in extractive work, resulting in reduced food supplies and slavelike conditions in the coltan mines.***

LETTER FROM BERNIE GRANT, MP, CHAIR, AFRICA REPARATIONS MOVEMENT (U.K.) TO MR. JULIAN SPALDING, DIRECTOR, ART GALLERY AND MUSEUM, KELVINGROVE, GLASGOW

December 10, 1996

Re: *African Religious and Cultural Objects*

Dear Mr. Spalding,

Thank you very much indeed for your recent correspondence about the above matter.

I write on behalf of the Oba of Benin,*** and on behalf of the Africa Reparations Movement (UK) of which I am the Chair. The subject of this letter is the Benin Bronzes, Ivories and other cultural and religious objects contained in the Glasgow Art Gallery and Museum ***

As you are aware, most of the Benin religious and cultural objects currently in British museums and other institutions, were looted in February 1897 from Benin City. The context of this was the battle for trade in the carve up of Africa, into "spheres of influence," by the European powers, and the launching of a military expedition by the British in 1897, to depose the King of Benin who insisted on preserving the independence and sovereignty of his kingdom.

The Benin religious and cultural objects belong to a living culture and have deep historic and social value, which go far beyond the aesthetic and monetary value which they hold in exile. I was recently informed by Prince Akenzua, the Oba's brother, who was in the UK on a quest to speak to MP's regarding the return of the Bronzes etc., that those officiating at the Oba's coronation ceremonies had forgotten the rituals. They had had to consult some of the Bronzes that are still in Benin, in order for them to wear the correct vestments and have the appropriate officials present.

Prince Akenzua explained that the previous coronation had been well over 50 years previously and because the ceremony is not written down, the officials had forgotten, and their only recourse to the proper rituals were the Bronzes which were made for that specific purpose. He went on to say that many of their ceremonies have not been performed satisfactorily because most of the Bronzes are missing. This situation is very distressing for the Benin people of today. Moreover, the objects have come to symbolise the intense sense of injustice widely felt in Africa, and indeed amongst many people of African origin in Britain, about the mis-appropriation of African art, cultural and religious objects, arising from the period of European colonisation.

There has for many years now, been a demand for these religious and cultural objects to be returned to Benin, and as the centenary of their looting approaches in February 1997, the strength of feeling around this has intensified.***

As Chair of the Africa Reparations Movement (UK), (ARM UK), at the recent meeting with Prince Akenzua, I discussed the plans for the centenary commemoration next year. The demand for the return of the Benin religious and cultural objects is clearly central to this occasion, and the Prince has formally authorised me to investigate the possibility of returning at least some of the objects at this time.*** I understand *** that [under Scottish Law] *** it is within the powers of individual local authorities to make decisions on the restitution of items from collections which they hold. I also understand that there are precedents for restitution where a formal request has been made.

The Royal Family of Benin has therefore authorised me to make such a formal request, and has asked me to draw an analogy with the recent return to Scotland of the Stone of Destiny. Just as the Stone is of such great significance to the people of Scotland, so the Benin treasures are significant to the people of Benin. Theirs was a rich, sophisticated, and advanced civilisation, which was in many ways far more developed than contemporary European societies. The denial and destruction of the history of the Benin people were acts of appalling racism, which need urgently to be rectified. These are indeed some of the most distasteful and abiding injustices arising out of the period of European colonisation of Africa.

Yours sincerely,

BERNIE GRANT MP

Notes and Questions

1. What kind of objects may be important to a culture or a nation? Should possession or historic title be determinative in assigning ownership of culturally valuable artifacts? Is this a human rights issue? Do citizens of Benin have a human right to the possession

of cultural artifacts removed from their country during colonialism? Would your analysis be different if a private collector held the object?

2. What kinds of international agreements could be developed for the protection and appreciation of cultural and religious objects?

DARRYL FEARS, AGING SONS OF SLAVES JOIN REPARATIONS BATTLE; FINANCIAL CORPORATIONS TARGETED BY LAWSUITS

WASHINGTON POST, September 30, 2002, at A3

Not long ago, Chester A. Hurdle opened a newspaper and read a commentary by a man who opposed paying reparations for slavery, partly because he believed that the victims and their immediate descendants were dead.

"I guess I'm a ghost," Hurdle said to himself, "and so is my brother and my sister."

Hurdle is the son of Andrew Jackson Hurdle, who was taken from his parents and sold in bondage in North Carolina at age 8, according to the family's genealogy and oral history. He escaped in his teenage years after being taken to Texas, where he eventually started his own farm, fathered 25 children by two wives and died in 1936, at age 88.

Now Chester Hurdle, 75, of San Francisco, and his last surviving brother, Timothy, 83, have filed a class action lawsuit in a California court, seeking reparations on behalf of their father and all slave descendants. Reparations advocates see the lawsuit as groundbreaking: a means of establishing a direct, living link to an institution that was outlawed in 1865. The Hurdles' lawsuit, filed earlier this month, is the first of its kind. In Mississippi, 119-year-old EddLee Bankhead of Corinth, near Memphis, who says his parents were slaves, filed a similar action in federal court. Attorneys who helped him and the Hurdles organize their cases say there will be others.

Historically, the reparations movement has struggled with the questions of who should pay and who is owed. In years past, claimants who were generations removed from slavery tried to seek damages from the government, and their claims were quickly dismissed.

But in these cases, the plaintiffs are direct descendants seeking unspecified damages from corporations, including Fleet Boston Financial Corp., Aetna Inc., New York Life Insurance Co., and Lloyds of London, that they say profited from the slave trade. Any damages awarded would be placed in trust to aid future generations of African Americans, advocates said.

"This is a radical departure from how reparations were demanded," said Vincene Verdun, an associate professor of law at Ohio State University. "It will be up to the plaintiffs to demonstrate that corporations did, in fact, gain from slavery."

One reparations activist has demonstrated that Aetna did, unearthing from company archives some insurance policies that indemnified slave owners against the loss of their slaves. Aetna has acknowledged and apologized for its role, but the activist, Deadria Farmer-Paellmann, has filed a lawsuit against the company at a federal court in Brooklyn. Aetna has challenged its merits.

The lawsuits have come when public discussion of reparations is more extended and intense than in recent memory—and 140 years to the month after President Abraham Lincoln issued the Emancipation Proclamation.

The public discussion, however, seems no closer to resolution than the litigation.***

A CNN/USA Today/Gallup poll conducted in February found that 9 out of 10 white Americans oppose government payments, while slightly more than half of black Americans support them. About 62 percent of white Americans oppose corporate payments, while 68 percent of African Americans support them.

Even some liberal African American commentators have said that black people should stop seeking compensation for slavery, however much it is deserved.

"They can't print enough money to compensate for the crime," wrote Miami Herald columnist Leonard Pitts Jr., an African American. "Even if they could, reparations would not happen because the mood of the country would not allow it."

David Horowitz, a white conservative analyst, is perhaps the most vocal opponent of reparations. "This will isolate the black community," he said. "Look at what reparations does. It says to the rest of America, 'You're involved with slavery and discrimination. Now, racists, first apologize and give us money.' Anyone with half a political brain knows this is not the way to go about things. Beyond all the merits of the claim itself are all these political problems."

Nevertheless, the reparations movement is creeping from the fringes of American activism into the mainstream.

Randall Robinson's 2000 book, "The Debt," began the discussion in earnest when it asked why reparations were provided to Native Americans who had been stripped of their lands during the Indian Wars, Japanese citizens who had been interned during World War II, and the relatives of Jews who had been interned, enslaved and exterminated by Germans in that same war.

Farmer-Paellmann's research of corporate ties to slavery inspired then-California state Sen. Tom Hayden to sponsor legislation that required insurance companies in his state to provide archives documenting their participation in the slave trade to government officials and any citizen who asked. Gov. Gray Davis signed the bill into law two years ago.

The November 2000 issue of Harper's magazine featured a 12-page roundtable discussion of slavery, its aftermath and reparations by some of the nation's most successful black attorneys.

"Every great lawsuit tries to tell a story of injustice in a way that will resonate," Alexander J. Pires Jr. said during the discussion. "There's a lot of work to do here. Slavery's the most unacknowledged story in America's history."

The story started with the first Africans who stepped off ships in Jamestown in the early 1600s and ended with waves of African Americans marching in protest against segregation about 350 years later. In between were the cruelties of subjugation—forced labor, violence, rape, the breaking apart of families. Estimates of the number of black people killed in that era range from 2 million to 30 million.

From forced labor, government and industry both benefited. The foundation of the U.S. Capitol was laid by slaves whose masters were compensated by the federal government for their work. The White House was also built by slaves. Rail companies used slave labor to lay thousands of miles of tracks. Tobacco companies used tobacco picked by slaves, and clothiers benefited from their toil in the cotton field.

Insurance companies compensated slavers for runaways and injured men and women. In some cases, historians said, insurers put prices on the heads of escaped slaves and financed bounty hunters to take them back to an owner even after they fled to states that had abolished the practice.

Then the Emancipation Proclamation ended slavery in some states before the close of the Civil War.

"Think about this," said Willie E. Gary, a Florida attorney known as "the giant killer" for the millions of dollars he's won in court against corporations. "In 1865 the government freed 4 million blacks. Without a dime, with no property, nearly all illiterate, they were let loose to wander. That's what begins the aftermath of slavery."

In the fields of Savannah, Ga., Union Gen. William Tecumseh Sherman issued an order setting aside land in South Carolina, Georgia and Florida for slaves and their descendants. They were allotted 40 acres and an Army mule.

After Lincoln's assassination, however, President Andrew Johnson rescinded the order, and the few former slaves who settled on land had it taken away. They were encouraged to work for their former masters, and many became sharecroppers, borrowers on land they had owned for a few days.

Demands for reparations began even before the war ended, said Verdun, the Ohio State law professor, but former slaves' claims were not given a fair hearing in a world of Jim Crow laws, black codes and lynchings.

Now, however, reparations advocates are focused on the courts again.[2]

Notes and Questions

1. The issue of reparations can be framed as providing a remedy for governmental complicity with slavery, as well as assigning liability to private actors, *viz.*, corporations directly linked to slave labor. Who were the beneficiaries of the slave trade? Do the benefits accrued through hundreds of years of unpaid labor persist today?

---

[2]   The Durban Declaration, a statement of principles resulting from the 2001 U.N. World Conference Against Racism, Racial Discrimination, Xenophobia, and Related Intolerance in South Africa, recognizes slavery and the slave trade as a "crime against humanity": "We acknowledge that slavery and the slave trade, especially the transatlantic slave trade, were appalling tragedies in the history of humanity . . . and further acknowledge that slavery and the slave trade were a crime against humanity and should always have been so, especially the transatlantic slave trade and are among the major sources and manifestations of racism, racial discrimination, xenophobia, and related intolerance." Durban Declaration and World Programme of Action, World Conference against Racism, Racial Discrimination, Xenophobia and Related Intolerance (Sept. 2001), para. 13, *available at* http://www.unhchr.ch/html/racism/02-documents-cnt.html (last visited Apr. 10, 2004).

2.   What is the role of reparations in redressing gross human rights violations? Is the decision to award reparations punitive, retributive or remedial? Is it a moral statement? How do the legal and moral issues related to reparations for slavery compare with reparations for Holocaust survivors, or for the WWII incarceration of people of Japanese descent in the United States?

3.   Assuming reparations for slavery are appropriate, who should receive them? Should compensation be paid to individuals? To all people whose ancestors were slaves? Only to families who can prove specific harm? What about families with slave ancestors from other parts of the Americas? Should they be compensated by the governments of countries from which they emigrated? Should the governments of those African countries in which certain groups or individuals participated in the slave trade pay reparations? Should the former colonial powers pay reparations to their former colonies? Is there another way to conceive of a remedy for hundreds of years of slavery? Is it just "too late?"

SELECTED WEB-BASED RESOURCES ON ECONOMIC, SOCIAL, AND CULTURAL HUMAN RIGHTS

There are now a large number of web-based resources on international human rights in general, and a growing number on economic, social and cultural rights in particular. The following is a selected list of helpful sites for further research.

U.N. Human Rights Bodies

Committee on Economic, Social and Cultural Rights (U.N. body responsible for implementing the International Covenant on Economic, Social and Cultural Rights): http://www.unhchr.ch/html/menu2/6/cescr.htm

Committee on the Elimination of All Forms of Racial Discrimination (CERD) (U.N. body responsible for implementing the International Convention on the Elimination of All Forms of Racial Discrimination): http://www.unhchr.ch/html/menu2/6/cerd.htm

Committee on the Elimination of All Forms of Discrimination Against Women (CEDAW) (U.N. body responsible for implementing the Convention on the Elimination of All Forms of Discrimination Against Women): http://www.un.org/womenwatch/daw/cedaw/index.html

Committee on the Rights of the Child (CRC) (U.N. body responsible for implementing the Convention on the Rights of the Child): http://www.unhchr.ch/html/menu2/6/crc/

U.N. Office of the High Commissioner for Human Rights (central site for U.N.-based human rights activities): http://www.unhchr.ch/hchr_un.htm

Commission on Human Rights (central U.N. body charged with overall promotion and protection of human rights): http://www.unhchr.ch/html/menu2/2/chr.htm

U.N. Specialized Agencies

Several U.N. specialized agencies address broader social, economic, and cultural issues that affect international human rights:

Food and Agricultural Organization (FAO): http://www.fao.org/

International Labour Organization (Rights and status of workers. Administers a variety of labor-related international conventions.): http://www.ilo.org/

U.N. Development Programme, Millennium Development Plan (U.N. initiative, agreed to by 191 nations, to work toward a variety of social and economic goals by the year 2015. Web site includes list of goals and data on progress toward goals): http://www.undp.org/

U.N. Development Programme, Human Develoment Report (annual report on the economic and social status of populations throughout the world): http:// hdr.undp.org/

UNAIDS (information on the Acquired Immune Deficiency Syndrome (AIDS) pandemic): http://www.unaids.org/en/default.asp

U.N. Economic, Scientific and Cultural Organization (UNESCO) (intellectual property and traditional knowledge, exchange of scientific knowledge and technical information, and issues related to violations of cultural rights.): http://www.unesco.org

UNIFEM (resources on the status of women in developing countries): http://www.unifem.org/

World Health Organization (WHO): http://www.who.int/en/

Non-Governmental Organizations

Center for Economic and Social Rights (U.S.-based human rights organization with a specific focus on social welfare rights. Website includes links to many other economic and social welfare rights organizations throughout the world): http://www.cesr.org/PROGRAMS/usprogram.htm

Center for Human Rights Education (U.S.-based human rights organization focused on human rights popular education in the United States): http://www.nchre.org/

Habitat for Humanity International (One of many international NGOs focusing on economic, social, and cultural rights. Organization builds housing for the poor and homeless in more than 90 countries): http://www.habitat.org

International Network for Economic, Social, and Cultural Rights (International activist resource and information-sharing network): http://www.escr-net.org/EngGeneral/home.asp.

Jubilee USA Network: Drop the Debt (NGO network on international debt relief/debt cancellation): http://www.jubileeusa.org/

Physicians for Human Rights (U.S.-based human rights NGO focusing on the right to health and the health implications of other human rights violations throughout the world): http://www.phrusa.org/

Poor Peoples' Economic Human Rights Campaign (U.S.-based NGOs and lawyers advocating for socio-economic and other human rights in the U.S.): http://www.marchforourlives.org/

TransAfrica Forum (NGO that addresses social justice issues in Africa, the Caribbean and other parts of the African Diaspora): http://www.transafricaforum.org/

Amnesty International: http://www.amnesty.org/

Global Justice (formerly International Human Rights Law Group): http://www.hrlaw-group.org/

Human Rights Watch: http://www.hrw.org/

Academic Sites

E-Book (A project of the University of Iowa, Center for International Finance and Development. Electronic text and bibliography on international economic and development issues, including economic and social rights.): http://www.uiowa.edu/ifde-book/ebook/main/main.shtml

David Weissbrodt and Marci Hoffman, *Bibliography for Research on International Human Rights Law* (A comprehensive research resource on international human rights based at the University of Minnesota School of Law library Web page): http://www1.umn.edu/humanrts/bibliog/BIBLIO.htm#N_1_

CHAPTER TWO

THEORETICAL PARADIGMS

A. HISTORICAL ROOTS

This section examines philosophical and political precursors to contemporary discourse on economic, social and cultural rights, from religious appeals to charity to the formalization of international legal instruments. The materials are selected to introduce our investigation of the theoretical debates over rights–based approaches to the fulfillment of basic human needs. Here we encounter themes that will be developed throughout the book: charity vs. justice; autonomy vs. interdependence; universality vs. cultural specificity.

1. Religious Traditions

Most religious traditions encourage believers to provide for the economic and social needs of the poor, the elderly, those who are sick or disabled, and indigent travelers. Commentators note, for example, the "Buddhist belief that one-fourth of one's income should be devoted to *dana,* or religious giving." Donald R. Price & Mark C. Rahdert, *Distributing the First Fruits: Statutory and Constitutional Implications of Tithing in Bankruptcy,* 26 U.C. DAVIS L. REV. 853, at n.142 (1993), *citing* Melford E. Spiro, BUDDHISM AND SOCIETY: A GREAT TRADITION AND ITS BURMESE VICISSITUDES 108–11 (1970). *See generally,* 14 THE ENCYCLOPEDIA OF RELIGION 537–38 (Mircea Eliade ed., 1987). In addition, certain traditions impose obligations on adherents to provide for the economic maintenance of religious representatives and sanctuaries.

What relationship do such traditions bear to contemporary conceptions of economic and social rights? These forms of giving are often characterized as duties that are owed to a Supreme Being, as demonstrations of the righteousness of the believer, or as beneficial for the moral development of the giver, rather than as rights of individuals that could be enforced against the wealthy or the community as a whole. Nevertheless, religious economic and social obligations to provide for the subsistence of the poor can also be viewed as antecedents of contemporary notions of economic and social rights such as the right to an adequate standard of living.

In some African spiritual traditions, such as the Akan of West Africa, reciprocal rights and duties arise from the inherent dignity and interdependency of human beings:

> The Akan conception of a person has both descriptive and normative aspects that are directly relevant not only to the idea that there are human rights but also to the question of what those rights are. In this conception a person is the result of the union of three elements, not necessarily sharply disparate ontologically, though each is different from the other. There is the life prin-

ciple (*okra*), [which] is held to come directly from God. It is supposed to be an actual speck of God that he gives out of himself as a gift of life along with a specific destiny.***

By virtue of possessing an *okra*, a divine element, all persons have an intrinsic value, the same in each, which they do not owe to any earthly circumstance. Associated with this value is a concept of human dignity, which implies that every human being is entitled in an equal measure to a certain basic respect.*** Directly implied in the doctrine of *okra* is the right of each person, as the recipient of a destiny, to pursue that unique destiny assigned to him by God.***

Through the possession of an *okra*, *mogya*, and *sunsum* a person is situated in a network of kinship relations that generate a system of rights and obligations. Because the Akans are matrilineal, the most important kinship group is the lineage ***. Its innermost circle comprises the grandmother, the mother, the mother's siblings, her own children, and the children of her sisters. To this group, with the mother as the principal personage, belongs the duty of nursing an Akan newborn. The Akans have an acute sense of the dependency of a human being. On first appearance in this world, one is totally defenseless and dependent. This is the time when there is the greatest need for the care and protection of others and also, to the Akan mind, the time of the greatest right to that help. But this right never deserts a human being, for one is seen at all times as insufficient unto oneself. The logic of this right may be simply phrased: a genuine human need carries the right to satisfaction. The right to be nursed, then, is the first human right. In the fullness of time it will be transformed dialectically into a duty, the duty to nurse one's mother in her old age. "If your mother nurses you to grow your teeth," says an Akan adage, "you nurse her to lose hers."***

Kwasi Wiredu, *An Akan Perspective on Human Rights*, *in* KWASI WIREDU, CULTURAL UNIVERSALS AND PARTICULARS: AN AFRICAN PERSPECTIVE 158–59 (1996).

Some Western traditions require that a specified portion of wealth or income be remanded to religious institutions as property belonging to a Supreme Being. The monies are used for the maintenance of the religious institutions and for the charitable and social roles that those institutions may play. Such required amounts are sometimes analogized to tax payments. Additional charitable contributions might well be encouraged, but would be considered voluntary. Many religious traditions also recognize the exploitation or oppression of the poor as violating religious law. The following excerpts from Talmudic sources, the Holy Bible, and the Qur'an provide illustrations of such economic and social obligations and duties from Jewish, Christian and Islamic traditions.

Judaism

Talmudic Sources

VaYikra 25:35

When your brother becomes poor and he slips down among you, you must come to his aid [even to] a convert and a [non-Jewish] settler, so that he can live with you.

Temurah 16a

If a poor person approaches a wealthy person and asks him for support, and the wealthier person refuses, then God will make the poor person wealthy and make the wealthy person poor.

Devarim 14:7–8

When any of your brothers is poor in any of your cities, in the land which HaShem your God is giving you, do not harden your heart or shut your hand from your poor brother. You shall open your hand, and you shall lend him whatever he needs, whatever he is lacking.

Eruvin 86a

The world will not be at peace before God until people are generous and provide food for the poor.

Judaism and Christianity

Holy Bible (King James Version)

Leviticus 27:32

And concerning the tithe of the herd, or of the flock, even of whatsoever passeth under the rod, the tenth shall be holy unto the Lord.

Isaiah 10:1

Woe unto them that decree unrighteous decrees, and that write grievousness which they have prescribed;

To turn aside the needy from judgment, and to take away the right from the poor of my people, that widows may be their prey and that they may rob the fatherless!

Isaiah 58:6–8

Is not this the fast that I have chosen? To loose the bands of wickedness, to undo the heavy burdens, and to let the oppressed go free, and that ye break every yoke?

Is it not to deal thy bread to the hungry, and that thou bring the poor that are cast out to thy house?

When thou seest the naked, that thou cover him; and that thou hide not thyself from thine own flesh?

Christianity

Holy Bible (King James Version)

II Corinthians 9:8

Every man according as he purposeth in his heart, so let him give; not grudgingly, or of necessity: for God loveth a cheerful giver.

Islam

The Qur'an

9:60

Charities shall go to the poor, the needy, the workers who collect them, the new converts, to free the slaves, to those burdened by sudden expenses, in the cause of ALLAH, and to the traveling alien. Such is ALLAH's commandment. . . .

7:156

> *My mercy encompasses all things, but I will specify it for the righteous who give Zakat.*

"Tithing" in Jewish (*ma'ser*) and Christian traditions refers to the religious obligation to give a tenth of one's income to religious causes (including maintenance of religious sanctuaries and religious workers). The traditions associated with tithing are complex and sometimes are associated with providing for the poor as well as for explicitly religious purposes. "*Zakat*" refers to a similar obligation under Islamic tradition to give 2.5 percent (approximately) of wealth and income annually to religious causes. At the same time, most religious traditions also require or encourage charitable giving to the poor (*e.g.*, "*Tzedaka*" or "charity" in Judaism, "charity" in Christianity, and "*sadaqa*" in Islam). Religious giving traditions are recognized in the domestic law of some nations, but raise complex issues about the relationship between religious communities and the state:

> In the present day, the [U.S.] Internal Revenue Code provides deductions for charitable givings. Such deductions date back to Roman and pre-Christian times. Charitable giving, or alms, is akin to tithing. Because a portion of the tithe supports social overheads, the tithe may be considered to partially support an activity that the government, or public purse, might otherwise have to support based on taxes. Furthermore, part of the theory underlying the special rights of nonprofit corporations is that these corporations serve a socially useful function which might otherwise fall on the governmental tax base and do not otherwise compete with the profit sector. The Bible, dictionaries, encyclopedias, and comparative religion texts all discuss tithes, alms, and charitable giving. There is also a link between Jewish, Christian, Muslim, and Buddhist practices regarding tithing and charitable giving ***.

Oliver B. Pollak, *"Be Just Before You're Generous": Tithing and Charitable Contributions in Bankruptcy*, 29 CREIGHTON L. REV. 527, 531 (1996).

The following excerpts from an encyclopedia of Jewish traditions summarize both charitable obligations and tithing obligations:

> Charity. The obligation to help the poor and the needy and to give them gifts is stated many times in the Bible and was considered by the rabbis of all ages to be one of the cardinal *mitzvot* of Judaism.
>
> The Bible itself legislates several laws which are in effect a sort of tax for the benefit of the poor. Among these are *leket, shikhhah*, and *pe'ah* as well as the special tithe for the poor (*ma'aser*). The institution of the sabbatical year . . . and Jubilee was in order "that the poor of the people may eat" (Exodus 23:11) as well as to cancel debts (Deuteronomy 15:7–10). The Pentateuch also insists that the needy be remembered when the festivals are celebrated.*** The Bible expects Israel to be aware of the needs of the poor and the stranger (who is considered to be in an inferior economic position) because Israel itself had experienced this situation in Egypt: "Love ye therefore the stranger; for ye were strangers in the land of Egypt" (10: 19) and promises "for this thing the Lord thy God will bless thee in all thy work and in all that thou puttest thy hand unto" (15:10).

5 ENCYCLOPAEDIA JUDAICA 338–39 (1971). *See, e.g.*, ELI M. SHEAR & CHAIM MILLER, THE RICH GO TO HEAVEN: GIVING CHARITY IN JEWISH THOUGHT (1998); JULIE SALAMON, RAMBAM'S LADDER: A MEDITATION ON GENEROSITY AND WHY IT IS NECESSARY TO GIVE (2003); MAASER KESAFIM: ON GIVING A TENTH TO CHARITY (Cyril Domb ed., 1982).

> The rendering of tithes of property for sacral purposes was common all over the Ancient Near East, though well-documented and firsthand evidence concerning tithes comes mainly from Mesopotamia.*** Although these Mesopotamian documents come from the neo-Babylonian period (sixth century B.C.E.) there is no doubt that the institution as such is much older. In the Syro-Palestine area the tithe (*ma'sartu*; cf. Heb. *ma'ser*) is found in Ugarit in the 14th century B.C. E. (Palais royal d'Ugarit, 3 (1955) 147: 9–11). The tithe was not assigned to temples only. As may be learned from I Samuel 8: 15, 17 and from Ugarit *** the tithe could also be a royal tax which the King could exact and give to his officials. This ambiguity of the tithe, as a royal due on the one hand and as a sacred donation on the other, is to be explained by the fact that the temples to which the tithe was assigned were royal temples (cf. esp. Amos 7:13) and, as such, the property and treasures in them were put at the king's disposal.*** As is well known, the kings controlled the treasures of palace and temple alike (I Kings 15:18; II Kings 12: 19; 18:15), which is understandable, since they were responsible for the maintenance of the sanctuary and its service not less than for the service of the court (cf. Ezek. 45:17, etc.). It stands to reason that the tithe, which originally was a religious tribute, came to be channeled to the court, and was therefore supervised by royal authorities.***

15 ENCYCLOPAEDIA JUDAICA 1156–58 (1971).

Raj Bhala has compared charitable giving requirements under Islamic and Catholic/Christian traditions and draws implications for international economic relations between developed and developing countries:

> The Catholic concept of almsgiving has a direct analog in Islamic belief and life. [Bhala notes that charitable giving is one of the Five Pillars of Islam to which faithful Muslims must adhere.] Almsgiving, in the sense of donating money or property to charitable causes, specifically to those in need, is an obligation set forth in the Qur'an.*** In Arabic, alms are referred to as "*zakat*" *** and understood as a "religious tax").

> *** Insofar as both Almsgiving Rules and *zakat* have a compulsory dimension to them, the underlying theological concepts concerning the giving of alms in Catholicism and Islam would seem to be all the closer. Rules in the Almsgiving category do not leave contributions to developing country WTO Members to the discretion of the developed country Members.*** Instead, the "call" of a true Almsgiving Rule is a mandate to help out, and it is the help that has a charitable benefit. Similarly, for *zakat*, religious obligation and charity—in a compulsory sense—are intertwined.

> Those who have much should help lift the burden of those who are less fortunate.*** The Koran introduced *** [this] basic principle in the seventh century by prescribing a graduated tax on the haves to relieve the circumstances of the have-nots.***

In contrast, *sadaqa* can be made at any time as a sign of gratitude to Allah. Typical instances of the optional payment include weddings, anniversaries, and personal milestones (be they happy or sad)—contexts not mandating righteous behavior toward the needy.

Raj Bhala, *Symposium: Globalization and Sovereignty: Theological Categories for Special and Differential Treatment,* 50 KAN. L. REV. 635, 689–91 (2002).

Legal historians differ about the extent to which religious law influenced modern human rights norms. Revisionist historians have examined the role of canon law in the development of Western human rights concepts:

[W]hen and how did natural human rights come to be recognized within the Western legal tradition?

Up until a few years ago, most scholarship on the subject located the origins of natural rights in the eighteenth century, specifically within the thought of the Enlightenment era, although natural rights may have been foreshadowed in the writing of the jurists of the seventeenth century.*** This view is reflected in much of the modern literature on human rights.***

The canon law, which held a significant place in European legal systems prior to the Enlightenment, has *** traditionally been widely regarded as indifferent to the idea of natural human rights. Ensuring that men and women held orthodox beliefs was the preeminent goal of the law of the church, and this goal entailed the exclusion of subjective rights. The church's acceptance of slavery, shared, of course, with the Roman law, is perhaps the most dramatic example of the church's indifference to natural rights. It is commonly said, therefore, that the language of human rights only "entered into philosophical writing in the seventeenth century in the work of Grotius and Locke. It was first invoked in practice by the leaders of the French and American revolutions in the interests of creating a new social and political order."

This traditional view has been challenged during the last twenty years by a strand of revisionist scholarship *** led by Professor Brian Tierney. [This scholarship has] examined the history of human rights and [has] found that the concept of natural rights in fact antedated the Enlightenment. In their view, its true origins are found within the medieval traditions of the *ius commune,* the amalgam of Roman and canon law that governed European legal education up to the time of codification and controlled much of the legal practice in the courts of church and state from the twelfth century to the eighteenth.*** Tierney argued that the idea of natural rights did not enter political life "with a clatter of drums and trumpets *** like the American Declaration of Independence or the French Declaration of the Rights of Man." Instead, "this central concept of Western political theory first grew into existence almost imperceptibly in the obscure glosses of the medieval jurists."***

Broadly speaking *** the medieval jurists did understand and develop the notion that fundamental human rights existed. These rights did not depend upon a grant by the sovereign, and they could be exercised in fact. Further examination does, however, suggest limitations to this view.*** When examined more closely, it becomes clear that the medieval law took a decidedly less individualistic approach to rights than is common today. In medieval law, rights were based upon the tenets of natural and divine law, laws that God himself had created and implanted in men's consciousness. The objective order found in the natural law did include the grant of natural rights. The reason for the existence of those rights, however, was not to vindicate human choice, to promote the sacredness of human life, or to allow men and women to flourish as they chose. It was to vindicate and promote God's plan for the world. This was a purportedly objective way of thinking about rights; it was quite distinct from the subjective approach that is characteristic of modern thought. The distinction between these two approaches had important consequences in fact.

[One] example is the right of the poor to sustenance in time of need. In such circumstances, Professor Tierney concluded, the canonists held that "the poor had a right to be supported from the superfluous wealth of the community." In traditional Christian thought, there was a moral duty, of course, upon all persons to give alms as they were able. Charity held a high place among the virtues. As Tierney has convincingly shown, however, there was more than an endorsement of the merits of charitable giving in the *ius commune*. The canon law took the position that poor men and women could themselves demand to be supported in case of need. It was a matter of *right*. The principle extended even to small children. Even though there was nothing like the modern welfare state in medieval Europe, the *ius commune* did contain a forerunner of modern rights to welfare.***

Closer examination of the canon law does not overturn this argument. It does, however, produce a more complicated picture. Almost every point upon which the argument rests was disputed among the medieval jurists. For example, none of them supported the position that the poor were given a direct action, as we would say, to compel the rich to support them. The poor could not sue the church or the government to secure an adequate standard of living. Some suggested, however, that the poor could reach this result indirectly by making use of the procedure known as *denunciatio evangelica*. This procedure allowed a poor Christian to "denounce" a rich man who refused to share his assets with the poor, and the church would, in turn, compel him to do so by ecclesiastical censure, and as a last resort, by excommunication. The availability of even this procedure was, however, a contentious issue. Some canonists held that giving alms was purely a matter of choice for the people affected. Whatever right the poor might have, it was not one that could be enforced by direct action in public courts. At the very least, under some circumstances, a case for an enforceable right to sustenance might be established under the classical canon law.

Upon what theory did this right rest? Was it an early recognition of the inherent right of each individual to flourish? The reasons given by the medieval jurists do not suggest that it was. They did, of course, mention the biblical precepts in favor of charitable giving. They did denounce avarice. These beliefs, however, could not be the foundation of the rights of the poor. The precepts about giving alms were not obligatory except as to tithes and a few other traditional obligations, none of which was destined for the poor. When commentators on the law of the church spoke about the existence of a right to sustenance per se, they instead rested their discussion upon an argument from natural law, one they shared with the civilians. Before society was organized, the argument ran, all things had been held in common. In times of extreme necessity, that situation recurred. When the worst did happen, the poor could take from that common mass without being guilty of theft. Because they were entitled to a share under natural law, the poor would only be taking what had been theirs anyway, and the breakdown of society's order would have effectively dissolved the societal regime under which the riches of other men had been acquired.***

R.H. Helmholz, *Natural Human Rights: The Perspective of the Ius Commune*, 52 CATH. U.L. REV. 301, 301–06 (2003).

Notes and Questions

1.   Should religious precepts play any role in the contemporary interpretation or implementation of economic and social rights? One article notes that "beyond the Judeo-Christian tradition *** the notion that sharing one's wealth and possessions with others as a component of religious inspiration has a wide, indeed nearly universal, appeal.***" Donald R. Price & Mark C. Rahdert, *Distributing the First Fruits: Statutory and Constitutional Implications of Tithing in Bankruptcy*, 26 U.C. DAVIS L. REV. 853 (1993). Do you agree? If such values have a "nearly universal appeal," why do widespread poverty and large disparities in economic wealth still exist in parts of the world (such as the United States) where religious values are said to be prevalent? Can governments committed to secularism in government (such as the constitutional separation of church and state in the United States) integrate these principles into their rights frameworks? What about societies with large religious minorities such as India? Would the state need to simply pick and choose among religious doctrines?

2.   Do developed countries have a legal obligation to provide aid to developing countries? Why, or why not? If not, do they have a moral obligation to do so? Under what circumstances? What guidelines or conditions, if any, would you impose on the giving of international economic aid? Can, or should international economic aid be considered a form of economic reparation for the devastating effects of slavery and colonialism on many developing countries? *See* Chapter 3, *infra* discussing the movement for slavery reparations in the United States.

3.   What difference does it make, if any, if the poor are said to have a "right" to food or housing or if the wealthy (or the state) can be said to have a "duty" or an "obligation" to provide food or housing to the poor?

2.   *Philosophical and Political Formulations*

JOHN LOCKE, FIRST TREATISE OF GOVERNMENT (1698)

JOHN LOCKE, TWO TREATISES OF GOVERNMENT (Peter Laslett et al., ed., 1988)

42.   But we know God hath not left one Man so to the Mercy of another, that he may starve him if he please; God the Lord and Father of all, has given no one of his Children such a Property, in his peculiar Portion of the things of this World, but that

he has given his needy Brother a Right to the Surplusage of his Goods; so that it cannot justly be denied him, when his pressing Wants call for it. And therefore no Man could ever have a just Power over the Life of another, by Right of property in Land or Possessions; since 'twould always be a Sin in any Man of Estate, to let his Brother perish for want of affording him Relief out of his Plenty. As *Justice* gives every Man a Title to the product of his honest Industry, and the fair Acquisitions of his Ancestors descended to him; so *Charity* gives every Man a Title to so much out of another's Plenty, as will keep him from extream want, where he has no means to subsist otherwise; and a Man can no more justly make use of another's necessity, to force him to become his Vassal, by with-holding that Relief God requires him to afford to the wants of his Brother, than he that has more strength can seize upon a weaker, master him to his Obedience and with a Dagger at his Throat offer him Death or Slavery.

Notes and Questions

1. John Locke (1632–1704) wrote his *First Treatise of Government* (written ca. 1680; published 1690) to refute Sir Robert Filmer's *Patriarcha, or the Natural Power of Kings* (written ca. 1638; published 1680). Locke argued against Filmer's defense of the "divine right of kings," maintaining that the state was a creation of a social contract, an agreement among autonomous, rational individuals, whose purpose was the protection of private property. Locke's First Treatise is viewed by some scholars as laying the theoretical groundwork for the modern welfare state. His better known exposition on property in the Second Treatise is excerpted in Section B, *infra*.

2. Locke argued that all people are born free, and the attempt to enslave any person creates a state of war (as opposed to the state of nature). Ironically, Locke himself had invested in the slave trade and drafted the *Fundamental Constitutions of Carolina* which enshrined slavery into law.

3. Locke's formulation grounds the rights to property and inheritance in justice, while granting the needy a right to "surplusage" based on charity. What is the basis of this distinction? Are justice and charity equally compelling norms?

PHILIP HARVEY, HUMAN RIGHTS AND ECONOMIC POLICY DISCOURSE: TAKING ECONOMIC AND SOCIAL RIGHTS SERIOUSLY

33 COLUM. HUM. RTS. L. REV. 363, 390–401 (2002)

*** *The Moral Legitimacy of Right To Work Claims*

The rights proclaimed in international human rights agreements are not based on a unified theory of human rights. Given the highly political nature of the process that led to their adoption it could hardly be otherwise. As Louis Henkin has noted, "[I]nternational human rights are not the work of philosophers, but of politicians and citizens, and philosophers have only begun to try to build conceptual justifications for them." Nevertheless, philosophical justifications for these rights do exist and their articulation has been an important part of the political process that has led to their formal recognition.

Early advocates of the right to work were strongly influenced by the social contract strain of natural rights theory. The writings of the French utopian theorist Charles

Fourier exemplify this tradition. Fourier argued that in the state of nature everyone had seven natural rights. Four of these—the right to hunt, to fish, to gather food, and to pasture animals—were rights to derive a subsistence from nature's bounty through work carried on in free association with others. It was society's obligation, he maintained to provide its members equivalent opportunities.

> To equal nature's bounty you must give us at least what it gives to the savages and the wild animals, a job which pleases them and to which they have become accustomed during the course of their lives, a job with creatures whose society suits them.

Fourier was well aware of the differences between his discussion of natural rights and that of earlier natural rights theorists. His recognition of the right to work was associated with express denunciations of what he perceived to be the inadequacies of classical liberalism.

> Our social compacts are utterly unable to provide the poor man with a decent level of subsistence consistent with his education. They cannot guarantee him the first of the natural rights, the RIGHT TO WORK!*** Politics *** vaunts the rights of man but fails to guarantee the right and the only useful one, which is the right to work.

The first task of politics, he maintained, was "to find a new social order that insures the poorest members of the working class sufficient well-being to make them constantly and passionately prefer their work to idleness and brigandage to which they now aspire."

Although Fourier's philosophical discussion of the right to work was the most extensive among early advocates of the right, he was not the first to suggest that access to work is a natural right that society has a duty to secure. That claim was advanced during the French Revolution by a number of people representing various tendencies on the left and culminated in its recognition in the revised Declaration of the Rights of Man included in the French Constitution of 1793.

The pre-revolutionary origin of the idea that society has an obligation to provide work to those who need it is unclear. It may lie in much older claims that all persons have a natural or God-given right to a share of the earth in order that they may secure their own existence—the right to existence being the most fundamental of all natural entitlements. In agrarian societies this claim has been the common currency of radical reformers for centuries, perhaps millennia. It was the rallying cry of Winstanley and the diggers in seventeenth century England, of supporters of the so-called 'agrarian law' (a redistribution of the property of the rich among the poor) in eighteenth century France, and of 'land reform' advocates in the Third World today.

In urban societies, the idea that everyone is entitled to enough land to be self-supporting is easily transmuted into the claim that everyone is entitled to enough work to be self-supporting. This obviously is what happened in urban France during the Revolution, since early proponents of the right to work such as Noel "Gracchus" Babeuf were ardent supporters of the "agrarian law" as well. If peasants received land in satisfaction of their natural rights, what should their urban compatriots, the *sans cullotes*, receive? A guarantee of work paying wages capable of supporting a reasonable subsistence seemed the natural equivalent.***

DECLARATION OF THE RIGHTS OF MAN AND CITIZEN: CONSTITUTION OF THE YEAR I (1793)

The Constitution and Other Selected Documents Illustrative of the History of France 1789–1901, 170–74 (Frank Maloy Anderson ed. 1904)
available at http://chnm.gmu.edu/revolution/d/297

The French people, convinced that forgetfulness and contempts of the natural rights of man are the sole causes of the miseries of the world, have resolved to set forth in a solemn declaration these sacred and inalienable rights, in order that all the citizens, being able to compare unceasingly the acts of the government with the aim of every social institution, may never allow themselves to be oppressed and debased by tyranny; and in order that the people may always have before their eyes the foundations of their liberty and their welfare, the magistrate the rule of his duties, the legislator the purpose of his commission.

In consequence, it proclaims in the presence of the supreme being the following declaration of the rights of man and citizen.

1. The aim of society is the common welfare. Government is instituted in order to guarantee to man the enjoyment of his natural and imprescriptible rights.

2. These rights are equality, liberty, security, and property.***

17. No kind of labor, tillage, or commerce can be forbidden to the skill of the citizens.

18. Every man can contract his services and his time, but he cannot sell himself nor be sold: his person is not an alienable property. The law knows of no such thing as the status of servant; there can exist only a contract for services and compensation between the man who works and the one who employs him.***

21. Public relief is a sacred debt. Society owes maintenance to unfortunate citizens, either procuring work for them or in providing the means of existence for those who are unable to labor.

22. Education is needed by all. Society ought to favor with all its power the advancement of the public reason and to put education at the door of every citizen.

23. The social guarantee consists in the action of all to secure to each the enjoyment and the maintenance of his rights: this guarantee rests upon the national sovereignty.***

Notes and Questions

1. How do the formulations of the French Declaration differ from Locke's theory? On what points are they in accord?

2. For further reading on the French Declaration, *see* GEORG JELLINEK, THE DECLARATION OF THE RIGHTS OF MAN AND OF CITIZENS: A CONTRIBUTION TO MODERN CONSTITUTIONAL HISTORY (Max Farrand trans., 1901); G.R. Elton, *Human Rights and the Liberties of Englishmen*, 1990 U. Ill. L. Rev. 329; Ulrich K. Preuss, *Judging and the Holocaust: The Human Rights Legacy: The Force, Frailty, and Future of Human Rights under Globalization*, 1 THEORETICAL INQ. L. 283 (2000).

IMMANUEL KANT, THE DOCTRINE OF VIRTUE

THE METAPHYSICS OF MORALS (1797) (Mary Gregor trans., 1991)

§24. When we are speaking of laws of duty (not laws of nature) and, among these, of laws governing men's external relations with one another, we are considering a moral (intelligible) world where, by analogy with the physical world, *attraction* and *repulsion* bind together rational beings (on earth). The principle of *mutual love* admonishes men constantly to *come nearer* to each other; that of the *respect* which they owe each other, to keep themselves at a *distance* from one another.***

§25. In this context, however, love is not to be taken as a *feeling* (aesthetic love), *i.e.* a pleasure in the perfection of other men; it does not mean *emotional love* (for others cannot oblige us to have feelings). It must rather be taken as a maxim of *benevolence* (practical love), which has beneficence as its consequence.

The same holds true of the *respect* to be shown to others: it is not to be taken merely as the *feeling* that comes from comparing one's own *worth* with another's (such as mere habit causes a child to feel toward his parents, a pupil toward his teacher, a subordinate in general toward his superior). Respect is rather to be taken in a practical sense (*observantia aliis praestanda*), as a *maxim* of limiting our self-esteem by the dignity of humanity in another person.

Moreover, the duty of free respect to others is really only a negative one (of not exalting oneself above others) and is thus analogous to the juridical duty of not encroaching on another's possessions. Hence, although respect is a mere duty of virtue, it is considered *narrow* in comparison with a duty of love, and it is the duty of love that is considered *wide*.

The duty of love for one's neighbour can also be expressed as the duty of making others' *ends* my own (in so far as these ends are only not immoral). The duty of respect for my neighbour is contained in the maxim of not abasing any other man to a mere means to my end (not demanding that the other degrade himself in order to slave for my end).

By the fact that I fulfill a duty of love to someone I obligate the other as well: I make him indebted to me. But in fulfilling a duty of respect I obligate only myself, contain myself within certain limits in order to detract nothing from the worth that the other, as a man, is entitled to posit in himself.

§30. It is every man's duty to be beneficent—that is, to promote, according to his means, the happiness of others who are in need, and this without hope of gaining anything by it.

For every man who finds himself in need wishes to be helped by other men. But if he lets his maxim of not willing to help others in turn when they are in need become public, *i.e.* makes this a universal permissive law, then everyone would likewise deny him assistance when he needs it, or at least would be entitled to. Hence the maxim of self-interest contradicts itself when it is made universal law—that is, it is contrary to duty. Consequently the maxim of common interest—of beneficence toward the needy—is a universal duty of men, and indeed for this reason: that men are to be considered fellow-men—that is, rational beings with needs, united by nature in one dwelling place for the purpose of helping one another.

Casuistical Questions

The ability to practice beneficence, which depends on property, follows largely from the injustice of the government, which favours certain men and so introduces an inequality of wealth that makes others need help. This being the case, does the rich man's help to the needy, on which he so readily prides himself as something meritorious, really deserve to be called beneficence at all?

Notes and Questions

1.   Immanuel Kant (1724–1804) was born in East Prussia the child of a poor saddler; he was raised as a follower of Pietism, a Lutheran revival movement stressing love and good works. Kant viewed reason as the source of human autonomy, arguing that both the laws of nature and the laws of morality are derived from the nature of rational, autonomous beings, and linking human dignity to the status of rational being.

2.   Kant is known for his quest for a single supreme principle of morality, which he called the Categorical Imperative: "Act externally in such a manner that the free exercise of thy will may be able to coexist with the freedom of all others, according to universal law." IMMANUEL KANT, THE PHILOSOPHY OF LAW (1797) (W. Hastie trans., 1887). According to Kant, ethical duties to others include both the prohibition of injuries to the dignity of others as free agents ("duties of respect") and efforts to improve the conditions for others to exercise their own freedom ("duties of love"). His application of his principles led him to criticize such violations as African slavery and the mistreatment of Native Americans. One student of Kant's work has proclaimed that "[o]ur legal discourse is the discourse of rights, and Kant is the first—perhaps the greatest—modern expositor of the concept of right. In this sense, we are all Kant's children." Ernest J. Weinrib, *Law as a Kantian Idea of Reason*, 87 COLUM. L. REV. 472 (1987).

3.   Compare Kant's "benevolence" with Locke's "charity." Are these legal principles, moral principles, or both? Is Kant's duty-based theory analogous to the Akan world-view, or the tenets of Chinese philosophy discussed below?

KWASI WIREDU, AN AKAN PERSPECTIVE ON HUMAN RIGHTS

KWASI WIREDU, CULTURAL UNIVERSALS AND PARTICULARS 159–60 (1996)

[I]n the Akan perception of things, people have [rights] simply because they are human beings. They are entitlements entailed by the intrinsic sociality of the human status. In viewing a human being in this light, the Akans perhaps went beyond Aristotle's maxim that human beings are political animals. To the Akans, a human being is already social at conception, for the union of the blood principle and the personality principle already defines a social identity. A person is social in a further sense. The social identity just alluded to is a kinship identity. But people live, move, and have their being in an environment that includes persons outside the kin group. They live in a town or city and they have to relate to that environment in definite ways. A well-known Akan maxim asserts that when a human being descends upon the earth from above, s/he lands in a town. Membership in town and state brings with it a wider set of rights and obligations embracing the whole race of humankind, for the possession of the *okra*, the speck of God in man, is taken to link all human beings together in one universal family. The immediate concerns here, however, are with the rights of persons in the context of Akan society. In that society an individual's status as a person is predicated on the fulfillment of certain roles that have a reference to circles of relationships transcending the kin group. There is an ambiguity here in the use of the word *person*, the resolution of which will bring us to the normative conception of a person.

In one sense the Akan word *onipa* translates into the English word *person* in the sense of a human being ***. In this sense everyone is born a person, an *onipa*. This is the descriptive sense of the word. But there is a further sense of the word *onipa* in which to call an individual a person is to commend him; it implies the recognition that s/he has attained a certain status in the community. Specifically, it implies that s/he has demonstrated an ability through hard work and sober thinking to sustain a household and make contributions to the communal welfare. In traditional Akan society, public works were always done through communal labor. Moreover, the defense of the state against external attack was the responsibility of all. Good contributions toward these ends stamped an individual in the community as an *onipa*. Inversely, consistent default distanced him from that title. In this sense, personhood is not something you are born with but something you may achieve, and it is subject to degrees, so that some are more *onipa* than others, depending on the degree of fulfillment of one's obligations to self, household, and community.

On the face of it, the normative layer in the Akan concept of person brings only obligations to the individual. In fact, however, these obligations are matched by a whole series of rights that accrue to the individual simply because s/he lives in a society in which everyone has those obligations. It is useful in this regard to recall the fact, noted earlier, that the Akans viewed a human being as essentially dependent. From this point of view, human society is seen as a necessary framework for mutual aid for survival and, beyond that, for the attainment of reasonable levels of well-being. A number of Akan sayings testify to this conception, which is at the root of Akan communalism. One is to the effect that a human being is not a palm tree so as to be sufficient unto himself. (The Akans were highly impressed by the number of things that could be got from a palm tree, not the least memorable among them being palm nut soup and palm wine.) A second saying points out that to be human is to be in need of help. Literally it says simply, "a human being needs help" (*onipa hia moa*). The Akan verb *hia* means "is in need of." In this context it also has the connotation of desert, so that the maxim may also be interpreted as asserting that a human being, simply because he is a human being, is entitled to help from others. A further saying explains that it is because of the need to have someone blow out the speck of dust in one's eye that antelopes go in twos. This saying obviously puts forward mutual aid as the rationale of society.

Although the rights deriving from the general human entitlement to the help of their kind did not have the backing of state sanctions, they were deeply enough felt in Akan society. In consequence, such rights may be said to have enjoyed the strong backing of public opinion, which in communalistic societies cannot be taken lightly.***

Notes and Questions

1. Professor Jeanne Woods observes that "[t]he Akan do not share the philosophical premise of the Lockean model; therefore, they view interdependence, not autonomy, as the essential characteristic of the human condition.*** [T]hey identify the jurisprudential source of rights not in the human capacity for reason, but in that very interde-

pendence." Jeanne M. Woods, *Rights as Slogans: A Theory of Human Rights Based on African Humanism*, 17 NAT'L BLACK L.J. 52, 56–57 (2003). What are the implications of such a worldview for human rights discourse?

2.   Woods posits an alternative human rights paradigm based on African humanism, which she defines as "the predominant philosophical outlook and way of life of traditional African societies." *Id.* at 53. She argues that

> [t]he conceptual constructs of African humanism contrast sharply with those of liberal discourse. Contemporary discourse posits rigid theoretical dichotomies (*e.g.*, public sphere vs. private sphere; positive rights vs. negative rights; moral duties vs. legal duties, etc.) that separate compatible ideas into contradictory and mutually exclusive categories, thereby narrowing the jurisprudential space in which rights can evolve. For example, only "negative" rights are assumed to be justiciable, hence truly rights, while "positive" rights are deemed mere aspirations. On the other hand *** African humanism affords a more harmonious interaction among the various dimensions of the legal, political, and social realms.
>
> *** [C]ontinuity and interconnectedness add depth and dimension to the construction of rights. There is a unity between the political person and the social person. Just as there is no contradiction in African ontology between the spiritual and material worlds, the public sphere and private sphere are not artificially distinguished. Instead, implicit in African humanism is the recognition that "the practices comprising the private sphere of life—the world of business, education, culture, the community, and the family—are inextricably linked to and at least partially constituted by politics and law," hence not preordained or immutable. This African worldview premised on inclusiveness, "places the individual within a continuum of the dead, the living, and the yet unborn."

Id. at 55–56. How might a theory of human rights based on African humanism inform the dominant discourse?

3.   For further reading on the philosophy of African humanism, *see* RICHARD H. BELL, UNDERSTANDING AFRICAN PHILOSOPHY: A CROSS-CULTURAL APPROACH TO CLASSICAL AND CONTEMPORARY ISSUES (2002); PAULIN J. HOUNTONDJ, AFRICAN PHILOSOPHY: MYTH AND REALITY (AFRICAN SYSTEMS OF THOUGHT) (2d ed. 1996); JAMES OGUDE, ED., ES'KIA: ES'KIA MPHAHLELE ON EDUCATION, AFRICAN HUMANISM AND CULTURE, SOCIAL CONSCIOUSNESS, LITERARY APPRECIATION (2003); V.Y. MUDIMBE, THE INVENTION OF AFRICA: GNOSIS, PHILOSOPHY AND THE ORDER OF KNOWLEDGE (AFRICAN SYSTEMS OF THOUGHT) (1988); PAUL A. MWAIPAYA, AFRICAN HUMANISM AND NATIONAL DEVELOPMENT: A CRITICAL ANALYSIS OF THE FUNDAMENTAL THEORETICAL PRINCIPLE OF ZAMBIAN HUMANISM (1981); JACQUES MAQUET, AFRICANITY (Joan Rayfield trans., 1972); KENNETH KAUNDA, A HUMANIST IN AFRICA (1966); Makau wa Mutua, *The Banjul Charter and the African Cultural Fingerprint: An Evaluation of the Language of Duties*, 35 VA. J. INT'L L. 339 (1995); Richard N. Kiwanuka, *Note: The Meaning of "People" in the African Charter on Human and Peoples' Rights*, 82 AM. J. INT'L L. 80 (1988); Riane Eisler, *Human Rights: Toward an Integrated Theory for Action*, 9 HUM. RTS. Q. 287 (1987); U.O. Umozurike, *Current Development: The African Charter on Human and Peoples' Rights*, 77 AM J. INT'L L. 902 (1983).

MARGARET Y.K. WOO, BIOLOGY AND EQUALITY: CHALLENGE FOR FEMINISM IN THE SOCIALIST AND THE LIBERAL STATE

42 EMORY L.J. 143, 177–78, 181–84 (1993)

*** Traditional Chinese attitudes toward the law have always fluctuated between two schools of legal thought—the Legalist School and the Confucian School. While the Legalists advocated a system of written law that relied on government enforcement, the Confucian school emphasized compliance through the internalization of li (rules of conduct), which embodied accepted values and norms. The Legalist School rose to prominence with the unification of China into the Qin Empire around the third century B.C., but Confucianism did not vanish completely. Confucianism reigned in the private sphere while the Legalist's formal law reigned in the public sphere. Even in the public sphere, however, Confucian values infiltrated and were codified into law, through a process known as the "Confucianization of law."

The Confucian definition of the self was primarily contextual, dependent on one's relationship to another. Similarly, male and female, as Confucian concepts, "always appeared as part of something else, defined not by essence but by context, marked by interdependency and reciprocal obligation rather than by autonomy and contradiction." Confucian values projected all social life as a series of relationships (lun), with the five prominent luns being father to son, monarch to subject, husband to wife, older to younger brother, and older to younger friend.

Chinese social theory thus contrasts with liberal Western notions that communities are composed of autonomous individuals who act out of self-interest, and that the desires of individuals inevitably clash with the needs of society. In the Confucian view, each person is defined by his or her experience as a person, but more importantly, as a member of his or her family and a broader community group.***

The socialist conception of rights and laws also emphasizes the imposition of duties on the individual citizen. In this view, law is designed not simply to protect individual interests, but rather to enable the individual to meet his or her duties to the state.*** The imposition of reciprocal duties, however, also means that the individual in Chinese society receives certain protections.

In contrast to the United States Constitution, the rights guaranteed by the Chinese Constitution concern the state's responsibility to liberate the working class. China's Constitution, like most socialist constitutions, contains a litany of positive social and economic rights guarantees. In contrast, the United States Constitution guarantees individual inalienable rights that the state cannot easily override. Thus, the essential freedom preserved by the United States Constitution is freedom from governmental impingement of the rights of individuals. As Louis Henkin explained, "Rights theory, in the United States, supports rights deriving from, and vindicating, individual freedom and autonomy, but not claims upon society to do for the individual what he cannot do for himself. It tells the government only what not to do, not what it must do." The "negative rights" tradition stands in stark contrast to the concept of "positive rights" where one is entitled to specific benefits of those rights.***

The socialist conception of collective rights is also quite different from the familiar notions of individual rights in the United States. The legal philosophy of the People's

Republic of China defines law as the state's will and rights as the state's creation. Rights may be expanded and contracted at will by the state based on the needs of the collective. Under this view of law and rights, the Chinese people have true freedom because their laws represent the will of the proletariat, as represented by the Chinese Communist Party. In contrast, captalist laws reflect only the will of the ruling class—the owners of production.***

This concept of rights is based on a combination of the traditional Confucian ethic of selflessness as well as the Marxist concept of law as an instrument of the ruling class. The Confucian ethic emphasized private interests as belonging to a group such as a family, lineage, or community. Similarly, "Chinese Marxism accepts the legitimacy of individual interests, but only in a limited sense, it argues that this interest both is, and should be, subordinated to the higher interests of party, class and nation." Hence, Mao wrote, "The individual is an element of the collective. When collective interests are increased, personal interests will subsequently be improved."***

Notes and Questions

1. The teachings of Confucius are embodied in brief narratives, or Analects. Consider the implications of the following Analects for economic, social and cultural rights and duties:

> A disciple said, "If one can be generous to people and can help the masses, how would that be? Could it be called humaneness?" Confucius said, "One would not only be humane; one would surely be a sage. Even [the legendary wise kings] Yao and Shun had trouble doing this." (6:30)
>
> A disciple asked Confucius about government. Confucius said, "See to it that there is enough food, enough arms, and the trust of the people in the government." The disciple asked, "If one of these unavoidably had to be omitted, which of the three would be first?" Confucius said, "Omit arms." The disciple asked, "If one of the remaining two unavoidably had to be omitted, which would go first?" Confucius said, "Omit food. Since ancient times people have died, but nothing can be established without the trust of the people." (12:7)
>
> Confucius said, "If people are not humane, what is the use of rites? If people are not humane, what is the use of music?" (3:3)

THE ESSENTIAL CONFUCIUS: THE HEART OF CONFUCIUS' TEACHINGS IN AUTHENTIC I CHING ORDER (Thomas Cleary Trans., 1992).

2. For further reading on Confucianism and human rights, *see* STEPHEN C. ANGLE, HUMAN RIGHTS AND CHINESE THOUGHT: A CROSS-CULTURAL INQUIRY (2002); JOANNE R. & DANIEL A. BELL EDS., THE EAST ASIAN CHALLENGE FOR HUMAN RIGHTS (1999); WM. THEODORE DE BARY, ASIAN VALUES AND HUMAN RIGHTS: A CONFUCIAN COMMUNITARIAN PERSPECTIVE (1998); PETER VAN NESS ED., DEBATING HUMAN RIGHTS: CRITICAL ESSAYS FROM THE UNITED STATES AND ASIA (1999); ROBERT WEATHERLEY, THE DISCOURSE OF HUMAN RIGHTS IN CHINA: HISTORICAL AND IDEOLOGICAL PERSPECTIVES (1999); Roger T. Ames, *Rites as Rights: The Confucian Alternative, in* LEROY S. ROUNER, HUMAN RIGHTS AND THE WORLD'S RELIGIONS 199–216 (1988); Chu, Ron Guey, *Rites and Rights in Ming China, in* WM. THEODORE DEBARY, & TU WEI-MING EDS., CONFUCIANISM AND HUMAN RIGHTS 169–78 (1998); William Theodore DeBary, *Neo-Confucianism and Human Rights, in* LEROY S. ROUNER ED., HUMAN RIGHTS AND THE WORLD'S RELIGIONS 183–98 (1988);

Chaihark Hahm, *Law, Culture, and the Politics of Confucianism*, 16 COLUM. J. ASIAN L. 253 (2003); Harriet Samuels, *Hong Kong on Women, Asian Values, and the Law*, 21 HUM. RTS. Q. 707 (1999).

THOMAS PAINE, AGRARIAN JUSTICE (1797)

THOMAS PAINE, COLLECTED WRITINGS, at 396–411 (Eric Foner ed., 1995)

To preserve the benefits of what is called civilized life, and to remedy, at the same time, the evils it has produced, ought to be considered as one of the first objects of reformed legislation.

Whether the state that is proudly, perhaps erroneously, called civilization, has most promoted or most injured the general happiness of man, is a question that may be strongly contested. On one side, the spectator is dazzled by splendid appearances; on the other he is shocked by extremes of wretchedness; both of which he has erected. The most affluent and the most miserable of the human race are to be found in the countries that are called civilized.

To understand what the state of society ought to be, it is necessary to have some idea of the natural and primitive state of man; such as it is at this day among the Indians of North America. There is not, in that state, any of those spectacles of human misery which poverty and want present to our eyes, in all the towns and streets of Europe. Poverty, therefore, is a thing created by that which is called civilized life. It exists not in the natural state. On the other hand, the natural state is without those advantages which flow from Agriculture, Arts, Science, and Manufactures.

The life of an Indian is a continual holiday, compared with the poor of Europe; and, on the other hand, it appears to be abject when compared to the rich; Civilization, therefore, or that which is so called, has operated two ways, to make one part of society more affluent, and the other part more wretched, than would have been the lot of either in a natural state.***

It is a position not to be controverted, that the earth, in its natural uncultivated state, was, and ever would have continued to be, the COMMON PROPERTY OF THE HUMAN RACE. In that state every man would have been born to property. He would have been a joint life-proprietor with the rest in the property of the soil, and in all its natural productions, vegetable and animal.

But the earth, in its natural state *** is capable of supporting but a small number of inhabitants compared with what it is capable of doing in a cultivated state. And as it is impossible to separate the improvement made by cultivation, from the earth itself, upon which that improvement is made, the idea of landed property arose from that inseparable connection; but it is nevertheless true, that it is the value of the improvement only, and not the earth itself, that is individual property. Every proprietor therefore of cultivated land, owes to the community a *ground-rent*; for I know no better term to express the idea by, for the land which he holds; and it is from this ground-rent that the fund proposed in this plan is to issue.***

There could be no such thing as landed property originally. Man did not make the earth, and, though he had a natural right to *occupy* it, he had no right to *locate* as *his* *property* in perpetuity any part of it; neither did the Creator of the earth open a land-office, from whence the first title-deeds should issue. From whence then arose the idea of landed property? I answer as before, that when cultivation began, the idea of landed property began with it, from the impossibility of separating the improvement made by cultivation from the earth itself upon which that improvement was made. The value of the improvement so far exceeded the value of the natural earth, at that time, as to absorb it; till, in the end, the common right of all became confounded into the culti-vated right of the individual. But they are nevertheless distinct species of rights, and will continue to be so as long as the earth endures.***

Cultivation is, at least, one of the greatest natural improvements ever made by human invention. It has given to created earth a tenfold value; But the landed monop-oly, that began with it, has produced the greatest evil. It has dispossessed more than half the inhabitants of every nation of their natural inheritance, without providing for them, as ought to have been done, as an indemnification for that loss, and has thereby cre-ated a species of poverty and wretchedness, that did not exist before.

In advocating the case of the persons thus dispossessed, it is a right and not a char-ity that I am pleading for.***

Having thus, in a few words, opened the merits of the case, I proceed to the plan I have to propose, which is,

To create a National Fund, out of which there shall be paid to every person, when arrived at the age of twenty-one years, the sum of Fifteen Pounds sterling; *as a compensation in part for the loss of his or her natural inheritance by the introduction of the system of landed property.*

AND ALSO,

The sum of Ten Pounds per annum, *during life, to every person now living of the age of fifty years, and to all others as they shall arrive at that age.*

MEANS BY WHICH THE FUND IS TO BE CREATED. ***

It is proposed that the payments, as already stated, be made to every person, rich or poor. It is best to make it so, to prevent invidious distinctions. It is also right it should be so, because it is in lieu of the natural inheritance, which, as a right, belongs to every man, over and above the property he may have created or inherited from those who did. Such persons as do not chuse to receive it, can throw it into the common fund.

Taking it then for granted, that no person ought to be in a worse condition when born under what is called a state of civilization, than he would have been, had he been born in a state of nature, and that civilization ought to have made, and ought still to make, provision for that purpose, it can only be done by subtracting from property a portion equal in value to the natural inheritance it has absorbed.

Various methods may be proposed for this purpose, but that which appears to be the best,*** is, at the moment that property is passing by the death of one person to the possession of another. In this case, the bequeather gives nothing; the receiver pays nothing. The only matter to him is, that the monopoly of natural inheritance, to which there never was a right, begins to cease in his person. A generous man would not wish it to continue, and a just man will rejoice to see it abolished.***

It is not charity but a right—not bounty but justice, that I am pleading for.*** The contrast of affluence and wretchedness continually meeting and offending the eye, is like dead and living bodies chained together. Though I care as little about riches as any man, I am a friend to riches because they are capable of good. I care not how affluent some may be, provided that none be miserable in consequence of it. But it is impossible to enjoy affluence with the felicity it is capable of being enjoyed, whilst so much misery is mingled in the scene.***

There are in every country some magnificent charities established by individuals. It is however but little that any individual can do when the whole extent of the misery to be relieved be considered. He may satisfy his conscience, but not his heart. He may give all that he has, and that all will relieve but little. It is only by organizing civilization upon such principles as to act like a system of pullies, that the whole weight of misery can be removed.***

[I]t is justice and not charity, that is the principle of the plan. In all great cases it is necessary to have a principle more universally active than charity; and with respect to justice, it ought not to be left to the choice of detached individuals, whether they will do justice or not.***

A plan upon this principle would benefit the revolution by the energy that springs from the consciousness of justice. It would multiply also the national resources; for property, like vegetation, increases by off-sets. When a young couple begins the world, the difference is exceedingly great whether they begin with nothing or with fifteen pounds apiece. With this aid they could buy a cow, and implements to cultivate a few acres of land; and instead of becoming burdens upon society, which is always the case, where children are produced faster than they can be fed, would be put in the way of becoming useful and profitable citizens.***

I have made the calculations, stated in this plan, upon what is called personal, as well as upon landed property. The reason for making it upon land is already explained; and the reason for taking personal property into the calculation, is equally well founded, though on a different principle. Land, as before said, is the free gift of the Creator in common to the human race. Personal property is the *effect of Society*; and it is as impossible for an individual to acquire personal property without the aid of Society, as it is for him to make land originally. Separate an individual from society, and give him an island or a continent, to possess, and he cannot acquire personal property. He cannot become rich. So inseparably are the means connected with the end, in all cases, that where the former do not exist, the latter cannot be obtained. All accumulation therefore of personal property, beyond what a man's own hands produce is derived to him by living in society; and he owes, on every principle of justice, of gratitude, and of civilization, a part of that accumulation back again to society from whence the whole came. This is putting the matter on a general principle, and perhaps it is best to do so; for if we examine the case minutely, it will be found, that the accumulation of personal property is, in many instances, the effect of paying too little for the labor that produced it the consequence of which is, that the working hand perishes in old age, and the employer abounds in affluence.***

The superstitious awe, the enslaving reverence, that formerly surrounded affluence, is passing away in all countries, and leaving the possessor of property to the convulsion of accidents. When wealth and splendour, instead of fascinating the multitude, excite emotions of disgust; when, instead of drawing forth admiration, it is beheld as an insult upon wretchedness: when the ostentatious appearance it makes serves to call the right of it in question, the case of property becomes critical, and it is only in a system of justice that the possessor can contemplate security.

To remove the danger, it is necessary to remove the antipathies, and this can only be done by making property productive of a national blessing, extending to every individual. When the riches of one man above another shall increase the national fund in the same proportion; when it shall be seen that the prosperity of that fund depends on the prosperity of individuals; when the more riches a man acquires, the better it shall be for the general mass; it is then that antipathies will cease and property be placed on the permanent basis of national interest and protection.***

Notes and Questions

1. Born in England in 1737, Thomas Paine was a poor, largely self-educated artisan when he immigrated to America in 1774. On January 10, 1776, he published his 50-page polemic, *Common Sense*, which sold 500,000 copies and almost overnight turned the country towards revolution. In this pamphlet and 16 essays on *The Crisis* (1776–83) written while serving as a soldier in the Continental Army, Paine advanced Locke's democratic ideas in pursuit of the goals of the American revolutionaries, in a style that spoke to the common man and woman. *Common Sense* convinced many Americans, including George Washington, to seek redress in political independence from Britain, and was instrumental in bringing about the Declaration of Independence. Paine also has the distinction of being the man who proposed the name *United States of America.*

2. *Agrarian Justice* was written in the winter of 1795–1796 in response to the Bishop of Llandaff's sermon praising the division between rich and poor as a sign of God's wisdom. Paine made the case for taking the revolution beyond liberal democracy to redistributive economic justice. Contemporary liberal scholars Bruce Ackerman and Anne Alstott have seized upon Paine's ideas to propose reforms of American capitalism based on "stakeholding." *See* BRUCE ACKERMAN & ANNE ALSTOTT, THE STAKEHOLDING SOCIETY (1999).

3. Unlike many of his contemporaries, Paine was a true democrat; many historians regard him as the country's first abolitionist. In an article for *The Pennsylvania Journal* published on March 8, 1775, Paine denounced slavery, leading to the formation of the first American anti-slavery society a month later in Philadelphia. Paine was also the drafter and signer of the March, 1780 Act of Pennsylvania, which made Pennsylvania the first state to abolish slavery. His first recorded writing was a short article in favor of better salaries and working conditions.

4. Compare Paine's vision of distributive justice with that of Locke's First Treatise. How do their concepts of rights differ? Does Paine have a social contract theory? If so, how would you describe it?

5. *Social Movements in the Nineteenth and Early 20th Centuries in Britain and the United States.* The 19th and early 20th centuries saw the flourishing of popular social movements in both Britain and the United States. Some, such as the Fabian socialist movement, were aimed at improving the condition of the poor as well as wages and working conditions for laborers. Abolitionists took direct action by supporting the "Underground Railroad" (a system of transporting and harboring escaped slaves) and lectured against

slavery and the slave trade. Suffragists fought for the rights of women to vote, to own property and to participate in public life. News of atrocities in the Belgian Congo and elsewhere led to anti-colonialist movements. Temperance and other religious movements organized to achieve a variety of religious and moral goals such as imposing a prohibition on alcohol. *See, e.g.,* FREDERICK DOUGLASS, MY BONDAGE AND MY FREEDOM (John David Smith Ed., 2003); BLACK WOMEN IN AMERICA: AN HISTORICAL ENCYCLOPEDIA (2 VOLUMES) (Darlene Clark Hine, et al. eds., 1994); ADAM HOCHSCHILD, KING LEOPOLD'S GHOST (1999); PAMPHLETS OF PROTEST: AN ANTHOLOGY OF EARLY AFRICAN-AMERICAN PROTEST LITERATURE, 1790–1860 (Richard Newman et al. eds. 2000); MICHAEL J.D. ROBERTS, MAKING ENGLISH MORALS: VOLUNTARY ASSOCIATION AND MORAL REFORM IN NINE-TEENTH-CENTURY ENGLAND (CAMBRIDGE SOCIAL AND CULTURAL HISTORIES, 2) (2004); ANN RUSSO & CHERIS KRAMARAE, THE RADICAL WOMEN'S PRESS OF THE 1850s (WOMEN'S SOURCE LIBRARY, V. 2) (2001); GEORGE BERNARD SHAW, FABIAN ESSAYS IN SOCIALISM (Peter Smith pub., 1981); ROSALYN TERBORG-PENN, AFRICAN AMERICAN WOMEN IN THE STRUGGLE FOR THE VOTE, 1850–1920 (1998); JoEllen Lind, *Dominance and Democracy: The Legacy of Woman Suffrage for the Voting Right,* 5 UCLA WOMEN'S L.J. 103 (FALL 1994); Edward L. Rubin, *Symposium: Social Movements and Law Reform: Passing Through the Door: Social Movement Literature and Legal Scholarship,* 150 U. PA. L. REV. 1 (2001).

PAPAL ENCYCLICALS

The papal social encyclicals embody formal statements of Catholic doctrine on social issues. The first such encyclical, issued in 1891, was a polemical response to the growing influence of socialist thought, and the perceived need to put forward a theistic theory of justice that proposed alternative solutions to the urgent social question of the day: the desperate condition of the working class. In the face of the socialist challenge to the existing order that envisioned a better life for all here on Earth, Pope Leo XIII issued *Rerum Novarum,* a vigorous defense of private property and a plea for better treatment of workers.

In the 1891 encyclical, Leo XIII decried the socialist notions of "class war" and the proposition that it is possible to eradicate human suffering. He tempered the socialist critique of capitalism and private property with calls for the modern state to assume certain responsibilities with respect to the needs of working men and women, calling upon states to recognize their duty to guarantee the right to work; the right to associate and to form unions; limitations on hours of work; a living wage; and distributive justice.

RERUM NOVARUM

Pope Leo XIII identified the cause of growing poverty as the greed of employers:

[T]he hiring of labor and the conduct of trade are concentrated in the hands of comparatively few; so that a small number of very rich men have been able to lay upon the teeming masses of the laboring poor a yoke little better than that of slavery itself.

RICHARD W. ROUSSEAU, S.J., HUMAN DIGNITY AND THE COMMON ROAD 26 (2002).

He criticized the socialist response to this problem and defended the institution of private property as one of the most important differences between man and beast:

> [Because] man alone among the animal creation is endowed with reason— it must be within his right to possess things not merely for temporary and momentary use, as other living things do, but to have and to hold them in stable and permanent possession.***

Id. at 27.

> Hence, man not only should possess the fruits of the earth, but also the very soil, inasmuch as from the produce of the earth he has to lay by provision for the future.

Id. at 28.

Having thus disposed of the argument for property redistribution, Pope Leo XIII turned to the role of the state in social matters. Among its responsibilities is the duty to treat all citizens as equal:

> It would be irrational to neglect one portion of the citizens and favor another, and therefore the public administration must duly and solicitously provide for the welfare and the comfort of the working classes; otherwise, that law of justice will be violated which ordains that each man shall have his due.

Id. at 39.

Within the sanctity of life, Pope Leo XIII found a natural right to work and to provide for oneself:

> The preservation of life is the bounden duty of one and all, and to be wanting therein is a crime. It necessarily follows that each one has a natural right to procure what is required in order to live, and the poor can procure that in no other way than by what they can earn through their work.

Id.

Justice further requires the state to keep watch over its laborers to ensure that they receive benefits from their work and that they are being

> housed, clothed, and bodily fit, [so that] they may find their life less hard and more endurable. It follows that whatever shall appear to prove conducive to the well-being of those who work should obtain favorable consideration.

Id.

Included in these labor rights is the right to limited working hours, rest, and the right of women and children to be treated differently in the kind and length of work.

To protect these rights Pope Leo XIII urged the formation of labor unions, defending the right to associate as a basic human right rooted in the natural "consciousness [of man] of his own weakness." *Id.* at 46.

CENTESIMUS ANNUS

On the 100th anniversary of *Rerum Novarum*, Pope John Paul II issued *Centesimus Annus*, an encyclical inspired in part by the apparent fall of socialism at the end of the Cold War. In reviewing the groundbreaking document that signaled the entry of the Church into social justice discourse, he elaborated on the twin themes of the parent document, of the interrelationship between work and private property.

Centesimus Annus extolled the contribution of *Rerum Novarum* toward defining human rights in the 20th century. Pope John Paul II noted that many of the ills addressed by Leo XIII still plague the world's toiling masses. Leo XIII had called for a workman's wages to be sufficient so as to allow him to take care of his family. John Paul II wrote that even today,

> one finds instances of contracts between employers and employees which lack reference to the most elementary justice regarding the employment of children or women, working hours, the hygienic condition of the workplace and fair pay; and this is the case despite international declarations and conventions on the subject and the internal laws of the states.

Id. at 465.

He warns that the free market system can reduce mankind to an economic creature ignoring spirituality and turning man into a mere consumer. Equating poverty with "hindrances to private ownership," John Paul II opined that the persistence of poverty calls for "deeper analysis."

Notes and Questions

1. Challenges to the Catholic Church hierarchy's flawed implementation of social policy arose among the clergy in Latin America in the 1960s, in response to the growing marginalization of the poor, indigenous peoples, blacks and mestizos. The following excerpt by Gustavo Gutiérrez, a leader of the movement known as "liberation theology," summarizes its principles:

> To speak about a theology of liberation is to seek an answer to the following question: what relation is there between salvation and the historical process of the liberation of man?***

> The "social problem" or the "social question" has been discussed in Christian circles for a long time, but it is only in the last few years that people have become clearly aware of the scope of misery and especially of the oppressive and alienating circumstances in which the great majority of mankind exists. This state of affairs is offensive to man and therefore to God. Moreover, today people are more deeply aware both of personal responsibility in this situation and the obstacles these conditions present to the complete fulfillment of all men, exploiters and exploited alike.

> People are also more keenly and painfully aware that a large part of the Church is one way or another linked to those who wield economic and political power in today's world. This applies to its position in the opulent and oppressive countries as well as in the poor countries, as in Latin America, where it is tied to the exploiting classes.

Under these circumstances, can it honestly be said that the Church does not interfere in "the temporal sphere"? Is the Church fulfilling a purely religious role when by its silence or friendly relationships it lends legitimacy to a dictatorial and oppressive government? We discover, then, that the policy of non-intervention in political affairs holds for certain actions which involve ecclesiastical authorities, but not for others. In other words, this principle is not applied when it is a question of maintaining the status quo, but it is wielded when, for example, a lay apostolic movement or a group of priests holds an attitude considered subversive to the established order.*** The dominant groups, who have always used the Church to defend their interests and maintain their privileged position, today—as they see "subversive" tendencies gaining ground in the heart of the Christian community—call for a return to the purely religious and spiritual function of the Church.***

[I]n the face of the immense misery and injustice, ought not the Church—especially in those areas such as Latin America where it has great social influence—intervene more and abandon the field of lyrical pronouncements?***

GUSTAVO GUTIERREZ, A THEOLOGY OF LIBERATION 45, 64–66 (1973).

2. Does liberation theology differ in its approach to social questions from the papal encyclicals? If so, how? Is one approach more suitable to a rights framework than the other?

International human rights have as their antecedents the humanitarian laws of war. *The Paquete Habana*, often cited for its unequivocal pronouncement that international customary law is law of the United States, is also a landmark decision of international humanitarian law. We consider it here for its protection of a key economic right: the right to livelihood.

THE PAQUETE HABANA

175 U.S. 677, 677–79, 686–91, 696–701, 707–08 (1900)

Mr. Justice Gray delivered the opinion of the court:

These are two appeals from decrees of the district court of the United States for the southern district of Florida condemning two fishing vessels and their cargoes as prize of war.

Each vessel was a fishing smack, running in and out of Havana, and regularly engaged in fishing on the coast of Cuba; sailed under the Spanish flag; was owned by a Spanish subject of Cuban birth, living in the city of Havana; was commanded by a subject of Spain, also residing in Havana; and her master and crew had no interest in the vessel, but were entitled to shares, amounting in all to two thirds, of her catch, the other third belonging to her owner. Her cargo consisted of fresh fish, caught by her crew from the sea, put on board as they were caught, and kept and sold alive. Until stopped by the blockading squadron she had no knowledge of the existence of the war or of any blockade. She had no arms or ammunition on board, and made no attempt to run the blockade after she knew of its existence, nor any resistance at the time of the capture.

The Paquete Habana *** had a crew of three Cubans, including the master, who had a fishing license from the Spanish government, and no other commission or license. She left Havana March 25, 1898; sailed along the coast of Cuba to Cape San Antonio, at the western end of the island, and there fished for twenty-five days *** within the territorial waters of Spain; and then started back for Havana, with a cargo of about 40 quintals of live fish. On April 25, 1898, about 2 miles off Mariel, and 11 miles from Havana, she was captured by the United States gunboat Castine.

[Another fishing smack, the Lola, was also captured.]

Each vessel was thereupon sold by auction; the Paquete Habana for the sum of $490; and the Lola for the sum of $800.***

We are then brought to the consideration of the question whether, upon the facts appearing in these records, the fishing smacks were subject to capture by the armed vessels of the United States during the recent war with Spain.

By an ancient usage among civilized nations, beginning centuries ago, and gradually ripening into a rule of international law, coast fishing vessels, pursuing their vocation of catching and bringing in fresh fish, have been recognized as exempt, with their cargoes and crews, from capture as prize of war.

This doctrine, however, has been earnestly contested at the bar; and no complete collection of the instances illustrating it is to be found, so far as we are aware, in a single published work although many are referred to and discussed by the writers on international law ***. It is therefore worth the while to trace the history of the rule, from the earliest accessible sources, through the increasing recognition of it, with occasional setbacks, to what we may now justly consider as its final establishment in our own country and generally throughout the civilized world.

The earliest acts of any government on the subject, mentioned in the books, either emanated from, or were approved by, a King of England.

In 1403 and 1406 Henry IV. issued orders to his admirals and other officers, entitled 'Concerning Safety for Fishermen-De Securitate pro Piscatoribus.' By an order of October 26, 1403, reciting that it was made pursuant to a treaty between himself and the King of France; and for the greater safety of the fishermen of either country, and so that they could be, and carry on their industry, the more safely on the sea, and deal with each other in peace; and that the French King had consented that English fishermen should be treated likewise, it was ordained that French fishermen might, during the then pending season for the herring fishery, safely fish for herrings and all other fish.*** And by an order of October 5, 1406, he took into his safe conduct and under his special protection, guardianship, and defense, all and singular the fishermen of France, Flanders, and Brittany, with their fishing vessels and boats, everywhere on the sea, through and within his dominions, jurisdictions, and territories, in regard to their fishery, while sailing, coming, and going, and, at their pleasure, freely and lawfully fishing, delaying, or proceeding, and returning homeward with their catch of fish, without any molestation or hindrance whatever; and also their fish, nets, and other property and goods soever ***.***

The treaty made October 2, 1521, between the Emperor Charles V. and Francis I. of France, through their ambassadors, recited that a great and fierce war had arisen between them, because of which there had been, both by land and by sea, frequent depredations and incursions on either side, to the grave detriment and intolerable injury of the innocent subjects of each; and that a suitable time for the herring fishery was at hand, and, by reason of the sea being beset by the enemy, the fishermen did not dare to go out, whereby the subject of their industry, bestowed by heaven to allay the hunger of the poor, would wholly fail for the year, unless it were otherwise provided ***. And it was therefore agreed that the subjects of each sovereign, fishing in the sea, or exercising the calling of fishermen, could and might, until the end of the next January, without incurring any attack, depredation, molestation, trouble, or hindrance soever, safely and freely, everywhere in the sea, take herrings and every other kind of fish ***.***

The herring fishery was permitted, in time of war, by French and Dutch edicts in 1536.***

France, from remote times, set the example of alleviating the evils of war in favor of all coast fishermen. In the compilation entitled 'Us et Coutumes de la Mer,' published by Cleirac in 1661, and in the third part thereof, containing 'Maritime or Admiralty Jurisdiction, la Jurisdiction de la Marine ou d' Admiraute—as well in time of peace, as in time of war,' article 80 is as follows: 'The admiral may in time of war accord fishing truces—tresves pescheresses—to the enemy and to his subjects; provided that the enemy will likewise accord them to Frenchmen.'***

The same custom would seem to have prevailed in France until towards the end of the seventeenth century.*** But by the ordinances of 1681 and 1692 the practice was discontinued, because, Valin says, of the faithless conduct of the enemies of France, who, abusing the good faith with which she had always observed the treaties, habitually carried off her fishermen, while their own fished in safety.***

The doctrine which exempts coast fishermen, with their vessels and cargoes, from capture as prize of war, has been familiar to the United States from the time of the War of Independence.

On June 5, 1779, Louis XVI, our ally in that war, addressed a letter to his admiral, informing him that the wish he had always had of alleviating, as far as he could, the hardships of war, had directed his attention to that class of his subjects which devoted itself to the trade of fishing, and had no other means of livelihood; that he had thought that the example which he should give to his enemies, and which could have no other source than the sentiments of humanity which inspired him, would determine them to allow to fishermen the same facilities which he should consent to grant; and that he had therefore given orders to the commanders of all his ships not to disturb English fishermen, nor to arrest their vessels laden with fresh fish *** provided they had no offensive arms, and were not proved to have made any signals creating a suspicion of intelligence with the enemy *** and the capture and ransom, by a French cruiser, of The John and Sarah, an English vessel, coming from Holland, laden with fresh fish, were pronounced to be illegal.

In the treaty of 1785 between the United States and Prussia, article 23 *** provided that, if war should arise between the contracting parties, "all women and children, scholars of every faculty, cultivators of the earth, artisans, manufacturers, and fishermen, unarmed and inhabiting unfortified towns, villages, or places, and in general all others whose occupations are for the common subsistence and benefit of mankind, shall be allowed to continue their respective employments, and shall not be molested in their persons, nor shall their houses or goods be burnt or otherwise destroyed, nor their fields wasted by the armed force of the enemy, into whose power, by the events of war, they may happen to fall; but if anything is necessary to be taken from them for the use of such armed force, the same shall be paid for at a reasonable price.***"

Since the United States became a nation, the only serious interruptions, so far as we are informed, of the general recognition of the exemption of coast fishing vessels from hostile capture, arose out of the mutual suspicions and recriminations of England and France during the wars of the French Revolution.***

In the war with Mexico, in 1846, the United States recognized the exemption of coast fishing boats from capture. In proof of this, counsel have referred to records of the Navy Department, which this court is clearly authorized to consult upon such a question. [Citations omitted.]

In the treaty of peace between the United States and Mexico, in 1848, were inserted the very words of the earlier treaties with Prussia, already quoted, forbidding the hostile molestation or seizure in time of war of the persons, occupations, houses, or goods of fishermen. 9 Stat. at L. 939, 940.

France in the Crimean War in 1854, and in her wars with Italy in 1859 and with Germany in 1870, by general orders, forbade her cruisers to trouble the coast fisheries, or to seize any vessel or boat engaged therein, unless naval or military operations should make it necessary.***

International law is part of our law, and must be ascertained and administered by the courts of justice of appropriate jurisdiction as often as questions of right depending upon it are duly presented for their determination. For this purpose, where there is no treaty and no controlling executive or legislative act or judicial decision, resort must be had to the customs and usages of civilized nations, and, as evidence of these, to the works of jurists and commentators who by years of labor, research, and experience have made themselves peculiarly well acquainted with the subjects of which they treat. Such works are resorted to by judicial tribunals, not for the speculations of their authors concerning what the law ought to be, but for trustworthy evidence of what the law really is. [Citation omitted.]

Wheaton places among the principal sources of international law 'text-writers of authority, showing what is the approved usage of nations, or the general opinion respecting their mutual conduct, with the definitions and modifications introduced by general consent.' As to these he forcibly observes: "Without wishing to exaggerate the importance of these writers, or to substitute, in any case, their authority for the principles of reason, it may be affirmed that they are generally impartial in their judgment. They are witnesses of the sentiments and usages of civilized nations, and the weight of their testimony increases every time that their authority is invoked by statesmen, and every year that passes without the rules laid down in their works being impugned by the avowal of contrary principles." Wheaton, International Law (8th ed.), 15.***

Carlos Testa, captain in the Portugese Navy and professor in the naval school at Lisbon, in his work on Public International Law, published in French at Paris in 1886, when discussing the general right of capturing enemy ships, says: "Nevertheless, in this, customary law establishes an exception of immunity in favor of coast fishing vessels. Fishing is so peaceful an industry, and is generally carried on by so poor and so hardworking a class of men, that it is likened, in the territorial waters of the enemy's country, to the class of husbandmen who gather the fruits of the earth for their livelihood. The examples and practice generally followed establish this humane and beneficent exception as an international rule, and this rule may be considered as adopted by customary law and by all civilized nations."***

[T]he distinguished Italian jurist, Pasquale Fiore, in the enlarged edition of his exhaustive work on Public International Law [says] 'The vessels of fishermen have been generally declared exempt from confiscation, because of the eminently peaceful object of their humble industry, and of the principles of equity and humanity. The exemption includes the vessel, the implements of fishing, and the cargo resulting from the fishery. This usage, eminently humane, goes back to very ancient times; and although the immunity of the fishery along the coasts may not have been sanctioned by treaties, yet it is considered to-day as so definitely established that the inviolability of vessels devoted to that fishery is proclaimed by the publicists as a positive rule of international law, and is generally respected by the nations.***

This review of the precedents and authorities on the subject appears to us abundantly to demonstrate that at the present day, by the general consent of the civilized nations of the world, and independently of any express treaty or other public act, it is an established rule of international law, founded on considerations of humanity to a poor and industrious order of men, and of the mutual convenience of belligerent states, that coast fishing vessels, with their implements and supplies, cargoes and crews, unarmed and honestly pursuing their peaceful calling of catching and bringing in fresh fish, are exempt from capture as prize of war.***

This rule of international law is one which prize courts administering the law of nations are bound to take judicial notice of, and to give effect to, in the absence of any treaty or other public act of their own government in relation to the matter.***

Notes and Questions

1. What kind of work is protected by this decision? Why is such protection afforded by international law? What implications might this decision have for the protection of other economic, social, or cultural rights?

2. Who is obligated to protect this work? Who might not be? Were the Spanish obligated to protect the livelihoods of their own fishermen under this doctrine? Does it make sense to obligate a belligerent power to protect the industries of their opponents? Is there a mutual interest in such protections?

THE CONSTITUTION OF MEXICO (1917)

TITLE VI

Labor and Social Security

Article 123. Every person is entitled to suitable work that is socially useful. Toward this end, the creation of jobs and social organization for labor shall be promoted in conformance with the law. The Congress of the Union, without contravening the following basic principles, shall enact labor laws which shall apply to:

A. Workers, day laborers, domestic servants, artisans (obreros, jornaleros, empleados, domésticos, artesanos) and in a general way to all labor contracts:

I. The maximum duration of work for one day shall be eight hours.

II. The maximum duration of nightwork shall be seven hours. The following are prohibited for minors under sixteen years of age: unhealthful or hazardous work, industrial nightwork, and work (of any kind) after ten o'clock at night.

III. The use of labor of minors under fourteen years of age is prohibited. Persons above that age and less than sixteen shall have a maximum work day of six hours.

IV. For every six days of work a worker must have at least one day of rest.

V. Women in a state of pregnancy shall not perform physical labor which requires considerable effort and which could be hazardous to their health.***

The general minimum wage must be sufficient to satisfy the normal material, social, and cultural needs of the head of a family and to provide for the mandatory education of his children. The minimum occupational wage shall be fixed by also taking into consideration the conditions of different industrial and commercial activities.***

Notes and Questions

1. How does Title VI of the Mexican Constitution protect working people? Are there any parts of it that appear open to broad interpretation by future governments?

2. Would you interpret Title VI to contain an individually enforceable right to a job? Does it include the right to choose the job?

3. How does Title VI function vis-à-vis the family? The individual? Society more generally?

PAOLO G. CAROZZA, FROM CONQUEST TO CONSTITUTIONS: RETRIEVING A LATIN AMERICAN TRADITION OF THE IDEA OF HUMAN RIGHTS

25 Hum. Rts. Q. 281, 303–13 (2003)

THE CONSTITUTION OF "SOCIAL LIBERALISM"

What was so uniquely important about the Mexican Constitution of 1917? Part of the answer lies simply in its timing. It was crafted at a time of global upheaval and was the first constitution to begin to take into account a world being reshaped by World War I, Russian unrest, significant economic globalization, and the growing power of Latin America's northern neighbor.***

But the importance of the Mexican Constitution of 1917 is due even more to its content, and specifically to its incorporation of extensive social and economic guarantees and protections. It preserves almost unchanged the traditional complement of classical civil and political liberties of the previous constitution of 1857, but adds to them detailed provisions on labor, agrarian reform, and the social dimensions of property rights. Articles 27 and 123 of the 1917 Constitution are its most famous. The former provides, among other things, that, "The Nation shall have at all times the right to impose on private property such limitations as the public interest may demand" and gives the government the power to, "take necessary measures to divide large landed estates." It recognizes the right to hold property privately, but subordinates that right to the public interest.***

These social and economic provisions were the first of their kind in any constitutional document, not just in Latin America but in all the world. The principles of the 1917 Constitution were borrowed or imitated in varying degree by virtually every Latin American constitution thereafter, and made themselves felt in the next wave of European constitutionalism, too.***

[I]t is a misleadingly simplistic reduction to see the 1917 Constitution as socialist in its original orientation. Neither the history of the Constitutional Congress nor the resulting text itself support such a view, and in fact it obscures the uniqueness of the Mexican developments, reinforcing again an implicit perception that Latin American developments are merely derivative of European creativity.***

Practically the only philosophical-juridicial theme that has been plausibly proposed as a consistent underlying idea of the 1917 Constitution at the time when it was drafted is "the conviction that the human being, as a human person, has rights prior to the state." It can reasonably be seen as a document about a certain vision of rights, one that encompasses social, economic, and cultural spheres as well as political and civil ones.***

The Constitution *** did not reject the basic liberal rights of the previous 1857 constitution, but instead added to them a solicitude for certain social concerns, especially labor, that sought to make constitutional rights more reflective of the reality of human life in all its factors. As one author puts it, "the concept of human dignity, called to be protected by law and by social institutions, was enriched by reaching concrete individuals, men in history with hunger and thirst, with material needs that are presuppositions for the exercise of their liberty."

This immediate, concrete concern for the conditions of the people stands out in the work of the Congress, and must be regarded as the first source of the 1917 Constitution's innovations. The delegates' reforms were not the product of a general theory, nor of the mechanical importation of foreign ideas but rather of the tangible experience of the Revolution. A human solidarity with the poor and the working class prevailed over abstract ideology: "In the heart of the congress, even on the lips of the distinguished members of the radical group,*** we observe only *** an authentic preoccupation for the concrete problems of the fields [*campo*] and of laborers, problems that were *** posed as burning realities of life, stripped of all conceptual clothing." These are not "natural rights" in the sense of being the result of understanding and reflecting on any theory of natural law, but natural rights in the existential sense of belonging to the human person as such, engaged in specific activities in which human dignity and freedom is at stake.

The second source, which goes more specifically to the actual language of the constitutional provisions of Article 123, was some of the progressive social and labor legislation of other countries.***

Finally, a third source for the Constitution's social guarantees [emanated from] the pervasive presence and influence of Catholic social doctrines that became prominent in the decades preceding 1917 ***. In the first papal encyclical on the "social question," *Rerum Novarum* in 1891, Pope Leo XIII addressed the conditions of workers, emphasizing the need for state intervention to protect them, guaranteeing for instance a just wage and the freedom to organize for collective bargaining.

The irony, of course, is that Mexico was a paradigmatically anticlerical state through-out most of the 19th century, and during the Revolutionary years between 1910 and 1917 the persecution of the Catholic Church was sometimes extreme. In the Constitutional Congress, aside from the social provisions of the constitution, nothing was more central to the debate and work of the assembly than the "Jacobin" hostility toward religion generally and the Catholic Church in particular. Yet, a closer look at the history shows that the air of Catholic social mobilization had nevertheless been quietly blowing since the turn of the century and had become a prominent part of the public discourse.***

*** The fact that the 1917 Constitution did have such a widespread impact on the region, even in many systems that were not necessarily socialist in ideological orienta-tion, attests to the fact that it tapped into the broadly shared understandings of human dignity and society that are the foundation of expressions of human rights. It was located within a history recognizable throughout Latin America. [T]he parallel between Mexican revolutionary social policies and Catholic social activism highlights the con-tinuation of one of the Latin American tradition's central themes: seeking to combine and balance the individual and the communal aspects of human rights ***.***

1936 CONSTITUTION OF THE USSR

CHAPTER X: FUNDAMENTAL RIGHTS AND DUTIES OF CITIZENS

ARTICLE 118. Citizens of the U.S.S.R. have the right to work, that is, are guaran-teed the right to employment and payment for their work in accordance with its quan-tity and quality.

The right to work is ensured by the socialist organization of the national economy, the steady growth of the productive forces of Soviet society, the elimination of the pos-sibility of economic crises, and the abolition of unemployment.

ARTICLE 119. Citizens of the U.S.S.R. have the right to rest and leisure. The right to rest and leisure is ensured by the reduction of the working day to seven hours for the overwhelming majority of the workers, the institution of annual vacations with full pay for workers and employees and the provision of a wide network of sanatoria, rest homes and clubs for the accommodation of the working people.

ARTICLE 120. Citizens of the U.S.S.R. have the right to maintenance in old age and also in case of sickness or loss of capacity to work. This right is ensured by the exten-sive development of social insurance of workers and employees at state expense, free medical service for the working people and the provision of a wide network of health resorts for the use of the working people.

ARTICLE 121. Citizens of the U.S.S.R. have the right to education. This right is ensured by universal, compulsory elementary education; by education, including higher education, being free of charge; by the system of state stipends for the overwhelming majority of students in the universities and colleges; by instruction in schools being con-ducted in the native language; and by the organization in the factories, state farms, machine and tractor stations and collective farms of free vocational, technical and agro-nomic training for the working people.

ARTICLE 122. Women in the U.S.S.R. are accorded equal rights with men in all spheres of economic, state, cultural, social and political life. The possibility of exercising these rights is ensured to women by granting them an equal right with men to work, payment for work, rest and leisure, social insurance and education, and by state protection of the interests of mother and child, prematernity and maternity leave with full pay, and the provision of a wide network of maternity homes, nurseries and kindergartens.

ARTICLE 123. Equality of rights of citizens of the U.S.S.R., irrespective of their nationality or race, in all spheres of economic, state, cultural, social and political life, is an indefeasible law. Any direct or indirect restriction of the rights of, or, conversely, any establishment of direct or indirect privileges for, citizens on account of their race or nationality, as well as any advocacy of racial or national exclusiveness or hatred and contempt, is punishable by law.

Notes and Questions

1. These Soviet constitutional provisions, like Title VI of the Mexican Constitution, contain various guarantees for working people. Do they appear to include the right to a job? If so, how is that right protected?

2. What other rights are protected by Chapter X? What mechanisms are needed to guarantee these rights?

3. Are these rights expressed in negative or positive terms? In particular, see Articles 122 and 123. Are these anti-discrimination provisions similar to those with which you are familiar? Does it appear that these articles apply only to government actions? Why or why not?

PRESIDENT FRANKLIN ROOSEVELT, 1944 STATE OF THE UNION ADDRESS

This Nation in the past two years has become an active partner in the world's greatest war against human slavery.

We have joined with like-minded people in order to defend ourselves in a world that has been gravely threatened with gangster rule.

But I do not think that any of us Americans can be content with mere survival. Sacrifices that we and our allies are making impose upon us all a sacred obligation to see to it that out of this war we and our children will gain something better than mere survival.***

The one supreme objective for the future, which [the Allies] discussed for each Nation individually, and for all the United Nations, can be summed up in one word: Security.

And that means not only physical security which provides safety from attacks by aggressors. It means also economic security, social security, moral security—in a family of Nations.

In the plain down-to-earth talks that I had with the Generalissimo [Chiang Kai-shek] and Marshal Stalin and Prime Minister Churchill, it was abundantly clear that they are all most deeply interested in the resumption of peaceful progress by their own peoples—progress toward a better life. All our allies want freedom to develop their lands and resources, to build up industry, to increase education and individual opportunity, and to raise standards of living.

All our allies have learned by bitter experience that real development will not be possible if they are to be diverted from their purpose by repeated wars—or even threats of war.

China and Russia are truly united with Britain and America in recognition of this essential fact:

The best interests of each Nation, large and small, demand that all freedom-loving Nations shall join together in a just and durable system of peace. [E]ssential to peace is a decent standard of living for all individual men and women and children in all Nations. Freedom from fear is eternally linked with freedom from want.***

It is our duty now to begin to lay the plans and determine the strategy for the winning of a lasting peace and the establishment of an American standard of living higher than ever before known. We cannot be content, no matter how high that general standard of living may be, if some fraction of our people—whether it be one-third or one-fifth or one-tenth—is ill-fed, ill-clothed, ill housed, and insecure.

This Republic had its beginning, and grew to its present strength, under the protection of certain inalienable political rights—among them the right of free speech, free press, free worship, trial by jury, freedom from unreasonable searches and seizures. They were our rights to life and liberty.

As our Nation has grown in size and stature, however—as our industrial economy expanded—these political rights proved inadequate to assure us equality in the pursuit of happiness.

We have come to a clear realization of the fact that true individual freedom cannot exist without economic security and independence. "Necessitous men are not free men." People who are hungry and out of a job are the stuff of which dictatorships are made.

In our day these economic truths have become accepted as self-evident. We have accepted, so to speak, a second Bill of Rights under which a new basis of security and prosperity can be established for all regardless of station, race, or creed.

Among these are:

The right to a useful and remunerative job in the industries or shops or farms or mines of the Nation;

The right to earn enough to provide adequate food and clothing and recreation;

The right of every farmer to raise and sell his products at a return which will give him and his family a decent living;

The right of every businessman, large and small, to trade in an atmosphere of freedom from unfair competition and domination by monopolies at home or abroad;

The right of every family to a decent home;

The right to adequate medical care and the opportunity to achieve and enjoy good health;

The right to adequate protection from the economic fears of old age, sickness, accident, and unemployment;

The right to a good education.

All of these rights spell security. And after this war is won we must be prepared to move forward, in the implementation of these rights, to new goals of human happiness and well-being.***

Notes and Questions

1.   What does Roosevelt mean by a second Bill of Rights? How do you think the rights enumerated in this speech have fared since 1944? To whom was Roosevelt trying to appeal? Why?

3.   *The Quest for Universalization*

AMERICAN ANTHROPOLOGICAL ASSOCIATION: STATEMENT ON HUMAN RIGHTS [1]

49 AMERICAN ANTHROPOLOGIST NEW SERIES, No. 4, at 539, 539–43 (Oct.–Dec. 1947)

THE problem faced by the Commission on Human Rights of the United Nations in preparing its Declaration on the Rights of Man must be approached from two points of view. The first, in terms of which the Declaration is ordinarily conceived, concerns the respect for the personality of the individual as such, and his right to its fullest development as a member of his society. In a world order, however, respect for the cultures of differing human groups is equally important.

These are two facets of the same problem, since it is a truism that groups are composed of individuals, and human beings do not function outside the societies of which they form a part. The problem is thus to formulate a statement of human rights that will do more than just phrase respect for the individual as an individual. It must also take into full account the individual as a member of the social group of which he is a part, whose sanctioned modes of life shape his behavior, and with whose fate his own is thus inextricably bound.

Because of the great numbers of societies that are in intimate contact in the modern world, and because of the diversity of their ways of life, the primary task confronting those who would draw up a Declaration on the Rights of Man is thus, in essence, to resolve the following problem: How can the proposed Declaration be applicable to all human beings, and not be a statement of rights conceived only in terms of the values prevalent in the countries of western Europe and America?***

If we begin, as we must, with the individual, we find that from the moment of his birth not only his behavior, but his very thoughts, his hopes, aspirations, the moral values which direct his action and justify and give meaning to his life in his own eyes and those of his fellows, are shaped by the body of custom of the group of which he becomes a member. The process by means of which this is accomplished is so subtle, and its effects are so far-reaching, that only after considerable training are we conscious of it. Yet if

---

[1]   Submitted to the Commission on Human Rights, United Nations (June 24, 1947).

the essence of the Declaration is to be, as it must, a statement in which the right of the individual to develop his personality to the fullest is to be stressed, then this must be based on a recognition of the fact that the personality of the individual can develop only in terms of the culture of his society.

Over the past fifty years, the many ways in which man resolves the problems of subsistence, of social living, of political regulation of group life, of reaching accord with the Universe and satisfying his aesthetic drives has been widely documented by the researches of anthropologists among peoples living in all parts of the world. All peoples do achieve these ends. No two of them, however, do so in exactly the same way, and some of them employ means that differ, often strikingly, from one another.

Yet here a dilemma arises. Because of the social setting of the learning process, the individual cannot but be convinced that his own way of life is the most desirable one. Conversely, and despite changes originating from within and without his culture that he recognizes as worthy of adoption, it becomes equally patent to him that, in the main, other ways than his own, to the degree they differ from it, are less desirable than those to which he is accustomed. Hence valuations arise, that in themselves receive the sanction of accepted belief.

The degree to which such evaluations eventuate in action depends on the basic sanctions in the thought of a people. In the main, people are willing to live and let live, exhibiting a tolerance for behavior of another group different than their own, especially where there is no conflict in the subsistence field. In the history of Western Europe and America, however, economic expansion, control of armaments, and an evangelical religious tradition have translated the recognition of cultural differences into a summons to action. This has been emphasized by philosophical systems that have stressed absolutes in the realm of values and ends. Definitions of freedom, concepts of the nature of human rights, and the like, have thus been narrowly drawn. Alternatives have been decried, and suppressed where controls have been established over non-European peoples. The hard core of *similarities* between cultures has consistently been overlooked.

The consequences of this point of view have been disastrous for mankind. Doctrines of the "white man's burden" have been employed to implement economic exploitation and to deny the right to control their own affairs to millions of peoples over the world— where the expansion of Europe and America has not meant the literal extermination of whole populations. Rationalized in terms of ascribing cultural inferiority to these peoples, or in conceptions of their backwardness in development of their "primitive mentality," that justified their being held in the tutelage of their superiors, the history of the expansion of the western world has been marked by demoralization of human personality and the disintegration of human rights among the peoples over whom hegemony has been established.

The values of the ways of life of these peoples have been consistently misunderstood and decried. Religious beliefs that for untold ages have carried conviction, and permitted adjustment to the Universe have been attacked as superstitious, immoral, untrue. And, since power carries its own conviction, this has furthered the process of demoralization begun by economic exploitation and the loss of political autonomy. The white man's burden, the civilizing mission, have been heavy indeed. But their weight has not been borne by those who, frequently in all honesty, have journeyed to the far places of the world to uplift those regarded by them as inferior.

We thus come to the first proposition that the study of human psychology and culture dictates as essential in drawing up a Bill of Human Rights in terms of existing knowledge:

1. *The individual realizes his personality through his culture, hence respect for individual differences entails a respect for cultural differences.*

There can be no individual freedom, that is, when the group with which the individual indentifies himself is not free. There can be no full development of the individual personality as long as the individual is told, by men who have the power to enforce their commands, that the way of life of his group is inferior to that of those who wield the power.***

2. *Respect for differences between cultures is validated by the scientific fact that no technique of qualitatively evaluating cultures has been discovered.*

This principle leads us to a further one, namely that the aims that guide the life of every people are self-evident in their significance to that people. It is the principle that emphasizes the universals in human conduct rather than the absolutes that the culture of Western Europe and America stresses. It recognizes that the eternal verities only seem so because we have been taught to regard them as such; that every people, whether it expresses them or not, lives in devotion to verities whose eternal nature is as real to them as are those of Euroamerican culture to Euroamericans. Briefly stated, this third principle that must be introduced into our consideration is the following:

3. *Standards and values are relative to the culture from which they derive so that any attempt to formulate postulates that grow out of the beliefs or moral codes of one culture must to that extent detract from the applicability of any Declaration of Human Rights to mankind as a whole.*

Ideas of right and wrong, good and evil, are found in all societies, though they differ in their expression among different peoples. What is held to be a human right in one society may be regarded as anti-social by another people or by the same people in a different period of their history. The saint of one epoch would at a later time be confined as a man not fitted to cope with reality. Even the nature of the physical world, the colors we see, the sounds we hear, are conditioned by the language we speak, which is part of the culture into which we are born.

The problem of drawing up a Declaration of Human Rights was relatively simple in the Eighteenth Century, because it was not a matter of *human* rights, but of the rights of men within the framework of the sanctions laid by a single society. Even then, so noble a document as the American Declaration of Independence, or the American Bill of Rights, could be written by men who themselves were slave-owners, in a country where chattel slavery was a part of the recognized social order. The revolutionary character of the slogan ''Liberty, Equality, Fraternity'' was never more apparent than in the struggles to implement it by extending it to the French slave-owning colonies.

Today the problem is complicated by the fact that the Declaration must be of worldwide applicability. It must embrace and recognize the validity of different ways of life. It will not be convincing to the Indonesian, the African, the Indian, the Chinese, if it lies on the same plane as like documents of an earlier period. The rights of Man in the Twentieth Century cannot be circumscribed by the standards of any single culture, or be dictated by the aspirations of any single people. Such a document will lead to frustration, not realization of the personalities of vast numbers of human beings.***

Even where political systems exist that deny citizens the right of participation in their government, or seek to conquer weaker peoples, underlying cultural values may be called on to bring the peoples of such states to a realization of the consequences of the acts of their governments, and thus enforce a brake upon discrimination and conquest. For the political system of a people is only a small part of their total culture.

World-wide standards of freedom and justice, based on the principle that man is free only when he lives as his society defines freedom, that his rights are those he recognizes as a member of his society, must be basic. Conversely, an effective world-order cannot be devised except insofar as it permits the free play of personality of the members of its constituent social units, and draws strength from the enrichment to be derived from the interplay of varying personalities.

*** Only when a statement of the right of men to live in terms of their own traditions is incorporated into the proposed Declaration, can the next step of defining the rights and duties of human groups as regards each other be set upon the firm foundation of the present-day scientific knowledge of Man.

Notes and Questions

1. The American Anthropological Association's statement is skeptical about the feasibility of drafting a declaration of rights that is truly universal. According to Professor Karen Engle,

> [t]he Statement was written in the context of colonialism and to oppose a dominant belief that the West (and, therefore, the United Nations at the time) and Western culture and biology were superior. That belief had earlier permitted slavery in the United States and had supported the colonialism that still existed in 1947. The Statement also focused on non-European peoples and the need to understand, rather than attempt to change, their cultures and values.
>
> Against this backdrop, the Statement cleverly argues both for *similarities* and *differences*. It suggests that no biological differences exist between the races, but that individuals are nevertheless formed by the communities in which they live. Although the Statement was clearly guided by the relativist, anti-colonialist, and anti-racist positions of its author, Melville Herskovits, the current movement in the AAA is to see the Statement, because of its relativist bent, as an unfortunate part of its history. Despite the attempts of some to resurrect the anti-colonialist motivation for the Statement, most contemporary pro-rights anthropologists have tried to separate the discipline of anthropology from the relativism they believe drove the Statement.

Karen Engle, *Culture and Human Rights: The Asian Values Debate in Context*, 32 N.Y.U. J. INT'L L. & POL. 291, 308–09 (2000). Do the concerns expressed in the AAA Statement remain valid today?

2. Consider whether all of the values expressed in the Declaration are truly applicable to all human societies. For example, does the right to "periodic holidays with pay" (Article 24) make sense in the context of indigenous communities pursuing traditional livelihoods? Does it matter?

UNIVERSAL DECLARATION OF HUMAN RIGHTS

General Assembly Resolution 217 A (III) (December 10, 1948)

PREAMBLE

Whereas recognition of the inherent dignity and of the equal and inalienable rights of all members of the human family is the foundation of freedom, justice and peace in the world,

Whereas disregard and contempt for human rights have resulted in barbarous acts which have outraged the conscience of mankind, and the advent of a world in which human beings shall enjoy freedom of speech and belief and freedom from fear and want has been proclaimed as the highest aspiration of the common people,

Whereas it is essential, if man is not to be compelled to have recourse, as a last resort, to rebellion against tyranny and oppression, that human rights should be protected by the rule of law,

Whereas it is essential to promote the development of friendly relations between nations,

Whereas the peoples of the United Nations have in the Charter reaffirmed their faith in fundamental human rights, in the dignity and worth of the human person and in the equal rights of men and women and have determined to promote social progress and better standards of life in larger freedom,

Whereas Member States have pledged themselves to achieve, in co-operation with the United Nations, the promotion of universal respect for and observance of human rights and fundamental freedoms,

Whereas a common understanding of these rights and freedoms is of the greatest importance for the full realization of this pledge,

Now, Therefore THE GENERAL ASSEMBLY proclaims THIS UNIVERSAL DECLARATION OF HUMAN RIGHTS as a common standard of achievement for all peoples and all nations, to the end that every individual and every organ of society, keeping this Declaration constantly in mind, shall strive by teaching and education to promote respect for these rights and freedoms and by progressive measures, national and international, to secure their universal and effective recognition and observance, both among the peoples of Member States themselves and among the peoples of territories under their jurisdiction.

Article 1.

All human beings are born free and equal in dignity and rights. They are endowed with reason and conscience and should act towards one another in a spirit of brotherhood.

Article 2.

Everyone is entitled to all the rights and freedoms set forth in this Declaration, without distinction of any kind, such as race, color, sex, language, religion, political or other opinion, national or social origin, property, birth or other status.***

Article 22.

Everyone, as a member of society, has the right to social security and is entitled to realization, through national effort and international co-operation and in accordance with the organization and resources of each State, of the economic, social and cultural rights indispensable for his dignity and the free development of his personality.

Article 23.

(1) Everyone has the right to work, to free choice of employment, to just and favorable conditions of work and to protection against unemployment.

(2) Everyone, without any discrimination, has the right to equal pay for equal work.

(3) Everyone who works has the right to just and favourable remuneration ensuring for himself and his family an existence worthy of human dignity, and supplemented, if necessary, by other means of social protection.

(4) Everyone has the right to form and to join trade unions for the protection of his interests.

Article 24.

Everyone has the right to rest and leisure, including reasonable limitation of working hours and periodic holidays with pay.

Article 25.

(1) Everyone has the right to a standard of living adequate for the health and well-being of himself and of his family, including food, clothing, housing and medical care and necessary social services, and the right to security in the event of unemployment, sickness, disability, widowhood, old age or other lack of livelihood in circumstances beyond his control.

(2) Motherhood and childhood are entitled to special care and assistance. All children, whether born in or out of wedlock, shall enjoy the same social protection.

Article 26.

(1) Everyone has the right to education. Education shall be free, at least in the elementary and fundamental stages. Elementary education shall be compulsory. Technical and professional education shall be made generally available and higher education shall be equally accessible to all on the basis of merit.

(2) Education shall be directed to the full development of the human personality and to the strengthening of respect for human rights and fundamental freedoms. It shall promote understanding, tolerance and friendship among all nations, racial or religious groups, and shall further the activities of the United Nations for the maintenance of peace.

(3) Parents have a prior right to choose the kind of education that shall be given to their children.

Article 27.

(1) Everyone has the right freely to participate in the cultural life of the community, to enjoy the arts and to share in scientific advancement and its benefits.

(2) Everyone has the right to the protection of the moral and material interests resulting from any scientific, literary or artistic production of which he is the author.

Article 28.

Everyone is entitled to a social and international order in which the rights and freedoms set forth in this Declaration can be fully realized.

Article 29.

(1) Everyone has duties to the community in which alone the free and full development of his personality is possible.

(2) In the exercise of his rights and freedoms, everyone shall be subject only to such limitations as are determined by law solely for the purpose of securing due recognition and respect for the rights and freedoms of others and of meeting the just requirements of morality, public order and the general welfare in a democratic society.

(3) These rights and freedoms may in no case be exercised contrary to the purposes and principles of the United Nations.***

Notes and Questions

1.   The Universal Declaration of Human Rights is not binding *qua* international convention. However, it does constitute "evidence of the interpretation and application of the relevant [United Nations] Charter provisions." *South West Africa Cases (Second Phase)* 1966 I.C.J. Rep. 293. The Declaration is also binding as a codification of customary international law. *Legal Consequences for States of the Continued Presence of South Africa in Namibia (South West Africa) Notwithstanding Security Council Resolution 276* (Request for Advisory Opinion), 1971 I.C.J. Rep. 12, 76.

2.   The promulgation of the UDHR followed the most brutal war in human history. How does the Preamble reflect that fact? Do any of the provisions look familiar? Is this a constitution? If so, for what entity?

3.   Article 28 states that "everyone is entitled to a social and international order in which the rights and freedoms set forth *** can be fully realized." Does that give more or less leeway to individual states? Should Article 28 itself be a right enforceable against the state? Should it be enforceable against the "international order?" How might Article 28 relate to the possible "rebellion against tyranny and oppression" mentioned in the Preamble?

4.   For further reading on the substantial influence of the Universal Declaration of Human Rights on the international human rights movement, *see, e.g.*, MARY ANN GLENDON, A WORLD MADE NEW (2001); PAUL GORDON LAUREN, THE EVOLUTION OF INTERNATIONAL HUMAN RIGHTS: VISIONS SEEN (1998); Hilary Charlesworth, *The Mid-Life Crisis of the universal Declaration of Human Rights*, 55 WASH. & LEE L. REV. 781 (1998); Hurst Hannum, *The Status and Future of Customary International Law of Human Rights: The Status of the Universal Declaration of Human Rights in National and International Law*, 25 GA. J. INT'L & COMP. L. 287 (1996); Tracy E. Higgins, *Symposium in Celebration of the Fiftieth Anniversary of the Universal Declaration of Human Rights: Regarding Rights: An Essay Honoring the Fiftieth Anniversary of Human Rights*, 30 COLUM. HUM. RTS. L. REV. 225 (1999).

MARY ANN GLENDON, THE SOURCES OF 'RIGHTS TALK'

28 COMMONWEAL, No. 17, at 11 (October 13, 2001)

During World War II, the idea began to percolate that there should be some kind of international bill of rights—a common standard to which all nations could aspire—and by which they could measure their own and each other's progress. One of the first suggestions came from Pope Pius XII, who, in a June 1941 radio address, called for an international bill recognizing the rights that flowed from the dignity of the person. Another came from the British writer H.G. Wells in a little pamphlet subtitled, "What Are We Fighting For?" But in practical terms, the most consequential support came from several Latin American countries, which composed twenty-one of the original fifty-five member nations of the UN when it was founded in 1945.

Largely due to the insistence of the Latin Americans, joined by other small nations, the UN established a Human Rights Commission composed of members from eighteen different countries. It was chaired by Eleanor Roosevelt who was just then making a new life for herself after the death of her husband. When the Human Rights Commission set to work in early 1947, its first major task was to draft a "bill of rights" to which persons of all nations and cultures could subscribe. But that assignment rested upon a couple of problematic assumptions: no one really knew whether there were any such common principles, or what they might be. So UNESCO asked a group of philosophers—some well known in the West, like Jacques Maritain, and others from Confucian, Hindu, and Muslim countries—to examine the question. These philosophers sent a questionnaire to still more leading thinkers, from Mahatma Gandhi to Teilhard de Chardin, and in due course, they reported that, somewhat to their surprise, they had found that there were a few common standards of decency that were widely shared, though not always formulated in the language of rights. Their conclusion was that this practical consensus was enough to enable the project to go forward.

The judgment of the philosophers was borne out by the experience of the delegates on the Human Rights Commission. This group, too, was highly diverse, but they had few disagreements over the content of the Declaration. Their disputes were chiefly political, and mainly involved the Soviet Union and the United States hurling accusations of hypocrisy against each other.

The framers of the UDHR *** drew many provisions from existing constitutions and rights instruments. They relied most heavily on two draft proposals for international bills that were themselves based on extensive cross-national research. One of these proposals was prepared under the auspices of the American Law Institute, and the other was a Latin American document that became the 1948 Bogota Declaration of the Rights and Duties of Man.

The final draft was a synthesis drawn from many sources—and thus a document that differed in many ways from our familiar Anglo-American rights instruments—most noticeably in its inclusion of social and economic rights, and in its express acknowledgment that rights are subject to duties and limitations. It also differed from socialist charters, notably with its strong emphasis on political and civil liberties.

Several features of the Declaration set it apart from both Anglo-American and Soviet-bloc documents, and these should be kept in mind as contests over the meanings of the

Declaration's provisions continue. Consider the following: its pervasive emphasis on the "inherent dignity" and "worth of the human person"; the affirmation that the human person is "endowed with reason and conscience"; the right to form trade unions; the worker's right to just remuneration for himself and his family; the recognition of the family as the "natural and fundamental group unit of society" entitled as such to "protection by society and the state"; the prior right of parents to choose the education of their children; and a provision that motherhood and childhood are entitled to "special care and assistance."

Where did those ideas come from? The immediate source was the twentieth-century constitutions of many Latin American and continental European countries. But where did the Latin Americans and continental Europeans get them? The proximate answer to that question is: mainly from the programs of political parties, parties of a type that did not exist in the United States, Britain, or the Soviet bloc, namely, Christian Democratic and Christian Social parties.

And where did the politicians get their ideas about the family, work, civil society, and the dignity of the person? The answer is: mainly from the social encyclicals Rerum novarum (1891) and Quadragesimo anno (1931). And where did the church get them? The short answer is that those encyclicals were part of the process through which the church had begun to reflect on the Enlightenment, the eighteenth-century revolutions, socialism, and the labor question in the light of Scripture, tradition, and her own experience as an "expert in humanity."

The most articulate advocate of this complex of ideas on the Human Rights Commission was a Lebanese Arab of the Greek Orthodox faith, Charles Malik. In reading the old UN transcripts, I was struck by Malik's frequent use of terms like the "intermediate associations" of civil society, and by his emphatic preference for the term "person" rather than "individual." When I had the opportunity to meet Charles Malik's son, Dr. Habib Malik, I asked him if he knew where his father had acquired that vocabulary. The answer was: from the heavily underlined copies of Rerum novarum and Quadragesimo anno, which Malik kept among the books he most frequently consulted.

Contrary to what is now widely supposed, the most zealous promoters of social and economic rights were not the Soviet bloc representatives but delegates from the Latin American countries. Except for the Mexican delegates, most of these people were inspired, not by Marx and Engels, but, like Malik, by Leo XIII and Pius XI. Their focus was not on the exploitation of man by man, but on the dignity of work and the preferential option for the poor.***

STATEMENT BY MRS. FRANKLIN D. ROOSEVELT[2]

Department of State Bulletin 1059, 1064–66 (December 31, 1951)

Three years ago in [Paris] the General Assembly proclaimed the Universal Declaration of Human Rights. That Declaration has already become the yardstick by which all can measure the conduct of governments. The language of that Declaration

---

2   Made before Committee III (Social, Humanitarian, and Cultural) on December 5 and released to the press by the U.S. Mission to the U.N. on the same date. Mrs. Roosevelt is a U.N.

has been written into the constitution of a number of states. The United Nations must now move ahead to develop new methods for advancing human liberty and for translating human rights and fundamental freedoms into action. One of these methods is the Draft International Covenant on Human Rights.

The task of drafting the Covenant, of putting human rights into treaty form, is not an easy one. We have been working in the United Nations on this draft Covenant since 1947.

I would like in particular to discuss the matter of economic, social, and cultural rights.

When the General Assembly last year called on the Commission on Human Rights to include economic, social, and cultural provisions in the Covenant on Human Rights, the United States fully cooperated in the 5-weeks' session of the Commission this spring in Geneva in drafting these provisions. The United States delegation voted last year in the General Assembly against the inclusion of economic, social, and cultural rights in the same Covenant with civil and political rights. At no time, however, did my delegation to the Commission on Human Rights question the responsibility of the Commission to prepare a draft with these provisions for the consideration of the General Assembly. The United States delegation to the Commission felt that, as a member of a technical commission, we should cooperate in doing that which the General Assembly had asked us to do at that time.

We did vote at the end of the Commission session for a resolution introduced by the delegate of India requesting a reconsideration by the General Assembly of the question of including economic, social, and cultural rights in the same Covenant with civil and political rights. This resolution did not, however, interrupt the technical work of the Commission. This Indian resolution pointed out that economic, social, and cultural rights, though equally fundamental and therefore important, formed a separate category of rights from that of the civil and political rights in that they were not justiciable rights and their method of implementation was different.

At this session of the General Assembly we have before us a resolution of the Economic and Social Council inviting the General Assembly to reconsider its decision of last year.***

Principal Provisions of the ECOSOC Resolution

The resolution of the Economic and Social Council points out that there are certain differences between the provisions on civil and political rights and the provisions on economic, social, and cultural rights and that these differences warrant a consideration of two covenants rather than a single covenant. The Council resolution also refers to the difficulties which may flow from embodying in one covenant two different kinds of rights and obligations.

Let us examine these differences which have been recognized by the Commission in a number of ways in drafting the provisions of the Covenant.

Delegate to the Sixth Session of the U.N. General Assembly at Paris and U.S. representative on the United Nations Commission on Human Rights.

In the first place, article 19 of the draft Covenant recognizes that the economic, social, and cultural provisions are objectives to be achieved "progressively." This obligation is to be distinguished from the obligation applicable to the civil and political rights in the Covenant. In the case of civil and political rights, states ratifying the Covenant will be under an obligation to take necessary steps fairly quickly to give effect to these rights. A much longer period of time is clearly contemplated under the Covenant for the achievement of the economic, social, and cultural provisions. This is obvious and is, of course, to be expected.

*** In contrast, in the case of civil and political rights, it is anticipated that these rights will be effectuated promptly. It is this time difference between these two types of rights that I am stressing.

A second difference between the civil and political provisions and the economic, social, and cultural provisions is the manner in which the obligation is expected to be performed. In the case of the civil and political rights, they can in general be achieved by the enactment of appropriate legislation, enforced under effective administrative machinery. On the other hand, it is recognized that economic, social, and cultural progress and development cannot be achieved simply by the enactment of legislation and its enforcement. Private as well as public action is necessary. The Commission on Human Rights repeatedly rejected the proposal by two members of the Commission to limit the achievement of economic, social, and cultural rights solely through state action. The Commission fully recognized the importance of private as well as governmental action for the achievement of these rights.

A third difference between the civil and political provisions and the economic, social, and cultural provisions relates to the difference in the implementation contemplated. Initially the Commission on Human Rights drafted provisions for the establishment of a Human Rights Committee to which complaints by one state against another state may be filed. The Commission did not then have time at its session this spring to decide whether this machinery should also be applicable to the economic, social, and cultural provisions, but there actually was general sentiment in the Commission that this complaint machinery should be limited to the civil and political provisions of the Covenant. It was felt by those with whom I discussed this matter in the Commission that this machinery is not appropriate for the economic, social, and cultural provisions of the Covenant, since these rights are to be achieved progressively and since the obligations of states with respect to these rights were not as precise as those with respect to the civil and political rights. These members of the Commission thought that it would be preferable, with respect to the economic, social, and cultural rights, to stress the importance of assisting states to achieve economic, social, and cultural progress rather than to stress the filing of complaints against states in this field.

Instead of a complaint procedure, a reporting procedure was devised by the Commission with respect to the progress made in the observance of the economic, social, and cultural provisions of the Covenant.

A fourth difference between the civil and political rights and the economic, social, and cultural rights relates to the drafting of these rights. The economic, social, and cultural provisions were necessarily drafted in broad language as contrasted to the civil and political provisions. For example, article 22 simply provides that "The States Parties to the Covenant recognize the right of everyone to social security." It was thought in the

Commission that since economic, social, and cultural provisions were being stated in terms of broad objectives, general language would be adequate.

It seems to my delegation that these four basic differences between the civil and political rights and the economic, social, and cultural rights warrant the separation of the present provisions of the Covenant into two covenants, one covenant on civil and political rights and another covenant on economic, social, and cultural rights. By a separation of these rights into two separate covenants we would avoid a great deal of confusion that is naturally inherent in a combination of all these different provisions in one covenant.

Equality of Importance in the Two Groups of Rights

Of course, I realize that some members of this Committee argue for a single covenant to include all the provisions now before us. The principal argument urged by those pressing this view is that there should be no differentiations in importance between civil and political rights and economic, social, and cultural rights. In the proposal that I wish to make to the Committee there is no question raised with respect to the importance of one group of rights as against another group of rights. I consider each group of rights of equal importance. My proposal would maintain this equality of importance.

My delegation proposes that two covenants of equal importance be completed in the United Nations simultaneously and be opened for signature and ratification at the same time. Neither one nor the other covenant would be called the first or the second covenant. Each of the two covenants would be on human rights, one setting forth the civil and political rights, and the other setting forth the economic, social, and cultural rights. We would request the Commission on Human Rights to prepare both of these covenants for the consideration of the General Assembly next year.***

Notes and Questions

1. What effect does the bifurcation of the International Bill of Rights into two covenants have on the implementation of these rights? What are the ideological bases for the separation? African-American feminist Lisa Crooms asserts that this division of rights into mutually exclusive categories undermines their protection:

> [T]he "both/and" conceptual stance reflected in the Charter and the UDHR is compromised by the existence of separate covenants, conventions, and declarations, the ranking of rights in an overarching hierarchy, and the procedures by which states choose which instruments to ratify and under what conditions they will do so. This paradox has proven particularly deleterious for women.***
>
> With respect to the constructed rights hierarchy and its impact on women's human rights, many of the "first-generation rights" associated with civil and political life do not reach much of what causes women's oppression. For example, in the area of state accountability for rights deprivations, the traditional distinction between public and private life, central to much of the civil and political rights discourse, has proven to be largely incompatible with many women's human-rights deprivations. Indeed, for most women, "there is little difference between the relationship of the citizen to government in exercising judgment and making laws, and the father and the husband who govern from 'natural' authority.

Lisa A. Crooms, *Indivisible Rights and Intersectional Identities or, "What Do Women's Human Rights Have to Do With the Race Convention?"* 40 HOWARD L.J. 619, 628–30 (1997). Do you agree?

2.   Are there any advantages that might be gained by separating human rights protections into separate agreements?

VIENNA DECLARATION AND PROGRAMME OF ACTION

Adopted by the World Conference on Human Rights, Vienna, June 25, 1993

(A/CONF. 157/24 (Part 1), chap. 111).

¶5. All human rights are universal, indivisible and interdependent and interrelated. The international community must treat human rights globally in a fair and equal manner, on the same footing, and with the same emphasis. While the significance of national and regional particularities and various historical, cultural and religious backgrounds must be borne in mind, it is the duty of States, regardless of their political, economic and cultural systems, to promote and protect all human rights and fundamental freedoms.

Notes and Questions

1.   What is the significance of the assertion that all human rights are "interdependent" and "equal"? Are some rights inherently incompatible? What status does the Vienna Declaration accord different cultural particularities?

B.   FOUNDATIONS OF LIBERAL RIGHTS DISCOURSE

ARISTOTLE, POLITICS

ARISTOTLE POLITICS (Benjamin Jowett, H. W. C. Davis eds.,
Dover Publications ed. 2000)

Book One

Part II

*** The family is the association established by nature for the supply of men's everyday wants.*** But when several families are united, and the association aims at something more than the supply of daily needs, the first society to be formed is the village.***

When several villages are united in a single complete community, large enough to be nearly or quite self-sufficing, the state comes into existence, originating in the bare needs of life, and continuing in existence for the sake of a good life. And therefore, if the earlier forms of society are natural, so is the state, for it is the end of them, and the nature of a thing is its end.***

Hence it is evident that the state is a creation of nature, and that man is by nature a political animal.***

Further, the state is by nature clearly prior to the family and to the individual, since the whole is of necessity prior to the part; for example, if the whole body be destroyed, there will be no foot or hand, except in an equivocal sense, as we might speak of a stone hand; for when destroyed the hand will be no better than that.*** The proof that the state is a creation of nature and prior to the individual is that the individual, when isolated, is not self-sufficing; and therefore he is like a part in relation to the whole. But he who is unable to live in society, or who has no need because he is sufficient for himself, must be either a beast or a god: he is no part of a state. A social instinct is implanted in all men by nature, and yet he who first founded the state was the greatest of benefactors. For man, when perfected, is the best of animals, but, when separated from law and justice, he is the worst of all ***. But justice is the bond of men in states, for the administration of justice, which is the determination of what is just, is the principle of order in political society.***

Book Three

Part VI

*** First, let us consider what is the purpose of a state, and how many forms of government there are by which human society is regulated. We have already said *** that man is by nature a political animal. And therefore, men, even when they do not require one another's help, desire to live together; not but that they are also brought together by their common interests in proportion as they severally attain to any measure of well-being. This is certainly the chief end, both of individuals and of states. And also for the sake of mere life *** mankind meet together and maintain the political community. And we all see that men cling to life even at the cost of enduring great misfortune, seeming to find in life a natural sweetness and happiness.***

Part IX

*** But a state exists for the sake of a good life, and not for the sake of life only: if life only were the object, slaves and brute animals might form a state, but they cannot, for they have no share in happiness or in a life of free choice. Nor does a state exist for the sake of alliance and security from injustice, nor yet for the sake of exchange and mutual intercourse;*** Nor does one state take care that the citizens of the other are such as they ought to be, nor see that those who come under the terms of the treaty do no wrong or wickedness at all, but only that they do no injustice to one another. Whereas, those who care for good government take into consideration virtue and vice in states. Whence it may be further inferred that virtue must be the care of a state which is truly so called, and not merely enjoys the name: for without this end the community becomes a mere alliance which differs only in place from alliances of which the members live apart; and law is only a convention, 'a surety to one another of justice,' as the sophist Lycophron says, and has no real power to make the citizens.***

It is clear then that a state is not a mere society, having a common place, established for the prevention of mutual crime and for the sake of exchange. These are conditions without which a state cannot exist; but all of them together do not constitute a state, which is a community of families and aggregations of families in well-being, for the sake of a perfect and self-sufficing life. Such a community can only be established among those who live in the same place and intermarry. Hence arise in cities family connections, brotherhoods, common sacrifices, amusements which draw men together. But these are created by friendship, for the will to live together is friendship. The end of the state is the good life, and these are the means towards it. And the state is the union of families and villages in a perfect and self-sufficing life, by which we mean a happy and honorable life.***

Notes and Questions

1.   A Greek philosopher who lived from 384–322 BC, Aristotle was a student of Plato, and teacher of Alexander the Great. In the *Politics*, Aristotle sought to describe a society that embodies the virtues necessary to attain the "good life." His works provided the basis for the natural law theory of Thomas Aquinas.

2.   Fundamental to Aristotle's thought is the concept of human beings as "political animals"—fulfilled and capable of pursuing the good life only in a political community. He viewed the state as a natural progression of the human need to associate, rather than an artificial construct created through a social contract. Membership in the political community was restricted, however, excluding women and slaves, whom he regarded as incapable of developing the necessary virtues of citizenship.

3.   If human beings are completely fulfilled only in a political community, does it follow that the individual's happiness must involve the good of fellow members of a community? Does this provide a theoretical basis for economic, social, and cultural rights?

4.   According to Aristotle, citizenship is an acquired status. Similarly, Confucius identified *ren*—literally "becoming a person"—as the recognition that personal character is the consequence of cultivating one's relationships with others. Later, Wiredu makes a similar point regarding Akan society (*see infra*). What are the implications of this view for human rights?

5.   Aristotle also believed the state has a duty to cultivate "virtue." What would such a duty entail? Is such a duty consistent with the concept of limited government? Does it suggest a potential conflict between some social values and traditional civil rights?

JOHN LOCKE, SECOND TREATISE OF GOVERNMENT

(1698)

Chapter V.

Of Property

25.   Whether we consider natural *Reason*, which tells us that Men, being once born, have a right to their Preservation consequently to Meat and Drink, and such other things as Nature affords for their subsistence; or *Revelation*, which gives us an account of those Grants God made of the World to *Adam*, and to *Noah*, and his Sons; 'tis very clear, that God *** *has given the Earth to the Children of Men*, given it to Mankind in common. But this being supposed, it seems to some a very great difficulty how anyone should ever come to have a Property in anything; *I will* not content myself to answer, That if it be difficult to make out *Property*, upon a supposition, That God gave the World to *Adam* and his Posterity in common; it is *impossible* that any Man, but one universal Monarch, should have any *Property* upon a supposition, That God gave the World to *Adam*, and his Heirs in Succession, exclusive of all the rest of his Posterity. But I still endeavor to show, how Men might come to have a property in several parts of that which God gave to mankind in common, and that without any express Compact of all the commoners.

26. God, who hath given the World to Men in common, hath also given them reason to make use of it to the best advantage of Life, and convenience. The Earth, and all that is therein, is given to men for the Support and Comfort of their being. And though all the Fruits it naturally produces, and Beasts it feeds, belong to Mankind in common, as they are produced by the spontaneous hand of Nature; and no body has originally a private Dominion, exclusive of the rest of Mankind, in any of them, as they are thus in their natural state: yet being given the use of Men, there must of necessity be a means to appropriate them some way or other before they can be of any use, or at all beneficial to any particular Man.***

27. Though the Earth, and all inferior Creatures be common to all Men, yet every Man has a *Property* in his own *Person*. This no Body has any Right to but himself. The *Labor* of his Body, and the *Work* of his hands, we may say, are properly his. Whatsoever then he removes out of the State that Nature hath provided, and left it in, he hath mixed his Labor with it, and joined to it something that is his own, and thereby makes it his Property. It being by him removed from the common state Nature placed it in, it hath by this labor something annexed to it, that excludes the common right of other Men. For this *Labor* being the unquestionable *Property* of the *Laborer*, no Man but he can have a right to what that is once joined to, at least where there is enough, and as good left in common for others.***

31. It will perhaps be objected to this, That if gathering the Acorns, or other Fruits of the Earth, etc. makes a right to them, then any one may engross as much as he will. To which I Answer, Not so. The same Law of Nature that does by this means gives us Property, does also bound that property too.*** As much as any one can make use of to any advantage of life before it spoils; so much he may by his labor fix a Property in. Whatever is beyond this, is more than his share, and belongs to others. Nothing was made by God for Man to spoil or destroy.***

32. *** As much Land as a Man Tills, Plants, Improves, Cultivates, and can use the Product of, so much is his Property. He by his Labor does, as it were, inclose it from the Common.*** God, when he gave the World in common to all Mankind, commanded Man also to labor, and the penury of his Condition required it of him. God and his Reason commanded him to subdue the Earth, *i.e.* improve it for the benefit of Life, and therein lay out something upon it that was his own, his labor. He that in Obedience to this Command of God, subdued, tilled and sowed any part of it, thereby annexed to it something that was his Property, which another had no Title to, nor could without injury take from him.

33. Nor was this appropriation of any parcel of land, by improving it, any prejudice to any other Man since there was still enough, and as good left, and more than the yet unprovided could use.***

Chapter IX.

Of the Ends of Political Society and Government

123. If Man in the State of Nature be so free, as has been said; if he be absolute Lord of his own Person and Possessions, equal to the greatest, and subject to no Body, why will he part with his Freedom? Why will he give up this Empire, and subject himself to the Dominion and Control of any other Power? To which 'tis obvious to Answer, that though in the state of Nature he hath such a right, yet the Enjoyment of it is very

uncertain, and constantly exposed to the Invasion of others; for all being Kings as much as he, every Man is Equal, and the greater part no strict Observers of Equity and Justice; the enjoyment of the property he has in this state is very unsafe, very unsecure. This makes him willing to quit this Condition, which however free, is full of fears and continual dangers: And 'tis not without reason, that he seeks out, and is willing to join in Society with others who are already united, or have a mind to unite for the mutual Preservation of their Lives, Liberties and Estates, which I call by the general Name, Property.

Notes and Questions

1. Locke's theory of property diverged from that of Hobbes, who had argued that rights of property only came into existence when states were created, and that no one held such rights against the sovereign. Locke argued that people acquired rights to things with which they have mixed their labor, thereby defending the property rights of the wealthy against royal encroachment. Nevertheless, his theory of natural rights and revolution influenced the American Declaration of Independence and subsequent ideas of constitutionalism. His development of the labor theory of value laid the groundwork for the economic theories of Adam Smith and Karl Marx.

2. What are the implications of Locke's account of the origins of private property as preceding civil society, rather than being a creation of law and society?

3. How does Locke's social contract theory differ from Aristotle's concept of the state as a natural entity? Which approach entails more protection for human rights?

4. Locke envisioned a state of nature comprised of individuals, as opposed to groups, such as tribes, clans, families, etc. What are the implications of this conception for human rights discourse?

5. Locke's theory of property and appropriation rationalized the conquest of Native American lands and resources. Grounding rights to land in its improvement and cultivation, Second Treatise at ¶ 31, Locke denied such rights to "the wild Indian, who knows no enclosure, and is still a tenant in common." *Id.* at ¶ 25. Indeed, in his thesis, any parcel of their land could be appropriated by improving it, even without the consent of the native inhabitants. *Id.* at ¶¶ 27, 32.

WESLEY NEWCOMB HOHFELD, SOME FUNDAMENTAL LEGAL CONCEPTIONS AS APPLIED IN JUDICIAL REASONING

23 Yale L.J. 16, 28–44 (1913)

One of the greatest hindrances to the clear understanding, the incisive statement, and the true solution of legal problems frequently arises from the express or tacit assumption that all legal relations may be reduced to "rights" and "duties," and that these latter categories are therefore adequate for the purpose of analyzing even the most complex legal interests, such as trusts, options, escrows, "future" interests, corporate interests, etc. Even if the difficulty related merely to inadequacy and ambiguity of terminology, its seriousness would nevertheless be worthy of definite recognition and persistent effort toward improvement; for in any closely reasoned problem, whether legal or non-legal, chameleon-hued words are a peril both to clear thought and to lucid expression. As a matter of fact, however, the above mentioned inadequacy and ambiguity of terms unfortunately reflect, all too often, corresponding paucity and confusion as regards actual legal conceptions.***

The strictly fundamental legal relations are, after all, *sui generis*; and thus it is that attempts at firm definition are always unsatisfactory, if not altogether useless. Accordingly, the most promising line of procedure seems to consist in exhibiting all of the various relations in a scheme of "opposites" and "correlatives," and then proceeding to exemplify their individual scope and application in concrete cases. An effort will be made to pursue this method:

Jural	rights	privilege	power	immunity
Opposites	no-rights	duty	disability	liability

Jural	right	privilege	power	immunity
Correlatives	duty	no-right	liability	disability

Rights and Duties. As already intimated, the term "rights" tends to be used indiscriminately to cover what in a given case may be a privilege, a power, or an immunity, rather than a right in the strictest sense.***

Recognizing, as we must, the very broad and indiscriminate use of the term, "right," what clue do we find, in ordinary legal discourse, toward limiting the word in question to a definite and appropriate meaning. That clue lies in the correlative "duty," for it is certain that even those who use the word and the conception "right" in the broadest possible way are accustomed to thinking of "duty" as the invariable correlative.***

In other words, if X has a right against Y that he shall stay off the former's land, the correlative (and equivalent) is that Y is under a duty toward X to stay off the place. If, as seems desirable, we should seek a synonym for the term "right" in this limited and proper meaning, perhaps the word "claim" would prove the best.***

Notes and Questions

1.   Wesley Hohfeld's noted analytic scheme of jural correlatives and jural opposites sought to establish the importance of applying the appropriate terminology in rights discourse. Hohfeld's premise was that the word "right" and other less precise terms are often used interchangeably, resulting in a lack of analytical clarity. In his system, terms denoting legal relationships are defined by their correlatives and opposites. Thus, the term "right" should be limited to claims in which a correlative duty could be identified, as distinguished from entitlements which do not impose such a duty, more appropriately labeled "privileges," "liberties," "powers" or "immunities."

2.   What are the implications of Hohfeld's system for human rights discourse? Does his system differentiate between "negative" rights and "positive" rights? Does his emphasis on the identification of a correlative duty-holder limit the range of rights-talk to a narrower category of values? Does the Hohfeldian "claim-right" confine the language of rights to instances in which a legal remedy is provided? Does this system take into account the potential inter-relatedness of claims?

3. *Cf.* JACK DONNELLY, UNIVERSAL HUMAN RIGHTS IN THEORY AND PRACTICE 8 (2d ed. 2003):

> Rights are not reducible to the correlative duties of those against whom they are held. If Anne has a right to *x* with respect to Bob, it is more than simply desirable, good, or even right that Anne enjoy *x*. She is entitled to it. Should Bob fail to discharge his obligations, besides acting improperly *** and harming Anne, he violates her rights, making him subject to special remedial claims and sanctions.

What is the significance of Donnelly's critique?

JOHN RAWLS, A THEORY OF JUSTICE 11–15 (1971)

My aim is to present a conception of justice which generalizes and carries to a higher level of abstraction the familiar theory of the social contract. [T]he guiding idea is that the principles of justice for the basic structure of society are the object of the original agreement. They are the principles that free and rational persons concerned to further their own interests would accept in an initial position of equality as defining the fundamental terms of their association. These principles *** specify the kinds of social cooperation that can be entered into and the forms of government that can be established. This way of regarding the principles of justice I shall call justice as fairness.

Thus we are to imagine that those who engage in social cooperation choose together, in one joint act, the principles which are to assign basic rights and duties and to determine the division of social benefits. Men are to decide in advance how they are to regulate their claims against one another and what is to be the foundation charter of their society. Just as each person must decide by rational reflection what constitutes his good, that is, the system of ends which it is rational for him to pursue, so a group of persons must decide once and for all what is to count among them as just and unjust. The choice which rational men would make in this hypothetical situation of equal liberty *** determines the principles of justice.

In justice as fairness the original position of equality corresponds to the state of nature in the traditional theory of the social contract. This original position is *** understood as a purely hypothetical situation characterized so as to lead to a certain conception of justice. Among the essential features of this situation is that no one knows his place in society, his class position or social status, nor does anyone know his fortune in the distribution of natural assets and abilities, his intelligence, strength, and the like. I shall even assume that the parties do not know their conceptions of the good or their special psychological propensities. The principles of justice are chosen behind a veil of ignorance. This ensures that no one is advantaged or disadvantaged in the choice of principles by the outcome of natural chance or the contingency of social circumstances. Since all are similarly situated and no one is able to design principles to favor his particular condition, the principles of justice are the result of a fair agreement or bargain. For given the circumstances of the original position, the symmetry of everyone's relations to each other, this initial situation is fair between individuals as moral persons, that is, as rational beings with their own ends and capable, I shall assume, of a sense of justice. The original position is, one might say, the appropriate initial status quo, and thus the fundamental agreements reached in it are fair.***

Justice as fairness begins, as I have said, with one of the most general of all choices which persons might make together, namely, with the choice of the first principles of a conception of justice.*** Then, having chosen a conception of justice, we can suppose that they are to choose a constitution and a legislature to enact laws, and so on, all in accordance with the principles of justice initially agreed upon. Our social situation is just if it is such that by this sequence of hypothetical agreements we would have contracted into the general system of rules which defines it. Moreover, assuming that the original position does determine a set of principles (that is, that a particular conception of justice would be chosen), it will then be true that whenever social institutions satisfy these principles those engaged in them can say to one another that they are cooperating on terms to which they would agree if they were free and equal persons whose relations with respect to one another were fair. They could all view their arrangements as meeting the stipulations which they would acknowledge in an initial situation that embodies widely accepted and reasonable constraints on the choice of principles. The general recognition of this fact would provide the basis for a public acceptance of the corresponding principles of justice. No society can, of course, be a scheme of cooperation which men enter voluntarily in a literal sense; each person finds himself placed at birth in some particular position in some particular society, and the nature of this position materially affects his life prospects. Yet a society satisfying the principles of justice as fairness comes as close as a society can to being a voluntary scheme, for it meets the principles which free and equal persons would assent to under circumstances that are fair. In this sense its members are autonomous and the obligations they recognize self-imposed.

One feature of justice as fairness is to think of the parties in the initial situation as rational and mutually disinterested. This does not mean that the parties are egoists, that is, individuals with only certain kinds of interests, say in wealth, prestige, and domination. But they are conceived as not taking an interest in one another's interests. They are to presume that even their spiritual aims may be opposed, in the way that the aims of those of different religions may be opposed. Moreover, the concept of rationality must be interpreted as far as possible in the narrow sense, standard in economic theory, of taking the most effective means to given ends. [O]ne must try to avoid introducing into it any controversial ethical elements. The initial situation must be characterized by stipulations that are widely accepted.***

I shall maintain *** that the persons in the initial situation would choose two rather different principles: the first requires equality in the assignment of basic rights and duties, while the second holds that social and economic inequalities, for example inequalities of wealth and authority, are just only if they result in compensating benefits for everyone and in particular for the least advantaged members of society. [T]here is no injustice in the greater benefits earned by a few provided that the situation of persons not so fortunate is thereby improved. The intuitive idea is that since everyone's well-being depends upon a scheme of cooperation without which no one could have a satisfactory life, the division of advantages should be such as to draw forth the willing cooperation of everyone taking part in it, including those less well situated. Yet this can be expected only if reasonable terms are proposed. The two principles mentioned seem to be a fair agreement on the basis of which those better endowed, or more fortunate in their social position, neither of which we can be said to deserve, could expect the willing cooperation of others when some workable scheme is a necessary condition of the welfare of all. Once we decide to look for a conception of justice that nullifies the accidents of natural endowment and the contingencies of social circumstance as counters in quest for political and economic advantage, we are led to these principles. They express the result of leaving aside those aspects of the social world that seem arbitrary from a moral point of view.***

TWO PRINCIPLES OF JUSTICE

I shall now state in a provisional form the two principles of justice that I believe would be chosen in the original position.***

First: each person is to have an equal right to the most extensive basic liberty compatible with a similar liberty for others.

Second: social and economic inequalities are to be arranged so that they are both (a) reasonably expected to be to everyone's advantage, and (b) attached to positions and offices open to all [the difference principle].***

[T]hese principles primarily apply, as I have said, to the basic structure of society. They are to govern the assignment of rights and duties and to regulate the distribution of social and economic advantages. As their formulation suggests, these principles presuppose that the social structure can be divided into two more or less distinct parts, the first principle applying to the one, the second to the other. They distinguish between those aspects of the social system that define and secure the equal liberties of citizenship and those that specify and establish social and economic inequalities. The basic liberties of citizens are, roughly speaking, political liberty (the right to vote and to be eligible for public office) together with freedom of speech and assembly; liberty of conscience and freedom of thought; freedom of the person along with the right to hold (personal) property; and freedom from arbitrary arrest and seizure as defined by the concept of the rule of law. These liberties are all required to be equal by the first principle, since citizens of a just society are to have the same basic rights.]

The second principle applies, in the first approximation, to the distribution of income and wealth and to the design of organizations that make use of differences in authority and responsibility, or chains of command. While the distribution of wealth and income need not be equal, it must be to everyone's advantage, and at the same time, positions of authority and offices of command must be accessible to all. One applies the second principle by holding positions open, and then, subject to this constraint, arranges social and economic inequalities so that everyone benefits.

These principles are to be arranged in a serial order with the first principle prior to the second. This ordering means that a departure from the institutions of equal liberty required by the first principle cannot be justified by, or compensated for, by greater social and economic advantages. The distribution of wealth and income, and the hierarchies of authority, must be consistent with both the liberties of equal citizenship and equality of opportunity.

[T]he two principles (and this holds for all formulations) are a special case of a more general conception of justice that can be expressed as follows.

All social values—liberty and opportunity, income and wealth, and the bases of self-respect—are to be distributed equally unless an unequal distribution of any, or all, of these values is to everyone's advantage.

Injustice, then, is simply inequalities that are not to the benefit of all.***

THE TENDENCY TO EQUALITY

I wish to conclude this discussion of the two principles by explaining the sense in which they express an egalitarian conception of justice. Also I should like to forestall the objection to the principle of fair opportunity that it leads to a callous meritocratic society. In order to prepare the way for doing this, I note several aspects of the conception of justice that I have set out.***

*** Now the difference principle is not of course the principle of redress. It does not require society to try to even out handicaps as if all were expected to compete on a fair basis in the same race. But the difference principle would allocate resources in education, say, so as to improve the long term expectation of the least favored. If this end is attained by giving more attention to the better endowed, it is permissible; otherwise not. And in making this decision, the value of education should not be assessed only in terms of economic efficiency and social welfare. Equally if not more important is the role of education in enabling a person to enjoy the culture of his society and to take part in its affairs, and in this way to provide for each individual a secure sense of his own worth.

Thus although the difference principle is not the same as that of redress, it does achieve some of the intent of the latter principle. It transforms the aims of the basic structure so that the total scheme of institutions no longer emphasizes social efficiency and technocratic values. We see then that the difference principle represents, in effect, an agreement to regard the distribution of natural talents as a common asset and to share in the benefits of this distribution whatever it turns out to be. Those who have been favored by nature, whoever they are, may gain from their good fortune only on terms that improve the situation of those who have lost out. The naturally advantaged are not to gain merely because they are more gifted, but only to cover the costs of training and education and for using their endowments in ways that help the less fortunate as well. No one deserves his greater natural capacity nor merits a more favorable starting place in society. But it does not follow that one should eliminate these distinctions. There is another way to deal with them. The basic structure can be arranged so that these contingencies work for the good of the least fortunate. Thus we are led to the difference principle if we wish to set up the social system so that no one gains or loses from his arbitrary place in the distribution of natural assets or his initial position in society without giving or receiving compensating advantages in return.***

Notes and Questions

1. Rawls' theory continues the project of the rights-based social contractarian school, which holds that just societies are formed by the agreement of their members. In *A Theory of Justice*, he attempts to fill in the gaps left by Locke and other contractarians by providing the details of the transition from the state of nature to civil society. (Rawls' "original position" is a hypothetical construct, whereas Locke viewed the state of nature as an actual historical era.) Rawls considers two major questions: the conditions under which the agreement will be negotiated, and the terms of the agreement that would be reached.

2. The express aim of *A Theory of Justice* is to present an alternative to utilitarianism, the concept that a just society ought to work toward the greatest possible good for the greatest number of people. In what way does Rawls' philosophy reject utilitarianism?

3. *The Veil of Ignorance.* What is the function of the "veil of ignorance" in Rawls' theory? How does it facilitate the construction of the equal liberty and difference principles? What social institutions might be imagined in the absence of such a device? Does the veil really establish a value-neutral approach to determining principles of justice? Does it contain an implicit conception of the good life? What conceptions of justice might be "intuitive" in a different paradigm, *e.g.*, a milieu characterized by communitarianism, social ownership, or matriarchy?

4. What is the effect on economic, social and cultural rights of giving priority to "basic" (*i.e.*, political) liberties and to equality of opportunity? David Kennedy argues that "[w]hile the powerful of any ideological stripe will prefer a system of free bargaining among procedural equals, this should never satisfy the weak." David Kennedy, *Book Review*, 21 HARV. INT'L L.J. 301, 301 (1980). Do you agree? What is the practical applicability of Rawls' principles? What reforms, if any, would be necessary in order to implement them?

5. Critics assert that Rawls' focus on the autonomous, rational individual excludes the interests of vulnerable sectors of society, such as children and the mentally disabled. Some also claim that he undervalues inequalities in the private sphere. For a feminist critique of Rawls, *see* Mari Matsuda, *Liberal Jurisprudence and Abstracted Visions of Human Nature: A Feminist Critique of Rawls' Theory of Justice*, 16 N.M. L. REV. 613 (1986). One commentator suggests that the concept "rational men" means "the elites throughout the system, including its periphery." Immanuel Wallerstein, *Civilizations and Modes of Production: Conflicts and Convergences, in* CULTURE, IDEOLOGY AND WORLD ORDER 66 (R.B.J. Walker ed., 1984).

6. *Justice as Fairness: A Restatement.* In this 2001 book, Rawls addresses some of the criticisms and ambiguities of his earlier work. He explains that his theory did not propose a universal, generally applicable conception of justice, but that it was premised on democratic institutions. What effect does this acknowledgement have on the construct of the "original position?"

7. Rawls further clarified that the goal of his account of justice was to articulate values relevant to political relationships as opposed to associations in the private realm. He revised his statement of the two principles of justice as follows:

> (a) Each person has the same indefeasible claim to a fully adequate scheme of equal basic liberties, which scheme is compatible with the same scheme of liberties for all; and

> (b) Social and economic inequalities are to satisfy two conditions: first, they are to be attached to offices and positions open to all under conditions of fair equality of opportunity; and second, they are to be to the greatest benefit of the least-advantaged members of society (the difference principle).

> [T]he first principle is prior to the second; also, in the second principle fair equality of opportunity is prior to the difference principle.***

RESTATEMENT, § 13.1.

8. How does Rawls' restatement differ from his original formulation? Does it offer more or less protection for economic, social and cultural rights? Does it adequately distinguish itself from utilitarianism?

9.   While focusing on the basic institutions of a just society, Rawls concludes that either a "property-owning democracy" or "liberal (democratic) socialism" would satisfy his two principles of justice. His concept of "property-owning democracy" distinguishes it from both laissez-faire capitalism and the welfare state:

> In property-holding democracy *** the aim is to realize in the basic institutions the idea of society as a fair system of cooperation between citizens regarded as free and equal. To do this, those institutions must, from the outset, put in the hands of citizens generally, and not only of a few, sufficient productive means for them to be fully cooperating members of society on a footing of equality. Among these means is human as well as real capital, that is, knowledge and an understanding of institutions, educated abilities, and trained skills. Only in this way can the basic structure realize pure background procedural justice from one generation to the next.

RESTATEMENT, § 42.4. What policies would be necessary in order to achieve such a society? What are its relative advantages and disadvantages? Does Rawls' ultimate acceptance of social inequalities contradict the goals of a just society?

LOUIS HENKIN, RIGHTS: HERE AND THERE

81 COLUM. L. REV. 1582, 1582–86 (1981)

*** By rights I mean what are now called human rights, claims which every individual has, or should have, upon the society in which he/she lives. To call them human suggests that they are universal: they are the due of every human being in every human society. They do not differ with geography or history, culture or ideology, political or economic system, or stage of development. They do not depend on gender or race, class or status. To call them "rights" implies that they are claims "as of right," not merely appeals to grace, or charity, or brotherhood, or love; they need not be earned or deserved. They are more than aspirations, or assertions of "the good," but claims of entitlement and corresponding obligation in some political order under some applicable law, if only in a moral order under a moral law.

When used carefully, "human rights" are not some abstract, inchoate "good." The rights are particular, defined, and familiar, reflecting respect for individual dignity and a substantial measure of individual autonomy, as well as a common sense of justice and injustice. Enumerated in international instruments, notably the Universal Declaration of Human Rights, they include: the right to one's life and to physical and psychological integrity, free from torture or mistreatment; to freedom from arbitrary physical restraint; to fair trial in the criminal process; to freedom from invasions of privacy; to freedom of conscience, expression, and association; to equal protection of the laws; the right to participate in government; as well as to have basic human needs satisfied—food and shelter, health care, education.

The Universal Declaration of Human Rights has now been accepted by all governments representing all societies. Human rights are also enshrined in the constitutions of virtually every one of today's 150 states—old states and new; religious, secular, or atheist; capitalist, socialist, or mixed; developed, developing, or less developed.***

*** Individual rights are at the heart of the theory of the American polity, articulated in our early national hagiography, notably the Declaration of Independence and the Virginia Declaration.*** They are not a gift from society or from any government. They are not merely concessions extracted from, and limitations imposed on, preexisting, established government, in the tradition of Magna Carta and subsequent English bills; rather, they are freedoms and entitlements of all men, everywhere, antecedent and superior to government. They do not derive from any constitution; they antecede constitutions. But they are retained under and protected by the constitution establishing a political society. In Virginia, in Massachusetts, and elsewhere, our ancestors wrote social compacts, according to their political faith. The United States Constitution, which came later, reflected the same theory: popular sovereignty, in "We the people *** ordain this Constitution"; rights, in the Bill of Rights, which does not grant rights but safeguards antecedent rights, as is made explicit in the ninth and tenth amendments.

The rights retained by our ancestors reflect their conceptions of the good society, of justice, and of other values accepted as axiomatic. Every human being is a person, entitled to the political, social, and legal implications of personhood. The family is the natural unit. The individual is essentially autonomous, free to pursue his happiness as he will. He is entitled to his property, acquired honestly by labor, trade, or inheritance. An individual accused of crime is entitled to a fair trial because it is, obviously, unjust to deprive him of his liberty without due process of law. The good society is the liberal society in which the individual enjoys his antecedent freedoms—religion, speech, press, assembly—giving up only a little to the needs of society.

What the people retained reflects also what they gave up to their governors—the authority their representatives needed for the purposes of governing. The purposes for which government was formed were commonly understood. Government was to be a watchman, a policeman. It would promote safety, health, and morals. It was not seen as the business of government to provide the people with the "welfare state" variety of welfare; government was to leave the individual free to pursue it himself. (Only the obligation to provide or promote education found its way early into state constitutions.)***

More serious is the charge, commonly heard around the world, that our eighteenth century theory of social contract and of rights is hardly sufficient for our century. Our rights theory supports rights deriving from, and vindicating, individual freedom and autonomy, but not claims upon society to do for the individual what he cannot do for himself. It tells government only what not to do, not what it must do. There is no constitutional right to freedom from want. The United States is a welfare state not by constitutional mandate but by grace of Congress, and subject to political and budgetary constraints.***

Notes and Questions

1.   Louis Henkin's work has had a significant influence on international human rights jurisprudence and scholarship. *See e.g.*, LOUIS HENKIN, THE AGE OF RIGHTS (1990); HUMAN RIGHTS (Louis Henkin, et al. eds., 1999); HUMAN RIGHTS: AN AGENDA FOR THE TWENTY-FIRST CENTURY (Louis Henkin & John Hargrove eds., 1994); Louis Henkin, *Economic Rights under the U.S. Constitution*, 32 COLUM. J. TRANSNAT'L L. 97 (1994) (discussing market-based economic rights in the U.S. constitution); Louis Henkin, *Human Rights and State Sovereignty* 25 GA. J. INT'L & COMP. L. 31 (1995) (discussing the weakening of national sovereignty and the role of the state in implementing human rights prin-

ciples); Louis Henkin, *The Universal Declaration at 50 and the Challenge of Global Markets*, 25 BROOK. J. INT'L L. 17 (1999) (reflections on the state of international human rights principles under globalization).

2.   What does Henkin mean when he says that human rights are antecedent to "any government" or state. Does this suggest that human rights have meaning even without implementation by states or international bodies? What is the value of viewing rights as pre-existing the mechanisms created to enforce them?

3.   Should "basic human needs" such as food, shelter, and health care have the same priority as due process rights and the right to participate in government?

Consider the following review of Henkin's influential book, *The Age of Rights*, by another leading international legal scholar, Henry Steiner:

HENRY J. STEINER, THE YOUTH OF RIGHTS

104 HARV. L. REV. 917, 923–30 (1991)

*** Great value resides in Henkin's primary project: the analysis of norms' ancestry, animating ideals, common principles, and interrelationships. By revealing human rights law's ideological formation and internal structure, such a project aids both scholars and advocates.***

These essays, however, go beyond the primary project to make claims about the sway of human rights in the world. This greater ambition requires a further level of description and analysis. To be sure, the essays do not ignore violations. At several points throughout the book, Henkin takes brief note of them through what I may term concessions. Thus, human rights born in the West have been universally accepted, "nominally at least" ***. The spread of national constitutions with human rights norms brought acceptance of those norms to all kinds of societies "at least in principle and rhetoric."*** Despite the universal consensus, the condition of human rights differs widely throughout the world and "leaves much to be desired in many countries" that are parties to the basic covenants ***.

*** In context *** such concessions have the character of brief qualifications that carry little weight compared with the book's major claims. Fragmentary rather than sustained, abstract rather than contextual, flat rather than graphic, these remarks do not form a subordinate or companion theme, let alone a countertheme.***

As a consequence, the worlds of international norms and states' violations remain apart in this book, the second brought in like an uncomfortable other dimension of the human rights movement that, if confined to discrete observations, allows the book's principal arguments to prevail. Henkin's several references to those questioning the meaning or efficacy of human rights as "skeptics"—people who instinctively or habitually doubt or disagree with assertions—rather than as realists, a happier characterization, suggests how their views embarrass the grand thesis of an "age of rights."

Does that thesis not require evaluation of the capacity of the human rights movement to advance its goals in relatively open societies and, more important, to achieve some significant measure of political change in oppressive ones? The value of the movement cannot lie in its contribution to moral thought (which long predated the positivization of rights through the postwar movement), but in its actual or potential influence on conduct.***

In many populous states the human rights situation remains consistently oppressive or, if it has improved, reveals risk of cyclical regression. We find ample evidence in Latin America (Guatemala, El Salvador, Argentina, Peru) and in Asia (China, Indonesia, India, Pakistan). Africa and the Middle East give rare cause for cheer. The potential for repression under new political forms in the [former] Soviet Union and Eastern European countries raises serious concerns. Ethnic conflicts rage in all these continents, often breeding brutal violations of rights by states and sometimes equivalent outrages by dissidents. From the perspective of the human rights movement's ideals, the picture is not relentlessly bleak, for recent advances may be confirmed and hopes may be realized. But it is bleak enough.

The question then is how to portray the significance of the human rights movement in a world of massive, cruel, and long-continuing violations, a world where international means of enforcement are, to use Henkin's apt term, primitive. It is instructive to set beside *The Age of Rights* a 1984 report by Amnesty International that contains accounts from ninety-eight countries of one of the ugliest of human rights violations. The report points out that no state legalizes torture, that indeed governments "universally and collectively" condemn it. Nonetheless, "more than a third of the world's governments have used or tolerated torture or ill-treatment of prisoners in the 1980s." Each of these books of radically different intentions tells an important part of the human rights story. Those parts complement each other by speaking to the ideal and the real, to norms and power, to law and politics.*** Together they expose the problematic character of [the human rights] movement. Do they in combination suggest that human rights is "the idea of our time," the "essential idea"?***

The essays reveal Professor Henkin's tendency to see the world harmoniously, both with respect to human rights' relationships to political order and their interrelationships. But these rights, viewed from the dual perspectives of their animating ideals and the world's political cultures, conflict with many governmental regimes for the root reason that one of their basic aims is to diffuse and limit power, partly by heightening political participation. Historically as well as today, rights often mean fights.***

[R]ights are often asserted *against* states and have often prevailed only over governments' violent resistance. Unlike many components of classical international law, the human rights movement was not meant to work out matters of reciprocal convenience among states—for example, sovereign or diplomatic immunities—or to aim only at regulating areas of historical conflict among states—for example, uses of the sea or airspace, or treatment by a state of its alien population. Rather it reached broad areas of everyday life within states that are vital to the internal rather than international distribution of political power. As international law's aspirations grew, as that law became more critical of and hence more distanced from states' behavior, the potential for conflict between human rights advocates within a state and that state's controlling elites escalated.

Even the most consensual of rights, the right not to be tortured, has a subversive potential. If, as the Amnesty International report suggests, torture amounts to the price of dissent because it is "most often used as an integral part of a government's security strategy," abolishing torture lowers that price. Oppressive regimes prefer to keep the price high.***

Notes and Questions

1.   Do you agree with Steiner's assertion that "[t]he value of the [human rights] movement cannot lie in its contribution to moral thought *** but in its actual or potential influence on conduct"? What do the continuous media reports of widespread human rights violations suggest about the influence and efficacy of the international human rights movement? Is there evidence that international human rights standards are becoming more widely recognized?

2.   The preamble to the Universal Declaration of Human Rights proclaims that, "it is essential, if man is not to be compelled to have recourse, as a last resort, to rebellion against tyranny and oppression, that human rights should be protected by the rule of law ***." Does Steiner's assertion that "[h]istorically as well as today, rights often mean fights" contradict this vision? Is human rights advocacy a fundamentally subversive enterprise from the perspective of state power? Does your answer depend on the category of rights being discussed, *i.e.*, whether the rights are classified as civil and political, or as economic, social, and cultural? Does the legal protection of human rights have a pacifying effect on political struggle? Do you believe that some governments ratify international human rights instruments for this reason? Why, then, would many governments fail to adhere to those commitments?

3.   Is it possible for the normative status of human rights to regress? For example, has the use of torture as an interrogation technique (perhaps under another name) been reasserted as a potentially legitimate national security tool after the events of September 11, 2001? *See e.g.*, Alan Dershowitz, *The Public Must Know If Torture Is Used*, THE AGE, (Melbourne) (Mar. 15, 2003) 9; Michael Ignatieff, *Evil under Interrogation: Is torture ever permissible?*, FIN. TIMES MAGAZINE May 15, 2004, 25 (noting that "Alan Dershowitz has suggested that investigators should be able to seek court-issued torture warrants in 'ticking bomb' cases" and revelations that U.S. and British soldiers had tortured and abused Iraqi prisoners); Andrew Maykuth, *Shift Seen in Public Views on Torture; Polls find that since Sept. 11, people have been more accepting*, MILWAUKEE J. SENTINEL May 16, 2004, 14A. Does the controversy on this issue provide support for Steiner's point about the potential conflict between human rights and the perceived interests of state authorities? Can you think of an economic, social, or cultural rights violation that has achieved the international significance of the prohibition on torture?

4.   Consider and compare the following statements on the nature and content of rights:

> Individual rights are political trumps held by individuals. Individuals have rights when, for some reason, a collective goal is not a sufficient justification for denying them what they wish, as individuals, to have or to do, or not a sufficient justification for imposing some loss or injury upon them. That characterization of a right *** does not suppose that rights have some special metaphysical character ***.

RONALD DWORKIN, TAKING RIGHTS SERIOUSLY xi (1977).

> Rights have been seen as a basis of protection not for all human interests but for those specifically related to choice, self-determination, agency, and independence. On this view, the duties correlative to rights are mainly negative in character; they are duties to refrain from obstructing action or interfering with choice, rather than duties to provide positive assistance.

JEREMY WALDRON, THEORIES OF RIGHTS 11 (1984).

> If human rights are the rights that one has simply as a human being, then only human beings have human rights; if one is not a human being, by definition one cannot have human rights. Because only individual persons are human beings, it would seem that only individuals can have human rights.
>
> Collectivities of all sorts have many and varied rights. But these are not—cannot be—human rights, unless we substantially recast the concept.

JACK DONNELLY, UNIVERSAL HUMAN RIGHTS IN THEORY AND PRACTICE 25 (2d ed. 2003).

> [T]he concept of a right belongs to that branch of morality which is specifically concerned to determine when one person's freedom may be limited by another's and so to determine what actions may appropriately be made the subject of coercive legal rules. [The morality of law] is occupied by the concepts of justice, fairness, rights and obligation ***. The most important common characteristic of this group of moral concepts is that there is no incongruity, but a special congruity in the use of force or the threat of force to secure that what is just or fair or someone's right to have done shall in fact be done; for it is in just these circumstances that coercion of another human being is legitimate.

H.L.A. Hart, *Are There Any Natural Rights?*, *in* JEREMY WALDRON, ED., THEORIES OF RIGHTS 77, 79–80 (1984).

> [A] philosophically respectable concept of human rights has been muddied, obscured and debilitated in recent years by an attempt to incorporate into it specific rights of a different logical category. The traditional human rights are political and civil rights, such as the right to life, liberty, and a fair trial. What are now being put forward as universal human rights are social and economic rights ***. I have both a philosophical and a political objection to this. The philosophical objection is that the new theory of human rights does not make sense. The political objection is that the circulation of a confused notion of human rights hinders the effective protection of what are correctly seen as human rights.

Maurice Cranston, *Human Rights, Real and Supposed*, *in* D.D. RAPHAEL ED., POLITICAL THEORY AND THE RIGHTS OF MAN 43 (1967).

> It makes no difference whether the legally enforced system of property where a given person lives is private, state, communal, or one of the many more typical mixtures and variants. Under all systems of property people are prevented from simply taking even what they need for survival. Whatever the property institutions and the economic system are, the question about rights to subsistence remains: if persons are forbidden by law from taking what they need to survive and they are unable within existing economic institutions and policies to provide for their own survival (and the survival of dependents for whose welfare they are responsible) are they entitled, as a last resort, to receive the essentials of survival from the remainder of humanity whose lives are not threatened?

HENRY SHUE, BASIC RIGHTS, SUBSISTENCE, AFFLUENCE AND U.S. FOREIGN POLICY 24 (1980).

> It is paradoxical, but hardly surprising, that the right to food has been endorsed more often and with greater unanimity and urgency than most other human

rights, while at the same time being violated more comprehensively and systematically than probably any other right. What is perhaps more surprising is that the widespread violation of the right to food in practice has been accompanied and even facilitated by the almost total neglect, for all practical intents and purposes, of its theoretical, normative and institutional aspects.

Philip Alston, *International Law and the Human Right to Food, in* P. ALSTON & K. TOMA-LEVSKI, EDS., THE RIGHT TO FOOD 9 (1984).

The protection of rights through law suits and regulatory proceedings imposes immense costs on ordinary transactions and elevates rights over responsibilities and individuals over communities. The existence of a safety net produces personal dependency and erodes savings, initiative and accountability; any means-tested program provides a strong incentive for people living near the cutoff point either to substitute welfare for work or to detest those who do.***

Income redistribution has never caught the fancy of Americans. Sidney Verba and his colleagues showed, in their important book, Elites and the Idea of Equality, that even the most liberal Americans are tolerant of income differences that would appall a conservative Swede. When American feminists, intellectuals and Democratic Party leaders are asked to define a fair ratio between the earnings of a top executive and a skilled worker in an auto company, on average they endorse a ratio of roughly six to one. Similar respondents in Sweden support a ratio closer to two to one. And when the comparison is between executives and elevator operators, the preferred ratio for American liberals is about ten to one, while for their Swedish counterparts it is about three to one. Democratic Party leaders in this country support as fair an income ratio that is more than twice as great as the income ratio thought fair by Swedish conservatives and business leaders.***

Elsewhere, the Enlightenment was modified—in France, by the tradition of a powerful central regime, in other countries, by the belief that government ought to preside over economic development and minimize the distinction between the public and private spheres. In the United States, however, the Enlightenment mentality came to us intact, protected by a tradition of limited government and a culture of legally defended rights.***

James Q. Wilson, *Liberal Ghosts*, A Review of ALAN BRINKLEY, NEW DEAL LIBERALISM IN RECESSION AND WAR, NEW REPUBLIC, May 22, 1995, at 31.

5.   For further reading on liberal rights theories, *see, e.g.,* MICHAEL J. SANDEL, LIBERAL-ISM AND THE LIMITS OF JUSTICE (1998); PETER JONES, RIGHTS (1994); MARY ANN GLENDON, RIGHTS TALK: THE IMPOVERISHMENT OF POLITICAL DISCOURSE (1991); JEREMY WALDRON, NONSENSE UPON STILTS: BENTHAM, BURKE, AND MARX ON THE RIGHTS OF MAN (1987); RONALD DWORKIN, A MATTER OF PRINCIPLE (1985); THEODORE M. BENDITT, RIGHTS (1982); JOHN FINNIS, NATURAL LAW AND NATURAL RIGHTS (1980); CHARLES FRIED, RIGHT AND WRONG (1978); RONALD DWORKIN, TAKING RIGHTS SERIOUSLY (1977); ROBERT NOZ-ICK, ANARCHY, STATE AND UTOPIA (1974); JOHN STUART MILL, ON LIBERTY AND OTHER ESSAYS (1859) (John Gray ed., 1991); THE SOCIAL CONTRACT AND DISCOURSES BY JEAN JACQUES ROUSSEAU (G.D.H. Cole trans., 1913); THOMAS PAINE, RIGHTS OF MAN (1791) (H. Collins ed., 1969); C.B. MACPHERSON, THE POLITICAL THEORY OF POSSESSIVE INDI-VIDUALISM (1962); Michael J. Sandel, *The Constitution of the Procedural Republic: Liberal*

Rights and Civic Virtues. 66 FORDHAM L. REV. 1 (1997); Jerome Shestack, *The Philosophic Foundations of Human Rights*, 20 HUM. RTS. Q. 6 (1998); Cass R. Sunstein, *Rights and their Critics*, 70 NOTRE DAME L. REV. 727 (1995); Cass R. Sunstein, *Liberal Constitutionalism and Liberal Justice*, 72 TEX. L. REV. 305 (1994); Mark Tushnet, *An Essay on Rights*, 62 TEX. L. REV. 1363 (1984).

C. CRITICAL VOICES

International law, including human rights law, is undergoing a continual process of development, change and contestation; several recent trends in international legal scholarship have generated substantial debate and controversy. One school, described by Professor David Kennedy as "New Approaches to International Law" (NAIL), draws on Critical Legal Studies and other theoretical approaches to expose and explore the contradictions and implications of liberal international legal theory. *See, e.g.*, David Kennedy, *A New Stream of International Law Scholarship, in* INTERNATIONAL RULES: APPROACHES FROM INTERNATIONAL LAW AND INTERNATIONAL RELATIONS 230 (Robert J. Beck et al. eds., 1996); MARTTI KOSKENNIEMI, FROM APOLOGY TO UTOPIA: THE STRUCTURE OF INTERNATIONAL LEGAL ARGUMENT (1989); Nathaniel Berman, *Sovereignty in Abeyance: Self-Determination and International Law*, 7 WIS. INT'L L.J. 51 (1988); David Kennedy, *The International Human Rights Movement: Part of the Problem?* 15 HARV. HUM. RTS. J. 99 (2002); David Kennedy, *When Renewal Repeats: Thinking Against the Box*, 32 N.Y.U. J. INT'L L. & POL. 335 (2000); David Kennedy & Chris Tennant, *New Approaches to International Law—A Bibliography*, 35 HARV. INT'L L.J. 417 (1994); Outi Korhonen, *New International Law: Silence, Defence, or Deliverance?* 7 EUR. J. INT'L L. 1 (1996); Nigel Purvis, *Critical Legal Studies in Public International Law*, 32 HARV. INT'L L.J. 81(1991); Phillip Trimble, *International Law, World Order and Critical Legal Studies*, 42 STAN. L. REV. 811 (1990).

Feminist approaches to international law, influenced by international feminist movements and efforts to mainstream gender analysis in international organizations, criticize sexism and other gender implications of traditional international legal theory and practice. Scholars in this vein argue that international law, including the traditional human rights framework, tends to reify the subordination of women through, among other things, a strict separation between "public" and "private" spheres of social organization. Feminist scholarship and activism has had a particularly significant influence on international human rights theory since the 1980s. *See, e.g.*, HUMAN RIGHTS OF WOMEN: NATIONAL AND INTERNATIONAL PERSPECTIVES (Rebecca J. Cook ed., 1994); WOMEN AND INTERNATIONAL HUMAN RIGHTS LAW (Kelly D. Askin & Dorean M. Koenig eds., 1999); WOMEN'S RIGHTS, HUMAN RIGHTS: INTERNATIONAL FEMINIST PERSPECTIVES (Julie Peters & Andrea Wolper eds., 1995); Hilary Charlesworth, *The Public/Private Distinction and the Right to Development in International Law*, 12 AUST. Y.B. INT'L L. 190 (1992); Hilary Charlesworth, Christine Chinkin & Shelley Wright, *Feminist Approaches to International Law*, 85 AM. J. INT'L L. 613 (1991); FEMINIST LEGAL THEORY AN ANTI-ESSEN-TIAL READER (Nancy E. Dowd & Michelle S. Jacobs eds., 2003); Karen Engle, *International Human Rights and Feminism: When Discourses Meet*, 13 MICH. J. INT'L L. 517 (1992); Karen Knop, *Re/statements: Feminism and State Sovereignty in International Law*, 3 TRANSNAT'L L. & CONTEMP. PROBS. 293 (1993); Joe Oloka-Onyango & Sylvia Tamale, *The Plight of the Larger Half: Human Rights Gender Violence and the Legal Status of Refugees and Internally Displaced Women in Africa*, 24 DENV. J. INT'L L. & POL'Y 349 (1996); Dianne Otto, *Challenging the "New World Order": International Law, Global Democracy and the Possibilities for Women*, 3 TRANSNAT'L L. & CONTEMP. PROBS. 371 (1993); Celina Romany, *State Responsibility Goes Private: A Feminist Critique of the Feminist Approaches to International Law*, 85 AM. J. INT'L L. 613 (1991); Saskia Sassen, *Toward a Feminist Analytics of the Global Economy*, 4 IND. J. GLOBAL LEGAL STUD. 7 (1996); Barbara Stark, *International Human Rights Law, Feminist Jurisprudence, and Nietzsche's "Eternal Return": Turning the Wheel*, 19 HARV. WOMEN'S L.J. 169 (1996); Uche U. Ewelukwa, *Women and International Economic Law: An Annotated Bibliography*, 8 L. & BUS. REV. AM. 603 (2002).

"Third World Approaches to International Law" (TWAIL), influenced by post-colonialist theory and the work of African, Asian, Latin American and Caribbean scholars, reexamine the origins, goals and framework of international law as it impacts, and is impacted by, encounters with the Third World. *See, e.g.*, Antony Anghie, *Finding the Peripheries: Sovereignty and Colonialism in Nineteenth-Century International Law*, 40 HARV. INT'L L.J. 1 (1999); Antony Anghie, *Time Present and Time Past: Globalization, International Financial Institutions, and the Third World*, 32 N.Y.U. J. INT'L L. & POL. 243 (2000); Ibrahim J. Gassama, *Reaffirming Faith in the Dignity of Each Human Being: The United Nations, NGOs, and Apartheid*, 19 FORDHAM INT'L L.J. 1464 (1996); Ibrahim J. Gassama, *Safeguarding the Democratic Entitlement: A Proposal for United Nations Involvement in National Politics*, 30 CORNELL INT'L L.J. 287 (1997); Ibrahim J. Gassama, *Social Justice Movements and LatCrit Community: Confronting Globalization: Lessons from the Banana Wars and the Seattle Protests*, 81 OR. L. REV. 707 (2002); James Thuo Gathii, *Alternative and Critical: The Contribution of Research and Scholarship on Developing Countries to International Legal Theory*, 41 HARV. INT'L L.J. 263 (2000); Carmen G. Gonzalez, *Institutionalizing Inequality: the WTO Agreement on Agriculture, Food Security, and Developing Countries*, 27 COLUM. J. ENVTL. L. 433 (2002); Ruth Gordon, *Saving Failed States: Sometimes a Neocolonialist Notion*, 12 AM. U. J. INT'L L. & POL'Y 903 (1997); Ratna Kapur, *The Tragedy of Victimization Rhetoric: Resurrecting the "Native" Subject in International/Post-Colonial Feminist Legal Politics*, 15 HARV. HUM. RTS. J. 1 (2002); Hope Lewis, *Lionheart Gals Facing the Dragon: The Human Rights of Inter/national Black Women in the United States*, 76 OR. L. REV. 567 (1997); Karin Mickelson, *Rhetoric and Rage: Third World Voices in International Legal Discourse*, 16 WIS. INT'L L.J. 353 (1998); Makau wa Mutua, *Hope and Despair for a New South Africa: The Limits of Rights Discourse*, 10 HARV. HUM. RTS. J. 63 (1997); Makau wa Mutua, *The Ideology of Human Rights*, 36 VA. J. INT'L L. 589 (1996); Makau Mutua, *What is TWAIl?*, 94 AM. SOC'Y INT'L L. PROC. 31 (2000); Vasuki Nesiah, *Toward A Feminist Internationality: A Critique of U.S. Feminist Legal Scholarship*, 16 HARV. WOMEN'S L.J. 189 (1993); Celestine Nyamu, *How Should Human Rights and Development Respond to Cultural Legitimization of Gender Hierarchy in Developing Countries?*, 41 HARV. INT'L L.J. 381 (2000); L. Amede Obiora, *Bridges and Barricades: Rethinking Polemics and Intransigence in the Campaign Against Female Circumcision*, 47 CASE W. RES. L. REV. 275 (1997); Balakrishnan Rajagopal, *From Resistance to Renewal: The Third World, Social Movements, and the Expansion of International Institutions*, 41 HARV. INT'L L.J. 529 (2000); Balakrishnan Rajagopal, *International Law and Social Movements: Challenges of Theorizing Resistance*, 41 COLUM. J. TRANSNAT'L L. 397 (2003); Jeanne M. Woods, *Justiciable Social Rights as a Critique of the Liberal Paradigm*, 38 TEX. INT'L L.J. 763 (2003); Jeanne M. Woods, *The Fallacy of Neutrality: Diary of an Election Observer*, 18 MICH. J. INT'L L. 475 (1997); Jeanne M. Woods, *Reconciling Reconciliation*, 3 UCLA J. INT'L L. & FOR. AFF. 81 (1998).

International legal scholars have also examined the role of race in transnational perspective. *See, e.g.*, Jeffrey M. Brown, *Black Internationalism: Embracing an Economic Paradigm*, 23 MICH. J. INT'L L. 807 (2002); Lennox S. Hinds, *The Gross Violation of Human*

Rights of the Apartheid Regime Under International Law, 1 RUTGERS RACE & L. REV. 231 (1999); Henry J. Richardson III, *The Gulf Crisis and African-American Interests under International Law*, 87 AM. J. INT'L L. 42 (1993).

"Critical Race Theory," a set of approaches to legal scholarship and activism that began by centering the roles that race and other forms of identity play in the subordination of racial minorities in the United States, has also addressed other forms of subordination internationally as well. *See, e.g.*, Penelope E. Andrews, *Making Room for Critical Race Theory in International Law: Some Practical Pointers*, 45 VILL. L. REV. 855 (2000); Ibrahim J. Gassama, *Transnational Critical Race Scholarship: Transcending Ethnic and National Chauvinism in the Era of Globalization*, 5 MICH. J. RACE & L. 133 (1999); Ruth Gordon, *Critical Race Theory and International Law: Convergence and Divergence*, 45 VILL. L. REV. 82 (2000); Gil Gott, *Critical Race Globalism?: Global Political Economy, And The Intersections Of Race, Nation, and Class*, 33 U.C. DAVIS L. REV. 1503 (2000); Tayyab Mahmud, *Colonialism and Modern Constructions of Race: A Preliminary Inquiry*, 53 U. MIAMI L. REV. 1219 (1999); Kevin R. Johnson, *Race Matters: Immigration Law and Policy Scholarship, Law in the Ivory Tower, and the Legal Indifference of the Race Critique*, 2000 U. ILL. L. REV. 525 (2000). Hope Lewis, *Reflections on "BlackCrit Theory": Human Rights*, 45 VILL. L. REV. 1075 (2000); Ediberto Roman, *LatCrit IV Symposium: A Race Approach to International Law (RAIL): Is there a Need for Yet Another Critique of International Law?*, 33 U.C. DAVIS L. REV. 1519 (2000); Natsu Taylor Saito, *Critical Race Theory as International Human Rights Law*, 93 AM. SOC'Y INT'L L. PROC. 228 (1999); Eric K. Yamamoto, *Race Apologies*, 1 J. GENDER, RACE & JUST. 47 (1997); *Symposium, Critical Race Theory and International Law*, 45 VILL. L. REV. 827 (2000). For a retrospective look at the Critical Race movement, *see* Kimberle Williams Crenshaw, *Critical Race Studies: The First Decade: Critical Reflections, or "A Foot in the Closing Door,"* 49 UCLA L. REV. 1343 (2002).

Several streams of legal scholarship and activism are associated with Critical Race Theory, but are also influenced by post-modernist and other intellectual movements. Among them are "AsianCrit," "LatCrit," and "QueerCrit" movements. For one overview of recent trends in LatCrit Theory, for example, *see* Elizabeth M. Iglesias & Francisco Valdes, *Afterword to LatCrit V Symposium; LatCrit at Five: Institutionalizing a Postsubordination Future*, 78 DENV. U. L. REV. (2001).

A related movement, "Global Critical Race Feminism" seeks to integrate the analysis of domestic Critical Race Theory (among scholars in North America and Europe) and feminist theory with some aspects of NAIL and TWAIL. *See, e.g.*, GLOBAL CRITICAL RACE FEMINISM: AN INTERNATIONAL READER (Adrien K. Wing ed., 2000); SHERENE RAZACK, LOOKING WHITE PEOPLE IN THE EYE: GENDER, RACE, AND CULTURE IN COURTROOMS AND CLASSROOMS (1998); Penelope E. Andrews, *Globalization, Human Rights and Critical Race Feminism: Voices from the Margins*, 3 J. GENDER, RACE & JUSTICE. 373 (2000); Lisa A. Crooms, *Indivisible Rights and Intersectional Identities, or "What Do Women's Human Rights Have to Do with the Race Convention?,"* 40 HOW. L.J. 619 (1997); Berta Esperanza Hernandez-Truyol, *Out of the Shadows: Traversing the Imaginary of Sameness, Difference, and Relationalism—A Human Rights Proposal*, 17 WIS. WOMEN'S L.J. 111 (2002); Hope Lewis, *Embracing Complexity: Human Rights in Critical Race Feminist Perspective*, 12 COLUM. J. GENDER & L. 510 (2003); Hope Lewis, *Global Intersections: Critical Race Feminist Human Rights and International Black Women*, 50 ME. L. REV. 309 (1998).

For an overview of a variety of critical movements in international legal scholarship, *see, e.g.*, William J. Aceves, *Critical Jurisprudence and International Legal Scholarship: A Study of Equitable Distribution*, 39 COLUM. J. TRANSNAT'L L. 299 (2001). While the works cited above are associated with various streams of scholarship and activism, the issues and themes emphasized by the individual authors can vary quite widely. Why is that the case? What role, if any, do race, gender, class, sexual orientation, culture, nation, disability, and other forms of identity play in the definition, promotion, and protection of human rights? Is a focus on specific, socially constructed identity categories overly divisive? Does it undermine efforts to identify a universally accepted and universally applicable set of human rights norms? Does it empower subordinated groups by focusing on previously hidden forms of oppression? Such questions will continue to be relevant as you explore specific human rights issues throughout this book.

JEANNE M. WOODS, JUSTICIABLE SOCIAL RIGHTS AS A CRITIQUE OF THE LIBERAL PARADIGM

38 TEX. INT'L L.J. 763, 763–71, 773–78 (2003)

I. INTRODUCTION

Postmodern discourse on the moral and political problems of the day—from Afghanistan to AIDS—is shaped by the rhetoric of human rights. The discourse promotes as its core value the ideal of human dignity, enshrined in the Universal Declaration of Human Rights. But human dignity may be too elusive a concept to provide a foundation on which to ground the full panoply of claims enumerated in the international catalogue of rights. While the Declaration posits as fundamental both the traditional tenets of individual liberty and so-called second-generation rights, the social, economic, and cultural preconditions of a dignified human life remain marginalized in the dominant rights discourse.

This article proposes human need as a more comprehensive framework for theorizing social rights claims, which are indispensable to the full development of the person represented by the concept of dignity. Social rights discourse is the assertion of collective claims to share in the abundance of our interdependent global civilization. The argument that social rights are inherently collective in nature embraces the following premises: that the human person is a socially constituted being; that community is a human need; that human need is the ultimate source of rights; that social rights are claims to communally produced resources; that such claims are exercised within society rather than against society, that is, they are non-adversarial insofar as they are not asserted against the repressive machinery of the state; that the resources required for the satisfaction of the minimum core of social rights are universally necessary and available goods; that the dutybearer is society as a whole, including individuals, states, and the international community; and that remedies for violations may be collective rather than individual.

Classic rights discourse distinguishes "negative" rights imposing constitutional restraints on the state from "positive" rights implicating affirmative state duties. The negative rights/positive rights distinction poses a false dichotomy; all human rights potentially contain both negative and positive dimensions. The assumed dichotomy blurs the true dilemma that social rights pose for the liberal paradigm: that rights implicating the redistribution of social resources are collective in character and rooted in the common needs of human beings in society. The collective nature of social rights contradicts the liberal conception of rights, which presumes that social living requires the surrender, not the creation, of rights. Social rights pose a significant conceptual difficulty and practical challenge to the construct of rights as individual entitlements that are antagonistic to and supercede the common good or collective will. Commentators observe that the special function of rights discourse is to "represent the individual interest against the general good or claims of others, to put limits on the pursuit of the general welfare or collective interest." Liberalism recognizes collective rights only to the extent that they "support the formation of autonomous individuals to be able to compete equally in economic markets." Since democracy is often viewed as synonymous with the free market and social rights entail interference with the market's distributive outcomes, such rights are deemed incompatible with a free society.

Thus, critics of social rights argue that they are not authentic rights in the normative sense but mere moral aspirations. Even scholars more supportive of the concept of positive state duties nevertheless rank the two sets of rights on the basis of their perceived sources. To these theorists, negative liberties such as freedom of speech represent higher values because they are intrinsic to the human condition. These liberties preexist society in a hypothetical "state of nature," the theoretical construct within which liberal rights are imagined. The right is not provided by the state; having a right simply means that the state must refrain from interference with its exercise. On the other hand, positive rights such as food are classified as rights of recipience. In other words, they are "rights to things not yet possessed." These rights are ranked lower in the hierarchy of rights because, presumably, they are not inherent characteristics of autonomous individuals, and having a right means that the state must provide some extrinsic good.

Arguably, however, rights are not readily distinguishable on this basis. The notion that freedom of speech precedes organized society is counterintuitive; expressive rights are wholly incomprehensible outside of a social context. At the same time, in a "state of nature," without social institutions such as private property, individuals and groups inherently have access to the means of basic subsistence. Organized society can also interfere with the exercise of such rights through its ordering of political, economic, and social relations as well as controlling and distributing the resources needed for self-sufficiency. To the extent that rights are to be distinguished and prioritized, the bifurcation into intrinsic and extrinsic categories seems artificial and unworkable.

Finally, some scholars who do not reject social rights on philosophical grounds nevertheless contend that they are nonjusticiable. This perceived dilemma is traceable to the classic view that rights are individualistic, adversarial, and negative, and therefore must be susceptible to a private judicial remedy. As articulated by the prominent liberal thinker Ronald Dworkin, rights are "political trumps held by individuals." Critics argue that judicial review is inappropriate in the case of positive rights, which, because of their budgetary implications, are deemed the sole province of the political branches. Thus, while formalized in many legal instruments, economic, social, and cultural rights remain the normatively underdeveloped stepchild of the human rights family.***

II. THE NATURE OF LIBERAL RIGHTS

Contemporary rights discourse is shaped by the classic liberal conception of the nature of the human person. It is a conception that imagines a solitary figure standing apart from society, jealously guarding her Lockean "property"—life, liberty, and estates—from a hostile community of others. As the philosopher Theodore Benditt explains, the individualistic character of rights discourse proceeds from its historical origins:

The idea of a right comes out of an era which saw the rise of the nation-state, and, as a concomitant, the rise of the individual, the citizen, a morally selfcontained atom shorn of all the ties of family, class and status which for so long defined people and their moral and social situations. The possession of a personal right means that people think of themselves as distinct from others, as having interests that differ from the interests of others.

In the individual rights paradigm, therefore, what defines the human person are her differences, not her shared commonalities. The Lockean fiction of the autonomous individual provided a theoretical foundation for the revolutionary demand for limitations on the powers of government in an age of monarchal tyranny. This fiction has long ceased to be recognized as an invention, or "presumption[] of reality," but is widely believed to have an independent existence. Notwithstanding the undeniable reality of interdependence in human society today—exemplified if not caused by pervasive social regulation and distribution of land and other means of self-sufficiency—Western culture perpetuates the myth of radical individual autonomy. The conception of the individual in modern liberal-democratic theory is "as essentially the proprietor of his own person or capacities, owing nothing to society for them.*** The human essence is freedom from dependence on the wills of others, and freedom is a function of possession." This fictional rendition of "human nature" presumes an adversarial relationship between the individual and organized society, nurturing a jurisprudence of rights that is inhospitable to claims to communal rights and confines the consideration of the collective good to narrowly defined exceptional circumstances.

The autonomous individual remains the centerpiece of contemporary liberalism across its ideological spectrum—from defenders of the welfare state like John Rawls to advocates of a minimal state such as Robert Nozick. The Rawlsian conceit posits a postmodern state of nature—the "original position"—within which individuals free of all social, political, economic, and cultural attachments choose the first principles of a just society. While this construct allows for social attachments in one's "private spheres," Rawls insists that in the "public sphere" individuals make moral choices and create political institutions based only on perceived self-interest, detached from their social contexts and consequences. To Rawls, autonomy means the reduction of moral values and social connections in public life to optional undertakings rather than critical components of self-identity. According to philosopher Michael Sandel, this conception of the self as constitutively independent from other individuals or groups, as well as from one's interests and values, ensures a subordinated status for community-oriented values. Sandel argues that since "a person's values and ends are always attributes and never constituents of the self, so a sense of community is only an attribute and never a constituent of a well-ordered society."

Libertarian Robert Nozick posits similarly detached, atomistic individuals represented by hypothetical Robinson Crusoes working alone on separate islands who owe nothing to one another that they do not voluntarily undertake. Nozick argues that there is no social entity apart from the individuals who comprise it: "There are only individual people, different individual people, with their own individual lives." This construct excludes the possibility of any rights against the collective beyond the negative rights held as to similarly situated "Robinson Crusoes." Nozick is also unsympathetic to the notion of individual duties to the community: "Using one of these people for the benefit of others, uses him and benefits the others. Nothing more."

The autonomous individual presents a substantial barrier to the development and implementation of a theory of social rights. He embodies a limited and incomplete concept of human dignity, which is the asserted normative premise of human rights discourse—a concept that omits the fundamental moral and material prerequisites to a dignified human life. Freedom is defined as the ability to engage in activity without external interference. The greater the detachment of the self from the community, its values, ends, and history, the more free one is deemed to be. Sandel opines that "[t]o imagine a person incapable of constitutive attachments *** is not to conceive an ideally free and rational agent, but to imagine a person wholly without character, without moral depth." He argues that this notion of freedom constrains our ability to imagine and create constitutive communities in which one's well-being is inextricably linked with that of the other members. The celebrated freedom of the pauper to "sleep under the bridges of Paris" makes a mockery of human dignity and compromises political freedom.

Critiquing the distinctive American flavor of rights discourse, Professor Mary Ann Glendon points out that the philosophy of the radically autonomous individual is accompanied by a "corresponding neglect of the social dimensions of human personhood." As Glendon observes, contemporary society internalizes "[a]n implicit anthropology— an encoded image of the human person as radically alone and as 'naturally' at odds with his fellows." Thus we are unable to fully accommodate this aspect of the self in legal and political discourse or to envision a theoretical foundation for social rights. Individual autonomy requires the moral neutrality of the state, further retarding the development of a theory of social rights. The liberal maxim, "the right is prior to the good" means not only that individual rights supercede the common good, but that the collective/state must be neutral as to the worth of the interests that underlie these rights. However, this notion of moral neutrality is another legal fiction; individualism is itself a conception of the good that is promoted by the liberal state. In its postmodern incarnation the individualist norm glorifies self-centeredness and greed, epitomized by the recent corporate scandals. Beyond the minimal social programs grudgingly provided by taxpayers, concern for one's fellow human being is largely relegated to the realm of private charity. Inequality in material wealth and access to resources is deemed not only natural, but a moral good. Ambivalent environmental policies reflect our unwillingness to make sacrifices for future generations. The language of choice permeates debates on public education, which faces eroding support. Competitiveness, consumption, and pleasure seeking are ranked high among our cultural values, rendering elusive a "genuine community capable of offering its members a just distribution of goods and a morally meaningful life." Individualist norms make the idea of social rights virtually incomprehensible to the liberal mindset.***

IV. THEORETICAL CONSTRUCTIONS OF SOCIAL RIGHTS

Two interconnected precepts characterize the liberal conception of the self: (1) it is capable of dispensing with collective identities and values; and (2) it is a free agent motivated primarily by self-interest. This conception undermines the development of a sense of community that entails nonconsensual obligations to the collective. The penultimate virtue of self-interested free choice overshadows communal values of generosity, reciprocity, and solidarity in public life, and the notion that it is possible (or desirable) to achieve "the good life" for all is virtually absent from public debate. The idea of social rights presupposes a conception of the human person as a predominantly socially constituted being. This "intersubjective conception" of the self contemplates the possibility that in some contexts the self could embrace more than one person, such as the family, community, or other relevant collective. Unlike the voluntarism of the liberal paradigm, this conception accepts that the "social attachments which determine the self are not necessarily chosen ones."

The notion that the community is structurally part of who we are as individuals suggests a commonality of interests between the individual and the collective. The assumption of an inherently antagonistic relationship is absent. In contrast to the Rawlsian construct, communal values are ineluctably entwined with the self in public as well as private life. The elevation of communal values likewise serves to elevate communal needs, and allows for the prioritization of these needs through their classification as legal rights. The goal of rights discourse is thus furthered not simply through negative freedoms, but through the recognition of positive freedoms to fulfill one's basic needs, thus embracing the totality of the human condition.

The importance of a social conception of the self that grounds rights in human need can be appreciated by examining efforts to theorize social rights without repudiating fully the individualistic bias of the liberal tradition. Some scholars agree that there is a category of "social rights," but reject the grounding of such rights in human need. Thus lacking a jurisprudential foundation, such rights do not generate correlative duties on the part of society.

For example, the philosopher Theodore Benditt posits a right to mutual aid—a "right to beneficence." While he acknowledges no general right to resources, he suggests that "a person may have a right, in some circumstances, to another person's making efforts to make needed resources available. This might take the form of a right to a change in individual institutional structures, so that needed resources might be available in the future."

To Benditt, the collective consists of "individuals engaged in primary economic activities." It is characterized by "the move from widespread self-sufficiency to large-scale specialization and division of labor.***" One becomes part of the collective by taking part in its economic life. For this economic self, the relationship between the individual and the community is dominated by self-interest.

Benditt suggests that the right to mutual aid may be grounded in the mutual dependency of the winners and losers in the economic life of the collective. Those who are successful need the continuous functioning of the collective life to maintain their success, which requires participation by others. The losers are unable to benefit on their own from the collective activity, and everyone is "virtually dependent on the collective" economy. In other words, total self-sufficiency is not possible. However, to Benditt need alone does not create rights; rights accrue only to the extent that the collective is directly responsible for the need—for example, unemployment or industrial-related disease. Thus, the collective has wide discretion as to which needs to meet, subject to limitations on resources.

Similarly, in his book *Right and Wrong*, Charles Fried argues that each individual has a positive right to a fair share of his community's scarce resources, a right grounded in the Kantian duty of beneficence. Fried argues that respect for persons and for our common humanity requires affirmative care for others and a positive contribution to their welfare. However, in his construct, rights are not generated by need. Fried sees positive rights as primarily enhancements of autonomy: they are "claims that men have on each other *** to help maintain and further their enterprise as free, rational beings pursuing their life plan." In deference to autonomy, one's positive right is not to any particular resource, such as education or medical care, but rather to a fair share of objective resources. In other words, the individual's positive right is to money, which represents an opportunity to obtain goods, leaving the individual free to choose among various wants and needs. Fried has no proposal for how to ascertain one's fair share, but he insists that state neutrality be maintained and that the claim is limited by scarcity. Moreover, the right is prior to the good; "negative rights constrain *** what may be taken *from* an individual to provide a fair share to others." Nevertheless, while accepting the basic postulates of the liberal model, he inserts into the construct the moral criterion that the polity be guided by "*aspirations* toward fairness, toward distributive justice." Fried freely concedes the indeterminacy of outcomes produced by such a model.

Like Fried, Alan Gewirth views individual autonomy as a primary normative value. However, he sees social rights not as unalterably opposed or incompatible, but as integral to the attainment of autonomy. Gewirth shares Dworkin's conception of rights as individual "trumps" over other policy considerations; like Nozick, he views the community as no more than an amalgam of individuals. But his goal is to achieve a discourse that promotes social solidarity, grounding rights in the moral principle "that all humans are equally entitled to have [the freedom and well-being that are the] necessary conditions to fulfill the general needs of human agency." By identifying a single normative principle underlying both political and social rights, this formulation serves to equalize them and transcends the dichotomy posited in liberal discourse between negative and positive rights. He also rises above the positivist state-centric bias, asserting that the duty-bearers of human rights "are all persons, not simply governments." Thus, "where basic well-being and equality of opportunity *** can be fostered only by collective action, the positive duties require advocacy of the basic rights of others and taking the necessary steps toward their support, including taxation."

But Gewirth's theory falls short of conceptualizing fundamental norms with equal status to traditional rights, because it attempts to squeeze social rights into the liberal mold. Significantly, the duty owed to the community is framed in terms of individual choice and contingent upon a meritocratic stipulation that belies a claim of right:

> For *** persons to have a duty of supplying A with food *** they must both be aware that he lacks food from causes *beyond his control* and be able to repair this lack. They must have sufficient resources to have a surplus from their own basic food needs so as to be able to transfer some to A. By virtue of this ability, it is within their control to determine by their own *unforced choice* whether or not A has food. If, under these circumstances, A lacks food and they withhold food from him, then they *voluntarily* interfere with his having food and hence inflict basic harm on him. Thereby they violate his right to have food.

Thus, the right to food is not an inalienable right of persons by virtue of their humanity or need, but is conditioned on the choices of both the right-holder and the duty-holder.

Similarly, Michael Walzer implicitly adopts the Lockean assumption that life and liberty are natural, self-evident norms, whereas rights beyond these are social constructions, which "do not follow from our common humanity [but] from shared conceptions of social goods." Walzer grounds such socially constructed rights in the primary function of human society, which he regards as the distribution of social goods. Walzer does move beyond the Rawlsian concept of the self, acknowledging social goods as key to distinct individual identities, and he abandons the negative Lockean version of the social contract, advancing the idea of an agreement for mutual provision of socially determined needs. Walzer envisions a moral bond that "connects the strong and the weak, the lucky and the unlucky, the rich and the poor, creating a union that transcends all differences of interest." This description suggests that the social contract may create a collective entity distinct from the individuals of which it is comprised, capable of being a positive rights-holder and duty-bearer.

But Walzer does not go this far. His implicit distinction between "self-evident" and "socially constructed" rights leads him to adopt a cultural relativist approach to social rights. While presumably he would reject such arguments with regard to life and liberty, he argues that "goods have different meanings in different societies," thus denying social rights the status of universal norms.

Yet if it is possible to establish nonderogable norms of liberty that cross cultural boundaries, it is possible to determine the minimum core content of social rights. All human beings need a certain minimum caloric intake to stay alive and healthy. All human societies need to educate their young. And, while the particulars of one's dwelling may vary widely from one society to the next, there is no gainsaying the basic human need for shelter. But to Walzer need is vague, elusive, and subject to an inevitable scarcity of resources. Therefore it is not a source of rights but a potential distributive principle, subject to political limitation.

The case for social rights from within the liberal tradition, then, is a modified endorsement of the liberal welfare state. While acknowledging that our common humanity and interdependence generate some sort of collective responsibility for one another, these arguments accept that there must be winners and losers in the game of life and seek a way to accommodate the minimal needs of the inevitable (potentially disruptive) losers. These accommodations, while significant, remain mere gratuitous entitlements. They are subject to the whim of the polity or—even less—simply moral aspirations for future distributive justice, rather than fundamental rights with normative force.***

Notes and Questions

1. Woods proposes that "human need" is a more promising basis for a rights system than "human dignity." How would you distinguish the two?

2. What does Woods mean when she says that the human person is a "socially constituted being?" What is the significance of this assertion for the concept of human rights?

3. How would Woods distinguish between "community," "society," and "state?" What purposes might such distinctions serve?

4. To which communities do you belong? How do you know? What and who defines those communities—ethnic heritage; language; religion; neighborhood? Are class distinctions relevant to how you identify your community? Do you find spatial considerations more or less important than personal, familial, or economic relationships in defining your community? How does law interact with the communities with which you identify?

5. Woods argues that it is impossible for liberal theorists to reach a comprehensive framework for social rights because they build from an individualistic base. She main-

tains that liberal recognition of basic human needs such as food, education, and shelter are always accompanied by the qualification that the fulfillment of such needs will be subject to the "whim of the polity." Presumably, those whose basic needs are already fulfilled will find budgetary and political reasons to deny the provision of resources to others. Do you agree? Are civil and political rights also subject to the "whim of the polity?" Consider the issues of gay marriage or abortion rights in the United States. How do democratic processes affect an individual's freedom to marry, or reproductive rights? Do these examples support or contradict the notion that social rights will not thrive without the "normative force" now accorded to individual rights? Alternatively, would these rights be more powerfully protected by a social need-based conceptualization?

KARL E. KLARE, LEGAL THEORY AND DEMOCRATIC RECONSTRUCTION: REFLECTIONS ON 1989

26 U.B.C. L. Rev. 69, 95–101 (1991)

Human rights guarantees are indispensable to any legal order committed to democracy. The project of fostering equality and human self-realization requires some point of reference from which to evaluate prevailing institutions, some vantage from which to criticize and condemn domination and injustice.***

How could there be any doubt of the central place of rights in democratic legal reconstruction? Yet, if not quite doubt, then at least a sense of complexity and unease on that score has been generated by recent debates among western legal scholars.***

The rights debate has caused considerable misunderstanding, owing in part to unexplored ambiguities in the concept of "rights." It is quite difficult to talk about autonomy, equality and democracy without invoking the concepts, so anyone who attempts to probe the conceptual and legal underpinnings of the idea of rights runs the risk of being incorrectly perceived as an opponent of justice or a critic of democracy. Lest I add to the confusion, let me say clearly at the outset what this debate is *not* about. It is not about whether we should be committed to liberty, due process, the protection of dissent or the other values customarily associated with the human rights tradition.***

So, what is the issue? Contemporary "rights skepticism" takes aim at two things: a certain strategy for achieving human freedom, and a certain way of thinking about social conflict. The *strategic* aspect of the critique questions the efficacy of relying centrally on human rights charters, doctrine, and litigation to bring about a just society. Rights skeptics consider human rights progress to be a necessary but not sufficient strategy to democratize the world and to achieve justice. Some go farther and assert that an overreliance on the rights tradition may deflect attention from or actually impede other valuable and needed approaches to social change. The *conceptual* aspect of the critique questions the coherence of the idea that social conflict can be resolved or that institutions can be designed solely by appeal to rights concepts. The skeptics challenge the implicit aspiration of rights discourse to supply neutral, self-revealing principles of social organization and an apolitical analytical method for resolving contested questions. The central critical argument in this connection *** is that rights discourse is too indeterminate and too internally contradictory to resolve contested social issues without recourse to conceptions of political philosophy and social vision external to rights discourse itself. The dilemma is that the appeal to social vision alters the character and status of rights arguments.

I will briefly summarize some of the major lines of criticism advanced by the rights skeptics. A first tack interrogates the philosophical orientation or "spin" of the human rights tradition. Some skeptics argue that conventional rights discourse is substantively limited by its natural law origins, and that the discourse bears an individualist, anti-communitarian stamp derived from the idea of the minimalist, "night-watchman" state. Or they argue that, until very recent times, rights rhetoric was systematically deployed to protect property rights of the rich and powerful from redistributive legislation. Linkage between rights discourse and vested interests endures, as in the example of contemporary white male claims that affirmative action programs violate human rights. A stronger version of the critique, influenced by postmodernist feminism and some aspects of critical race theory, holds that the rights tradition is indelibly tainted by its Enlightenment roots as a white and male deployed discourse, one that is insufficiently sensitive to social context and the needs of women and people of colour.

There is much to be said for these criticisms, although critics of the critics correctly insist that, for all its flaws, the rights tradition has long inspired, empowered and mobilized dominated and disenfranchised groups. Perhaps the best conclusion is that rights discourse needs to be transformed, not abandoned; that its individualism should be tempered by an infusion of communitarian and egalitarian values; and that rights discourse must be made more sensitive to issues of gender and cultural difference. For present purposes it is enough to note that the very existence of this debate shows that rights discourse is socially constructed, that conceptions of rights are embedded within and framed by particular political and social visions.

A second branch of rights skepticism concerns the efficacy and limitations of the rights tradition in relationship to social change. There is much discussion of the gap between "rights on the books" and "rights in the real world." Additionally, the skeptics call attention to certain self-imposed limitations internal to rights discourse stemming from its embrace of the public/private distinction. Rights thinking has predominantly concerned the relationship between the individual and the state. As traditionally understood, the human rights project is to erect barriers between the individual and the state, so as to protect human autonomy and self-determination from being violated or crushed hy governmental power.

Unquestionably, a just society requires such protections, but human freedom can also be invaded or denied by nongovernmental forms of power, by domination in the so-called "private sphere."[a] Human dignity is denied by *de jure* racial segregation, but it is also denied by employers who discriminate on the basis of race. Laws barring adult homosexuals from privately and consensually expressing their sexuality deny freedom and autonomy, but so, too, do homophobic social practices such as housing discrimination and gay bashing. The expression of dissent can be inhibited by the cost of media access as well as by abuses of state power. Rights charters almost invariably concern restrictions on state power and therefore leave intact many forms of "private" domination, including hierarchies of class, race, gender and sexual preference. The skeptics argue that the vision of freedom embodied in the rights tradition is for this reason par-

---

[a]   "So called," because *** in establishing background rules of law, the state assumes responsibility for structuring power relations in economic and social life.

tial and incomplete.*** A strong version of rights skepticism suggests that the fixation on the individual/state relationship in the rights tradition actually diverts intellectual and political resources from other, needed approaches to social justice.[b]

Here again, it is conceivable that rights discourse can he transformed to accommodate these criticisms; that we can articulate a panoply of self-determination rights in social and economic life. Indeed, some western European nations have taken steps in this direction, although much more needs to be done. [F]or rights discourse to provide expanded foundations for human freedom, it must be pushed beyond its intellectual origins in liberal political theory. This conclusion, too, reinforces my point that the social vision brought to interpretation and implementation crucially influences the scope and power of rights concepts as instruments for democratizing the world.

This brings us to a third aspect of contemporary rights skepticism, the so-called "indeterminacy cricique." In its strongest versions, rights discourse purports to supply apolitical criteria for evaluating institutions and practices and for resolving social conflict. The very power of a claim of right is that it is founded upon universal values, that it transcends all particular understandings of appropriate social organization. A successful rights claimant trumps majoritarian sentiment regarding the good life. The fact that a practice is settled, widely approved and adopted in accordance with applicable legal procedures is ordinarily no answer at all to a claim that the practice nonetheless violates someone's *rights*. Accordingly, it would appear that rights claims would lose critical bite and moral force if they turn out to be dependent on controversial assumptions and arguments of political philosophy.***

*** The initial problem is that many of the most important rights concepts are formulated at an exceedingly high level of abstraction. Because human rights concepts tend to be very elastic and open-ended, they are capable of being given a wide range of meanings, including inconsistent meanings. Take freedom of speech, for example. One meaning is the right to dissent and to criticize the powers that be. Yet the right to free speech can also be given quite a different meaning, as, *e.g.*, in the American cases barring government from trying to prevent the distortion of the electoral process by corporate campaign contributions. In the former interpretation, free speech permits individuals to unfreeze hierarchy and open up political debate, whereas in the latter case, the right to free speech is mobilized to reinforce domination by entrenched power. Or, take the right to privacy, the right to be left alone by government with regard to certain intimate matters. For most feminists, this connotes a right to choice about reproduction and abortion. But the right to privacy regarding intimate personal matters has long had a less savory invocation as a justification for why courts should not intervene to prevent or punish domestic violence. An interesting aspect of rights-fixated political

---

[b] A related, but different, criticism is that rights thinking encourages an emphasis on litigation and lobbying as methods of bringing about social change and on the promulgation and enforcement of legal guarantees as the goal of social change movements, and that these legal preoccupations elicit and detract from other valuable goals such as grassroots empowerment and participation. Strictly speaking, this point is not a criticism of "rights discourse" (as opposed to other legal modalities, such as precedential or consequentialist thinking), but a criticism of "legal strategies" in general. For reasons growing out of my view of the "constitutive role" of law in social order, I take for granted that legal strategies must be at least an aspect of any project of social transformation, although only an aspect, and one that ought not to be at the expense of popular participation and democratic institution-building.

cultures, such as we have in the United States, is that anybody and everybody can and does formulate their political claims in rights terms.

Thus, rights concepts are sufficiently elastic so that they can mean different things to different people. People who seek to reinforce hierarchy and perpetuate domination can speak the language of rights, often with sincerity. But there is an even deeper problem. Even those who would consistently invoke rights in the service of self-determination, autonomy and equality find that rights concepts are internally contradictory. That is because, like all of legal discourse, rights theory is an arena of conflicting conceptions of justice and human freedom. For example, democratic thinking, particularly within the liberal tradition, contains conceptions of rights as freedom of action and also of rights as guarantors of security. It contains conceptions of rights as protection from state power and also of rights to invoke state power to protect the individual from powerful private groups. Proponents of democracy have advanced conceptions of rights to freedom of association and also conceptions of rights of excluded minorities to insist on membership in important groups. Rights theories contain conceptions of equality as identical treatment of those similarly situated and also theories of equality as protection for those not similarly situated. Human rights discourse holds that its claims are universal yet also embodies a belief in the right of all peoples to cultural autonomy and self-determination.

Thus, choices must be made in elaborating any structure of human rights guarantees *** and the choices bear socially and politically significant consequences.

The problem is that rights discourse itself does not provide neutral decision procedures with which to make such choices.

This does not mean that principled choices are impossible. There is a common but completely mistaken view that rights skepticism is a species of nihilism. On certain questions, principled choice seems within easy reach. Most of the rights skeptics would feel justified in reaching such conclusions as that the right to privacy encompasses reproductive choice but not legal immunity for domestic violence, and that "free speech" means (among other things) protecting dissent by persons but not necessarily unlimited corporate campaign contributions. Other issues pose more difficult questions, such as whether and when universalistic claims should trump rights of cultural autonomy, or how to define equality so as to respect gender differences without risking gender stereotyping.

Resolving these sorts of questions requires complex theoretical work and a keen sense of judgment about social context. People committed to democracy can be expected to disagree sharply about such matters. My point here is that, by itself, rights discourse does not and probably cannot provide us with the criteria for deciding between conflicting claims of right. In order to resolve rights conflicts, it is necessary to step outside the discourse. One must appeal to more concrete and therefore more controversial analyses of the relevant social and institutional contexts than rights discourse offers; and one must develop and elaborate conceptions of and intuitions about human freedom and self-determination by reference to which one seeks to assess rights claims and resolve rights conflicts.***

The challenge *** becomes to create a new conception of legality. Critical scholarship on law challenges the traditional image of legal argument as a process which derives institutional solutions by applying a neutral apparatus of analytical techniques to a set of shared general principles. However, critical legal theory does not conclude with a call to abandon the idea of legality, but rather to re-imagine and redefine it. We seek a conception of legality that is more open and honest about the political and social presuppositions of legal argument; a conception of legality that is committed to self-realization, democracy and equality, but that views broad generalizations skeptically and seeks to import a sensitivity to social context and gender and cultural difference into legal discourse; a conception that does not regard the legal foundations of human free-dom as self-evident, but rather seeks to encourage practices in which lawyers and oth-ers constantly re-examine and revise their understanding of the institutional and social preconditions of freedom; a conception that is less elitist and more open and accessi-ble to popular understanding and input. Critical legal theory points toward a revised conception of legal argument that acknowledges conflict and embraces dialogue between competing visions of justice and social organization.

ISSA SHIVJI, HUMAN RIGHTS IDEOLOGY: PHILOSOPHICAL IDEALISM AND POLITICAL NIHILISM

ISSA SHIVJI, THE CONCEPT OF HUMAN RIGHTS IN AFRICA 45–49 (1989)

Conceptually, the dominant outlook on 'human rights' centers around the concept of 'human nature.' Human nature is an abstraction both from history as well as society. The historically determined social being, abstracted from social-history, is transformed into a human being in general while material social relations, abstracted from political economy, are metamorphosed into a bundle of ideal qualities and characteristics called 'human nature.' The 'human nature' so arrived at philosophically is ideologically declared more-or-less eternal, more-or-less immutable, at least in its fundamentals. The discourse is strictly compartmentalised as philosophical and therefore politically and ideologically neutral while morally and ethically it is preached as righteous. The process of positivising these moral rights into statutory/treaty law is part of human rights activ-ity in which the human rights community is engaged. The human rights community is constituted by an amalgam of supposedly non-political philosophers, jurists, political scientists, academics etc. in collectives called non-governmental organisations.

Within Western idealist philosophy, human rights concepts have been broadly located in two major traditions—natural law and positivism. The development of natu-ral law itself may be periodized into four periods—the classical, the medieval, renais-sance and enlightenment and the post-World War II revivalism. Arguing that justice is the most abstract form of natural right, Engels notes that 'justice is but the ideologised, glorified expression of the existing economic relations, now from their conservative, and now from their revolutionary angle.'

The same can be said of natural law. In its conservative role, natural law justifies the existing order by providing a divine sanctity to the rulers and their laws while, in its rev-olutionary role, it provides a mobilizing ideology to the rising classes for the overthrow of the existing order. In both cases, natural law theories, and their latter-day derivative, 'natural rights' theories, are essentially political, class-based ideologies, here playing a legitimising and there playing a mobilising role.

In the classical and medieval periods, natural law played largely a conservative role to justify the existing order of political and economic inequalities. The philosopher-king of Plato is naturally endowed as a ruler while the equality of the Athenian city-state naturally does not extend to its slave population. Under the Greeks, natural law is still parochial. It is only under Roman imperialism that the needs of commerce, conquest and rule over foreigners lend it a universalistic character in the form of *jus gentium*. The Roman rulers applied their *jus civile*, stripped of formalities, to their Empire and the Roman jurists/ideologists obliged by giving it the legitimacy of the law of nature which the Stoics had earlier declared to be universally applicable. During the middle ages, perched on the edifice of feudalism, natural law sanctified hierarchy as well as justified the supremacy of the Catholic Church. And Thomas Aquinas worked out a neat compromise which, while maintaining the supremacy of the Church, removed the stigma of the original sin from the civil government. But this was a tenuous compromise for tension between the Church and the state remained. It is important to stress that the natural laws of the classical and medieval periods had little in common between them except the name and they in turn are far removed, both in content and social character, from the natural rights theories of the bourgeois revolutions.

During the long drawn-out bourgeois revolutions, natural law, and its derivative natural rights, played a revolutionary role against the *status quo* and in the interests of the rising middle classes. The compromises reached between the English aristocracy and the English bourgeoisie facilitated the entry of the English bourgeois revolution onto the historical stage through the parliament bringing with it the whole traditional baggage, including the Englishman's feudal parochialism. Thus the English Petition of Rights, 1627 and the English Bill of Rights of 1679 were exclusively for the Englishman. Locke used natural law as the foundation of his theory of natural rights to life, liberty and property providing ideological justification for the Glorious Revolution (1688) and for the rights of the Englishmen. A century later, the much more decisive French revolution, taking place against the background of absolutism, universalized the language of rights by declaring the Rights of Man and Citizen in 1789.

The American Declaration too adopted a universal language. But the declared universality was fundamentally ideological. Language did not correspond to life. 'Man' did not include 'woman' nor 'slave.' If the eighteenth century declarations of rights of man did not include all men, the twentieth century conceptions have not been that universalistic either. In the era of colonialism, the definition of 'man' has not included the 'colonial man' and the 'native' has been excluded from the notion of 'citizen.'

The rise of the concept of an autonomous individual with the advent of capitalism has often been noted. In the liberal conceptions of human rights, rights attach to the erstwhile individual. The commodity owner of the market thus becomes the juristic subject of law and bearer of rights, simultaneously constituting the human being of moral philosophy and the glorious individual of liberalism. The concept and language of rights in law and morality, whose fundamental basis is the standard of equality, is an expression of the equivalence of exchange in the sphere of commodity circulation. The free and equal commodity-owner of the market, who enters into equally free and equal exchange relations, translates itself into the free and equal juristic person as the holder of a bundle of rights, who freely enters into legal relations through a contract.***

If the ideology of natural-rights was the rallying cry of the rising bourgeoisie against feudalism, positivism became the ideology of the triumphant bourgeoisie. Through it the bourgeoisie declared not only its victory but its resolution to stay and build the world in its own image. There were no more ideals to fight for, the 'is' was the 'ought' and therefore there was no need to look beyond the existing law and state. Rights were those granted by the state and all talk about inherent rights was nothing but metaphysical.***

*** If the natural rights ideology of the Enlightenment was an instrument of change to establish bourgeois rule, positivism is eminently an ideology of the *status quo* to protect bourgeois rule. Natural law in its conservative form justified the political and economic inequalities of the classical and medieval periods, while positivism, which has never had any revolutionary angle, provides justification for the social and economic inequalities of the capitalist era as at the same time majestically proclaiming to be the theoretical fountain-head of political and legal equality.***

To be sure, positivism received its rudest shock in Nazism and fascism which found the bourgeoisie seeking refuge, once again, in natural law ideologies. In the first or so decade after the second world war, the so-called revival of natural law was at its highest. Yet it must be understood that this was not a resurrection of the natural law from a 'revolutionary angle.' Rather it was, and probably still is, an attempt to salvage positivism by modifying it with certain natural law elements. In both respects, the resultant amalgam was and is an ideology of the *status quo*. For instance, Fuller's 'internal morality of law,' the natural-law element in his positivism, is in sum nothing but an ideologised version of the various procedural rules against arbitrariness found and observed in Anglo-American jurisdictions.

Dworkin's and Rawls' attempts are of a similar genre. They may have resuscitated the 'social contract' and the 'original position' techniques of the philosophers of Enlightenment but have forcefully retained the positivist methodology of abstracting from state and society and asserting the primacy of law. Given the historical and social specificity of the present conjuncture, this amalgam has proved to be an ideal ideological defense of the *status quo*, promulgating welfarism at home and practicing imperialism abroad.

Notes and Questions

1.   Do you agree with Shivji that the concept of human rights assumes a particular concept of "human nature?" If so, what does that concept entail? What purpose is served by this construct?

2.   What is the difference between positivism and natural rights theory? How does Shivji conceptualize the connections between the two in the period immediately following World War II? Looking back on the Universal Declaration of Human Rights, does Shivji's account ring true?

3.   How might Shivji view Karl Klare's statement that "legal strategies must be at least part of any project of social transformation"? In Shivji's conception, is a "less elitist" legality possible?

4.   What do you make of Shivji's claim that liberal rights theorists have formulated an "ideal ideological defense of the *status quo*, promulgating welfarism at home and practicing imperialism abroad"? Are international human rights imperialistic? Do they generally promote a deceptive façade of social change possibilities or enable real transformation of the structures of society?

MAKAU WA MUTUA, THE IDEOLOGY OF HUMAN RIGHTS

36 Va. J. Int'l L. 589, 589–620, 626–29, 637–53 (1996)

Introduction

Over the last fifty years the international law of human rights has steadily achieved a moral plateau rarely associated with the law of nations. A diverse and eclectic assortment of individuals and entities now invoke human rights norms and the attendant phraseology with the intent of cloaking themselves and their causes in the paradigm's perceived power and righteousness.***

[A]lthough it seems implausible to openly deny that the human rights corpus is the construction of a political ideology, the discourse's major authors present it as non-ideological. They use a vocabulary that paints the movement as both impartial and the quintessence of human goodness.*** In reality, however, the human rights corpus is not a creed or a set of normative principles suspended in outer space; the matters that it affects are earthly and concern immediate routine politics. The larger political agenda of the human rights regime has, however, been blurred by its veneration and by attempts to clean it of the taint of partisanship.***

Since World War II, the United Nations, non-governmental organizations, and scholarly writers have created a thicket of norms, processes, and institutions that purport to promote and protect human rights. Working with the so-called International Bill of Rights as their basis, the key but diverse collection of organizations and scholars has tended to agree on an irreducible human rights core. This core, although stated in human rights terms, is now being formulated into the emergent norm of democratic governance in international law. The routes different authors of human rights have taken to arrive at these conclusions are, of course, varied. Nevertheless, I have identified the four defining approaches or schools of thought into which I believe all the paramount voices writing and acting in the human rights discourse fall. I believe that these voices express the synonymity and close fit of the human rights corpus with its parent, Western liberalism.

The proponents of and adherents to the four dominant schools of thought may be classified as (i) conventional doctrinalists, (ii) constitutionalists or conceptualizers, (iii) cultural agnostics or multiculturalists, and (iv) political strategists or instrumentalists. Although most of these voices differ—in some instances radically—on the content of the human rights corpus and whether or how the contents should be ranked, they are nevertheless united by the belief that there are basic human rights. They also believe that these human rights should be promoted and where possible protected by the state, the basic obligor of human rights law.***

The first two approaches, which are espoused by conventional doctrinalists and conceptualizers or constitutionalists, are closest in ideological orientation and share an unequivocal belief in the redemptive quality and power of human rights law. Admittedly, there is a wide and contrasting diversity of attitudes towards the human rights corpus within the two schools. While the doctrinalists tend to be statisticians of violence, conceptualizers are at their core systematizers of the human rights corpus. For the latter, human rights norms arise out of the liberal tradition, and their application should achieve a type of a constitutional system broadly referred to as constitutionalism. Such a system generally has the following characteristics, although the weight accorded to each differs from one state to the next: (i) political society is based on the concept of popular sovereignty; (ii) the government of the state is constitutionally required to be accountable to the populace through various processes such as periodic, genuine, multi-party elections; (iii) government is limited in its powers through checks and balances and the separation of powers, a central tenet of the liberal tradition; (iv) the judiciary is independent and safeguards legality and the rule of law; and (v) the formal declaration of individual civil and political rights is an indispensable facet of the state.***

Both schools enjoy a spirited supporting cast in the non-Western world. In the last several decades, the number of national human rights NGOs and human rights academics has mushroomed in the South. In virtually all cases, they reproduce intellectual patterns and strategies of advocacy similar to those in the West. Although there are some significant differences on the emphasis placed on certain rights, there has been little originality as the corpus has conquered new territory outside the West.

Substantively, doctrinalists stress the primacy of civil and political rights over all other classes of rights. Thus, only a small number of "traditional" civil and political rights comprise the heart of the human rights regime. In addition, doctrinalists seek immediate and "blind" application of these rights without regard to historical, cultural, or developmental differences among states and societies. Many constitutionalists, on the other hand, recognize the supremacy of these "core" rights but point out that the list could or should be expanded. They see the difficulties of "immediate" implementation and prefer a more nuanced approach, staggered to take into account variables of culture, history, and other cleavages. Although many who adopt this approach are positivist, some are critical thinkers who subject the human rights regime to a probing critique. I call them constitutionalists because they believe that, as a whole, human rights law is or should be a constitutional regime and a philosophy that is constitutive of a liberal democratic society, along a spectrum that stretches from a bare republican state to the social democratic state.***

Cultural agnostics are generally outsiders who see the universality or convergence of some human rights norms with certain non-Western norms and as a result partially embrace the human rights corpus. Many are scholars and policymakers of multicultural heritage or orientation who, though familiar and sometimes even comfortable with the West, see cross-cultural referencing as the most critical variable in the creation of a universal corpus of human rights. They critique the existing human rights corpus as culturally exclusive in some respects and therefore view parts of it as illegitimate or, at the very least, irrelevant in non-Western societies.*** Many proponents of the first two schools who regard themselves as universalists have labelled many cultural agnostics "cultural relativists," a form of type-casting or human rights name-calling that has generally had the effect of stigmatizing those who resist the Eurocentric formulation of human rights.***

The last school, that of political strategists or instrumentalists, abounds with governments and institutions that selectively and inconsistently deploy human rights discourse for strategic and political ends. While all states—socialist or capitalist, developed or underdeveloped—are generally cynical in their deployment of human rights norms, my focus here is not on all states.*** I am only interested in Western democracies and their institutions which alone rhetorically champion the universalization of human rights. Such institutions include the World Bank and the North Atlantic Treaty

Organization (NATO), whose primary purposes are related to the preservation or the enhancement of liberalism and free markets.***

I.   *Liberalism, Democracy, and Human Rights: A Holy Trinity?*

Liberalism is distinguished from other traditions by its commitment to formal autonomy and abstract equality. It is a tradition that in its contemporary expression requires a constitutional state with limited powers, a state that is moreover accountable to the broad public. These aspirations are the basis for the development and elaboration of liberal democracy and, as this Article contends, the construction and universalization of the jurisprudence of human rights. In the historical continuum, therefore, liberalism gave birth to democracy, which, in turn, now seeks to present itself internationally as the ideology of human rights.***

The minimalist definition of democracy *** responds to liberalism's basic commitment to guarantee citizens their formal autonomy and political and legal equality. Thus, as Henry Steiner puts it, the traditional liberal understanding of the state requires that it "protect citizens in their political organizations and activities,"*** but does not require that it remove impediments to actual equality which may result from lack of resources and status. Steiner says it clearly:

> Choices about types and degrees of [political] participation may depend on citizens' economic resources and social status. But it is not the government's responsibility to alleviate that dependence, to open paths to political participation which lack of funds or education or status would otherwise block.

In reality, of course, participation in the political process requires more than the state's permission and protection. Increasingly, states not only provide these two services but also expend enormous resources constructing the electoral machinery for participation; legislative reforms in many democracies now attempt to address historical, socioeconomic, and ethnic, racial, and gender-related barriers to participation. Such interpretations of political democracy have attempted to build into their frameworks notions of social or economic democracy. In human rights law, the International Covenant on Economic, Social and Cultural Rights (ICESCR) most closely resembles this aspiration.

The main focus of human rights law, however, has been on those rights and programs that seek to strengthen, legitimize, and export political or liberal democracy. Inversely, most of the human rights regime is derived from bodies of domestic jurisprudence developed over several centuries in the West. The emphasis, by academics and practitioners, in the development of human rights law has been on civil and political rights. In fact the currency of civil and political rights has been so strong that they have become synonymous with the human rights movement.***

There is virtual agreement that the early formulation and codification of human rights standards was dominated by Western cultural and political norms. This was particularly true with the formulation and adoption of the Universal Declaration on Human Rights (UDHR), the "spiritual parent of and inspiration for many human rights treaties." As one author has remarked, the West was able to "impose" its philosophy of human rights on the rest of the world because in 1948 it dominated the United Nations. The minority socialist bloc abstained after it put up ineffectual resistance on grounds that economic, social, and cultural rights were downgraded. More important, non-Western views were largely unrepresented because the so-called Third World at the United Nations was mainly composed of Latin American countries whose dominant worldview was European.***

Although non-Western perspectives on human rights, such as the African conceptions of peoples' rights and duties and the more celebrated right to development, have acquired some notoriety in human rights debates, they remain marginal to the mainstream practice of human rights. The same has been true of economic, social, and cultural rights since their relegation to the "other" human rights treaty.***

II. *Conventional Doctrinalism: Content and Context* ***

The most active element in the internationalization of the human rights movement has been the so-called international non-governmental organization (INGO), the movement's prime engine of growth. The most prominent INGOs in this regard are based in the West and seek to enforce the application of human rights norms internationally, particularly towards repressive states in the South. They are ideological analogues, both in theory and in method, of the traditional civil rights organizations which preceded them in the West. The American Civil Liberties Union (ACLU), one of the most influential civil rights organizations in the United States, is the classic example of the Western civil rights organization. Two other equally important domestic civil rights organizations in the United States are the National Association for the Advancement of Colored People (NAACP) and the NAACP Legal Defense and Educational Fund (LDF). Although these organizations are called civil rights groups by Americans, they are in reality human rights organizations. The historical origin of the distinction between a "civil rights" group and a "human rights" group in the United States remains unclear. The primary difference is that Western human rights groups focus on abusive practices and traditions in what they see as relatively repressive, "backward" foreign countries and cultures, while the agenda of civil rights groups concentrates on domestic issues. Thus, although groups such as Human Rights Watch publish reports on human rights abuses in the U.S., the focus of their activity is the human rights "problems" or "abuses" of other countries.

In American popular culture, several assumptions are implicit in this thinking: "human rights problems" do not apply to "people like us," but rather to "backward" peoples or those who are "exotic;" these "problems" arise where the political and legal systems do not work or cannot correct themselves; and "we are lucky" and should "help those less fortunate" overcome their history of despotism. Unfortunately, this dichotomy has calcified in academic institutions where civil rights questions are taught and explored under the rubric of "American" courses while human rights offerings and activities are treated under the rubric "foreign" or "international" disciplines and classifications.*** This organizational format could lead to a sense of cultural superiority and may exacerbate problems of nationalism.***

Some structural factors provide further evidence of the ideological orientation of INGOs. They concern the sources of their moral, financial, and social support. The founding fathers of major INGOs—they have all been White males—were Westerners who either worked on or had an interest in domestic civil and political rights issues; they sought the reform of governmental laws, policies, and processes to bring about compliance with American and European conceptions of liberal democracy and equal protection. Although the founders of the INGOs did not explicitly state their "mission" as a crusade for the globalization of these values, they nevertheless crafted organizational mandates that promoted liberal ideals and norms. In any case, the key international human rights instruments such as the UDHR and the ICCPR pierced the sovereign veil for the purposes of protecting and promoting human rights. The mandates of INGOs are lifted, almost verbatim, from such instruments.***

Substantively, conventional doctrinalists stress a narrow range of civil and political rights, as is reflected by the mandates of leading INGOs like Amnesty International and Human Rights Watch. Throughout the Cold War period, INGOs concentrated their attention on the exposure of violations of what they deemed "core" rights in Soviet bloc countries, Africa, Asia, and Latin America. In a reflection of this ideological bias, INGOs mirrored the position of the industrial democracies and generally assumed an unsympathetic, and at times, hostile posture towards calls for the expansion of their mandates to include economic and social rights.

In the last few years since the collapse of the Soviet bloc, however, several INGOs have started to talk about the "indivisibility" of rights; a few now talk about their belief in the equality of the ICESCR and the ICCPR, although their rhetoric has not been matched by action and practice. Many, in particular Human Rights Watch, for a long time remained hostile, however, to the recognition of economic and social rights as "rights." HRW, which considered such rights "equities," instead advanced its own nebulous interpretation of "indivisible human rights" which related civil and political rights to survival, subsistence, and poverty, "assertions" of good that it did not explicitly call rights. It argued that subsistence and survival are dependent on civil and political rights, especially those related to democratic accountability.

In September 1996, however, Human Rights Watch tentatively abandoned its long-standing opposition to the advocacy of economic and social rights. It passed a highly restrictive and qualified one-year policy—effective January 1997—to investigate, document, and promote compliance with the ICESCR. Under the terms of the new policy, HRW's work on the ICESCR will be limited to two situations: where protection of the ICESCR right is "necessary to remedy a substantial violation of an ICCPR right," and where "the violation of an ICESCR right is the direct and immediate product of a substantial violation of an ICCPR right." Furthermore, HRW will only intervene to protect ICESCR rights where the violation is a "direct product of state action, whether by commission or omission;" where the "principle applied in articulating an ICESCR right is one of general applicability;" and where "there is a clear, reasonable and practical remedy that HRW can advocate to address the ICESCR violation."

While an important step by HRW, this policy statement can be seen as a continuation of the history of skepticism toward economic and social rights HRW has long demonstrated; it sees economic and social rights only as an appendage of civil and political rights.*** The policy also continues HRW's stress on state-related violations, an orientation that overlooks other important violators, such as businesses and international corporations.***

III. The Conceptualizers: Constitutionalizing Human Rights

Constitutionalists, as the label suggests, see, or would like to see, the human rights corpus as a constitutional framework: a set of norms, ideals, and principles—moral, philosophical, legal, even cultural—that cohere to determine the fundamental character of a state and its society. They do not openly distinguish or distance themselves from

doctrinalists whom they see as the human rights movement's critical core, its foot soldiers, those on whom the practical advocacy, proselytization, and universalization of its
creed depend. Rather, constitutionalists are the "thinking" corps of the movement; as
its ideologues they provide intellectual direction and rigor.***

Principal among the constitutionalists has been Louis Henkin. Perhaps more than
any other proponent in this school, Henkin has combined extensive and authoritative
scholarship with active association with the "nerve center" of the American human rights
community in New York.***

In the preface to The Age of Rights, a collection of essays that crystallizes his ideas
on human rights, Henkin underlines his belief in the omnipotence of human rights by
elevating them to a near-mythical, almost biblical plateau. To him, the universality of
the acceptance of the idea of human rights sets it apart from all other ideas and puts it
in a most distinctive place in modern times. He boldly states:

> Ours is the age of rights. Human rights is the idea of our time, the only
> political-moral idea that has received universal acceptance. The Universal
> Declaration of Human Rights, adopted by the United Nations General Assembly
> in 1948, has been approved by virtually all governments representing all soci-
> eties. Human rights are enshrined in the constitutions of virtually every one of
> today's 170 states.***

This celebratory and triumphant passage uses a quantitative approach—the idea's
dissemination and diffusion to most corners of the earth—as the standard for determining the superiority of human rights over other ideas. But the quantitative approach,
while persuasive, has its own problems. One might plausibly argue, based on this criterion, that ideas about free markets as the engine of economic development, among others, are equally, if not more universally accepted, than human rights. Furthermore,
depending on how universal acceptance is calibrated, and who the participants are,
might it not have been possible to argue at the close of the last century that colonialism enjoyed a similar status? ***

Like other Western pioneers of the concept of human rights, Henkin rejects claims
of "cultural relativism" or a multicultural approach to the construction of human rights.
He accuses those who advocate cultural and ideological diversity in the creation of the
human rights corpus of desiring a vague, broad, ambiguous, and general text of human
rights.***

Henkin draws many parallels between human rights and American or Western constitutionalism but concludes, surprisingly, that the human rights corpus does not require
a particular political ideology. This conclusion, with which this Article disagrees, has
been popular among the pioneers of the human rights movement for a number of reasons, including their basic assertion that human rights are distinct from politics—defined
here as a particular ideology—and can be achieved in different political traditions such
as socialist, religious, or free market systems.***

Among the constitutionalists, few have had the rare combination of high-level practical and scholarly experience that has characterized the work of Philip Alston. A leading advocate of a broader conception of human rights, one that treats economic, social,
and cultural rights as an integral part of the corpus, Alston has stated with approval
that "the characterization of a specific goal as a human right elevates it above the rank

and file of competing societal goals, gives it a degree of immunity from challenge and generally endows it with an aura of timelessness, absoluteness and universal validity." Hence, Alston's efforts to promote the legitimacy of rights such as the right to development, and other economic, social and cultural rights whose status as "rights" remains contested.

In a statement to the 1993 World Conference on Human Rights, Alston's Committee on Economic, Social and Cultural Rights lamented that the massive violations of economic and social rights would have provoked "horror and outrage" if they had occurred to civil and political rights. The Committee noted that it was "inhumane, distorted and incompatible with international standards" to exclude the one-fifth of the global population which suffered from poverty, hunger, disease, illiteracy, and insecurity from human rights concerns. It noted that although "political freedom, free markets and pluralism" had been chosen by a large percentage of the global population in recent years because they were seen as the best routes for attaining economic, social and cultural rights, democracy will inevitably fail and societies will revert to authoritarianism unless those rights are respected. The Statement, which underlines Alston's central goal, seeks the globalization of more humane economic and social structures—a social democracy—to complement the open political society of liberal democracy.***

IV. The Dilemmas of the Agnostic

One of the most probing critiques of the human rights corpus has come from non-Western thinkers who, though educated in the West or in Western-oriented educational systems, have philosophical, moral, and cultural questions about the distinctly Eurocentric formulation of human rights discourse. They have difficulties accepting the specific cultural and historical experiences of the West as the standard for all humanity. As outsider-insiders, cultural agnostics understand and accept certain contributions of Western (largely European) civilization to the human rights movement but reject the wholesale adoption or imposition of Western ideas and concepts of human rights. Instead, they present external critiques to human rights discourse, while generally applying language internal to that discourse. By agnostics, I do not refer to external critiquers who think that as a Western project the human rights system is irredeemable and cannot rearrange its priorities or be transformed by other cultural milieus to reflect a genuinely universal character and consensus. Rather, I mean those who advocate a multicultural approach in the reconstruction of the entire edifice of human rights. They could also be termed human rights pluralists.

There is no dispute about the European origins of the philosophy of the human rights movement; even Westerners who advocate its universality accept this basic fact. Refuge from this disturbing reality is taken in the large number of states, from all cultural blocs, which have indicated their acceptance of the regime by becoming parties to the principal human rights instruments.***

Cultural agnostics do not reject the Western conception of human rights in toto; nor do they even deny that a universal corpus may ultimately yield societal typologies and structures similar to those imagined by the present human rights regime. At stake for them is the availability of the opportunity for all major cultural blocs of the world to negotiate the normative content of human rights law and the purposes for which the discourse should be legitimately deployed. Many African agnostics and some Africanists, for example, have demonstrated the similarity of human rights norms in Western states to pre-colonial African states and societies.***

V. Political Strategists: Instrumentalism in Human Rights

The school of political strategists, of all the four typologies explored here, is the least principled and the most open-textured in the manner and the purposes for which it deploys human rights discourse. Apart from the United Nations, whose Center for Human Rights is responsible for human rights matters, Western governments, and particularly the United States, have been the principal advocates for the use of human rights as a tool of policy against other states. In this respect, human rights standards have been viewed as norms with which non-Western, non-democratic states must comply.***

The United States was a principal player in the drafting of the major international human rights instruments, although it has been reluctant to become a party to most of them. It was not until the 1970s that the United States started institutionalizing human rights within its foreign policy bureaucracy.*** As a result, laws were amended to restrict assistance to countries with particular levels of human rights abuses. In 1977, President Jimmy Carter elevated the head of the Human Rights Bureau within the Department of State to the rank of Assistant Secretary of State for Human Rights and Humanitarian Affairs.***

While Carter was inconsistent and continued American support for abusive client states, the Reagan administration found the "perfect" use for human rights in American foreign policy. Rather than push for the unlikely repeal of human rights concerns from American policy, which many human rights advocates feared, the administration quickly enlisted human rights as a key ally in the greater struggle against Communism, which many officials saw as the prime evil of the day.***

This policy was outlined as the promotion of "democratic processes in order to help build a world environment more favorable to respect for human rights." It was billed as a dual policy that opposed human rights violations while strengthening democracy. The policy aimed singularly at the promotion of democracy "as the human right, rejecting in principle not only military 'juntas' but the many one-party states of Africa and Asia." In reality, of course, the administration coddled right-wing dictatorships and oppressive pro-Western regimes, including apartheid South Africa. With the end of the Cold War, however, political conditionality has frequently been used to push one-party states towards the creation of more open, democratic political structures.

The Bush administration did not dramatically depart from the substance of the Reagan policy, although it countenanced the withdrawal of knee-jerk U.S. support for some pro-Western regimes primarily because of the collapse of Communism. Despite its rhetorical defense of human rights, the Clinton administration has been more concerned with the promotion of democratic initiatives and trade opportunities than with the principled application of human rights norms.***

International financial institutions and donor agencies also constitute an increasingly important component of the political strategy approach. World Bank-led groups of donors that keep many states in the South from total economic collapse have used human rights conditionalities to force economic liberalization, a measure of public accountability, and political pluralism. But the World Bank's concern with "good governance" has not been altruistic. That attitudinal change came after the Bank's utter failure to reverse economic decline in Africa. Overlooking its own role in exacerbating Africa's underdevelopment, the Bank concluded in 1989 that "underlying the litany of Africa's development problems is a crisis of governance." In what amounted to a prescription for liberal democracy, it defined governance in the following familiar language:

> By governance is meant the exercise of political power to manage a nation's affairs. Because countervailing power has been lacking, state officials in many countries have served their own interests without fear of being called to account.*** This environment cannot readily support a dynamic economy. At worst the state becomes coercive and arbitrary. These trends, however, can be resisted.*** It requires a systematic effort to build a pluralistic institutional structure, a determination to respect the rule of law, and vigorous protection of the freedom of the press and human rights.***

The significance of the Bank's general attitude lies in its conclusions: economic liberalization and free markets are less likely in undemocratic regimes that abuse basic liberal freedoms.*** The trademark of political strategists is their unabashed deployment of human rights and democracy interchangeably for the advancement of a variety of interests: strategic, tactical, geopolitical, security, "vital," economic, and political.***

Notes and Questions

1. *Is there a human rights ideology?* What are the implications of Mutua's view that the international human rights movement is guided by a dominant ideology or set of ideologies? Do you agree with this proposition? If so, do you find this problematic? Why, or why not?

2. *Consequences of the Critique.* Does Mutua's analysis challenge the human rights project entirely, or does it critique only cross-cultural discourses on human rights? What are the possible advantages of local or regional approaches to human rights? What are the disadvantages or limitations of such alternative approaches?

3. *NGOs and Second Generation Rights.* Mutua criticizes major Western human rights NGOs for, among other things, failing to adequately monitor and report on violations of economic, social and cultural rights. In recent years, however, the major human rights NGOs, like Human Rights Watch, Amnesty International and Human Rights First (formerly Lawyers Committee for Human Rights) have begun to address such issues. Consider the following statement on second generation rights by Human Rights Watch, one of the largest and most influential human rights NGOs:

> Since its formation in 1978, Human Rights Watch has focused mainly on upholding civil and political rights, but in recent years we have increasingly addressed economic, social and cultural rights as well. We focus particularly on situations in which our methodology of investigation and reporting is most effective, such as when arbitrary or discriminatory governmental conduct lies behind an economic, social and cultural rights violation.

> We pay special attention to economic, social and cultural rights violations when they result from violations of civil and political rights or must be remedied as part of a plan for ending violations of civil and political rights. ***

Human Rights Watch, Economic, Social, and Cultural Rights, *available at* http://www. hrw.org/esc/ (last visited July 24, 2004).

A review of current agenda items monitored by Human Rights Watch reveals that the group reports on labor rights (including the rights of sex workers and domestic workers), public health issues (including environmental justice and the rights of persons with HIV/AIDS), and other social and cultural concerns (including discrimination in education and in caste systems). See Human Rights Watch Web site at http://www.hrw.org. Amnesty International, which once focused primarily on the rights of political prisoners and on organizing against capital punishment, now investigates and reports on a wide range of economic, social, and cultural issues as well: globalization and human rights, business and human rights, violence and the trade in "conflict diamonds" and small arms, women and development, the rights of indigenous peoples and the economic rights of women. *See* Amnesty International Web site at http://www.amnesty.org. *See also* Amnesty International, Women's Rights: A Fact Sheet on Economic, Social, and Cultural Rights (ESCR) and Women, *available at* http://www.amnestyusa.org/women/economicrights.html (last visited July 24, 2004). Similarly, Human Rights First now works on issues of corporate accountability and workers' rights as well as traditional civil and political rights. *See* Human Rights First Web site, *at* http://www.humanrightsfirst.org. *See also* the Web site of Global Rights (formerly International Human Rights Law Group), *at* http://www.hrlawgroup.org/ (including focus on human trafficking, women's rights, and affirmative action in education).

In addition, there are a growing number of international and local NGOs that focus specifically on violations of socio-economic rights, such as Physicians for Human Rights (http://www.phrusa.org) (the right to health), Treatment Action Campaign (South Africa) http://www.tac.org.za) (the right to affordable treatment for HIV/AIDS), Center on Economic and Social Rights http://www.cesr.org) (economic and social rights generally), Cultural Survival (http://www.cs.org), Women and the Economy (http://www.unpac.ca) (gender and economic rights), Global Exchange (http://www.globalexchange.org) (human rights and economic development), Human Rights in China (http://iso.hrichina.org/iso/) (includes focus on economic, social and cultural rights in China) and the Kensington Welfare Rights Union (http://www.kwru.org) (economic, social and cultural rights of the poor in the United States). The International Network for Economic, Social, and Cultural Rights-NET, *at* http://www.escr-net.org, provides an excellent portal site on these issues. In addition to providing links organized by issue, this site has a search engine on U.S. domestic, foreign and international judicial and administrative decisions in the field.

What might explain the fact that major Western NGOs that once explicitly rejected the need to monitor second generation rights violations began to broaden their focus in the late 1990s and the early 21st century? Is this a response to changing global realities, a response to changing global politics, or both? What are the benefits or drawbacks of such an expanded emphasis? If you were a member of the board of a human rights NGO, what criteria would you use to decide on the organization's focus?

4. As you conduct research on specific violations of economic, social or cultural rights, consider the differences in emphasis, methodology or coverage you observe among the various human rights NGOs. Can these differences be classified along identifiable ideological lines as Mutua would suggest? Do they break down along geopolitical lines between North and South or West and East?

**HILARY CHARLESWORTH, CHRISTINE CHINKIN AND SHELLEY WRIGHT,
FEMINIST APPROACHES TO INTERNATIONAL LAW**

85 Am. J. Int'l L. 613, 614–30, 634–35 (1991)

I. INTRODUCTION ***

International law has thus far largely resisted feminist analysis. The concerns of public international law do not, at first sight, have any particular impact on women: issues of sovereignty, territory, use of force and state responsibility, for example, appear gender free in their application to the abstract entities of states. Only where international law is considered directly relevant to individuals, as with human rights law, have some specifically feminist perspectives on international law begun to be developed.***

By challenging the nature and operation of international law and its context, feminist legal theory can contribute to the progressive development of international law. A feminist account of international law suggests that we inhabit a world in which men of all nations have used the statist system to establish economic and nationalist priorities to serve male elites, while basic human, social and economic needs are not met. International institutions currently echo these same priorities. By taking women seriously and describing the silences and fundamentally skewed nature of international law, feminist theory can identify possibilities for change.***

Feminism in the First and Third Worlds

An alternative, feminist analysis of international law must take account of the differing perspectives of First and Third World feminists. Third World feminists operate in particularly difficult contexts. Not only does the dominant European, male discourse of law, politics and science exclude the kind of discourse characterized by the phrase "a different voice," both female and non-European, but also feminist concerns in the Third World are largely ignored or misunderstood by western feminists. Western feminism began as a demand for the right of women to be treated as men. Whether in campaigns for equal rights or for special rights such as the right to abortion, western feminists have sought guarantees from the state that, as far as is physically possible, they will be placed in the same position as men. This quest does not always have the same attraction for nonwestern women. For example, the western feminist preoccupation with a woman's right to abortion is of less significance to many Third World women because population-control programs often deny them the chance to have children. Moreover, "nonpositivist" cultures, such as those of Asia and Africa, are just as masculinist, or even more so, than the western cultures in which the language of law and science developed. In the context of international law (and, indeed, domestic law), then, Third World feminists are obliged to communicate in the western rationalist language of the law, in addition to challenging the intensely patriarchal "different voice" discourse of traditional non-European societies. In this sense, feminism in the Third World is doubly at odds with the dominant male discourse of its societies.

The legacy of colonial rule has been particularly problematic for many women in the Third World. Local women were seen as constituting a pool of cheap labor for industries, agriculture and domestic service, and local men were often recruited to work away from their families. Local women also provided sex to the colonizers, especially where there was a shortage of women from home. To local men, the position of their women was symbolic of and mirrored their own domination: while colonialism meant allowing the colonial power to abuse colonized women, resistance to colonialism encompassed reasserting the colonized males' power over their women.

Nationalist movements typically pursued wider objectives than merely to transfer power from white colonial rulers to indigenous people: they were concerned with restructuring the hierarchies of power and control, reallocating wealth within society, and creating nothing less than a new society based on equality and nonexploitation. It was inevitable that feminist objectives, including the restructuring of society across gender lines, would cause tension when set beside nationalist objectives that sounded similar but so frequently discounted the feminist perspective.***

III. THE MASCULINE WORLD OF INTERNATIONAL LAW ***

The structure of the international legal order reflects a male perspective and ensures its continued dominance. The primary subjects of international law are states and, increasingly, international organizations. In both states and international organizations the invisibility of women is striking. Power structures within governments are overwhelmingly masculine: women have significant positions of power in very few states, and in those where they do, their numbers are minuscule. Women are either unrepresented or underrepresented in the national and global decision-making processes.

States are patriarchal structures not only because they exclude women from elite positions and decision-making roles, but also because they are based on the concentration of power in, and control by, an elite and the domestic legitimation of a monopoly over the use of force to maintain that control. This foundation is reinforced by international legal principles of sovereign equality, political independence and territorial integrity and the legitimation of force to defend those attributes.

International organizations are functional extensions of states that allow them to act collectively to achieve their objectives. Not surprisingly, their structures replicate those of states, restricting women to insignificant and subordinate roles. Thus, in the United Nations itself, where the achievement of nearly universal membership is regarded as a major success of the international community, this universality does not apply to women.***

Women are excluded from all major decision-making by international institutions on global policies and guidelines, despite the often disparate impact of those decisions on women. Since 1985, there has been some improvement in the representation of women in the United Nations and its specialized agencies. It has been estimated, however, that "at the present rate of change it will take almost 4 more decades (until 2021) to reach equality (i.e.: 50% of professional jobs held by women)." This situation was recently described as "grotesque."***

The normative structure of international law has allowed issues of particular concern to women to be either ignored or undermined. For example, modern international law rests on and reproduces various dichotomies between the public and private spheres, and the "public" sphere is regarded as the province of international law. One such distinction is between public international law, the law governing the relations between nation-states, and private international law, the rules about conflicts between national legal systems. Another is the distinction between matters of international "public" concern and matters "private" to states that are considered within their domestic jurisdiction, in which the international community has no recognized legal interest. Yet another is the line drawn between law and other forms of "private" knowledge such as morality.

At a deeper level one finds a public/private dichotomy based on gender. One explanation feminist scholars offer for the dominance of men and the male voice in all areas of power and authority in the western liberal tradition is that a dichotomy is drawn between the public sphere and the private or domestic one. The public realm of the work place, the law, economics, politics and intellectual and cultural life, where power and authority are exercised, is regarded as the natural province of men; while the private world of the home, the hearth and children is seen as the appropriate domain of women. The public/private distinction has a normative, as well as a descriptive, dimension. Traditionally, the two spheres are accorded asymmetrical value: greater significance is attached to the public, male world than to the private, female one. The distinction drawn between the public and the private thus vindicates and makes natural the division of labor and allocation of rewards between the sexes. Its reproduction and acceptance in all areas of knowledge have conferred primacy on the male world and supported the dominance of men.***

The assumption that underlies all law, including international human rights law, is that the public/private distinction is real: human society, human lives can be separated into two distinct spheres. This division, however, is an ideological construct rationalizing the exclusion of women from the sources of power. It also makes it possible to maintain repressive systems of control over women without interference from human rights guarantees, which operate in the public sphere. By extending our vision beyond the public/private ideologies that rationalize limiting our analysis of power, human rights language as it currently exists can be used to describe serious forms of repression that go far beyond the juridically narrow vision of international law. For example, coercive population control techniques, such as forced sterilization, may amount to punishment or coercion by the state to achieve national goals.***

Critique of Rights

The feminist critique of rights questions whether the acquisition of legal rights advances women's equality. Feminist scholars have argued that, although the search for formal legal equality through the formulation of rights may have been politically appropriate in the early stages of the feminist movement, continuing to focus on the acquisition of rights may not be beneficial to women. Quite apart from problems such as the form in which rights are drafted, their interpretation by tribunals, and women's access to their enforcement, the rhetoric of rights, according to some feminist legal scholars, is exhausted.

Rights discourse is taxed with reducing intricate power relations in a simplistic way. The formal acquisition of a right, such as the right to equal treatment, is often assumed to have solved an imbalance of power. In practice, however, the promise of rights is thwarted by the inequalities of power: the economic and social dependence of women on men may discourage the invocation of legal rights that are premised on an adversarial relationship between the rights holder and the infringer. More complex still are rights designed to apply to women only such as the rights to reproductive freedom and to choose abortion.

In addition, although they respond to general societal imbalances, formulations of rights are generally cast in individual terms. The invocation of rights to sexual equality may therefore solve an occasional case of inequality for individual women but will leave the position of women generally unchanged. Moreover, international law accords priority to civil and political rights, rights that may have very little to offer women generally. The major forms of oppression of women operate within the economic, social and cultural realms. Economic, social and cultural rights are traditionally regarded as a lesser form of international right and as much more difficult to implement.

A second major criticism of the assumption that the granting of rights inevitably spells progress for women is that it ignores competing rights: the right of women and children not to be subjected to violence in the home may be balanced against the property rights of men in the home or their right to family life. Furthermore, certain rights may be appropriated by more powerful groups: Carol Smart relates that provisions in the European Convention on Human Rights on family life were used by fathers to assert their authority over *ex nuptial* children.***

Notes and Questions

1.   How is partriarchy defined? What is inherently patriarchal about "the concentration of power in *** an elite and *** monopoly over the use of force ***?" Is it inconceivable that women could willingly participate in and even someday dominate such structures?

2.   The authors suggest that individual rights may be inadequate to address women's needs. How would collective rights based on gender be framed? How would they be implemented? Could collective rights address the complexity of issues faced by working class women, women of color, Third World women, etc.? Consider the following critique of some contemporary feminist analyses:

> The critique of [the] individualism underlying traditional liberal thought is applicable to the gender debate and has been extended to feminism, most notably to conventional liberal feminism. As noted by Elizabeth Fox-Genovese, "individualism remains fully ingrained in most feminist thought." This is evident in both the language and goals pursued by feminists: in analyzing the choice rhetoric in the family/work context, Joan Williams has pointed out that feminists "in their demands for liberation use the standard legal language of autonomous individuals with rights making choices in their own self interest." Deriving from a historical and cultural tradition of individualism, the focus of American feminists continues to be on achieving women's selfhood and the liberty to shape their own lives. Even the difference school feminists, who come closest to a critique of individualism in focusing on the importance of relationships in constituting the self, are rightly criticized as developing a theory of female individualism or "individualism with a human face." The issue for communitarians and feminists alike, then, is how to reconcile "claims of constitutiveness of social relations with values of self-determination."

Margaret Y.K. Woo, *Biology and Equality: Challenge for Feminism in the Socialist and the Liberal State*, 42 EMORY L.J. 143, 188–89 (1993).

D. CULTURAL RELATIVISM

The foundational instruments of the international human rights legal regime presume a universal understanding of rights—common ground—among the world's peoples. At the same time, the Universal Declaration of Human Rights and the two human rights covenants recognize individual and collective rights to cultural enjoyment, language, religion and the self-determination of peoples. How are the tensions between universal standards and culturally specific values to be resolved, if at all? To some extent, the human rights norms elaborated in the International Bill of Rights are broadly stated so that individual states can implement them in accordance with local political, economic, cultural and social contexts. Simultaneously, these instruments are intended to reflect common guarantees upon which any human being can rely regardless of nationality, race, religion, gender or other social status.

Some voices critical of universalist claims emphasize the importance of the cultural particularity of rights and of the values associated with them. Many point to the hegemonic influence of colonial, neo-colonial, and imperial cultures on non-Western peoples. As seen in the American Anthropological Association's Statement on Human Rights, excerpted in Section A.3. *supra*, even some Western cultural anthropologists questioned whether it was possible to accurately identify any truly universal list of human rights, particularly by states with a history of slavery, colonialism, and imperialism.

To the extent that important values such as rights exist in a particular culture, how likely is it that such rights would be culturally-specific rather than cross-cultural? Is an emphasis on rights (as opposed to, say, duties) itself a cultural construct? Does the prioritization of rights categories break down along cultural lines?

The following materials examine some of these fundamental questions raised by the universalist/relativist debate. In particular, they examine the "Asian Values" debate—in broad terms, the notion that Asian cultures place greater value on the collective good rather than individual rights, on economic and social priorities over civil liberties, and on the notion that the rule of law should work hand in hand with cultural constraints.

Even the terms of the debate are fluid and contestable. How does one define "culture" or "religion"? Does culture include choices about political and economic systems and priorities? How is membership in a particular culture or religion regulated? What is the relationship between religion and culture? Does the International Bill of Rights reflect a "floor" of values that are (or should be) truly universal? Or, are the norms in human rights instruments the historically and socially constructed legacy of Western liberalism? How are the values of "West" and "East" to be defined and differentiated? Should the goal of rights discourse be to find a balance between extant cultural norms?

FINAL DECLARATION OF THE REGIONAL MEETING FOR ASIA OF THE WORLD CONFERENCE ON HUMAN RIGHTS (THE BANGKOK DECLARATION)

Available at http://www.unhchr.ch/html/menu5/wcbankg.htm

Emphasizing the significance of the World Conference on Human Rights, which provides an invaluable opportunity to review all aspects of human rights and ensure a just and balanced approach thereto,

Recognizing the contribution that can be made to the World Conference by Asian countries with their diverse and rich cultures and traditions,***

Noting the progress made in the codification of human rights instruments, and in the establishment of international human rights mechanisms, while *expressing concern* that these mechanisms relate mainly to one category of rights,***

Recognizing that the promotion of human rights should be encouraged by cooperation and consensus, and not through confrontation and the imposition of incompatible values,

Reiterating the interdependence and indivisibility of economic, social, cultural, civil and political rights, and the inherent interrelationship between development, democracy, universal enjoyment of all human rights, and social justice, which must be addressed in an integrated and balanced manner,

Recalling that the Declaration on the Right to Development has recognized the right to development as a universal and inalienable right and an integral part of fundamental human rights,

Emphasizing that endeavours to move towards the creation of uniform international human rights norms must go hand in hand with endeavours to work towards a just and fair world economic order,***

1.   *Reaffirm* their commitment to the principles contained in the Charter of the United Nations and the Universal Declaration on Human Rights as well as the full realization of all human rights throughout the world;***

3.   *Stress* the urgent need to democratize the United Nations system, eliminate selectivity and improve procedures and mechanisms in order to strengthen international cooperation, based on principles of equality and mutual respect, and ensure a positive, balanced and non-confrontational approach in addressing and realizing all aspects of human rights;

4.   *Discourage* any attempt to use human rights as a conditionality for extending development assistance;

5.   *Emphasize* the principles of respect for national sovereignty and territorial integrity as well as non-interference in the internal affairs of States, and the non-use of human rights as an instrument of political pressure;

6.   *Reiterate* that all countries, large and small, have the right to determine their political systems, control and freely utilize their resources, and freely pursue their economic, social and cultural development;

7.   *Stress* the universality, objectivity and non-selectivity of all human rights and the need to avoid the application of double standards in the implementation of human rights and its politicization, and that no violation of human rights can be justified;

8.   *Recognize* that while human rights are universal in nature, they must be considered in the context of a dynamic and evolving process of international norm-setting, bearing in mind the significance of national and regional particularities and various historical, cultural and religious backgrounds; ***

10.   *Reaffirm* the interdependence and indivisibility of economic, social, cultural, civil and political rights, and the need to give equal emphasis to all categories of human rights;

11. *Emphasize* the importance of guaranteeing the human rights and fundamental freedoms of vulnerable groups such as ethnic, national, racial, religious and linguistic minorities, migrant workers, disabled persons, indigenous peoples, refugees and displaced persons;

12. *Reiterate* that self-determination is a principle of international law and a universal right recognized by the United Nations for peoples under alien or colonial domination and foreign occupation, by virtue of which they can freely determine their political status and freely pursue their economic, social and cultural development, and that its denial constitutes a grave violation of human rights;

13. *Stress* that the right to self-determination is applicable to peoples under alien or colonial domination and foreign occupation, and should not be used to undermine the territorial integrity, national sovereignty and political independence of States;

14. *Express concern* over all forms of violation of human rights, including manifestations of racial discrimination, racism, apartheid, colonialism, foreign aggression and occupation, and the establishment of illegal settlements in occupied territories, as well as the recent resurgence of neo-nazism, xenophobia and ethnic cleansing;

15. *Underline* the need for taking effective international measures in order to guarantee and monitor the implementation of human rights standards and effective and legal protection of people under foreign occupation;[3]

16. *Strongly affirm* their support for the legitimate struggle of the Palestinian people to restore their national and inalienable rights to self-determination and independence, and demand an immediate end to the grave violations of human rights in the Palestinian, Syrian Golan and other occupied Arab territories including Jerusalem;

17. *Reaffirm* the right to development, as established in the Declaration on the Right to Development, as a universal and inalienable right and an integral part of fundamental human rights, which must be realized through international cooperation, respect for fundamental human rights, the establishment of a monitoring mechanism and the creation of essential international conditions for the realization of such right;[4]

18. *Recognize* that the main obstacles to the realization of the right to development lie at the international macroeconomic level, as reflected in the widening gap between the North and the South, the rich and the poor;

19. *Affirm* that poverty is one of the major obstacles hindering the full enjoyment of human rights;

20. *Affirm also* the need to develop the right of humankind regarding a clean, safe and healthy environment;***

22. *Reaffirm* their strong commitment to the promotion and protection of the rights of women through the guarantee of equal participation in the political, social, economic and cultural concerns of society, and the eradication of all forms of discrimination and of gender-based violence against women;

23. *Recognize* the rights of the child to enjoy special protection and to be afforded the opportunities and facilities to develop physically, mentally, morally, spiritually and socially in a healthy and normal manner and in conditions of freedom and dignity;***

---

3   *See infra* Ch. 6.
4   *See infra* Ch. 5.

30. *Call for* increased representation of the developing countries in the Centre for Human Rights.

Notes and Questions

1.   What are the concerns expressed in the Declaration regarding the formulation and implementation of human rights norms? How should the international community respond to these concerns? Is the undemocratic nature of the U.N. Security Council a human rights issue? Should human rights be depoliticized, as urged in the Bangkok Declaration? If so, how might the goals of the human rights movement be achieved?

2.   *The NGO Response to the Bangkok Declaration.* On the eve of the Preparatory Meeting of Asian Governments, representatives of more than 110 non-governmental organizations from about 26 Asian-Pacific countries met to advance their vision for human rights in the region. The NGOs challenged their governments to implement fully and immediately a human rights agenda that embraces the "emerging *** new understanding of universalism encompassing the richness and wisdom of Asia-Pacific cultures."

While acknowledging cultural pluralism, the NGOs disputed governmental claims of exemption from certain norms based on sovereignty and culture. The groups emphasized that the premise of universality invalidates a view of human rights advocacy as an encroachment upon national sovereignty. They also challenged the classic state defense of human rights violations based on the bifurcation and "prioritization" of rights categories, stressing that the principle of indivisibility and interdependence of rights means that "one set of rights cannot be used to bargain for another."

Criticizing governments for not prominently featuring the issue of women's rights, the groups stressed the interrelationship between these rights and "balanced and sustainable development," and called for the democratization of the development process "so as to ensure a harmonious relationship between humanity and the natural environment, and to create processes to enhance the empowerment of women and gender equality."

The NGOs expressed "deep concern over the increasing militarization throughout the region and the diversion of resources," noting the interdependence of peace and human rights. They also pointed out that the right of self-determination imposed obligations on governments to recognize and respect the rights of indigenous peoples within their borders.

Reviewing the NGO Statement, Professor Yash Ghai observes:

> If in these perspectives the views of the NGOs are at variance with those of governments, there is some common ground on other points. The NGOs attribute the poor state of human rights to the international economic order, whose reform through several structural changes as well as the adoption of a Convention on the Right to Development, they urge. Unlike the governments, they see a much closer connection with domestic oppression and international exploitation, in the collaboration of local economic and political elites with multinational corporations and aid agencies. Unlike the governments, they are critical of the market system. They share with governments the desire to establish a broad framework for the analysis of human rights, but their framework (unlike that of governments which is informed by a statist view of development) is suffused with notions of social justice, eradication of poverty through equitable distribution of resources and the empowerment of people, especially women and other disadvantaged communities.***

Yash Ghai, *Human Rights and Governance: The Asia Debate*, 15 Aust. Y.B. Int'l L. 1, 14 (1993).

BILAHARI KAUSIKAN, AN ASIAN APPROACH TO HUMAN RIGHTS[5]

Symposium: Structure of World Order: East Asian Approaches to Human Rights,
89 AM. SOC'Y INT'L L. PROC. 146, 146–52, 165–67 (1995)

Is there, can there be, a distinctively Asian approach to human rights? The answer is more complex than is sometimes assumed.

At one level the answer logically must be negative if human rights are rights everyone has simply as a human being. Yet cultural diversity is also real. As a matter of empirical record, rights, order and justice are obtained in diverse ways in different countries at different times. Japan and India are two Asian countries that profess adherence to democracy and human rights in terms almost indistinguishable from the West. Nevertheless, there are great differences in the way rights are conceived and laws implemented in Japan and India, and between both and the West; differences that can be attributed to culture and the level of development.

Reference to cultural diversity as an empirical fact points to the core difficulty of conceiving of a single Asian approach to human rights. Asia is a vast and diverse continent. There are different voices saying different things with different motivations. The clamor is even greater if we take into account not just governments, but NGOs and some minority ethnic or religious groups. The debate is not just between Asia and the West, but between Asian countries and within Asian countries.

My emphasis is on the governmental perspective in this ongoing human rights debate. From this viewpoint, an Asian approach to human rights is perhaps more a matter of process rather than particular outcomes or positions. There is a general disquiet across the region, and not just among governments, with letting the West determine the international human rights agenda, as it has done for so long. Common sets of questions are being asked across Asia, even if there are no common answers.

I want to deal with four aspects of this complex debate: First, the central question of universality; second, the relationship of development to human rights; third, the Western reaction to this debate; and fourth, how the West and Asian governments can find a more common ground. Needless to say, mine is only one Asian point of view.

The Ideal of Universality

A key question is whether or not all human rights are truly universal. This is often, somewhat crudely, posed in the form of a dichotomy between universality and cultural relativism, provoking fierce disputes with a pronounced theological flavor. I believe that this is a false and sterile dichotomy.

---

[5] Ambassador Kausikan's remarks were delivered as part of a panel chaired by Professor Timothy Kearley on "Structure of World Order: East Asian Approaches to Human Rights" at the annual meeting of the American Society of International Law. See also an expanded version in Bilahari Kausikan, Symposium: East Asian Approaches To Human Rights. Selected Panelists From The 1995 Annual Meeting Of The American Society Of International Law: An East Asian Approach To Human Rights, 2 BUFF. J. INT'L L. 263 (1995). This excerpt also includes remarks in response to Kausikan by Sharon Hom, then Professor of Law at the City University of New York School of Law and now Executive Director of Human Rights in China, a human rights NGO based in the United States.

To many in the West, cultural relativism is nothing more than a shield for dictators. It cannot be denied that gross violators of human rights are among those who advance the cultural diversity argument. There is a global culture of modernity of which the ideal of human rights is part. No traditional culture exists in a pure form anymore, anywhere. No country has rejected the Universal Declaration of Human Rights. Recognition of diversity as an empirical fact cannot justify gross violation of human rights. Murder is murder whether perpetrated in America, Asia or Africa. No one claims torture as part of his cultural heritage.***

Universality is not uniformity. The extent and exercise of rights and freedoms must necessarily vary from one culture or political community to another, and over time, because they are the products of historical experiences of particular peoples. Many Asian societies are more group-oriented and accept a wider sphere of governmental responsibility and intervention than is common elsewhere. But societal differences are a reality even within the West. The United States has no state church nor religion. Many European countries do. Are we therefore to conclude that freedom of religion is less protected in Europe than in the United States? This would be absurd.

Upon examination, the "Asian challenge to universality" is often no more than a similar assertion of the freedom for each country to find its own best social and political arrangements. Curiously this fundamentally pluralist approach is often contested by otherwise liberal and tolerant individuals in the West who would instinctively take a multiculturalist perspective if similar issues were raised in a domestic context.

How rights were defined in Europe or America a hundred years ago is certainly not how they are defined today. And they will be defined differently a hundred years hence.

Almost fifty years after the Universal Declaration was adopted as a "common standard of achievement," debate over the meaning of many of its thirty articles continues. The debate is not just between the West and Asia. Not every country in the West will agree on the specific meaning of every one of the Universal Declaration's thirty articles. Not everyone will agree that all of them are really rights. Not even every state of the fifty states of the United States will interpret the Universal Declaration in the same way. But the multiplicity of national, state and local laws and practices in the United States is not decried as a retreat from universalism. On the contrary, the clash and clamor of contending interests is held up as a shining model of democratic freedom.

Universality is not a static concept. Rights, like all human norms, evolve in response to changing configurations of interests and needs. Irrelevant norms are discarded or modified. The right to asylum, for instance, has been progressively restricted by most Western countries in the last few years. If it had not, the very principle may have been discarded under the political, economic, cultural and social pressures of new mass population movements. It is not difficult to trace a similar evolutionary process for many other rights and international norms.

Yet an attempt to reflect this commonplace process in a diplomatic document aroused fierce accusations of Asians undermining universality in the preparatory activities for the World Conference on Human Rights held in Vienna in June 1993.

Article 8 of the Final Declaration of the Regional Meeting for Asia of the World Conference on Human Rights, known as the Bangkok Declaration of 2 April 1993, reads:

[Ministers and representatives of Asian governments] recognise that while human rights are universal in nature, they must be considered in the context of a dynamic and evolving process of international norm-setting, bearing in mind the significance of national and regional particularities and various historical, cultural and religious backgrounds.

Western over-reaction to this simple description of reality—that moreover explicitly recognized the ideal of universality—led to much of the acrimony that characterized the debate between the West and Asia at the Vienna Conference. It still poisons the atmosphere and fuels misunderstanding.

The controversy underscores the essential problem with universality as an ideal. Acceptance of the ideal prescribes nothing useful about how allegedly universal rights are to be implemented in the real world. Nor does it imply anything practical about how this dynamic process of international norm-setting is to be managed.

Singapore has had differences of opinion with several Western governments as regards capital punishment, corporal punishment and limits to the freedom of expression. How are such disagreements to be resolved? International law prescribes no single international standard that can be applied to any of these issues. Capital punishment is hotly debated, not just in the international community but even within the United States. Nine American states are contemplating introducing corporal punishment. Several European countries have limited freedom of expression through such measures as the Official Secrets Act and stricter libel and contempt of court laws than exist in the United States. The days are gone when any single country can insist on its own practices as a "universal norm." ***

I am not arguing that national sovereignty precludes all international discussions on human rights. International law has evolved to the point that how a country treats its citizens is no longer a matter for its exclusive determination. But international human rights law still co-exists uneasily, and in as yet an unresolved manner, with the fundamental principle of national sovereignty. It would thus be prudent to restrict such discussions to gross and egregious violations of human rights, which clearly admit of no derogation on the grounds of national sovereignty. Attempting to expand the debate to areas where there are legitimate national differences of interpretation or implementation only exacerbates misunderstanding and prevents consensus.

Development and Human Rights

The relationship between development and human rights is another aspect of the debate that is often misrepresented. The crude argument that the enjoyment of human rights must await a certain standard of economic development is often attributed to Asians—to be sure, some Asians do make this argument, but I do not agree with them and I do not think that those who advance this crude argument are in the majority.

It is certainly meaningless to speak of human rights while in conditions of abject misery. There are nevertheless certain core rights that ought not be derogated under any circumstances. Poverty cannot justify murder or torture. But the relationship between development and human rights is perhaps more subtle than is sometimes appreciated.

Repression is morally wrong and unhealthy. Our experience is that growth both promotes and is promoted by the ability of the individual to live with dignity.

What we dispute is the simplistic belief that the extension of individual political and civil liberties will necessarily and inevitably lead to economic development. Nothing is inevitable. Growth and stability are linked by a more complex and subtle dynamic—an unremitting search for an equilibrium between the rights of the individual, the claims of the community to which every individual must belong, and the no less urgent need for governments to govern effectively and for society to develop. This requires, on occasion, a firm hand and a limitation of some individual rights in the public interest. For experience has equally convinced us that stability is also an imperative for growth and the extension of human rights.***

Several Asian societies are searching for their own distinctive mix of capitalism, state and society. But in talking about "Asian values," they are also often only examining such issues as the responsibility of individuals to society, or the role of the family and the maintenance of law and order. These issues also are being discussed and debated by significant sections of Western societies who now feel that the exaggeration of liberal values has led to serious problems.***

The key question raised by the debate over Asian values is complex: As societies develop economically, must they necessarily follow the particular path of political development that many in the West would define as "democracy"?***

Things inevitably change. Whether change necessarily leads to a particular form of political system is still an open question. Indeed, whether the specific political system that many in the West understand by the term "democracy" is intrinsically desirable if it requires all societies to face the serious problems of governance confronted by the mature democracies is also an open question.

This is not to say that governments should not be accountable to the people through periodic free and fair elections. Accountability is clearly an essential condition for good government and growth, but this does not impel any particular set of political institutions or arrangements.

The question is simply what works, not what is prescribed by one set of political ideals or another. The first duty of a government is to govern fairly, and in a way that increases the general welfare. Communism failed, not because it lacked a lofty ideal, but because in the final analysis it could not deliver. So also will any political system fail if it becomes, or is perceived to be, dysfunctional. No political system or ideal is sacrosanct. Liberal democracy is certainly not the "end of history."

The Western Response

The Western response to the Asian human rights debate bears examination because, in my view, it has been disproportiontely vehement in relation to what is actually being said by some Asians.

To be sure, the universality and individuality of rights is deeply ingrained in Western political culture and the Western definition of its own identity. It is only to be expected that anything that is regarded as even mildly questioning these "idols of the tribe" would provoke a strong reaction. Still, the response often seems insensitive to the nuances of different Asian voices; indeed, it often appears that many in the West are responding not so much to what is actually being said, as to their own worst fears and insecurities.

The end of the Cold War deprived the West of the convenient ability to define its own identity in opposition to the Eastern bloc. Fighting global Communism made it easy for Europeans and Americans to believe that their common values were true and beneficial, not only for the West, but for the whole world. This cozy assumption has now evaporated. Economic success and the removal of the Cold War straightjacket now allow Asian countries greater freedom to find their own way. The West is also freed to pursue its own values, but is not yet entirely comfortable with the post-Cold War world. Some in the West occasionally seem disquieted by the rise of several Asian countries as major international players that, while friendly to the West, have no wish to become good westerners and are strong economic competitors. The problems are particularly acute for those Western societies that define themselves in relation to a universal mission.

Some have responded by trying to recreate the comfortable verities of the Cold War by postulating a "clash of civilizations." Others appear disheartened by the loss of economic competitiveness and seemingly intractable social and political problems. They seem to have lost the confidence to believe that their own way of life is worth living without seeing it as obligatory for the entire human race.

I believe that the debate on "Asian values" or "Asian human rights" has provoked such strong responses in the West precisely because it resonates deeply and uncomfortably with an ongoing process of questioning of once widely accepted values within many Western societies.***

Conclusion: Toward Convergence ***

The key problem is to find a balance between an often ethnocentric universalism and a paralyzing cultural relativism. This will require a modest and pragmatic approach that seeks to consolidate what common ground can be agreed, while agreeing to disagree when necessary. It will require both sides to eschew self-righteousness of any variety, respect diversity and accept that disagreement is not always evidence of bad faith or malign intent.

REMARKS BY SHARON HOM

*** I would describe my own approach as a discursive strategy situated in "shifting material cartographies." That is just a warning that discursive victories do not necessarily signify real changes in people's lives. I would further describe my approach as derived from physics, specifically the Heisenberg principle of uncertainty. This is the idea that one cannot observe something without changing it.***

Human rights is ultimately about justice, and the contest is over content, meaning and implementation. An example of one of these very significant contests is the struggle, since 1975, for the recognition of women's rights as human rights. One of the major theoretical and practical accomplishments has been to move women's rights onto the human rights agenda—to challenge the bifurcation of civil and political rights, and economic, social and cultural rights; to challenge the marginalization of women's issues; and to reconceptualize human rights as inclusive of the specific human rights of women.

The 1993 Conference on Human Rights recognized the importance of these issues. It issued the Vienna Declaration, a statement on integrating the rights of women into the human rights of the United Nations. It adopted many recommendations, including that of appointing a special rapporteur for an initial three-year period on the issue of violence against women—one of the major areas of concern to many of the NGOs that had been lobbying.

*** I would like to outline briefly what I mean by "shifting material cartographies." Second, I would like to say something about deconstructing the concept of "Asian." And third, I would like to take that discussion and use China as an example of the limits of speaking about an Asian perspective.

By shifting material cartographies I mean the material cartographies of ethnic violence and dislocations, the dissolution of the post-Cold War national boundaries, the undermining of the privileged position of the state as the primary actor in the global arena by the vast power of transnationals, the increasing interpenetration of the local and the global dimensions of economic development, the globalization of an array of areas of capital-productive processes, and the homogenization of culture.

When I was in China in 1986, McDonalds had not arrived yet, although the Kentucky Fried Chicken Colonel was looking ironically toward Mao's mausoleum. Now the golden arches dot the Beijing landscape. We have witnessed the Western media gleefully reporting the "collapse of socialist economic systems," and the extension of market-oriented types of economic policies godfathered by, in some cases, shock treatment advocates like Alan Greenspan. I refer also to the emergence of the larger trading blocs—the Pacific (Japan as the center), the European Union, NAFTA and the shift away from individual states as the major domestic international economic actors. Now the range of international actors in global and national politics include multilateral institutions; transnational corporations; multinational corporations; and local, regional and international NGOs.

*** I think that what is often lost in discursive debates is not the headline news that we read every morning, but the micro-human dimensions of these trends and what this new global order looks like from a human development perspective. The first thing I would like to suggest through this brief description of some of these cartographies is that we put the "human" back in human rights. Specifically, I suggest that "human" does not refer to a neutered, genderless, raceless, languageless group of entities—that gender, culture, religion and ethnicity are the numerous axes along which one needs to begin replotting both the discourse and the practice, and that to keep the discourse plotted along the exclusive or primary axes of states and governments is partial, incorrect and will not lead to any transformative strategies.***

Moving to my second point about deconstructing the concept of "Asian," the dominant human rights discourse is still shaped by an implicit acceptance of a paradigm of "Asian as Asian," and by a universal/relativist dichotomy. A problem that I see in this discourse about "Asian" is the problem of reification—simply that "Asian" is really an idea, a cultural construct, a concept of identity, historically situated and contingent. Despite its contested meanings, the reification of "Asian"—endowing this concept with the status of thingness—continues. This applies to official state articulations of human rights approaches and to attacks from different quarters. I also note that parallel to this reification of "Asian" the "West" is, ironically, simultaneously reified and becomes a monolithic, convenient oppositional target, despite the calls for a more complex dialogue for understanding by Asian government leaders. This underscores the difficulty of open dialogue and developing mutual understanding across such discursive obstacles.

Let me talk more specifically about both this concept of "Asian" and the limits of universalist and relativist discourse in the context of China. There are at least three grounds for problematizing the reified concept of "Asian" and for exposing the limits of universalist and relativist discourse for China. The grounds include an empirical, an ideological and a partiality critique. Regarding the first, we can take the events of June 4 at Tiananmen Square as an example. It is commonly suggested that the "Asian" perspective revolves around collective and community notions as basic values, and that consensus-building is the primary methodology that characterizes this "Asian" approach, in opposition to the Western focus on individualistic rights as values and adversarial institutions as process. It doesn't take much theoretical analysis, however, to see that the Tiananmen Square episode wasn't very much of a consensus-building approach to solving an "internal" problem, as designated by the government. That is, this theoretical paradigm of an "Asian" model is not borne out by empirical evidence of state action and evidence of challenge to this action. China is beginning to play the human rights game—and I would underscore "game." The role of NGOs and the role of human rights scholars and activists becomes increasingly important. With the emergence of a civil sphere and dissident voices within China, the state can no longer claim sole legitimacy to define "Chinese" or "Asian."

A brief look at the social costs of China's economic policies exposes some of the disjunctures between state policy, macro-indicators and micro/human "indicators."

The effect of economic liberalization on China can best be reflected in an expression that is currently prevalent in China, especially in the coastal and developed urban areas. The expression is that China currently has *sanwu, wu* meaning "lacking," "without," "something missing." So *sanwu* means the "three lacks." The three lacks are *wu liangxin, wu daode,* and *wu wenming,* that is, China now has no conscience, no ethics, and no civilization. This expression reflects the depth and the complexity of the spiritual despair involved in the current economic reform process.***

*** I want to suggest a series of questions with which we might complicate and add texture to the debate and to our strategies on human rights. These questions also reflect a critique of the partiality of dominant discourses. Who benefits from these assertions of difference? Who asserts these differences, and on whose behalf? Whose voices and experiences are marginalized or made invisible to ensure the clarity of the oppositional East-West, universalist-relativist paradigms? Which issues are foreclosed by claims of Western imperialism? When the banner of cultural imperialism is raised, who benefits?

Ambassador Kausikan said that the real question is, What works? I would add: What is working—for whom? Who decides what is working? Or to put a Chinese spin on it, what "mice" do we want to catch? Who is going to get the opportunity to catch the mice? And who gets to set the ground rules? These are some of the questions that I suggest are missing from the privileged focus on governments and states as international actors. Human rights is too important an issue to be left to governments, at least exclusively.***

KAREN ENGLE, CULTURE AND HUMAN RIGHTS: THE ASIAN VALUES DEBATE IN CONTEXT

32 N.Y.U. J. Int'l L. & Pol. 291, 292–96, 311–21, 329–32 (2000)

*** As we enter the new millennium, assertions of culture continue to dominate the scene of human rights law and discourse. The claims to cultural protection, however, are made in many different ways and with varying degrees of success.***

I. Women's Human Rights

Perhaps women's human rights pose the quintessential, or at least most commonly invoked, example of the clash between culture and rights. Although in other contexts culture is often considered to be protected by human rights, its oppositional stance vis-à-vis human rights most commonly is seen in challenges to at least some interpretations of women's human rights. Indeed, in a survey of literature and legal cases on claims by minority groups in the United States and Western Europe to legal protection based on culture, Susan Moller Okin has recently concluded that the majority of claims, or examples given, involve issues related to gender, such as child and forced marriages, divorce, adultery, polygamy, abortion, sexual harassment, domestic violence, clitoridectomy, and purdah. While minority groups in the West and minority or majority groups elsewhere certainly could assert a right to cultural protection, they rarely do with regard to women's rights. Rather, their claims generally arise as a defense to claims that they have violated the individual human rights of some of their members. In other words, culture is not affirmatively asserted as a human right; instead, culture is pitted against human rights. This failure to articulate a right to culture is particularly surprising in light of the extent to which other advocates, particularly indigenous rights advocates, argue for a human right to culture.

This sense of opposition between culture and rights is manifested in the arguments made by opponents of particular claims of women's human rights as well as by women's human rights advocates. Both opponents and proponents of different rights claims, then, acknowledge that such rights conflict with the culture of a particular ethnic group, religion, or even state or region. The primary difference is in their responses to it. While opponents believe that culture should serve to limit women's human rights, proponents argue that culture must be changed to protect women's rights. Again, rarely does either side discuss culture as a legal right.

A good example of this dynamic can be found in debates over what is often seen as the expansive nature of the Convention on the Elimination of All Forms of Discrimination Against Women (Women's Convention), which prohibits discrimination "in the political, economic, social, cultural, civil or any other field." Some of the most controversial provisions require states "[t]o take all appropriate measures, including legislation, to modify or abolish existing laws, regulations, customs and practices which constitute discrimination against women" and grant women rights to be free from discrimination in the family. Indeed, many states that have ratified the Women's Convention have specifically reserved from one or both of these provisions, often citing religion as the basis for their reservation. Further, Article 5 of the Women's Convention requires states to make all efforts to change their culture where necessary to protect women's rights, thereby specifically recognizing that culture might be in opposition to women's human rights. That said, few states take the position that they are against human rights for women. Rather, they believe that human rights should not be interpreted to conflict with culture. Despite, or perhaps because of, the many reservations, the Women's Convention is one of the international conventions with the highest number of signatories to date.

The reservations to the Women's Convention provide a means for states to argue against an interpretation of women's rights that they see as conflicting with their culture. Even if many states have reserved to the Women's Convention, though, they do not generally push the conflict. Indeed, the most recent document concerning women's human rights, the Beijing Declaration and Platform for Action (Beijing Declaration and Platform), contains language protecting a surprising number of rights that might have been challenged by the culture argument.***

III. Asian Values Debate

Beginning in the early 1990s, a newly articulated cultural challenge to human rights emerged. This time, the challenge did not come from human rights advocates, groups, or populations within states who opposed the protection of certain rights. Rather, the challenge came from states themselves. Southeast Asian countries, in particular Singapore, Malaysia, and Indonesia, began to argue that international human rights law should not necessarily be applied to them because it was Western and did not conform to Asian culture or, as was sometimes argued, Confucianism. Although a similar argument had been made by China for some time, it was the use of the rhetoric by Western allies from the Cold War that many participants in the ensuing debate found surprising and troubling. At the very moment that the Cold War, East/West division, on human rights was disappearing, a new assertion of difference was developing.

[The] interrelationship between culture and economics or politics, as well as the use of culture by Asian states to argue both for and against human rights, has been missed by many of the commentators who have written about the debate. That is, the common understanding of the position put forth by Asian states is that human rights should not apply to them because of their unique, or at least non-Western, cultural situations. That argument is then either tackled as a debate about universalism versus relativism or is seen as a mere political maneuver by some Asian governments to attempt to avoid scrutiny of their undemocratic regimes. Related to both attacks, the argument is deconstructed by demonstrating that there is no such thing as an Asian value. As Yash Ghai has argued, "[it] would be surprising if there were indeed one Asian perspective, since neither Asian culture nor Asian realities are homogenous throughout the continent." I suggest that while scholars have been persuasive in the deconstruction of Asian values, they have failed to get to the heart of the debate. Although the debate is about both the significance of culture and the economic hegemony of the West (North), neither factor alone provides a sufficient explanation. When Asian states asserted the claim to Asian values, they were arguing for an interpretation of human rights law different from that which the West was perpetuating. They also aimed to pursue their interest in economic development—done in their "own way"—which at the time seemed to be working for at least most of the Association of Southeast Asian Nations (ASEAN). Talking about culture and asserting an Asian group identity seemed the best strategy for arguing for this different interpretation. Culture provided the vocabulary for the argument both because it had been well-rehearsed (with some success) and because it provided a means by which otherwise disparate states could present a united front. The fact that states with such different histories and politics were willing to endorse the Bangkok Declaration attests to the strength of the Asian values argument and the extent to which the culture argument resonates.***

A. Comparing the Asian Values Debate with the Women's Rights Debate ***

Double Standard Argument: Paragraph 7 of the Bangkok Declaration [stresses] "the need to avoid the application of double standards in the implementation of human rights and its politicization." The same provision also "[s]tresses the universality, objectivity and non-selectivity of all human rights." Much as some opponents of women's human rights critique the West for its focus on what they identify as problems for women in the non-Western world rather than on violations of women's rights in the West, this provision argues against picking and choosing among human rights principles. Because *** the document calls for an expansive interpretation of human rights discourse—one that includes the right to economic development, for example—the suggestion here is that the West could be found in violation of many human rights standards and that it should not focus on particular civil and political rights that it might consider Asian countries to be violating.

While Paragraph 7 specifically uses double standard language, other parts of the Bangkok Declaration point to the same concern. Paragraph 3, for example, calls for a democratized U.N. system, suggesting that the United Nations does not abide by the very standards it endorses for other countries. This provision is particularly charged for Southeast Asian countries, which are often criticized for their autocratic, rather than democratic, rule. Paragraph 30 continues the same concern in calling for increased representation of developing countries in the Center for Human Rights.***

Priorities Argument: *** For these critics, whether a country is democratic is less important than the level of poverty in the country. Moreover, the argument suggests that it is premature to begin thinking about civil and political rights before development is achieved, as "poverty is one of the major obstacles hindering the full enjoyment of human rights." Poverty and lack of development, the Bangkok Declaration suggests, are directly attributable to macroeconomic policies that increase "the widening gap between the North and the South, the rich and the poor." This latter concern suggests that the right to development should be given priority over civil and political rights.***

Singapore's patriarch and former Prime Minister Lee Kuan Yew has made a slightly different argument about priorities in defending policies and practices of his country that have been challenged as violations of human rights. Pointing to problems in the United States such as "guns, drugs, violent crime, vagrancy, unbecoming behavior in public—in sum, the breakdown of civil society," Lee argues that "[t]he expansion of the right of the individual to behave or misbehave as he pleases has come at the expense of orderly society." By contrast, he asserts, the East places emphasis on a well-ordered society. Only with such a society will everyone have "maximum enjoyment of his freedoms." Again, the argument seems to be that the West has its priorities reversed by not valuing social order over individual rights.

Context Argument: Paragraph 8 of the Bangkok Declaration states "that while human rights are universal in nature, they must be considered in the context of a dynamic and evolving process of international norm-setting, bearing in mind the significance of national and regional particularities and various historical, cultural and religious backgrounds."*** As Indonesia's representative explained during the Vienna Conference, "[m]any developing countries, some endowed with ancient and highly developed cultures, have not gone through the same history and experiences as the Western nations in developing their ideas on human rights and democracy."*** What seemed to be controversial about the position is that it suggests a contradiction; the rights cannot be both viewed as universal and interpreted differently according to one's culture.***

C. The Function of Culture in the Asian Values Debate

[C]ulture is a proxy for many different ideas in the debate over Asian values.*** Sometimes culture is a synonym for sovereignty ***. At other times, culture refers to particular, local knowledge, such as Lee's understanding of the Southeast Asian family structure or assertions about the role of the individual within Asian society. Connected to this last meaning, Asian culture often refers to communal over individual values or duties over rights.

Relying (sometimes simultaneously) on these various meanings, the argument for Asian values or the assertion of culture functions in a variety of ways in the debate over human rights. Culture is deployed to argue for the right to development, for economic and social rights and their indivisibility from civil and political rights, for eliminating poverty, and for decreasing the wealth gap between the North and the South. It is also used to argue against certain "Western" human rights and double standards and for a different prioritization of rights.

[N]one of these arguments is new. Moreover, they reveal how the Cold War debate over the priority of economic and social versus civil and political rights is very much alive in the culture debate; the debate over culture in many ways provides a new focus for old debates.***

Sovereignty, context, and attention to rights (versus duties) were the three primary objections raised by the Soviet Union in opposition to the Universal Declaration. It would seem that those arguments were soundly defeated by the ensuing passage of the Universal Declaration, the proliferation of human rights instruments during the Cold War, and the end of the Cold War itself.***

Why, then, would Asian states have resurrected these arguments, with any hope of being listened to by the West? Did putting the arguments into the cloak of Asian values make them more palatable?***

Because the culture argument had currency, and because rights discourse has long been the site of political struggles, the debate between culture and rights became a site for a renewed debate between the North and the South. This time, however, the proponents of the South were largely capitalist and economically successful countries. Southeast Asian countries, speaking for the South, used the debate to question the North's focus on a particular conception of rights that, they argued, was not only too narrow, but also could prevent the economic development of struggling countries. They used the debate, coupled with their recent economic success, to demonstrate that capitalism and liberalism were not necessarily linked and to question Northern policies that tied economic assistance to human rights records.

To the extent that ASEAN states (and their allies) might have hoped to make a dent in Western/Northern economic domination, it is important to recognize that they did not aim to upset the hegemony of the capitalist model. In his thoughtful article setting forth and critiquing the three main positions in the Asian values debate—those of Western capitalist countries, Asian governments, and Asian NGOs—Pheng Cheah argues that all of the positions were "contaminated" by global capitalism. Indeed, for him, the debate did not challenge global capitalism. To the contrary,

> [t]he two poles of that binary opposition are complicitous. The fight is between different globalising models of capitalist development attempting to assert economic hegemony. The coding of this fight in terms of cultural difference diverts our attention from the subtending line of force of global capital that brings the two antagonists into an aporetic embrace against the possibility of other forms of development, feminist or ecological subalternist.***

Even if they did not alter the discourse on global capitalism, proponents of Asian values did succeed in altering the mainstream discourse on the relationship between rights and culture. They did so by oscillating between a position that used culture to argue against a neoliberal set of rights and one that argued that culture (or development) was protected by human rights. Only time will tell whether they succeeded in their related aim of unsettling Western (Northern) economic hegemony.***

Notes and Questions

1. Does contemporary globalization make it more difficult to identify cultural boundaries? Does globalization encourage community leaders to interpret cultural or religious norms more strictly as a defense against global popular culture?

2. Is the right of individual dissent a culturally specific concept? Is tolerance a culturally specific concept? *See, e.g.,* ALISON DUNDES RENTELN, INTERANTIONAL HUMAN RIGHTS: UNIVERSALISM VS. RELATIVISM (1990).

3. What values would you identify as Navajo, Kikuyu, Japanese, African, Asian, American, Latino, etc.? What are the similarities and differences among the values you identified? Is the search for definitions of group-identity futile? What positive and negative roles does cultural and religious identity play in society and in an individual's development? How should those roles be addressed in the law? *See, e.g.,* Professor Leti Volpp's discussion of the "cultural defense" in U.S. law in Chapter 6, *infra.*

4. Are there "cultural" patterns among activists in the large human rights NGOs? For a provocative commentary by an "insider/outsider," *see* Makau Mutua, *Savages, Victims, and Saviors: The Metaphors of Human Rights,* 42 HARV. INT'L L.J. 201 (2001).

5. Gender, and the regulation of gender norms in the family and community, is often the focus of heated disputes about universal or culturally relative approaches to human rights. See the discussions of appearance regulation of women, traditional and religious practices and same-sex marriage in Chapter 6. Why is gender a particular cause of cultural conflict?

6. The literature on human rights and cultural relativism and human rights and religion is extensive. *See, e.g.,* Adeno Addis, *Cultural Integrity and Political Unity: The Politics of Language in Multilingual States,* 33 ARIZ. ST. L.J. 719 (2001); Adeno Addis, *Individualism, Communitarianism, and the Rights of Ethnic Minorities,* 67 NOTRE DAME L. REV. 615 (1992); HUMAN RIGHTS IN AFRICA. CROSS-CULTURAL PERSPECTIVES. (Abdullahi Ahmed An-Na'im & Francis Deng eds., (1992); HUMAN RIGHTS IN CROSS-CULTURAL PERSPECTIVE (Abdullahi

An-Na'im ed., 1992); ABDULLAHI AN-NA'IM, TOWARD AN ISLAMIC REFORMATION: CIVIL LIBERTIES, HUMAN RIGHTS, AND INTERNATIONAL LAW (1990); KWAME ANTHONY APPIAH, IN MY FATHER'S HOUSE. AFRICA IN THE PHILOSOPHY OF CULTURE (1992); RELIGIOUS DIVERSITY AND HUMAN RIGHTS (Irene Bloom, J. Paul Martin & Wayne L. Proudfoot eds., 1996); WILLIAM THEORDORE DE BARY, ASIAN VALUES AND HUMAN RIGHTS: A CONFUCIAN COMMUNITARIAN PERSPECTIVE (1998); CONFUCIANISM AND HUMAN RIGHTS (Wm. Theodore de Bary & Tu Weiming eds., 1998); THE EAST ASIAN CHALLENGE FOR HUMAN RIGHTS (Joanne R. Bauer & Daniel A. Bell eds., 1999); ROSEMARY COOMBE, THE CULTURAL LIFE OF INTELLECTUAL PROPERTIES: AUTHORSHIP, APPROPRIATION, AND THE LAW (POSTCONTEMPORARY INTERVENTIONS) (1998); JACK DONNELLY, UNIVERSAL HUMAN RIGHTS IN THEORY AND PRACTICE (1989); Clifford Geertz, *Anti Anti-Relativism.* in RELATIVISM. INTERPRETATION AND CONFRONTATION (Michael Krausz ed., 1989); YASH GHAI, AUTONOMY AND ETHNICITY: NEGOTIATING COMPETING CLAIMS IN MULTIETHNIC STATES, (2000); YASH GHAI, ETHNICITY, DEMOCRACY AND HUMAN RIGHTS (2000); Yash Ghai, *Human Rights and Governance: The Asia Debate,* 15 AUST. Y.B. INT'L L. 1 (1994); MELVILLE HERSKOVITS, CULTURAL RELATIVISM (1973); PAULIN HOUNTONDJI, AFRICAN PHILOSOPHY. MYTH & REALITY (2d ed. 1996); HUMAN RIGHTS AND ASIAN VALUES: CONTESTING NATIONAL IDENTITIES AND CULTURAL REPRESENTATIONS IN ASIA (Michael Jacobsen & Ole Bruun eds., 2000); Bilhari Kausikan, *Asia's Different Standard,* 92 FOR. POLC'Y 24 (1993); KAREN KNOP, DIVERSITY AND SELF-DETERMINATION IN INTERNATIONAL LAW (2002); WILL KYMLYCKA, POLITICS IN THE VERNACULAR: NATIONALISM, MULTICULTURALISM, AND CITIZENSHIP (2000); MAKAU MUTUA, HUMAN RIGHTS: A POLITICAL AND CULTURAL CRITIQUE (2002); SUSAN MOLLER OKIN WITH RESPONDENTS, IS MULTICULTURALISM BAD FOR WOMEN? (Joshua Cohen, Matthew Howard & Martha C. Nussbaum eds., 1999); Raimundo Pannikar, *Is the Notion of Human Rights A Western Concept?,* 120 DIOGENES 75 (1982); Adamantia Pollis & Peter Schwab, *Human Rights: A Western Construct With Limited Applicability in* HUMAN RIGHTS: CULTURAL AND IDEOLOGICAL PERSPECTIVES 1 (Adamantia Pollis & Peter Schwab eds., 1979); ALISON DUNDES RENTELN, INTERNATIONAL HUMAN RIGHTS: UNIVERSALISM VS. RELATIVISM (1990); Ann-Belinda Preis, *Human Rights as Cultural Practice: An Anthropological Critique,* 18 HUM. RTS. Q. 286 (1996); EMERGING HUMAN RIGHTS. THE AFRICAN POLITICAL CONTEXT (George Shepherd, Jr. & Mark Anikpo eds., 1990); ISSA SHIVJI, THE CONCEPT OF HUMAN RIGHTS IN AFRICA (1989); INTERNATIONAL HUMAN RIGHTS IN CONTEXT: LAW, POLITICS, MORALS 445–553 (Henry J. Steiner & Philip Alston eds., 2d ed. 2000); NGUGI WA THIONG'O, DECOLONISING THE MIND (1986); HUMAN RIGHTS, CULTURE & CONTEXT (Richard Wilson ed., 1997); KWASI WIREDU, CULTURAL UNIVERSALS AND PARTICULARS. AN AFRICAN PERSPECTIVE (1996); Jeanne M. Woods, *Rights as Slogans: A Theory of Human Rights Based on African Humanism,* 17 NAT'L BLACK L.J. 52 (2003).

E. JUSTICIABILITY AND DEMOCRATIC ACCOUNTABILITY

1. *The Justiciability Debate*

HERMAN SCHWARTZ, DO ECONOMIC AND SOCIAL RIGHTS BELONG IN A CONSTITUTION?

10 AM. U. J. INT'L L. & POL'Y 1233, 1233–41 (1995)

[T]he competing arguments [as to whether social and economic rights should be constitutionalized] can roughly be divided into what might loosely be called practical and philosophical. The former focuses on whether economic and social rights are judicially enforceable, the latter on whether placing economic and social rights in a constitution is consistent in principle with the establishment of a free, democratic, market-oriented civil society. Put another way, the first question turns on a supposed dichotomy between positive and negative rights, the second on the kind of society that is most desirable.

To most American lawyers, putting economic and social rights in a constitution verges on the unthinkable. Americans are taught to think that constitutional rights depend on judicial enforceability almost by definition. No matter that, in practice, courts refrained from enforcing these rights for most of the first 150 years of our existence. Formally, the courts were available as an appropriate forum. In a nation that relies on legal resolution of disputed issues more than any other, including the protection of rights, the presumed inappropriateness of a conventional judicial resolution seems to imply as a matter of linguistic logic that the concept of "right" may not be used for something that does not lend itself readily to such resolution.

There is also the related belief that courts can effectively enforce only negative rights, only those rights that deny power. Our Bill of Rights seems to contain only such denials. Although there is no shortage of demands on government for everything from tariff protection to outright subsidies and social protection, these are not considered a matter of right. To the contrary, the national ethos has always been anti-government and negative, especially where social rights are concerned, as we are seeing today. Today, no serious person would suggest establishing economic and social rights as a matter of American constitutional law.

Before turning to these questions, a preliminary clearing away is necessary. The central issue is not really about social and economic rights, but primarily about social rights. More precisely, it is about social and certain economic rights. There seems to be no controversy, certainly on the part of opponents of constitutionalizing such rights, about the appropriateness of protecting property and other forms of private economic activity against governmental action. This is justified (or perhaps rationalized) on the ground that this involves only a negative right; that is, preventing the state from interfering with property. That, of course, overlooks the vast panoply of protections that property owners expect the state to provide—police, courts, a legal structure—in order to give substance to property rights.

Insofar as the issue is put in terms of the contrast between positive and negative rights, it should first be noted that many of the social rights involved are themselves negative rights. The rights under discussion, as set out for example in the International Covenant on Economic, Social, and Cultural Rights, include the right to work as variously defined; the right to just and favorable conditions of work; the right to form trade unions and to strike; the right to social security, adequate food, clothing, housing, education, health and health care; and the right to special protection for mothers and children. Some of these, such as the right to form unions, are just variations of the right to associate, a traditional negative right. Similarly, the right to strike includes a right to be free from interference with strikes, also a negative right. Even so "outlandish" a right as the right to a clean environment, a so-called "third generation" right, will often call for stopping governments and others from polluting the atmosphere or the home, something that is not too different from traditional public nuisance litigation.

Moreover, some social rights that require courts to order affirmative remedial measures involve only traditional judicial functions. The right to safe working conditions is a good example. Courts enforce this right all the time in statutory, common law, and even constitutional cases. Thus, prisoner litigation in the 1970s frequently challenged unsafe and unhealthy conditions in prison workshops under so vague a rubric as the Eighth Amendment's cruel and unusual punishment clause, with a good deal of success.

The courts' role in issuing orders commanding specific positive actions and not just prohibitions, discussed earlier, raises a larger consideration. As Professor Abram Chayes pointed out over twenty years ago, courts today are far beyond the narrow roles they used to play. The modern court engages in a wide variety of affirmative activities, ranging from the supervision of school desegregation, prisons, and nursing homes, to the monitoring of corrupt unions. Courts have always supervised the administration of estates, bankruptcies, and receiverships. In all these cases, courts are doing much more than merely saying no—they are actually setting standards and in many cases requiring the expenditure of public money.

It is this latter point—court-ordered expenditures of public money—that raises the problems to which the criticism of constitutionalizing rights is primarily addressed. Suppose there is no health care or housing or education system. By what authority does a court tell a legislature that it must create a health care or education system, a welfare program, or some other kind of benefit system? This certainly raises issues relating to budgetary priorities, separation of powers, judicial authority, and competence.*** [T]hese issues will induce conflicts within societies, for they involve reordering fundamental priorities. How can courts reorder the priorities established by a democratically elected legislature and executive? And suppose there is little or no money so that the programs cannot be established? Won't there be disillusionment with democracy if such rights are not implemented?

As noted, this problem is usually more theoretical than real. Almost all modern nations already have governmental health care, education, social security, and similar programs. Where established programs exist, the usual problems revolve around the discriminatory or arbitrary administration of these programs.*** Courts have been dealing with such problems in Europe and the United States for a long time.

Moreover, many European constitutional courts do not seem at all reluctant to tell legislatures that they must adopt specific legislation. The Hungarian Court recently told the Parliament that it must pass legislation protecting minorities. This is not unusual in Europe and is often constitutionally authorized, though foreign to Americans.

One final point: Positive rights are not unknown to American constitutional law. Almost all state constitutions provide for a right to an education, and some states recognize constitutional rights to welfare, housing, health, and abortions. For example, some twelve state constitutions set forth a state constitutional obligation to care for the sick and needy. Although some state courts virtually ignore such provisions, New York's highest court ruled that the New York State Constitution Article XVII, § 1 which provides that "[t]he aid, care and support of the needy are public concerns and shall be provided by the State and by such of its subdivisions and in such manner and by such means as the legislature may from time to time determine," requires that the legislature not deny aid to needy individuals on the basis of criteria unrelated to need.[6]

---

6   *See* the materials in Ch. 10.B *infra.*

Notes and Questions

1. Schwartz asserts that "for most of the 150 years of our existence" U.S. courts refrained from enforcing the Bill of Rights. Indeed, the first case in which a federal statute was struck down as violative of the First Amendment was *Lamont v. Postmaster General*, 381 U.S. 301 (1965). Jurisprudence protecting freedom of expression blossomed in the wake of the mass social movements for Black civil rights and in opposition to the war in Vietnam. *See, e.g., NAACP v. Alabama*, 357 U.S. 449 (1958) (holding freedom of association is fundamental right protected by First Amendment); *NAACP v. Button*, 371 U.S. 415 (1963) (striking down Virginia law prohibiting attorneys from soliciting clients that had been used against NAACP for informing people of their rights); *New York Times v. United States*, 403 U.S. 713 (1971) (upholding right of press to publish the Pentagon Papers); *Cohen v. California*, 403 U.S. 15 (1971) (overturning conviction for disturbing the peace based on being in courtroom with jacket that said, "Fuck the Draft"); and *Spence v. Washington*, 418 U.S. 405 (1974) (reversing conviction for taping peace sign on American flag after Kent State killings). *But see United States v. O'Brien*, 391 U.S. 367 (1968) (upholding federal statute criminalizing burning of draft cards to protest Vietnam War).

2. Schwartz contends that most American lawyers believed that the "national ethos" has always been anti-government, an ethic that is unsympathetic to constitutional inter-pretations that entrench economic and social rights. Conservative economist James Q. Wilson agrees:

> American liberalism, like America in general, is different. Created by the New Deal but drawing on features of the earlier Progressive movement, liberalism here, unlike the liberalism found in many European nations, never took seri-ously the idea of nationalizing major industries, only occasionally and then with-out much conviction proposed any major redistribution of income, and merely flirted with centralized economic planning. A welfare state was created, but compared to the welfare state in many other industrialized nations, the American version offered less generous benefits to the unemployed, provided no children's allowances and restricted tax-supported medical care to veterans, the elderly and the very poor.***
>
> [L]iberalism was transformed by the New Deal from a Progressive preoc-cupation with economic reform to a postwar interest in rights, from an early discussion of planning production to a later commitment to encouraging con-sumption, from an attack on "economic royalists" to the recruitment of busi-ness executives. Some obvious historical factors help to account for this change. The depression of 1937, coming right on the heels of the great Democratic vic-tories in the 1936 elections *** was of a magnitude that rivaled the Depression of 1929–1932 ***. [T]he New Deal had not ended the Depression.***
>
> [Yet] liberals in other democratic nations struggled with depressions and the war without abandoning—in fact, while strengthening—their commitment to central planning and income equalization. Great Britain entered the post war era under the control of a Labor Party that nationalized much of British industry, including the health care system. When Germany began its postwar reconstruction, it did so by linking free-market economics with a welfare state [more expansive] than anything contemplated here. Sweden, though not a

combatant . . . combined private ownership of property with very high taxes and substantial income redistribution. Almost everywhere in Europe and Japan one finds economic planning, government-business partnerships and cradle-to-grave public assistance. But not here.

Brinkley's explanation of this aspect of American exceptionalism rests precisely on those aspects of political culture that have always been central to our public life. Americans retained throughout the 1930s their deep suspicion of institutional power. "For all the efforts of New Dealers to celebrate and legitimize the new functions they were creating for the state," he writes, "a broad suspicion of centralized bureaucratic power—rooted in traditions of republicanism and populism stretching back to the earliest years of the American polity—remained a staple of popular discourse and constant impediment to liberal aims." Even when people were praising Roosevelt for sending them federal money and government jobs, they were attacking him for trying to pack the Court and for regulating their lives. The farmers cashed their agricultural assistance checks, but began increasingly to vote Republican.

James Q. Wilson, *Liberal Ghosts*, A review of ALAN BRINKLEY, NEW DEAL LIBERALISM IN RECESSION AND WAR, NEW REPUBLIC, May 22, 1995, at 31.

If Wilson is correct, does this mean that this ethos is a permanent, immutable feature of U.S. culture? What factors influence such normative developments? Could suspicion of governmental power actually enhance the attainment of the goals of economic and social rights discourse? Might it point us in other, equally forward-looking directions?

3.   Why does Schwartz make a point of distinguishing social rights from economic rights? In 1995, he pessimistically opined that "no serious person would suggest establishing economic and social rights as a matter of American constitutional law." However, he does note that such proposals have, in fact, been put forward by very serious scholars. *See, e.g.,* Charles L. Black, Jr., *Further Reflections on the Constitutional Justice of Livelihood*, 86 COLUM. L. REV. 1103 (1986) (arguing that the Ninth Amendment provides a basis for protecting rights not expressly enumerated in the Constitution); Peter B. Edelman, *The Next Century of Our Constitution: Rethinking Our Duty to the Poor*, 39 HASTINGS L.J. 1 (1987) (arguing for a constitutional right to a subsistence income); Frank J. Michelman, *Forward: On Protecting the Poor Through the Fourteenth Amendment*, 83 HARV. L. REV. 7 (1969) (arguing that government has duty to alleviate discriminatory deprivation). *See also* Philip Harvey, *Human Rights and Economic Policy Discourse: Taking Econmic and Social Rights Seriously*, 33 COLUM. HUM. RTS. L. REV. 363 (2002) (economic rights entail government duty to adopt macroeconomic policies that prioritize rights over other policy goals).

4.   What is fundamentally distinct about expenditures of public monies? Would a court order setting budgetary priorities "induce conflicts within societies" any more than an order regarding abortion, for example, or any other personal right? If so, why?

ASBJORN EIDE, ECONOMIC, SOCIAL AND CULTURAL RIGHTS AS HUMAN RIGHTS

A. EIDE, C. KRAUS AND A. ROSAS (EDS.), ECONOMIC, SOCIAL AND CULTURAL RIGHTS 9, at 23–25 (2001)

A widely spread misunderstanding has been that all economic, social and cultural rights must be provided by the State, and that they are costly and lead to an overgrown state apparatus. This view results from a very narrow understanding of the nature of these rights and of the corresponding state obligations; consequently, some words about their nature is required.

Fundamental to a realistic understanding of state obligations is that the individual is the active subject of all economic and social development, as stated in the Declaration on the Right to Development (Article 2). The individual is expected, whenever possible through his or her own efforts and by use of own resources, to find ways to ensure the satisfaction of his or her own needs, individually or in association with others. Use of his or her own resources, however requires that the person has resources that can be used—typically land or other capital, or labour. This could include the shared right to use communal land, and the land rights held by indigenous peoples. Furthermore, the realization of economic, social and cultural rights of an individual will usually take place within the context of a household as the smallest economic unit, although aspects of female and male division of labour and control over the production, as well as various forms of wider kinship arrangements may present alternative alliances.

State obligations must be seen in this light. States must, at the primary level, *respect* the resources owned by the individual, her or his freedom to find a job of preference and the freedom to take the necessary actions and use the necessary resources—alone or in association with others—to satisfy his or her own needs. It is in regard to the latter that *collective* or group rights become important: the resources belonging to a collective of persons, such as indigenous populations, must be respected in order for them to be able to satisfy their needs. Consequently, as part of the obligation to respect these resources the State should take steps to recognize and register the land rights of indigenous peoples and land tenure of small holders whose title is uncertain. By doing so, the State will have assisted them in making use of their resources in greater safety in their pursuit to maintain an adequate standard of living. Similarly, the rights of peoples to exercise permanent sovereignty over their natural resources may be essential for them to be able, through their own collective efforts, to satisfy the needs of the members of that group.

State obligations consist, at a secondary level, of, for example, the protection of the freedom of action and the use of resources against other, more assertive or aggressive subjects, more powerful economic interests, protection against fraud, against unethical behaviour in trade and contractual relations, against the marketing and dumping of hazardous or dangerous products. This protective function of the State is the most important aspect of state obligations also with regard to economic, social and cultural rights, and it is similar to the role of the State as protector of civil and political rights.

Significant components of the obligation to *protect* are spelled out in existing law. Such legislation becomes manageable for judicial review, and therefore belies the argument that economic and social rights are inherently non-justiciable. Legislation of this kind, must, of course, be contextual—that is, it must be based on the specific requirements in the country concerned. To take one example: legislation requiring that land can be owned only by the tiller of the land is essential where agriculture is the major basis of income, but may be much less relevant in highly industrialized technological societies where only a small percentage of the population lives off the land. For groups of people whose culture requires a close link to the use of land, protection of that land is even more important as an obligation to realize the right to food—again, the indigenous peoples serve as the clearest example.

At the tertiary level, the State has the obligations to assist and to fulfill the rights of everyone under economic, social and cultural rights. The obligation to assist takes many forms, some of which are spelled out in the relevant instruments. For example, under the CESCR (Article 11(2)), the State shall take measures to improve measures of production, conservation and distribution of food by making full use of technical and scientific knowledge and by developing or reforming agrarian systems. The obligation to fulfill could consist of the direct *provisions* of basic needs, such as food or resources which can be used for food (direct food aid, or social security) when no other possibility exists, such as, for example: (1) when unemployment sets in (such as under recession); (2) for the disadvantaged, and the elderly; (3) during sudden situations of crisis or disaster; and (4) for those who are marginalized (for example, due to structural transformations in the economy and production).

[T]he allegation that economic and social rights differ from the civil and political is that the former requires the use of resources by the State, while the obligation for States to ensure the enjoyment of civil and political rights does not require resources. This is a gross oversimplification. The argument is tenable only in situations where the focus on economic and social rights is on the tertiary level (the obligation to fulfill), while civil and political rights are observed on the primary level (the obligation to respect). This scenario is, however, arbitrary. Some civil rights require state obligations at all levels—also the obligation to provide direct assistance, when there is a need for it. Economic and social rights, on the other hand, can in many cases best be safeguarded through non-interference by the State with the freedom and use of resources possessed by the individuals.

JEANNE M. WOODS, JUSTICIABLE SOCIAL RIGHTS AS A CRITIQUE OF THE LIBERAL PARADIGM

38 Tex. Int'l L.J. 763, 771–73 (2003)

The conception of rights as individualistic, negative claims against government underlies the argument that social rights are not judicially enforceable. For example, in her work on the social rights in the South African Constitution, Erica De Wet argues that meaningful judicial review is possible only if these rights are guaranteed as individual subjective rights, in other words, only if having the right to housing means that an individual can go to court and receive an order awarding him a house. Furthermore, she contends that if such an order were to be issued, it would implicate the court in matters reserved to the political branches, violating a cardinal principle of democratic governance—the separation of powers.

De Wet asserts that the normative contents of social rights are too vague to be legally enforceable, assuming that a court would have no judicially discoverable standards by which to measure the state's compliance. She contrasts this presumed state of affairs with political and civil rights, arguing that their core values are more easily ascertained, given the "wealth of political and historical knowledge, experience and significance" behind them.

This argument overlooks the valuable work that is being done on the international level to define these norms as well as the collective judicial expertise in constitutional construction. In many jurisdictions, courts routinely apply well-established interpretive principles to define constitutional norms. Interpretive techniques include parsing the language of the provision; examining the legislative history and intent of the drafters; considering the community's history and traditions; and analyzing the relation of the provision to other relevant norms, enabling courts to implement the core values of constitutional guarantees. Courts are equally competent to apply these techniques to develop a jurisprudence of social rights. Without judicial review these rights would remain in the normatively underdeveloped state of which she complains. De Wet further argues that the content of social rights is indeterminate because "the socio-economic circumstances of the day constantly determine new state priorities." But political and civil rights are not static either.

What lies at the heart of the justiciability debate is the redistributive nature of the remedial measures. The allocation of resources is typically deemed the province of the legislature, which has both the political legitimacy of being an elected body and the institutional capacity to weigh and accommodate competing demands on the public purse. Since rights override other legislative priorities, a judicial power of review positions an unelected judiciary to overrule majority decisions, raising accountability concerns.

The concept of a judicially enforceable bill of rights is inherently countermajoritarian. We have learned to live with this democratic contradiction when it comes to political and civil rights because they are viewed as shielding fundamental minority interests from the political majority. Because the Lockean paradigm conflates property and liberty, we are more uncomfortable with judges openly making decisions affecting fiscal policy. However, there are always legislative dimensions to judicial interpretation, and courts affect the distribution of resources in myriad ways, for example, by allocating risk through tort policy. I argue that judicial enforcement of collective legislative commands does not entail a significant divergence from the classic judicial role.

Separation of powers as a normative principle is not an end in itself—it is a means of keeping the government in check in order to ensure the protection of preferred rights. In the case of social rights, judicial review serves the function of checking the political branches to ensure that they are responsive to the constitutional rights of the least privileged in society, and that policymakers do not lose sight of their suffering in the inevitable political games of compromise and horse-trading. In some instances, especially where free legal services are available, a court may actually be more accessible than a legislative or executive body; a judicial forum "keep[s] the plight and pain of marginalized members of the community on the political agenda."

Finally, De Wet warns that constitutional entrenchment of social rights can generate unreasonable expectations on the part of the poor for immediate provision of basic needs: "It would be extremely disillusioning if the members of the public were to find out that their constitutional right was, in fact, only a right to judicial review." This point is well taken given the liberal focus on individual remedies. [H]owever, the South African experience suggests that, rather than being discouraged, litigants will simply become more sophisticated in fashioning social rights claims.[7]

---

[7]   *See* the materials in Ch. 8 *infra*.

CRUZ DEL VALLE BERMUDEZ V. MINISTRY OF HEALTH AND SOCIAL ASSISTANCE

Supreme Court of Justice of Venezuela
(July 15, 1999) File No. 15.789, Judgment No. 916.

EXAMINATION (ANALYSIS) OF THE SITUATION

[A]n action for protection has been brought forth before this Political Administrative Section [of the Supreme Court of Justice] against the Ministry of Health and Social Assistance, in light of said entity's failure to give the HIV/AIDS sick plaintiffs the necessary medicines for the treatment of said illness.***

[Plaintiffs] denounce the violation of the rights to life, health, freedom and personal safety, rights against discrimination and rights to the benefits of science and technology, as set forth in articles 50, 58, 60, 61 (3) and 76 of the Constitution and in the terms of the international treaties relating to human rights, as they related to the mentioned constitutional articles.***

Right to health, life and the access to science and technology:

[T]he rights to health, life and the access to science and technology are closely linked in this case, and the analysis will be made together. Such closeness may be explained in the following manner: The right of access to the advances of science and technology would permit those ill with HIV/AIDS a guarantee of the preservation of the minimum vital conditions (right to health), which, in these cases, would mean the possibility of lengthening the life of these patients and, long term, an eventual cure of the illness [from] which they suffer.

The most supreme of the juridical possessions of the individual (life) is protected as a human right in the most ample form possible, not only nationally but internationally. The fundamental right to life, a substantive right, gives those who possess it the possibility of obtaining judicial protection and, in the end, [protection by] this Supreme Tribunal, against all acts of public powers which threaten life or integrity. In the same manner, the preservation of this right at any cost is an end which the law imposes on those same public powers and especially on the legislator, who must adopt the necessary measures to protect those possessions, life and physical integrity, against the attacks of third parties *** and in fact, [must do so] with strict rigor. It must be said therefore, that the configuration of the right to life contains a positive protection.*** It is in the guarantee of that prized possession, that the politics of the State play a fundamental role in questions of public health. Because of that, in the present case, the obligations imposed on the public power in matters of prevention and treatment of HIV/AIDS become fundamental.

The Venezuelan Constitution recognizes in article 76 that "all have the right to protection of Health," and to effectively safeguard this right,*** "the authorities will take care of maintaining the public health and will provide the means for the prevention and assistance to those who may lack it."

The right to health claimed by those ill with HIV/AIDS has been recognized by this Court. [Citations omitted.] In that [case we] signaled that, *"the obligation to provide physical, psychological, economic and social assistance to those infected is the concern of the State; in fact, the State must adopt an attitude of recognizing the dignity of the human being affected with this suffering.*"

[H]aving recognized the right which all citizens have—including the petitioners in the present case—to the protection of health, and the corresponding obligation of the State to ensure that that right is effectively realized above all in the case of those who lack sufficient means, this Court observes that *** said obligation is not being met, which immediate consequence is to put at risk the health and life of the petitioners. In effect, there exists proof that the doctors, specializing in immunology and infectious diseases from the different centers of the Ministry of Health and Social Assistance, prescribe the [required] medicines *** and on the other hand, there is no proof the administration of such is being done regularly and correctly as to those ill with HIV/AIDS ***. This circumstance puts at risk the life of those affected and, as it is generally known, despite the efforts made at the global level, still no cure has been found.

The alleged transgressor does not deny this situation. In fact it recognizes expressly that: given the costs, "it is evident that it will not be able to satisfy all the needs of those ill with HIV/AIDS," with the budget currently assigned. As a result, the failure to comply with its obligation by the Ministry of Health and Social Assistance, is plainly proven, elements which, in principle, would be sufficient in order to issue the protection as sought by the plaintiffs.

From another side, it is fitting to note that, as human persons, those ill with HIV/AIDS also are protected by the *** norms regarding fundamental rights which have been set forth at the international level. Said principles are set forth in the jurisprudence of the Court which includes the most current and relevant pronouncements of the entities which have faced the situation of those affected by HIV/AIDS, such as *** "The United Kingdom Declaration of the Rights of People with HIV and AIDS" of 1990.

[T]his Court cannot issue an order of protection looking askance at the defenses that might be made by [the defendant] denying that the alleged conduct of omission by the Ministry of Health and Social Assistance is deliberate.***

In the current case, the alleged injurious conduct would take place if the Ministry of Health and Social Assistance, having provided in the budget for those ill with HIV/AIDS, had not proceeded to acquire the equipment and necessary medicines to render assistance to the sick.

In the matter at hand, the representative for the Ministry asserts that it is impossible for the Ministry of Health and Social Assistance to pay for the treatment in question for the universe of people who suffer from HIV/AIDS, so that in light of this crisis situation confronting the country, it must be determined who can and who cannot pay for the required treatment.

[T]his Court understands that the failure to meet its constitutional obligations of prevention and health assistance is not deliberate as within its budgetary constraints [the Ministry] has provided for the exigencies of this high risk illness and high costs. Therefore, we do not deal with—in the strict juridical sense—a conduct of omission on the part of the Administration.***

[T]he matter debated is reduced to a problem of the budgetary type. With respect to the costs, a curative treatment not being in existence, it is difficult to make an estimate of the exact economic aspects which this implies ***. To calculate the costs in this country, for a patient with HIV/AIDS the following would have to be considered:

— Expenses for consultations prior to the diagnosis.***

— Costs of the tests for verification of the diagnosis.

— Prices of the medicines used.

— Vigilance during the treatment (consultations, laboratory tests, periodic immunological evaluations, hospitalizations in the case of complications, including in admittance to units of intensive care, etc.***).

It is estimated that at the international level, the global cost of an HIV/AIDS case during the life of the patient reaches some One Hundred Twenty Thousand Dollars ($120,000.00), which are equivalent currently to approximately Seventy Two Million Bolivars (Bs. 72,000,000.00). This is an approximate amount and many variables influence this amount, especially the age of the patient.

As has been noted before, the budgetary capacity of the transgressing party (Ministry of Health and Social Assistance) has been insufficient to meet the obligations of assistance to those sick with HIV/AIDS.

[T]here exist two possibilities which might permit resolving the demands of those sick with HIV/AIDS: On the one hand, the budget correction provided for in article 32 of the Fundamental Law of the Budget Regimen, which is a method designed to: 1) provide for unforeseen costs which come up in the course of the fiscal period; or, 2) increase the budget credits which might prove to be insufficient.*** On the other hand, the National Executive could decree, in accordance with the provisions of article 33 of the Fundamental Law of the Budget Regimen, additional credits for the costs in the budget previously authorized *** to cover those which were unforeseen.

Given the budget insufficiency, the Ministry of Health and Social Assistance could make use of the methods noted above, for the purpose of satisfying the demands of those sick with HIV/AIDS, and ask from the President of the Republic the resources deemed necessary, with the aim of preserving the right to health and life of the persons infected with HIV/AIDS. It is so declared.

From another side, since there is no curative treatment and the medical costs are high, this Court considers that the fight against that illness must be focused principally toward prevention ***. [T]he Ministry of Health and Social Assistance, by means of the National Program [on] HIV/AIDS and Sexually Transmitted Infections, is implementing a program of prevention and medical attention in all the national territories, for which the necessary economic resources are being obtained. Said program is undertaking to achieve the following:

1. Review the Programs of prevention directed to the youth and sexual workers (prostitutes).

2. Re-edit 5,000 pamphlets for the prevention of HIV/AIDS to be distributed in different regions.

3. Distribution of 100,000 condoms *** to organizations which are not governmental or Public Institutions.

4. Enter into Agreements of Cooperation with the Youth and Change Foundation, Commission for the National Prevention of Teenage Pregnancy, Committee for the Support of the Child and the Family, Fund for the "Libertador" Medical Attention and Secondary and University Pedagogic Education.

5. National Campaign for the promotion of safe sex, adding to the amount of this Plan, approximately ONE HUNDRED EIGHTY MILLION BOLIVARS (Bs. 180,000,000.00).

[T]his Court considers that this constitutes a positive initiative and must continue and be intensified.***

To that end, the Ministry of Health and Social Assistance must conduct a real study of what are the minimum needs which require priority in connection with those patients and the programs destined to prevent the growth of the percentage of those infected, taking into consideration the elements previously discussed, [which the Ministry] must present to the President of the Republic and the Council Ministers, so that they may take this into consideration in the *** formulation of the *** Budgets for the next fiscal year.

Once this Court declares the violation of the rights to health *** *"the recognized benefits are extended to all the citizens who live in Venezuela who suffer from HIV/AIDS, who require treatment prescribed by the medical specialists, without having the imperative need to constantly seek constitutional protection."* ***

DECISION

Given the previously discussed considerations, this Political-Administrative Section of the Supreme Court of Justice, DECLARES (VALID) the petition for protection against the Ministry of Health and Social Assistance in the following respects:

1. [T]he Ministry of Health and Social Assistance is ordered to issue regularly the medicines known as Inhibitors such as: AZT or Zidovudine, DDI or Didanosine, DDC or Zalcitabine, D4T or Stavudine, 3TC or Lamivudine, Crixivan or Indinavir, Saquinavir or Invirase and Ritonavir or Norvir on behalf of the plaintiffs ***, in accordance with the combined prescriptions of the specialist doctors of the Immunology and Infectious Diseases Services of the hospitals and health centers known as MSAS;

2. [T]he Ministry of Health and Social Assistance is ordered to effect or cover the specialized exams on behalf of the plaintiffs, such as "Viral Charge, Lymphocyte Count, Platelet Count and all those exams related not only to the collateral illnesses, but those necessary for gaining access to the combined treatments of the Inhibitors of (Trascriptasa and Proteasa);"

3. [T]he Ministry of Health and Social Assistance is ordered to develop a body of information, treatment, and complete medical assistance in favor of the plaintiffs;

4. [T]he Ministry of Health and Social Assistance is ordered to issue to the plaintiffs all of the medicines for the treatment of the collateral illnesses, such as antibiotics, anti-diarrhea, chemotherapy, and all of those others which may be necessary due to their derivation from the condition of HIV/AIDS.

As a result of the previously set forth declarations, the following *order of protection* is issued:

1) The Ministry of Health and Social Assistance is ORDERED to issue the necessary orders so that the organizations under its authority comply with the petition of the plaintiffs which has been declared as valid in the current judgment.

2) The Ministry of Health and Social Assistance is ORDERED to petition the President of the Republic *** immediately for a correction of the budgets corresponding to the prevention and control of AIDS or the consideration of an additional credit, with the purpose of guaranteeing the level and timely compliance with that ordered in the current judgment, for the time left in the current fiscal year; also, complete the measures necessary for the inclusion of the necessary resources for the next [fiscal year's] budgets.

3) The Ministry of Health and Social Assistance is ORDERED to conduct a real study of what are the minimum needs which require priority in connection with those ill with HIV/AIDS and the programs destined to prevent the growth of the percentage of those infected, with the purpose of developing a preventive policy of information, awareness, education, and a total assistance in favor of those persons living with HIV/AIDS.

4) The Ministry of Health and Social Assistance is ORDERED to act in conformity with the present judgment of protection as long as the following requirements are met:

    1. Verification that the petitioner *** is suffering [from] HIV/AIDS.

    2. Verification of the need for treatment.

    3. Lack of economic resources to pay for the expenses related to treatment of said illness.

    4. Must be Venezuelan or a resident in the territory of the Republic.

The current judgment of protection must be obeyed immediately by all authorities, under penalty of contempt.

Notes and Questions

1. Does the *Bermudez* decision demonstrate that courts are competent to adjudicate social rights disputes? Does it support Herman Schwartz's contention that a court order setting budgetary priorities would "induce conflicts within societies"? Would such conflicts be more likely to arise in the context of an issue like AIDS than it would with a claim involving housing, for example? What are the implications of the court's order that the Ministry of Health essentially find the resources wherever it can? How does the ability of the court to enforce its ruling bear on justiciability?

2. Are justiciable social rights contrary to democratic values? Nicholas Haysom summarizes arguments from both left and right:

> [One] argument associated with a 'left' European tradition whose opposition to socio-economic rights is part of a broader rights skepticism [maintains] that the judges are unaccountable and inherently conservative, [and] that the courts are not a democratic institution and should not be vested with any power over

parliament. This majoritarian position asserts more than a simple parliamentary sovereignty, but that judges especially should not have the authority to prioritise government expenditure, for example, by compelling government to build a clinic from funds designated for housing. The majority is subject to the rule, the final word of unaccountable 'wise men.' This constitutionalisation of socio-economic rights is particularly dangerous because of the judicial discretion that is inevitably required to be exercised when adjudicating on these rights. The courts will make policy not only on the reach of such rights but also on the method of implementation. Socio-economic rights thus politicise justice and judicialise politics. They allow the courts, by enforcing socio-economic rights, to stray onto the political terrain, at the expense of the democratic process—and political life is inevitably impoverished.

Support for this argument is also found amongst the free-market theorists for whom socio-economic rights will create *inter alia* an artificial distortion of the market, and for whom the reach of the state is to be curtailed at all costs. Private power is to be insulated from public power. The convergence of the conclusions thus reached by both the right libertarians and the left majoritarians frequently renders their arguments indistinguishable.***

Nicholas Haysom, *Constitutionalism, Majoritarian Democracy and Social-Economic Rights*, 8 S. Afr. J. Hum. Rts. 451, 455–56 (1992).

3. The Supreme Court of Venezuela held that it was possible to violate a human right by inaction, and identified a positive dimension of the right to life. What is the content of this right? What implications does this finding have for other state duties? What duties does the finding impose on the state vis-à-vis private actors?

4. How does the decision reflect the concept of indivisibility of human rights?

5. Other national and regional judicial bodies in Latin America have been forced to respond to the AIDS pandemic. *See, e.g., William Garcia v. Caja de Salud*, Sala Constitucional de la Corte Suprema de Justicia (Costa Rica), Sept. 23, 1997, Expedient No. 5778-V-97, N 5934–97 (provision of medical care for AIDS-affected people is state obligation); *Jose Luis Castro Ramirez v. Instituto Mexicano del Seguro Social*, Tribunal Pleno, Suprema Corte de Jjusticia, Amparo 223/97 (ordering Mexican Social Security Institute to treat "any disease, no matter what it is"); *Jorge Odir Miranda v. El Gobierno de El Salvador*, Inter-American Commission on Human Rights, Case No. 12.249 (ordering government of El Salvador to provide antiretroviral medications). *See also Government of South Africa v. Treatment Action Campaign*, excerpted in *infra* Ch. 8.

2. Democracy or Disenfranchisement?

NICHOLAS HAYSOM, CONSTITUTIONALISM, MAJORITARIAN DEMOCRACY AND SOCIO-ECONOMIC RIGHTS

8 S. Afr. J. Hum. Rts. 451, 452, 454, 458–62 (1992)

*** Recent political developments in Africa and Eastern Europe have underlined one linkage between political/civil and socio-economic rights: without political/civil rights there can be no socio-economic rights. In short, it is argued, third world and socialist constitutions which have asserted the primacy of economic rights have done so at the expense of political rights. These political systems have invariably created vacuous political forms, devoid of civil liberties and democratic freedoms. The lesson from this experience is that political/civil rights are the guarantees both of political democracy and of an independent, robust civil society which is essential for the attainment, entrenchment and development of socio-economic rights. Without freedom of association there may be no trade unions. Without trade unions there can be no workers' rights.***

However, the reciprocal linkage between the two categories of rights is no longer asserted with equal conviction: that without socio-economic rights these political/civil rights cannot exist in a meaningful way. [I argue] that rights are not anti-democratic, but rather that a constitutional democracy requires both political/civil and socio-economic rights as a condition for its existence and survival.***

[I]t is eloquently acknowledged by both protagonists and antagonists alike that, for a constitution to have a meaningful place in the hearts and minds of the citizenry, it must address the pressing needs of ordinary people. It cannot be seen to institutionalise and guarantee only political/civil rights and ignore the real survival needs of the people—it must *promise* both bread and freedom. If it does not do so, it will find no lasting resonance amongst the true guardians of the constitution—which are not the courts but the citizens.***

Majoritarianism, constitutionalism and socio-economic rights

Those who adopt the vulgar majoritarian opposition to the politicisation of law should oppose the constitutionalist project altogether, and not just the constitutionalisation of socio-economic rights.*** They should argue that the notion of a democratically elected parliament rendered subject to constitutional rules, judicial review, and a bill of rights is undemocratic. However the contrary assertion—that these institutions (amongst many others) guarantee the rules of the game, create democratic space and establish the ground for vigorous politics, informed and shaped by the institutions of civil society, is now widely accepted by democratic majoritarians as historically justified. In this view the constitutionalist project is designed to create the conditions for democracy, not undermine it.*** Fundamental rights guaranteeing the equal participation of citizens in social and political life are accordingly not only consistent with democracy, they are also the precondition for real majoritarianism—even though the powers of the majority to remove those rights are limited.***

*** It may still be argued that it is one thing to argue for process rights—'the rules of the game'—to be institutionalised in a legal 'place' beyond the reach of temporary and narrow majorities, but it is another to place the purported outcomes of the democratic contest beyond the reach of the political process. This is, in my view, the sharpest edge of the argument against socio-economic rights.***

Why, in a constitutionalist vision, should economic rights be a critical component of the rights charter? One important foundation for these rights, as discussed above, is that such rights will legitimise the whole constitution. But the 'legitimation' argument is, whatever its merits, an inadequate foundation for the constitutionalisation of socio-economic rights.***

Process rights and civil equality

There is another reason for constitutionalising socio-economic rights. The constitutionalist vision is premised on the need to guarantee political and civil equality—to make clear that all citizens are equal social and political participants. This notion of citizens as equals can be construed as a *formal equality of opportunity* to vote, to impart and to receive opinions. But rights charters do not confine themselves only to the narrow formal requirements of the democratic process. They establish a prior dignity and equality of citizens—the right to cultural identity, to be free from racial and gender discrimination and not to be exposed to other deprivations unconnected on the face of it to the democratic process. In short, even within the narrow world of political/civil rights there is a recognition that citizens need more than access to a ballot box to be empowered to act as citizens.*** It is for this same reason that certain socio-economic rights need to be treated as fundamental rights. Can an illiterate, hungry person participate in the political process let alone social life? Does a marginalised, rural woman—untrained and unemployed—have anything remotely akin to civic equality to her urban, middle-class male compatriot? The question barely needs an answer. Those who argue against all socio-economic rights per se, are akin to those who argue for the right to a fair trial but oppose the provision of any assistance to those who cannot afford a lawyer. We may quibble as to how far a legal aid programme may go, but can one still argue in principle for a right without substance?

[T]his is not a novel proposition. Franklin Roosevelt argued in the 1940's that for the survival of democracy, freedom from hunger was as important as freedom of speech.[8] Like affirmative action, socio-economic rights are based on an assertion that formal equality of opportunity does not mean real equality. Indeed, some argue that it is a device to allow structural inequality to manifest itself in the unequal enjoyment of the benefits of citizenship. One strand of legal thinking that has contributed to a richer understanding of civic equality is the feminist critique of equality of opportunity. In asserting, *inter alia*, a basis for affirmative action and a right to interfere with practices and relations in the private or personal sphere, they have pointed out that it is precisely in this unregulated world that the patterns of domination and subordination are established and which limit or cap gender equality programmes in the public sphere.

By constitutionalising selected socio-economic rights, society is elevating certain rights to a necessary condition for the existence of a *minimum* civic equality. This, in turn, establishes the conditions for democracy for the effective use of political/civil rights. In this way the reciprocal linkage between socio-economic and political/civil rights is reinstated. This is to go further than justifying egalitarian claims on an expanded process argument. It is to root the notion of rights on a fuller conception of equal citizenship. It is on just such a basis that the argument for gender equality, non-discrimination on grounds of sexual orientation or the protection of minority rights of disadvantaged groups are based. Just as *** the treatment of these groups constitutes a test of the integrity of the constitution, so too is the commitment to civil equality for the economically marginalised through guaranteed socio-economic rights.***

---

8   *See supra* Ch. 2.A.

Notes and Questions

1.   This article was written in the context of the debate on the inclusion of socio-eco-nomic rights in the post-apartheid South African Constitution. The drafters decided that the South African social contract should reflect the aspirations of those who waged the struggle against apartheid, and address the vast poverty, social indignities and inequalities that are its legacy. *See* Chapter 8, *infra*.

2.   Consider Haysom's thesis that the constitutional entrenchment of economic and social rights enhances civic equality in light of the following article on the role of wealth in the American political process.

BURT NEUBORNE, IS MONEY DIFFERENT?

77 Tex. L. Rev. 1609, 1609–21 (1999)

I.   Introduction

We can never be true political equals. Some people are smarter, or more ambitious, or more committed, or more unscrupulous, or better able to gauge the public's needs or wants, or better speakers, or better known, or better educated, or better looking, or better born, or just plain luckier. Someone who displays one or more of these attributes will probably be more influential politically than someone who lacks these attributes, even when everyone enjoys equal formal political rights.*** Why, then, should we balk at significant political inequality caused by wealth? Is wealth-based political inequality different from the inevitable political inequality that flows from differences in personal attributes? I think so, but I wonder whether my view is as widely shared as I once believed.

When one contrasts our formal rules and rhetoric, both of which vigorously reject the legitimacy of wealth as a criteria for allocating political power, with our political real-ity in which wealth plays a huge role in allocating political power, the disconnect is mas-sive. As a constitutional matter, we have resoundingly rejected the notion that disparities of wealth should be reflected in formal disparities in political power. Similarly, as a mat-ter of political rhetoric, virtually no one openly argues that rich people should have more political power merely because they have more money. Why, then, do we tolerate so much wealth-driven political inequality in our political system? Could it be that, deep down, we want to tilt the political playing field towards the rich (or away from the poor) because, despite formal and rhetorical protests to the contrary, our political culture still regards wealth as a proxy for talent, and poverty as a mark of inferiority?

II.   The Three Tiers of Citizenship

Despite our formal and rhetorical acceptance of the idea that rich and poor should exercise equal political rights, we operate a three-tier democratic process that dramat-ically discriminates on the basis of wealth. The top tier, made up of "super-citizens," is comprised of the wealthiest and most influential segment of the population. Membership in the top tier is restricted to people who control enough wealth to play a significant role in the laissez faire funding of political campaigns, or those few individ-uals whose personal attributes (brains, for example) are sufficiently impressive to com-mand significant attention regardless of wealth.

Super-citizens fund the political process with their money, and define it with their ideas. By deciding who and what to fund and what to talk about, members of the top tier play hugely disproportionate roles in deciding who runs for office, what the issues will be, and who will be elected. Despite efforts to control the size and source of campaign contributions, massive loopholes exist that permit corporations and extremely wealthy individuals to pour unlimited sums into the electoral process. Incumbents regularly outraise and outspend challengers by overwhelming percentages. Indeed, fully twenty-five percent of House seats, and an even greater number of state legislative seats, are uncontested, in part because no challenger can raise enough money to wage a credible campaign. Access to the mass media is beyond the financial means of most candidates challenging the reigning party duopoly, and beyond the means of many major party challengers seeking to unseat an entrenched figure.

The second tier, made up of ordinary citizens, is comprised of the forty to fifty percent of the population that votes in major elections, but that lacks the disposable income or personal attributes needed to propel them into the first tier. Ordinary citizens choose among the alternatives proposed by super-citizens. Ordinary citizens decide the outcome of elections, and determine which items on the proposed agenda will become law. Of course, a feedback effect exists between super-citizens and ordinary citizens. Super-citizens are likely to support candidates and issues based, in part, on assumptions about what ordinary citizens will support; ordinary citizens are influenced by the money provided by super-citizens.

The third tier, made up of spectator-citizens, is comprised of the fifty percent of the eligible electorate that does not vote. Spectator-citizens are formally entitled to participate in the democratic process, and may occasionally be drawn into the voting population. Ordinarily, however, spectators do not perceive themselves as players in the game of politics. Ominously, while the top tier has been relatively stable at two to five percent, the third tier has grown steadily throughout the twentieth century from approximately twenty-five percent of the voting population in 1900 to more than half the voting population in 1996.

A. *Money and the First Tier*

If the political tiers corresponded to functional personal attributes, the differences in political power would be troublesome, but defensible. But the tiers do not track personal attributes. Rather, they are driven principally by a relationship between wealth and law. The disproportionate power of the top tier is a direct consequence of our choice to fund the democratic process almost exclusively from contributions by interested participants. As the Supreme Court noted in *Buckley v. Valeo*, effective political speech in our system is a function of how much money the speaker can command. Once money becomes crucial to effective political speech, disproportionate political power in the system inevitably gravitates to the people who control the money. How could it be otherwise? That massive inequalities tied to wealth exist in our political funding system is beyond dispute. Under our existing campaign financing system, American political campaigns are funded almost exclusively by the top ten percent of the economic ladder. This presents dramatic consequences for skewing the political agenda, selecting the candidates, affecting the outcome of elections, changing the course of legislative debate, and altering patterns of access to public officials.

Were money randomly distributed across the political spectrum, the increased political power of the rich would pose issues of individual equity, but would not threaten the basic fairness of the political system. But money is not randomly distributed across the political system. The "haves" tend to possess a set of political beliefs and policies that are dramatically different from the political beliefs generally held by the "have nots." While there are wealthy left-wing radicals, and impoverished right-wing conservatives, by and large, the wealthy are likely to cluster at given points on the political spectrum that do not overlap with the places where the poor cluster. If I am right, the top tier will not only be disproportionately rich, it will be significantly slanted toward a particular set of political beliefs associated with the best interests of the rich.***

B.   Money and the Third Tier

Concern over the link between law, money, and power at the level of the first tier is a staple of American political debate. But the makeup of the third tier is similarly a legal construct. An equally potent, if less obvious, wealth advantage flows from laws governing registration and voting that, alone among the world's developed democracies, place the inertial obligation on the prospective voter to register in advance of the election, and force working people to vote on a workday. Burdening voting with significant transaction costs does more than diminish voter participation; it gives an advantage to wealthy and educated voters who are more likely to overcome multiple transaction costs in order to vote. Not surprisingly, American elections are characterized by low voter turnouts, with disproportionately high participation by wealthy, well-educated voters, and disproportionately low participation by the poor and less well-educated. In fact, the very existence of a third tier is a matter of political choice and legal construction. We compel jury service, school attendance, vaccination, military service, census cooperation, and the payment of taxes. Why don't we compel voting or, at least, voter registration? Several states have either abandoned voter registration entirely or adopted same-day registration. At a minimum, why do we insist on holding elections on a workday?

III.   Must We Permit the Wealthy to Exercise Unequal Political Power as a Matter of Constitutionally Compelled Deference to Individual Political Autonomy?

Why is our political system so rigged in favor of wealth? The story we usually tell ourselves is that wealth-driven political inequality is a necessary consequence of our liberal constitutional system. We can't cut back on the ability of the wealthy to dominate the first tier of electoral politics because it would be a violation of our First Amendment commitment to political autonomy. At least that's what *Buckley* says. Similarly, we can't prevent skewing the voting rolls in the direction of the wealthy, because the idea of a legal duty (as opposed to a formal right) to vote would be a constitutionally impermissible violation of political autonomy. This is true despite the fact that we tolerate compulsory jury service, compulsory education, compulsory military service, compulsory taxation, and compulsory cooperation with the census. We even tell ourselves that, alone among the world's established democracies, we can't eliminate the double transaction costs for registration and voting on a workday because it would risk electoral fraud and insert the government too directly into the political process.***

In an earlier time, the belief that democracy worked best if greater power was given to the wealthy was so widely shared that, in virtually every democracy, the poor and uneducated were formally excluded from political power. In every democracy, including ours, until very recently, political power was formally concentrated in the hands of the economically successful. American democracy, responding to the ethos of an egalitarian age, has abandoned almost all formal wealth qualifications for voting and running for office. But we appear to have substituted a system of de facto wealth advantage that continues to skew political power towards the economically comfortable.***

A. Campaign Financing

Apologists for our current laissez faire system of campaign financing argue that any effort to regulate campaign spending in an effort to level the political playing field is fundamentally inconsistent with our commitment to individual political autonomy. In a conflict between political autonomy and political equality, autonomy is privileged, they argue, by our liberal First Amendment tradition. Defenders of the current laissez faire system have excellent judicial authority for their position: Justice Brennan persuaded the Supreme Court to adopt it in *Buckley*. The Court held in *Buckley* that while an interest in political equality might justify subsidizing the weak, it could not justify limiting the strong. The *Buckley* decision is a paean to political autonomy, even when its exercise seriously compromises political equality. But is *Buckley* really a net gain for political autonomy?***

Buckley's effect on political autonomy is *** far more complex than the Court appeared to imagine. A laissez faire system enhances the autonomy of those extremely wealthy individuals for whom no ceiling exists on the amount they are prepared to spend. But it restricts the autonomy of those who wish to place any limits on their fundraising and spending. Candidates in such a position are at the mercy of a prisoners' dilemma, supporters in such a position are at the mercy of powerful pressures to give more than they wish, and officials in that position are under intense pressure from their monied constituents. What *Buckley* does, therefore, in the name of autonomy, is to privilege the autonomy of those with limitless wealth over the autonomy of those with limited funds. That is, of course, a permissible choice, but it is not compelled by respect for individual autonomy.***

B. Defining the Electorate

Although the Founders' electorate formally excluded women, African-Americans, and the poor, the history of American democracy is the steady expansion of the formal electorate. Many property qualifications were relaxed by 1824, but significant wealth restrictions persisted until the 1970s. The Fifteenth Amendment ended formal racial discrimination in allocating voting rights, but it was not until the passage of the Voting Rights Act of 1965 that many members of racial minorities were able to exercise the franchise. Women obtained the vote in 1919 with the passage of the Nineteenth Amendment, but continue to be radically underrepresented in positions of political influence.

As formal restrictions on the definition of the electorate were lifted, de facto substitutes arose that continued to skew the voting rolls toward the wealthy and educated.*** Beginning in 1900, ostensible concerns with fraud led to the adoption of voter registration requirements in the nation's major cities, and, quickly, in every state. The imposition of voter registration had a catastrophic effect on voter turnout. Turnout went from seventy-nine percent in the 1896 presidential election, to forty-nine percent in 1924. Since the imposition of voter registration, it has never gone above sixty-five percent in a presidential election and tends to be lower in off-year Congressional elections. Moreover, the impact on voting turnout has been far greater on poor and less-educated voters. In fact, the shift from formal disenfranchisement to de facto exclusion has allowed significant numbers of poor persons to enter the political process, but has retained ultimate voting control in the hands of propertied, better-educated voters.

The disproportionate exclusion of poor voters caused by voter registration rules cannot plausibly be defended as necessary. No other developed democracy imposes a similar transaction cost on voting. Most democracies place the responsibility for assembling the voting rolls on the state. In fact, several states have abandoned pre-election voter registration in favor of same-day registration. Some democracies—Australia, Belgium and Italy—even view voting as a duty, not an option.

If voting were a duty, the actual voting population would be less well-educated, less white, less male, and much poorer. But, argue libertarians, it would also be less free. Compulsory voting, they argue, is a blatant interference with political autonomy. If individuals were actually forced to vote, autonomy values would be seriously compromised, although the violation would be no greater than our accepted practices of compelling jury service, education, military service, taxation, and census cooperation. However, if individuals were empowered to remove their names from the voting rolls at will, reversing the inertial burden on whether to vote would not violate norms of political autonomy. Moreover, whatever the libertarian objection to viewing voting as a duty, there is no autonomy-based objection to placing the initial responsibility for assembling the voting rolls on the state. We already do it for jury service. Why not for elections as well? And, given the success of same-day registration in several states, there simply is no justification for retaining the traditional pattern of pre-election registration. Finally, no reason exists to force working people to vote on a workday. Many democracies schedule elections on the weekend, allowing voters to go to the polls on either Saturday or Sunday. Oregon has begun to experiment with an even longer voting period of two weeks, during which voting by mail is permitted. If we retain the present system of constructing a third tier of citizens who are poorer, less educated, and less white than the first and second tiers, it is because we want to.***

Notes and Questions

1. Is Neuborne's distinction between ordinary citizens and spectator-citizens based solely on wealth? What other factors might be relevant? David Copp agrees that the wealthy exercise disproportionate power over political outcomes, identifying the following three reasons:

> First is the cost of political campaigning in large complex societies. In the United States, for example, the *New York Times* estimated that the 1996 presidential campaign cost between $600 million and $1 billion and that a successful campaign for a seat in the Senate cost at least $5 million and went as high as $30 million in some states. Even a campaign for a seat in the House of Representatives can cost $2 million. Given this, a wealthy person obviously has immediate advantages over less wealthy people who might be interested in running for office. If she is sufficiently wealthy, she can simply attempt a campaign without being dependent on contributions from sources other than her own bank account, and if she does this, she will not be forced to modify her platform in order to gain financial backing for her campaign.***

> Given the cost of campaigning for office, moreover, every candidate who is not personally wealthy is dependent in part on wealthy people and capitalist

business to finance his campaign. According to a private research group, 'business' was the largest source of campaign contributions in the 1996 federal elections in the United States, contributing an estimated $242 million.*** Organized labour contributed about $35 million to the campaign. But this is not really an example of a way that ordinary people can influence politics under capitalism, since *** the rank and file does not really control the budgets of organized labour.***

Second, those who control the productive apparatus of a capitalist economy have an extra measure of power, for they can use covert threats and promises in attempts to achieve political results that are favourable to them. In some cases they can use explicit threats and promises. If political outcomes are contrary to their interests, they can often move their assets to another jurisdiction, and often be welcomed there for the jobs and tax dollars they bring with them. For example, an entrepreneur can threaten to close a factory that is a major employer of the voters in a particular community, and such threats obviously can affect people's votes or the policy of the government. Since government in a capitalist economy has no direct control over industry, it may need to offer incentives to industry, so-called corporate welfare, such as special tax breaks for industries that remain in regions where there is high unemployment.***

Third, the wealthy can affect the political process by buying special access to or control of the mass media, such as television stations and networks and newspapers, and by creating, or controlling through contributions, other institutions that shape political opinion, such as the 'think tanks.'***

David Copp, *Capitalism Versus Democracy: The Marketing of Votes and the Marketing of Political Power, in* JOHN DOUGLAS BISHOP, ED., ETHICS AND CAPITALISM 91–95 (2000).

2.   Is voting distinguishable from the other obligatory activities cited by Neuborne, such as paying taxes or jury service? How does compulsory voting actually work? How is it enforced? Over twenty countries—including Australia, Argentina, Brazil, Greece and Italy—have some form of requirement to register to vote and turn out on election day. What are the advantages and disadvantages of such an approach? Are fines appropriate for failure to perform this civic duty? Would compulsory turn-out promote or impede voter education? Would it eliminate voter apathy? Would enforcement of the requirement be unduly costly?

3.   What are the implications of the three-tier citizenry for democratic accountability? Does it render the political process a less viable means of addressing economic, social, and cultural inequities? Does it render the courts more attractive for such purposes?

PART II

INTERNATIONAL INSTRUMENTS AND THEIR IMPLEMENTATION

The materials in Part II introduce the major international and regional instruments that elaborate economic, social and cultural human rights norms and their associated implementation mechanisms. Our main focus will be on human rights as specified in treaty law. "Treaty" is defined in the Vienna Convention on the Law of Treaties to mean "an international agreement concluded between States in written form and governed by international law." *See* Vienna Convention on the Law of Treaties, art. 2, 1155 U.N.T.S. 336 (1969). Treaty law is one of the primary "sources" of international law listed in classic statements such as Article 38 of the Statute of the International Court of Justice, which includes:

    a.   international conventions, whether general or particular, establishing rules expressly recognized by the contesting states;

    b.   international customs, as evidence of a general practice accepted as law;

    c.   the general principles of law recognized by civilized nations; [and]

    d.   *** judicial decisions and the teachings of the most highly qualified publicists of the various nations, as subsidiary means for the determination of rules of law.

Statute of the International Court of Justice, Art. 38(1), as annexed to the Charter of the United Nations, 59 Stat. 1055 T.S. No. 993, 3 Bevans 1153, 1 U.N.T.S. (signed at San Francisco, June 26, 1945, *entered into force* October 24, 1945). For an overview of the meanings and roles of treaty law (also referred to as "conventional law"); international customary law; general principles of law; and the interpretive role of the judiciary and legal scholars, *see* MARK W. JANIS, AN INTRODUCTION TO INTERNATIONAL LAW, at 9–83 (4th ed. 2003).

The formulation of international legal sources in Article 38, while highly influential, was originally intended to apply specifically to the jurisprudence of the ICJ (World Court). Subsequently, international legal scholars have also elaborated on the role of "soft law" (*i.e.*, U.N. General Assembly resolutions, the resolutions of other international organizations and conferences, and corporate codes of conduct) and other sources of international legal norms. *Id.* at 52–53.

While the goal of universal respect for human rights was articulated in Article 55 of the Charter of the United Nations, no concrete mechanisms for achieving this goal were incorporated into the Charter itself. Our discussion of the implementation of economic, social and cultural rights begins with the foundational human rights instruments under the U.N. system—the International Bill of Rights. That section is followed by examination of human rights treaties that focus on the rights of specified groups—the Race Convention, the Women's Convention and the Children's Convention. Each of those instruments addresses the full panoply of rights, including the economic, social and cultural dimensions of human dignity. Finally, we look at the regional instruments and systems created to address human rights violations. Such regional systems have been adopted in the Americas, Europe and Africa. Asia, however, has not yet created such a human rights-based regional system for complex cultural, historical and political reasons. *See* the discussion of the "Asian Values Debate" in Chapter 2, *supra.*

Note that treaty law (as opposed to customary law for example) might seem to have the advantage of interpretive certainty because its terms are written, negotiated, and directly consented to by states. However, as we will see throughout the book, there is considerable room for interpretation and dispute in the application of treaty provisions. This seems to be particularly true of international human rights treaties, which are often drafted in broad and vague terms. As you read these materials, consider whether the problems of interpretation are even more significant with regard to treaty provisions addressing economic, social, and cultural rights. Consider, as well, whether rights discourse is an effective approach to the social, political and economic transformation that must precede the full realization of human dignity for the majority of the world's people, or, as some critics assert, serves instead to distract activists from more radical forms of struggle:

> Even very broad social movements of emancipation—for women, for minorities of various sorts, for the poor—have their vision blinkered by the promise of recognition in the vocabulary and institutional apparatus of human rights. They will be led away from the economy and toward the state, away from political/social conditions and toward the forms of legal recognition. It has been claimed, for example, that promoting a neutral right to religious expression in Africa without acknowledging the unequal background cultural, economic and political authority of traditional religions and imported evangelical sects will dramatically affect the distribution of religious practice.***

David Kennedy, *The International Human Rights Movement: Part of the Problem?*, 15 HARV. HUM. RTS. J. 101 (2002).

Others argue that the abundance of norms codified in legal instruments may actually undermine the protection of fundamental rights:

> [A] serious problem that is seldom acknowledged by the human rights community must be confronted—the sheer proliferation of ideals claimed or asserted to be rights. The rapid multiplication of international human rights instruments encourages a sterile formalism as more and more states are encouraged to accede to these treaties without the intention or capability to comply. Proliferation of rights merely compounds the occasions for conflicts of interpretation or implementation without really enlarging the consensus on human rights. The very language of rights fuels sterile debate because it frames issues in stark, universalist and static terms, leaving little room for compromise.

Bilahari Kausikan, *An Asian Approach to Human Rights*, 89 AM. SOC'Y INT'L L. PROC. 146 (1995). Do you agree with this analysis? Should there be "room to compromise" on which rights are fundamental? What alternatives to rights discourse may be viable options?

CHAPTER THREE

INTERNATIONAL TREATIES

A. THE INTERNATIONAL BILL OF RIGHTS

The International Bill of Rights, consisting of the Universal Declaration of Human Rights, the International Covenant on Civil and Political Rights and the International Covenant on Economic, Social and Cultural Rights, sets forth the fundamental norms of human rights under the U.N. system. The Charter of the United Nations recognized the obligation of member states to respect and promote "human rights and fundamental freedoms" (see below), but did not elaborate on the specific rights to be protected. The Universal Declaration of Human Rights (UDHR), adopted by the U.N. General Assembly in 1948, was the first authoritative statement of the content of a universal human rights framework. However, as a "declaration," the UDHR was not intended to have the legally binding effect of a multi-lateral treaty. Rather, its purpose was to elaborate the norms that were later to become the basis for a legally binding Covenant to follow. As the leading authoritative statement of international human rights, however, the UDHR, or some of its provisions at least, arguably have achieved customary law status.

In any case, while the UDHR included both economic, social and cultural rights and civil and political rights, Cold War politics resulted in the adoption of a separate Covenant for each category of rights. While both Covenants have now been widely ratified, the implementation of economic, social and cultural rights has lagged behind that of the traditional "first generation" rights. Nevertheless, a significant body of jurisprudence is being developed; this chapter examines these emerging norms.

CHARTER OF THE UNITED NATIONS, ARTICLES 55 AND 56

59 Stat. 1031, T.S. No. 993, 3 Beavans 1153 (*entered into force* October 24, 1945)

CHAPTER IX. INTERNATIONAL ECONOMIC AND SOCIAL CO-OPERATION

Article 55

With a view to the creation of conditions of stability and well-being which are necessary for peaceful and friendly relations among nations based on respect for the principle of equal rights and self-determination of peoples, the United Nations shall promote:

(A) higher standards of living, full employment, and conditions of economic and social progress and development;

(B) solutions of international economic, social, health, and related problems; and international cultural and educational co-operation; and

(C) universal respect for, and observance of, human rights and fundamental freedoms for all without distinction as to race, sex, language, or religion.

Article 56

All members pledge themselves to take joint and separate action in cooperation with the Organization for the achievement of the purposes set forth in Article 55.

INTERNATIONAL COVENANT ON CIVIL AND POLITICAL RIGHTS, ARTICLE 1

G.A. Res. 2200A (XXI), Dec. 16, 1966, 21 U.N. GAOR Supp. (No. 16) at 52, U.N. Doc. A/6316 (1966), 999 U.N.T.S. 171, *entered into force* March 23, 1976

Article 1

1. All peoples have the right of self-determination. By virtue of that right they freely determine their political status and freely pursue their economic, social and cultural development.

2. All peoples may, for their own ends, freely dispose of their natural wealth and resources without prejudice to any obligations arising out of international economic cooperation, based upon the principle of mutual benefit, and international law. In no case may a people be deprived of its own means of subsistence.

Notes and Questions

1. *Implementation of the Covenant.* The Human Rights Committee, the U.N. body charged with implementing the International Covenant on Civil and Political Rights, reviews the periodic reports of states parties to the Covenant. At the end of the review process, it issues "Concluding Observations" on the states' compliance with the treaty's requirements. *See e.g.*, Concluding Observations on the Fourth Periodic Report of Canada, U.N. Hum. Rts. Comm., 65th Sess., 1747th mtg., para 8, U.N. Doc. CPR/C/79/ Add. 105 (1999) criticizing the Canadian government's policies on aboriginal rights as incompatible with Article 1. In addition, under the Optional Protocol, individuals in states that are parties to the Protocol have the right to petition the Human Rights Committee alleging breaches of the Covenant.

2. Does the language of Articles 55 and 56 reflect a strong commitment to the protection of human rights? Is it merely hortatory?

INTERNATIONAL COVENANT ON ECONOMIC, SOCIAL AND CULTURAL RIGHTS

G.A. Res. 2200A (XXI), 21 U.N. GAOR (No. 16), U.N. Doc. A/6316 (1966), 993 U.N.T.S. 3, *entered into force* January 3, 1976

THE STATES PARTIES TO THE PRESENT COVENANT,

Considering that, in accordance with the principles proclaimed in the Charter of the United Nations, recognition of the inherent dignity and of the equal and inalienable rights of all members of the human family is the foundation of freedom, justice and peace in the world.

Recognizing that these rights derive from the inherent dignity of the human person,

Recognizing that, in accordance with the Universal Declaration of Human Rights, the ideal of free human beings enjoying freedom from fear and want can only be achieved if conditions are created where by everyone may enjoy his economic, social and cultural rights, as well as his civil and political rights,

Considering the obligation of States under the Charter of the United Nations to promote universal respect for, and observance of, human rights and freedoms,

Realizing that the individual, having duties to other individuals and to the community to which he belongs, is under a responsibility to strive for the promotion and observance of the rights recognized in the present Covenant,

Agree upon the following articles:

PART I

Article 1

1. All peoples have the right of self-determination. By virtue of that right they freely determine their political status and freely pursue their economic, social and cultural development.

2. All peoples may, for their own ends, freely dispose of their natural wealth and resources without prejudice to any obligations arising out of international economic co-operation, based upon the principle of mutual benefit, and international law. In no case may a people be deprived of its own means of subsistence.

3. The States Parties to the present Covenant, including those having responsibility for the administration of Non-Self-Governing and Trust Territories, shall promote the realization of the right of self-determination, and shall respect that right, in conformity with the provisions of the Charter of the United Nations.

PART II

Article 2

1. Each State Party to the present Covenant undertakes to take steps, individually and through international assistance and co-operation, especially economic and technical, to the maximum of its available resources, with a view to achieving progressively the full realization of the rights recognized in the present Covenant by all appropriate means, including particularly the adoption of legislative measures.

2. The States Parties to the present Covenant undertake to guarantee that the rights enunciated in the present Covenant will be exercised without discrimination of any kind as to race, color, sex, language, religion, political or other opinion, national or social origin, property, birth or other status.

3. Developing countries, with due regard to human rights and their national economy, may determine to what extent they would guarantee the economic rights recognized in the present Covenant to non-nationals.

Article 3

The States Parties to the present Covenant undertake to ensure the equal right of men and women to the enjoyment of all economic, social and cultural rights set forth in the present Covenant.

Article 4

The States Parties to the present Covenant recognize that, in the enjoyment of those rights provide by the State in conformity with the present Covenant, the State may subject such rights only to such limitations as are determined by law only in so far as this may be compatible with the nature of these rights and solely for the purpose of promoting the general welfare in a democratic society.

Article 5

1. Nothing in the present Covenant may be interpreted as implying for any State, group or person any right to engage in any activity or to perform any act aimed at the destruction of any of the rights of freedoms recognized herein, or at their limitation to a greater extent than is provided for in the present Covenant.

2. No restriction upon or derogation from any of the fundamental human rights recognized or existing in any country in virtue of law, conventions, regulations or custom shall be admitted on the pretext that the present Covenant does not recognize such rights or that it recognizes them to a lesser extent.

PART III

Article 6

1. The States Parties to the present Covenant recognize the right to work, which includes the right of everyone to the opportunity to gain his living by work which he freely chooses or accepts, and will take appropriate steps to safeguard this right.

2. The steps to be taken by a State Party to the present Covenant to achieve the full realization of this right shall include technical and vocational guidance and training programmes, policies and techniques to achieve steady economic, social and cultural development and full and productive employment under conditions safeguarding fundamental political and economic freedoms to the individual.

Article 7

The States Parties to the present Covenant recognize the right of everyone to the enjoyment of just and favourable conditions of work which ensure, in particular:***

(e) Remuneration which provides all workers, as a minimum, with:

  (i) Fair wages and equal remuneration for work of equal value without distinction of any kind, in particular women being guaranteed conditions of work not inferior to those enjoyed by men, with equal pay for equal work;

  (ii) A decent living for themselves and their families in accordance with the provisions of the present Covenant;

(f) Safe and healthy working conditions;

(g) Equal opportunity for everyone to be promoted in his employment to an appropriate higher level, subject to no considerations other than those of seniority and competence;

(h) Rest, leisure and reasonable limitation of working hours and periodic holidays with pay, as well as remuneration for public holidays.

Article 8

1. The States Parties to the present Covenant undertake to ensure:

(a) The right of everyone to form trade unions and join the trade union of his choice, subject only to the rules of the organization concerned, for the promotion and protection of his economic and social interests. No restrictions may be placed on the exercise of this right other than those prescribed by law and which are necessary in a democratic society in the interests of national security or public order or for the protection of the rights and freedoms of others;

(b) The right of trade unions to establish national federations or confederations and the right of the latter to form or join international trade-union organizations;

(c) The right of trade unions to function freely subject to no limitations other than those prescribed by law and which are necessary in a democratic society in the interests of national security or public order or for the protection of the rights and freedoms of others;

(d) The right to strike, provided that it is exercised in conformity with the laws of the particular country.

2. This article shall not prevent the imposition of lawful restrictions on the exercise of these rights by members of the armed forces or of the police or of the administration of the State.

3. Nothing in this article shall authorize States Parties to the International Labor Organisation Convention of 1948 concerning Freedom of Association and Protection of the Right to Organize to take legislative measures which would prejudice, or apply the law in such a manner as would prejudice, the guarantees provided for in that Convention.

Article 9

The States Parties to the present Covenant recognize the right of every one to social security, including social insurance.

Article 10

The States Parties to the present Covenant recognize that:

1. The widest possible protection and assistance should be accorded to the family, which is the natural and fundamental group unit of society, particularly for its establishment and while it is responsible for the care and education of dependent children. Marriage must be entered into with the free consent of the intending spouses.

2. Special protection should be accorded to mothers during a reasonable period before and after childbirth. During such period working mothers should be accorded paid leave or leave with adequate social security benefits.

3. Special measures of protection and assistance should be taken on behalf of all children and young persons without any discrimination for reasons of parentage or other conditions. Children and young persons should be protected from economic and social exploitation. Their employment in work harmful to their morals or health or dangerous to life or likely to hamper their normal development should be punishable by

law. States should also set age limits below which the paid employment of child labor should be prohibited and punishable by law.

Article 11

1. The States Parties to the present Covenant recognize the right of everyone to an adequate standard of living for himself and his family, including adequate food, clothing and housing, and to the continuous improvement of living conditions. The States Parties will take appropriate steps to ensure the realization of this right, recognizing to this effect the essential importance of international co-operation based on free consent.

2. The States Parties to the present Covenant, recognizing the fundamental right of everyone to be free from hunger, shall take, individually and through international co-operation, the measures, including specific programs, which are needed:

(a) To improve methods of production, conservation and distribution of food by making full use of technical and scientific knowledge, by disseminating knowledge of the principles of nutrition and by developing or reforming agrarian systems in such a way as to achieve the most efficient development and utilization of natural resources;

(b) Taking into account the problems of both food-importing and food-exporting countries, to ensure an equitable distribution of world food supplies in relation to need.

Article 12

1. The States Parties to the present Covenant recognize the right of everyone to the enjoyment of the highest attainable standard of physical and mental health.

2. The steps to be taken by the States Parties to the present Covenant to achieve the full realization of this right shall include those necessary for:

(a) The provision for the reduction of the stillbirth-rate and of infant mortality and for the healthy development of the child;

(b) The improvement of all aspects of environmental and industrial hygiene;

(c) The prevention, treatment and control of epidemic, endemic, occupational and other diseases;

(d) The creation of conditions which would assure to all medical service and medical attention in the event of sickness.

Article 13

1. The States Parties to the present Covenant recognize the right of everyone to education. They agree that education shall be directed to the full development of the human personality and the sense of its dignity, and shall strengthen the respect for human rights and fundamental freedoms. They further agree that education shall enable all persons to participate effectively in a free society, promote understanding, tolerance and friendship among all nations and all racial, ethnic or religious groups, and further the activities of the United Nations for the maintenance of peace.

2. The States Parties to the present Covenant recognize that, with a view to achieving the full realization of this right:

(a) Primary education shall be compulsory and available free to all;

(b) Secondary education in its different forms, including technical and vocational secondary education, shall be made generally available and accessible to all by every appropriate means, and in particular by the progressive introduction of free education;

(c) Higher education shall be made equally accessible to all, on the basis of capacity, by every appropriate means, and in particular by the progressive introduction of free education;

(d) Fundamental education shall be encouraged or intensified as far as possible for those persons who have not received or completed the whole period of their primary education;

(e) The development of a system of schools at all levels shall be actively pursued, an adequate fellowship system shall be established, and the material conditions of teaching staff shall be continuously improved.

3. The States Parties to the present Covenant undertake to have respect for the liberty of parents and, when applicable, legal guardians to choose for their children schools, other than those established by the public authorities, which conform to such minimum educational standards as may be laid down or approved by the State and to ensure the religious and moral education of their children in conformity with their own convictions.

4. No part of this article shall be construed so as to interfere with the liberty of individuals and bodies to establish and direct educational institutions, subject always to the observance of the principles set forth in paragraph 1 of this article and to the requirement that the education given in such institutions shall conform to such minimum standards as may be laid down by the State.

Article 14

Each State Party to the present Covenant which, at the time of becoming a Party, has not been able to secure in its metropolitan territory or other territories under its jurisdiction compulsory primary education, free of charge, undertakes, within two years, to work out and adopt a detailed plan of action for the progressive implementation, within a reasonable number of years, to be fixed in the plan, of the principle of compulsory education free of charge for all.

Article 15

1. The States Parties to the present Covenant recognize the right of everyone:

(a) To take part in cultural life;

(b) To enjoy the benefits of scientific progress and its applications;

(c) To benefit from the protection of the moral and material interests resulting from any scientific, literary or artistic production of which he is the author.

2. The steps to be taken by the States Parties to the present Covenant to achieve the full realization of this right shall include those necessary for the conservation, the development and the diffusion of science and culture.

3. The States Parties to the present Covenant undertake to respect the freedom indispensable for scientific research and creative activity.

4. The States Parties to the present Covenant recognize the benefits to be derived from the encouragement and development of international contracts and co-operation in the scientific and cultural fields.

PART IV

Article 16

1. The States Parties to the present Covenant undertake to submit in conformity with this part of the Covenant reports on the measures which they have adopted and the progress made in achieving the observance of the rights recognized herein.

2. (a) All reports shall be submitted to the Secretary-General of the United Nations, who shall transmit copies to the Economic and Social Council for consideration in accordance with the provisions of the present Covenant.

(b) The Secretary-General of the United Nations shall also transmit to the specialized agencies copies of the reports, or any relevant parts therefrom, from States Parties to the present Covenant which are also members of these specialized agencies in so far as these reports, or parts therefrom, relate to any matters which fall within the responsibilities of the said agencies in accordance with their constitutional instruments.

Article 17

1. The States Parties to the present Covenant shall furnish their reports in stages, in accordance with a program to be established by the Economic and Social Council within one year of the entry into force of the present Covenant after consultation with the States Parties and the specialized agencies concerned.

2. Reports may indicate factors and difficulties affecting the degree of fulfilment of obligations under the present Covenant.

3. Where relevant information has previously been furnished to the United Nations or to any specialized agency by any State Party to the present Covenant, it will not be necessary to reproduce that information, but a precise reference to the information so furnished will suffice. ***

Article 23

The States Parties to the present Covenant agree that international action for the achievement of the rights recognized in the present Covenant includes such methods as the conclusion of conventions, the adoption of recommendations, the furnishing of technical assistance and the holding of regional meetings and technical meetings for the purpose of consultation and study organized in conjunction with the Governments concerned.

Article 24

Nothing in the present covenant shall be interpreted as impairing the provisions of the Charter of the United Nations and of the constitutions of the specialized agencies which define the respective responsibilities of the various organs of the United Nations and of the specialized agencies in regard to the matters dealt with in the present Covenant.

Article 25

Nothing in the present Covenant shall be interpreted as impairing the inherent right of all peoples to enjoy and utilize fully and freely their natural wealth and resources.

PART V

Article 26

1. The present Covenant is open for signature by any State Member of the United Nations or member of any of its specialized agencies, by any State Party to the Statute of the International Court of Justice, and by any other State which has been invited by the General Assembly of the United Nations to become a party to the present Covenant.

2. The present Covenant is subject to ratification. Instruments of ratification shall be deposited with the Secretary-General of the United Nations.

3. The present Covenant shall be open to accession by any State referred to in paragraph 1 of this article.

4. Accession shall be effected by the deposit of an instrument of accession with the Secretary-General of the United Nations.

5. The Secretary-General of the United Nations shall inform all States which have signed the present Covenant or acceded to it of the deposit of each instrument of ratification or accession.

Article 27

1. The present Covenant shall enter into force three months after the date of the deposit with the Secretary-General of the United Nations of the thirty-fifth instrument of ratification or instrument of accession.

2. For each State ratifying the present Covenant or acceding to it after the deposit of the thirty-fifth instrument of ratification or instrument of accession, the present Covenant shall enter into force three months after the date of the deposit of its own instrument of ratification or instrument of accession.

Article 28

The provisions of the present Covenant shall extend to all parts of federal States without any limitations or exceptions.

Article 29

1. Any State Party to the present Covenant may propose an amendment and file it with the Secretary-General of the United Nations. The Secretary-General shall thereupon communicate any proposed amendments to the States Parties to the present Covenant with a request that they notify him whether they favor a conference of States Parties for the purpose of considering and voting upon the proposals. In the event that at least one third of the States Parties favors such a conference, the Secretary-General shall convene the conference under the auspices of the United Nations. Any amendment adopted by a majority of the States Parties present and voting at the conference shall be submitted to the General Assembly of the United Nations for approval.

2. Amendments shall come into force when they have been approved by the General Assembly of the United Nations and accepted by a two-thirds majority of the States Parties to the present Covenant in accordance with their respective constitutional processes.

3. When amendments come into force they shall be binding on those States Parties which have accepted them, other States Parties still being bound by the provisions of the present Covenant and any earlier amendment which they have accepted.

Article 30

Irrespective of the notifications made under article 26, paragraph 5, the Secretary-General of the United Nations shall inform all States referred to in paragraph 1 of the same article of the following particulars:

(a) Signatures, ratifications and accessions under article 26;

(b) The date of the entry into force of the present Covenant under article 27 and the date of the entry into force of any amendments under article 29.

Article 31

1. The present Covenant, of which the Chinese, English, French, Russian and Spanish texts are equally authentic, shall be deposited in the archives of the United Nations.

2. The Secretary-General of the United Nations shall transmit certified copies of the present Covenant to all States referred to in article 26.

Notes and Questions

1. *State Obligations.* What are the overall obligations of states parties to the ICESCR? What does Article 2(2) require? Are the legal obligations imposed on states parties different for some rights than for others? What is the difference between language that requires a state to "undertake to ensure" a right as opposed to language requiring it to "recognize" a right? Does the nature of the obligation on states parties to the ICESCR depend on the nature of the right in question? If so, in what ways, and why?

2. *Philosophical Foundations.* What are the philosophical foundations of the ICESCR? Compare the rights and principles elaborated in the Covenant to the philosophical, religious and political principles described in Chapter 2.

3. *Individual Duties.* The Preambular paragraphs refer to duties that the individual owes "to other individuals and to the community." What are these duties? How are they identified? How are they enforced?

4. Consider the following:

Is there a human right to water under the ICESCR? Article 11 requires states parties to "take appropriate steps to ensure the realization of" the right to an adequate standard of living. That right includes, among other things, "food, clothing, and housing, and *** the continuous improvement of living conditions." Article 12 recognizes the right "to the enjoyment of the highest attainable standard of physical and mental health." Do such rights include access to a clean and safe water supply?

No resource is more basic than water. Water is essential for life, crucial for relieving poverty, hunger and disease and critical for economic development. Despite enormous improvements over the past 15 years, hundreds of millions of men, women and children still do not have proper water for drinking and sanitation.*** Water problems ultimately end up as "people" problems.

Stephen C. McCaffrey, *A Human Right to Water: Domestic and International Implications*, 5 GEO. INT'L ENVTL. L. REV. 1, 5 (1992).

Although the UDHR, the ICESCR, and the ICCPR do not explicitly reference access to clean water as a human right, the privatization of water distribution has increasingly been characterized as a human rights issue. Access to clean and safe water has particularly important implications for the Global South. Poor women, who are often primarily responsible for obtaining and distributing water for family use, often must walk for hours per day to obtain clean water. Poor people without any access to safe water must often use the same stagnant water sources for drinking, bathing, washing clothes and removing sewage. As is the case in South Africa, a new government's initial priority often may be the creation of the infrastructure and distribution systems in order to provide equitable local access. However, even when distribution facilities are put in place, many poor communities do not have the means to pay the drastic increases in water fees resulting from privatization. In an influential *New Yorker* article, journalist William Finnegan described local efforts among indigenous peoples, students, and others to resist water privatization in Cochabamba, Bolivia:

> The chief demand of the water warriors, as they were called, was the removal of a private, foreign-led consortium that had taken over Cochabamba's water system. For the Bolivian government, breaking with the consortium—which was dominated by the United States-based Bechtel Corporation—was unthinkable, politically and financially. Bolivia had signed a lucrative, long-term contract. Renouncing it would be a blow to the confidence of foreign investors in a region where national governments and economies depend such confidence for their survival. (Argentina's recent bankruptcy was caused in large part by a loss of credibility with international bankers.) The rebellion in Cochabamba was setting off loud alarms, particularly among the major corporations in the global water business. This business has been booming in recent years—Enron was a big player, before its collapse—largely because of the worldwide drive to privatize public utilities.

> For opponents of privatization, who believe that access to clean water is a human right, the Cochabamba Water War became an event of surpassing interest. There are many signs that other poor communities, especially in Third World cities, may start refusing to accept deals that put a foreign corporation's hand on the neighborhood pump or the household tap. Indeed, water auctions may turn out to test the limits of the global privatization gold rush. And while the number of populists opposing water privatization seems effectively inexhaustible *** the same cannot be said of the world's water supply.***

> The world is running out of fresh water. There's water everywhere, of course, but less than three per cent of it is fresh, and most of that is locked up in polar ice caps and glaciers, unrecoverable for practical purposes. Lakes, rivers, marshes, aquifers, and atmospheric vapor make up less than one per

cent of the earth's total water, and people are already using more than half of the accessible runoff. Water demand, on the other hand, has been growing rapidly.*** By 2025, the demand for water around the world is expected to exceed supply by fifty-six per cent.***

Meanwhile, more than a billion people have no access to clean drinking water, and nearly three billion live without basic sanitation. Five million people die each year from waterborne diseases such as cholera, typhoid, and dysentery.***

Arid regions with the means to pay (Southern California, the Persian Gulf States) already pipe water in from wetter areas. New technologies are being hurriedly developed: huge fabric bags holding millions of gallons of fresh water are being hauled by barges across the Mediterranean, and there are businessmen in Alaska who believe that the state's earnings from fresh water will eventually dwarf its earnings from oil.***

But the main push is in the Global South, where, over the past twenty years, the World Bank and the International Monetary Fund have effectively taken control of the economies of scores of nations that are heavily in debt. The Bank and the I.M.F. have been requiring these countries to accept "structural adjustment," which includes opening markets to foreign firms and privatizing state enterprises, including utilities.*** The Bank is now getting out of the dam business and into water privatization. It often works closely with the conglomerates, helping them to acquire the water assets of debtor nations.***

William Finnegan, *Leasing the Rain*, NEW YORKER, Apr. 8, 2002, at 43.

5. Is effective access to clean water an aspect of the right to an adequate standard of living and the right to health? Should it be? Why was the right to water not expressly protected in the Covenant? Does this suggest an oversight on the part of the drafters? Could it reflect a "Western" orientation? How best could such rights be protected given limited resources? What are the responsibilities of an individual state party? Are there international obligations in this regard? *See* Committee on Economic, Social and Cultural Rights, *General Comment No. 15: The Right to Water*, U.N. Doc. E/C.12/2002/11 (Nov. 26, 2002) (interpreting Arts. 11 and 12), *available at* http://193.194.138.190/html/menu2/6/gc15.doc (last visited Apr. 20, 2004):

The human right to water entitles everyone to sufficient, safe, acceptable, physically accessible and affordable water for personal and domestic uses. An adequate amount of safe water is necessary to prevent death from dehydration, to reduce the risk of water-related disease and to provide for consumption, cooking, personal and domestic hygienic requirements.***

States parties should ensure that the right to water is given due attention in international agreements and, to that end, should consider the development of further legal instruments. With regard to the conclusion and implementation of other international and regional agreements, States parties should take steps to ensure that these instruments do not adversely impact upon the right to water. Agreements concerning trade liberalization should not curtail or inhibit a country's capacity to ensure the full realization of the right to water.

6.   *Sovereignty and Water.* Article 1 of the ICESCR (and Article 1 of the ICCPR) provides that "in no case may a people be deprived of its own means of subsistence" and that "[n]othing in the present Covenant shall be interpreted as impairing the inherent right of all peoples to enjoy and utilize fully and freely their natural wealth and resources." What does this principle of permanent sovereignty over natural resources imply for access to water and the controversies surrounding the privatization of water distribution? *Cf.* Gamal Abouali, *Natural Resources Under Occupation: The Status of Palestinian Water Under International Law*, 10 PACE INT'L L. REV. 411, 496–536 (1998), discussing applicability of ICESCR Articles 1 (sovereignty); 2 (non-discrimination); 6 (right to work); 11 (housing); and 12 (health) to Palestinian water rights.

7.   *Efficacy of "Rights-Talk."* Do rights-based approaches to economic, social, and cultural goals preempt alternative strategies for achieving these goals, such as individual responsibility, political activism or restructuring of a state's socio-economic system?

8.   *A Patriarchal Concept of Family?* Article 10 recognizes that the "widest possible protection and assistance should be accorded to the family, which is the natural and fundamental group unit of society particularly for its establishment and while it is responsible for the care and education of dependent children." Do you agree? Should states parties provide special protections for families? What definition of "family," if any, does the article seem to recognize? Might the rights of individuals within the family sometimes conflict with those of the family unit as a whole? If so, how should such conflicts be resolved?

9.   *The Right of Petition.* In 1993, the Vienna Declaration and Programme of Action affirmed the importance of economic, social and cultural rights and called on the U.N. Commission on Human Rights to explore the adoption of an optional protocol to the ICESCR that would provide the right of individual petition. The delegates recognized that the protection of economic, social and cultural rights under international instruments had not been as effective as those protecting civil and political rights. In a statement to the Economic and Social Council, Amnesty International outlined the potential benefits:

— An optional protocol to the ICESCR would provide individuals and groups with international recourse with respect to violations of economic, social and cultural rights;

— It would mark an important step towards strengthening the principle of progressive realization of social, economic and cultural rights to which states parties to ICESCR have committed themselves;

— The consideration of specific cases of violations of economic, social and cultural rights would contribute to the development of the jurisprudence;

— It would strengthen the relationship between the Committee on Economic, Social and Cultural Rights and states parties by creating an impetus at the national level for states parties to ensure effective national implementation of the rights guaranteed in the ICESCR; and,

— It would further support the interdependence and indivisibility of civil, political, economic, social and cultural rights.

Written Statement Submitted by Amnesty International, U.N. Doc. E/CN.4/2003/NGO/182 (Mar. 17, 2003).

The Committee on Economic, Social and Cultural Rights submitted a Draft Optional Protocol to the Commission on Human Rights in 1997. *See Draft Optional Protocol to the International Covenant on Economic, Social and Cultural Rights*, U.N. Doc. E/CN.4/1997/105. Since then, the Commission has received comments and reports on the draft from states, the U.N. High Commissioner on Human Rights, NGOs, and an independent expert. *See, e.g., Report of the High Commissioner for Human Rights on Economic, Social and Cultural Rights*, U.N. Doc. E/CN.4/2000/49 (Jan. 14, 2000); *Report of the Independent Expert to Examine the Question of a Draft Optional Protocol to the International Covenant on Economic, Social and Cultural Rights*, U.N. Doc. E/CN.4/2002/57 (Feb. 12, 2002). In 2003, the Commission organized a Working Group to continue efforts toward implementation (anticipated in four to five years from that time). Commission on Human Rights Resolution 2003/18, *Question of the Realization in all Countries of the Economic, Social and Cultural Rights Contained in the Universal Declaration of Human Rights and in the International Covenant on Economic, Social and Cultural Rights, and Study of Special Problems which the Developing Countries Face in their Efforts to Achieve these Human Rights*, U.N. Doc. E/CN.4/2003/L.11/Add.3 (Apr. 22, 2003).

The complaints procedures available under the Optional Protocol, when finalized, are likely to be similar to existing mechanisms recently adopted under other human rights instruments such as CEDAW (*see* discussion of Optional Protocol to CEDAW in Section C *infra*). As an "optional" instrument, the Protocol would be available only with regard to complaints against those states that have ratified the Protocol itself. Further, it was recommended that no inter-state complaints procedure be included in the draft. It should be noted, however, that such state-to-state complaint mechanisms are generally met with deafening silence despite their availability in other international human rights instruments. In its current form, the draft allows individuals as well as third parties such as NGOs to submit complaints on behalf of other individuals or groups affected by violations of the ICESCR. *See generally*, Kitty Arambulo, *Drafting an Optional Protocol to the International Covenant on Economic, Social and Cultural Rights: Can an Ideal Become Reality?*, 2 U.C. Davis J. Int'l L. & Pol'y 111 (1996). A group of NGOs has created a Coalition for the Adoption of the Optional Protocol to the International Covenant on Economic, Social and Cultural Rights. *See* http://www.escr-net.org/EngGeneral/disp-breakingnews.asp?tbnid=10 (last visited July 15, 2003).

10. The United States has signed, but not ratified, the Covenant. The following article discusses the ambivalence that still impedes the full implementation of these rights.

ALICIA ELY YAMIN, REFLECTIONS ON DEFINING, UNDERSTANDING, AND MEASURING POVERTY IN TERMS OF VIOLATIONS OF ECONOMIC AND SOCIAL RIGHTS UNDER INTERNATIONAL LAW

4 Geo. J. Fighting Poverty 273, 294–95 (1997)

Historical Context: The Twin Regimes Under International Human Rights Law

At the 1993 World Conference on Human Rights, held in Vienna, a statement on behalf of the Committee on Economic, Social and Cultural Rights lamented:

The shocking reality *** is that States and the international community as a whole continue to tolerate all too often breaches of economic, social and cultural rights which, if they occurred in relation to civil and political rights, would provoke expressions of horror and outrage and would lead to concerted calls for immediate remedial action. In effect, despite the rhetoric, violations of civil and political rights continue to be treated as though they were far more serious, and more patently intolerable, than massive and direct denials of economic and social rights.

At that conference, held at a time when hopes were high due to the end of the Cold War and the emergence of a new and potentially more fruitful role for the United Nations, there were vehement reaffirmations of the nature of all human rights as "universal, indivisible, and interdependent and interrelated." At the same time, fears were expressed that "democracy, stability and peace cannot long survive in conditions of chronic poverty, dispossession and neglect." To understand the significance of capability theory for measuring compliance with and furthering the implementation of economic and social rights necessary to combat poverty, it is worth revisiting the evolution of the two distinct sets of rights—civil and political, constructed separately from economic, social, and cultural—whose equality "has often been more honored in the breach than in observance."

After the Universal Declaration of Human Rights was adopted unanimously by the United Nations General Assembly in 1948, eighteen years passed before the rest of the so-called International Bill of Rights came into existence in 1966, and another ten years passed before it entered into force in 1976. The International Covenant on Civil and Political Rights (ICCPR) and its twin, the ICESCR, at once proclaimed their interdependence while establishing separate and distinctly unequal regimes, which were to have relevance not only for the provisions in those respective covenants, but also for civil and political versus economic and social rights generally.

For example, in contrast to the ICCPR, which imposes an immediate obligation "to respect and ensure" the rights it contains and thereby to take any action necessary to make those rights effective in fact as well as law, the ICESCR commits states to take steps towards "achieving progressively the full realization of the rights" included in the Covenant. The assumption of the obligations is instructive: civil and political rights were framed as uncompromising, while economic, social and cultural rights were framed as essentially hortatory because of their contingency upon the "available resources" of the state. Moreover, not only did the Western nations that appropriated the international human rights movement relegate economic and social norms to a lesser status conceptually, but they also ensured the paralysis of the promotion of such claims as rights by crippling the mechanisms through which the ICESCR could be monitored. The responsibility for monitoring compliance with the ICESCR was placed initially in a Working Group composed of governmental representatives and later of government-appointed experts. As a result, supervising implementation was entirely politicized and only added to the general perception of economic and social rights not as real rights but as tools of political agendas.

The Economic, Social, and Cultural Rights Committee (the Committee), which replaced the Working Group in 1986, did away with many of the most glaring flaws that had plagued its predecessor. Indeed, as Matthew Craven observed, "it is undoubtedly the case that in the relatively short period of time that the Committee on Economic, Social, and Cultural Rights has been charged with monitoring and implementation of the Covenant, it has transformed the supervision system beyond recognition." The

Committee has made remarkably rapid and significant modifications in its functions, such as: receiving written and oral communications from non-governmental organizations (NGOs); providing state-specific observations when considering state reports; engaging in discussion and interchange with experts from varied disciplines; and drafting General Comments to elucidate the meaning of the obligations under different articles of the ICESCR. ***

DEVELOPMENT OF THE LAW OF THE COVENANT

In 1986, a group of international law experts, convened by the International Commission of Jurists, the Faculty of Law of the University of Limburg and the Urban Morgan Institute for Human Rights, met to discuss the nature and scope of the obligations of State Parties to the International Covenant on Economic, Social and Cultural Rights. The document that resulted—The *Limburg Principles on the Implementation of the International Covenant on Economic, Social and Cultural Rights*[1] ("Limburg Principles") confirms that violations of the Covenant implicate the law of state responsibility, and specifies conduct that constitutes a violation.

While the Limburg Principles have no legally binding force, they draw upon the expert opinion of prominent leaders in the human rights field including lawyers, members of the United Nations Committee on Economic, Social and Cultural Rights, and members of academia, thus representing an authoritative summary of the state of international human rights law as relevant to the Covenant.

In 1997, another group of human rights scholars met in the Netherlands to reaffirm and update the Limburg Principles. The Maastricht Guidelines[2] affirm that "as in the case of civil and political rights, the failure by a state party to comply with a treaty obligation concerning economic, social, and cultural rights is, under international law, a violation of that treaty." Like the Limburg Principles, The Maastricht Guidelines include minimum core obligations of the state parties, emphasize the significance of the Covenant on Economic and Social Rights, and propose remedies in response to violations of the Covenant.

THE MAASTRICHT GUIDELINES ON VIOLATIONS OF ECONOMIC, SOCIAL AND CULTURAL RIGHTS

U.N. Doc. E/C.12/2000/13, at 16–22

I.   The Significance of Economic, Social and Cultural Rights

1. Since the Limburg Principles were adopted in 1986, the economic and social conditions have declined at alarming rates for over 1.6 billion people, while they have advanced also at a dramatic pace for more than a quarter of the world's population. The gap between rich and poor has doubled in the last three decades, with the poorest fifth of the world's population receiving 1.4 per cent of the global income and the

---

[1]   U.N. Doc. E/CN.4/1987/17 (1987), *reprinted in* 9 HUM. RTS. L.J. 122 (1987).

[2]   The Maastricht Guidelines are *reprinted in* INT'L COMM'N OF JURISTS, ECONOMIC, SOCIAL, AND CULTURAL RIGHTS: A COMPILATION OF ESSENTIAL DOCUMENTS, 82–86 (1997).

richest fifth 85 per cent. The impact of these disparities on the lives of people—especially the poor—is dramatic and renders the enjoyment of economic, social and cultural rights illusory for a significant portion of humanity.

2. Since the end of the Cold War, there has been a trend in all regions of the world to reduce the role of the State and to rely on the market to resolve problems of human welfare, often in response to conditions generated by international and national financial markets and institutions and in an effort to attract investments from the multinational enterprises whose wealth and power exceed that of many States.***

3. There have also been significant legal developments enhancing economic, social and cultural rights since 1986, including the emerging jurisprudence of the Committee on Economic, Social and Cultural Rights and the adoption of instruments, such as the revised European Social Charter of 1996 and the Additional Protocol to the European Charter providing for a System of Collective Complaints, and the San Salvador Protocol to the American Convention on Human Rights in the Area of Economic, Social and Cultural Rights of 1988. Governments have made firm commitments to address more effectively economic, social and cultural rights within the framework of seven United Nations world summit conferences (1992–1996). Moreover, the potential exists for improved accountability for violations of economic, social and cultural rights through the proposed optional protocols to the International Covenant on Economic, Social and Cultural Rights and the Convention on the Elimination of All Forms of Discrimination against Women. [*See* discussion of CEDAW, in Section C *infra*.] Significant developments within national civil society movements and regional and international NGOs in the field of economic, social and cultural rights have taken place.

4. It is now undisputed that all human rights are indivisible, interdependent, interrelated and of equal importance for human dignity. Therefore, States are as responsible for violations of economic, social and cultural rights as they are for violations of civil and political rights.***

II.   The Meaning Of Violations Of Economic, Social And Cultural Rights

Obligations to respect, protect and fulfil

6. [E]conomic, social and cultural rights impose three different types of obligations on States: the obligations to respect, protect and fulfil. Failure to perform any one of these three obligations constitutes a violation of such rights. The obligation to respect requires States to refrain from interfering with the enjoyment of economic, social and cultural rights. Thus, the right to housing is violated if the State engages in arbitrary forced evictions. The obligation to protect requires States to prevent violations of such rights by third parties. Thus, the failure to ensure that private employers comply with basic labour standards may amount to a violation of the right to work or the right to just and favourable conditions of work. The obligation to fulfil requires States to take appropriate legislative, administrative, budgetary, judicial and other measures towards the full realization of such rights. Thus, the failure of States to provide essential primary health care to those in need may amount to a violation.

Obligations of conduct and of result

7. The obligations to respect, protect and fulfil each contain elements of obligation of conduct and obligation of result. The obligation of conduct requires action reasonably calculated to realize the enjoyment of a particular right. In the case of the right

to health, for example, the obligation of conduct could involve the adoption and implementation of a plan of action to reduce maternal mortality. The obligation of result requires States to achieve specific targets to satisfy a detailed substantive standard. With respect to the right to health, for example, the obligation of result requires the reduction of maternal mortality to levels agreed at the 1994 Cairo International Conference on Population and Development and the 1995 Beijing Fourth World Conference on Women.

Margin of discretion

8. [T]he burden is on the State to demonstrate that it is making measurable progress toward the full realization of the rights in question. The State cannot use the "progressive realization" provisions in article 2 of the Covenant as a pretext for non-compliance. Nor can the State justify derogations or limitations of rights recognized in the Covenant because of different social, religious and cultural backgrounds.

Minimum core obligations

9. Violations of the Covenant occur when a State fails to satisfy what the Committee on Economic, Social and Cultural Rights has referred to as a "minimum core obligation" to ensure the satisfaction of, at the very least, minimum essential levels of each of the rights.*** Thus, for example, a State party in which any significant number of individuals is deprived of essential foodstuffs, of essential primary health care, of basic shelter and housing, or of the most basic forms of education is, prima facie, violating the Covenant. Such minimum core obligations apply irrespective of the availability of resources of the country concerned or any other factors and difficulties.

Availability of resources

10. [F]ull realization of the rights may depend upon the availability of adequate financial and material resources. Nonetheless,*** resource scarcity does not relieve States of certain minimum obligations ***.

State policies

11. A violation *** occurs when a State pursues, by action or omission, a policy or practice which deliberately contravenes or ignores obligations of the Covenant ***. Furthermore, any discrimination on grounds of race, colour, sex, language, religion, political or other opinion, national or social origin, property, birth or other status with the purpose or effect of nullifying or impairing the equal enjoyment or exercise of economic, social and cultural rights constitutes a violation of the Covenant.***

Inability to comply

13. *** A State claiming that it is unable to carry out its obligations for reasons beyond its control has the burden of proving that this is the case.***

Violations through acts of commission

14. Violations of economic, social and cultural rights can occur through the direct action of States or other entities insufficiently regulated by States. Examples of such violations include:

(a) The formal removal or suspension of legislation necessary for the continued enjoyment of an economic, social and cultural right that is currently enjoyed;

(b) The active denial of such rights to particular individuals or groups, whether through legislated or enforced discrimination;

(c) The active support for measures adopted by third parties which are inconsistent with economic, social and cultural rights;***

(e) The adoption of any deliberately retrogressive measure that reduces the extent to which any such right is guaranteed;***

Violations through acts of omission

15. Violations of economic, social and cultural rights can also occur through the omission or failure of States to take necessary measures stemming from legal obligations. Examples of such violations include: ***

(b) The failure to reform or repeal legislation which is manifestly inconsistent with an obligation of the Covenant;

(c) The failure to enforce legislation or put into effect policies designed to implement provisions of the Covenant;

(d) The failure to regulate activities of individuals or groups so as to prevent them from violating economic, social and cultural rights;

(e) The failure to utilize the maximum of available resources towards the full realization of the Covenant;

(f) The failure to monitor the realization of economic, social and cultural rights, including the development and application of criteria and indicators for assessing compliance;***

(h) The failure to implement without delay a right which it is required by the Covenant to provide immediately;

(i) The failure to meet a generally accepted international minimum standard of achievement, which is within its powers to meet;

(j) The failure of a State to take into account its international legal obligations in the field of economic, social and cultural rights when entering into bilateral or multilateral agreements with other States, international organizations or multinational corporations.

III. Responsibility for Violations

State responsibility

16. The violations referred to in section II are in principle imputable to the State within whose jurisdiction they occur. As a consequence, the State responsible must establish mechanisms to correct such violations, including monitoring investigation, prosecution, and remedies for victims.

Alien domination or occupation

17. Under circumstances of alien domination, deprivations of economic, social and cultural rights may be imputable to the conduct of the State exercising effective control over the territory in question. This is true under conditions of colonialism, other forms of alien domination and military occupation. The dominating or occupying power bears

responsibility for violations of economic, social and cultural rights. There are also circumstances in which States acting in concert violate economic, social and cultural rights.

Acts by non-State entities

18. The obligation to protect includes the State's responsibility to ensure that private entities or individuals, including transnational corporations over which they exercise jurisdiction, do not deprive individuals of their economic, social and cultural rights. States are responsible for violations of economic, social and cultural rights that result from their failure to exercise due diligence in controlling the behaviour of such non-State actors.

Acts by international organizations

19. The obligations of States to protect economic, social and cultural rights extend also to their participation in international organizations, where they act collectively. It is particularly important for States to use their influence to ensure that violations do not result from the programmes and policies of the organizations of which they are members. It is crucial for the elimination of violations of economic, social and cultural rights for international organizations, including international financial institutions, to correct their policies and practices so that they do not result in deprivation of economic, social and cultural rights.

IV. Victims of Violations

Individuals and groups

20. [B]oth individuals and groups can be victims of violations of economic, social and cultural rights. Certain groups suffer disproportionate harm in this respect, such as lower-income groups, women, indigenous and tribal peoples, occupied populations, asylum seekers, refugees and internally displaced persons, minorities, the elderly, children, landless peasants, persons with disabilities and the homeless.

Criminal sanctions

21. Victims of violations of economic, social and cultural rights should not face criminal sanctions purely because of their status as victims, for example, through laws criminalizing persons for being homeless.***

V. Remedies and Other Responses to Violations

Access to remedies

22. Any person or group who is a victim of a violation of an economic, social or cultural right should have access to effective judicial or other appropriate remedies at both national and international levels.

Adequate reparation

23. All victims of violations of economic, social and cultural rights are entitled to adequate reparation, which may take the form of restitution, compensation, rehabilitation and satisfaction or guarantees of non-repetition.***

National institutions

25. Promotional and monitoring bodies such as national ombudsman institutions and human rights commissions, should address violations of economic, social and cultural rights as vigorously as they address violations of civil and political rights.***

Notes and Questions

1. *Classification of State Obligations.* The classification of state obligations in terms of duties to respect, protect, assist and fulfill is generally attributed to HENRY SHUE, BASIC RIGHTS: SUBSISTENCE, AFFLUENCE, AND U.S. FOREIGN POLICY (1980). Shue's analysis debunked the negative rights/positive rights dichotomy by showing that both categories of rights evoke similar correlative duties.

2. *Comparison of Rights Categories.* List examples of how the state can satisfy its obligations to (a) respect; (b) protect; and (c) fulfill the right to food. Do the same with a classic first generation right, *e.g.*, freedom of speech, or the right to a fair trial. What analogies can be drawn?

COMMITTEE ON ECONOMIC, SOCIAL, AND CULTURAL RIGHTS, GENERAL COMMENT NO. 3: THE NATURE OF STATES PARTIES OBLIGATIONS

U.N. Doc. E/1991/23 (Fifth Session, 1990)

1. Article 2 is of particular importance to a full understanding of the Covenant and must be seen as having a dynamic relationship with all of the other provisions of the Covenant. It describes the nature of the general legal obligations undertaken by States parties to the Covenant. Those obligations include both what may be termed *** obligations of conduct and obligations of result. While the Covenant provides for progressive realization and acknowledges the constraints due to the limits of available resources, it also imposes various obligations which are of immediate effect.***

2. [T]he undertaking in article 2 (1) "to take steps" *** is not qualified or limited by other considerations. The full meaning of the phrase can also be gauged by noting some of the different language versions. In English the undertaking is "to take steps," in French it is "to act" ("s'engage à agir") and in Spanish it is "to adopt measures" ("a adoptar medidas"). Thus while the full realization of the relevant rights may be achieved progressively, steps towards that goal must be taken within a reasonably short time after the Covenant's entry into force for the States concerned.***

3. The means which should be used in order to satisfy the obligation to take steps are stated in article 2 (1) to be "all appropriate means, including particularly the adoption of legislative measures."***

4. The Committee *** wishes to emphasize, however, that the adoption of legislative measures, as specifically foreseen by the Covenant, is by no means exhaustive of the obligations of States parties. Rather, the phrase "by all appropriate means" must be given its full and natural meaning.***

5. Among the measures which might be considered appropriate, in addition to legislation, is the provision of judicial remedies with respect to rights which may, in accordance with the national legal system, be considered justiciable. The Committee notes, for example, that the enjoyment of the rights recognized, without discrimination, will often be appropriately promoted, in part, through the provision of judicial or other effective remedies ***. In addition, there are a number of other provisions in the International Covenant on Economic, Social and Cultural Rights, including articles 3, 7 (a) (i), 8, 10 (3), 13 (2) (a), (3) and (4) and 15 (3) which would seem to be capable of immediate application by judicial and other organs in many national legal systems.

Any suggestion that the provisions indicated are inherently non-self-executing would seem to be difficult to sustain.***

7. Other measures which may also be considered "appropriate" for the purposes of article 2 (1) include, but are not limited to, administrative, financial, educational and social measures.

8. The Committee notes that the undertaking "to take steps *** by all appropriate means including particularly the adoption of legislative measures" neither requires nor precludes any particular form of government or economic system being used as the vehicle for the steps in question, provided only that it is democratic and that all human rights are thereby respected. Thus, in terms of political and economic systems the Covenant is neutral and its principles cannot accurately be described as being predicated exclusively upon the need for, or the desirability of a socialist or a capitalist system, or a mixed, centrally planned, or laissez-faire economy, or upon any other particular approach. In this regard, the Committee reaffirms that the rights recognized in the Covenant are susceptible of realization within the context of a wide variety of economic and political systems, provided only that the interdependence and indivisibility of the two sets of human rights, as affirmed *inter alia* in the preamble to the Covenant, is recognized and reflected in the system in question. The Committee also notes the relevance in this regard of other human rights and in particular the right to development.

9. The principal obligation of result reflected in article 2 (1) is to take steps "with a view to achieving progressively the full realization of the rights recognized" in the Covenant. The term "progressive realization" is often used to describe the intent of this phrase. The concept of progressive realization constitutes a recognition of the fact that full realization of all economic, social and cultural rights will generally not be able to be achieved in a short period of time.*** Nevertheless, the fact that realization over time, or in other words progressively, is foreseen under the Covenant should not be misinterpreted as depriving the obligation of all meaningful content. It is on the one hand a necessary flexibility device, reflecting the realities of the real world and the difficulties involved for any country in ensuring full realization of economic, social and cultural rights. On the other hand, the phrase *** imposes an obligation to move as expeditiously and effectively as possible towards that goal. Moreover, any deliberately retrogressive measures in that regard would require the most careful consideration and would need to be fully justified by reference to the totality of the rights provided for in the Covenant and in the context of the full use of the maximum available resources.

10. On the basis of the extensive experience gained by the Committee, as well as by the body that preceded it, over a period of more than a decade of examining States parties' reports the Committee is of the view that a minimum core obligation to ensure the satisfaction of, at the very least, minimum essential levels of each of the rights is incumbent upon every State party. Thus, for example, a State party in which any significant number of individuals is deprived of essential foodstuffs, of essential primary health care, of basic shelter and housing, or of the most basic forms of education is, *prima facie*, failing to discharge its obligations under the Covenant.*** By the same token, it must be noted that any assessment as to whether a State has discharged its minimum core obligation must also take account of resource constraints applying within the country concerned. Article 2 (1) obligates each State party to take the necessary steps "to the maximum of its available resources." In order for a State party to

be able to attribute its failure to meet at least its minimum core obligations to a lack of available resources it must demonstrate that every effort has been made to use all resources that are at its disposition in an effort to satisfy, as a matter of priority, those minimum obligations.

11. The Committee wishes to emphasize, however, that even where the available resources are demonstrably inadequate, the obligation remains for a State party to strive to ensure the widest possible enjoyment of the relevant rights under the prevailing circumstances. Moreover, the obligations to monitor the extent of the realization, or more especially of the non-realization, of economic, social and cultural rights, and to devise strategies and programmes for their promotion, are not in any way eliminated as a result of resource constraints.***

12. Similarly, the Committee underlines the fact that even in times of severe resources constraints whether caused by a process of adjustment, of economic recession, or by other factors the vulnerable members of society can and indeed must be protected by the adoption of relatively low-cost targeted programmes.***

13. A final element of article 2 (1), to which attention must be drawn, is that the undertaking given by all States parties is "to take steps, individually and through international assistance and cooperation, especially economic and technical ***." The Committee notes that the phrase "to the maximum of its available resources" was intended by the drafters of the Covenant to refer to both the resources existing within a State and those available from the international community through international cooperation and assistance.***

14. The Committee wishes to emphasize that in accordance with Articles 55 and 56 of the Charter of the United Nations, with well-established principles of international law, and with the provisions of the Covenant itself, international cooperation for development and thus for the realization of economic, social and cultural rights is an obligation of all States. It is particularly incumbent upon those States which are in a position to assist others in this regard. The Committee notes in particular the importance of the Declaration on the Right to Development adopted by the General Assembly in its resolution 41/128 of 4 December 1986 and the need for States parties to take full account of all of the principles recognized therein. It emphasizes that, in the absence of an active programme of international assistance and cooperation on the part of all those States that are in a position to undertake one, the full realization of economic, social and cultural rights will remain an unfulfilled aspiration in many countries.***

THE ICESCR COMMITTEE

The ICESCR Committee was established in 1986 to supervise compliance by states parties with their obligations under the ICESCR. The Committee has issued Reporting Guidelines for states to follow when submitting their regular reports. Also, through the drafting of General Comments, the ICESCR Committee seeks to achieve three principal objectives: (1) development of the normative content of the rights recognized in the Covenant; (2) acting as a catalyst to state action in developing national 'benchmarks' and devising appropriate mechanisms for establishing accountability, and providing means of vindication to aggrieved individuals and groups at the national level; and (3) holding states accountable at the international level through the examination of reports.

COMMITTEE ON ECONOMIC, SOCIAL AND CULTURAL RIGHTS, REPORTING GUIDELINES

U.N. Doc. E/1991/23, Annex IV

[These guidelines, adopted by Committee in 1991 and subject to revision over time, regulate the form and contents of the reports that states parties to the ICESCR are required to submit. An initial report is required within two years of ratification and periodic reports are due every five years thereafter.]

The right to adequate housing

1. Please furnish detailed statistical information about the housing situation in your country.

2. Please provide detailed information about those groups within your society that are vulnerable and disadvantaged with regard to housing. Indicate in particular:

   (i) The number of homeless individuals and families;

   (ii) The number of individuals and families currently inadequately housed and without ready access to basic amenities ***;

   (iii) The number of persons currently classified as living in 'illegal' settlements or housing;

   (iv) The number of persons evicted within the last five years.***

3. (c) Please provide information on the existence of any laws affecting the realization of the right to housing.

   (d) Please provide information on all other measures taken to fulfil the right to housing, including:

      (i) Measures taken to encourage 'enabling strategies' whereby local community-based organizations and the 'informal sector' can build housing and related services. Are such organizations free to operate? Do they receive Government funding?

      (ii) Measures taken by the State to build housing units and to increase other construction of affordable, rental housing.

      (iii) Measures taken to release unutilized, under-utilized or mis-utilized land;

      (iv) Financial measures taken by the State including details of the budget of the Ministry of Housing or other relevant Ministry.***

4. Please give details on any difficulties or shortcomings encountered in the fulfilment of the rights enshrined in article 11 and on the measures taken to remedy these situations (if not already described in the present report).

PROBLEM ON THE RIGHT TO HOUSING IN THE DOMINICAN REPUBLIC

The following problem on the right to housing in the Dominican Republic illustrates this procedure of state reporting, provision of data by NGOs, and release of Concluding Observations to the government and the public.

I. Background

Arawak-speaking people, known as the Tainos, originally occupied the island of Hispaniola, of which the Dominican Republic forms the eastern two-thirds and Haiti the remainder. In 1492, the Tainos welcomed Columbus in his first voyage to the Americas. Columbus arrived at the island which he called *La Espaniola* and established it as his main base for the further conquest of the region. After failing to successfully enslave the Tainos, beginning in 1503 the Spanish brought African slaves to the Dominican Republic to provide labor for the plantations. By 1548 the Spanish had virtually exterminated the peaceful Taino Indians. In 1697, the Western part of the island came under French control, with the east remaining under Spanish control. In 1844, the Dominican Republic was established as an independent state.

Today, the Dominican Republic is a representative democracy that divides its national powers among three branches: the independent executive, legislative and judicial branches. Similar to the United States executive branch, the President appoints the cabinet, executes laws passed by the legislative branch, and is commander-in-chief of the armed forces. The President and Vice President run for office on the same ticket and are elected by direct vote for four-year terms. Legislative power is exercised by a bicameral Congress made up of a 30-member Senate and 120-member Chamber of Deputies. The 16-member Supreme Court is appointed by a National Judicial Council, which is nominated by the three major political parties in the Dominican Republic. The Supreme Court hears appeals from lower courts and chooses members of the lower courts.

With a population of 8.4 million, the Dominican Republic is classified as a middle-income developing country primarily dependent on agriculture, trade and services. The most important service in the Dominican Republic is tourism, which accounts for more than $1 billion in annual earnings. The largest exports are sugar, coffee, gold, silver, ferronickel, cacao, tobacco and meats, which account for $661 million. The largest imports are foodstuffs, petroleum, industrial raw materials and capital goods, which account for $6.6 billion.

II. Forced Evictions

The right to adequate housing is established under Article 8 of the Dominican Republic Constitution. As tourism increasingly became a major industry, the government realized that a visitor's first view of Santo Domingo consisted of a large number of slums built by the riverbanks. Between 1986 and 1992, the city of Santo Domingo initiated an "urban renewal" campaign that ousted over 30,000 families from their homes in the poorer districts of the city. The government forcibly evicted persons without providing any alternative housing for them, or removed them to distant places where they were separated from their communities. Many families waiting to be relocated to new housing found their "new" homes were given to other families who were not homeless; those responsible for the allocation of housing units had given the apartments to their political friends.

Most of the housing in the barrios and poor "shantytowns" that made up the "informal sector" of the city was built on state-owned land. Because the people were poor, the state permissively allowed the squatter settlements to spring up on state property. Once the land value increased, the state began evicting the people; arguing that the settlements were unhealthy, polluted, dangerous, and uninhabitable, the state sent the army into the *barrios*.

The most characteristic feature of the evictions was violence. Houses were demolished while inhabitants were still inside; shock troops were used to intimidate and terrorize people; the police took the place of judges; household goods were vandalized or stolen; public services to the barrios were cut off; and notice of eviction was given on the day a family was to be thrown out.

III. International Oversight

The government of the Dominican Republic received the following concluding Observations on its Housing Report from the United Nations Committee on Economic, Social and Cultural Rights:

COMMITTEE ON ECONOMIC, SOCIAL AND CULTURAL RIGHTS, CONCLUDING OBSERVATIONS ON THE REPORT OF THE DOMINICAN REPUBLIC

U.N. Doc. E/C.12/1994/15, at 3.

[The ICESCR Committee notes that the "detailed and precise information" that it has received over several years from NGO sources indicates, *inter alia*, that: 30,000 families in the Zona Norte are threatened with forced eviction; thousands of families have already been evicted from Faro a Colon and from other specified cities; 3,000 relocated families received neither compensation nor relocation allowances; and the housing conditions of some 750 families relocated after Hurricane David in 1979 are grossly inadequate. That information was relayed to the Government by the Committee.]

10. While the Government presented the Committee with information as to the achievements and shortcomings of its various policies in relation to housing, the Committee did not receive any information which would lead it to conclude that these problems do not exist or have been adequately addressed.

11. It therefore expresses its serious concern at the nature and magnitude of the problems relating to forced evictions and calls upon the Government of the Dominican Republic to take urgent measures ***. [W]henever an inhabited dwelling is either demolished or its inhabitants evicted, the Government is under an obligation to ensure that adequate alternative housing is provided.***

13. [T]he Committee was also informed that less than 17 percent of Government-built housing units are provided to the poorest sectors of society.

14. On the basis of the detailed information available to it the Committee also wishes to emphasize its concern at the 'militarization' of La Cienaga—Los Guandules, the long-standing prohibition on improving or upgrading existing dwellings for the more than 60,000 residents of the area, and the inadequate and heavily polluted living conditions. The situation is especially problematic given that these communities were originally established as relocation areas for evictees in the 1950s. Since that time the Government has failed to confer legal security of tenure on residents or to provide basic civic services.***

16. The Committee is also concerned at the effects presidential decrees can and do have upon the enjoyment of the rights recognized in the Covenant. It wishes to emphasize in this regard the importance of establishing judicial remedies which can be

invoked, including in relation to Presidential decrees, in order to seek redress for housing rights violations. The Committee is not aware of any housing rights matters that have been considered by the Supreme Court in relation to article 8(15)(b) of the Constitution [establishing a right to housing].***

19. All persons residing in extremely precarious conditions such as those residing under bridges, on cliff sides, in homes dangerously close to rivers, ravine dwellers, residents of Barrancones and Puente Durate, and the more than 3,000 families evicted between 1986–1994 who have yet to receive relocation sites *** should all be ensured, in a rapid manner, the provision of adequate housing in full conformity with the provisions of the Covenant.

20. The Government should confer security of tenure on all dwellers lacking such protection at present, with particular reference to areas threatened with forced eviction.***

23. The Committee requests the Government to apply existing housing rights provisions in the Constitution and for that purpose to take measures to facilitate and promote their application. Such measures could include: (a) adoption of comprehensive housing rights legislation; (b) legal recognition of the right of affected communities to information concerning any governmental plans actually or potentially affecting their rights; (c) adoption of urban reform legislation which recognizes the contribution of civil society in implementing the Covenant and addresses questions of security of tenure, regularization of land-ownership arrangements, etc.

24. In order to achieve progressively the right to housing, the Government is requested to undertake, to the maximum of available resources, the provision of basic services (water, electricity, drainage, sanitation, refuse disposal, etc.) to dwellings and ensure that public housing is provided to those groups of society with the greatest need.***

25. [T]he Government is urged to give consideration to initiatives designed to promote the participation of those affected in the design and implementation of housing policies. Such initiatives could include: (a) a formal commitment to facilitating popular participation in the urban development process; (b) legal recognition of community-based organizations; (c) the establishment of a system of community housing finance designed to open more lines of credit for poorer social sectors; (d) enhancing the role of municipal authorities in the housing sector; (e) improving coordination between the various governmental institutions responsible for housing and considering the creation of a single governmental housing agency.

IV. Problem

You are the government official charged with responding to the Observations. You have been asked to submit proposals to the President of the Republic on how the government can (1) respect, (2) protect, and (3) fulfill the right to housing. Your proposals should address the specific problems raised in the Observations, and include both legislative and programmatic initiatives for resolving them. Consider the ESC Committee's General Comment on Housing below for guidance as to the content of the right to housing.

COMMITTEE ON ECONOMIC, SOCIAL AND CULTURAL RIGHTS, GENERAL COMMENT NO. 4 (1991), THE RIGHT TO ADEQUATE HOUSING

U.N. Doc. E/1992/23, Annex III

The right to adequate housing (art. 11 (1) of the Covenant)

1. Pursuant to article 11(1) of the Covenant, States parties 'recognize the right of everyone to an adequate standard of living for himself and his family, including adequate food, clothing and housing, and to the continuous improvement of living conditions.'***

7. In the Committee's view, the right to housing should not be interpreted in a narrow or restrictive sense which equates it with, for example, the shelter provided by merely having a roof over one's head or views shelter exclusively as a commodity. Rather it should be seen as the right to live somewhere in security, peace and dignity.***

8. *** While adequacy is determined in part by social, economic, cultural, climatic, ecological and other factors, [there are] certain aspects of the right that must be taken into account ***. They include the following:

(a) *Legal security of tenure.* Tenure takes a variety of forms, including rental (public and private) accommodation, cooperative housing, lease, owner-occupation, emergency housing and informal settlements ***. Notwithstanding the type of tenure, all persons should possess a degree of security of tenure which guarantees legal protection against forced eviction, harassment and other threats.***

(b) *Availability of services, materials, facilities and infrastructure.**** All [persons] should have sustainable access to natural and common resources, safe drinking water, energy for cooking, heating and lighting, sanitation and washing facilities, means of food storage, refuse disposal, site drainage and emergency services;

(c) *Affordability.* [F]inancial costs associated with housing should be at such a level that the attainment and satisfaction of other basic needs are not threatened or compromised.***

(d) *Habitability.* Adequate housing must be habitable, in terms of providing the inhabitants with adequate space and protecting them from cold, damp, heat, rain, wind or other threats to health, structural hazards, and disease vectors .***

(e) *Accessibility.* Adequate housing must be accessible to those entitled to it. Disadvantaged groups must be accorded full and sustainable access to adequate housing resources .***

(f) *Location.* Adequate housing must be in a location which allows access to employment options, health-care services, schools, child-care centers and other social facilities. *** Similarly, housing should not be built on polluted sites nor in immediate proximity to pollution sources that threatens the right to health of the inhabitants;

(g) *Cultural adequacy.* The way housing is constructed, the building materials used and the policies supporting these must appropriately enable the expression of cultural identity and diversity of housing.

10. Regardless of the state of development of any country, there are certain steps which must be taken immediately. [M]any of the measures required to promote the right to housing would only require the abstention by the Government from certain practices and a commitment to facilitating 'self-help' by affected groups. To the extent that any such steps are considered to be beyond the maximum resources available to a State party, it is appropriate that a request be made as soon as possible for international cooperation *** and that the Committee be informed thereof.

12. [T]he Covenant clearly requires the adoption of a national housing strategy. [S]uch a strategy should reflect extensive genuine consultation with, and participation by, all of those affected, including the homeless, the inadequately housed and their representatives.***

13. Effective monitoring of the situation with respect to housing is another obligation of immediate effect. [A] State party *** must demonstrate, *inter alia*, that it has taken whatever steps are necessary *** to ascertain the full extent of homelessness and inadequate housing within its jurisdiction.***

The following sections introduce U.N. treaties that supplement the International Bill of Rights, providing implementation mechanisms that focus on specific, identity-based human rights violations. In examining these materials, consider the advantages and disadvantages of categorizing human rights protections in this way.

B. THE RACE CONVENTION

INTERNATIONAL CONVENTION ON THE ELIMINATION OF ALL FORMS OF RACIAL DISCRIMINATION

Adopted and opened for signature and ratification by General Assembly Resolution 2106 (XX) of Dec. 21, 1965 (*entered into force* Jan. 4, 1969)[3]

The States Parties to this Convention,***

Alarmed by manifestations of racial discrimination still in evidence in some areas of the world and by governmental policies based on racial superiority or hatred, such as policies of apartheid, segregation or separation,

Resolved to adopt all necessary measures for speedily eliminating racial discrimination in all its forms and manifestations,***

Have agreed as follows:

PART I

Article I

1. In this Convention, the term "racial discrimination" shall mean any distinction, exclusion, restriction or preference based on race, colour, descent, or national or ethnic origin which has the purpose or effect of nullifying or impairing the recognition, enjoyment or exercise, on an equal footing, of human rights and fundamental freedoms in the political, economic, social, cultural or any other field of public life.

---

3   The United States ratified the Treaty on Oct. 21, 1994.

2. This Convention shall not apply to distinctions, exclusions, restrictions or preferences made by a State Party to this Convention between citizens and non-citizens.***

4. Special measures taken for the sole purpose of securing adequate advancement of certain racial or ethnic groups or individuals requiring such protection as may be necessary in order to ensure such groups or individuals equal enjoyment or exercise of human rights and fundamental freedoms shall not be deemed racial discrimination ***.

Article 5

*** States Parties undertake to prohibit and to eliminate racial discrimination in all its forms and to guarantee the right of everyone, without distinction as to race, colour, or national or ethnic origin, to equality before the law, notably in the enjoyment of the following rights:

(e) Economic, social and cultural rights, in particular:

(i) The rights to work, to free choice of employment, to just and favourable conditions of work, to protection against unemployment, to equal pay for equal work, to just and favourable remuneration;

(ii) The right to form and join trade unions;

(iii) The right to housing;

(iv) The right to public health, medical care, social security and social services;

(v) The right to education and training;

(vi) The right to equal participation in cultural activities;***

Article 9

1. States Parties undertake to submit to the Secretary-General of the United Nations, for consideration by the Committee, a report on the legislative, judicial, administrative or other measures which they have adopted and which give effect to the provisions of this Convention:

(a) within one year after the entry into force of the Convention for the State concerned; and

(b) thereafter every two years and whenever the Committee so requests. The Committee may request further information from the States Parties.***

Article 11

1. If a State Party considers that another State Party is not giving effect to the provisions of this Convention, it may bring the matter to the attention of the Committee. The Committee shall then transmit the communication to the State Party concerned. Within three months, the receiving State shall submit to the Committee written explanations or statements clarifying the matter and the remedy, if any, that may have been taken by that State.***

Article 14

1. A State Party may at any time declare that it recognizes the competence of the Committee to receive and consider communications from individuals or groups of indi-

viduals within its jurisdiction claiming to be victims of a violation by that State Party of any of the rights set forth in this Convention. No communication shall be received by the Committee if it concerns a State Party which has not made such a declaration.***

OFFICE OF THE HIGH COMMISSIONER FOR HUMAN RIGHTS, RACIAL DISCRIMINATION: THE UNITED NATIONS TAKES ACTION

Available at http://www.unhchr.ch/html/menu6/2/fs12.htm

*** The Committee on the Elimination of Racial Discrimination (CERD) was the first body created by the United Nations to monitor and review actions by States to fulfil their obligations under a specific human rights agreement.*** This was a precedent. Five other committees with comparable constitutions and functions have since been created: the Human Rights Committee (which has responsibilities under the International Covenant on Civil and Political Rights), the Committee on the Elimination of Discrimination against Women, the Committee against Torture, the Committee on Economic, Social and Cultural Rights, and the Committee on the Rights of the Child.***

The Convention establishes three procedures to make it possible for CERD to review the legal, judicial, administrative and other steps taken by individual States to fulfill their obligations to combat racial discrimination. The first is the requirement that all States which ratify or accede to the Convention must submit periodic reports to CERD. A second procedure in the Convention provides for State-to-State complaints. The third procedure makes it possible for an individual or a group of persons who claim to be victims of racial discrimination to lodge a complaint with CERD against their State. This may only be done if the State concerned is a party to the Convention and has declared that it recognizes the competence of CERD to receive such complaints. This declaration had been made by 42 States as of June 9, 2004.

The Convention also provides that States which have made the declaration may establish or indicate a national body competent to receive petitions from individuals or groups who claim to be victims of violations of their rights and who have exhausted other local remedies. Only if petitioners fail to obtain satisfaction from the body indicated may they bring the matter to the Committee's attention.

(In the Programme of Action adopted by the Second World Conference to Combat Racism and Racial Discrimination in 1983, States were asked to make access to their national procedures for dealing with complaints of this kind as easy as possible. The procedures should be publicized and victims of racial discrimination should be helped to make use of them. The rules for making complaints should be simple, and complaints should be dealt with promptly. Legal aid should be available for poor victims of discrimination in civil or criminal proceedings and there should be the right to seek reparation for damages suffered.)***

CERD, in the words of the Convention, is composed of "18 experts of high moral standing and acknowledged impartiality." The members are elected for a term of four years by the States parties to the Convention. Elections take place for half the membership at two-year intervals.

The composition of CERD takes into account a fair representation of the geographical regions of the world, as well as of different civilizations and legal systems.***

States parties are required to submit comprehensive reports to the Committee every four years, with brief updating reports at intervening two-year periods. When a report comes before the Committee for examination, a representative of the country concerned may introduce it, answer questions from the experts, and comment on the observations they make. The Committee's report to the General Assembly summarizes these proceedings, and offers suggestions and recommendations.***

CERD has provided guidelines to the States parties on the preparation of their reports, and has frequently asked them for additional information. The Committee has also made general recommendations to the States parties when it has found that information on specific articles of the Convention useful to the experts in establishing the facts and summarizing their views is broadly lacking.***

The entering into force of the International Convention on the Elimination of All Forms of Racial Discrimination and the periodic review by CERD over the past 20 years of the reports of action taken by the States parties to fulfill their obligations have had positive results. In various countries these included:

Amendments to national constitutions to include provisions prohibiting racial discrimination;

Systematic reviews of existing laws and regulations to amend those which tend to perpetuate racial discrimination, or the passing of new laws to satisfy the requirements of the Convention;***

Making racial discrimination a punishable offence;

Legal guarantees against discrimination in justice, security, political rights, or access to places intended for use by the general public;

Educational programmes;

Creation of new agencies to deal with problems of racial discrimination and to protect the interests of indigenous groups;***.

Notes and Questions

1. The Race Convention addresses racial discrimination as it impacts economic, social and cultural rights as well as civil and political rights. How does this contrast with the approach to domestic anti-discrimination law in, for example, the United States? The United States ratified the Race Convention in 1994. *See* Initial Report of the United States of America to the United Nations Committee on the Elimination of Racial Discrimination, September 2000, *available at* http://www.state.gov/www/global/human_rights/cerd_report/cerd_index.html (last visited Apr. 20, 2004).

2. What role do violations of economic, social and cultural rights play in racial discrimination? Do persistent patterns of violations of such rights further marginalize and subordinate racial minorities?

3. The CERD Committee has issued significant "General Recommendations" discussing racism and other forms of intolerance as they apply to specific contexts. *See, e.g.,* Committee on the Elimination of Racial Discrimination, General Recommendation

XXIII: Indigenous Peoples (Fifty-first session, 1997) U.N. Doc. A/52/18, annex V, and Committee on the Elimination of Racial Discrimination, General Recommendation XXV: Gender Related Dimensions of Racial Discrimination U.N. Doc. A/55/18, Annex V (56th Session, 2000).

4. In 2001, the United Nations organized the World Conference Against Racism, Racial Discrimination, Xenophobia, and Related Intolerance in Durban, South Africa (August 31–September 7, 2001). Among the many important issues addressed at the conference were the implications of racism for the implementation of economic, social and cultural rights. The text of the Durban Declaration, the official final statement coming out of the conference, is *available at* http://www.unhchr.ch/html/racism/02-documents-cnt.html.

5. The World Conference provided a forum for renewed calls for reparations with regard to slavery in the United States, the Trans-Atlantic slave trade and slavery in other parts of the world. As you read the excerpts below from Randall Robinson's *The Debt: What America Owes to Blacks* and from a speech by U.S. President Bush, consider the following: Are modern states accountable under international law for slavery or the slave trade? If so, to whom should reparations be paid? By whom should they be paid? What impact does the legacy of slavery and other race-based atrocities have on contemporary implementation of economic, social, and cultural rights? What is the legal effect, if any, of President Bush's statements about the status of slavery and the slave trade?

RANDALL ROBINSON, THE DEBT: WHAT AMERICA OWES TO BLACKS 201–209 (2000)

ON JANUARY 5, 1993, Congressman John Conyers, a black Democrat from Detroit, introduced in Congress a bill to "acknowledge the fundamental injustice, cruelty, brutality, and inhumanity of slavery in the United States and the 13 American colonies between 1619 and 1865 and to establish a commission to examine the institution of slavery, subsequent *de jure* and *de facto* racial and economic discrimination against African Americans, and the impact of these forces on living African Americans, to make recommendations to the Congress on appropriate remedies, and for other purposes."

The bill, which did not ask for reparations for the descendants of slaves but merely a commission to study the effects of slavery; won from the 435-member U.S. House of Representatives only 28 cosponsors, 18 of whom were black.

The measure was referred to the House Committee on the Judiciary and from there to the House Subcommittee on Civil and Constitutional Rights. The bill has never made it out of committee.

More than twenty years ago, black activist James Foreman interrupted the Sunday morning worship service of the largely white Riverside Church in New York City and read a *Black Manifesto* which called upon American churches and synagogues to pay $500 million as "a beginning of the reparations due us as people who have been exploited and degraded, brutalized, killed and persecuted." Foreman followed by promising to penalize poor response with disruptions of the churches' program agency operations. Though Foreman's tactics were broadly criticized in the mainstream press, the issue of reparations itself elicited almost no thoughtful response. This had been the case by then for nearly a century; during which divergent strains of black thought had offered a variety of reparations proposals. The American white community had turned a deaf ear almost uniformly.

Gunnar Myrdal, a widely respected thinker, wrote of dividing up plantations into small parcels for sale to ex-slaves on long-term installment plans. He theorized that American society's failure to secure ex-slaves with an agrarian economic base had led ultimately to an entrenched segregated society; a racial caste system. But while Myrdal had seen white landowners being compensated for their land, he never once proposed recompense of any kind for the ex-slave he saw as in need of an economic base. In fact, in his book on the subject, *An American Dilemma*, Myrdal never once uses the words: reparation, restitution, indemnity or compensation.

In the early 1970s Boris Bittker, a Yale Law School professor, wrote a book, *The Case for Black Reparations*, which made the argument that slavery; Jim Crow, and a general climate of race-based discrimination in America had combined to do grievous social and economic injury to African Americans. He further argued that sustained government-sponsored violations had rendered distinctions between *de jure* and *de facto* segregation meaningless for all practical purposes. Damages, in his view, were indicated in the form of an allocation of resources to some program that could be crafted for black reparations. The book evoked little in the way of scholarly response or follow-up.***

Derrick Bell, who was teaching at Harvard Law School while I was a student there in the late 1960s, concluded [in] his review of Bittker's book [that]

> Short of a revolution, the likelihood that blacks today will obtain direct payments in compensation for their subjugation as slaves before the Emancipation Proclamation, and their exploitation as quasi-citizens since, is no better than it was in 1866, when Thaddeus Stevens recognized that his bright hope of "forty acres and a mule" for every freedman had vanished "like the baseless fabric of a vision."

If Bell is right that African Americans will not be compensated for the massive wrongs and social injuries inflicted upon them by their government, during and after slavery then there is *no* chance that America can solve its racial problems—if solving these problems means, as I believe it must, closing the yawning economic gap between blacks and whites in this country. The gap was opened by the 246-year practice of slavery. It has been resolutely nurtured since in law and public behavior. It has now ossified. It is structural. Its framing beams are disguised only by the counterfeit manners of a hypocritical governing class.

For twelve years Nazi Germany inflicted horrors upon European Jews. And Germany paid. It paid Jews individually. It paid the state of Israel. For two and a half centuries, Europe and America inflicted unimaginable horrors upon Africa and its people. Europe not only paid nothing to Africa in compensation, but followed the slave trade with the remapping of Africa for further European economic exploitation. (European governments have yet even to accede to Africa's request for the return of Africa's art treasures looted along with its natural resources during the century-long colonial era.)[4]

While President Lincoln supported a plan during the Civil War to compensate slave owners for their loss of "property" his successor, Andrew Johnson, vetoed legislation that would have provided compensation to ex-slaves.

---

4   *See supra* Ch. 1 for discussion of the issue of stolen cultural treasures.

Under the Southern Homestead Act, ex-slaves were given six months to purchase land at reasonably low rates without competition from white southerners and northern investors. But, owing to their destitution, few ex-slaves were able to take advantage of the homesteading program. The largest number that did were concentrated in Florida, numbering little more than three thousand. The soil was generally poor and unsuitable for farming purposes. In any case, the ex-slaves had no money on which to subsist for months while waiting for crops, or the scantest wherewithal to purchase the most elementary farming implements. The program failed. In sum, the United States government provided no compensation to the victims of slavery.

Perhaps I should say a bit here about why the question of reparations is critical to finding a solution to our race problems.

This question—and how blacks gather to pose it—is a good measure of our psychological readiness as a community to pull ourselves abreast here at home and around the world. I say this because no outside community can be more interested in solving our problems than we. Derrick Bell suggested in his review of Bittker's book that the white power structure would never support reparations because to do so would operate against its interests. I believe Bell is right in that view. The initiative must come from blacks, broadly, widely implacably.

But what exactly will black enthusiasm, or lack thereof, measure? There is no linear solution to any of our problems, for our problems are not merely technical in nature. By now, after 380 years of unrelenting psychological abuse, the biggest part of our problem is inside us: in how we have come to see ourselves, in our damaged capacity to validate a course for ourselves without outside approval.***

The issue here is not whether or not we can, or will, win reparations. The issue rather is whether we will fight for reparations, because we have decided for ourselves that they are our due. In 1915, into the sharp teeth of southern Jim Crow hostility Cornelius J. Jones filed a lawsuit against the United States Department of the Treasury in an attempt to recover sixty-eight million dollars for former slaves. He argued that, through a federal tax placed on raw cotton, the federal government had benefitted financially from the sale of cotton that slave labor had produced, and for which the black men, women, and children who had produced the cotton had not been paid. Jones's was a straightforward proposition. The monetary value of slaves' labor, which he estimated to be sixty-eight million dollars, had been appropriated by the United States government. A debt existed. It had to be paid to the, by then, ex-slaves or their heirs.

Where was the money?

A federal appeals court held that the United States could not be sued without its consent and dismissed the so-called Cotton Tax case. But the court never addressed Cornelius J. Jones's question about the federal government's appropriation of property—the labor of blacks who had worked the cotton fields—that had never been compensated.

Let me try to drive the point home here: through keloids of suffering, through coarse veils of damaged self-belief, lost direction, misplaced compass, shit-faced resignation, racial transmutation, black people worked long, hard, killing days, years, centuries—and they were never *paid*. The value of their labor went into others' pockets—plantation owners, northern entrepreneurs, state treasuries, the United States government.

Where was the money?

Where *is* the money?

There is a debt here.

I know of no statute of limitations either legally or morally that would extinguish it. Financial quantities are nearly as indestructible as matter. Take away here, add there, interest compounding annually, over the years, over the whole of the twentieth century.

Where is the money?

Jews have asked this question of countries and banks and corporations and collectors and any who had been discovered at the end of the slimy line holding in secret places the gold, the art, the money that was the rightful property of European Jews before the Nazi tenor. Jews have demanded what was their due and received a fair measure of it.

Clearly, how blacks respond to the challenge surrounding the simple demand for restitution will say a lot more about us *and do a lot more for us* than the demand itself would suggest. We would show ourselves to be responding as any normal people would to victimization were we to assert collectively in our demands for restitution that, for 246 years and with the complicity of the United States government, hundreds of millions of black people endured unimaginable cruelties—kidnapping, sale as livestock, deaths in the millions during terror-filled sea voyages, backbreaking toil, beatings, rapes, castrations, maimimgs, murders. We would begin a healing of our psyches were the most public case made that whole peoples lost religions, languages, customs, histories, cultures, children, mothers, fathers. It would make us more forgiving of ourselves, more self-approving, more self-understanding to see, *really see*, that on three continents and a string of islands, survivors had little choice but to piece together whole new cultures from the rubble shards of what theirs had once been. And they were never made whole. And never compensated. Not one red cent.

Left behind to gasp for self-regard in the vicious psychological wake of slavery are history's orphans played by the brave black shells of their ancient forebears, people so badly damaged that they cannot *see* the damage, or how their government may have been partly, if not largely, responsible for the disabling injury that by now has come to seem normal and unattributable.

Until America's white ruling class accepts the fact that the book never closes on massive unredressed social wrongs, America can have no future as one people. Questions must be raised, to American private, as well as, public institutions. Which American families and institutions, for instance, were endowed in perpetuity by the commerce of slavery? And how do we square things with slavery's modem victims from whom all natural endowments were stolen? What is a fair measure of restitution for this, the most important of all American human rights abuses? ***

REMARKS BY PRESIDENT BUSH ON GORÉE ISLAND, SENEGAL (JULY 8, 2003)

Available at www.whitehouse.gov/news/releases/2003/07/20030708-1.html
(last visited April 27, 2004)

*** For hundreds of years on this island peoples of different continents met in fear and cruelty. Today we gather in respect and friendship, mindful of past wrongs and dedicated to the advance of human liberty.

At this place, liberty and life were stolen and sold. Human beings were delivered and sorted, and weighed, and branded with the marks of commercial enterprises, and loaded as cargo on a voyage without return. One of the largest migrations of history was also one of the greatest crimes of history.

Below the decks, the middle passage was a hot, narrow, sunless nightmare; weeks and months of confinement and abuse and confusion on a strange and lonely sea. Some refused to eat, preferring death to any future their captors might prepare for them. Some who were sick were thrown over the side. Some rose up in violent rebellion, delivering the closest thing to justice on a slave ship. Many acts of defiance and bravery are recorded. Countless others, we will never know.

Those who lived to see land again were displayed, examined, and sold at auctions across nations in the Western Hemisphere. They entered societies indifferent to their anguish and made prosperous by their unpaid labor. There was a time in my country's history when one in every seven human beings was the property of another. In law, they were regarded only as articles of commerce, having no right to travel, or to marry, or to own possessions. Because families were often separated, many were denied even the comfort of suffering together.

For 250 years the captives endured an assault on their culture and their dignity. The spirit of Africans in America did not break. Yet the spirit of their captors was corrupted. Small men took on the powers and airs of tyrants and masters. Years of unpunished brutality and bullying and rape produced a dullness and hardness of conscience.*** A republic founded on equality for all became a prison for millions.***

*** Down through the years, African Americans have upheld the ideals of America by exposing laws and habits contradicting those ideals. The rights of African Americans were not the gift of those in authority. Those rights were granted by the Author of Life, and regained by the persistence and courage of African Americans, themselves.***

*** At every turn, the struggle for equality was resisted by many of the powerful. And some have said we should not judge their failures by the standards of a later time. Yet, in every time, there were men and women who clearly saw this sin and called it by name.

We can fairly judge the past by the standards of President John Adams, who called slavery "an evil of collossal magnitude." We can discern eternal standards in the deeds of William Wilberforce and John Quincy Adams, and Harriet Beecher Stowe, and Abraham Lincoln. These men and women, black and white, burned with a zeal for freedom, and they left behind a different and better nation. Their moral vision caused Americans to examine our hearts, to correct our Constitution, and to teach our children the dignity and equality of every person of every race. By a plan known only to Providence, the stolen sons and daughters of Africa helped to awaken the conscience of America. The very people traded into slavery helped to set America free.

My nation's journey toward justice has not been easy and it is not over. The racial bigotry fed by slavery did not end with slavery or with segregation. And many of the issues that still trouble America have roots in the bitter experience of other times. But however long the journey, our destination is set: liberty and justice for all.***

We know that these challenges can be overcome, because history moves in the direction of justice. The evils of slavery were accepted and unchanged for centuries. Yet, eventually, the human heart would not abide them. There is a voice of conscience and hope in every man and woman that will not be silenced—what Martin Luther King called a certain kind of fire that no water could put out. That flame could not be extinguished at the Birmingham jail. It could not be stamped out at Robben Island Prison. It was seen in the darkness here at Gorée Island, where no chain could bind the soul. This untamed fire of justice continues to burn in the affairs of man, and it lights the way before us.***

UNITED STATES INITIAL REPORT TO THE UNITED NATIONS COMMITTEE ON THE CONVENTION ON THE ELIMINATION OF ALL FORMS OF RACIAL DISCRIMINATION (SUBMITTED SEPTEMBER 2000)

Available at http://www1.umn.edu/humanrts/usdocs/cerdinitial.html

PART I—GENERAL ***

E. Factors Affecting Implementation

Although there has been significant progress in the improvement of race relations in the United States over the past half-century, serious obstacles remain to be overcome. Overt discrimination is far less pervasive than it was thirty years ago, yet more subtle forms of discrimination against minority individuals and groups persists in American society.*** Among the principal causative factors are:

The persistence of attitudes, policies and practices reflecting a legacy of segregation, ignorance, stereotyping, discrimination and disparities in opportunity and achievement. Inadequate enforcement of existing anti-discrimination laws due to under-funding of federal and state civil rights agencies.***

Ineffective use and dissemination of data on racial and ethnic issues and information on civil rights protection. Too many persons do not believe that racial discrimination is a common or active form of mistreatment and are therefore less supportive of race conscious remedial actions. Moreover, many minority groups do not have adequate information about government-funded programs and activities because information is not distributed in languages they can understand in often remote areas throughout the United States. This is particularly true for some American Indian and Alaska Native populations.

Economic disadvantage. In the contemporary United States, persons belonging to minority groups are disproportionately at the bottom of the income distribution curve. While it is inaccurate to equate minority status with poverty, members of minority groups are nonetheless more likely to be poor than are non-minorities. It is also true, in the United States as elsewhere, that almost every form of disease and disability is more prevalent among the poor, that the poor face higher levels of unemployment, that they achieve lower educational levels, that they are more frequently victimized by crime, and that they tend to live in environments (both urban and rural) which exacerbate these problems.

Persistent discrimination [exists] in employment and labor relations, especially in the areas of hiring, salary and compensation, but also in tenure, training, promotion, layoff and in the work environment generally. Over the past few years, for example, complaints have been leveled against several major employers including Texaco, Shoney's, General Motors, Pitney Bowes and Avis. Continued segregation and discrimination [prevail] in housing, rental and sales of homes, public accommodation and consumer goods. Even where civil rights laws prohibit segregation and discrimination in these areas, such practices continue.

Lack of equal access to business capital and credit markets. Minorities continue to have difficulty raising capital or securing loans to finance a business. Without sufficient access to such financial markets, minority entrepreneurs will continue to start and grow businesses at a much slower rate than their White counterparts. This problem further lessens the prospects of wealth creation in under-served communities, thus perpetuating the cycle of poverty that disproportionately affects minorities.

Lack of access to technology and high technology skills. Despite the rapid development of the Internet and other information technologies, minorities have participated at lower rates in the so-called "new economy" because they lack the skills necessary to fill the numerous technology jobs created everyday.***

Lack of educational opportunities. Largely because of the persistence of residential segregation and so-called "White flight" from the public school systems in many larger urban areas, minorities often attend comparatively under-funded (and thus lower-quality) primary and secondary schools. Thus minority children are often less prepared to compete for slots in competitive universities and jobs.***

Discrimination in the criminal justice system. The negative overall impact of the criminal justice system on Blacks, Hispanics and members of other minority groups is another barrier to our achieving the goals of the Convention. Various studies indicate that members of minority groups, especially Blacks and Hispanics, may be disproportionately subject to adverse treatment throughout the criminal justice process. High incarceration rates for minorities have led to the political disenfranchisement of a significant segment of the U.S. population. Moreover, many have raised concerns that incidents of police brutality seem to target disproportionately individuals belonging to racial or ethnic minorities.

Disadvantages for women and children of racial minorities. Often, the consequences of racism and racial discrimination are heightened for women and children. Whether in the criminal justice system, education, employment or health care, women and children suffer discrimination disproportionately. Startlingly high incarceration rates for minority women and children have placed them at a substantial social, economic and political disadvantage.

Health care. Persons belonging to minority groups tend to have less adequate access to health insurance and health care. Historically, ethnic and racial minorities were excluded from obtaining private insurance, and although such discriminatory practices are now prohibited by law, statistics continue to reflect that persons belonging to minority groups, particularly the poor, are less likely to have adequate health insurance than White persons. Racial and ethnic minorities also appear to have suffered disproportionately the effects of major epidemics like AIDS. For example, in 1999, 54 percent of new cases of HIV infection occurred among Blacks, even though they make up less than 15 percent of the population.

Voting. While the Voting Rights Act has made it possible for Blacks and Hispanics to obtain an equal opportunity to elect their candidates of choice to local, state, and federal office, the federal courts—since the early 1990s—have become more restrictive in permitting race-conscious apportionment of voting districts. Thus, many of the gains made by minority voters in the1970s and 1980s have been jeopardized.

Discrimination against immigrants. Whether legal or illegal, recent immigrants often encounter discrimination in employment, education and housing as a result of persistent racism and xenophobia. Some also contend that U.S. immigration law and policy is either implicitly or explicitly based on improper racial, ethnic and national criteria. Language barriers have also created difficulties of access, inter alia, to health care, education and voting rights for some.

Specific examples of these shortcomings include the following incidents:

On June 8, 1998, James Byrd, Jr., a Black man, was chained to the back of a pickup truck and dragged to his death in Jasper, Texas. Two of the three young White men who killed James Byrd were connected with White supremacist groups. The three men accused of committing this crime were successfully prosecuted under Texas law by the state of Texas, with the assistance of the U.S. Department of Justice. Two received the death penalty; the third was sentenced to life imprisonment.

One of the most high-profile cases in recent years was the videotaped beating of Rodney King by officers of the Los Angeles Police Department. After the police officers were acquitted on state charges, riots broke out in Los Angeles and in other cities throughout the country. Subsequent to these acquittals, however, two of the four officers involved were convicted on federal charges and sentenced to thirty months in prison.

In 1999, Black guests of the Adams Mark Hotel during the Black College Reunion in Daytona Beach, Florida were allegedly mistreated, including being required to wear wrist bands identifying them as guests of the hotel, while White guests did not receive such treatment. The Department of Justice filed suit against the hotel, and pursuant to a proposed settlement, the hotel chain will agree, inter alia, to adopt a comprehensive plan to ensure every hotel will be operated in a non-discriminatory fashion.

The Civil Rights Division of the U.S. Department of Justice has initiated several investigations into allegations of discriminatory highway traffic stops and discriminatory stops of persons traveling in urban areas (so-called "racial profiling") by state and local law enforcement authorities. Its investigation of the New Jersey state police led to a lawsuit and consent decree emphasizing non-discrimination in policy and practices as well as improved data collection, training, supervision and monitoring of officers. A similar agreement was reached with the Montgomery County, Maryland Police Department.

In Jackson, Mississippi more than 200 Blacks were allegedly denied home improvement loans even though they received passing scores on credit scoring systems. Black applicants were more than three times more likely to have their loan applications denied than similarly situated White applicants. The United States filed a lawsuit, which was settled in the amount of $3 million, to be paid to Black applicants who had been denied loans.

Throughout the United States, primary and secondary schools, colleges and universities, and professional sports teams use depictions of Native Americans as mascots. Native American groups have challenged these uses on the basis that they are demeaning and offensive.***

PART II (C)—IMPLEMENTATION OF SPECIFIC ARTICLES

Article 5(e) Economic Social and Cultural Rights

Economic Social and Cultural Rights. Article 5(e)(i) guarantees equality and non-discrimination with regard to the right to work, to free choice of employment, to just and favorable conditions of work, to protection against unemployment, to equal pay for equal work, and to just and favorable remuneration. As a matter of law and regulation, this obligation is met; in practice, however, significant disparities continue.***

Although some narrowing of economic status among various racial and ethnic groups has occurred in recent years, substantial gaps persist. For example, in 1998 the median incomes of White non-Hispanic households and of Asian and Pacific Islander households ($42,400 and $46,600, respectively) were much higher than those of Black and Hispanic households ($25,400 and $28,300, respectively). By one 1993 measure, the median wealth (net worth) of White households was nearly 10 times that of Black and Hispanic households. In 1998, the poverty rate among Blacks (26.1 percent) was more than triple the poverty rate of White non-Hispanics (8.2 percent). The poverty rate among Hispanics (25.6 percent) was not statistically different from that of Blacks. According to data from the 1990 decennial census, the poverty rate for American Indians, Eskimos and Aleuts was 30.9 percent in 1989. In the same year, the poverty rate was 9.8 percent for Whites, 29.5 percent for Blacks, and 14.1 percent for Asians and Pacific Islanders.

The pervasiveness of child poverty is of particular concern. Since 1993, poverty rates for children under 18 years within the United States have fallen, but differences among racial and ethnic groups remain high. Between 1993 and 1998, the poverty rate for White children fell 2.7 percentage points to 15.1 percent. The rate for Black children fell even more, from 46.1 percent to 36.7 percent, but was still twice as high as the rate for White children. The rate for Hispanic children fell from 40.9 percent in 1993 to 34.4 percent in 1998, but was not statistically different from the rate for Black children in 1998. By comparison, the rate for Asian and Pacific Islander children in 1998 was 18.0 percent, not statistically different from the rate for White children, and the same as in 1993 (18.2 percent).

In 1989, the poverty rate for American Indian, Eskimo and Aleut children was 38.3 percent. In the same year, the poverty rate was 12.1 percent for White children, 39.5 percent for Black children, and 16.7 percent for Asian and Pacific Islander children.***

With regard to other social and cultural rights, as the percentage of immigrants living in the United States has increased in recent years, larger numbers of individuals primarily speak languages other than English. While the number of individuals who speak or understand English and another language is also increasing, this diversity in languages has been met with calls for official language policies or legislation that requires that only English be spoken in the workplace. The present administration has taken the position that an "Official English" law would effectively exclude Americans who are not fully proficient in English from employment, voting, and equal participation in society and be subject to serious constitutional challenge. (Statement of Administration Policy, H.R. 123, 104th Congress).***

WILLIAM F. FELICE, THE UN COMMITTEE ON
THE ELIMINATION OF ALL FORMS OF RACIAL DISCRIMINATION:
RACE AND ECONOMIC AND SOCIAL HUMAN RIGHTS

24 Hum. Rts. Q. 205, 205–209 (2002)

*** Simplified racial categories can be misleading and dangerous, since individuals are not only a race, but also a class, gender, and sexuality. Thus, broad generalizations about race can be deceptive and groundless in individual cases. In the real world, a person does not exist only as a racial category.

According to the International Convention on the Elimination of All Forms of Racial Discrimination (CERD), race encompasses color, descent, and national or ethnic origin. "Descent" suggests social origin, such as heritage, lineage, or parentage. "National or ethnic origin" denotes linguistic, cultural, and historical roots. Thus, this broad concept of race clearly is not limited to objective, mainly physical elements, but also includes subjective and social components. The ingredients considered central to a person's "race" may, in fact, vary from place to place. Some may emphasize linguistic and cultural factors while others emphasize social reasons, but not ethnic reasons. Furthermore, nothing is permanent about all these aspects of race. Anthropologists have shown that environmental influences can profoundly change even the physical appearance of a human being in a relatively short time.

Recent scientific research on the human genome—the aggregate of genetic material encased in the heart of almost every cell of the body—has confirmed that the racial categories recognized by society are not reflected on the genetic level. Most of the scientists studying the human genome are convinced that the standard labels used to distinguish people by race have little or no biological meaning.***

A definition and understanding of race and racial discrimination analysis should, therefore, include more than a mere difference of skin color. Race is also tied to power differentials, social status, and other distinctions. Differences in power give one group the ability to declare the less powerful group "inferior." In fact, those in power may share the same skin color and ethnic characteristics as those they oppress, yet use "race" and "ethnic" differences to consolidate their rule.

Those most vulnerable to economic and social deprivations (hunger, illiteracy, disease, and so on) are those groups without wealth and political power, the majority of whom are women and children. Skin color alone will not tell who will suffer. For example, the majority of US citizens living in poverty are white, the color of most US policy makers.

Yet, most of the people in the world who experience a life of severe destitution are people of color. Suffering clearly continues to be related to the politics of race. According to the administrator of the United Nations Development Programme (UNDP), among the 4.4 billion people in developing countries around the world at the end of the twentieth century, three-fifths lived in communities lacking basic sanitation; one-third went without safe drinking water; one-quarter lacked adequate housing; and one-fifth were undernourished. In addition, nearly one-third of the people in the poorest countries, mostly in sub-Saharan Africa, could expect to die by age forty. According to the World Bank, of the world's 6 billion people, 2.8 live on less than $1 a day; with

44 percent living in South Asia. Overwhelmingly, these impoverished people are people of color. A glance at a map of global hunger, for example, graphically shows that the preponderance of the chronically undernourished are peoples in Africa, Asia, and parts of Latin America and the Caribbean. In early 2001, the UN World Food Program distributed a map calling attention to "hot spots" where hunger is most severe. The map identifies huge areas in Asia and sub-Saharan Africa, where tens of millions of people of color, most of them women and children, cannot get enough to eat. The UN agency estimates that of the 830 million undernourished people in the world, 791 million live in developing countries.

Racial minorities inside the US also continue to suffer a lack of economic security compared to their white counterparts, despite a "booming" economy at the end of the twentieth century. The following statistics from the 1990s reveal the economic divide between black and white Americans. According to Census Bureau statistics, there was a stark $14,000-per-household income gap between blacks and whites ($25,050 a year vs. $38,970; income stated in 1997 US dollars). The unemployment rate for young black men at all education levels was more than twice that for young white men. In addition, twice the number of young black men between the ages of sixteen and twenty-four were not in school or working. One out of every three black men in their twenties was under the supervision of the criminal justice system, either imprisoned or on probation or parole. Blacks in the US were six times more likely than whites to be held in jail. This vast disparity in economic opportunity between blacks and whites in the US continues in the new century.

The same disparity in economic security exists between white and Hispanic Americans. The National Council of La Raza reports that Hispanic workers were disproportionately concentrated in low-wage jobs that offered few benefits throughout the 1990s. As a result, married Hispanics with children continued to have higher poverty rates compared to black and white families. In 1997, for example, 21 percent of Hispanic married couples with children were poor, compared with 6 percent of white and 9 percent of black families. That same year only 55 percent of Hispanics twenty-five and older had graduated from high school, and 7.4 percent had graduated from college.

Any serious program for the protection of economic and social rights must address this reality. These conditions are the result of history, especially the heritage of four major historical processes: conquest, state building, migration, and economic development. Modern states have been built by powerful groups at the expense of the less powerful, with racial prejudice underlying the entire process. For those concerned with economic justice, the questions to be confronted today include the following: How is it possible to overcome and reverse this historical record of racial bias? What political and economic structures perpetuate racial bias in economic outcomes? What policies can be implemented at the national and international levels to create real economic opportunity for all races?

Notes and Questions

1. *Race in the Global Economy.* How would you respond to the questions raised at the end of the Felice article? The linkage between global economic and social violations and racism is rarely discussed in the literature on international economic and social rights. For some exceptions, *see, e.g.*, Jeffrey M. Brown, *Black Internationalism: Embracing an Economic Paradigm*, 23 MICH. J. INT'L L. 807 (2002); Lennox S. Hinds, *The Gross*

Violation of Human Rights of the Apartheid Regime Under International Law, 1 RUTGERS RACE & L. REV. 231 (1999); Ibrahim J. Gassama, *Transnational Critical Race Scholarship: Transcending Ethnic and National Chauvinism in the Era of Globalization*, 5 MICH. J. RACE & L. 133 (1999); Gil Gott, *Critical Race Globalism?: Global Political Economy, And The Intersections Of Race, Nation, and Class*, 33 U.C. DAVIS L. REV. 1503 (2000); Hope Lewis, *Reflections on "BlackCrit Theory": Human Rights*, 45 VILL. L. REV. 1075 (2000); Gay McDougall, *The Durban Racism Conference Revisited: The World Conference Through a Wider Lens*, 26 FLETCHER F. WORLD AFF. 135 (2002); Natsu Taylor Saito, *Critical Race Theory as International Human Rights Law*, 93 AM. SOC'Y INT'L L. PROC. 228 (Mar. 24–27, 1999).

2. *Defining Race.* Felice argues that "race" is largely a social construction. Do you agree? What physical, cultural or social characteristics do you associate with race? For example, the Race Convention defines racial discrimination more broadly than discrimination associated with skin color. Are you comfortable with that approach? How might people from the United States, Canada, England, China, Japan, Denmark, Brazil, the Dominican Republic or Mexico construe "race" differently? What roles do relative differences in economic, social, or political power play in your analysis?

3. What are the legal and practical implications of the statements in the initial report of the United States to the CERD Committee describing the nature and extent of racial discrimination in the United States? How might the report be used by lawyers representing individual clients? NGOs? Civil rights groups? Will U.S. ratification of CERD have a significant impact on racial discrimination in that country? For a critique of the United States initial report, *see* Human Rights Watch, United States of America, *in* WORLD REPORT 2001, *available at* http://hrw.org/wr2k1/usa/.

4. Under traditional international law doctrine, customary norms can be evidenced by widespread and persistent state practice coupled with evidence that the states engage in the practice from a sense of legal obligation (*opinio juris*). Can President Bush's Goree Island statements about the criminality and brutality of slavery be read as an acknowledgement of U.S. responsibility under international law? Why, or why not? (For a discussion of the elements of international customary law, *see, e.g.*, MARK W. JANIS, AN INTRODUCTION TO INTERNATIONAL LAW, at 41–55 (4th ed. 2003).

5. For further readings on reparations for U.S. slavery, abuses against Native Americans, and colonial abuses, *see, e.g.*, William Bradford, *"With a Very Great Blame on Our Hearts": Reparations, Reconciliation, and an American Indian Plea for Peace with Justice*, 27 AM. INDIAN L. REV. 1 (2002/2003); Robert Westley, *Many Billions Gone: Is It Time to Reconsider the Case for Black Reparations?*, 40 B.C. L. REV. 429, 450 (1998); John Donnelly, *Wounds of Colonialism Reopen in Namibia: German Apology for Massacres Poses Questions*, BOSTON GLOBE, Feb. 8, 2004, at A10.

6. How does racial discrimination intersect with other forms of discrimination? Does CERD address multiple forms of identity-based discrimination? *See, e.g.*, WILD for Human Rights, Gender, Race, Ethnicity and Human Rights: Putting Gender on the Agenda, Statement to the Preparatory Committee of The World Conference Against Racism, Racial Discrimination, Xenophobia, and Related Intolerance: September 2001, *available at* http://www.wildforhumanrights.org/WILD_statement.html (last visited June 6, 2004). *See also* GLOBAL CRITICAL RACE FEMINISM: AN INTERNATIONAL READER (Adrien K. Wing ed., 2000); SHERENE RAZACK, LOOKING WHITE PEOPLE IN THE EYE: GENDER, RACE, AND CULTURE IN COURTROOMS AND CLASSROOMS (1998); Penelope E. Andrews,

Globalization, Human Rights and Critical Race Feminism: Voices from the Margins, 3 J. GEN-DER, RACE & JUSTICE 373 (2000); Johanna E. Bond, *International Intersectionality: A Theoretical and Pragmatic Exploration of Women's International Human Rights Violations,* 52 EMORY L.J. 71 (2003); Lisa A. Crooms, *Indivisible Rights and Intersectional Identities, or "What Do Women's Human Rights Have to Do with the Race Convention?,"* 40 HOW. L.J. 619 (1997); Berta Esperanza Hernandez-Truyol, *Out of the Shadows: Traversing the Imaginary of Sameness, Difference, and Relationalism—A Human Rights Proposal,* 17 WIS. WOMEN'S L.J. 111 (2002). Hope Lewis, *Embracing Complexity: Human Rights in Critical Race Feminist Perspective,* 12 COLUM. J. GENDER & L. 510 (2003); Hope Lewis, *Global Intersections: Critical Race Feminist Human Rights and International Black Women,* 50 ME. L. REV. 309 (1998).

C. THE WOMEN'S CONVENTION

CONVENTION ON THE ELIMINATION OF ALL FORMS OF DISCRIMINATION AGAINST WOMEN

19 I.L.M. 33 (1980)

[The text of the Convention is annexed to U.N. General Assembly Resolution 34/180 of December 18, 1979. The Resolution was adopted by a vote of 130 in favor to none against, with 10 abstentions. The Convention [was] opened for signature on March 1, 1980.]

Thirty-fourth session Agenda item 75 RESOLUTION ADOPTED BY THE GENERAL ASSEMBLY [on the report of the Third Committee (A/34/830 and A/34/L.61] 34/180. Convention on the Elimination of All Forms of Discrimination against Women

PREAMBLE***

The States Parties to the present Convention,***

Noting that the Universal Declaration of Human Rights affirms the principle of the inadmissibility of discrimination and proclaims that all human beings are born free and equal in dignity and rights and that everyone is entitled to all the rights and freedoms set forth therein, without distinction of any kind, including distinction based on sex,

Noting that the States Parties to the International Covenants on Human Rights have the obligation to ensure the equal right of men and women to enjoy all economic, social, cultural, civil and political rights,***

Recalling that discrimination against women *** is an obstacle to the participation of women, on equal terms with men, in the political, social, economic and cultural life of their countries, hampers the growth of the prosperity of society and the family and makes more difficult the full development of the potentialities of women in the service of their countries and of humanity,

Concerned that in situations of poverty women have the least access to food, health, education, training and opportunities for employment and other needs,

Convinced that the establishment of the new international economic order based on equity and justice will contribute significantly towards the promotion of equality between men and women,

Emphasizing that the eradication of apartheid, of all forms of racism, racial discrimination, colonialism, neo-colonialism, aggression, foreign occupation and domination and interference in the internal affairs of States is essential to the full enjoyment of the rights of men and women,***

Convinced that the full and complete development of a country, the welfare of the world and the cause of peace require the maximum participation of women on equal terms with men in all fields,

Bearing in mind the great contribution of women to the welfare of the family and to the development of society, so far not fully recognized, the social significance of maternity and the role of both parents in the family and in the upbringing of children, and aware that the role of women in procreation should not be a basis for discrimination but that the upbringing of children requires a sharing of responsibility between men and women and society as a whole,

Aware that a change in the traditional role of men as well as the role of women in society and in the family is needed to achieve full equality between men and women,***

Have agreed on the following:

Article 1

[T]he term "discrimination against women" shall mean any distinction, exclusion or restriction made on the basis of sex which has the effect or purpose of impairing or nullifying the recognition, enjoyment or exercise by women, irrespective of their marital status, on a basis of equality of men and women, of human rights and fundamental freedoms in the political, economic, social, cultural, civil or any other field.

Article 2

States Parties condemn discrimination against women in all its forms, agree to pursue by all appropriate means and without delay a policy of eliminating discrimination against women ***.

Article 3

States Parties shall take in all fields, in particular in the political, social, economic and cultural fields, all appropriate measures, including legislation, to ensure the full development and advancement of women ***.

Article 4

1. Adoption by States Parties of temporary special measures aimed at accelerating de facto equality between men and women shall not be considered discrimination as defined in the present Convention, but shall in no way entail as a consequence the maintenance of unequal or separate standards; these measures shall be discontinued when the objectives of equality of opportunity and treatment have been achieved.

2. Adoption by States Parties of special measures, including those measures contained in the present Convention, aimed at protecting maternity shall not be considered discriminatory.

Article 5

States Parties shall take all appropriate measures:

(a) To modify the social and cultural patterns of conduct of men and women, with a view to achieving the elimination of prejudices and customary and all other practices which are based on the idea of the inferiority or the superiority of either of the sexes or on stereotyped roles for men and women;

(b) To ensure that family education includes a proper understanding of maternity as a social function and the recognition of the common responsibility of men and women in the upbringing and development of their children, it being understood that the interest of the children is the primordial consideration in all cases.

Article 6

States Parties shall take all appropriate measures, including legislation, to suppress all forms of traffic in women and exploitation of prostitution of women.***

Article 9

1. States Parties shall grant women equal rights with men to acquire, change or retain their nationality. They shall ensure in particular that neither marriage to an alien nor change of nationality by the husband during marriage shall automatically change the nationality of the wife, render her stateless or force upon her the nationality of the husband.

2. States Parties shall grant women equal rights with men with respect to the nationality of their children.

Article 10

States Parties shall take all appropriate measures to eliminate discrimination against women in order to ensure to them equal rights with men in the field of education ***:

(a) The same conditions for career and vocational guidance, for access to studies and for the achievement of diplomas in educational establishments of all categories in rural as well as in urban areas ***;

(c) The elimination of any stereotyped concept of the roles of men and women at all levels and in all forms of education ***;***

(e) The same opportunities for access to programmes of continuing education ***;

(f) The reduction of female student drop-out rates and the organization of programmes for girls and women who have left school prematurely;

(g) The same opportunities to participate actively in sports and physical education;

(h) Access to specific educational information to help to ensure the health and well-being of families, including information and advice on family planning.

Article 11

1. States Parties shall take all appropriate measures to eliminate discrimination against women in the field of employment in order to ensure ***;

(a) The right to work as an inalienable right of all human beings;

(b) The right to the same employment opportunities, including the application of the same criteria for selection in matters of employment;

(c) The right to free choice of profession and employment, the right to promotion, job security and all benefits and conditions of service and the right to receive vocational training and retraining, including apprenticeships, advanced vocational training and recurrent training;

(d) The right to equal remuneration, including benefits, and to equal treatment in respect of work of equal value, as well as equality of treatment in the evaluation of the quality of work;

(e) The right to social security,*** as well as the right to paid leave;

(f) The right to protection of health and to safety in working conditions, including the safeguarding of the function of reproduction.

2. In order to prevent discrimination against women on the grounds of marriage or maternity and to ensure their effective right to work, States Parties shall take appropriate measures:

(a) To prohibit, subject to the imposition of sanctions, dismissal on the grounds of pregnancy or of maternity leave and discrimination in dismissals on the basis of marital status;

(b) To introduce maternity leave with pay or with comparable social benefits without loss of former employment, seniority or social allowances;

(c) To encourage the provision of the necessary supporting social services to enable parents to combine family obligations with work responsibilities ***;

(d) To provide special protection to women during pregnancy in types of work proved to be harmful to them.***

Article 12

1. States Parties shall take all appropriate measures to eliminate discrimination against women in the field of health care in order to ensure, on a basis of equality of men and women, access to health care services, including those related to family planning.

2. Notwithstanding the provisions of paragraph 1 of this article, States Parties shall ensure to women appropriate services in connexion with pregnancy, confinement and the post-natal period, granting free services where necessary, as well as adequate nutrition during pregnancy and lactation.

Article 13

States Parties shall take all appropriate measures to eliminate discrimination against women in other areas of economic and social life in order to ensure ***;

(a) The right to family benefits;

(b) The right to bank loans, mortgages and other forms of financial credit;

(c) The right to participate in recreational activities, sports and all aspects of cultural life.

Article 14

1. States Parties shall take into account the particular problems faced by rural women and the significant roles which rural women play in the economic survival of their families, including their work in the non-monetized sectors of the economy ***.

2. States Parties shall take all appropriate measures to eliminate discrimination against women in rural areas in order to ensure ***; that they participate in and benefit from rural development and, in particular, shall ensure to such women the right:

(a) To participate in the elaboration and implementation of development planning at all levels;

(b) To have access to adequate health care facilities, including information, counselling and services in family planning;

(c) To benefit directly from social security programmes;

(d) To obtain all types of training and education, formal and non-formal ***;

(e) To organize self-help groups and co-operatives in order to obtain equal access to economic opportunities through employment or self-employment;

(f) To participate in all community activities;

(g) To have access to agricultural reform as well as appropriate technology and equal treatment in land and a in land resettlement schemes;

(h) To enjoy adequate living conditions, particularly in relation to housing, sanitation, electricity and water supply, transport and communications.***

Article 16

1. States Parties shall take all appropriate measures to eliminate discrimination against women in all matters relating to marriage and family relations and *** shall ensure ***:

(a) The same right to enter into marriage;

(b) The same right freely to choose a spouse and to enter into marriage only with their free and full consent;

(c) The same rights and responsibilities during marriage and at its dissolution;

(d) The same rights and responsibilities as parents, irrespective of their marital status, in matters relating to their children; in all cases the interests of the children shall be paramount;

(e) The same rights to decide freely and responsibly on the number and spacing of their children and to have access to the information, education and means to enable them to exercise these rights;

(f) The same rights and responsibilities with regard to guardianship, wardship, trusteeship and adoption of children, or similar institutions ***;

(g) The same personal rights as husband and wife, including the right to choose a family name, a profession and an occupation;

(h) The same right for both spouses in respect of the ownership, acquisition, management, administration, enjoyment and disposition of property, whether free of charge or for a valuable consideration.

2. The betrothal and the marriage of a child shall have no legal effect, and all necessary action, including legislation, shall be taken to specify a minimum age for marriage and to make the registration of marriages in an official registry compulsory.

Article 17

1. For the purpose of considering the progress made in the implementation of the present Convention, there shall be established a Committee on the Elimination of Discrimination against Women *** consisting *** of twenty-three experts of high moral standing and competence in the field covered by the Convention. The experts shall be elected by States Parties from among their nationals and shall serve in their personal capacity, consideration being given to equitable geographical distribution and to the representation of the different forms of civilization as well as the principal legal systems.***

9. The Secretary-General of the United Nations shall provide the necessary staff and facilities for the effective performance of the functions of the Committee under the present Convention.

Article 18

1. States Parties undertake to submit to the Secretary-General of the United Nations, for consideration by the Committee, a report on the legislative, judicial, administrative or other measures which they have adopted to give effect to the provisions of the present Convention and on the progress made in this respect:

(a) Within one year after the entry into force for the State concerned; and

(b) Thereafter at least every four years and further whenever the Committee so requests.

2. Reports may indicate factors and difficulties affecting the degree of fulfillment of obligations under the present Convention.***

Article 20

1. The Committee shall normally meet for a period of not more than two weeks annually in order to consider the reports submitted in accordance with article 18 of the present Convention.***

Article 21

1. The Committee shall, through the Economic and Social Council, report annually to the General Assembly of the United Nations on its activities and may make suggestions and general recommendations based on the examination of reports and information received from the States Parties. Such suggestions and general recommendations shall be included in the report of the committee together with comments, if any, from States Parties.***

Article 23

Nothing in this Convention shall affect any provisions that are more conducive to the achievement of equality between men and women which may be contained:

    (a) In the legislation of a State Party; or

    (b) In any other international convention, treaty or agreement in force for that State.

Article 24

States Parties undertake to adopt all necessary measures at the national level aimed at achieving the full realization of the rights recognized in the present Convention.***

Article 28

*** 2. A reservation incompatible with the object and purpose of the present Convention shall not be permitted.***

Article 29

1. Any dispute between two or more States Parties concerning the interpretation or application of the present Convention which is not settled by negotiation shall, at the request of one of them, be submitted to arbitration. If within six months from the date of the request for arbitration the parties are unable to agree on the organization of the arbitration, any one of those parties may refer the dispute to the International Court of Justice by request in conformity with the Statute of the Court.

2. Each State Party may at the time of signature or ratification of this Convention or accession thereto declare that it does not consider itself bound by paragraph 1 of this article. The other States Parties shall not be bound by that paragraph with respect to any State Party which has made such a reservation.

3. Any State Party which has made a reservation in accordance with paragraph 2 of this article may at any time withdraw that reservation by notification to the Secretary-General of the United Nations.***

Notes and Questions

1. Some feminist scholars criticize the approach to women's rights adopted in CEDAW:

> The Women's Convention is the most prominent international normative instrument recognizing the special concerns of women. But the terms of the Convention and the way it has been accepted by states prompt us to ask whether it offers a real or chimerical possibility of change.***
>
>   Although the Convention goes further than simply requiring equality of opportunity and covers the more contentious concept of equality of result, which justifies affirmative action programs and protection against indirect discrimination, the underlying assumption of its definition of discrimination is that women and men are the same. Most international commentators treat this model of equality as uncontroversial. But the notions of both equality of opportunity and equality of result accept the general applicability of a male standard (except in special circumstances such as pregnancy) and promise a very limited form of equality: equality is defined as being like a man. "Man," writes Catharine MacKinnon, "has become the measure of all things." On this analysis, equality can be achieved in a relatively straightforward way by legally requiring the removal of identifiable barriers to the rise of women to the same status as men: equality is achievable within the social and legal structures as they are

now. This assumption ignores the many real differences and inequities between the sexes and the significant barriers to their removal.***

Hilary Charlesworth, Christine Chinkin & Shelley Wright, *Feminist Approaches to International Law*, 85 AM. J. INT'L L. 613 (1991).

Are these criticisms valid? How could legally defined norms be formulated differently to take these concerns into account?

THE OPTIONAL PROTOCOL TO THE CONVENTION ON THE ELIMINATION OF ALL FORMS OF DISCRIMINATION AGAINST WOMEN

As originally adopted, the Women's Convention did not include a mechanism for individual complaints. The Convention provided for two means of enforcement: (1) reporting by states parties to the Committee on the Elimination of Discrimination Against Women (CEDAW or "the Committee"); and (2) an inter-state complaints procedure under Article 29. These procedures were regarded by many human rights groups as inadequate for the full implementation of women's rights against discrimination. For example, many states parties to the Convention are notoriously late in fulfilling their reporting obligations as required within one year of accession or ratification and thereafter every four years (or upon Committee request). Further, states parties lacked the political will to make use of the inter-state complaints procedure and made significant reservations to its application. United Nations, Division for the Advancement of Women, *Why an Optional Protocol?*, *available at* http://www.un.org/womenwatch/daw/cedaw/why.htm (last visited Nov. 12, 2003).

Further, while discrimination against women can, and has, been a subject of communications and complaints under other human rights treaties and U.N. Charter-based procedures, none of them (with the exception of the weak complaints mechanism administered by the Commission on the Status of Women) was intended to focus specifically on violations of the rights of women. *Id.* As a result, human rights activists, U.N. officials and academics lobbied for the adoption of an Optional Protocol to the Women's Convention. The following excerpt from an Amnesty International report describes the events leading up to the eventual adoption of the Optional Protocol in 2000.

AMNESTY INTERNATIONAL, CLAIMING WOMEN'S RIGHTS: THE OPTIONAL PROTOCOL TO THE UN WOMEN'S CONVENTION[5]

The entry into force on 22 December 2000 of the Optional Protocol to the Women's Convention [is] a significant advancement in the promotion and protection of the human rights of women. The Optional Protocol offers women direct means to seek redress at the international level for violations of their rights under the Women's Convention: it opens the door to the UN committee that monitors implementation of the Convention, enabling the Convention to be applied directly to actual situations that women in all parts of the world face in their daily lives, ensuring that it does not remain a distant and abstract set of rules and principles for them.***

<p>[5]   INDEX: IOR 51/008/2002, July 1, 2002, *available at* http://web.amnesty.org/library/Index/ENGIOR510082002?open&of=ENG-200.</p>

1. Background ***

During the drafting of the Women's Convention some thought was given to including an individual complaints procedure to supplement the reporting system. Three of the major international human rights treaties in force had complaints procedures—the First Optional Protocol of the International Covenant on Civil and Political Rights; Article 14 of the International Covenant on the Elimination of All Forms of Racial Discrimination; Article 22 of the Convention against Torture and Other Cruel, Inhuman or Degrading Treatment or Punishment—mandating their monitoring committees to receive and consider individual petitions. However, no such mandate was provided for in the Convention, a situation that over time served to limit CEDAW's ability to respond to specific violations of the Convention.

In 1991, when an expert group was convened by the United Nations Division for the Advancement of Women on the issue of violence against women in all its forms, the prospect of considering an optional protocol *** to the Women's Convention began to gather force. In 1993 the adoption of an optional protocol *** was one of the commitments made by states at the World Conference on Human Rights in Vienna. At the Fourth World Conference on Women held in Beijing in September 1995 governments committed themselves to supporting "'the elaboration (of) a draft optional protocol to the Women's Convention that could enter into force as soon as possible." Work on drafting the Optional Protocol began in 1996, when the United Nations Commission on the Status of Women (CSW) established an open-ended working group for this purpose. In March 1999 governments represented in the working group were able to agree on a draft text by consensus; this was subsequently passed to the UN General Assembly ***.

[The General Assembly adopted the Optional Protocol in its 54th Session on Oct. 6, 1999.

The Optional Protocol was opened for signature on Dec. 10, 1999, and *entered into force* on Dec. 22, 2000. As of Oct. 26, 2003, there were 75 signatories and 57 state parties to the Optional Protocol.]

2. A summary of guarantees under the Women's Convention

When a government becomes a state party to the Women's Convention it is under an obligation to bring its laws and practices into compliance with the Convention's provisions. This means *de facto* as well as *de jure* compliance,(6) and includes the whole range of civil, cultural, economic, political and social rights for women guaranteed by the Convention.***

The Convention protects women against discrimination by public authorities or agents of the state. In addition—and very significantly—it holds a state party responsible for discriminatory acts committed by private individuals or organizations. This is relevant in many aspects of women's lives, but no more so than when it applies to their physical and psychological integrity and well-being, especially when practices that threaten these are supported by long-standing traditions, customs and attitudes; for example, the practice of female genital mutilation, "honour" killings and dowry deaths; or rape, including rape in armed conflict or marital rape, and domestic violence. This means that if the state authorities fail to offer protection against such practices and abuses through, for example, legislation and public education, or to bring to justice those who commit such abuses and to compensate the victims, the state is in breach of its obligations under the Convention.

The Women's Convention has been ratified (or acceded to) by [174] states to date. Despite this high figure, Amnesty International notes with concern that more reservations have been entered by states parties than to any of the other international human rights treaties ***.***

3. What difference does the Optional Protocol make to women

Since the Women's Convention's entry into force CEDAW has been limited to monitoring compliance by states parties by receiving, reviewing and issuing observations and recommendations on the periodic reports governments are obliged to submit. Now, under the Optional Protocol, CEDAW is mandated to act on individual complaints and also to initiate inquiries, bringing the Committee into line with other committees monitoring international human rights treaties. This serves most importantly to supplement CEDAW's monitoring strength and allows the Committee to focus on cases and situations that it cannot address through the standard reporting system.***

4. Procedures under the Optional Protocol

a) The individual complaints procedure

Under the Optional Protocol any individual woman or group of women whose rights under the Convention have been violated in a state that has ratified the Optional Protocol will be able to present a complaint to CEDAW, on condition that all *effective* means of domestic redress have been exhausted. In practical terms this can mean that if violations against women occur in countries where access to domestic remedies is denied or significantly restricted they may bring their cases immediately to the attention of CEDAW.

A further significant feature of the individual complaints procedure is that individuals other than victims themselves, and organizations including NGOs, can bring a complaint on behalf of victims. This feature is important because of the political, economic, social and cultural factors that so often restrict access by women to information and to practical opportunities to claim their rights. Women's organizations are well placed to make submissions on their behalf.***

b) The inquiry procedure

The Optional Protocol provides also for an inquiry procedure, which allows CEDAW to undertake investigation of grave or systematic violations of women's human rights. The inquiry procedure allows CEDAW to focus attention on widespread practices affecting women such as lack of equal opportunities in education, politics or the work place; sexual exploitation; or abuses that cross borders and involve multiple governments such as in trafficking or violence against women in situations of armed conflict. It provides for an in-depth examination of the underlying causes of discrimination against women and can focus on abuses that would not normally be submitted to CEDAW by means of the individual complaints procedure.

With the inquiry procedure, CEDAW can act on its own initiative, on the basis of reliable information. Women's organizations and NGOs can provide CEDAW with information on grave or systematic violations of the Convention, requesting the committee to investigate, and are well-placed to do so on wide-scale practices that affect women's rights. While the conduct of such investigation is confidential, CEDAW may publish the findings once the inquiry is concluded. This can put effective pressure on governments to end the worst forms of discrimination against women.***

The Opt-out clause (Article 10)

The Optional Protocol does not permit states to enter reservations (Article 17). However, one of the compromises agreed during negotiations on the text of the Optional Protocol was to allow a state party to "opt-out" the inquiry procedure, simply by declaring that it does not recognize the competence of CEDAW to carry out such inquiry.

Amnesty International strongly opposed this compromise during the drafting process. The organization urges states parties ratifying the Optional Protocol not to make a declaration under Article 10.***

Notes and Questions

1. *Implementation of the Women's Convention.* Why do you think CEDAW was originally adopted without a procedure for individual complaints? Do you agree with Amnesty International's view that the Optional Protocol will significantly advance the rights of women, including their economic, social, and cultural rights? Why or why not?

2. The Women's Convention requires states parties to take "all appropriate measures" to prevent and prohibit discrimination against women including discrimination by private actors. What might be some of the implications for states parties in terms of their regulation of the activities of corporations, private educational institutions or social clubs, for example?

3. The Amnesty International report notes that CEDAW, in General Recommendation No. 19, has interpreted the Women's Convention to prohibit violence against women and lists "the practice of female genital mutilation, 'honour' killings and dowry deaths; or rape, including rape in armed conflict or marital rape, and domestic violence" as particular causes of concern. Article 5 of the Women's Convention requires states parties to "take all appropriate measures: (a) To modify the social and cultural patterns of conduct of men and women, with a view to achieving the elimination of prejudices and customary and all other practices which are based on the idea of the inferiority or the superiority of either of the sexes or on stereotyped roles for men and women***". If you were a government official in a country that had ratified the Women's Convention, what kinds of measures would you suggest for implementing this provision? What customs and practices would be of most concern to you? How should this provision be implemented in light of rights to religious and cultural freedom?

4. The United Nations Division for the Advancement of Women contains information about the background and implementation of the Women's Convention and its Optional Protocol. *See* http://www.un.org/womenwatch/daw. The Web site of the International Women's Rights Action Watch (IWRAW), a U.S.-based NGO, promotes implementation of the Women's Convention by providing information helpful to NGOs in developing countries: www.igc.org/iwraw.

5. For further reading on the legal and political process leading to the adoption of an Optional Protocol to CEDAW, *see* Amnesty International, *The Optional Protocol to the Women's Convention: Enabling Women to Claim their Rights at the International Level,* Dec. 1997; Andrew Byrnes, *Slow and Steady Wins the Race? The Development of an Optional Protocol to the Women's Convention.* 91 ASIL PROC. 383 (1997); Andrew Byrnes & Jane Connors, *Enforcing the Human Rights of Women: A Complaints Process for the Women's Convention?,* 21 BROOK. J. INT'L L. 682 (1996).

6. Like other human rights treaty bodies, CEDAW is authorized to make General Recommendations with regard to the interpretation and implementation of the human rights treaty that created it. CEDAW has taken quite an activist approach in this regard. A number of CEDAW's General Recommendations have focused on the economic, social and cultural rights of women: General Recommendation No. 5 (7th session, 1988) (recommending greater use of "temporary special measures" such as positive action, preferential treatment or quota systems to advance women's integration into education, the economy, politics and employment); General Recommendation No. 13: Equal Remuneration for Work of Equal Value (8th session, 1989); General Recommendation No. 14: Female Circumcision (9th session, 1990); General Recommendation No. 15: Avoidance of Discrimination Against Women in National Strategies for the Prevention and Control of Acquired Immunodeficiency Syndrome (AIDS) (9th session, 1990); General Recommendation No. 16: Unpaid Women Workers in Rural and Urban Family Enterprises (10th session, 1991); General Recommendation No. 17: Measurement and Quantification of the Unremunerated Domestic Activities of Women and Their Recognition in the Gross National Product (10th session, 1991); General Recommendation No. 18: Disabled Women (10th session, 1991); General Recommendation No. 21: Equality in Marriage and Family Relations (13th session, 1994); General Recommendation No. 24: Women and Health (20th session, 1999). For the text of CEDAW General Recommendations, *see* United Nations, Division for the Advancement of Women, *General Recommendations Made by the Committee on the Elimination of Discrimination Against Women, available at* http://www.un.org/womenwatch/daw/cedaw/recomm.htm.

General Recommendation No. 19: Violence Against Women, is, arguably, the most influential of the statements issued by CEDAW. A focus on the theme of violence against women had been chosen strategically by international women's rights activists as a means of using the international human rights framework to bring attention to the seriousness of violations of women's rights. Activists also hope to provide a cross-cultural umbrella that would characterize a range of violations and minimize cross-cultural conflicts among women's rights advocates.

Women's NGOs also adopted this approach as part of a well organized and successful media and organizing campaign to influence proceedings at the 1993 World Conference on Human Rights in Vienna and the 1995 World Conference on Women in Beijing. Their efforts resulted in, among other things, the adoption by the General Assembly of a Declaration on the Elimination of Violence Against Women, the appointment of a Special Rapporteur on Violence Against Women (Radhika Coomaraswamy), and CEDAW's issuance of General Recommendation No. 19.

GENERAL RECOMMENDATION NO. 19: VIOLENCE AGAINST WOMEN

U.N. CEDAW Comm. 11th Sess., U.N. Doc. A/47/38 (1992)

Background

1. Gender-based violence is a form of discrimination that seriously inhibits women's ability to enjoy rights and freedoms on a basis of equality with men.***

5. The Committee suggested to States parties that in reviewing their laws and policies, and in reporting under the Convention, they should have regard to the following comments of the Committee concerning gender-based violence.

General comments

6. The Convention in article 1 defines discrimination against women. The definition of discrimination includes gender-based violence, that is, violence that is directed against a woman because she is a woman or that affects women disproportionately. It includes acts that inflict physical, mental or sexual harm or suffering, threats of such acts, coercion and other deprivations of liberty. Gender-based violence may breach specific provisions of the Convention, regardless of whether those provisions expressly mention violence.

7. Gender-based violence, which impairs or nullifies the enjoyment by women of human rights and fundamental freedoms under general international law or under human rights conventions, is discrimination within the meaning of article 1 of the Convention. These rights and freedoms include:

(a) The right to life;

(b) The right not to be subject to torture or to cruel, inhuman or degrading treatment or punishment;

(c) The right to equal protection according to humanitarian norms in time of international or internal armed conflict;

(d) The right to liberty and security of person;

(e) The right to equal protection under the law;

(f) The right to equality in the family;

(g) The right to the highest standard attainable of physical and mental health;

(h) The right to just and favourable conditions of work.

8. The Convention applies to violence perpetrated by public authorities. Such acts of violence may breach that State's obligations under general international human rights law and under other conventions, in addition to breaching this Convention.

9. It is emphasized, however, that discrimination under the Convention is not restricted to action by or on behalf of Governments ***. Under general international law and specific human rights covenants, States may also be responsible for private acts if they fail to act with due diligence to prevent violations of rights or to investigate and punish acts of violence, and for providing compensation.

Comments on specific articles of the Convention

Articles 2 and 3

10. Articles 2 and 3 establish a comprehensive obligation to eliminate discrimination in all its forms in addition to the specific obligations under articles 5–16.

Articles 2 (f), 5 and 10 (c)

11. Traditional attitudes by which women are regarded as subordinate to men or as having stereotyped roles perpetuate widespread practices involving violence or coercion, such as family violence and abuse, forced marriage, dowry deaths, acid attacks and female circumcision. Such prejudices and practices may justify gender-based violence as a form of protection or control of women. The effect of such violence on the physi-

cal and mental integrity of women is to deprive them of the equal enjoyment, exercise and knowledge of human rights and fundamental freedoms. While this comment addresses mainly actual or threatened violence the underlying consequences of these forms of gender-based violence help to maintain women in subordinate roles and contribute to their low level of political participation and to their lower level of education, skills and work opportunities.***

Article 6

13. States parties are required by article 6 to take measures to suppress all forms of traffic in women and exploitation of the prostitution of women.

14. Poverty and unemployment increase opportunities for trafficking in women. In addition to established forms of trafficking there are new forms of sexual exploitation, such as sex tourism, the recruitment of domestic labour from developing countries to work in developed countries, and organized marriages between women from developing countries and foreign nationals. These practices are incompatible with the equal enjoyment of rights by women and with respect for their rights and dignity. They put women at special risk of violence and abuse.

15. Poverty and unemployment force many women, including young girls, into prostitution. Prostitutes are especially vulnerable to violence because their status, which may be unlawful, tends to marginalize them. They need the equal protection of laws against rape and other forms of violence.***

Article 11

17. Equality in employment can be seriously impaired when women are subjected to gender-specific violence, such as sexual harassment in the workplace.***

Article 12

19. States parties are required by article 12 to take measures to ensure equal access to health care. Violence against women puts their health and lives at risk.

20. In some States there are traditional practices perpetuated by culture and tradition that are harmful to the health of women and children. These practices include dietary restrictions for pregnant women, preference for male children and female circumcision or genital mutilation.

Article 14

21. Rural women are at risk of gender-based violence because traditional attitudes regarding the subordinate role of women that persist in many rural communities. Girls from rural communities are at special risk of violence and sexual exploitation when they leave the rural community to seek employment in towns.

Article 16 (and Article 5)

22. Compulsory sterilization or abortion adversely affects women's physical and mental health, and infringes the right of women to decide on the number and spacing of their children.

23. Family violence is one of the most insidious forms of violence against women. It is prevalent in all societies. Within family relationships women of all ages are subjected to violence of all kinds, including battering, rape, other forms of sexual assault,

mental and other forms of violence, which are perpetuated by traditional attitudes. Lack of economic independence forces many women to stay in violent relationships. The abrogation of their family responsibilities by men can be a form of violence, and coercion. These forms of violence put women's health at risk and impair their ability to participate in family life and public life on a basis of equality.

Specific recommendations

24. In light of these comments, the Committee on the Elimination of Discrimination against Women recommends:

(a) States parties should take appropriate and effective measures to overcome all forms of gender-based violence, whether by public or private act;

(b) States parties should ensure that laws against family violence and abuse, rape, sexual assault and other gender-based violence give adequate protection to all women, and respect their integrity and dignity. Appropriate protective and support services should be provided for victims. Gender-sensitive training of judicial and law enforcement officers and other public officials is essential for the effective implementation of the Convention;

(c) States parties should encourage the compilation of statistics and research on the extent, causes and effects of violence, and on the effectiveness of measures to prevent and deal with violence;

(d) Effective measures should be taken to ensure that the media respect and promote respect for women;

(e) States parties in their reports should identify the nature and extent of attitudes, customs and practices that perpetuate violence against women, and the kinds of violence that result. They should report the measures that they have undertaken to overcome violence, and the effect of those measures;

(f) Effective measures should be taken to overcome these attitudes and practices. States should introduce education and public information programmes to help eliminate prejudices which hinder women's equality ***.

(g) Specific preventive and punitive measures are necessary to overcome trafficking and sexual exploitation;

(h) States parties in their reports should describe the extent of all these problems and the measures, including penal provisions, preventive and rehabilitation measures, that have been taken to protect women engaged in prostitution or subject to trafficking and other forms of sexual exploitation. The effectiveness of these measures should also be described;

(i) Effective complaints procedures and remedies, including compensation, should be provided;

(j) States parties should include in their reports information on sexual harassment, and on measures to protect women from sexual harassment and other forms or violence of coercion in the workplace;

(k) States parties should establish or support services for victims of family violence, rape, sex assault and other forms of gender-based violence, including refuges, specially trained health workers, rehabilitation and counselling;

(l) States parties should take measures to overcome such practices and should take account of the Committee's recommendation on female circumcision . . . in reporting on health issues;

(m) States parties should ensure that measures are taken to prevent coercion in regard to fertility and reproduction, and to ensure that women are not forced to seek unsafe medical procedures such as illegal abortion because of lack of appropriate services in regard to fertility control;

(n) States parties in their reports should state the extent of these problems and should indicate the measures that have been taken and their effect;

(o) States parties should ensure that services for victims of violence are accessible to rural women and that where necessary special services are provided to isolated communities;

(p) Measures to protect them from violence should include training and employment opportunities and the monitoring of the employment conditions of domestic workers;

(q) States parties should report on the risks to rural women, the extent and nature of violence and abuse to which they are subject, their need for and access to support and other services and the effectiveness of measures to overcome violence;

(r) Measures that are necessary to overcome family violence should include:

   (i) Criminal penalties where necessary and civil remedies in case of domestic violence;

   (ii) Legislation to remove the defence of honour in regard to the assault or murder of a female family member;

   (iii) Services to ensure the safety and security of victims of family violence, including refuges, counselling and rehabilitation programmes;

   (iv) Rehabilitation programmes for perpetrators of domestic violence;

   (v) Support services for families where incest or sexual abuse has occurred;

(s) States parties should report on the extent of domestic violence and sexual abuse, and on the preventive, punitive and remedial measures that have been taken;

(t) That States parties should take all legal and other measures that are necessary to provide effective protection of women against gender-based violence, including, *inter alia:*

   (i) Effective legal measures, including penal sanctions, civil remedies and compensatory provisions ***;

   (ii) Preventive measures, including public information and education rogrammes ***;

   (iii) Protective measures, including refuges, counselling, rehabilitation and support services for women ***;

(u) That States parties should report on all forms of gender-based violence, and that such reports should include all available data on the incidence of each form of violence, and on the effects of such violence on the women who are victims;

(v) That the reports of States parties should include information on the legal, preventive and protective measures that have been taken to overcome violence against women, and on the effectiveness of such measures.

Notes and Questions

1. *General Recommendation No. 19 and the Interdependency of Rights.* Many people associate violence against women only with violations of civil and political rights. How does General Recommendation No. 19 establish links to violations of the economic, social and cultural rights of women? Do you think that establishing connections between violence and violations of socio-economic rights is an appropriate strategy for furthering women's human rights? Why or why not?

2. *Affirmative Obligations.* As illustrated by General Recommendation No. 19, states parties to the Women's Convention ostensibly agree to take an interventionist approach to protecting women against discrimination in public and private life. For example, CEDAW recommends that states parties not only adopt appropriate legislation and enforcement measures, but also that they set up shelters, rehabilitation programs, employment opportunities, and promote positive images of women in the media. Are there drawbacks to such an approach? Do the potential benefits outweigh the drawbacks?

3. For more on international human rights responses to violence against women, *see, e.g., Report of the Special Rapporteur on Violence Against Women, Its Causes and Consequences,* U.N. ESCOR Hum. Rts. Comm., 56th Sess., Provisional Agenda Item 12(a), U.N. Doc. E/CN.4/2000/68 (2000); Penelope E. Andrews, *Violence Against Aboriginal Women in Australia: Possibilities for Redress Within the International Human Rights Framework,* 60 ALB. L. REV. 917 (1997); Berta Esperanza Hernandez-Truyol, *Sex, Culture, and Rights: A Reconceptualization of Violence for the Twenty-First Century,* 60 Alb. L. Rev. 607 (1997).

REPORTING OBLIGATIONS UNDER THE WOMEN'S CONVENTION

States parties to the Women's Convention are required to submit periodic reports to CEDAW on the status of their efforts to comply with the Convention. The reports of many countries can be years overdue or are only cursory in nature. The following country report by the government of Jamaica provides an illustration of the nature and scope of such reports. Note that this report was issued as a combination report after the government failed to submit previous reports on time. Jamaica ratified the Women's Convention on October 19, 1984.

COMMITTEE ON THE ELIMINATION OF DISCRIMINATION AGAINST WOMEN, CONSIDERATION OF REPORTS SUBMITTED BY STATES PARTIES UNDER ARTICLE 18 OF THE CONVENTION ON THE ELIMINATION OF ALL FORMS OF DISCRIMINATION AGAINST WOMEN: SECOND, THIRD, AND FOURTH PERIODIC REPORTS OF STATES PARTIES: JAMAICA

U.N. Doc. CEDAW/C/JAM/2-4 (1998)

Article 2

28. Discrimination is proscribed when it is seen or shown to be evident in intent or effect. In accordance with this policy, several Acts have been passed ***:

(a) The Equal Pay for Men and Women Act

*** to proscribe the practice of paying women less than men for comparable work;

(b) The Maternity Leave Act

*** to safeguard the position of employed pregnant women;

29. Legislation passed in the period being covered by this report include:

(a) The Matrimonial Causes Act 1989

*** to update the law relating to matrimonial causes, the following of which are of particular significance to women:

   (i) A husband's claim to damages for adultery has been abolished. This claim was based on the notion that a wife is the property of her husband

   (ii) [T]he domicile of a married woman is to be determined as if she were a single woman.***

(d) Domestic Violence Act ***

Article 3

32. *** [T]he National Policy Statement on Women represents a major milestone in securing the advancement of women. The goals of the document include:

   (i) Recognizing the existing high levels of unemployment among women, and that women's employment and income have an immediate impact on the living standards of children;

   (ii) Recognizing that many areas of employment in which women predominate are also those which receive low remuneration and have poor working conditions;

   (iii) Recognizing that appropriate child care arrangements not only increase the efficiency of women workers but are an investment in the children and future of Jamaica;

   (iv) Recognizing that legal and administrative reforms are still required to achieve adequate protection and treatment of women under the law;

   (v) Recognizing that women are unique in their capacity to bear children and that many of our women remain unaware or powerless in controlling the frequency of conception and pregnancy, with detrimental effects on themselves and their families.***

Article 4

Temporary Special Measures:

34. *** Bureau of Women's Affairs current priorities are geared towards young women (14–24 years), elderly women and domestic workers. These priorities include: education and training in non-traditional skills to reduce unemployment levels, particularly among young women and gender sensitivity training.

35. Workshops and educational audio-visual material are being used to achieve these objectives.***

37. *** [T]he Prime Minister announced the Government's intention to establish a Commission on Gender and Social Equity. A Steering Committee has also been set up within the Policy Support Unit of the Prime Minister to recommend a framework for which gender equity can be achieved as a social policy goal and an empowerment process which can be sustained over time. The Commission works simultaneously with government organizations to incorporate gender and social equity in its machinery ***.

40. The Government of Jamaica *** also provides comprehensive maternal and child health care services *** and post-natal services, child health, immunization and family planning ***.

Article 5(a)

42. *** Among measures undertaken to combat the idea of female inferiority and break-down stereotypical role images are: the development of appropriate school curricula; media awareness efforts (including the use of non-sexist advertisement); and the use of drama ***.***

47. The conceptualization of education as predominantly a male domain has been affected by such affirmative actions as:

(a) The elimination of fees up to the tertiary level which has enabled many women to improve their economic status through improved educational opportunities.

(b) Amendments to the Education Regulations in 1980 and 1981 allowed pregnant school girls to sit examinations and gave maternity leave with pay to married and unmarried female teachers.

(c) The government of Jamaica has also expanded its subsidy to the Woman's Centers Foundation which provides continuing education for pregnant school girls and also offers child care in order to allow young mothers to return to school after their babies are born.***

50. Mass media has been particularly destructive in the conception of "being female" over the years with the female's anatomy *** being commodified ***. During the 1980s, space was created for women's issues in the print media.*** [T]here has been an obvious effort in advertising to present images of women which are motivating and positive.***

Article 6

57. Exploitation of women through trafficking and prostitution is addressed by the Offenses Against the Person Act ***.***

Article 7

65. *** [F]or every 100 working women, only about eight have some kind of administrative position and a good portion of this number is to be found in teaching and nursing.

66. Women are just now becoming more visible in the trade unions ***.***

Article 10

74. (g) The government of Jamaica expanded subsidy to the Women's Center Foundation, which provides continuing education for pregnant school girls and also offers child care in order to allow them to return to school after their baby is born.***

84. The rate of female student drop-out has been positively affected by such organizations as the Women's Center which assists pregnant school girls to continue their education, learn parenting and vocational skills and which also encourages the participation of fathers. There has also been a reduction in the number of second pregnancies among high school girls who come to the Center. Many of these young women have been able to complete their education and go on to successful careers.***

Article 11

88. Provisions have been made under the law which speak to the conditions and terms under which men and women work ***.***

94. The 1975 Employment (Equal Pay For Men and Women) Act had as it's main object the elimination of discrimination between the sexes in the payment for performance of similar work for the same employer. There has, however, been no attempt to create an analogue of the diverse forms of employment to affect a semblance of parity. For example, a title may protect the employer from prosecution.*** Further, 'male' fields of employment attract a higher level of remuneration than primarily 'female' fields.

95. *** Maternity Leave With Pay Act, 1979 *** to safeguard the position of women when pregnancy interrupts their employment.

96. The Act grants such women the right to three months maternity leave, two at which they obtain normal wages ***.***

98. *** Domestic Helpers fall into their own special category. Maternity leave with pay for this group would be the minimum wage for eight weeks, provided that the necessary contributions to the National Insurance Scheme have been made ***.

99. Few Helpers agree to the deductions, few employers trouble to make them. Helpers, by and large, tend to have no National Insurance Benefit or National Housing Trust Benefit, and are left without pension when they are no longer able to work.

100. To ensure parity between working men and women, attempts have to be made to create an analogue of areas of employment so that covert discrimination by ways of title be impermissible.***

102. Maternity leave for Helpers need also to be placed on par with that of other categories of workers.***

Article 12

Access to Health Care Services:

137. The Government of Jamaica *** provides comprehensive maternal and child health services which include ante, intra and postnatal services, child health, immunization and family planning. The government's endorsement of the primary health care strategy in 1978 is well established in its organization of basic care for women and children in the population.***

Article 13

146. The social security system of Jamaica allows men and women equal access to family benefits ***.

147. Public Assistance programs in Jamaica are also equally accessible to men and women ***.

Food Aid Program

148. The Food Aid Program *** provides improved nutritional levels for school children, pregnant and lactating mothers and children aged 0–6 years.***

Loans, Mortgages and Credit

150. The economic situation of the 1980s challenged the initiative of Jamaican women, many of whom became entrepreneurs—either establishing their own micro-enterprises, such as hairdressing, street vending, handicraft and garment making, or else becoming Informal Commercial Importers (ICIs)—traders in consumer goods for sale locally and/or selling Jamaican goods overseas. These women have been able to use these strategies to help their families survive, and to ensure that their children are fed, clothed and sent to school.

151. Some financial institutions have increased women's access to credit for establishing small businesses ***.***

155. Some women farm land that they do not own, either because they lack the financial resources, the information on how to purchase the land, or because it belongs to a relative who allows them to use the portion of land which they farm. Other women farm on government lands only to find themselves without a holding if and when the land is required for some other purpose.

156. The National Housing Trust has *** initiated housing schemes targeted at the lower end of the middle income bracket. A number of purchases in these schemes have been made by women heads of households ***.

Article 14

159. [I]ncreased efforts to recognize and document women's contribution to the rural economy through agricultural production, which is still the principal economic activity in most rural areas.

160. [W]omen still constitute an important force in the production and marketing of agricultural commodities in Jamaica.

161. *** 22 percent of the holdings were managed principally by women [and] even where they are not the principal farm operators, women participate regularly in farm production activities at every level *** 27 percent of the households [have] women who independently make decisions concerning changes in farming practices.***

163. The increasing focus on women's role in the agricultural and rural development process has not only served to highlight the value of their contribution but also to identify the factors which limit their participation.

164. In Jamaica, underlying social and cultural values influencing attitude and behavior, are much greater barriers to women than institutional factors. Agricultural programs, for example, are generally open to both men and women but in certain types of projects women tend to be under-represented.***

166. *** [T]raditional land inheritance practices which favor male relatives, give women less access to landed security; which, in many instances largely determines one's capability to meet loan eligibility requirements. Evidence that women have less access to land is borne out in the fact that average farm size is generally lower for them than for men.***

168. The adverse socio-economic and ecological factors facing female farmers *** are very often the same ones experienced by their male counterparts. However, in many instances, it is a question of degree, so that while men and women face the same problems, the situation of women is generally worse. This is borne out in data on access to credit and land ownership.***

Contribution of Women to Family Income

170. Among the rural, poor female-headed households are considered to be one of the most vulnerable groups. This includes women farmers and wage laborers ***.

Participation in Development

174. *** The factors which account for this state of affairs are largely related to cultural traditions which are sometimes reinforced by stereotypes held by certain officials involved in rural development, for example, the complaint by some women that male extension officers do not regard them as "serious" farmers.

175. The lack of awareness of policies and programs, on the part of women themselves, has also been a contributory factor to their limited access to agricultural development benefits ***.

Policies Directed Specifically at Rural Women

176. *** The National Policy Statement on Women *** represented a major step in recognizing the need for a gender approach in policy formation ***. Four principles were outlined as essential to policy development in all sectors:

i)   All policies of the Government must reflect full recognition of the equal and complementary partnership of women and men.

ii) Economic and social development policies and programs must provide for equality of access to resources by both men and women.

iii) In policy planning, special consideration must be given to women's multiple responsibilities in the household. In particular, policies must take account of the high percentage of women of all ages who are single parents and sole supporters of their families.

iv) Special measures must be developed to compensate for historic and current disadvantages experienced by women.

177.   *** Certain immediate goals were identified for various sectors, including agriculture. With specific regard to this sector, it was stated that:

*** [T]he Government will promote the identification and upgrading of women's existing skills and promote new opportunities, and will also take measures to address constraints such as access to credit, access to markets and the need for support services.***

179.   Specific program and project areas suggested included *** the targeting of small farmers with special emphasis on giving women farmers access to land, credit and co-operatives.***

190.   For many years, the Rural Family Development Program *** has placed special emphasis on the training of women farmers ***. [C]onsideration was also given to the needs of women farmers, but the impact to date has not been significant.

191.   Academic educational programs aimed at providing functional literacy, primary, and secondary programs are also accessible to rural women.

Self help groups, co-operatives and community activities

192.   In some areas rural women have organized themselves into self-help groups and co-operatives in order to make use of economies of scale in purchasing inputs and marketing agricultural produce. Organizations in which this group of women are involved in include: sports clubs, social clubs, church clubs, farmer organizations, community groups and parent/teachers associations.

Land and Credit Policies

193.   In respect of land ownership and use under the law, men and women have equal access ***. However, in practice there is evidence of unequal access between men and women in the ownership and use of land resources.***

196.   Gender is not a written consideration for receiving a loan through the bank.***

*Article 15 ***

Family Property (Bill in Draft)

206.   This Act will provide for a more equitable division of property between spouses upon breakdown of marriage or the termination of a common law union.***

COMMITTEE ON THE ELIMINATION OF DISCRIMINATION AGAINST WOMEN, CONCLUDING OBSERVATIONS: JAMAICA (2001)

24th Session, January 15–February 2, 2001
U.N. Doc. CEDAW/C/JAM/2-4 (2001)

(a) Introduction by the State party

196.   In introducing the report the representative of Jamaica informed the Committee of some of the legal, political, social and economic challenges facing her country in the implementation of the Convention ***.***

198.   Despite the fact that many women had high academic qualifications, they remained largely under-represented in positions of influence, power and decision-making.*** Similarly, women tended to be under-represented in decision-making positions in the private sector ***. [W]omen still encountered difficulties in finding employment commensurate with the level of their qualifications.

199.   The representative described her Government's programs to address poverty, violence against women, prostitution and the spread of HIV/AIDS, pointing out particular progress in the areas of education and health ***.

200.   Noting that poverty continued to affect all aspects of women's lives, the representative stated that poverty eradication programs were a national priority ***. The Government was seeking to ensure the wider integration of women in the tourism field, although the negative aspects associated with that sector, such as sex tourism, prostitution and sexual exploitation of young girls, would be monitored.

201.   *** The representative noted that despite the significant achievements in the area of women's health, HIV/AIDS had become an issue requiring urgent national attention. Women were contracting the virus at a faster rate than men ***.

202.   The representative explained that achievements had been made in addressing the issues of domestic and other forms of gender-based violence ***.

203.   *** The goals of justice and equity faced challenges because of joblessness, lack of growth and feminization of poverty. It was a priority for the Government to target the most marginalized and poorest in the society, especially women and children, to give them autonomy and choice ***.***

(b) Concluding comments of the Committee

Factors and difficulties affecting the implementation of the Convention

210. The Committee notes that the entrenched stereotypical attitudes with regard to the role of women and men and the persistence of gender-based violence within the society constitute obstacles to the full implementation of the Convention.***

Principal areas of concern and recommendation

212.   *** The Committee urges the Government to reform existing legislation and to create new legislation to protect the equal rights of women and men in regard to labor, social, family and property.***

215.   The Committee expresses its concern that the Maternity Leave with Pay Act of 1979 does not cover domestic workers. It also expresses its concern with the disparity of eligibility and benefits to domestic workers under the National Insurance Scheme ***.***

217.   The Committee expresses its concern that stereotypical attitudes and behavioral patterns about the roles of women and men in the family and in society persist.

218.   The Committee urges the Government to implement awareness-raising campaigns to change stereotypical and discriminatory attitudes concerning the roles of women and girls.***

223.   The Committee expresses its concern about the high rate of teenage pregnancies.

225. The Committee expresses its concern about the persistence of gender-based violence and domestic violence, including marital rape. The Committee also expresses its concern about the high incidence of incest and rape, and the lack of a holistic governmental strategy to identify and eradicate gender-based violence.

226. The Committee urges the Government to place a high priority on measures to address violence against women in the family and in society ***. The Committee recommends that the Government raise public awareness about violence against women and urges the Government to strengthen its activities and programs to focus on sexual violence, sexual crimes, incest and prostitution, especially prostitution associated with tourism ***.

227. The Committee expresses its concern at the high incidence of poverty among various groups of women, in particular in households headed by females. The Committee recognizes that those households have been negatively affected by structural adjustment programs and the changing global situation.***

229. The Committee expresses its concern about the working conditions of female laborers in the free-trade zone areas.

Notes and Questions

1. *Impact of Structural Adjustment.* In paragraph 227 of its Concluding Observations on the Jamaica Country Report, CEDAW expresses concern about "the high incidence of poverty among various groups of women" and "recognizes that those households have been negatively affected by structural adjustment programs and the changing global situation." How should the government of Jamaica respond to such concerns?

2. *Role of Government.* How far should government policy go in attempting to address stereotyped roles for women and men in political, economic, and social life? What are the implications for educational policy and freedom of the press?

3. For more on the economic, social and cultural status of Jamaican women, some of whom work as migrant domestic workers, health care workers or assembly workers, *see, e.g.*, Hope Lewis, *Lionheart Gals Facing the Dragon: The Human Rights of Inter/National Black Women in the United States*, 76 OR. L. REV. 567 (1997); Hope Lewis, *Universal Mother: Transnational Migration and the Human Rights of Black Women in the Americas*, 5 J. GENDER, RACE & JUSTICE 197 (2001); Camille Nelson, *Carriers of Globalization: Loss of Home and Self within the African Diaspora*, 55 FLA. L. REV. 539 (2003); Sherrie L. Russell-Brown, *Labor Rights as Human Rights: The Situation of Women Workers in Jamaica's Export Free Zones*, 1 BERKELEY J. EMP. & LAB. L. 179 (2003).

4. Feminist legal scholars have criticized the longstanding failure of public international law to fully address the concerns of women, *see* Hilary Charlesworth, *et al.*, *Feminist Approaches to International Law*, 85 AM. J. INT'L L. 613 (1991). In recent years, however, the literature on gender and international human rights law has become voluminous. For further reading on the implementation of the human rights of women under the Women's Convention and other instruments, *see, e.g.*, GLOBAL CRITICAL RACE FEMINISM: AN INTERNATIONAL READER (Adrien Katherine Wing ed., 2000); HUMAN RIGHTS OF WOMEN: NATIONAL AND INTERNATIONAL PERSPECTIVES (Rebecca Cook ed., 1994); WOMEN AND INTERNATIONAL HUMAN RIGHTS LAW (Kelly D. Askin & Dorean M. Koenig eds., 1999).

D. THE CONVENTION ON THE RIGHTS OF THE CHILD

INTRODUCTION

With 192 states parties (as of June 2004), the Convention on the Rights of the Child is now the most widely ratified international human rights instrument. Only the United States and Somalia failed to ratify the Children's Convention, although both have signed it. Ironically, and despite what appears to be an almost universal commitment to the rights and interests of children, massive violations of their rights occur daily in all parts of the world. Recent reports by NGOs and U.N. agencies list a panoply of abuses. Street children are killed or tortured by police or paramilitary groups. In some regions, young children are forced to serve in military, paramilitary or insurgent armies. Globalization has extended an already disturbing trend in the trafficking of children for sex and other labor. The International Labour Organization reports that more than "246 million children between 5 and 17 years old are working instead of attending school." International Labour Organization, World Day Against Child Labour (June 12, 2002), *available at* http://www.ilo.org/public/english/bureau/inf/childlabour/index.htm. Children work in domestic, agricultural and manufacturing settings, often under exploitative and dangerous conditions. Many of the world's poorest children lack access to clean water, basic nutrition, health care, and education. Some juveniles are still subjected to the death penalty. *See, e.g.,* Human Rights Watch, *Children's Rights, available at* http://www.hrw.org/children/ (last visited June 23, 2004); *and* Human Rights Watch, *Promises Broken: an Assessment of Children's Rights on the 10th Anniversary of the Convention on the Rights of the Child* (December 1999), *available at* http://www.hrw.org/campaigns/crp/promises/ (last visited June 23, 2004).

While the interests of children were recognized in the International Bill of Rights and other human rights instruments, their rights arguably were seen primarily as derivatives of their parents' rights. In the 1980s and 1990s, a large and active international children's rights movement successfully advocated for the drafting, adoption and global ratification of a special convention recognizing children as individual and direct subjects of human rights. The Convention, drafted in the ten years following the International Year of the Child in 1979, addresses the full range of human rights—civil, political, economic, social and cultural—as well as rights based in international humanitarian law. Observers note that "the text of the Convention is drafted in language that strongly emphasizes rights of the individual child, rather than the child as a member of a family or group." CYNTHIA PRICE COHEN & HOWARD A. DAVIDSON EDS., CHILDREN'S RIGHTS IN AMERICA: U.N. CONVENTION ON THE RIGHTS OF THE CHILD COMPARED WITH UNITED STATES LAW (1990).

As you read the Convention, consider the following: What are the structural similarities and differences as compared to other human rights instruments such as the Race Convention or the Women's Convention? What unique human rights concerns do children face? How might those concerns vary across cultures and economic class, if at all? Do you agree that the Convention emphasizes individual rights as opposed to family or other group rights? If so, is this emphasis appropriate? What social, political, economic and cultural values does such an approach promote? To the extent that there are potential conflicts between the rights of children and the rights of their parents, how should such conflicts be resolved?

CONVENTION ON THE RIGHTS OF THE CHILD

Adopted and opened for signature, ratification and accession by General Assembly Resolution 44/25 of November 20, 1989 (*entered into force* September 2, 1990)

Preamble

The States Parties to the present Convention,***

Recalling that, in the Universal Declaration of Human Rights, the United Nations has proclaimed that childhood is entitled to special care and assistance,***

Recognizing that, in all countries in the world, there are children living in exceptionally difficult conditions, and that such children need special consideration,

Taking due account of the importance of the traditions and cultural values of each people for the protection and harmonious development of the child,

Recognizing the importance of international co-operation for improving the living conditions of children in every country, in particular in the developing countries,

Have agreed as follows:

PART I

Article 1

For the purposes of the present Convention, a child means every human being below the age of eighteen years unless under the law applicable to the child, majority is attained earlier.

Article 2

1. States Parties shall respect and ensure the rights set forth in the present Convention to each child within their jurisdiction without discrimination of any kind, irrespective of the child's or his or her parent's or legal guardian's race, colour, sex, language, religion, political or other opinion, national, ethnic or social origin, property, disability, birth or other status.***

Article 3

1. In all actions concerning children, whether undertaken by public or private social welfare institutions, courts of law, administrative authorities or legislative bodies, the best interests of the child shall be a primary consideration.***

Article 4

*** With regard to economic, social and cultural rights, States Parties shall undertake [all appropriate legislative, administrative, and other] measures to the maximum extent of their available resources and, where needed, within the framework of international co-operation.

Article 5

States Parties shall respect the responsibilities, rights and duties of parents or, where applicable, the members of the extended family or community as provided for by local custom, legal guardians or other persons legally responsible for the child ***.***

Article 7

1. The child shall be registered immediately after birth and shall have the right from birth to a name, the right to acquire a nationality and. as far as possible, the right to know and be cared for by his or her parents.***

Article 8

1. States Parties undertake to respect the right of the child to preserve his or her identity, including nationality, name and family relations as recognized by law without unlawful interference.***

Article 9

1. States Parties shall ensure that a child shall not be separated from his or her parents against their will, except when competent authorities subject to judicial review determine, in accordance with applicable law and procedures, that such separation is necessary for the best interests of the child.***

Article 17

States Parties recognize the important function performed by the mass media and shall ensure that the child has access to information and material from a diversity of national and international sources, especially those aimed at the promotion of his or her social, spiritual and moral well-being and physical and mental health.***

*Article 18****

2. For the purpose of guaranteeing and promoting the rights set forth in the present Convention, States Parties shall render appropriate assistance to parents and legal guardians in the performance of their child-rearing responsibilities and shall ensure the development of institutions, facilities and services for the care of children.

3. States Parties shall take all appropriate measures to ensure that children of working parents have the right to benefit from child-care services and facilities for which they are eligible.***

Article 20

1. A child temporarily or permanently deprived of his or her family environment, or in whose own best interests cannot be allowed to remain in that environment, shall be entitled to special protection and assistance provided by the State.

2. States Parties shall in accordance with their national laws ensure alternative care for such a child.

3. Such care could include, inter alia, foster placement, kafalah of Islamic law, adoption or if necessary placement in suitable institutions for the care of children. When considering solutions, due regard shall be paid to the desirability of continuity in a child's upbringing and to the child's ethnic, religious, cultural and linguistic background.***

Article 23

1. States Parties recognize that a mentally or physically disabled child should enjoy a full and decent life, in conditions which ensure dignity, promote self-reliance and facilitate the child's active participation in the community.

2. States Parties recognize the right of the disabled child to special care and shall encourage and ensure the extension, subject to available resources, to the eligible child and those responsible for his or her care, of assistance for which application is made and which is appropriate to the child's condition and to the circumstances of the parents or others caring for the child.***

Article 24

1. States Parties recognize the right of the child to the enjoyment of the highest attainable standard of health and to facilities for the treatment of illness and rehabilitation of health. States Parties shall strive to ensure that no child is deprived of his or her right of access to such health care services.

2. States Parties shall pursue full implementation of this right and, in particular, shall take appropriate measures:

(a) To diminish infant and child mortality;

(b) To ensure the provision of necessary medical assistance and health care to all children with emphasis on the development of primary health care;

(c) To combat disease and malnutrition, including within the framework of primary health care, through, inter alia, the application of readily available technology and through the provision of adequate nutritious foods and clean drinking-water, taking into consideration the dangers and risks of environmental pollution;

(d) To ensure appropriate pre-natal and post-natal health care for mothers;

(e) To ensure that all segments of society, in particular parents and children, are informed, have access to education and are supported in the use of basic knowledge of child health and nutrition, the advantages of breastfeeding, hygiene and environmental sanitation and the prevention of accidents;

(f) To develop preventive health care, guidance for parents and family planning education and services.

3. States Parties shall take all effective and appropriate measures with a view to abolishing traditional practices prejudicial to the health of children.

4. States Parties undertake to promote and encourage international co-operation with a view to achieving progressively the full realization of the right recognized in the present article. In this regard, particular account shall be taken of the needs of developing countries.***

Article 27

1. States Parties recognize the right of every child to a standard of living adequate for the child's physical, mental, spiritual, moral and social development.

2. The parent(s) or others responsible for the child have the primary responsibility to secure, within their abilities and financial capacities, the conditions of living necessary for the child's development.

3. States Parties, in accordance with national conditions and within their means, shall take appropriate measures to assist parents and others responsible for the child to

implement this right and shall in case of need provide material assistance and support programmes, particularly with regard to nutrition, clothing and housing.***

Article 28

1. States Parties recognize the right of the child to education, and with a view to achieving this right progressively and on the basis of equal opportunity, they shall, in particular:

(a) Make primary education compulsory and available free to all;

(b) Encourage the development of different forms of secondary education, including general and vocational education, make them available and accessible to every child, and take appropriate measures such as the introduction of free education and offering financial assistance in case of need;

(c) Make higher education accessible to all on the basis of capacity by every appropriate means;

(d) Make educational and vocational information and guidance available and accessible to all children;

(e) Take measures to encourage regular attendance at schools and the reduction of drop-out rates.***

Article 30

In those States in which ethnic, religious or linguistic minorities or persons of indigenous origin exist, a child belonging to such a minority or who is indigenous shall not be denied the right, in community with other members of his or her group, to enjoy his or her own culture, to profess and practise his or her own religion, or to use his or her own language.

Article 31

1. States Parties recognize the right of the child to rest and leisure, to engage in play and recreational activities appropriate to the age of the child and to participate freely in cultural life and the arts.

2. States Parties shall respect and promote the right of the child to participate fully in cultural and artistic life and shall encourage the provision of appropriate and equal opportunities for cultural, artistic, recreational and leisure activity.

Article 32

1. States Parties recognize the right of the child to be protected from economic exploitation and from performing any work that is likely to be hazardous or to interfere with the child's education, or to be harmful to the child's health or physical, mental, spiritual, moral or social development.

2. States Parties shall take legislative, administrative, social and educational measures to ensure the implementation of the present article. To this end, and having regard to the relevant provisions of other international instruments, States Parties shall in particular:

(a) Provide for a minimum age or minimum ages for admission to employment;

(b) Provide for appropriate regulation of the hours and conditions of employment;

(c) Provide for appropriate penalties or other sanctions to ensure the effective enforcement of the present article.***

Notes and Questions

1. What could explain the U.S. failure to ratify the Children's Convention? Should it ratify? If so, would you recommend attaching reservations limiting the domestic application of any provisions? How is the approach taken by the Convention different from the legal treatment of children in the United States?

2. While Somalia's failure to ratify the Children's Convention might be explained by the instability and civil unrest in that country following the end of the Cold War, the reasons for U.S. objections to ratification are complex and controversial. Some object to the treaty's provisions that would conflict with current interpretations of U.S. law. The United States, for example, is one of very few countries that continue to impose the death penalty for crimes committed prior to adulthood. Further, the treatment of juveniles in the highly racialized U.S. criminal justice system has been strongly condemned by human rights monitoring organizations. *See, e.g.*, Human Rights Watch, *Children in the U.S.*, *available at* http://www.hrw.org/about/projects/crd/child-usa.htm (last visited June 22, 2004). Some fear the increased international scrutiny and criticism to which U.S. law and policy would be exposed upon ratification. Others argue that the Convention would undermine family unity or even encourage children to sue for the legal termination of parental rights. In addition, some object to the potential implications of the Convention for the sexual and reproductive rights of children and adolescents. *See, e.g.*, Children's Rights Caucus, An Open Letter to the Honorable Tommy Thompson, US Secretary of Health and Human Services and the United States delegation to the UN Special Session on Children, *available at* http://www.hrw.org/press/2002/05/unkids0509.htm (last visited June 23, 2004) (objecting to U.S. delegation's advocacy of an abstinence approach to children's sexual and reproductive health and the continuing failure to outlaw the death penalty for juvenile offenses in the United States). For a general discussion of reservations to the Convention, *see* William Schabas, *Reservations to the Convention on the Rights of the Child*, 18 Hum. Rts. Q. 472 (1996).

3. Interestingly, the United States has ratified the two Optional Protocols to the Children's Convention, the Optional Protocol on the Rights of the Child on the Involvement of Children in Armed Conflicts, GA Res. A/RES/54/263, *entered into force* Feb. 12, 2002, and the Optional Protocol to the Convention on the Rights of the Child on the Sale of Children, Child Prostitution and Child Pornography, GA Res. A/RES/54/263, *entered into force* Jan. 18, 2002. For a discussion of the controversies surrounding the adoption of the optional protocols, including U.S. objections, *see, e.g.*, Cris R. Revaz, *The Optional Protocols to the UN Convention on the Rights of the Child on Sex Trafficking and Child Soldiers*, 9 Hum. Rts. B. (No. 1) (Fall 2001), *available at* http://www.wcl.american.edu/hrbrief/09/1child.cfm.

4. Article 24 of the Convention imposes obligations on states parties to work toward the elimination of traditional practices, such as "female circumcision" (also known as "female genital mutilation" or "female genital cutting") that are harmful to children. Has the widespread ratification of the CRC eliminated the controversy over the human rights status of these and other traditional practices? If not, why not? *See* the discussion of traditional practices in Chapter 6, *infra*.

5.   Why was the Children's Convention so widely ratified? If the vast majority of countries were able to agree on cross-cultural standards applicable to children, why does it seem so much more difficult to agree on the treatment of adults? If children are considered to be of "special" importance in most, if not all, cultures, why are their rights violated on such a massive scale?

6.   Is it useful to focus human rights monitoring on particular groups such as women, children, or ethnic minorities? Why or why not?

INTERPRETATION OF THE CONVENTION

The decisions below illustrate differences in approach to the interpretation of the Convention on the Rights of the Child in domestic law. The cases involve somewhat similar factual backgrounds—arguments that, in deportation proceedings against a noncitizen, the best interests of a native-born child should be considered.

MAVIS BAKER v. MINISTER OF CITIZENSHIP AND IMMIGRATION[6]

Supreme Court of Canada
1999 Can. Sup. Ct. LEXIS 44

1.   Regulations made pursuant to §114(2) of the Immigration Act, R.S.C., 1985, c. I-2, empower the respondent Minister to facilitate the admission to Canada of a person where the Minister is satisfied, owing to humanitarian and compassionate considerations, that admission should be facilitated or an exemption from the regulations made under the Act should be granted. ***

I.   Factual Background

2.   Mavis Baker is a citizen of Jamaica who entered Canada as a visitor in August of 1981 and has remained in Canada since then. She never received permanent resident status, but supported herself illegally as a live-in domestic worker for 11 years. She has had four children (who are all Canadian citizens) while living in Canada: Paul Brown, born in 1985, twins Patricia and Peter Robinson, born in 1989, and Desmond Robinson, born in 1992. After Desmond was born, Ms. Baker suffered from post-partum psychosis and was diagnosed with paranoid schizophrenia. She applied for welfare at that time. When she was first diagnosed with mental illness, two of her children were placed in the care of their natural father, and the other two were placed in foster care. The two who were in foster care are now again under her care, since her condition has improved.

3.   The appellant was ordered deported in December 1992, after it was determined that she had worked illegally in Canada and had overstayed her visitor's visa. In 1993, Ms. Baker applied for an exemption from the requirement to apply for permanent residence outside Canada, based upon humanitarian and compassionate considerations, pursuant to §114(2) of the Immigration Act. She had the assistance of counsel in filing

---

6   The Canadian Council of Churches, the Canadian Foundation for Children, Youth and the Law, the Defence for Children International-Canada, the Canadian Council for Refugees, and the Charter Committee on Poverty Issues, were Interveners in this case.

this application, and included, among other documentation, submissions from her lawyer, a letter from her doctor, and a letter from a social worker with the Children's Aid Society. The documentation provided indicated that although she was still experiencing psychiatric problems, she was making progress. It also stated that she might become ill again if she were forced to return to Jamaica, since treatment might not be available for her there. Ms. Baker's submissions also clearly indicated that she was the sole caregiver for two of her Canadian-born children, and that the other two depended on her for emotional support and were in regular contact with her. The documentation suggested that she too would suffer emotional hardship if she were separated from them.

4. The response to this request was contained in a letter, dated April 18, 1994, and signed by Immigration Officer M. Caden, stating that a decision had been made that there were insufficient humanitarian and compassionate grounds to warrant processing Ms. Baker's application for permanent residence within Canada. This letter contained no reasons for the decision.***

[handwritten: Application denied]

6. Following the refusal of her application, Ms. Baker was served, on May 27, 1994, with a direction to report to Pearson Airport on June 17 for removal from Canada. Her deportation has been stayed pending the result of this appeal.

II. Relevant Statutory Provisions and Provisions of International Treaties ***

Immigration Regulations, 1978, SOR/78-172, as amemded by SOR/93-44 ***

2.1 The Minister is hereby authorized to exempt any person from any regulation made under subsection 114(1) of the Act or otherwise facilitate the admission to Canada of any person where the Minister is satisfied that the person should be exempted from that regulation or that the person's admission should be facilitated owing to the existence of compassionate or humanitarian considerations.

Convention on the Rights of the Child, Can. T.S. 1992 No. 3

Article 3

1. In all actions concerning children, whether undertaken by public or private social welfare institutions, courts of law, administrative authorities or legislative bodies, the best interests of the child shall be a primary consideration.

2. States Parties undertake to ensure the child such protection and care as is necessary for his or her well-being, taking into account the rights and duties of his or her parents, legal guardians, or other individuals legally responsible for him or her, and, to this end, shall take all appropriate legislative and administrative measures.***

Article 9

1. States Parties shall ensure that a child shall not be separated from his or her parents against their will, except when competent authorities subject to judicial review determine, in accordance with applicable law and procedures, that such separation is necessary for the best interests of the child. Such determination may be necessary in a particular case such as one involving abuse or neglect of the child by the parents, or one where the parents are living separately and a decision must be made as to the child's place of residence.

2. In any proceedings pursuant to paragraph 1 of the present article, all interested parties shall be given an opportunity to participate in the proceedings and make their views known.

3. States Parties shall respect the right of the child who is separated from one or both parents to maintain personal relations and direct contact with both parents on a regular basis, except if it is contrary to the child's best interests.

4. Where such separation results from any action initiated by a State Party, such as the detention, imprisonment, exile, deportation or death (including death arising from any cause while the person is in the custody of the State) of one or both parents or of the child, that State Party shall, upon request, provide the parents, the child or, if appropriate, another member of the family with the essential information concerning the whereabouts of the absent member(s) of the family unless the provision of the information would be detrimental to the well-being of the child. States parties shall further ensure that the submission of such a request shall of itself entail no adverse consequences for the person(s) concerned.***

Article 12

1. States Parties shall assure to the child who is capable of forming his or her own views the right to express those views freely in all matters affecting the child, the views of the child being given due weight in accordance with the age and maturity of the child.

2. For this purpose, the child shall in particular be provided the opportunity to be heard in any judicial and administrative proceedings affecting the child, either directly, or through a representative or an appropriate body, in a manner consistent with the procedural rules of national law.

[The trial court ruled that the Convention on the Rights of the Child was inapplicable and dismissed Ms. Baker's application. The appellate court held that the CRC was non-self-executing, and that applying it to immigration matters would violate the separation of powers. It further concluded that the deportation of a parent was not a decision "concerning" children within the meaning of Article 3 of the Convention. The Canadian Supreme Court framed the issues in terms of, *inter alia*, potential violations of the principles of procedural fairness and abuse of discretion by immigration officials.]

*IV. Analysis ***

*B. The Statutory Scheme and the Nature of the Decision ***

14. *** The Minister's power to grant an exemption based on humanitarian and compassionate (H & C) considerations arises from § 2.1 of the Immigration Regulations.***

15. Applications for permanent residence must, as a general rule, be made from outside Canada, pursuant to §9(1) of the Act. One of the exceptions to this is when admission is facilitated owing to the existence of compassionate or humanitarian considerations. *** It is an important decision that affects in a fundamental manner the future of individuals' lives. In addition, it may also have an important impact on the lives of any Canadian children of the person whose humanitarian and compassionate application is being considered, since they may be separated from one of their parents and/or uprooted from their country of citizenship, where they have settled and have connections.

16. Immigration officers who make H & C decisions are provided with a set of guidelines *** Guideline 9.05 emphasizes that officers have a duty to decide which cases should be given a favourable recommendation, by carefully considering all aspects of the case, using their best judgment and asking themselves what a reasonable person would do in such a situation. It also states that although officers are not expected to "delve into areas which are not presented during examination or interviews, they should attempt to clarify possible humanitarian grounds and public policy considerations even if these are not well articulated."

17. The guidelines also set out the bases upon which the discretion conferred by § 114(2) and the regulations should be exercised. Two different types of criteria that may lead to a positive § 114(2) decision are outlined—public policy considerations and humanitarian and compassionate grounds. Immigration officers are instructed, under guideline 9.07, to assure themselves, first, whether a public policy consideration is present, and if there is none, whether humanitarian and compassionate circumstances exist. Public policy reasons include marriage to a Canadian resident, the fact that the person has lived in Canada, become established, and has become an "illegal de facto resident," and the fact that the person may be a long-term holder of employment authorization or has worked as a foreign domestic. Guideline 9.07 states that humanitarian and compassionate grounds will exist if "unusual, undeserved or disproportionate hardship would be caused to the person seeking consideration if he or she had to leave Canada." The guidelines also directly address situations involving family dependency, and emphasize that the requirement that a person leave Canada to apply from abroad may result in hardship for close family members of a Canadian resident, whether parents, children, or others who are close to the claimant, but not related by blood. They note that in such cases, the reasons why the person did not apply from abroad and the existence of family or other support in the person's home country should also be considered.***

C. Procedural Fairness ***

(2) Legitimate Expectations ***

29. *** I will first determine whether the duty of procedural fairness that would otherwise be applicable is affected, as the appellant argues, by the existence of a legitimate expectation based upon the text of the articles of the Convention and the fact that Canada has ratified it. In my view, however, the articles of the Convention and their wording did not give rise to a legitimate expectation on the part of Ms. Baker that when the decision on her H & C application was made, specific procedural rights above what would normally be required under the duty of fairness would be accorded, a positive finding would be made, or particular criteria would be applied. This Convention is not, in my view, the equivalent of a government representation about how H & C applications will be decided, nor does it suggest that any rights beyond the participatory rights discussed below will be accorded. Therefore, in this case there is no legitimate expectation affecting the content of the duty of fairness ***.***

(5) Reasonable Apprehension of Bias

45. Procedural fairness also requires that decisions be made free from a reasonable apprehension of bias, by an impartial decision-maker. ***

48. In my opinion, the well-informed member of the community would perceive bias when reading Officer Lorenz's comments. His notes, and the manner in which they

are written, do not disclose the existence of an open mind or a weighing of the particular circumstances of the case free from stereotypes. Most unfortunate is the fact that they seem to make a link between Ms. Baker's mental illness, her training as a domestic worker, the fact that she has several children, and the conclusion that she would therefore be a strain on our social welfare system for the rest of her life. In addition, the conclusion drawn was contrary to the psychiatrist's letter, which stated that, with treatment, Ms. Baker could remain well and return to being a productive member of society. Whether they were intended in this manner or not, these statements give the impression that Officer Lorenz may have been drawing conclusions based not on the evidence before him, but on the fact that Ms. Baker was a single mother with several children, and had been diagnosed with a psychiatric illness. His use of capitals to highlight the number of Ms. Baker's children may also suggest to a reader that this was a reason to deny her status. Reading his comments, I do not believe that a reasonable and well-informed member of the community would conclude that he had approached this case with the impartiality appropriate to a decision made by an immigration officer. It would appear to a reasonable observer that his own frustration with the "system" interfered with his duty to consider impartially whether the appellant's admission should be facilitated owing to humanitarian or compassionate considerations. I conclude that the notes of Officer Lorenz demonstrate a reasonable apprehension of bias.

D. *Review of the Exercise of the Minister's Discretion*

49. *** Since it is important to address the central questions which led to this appeal, I will also consider whether, as a substantive matter, the H & C decision was improperly made in this case.

50. The appellant argues that the notes provided to Ms. Baker show that, as a matter of law, the decision should be overturned on judicial review. She submits that the decision should be held to a standard of review of correctness, that principles of administrative law require this discretion to be exercised in accordance with the Convention, and that the Minister should apply the best interests of the child as a primary consideration in H & C decisions. The respondent submits that the Convention has not been implemented in Canadian law, and that to require that §114(2) and the regulations made under it be interpreted in accordance with the Convention would be improper, since it would interfere with the broad discretion granted by Parliament, and with the division of powers between the federal and provincial governments.***

(2) *The Standard of Review in this Case* ***

I conclude that considerable deference should be accorded to immigration officers exercising the powers conferred by the legislation, given the fact-specific nature of the inquiry, its role within the statutory scheme as an exception, the fact that the decision-maker is the Minister, and the considerable discretion evidenced by the statutory language. Yet the absence of a privative clause, the explicit contemplation of judicial review by the Federal Court Trial Division and the Federal Court of Appeal in certain circumstances, and the individual rather than polycentric nature of the decision, also suggest that the standard should not be as deferential as "patent unreasonableness." I conclude, weighing all these factors, that the appropriate standard of review is reasonableness simpliciter.

(3) Was this Decision Unreasonable? ***

64. The notes of Officer Lorenz, in relation to the consideration of "H&C factors," read as follows:

> The PC is a paranoid schizophrenic and on welfare. She has no qualifications other than as a domestic. She has FOUR CHILDREN IN JAMAICA AND ANOTHER FOUR BORN HERE. She will, of course, be a tremendous strain on our social welfare systems for (probably) the rest of her life. There are no H&C factors other than her FOUR CANADIAN-BORN CHILDREN. So we let her stay because of that? I am of the opinion that Canada can no longer afford this kind of generosity.

65. In my opinion, the approach taken to the children's interests shows that this decision was unreasonable in the sense contemplated in [prior cases]. The officer was completely dismissive of the interests of Ms. Baker's children. As I will outline in detail in the paragraphs that follow, I believe that the failure to give serious weight and consideration to the interests of the children constitutes an unreasonable exercise of the discretion conferred by the section, notwithstanding the important deference that should be given to the decision of the immigration officer. ***

67. *** Children's rights, and attention to their interests, are central humanitarian and compassionate values in Canadian society. Indications of children's interests as important considerations governing the manner in which H & C powers should be exercised may be found, for example, in the purposes of the Act, in international instruments, and in the guidelines for making H & C decisions published by the Minister herself.

(a) The Objectives of the Act

68. The objectives of the Act include, in §3(c):

> to facilitate the reunion in Canada of Canadian citizens and permanent residents with their close relatives from abroad;

Although this provision speaks of Parliament's objective of reuniting citizens and permanent residents with their close relatives from abroad, it is consistent, in my opinion, with a large and liberal interpretation of the values underlying this legislation and its purposes to presume that Parliament also placed a high value on keeping citizens and permanent residents together with their close relatives who are already in Canada. The obligation to take seriously and place important weight on keeping children in contact with both parents, if possible, and maintaining connections between close family members is suggested by the objective articulated in §3(c).

(b) International Law

69. Another indicator of the importance of considering the interests of children when making a compassionate and humanitarian decision is the ratification by Canada of the Convention on the Rights of the Child, and the recognition of the importance of children's rights and the best interests of children in other international instruments ratified by Canada. International treaties and conventions are not part of Canadian law unless they have been implemented by statute [Citations omitted.] I agree with the respondent and the Court of Appeal that the Convention has not been implemented by Parliament. Its provisions therefore have no direct application within Canadian law.

[Handwritten margin note: CRC not implemented in Canada]

70. Nevertheless, the values reflected in international human rights law may help inform the contextual approach to statutory interpretation and judicial review. As stated in R. Sullivan, Driedger on the Construction of Statutes (3rd ed. 1994), at p. 330:

> [T]he legislature is presumed to respect the values and principles contained in international law, both customary and conventional. These constitute a part of the legal context in which legislation is enacted and read. In so far as possible, therefore, interpretations that reflect these values and principles are preferred.***

The important role of international human rights law as an aid in interpreting domestic law has also been emphasized in other common law countries: *see*, for example, *Tavita v. Minister of Immigration*, [1994] 2 N.Z.L.R. 257 (C.A.), at p. 266; *Vishaka v. Rajasthan*, [1997] 3 L.R.C. 361 (S.C. India), at p. 367. It is also a critical influence on the interpretation of the scope of the rights included in the Charter: *Slaight Communications, supra; R. v. Keegstra*, [1990] 3 S.C.R. 697.

71. The values and principles of the Convention recognize the importance of being attentive to the rights and best interests of children when decisions are made that relate to and affect their future. In addition, the preamble, recalling the Universal Declaration of Human Rights, recognizes that "childhood is entitled to special care and assistance." A similar emphasis on the importance of placing considerable value on the protection of children and their needs and interests is also contained in other international instruments. The United Nations Declaration of the Rights of the Child (1959), in its preamble, states that the child "needs special safeguards and care." The principles of the Convention and other international instruments place special importance on protections for children and childhood, and on particular consideration of their interests, needs, and rights. They help show the values that are central in determining whether this decision was a reasonable exercise of the H & C power.

(c) The Ministerial Guidelines

72. Third, the guidelines issued by the Minister to immigration officers recognize and reflect the values and approach discussed above and articulated in the Convention. As described above, immigration officers are expected to make the decision that a reasonable person would make, with special consideration of humanitarian values such as keeping connections between family members and avoiding hardship by sending people to places where they no longer have connections. ***

73. The above factors indicate that emphasis on the rights, interests, and needs of children and special attention to childhood are important values that should be considered in reasonably interpreting the "humanitarian" and "compassionate" considerations that guide the exercise of the discretion. I conclude that because the reasons for this decision do not indicate that it was made in a manner which was alive, attentive, or sensitive to the interests of Ms. Baker's children, and did not consider them as an important factor in making the decision, it was an unreasonable exercise of the power conferred by the legislation, and must, therefore, be overturned. In addition, the reasons for decision failed to give sufficient weight or consideration to the hardship that a return to Jamaica might cause Ms. Baker, given the fact that she had been in Canada for 12 years, was ill and might not be able to obtain treatment in Jamaica, and would necessarily be separated from at least some of her children.

74. *** [A]ttentiveness and sensitivity to the importance of the rights of children, to their best interests, and to the hardship that may be caused to them by a negative decision is essential for an H & C decision to be made in a reasonable manner. While deference should be given to immigration officers on s. 114(2) judicial review applications, decisions cannot stand when the manner in which the decision was made and the approach taken are in conflict with humanitarian and compassionate values. The Minister's guidelines themselves reflect this approach. However, the decision here was inconsistent with it.

75. *** [F]or the exercise of the discretion to fall within the standard of reasonableness, the decision-maker should consider children's best interests as an important factor, give them substantial weight, and be alert, alive and sensitive to them. That is not to say that children's best interests must always outweigh other considerations, or that there will not be other reasons for denying an H & C claim even when children's interests are given this consideration. However, where the interests of children are minimized, in a manner inconsistent with Canada's humanitarian and compassionate tradition and the Minister's guidelines, the decision will be unreasonable.

E. Conclusions and Disposition

76. Therefore, both because there was a violation of the principles of procedural fairness owing to a reasonable apprehension of bias, and because the exercise of the H & C discretion was unreasonable, I would allow this appeal *** and set aside the decision of Officer Caden of April 18, 1994, with party-and-party costs throughout. The matter will be returned to the Minister for redetermination by a different immigration officer.***

[handwritten: Conclusion]

IACOBUCCI J.—

[handwritten: Dissent]

78. I agree with L'Heureux-Dube J.'s reasons and disposition of this appeal, except to the extent that my colleague addresses the effect of international law on the exercise of Ministerial discretion pursuant to §114(2) of the Immigration Act, R.S.C., 1985, c. I-2. The certified question at issue in this appeal concerns whether federal immigration authorities must treat the best interests of the child as a primary consideration in assessing an application for humanitarian and compassionate consideration under §114(2) of the Act, given that the legislation does not implement the provisions contained in the Convention of the Rights of the Child, Can. T.S. 1992 No. 3, a multilateral convention to which Canada is party. In my opinion, the certified question should be answered in the negative.

79. It is a matter of well-settled law that an international convention ratified by the executive branch of government is of no force or effect within the Canadian legal system until such time as its provisions have been incorporated into domestic law by way of implementing legislation: *Capital Cities Communications Inc. v. Canadian Radio-Television Commission*, [1978] 2 S.C.R. 141. I do not agree with the approach adopted by my colleague, wherein reference is made to the underlying values of an unimplemented international treaty in the course of the contextual approach to statutory interpretation and administrative law, because such an approach is not in accordance with the Court's jurisprudence concerning the status of international law within the domestic legal system.

80. In my view, one should proceed with caution in deciding matters of this nature, lest we adversely affect the balance maintained by our Parliamentary tradition, or inad-

vertently grant the executive the power to bind citizens without the necessity of involving the legislative branch.***

81. The primacy accorded to the rights of children in the Convention, assuming for the sake of argument that the factual circumstances of this appeal are included within the scope of the relevant provisions, is irrelevant unless and until such provisions are the subject of legislation enacted by Parliament.***

BEHARRY V. RENO

183 F. Supp. 2d 584 (E.D.N.Y. 2002)

WEINSTEIN, Senior District Judge

I. Introduction

Petitioner seeks relief from deportation under the Immigration and Naturalization Act, 8 U.S.C. §§1101 *et seq.* (INA), or under principles of international law. Because of treaty and international law requirements, applicable immigration statutes must be interpreted to require that petitioner be granted a hearing where he can attempt to show the effect his deportation would have on his family (both citizen and lawful permanent resident aliens) and himself, as against the risks of his continued presence in this country. If the statutes are not so interpreted, then in this instance treaties and international law override the statutes and require such a hearing.

II. Facts

A. Background

Petitioner entered the United States from Trinidad as a lawful permanent resident in April of 1982, when he was seven years old. He has resided here without interruption since that time. He completed an eleventh-grade education in the United States and has worked here at a variety of jobs.

Many of petitioner's immediate family live in the United States, including his mother, a lawful permanent resident, and his sister, a United States citizen. He has a six-year-old daughter who is a United States citizen.

In November 1996 petitioner was convicted of robbery in the second degree for an alleged July 1996 theft of $714 from a coffee shop. According to facts presented at his deportation hearing, petitioner acted with the aid of an accomplice and the help of a friend working at the store. He and his accomplice took the money from the cash register.***

Petitioner had unrelated prior criminal violations, including two convictions for petty larceny (one as a juvenile), a conviction for criminal mischief, and a conviction for second degree riot. None resulted in incarceration.

A sentence of two-and-a-quarter to four-and-a-half years was imposed for the robbery. ***

B. Procedural History

While petitioner was incarcerated, the Immigration and Naturalization Service (I.N.S.) commenced deportation proceedings in February of 1997.***

The immigration judge found him 1) statutorily ineligible for 212(c) relief as an excludee; 2) statutorily ineligible for asylum; and 3) not covered by section 243(h) since he did not fall within the special classes enumerated in that section.

*** The BIA reversed the finding of the immigration judge that petitioner's robbery was not a "serious crime," thus providing another bar to section 243(h) relief.

This petition for a writ of habeas corpus in federal district court followed. Petitioner is presently being detained by I.N.S. awaiting deportation.

III. Law

5. Other Statutory Provisions for Relief from Removal ***

Section 212(h) of the INA allows waiver of deportation under special circumstances for aliens whose deportation would result in substantial hardship to a citizen spouse or children. Section 212(h) does not apply to a lawful permanent resident alien convicted of an aggravated felony.***

A. International Covenant on Civil and Political Rights

Article 13 of the ICCPR requires that an alien lawfully residing in a territory "be allowed to submit the reasons against his expulsion" unless compelling interests of national security require otherwise. The ICCPR is particularly forceful in defense of the rights to privacy and family integrity.*** The ICCPR also states that "the family is the natural and fundamental group unit of society and is entitled to protection by society and the State." ICCPR Article 23(1). Separating a parent from a citizen child by forced deportation can be considered a violation of the ICCPR if no adequate hearing is afforded.

Article 7 of the ICCPR prohibits "cruel, inhuman, or degrading treatment." Arbitrary separation from one's family and longtime home can reasonably be interpreted to fall within that general category.

The ICCPR is a signed, ratified treaty. It came with attached reservations of non-self-execution. This has led some courts to disregard some of its parts. *See e.g., Beazley,* 242 F.3d at 263–68; *but see* Maria, 68 F.Supp.2d at 231–35 (reliance on the ICCPR to interpret provisions of the 1996 Acts). It is significant that the Senate Committee on Foreign Relations stated that "existing U.S. law generally complies with the Covenant." Sen. Exec. Rep. 102–23 (Mar. 24, 1992).

B. Universal Declaration of Human Rights

The UDHR contains a provision prohibiting the imposition of "arbitrary . . . exile." *See* UDHR, Article 9. It also states that "everyone is entitled in full equality to a fair and public hearing by an independent and impartial tribunal, in the determination of his rights and obligations." UDHR, Article 10. ***

While the UDHR is not a treaty, it has an effect similar to a treaty. *See Filartiga,* 630 F.2d at 883 (The UDHR is "an authoritative statement of the international community"). It is a declaration published by the General Assembly of the United Nations "as a common standard of achievement for all peoples and all nations." *See* Preamble, Universal Declaration of Human Rights; Restatement (Third) of Foreign Relations Law §701, Reporter's Note 6 ("The Declaration has become the accepted general articulation of recognized rights.") U.S. Dept. of State, "Human Rights," available at www.state. gov/g/drl/hr/ ("A central goal of U.S. foreign policy has been the promotion of respect for human rights, as embodied in the Universal Declaration of Human Rights."). Provisions of the UDHR may be used in statutory construction. *See Mojica*, 970 F.Supp. at 146–48 (using the UDHR in statutory construction). The UDHR is helpful in resolving questions of international human rights law. *See Rodriguez-Fernandez v. Wilkinson*, 654 F.2d 1382 (10th Cir.1981) (using UDHR provisions as well as other methods of interpretation to conclude that indefinite detention of aliens was not permissible); *Fernandez v. Wilkinson*, 505 F.Supp. 787, 795–96 (D.Kan.1980). The UDHR has also been utilized in weighing the constitutionality of provisions of the 1996 Acts. [Citations omitted.]

C. *Convention on the Rights of the Child*

The CRC declares in its preamble that "the family, as the fundamental group of society and the natural environment for the growth and well-being of all its members and particularly children, should be afforded the necessary protection and assistance. [T]he child[s]hould grow up in a family environment." Article 3 states that "[i]n all actions concerning children, whether undertaken by private or public social welfare institutions, courts of law, administrative authorities or legislative bodies, the best interests of the child shall be a primary consideration." Article 7 provides children with, "as far as possible, the right to know and be cared for by his or her parents."***

The United States signed the CRC on February 16, 1995; it has never been sent to the Senate for ratification, but every other nation except Somalia—which is effectively without a government—has ratified the CRC. The CRC does not have the force of domestic law under the treaty clause of the Constitution. Non-ratification does not, however, eliminate its impact on American law.***

D. *Customary International Law*

1. *Definition of Customary International Law*

Customary international law is not static. It is subject to change as customs change. Customs are not always well-defined. "Evidence of customary international law is found in (1) the general usage and practice among nations, (2) the works of jurists and writers, and (3) judicial decisions recognizing and enforcing that law." *Maria*, 68 F.Supp.2d at 233. ***

In terms of "tradition" and "custom" and their definition as a chronological matter, the courts take into account several new factors. These include the rapidity with which norms of personal rights have changed since World War II, the creation of the United Nations, and the increased influence on international affairs by the United States—founded on the protection of human rights—as a superpower.

2. *Authority of Customary International Law*

United States courts may not ignore the precepts of customary international law. *See e.g., Charming Betsy*, 6 U.S. at 118, 2 Cranch 64; *The Paquete Habana*, 175 U.S. 677, 694–700, 20 S.Ct. 290, 297–300, 44 L.Ed. 320, 326–29 (1900); *The Nereide*, 13 U.S. (9 Cranch) 388, 423, 3 L.Ed. 769, 780 (1815); *Filartiga*, 630 F.2d at 881; *Mojica*, 970 F.Supp. at 146–52; *Maria*, 68 F.Supp.2d at 233–35.***

Since Congress's power over aliens rests at least in part on international law, it should come as no shock that it may be limited by changing international law norms.***

It is inappropriate to sustain such plenary power based on a 1920 understanding of international law, when the 2002 conception is radically different. *See Patterson v. McLean Credit Union*, 491 U.S. 164, 173, 109 S.Ct. 2363, 2370, 105 L.Ed.2d 132 (1989) (courts must reevaluate past precedents where the "intervening development of the law" has "weakened the conceptual underpinnings from the prior decision").***

United States courts should interpret legislation in harmony with international law and norms wherever possible. "An act of Congress ought never to be construed to violate the law of nations if any other possible construction remains." *Charming Betsy*, 6 U.S. at 118, 2 Cranch 64.***

Congress may override provisions of customary international law. See The Paquete Habana, 175 U.S. at 694, 20 S.Ct. 290. This rule interacts with the "Charming Betsy" principle to create a principle of clear statement: since Congress may overrule customary international law (Paquete Habana), but laws are to be read in conformity with international law where possible (Charming Betsy), it follows that in order to overrule customary international law, Congress must enact domestic legislation which both postdates the development of a customary international law norm, and which clearly has the intent of repealing that norm. [Citations omitted].

The need to harmonize domestic and international law is well recognized.***

[I]t is appropriate for courts to balance domestic and international law concerns when these conflict, treating the international community as a distinct legal entity, but remembering that in the deportation context these cases tend to represent a two nation problem—the United States as a nation of real long-term domicile and the foreign country as a nation of technical citizenship. Analyzing these international law matters in a way similar to conflicts cases would complement the clear statement rule. A clear statement from Congress on an issue would control because it would show the overriding interest of the local forum (the United States) on that issue.

Where a statute appears to contradict international law, an appropriate remedy is to construe the statute so as to resolve the contradiction.*** Customary international law is legally enforceable unless superceded by a clear statement from Congress. Such a statement must be unequivocal. Mere silence is insufficient to meet this standard.***

3. *Provisions of the Convention on the Rights of the Child as Customary International Law*

The CRC has been adopted by every organized government in the world except the United States. This overwhelming acceptance is strong reason to hold that some CRC provisions have attained the status of customary international law. As at least one court of appeals had explicitly stated, "international human rights instruments *** are evidence of customary international law." Alvarez-Machain v. United States, 266 F.3d 1045 (9th Cir. 2001), citing Siderman de Blake v. Argentina, 965 F.2d 699 (9th Cir. 1991).

While the CRC is relatively new, it contains many provisions codifying longstanding legal norms. It states that "the family *** should be afforded the necessary protection and assistance" and that "in all actions concerning children *** the best interests of the child shall be a primary consideration." CRC, Preamble and Art. 3. These provisions of the CRC are not so novel as to be considered outside the bounds of what is customary. Similar doctrines have long been a part of our law. *See e.g., Tenenbaum*, 193 F.3d at 594 (noting that in family law situations of abuse, "the child's welfare predominates over other interests."); 59 Am.Jur.2d Parent and Child §10 (1987) (general tenets of family law including best interests of the child); 2 Am.Jur.2d Adoption § 136 (1994) (in adoption, "best interests of the child" is the paramount consideration). As already noted, they are related to the constitutional right to privacy under United States law. They are also applied by other nations.*** Given its widespread acceptance, to the extent that it acts to codify longstanding, widely-accepted principles of law, the CRC should be read as customary international law. "The rights to be free from arbitrary interference with family life and arbitrary expulsion are part of customary international law." *Maria*, 68 F.Supp.2d at 234.***

E. Policy Reasons for Honoring International Human Rights Obligations

This nation's credibility would be weakened by non-compliance with treaty obligations or with international norms. The United States seeks to impose international law norms—including, notably, those on terrorism—upon other nations. It would seem strange, then, if the government would seek to avoid enforcement of such norms within its own borders.***

The United States cannot expect to reap the benefits of internationally recognized human rights—in the form of greater worldwide stability and respect for people—without being willing to adhere to them itself. As a moral leader of the world, the United States has obligated itself not to disregard rights uniformly recognized by other nations. Thus, United States courts act appropriately when they construe statutory programs in accordance with international law; they avoid a construction which, "if given its literal application, would threaten the interests of the United States by placing the Nation in violation of international standards or embarrassing the political branches in their conduct of foreign relations." Steinhardt, *supra*, at 1197. The United States also recognizes the problems of the potential receiving state which may not welcome a long-term United States resident, particularly one convicted of a crime; in effect, such a person will be in limbo. *Cf. Zadvydas*, 121 S.Ct. at 2502 (striking down I.N.S. policy of indefinite detention where there is no convenient receiving state).

A second consideration is the need to justify the radical disparity in the punishment meted out to citizens as compared to non-citizens under the statute. Petitioner has been convicted of a non violent second degree robbery of $714. He was also convicted of a drug offense. The total prison sentence he received for all his crimes was 27 to 54 months. Amicus notes that, due to the operation of INA section 212(a)(2)(C), petitioner is inadmissible for reentry to the United States. Amicus Brief at 3. His actual sentence is a probable life term of separation from his home, family, job, and adopted country.*** Likening deportation to a life sentence is not hyperbole; the Supreme Court has, as already noted, recognized on more than one occasion that "deportation may result in the loss 'of all that makes life worth living.'" *Bridges v. Wixon*, 326 U.S. 135, 147, 65 S.Ct. 1443, 1449, 89 L.Ed. 2103, 2112 (1945), citing *Ng Fung Ho v. White*, 259 U.S. 276, 284, 42 S.Ct. 492, 495, 66 L.Ed. 938, 943 (1922).***

Draconian punishment of aliens, as compared to citizens, is based on formal legal status. It ignores the claims of all people, including aliens, to universal rights of "personhood." *See Schuck*, *supra*, at 202; *see also* Harry S. Truman, Inaugural Address, January 1949 ("Decent, satisfying life . . . is the right of all people"). Unusually cruel and harsh treatment of aliens is directly tied to their status as a relatively weak minority group. Such groups require diligent attention by courts to ensure that their rights are not unnecessarily violated by the majority. *See United States v. Carolene Products Co.*, 304 U.S.

144, 152 n. 4, 58 S.Ct. 778, 783 n. 4, 82 L.Ed. 1234, 1241 n. 4 (1938) (courts must be diligent to guard the rights of "discrete and insular" minorities); Lewis F. Powell, *Carolene Products Revisited,* 82 COLUM. L. REV. 1087, 1088 (1982); Louis Lusky, *Footnote Redux: A Carolene Products Reminiscence,* 82 COLUM. L. REV. 1093, 1095–1100 (1982); JOHN HART ELY, DEMOCRACY AND DISTRUST 77–79 (1980) (explaining and elaborating the rule of *Carolene Products*).

*** This case presents another of the many situations in which courts are obliged to "integrate . . . classical doctrines and practices into a public law committed to protecting the rights of individuals, including immigrants, against government overreaching and procedural unfairness."

IV. Application of Law to Facts

A. Relief Under the Immigration and Naturalization Act

Petitioner is ineligible for relief under a narrow and wooden construction of the INA. As an aggravated felon (as now defined), he would not qualify for relief under section 212(h), section 240A, or for asylum under section 208. Because his plea came after the 1996 Acts, he would not be eligible *** for section 212(c) relief. Petitioner would not qualify for section 243(h) relief because he is not a member of a protected class under that section. Even if he were a member of a 243(h) class, his "serious" crime would now preclude relief under that section.***

B. Relief Under the International Covenant on Civil and Political Rights ***

Summary deportation of this long term legal alien without allowing him to present the reasons he should not be deported violates the ICCPR's guarantee against arbitrary interference with one's family, and the provision that an alien shall "be allowed to submit the reasons against his expulsion." The statute must be interpreted in a way not inconsistent with international law to permit a compassionate hearing.

Interpreting the statute in conformity with the ICCPR will also remedy any possible incompatibility with the UDHR, which prohibits "arbitrary *** exile," UDHR Art. 9, and also requires that parties be allowed a full and fair hearing. UDHR, Art. 10. *See also, supra* Part III.C.2.B (rights under UDHR).

C. Relief Under Customary International Law

*** If read as the government suggests, the INA would violate the principles of customary international law that the best interests of the child must be considered where possible. Categoric denial of a hearing and thus of any consideration of the child's interests in all cases of theft where the sentence exceeds a year is not in compliance with that international mandate.

It is not disputed that Congress could override this norm of customary international law if it chose to do so. It has not expressed a clear intent to overrule this principle of customary international law which is otherwise binding upon United States courts. "The statutes under which Mr. Beharry is being deported [do] not explicitly authorize the separation of an alien from immediate family members." Amicus Brief at 18. The court construes the statute in conformity with international law, as mandated by the *Charming Betsy* doctrine.

D. *Appropriate Remedy*

As now interpreted and implemented against this petitioner, the statute would violate treaty obligations and customary international law. It is appropriate to interpret the statute in a way which does not violate international law. Since both statutes and international law are enforceable under the Constitution's Supremacy Clause, the statute should be construed in conformity with international law to avoid a constitutional issue if "fairly possible." *See e.g., Crowell v. Benson,* 285 U.S. 22, 62, 52 S.Ct. 285, 76 L.Ed. 598 (1932); *Zadvydas,* 121 S.Ct. at 2501. In this task the court should make the minimal changes necessary to bring the statute into compliance.***

The most narrowly targeted way to bring the INA into compliance with international law requirements is to read into section 212(h) a requirement of compliance with international law. *** That can be done by ruling that section 212(h) waivers are available for aliens, including petitioner, who meet its stringent requirements of seven years residence and "extreme hardship" to family—if these aliens have been convicted of an "aggravated felony" as defined after they committed their crime, but which was not so categorized when they committed the crime.

It should be emphasized that such an interpretation does not constitute a ruling that petitioner cannot be deported. He is only entitled to a hearing at which a broad discretion to exclude may be exercised by the INS. *See Palmer v. I.N.S.,* 4 F.3d 482, 487 (7th Cir.1993) (in a 212(h) hearing, the alien bears the burden of showing "equities meriting favorable exercise of the Attorney General's discretion").

This interpretation will affect only a small subset of the aliens who would otherwise be ineligible for section 212(h) relief. It fulfills the goal of bringing the statute into compliance with international law, while doing so in the least intrusive way possible. For example, this statute already contains a separate provision prohibiting 212(h) relief for aliens convicted of murder, torture, or who are a security threat to the United States, provisions which are unchallenged and unaffected by this ruling.***

Notes and Questions

1. *Reversed on Appeal.* The Attorney General appealed the ruling to the Second Circuit Court of Appeals, which dismissed Beharry's *habeas* petition. The appellate court ruled that the federal courts lacked subject matter jurisdiction to consider his claim that he is entitled to a hearing on the availability of discretionary relief under § 212(h) because he had not raised the issue in the administrative proceedings. Instead, the issue was raised by the district court *sua sponte.* Thus, the Court concluded that Beharry failed to exhaust his administrative remedies. *Beharry v. Ashcroft,* 329 F.2d 51, 59 (2d Cir. 2003).

2. Which of the decisions do you find most persuasive with regard to the interpretation of a state's legal obligations under the Children's Convention? Are you persuaded that all or some of the provisions of the Convention have achieved the status of customary law? For example, is the "best interests of the child" standard a rule of customary international law? Is it a general principle of municipal law? *See* Article 38 of the ICJ statute in introductory text to Part II, *supra.*

3. The primary focus of the decisions above was, of course, on the implications of a parent's deportation on native-born children in the host country. Many "economic" migrants must leave children and other family members in their country of origin and may have additional children born in the host country. Should courts interpreting the

Convention on the Rights of the Child consider the implications of domestic legal decisions on children born outside of the country in which the migrant parent is now located? *Cf,* Hope Lewis, *Universal Mother: Transnational Migration and the Human Rights of Black Women in the Americas,* 5 J. GENDER, RACE & JUSTICE 197 (2001).

4.   Like other human rights treaty bodies, the Committee on the Rights of the Child reviews periodic reports by states parties, issues "general comments" interpreting the nature and scope of convention provisions and administers the two optional protocols under the Convention. *See, e.g.,* Office of the UN High Commissioner for Human Rights, The Committee on the Rights of the Child, *available at* http://www.unhchr.ch/html/menu2/6/crc; and Optional Protocol to the Convention on the Rights of the Child on the Sale of Children, Child Prostitution and Child Pornography, adopted and opened for signature, ratification and accession by General Assembly Resolution a/res/54/263, May 25, 2000 (*entered into force* Jan. 18, 2002).

GENERAL COMMENT NO. 3 (2003):
HIV/AIDS AND THE RIGHTS OF THE CHILD

U.N. Doc. CRC/GC/2003/3 (March 17, 2003)

I.   INTRODUCTION[7]

1.   The HIV/AIDS epidemic has drastically changed the world in which children live. Millions of children have been infected and have died and many more are gravely affected as HIV spreads through their families and communities. The epidemic impacts on the daily life of younger children, the victimization and marginalization of children, especially those living in particularly difficult circumstances. HIV/AIDS is not a problem of some countries but of the entire world. To truly bring its impact on children under control will require concerted and well-targeted efforts from all countries at all stages of development.

---

[7]   At its seventeenth session (1998), the Committee on the Rights of the Child held a day of general discussion on the theme of HIV/AIDS and children's rights, in which it recommended that a number of actions be taken, including facilitating the engagement of States parties on HIV/AIDS issues in relation to the rights of the child. Human rights in relation to HIV/AIDS has also been discussed at the Eighth Meeting of Persons Chairing the Human Rights Treaty Bodies in 1997 and has been taken up by the Committee on Economic, Social and Cultural Rights and the Committee on the Elimination of Discrimination against Women. Similarly, HIV/AIDS has been discussed annually by the Commission on Human Rights for over a decade. UNAIDS and the United Nations Children's Fund (UNICEF) have emphasized the rights of the child in relation to HIV/AIDS in all aspects of their work, and the World AIDS Campaign for 1997 focused on "Children Living in a World with AIDS" and for 1998 on "Force for Change: World AIDS Campaign with Young People." UNAIDS and the Office of the United Nations High Commissioner for Human Rights have also produced *The International Guidelines on HIV/AIDS and Human Rights* (1998) and its *Revised Guideline 6* (2002) to promote and protect human rights in the context of HIV/AIDS. At the international political level, HIV/AIDS-related rights have been recognized in the *Declaration of Commitment on HIV/AIDS,* adopted at the United Nations General Assembly special session, *A World Fit for Children,* adopted at the United Nations General Assembly special session on children, and in other international and regional documents.

2. Initially children were considered to be only marginally affected by the epidemic. However, the international community has discovered that, unfortunately, children are at the heart of the problem. According to the Joint United Nations Programme on HIV/AIDS (UNAIDS), the most recent trends are alarming: in most parts of the world the majority of new infections are among young people between the ages of 15 and 24, sometimes younger. Women, including young girls, are also increasingly becoming infected. In most regions of the world, the vast majority of infected women do not know that they are infected and may unknowingly infect their children. Consequently, many States have recently registered an increase in their infant and child mortality rates. Adolescents are also vulnerable to HIV/AIDS because their first sexual experience may take place in an environment in which they have no access to proper information and guidance. Children who use drugs are at high risk.

3. Yet, all children can be rendered vulnerable by the particular circumstances of their lives, especially (a) children who are themselves HIV-infected; (b) children who are affected by the epidemic because of the loss of a parental caregiver or teacher and/or because their families or communities are severely strained by its consequences; and (c) children who are most prone to be infected or affected.

II. THE OBJECTIVES OF THE PRESENT GENERAL COMMENT

4. The objectives of the present General Comment are:

(a) To identify further and strengthen understanding of all the human rights of children in the context of HIV/AIDS;

(b) To promote the realization of the human rights of children in the context of HIV/AIDS, as guaranteed under the Convention on the Rights of the Child (hereafter "the Convention");

(c) To identify measures and good practices to increase the level of implementation by States of the rights related to the prevention of HIV/AIDS and the support, care and protection of children infected with or affected by this pandemic;

(d) To contribute to the formulation and promotion of child-oriented plans of action, strategies, laws, polices and programmes to combat the spread and mitigate the impact of HIV/AIDS at the national and international levels.

III. THE CONVENTION'S PERSPECTIVES ON HIV/AIDS: THE HOLISTIC CHILD RIGHTS-BASED APPROACH

5. The issue of children and HIV/AIDS is perceived as mainly a medical or health problem, although in reality it involves a much wider range of issues. In this regard, the right to health (article 24 of the Convention) is, however, central. But HIV/AIDS impacts so heavily on the lives of all children that it affects all their rights—civil, political, economic, social and cultural. The rights embodied in the general principles of the Convention—the right to non-discrimination (art. 2), the right of the child to have his/her interest as a primary consideration (art. 3), the right to life, survival and development (art. 6) and the right to have his/her views respected (art. 12)—should therefore be the guiding themes in the consideration of HIV/AIDS at all levels of prevention, treatment, care and support.

6. Adequate measures to address HIV/AIDS can be undertaken only if the rights of children and adolescents are fully respected. The most relevant rights in this regard, in addition to those enumerated in paragraph 5 above, are the following: the right to access information and material aimed at the promotion of their social, spiritual and moral well-being and physical and mental health (art. 17); the right to preventive health care, sex education and family planning education and services (art. 24 (f)); the right to an appropriate standard of living (art. 27); the right to privacy (art. 16); the right not to be separated from parents (art. 9); the right to be protected from violence (art. 19); the right to special protection and assistance by the State (art. 20); the rights of children with disabilities (art. 23); the right to health (art. 24); the right to social security, including social insurance (art. 26); the right to education and leisure (arts. 28 and 31); the right to be protected from economic and sexual exploitation and abuse, and from illicit use of narcotic drugs (arts. 32, 33, 34 and 36); the right to be protected from abduction, sale and trafficking as well as torture or other cruel, inhuman or degrading treatment or punishment (arts. 35 and 37); and the right to physical and psychological recovery and social reintegration (art. 39). Children are confronted with serious challenges to the above-mentioned rights as a result of the epidemic. The Convention, and in particular the four general principles with their comprehensive approach, provide a powerful framework for efforts to reduce the negative impact of the pandemic on the lives of children. The holistic rights-based approach required to implement the Convention is the optimal tool for addressing the broader range of issues that relate to prevention, treatment and care efforts.***

Notes and Questions

1.   Do you agree that a rights-based approach would be helpful in addressing problems such as HIV/AIDS in children? What specific rights, other than the right to health, might be relevant? Could a rights approach shift the focus away from treatment and prevention? Should such approaches be pursued in tandem?

2.   For overall data on the status of children, *see, e.g.*, The State of the World's Children 2004 (updated annually), *available at*, http://www.unicef.org/sowc04/index.html; and UNICEF, Monitoring the Situation of Women and Children, *available at* http://www.childinfo.org/ (last visited June 22, 2004).

3.   For U.N. activities related to the implementation of the Convention on the Rights of the Child, *see, e.g.*, Office of the High Commissioner for Human Rights, The Convention on the Rights of the Child, *available at* http://www.unhchr.ch/html/menu3/b/k2crc.htm (last visited June 22, 2004);

4.   The elimination of child labor is one of four "fundamental principles" elaborated by the International Labour Organization. *See* International Labour Organization, Fundamental Principles and Rights at Work, *available at* http://www.ilo.org/dyn/declaris/DECLARATIONWEB.INDEXPAGE (last visited June 23, 2004). For data on child labor and a discussion of the approaches adopted by the International Labour Organization, *see, e.g.*, International Labour Organization, Global Report: A Future without Child Labour (Mar. 2002); and World Day against Child Labour (June 12, 2002), *available at* http://www.ilo.org/public/english/bureau/inf/childlabour/index.htm. *See also* the discussion on child labor in Chapter 7, *infra*.

5.   *Reparations and the rights of children.* In 2001, the Inter-American Court of Human Rights ordered the Guatemalan government to pay reparations for the murder of five

street children: "The Court ordered Guatemala to pay financial reparations to the families of the victims, to establish a school for street children, and to implement internal laws in accordance with Article 19 (Rights of the Child) of the American Convention on Human Rights *** requiring respect and protection of minors by family, society, and the state." Ismene Zarifis, *Guatemala: Children's Rights Case Wins Judgment at Inter-American Court of Human Rights*, 9(1) HUM. RTS. B. (Fall 2001), *available at* http://www.wcl.american.edu/hrbrief/09/1guatemala.cfm.

E. THE INTERNATIONAL LABOUR ORGANIZATION

The recognition of workers' rights in an international context preceded the founding of the United Nations and the adoption of the International Bill of Rights. The rise of industrialization led not only to increased efficiency in production of goods, but also to increased potential for the exploitation and abuse of workers. New technology made mass production possible, but also exposed workers to new forms of injury. A convergence of interests—those of the workers, employers and the international community—resulted in the creation of one of the earliest and structurally most influential of the international economic and social rights organizations. The International Labour Organization (ILO) now operates as an agency of the United Nations. Note, however, that the agency has a complex governance structure of its own; it promulgates and implements many conventions on the rights of workers and on related human rights issues. *See* the "further reading" list at the end of this section for more detailed explorations of labor rights as human rights.

The following document, known as the "Declaration of Philadelphia," states the principles that guide the ILO's operations and is now appended to the Constitution of the International Labour Organization:

DECLARATION CONCERNING THE AIMS AND PURPOSES OF THE INTERNATIONAL LABOUR ORGANIZATION

Available at http://www.ilo.org/public/english/about/iloconst.htm#annex

I

The Conference reaffirms the fundamental principles on which the Organization is based and, in particular, that—

(a) labour is not a commodity;

(b) freedom of expression and of association are essential to sustained progress;

(c) poverty anywhere constitutes a danger to prosperity everywhere;

(d) the war against want requires to be carried on with unrelenting vigor within each nation, and by continuous and concerted international effort in which the representatives of workers and employers, enjoying equal status with those of governments, join with them in free discussion and democratic decision with a view to the promotion of the common welfare.

II

Believing that experience has fully demonstrated the truth of the statement in the Constitution of the International Labour Organization that lasting peace can be established only if it is based on social justice, the Conference affirms that—

(a) all human beings, irrespective of race, creed or sex, have the right to pursue both their material well-being and their spiritual development in conditions of freedom and dignity, of economic security and equal opportunity;

(b) the attainment of the conditions in which this shall be possible must constitute the central aim of national and international policy;

(c) all national and international policies and measures, in particular those of an economic and financial character, should be judged in this light and accepted only in so far as they may be held to promote and not to hinder the achievement of this fundamental objective;

(d) it is a responsibility of the International Labour Organization to examine and consider all international economic and financial policies and measures in the light of this fundamental objective;

(e) in discharging the tasks entrusted to it the International Labour Organization, having considered all relevant economic and financial factors, may include in its decisions and recommendations any provisions which it considers appropriate.***

III

The Conference recognizes the solemn obligation of the International Labour Organization to further among the nations of the world programmes which will achieve:

(a) full employment and the raising of standards of living;

(b) the employment of workers in the occupations in which they can have the satisfaction of giving the fullest measure of their skill and attainments and make their greatest contribution to the common well-being;

(c) the provision, as a means to the attainment of this end and under adequate guarantees for all concerned, of facilities for training and the transfer of labour, including migration for employment and settlement;

(d) policies in regard to wages and earnings, hours and other conditions of work calculated to ensure a just share of the fruits of progress to all, and a minimum living wage to all employed and in need of such protection;

(e) the effective recognition of the right of collective bargaining, the cooperation of management and labour in the continuous improvement of productive efficiency, and the collaboration of workers and employers in the preparation and application of social and economic measures;

(f) the extension of social security measures to provide a basic income to all in need of such protection and comprehensive medical care;

(g) adequate protection for the life and health of workers in all occupations;

(h) provision for child welfare and maternity protection;

(i) the provision of adequate nutrition, housing and facilities for recreation and culture;

(j) the assurance of equality of educational and vocational opportunity.

IV

Confident that the fuller and broader utilization of the world's productive resources necessary for the achievement of the objectives set forth in this Declaration can be secured by effective international and national action, including measures to expand production and consumption, to avoid severe economic fluctuations to promote the economic and social advancement of the less developed regions of the world, to assure greater stability in world prices of primary products, and to promote a high and steady volume of international trade, the Conference pledges the full cooperation of the International Labour Organization with such international bodies as may be entrusted with a share of the responsibility for this great task and for the promotion of the health, education and well-being of all peoples.***

V

The conference affirms that the principles set forth in this Declaration are fully applicable to all peoples everywhere and that, while the manner of their application must be determined with due regard to the stage of social and economic development reached by each people, their progressive application to peoples who are still dependent, as well as to those who have already achieved self-government, is a matter of concern to the whole civilized world.

Notes and Questions

1.   *Inspiration for the ILO.* The International Labor Organization emerged from the ashes of the First World War; its Constitution was adopted by the Paris Peace Conference in April of 1919. Its creation was prompted by humanitarian, political and economic motivations. While the horrendous exploitation of the growing working class threatened to precipitate demands for radical social change, the economic cost of labor standards provided an incentive to the industrial class to promote uniformity. The Preamble to the Constitution states that "the failure of any nation to adopt humane conditions of labour is an obstacle in the way of other nations which desire to improve the conditions in their own countries." Do you agree with this statement? Does the experience of developing countries under globalization affirm or negate its validity? *See* Chapter 5, *infra.*

2.   How do the goals of the Declaration of Philadelphia compare with those in President Franklin Roosevelt's 1944 State of the Union Address, excerpted in Chapter 2, *supra*? How is the experience of global war reflected in these pronouncements? Were the drafters attempting to acknowledge the contributions of working people to the war efforts? If so, why might this have been deemed necessary? Compare the view in the ILO Constitution that "universal and lasting peace can be established only if it is based upon social justice" with Roosevelt's assertion that "true individual freedom cannot exist without economic security and independence." The United States became a member of the ILO in 1934, under Roosevelt's presidency.

3. *Development of Normative Standards.* The first six International Labour Conventions, setting minimum standards for working hours, unemployment, maternity protection, night work for women and youth and child labor, were adopted in October, 1919. In less than two years, 16 International Labour Conventions and 18 Recommendations had been adopted. In 1926, the International Labour Conference set up a supervisory reporting system, with a Committee of Experts responsible for examining government reports. The ILO is unique within the U.N. system, with workers and employers enjoying equal participation with governments in its work. The organization was awarded the Nobel Peace Prize in 1969. For more information on the history of the ILO, *see* http://www.ilo.org/public/english/about/history.htm (last visited May 31, 2004).

EMILY A. SPIELER, THE CASE FOR OCCUPATIONAL SAFETY AND HEALTH AS A CORE WORKER RIGHT

JAMES A. GROSS ED., WORKERS RIGHTS AS HUMAN RIGHTS 78, 78–89, 115–17 (2003)

My foreman said, 'You be sure you don't get that mule where no rock can fall on him.' I asked, 'What about me?' He said, 'We can always hire another man, you have to buy another mule.'"

> —A story sometimes told by older coal miners in the United States.

A law student in West Virginia suggested that health and safety was the most important arena for continued employment regulation in the United States in the twenty-first century. 'Why?' I asked her. 'Because you can always quit *** but you need two legs to walk out on,' she answered.***

Hazards at work pose risks to both the physical and economic health of workers. Although occupational injury and fatality rates have declined in the United States, a significant number of people are still killed or injured. An estimated 65,000 workers die each year from work-related illnesses and injuries, a total of more than 180 deaths each day. Of these, approximately 6,000 workers die from traumatic work injuries, an annual rate of about 5.3 per 100,000 workers. In 1999, the last year for which data are available, there were 1.7 million reported injuries and illnesses in private industry that required workers to take time off from work, and more than 1 million additional cases of workers who remained at work, but with restricted work activities, during that same year. Official record keepers acknowledge that at least an additional 25 percent of these injuries occur but are not reported to government authorities. Uncounted numbers of injured workers end up without employment as a result of their injuries; the social and economic costs associated with these events are huge.

Not surprisingly, the occupational fatality and injury rates in advanced industrial countries are substantially lower than the rates in less developed parts of the world. The U.S. fatality rate compares favorably to the death rates in Latin America and the Caribbean (13.5 deaths per 100,000 workers), the Republic of Korea (34 per 100,000), or Thailand (19 per 100,000 workers). The International Labour Organization (ILO) has estimated that 1.1 million people per year die worldwide from occupational diseases, a number surpassing the average annual number of deaths from road accidents (999,000) and war (502,000). There are reports as well that the number of workplace injuries is increasing with industrialization at alarming rates in developing countries.

Although serious hazards are less common in developed countries with stronger economies and legal regimes, workers and commentators suggest that the protections are nevertheless not adequate. In recent years, workers have died in fires because escape doors were intentionally locked in countries as economically and politically diverse as Thailand, China, and the United States. In the United States, workers report that the Occupational Safety and Health Act (OSHA) is inadequate, that hazards are sometimes intentionally created or tolerated by management, and that these hazards and resulting injuries often go unreported. Injured workers paint a dismal picture of every aspect of the workers' compensation system. Workers feel that their employers expend their resources mounting successful political campaigns against workers' compensation and OSHA to the detriment of workers.***

In the end, those of us who believe that labor rights are human rights must be prepared to confront the neoclassical economic argument that assertions of rights damage not only the aggregate wealth of a society but also the well-being of workers. In responding to these arguments, we are forced to consider three questions. First, does the current system of laws, norms, and markets in fact maximize aggregate wealth? Second, does this current system achieve a distribution of wealth that meets our normative views about equality and fairness?*** Finally, can practices, norms, or laws be changed by assertions of rights?

This last question demands that we consider the real-world utility of this entire discussion. It is my hope that the exploration of the application of rights to risks may provide an important rhetorical foundation to confront abusive working conditions in both developed and developing countries. Without a clear statement that workers have a human right to safe workplaces, international and national discussions can continue without any concern for the persistence of sometimes astonishingly abusive conditions (while we wait for proof of the hypothesis that the market will improve the working conditions of the most oppressed workers). One can imagine meetings at which serious and concerned people, including trade unionists, agree to put aside stories of extreme abuse on the basis that these issues are not within enumerated international concerns. But if there is acceptance that workers have some right to safety at work, national laws and international agreements (as well as changed social expectations that develop) will begin to transform abstract theory into enforceable rights. In contrast, the currently dominant rhetoric of the market masks, or is used to justify, fundamental inequalities of the employment relationship, supports the perpetuation of working conditions that are abusive, and obscures the need for basic principles or standards to correct for inequalities within the labor market.

Health and Safety in International Human Rights Discourse

A long history of inclusion of health and safety in international and national laws, declarations, and treaties reflects deep concern about hazardous working conditions resulting from industrialization. Recently, however, pressure has mounted to increase reliance on market forces in order to encourage economic development. This has occurred at the same time that the battle over inclusion of labor and environmental standards in international treaties has grown. In response, a new articulation of labor rights has emerged, separating general labor rights, including all working conditions, from core human rights at work.***

The Exclusion of Health and Safety from Core Labor Rights

As the dominance of neoclassical market theory has grown, international consensus appears to be relegating economic and social rights, and particularly those involving working conditions, to a lower tier of importance in human rights discourse. There is an inevitable political tension between those who would expand social and economic rights, including workplace and health rights, and those who resist this expansion based on ideological reliance on market solutions for human problems.

In 1998, after a number of years of debate, the ILO adopted the Declaration on Fundamental Principles and Rights at Work. Faced with a growing and arguably unwieldy and unenforceable list of ILO conventions, as well as international resistance t o principles regarding working conditions, the ILO and member states chose to name four rights as "basic" or "core" worker rights: freedom of association and the right to collective bargaining; elimination of forced or compulsory labor; abolition of child labor; and elimination of discrimination in employment. These core rights have now been characterized as human rights, as opposed to labor rights. Other organizations, including the Organization for Economic Cooperation and Development (OECD), the International Monetary Fund (IMF), and the World Bank followed the ILO's lead and accepted that these core rights constitute the critical labor rights for international discussion. It is important to be clear that this emerging consensus does not mean that the four core rights will automatically be included in trade agreements or be made enforceable through either governmental or nongovernmental means. Rather, this consensus suggests that, to the extent that any labor rights are to be recognized and enforced, it is these core rights that merit consideration. Working conditions, including wages, hours, and safety, are excluded from these core rights.

The decision to relegate working conditions to a second tier of rights is both understandable and troubling. It is understandable because the decision makes strategic and political sense and is grounded in commonly accepted economic arguments. All four of the ILO's core principles focus on the formation of the labor market and not on the establishment of any minimum standards within the employment contract. These identified "core" rights authorize managerial or corporate control of workplace decision-making, subject only to equality principles (*i.e.*, all workers must be treated equally), protection of young people, and the right to bargain individually or collectively. The individual right to bargain is rooted, as it is in U.S. law, in the prohibition on forced labor that establishes the right of the individual to quit—the equivalent, in U.S. terms, of the employment-at-will doctrine. These core rights avoid any assertion of a right to a minimum level of protection within the employment relationship itself, and therefore set no expectations regarding working conditions, including health and safety. Instead, the actual conditions of work are left to employers, as controlled by local economic conditions and the local legal system, much as they were in the now developed world at the turn of the last century.

The apparent underlying assumptions are that working conditions, including occupational safety, are context driven, difficult to define, and contingent on local levels of economic development and productivity. Thus, improved working conditions and better distributional outcomes are best achieved in a market environment in which the four core rights can be exercised. In fact, this argument may be stronger in the arena of health and safety, for which scientific and engineering expertise are essential in both quantifying risk and proposing interventive strategies. Moreover, advocates characterize these four rights as sufficiently concrete and self-defining to be easily understandable and enforceable.

Advocates for the limitation to these four core rights also assert that this approach of limited market-forming rights means that poorer regions will retain critical competitive advantage through lower labor costs, thus nurturing potential for economic growth and allowing for maximum flexibility in the specific labor market conditions in any given region. The costs involved in guaranteeing wages and working conditions might have adverse effects by reducing the number of jobs and by creating downward pressure on wages (as employers treat newly imposed standards as exogenous wage increases). In particular, health and safety often requires application of capital resources and, according to some economists, the market (rather than regulatory intervention) produces more optimal levels of investment in health and safety. As the economy strengthens, workers can exert pressure through association, through choice in the labor market, and through exercise of political rights; as workers gain in both productivity and strength, the more contingent components of the labor contract—including wages and health and safety conditions—will improve.

Poorer countries see an assertion of rights regarding working conditions as intrusive and potentially damaging to fledgling economies (which need to retain their comparative advantage in some industries for a sustained period of time if they are to become developed). Spokespersons for these poor countries doubt the motivation of those in developed countries who argue in favor of broader labor rights, seeing these assertions as protectionist and paternalistic, forcing workers to accept the costs of improved working conditions in a depressed labor market. At the same time, developing countries are anxious to encourage economic development and expansion of employment opportunities to assist in fighting all aspects of poverty. They fear that minimum standards for working conditions will discourage investment by limiting the comparative competitive edge based upon lower labor costs.

Moreover, the selection of these four rights represents broad consensus among private parties, developing states, and the developed world. Parties across the political spectrum, including a wide range of international business organizations as well as trade unions, support this articulation of core rights. At the same time, large employers and multinational corporations benefit from the lack of any enforcement of minimum standards in the developing economies. Thus, these core rights support corporate flexibility, garnering the support of business and political conservatives.

Current dominant political ideology suggests that improved working conditions are best secured through the operation of market forces. Consensus concerning specific minimum standards was unlikely to emerge in the tripartite ILO discussions that involve developed and undeveloped states, businesses, and trade unions. To expand the list of core rights to include working conditions would also re-create the fundamental "laundry list" problem of the ILO conventions and related labor standards. While not denying the existence of deplorable working conditions, the apparent assumption is that wages and working conditions will improve with economic development and the emergence of viable trade unions: that is, their boat will rise with the economic tide as the economies develop. And while this compromise may abandon vulnerable workers in developing countries to abhorrent conditions, trade unionists value the strong international consensus around basic organizing principles.

It is true that the power of this broad endorsement of core labor principles as rights should not be underestimated, particularly if enforcement mechanisms can be established and these rights can be successfully incorporated into trade agreements. But this creation of a hierarchy of labor rights is also deeply troubling. Elimination of other labor rights involving working conditions encourages regulatory competition as countries compete to decrease labor costs in order to attract business, thus encouraging a race to the bottom. The drive for consensus also leads to a continuing search for the least common denominator: only the most serious abuses of even these four core rights become recognized as serious enough to merit the status of human rights violations. Further, this approach relegates subminimum wages, excessive hours, and sometimes brutally dangerous conditions to a lower level of importance in human rights discourse: it ratifies the view that labor is a commodity that is fully subject to market forces, no matter how abusive the resulting working conditions. These core market-forming rights essentially endorse the traditional American common law default rules governing employment, presumptively giving managerial control over all aspects of the employment relationship to the employer. It may be true that conditions are often better in facilities owned by multinational corporations than in facilities owned and operated by local entrepreneurs. Nevertheless, in the context of the current world economy, inadequate working conditions are sometimes supported (directly, covertly, or indirectly) by multinational corporations. The lack of insistence on some minimal level of worker rights is disquieting: it serves the interests of powerful private parties, but enables and justifies significant oppression of workers in undeveloped labor markets where unions are (and may remain) weak. This concern is especially justified when one considers the particular problems posed by health and safety hazards.

Does Health and Safety Belong among Core Labor Rights?

The powerful arguments in favor of exclusion of health and safety from core rights (whether called "human rights" or "labor rights") must be addressed carefully. While some advocates of these positions may be boldly attempting to enable international labor exploitation, many people who support the new core rights are in fact concerned about the best way to achieve advancement for people in developing countries.***

The Basis in International Law for Viewing Health and Safety as a Core Right

The right to health and safety has been dually rooted in rights to workplace fairness and to preservation of physical health. Until the recent development of the four core principles, working conditions, including health and safety, were consistently included in both national and international declarations. The more general right to health is increasingly recognized as a necessary component of social and economic rights that guarantee physical security. Occupational safety and health brings these two concerns together.***

At the urging of trade unions, the 1944 Declaration of Philadelphia proclaimed that "labour is not a commodity" and further recognized "the solemn obligation" of the International Labour Organization to advance a world program that would achieve "adequate protection for the life and health of workers in all occupations." The human rights status of workers' rights was again affirmed in the Universal Declaration of Human Rights in 1948: "Everyone has the right to work, to free choice of employment, to just and favourable conditions of work and to protection against unemployment." Recognizing that "these rights derive from the inherent dignity of the human person," the International Covenant on Economic, Social, and Cultural Rights states, more specifically, "The States Parties to the present Covenant recognize the right of everyone to the enjoyment of just and favourable conditions of work which ensure, in particular:*** (b) Safe and healthy working conditions." This covenant, entered into in 1976, articulates the most comprehensive protection of labor rights that exists in international law.

Drawing from the foundation established by the Universal Declaration and the International Covenant, the ILO has adopted specific standards governing occupational health and safety. Guiding principles are set out in standards such as the Occupational Safety and Health Convention, which aims "to prevent accidents and injury to health arising out of, linked with or occurring in the course of work, by minimizing, so far as is reasonably practicable, the causes of hazards inherent in the working environment." This convention also calls for inspection systems, provision of protective clothing, and protection for workers who remove themselves from work situations that they believe are too dangerous to health or life. In addition, more specific conventions regulate economic sectors (such as construction and mining) and designated risks (such as chemicals and asbestos) or require specific measures of protection (such as medical examinations).

Despite the recent narrowing of ILO core rights and the current failure to condition world trade on compliance with labor standards, regional treaties and trade agreements acknowledge the central importance of workers' rights, including the right to humane and safe working conditions. For example, in 1984 the U.S. Congress amended the General System of Preferences program to include whether a country "has taken or is taking steps to afford to workers *** internationally recognized worker rights." Among these rights were "acceptable conditions of work with respect to minimum wages, hours of work, and occupational safety and health." The North American Agreement on Labor Cooperation, a complementary side agreement to the North American Free Trade Agreement, specifically targets both occupational safety and health and compensation for work-related injuries among eleven enumerated labor rights, European treaties set out very strong requirements for working conditions, including health and safety, as well as social benefits. In fact, workplace health and safety is one of the few areas of labor rights susceptible to Europe-wide regulation through directives adopted by a qualified majority vote.

The right to safe working conditions is also strongly supported by the more general right to health that appeals in numerous international rights covenants, including the United Nations Charter and the Universal Declaration of Human Rights. The 1946 constitution of the World Health Organization recognized that the "enjoyment of the highest attainable standard of health" is a fundamental right of every human being. The International Covenant Economic, Social, and Cultural Rights includes the most explicit guarantee of the right to health, including occupational health. It states:

(1) The States Parties to the present Covenant recognize the right of everyone to the enjoyment of the highest attainable standard of physical and mental health.

(2) The steps to be taken *** to achieve the full realization of this right shall include those necessary for: *** the improvement of all aspects of environmental and industrial hygiene [and] the prevention, treatment and control of *** occupational *** diseases.

A growing health and human rights movement in the last decade is rooted in the principle that "promoting and protecting human rights is inextricably linked with promoting and protecting health." The broad right to health is viewed as encompassing the social and economic roots of poor health status and is not limited to the provision of personal health care services. Building on rights to public health, other commentators have suggested that rights to workplace safety and health may be rooted in this general right to health. The recent development of a literature on the right to health challenges the relegation of occupational safety and health to a lower tier of importance in labor rights discussions. In view of the fact that workplace risks are a significant source of morbidity, mortality, and disability, the right to health cannot be achieved without a reduction of risks in the workplace.***

Conclusion

The emerging international consensus to view health and safety as a secondary labor right is deeply troubling. In fact, the toleration of high levels of workplace risk permits a continuation of abusive conditions that in many ways minor abuses that are viewed as human rights violations in the political sphere. Workplace risks need to be recognized and evaluated based on an understanding that workers must have a right to information, a right to be free from retaliation, and a right to working environments that are free from recognized and preventable risks.

This right may vary somewhat depending on the specific conditions and the level of economic development of a country. In developed countries like the United States and other OECD countries, a fully realized right to safety at work should not be open to question. Yet, in the United States, a strong legal regime and economic strength mask serious problems for some workers. While health and safety abuses in the United States are less common and generally less severe than in many developing countries, there are nevertheless important lessons to be drawn from the continuing occupational safety and health problems that confront workers.

First, apparent successes reported in aggregate data and averages may mask significant distributional injustices. Even in developed countries, there is not uniform enforcement of important labor rights, including health and safety, for all workers in all sectors of the economy. Both aspirational laws (like OSHA) and data reports sometimes hide significant problems for distinct populations of workers. Sectors of the labor force that are vulnerable to discrimination and low wages, particularly racial minorities and immigrants, are also vulnerable to bad, even deplorable or criminal, working conditions that pose serious and immediate risks of bodily harm. Workers in the apparel industry, for example, are at serious risk whether they work in China or in the United States. The human right to working conditions that are free from preventable and predictable risks is important to workers in both developed and developing countries.

Second, because of the continuing vulnerability of these populations, there is a strong link between improving occupational safety and health and enforcing other fundamental labor rights. In particular, the health and safety of these vulnerable populations suffers when there is also a failure to provide effective enforcement of other rights: rights against discrimination for minorities and immigrants; rights to free speech at work, to association, to engage in concerted activity, and to organize trade unions; and any evolving rights to job security and social benefits. Failure of a country to support these other rights will result in occupational hazards, injuries at work, and possible destitution for vulnerable populations. This does not mean that the right to safety and health is simply contingent on these other rights. But as the legal and social norms at work change to allow for expanded demands of workers, there is no question that working conditions will also improve.

Third, complete dependence on the economic market to correct abusive working conditions would be misguided. During the 1990s, unemployment in the United States was at historical lows and wages rose for even the lowest paid workers. Nevertheless, some workers continued to face unacceptable health risks at work. This is a function of a number of factors. These include the fact that the labor laws do not provide adequate protections and that the current system of compensation allows firms to externalize the costs of injuries and illnesses, leaving workers, their families, and other social programs to pay for these costs. The failure of the economic market to provide adequate protections to all workers also highlights the problem with the four core labor rights that are currently endorsed in international law.

Fourth, and perhaps most obviously, the existence of aspirational laws does not guarantee effective enforcement. Workers in countries with theoretically strong legal protections are still subjected to continuing abuses. The abuses of workers in both poor and wealthy countries are persistent, troubling, and worthy of investigation and exposure.***

Notes and Questions

1.   What is the difference between a "labor right" and a "human right"? Should occupational health and safety be considered core rights? Imagine that you are a member of a working group made up of labor representatives, employers and government officials. Your group plans to present arguments on this question. Group A should make arguments on behalf of a country in the Global South. Group B should make arguments on behalf of a country in the Global North. What are the competing interests of the two groups? What are the competing interests of different members of each group?

2.   What do you think of the strategy of achieving broad consensus on core rights? Is it better to obtain broad buy-ins on a few human rights standards initially, or is it more effective to build agreement over a longer period on a broader range of standards? Could the proliferation of treaties establishing labor standards actually impede the struggle for workers' rights?

3.   As noted above, the International Labour Organization was one of the first international organizations charged with the elaboration and implementation of socio-economic rights. The literature on the ILO, and on the human rights of workers, is extensive. For further reading, *see, e.g.*, Harry Arthurs, *Reinventing Labor Law for the Global Economy: The Benjamin Aaron Lecture*, 22 BERKELEY J. EMP. & LAB. L. 271 (2001); HECTOR G. BARTOLOMEI DE LA CRUZ, ET AL., THE INTERNATIONAL LABOR ORGANIZATION: THE INTERNATIONAL STANDARDS SYSTEM AND BASIC HUMAN RIGHTS (1996); Adelle Blackett, *Whither Social Clause? Human Rights, Trade Theory and Treaty Interpretation*, 31 COLUM. HUM. RTS. L. REV. 1 (1999); RYSZARD CHOLEWINSKI, MIGRANT WORKERS IN INTERNATIONAL HUMAN RIGHTS LAW: THEIR PROTECTION IN COUNTRIES OF EMPLOYMENT (1997); LANCE A. COMPA & STEPHEN F. DIAMOND, EDS., HUMAN RIGHTS, LABOR RIGHTS, AND INTERNATIONAL TRADE: LAW AND POLICY PERSPECTIVES (1996); JOANNE CONAGHAN, ET AL. EDS., LABOUR LAW IN AN ERA OF GLOBALIZATION (2002); Benjamin N. Davis & Donald C. Dowling, Jr., *Human Rights, Corporate Responsibility, and Economic Sanctions: The Multinationals' Manifesto on Sweatshops, Trade/Labor Linkage, and Codes of Conduct*, 8 TULSA J. COMP. & INT'L L. 27 (2000); Christine Haight Farley, *Men May Work From Sun to Sun, But Women's Work is Never*

Done: International Law and the Regulation of Women's Work at Night, 4 CIRCLES BU. W. J. L. & SOC. POL. 44 (1996); M. Patricia Fernandez-Kelly, *Underclass and Immigrant Women as Economic Actors: Rethinking Citizenship in a Changing Global Economy*, 9 AM. U. J. INT'L L. & POL'Y 151 (1993); James A. Gross, *Worker Rights as Human Rights: Wagner Act Values and Moral Choices*, 4 U. PA. J. LAB. & EMP. L. 479 (2002); Laura Ho et al., *(Dis)assembling Rights of Women Workers Along the Global Assembly Line: Human Rights and the Garment Industry*, 31 HARV. C.R.-C.L. L. REV. 383 (1996); Karl E. Klare, *The Public/Private Distinction in Labor Law*, 130 U. PA. L. REV. 1358 (1982); Virginia A. Leary, *Workers' Rights and International Trade: The Social Clause (GATT, ILO, NAFTA, U.S. Laws)*, *in* 2 FAIR TRADE AND HARMONIZATION: PREREQUISITES FOR FREE TRADE?—LEGAL ANALYSIS 177 (Jagdish Bhagwati & Robert E. Hudec eds., 1996); Eddy Lee, *Globalization and Labor Standards: A Review of Issues*, 1997 INT'L LAB. REV. 172; Saskia Sassen, *The Informal Economy: Between New Developments and Old Regulations*, 103 YALE L.J. 2289 (1994); James J. Silk & Meron Makonnen, *Economic Exploitation of Children: Ending Child Labor: A Role for International Human Rights Law?* 22 ST. LOUIS U. PUB. L. REV. 359 (2003); PETER STALKER, THE WORK OF STRANGERS: A SURVERY OF INTERNATIONAL LABOUR MIGRATION (1994); John T. Suttles, Jr., *Transmigration of Hazardous Industry: The Global Race to the Bottom, Environmental Justice, and the Asbestos Industry*, 16 TUL. ENVTL. L.J. 1 (2002); United Nations Conference on Trade and Development (UNCTAD), World Investment Report 1994—Transnational Corporations, Employment and the Workplace (New York/Geneva: United Nations, 1994); Leti Volpp, *Migrating Identities: On Labor, Culture, and Law*, 27 N.C.J. INT'L L. & COM. REG. 507 (2002); Lucy A. Williams & Margaret Y.K. Woo, *The "Worthy" Unemployed: Societal Stratification and Unemployment Insurance Programs in China and the United States*, 33 COLUM. J. TRANSNAT'L L. 457 (1995); STOPPING FORCED LABOUR: REPORT OF THE DIRECTOR-GENERAL. GLOBAL REPORT UNDER THE FOLLOW-UP TO THE ILO DECLARATION ON FUNDAMENTAL PRINCIPLES AND RIGHTS AT WORK, REPORT I(B) (International Labour Conference. 89th Session 2001).

CHAPTER FOUR

REGIONAL CHARTERS

A. THE INTER-AMERICAN SYSTEM

1. The Organization of American States and Human Rights

The Organization of American States is the primary inter-governmental organization for countries in North, Central and South America, and is the focal point of the evolving Inter-American human rights system. The normative components of this system include three interlocking instruments: the OAS Charter, the American Declaration of the Rights and Duties of Man and the American Convention on Human Rights. As of March 2004, the American Convention on Human Rights has been ratified by Argentina, Barbados, Bolivia, Brazil, Chile, Colombia, Costa Rica, Dominica, the Dominican Republic, Ecuador, El Salvador, Grenada, Guatemala, Haiti, Honduras, Jamaica, Mexico, Nicaragua, Panama, Paraguay, Peru, Suriname, Uruguay and Venezuela.

The enforcement of human rights in OAS member states is conducted by the Inter-American Commission on Human Rights and the Inter-American Court of Human Rights. The Commission, an official organ of the OAS, hears individual petitions, reports on findings, and makes non-binding recommendations to states. Its structure and procedures were clarified in the post-OAS American Convention on Human Rights. The Commission may also visit a consenting state to assess compliance with human rights obligations. The Court hears cases on human rights violations and can issue advisory as well as binding judgments; all current signatories to the Convention—except Dominica and Grenada—have consented to the jurisdiction of the Court.

For more information on the OAS and human rights, *see* http://www.oas.org/main/main.asp?sLang=E&sLink=http://www.oas.org/key_issues/eng (last visited Apr. 25, 2004)).

CHARTER OF THE ORGANIZATION OF AMERICAN STATES

33 I.L.M. 981 (1994) (*entered into force* December 13, 1951)

Article 45

The Member States, convinced that man can only achieve the full realization of aspirations within a just social order, along with economic development and true peace, agree to dedicate every effort to the application of the following principles and mechanisms:

(a) All human beings, without distinction as to race, sex, nationality, creed, or social condition, have a right to material well-being and to their spiritual

development, under circumstances of liberty, dignity, equality of opportunity, and economic security;

(b) Work is a right and a social duty; it gives dignity to the one who performs
it, and it should be performed under conditions, including a system of fair
wages, that ensure life, health, and a decent standard of living for the
worker and his family, both during his working years and in his old age, or
when any circumstance deprives him of the possibility of working;

(c) Employers and workers, both rural and urban, have the right to associate
themselves freely for the defense and promotion of their interests, including the right to collective bargaining and the workers' right to strike, and
recognition of the juridical personality of associations and the protection
of their freedom and independence ***;

(f) The incorporation and increasing participation of the marginal sectors of
the population, in both rural and urban areas, in the economic, social, civic,
cultural, and political life of the nation, in order to achieve the full integration of the national community, acceleration of the process of social
mobility, and the consolidation of the democratic system; ***

(h) Development of an efficient social security policy; and

(i) Adequate provision for all persons to have due legal aid in order to secure
their rights.

AMERICAN DECLARATION OF THE RIGHTS AND DUTIES OF MAN

(Approved by the Ninth International Conference of
American States, Bogotá, Colombia, 1948)

Preamble

All men are born free and equal, in dignity and in rights, and, being endowed by
nature with reason and conscience, they should conduct themselves as brothers one to
another.

The fulfillment of duty by each individual is a prerequisite to the rights of all. Rights
and duties are interrelated in every social and political activity of man. While rights exalt
individual liberty, duties express the dignity of that liberty.

CHAPTER ONE

Rights

Article I. Right to life, liberty and personal security. Every human being has the
right to life, liberty and the security of his person.***

Article VII. Right to protection for mothers and children. All women, during pregnancy and the nursing period, and all children have the right to special protection, care
and aid.***

Article XI. Right to the preservation of health and to well-being. Every person has
the right to the preservation of his health through sanitary and social measures relat-

ing to food, clothing, housing and medical care, to the extent permitted by public and community resources.

Article XII.   Right to education. Every person has the right to an education, which should be based on the principles of liberty, morality and human solidarity.

Likewise every person has the right to an education that will prepare him to attain a decent life, to raise his standard of living, and to be a useful member of society.***

Every person has the right to receive, free, at least a primary education.

Article XIII.   Right to the benefits of culture. Every person has the right to take part in the cultural life of the community, to enjoy the arts, and to participate in the benefits that result from intellectual progress, especially scientific discoveries.

He likewise has the right to the protection of his moral and material interests as regards his inventions or any literary, scientific or artistic works of which he is the author.

Article XIV.   Right to work and to fair remuneration. Every person has the right to work, under proper conditions, and to follow his vocation freely, insofar as existing conditions of employment permit.

Every person who works has the right to receive such remuneration as will, in proportion to his capacity and skill, assure him a standard of living suitable for himself and for his family.

Article XV.   Right to leisure time and to the use thereof. Every person has the right to leisure time, to wholesome recreation, and to the opportunity for advantageous use of his free time to his spiritual, cultural and physical benefit.

Article XVI.   Right to social security. Every person has the right to social security which will protect him from the consequences of unemployment, old age, and any disabilities arising from causes beyond his control that make it physically or mentally impossible for him to earn a living.***

Article XXIII.   Right to property. Every person has a right to own such private property as meets the essential needs of decent living and helps to maintain the dignity of the individual and of the home.

CHAPTER TWO

*Duties***

Article XXX.   Duties toward children and parents. It is the duty of every person to aid, support, educate and protect his minor children, and it is the duty of children to honor their parents always and to aid, support and protect them when they need it.

Article XXXI.   Duty to receive instruction. It is the duty of every person to acquire at least an elementary education.***

Article XXXV.   Duties with respect to social security and welfare. It is the duty of every person to cooperate with the state and the community with respect to social security and welfare, in accordance with his ability and with existing circumstances.

Article XXXVI.   Duty to pay taxes. It is the duty of every person to pay the taxes established by law for the support of public services.

Article XXXVII. Duty to work. It is the duty of every person to work, as far as his capacity and possibilities permit, in order to obtain the means of livelihood or to benefit his community.***

AMERICAN CONVENTION ON HUMAN RIGHTS "PACT OF SAN JOSÉ, COSTA RICA"

9 I.L.M. 673 (1970)

ECONOMIC, SOCIAL, AND CULTURAL RIGHTS

Article 26. Progressive Development

The States Parties undertake to adopt measures, both internally and through international cooperation, especially those of an economic and technical nature, with a view to achieving progressively, by legislation or other appropriate means, the full realization of the rights implicit in the economic, social, educational, scientific, and cultural standards set forth in the Charter of the Organization of American States as amended by the Protocol of Buenos Aires.

Notes and Questions

1. Although the American Declaration of the Rights of Man is not a treaty, it effectively functions as one in the OAS context because parties to the OAS are automatically bound by its provisions. How is this approach different from other types of human rights treaties? What are its benefits and drawbacks? The OAS Charter also incorporates by reference the American Convention on Human Rights. However, not all members of the OAS are parties to the Convention. This unique circumstance creates a dual inter-American human rights system: one based on the provisions set forth in the OAS Charter and the other based on the provisions of the American Convention on Human Rights. *See* Thomas Buergenthal, *The OAS Charter After Forty Years*, 82 Am. Soc'y Int'l L. Proc. 101, 116 (1988). What challenges are posed by the application of disparate standards to members of the same political entity? What possible advantages might there be, if any?

2. Chapter 2 of the Declaration outlines legal duties incumbent on individuals, including duties to "aid, support, educate, and protect" children; to "honor,*** aid, support, and protect" parents; to "receive instruction" and to obtain, at minimum, an elementary education; to "cooperate with the state *** with respect to social security and welfare;" to pay taxes; to work for a livelihood; and to benefit the community. Are these duties consistent with a human rights regime? Which of these duties, if any, are enforceable? What are the advantages and disadvantages of including individual duties in addition to state duties in human rights treaties?

3. Is the efficacy of a regional human rights system correlated with successful representative democracy? Can a regional system substitute for domestic human rights protection? Many OAS member states have experienced persistent economic instability and political upheaval, characterized by coups and repressive regimes. These factors inhibit the flourishing of a human rights culture. *See* Cecilia Medina, *Toward Effectiveness in the Protection of Human Rights in the Americas*, 8 Transnat'l L. & Contemp. Probs. 337, 338–39 (1998). How is effective democracy defined? Obviously, merely holding elections and

creating parliamentary regimes are insufficient to institutionalize democratic norms. Can a regional organization find a common definition of democracy and provide assistance to members in building and supporting democratic institutions? *See* Helen L. Lutz, *Strengthening Core Values in the Americas: Regional Commitment to Democracy and the Protection of Human Rights*, 19 HOUS. J. INT'L L. 643, 650 (1997). In 2001, the OAS undertook specific initiatives to bolster human rights protection in member states. These steps include seeking to ensure that all OAS members ratify important human rights treaties, strengthening accountability in enforcing Court judgments and adhering to Commission recommendations, and increasing access to the Court and Commission.

4. Latin America suffers the greatest inequalities between rich and poor in the world. Are the poor inherently more vulnerable to violations of fundamental rights? Economic, social and cultural rights are guaranteed in almost all Latin American constitutions. How would the enforcement of these rights contribute to the protection of civil and political rights, and to the overall development of a human rights culture in the region? Consider the implications of guaranteeing universal education; enforcing minimum state obligations regarding basic needs such as food, water, and shelter; and demarginalizing women, blacks, mestizos and indigenous people in Latin American society. *See* Chapter 5 *infra*, on Human Rights and Human Development.

5. International human rights treaties are particularly significant in the context of the OAS. Consider the scenario in which an OAS member state may be a party to the U.N. Covenants on Civil and Political Rights and/or Economic, Social and Cultural Rights, but not to the American Convention on Human Rights. The Inter-American Commission has utilized the provisions of these Covenants to attempt to hold its own members accountable for violations of international human rights obligations. *See* Thomas Buergenthal, *Human Rights: The 1966 Covenants Twenty Years Later*, 80 AM. SOC'Y INT'L L. PROC. 408, 424 (1986) (citing Commission action against Suriname and Nicaragua as examples).

6. For further reading on the American Convention on Human Rights, *see* THOMAS BUERGENTHAL & ROBERT E. NORRIS EDS., HUMAN RIGHTS: THE INTER-AMERICAN SYSTEM (1982); THOMAS BUERGENTHAL, ROBERT NORRIS & DINAH SHELTON, PROTECTING HUMAN RIGHTS IN THE AMERICAS: SELECTED PROBLEMS (1982); ALI YILMAZ, THE EUROPEAN AND INTER-AMERICAN CONVENTIONS ON HUMAN RIGHTS: A COMPARATIVE STUDY OF REGIONAL ARRANGEMENTS [microform] (1980); Richard J. Wilson & Jan Perlin, *The Inter-American Human Rights System: Activities During 1999 through October 2000*, 16 AM. U. INT'L L. REV. 315 (2001); Victor Rodriguez Rescia & Marc David Seitles, *The Development of the Inter-American Human Rights System: A Historical Perspective and a Modern-Day Critique*, 16 N.Y. L. SCH. J. HUM. RTS. 593 (2000); Antonio Augusto Cancado Trindade, *Current State and Perspectives of the Inter-American System of Human Rights Protection at the Dawn of the New Century*, 8 TUL. J. INT'L & COMP. L. 5 (2000).

THE YANOMAMI INDIANS CASE

Inter-American Commission on Human Rights Case No. 7615 (March 5, 1985)

BACKGROUND:

1. On December 15, 1980, a petition against the Government of Brazil was presented to the Inter-American Commission on Human Rights, in which the petitioners,

Tim Coulter (Executive Director, Indian Law Resource Center); Edward J. Lehman (Executive Director, American Anthropological Association); Barbara Bentley (Director, Survival International); and other persons, allege violations of the human rights of the Yanomami Indians, citing in particular the following articles of the American Declaration of the Rights and Duties of Man: Article I (Right to Life, Liberty, and Personal Security); Article II (Right to Equality before the Law); Article III (Right to Religious Freedom and Worship); Article XI (Right to the Preservation of Health and to Well-being); Article XII (Right to Education); Article XVII (Right to Recognition of Juridical Personality and of Civil Rights); and Article XXIII (Right to Property).

2.   From examination of the documents and testimony submitted to the Commission, the following antecedents of fact and law can be inferred:

   a.   Between 10,000 and 12,000 Yanomami Indians live in the State of Amazonas and the Territory of Roraima, on the border with Venezuela;

   b.   The Brazilian Constitution guarantees the right of the Indians to their own territory and stipulates that this constitutes permanent and inalienable ownership ***. It also establishes the right of the Indians to the exclusive use of the natural resources of their territory;

   c.   Article 23 of the *Estatuto do Indio* (Statute of the Indians Law 6,001 of 1973) establishes that "the lands occupied by them in accordance with their tribal usage, customs and tradition, including territories where they carry on activities essential for their subsistence or that are of economic usefulness" constitute territory of the Indians;

   d.   Article 2 of Law 6,001 also guarantees the right of the Indians and of the Indian communities to "possess permanently the lands they occupy, recognizing to them the right to the exclusive usufruct of the natural resources and all useful things therein existing";

   e.   Article 6 of the Brazilian Civil Code establishes that the Indians are considered "relatively incompetent" and are under the "guardianship" of the Fundação Nacional do Indio (FUNAI—National Indian Foundation). That institution is under the Ministry of the Interior and was established for the defense, protection, and preservation of the interest and cultural heritage of the Indians and also to promote programs and projects related to their social and economic development;

   f.   In the decade of the 1960s the Government of Brazil approved a plan of exploitation of the vast natural resources in and development of the Amazon region. In 1973 construction began on highway BR-210 (the Northern Circumferential Highway), which, when it passed through the territory of the Yanomami Indians, compelled them to abandon their habitat and seek refuge in other places;

   g.   During the decade of the 1970s, rich mineral deposits were discovered in the territories of the Yanomamis which attracted mining companies and independent prospectors (*garimpeiros*), thus aggravating the displacement of thousands of Indians;

   h.   Between 1979 and 1984 various efforts were made and various projects presented aimed at marking the boundaries of a Yanomami Park as Indian territory;

i. In March 1982, after an intensive campaign of protest by national and international human rights and Indian defense organizations, the Government of Brazil, by ministerial decree GM/N° 025, established the interdiction (absolute reservation) of a continuous territory of 7,000,000 hectares in the Federal Territory of Roraima and the State of Amazonas for the Yanomami Indians. Among other provisions, that decree assigned to the FUNAI the responsibility for taking the following five measures for protection of the Yanomami Indians:

    i.   the interdiction (absolute reservation) of a continuous area of land;

    ii. the establishment of an administrative structure with enough control posts to coordinate and implement the assistance to the Yanomamis;

    iii. the construction of landing strips at the control posts and various areas for the purposes of attracting isolated groups of Indians as well as establishing an infrastructure for building roads and highways;

    iv. the adoption of measures to protect the Indian groups, especially those related to the reserved areas, to protect the natural environment and preserve the existing buildings and equipment; and

    v.   to coordinate and direct the activities of the religious missions.

j. On September 12, 1984, the then President of the FUNAI, Mr. Jurundy Marcos da Fonseca, submitted a new proposal to the inter ministerial Working Group that had been established in 1983 through Decree 88,118. It aimed at defining the future Yanomami Indian Park with an area of 9,419,108 hectares, which would include practically all the territory and the villages that the Yanomamis inhabit. Up to now, however, that proposal has not been implemented.

3. In the presentation made by the petitioners and in subsequent testimony and reports given to the Commission by them, the following allegations were made:

a. The massive penetration of outsiders into the area has had devastating physical and psychological consequences for the Indians; it has caused the break-up of their age-old social organization; it has introduced prostitution among the women, something that was unknown; and it has resulted in many deaths, caused by epidemics of influenza, tuberculosis, measles, venereal diseases, and others.

b. Despite repeated interventions in behalf of the Indians by many humanitarian, religious, and pro-Indian organizations, the authorities responsible for the Indians' health and for ensuring the implementation of the provisions of the Constitution and the law have done little.

c. The agricultural development projects carried out by the National Institute for Settlement and Agrarian Reform, established for the benefit of the Indians displaced from their lands, have not produced the desired effects. The result, on the contrary, has been the loss of their lands and their compulsory transfer to agricultural communities that do not correspond to their customs and traditions.

d.   The process of integration of the Indians,*** tends toward the disintegration and destruction of the Indian communities, instead of contributing to their economic and social well-being.

e.   The occupation and development of the area of Amazonas and the Territory of Roraima has resulted in the destruction of encampments and the disappearance and death of hundreds of Yanomami Indians and threatens to make them extinct.

f.   The proposal for the establishment of the "Yanomami Indian Park," while it has received the support of the Federal Government, on the other hand has been objected to by sectors primarily interested in the economic development of the State and the Territory of Roraima,*** and so far this has resulted in noncompliance with Law 6,001, which provided for the reservation of the Indians lands.

CONSIDERING:***

2.   That the reported violations have their origin in the construction of the trans-Amazonian highway BR-210 that goes through the territory where the Indians live; in the failure to establish the Yanomami Park for the protection of the cultural heritage of this Indian group; in the authorization to exploit the resources of the subsoil of the Indian territories; in permitting the massive penetration into the Indians' territory of outsiders carrying various contagious diseases that have caused many victims within the Indian community and in not providing the essential medical care to the persons affected; and finally, in proceeding to displace the Indians from their ancestral lands, with all the negative consequences for their culture, traditions, and costumes.

3.   That the Federal Constitution of the Republic stipulates in Article 4.IV that the patrimony of the Union includes "the lands occupied by forest-dwelling aborigenes," and that, moreover, in Article 198 it states:

Lands inhabited by forest-dwelling aborigenes are inalienable under the terms that federal law may establish; they shall have permanent possession of them, and their right to the exclusive usufruct of the natural resources and of all useful things therein existing is recognized.

4.   That for legal purposes, Law 6,001 in its Article 3, established two groups of Indians:

a.   the "Indians or Forest-dwelling Aborigenes," that is to say, individuals of pre-Colombian origin whose cultural characteristics distinguish them from the national society; and;

b.   the "Indian Community or Tribal Group," which refers to groups that may live isolated from, or in any case not integrated into, the national community.***

7.   That international law in its present state, and as it is found clearly expressed in Article 27 of the International Covenant on Civil and Political Rights, recognizes the right of ethnic groups to special protection on their use of their own language, for the practice of their own religion, and, in general, for all those characteristics necessary for the preservation of their cultural identity.

8. That on the subject of indigenous populations the Commission, in an earlier recommendation it adopted, has pointed out:

That for historical reasons and because of moral and humanitarian principles, special protection for indigenous populations constitutes a sacred commitment of the states;

That on various occasions this Commission has had to take cognizance of cases in which it has been verified that abuses of power committed by government officials responsible for administrative work in connection with indigenous communities have caused very serious injury to the human rights of their members;

That these offenses against human rights are all the more reprehensible considering that they are committed by agents of the public power and have as their victims persons or groups for whom the effective exercise of the means of defense established by the laws of the respective states is particularly difficult;***

9. That the Organization of American States has established, as an action of priority for the member states, the preservation and strengthening of the cultural heritage of these ethnic groups and the struggle against the discrimination that invalidates their members' potential as human beings through the destruction of their cultural identity and individuality as indigenous peoples.

10. That from the careful examination made by the Commission of the facts, including the replies from the Government of Brazil, it finds the following:

a. That on account of the beginning, in 1973, of the construction of highway BR-210 (the Northern Circumferential Highway), the territory occupied for ages beyond memory by the Yanomami Indians was invaded by highway construction workers, geologists, mining prospectors, and farm workers desiring to settle in that territory;

b. That those invasions were carried out without prior and adequate protection for the safety and health of the Yanomami Indians, which resulted in a considerable number of deaths caused by epidemics of influenza, tuberculosis, measles, venereal diseases, and others;

c. That Indian inhabitants of various villages near the route of highway BR-210 (the Northern Circumferential Highway) abandoned their villages and were changed into beggars or prostitutes, without the Government of Brazil's taking the necessary measures to prevent this; and

d. That after the discovery in 1976 of ores of tin and other metals in the region where the Yanomamis live, serious conflicts arose that led to acts of violence between prospectors and miners of those minerals, on one side, and the Indians, on the other. Such conflicts,*** affected the lives, security, health, and cultural integrity of the Yanomamis.

11. That from the facts set forth above a liability of the Brazilian Government arises for having failed to take timely and effective measures to protect the human rights of the Yanomamis.

12. That the Government of Brazil, in the last few years, has taken various measures to overcome or alleviate the problems that have come up with the Yanomami

Indians. In that direction, the Government of Brazil has reported, through a note from its Permanent Representative to the Organization of American States dated February 13, 1985, that it has taken the following measures to protect the security, health, and integrity of the Yanomamis:

a) The President of the FUNAI sent a proposal to the inter ministerial working group on September 12, 1984, requesting the definition and demarcation of the boundaries of the future Yanomami Park, which would have an area of 9,419,108 hectares;

b) The area proposed for that Park would cover the isolated areas of Ajarani, Catrimani, and Pacu, as well as four control posts, three surveillance posts, and a number of religious missions that would be able to provide medical and other services to the Indians;

c) The FUNAI, with the cooperation of the French association "Médecins du Monde" and the Committee for the Establishment of the Yanomami Park, is carrying out a health program among the Yanomamis, which especially includes mass vaccinations and control of epidemics;

d) The President of the FUNAI has prohibited the transits or stay of non-Indian individual or groups, especially mining prospectors, in the area proposed for the establishment of the Yanomami Park;

e) Up to now, no mining company has entered the Yanomami's region; and

f) The plan for aid and assistance to the Yanomamis continues being carried out ***.

THE INTER-AMERICAN COMMISSION ON HUMAN RIGHTS, RESOLVES:

1. To declare that there is sufficient background information and evidence to conclude that, by reason of the failure of the Government of Brazil to take timely and effective measures in behalf of the Yanomami Indians, a situation has been produced that has resulted in the violation, injury to them, of the following rights recognized in the American Declaration of the Rights and Duties of Man: the right to life, liberty, and personal security (Article I); the right to residence and movement (Article VIII); and the right to the preservation of health and to well-being (Article XI).

2. To recognize the important measures that the Government of Brazil has taken in the last few years, particularly since 1983, to protect the security, health, and integrity of the Yanomami Indians.

3. To recommend:

a) That the Government of Brazil continue to take preventive and curative health measures to protect the lives and health of Indians exposed to infectious or contagious diseases;

b) That the Government of Brazil, through the FUNAI and in conformity with its laws, proceed to set and demarcate the boundaries of the Yanomami Park, in the manner that the FUNAI proposed to the inter ministerial working group on September 12, 1984;

c) That the programs of education, medical protection, and social integration of the Yanomamis be carried out in consultation with the indigenous population affected and with the advisory service of competent scientific, medical, and anthropological personnel; and

d) That the Government of Brazil inform the Commission of the measures taken to implement these recommendations.***

Notes and Questions

1. The non-binding IACHR decision has thus far proven of little value to the Yanomami. According to the American Anthropological Association:

> [T]he Brazilian government *** has not only continued and intensified the policies but failed to take effective measures to ameliorate their massively disruptive and increasingly lethal effects on the Yanomami. Instead, it has actively sought to prevent others (religious missions, indigenous peoples' organizations, non-governmental organizations, medical doctors, ecological researchers and anthropologists) from gaining access or rendering assistance to the Yanomami, while going to great lengths to misrepresent the real nature, purpose, and effects of its policies toward them. The cumulative effects of these policies have now brought the Brazilian Yanomami to the brink of physical, not to mention social and cultural extinction.
>
> By 1990 the devastation of the environment, health, social organization and culture of the Yanomami, particularly in the State of Roraima but also increasingly in the state of Amazonas, had reached a scale and intensity that the Procurador Federal (Federal Prosecutor, the equivalent of the U.S. Attorney General) of Brazil frankly described as "genocidal."

American Anthropological Association, *Report of the Special Commission to Investigate the Situation of the Brazilian Yanomami* (1991). The AAA was one of the NGOs that petitioned for the IACHR opinion. The Report describes the impact of mining in this area, and the fate of the Park:

> In August 1987 there began a massive invasion of Yanomami territory by miners eager to exploit the area's gold and cassiterite. The army at first made a few feeble and unconvincing efforts to interfere, but moved into active complicity with the miners in 1988–89. The killing of four Yanomami and mutilation of their corpses by miners shortly after the beginning of the invasion was seized upon by the government as a pretext to suspend its working agreement with the Commission for the Creation of a Yanomami Park to permit the latter's medical personnel to carry on medical and public health work among the Yanomami, and to expel the Catholic medical mission at the Yanomami village of Catrimani. FUNAI and the military argued that all outsiders (i.e., medical workers, anthropologists, and other independent observers) should leave the area "for their own safety"; the key "outsiders" involved, the miners, were ironically exempt from this policy. Anthropologists were also refused entry into the area. Neither medical personnel nor anthropologists were involved in any incidents of conflict, and no effort was made to impede entry of those responsible for the increasingly frequent acts of violence, the miners. These selective expulsions served only to cut off the Yanomami from contact with their only outside supporters, and to prevent news of what was happening to them from reaching the outside world.

On September 13, 1988, the government issued interministerial order number 160, which divided Yanomami land into 19 small, discontinuous areas separated by "corridors" designed to allow unobstructed access by the miners who were invading their country in ever increasing numbers. Only 29% of the Yanomami area originally delimited by the government in 1985 was included in these areas. The remaining 71% was placed in two "National Forests" and a "National Park." The order was given the force of law by Presidential decree in early 1989, even though neither the Yanomami themselves or the National Congress had been consulted, as required by the constitution. This document was followed only two months later by a second interministerial order (number 250) superceding the earlier decision (160). It repeated all the key features of the former decision, such as the division of Yanomami territory into discontinuous areas, but amended it in one crucial respect, which was the deletion of the earlier document's characterization of the "National Park" and "National Forests" that now contained 71% of the originally recognized area of Yanomami country as "Indigenous Lands" under Yanomami control. This portentous change betrayed the real purpose of these deceptively named entities: the expropriation of the greater part of Yanomami territory from the Yanomami themselves, in order to make it freely available to exploitation by the miners.

The ominous threat to Brazil's indigenous peoples posed by the "Northern Headwaters Project," and the horrific example of what was already happening to the Yanomami as a result of the government-encouraged invasion of their territory by the miners, contributed to the successful mobilization of indigenous and democratic forces to demand a strong section on the rights of indigenous peoples in the new Brazilian constitution drawn up in 1988. This campaign, with important participation by indigenous Brazilian nations like the Kayapo and the Union of Indigenous Nations (UNI), was successful in obtaining an excellent set of Constitutional safeguards of indigenous rights. Article 231 of the new constitution, proclaimed on Oct. 5, 1988, defines "indigenous lands" as the total area necessary for the physical and cultural subsistence of the Indians and the protection of their environment. It also provides that any exploitation of indigenous territory for mining must first be approved by the National Congress and by the native communities affected. It further explicitly removes indigenous lands from those areas in which the State may stimulate the organization of miners' cooperatives or give their work priority over other uses.

These provisions clearly rendered unconstitutional the interministerial decisions 160 and 250 that had divided up Yanomami country into areas too small to support the native communities located in them, and which rendered impossible the inter-communal ritual visits and affinal exchanges that form an essential part of Yanomami social relations. They are likewise inconsistent with the government-encouraged expropriation of Yanomami land and resources by the invading miners. Above all, they are clearly contradictory with the way both the territorial division and the tacit acquiescence in the miners' invasion were implemented as federal government policy without the constitutionally prescribed consultation with the native people concerned and the National Congress. When pressed on the point, the general at the head of the National Security Council succinctly replied, "The constitution does not apply in the Northern Headwaters area." He could not easily have made it clearer that the National

Security Council and the political-economic forces it represents saw their policy toward the native peoples of the Northern Headwaters region in general, and the Yanomami in particular, as a direct challenge to constitutional legality and the democratic, indigenist and environmentalist forces that had mobilized behind it. Meanwhile, the National Security Council fomented spurious charges that criticisms of the Brazilian government's environmental and indigenous policies in Amazonia by NGO's and anthropologists were threats to "national security" inspired by foreign interests attempting to get control of Amazonia for their own ends. These charges have been widely repeated by Brazilian government spokespersons and media.

By 1989 an estimated 40,000 miners had flooded into Yanomami territory. The impact of this invasion on the Yanomami was shattering.***

2. The IACHR takes up the story in its own follow-up report on this problem:

69. Starting in 1988, the federal courts decided on various occasions in favor of the Yanomami's rights. To begin with, they annulled the break-up of their continuous area into separate "reserves," forming a sort of archipelago. At the same time, the courts ruled in defense of the right of this group and others, to the effect that their territories would no longer be subject to usurpation by unlawful mining and lumbering operations and specified measures that would be used to oust them.

70. When the indigenous rights were set forth in the 1988 constitution, the federal agencies began to cut down on the invasion of this area and reduced the number thereof to a few thousand by the early 90s.

71. In subsequent years, the commission received information that the recommendations it had issued in 1985 had been implemented and that the demarcation and definitive titling of the Yanomani area had been completed. During their visit, its members were able to confirm the existence of health care posts and the establishment of federal inspection stations in the indigenous area, along with the efficient service being provided at that time by the federal national police force in protecting the territory and defending it against the stealthy incursion of *garimpeiros*.

72. During its visit in December of 1995, the Commission obtained coinciding accounts from different sources—including state agents—placing the number of *garimpeiros* at less than three hundred in Brazilian territory, plus an undetermined number in the Yanomami area in Venezuela: most of the latter group were Brazilian and received their supplies from the Brazilian State of Roraima.

73. But the vigilance performed by FUNAI and federal agencies in the Yanomami was plagued by a series of ongoing changes. Early in March 1996, the helicopter watch performed by the Federal Police was suspended. As a result, a new shipment of *garimpeiros* and machinery was brought into the area by plane. It is estimated that some 2,000 *garimpeiros* have now settled there, and that 24 secret landing strips resulted from that operation. At the end of March, officials of the Justice Ministry announced that they would conduct a renewed campaign of expulsion and vigilance. The campaign has not been reinstated, nor had the intruders been evicted at the time this report was written.

Report on the Situation of Human Rights in Brazil, 1997.

3.   In the inter-American system, the recommendations of the Commission and judgments of the Court are enforced by bodies composed of non-independent government representatives. Could this explain the lack of efficacy evidenced by the *Yanomami* case? How could this structure be strengthened? What was the value, if any, of pursuing this petition in the Inter-American Commission? Could a litigation strategy actually work against the interests of the Yanomami? What other viable alternatives exist? For a critique of the IACHR's operational structure, *see* Kimberly D. King-Hopkins, *Inter-American Commission on Human Rights: Is Its Bark Worse Than its Bite in Resolving Human Rights Disputes?*, 35 TULSA L.J. 421, 439–40 (2000).

QUITO DECLARATION

On the enforcement and realization of economic,
social, and cultural rights in Latin America and the Caribbean
(July 24, 1998)

PREAMBLE

1.   RECOGNIZING that economic, social, and cultural rights (ESCR), like civil and political rights, are an indivisible part of human rights and international human rights law.***

5.   OBSERVING that the failure to respect and fulfill ESCR is clearly demonstrated by the growing poverty, hunger, absence of basic services, and discrimination prevalent in our region. Latin America is the area with the highest socio-economic inequalities in the world and suffers hundreds of thousands of avoidable deaths each year.

6.   UNDERSCORING that ignorance about ESCR in Latin America often comes from reducing the problem to a vicious circle whereby poverty, inequality, and the absence of development are seen as necessary or regrettable consequences of immutable economic reality that cannot be modified, when in fact human rights, as universally accepted principles, must establish the framework in which an economy should function.

7.   SIGNALING that market globalization, economic integration arising from the pressures of powerful economic interest groups in the North, the tremendous amounts of resources designated to repaying the region's external debt, structural adjustment programs, and development based on the neo-liberal model all constitute major threats to ESCR.

8.   DENOUNCING the social exclusion that is severing the basic ties of integration, threatening the cultural identity of indigenous and Afro-American minorities, and fostering social apartheid and violence.***

11. RECOGNIZING that violations of ESCR threaten both the domestic peace of States and world peace, and that the lack of respect for ESCR is one of the causes of public insecurity which has led to the militarization of police forces and a further deterioration of civil and political rights.***

II. PRINCIPLES ON THE ENFORCEMENT AND REALIZATION OF ESCR***

19. *** ESCR are subjective rights whose enforceability can be exercised individually or collectively.

20. ESCR set the minimum standards that the State must meet in economic and social terms to guarantee the functioning of a just society and to legitimate its own existence.***

22. The State has the obligation to prevent and sanction ESCR violations by private actors.***

III. OBLIGATIONS OF THE STATE AND OTHER ACTORS

A. *Obligations of the State ****

27. ESCR set limits to the State's discretionary powers in public policy-making. The State must make it a priority and must employ the "maximum available resources" towards fulfilling its commitments to ESCR (Article 2.1 of the ICESCR) ***

29. In addition, the State has the following obligations:

a. Obligation of non-discrimination: In addition to the obligations of equal treatment and non-discrimination, the State's obligation extends to the adoption of special measures, including differential legislative and political measures, for women, vulnerable groups and historically unprotected sectors such as the elderly, children, physically handicapped persons, the terminally ill, persons with chronic medical problems, persons suffering from mental illness, natural disaster victims, persons living in high-risk areas, indigenous communities, or/and groups living in conditions of extreme poverty.

b. Obligation to adopt immediate measures: The State is obligated to adopt measures in a reasonably short period of time from the very moment they ratify the instruments relating to ESCR.*** The following are among its immediate obligations:

  i. The obligation to adjust the legal framework ***.

  ii. Obligation to produce and disseminate information ***.

  iii. The obligation to provide legal recourse and other effective resources ***.

c. The obligation of guaranteeing essential levels of rights ***. This obligation is applicable even in periods of severe resource constraints ***.

d. The obligation of progressiveness and the correlative prohibition against regressiveness ***.***

30. All persons must be guaranteed the capacity to exercise their rights as citizens, and their equality, both formally and materially, in order to ensure the full realization of ESCR.

31. Opportunities to participate must be created for citizens in the budgetary process, the design, implementation, and oversight of development plans, and the monitoring of compliance with international treaties and human rights instruments.***

32. The States are directly responsible if they allow natural or legal "persons," such as national or foreign companies, to undertake activities in their territory that infringe the ESCR of the population located in their jurisdiction; or if they protect or permit

the abusive and discriminatory exercise of some rights that involve the violation of other rights, such as food or work, or lead to the exploitation of women or child labor.***

34. With an eye towards fully satisfying ESCR, public policies must be aimed at an equitable redistribution of income, by levying preferential and selective taxes on assets, large wealth, and commercial transactions, before taxing salaries or incomes of individual labor with undifferentiated or regressive consumption or value-added taxes.

36. A serious commitment to the obligations of the States with respect to ESCR requires that commitments to pay external creditors must be subordinated to the duty of promoting full access to, and enjoyment of, ESCR by citizens, so that structural adjustment programs agreed upon with international financial organizations must be subordinated to social development and, in particular, to the eradication of poverty, the generation of full, productive employment, and the promotion of social integration mindful of gender and cultural diversity.***

Notes and Questions

1. In July, 1998, more than 50 regional NGOs came together in Quito, Ecuador, for the Latin American Convention on the Promotion of Economic, Social and Cultural Rights. The Convention was organized by the South American Platform for Democracy, Human Rights, and Development; the Latin American Association of Promoter Organizations (ALOP); the Latin American League of the International Federation of Human Rights (FIDH); and the Center for Economic and Social Rights. Other major participants included the Inter-American Regional Organization of Workers (ORIT) and the Latin American Center on the Defense of the Rights of Women (CLADEM).

2. What are the benefits of cross-sectoral collaboration for promoting ESC rights? What seems to be the primary goal of the Declaration? Is it to offer a comprehensive analysis of the legal obligations of states and other actors? To formulate urgent socio-economic problems in terms of rights violations? To serve as a call to action? All of the above? Which of these goals might be the most effective in promoting ESC rights?

3. NGOs already play an active role in the inter-American system: filing petitions with the Commission on behalf of individuals; submitting *amicus* briefs in contentious and advisory proceedings in the Court; serving as legal advisors to the Commission; and acting on behalf of victims in Court cases. *See* Martin A. Olz, *Non-Governmental Organizations in Regional Human Rights Systems*, 28 COLUM. HUM. RTS. L. REV. 307, 356–60 (1997).

ADDITIONAL PROTOCOL TO THE AMERICAN CONVENTION ON HUMAN RIGHTS IN THE AREA OF ECONOMIC, SOCIAL AND CULTURAL RIGHTS "PROTOCOL OF SAN SALVADOR"

Adopted at San Salvador, El Salvador on November 17, 1988,
at the eighteenth regular session of the General Assembly of the
Organization of American States

OAS Treaty Series, No. 69, *entered into force* November 16, 1999

Preamble

The States Parties to the American Convention on Human Rights "Pact of San José, Costa Rica,"

Reaffirming their intention to consolidate in this hemisphere, within the framework of democratic institutions, a system of personal liberty and social justice based on respect for the essential rights of man;***

Considering the close relationship that exists between economic, social and cultural rights, and civil and political rights, in that the different categories of rights constitute an indivisible whole based on the recognition of the dignity of the human person, for which reason both require permanent protection and promotion if they are to be fully realized, and the violation of some rights in favor of the realization of others can never be justified;***

Bearing in mind that, although fundamental economic, social and cultural rights have been recognized in earlier international instruments of both world and regional scope, it is essential that those rights be reaffirmed, developed, perfected and protected in order to consolidate in America, on the basis of full respect for the rights of the individual, the democratic representative form of government as well as the right of its peoples to development, self-determination, and the free disposal of their wealth and natural resources; and

Considering that the American Convention on Human Rights provides that draft additional protocols to that Convention may be submitted for consideration to the States Parties, meeting together on the occasion of the General Assembly of the Organization of American States, for the purpose of gradually incorporating other rights and freedoms into the protective system thereof,

Have agreed upon the following Additional Protocol to the American Convention on Human Rights:

Article 1

Obligation to Adopt Measures

The States Parties to this Additional Protocol to the American Convention on Human Rights undertake to adopt the necessary measures, both domestically and through international cooperation, especially economic and technical, to the extent allowed by their available resources, and taking into account their degree of development, for the purpose of achieving progressively and pursuant to their internal legislations, the full observance of the rights recognized in this Protocol.***

Article 3

Obligation of Nondiscrimination

The State Parties to this Protocol undertake to guarantee the exercise of the rights set forth herein without discrimination of any kind for reasons related to race, color, sex, language, religion, political or other opinions, national or social origin, economic status, birth or any other social condition.***

Article 6

Right to Work

1.   Everyone has the right to work, which includes the opportunity to secure the means for living a dignified and decent existence by performing a freely elected or accepted lawful activity.

2.   The State Parties undertake to adopt measures that will make the right to work fully effective, [and] to implement and strengthen programs that help to ensure suitable family care, so that women may enjoy a real opportunity to exercise the right to work.

Article 7

Just, Equitable, and Satisfactory Conditions of Work

The States Parties to this Protocol recognize that the right to work to which the foregoing article refers presupposes that everyone shall enjoy that right under just, equitable, and satisfactory conditions,*** particularly with respect to:

a.   Remuneration which guarantees, as a minimum, to all workers dignified and decent living conditions for them and their families and fair and equal wages for equal work, without distinction;

b.   The right of every worker to follow his vocation and to devote himself to the activity that best fulfills his expectations and to change employment in accordance with the pertinent national regulations;***

e.   Safety and hygiene at work;

f.   The prohibition of night work or unhealthy or dangerous working conditions and, in general, of all work which jeopardizes health, safety, or morals, for persons under 18 years of age. As regards minors under the age of 16, the work day shall be subordinated to the provisions regarding compulsory education and in no case shall work constitute an impediment to school attendance or a limitation on benefiting from education received;

g.   A reasonable limitation of working hours, both daily and weekly. The days shall be shorter in the case of dangerous or unhealthy work or of night work;

h.   Rest, leisure and paid vacations as well as remuneration for national holidays.

Article 8

Trade Union Rights

1.   The States Parties shall ensure:

a.   The right of workers to organize trade unions and to join the union of their choice for the purpose of protecting and promoting their interests.***

b.   The right to strike.***

3.   No one may be compelled to belong to a trade union.

Article 9

Right to Social Security

1.   Everyone shall have the right to social security protecting him from the consequences of old age and of disability which prevents him, physically or mentally, from securing the means for a dignified and decent existence.***

2.   In the case of persons who are employed, the right to social security shall cover at least medical care and an allowance or retirement benefit in the case of work accidents or occupational disease and, in the case of women, paid maternity leave before and after childbirth.

Article 10

Right to Health

1. Everyone shall have the right to health, understood to mean the enjoyment of the highest level of physical, mental and social well-being.

2. In order to ensure the exercise of the right to health, the States Parties agree to recognize health as a public good and, particularly, to adopt the following measures to ensure that right:

    a.   Primary health care, that is, essential health care made available to all individuals and families in the community;

    b.   Extension of the benefits of health services to all individuals subject to the State's jurisdiction;

    c.   Universal immunization against the principal infectious diseases;

    d.   Prevention and treatment of endemic, occupational and other diseases;

    e.   Education of the population on the prevention and treatment of health problems, and

    f.   Satisfaction of the health needs of the highest risk groups and of those whose poverty makes them the most vulnerable.

Article 11

Right to a Healthy Environment

1. Everyone shall have the right to live in a healthy environment and to have access to basic public services.

2. The States Parties shall promote the protection, preservation, and improvement of the environment.

Article 12

Right to Food

1. Everyone has the right to adequate nutrition which guarantees the possibility of enjoying the highest level of physical, emotional and intellectual development.

2. In order to promote the exercise of this right and eradicate malnutrition, the States Parties undertake to improve methods of production, supply and distribution of food, and to this end, agree to promote greater international cooperation in support of the relevant national policies.

Article 13

Right to Education

1. Everyone has the right to education.

2. The States Parties to this Protocol agree that education should be directed towards the full development of the human personality and human dignity and should strengthen respect for human rights, ideological pluralism, fundamental freedoms, justice and peace. They further agree that education ought to enable everyone to partici-

pate effectively in a democratic and pluralistic society and achieve a decent existence and should foster understanding, tolerance and friendship among all nations and all racial, ethnic or religious groups and promote activities for the maintenance of peace.

3. The States Parties to this Protocol recognize that in order to achieve the full exercise of the right to education:

a.   Primary education should be compulsory and accessible to all without cost;

b.   Secondary education in its different forms, including technical and vocational secondary education, should be made generally available and accessible to all by every appropriate means, and in particular, by the progressive introduction of free education;

c.   Higher education should be made equally accessible to all, on the basis of individual capacity, by every appropriate means, and in particular, by the progressive introduction of free education;

d.   Basic education should be encouraged or intensified as far as possible for those persons who have not received or completed the whole cycle of primary instruction;

e.   Programs of special education should be established for the handicapped, so as to provide special instruction and training to persons with physical disabilities or mental deficiencies.

4. In conformity with the domestic legislation of the States Parties, parents should have the right to select the type of education to be given to their children, provided that it conforms to the principles set forth above.

5. Nothing in this Protocol shall be interpreted as a restriction of the freedom of individuals and entities to establish and direct educational institutions in accordance with the domestic legislation of the States Parties.

Article 14

Right to the Benefits of Culture

1. The States Parties to this Protocol recognize the right of everyone:

a.   To take part in the cultural and artistic life of the community;

b.   To enjoy the benefits of scientific and technological progress;

c.   To benefit from the protection of moral and material interests deriving from any scientific, literary or artistic production of which he is the author.***

Article 15

Right to the Formation and the Protection of Families

1. The family is the natural and fundamental element of society and ought to be protected by the State, which should see to the improvement of its spiritual and material conditions.

2. Everyone has the right to form a family, which shall be exercised in accordance with the provisions of the pertinent domestic legislation.

3. The States Parties hereby undertake to accord adequate protection to the family unit and in particular:

a. To provide special care and assistance to mothers during a reasonable period before and after childbirth;

b. To guarantee adequate nutrition for children at the nursing stage and during school attendance years;

c. To adopt special measures for the protection of adolescents in order to ensure the full development of their physical, intellectual and moral capacities;

d. To undertake special programs of family training so as to help create a stable and positive environment in which children will receive and develop the values of understanding, solidarity, respect and responsibility.

Article 16

Rights of Children

Every child, whatever his parentage, has the right to the protection that his status as a minor requires from his family, society and the State. Every child has the right to grow under the protection and responsibility of his parents; save in exceptional, judicially-recognized circumstances, a child of young age ought not to be separated from his mother. Every child has the right to free and compulsory education, at least in the elementary phase, and to continue his training at higher levels of the educational system.

Article 17

Protection of the Elderly

Everyone has the right to special protection in old age. With this in view the States Parties agree to take progressively the necessary steps to make this right a reality and, particularly, to:

a. Provide suitable facilities, as well as food and specialized medical care, for elderly individuals who lack them and are unable to provide them for themselves;

b. Undertake work programs specifically designed to give the elderly the opportunity to engage in a productive activity suited to their abilities and consistent with their vocations or desires;

c. Foster the establishment of social organizations aimed at improving the quality of life for the elderly.

Article 18

Protection of the Handicapped

Everyone affected by a diminution of his physical or mental capacities is entitled to receive special attention designed to help him achieve the greatest possible development of his personality. The States Parties agree to adopt such measures as may be necessary for this purpose and, especially, to:

a. Undertake programs specifically aimed at providing the handicapped with the resources and environment needed for attaining this goal, including work programs consistent with their possibilities and freely accepted by them or their legal representatives, as the case may be;

b. Provide special training to the families of the handicapped in order to help them solve the problems of coexistence and convert them into active agents in the physical, mental and emotional development of the latter;

c. Include the consideration of solutions to specific requirements arising from needs of this group as a priority component of their urban development plans;

d. Encourage the establishment of social groups in which the handicapped can be helped to enjoy a fuller life.

Article 19

Means of Protection

1. Pursuant to the provisions of this article and the corresponding rules to be formulated for this purpose by the General Assembly of the Organization of American States, the States Parties to this Protocol undertake to submit periodic reports on the progressive measures they have taken to ensure due respect for the rights set forth in this Protocol.

2. All reports shall be submitted to the Secretary General of the OAS, who shall transmit them to the Inter-American Economic and Social Council and the Inter-American Council for Education, Science and Culture ***.***

6. Any instance in which the rights established in paragraph a) of Article 8 and in Article 13 are violated by action directly attributable to a State Party to this Protocol may give rise, through participation of the Inter-American Commission on Human Rights and, when applicable, of the Inter-American Court of Human Rights, to application of the system of individual petitions governed by Article 44 through 51 and 61 through 69 of the American Convention on Human Rights.

7. Without prejudice to the provisions of the preceding paragraph, the Inter-American Commission on Human Rights may formulate such observations and recommendations as it deems pertinent concerning the status of the economic, social and cultural rights established in the present Protocol in all or some of the States Parties, which it may include in its Annual Report to the General Assembly or in a special report, whichever it considers more appropriate.

8. The Councils and the Inter-American Commission on Human Rights, in discharging the functions conferred upon them in this article, shall take into account the progressive nature of the observance of the rights subject to protection by this Protocol.***

2. The Human Rights of Persons with Disabilities

The inter-American system has also adopted a human rights treaty that promotes the fundmental rights of persons with disabilities. Efforts to draft and adopt a similar treaty are being made at the U.N. level. The Office of the U.N. High Commissioner for Human Rights has recognized the importance of a human rights perspective in improving the status of persons with disabilities:

Over 600 million people—or approximately 10 per cent of the world's total population—have a disability of one form or another. Over two thirds of them live in developing countries. While their living conditions vary, they are united in one common experience: being exposed to various forms of discrimination and social exclusion. This negative attitude, which is rooted in ignorance, low expectations and prejudice, leads to exclusion and marginalisation of persons with disabilities. This phenomenon also deprives societies of active participation and contribution by a significant societal group.

Persons with disabilities are entitled to the enjoyment of the full range of civil, cultural, economic, political and social rights embodied in international human rights instruments on an equal basis with other persons. Yet, the reality is different. In all societies of the world, including countries which have a relatively high standard of living, persons with disabilities often encounter discriminatory practices and impediments which prevent them from exercising their rights and freedoms and make it difficult for them to participate fully in the activities of their societies.

The disability rights debate is not about the enjoyment of specific rights. Rather, it is about ensuring the equal effective enjoyment of all human rights, without discrimination, by people with disabilities. The non discrimination principle helps make human rights relevant in the specific context of disability, just as it does in the contexts of age, sex and children. Non discrimination, and the equal effective enjoyment of all human rights by people with disabilities are therefore the dominant theme of the long overdue reform in the way disability and persons with disabilities are viewed throughout the world.***

In the past, persons with disabilities suffered from a relative "invisibility," and tended to be viewed as "objects" of protection, treatment and assistance rather than subjects of rights. As a result of this approach, persons with disabilities were excluded from mainstream society, and provided with special schools, sheltered workshops, and separate housing and transportation on the assumption that they were incapable of coping with either society at large or all or most major life activities. They were denied equal access to those basic rights and fundamental freedoms (e.g. health care, employment, education, vote, participation in cultural activities) that most people take for granted.

A dramatic shift in perspective has been taking place over the past two decades, and persons with disabilities have started to be viewed as holders of rights. This process is slow and uneven, but it is taking place in all economic and social systems.

The rights-based approach to disability essentially means viewing persons with disabilities as subjects of law. Its final aim is to empower disabled persons, and to ensure their active participation in political, economic, social, and cultural life in a way that is respectful and accommodating of their difference. This approach is normatively based on international human rights standards and operationally directed to enhancing the promotion and protection of the human rights of persons with disabilities. Strengthening the protection of human rights is also a way to prevent disability.

Four core values of human rights law are of particular importance in the context of disability:

- the dignity of each individual, who is deemed to be of inestimable value because of his/her inherent self-worth, and not because s/he is economically or otherwise "useful";

- the concept of autonomy or self-determination, which is based on the presumption of a capacity for self-directed action and behaviour, and requires that the person be placed at the centre of all decisions affecting him/her;

- the inherent equality of all regardless of difference;

- and the ethic of solidarity, which requires society to sustain the freedom of the person with appropriate social supports.

UN Office of the High Commissioner for Human Rights, *Human Rights and Disability, available at* http://www.Unhchr.ch/disability/intro.htm (last visited Apr. 18, 2004).

After adopting a "World Programme of Action concerning Disabled Persons" in 1982, the U.N. General Assembly adopted Standard Rules on the Equalization of Opportunities for Persons with Disabilities in 1993. The Standard Rules, a set of persuasive guidelines, made specific reference to human rights treaties as the moral basis of the Rules. *See* UN Standard Rules on the Equalisation of Opportunities for Persons with disabilities, General Assembly Resolution 48/96, Dec. 20, 1993. A Special Rapporteur on the Standard Rules was appointed, but reported to the Commission for Social Development rather than to the Commission on Human Rights, implying that disability issues were primarily social policy issues rather than rights issues. Since then, the U.N. Commission on Human Rights has authorized further U.N. efforts to enhance the rights of disabled persons, including "the elaboration of a new thematic Convention on the human rights and dignity of persons with disabilities." U.N. Office of the High Commissioner for Human Rights, *Human Rights and Disability, supra.* The planned convention was still in process at the time of writing (April 2004), but an expert Working Group has produced a draft text. For the text of the Working Group draft, *see Draft Comprehensive and Integral International Convention on the Protection and Promotion of the Rights and Dignity of Persons with Disabilities,* Final text compiled as adopted, U.N. Doc. CRP.4, plus CRP.4/Add.1, Add.2, Add.4 and Add.5, *available at* http://www.rightsforall.org/ (last visited Apr. 18, 2004).

The Commission on Human Rights also authorized the Office of the High Commissioner to conduct a groundbreaking and comprehensive study of existing aspects of human rights protections for persons with disabilities. *See* GERARD QUINN & THERESIA DEGENER, ET AL., HUMAN RIGHTS AND DISABILITY: THE CURRENT USE AND FUTURE POTENTIAL OF UNITED NATIONS HUMAN RIGHTS INSTRUMENTS IN THE CONTEXT OF DISABILITY (2002). In addition, the U.N. Committee on Economic, Social and Cultural Rights has discussed the application of the International Covenant on Economic, Social and Cultural Rights to persons with disabilities. *See* UN Committee on Economic, Social and Cultural Rights, General Comment No. 5, *Persons with disabilities,* U.N. Doc. E/C.12/1994/13 (1994), *available at* http://www1.umn.edu/humanrts/gencomm/ epcomm5e.htm (last visited Apr. 18, 2004).

INTER-AMERICAN CONVENTION ON THE ELIMINATION OF ALL FORMS OF DISCRIMINATION AGAINST PERSONS WITH DISABILITIES

Adopted at Guatemala City, Guatemala, 06/07/99, CONF/ASSEM/Meeting, Twenty-ninth Regular Session of the General Assembly of the Organization of American States (*entered into force* September 4, 2001), *available at* http://www.oas.org/Juridico/english/sigs/a-65.html (last visited April 19, 2004)

THE STATES PARTIES TO THIS CONVENTION,

REAFFIRMING that persons with disabilities have the same human rights and fundamental freedoms as other persons; and that these rights, which include freedom from discrimination based on disability, flow from the inherent dignity and equality of each person;

CONSIDERING that the Charter of the Organization of American States, in Article 3.j, establishes the principle that "social justice and social security are bases of lasting peace";

CONCERNED by the discrimination to which people are subject based on their disability;

BEARING IN MIND the agreement of the International Labour Organisation on the vocational rehabilitation and employment of disabled persons (Convention 159); the Declaration of the Rights of Mentally Retarded Persons (UN General Assembly resolution 2856 (XXVI) of December 20, 1971); the Declaration on the Rights of Disabled Persons (UN General Assembly resolution 3447 (XXX) of December 9, 1975); the World Programme of Action concerning Disabled Persons (UN General Assembly resolution 37/52 of December 3, 1982); the Additional Protocol to the American Convention on Human Rights in the area of Economic, Social, and Cultural Rights, "Protocol of San Salvador" (1988); the Principles for the Protection of Persons with Mental Illness and for the Improvement of Mental Health Care (UN General Assembly resolution 46/119 of December 17, 1991); the Declaration of Caracas of the Pan American Health Organization; resolution AG/RES. 1249 (XXIII-O/93), "Situation of Persons with Disabilities in the American Hemisphere"; the Standard Rules on the Equalization of Opportunities for Persons with Disabilities (UN General Assembly resolution 48/96 of December 20, 1993); the Declaration of Managua (December 1993); the Vienna Declaration and Programme of Action, adopted by the UN World Conference on Human Rights (157/93); resolution AG/RES. 1356 (XXV-O/95), "Situation of Persons with Disabilities in the American Hemisphere"; and AG/RES. 1369 (XXVI-O/96), "Panama Commitment to Persons with Disabilities in the American Hemisphere"; and

COMMITTED to eliminating discrimination, in all its forms and manifestations, against persons with disabilities,

HAVE AGREED as follows:

ARTICLE I

For the purposes of this Convention, the following terms are defined:

1. Disability

The term "disability" means a physical, mental, or sensory impairment, whether permanent or temporary, that limits the capacity to perform one or more essential activities of daily life, and which can be caused or aggravated by the economic and social environment.

2. Discrimination against persons with disabilities

a. The term "discrimination against persons with disabilities" means any distinction, exclusion, or restriction based on a disability, record of disability, condition resulting from a previous disability, or perception of disability, whether present or past, which has the effect or objective of impairing or nullifying the recognition, enjoyment, or exercise by a person with a disability of his or her human rights and fundamental freedoms.

b. A distinction or preference adopted by a state party to promote the social integration or personal development of persons with disabilities does not constitute discrimination provided that the distinction or preference does not in itself limit the right of persons with disabilities to equality and that individuals with disabilities are not forced to accept such distinction or preference. If, under a state's internal law, a person can be declared legally incompetent, when necessary and appropriate for his or her well-being, such declaration does not constitute discrimination.

ARTICLE II

The objectives of this Convention are to prevent and eliminate all forms of discrimination against persons with disabilities and to promote their full integration into society.

ARTICLE III

To achieve the objectives of this Convention, the states parties undertake:

1. To adopt the legislative, social, educational, labor-related, or any other measures needed to eliminate discrimination against persons with disabilities and to promote their full integration into society, including, but not limited to:

a. Measures to eliminate discrimination gradually and to promote integration by government authorities and/or private entities in providing or making available goods, services, facilities, programs, and activities such as employment, transportation, communications, housing, recreation, education, sports, law enforcement and administration of justice, and political and administrative activities;

b. Measures to ensure that new buildings, vehicles, and facilities constructed or manufactured within their respective territories facilitate transportation, communications, and access by persons with disabilities;

c. Measures to eliminate, to the extent possible, architectural, transportation, and communication obstacles to facilitate access and use by persons with disabilities; and

d. Measures to ensure that persons responsible for applying this Convention and domestic law in this area are trained to do so.

2. To work on a priority basis in the following areas:

a. Prevention of all forms of preventable disabilities;

b. Early detection and intervention, treatment, rehabilitation, education, job training, and the provision of comprehensive services to ensure the optimal level of independence and quality of life for persons with disabilities; and

c. Increasing of public awareness through educational campaigns aimed at eliminating prejudices, stereotypes, and other attitudes that jeopardize the right of persons to live as equals, thus promoting respect for and coexistence with persons with disabilities;

ARTICLE IV

To achieve the objectives of this Convention, the states parties undertake to:

1. Cooperate with one another in helping to prevent and eliminate discrimination against persons with disabilities;

2. Collaborate effectively in:

a. Scientific and technological research related to the prevention of disabilities and to the treatment, rehabilitation, and integration into society of persons with disabilities; and

b. The development of means and resources designed to facilitate or promote the independence, self-sufficiency, and total integration into society of persons with disabilities, under conditions of equality.

ARTICLE V

1. To the extent that it is consistent with their respective internal laws, the states parties shall promote participation by representatives of organizations of persons with disabilities, nongovernmental organizations working in this area, or, if such organizations do not exist, persons with disabilities, in the development, execution, and evaluation of measures and policies to implement this Convention.

2. The states parties shall create effective communication channels to disseminate among the public and private organizations working with persons with disabilities the normative and juridical advances that may be achieved in order to eliminate discrimination against persons with disabilities.

ARTICLE VI

1. To follow up on the commitments undertaken in this Convention, a Committee for the Elimination of All Forms of Discrimination against Persons with Disabilities, composed of one representative appointed by each state party, shall be established.

2. The committee shall hold its first meeting within the 90 days following the deposit of the 11th instrument of ratification. Said meeting shall be convened by the General Secretariat of the Organization of American States and shall be held at the Organization's headquarters, unless a state party offers to host it.

3. At the first meeting, the states parties undertake to submit a report to the Secretary General of the Organization for transmission to the Committee so that it may be examined and reviewed. Thereafter, reports shall be submitted every four years.

4. The reports prepared under the previous paragraph shall include information on measures adopted by the member states pursuant to this Convention and on any progress made by the states parties in eliminating all forms of discrimination against persons with disabilities. The reports shall indicate any circumstances or difficulties affecting the degree of fulfillment of the obligations arising from this Convention.

5. The Committee shall be the forum for assessment of progress made in the application of the Convention and for the exchange of experience among the states parties. The reports prepared by the committee shall reflect the deliberations; shall include information on any measures adopted by the states parties pursuant to this Convention, on any progress they have made in eliminating all forms of discrimination against per-

sons with disabilities, and on any circumstances or difficulties they have encountered in the implementation of the Convention; and shall include the committee's conclusions, its observations, and its general suggestions for the gradual fulfillment of the Convention.***

Notes and Questions

1. Why is it necessary to adopt a separate convention on the rights of persons with disabilities?

2. What specific legal obligations are created under the Inter-American Convention? What role should the economic resources of a state party play in fulfilling its obligations, if any?

3. Uganda has implemented a variety of progressive policies aimed at promoting the economic, social, and political rights of persons with disabilities:

> KAMPALA, UGANDA—In Uganda's recent national election, the polling instructions offered a portrait of a nation. After casting their ballots, citizens' thumbs were dipped in ink to show that they had voted.
>
> "If you do not have a thumb, you can have another finger dipped," says the voter's guide. "If you do not have any hands," it continues, "the process shall be applied to any other body part as a polling assistant may determine."
>
> The detailed directions underscore both problems and progress here. Disease, war, poverty, and frequent traffic accidents have left some 15 percent of the population disabled—a hardship mirrored in several parts of Africa. But in Uganda, efforts are being made to help those with disabilities out of the shadows and into the mainstream.
>
> During the past 15 years under the leadership of Yoweri Museveni—who was reelected to a fourth term March 12—Uganda has instituted some of the most advanced disability laws in Africa.
>
> The country's affirmative-action policy states that at least two disabled people—a man and a woman—must sit on every decisionmaking body (which typically has nine members) from the village to the district level.
>
> In total, there are 27,000 disabled leaders, including five members of Parliament and a minister for the disabled—Florence Naiga Sekabira. Ms. Sekabira walks with a crutch because of a bout with polio, which is still common in Uganda and the leading cause of disability here.
>
> New buildings must accommodate those with handicaps; libraries have Braille sections; the nightly news is signed for the deaf. Parents, who traditionally kept disabled children hidden at home, get incentives to send them to school.
>
> Richard Engorok Obin, the assistant program manager of Action on Disability and Development in Uganda, a British-based nongovernmental organization (NGO) that has been advocating for the rights of the disabled in Uganda and elsewhere in Africa, credits presidential policy with the changed approach to disability. "Museveni created a conducive environment for free association and free organization. And we saw a way to begin creating a group to articulate our needs," he says.

While public attitudes are still catching up to the country's progressive policies, they are nonetheless shifting.***

"Most of us were marginalized as children. Only now are we realizing we are of some use," says Mirembe. "At first, I was afraid to work with heavy materials. But I got used to it, and it has given me strength. I have made myself what I am," she says.

"We are not asking for any handouts or to be treated as appendages of existing structures. Rather, we want to change society completely so that we are equals within the system," says advocate Mr. Obin.

It was his group that pushed for the formation of the National Union of Disabled People (NUDP) of Uganda, which in turn did much of the lobbying that resulted in the new legislation.

NUDP is using as a model the Ugandan women's movement, which counts among its successes four female government ministers, 40 members of Parliament, various affirmative-action programs to integrate women into the workforce, and incentive programs urging families to send daughters to school.

NUDP has since gone about creating chapters at various levels and campaigning for more sensitivity to the needs of the disabled, as well as better laws to protect them. Says Obin: "Every program now in Uganda is gender-sensitive, and we hope to create a similar revolution."***

Danna Harman, *In Uganda, Disability is Less of a Burden*, CHRISTIAN SCI. MONITOR, Apr. 9, 2001.

4. Does, or should, the international community have an obligation to assist in the protection and implementation of disability rights?

5. Are rights-based approaches the most effective strategies for improving the status of persons with disabilities? How should disability activists build political will in this area? (*See* list of disability organizations in Section 6.C.6 and discussion of "disability culture.")

6. The Americans with Disabilities Act, a U.S. federal statute prohibiting certain forms of discrimination against persons with disabilities, had an influential impact on international law and activism in this area. *See, e.g.*, AMERICAN SOCIETY OF INTERNATIONAL LAW, PROCEEDINGS OF THE NINETY-THIRD ANNUAL MEETING, Panel Summary: *Is the Americans with Disabilities Act Exportable? Disability Rights in International Perspective*, Mar. 24–27, 1999, at 332. Domestic implementation of the ADA has had far-reaching implications for the rights of persons with disabilities in the United States. Nevertheless, the potential reach of the Act has been limited by Supreme Court interpretation. *See generally*, AMERICANS WITH DISABILITIES: EXPLORING IMPLICATIONS OF THE LAW FOR INDIVIDUALS AND INSTITUTIONS (Anita Silvers & Leslie Francis eds., 2000); Wendy E. Parmet, *Individual Rights and Class Discrimination: The Fallacy of an Individualized Analysis of Disability*, 9 TEMPLE POL. & CIV. RIGHTS L. REV. 283 (2000); Wendy E. Parmet, *Plain Meaning and Mitigating Measures: Judicial Interpretations of the Meaning of Disability*, 21 BERKELEY J. EMP. & LAB. L. 53 (2000).

B. THE EUROPEAN SYSTEMS

1. *The Council of Europe*

The European human rights system is considered to be one of the most highly effective human rights regimes in terms of its jurisprudence and implementation mechanisms. The Council of Europe is the primary regional organization through which normative principles are elaborated. The Council is a political organization founded in the aftermath of World War II to, among other things, guarantee democracy, human rights and the rule of law. All European states that are prepared to respect its principles may become members. New challenges are posed by the recent accession of 22 Central and Eastern European states, doubling the size of the Council.

Among the most significant human rights treaties promulgated by the Council are the European Convention on Human Rights and the Framework Convention for the Protection of National Minorities (considered in Chapter 9, *infra*), and the European Social Charter. The European Social Charter serves as a counterpart to the European Convention on Human Rights. All members of the Council of Europe have either ratified or signed the 1961 Charter or the 1996 Revised Charter, which entered into force in 1999 and will gradually replace the first Charter.

For further reading, *see, e.g.*, MARK JANIS, AN INTRODUCTION TO INTERNATIONAL LAW, at 261–75 (4th ed. 2003); Council of Europe, *Human Rights: Protection, Promotion and Prevention available at* http://www.coe.int/T/E/Com/About_Coe/Human_rights.asp.

EUROPEAN SOCIAL CHARTER

529 U.N.T.S. 89 (*entered into force* February 26, 1965)

Preamble

The governments signatory hereto, being members of the Council of Europe,***

Considering that in the European Convention for the Protection of Human Rights and Fundamental Freedoms signed at Rome on 4th November 1950, and the Protocol thereto signed at Paris on 20th March 1952, the member States of the Council of Europe agreed to secure to their populations the civil and political rights and freedoms therein specified;

Considering that the enjoyment of social rights should be secured without discrimination on grounds of race, colour, sex, religion, political opinion, national extraction or social origin;

Being resolved to make every effort in common to improve the standard of living and to promote the social well-being of both their urban and rural populations by means of appropriate institutions and action,

Have agreed as follows:

Part I

The Contracting Parties accept as the aim of their policy, to be pursued by all appropriate means, both national and international in character, the attainment of conditions in which the following rights and principles may be effectively realised:

1. Everyone shall have the opportunity to earn his living in an occupation freely entered upon.

2. All workers have the right to just conditions of work.

3. All workers have the right to safe and healthy working conditions.

4. All workers have the right to a fair remuneration sufficient for a decent standard of living for themselves and their families.

5. All workers and employers have the right to freedom of association in national or international organizations for the protection of their economic and social interests.

6. All workers and employers have the right to bargain collectively.

7. Children and young persons have the right to a special protection against the physical and moral hazards to which they are exposed.

8. Employed women, in case of maternity, and other employed women as appropriate, have the right to a special protection in their work.

9. Everyone has the right to appropriate facilities for vocational guidance with a view to helping him choose an occupation suited to his personal aptitude and interests.

10. Everyone has the right to appropriate facilities for vocational training.

11. Everyone has the right to benefit from any measures enabling him to enjoy the highest possible standard of health attainable.

12. All workers and their dependents have the right to social security.

13. Anyone without adequate resources has the right to social and medical assistance.

14. Everyone has the right to benefit from social welfare services.

15. Disabled persons have the right to vocational training, rehabilitation and resettlement, whatever the origin and nature of their disability.

16. The family as a fundamental unit of society has the right to appropriate social, legal and economic protection to ensure its full development.

17. Mothers and children, irrespective of marital status and family relations, have the right to appropriate social and economic protection.

18. The nationals of any one of the Contracting Parties have the right to engage in any gainful occupation in the territory of any one of the others on a footing of equality with the nationals of the latter, subject to restrictions based on cogent economic or social reasons.

19. Migrant workers who are nationals of a Contracting Party and their families have the right to protection and assistance in the territory of any other Contracting Party.

Part II

The Contracting Parties undertake, as provided for in Part III, to consider themselves bound by the obligations laid down in the following articles and paragraphs.***

Article 13—The right to social and medical assistance

With a view to ensuring the effective exercise of the right to social and medical assistance, the Contracting Parties undertake:

1. To ensure that any person who is without adequate resources and who is unable to secure such resources either by his own efforts or from other sources, in particular by benefits under a social security scheme, be granted adequate assistance, and, in case of sickness, the care necessitated by his condition;

2. To ensure that persons receiving such assistance shall not, for that reason, suffer from a diminution of their political or social rights;

3. To provide that everyone may receive by appropriate public or private services such advice and personal help as may be required to prevent, to remove, or to alleviate personal or family want;

4. To apply the provisions referred to in paragraphs 1, 2 and 3 of this article on an equal footing with their nationals to nationals of other Contracting Parties lawfully within their territories, in accordance with their obligations under the European Convention on Social and Medical Assistance, signed at Paris on 11th December 1953.***

Part III

Article 20—Undertakings

1. Each of the Contracting Parties undertakes:

   a. To consider Part I of this Charter as a declaration of the aims which it will pursue by all appropriate means, as stated in the introductory paragraph of that part;

   b. To consider itself bound by at least five of the following articles of Part II of this Charter: Articles 1, 5, 6, 12, 13, 16 and 19;

   c. In addition to the articles selected by it in accordance with the preceding sub-paragraph, to consider itself bound by such a number of articles or numbered paragraphs of Part II of the Charter as it may select, provided that the total number of articles or numbered paragraphs by which it is bound is not less than 10 articles or 45 numbered paragraphs.***

IMPLEMENTATION OF THE CHARTER

The European Social Charter is not directly enforceable by individuals. However, several member states apply its provisions in their courts, recognizing the rights provided under the Charter as binding under their national law. In most states, the Charter is applied through the enactment of domestic regulations and laws designed to implement its provisions.

States are required to present proof of adherence to the principles of the Charter through the submission of reports, which are scrutinized by the European Committee of Social Rights (ECSR), formerly the Committee of Independent Experts, to determine whether the states have respected the Charter. In 11 of the states parties, labor unions, employers' associations and non-governmental organizations have the right to apply to the ECSR when they believe that a provision of the Charter is not respected in their state. The findings of the ECSR are provided to the Governmental Committee, composed of state representatives, which works to ensure that each state undertakes the measures necessary to bring it into compliance with the Charter. In situations involving serious non-conformity, the Committee of Ministers, the decision-making body of the Council of Europe, makes recommendations to states that they change the legislation, regulations, or practices not in conformity with the Charter's obligations. These recommendations are non-binding.

Enforcement has been especially problematic with regard to the entitlement of non-nationals to social and medical benefits under local law, which remains controversial in Europe despite the codification of such rights. The resistance to extending benefits to persons legally residing in the country persists notwithstanding the asserted goal of European "integration." The following "Conclusions" regarding the application of Article 13 of the Charter are illustrative:

COMMITTEE OF INDEPENDENT EXPERTS, CONCLUSIONS XIII-4, AT 61–62 (1996)

*** Material scope of Article 13 as regards nationals of other Contracting Parties

1. *Article* 13 *para.* 1

[T]his provision requires that nationals of Contracting Parties working regularly or residing legally in the territory of another Contracting Party must be entitled to social and medical assistance as of right on an equal basis with nationals in accordance with Article 13 para. 1. This implies that no length of residence requirement may be demanded and that repatriation on the sole ground that those nationals are asking for social or medical assistance is excluded as long as their regular work or lawful residence on the territory of the Contracting Party concerned lasts.

2. *Article* 13 *para.* 2

Nationals of Contracting Parties working regularly or residing legally in the territory of another Contracting Party must not, in accordance with Article 13 para. 2, suffer any diminution of their political or social rights on the sole ground that they are receiving assistance. The assessment of a possible discrimination on this basis must of course be made in the light of the political rights these foreigners may claim under domestic law, it being understood that foreigners with a certain length of residence may enjoy more extensive rights.

3. *Article* 13 *para.* 3

Nationals of Contracting Parties working regularly or residing legally within the territory of another Contracting Party must have access to advice and personal help offered by social services on the same conditions as nationals in accordance with Article 13 para. 3.

4. *Article* 13 *para.* 4

With regard to the scope of assistance which has to be granted to those lawfully present in the territory of a Contracting Party without regularly working or lawfully residing,[a] the Committee stresses that as their stay is essentially temporary, the most appropriate form of assistance would be emergency aid to enable them to cope with an immediate state of need (accommodation, food, emergency care and clothing). In this way the grant of a guaranteed minimum income to someone who is only temporarily staying in the territory of a Contracting Party cannot be regarded as assistance under Article 13 para. 4.***

**COMMITTEE OF INDEPENDENT EXPERTS,
CONCLUSIONS XIV-1, VOL. 1, AT 193–95 (1998)**

[Report submitted by Denmark]

Article 13—The right to social and medical assistance

Paragraph 1—Social and medical assistance for those in need

The Danish report recalls, with respect to *social assistance*, that under Section 37 of the Act of 19 June 1974 on social assistance, subsistence benefit *(kontanthjaelp til underhold)* is payable to persons who cannot provide for themselves or their families, and confirms that this applies not just to nationals, but to all persons present in the country. The report clarifies that this form of assistance is categorised as temporary assistance if it lasts for less than one year. Longer periods are considered as constituting permanent assistance. The Danish authorities do not consider that the Charter confers a right to receive permanent social assistance benefit on non-nationals. The Committee observes that this view contradicts the wording of the Charter and the Appendix to the Charter.

According to the report, where a non-national is found to be in need of permanent assistance, the possibility of repatriation may be envisaged, subject to the restrictions laid down by international agreements. Section 4.2 of the Social Assistance Act provides that non-nationals who have been lawfully resident in the state for at least three years and anticipate obtaining a permanent residence permit are not subject to repatriation. The Committee refers the Danish authorities to its case law on the obligations of Contracting Parties towards nationals of other Contracting Parties who are legally resident or regularly working within their territory: such persons must enjoy the same rights as nationals to social and medical assistance, no length of residence requirement may be imposed and such persons may not be repatriated on the sole ground that they are in need of assistance (Conclusions XIII-4, p. 61). The situation in Denmark, as outlined above, clearly fails to respect these requirements.***

With respect to the assistance for specific costs *** the report lists the circumstances in which it may be granted and confirms that these payments may be claimed by nationals of other contracting Parties legally resident or regularly working in Denmark and by refugees. The Committee asks whether there is any length of residence requirement.

Special support may be granted *** where a person's accommodation expenses exceed certain thresholds. Again, the Committee seeks confirmation that such benefits are equally available to nationals of other Contracting Parties legally resident or regularly working in Denmark.

---

a   Those legally within the territory of a Contracting Party for a short stay, in particular students and tourists.

The report provides information on "specific activation" programmes organized by municipalities. These programmes, which *** authorities are required to offer to social assistance claimants, comprise education and training suitable to the needs and ability of the person. Where activation takes the form of job training, the person is paid the normal working wage. Participants in the programmes are entitled to a start-up subsidy if they wish to establish their own business.

The Committee inquires whether participation in such programmes is compulsory for social assistance recipients, whether there are sanctions for refusal to participate and, if so, whether a person may appeal against such sanctions to an independent body.

The Committee regrets that no further information has been supplied on re-establishment centres, despite its request in the previous Conclusion. As these centres cater for persons in need who are not eligible for cash assistance, they clearly play an important role in the social assistance infrastructure. Therefore, the Committee insists that a full account of the structure, operation, staffing and competence of these centres be supplied in the next report, along with statistics on the number of persons assisted in this way.***

As regards medical assistance, the Committee recalls that most forms of health care in Denmark are free of charge to all residents. Assistance for other health care costs may be granted under Section 46(a) of the Social Assistance Act. The report states that this provision also applies to nationals of other Contracting Parties legally resident or regularly working in Denmark. Applications are assessed on a case-by-case basis. The payments granted cover all or part of the cost of the treatment required, depending on the resources of the individual. The Committee notes that 37,831 persons received health care benefit in 1996. It asks that the next report also indicate how many people were refused this benefit and whether any of these refusals were linked to length of residence in Denmark.***

The Committee therefore concludes that, as nationals of other Contracting Parties legally resident or regularly working in Denmark do not enjoy the same rights to "permanent" social assistance (for over one year) as Danish nationals, and as they are also subject to repatriation if they are in need of such assistance, Denmark fails to comply with this provision of the Charter.

EUROPEAN COMMITTEE OF SOCIAL RIGHTS, CONCLUSIONS XV-1, VOL. 1, AT 164–67 (2000)

[Report submitted by Denmark]

Article 13—The right to social and medical assistance

Paragraph 1—Social and medical assistance for those in need

The Danish report states that a new Act on Active Social Policy (Act 1 No. 455/1997) has replaced the Act of 19 June 1974 on social assistance, and underlines the most significant changes introduced by this legislation.

According to Section 8(3), local authorities must assess the circumstances of persons in receipt of social assistance within eight weeks of the first payment of benefit, to determine whether the claimant is receiving the most appropriate form of aid. Activation (which comprises counseling, vocational guidance and various forms of training) must be offered to claimants under the age of 30 within 13 weeks of first payment. Activation must now be offered to all persons under 25, not just those whose principal difficulty is unemployment.***

[A] voluntary scheme has been introduced to allow a claimant's spouse to choose to continue to work at home. The condition of availability for employment no longer applies to such persons.***

The Committee recalls that it previously concluded that Denmark failed to comply with this provision of the Charter because of a restriction on the entitlement of non-nationals to social assistance. It notes that the new legislation retains this restriction. According to Section 3(1) of the Act, assistance may be granted to all persons lawfully residing in *** Denmark. However, "continued assistance," *i.e.* in excess of one year's duration, is reserved to Danish nationals, nationals of European Union ***, or parties to the Agreement on the European Economic Area, and foreigners who are covered by international agreements on this topic. Previous reports have indicated that the Charter is not among the international agreements contemplated by Section 4 of the Act. A non-national who is not entitled to continued assistance may be returned to their home state, but not if they have been lawfully resident for more than three years with a view to permanent residence (Section 3(4)). As *** the situation is unchanged, the Committee is obliged to reiterate its negative conclusion. It once again recalls that under the Appendix to *** the Charter, nationals of other Contracting Parties to the Charter who ***, are legally resident or regularly working in the state are entitled to be *** treated on the same basis as nationals of the host state. Their exclusion from "continued assistance" under Section 3 of the 1997 Act is determined essentially by their length of residence in Denmark, a restriction which is incompatible with Article 13 para. 1 of the Charter.*** Deporting such persons on the basis that they are without adequate resources is not compatible with the Charter (Conclusions XIII-4, p. 61). The Committee seeks confirmation that non-nationals who have been lawfully resident for more than three years may receive "continued assistance" if they are without adequate resources.***

Finally, the Committee notes from another source that there is a six week qualifying period for new residents before they become eligible for health care under the national public scheme. It asks the Danish authorities to clarify whether this is indeed the case.

The Committee concludes that the situation is not in conformity with Article 13 para. 1 of the Charter on the ground that non-nationals who are lawfully resident in Denmark do not enjoy the same entitlement to social assistance as nationals.

Notes and Questions

1. What is the purpose of the Charter's requirement that non-nationals enjoy the same entitlements as nationals? Why would member states that have ratified such a provision refuse to comply with it? What else could be done to ensure compliance?

2. One of the suggested explanations for the relative success of the European human rights system has been the similarities in political organization among Western European member states. To the extent that membership in the Council of Europe has rapidly expanded after the collapse of the Soviet Union, consider the concerns expressed by Professor Mark Janis:

Russian accession, as well as that of perhaps some of the other new states, raises at least three new kinds of problems for Strasbourg. First, it is clear that the Russian legal system is not presently in compliance with the minimum standards of European human rights law. Second, given the ongoing tumult in Russia, it is likely that the number of possible complaints from Russia for Strasbourg will be immense and that Strasbourg's judgments will not be effectively implemented. Third, and in a way the most troubling, there will be a strong temptation for the Strasbourg institutions to fashion a two-tier legal order, allowing lower than normal expectations for Russia.

MARK JANIS, AN INTRODUCTION TO INTERNATIONAL LAW 274–75 (4th ed. 2003). Could the "widening" of a European human rights system to include Eastern European states have a detrimental effect on human rights?

3. Why did the Council of Europe create a separate Social Charter? Should the substantive provisions of the Charter have been part of the European Convention on Human Rights? What difference would that have made?

4. For further reading on the European Social Charter, *see* DAVID JOHN HARRIS & JOHN DARCY, THE EUROPEAN SOCIAL CHARTER (2001); DONNA GOMIEN, DAVID HARRIS & LEO ZWAAK, LAW AND PRACTICE OF THE EUROPEAN CONVENTION ON HUMAN RIGHTS AND THE EUROPEAN SOCIAL CHARTER (1996); KRZYSZTOF DRZEWICKI, CATARINA KRAUSE & ALLAN ROSAS EDS., SOCIAL RIGHTS AS HUMAN RIGHTS: A EUROPEAN CHALLENGE (1994); Richard Burchill, *The EU and European Democracy—Social Democracy or Democracy with a Social Dimension?* 17 CAN. J.L. & JURIS. 185 (2004); Anne Theodore Briggs, *Waking "Sleeping Beauty": The Revised European Social Charter*, 7 HUM. RTS. BR. 24 (2000).

2. *The European Union*

The European Union (EU) (formerly the "European Community") is an economic and political organization that, like the Council of Europe, originated in the post-World War II period. However, the EU/EC only recently began to make clear the organization's commitment to human rights as applied to its many institutions. The culmination of this effort was the adoption in October 2000 of the Charter of Fundamental Rights of the European Union. According to Dana Neascu:

The need for such a Charter arose because the [Treaty on European Union] does not contain a "Community 'Bill of Rights.'" Thus, the TEU does not formally provide for judicial review of violations of human rights [by EU institutions]. In these circumstances, it is the European Court that has exercised jurisdiction over cases of human rights violations, in what experts call a "constitution-building" exercise. The first step towards adopting a Charter took place in March 1996, when the European Commission's *Comites des Sages* presented a report in support of incorporating fundamental civil and social rights into the TEU. More decisively, in June 1999, at the Cologne Summit, the European Council decided to authorize the drafting of the above-mentioned Charter of Fundamental Rights of the European Union, to be applicable at the EU level. The Charter was to emphasize that "protection of fundamental rights is a founding principle of the Union and an indispensable prerequisite for her legitimacy."***

[W]hile the opening articles are devoted to rights that are frequently found in human rights instruments, such as human dignity, the right to life, the right to integrity of the human person, freedom of expression, and the right to conscientious objection, the so-called "Solidarity" portion, Chapter Four, contains novel individual rights, especially by US standards.***

The chapter on solidarity is without doubt the most innovative one, incorporating social and economic rights such as the right to strike, the right of workers to information and consultation, the right to reconcile family and working life, the right to social security benefits and to social services and the right to health care.***

Formally and purportedly, the Charter does not create new rights for the Member States' citizens; it will only ensure judicial review for rights within existing national legal arrangements. For example, while "everyone has the right of access to preventive health care and the right to benefit from medical treatment," that right will be enforced according to the "conditions established by national laws and practices." It merits attention that the Charter seems to break with the distinction made [in] European, US, and international documents between civil and political rights, on the one hand, and economic and social rights, on the other. Additionally, the Charter, if endorsed by all Member States, becomes a legitimizing instrument of the Union, bringing it "closer to its citizens for whom fundamental rights matter a great deal," and transforming it from a purely economic entity into a political one as well.

E.   Dana Neacsu, *The Draft of the EU Charter of Fundamental Rights: A Step in the Process of Legitimizing the EU as a Political Entity, and Economic-Social Rights as Fundamental Human Rights,* 7 COLUM. J. EUR. L. 141 (2001).

CHARTER OF FUNDAMENTAL RIGHTS
OF THE EUROPEAN UNION

PREAMBLE

The people of Europe, in creating an ever closer union among them, are resolved to share a peaceful future based on common values.***

To this end, it is necessary to strengthen the protection of fundamental rights in the light of changes in society, social progress and scientific and technological developments by making those rights more visible in a Charter.***

Enjoyment of these rights entails responsibilities and duties with regard to other persons, to the human community and to future generations.

The Union therefore recognizes the rights, freedoms and principles set out hereafter.***

Chapter IV

SOLIDARITY

Article 27

Workers' right to information and consultation within the undertaking

Workers or their representatives must, at the appropriate levels, be guaranteed information and consultation in good time in the cases and under the conditions provided for by Community law and national laws and practices.

Article 28

Right of collective bargaining and action

Workers and employers, or their respective organizations, have, in accordance with Community law and national laws and practices, the right to negotiate and conclude collective agreements at the appropriate levels and, in cases of conflicts of interest, to take collective action to defend their interests, including strike action.

Article 29

Right of access to placement services

Everyone has the right of access to a free placement service.

Article 30

Protection in the event of unjustified dismissal

Every worker has the right to protection against unjustified dismissal, in accordance with Community law and national laws and practices.

Article 31

Fair and just working conditions

1. Every worker has the right to working conditions which respect his or her health, safety and dignity.

2. Every worker has the right to limitation of maximum working hours, to daily and weekly rest periods and to an annual period of paid leave.

Article 32

Prohibition of child labour and protection of young people at work

The employment of children is prohibited. The minimum age of admission to employment may not be lower than the minimum school-leaving age ***.

Young people admitted to work must have working conditions appropriate to their age and be protected against economic exploitation and any work likely to harm their safety, health or physical, mental, moral or social development or to interfere with their education.

Article 33

Family and professional life

1. The family shall enjoy legal, economic and social protection.

2. To reconcile family and professional life, everyone shall have the right to protection from dismissal for a reason connected with maternity and the right to paid maternity leave and to parental leave following the birth or adoption of a child.

Article 34

Social security and social assistance

1. The Union recognizes and respects the entitlement to social security benefits and social services providing protection in cases such as maternity, illness, industrial accidents, dependency or old age, and in the case of loss of employment, in accordance with the rules laid down by Community law and national laws and practices.

2. Everyone residing and moving legally within the European Union is entitled to social security benefits and social advantages in accordance with Community law and national laws and practices.

3. In order to combat social exclusion and poverty, the Union recognises and respects the right to social and housing assistance so as to ensure a decent existence for all those who lack sufficient resources, in accordance with the rules laid down by Community law and national laws and practices.

Article 35

Health care

Everyone has the right of access to preventive health care and the right to benefit from medical treatment under the conditions established by national laws and practices. A high level of human health protection shall be ensured in the definition and implementation of all Union policies and activities.***

Article 37

Environmental protection

A high level of environmental protection and the improvement of the quality of the environment must be integrated into the policies of the Union and ensured in accordance with the principle of sustainable development.

Article 38

Consumer protection

Union policies shall ensure a high level of consumer protection.***

Article 51

Scope

The provisions of this Chapter are addressed to the institutions and bodies of the Union with due regard for the principle of subsidiarity and to the Member States only when they are implementing Union law. They shall therefore respect the rights, observe the principles and promote the application thereof in accordance with their respective powers.***

Article 52

Scope of guaranteed rights

Any limitation on the exercise of the rights and freedoms recognised by this Charter must be provided for by law and respect the essence of those rights and freedoms. Subject to the principle of proportionality, limitations may be made only if they are necessary and genuinely meet objectives of general interest recognised by the Union or the need to protect the rights and freedoms of others.***

Notes and Questions

1. Why is a comprehensive rights charter deemed necessary to "legitimize" the European Union? What is the significance of the fact that the drafters included both "categories" of rights in the Charter of Fundamental Rights? Does this suggest that the status of economic, social and cultural (or "solidarity") rights has been elevated? Further information on the Charter is *available at* http://www.europarl.eu.int/charter/ default_ en.htmIntroduction; and http://europa.eu.int/abc/indix en.htm.

2. What advantages (or disadvantages) do regional approaches to human rights have over universal approaches? Do you believe that regional approaches are likely to be more effective? Why, or why not?

3. How does the European model compare to the inter-American system? What structural differences do you see? Is one system more effective than the other? Why or why not?

4. For further reading on the Charter of Fundamental Rights of the European Union, *see* TAMARA HERVEY & JEFF KENNER EDS., ECONOMIC AND SOCIAL RIGHTS UNDER THE EU CHARTER OF FUNDAMENTAL RIGHTS: A LEGAL PERSPECTIVE (2003); KIM FEUS ED., AN EU CHARTER OF FUNDAMENTAL RIGHTS (2000); LAMMY BETTEN & DELMA MAC DEVITT EDS., THE PROTECTION OF FUNDAMENTAL SOCIAL RIGHTS IN THE EUROPEAN UNION (1996); Grainne de Burca & Jo Beatrix Aschenbrenner, *The Development of European Constitutionalism and the Role of the EU Charter of Fundamental Rights*, 9 COLUM. J. EUR. L. 355 (2003); Pernice Ingolf, *Integrating the Charter of Fundamental Rights into the Constitution of the European Union: Practical and Theoretical Propositions*, 10 COLUM. J. EUR. L. 5–48 (2003). Giorgio Sacerdoti, *The European Charter of Fundamental Rights: From a Nation-State Europe to a Citizens' Europe*, 8 COLUM. J. EUR. L. 37 (2002); Web site on EU Human Rights Policy, *available at* http://europa.eu.int/comm/external_relations/human_rights/intro/ index. htm.

C. THE AFRICAN UNION

INTRODUCTION

Pan-Africanism—a political and cultural ideology emphasizing solidarity among people of African descent—has a long history predating the colonial conquest of Africa. During the struggle for independence, unification of the continent was seen as key to its liberation by leaders such as Kwame Nkrumah, the first post-colonial president of Ghana. Inspired by this vision, the Organization of African Unity (OAU) was established in 1963 in Addis Ababa, Ethiopia, the only African nation to escape European colonialism. African unity was furthered in 1994 with the entry into force of the Abuja Treaty establishing the African Economic Community (AEC). In 2001 the African Union was formed with the objective of combining these two institutions into a cohesive federation to promote development, peace and political and economic integration. Long-term goals include a legislative parliament, a supreme court of justice and a single currency.

The African Charter on Human and Peoples' Rights was adopted by the OAU in 1981. The Charter combines "first generation" political and civil rights, "second generation" economic, social and cultural rights, and "third generation" solidarity rights into one instrument. It provides the same enforcement mechanism—a complaint system with standing for individuals and NGOs—for all categories. A Protocol on the Establishment of an African Court on Human and Peoples' Rights entered into force on January 25, 2004. The Protocol empowers the court to award damages and provide other forms of relief; its decisions are legally binding and enforceable.

Other continent-wide human rights instruments include the Convention Governing the Specific Aspects of Refugee Problems in Africa, 1001 U.N.T.S. 45, *entered into force* June 20, 1974; the African Charter on the Rights and Welfare of the Child, adopted on July 11, 1990, OAU Doc. CAB/LEG/24.9/49 (1990), *entered into force* Nov. 29, 1999; and the Cultural Charter for Africa, *entered into force* Sept. 19, 1990, *available at* http://www.africa-union.org/official-documents/treaties-%20Conventions.

AFRICAN CHARTER ON HUMAN AND PEOPLES' RIGHTS[1]

O.A.U. Doc. CAB/LEG/67/3 Rev. 5, 21 I.L.M. 58 (1982),
entered into force October 21, 1986

PREAMBLE

The African States members of the Organization of African Unity, parties to the present convention entitled "African Charter on Human and Peoples' Rights,"***

Reaffirming the pledge they solemnly made in [the OAU Charter] to eradicate all forms of colonialism from Africa, to coordinate and intensify their cooperation and efforts to achieve a better life for the peoples of Africa and to promote international cooperation having due regard to the Charter of the United Nations and the Universal Declaration of Human Rights;

---

[1]   Adopted by the 18th Assembly of the Heads of State and Government of the Organization of African Unity, Nairobi, Kenya, June 27, 1981.

Taking into consideration the virtues of their historical tradition and the values of African civilization which should inspire and characterize their reflection on the concept of human and peoples' rights;***

Considering that the enjoyment of rights and freedoms also implies the performance of duties on the part of everyone;

Convinced that it is henceforth essential to pay a particular attention to the right to development and that civil and political rights cannot be dissociated from economic, social and cultural rights in their conception as well as universality and that the satisfaction of economic, social and cultural rights is a guarantee for the enjoyment of civil and political rights;***

Firmly convinced of their duty to promote and protect human and peoples' rights and freedoms taking into account the importance traditionally attached to these rights and freedoms in Africa;

Have agreed as follows:

PART I: RIGHTS AND DUTIES
CHAPTER I—HUMAN AND PEOPLES' RIGHTS***

Article 2

Every individual shall be entitled to the enjoyment of the rights and freedoms recognized and guaranteed in the present Charter without distinction of any kind such as race, ethnic group, color, sex, language, religion, political or any other opinion, national and social origin, fortune, birth or other status.***

Article 4

Human beings are inviolable. Every human being shall be entitled to respect for his life and the integrity of his person. No one may be arbitrarily deprived of this right.

Article 5

*** All forms of exploitation and degradation of man particularly slavery, slave trade, torture, cruel, inhuman or degrading punishment and treatment shall be prohibited.***

Article 14

The right to property shall be guaranteed. It may only be encroached upon in the interest of public need or in the general interest of the community and in accordance with the provisions of appropriate laws.

Article 15

Every individual shall have the right to work under equitable and satisfactory conditions, and shall receive equal pay for equal work.

Article 16

1. Every individual shall have the right to enjoy the best attainable state of physical and mental health.

2. States parties to the present Charter shall take the necessary measures to protect the health of their people and to ensure that they receive medical attention when they are sick.

Article 17

1. Every individual shall have the right to education.

2. Every individual may freely take part in the cultural life of his community.

3. The promotion and protection of morals and traditional values recognized by the community shall be the duty of the State.

Article 18

1. The family shall be the natural unit and basis of society. It shall be protected by the State which shall take care of its physical and moral health.

2. The State shall have the duty to assist the family which is the custodian of morals and traditional values recognized by the community.

3. The State shall ensure the elimination of every discrimination against women and also ensure the protection of the rights of the woman and the child as stipulated in international declarations and conventions.

4. The aged and the disabled shall also have the right to special measures of protection in keeping with their physical or moral needs.

Article 19

All peoples shall be equal; they shall enjoy the same respect and shall have the same rights. Nothing shall justify the domination of a people by another.

Article 20

1. All peoples shall have the right to existence. They shall have the unquestionable and inalienable right to self-determination. They shall freely determine their political status and shall pursue their economic and social development according to the policy they have freely chosen.

2. Colonized or oppressed peoples shall have the right to free themselves from the bonds of domination by resorting to any means recognized by the international community.

3. All peoples shall have the right to the assistance of the States parties to the present Charter in their liberation struggle against foreign domination, be it political, economic or cultural.

Article 21

1. All peoples shall freely dispose of their wealth and natural resources. This right shall be exercised in the exclusive interest of the people. In no case shall a people be deprived of it.

2. In case of spoliation the dispossessed people shall have the right to the lawful recovery of its property as well as to an adequate compensation.

3. The free disposal of wealth and natural resources shall be exercised without prejudice to the obligation of promoting international economic cooperation based on mutual respect, equitable exchange and the principles of international law.***

5. States parties to the present Charter shall undertake to eliminate all forms of foreign economic exploitation particularly that practiced by international monopolies so as to enable their peoples to fully benefit from the advantages derived from their national resources.

Article 22

1. All peoples shall have the right to their economic, social and cultural development with due regard to their freedom and identity and in the equal enjoyment of the common heritage of mankind.

2. States shall have the duty, individually or collectively, to ensure the exercise of the right to development.

Article 23

1. All peoples shall have the right to national and international peace and security.***

Article 24

All peoples shall have the right to a general satisfactory environment favorable to their development.

Article 25

States parties to the present Charter shall have the duty to promote and ensure through teaching, education and publication, the respect of the rights and freedoms contained in the present Charter and to see to it that these freedoms and rights as well as corresponding obligations and duties are understood.

Article 26

States parties to the present Charter shall have the duty to guarantee the independence of the courts and shall allow the establishment and improvement of appropriate national institutions entrusted with the promotion and protection of the rights and freedoms guaranteed by the present Charter.

CHAPTER II—DUTIES

Article 27

1. Every individual shall have duties towards his family and society, the State and other legally recognized communities and the international community.***

Article 28

Every individual shall have the duty to respect and consider his fellow beings without discrimination, and to maintain relations aimed at promoting, safeguarding and reinforcing mutual respect and tolerance.

Article 29

The individual shall also have the duty:

1. To preserve the harmonious development of the family and to work for the cohesion and respect of the family, to respect his parents at all times, to maintain them in case of need;

2. To serve his national community by placing his physical and intellectual abilities at its service;

3. Not to compromise the security of the State whose national or resident he is;

4. To preserve and strengthen social and national solidarity, particularly when the latter is threatened;

5. To preserve and strengthen the national independence and the territorial integrity of his country and to contribute to its defense in accordance with the law;

6. To work to the best of his abilities and competence, and to pay taxes imposed by law in the interest of the society;

7. To preserve and strengthen positive African cultural values in his relations with other members of the society, in the spirit of tolerance, dialogue and consultation and, in general, to contribute to the promotion of the moral well being of society;

8. To contribute to the best of his abilities, at all times and at all levels, to the promotion and achievement of African unity.

Notes and Questions

1. The Preamble of the African Charter states that "civil and political rights cannot be dissociated from economic, social, and cultural rights in their conception as well as universality." What does this mean? What are the practical implications of this view?

2. How does the Charter's formulation of economic, social, and cultural rights differ from that of the International Covenant? What are the implications of the Charter's approach for the nature and scope of state obligations; applicability to non-state actors; and the standards for determining violations?

3.   The African Charter was the first international human rights instrument to protect "third generation" rights, also referred to as solidarity rights. These norms include the right to development (Article 22); the right to peace (Article 23); and the right to a satisfactory environment (Article 24). What is the significance of solidarity rights for the protection of "first" and "second generation" rights? Do these rights have a determinable content? If so, what is it? If not, what is the value of including them in a human rights instrument? *See* Chapter 5, *infra*, for discussion of the right to development.

4.   Does the African Charter reflect values or belief systems that are identifiably "African"? What are they? Can you identify the influence of regional value systems in human rights instruments under the inter-American system or the European human rights system?

5.   What are the implications of the African Charter for the rights of women and girls? African women have been important participants in the development of African human rights law as well as in African societies in general. However, as in all parts of the world, gender discrimination, violence against women and other gender-specific violations occur throughout the continent. The African Union has addressed this issue in part by the adoption of a gender-specific Protocol. *See Protocol to the African Charter on Human and Peoples' Rights on the Rights of Women in Africa, available at* http://www.africa-union. org/home/Welcome.htm (last visited Apr. 27, 2004). African women's NGOs and other women's rights activists were important players in the development of the Protocol. A regional newsletter notes that "Women activists have made significant contributions to the [Protocol's] text, aimed at expanding the meaning of terms used as well as broadening the nature and scope of rights contained therein." The GAD Exchange: A Gender and Development Newsletter for Southern Africa, published by Women in Development —Southern Africa Awareness (WIDSAA), Issue No. 26, Nov. 2001.

Upon recommendation by the Executive Council of the African Union, this protocol was adopted on July 11, 2003, by the AU Assembly in Maputo, Mozambique. The Protocol will enter into force 30 days after the 15th country has ratified it. Claims of violations of the Protocol that are referred by the African Commission on Human and Peoples' Rights can be heard by the African Court on Human and Peoples' Rights. In Article 26 states parties to the Protocol commit themselves to issuing periodic reports to the African Commission on their progress in ensuring the "full realization of the rights" recognized in the Protocol.

The Protocol supplements the African Charter on Human and Peoples' Rights. The Report of the Interim Chairperson on the Proceedings of the Ministerial Meeting on the Draft Protocol concluded that the Protocol on the Rights of Women "will fill the vacuum in the African Charter on Human and Peoples' Rights in respect of the rights of women ***[,] complement the existing universal legal instruments dealing with the principles of equality between men and women *** [and] will constitute for the African Woman a legal tool that will shelter her from all kinds of abuses and surely make her an indispensable partner in the harmonious management of African societies."

The economic, social and cultural rights of women can be found throughout the Protocol, including in Articles 12 (right to education and training), 13 (economic and social welfare rights), 14 (health and reproductive rights), 15 (right to food security), 16 (right to adequate housing), 17 (right to positive cultural context), 18 (right to a healthy and sustainable environment), 19 (right to sustainable development), 21 (right to inheritance), and 24 (special protection of women in distress).

Women in Law and Development in Africa (WiLDAF), a "pan-African women's rights network" identifies the significance of the Protocol as "rest[ing] in the fact that it goes one step beyond the African Charter by exposing the specific inequalities that plague women's lives. In doing so, the Additional Protocol explicitly acknowledges what the African Charter does not: that women's rights as human rights must be respected and observed." WiLDAF News, The African Charter on Human and People's Rights & the Additional Protocol on Women's Rights, *available at* http://site.mweb.co.zw/wildaf/news5.html.

Equality Now, an international human rights NGO with a regional office in Nairobi, Kenya had the following reaction:

> For the first time in international law, [the Protocol] explicitly sets forth the reproductive right of women to medical abortion when pregnancy results from rape or incest or when the continuation of pregnancy endangers the health or life of the mother. [See Article 14(2)(c).] In another first, the Protocol explicitly calls for the legal prohibition of female genital mutilation.
>
> In other equality advances for women, the Protocol calls for an end to all forms of violence against women including unwanted or forced sex, whether it takes place in private or in public, and a recognition of protection from sexual and verbal violence as inherent in the right to dignity. It endorses affirmative action to promote the equal participation of women, including the equal representation of women in elected office, and calls for the equal representation of women in the judiciary and law enforcement agencies as an integral part of equal protection and benefit of the law. Articulating a right to peace, the Protocol also recognizes the right of women to participate in the promoting and maintenance of peace.***
>
> The final Protocol is indicative of the achievements that can be made when governments and civil society use their collective resources to advance the cause of human rights.

Equality Now Press Release, July 14, 2003, *available at* www.hrea.org/lists/hr-headlines/markup/msg01141.html.

Amnesty International calls the Protocol "a significant step in the efforts to promote and ensure respect for the rights of African women.*** If fully ratified and implemented, the Protocol could become an important framework for ending impunity for all attacks on human rights of women in Africa."

Article 2 instructs that states parties *shall* incorporate into their national constitutions and other legislative instruments "the principle of equality between women and men." They shall also enact and implement legislative and regulatory measures to prevent "all forms of discrimination" against women. Furthermore, States Parties are required to incorporate "a gender perspective in their policy decisions, legislation, development plans, programmes and activities and in all other spheres of life."

With regard to the "intersection" of gender and other identity status, legal scholar Johanna E. Bond notes that:

Article 22 of the Draft Protocol addresses the necessity of "special protection" for elderly women and women with disabilities.*** Although the Protocol does not incorporate intersectional analysis into its text, the recognition of different communities of women and the differences in their experiences of discrimination suggest that the Protocol reflects a move in the direction of intersectional analysis.

Joanna E. Bond, *International Intersectionality: A Theoretical and Pragmatic Exploration of Women's International Human Rights Violations*, 52 EMORY L.J. 71 (2003) at n. 106.

THE SOCIAL AND ECONOMIC RIGHTS ACTION CENTER AND THE CENTER FOR ECONOMIC AND SOCIAL RIGHTS/NIGERIA AFRICAN COMMISSION ON HUMAN RIGHTS,

30th Ordinary Session, Banjul, The Gambia (October 13–27, 2001)

Summary of Facts:

1. The Communication alleges that the military government of Nigeria has been directly involved in oil production through the State oil company, the Nigerian National Petroleum Company (NNPC), the majority shareholder in a consortium with Shell Petroleum Development Corporation (SPDC), and that these operations have caused environmental degradation and health problems resulting from the contamination of the environment among the Ogoni People.

2. The Communication alleges that the oil consortium has exploited oil reserves in Ogoniland with no regard for the health or environment of the local communities, disposing toxic wastes into the environment and local waterways in violation of applicable international environmental standards. The consortium also neglected and/or failed to maintain its facilities causing numerous avoidable spills in the proximity of villages. The resulting contamination of water, soil and air has had serious short and long-term health impacts, including skin infections, gastrointestinal and respiratory ailments, and increased risk of cancers, and neurological and reproductive problems.

3. The Communication alleges that the Nigerian Government has condoned and facilitated these violations by placing the legal and military powers of the State at the disposal of the oil companies.***

4. The Communication alleges that the Government has neither monitored operations of the oil companies nor required safety measures that are standard procedure within the industry. The Government has withheld from Ogoni Communities information on the dangers created by oil activities. Ogoni Communities have not been involved in the decisions affecting the development of Ogoniland.

5. The Government has not required oil companies or its own agencies to produce basic health and environmental impact studies regarding hazardous operations and materials relating to oil production, despite the obvious health and environmental crisis in Ogoniland. The government has even refused to permit scientists and environmental organisations from entering Ogoniland to undertake such studies. The government has also ignored the concerns of Ogoni Communities regarding oil

development, and has responded to protests with massive violence and executions of Ogoni leaders.

6. The Communication alleges that the Nigerian government does not require oil companies to consult communities before beginning operations, even if the operations pose direct threats to community or individual lands.

7. The Communication alleges that in the course of the last three years, Nigerian security forces have attacked, burned and destroyed several Ogoni villages and homes under the pretext of dislodging officials and supporters of the Movement of the Survival of Ogoni People (MOSOP). These attacks have come in response to MOSOP's non-violent campaign in opposition to the destruction of their environment by oil companies. Some of the attacks have involved uniformed combined forces of the police, the army, the air-force, and the navy, armed with armoured tanks and other sophisticated weapons. In other instances, the attacks have been conducted by unidentified gunmen, mostly at night. The military-type methods and the calibre of weapons used in such attacks strongly suggest the involvement of the Nigerian security forces. The complete failure of the Government of Nigeria to investigate these attacks, let alone punish the perpetrators, further implicates the Nigerian authorities.

8. The Nigerian Army has admitted its role in the ruthless operations which have left thousands of villagers homeless. The admission is recorded in several memos exchanged between officials of the SPDC and the Rivers State Internal Security Task Force, which has devoted itself to the suppression of the Ogoni campaign. One such memo calls for "ruthless military operations" and "wasting operations coupled with psychological tactics of displacement." At a public meeting recorded on video, Major Okuntimo, head of the Task Force, described the repeated invasion of Ogoni villages by his troops, how unarmed villagers running from the troops were shot from behind, and the homes of suspected MOSOP activists were ransacked and destroyed. He stated his commitment to rid the communities of members and supporters of MOSOP.

9. The Communication alleges that the Nigerian government has destroyed and threatened Ogoni food sources through a variety of means. The government has participated in irresponsible oil development that has poisoned much of the soil and water upon which Ogoni farming and fishing depended. In their raids on villages, Nigerian security forces have destroyed crops and killed farm animals. The security forces have created a state of terror and insecurity that has made it impossible for many Ogoni villagers to return to their fields and animals. The destruction of farmlands, rivers, crops and animals has created malnutrition and starvation among certain Ogoni Communities.

Complaint:

10. The communication alleges violations of Articles 2, 4, 14, 16, 18(1), 21, and 24 of the African Charter.***

Merits:

43. The present Communication alleges a concerted violation of a wide range of rights guaranteed under the African Charter for Human and Peoples' Rights. Before we venture into the inquiry whether the Government of Nigeria has violated the said rights as alleged in the Complaint, it would be proper to establish what is generally expected of governments under the Charter and more specifically vis-a-vis the rights themselves.

44. Internationally accepted ideas of the various obligations engendered by human rights indicate that all rights both civil and political rights and social and economic generate at least four levels of duties for a State that undertakes to adhere to a rights regime, namely the duty to respect, protect, promote, and fulfil these rights. These obligations universally apply to all rights and entail a combination of negative and positive duties.***

45. At a primary level, the obligation to respect entails that the State should refrain from interfering in the enjoyment of all fundamental rights ***. With respect to socio economic rights, this means that the State is obliged to respect the free use of resources owned or at the disposal of the individual alone or in any form of association with others, including the household or the family, for the purpose of rights-related needs. And with regard to a collective group, the resources belonging to it should be respected ***.

46. At a secondary level, the State is obliged to protect right-holders against other subjects by legislation and provision of effective remedies.*** Protection generally entails the creation and maintenance of an atmosphere or framework by an effective interplay of laws and regulations so that individuals will be able to freely realize their rights and freedoms. This is very much intertwined with the tertiary obligation of the State to promote the enjoyment of all human rights *** for example, by promoting tolerance, raising awareness, and even building infrastructures.

47. The last layer of obligation requires the State to fulfil the rights and freedoms it freely undertook under the various human rights regimes. It is more of a positive expectation on the part of the State to move its machinery towards the actual realisation of the rights.*** It could consist in the direct provision of basic needs such as food or resources that can be used for food (direct food aid or social security).***

49. *** The Commission thanks the two human rights NGOs who brought the matter under its purview: the Social and Economic Rights Action Center (Nigeria) and the Center for Economic and Social Rights (USA). Such is a demonstration of the usefulness to the Commission and individuals of *actio popularis*, which is wisely allowed under the African Charter. It is a matter of regret that the only written response from the government of Nigeria is an admission of the gravamen the complaints which is contained in a *note verbale*.*** In the circumstances, the Commission is compelled to proceed with the examination of the matter on the basis of the uncontested allegations of the Complainants, which are consequently accepted by the Commission.***

51. [The rights set forth in Articles 16 (health) and 24 (satisfactory environment) of the Charter] recognise the importance of a clean and safe environment that is closely linked to *** the quality of life and safety of the individual. As has been rightly observed by Alexander Kiss, "an environment degraded by pollution and defaced by the destruction of all beauty and variety is as contrary to satisfactory living conditions and development as the breakdown of the fundamental ecologic equilibria is harmful to physical and moral health."

52. The right to a general satisfactory environment, as guaranteed under Article 24 of the African Charter *** imposes clear obligations upon a government. It requires the State to take reasonable and other measures to prevent pollution and ecological degradation, to promote conservation, and to secure an ecologically sustainable development and use of natural resources.*** The right to enjoy the best attainable state of physical and mental health enunciated in Article 16(1) *** obligate[s] governments to desist from directly threatening the health and environment of their citizens.***

53. Government compliance with the spirit of Articles 16 and 24 of the African Charter must also include ordering or at least permitting independent scientific monitoring of threatened environments, requiring and publicising environmental and social impact studies prior to any major industrial development, undertaking appropriate monitoring and providing information to those communities exposed to hazardous materials and activities and providing meaningful opportunities for individuals to be heard and to participate in the development decisions affecting their communities.

54. *** Undoubtedly and admittedly, the government of Nigeria, through NNPC has the right to produce oil, the income from which will be used to fulfil the economic and social rights of Nigerians. But the care that should have been taken [to protect] the rights of the victims of the violations complained of was not taken. To exacerbate the situation, the security forces of the government engaged in conduct in violation of the rights of the Ogonis by attacking, burning and destroying several Ogoni villages and homes.

55. The Complainants also allege a violation of Article 21 of the African Charter by the government of Nigeria. The Complainants allege that the Military government of Nigeria was involved in oil production and thus did not monitor or regulate the operations of the oil companies and in so doing paved a way for the Oil Consortiums to exploit oil reserves in Ogoniland. Furthermore, in all their dealings with the Oil Consortiums, the government did not involve the Ogoni Communities in the decisions that affected the development of Ogoniland. The destructive and selfish role-played by oil development in Ogoniland, closely tied with repressive tactics of the Nigerian Government, and the lack of material benefits accruing to the local population, may well be said to constitute a violation of Article 21.

Article 21 provides

*1. All peoples shall freely dispose of their wealth and natural resources. This right shall be exercised in the exclusive interest of the people. In no case shall a people be deprived of it.****

56. The origin of this provision may be traced to colonialism, during which the human and material resources of Africa were largely exploited for the benefit of outside powers, creating tragedy for Africans themselves, depriving them of their birthright and alienating them from the land. The aftermath of colonial exploitation has left Africa's precious resources and people still vulnerable to foreign misappropriation.***

57. Governments have a duty to protect their citizens *** from damaging acts that may be perpetrated by private parties *(See Union des Jeunes Avocats/Chad)*. This duty calls for positive action on part of governments ***. The practice before other tribunals also enhances this requirement as is evidenced in the case *Velasquez Rodriguez v. Honduras*. In this landmark judgment, the Inter-American Court of Human Rights held that when a State allows private persons or groups to act freely and with impunity to the detriment of the rights recognised, it would be in clear violation of its obligations to protect the human rights of its citizens. Similarly, this obligation of the State is further emphasised in the practice of the European Court of Human Rights, in *X and Y v. Netherlands*. [*See* Part IV, Chapter 9, *infra.*]

58. [I]n the present case,*** the Government of Nigeria facilitated the destruction of the Ogoniland. Contrary to its Charter obligations and despite such internationally established principles, the Nigerian Government has given the green light to private actors,

and the oil Companies in particular, to devastatingly affect the well-being of the Ogonis. By any measure of standards, its practice falls short of the minimum conduct expected of governments, and therefore, is in violation of Article 21 of the African Charter.

59. The Complainants also assert that the Military government of Nigeria massively and systematically violated the right to adequate housing of members of the Ogoni community under Article 14 [right to property] and implicitly recognised by Articles 16 [health] and 18(1) [protection of family] of the African Charter.***

60. Although the right to housing or shelter is not explicitly provided for under the African Charter, the corollary of the combination of the provisions protecting the right to enjoy the best attainable state of mental and physical health,*** the right to property, and the protection accorded to the family forbids the wanton destruction of shelter because when housing is destroyed, property, health, and family life are adversely affected. It is thus noted that the combined effect of Articles 14, 16 and 18(1) reads into the Charter a right to shelter or housing which the Nigerian Government has apparently violated.

61. At a very minimum, the right to shelter obliges the Nigerian government not to destroy the housing of its citizens and not to obstruct efforts by individuals or communities to rebuild lost homes.*** Its obligation to protect obliges it to prevent the violation of any individual's right to housing by any other individual or non-state actors like landlords, property developers, and land owners, and where such infringements occur, it should act to preclude further deprivations as well as guaranteeing access to legal remedies. The right to shelter even goes further than a roof over one's head. It extends to embody the individual's right to be let alone and to live in peace—whether under a roof or not.

62. [T]he Government of Nigeria has failed to fulfill these two minimum obligations. The government has destroyed Ogoni houses and villages and then, through its security forces, obstructed, harassed, beaten and, in some cases, shot and killed innocent citizens who have attempted to return to rebuild their ruined homes. These actions constitute massive violations of the right to shelter, in violation of Articles 14, 16, and 18(1) of the African Charter.

63. The *** right to adequate housing *** also encompasses the right to protection against forced evictions. The African Commission draws inspiration from the definition of the term "forced evictions" by the Committee on Economic Social and Cultural Rights which defines this term as "the permanent removal against their will of individuals, families and/or communities from the homes they occupy, without the provision of, and access to, appropriate forms of legal or other protection." Wherever and whenever they occur, forced evictions are extremely traumatic. They cause physical, psychological and emotional distress; they entail losses of means of economic sustenance and increase impoverishment. They can also cause physical injury and in some cases sporadic deaths. Evictions break up families and increase existing levels of homelessness. The conduct of the Nigerian government clearly demonstrates a violation of this right enjoyed by the Ogonis as a collective right.

64. The Communication argues that the right to food is implicit in the African Charter, in such provisions as the right to life (Art. 4), the right to health (Art. 16) and the right to economic, social and cultural development (Art. 22). By its violation of these

rights, the Nigerian Government trampled upon not only the explicitly protected rights but also upon the right to food implicitly guaranteed.

65. The right to food is inseparably linked to the dignity of human beings and is therefore essential for the enjoyment and fulfillment of such other rights as health, education, work and political participation. The African Charter and international law require and bind Nigeria to protect and improve existing food sources and to ensure access to adequate food for all citizens. Without touching on the duty to improve food production and to guarantee access, the minimum core of the right to food requires that the Nigerian Government should not destroy or contaminate food sources. It should not allow private parties to destroy or contaminate food sources, and prevent peoples' efforts to feed themselves.

66. The government's treatment of the Ogonis has violated all three minimum duties of the right to food. The government has destroyed food sources through its security forces and State Oil Company; has allowed private oil companies to destroy food sources; and, through terror, has created significant obstacles to Ogoni communities trying to feed themselves.***

67. The Complainants also allege that the Nigerian Government has violated Article 4 of the Charter which guarantees the inviolability of human beings and everyone's right to life and integrity of the person respected. Given the wide-spread violations perpetrated by the Government of Nigeria and by private actors (be it following its clear blessing or not), the most fundamental of all human rights, the right to life has been violated. The Security forces were given the green light to decisively deal with the Ogonis, which was illustrated by the wide-spread terrorisations and killings. The pollution and environmental degradation to a level humanly unacceptable has made living in Ogoniland a nightmare. The survival of the Ogonis depended on their land and farms that were destroyed by the direct involvement of the Government. These and similar brutalities not only persecuted individuals in Ogoniland *** affected the life of the Ogoni Society as a whole. The Commission conducted a mission to Nigeria from the 7th–14th March 1997 and witnessed first hand the deplorable situation in Ogoniland including the environmental degradation.

68. The uniqueness of the African situation and the special qualities of the African Charter on Human and Peoples' Rights imposes upon the African Commission an important task. International law and human rights must be responsive to African circumstances. Clearly, collective rights, environmental rights, and economic and social rights are essential elements of human rights in Africa. The African Commission *** welcomes this opportunity to make clear that there is no right in the African Charter that cannot be made effective.***

69. The Commission does not wish to fault governments that are labouring under difficult circumstances to improve the lives of their people. The situation of the people of Ogoniland, however, requires, in the view of the Commission, a reconsideration of the Government's attitude to the allegations contained in the instant communication. The intervention of multinational corporations may be a potentially positive force for development if the State and the people concerned are ever mindful of the common good and the sacred rights of individuals and communities. The Commission however takes note of the efforts of the present civilian administration to redress the atrocities that were committed by the previous military administration.***

For the above reasons, the Commission,

Finds the Federal Republic of Nigeria in violation of Articles 2, 4, 14, 16, 18(1), 21 and 24 of the African Charter on Human and Peoples' Rights;

Appeals to the government of the Federal Republic of Nigeria to ensure protection of the environment, health and livelihood of the people of Ogoniland by:

— Stopping all attacks on Ogoni communities and leaders by the Rivers State Internal Securities Task Force and permitting citizens and independent investigators free access to the territory;

— Conducting an investigation into the human rights violations described above and prosecuting officials of the security forces, NNPC and relevant agencies involved in human rights violations;

— Ensuring adequate compensation to victims of the human rights violations, including relief and resettlement assistance to victims of government sponsored raids, and undertaking a comprehensive cleanup of lands and rivers damaged by oil operations;

— Ensuring that appropriate environmental and social impact assessments are prepared for any future oil development and that the safe operation of any further oil development is guaranteed through effective and independent oversight bodies for the petroleum industry; and

— Providing information on health and environmental risks and meaningful access to regulatory and decision-making bodies to communities likely to be affected by oil operations.

Urges the government of the Federal Republic of Nigeria to keep the African Commission informed of the out come of the work of:

— The Federal Ministry of Environment which was established to address environmental and environment related issues prevalent in Nigeria, and as a matter of priority, in the Niger Delta area including the Ogoniland;

— The Niger Delta Development Commission (NDDC) enacted into law to address the environmental and other social related problems in the Niger Delta area and other oil producing areas of Nigeria; and

— The Judicial Commission of Inquiry inaugurated to investigate the issues of human rights violations.

Notes and Questions

1. *Implied Right of Privacy.* Paragraph 61 of the decision implies that the right to shelter includes associated privacy rights: "The right to shelter even goes further than a roof over one's head. It extends to embody the individual's right to be let alone and to live in peace—whether under a roof or not." Is this an overly expansive reading of the Charter? Why or why not?

2. *Non-State Actors.* What are the implications of the decision for non-democratic governments who violate human rights in order to advance the interests of transnational corporations? Does the decision impute liability to states for the acts of private actors such as the TNCs?

3. *Collective Rights to Housing?* Paragraph 63 indicates that the right to adequate housing encompasses a collective right of the Ogoni not to be subject to forced evictions. The term "peoples" used in Article 21 can be difficult to define and has been the subject of controversy in international law. Does the decision recognize the status of the Ogonis as a "people"? If so, what are the implications of such a finding? *Compare* the right to housing under the International Covenant on Economic, Social and Cultural Rights. *See* Problem on Housing in Chapter 3 and the related materials on the Dominican Republic.

4. Note the Commission's discussion in paragraph 66 of the importance of the right to food and the ways in which the Nigerian government violated that right through action and inaction. Should it matter whether an alleged violation is characterized as action or inaction in assessing such violations?

5. How might the Commission's analysis inform constitutional interpretation in the other African nations that have included economic, social and cultural rights in their constitutions?

6. For further reading on the African Charter on Human and Peoples' Rights, *see* FATSAH OUGUERGOUZ, THE AFRICAN CHARTER ON HUMAN AND PEOPLES' RIGHTS: A COMPREHENSIVE AGENDA FOR HUMAN DIGNITY AND SUSTAINABLE DEMOCRACY IN AFRICA (2003); MALCOLM D. EVANS & RACHEL MURRAY EDS., THE AFRICAN CHARTER ON HUMAN AND PEOPLES' RIGHTS: THE SYSTEM IN PRACTICE, 1986–2000 (2002); Nsongurua J. Udombana, *Between Promise and Performance: Revisiting States' Obligations Under the African Human Rights Charter*, 40 STAN. J INT'L L. 105 (2004); Christof Heyns, *The African Regional Human Rights System: The African Charter*, 108 PENN ST. L. REV. 679 (2004); Vincent O. Nmehielle, *A Decade in Human Rights Law: Development of the African Human Rights System in the Last Decade*, 11 HUM. RTS. BR. 6 (2004); Curtis F.J. Doebbler, *A Complex Ambiguity: The Relationship Between the African Commission on Human and Peoples' Rights and other African Union Initiatives Affecting Respect for Human Rights*, 13 TRANSNAT'L L. & CONTEMP. PROBS. 7–31 (2003). Yemi Akinseye-George, *Africa at the Crossroads: Current Themes in African Law: VI. Conflict Resolution in Africa: New Trends in African Human Rights Law: Prospects of an African Court of Human Rights*, 10 U. MIAMI INT'L & COMP. L. REV. 159 (2001/02); Nsongurua J. Udombana, *Toward the African Court on Human and Peoples' Rights: Better Late than Never*, 3 YALE HUM. RTS. & DEV. L.J. 45 (2000); Web sites: African Commission on Human and Peoples' Rights: http://www1.umn.edu/humanrts/africa/comision.html; African Human Rights Resource Center: http://www1.umn.edu/humanrts/africa/.

BEN SAUL, IN THE SHADOW OF HUMAN RIGHTS: HUMAN DUTIES, OBLIGATIONS, AND RESPONSIBILITIES

32 COLUM. HUM. RTS. L. REV. 565, 588–601 (2001)

Duties and Limits in Regional Instruments

The recognition of duties in the International Bill of Rights is expanded in a number of regional human rights treaties, which indicate the creative possibilities open to local communities to elaborate upon, and particularize, the general duties contained in international instruments. Most prominently, Article 27(1) of the 1981 African Charter on Human and Peoples' Rights (African Charter) recognizes duties of an individual "towards his family and society, the State and other legally recognized communities and the international community." Article 28 of the African Charter states that "every individual shall have the duty to respect and consider his fellow beings without discrimination, and to maintain relations aimed at promoting, safeguarding and reinforcing mutual respect and tolerance." Article 29 particularizes an extensive range of "African" duties ***.

As Steiner and Alston note, the African Charter goes radically beyond the conventional notion that duties are correlative to rights, by "defining duties *** that run from individuals to the state as well as to other groups and individuals." Although the African Charter claims to reflect "African" culture, closer scrutiny reveals that it is in fact a product of drafting compromises, drawing on responsibilities to the community in "African tradition," neo-marxist obligations (at the insistence of Mozambique and Ethiopia), and the needs of post-colonial, modern African states. [According to critics] the African Charter "incorrectly assumes the existence of a permanent and static African culture' that it has the task of preserving," and it "fails to recognize that cultural values are socially and historically constructed *** in the context of continuous and permanent social and political struggles over resources and power relations in a given society."

The key difficulty is that the African Charter does not specify the means of enforcing its duties, interpreting their scope, or binding individuals. The duties are so broad and ambiguous that practical enforcement would be almost impossible. Nebulous terms in the treaty remain undefined in an "African" context: family, society, harmonious, cohesion, community, security, social and national solidarity, territorial integrity, positive African cultural values, moral well-being of society, and African unity. The African Charter's duties present "a general philosophy and principles of behavior rather than operational legal concepts"***. As a result, the imprecision of the enumerated duties may adversely affect the definition of rights under the African Charter, requiring, according to one African critic, "the domination and subjection of the individual to the authoritarian state."

To a lesser extent, the American Declaration of the Rights and Duties of Man of 1948 (American Declaration) has long stood as a prescriptive counterpoint to the brief duties in the International Bill of Rights. The American Declaration begins with a detailed preamble addressing the inter-relationship of rights and duties: "The fulfillment of duty by each individual is a prerequisite to the rights of all. Rights and duties are interrelated in every social and political activity of man. While rights exalt individual liberty, duties express the dignity of that liberty." The preamble argues that "juridical" duties presuppose "moral" duties "which support them in principle and constitute their basis." It then makes a chain of assumptions about the "supreme end of human existence" being achieved by the individual duty of "spiritual development," expressed in culture and constituted by morality:

> Inasmuch as spiritual development is the supreme end of human existence and the highest expression thereof, it is the duty of man to serve that end with all his strength and resources.
>
> Since culture is the highest social and historical expression of that spiritual development, it is the duty of man to preserve, practice and foster culture by every means within his power.
>
> And, since moral conduct constitutes the noblest flowering of culture, it is the duty of every man always to hold it in high respect.

The American Declaration also proclaims specific human duties, including the duties to develop one's personality (Article 29), support one's children and honor one's parents (Article 30), acquire at least an elementary education (Article 31), cooperate with the state and the community with respect to social security and welfare (Article 35), and refrain from political activities in foreign states which are reserved to foreign citizens (Article 38).***

In a world subject to the homogenizing effects of globalization—including the globalization of dominant strands of legal thought—regional instruments are potentially a conceptually useful means by which to particularize local differences including, for example, greater local emphases on human duties and responsibilities. There has been significant debate, for example, about whether some so-called "obligation societies" balance individual rights and personal responsibilities differently from Western societies, particularly in relation to the "Asian values" debate. [*See* Chapter 2, *supra.*] Regional instruments potentially provide a mechanism through which regional particularity can be acknowledged and therefore protected from erosion by the excessive, arguably imperialistic, effects of the expanding global consumer economy.

In relation to the African Charter and the American Declaration, however, the conceptual possibility of recognizing local difference is defeated by its practical realization. Neither treaty is demonstrably reflective of the diversity of local cultural traditions it purports to represent, and there is considerable opposition to the duties in the African Charter by many Africans themselves. Legitimate regional instruments must be firmly grounded in popular consent, reached through agreement and negotiation with the local communities whose values they purport to represent and protect. Both the African and American instruments have had little or no binding legal effect in their respective regions due to a lack of enforcement or enforceability ***. Nonetheless, even as moral exhortations they can potentially detract from, confuse, and dilute human rights protection.

Notes and Questions

1. Why do the African Charter and American Declaration emphasize duties to the community? Is this merely a reflection of an authoritarian approach, or is it rooted in cultural traditions or world-view? On what basis does a society determine whether the individual or the collective is primary? Is either choice morally unsound?

2. What are concrete examples of situations in which a treaty-based duty could "detract from, confuse, and dilute human rights protection"? Should there be a rule of construction requiring duties to be interpreted to be consistent with rights? Are there any duties that should always (or sometimes) supercede individual rights?

PART III

POWER, POLITICS AND POVERTY: STRUCTURAL CHALLENGES TO THE REALIZATION OF ECONOMIC, SOCIAL AND CULTURAL RIGHTS

Having surveyed the international and regional legal mechanisms established to address human rights violations, Part III explores important underlying causes of economic, social and cultural rights violations, examining various structural impediments to the effective implementation of international norms.

Often the poverty and immense human suffering plaguing two-thirds of the world's people is attributed to "underdevelopment." Development strategies themselves are fraught with human rights implications, depending largely on how the term is defined and the processes by which powerful actors put this definition into play. Chapter 5 begins with the question: what is development—an economic process, a social process or a "right" in and of itself? In the context of contemporary globalization, we examine the impact of neoliberal trade, investment and lending policies on the Global South, the status of women, public health (*e.g.*, the HIV/AIDS pandemic), democratic accountability and national sovereignty.

Chapter 6 engages an enduring and contentious issue in the struggle for human rights: the implications of cultural difference. What is the role of significant markers of social identity in defining and implementing normative standards? What is the relationship between culture and self-determination? When does recognition of cultural rights imperil other human rights? How should such conflicts be resolved? What is the relationship between individual rights and collective rights?

Indigenous peoples, many of whom have experienced the devastating effects of imperialism, colonialism, genocide and cultural genocide, now seek some forms of protection and reparation through the international human rights framework. What tensions does this strategy reveal? What are the economic, social and cultural dimensions of foreign occupation? How is the right to speak one's own language and to teach it to future generations connected to the integrity and survival of a people or cultural group? What are the views of the "Exotic Others"—those women and men of different cultures, traditions, religions and sexual orientations whose experiences are often viewed as so fundamentally different from the "norm"—on the claims of universality advanced by the dominant human rights discourse?

CHAPTER FIVE

HUMAN DEVELOPMENT AND HUMAN RIGHTS

INTRODUCTION: PERSPECTIVES ON POVERTY AND DEVELOPMENT

Contemporary political discourse often divides the world between "developed" and "developing" countries. This attempted categorization seems to assume that countries in the latter category (members of the Global South) aspire to the status of the states in the Global North. But exactly what development entails is controversial. Is there a universal definition? Is development synonymous with economic growth? Is it measured by per capita income, or by the degree of modernization and industrialization? The U.N. Development Programme's Human Development Report, excerpted in Chapter 1, includes such indicia of well-being as access to water, literacy, infant mortality and pollution. What additional factors should be taken into account?

This chapter explores the implications of development discourse for human rights, and the extent to which policies imposed in the name of development may actually violate basic norms. Consider the following:

a. The World Bank's 2000 World Development Report embodies the approach to poverty and development that has become known as the "*Washington Consensus*":

> Markets matter for the poor because poor people rely on formal and informal markets to sell their labor and products, to finance investment, and to insure against risks. Well-functioning markets are important in generating growth and expanding opportunities for poor people. That is why market-friendly reforms have been promoted by international donors and by developing country governments, especially those democratically elected.
>
> In the 1950s and 1960s many of those shaping policy believed that economic development and poverty reduction required active participation of the state and protection of local industry. This inward-looking, state-led development path was adopted by a wide array of countries throughout the world, with varying degrees of success. Many countries adopted protectionism, government control of investment, and state monopolies in key sectors.***
>
> The increasing disenchantment with inward-looking, state-led development led national governments to implement reforms that replaced state intervention in markets with private incentives, public ownership with private ownership, and protection of domestic industries with competition from foreign producers and investors. Where such market-friendly reforms have been successfully implemented, on average economic stagnation has ended and growth has resumed.***

WORLD BANK, WORLD DEVELOPMENT REPORT 61–62 (2000), *available at* http://www.world-bank.org/poverty/wdrpoverty/report/index.htm.

b. *What are the causes of underdevelopment?* According to Professor Mohammed Bedjaoui:

> *** Underdevelopment is not a phenomenon of backwardness attributable to purely national factors such as domestic constraints of various kinds, the ineptitude of rulers, or the corruption and prevarication of local officials. These factors certainly have a part to play in national development, sometimes, alas, a major part, but one must avoid invoking them as excuses to conceal another more decisive fact: *underdevelopment is a structural phenomenon linked to a given form of international economic relations and to a particular international division of labour.* Underdevelopment is even the direct consequence of this international divide. Even with the best Government imaginable in a country with the most favourable prospects on the basis of the wealth of its resources, it is certain that *** this international division of labour will act like a leech, sucking out the lifeblood of the country.

Mohammed Bedjaoui, *The Right to Development in* INTERNATIONAL LAW: ACHIEVEMENTS AND PROSPECTS 1177, 1181 (MOHAMMED BEDJAOUI ED., 1991).

Compare the following formulation adopted by the U.N. General Assembly in 1974 at the urging of the Nonaligned Movement:

> *** [T]he remaining vestiges of alien and colonial domination, foreign occupation, racial discrimination, *apartheid* and neo-colonialism in all its forms continue to be among the greatest obstacles to the full emancipation and progress of the developing countries and all the peoples involved. The benefits of technological progress are not shared equitably by all members of the international community. The developing countries, which constitute 70 per cent of the world's population, account for only 30 per cent of the world's income. It has proved impossible to achieve an even and balanced development of the international community under the existing international economic order. The gap between the developed and the developing countries continues to widen in a system which was established at a time when most of the developing countries did not even exist as independent States and which perpetuates inequality.

Declaration on the Establishment of a New International Economic Order, G.A. Res. 3201 (S-VI), U.N. GAOR, Sixth Special Sess., Agenda Item 6, 2229th Dlen, mtg., at 1, U.N. Doc. A/RES/3201 (S-VI) (1974).

A contrary view is advanced by Canadian professor Rhoda Howard-Hassmann:

> *** The underdevelopment of Commonwealth Africa is caused by both external and internal, historical and contemporary factors. Not only world systems and world markets are responsible for its underdevelopment, but also self-interested *people*, who can be identified as members of ruling classes. Even if they are able to extract economic concessions from the Western world in the name of a state-oriented "right to development," the ruling classes of Africa cannot be relied upon to distribute the benefits of such concessions to ordinary African men and women. In other words, the "right to development" is not necessarily tied to economic rights. It is possible to implement the former while denying the latter to large numbers of the world's poor. Economic rights of individuals, then, are in my view prior to development rights of collectivities. The economic

rights of individuals cannot be negotiated internationally; they must be created and distributed at the national level. Often the creation and distribution of the means to implement economic rights at the national level entails political competition, class struggle and even revolution against ruling classes. Economic development does not, logically or in fact, mean economic rights.***

Rhoda Howard, *Law and Economic Rights in Commonwealth Africa*, 15 CAL. WEST INT'L L.J. 607, 610 (1985).

    c. If, as Howard suggests, economic development does not necessarily entail economic rights, what is the relationship between growth and the eradication of poverty? Amartya Sen, winner of the Nobel Prize in economics, urges that development policy must distinguish between *income poverty* and *capability poverty*, suggesting that growth alone is insufficient:

> *** [T]he reduction of income poverty alone cannot possibly be the ultimate motivation of antipoverty policy. There is a danger in seeing poverty in the narrow terms of income deprivation, and then justifying investment in education, health care and so forth on the ground that they are good means to the end of reducing income poverty. That would be a confounding of ends and means. The basic foundational issues force us *** toward understanding poverty and deprivation in terms of lives people can actually lead and the freedoms they do actually have. The expansion of human capabilities fits directly into these basic considerations. It so happens that the enhancement of human capabilities also tends to go with an expansion of productivities and earning power. That connection establishes an important indirect linkage through which capability improvement helps both directly and indirectly in enriching human lives and in making human deprivations more rare and less acute.***

AMARTYA SEN, DEVELOPMENT AS FREEDOM 92 (1999).

    d. How does Sen's thesis accord with the following illustration provided by another Nobel laureate, Joseph Stiglitz, former vice-president of the World Bank:

> *** [T]he IMF/Washington Consensus approach *** does not acknowledge that development requires a transformation of society. Uganda grasped this in its radical elimination of all school fees, something that budget accountants focusing solely on revenues and costs simply could not understand. Part of the mantra of development economics today is a stress on universal primary education, including educating girls. Countless studies have shown that countries, like those in East Asia, which have invested in primary education, including education of girls, have done better. But in some very poor countries, such as those in Africa, it has been very difficult to achieve high enrollment rates, especially for girls. The reason is simple: poor families have barely enough to survive; they see little direct benefit from educating their daughters, and the education systems have been oriented to enhancing opportunities mainly through jobs in the urban sector considered more suitable for boys. Most countries, facing severe budgetary constraints, have followed the Washington Consensus advice that fees should be charged. Their reasoning: statistical studies showed that small fees had little impact on school enrollment. But Uganda's President Museveni thought otherwise. He knew that he had to create a culture in which the expectation was that everyone went to school. And he knew

he couldn't do that so long as there were any fees charged. So he ignored the advice of the outside experts and simply abolished all school fees. Enrollments soared. As each family saw others sending all of their children to school, it too decided to send its girls to school. What the simplistic statistical studies ignored is the power of systemic change.***

JOSEPH STIGLITZ, GLOBALIZATION AND ITS DISCONTENTS 76 (2003).

e. *What are the qualitative indices of development?* What other factors should the discourse take into account? Is it possible that a country with a low per capita income and a modest technological sector, could be more "developed" in an existential sense, than a modern industrial state? Consider the following:

*** Common views of what constitutes development in contemporary Africa are narrow and inadequate: for example, the view that development is coterminous with a buoyant economy or technological advancement.***

*** [In the view of post-colonial African leaders] economic development was indispensable; we must catch up with the industrialized West. They were right; for by the standards of the West, where they themselves were educated, conditions in Africa, whence the Western nations had siphoned their wealth, were deplorable. There would be no real independence for the new nations if their economies remained 'undeveloped.' Furthermore, economic development was seen as the means to an attainment of higher standards of living. Therefore, the new nations saw the path to development as consisting in establishing industries, constructing new buildings and roads, and laying a whole host of infrastructure.

We came to accept this concept of development. The indices used to measure a country's development are such things as the types of building, highways, forms of transportation and communication, the number of high-technology industries, sources of energy, forms of entertainment, etc. The more these approximate European patterns and standards then, the more developed a society is supposed to be. This view sees development in 'quantitative' and 'external' terms only.

We consider this a narrow and inadequate concept, for development is total; it has to do with the whole of the inhabited world and the environment including society, human beings themselves, as well as social systems and institutions. The above concept leaves out the more 'qualitative' and 'internal,' i.e., the humanistic and spiritual components of development—such as humaneness, integrity, justice, freedom of the individual, harmony, community, self-fulfillment, contentment, etc.***

J.N. Kudadjie, *Towards Moral and Social Development in Contemporary Africa: Insights from Dangme Traditional Moral Experience* in KWASI WIREDU & KWAME GYEKYE EDS., PERSON AND COMMUNITY, GHANAIAN PHILOSOPHICAL STUDIES, 207, 207–208 (1992).

f. *Is it possible for a society to be "overdeveloped"?* Consider this critique of postmodern society by Luther Ivory:

[A] prominent feature of postmodern culture is the unprecedented impact of market and commercial forces on every facet of American life, especially the everyday lives of ordinary people: careers, professions, values, knowledge, religion, technology, language, music, ideology, politics, and sexuality. The upshot is that a unique capitalist culture has been created in which powerful market forces reduce human beings to a mass of consumption-oriented, pleasure-seeking, addictive personalities. The powers of decision making, resource distribution, and image production, however, are concentrated in the hands of a small minority of wealthy business corporations, institutional complexes, and managerial elites. These forces are driven fundamentally by a motive of profit maximization.***

All this points to the second feature of postmodernism, which constitutes a major paradox. As the cultural masses become susceptible and vulnerable to market forces seeking pleasurable release and stimulation, they spend increased amounts of time, energy and resources trying to achieve what ultimately proves to be elusive. Market forces refuse to be satiated, and the more folk taste and acquire, the more they need and desire. Hence, a perpetual and insatiable fixation on conspicuous consumption aimed at the maximization of pleasure, comfort, and technological convenience. This is testament to the power of raw, market values to seize, subdue, and subtly regulate the thought processes, and decisively shape the values and priorities of consumers. As the messages of the market culture are transmitted continuously, on a daily basis, the culture is able to engender intense loyalty, even from those who suffer most and benefit least from these arrangements of power and wealth. Even the poor and marginalized in the culture often tenaciously defend the "system" as the best of what is possible. While the masses are distracted with matters of survival, market culture stimuli simultaneously provide technological and consumer anodynes that deaden revolutionary sensibilities. As persons become increasingly energized by market forces, the more they become desensitized to ways the culture anesthetizes the analytical impulse.***

[M]arket forces have had a devastating impact on the ability of ordinary working poor folk to meet basic subsistence necessities. At the same time, we witness the withdrawing of public provisions designed to mitigate the effect of corporate downsizing, increased unemployment, and rising levels of impoverishment. While the culture sustains significant increases in the number of poor, the government plays a decreasing role in public assistance for the needy. Moreover, the master narratives that once guided people's interpretation of reality and provided a way to make sense and meaning of life have been replaced by the seductive, fashionable narratives of the marketplace. And yet, these market-driven narratives lack the power to either provide meaning or to sustain hope in the cultural wasteland.

LUTHER D. IVORY, TOWARD A THEOLOGY OF RADICAL INVOLVEMENT: THE THEOLOGICAL LEGACY OF DR. MARTIN LUTHER KING, JR., 152–53 (1997).

g. *"Development" vs. "human development."* The following statement introduces readers to the United Nations Development Programme's annual Human Development Report, which provides extensive data and analysis on the economic and social status of people around the world:

The range of human development in the world is vast and uneven, with astounding progress in some areas amidst stagnation and dismal decline in others. Balance and stability in the world will require the commitment of all nations, rich and poor, and a global development compact to extend the wealth of possibilities to all people.

UNITED NATIONS DEVELOPMENT PROGRAMME, HUMAN DEVELOPMENT REPORT 2003: MILLENNIUM DEVELOPMENT GOALS: A COMPACT AMONG NATIONS TO END HUMAN POVERTY, *at* http://hdr.undp.org/.

How is the broad goal of ending poverty related to the implementation of human rights? How is "human development" to be distinguished from "development," if at all?

A. THE IFIS: ENFORCING THE WASHINGTON CONSENSUS

Toward the end of World War II, the Western Allied powers convened in Bretton Woods, New Hampshire, where they constructed a neoliberal regime of global economic governance, focused on trade and monetary policy. The goal of the new regime was to prevent another catastrophic economic crisis like the global depression of the 1930s. At this 1944 conference two multi-lateral financial institutions were born. The International Monetary Fund (IMF) was established to ensure the stability of the monetary system, by making foreign exchange capital available to members to relieve short-term balance of payments deficits, thus preventing resort to protectionist solutions to such crises. The International Bank for Reconstruction and Development (IBRD or World Bank) was created to finance the rebuilding of post-war Europe.

Since the emancipation of the former colonial peoples, the role of the international financial institutions (IFIs) has greatly expanded from short-term crisis management to long-term intervention into economic policymaking in post-colonial states; these states have had to turn to the IFIs for capital to finance infrastructure development and other social needs for which they are unable to attract private capital. Under Article V(3) of the IMF's Articles of Agreement, the organization is empowered to condition its financial support upon the adoption of specified macroeconomic policies. Similarly, the World Bank conditions its funding of development projects on the promulgation of specific macroeconomic "structural adjustment programs" by recipient governments. Under this mandate, the IFIs are major catalysts of neoliberal development strategies emphasizing trade and capital market liberalization, privatization, and fiscal austerity known as the "Washington Consensus." These policies are integral components of the controversial process of "globalization."

1. Globalization, Development and Human Rights

What is globalization? A comprehensive definition is provided in the following statement by the United Nations Committee on Economic, Social and Cultural Rights:

U.N. COMMITTEE ON ECONOMIC, SOCIAL AND CULTURAL RIGHTS, GLOBALIZATION AND THE ENJOYMENT OF ECONOMIC, SOCIAL AND CULTURAL RIGHTS

U.N. Comm. on Economic, Social and Cultural Rights, 18th Session (May 11, 1998)

1. *** Although it is capable of multiple and diverse definitions, globalization is a phenomenon which has wrought fundamental changes within every society.

2. It is usually defined primarily by reference to the developments in technology, communications, information processing and so on that have made the world smaller and more interdependent in very many ways. But it has also come to be closely associated with a variety of specific trends and policies including an increasing reliance upon the free market, a significant growth in the influence of international financial markets and institutions in determining the viability of national policy priorities, a diminution in the role of the state and the size of its budget, the privatization of various functions previously considered to be the exclusive domain of the state, the deregulation of a range of activities with a view to facilitating investment and rewarding individual initiative, and a corresponding increase in the role and even responsibilities attributed to private actors, both in the corporate sector, in particular to the transnational corporations, and in civil society.

3. None of these developments in itself is necessarily incompatible with the principles of the Covenant or with the obligations of governments thereunder. Taken together, however, and if not complemented by appropriate additional policies, globalization risks downgrading the central place accorded to human rights by the United Nations Charter in general and the International Bill of Human Rights in particular. This is especially the case in relation to economic, social and cultural rights. Thus, for example, respect for the right to work and the right to just and favorable conditions of work is threatened where there is an excessive emphasis upon competitiveness to the detriment of respect for the labor rights contained in the Covenant. The right to form and join trade unions may be threatened by restrictions upon freedom of association, restrictions claimed to be "necessary" in a global economy, or by the effective exclusion of possibilities for collective bargaining, or by the closing off of the right to strike for various occupational and other groups. The right of everyone to social security might not be ensured by arrangements which rely entirely upon private contributions and private schemes. Respect for the family and for the rights of mothers and children in an era of expanded global labor markets for certain individual occupations might require new and innovative policies rather than a mere laissez-faire approach. If not supplemented by necessary safeguards, the introduction of user fees, or cost recovery policies, when applied to basic health and educational services for the poor can easily result in significantly reduced access to services which are essential for the enjoyment of the rights recognized in the Covenant. An insistence upon higher and higher levels of payment for access to artistic, cultural and heritage-related activities risks undermining the right to participate in cultural life for a significant proportion of any community.

4. All of these risks can be guarded against, or compensated for, if appropriate policies are put in place. The Committee is concerned, however, that while much energy and many resources have been expended by governments on promoting the trends and policies that are associated with globalization, insufficient efforts are being made to devise new or complementary approaches which could enhance the compatibility of those trends and policies with full respect for economic, social and cultural rights. Competitiveness, efficiency and economic rationalism must not be permitted to become the primary or exclusive criteria against which governmental and inter-governmental policies are evaluated.

5. In calling for a renewed commitment to respect economic, social and cultural rights, the Committee wishes to emphasize that international organizations, as well as the governments that have created and manage them, have a strong and continuous responsibility to take whatever measures they can to assist governments to act in ways which are compatible with their human rights obligations and to seek to devise policies

and programmes which promote respect for those rights. It is particularly important to emphasize that the realms of trade, finance and investment are in no way exempt from these general principles ***.

7. The Committee calls upon the International Monetary Fund and the World Bank to pay enhanced attention in their activities to respect for economic, social and cultural rights, including through encouraging explicit recognition of these rights, assisting in the identification of country-specific benchmarks to facilitate their promotion, and facilitating the development of appropriate remedies for responding to violations. Social safety nets should be defined by reference to these rights and enhanced attention should be accorded to such methods to protect the poor and vulnerable in the context of structural adjustment programs.*** Similarly the World Trade Organization (WTO) should devise appropriate methods to facilitate more systematic consideration of the impact upon human rights of particular trade and investment policies.***

Notes and Questions

1. *The IFIs and Democratic Accountability.* Who makes the decisions in the IFIs? IMF member countries pay a subscription to the Fund in accordance with assigned quotas, which are based on their economic status. Decisions by the World Bank and the IMF are based on a voting system weighted according to the contribution of the member. Thus, the United States exercises 17 percent of the vote, the largest share of any member.

2. What impact might a statement by the ESCR Committee have on the operational policies of the IFIs? Both the World Bank and the IMF are statutorily independent of the control of the United Nations. Immunity from interference by the international community was deemed necessary to insulate these economic organizations from political pressure. Antony Anghie observes that these institutions are operating under a democracy deficit:

> *** The IFIs, and in particular the Bank, have extolled the virtues of good governance, democracy, accountability, and the rule of law, but as a study of the governance structure and the operations of the IFIs indicates, they are fundamentally undemocratic institutions. The interference in the affairs of sovereign states, the expansion of the mandate of the IFIs to encompass a huge range of issues, and the apparent operation of the IFIs according to the interests of major shareholders all raise complex questions as to whether the IFIs are acting within the scope of their Articles of Agreement ***.

Antony Anghie, *Time Present and Time Past: Globalization, International Financial Institutions, and the Third World,* 32 N.Y.U. J. INT'L L. & POL. 243, 270 (2000).

BALAKRISHNAN RAJAGOPAL, FROM RESISTANCE TO RENEWAL: THE THIRD WORLD, SOCIAL MOVEMENTS, AND THE EXPANSION OF INTERNATIONAL INSTITUTIONS

41 HARV. INT'L L.J. 529, 531–50 (2000)

In some ways, international institutions and the Third World are like Siamese twins: One can not even imagine them as separate from one another because development, human rights, environmental, and other institutions operate mostly in the Third World.

As the Third World decolonized and entered international society in the middle of the century, international institutions were truly becoming consolidated in a wave of pragmatism. Despite this temporal coincidence, leading accounts of international institutions say nothing about the influence that the Third World may have had on their evolution or vice versa. In this view, institutions evolve due to their own functionalist logic, while grand politics of decolonization and development take place elsewhere. Indeed, to the extent that the Third World is discussed as an entity in relation to institutions, it is criticized for politicizing them and preventing their effective operation. The failure of Third World resistance to achieve its objectives—such as the New International Economic Order (NIEO) proposals of the 1970s at the United Nations— is explained away by the unrealistic radicalism of its proposals.***

It is my argument that the expansion and renewal of international institutions cannot be understood in isolation from Third World resistance. Indeed, I claim that social movements from the Third World such as peasant rebellions, environmental movements, and human rights movements, have propelled the expansion of international institutions since the late 1960s.***

*** [The] Third World that international institutions deal with now is no longer the Third World of the post-independence period. Indeed, the very meaning of "the Third World" has undergone a radical change since the 1950s and 1960s, when it meant only an agglomeration of newly independent states. Now, it means a collection of peasant, environmental, and feminist movements, and a host of others who are in global and regional alliances with states, individuals, international institutions, and private groups. It is this Third World from which international institutions such as the BWIs [Bretton Woods Institutions] are now facing opposition and resistance. As the recent collapse of the WTO talks in Seattle shows, international institutions are now openly confronted with mass resistance. But of equal importance was the invocation of the "Third World masses" as the key driving force behind the expansion of the BWIs, even during the apogee of Third World radicalism at the United Nations in the 1960s and 1970s.***

*** I propose that the architecture of modern international law has been ineluctably shaped by popular, grassroots resistance from the Third World. This contrasts with traditional accounts of the birth of international institutions that emphasize the role of leading individuals, or states, or simply functional needs that propelled institutional behavior.***

II. WRITING RESISTANCE: BRETTON WOODS INSTITUTIONS AND THE EVOLUTION OF THEIR "NEW" DEVELOPMENT AGENDA ***

A. *Introduction: Beyond Benevolent Liberalism and Denunciatory Radicalism*

There have been basically two kinds of critiques of the BWIs. The first of these, which may be termed "liberal," essentially admits the beneficent character of development and the role of these institutions in the development process, which is defined as the collective effort to eradicate poverty and raise standards of living. The writers adopting this position may concede that sometimes these institutions do not achieve their objectives, but that is all the more reason to reform and improve them.***

A second line of critique of the BWIs draws from radical neo-Marxist and dependency theories. According to this critique, capitalism is a reactionary force in the Third

World and therefore the cause of poverty, not a cure for it. Given this premise, these critics view the BWIs as mechanisms that enable exploitation of the periphery by the core, and BWI development intervention as the result of the logic of capital.

While both of these critiques have served important purposes, they nevertheless appear to lack explanatory power. The liberal critique is politically naive since it assumes that BWI development intervention occurs in a class-neutral manner—in other words, during intervention, class relations are simply reproduced and not made worse. However, this does not explain either the popular resistance (if such intervention is so beneficent, why does it encounter such opposition) or the consistent failure to achieve its goals (such as the reduction of poverty). On the other hand, the dependency critique assumes too much: that every intervention by the BWIs is a core-periphery relation that mechanically reproduces unjust capitalistic relations between the West and the Third World. This overkill leads dependency critiques to policy paralysis as well as to a homogenizing tendency that ignores the actual process of resistance to development by different actors such as women or indigenous people (since the class character of the struggle has been assumed already) and the resultant heterogeneity of voices. Neither approach seems satisfactory ***.***

B. Cold War and the "Other" Third World Resistance

I begin with the role the BWIs played in furthering the Cold War objective of containing Third World mass radicalism since that role is essential for understanding the later emergence of poverty alleviation programs. It is often forgotten that during the few years after the establishment of the BWIs, their lending focus was substantially on developed countries such as Japan and Australia. Thus, from January 1949 to the approval of the first credit of the International Development Association (IDA) in April 1961, the World Bank lent these countries $1.7 billion, or one-third of a total $5.1 billion. Australia ($317 million by June 1961), Japan ($447 million), Norway ($120 million), Austria ($101 million), Finland ($102 million), France ($168 million), and Italy ($229 million) all received World Bank funding for reconstruction and development. This situation continued until the establishment of the IDA in 1961, even though several large loans had been made to India and Latin America. At the end of this key period from 1947 to 1961, which also witnessed the height of the Cold War, it was becoming obvious to the West that it was "losing the poor," and that explicit programs had to be invented that would contain the rebellion from the bottom. This Cold War imperative had a major impact on the evolution of the BWIs, for now there was a security rationale to their developmental work. In particular, the World Bank moved from its reconstruction phase to its development phase as the Cold War intensified.***

This technique of combining security and development was not entirely new; colonial regimes had perfected it in their handling of anti-colonial nationalist movements by designing welfare schemes for the protesting natives. The "dual mandate," articulated by colonial administrators like Sir Frederic Lugard was based on the idea that the native had to be cared for, not simply exploited.*** In this view, caring for the welfare of the natives was a crucial aspect of colonial dominance. Welfare spending was becoming necessary to achieve the dual purposes of sustaining production by fully constituting the *homo oeconomicus* in the Third World, and containing dissatisfaction and rebellion from the masses.

The Cold War reinforced this historically crucial link between security and development, and had a major impact on the evolution and expansion of the BWIs, especially the World Bank. Looked at this way, these international institutions are neither simply benevolent vehicles for development, nor ineluctably exploitative mechanisms of global capitalism; but rather, a terrain on which multiple ideological and other forces intersected, thus producing the expansion and reproduction of these very institutions.***

In the practice of the World Bank, the security dimension of development began to have a major impact. Thus, Nicaragua, a nation of one million inhabitants, received ten World Bank loans between 1951 and 1960 because of the close connection between the U.S. military and covert operations in the region, and the ruling Somoza family. By contrast, Guatemala, with three times the population, did not receive a loan until the overthrow of its supposedly communist regime in 1955. This coincided with the then U.S. preference for hard regimes over liberal ones. As George Kennan said in 1950, "[i]t is better to have a strong regime in power than a liberal government if it is indulgent and relaxed and penetrated by Communists."

In addition to being used to fund anticommunist actions in the Third World, the Bank was also deeply affected in its internal workings by the political strategies that were adopted by the United States to fight the Cold War. This is evident on at least two important fronts. First, under political influence, the lending portfolio of the Bank began to shift from a legalistic, cautious, and Wall Street oriented approach to project lending, to a more political and ad hoc approach to program lending.***

The second level at which the Bank was internally affected by the political necessities of the Cold War was in its sectoral allocation. Eighty-three percent of the lending until 1961 for developing countries was for power and transportation projects. Agriculture and social sector activities, such as health and education, were neglected. This lending portfolio was based on a biased understanding of development as capital accumulation and physical modernization, as opposed to human development. This not only reflected the dominant thinking toward development at that time, which emphasized investment in infrastructure rather than human beings, but it also followed from the Bank's status as a conservative institution, dependent upon Wall Street for its financing, which placed it in a much harder position to justify unproductive or fuzzy investments like education or even urban water supply. Agriculture fared worse: Only three percent of all development lending to developing countries through 1961 was for agriculture. This was mainly due to the Bank's wish to remain attractive to Wall Street financing. In the end, with the establishment of the IDA and the expansion into poverty alleviation, the Bank's sectoral allocation expanded dramatically to embrace health, education, rural development, and agriculture. While this changed focus has not actually reduced poverty, improved health, or made agriculture more efficient as much as had been intended, the instrumental effects of the change have involved a dramatic expansion of the BWIs into every conceivable sphere of human activity in the Third World.***

C. The "Discovery" of Poverty and the Establishment of the IDA: Rejuvenating the BWIs

[T]he Articles of Agreement of the BWIs do not refer to poverty or justice explicitly. Yet, in 1991, the World Bank declared in an Operational Directive that "sustainable poverty reduction is the Bank's overarching objective." This new faith was not the result of a smooth evolution toward rational objectives that resulted from a learning process, though the Bank itself has recently portrayed it as such.***

*** In contrast *** the Bank's mandate was an explicitly political one that was gradually crafted in complex struggles: between the two Cold War power blocs, between the Third World and the West, between leftist and reactionary politics, between peasant rebellions and authoritarian governments, between mass movements and elite manipulation, between colonial and anti-colonial forces, and between multiple conceptions of development. Still, it is important to focus on the process by which poverty came to constitute the governing logic or the episteme of development: the BWIs. This is because it is in the course of "discovering" poverty that the BWIs, particularly the Bank, discovered themselves as international institutions. In other words, if the Cold War provided a security dimension to the constitution of the BWIs as development institutions, the objective of poverty reduction provided the moral, the humanitarian dimension.

1. "Discovering" Poverty: Engaging the "Poor, Dark, and Hungry Masses"

In order to grasp the process that led to the crowning of the BWIs as poverty-reducers, one must analyze the establishment of the IDA in 1961, for it was the first major international institutional milestone in the turn to poverty as an international objective, and to the "poor, dark, and hungry masses" of the Third World as the target group of international interventions. There were several factors which were responsible for this turn. First, there was a realization that in the Cold War-driven competition for allegiance of regimes, it was essential to promote intra-country redistribution to pacify the masses that were becoming restive due to rising anti-colonialism and nationalism. Indeed, it was a commonplace in development thinking in the late 1950s and early 1960s that poor countries would succumb to Communism if they were not rescued from poverty. Aid began to be seen as a way of rescue. The importance of redistribution as a policy goal of foreign assistance in order to pacify the masses was clearly spelled out, for example, by Undersecretary of State Douglas Dillon while speaking to the U.S. Senate Foreign Relations Committee in the aftermath of Fidel Castro's victory: "While there has been a steady rise in national incomes throughout [Latin America], millions of underprivileged have not benefited."

Second, there was also an awareness that traditional foreign lending was too focused on accumulation of capital (mainly through infrastructure and power projects) and too little on so-called social lending. This was true not only due to the fact that Wall Street financiers considered social lending unproductive and fuzzy, but also because social lending seemed too political and therefore violative of the principle of nonintervention in international law and relations. The BWIs provided a way around this impasse.***

Third—and connected to the first two—the World Bank itself was clearly realizing the politically quiescent effect that its loans were having on Third World peoples. Though this could not be articulated as an economic rationale to justify social lending, the Bank was nevertheless widely aware of and influenced by this in lending to Third World countries.***

Fourth, the discovery of so-called underdevelopment as a domain of intervention in the 1950s had put poverty squarely on the international agenda. Before World War II, the poverty of the natives was taken as natural because they were seen to lack the capacity for science and technology and the will to economic progress.*** In this new conception, the poor were seen to lack in particular social domains, which called for technical interventions in education, health, hygiene, morality, savings, and so on.***

[A] very important factor responsible for the evolution of the poverty discourse, with its focus upon Third World peoples, was the inter-war experience of colonialism and the mandate system of the League of Nations, both of which attempted to construct a new, so-called humanitarian approach to the rule of natives, moving away (rhetorically at least) from exploitative colonialism. This experience provided institutional continuity to the "rule of the natives" after World War II when many colonial administrators joined the World Bank.

However, the internationalization of the social domain did not occur in a true sense until after World War II, following the establishment of the BWIs. The World Bank, for example, invented "per capita income" as a tool to compare countries in 1948. As a result, they magically converted almost two-thirds of the world's population into the "poor" because their annual per capita income was less than $100. Along with the invention of the notion of Third World as a terrain of intervention in the 1950s, the discovery of poverty emerged as a working principle of the process whereby the domain of interaction between the West and the non-West was defined.***

As a result, it must be recognized that contrary to popular viewpoints, the BWIs were neither benevolent do-gooders nor mechanistic tools in the hands of global capital opposed to social justice and equity. Rather, they constituted a complex space in which power, justice, security, and humanitarianism functioned in contradictory and complementary ways. Indeed, these phenomena could not exist without each other.***

Notes and Questions

1.   Rajagopal refers to the dual mandate of colonialism—to exploit the natives and, simultaneously, to care for them. Consider the ways in which the "natives" and other marginalized or oppressed groups might be maintained by rich nations at a level of bare survival. Does such a model help perpetuate the status quo among rich and poor nations? Would a successful, thriving Third World threaten the standard of living in the First World? If so, why? What concessions would the First World need to make in order to abandon the exploit/care model of colonialism?

2.   What is problematic about the selective lending practices described by Rajagopal? What roles might the IMF and World Bank lending policies play in the larger picture of decisionmaking about bilateral aid or even military interventions?

ANTONY ANGHIE, TIME PRESENT AND TIME PAST: GLOBALIZATION, INTERNATIONAL FINANCIAL INSTITUTIONS, AND THE THIRD WORLD

32 N.Y.U. J. INT'L L. & POL. 243, 249–258 (2000)

Globalization, Human Rights, and the Third World State ***

[T]he human rights community appears in many respects ambivalent about globalization, seeing it as a means by which human rights can be both furthered and undermined. Thus, while institutions and actors furthering globalization are single-minded in their task, important international bodies whose function it is to protect human rights and social welfare appear hesitant, more intent on placating rather than challenging globalization. Thus the Copenhagen Declaration on Social Development, while expressing a number of reservations about the effects of globalization, also reiterates that globalization "opens new opportunities for sustained economic growth and development of the world economy, particularly in developing countries." From this perspective, globalization, whatever negative effects it may have, is nevertheless essential for development. The task then is to "manage the process [of globalization] and threats so as to enhance their benefits and mitigate their negative effects." What is required is the formation of an alliance between globalization and its focus on economic growth and progress on the one hand, and human rights and its concern to protect human dignity on the other. Implicitly, this model of alliance suggests that human rights should attempt to adjust the outcomes of globalization rather than determine the manner in which globalization occurs in the first place. There is a danger that, under globalization, the promotion of the market becomes an end in itself rather than a means of promoting human welfare and social goals.

Proponents of globalization, by contrast, forcefully argue that it is through globalization that the principal goals of human rights may be realized. Thus, scholars argue that the best way of protecting human rights is through the actions of multinational corporations and that the intensification of multinational activity corresponds with an enhancement in the protection of human rights. Indeed, it is further argued that there is a "right to globalization."

From a third world perspective, perhaps the most elaborate and important arguments as to how globalization promotes human rights are being formulated by institutions such as the [World] Bank. The Bank plays an extremely vital role in fostering globalization in third world countries and, additionally, is developing an elaborate and comprehensive set of arguments as to how its policies further the cause of human rights.***

The Bank's central purpose is the promotion of international development. In recent times, the Bank has made notable attempts to focus on the social dimensions of development rather than on economic growth alone. Nevertheless, the Bank remains fundamentally committed to neo-liberal economic policies of privatization and liberalization as a means of achieving development. And it is by furthering this problematic model of development that the Bank claims it is advancing the cause of human rights: "The world now accepts that sustainable development is impossible without human rights. What has been missing is the recognition that the advancement of an interconnected set of human rights is impossible without development."

Basically, it seems, human rights law is not an independent category of norms and principles that govern the way in which development should take place. Rather, human rights is assimilated into development, achieved through development. The same primacy of development is evident in the Bank's articulation of the doctrine of "good governance," which it uses as justification for seeking to shape the political and legal institutions of a country, arguing that proper implementation of Bank-formulated development programs can only be achieved by accountable, transparent, and democratic government. Thus the Bank's promotion of good governance complements the efforts of human rights law to make government accountable. As [James] Gathii points out, however, this association between good governance and human rights could serve another purpose: "This association has given a measure of credibility to the neo-liberal macro-economic programs of the Bretton Woods institutions and their powerful western industrial members."

The basic problem here is that the neo-liberal development programs formulated by the Bank and the IFIs seem notorious for augmenting inequality and impoverishment among the most vulnerable groups in the third world countries in which these programs are implemented. The Bank elaborates its claim that it furthers human rights, not only by promoting development, but also, more specifically, by providing loans for health and education. While these loans may achieve some worthwhile purposes, they are often one element of a much more far-reaching process of privatizing health and education systems. These loans are often part of an "adjustment lending process" and are supposed to ameliorate some of the consequences of the fundamental changes that the Bank requires countries to undertake. Many scholars have argued persuasively that Bank/IMF formulated structural adjustment programs have led to a severe deterioration in living standards in countries that adopted such programs. Indeed, human rights scholars have documented in considerable detail the extent to which these programs have effectively violated economic and social rights. The assumption, then, that the economic development and structural adjustment programs fostered by the IFIs with the aim of improving living standards will in themselves better human welfare, and hence human rights, is highly questionable.

Equally significant, the marketized version of human rights appears to appropriate and reverse traditional understandings of important human rights doctrines and the uses for which they were formulated. This is evident, for example, in the Bank's claim to further the "Right to Development." There is a special poignancy in the invocation by the Bank of the "Right to Development," which was proposed by third world countries as an element of the campaign to establish a New International Economic Order that would attempt to bring about fundamental changes to the international economy and that would enhance the economic sovereignty of developing country states.[1] None of those aspirations has been realized in any significant way, and it is somewhat ironic that the Bank, which has adopted a very different idea of the international economic order, should be invoking precisely this right. Also, economic and social rights were created as a means of achieving important social goals and balancing civil and political rights which appeared less sensitive to questions of equity and social welfare. Within the new human rights discourse proposed by the Bank, however, the tensions between civil and political rights on the one hand, and economic and social rights on the other, appear to have been resolved. The market provides the answer, for the market calls into being the "good government," one which protects civil and political rights and provides the economic growth that is essential to securing economic and social goods. Whereas previously, economic and social rights were criticized because these rights apparently required an interventionary state, the economic and social rights articulated by the Bank seem to be achieved by the minimization of the state and the expansion of the market. The market becomes the ultimate good.

Complex and troubling issues arise as to whether the fundamental goals of human rights law are being furthered or distorted by the Bank's activities. More broadly, the principal danger is that important economic actors who are primarily concerned with profit and promotion of a problematic form of economic development are increasingly appropriating and distorting the language of rights to justify and legitimize their own actions. These actions often produce results completely contrary to the human rights goals of preserving and protecting human dignity. Consequently, any alliance between

---

[1] *See* Section A.2 *infra.*

human rights and globalization could result in the assimilation of human rights and its ideals by the formidable forces of globalization.***

The Third World State and the Contradictions of Globalization

A second major issue confronting third world countries lies in the contradictory demands that globalization appears to make of these countries. This contradiction is exacerbated by the role that the IFIs play in actively furthering globalization by profoundly influencing the economic and political policies of third world countries.

Even scholars who assert that globalization is largely beneficial argue that globalization causes extensive social dislocation that needs to be remedied by increased state-sponsored social welfare programs. Dani Rodrik, for example, in analyzing the relationship between freer trade policies and government activity, points out that: "Indeed, a key component of the implicit postwar social bargain in the advanced industrial countries has been the provision of social insurance and safety nets at home (unemployment compensation, severance payments, and adjustment assistance, for example) in exchange for the adoption of freer trade policies."

Basically, then, "the social welfare state has been the flip side of the open economy." There are grave concerns as to whether the states of advanced, industrialized countries can adequately meet this challenge in a situation where globalization has limited the policy options available to states intent on maintaining "global competitiveness." Far less politically established, far less wealthy post-colonial states confront a much more extreme version of this same problem which, compounded by their desperate need to attract foreign capital, often compels them to make significant financial concessions. Unlike the advanced industrialized countries, many developing countries are subject not only to the competition generated by the forces of economic globalization in general, but also to IMF/Bank structural adjustment programs that explicitly require them to adopt privatization and liberalization programs that further increase the powers of capital and that also reduce social spending.

The pressures of globalization require the post-colonial state to respond to a number of complex and contradictory demands. On the one hand, it is urged if not compelled by IFIs to create the conditions that enable globalization to further itself: by commercial law reforms, by creating favorable investment climates, by privatizing, and so forth. Most recently, developing countries are being pressured to allow complete currency convertibility in order to enable portfolio capital to move in and out of countries with little restriction. The effect of all these initiatives is to enhance the power of international capital by facilitating the mobility of capital and expanding the protection granted to multinational enterprises and their activities, even while diminishing the regulations to which capital is subjected in an attempt to attract much needed investment in an extraordinarily competitive global economy. In all these different ways, the post-colonial state is required, first, to intensify and accelerate globalization by creating the conditions in which the market can operate, and second, to minimize and transfer its own powers.

At the same time, it is the same post-colonial state that, using Rodrik's analysis, is expected to play the vital role of minimizing the social impact of globalization by providing the social programs necessary to prevent immense human suffering. On the one hand, the Bank furthers the process of globalization that undermines the third world state; on the other, the Bank simultaneously allocates to the state the responsibility of securing the basics of social welfare for its people and, hence, of addressing and in some measure resolving the problem of globalization. Apart from this tension, the argument that developing country states should do more to provide education and health to their people should be seen in the context of the realities that these countries confront:

Today in Ethiopia a hundred thousand children die annually from easily preventable diseases while debt repayments are four times more than public spending on health care. In Tanzania, where 40 percent of people die before the age of 35, debt payments are six times greater than spending on health care. In Africa, where one in every two children of primary-school age is not in school, governments transfer four times more to northern creditors in debt payments than they spend on the health and education of their citizens.

The further irony is that the debt crises afflicting many third world countries and profoundly undermining their development prospects has been exacerbated by the actions of the same IFIs that now call upon the state to remedy an intensifying number of social problems. Debt repayment was a priority for the IFIs to the extent that "[f]lows of finance from the IFIs, which were given on condition that countries respected their debt obligations, tightened the debt straitjacket and delayed serious consideration of debt write-off." Furthermore, it is precisely IFI-formulated structural adjustment programs implemented in many developing countries that significantly reduce social spending and that have terminated or minimized social programs, generally regarded as inefficient by the IFIs, already in place in many developing countries.

Post-colonial states, lacking resources and abdicating the few powers they have to capital, are incapable of addressing these contradictions. As a consequence, it is extremely likely that, in the vast majority of developing countries, poverty will increase, social and political tensions will be exacerbated, and ethnic and class conflicts—already a significant presence in many developing countries—will intensify. The violence that results, in all likelihood, will be seen as originating in purely endogenous factors, in the pathology of post-colonial societies unable to govern themselves.***

Notes and Questions

1. *Ethnic Violence and Globalization.* What influence might global economic trends have had on the outbreak of violent ethnic conflicts in Eastern Europe, Africa and Asia following the end of the Cold War? *See, e.g.,* AMY CHUA, WORLD ON FIRE: HOW EXPORTING FREE MARKET DEMOCRACY BREEDS ETHNIC HATRED AND GLOBAL INSTABILITY (2003) for a discussion of the catastrophic effects of globalization, free markets, and democracy on racial, ethnic and class disparity around the globe.

2. *The Third World Debt Crisis.* The international debt crisis is intimately related to the realization of human rights in developing countries. The U.N. Commission on Human Rights has articulated this relationship by noting that "despite repeated rescheduling of debt, developing countries continue to pay out more each year than the actual amount they receive in official development assistance." *See* United Nations High Commissioner For Human Rights, *Effects of Structural Adjustment Policies and Foreign Debt on the Full Enjoyment of all Human Rights, Particularly Economic, Social and Cultural,* Commission on Human Rights resolution 2000/82 (2000), *available at* http://www.unhchr.ch/Huridocda/Huridoca.nsf/0/358cd202aca1229c802568d6004432bf?Opendocument (last visited on June 11, 2004). Thus, servicing international debt prevents some governments in the Global South from fulfilling basic needs, including providing basic health care, education, nutrition, clean water, adequate shelter and other human rights.

For example, Tanzania spent $189.2 million on debt service payments in 1997, while it spent only $163.4 million on education and $65.8 million on health care. In 1998, Zambia spent over 69 percent more on debt service than it spent on health and education combined. *See* Eric A. Friedman, *Debt Relief in 1999: Only One Step on a Long Journey*, 3 YALE HUM. RTS. & DEV. L.J. 191 (2000). For a discussion of the specific effects of Third World debt and structural adjustment policies on women and children, *see* "Feminist Critiques of Development" Section B.1, *infra*.

3.   *Why Borrow?* All countries borrow in order to provide for domestic and international purposes. However, governments of developing countries sometimes amass unserviceable debt loads in response to a variety of internal or external pressures and needs. For example, public officials may hope to make large investments in infrastructure or modernization; they may try to address the effects of historical economic exploitation and underdevelopment; or they may hope to use the funds for military or political purposes. Often, large loans are taken out in response to spikes in oil prices or other necessary import commodities, or in response to fluctuating export commodity prices. Governments may approach a variety of lending sources, including private commercial banks and investment funds, but private capital is often unavailable for infrastructural needs. When technically available, the loans are often linked to the lending criteria and structural adjustment policies established by the international financial institutions (IFIs) such as the World Bank, the IMF, and regional development banks. A country's ability to tap into private lending sources, therefore, likely depends on its ability to meet the conditions established by the IFIs as well as by the private lenders.

World Bank officials maintain that the loans they provide will stimulate economic growth so beneficial that borrowers will be able to repay the loans and use the excess for domestic social programs and investment. *See e.g.*, News Release No:99/2278/LAC, World Bank Approves US$300 Million for Financial Sector Reform in Peru (June 23, 1999), *available at* web.worldbank.org/WBSITE/EXTERNAL/NEWS/0,,contentMDK: 20015618~menuPK:34466~pagePK:64003015~piPK:64003012~. But the reality has been much bleaker: many Bank projects have failed, and borrowers can only make payments by more borrowing. Critics of World Bank lending policies note that, with the economies of many poor countries in shambles, the only lender willing to risk supplying new loans is the Bank itself. The more "aid" countries take on, the more they need. *See, e.g.*, MICHEL CHOSSUDOVSKY, THE GLOBALISATION OF POVERTY: IMPACTS OF IMF AND WORLD BANK REFORMS 21 (1997).

The consequences of such a perennial cycle of lending and debt are enormous. According to Chossudovsky, "[t]he total outstanding long-term debt of developing countries (from official and private sources) stood at approximately US$62 billion in 1970. It increased sevenfold in the course of the 1970s to reach $481 billion in 1980." *Id.* at 45. By 1996, poor countries owed in excess of $2 trillion. *Id.* "By the mid-1980s, developing countries had become net exporters of capital in favour of the rich countries." *Id.* at 51. Many such governments believed that they had no choice but to accede to the "structural adjustment" demands of the Bank and the IMF. As discussed throughout this chapter, such policies often have a devastating effect on the human rights of people in the borrowing countries. Labor standards are suppressed to attract foreign investment. Natural resources are extracted and sold to further "development." National budget priorities are shifted from meeting the needs of people, such as food, education, health care, and housing, to meeting the needs of financial institutions. The foreign exchange needed to repay loans is obtained by using land previously devoted to domestic food production for cultivation of exotic export crops instead.

Are these approaches the best way to ensure economic growth in developing countries? Is growth a reliable indicator of progress? Traditional growth indicators such as the gross national product do not take into account the economic and human costs of development policies, such as environmental damage, physical and mental health consequences, etc. Is replication of rich-nation lifestyles a realistic or desirable goal for the developing world? Who should bear the financial cost of making development in poor countries ecologically feasible?

4. *Responses to the Debt: Resistance or Relief?* By 1996, the World Bank and the IMF had responded to criticisms about the devastating human and economic impact of massive Third World debt by adopting the Heavily Indebted Poor Countries (HIPC) Initiative. *See* International Bank for Reconstruction and Development (World Bank), *Debt Initiative for Heavily Indebted Poor Countries, available at* www.worldbank.org/hipc (last visited June 11, 2004) *and* International Monetary Fund, *Debt Relief under the Heavily Indebted Poor Counties (HIPC) Initiative, available at* http://www.imf.org/external/np/exr/facts/hipc. htm (last visited June 11, 2004). While the stated principle objective of the HIPC Initiative was to bring the debt of the most heavily indebted poor nations to a sustainable level, there were serious criticisms of the program. Critics argued that (1) few countries were able to qualify for the HIPC initiative;(2) debt relief for qualifying countries is made contingent on IMF and World Bank structural adjustment criteria which almost always mandate reduction in spending intended to fulfill basic economic and social human rights; and (3) debt relief may reduce overall debt but does not reduce debt servicing sufficiently to allow for significant increases in human rights-related spending. *See e.g.*, Eric A. Friedman, *Debt Relief in 1999: Only One Step on a Long Journey,* 3 YALE HUM. RTS. & DEV. L.J. 191 (2000). Jubilee 2000, an international religious and political advocacy organization, has drawn considerable attention to the issue of debt relief and human rights through its "Drop the Debt" campaign. *See* http://www.jubileeusa. org (U.S. Web site). What are the historical, moral, and legal underpinnings of the worldwide call for the cancellation of the international debt of poor countries? Do developed nations have an obligation to aid the developing world? If so, is this a positive or negative duty, or both?

Increasingly, the pressure exerted by the IFIs is met with resistance by the poor and working-class people hardest hit by the policy changes related to overwhelming foreign debt loads. Countries in Latin America and Southeast Asia, for example, have experienced "IMF riots," involving sometimes peaceful, sometimes violent revolts against governments that accede to IFI demands. *See e.g.*, World Development Movement, Press Release, *Anti-IMF Riots Sweep Developing World: IMF Policies are Linked to Widespread Protests in Poor Countries* (Sept. 25, 2000), *available at* http://www.wdm.org.uk/presrel/current/anti_IMF.htm (last visited July 31, 2004). Grassroots groups throughout the Third World are challenging the assertion that Washington Consensus reforms are the only solution to the problems facing poor people. Indeed, since 2001, hundreds of thousands of activists have gathered for the annual World Social Forum, a conference and network of social justice groups, challenging globalization and war under the banner of "Another World Is Possible." For information on a documentary on the 2004 World Social Forum in Mumbai, India, *see* www.pinholepictures.com/rumblemovie.

For further reading on the debt crisis, *see e.g,*. David Korten, When Corporations Rule the World 133–81 (1995); Bruce Rich, *The Cuckoo in the Nest: Fifty Years of Political Meddling by the World Bank*, 24(1) ECOLOGIST (Jan./Feb. 1994); Jonathan Cahn, *Challenging the New Imperial Authority: The World Bank and the Democratization of Development*, 6 HARV. HUM. RTS J. 160 (1993).

CHRISTIAN BARRY, DEALING JUSTLY WITH DEBT

INPRINT, Carnegie Council of Ethics and International Affairs Newsletter Jan./Feb. 2003, *available at* http://www.cceia.org/viewMedia.php/prmID/825

On October 27, 2002, former factory worker Luis Inácio Lula da Silva (popularly known as "Lula") achieved a landslide victory in the Brazilian presidential election. His platform included pledges to lower Brazil's domestic interest rates, *** revive national industry, invest in public infrastructure, and establish a "zero-hunger" program that will include food stamps for the poor.

It is far from clear, however, that Brazilian voters can get the progressive policies that they asked for. This is due in large part to the country's looming debt crisis. During the past eight years of the administration of Lula's predecessor, Fernando Henrique Cardoso, Brazil's public debt has grown from 29% of the gross domestic product to more than 62%, and in October of 2002, the Brazilian government accepted a $30 billion dollar loan package from the International Monetary Fund (IMF). The loan was conditioned on the Brazilian government maintaining policies such as high interest rates, a strict schedule of debt repayments, and large budget surpluses, all of which make increased investment in infrastructure and basic social services difficult at best.

Brazil strikingly illustrates how debt can lead to increased dependence of developing countries on foreign creditors and international institutions, limiting the capabilities of local citizens to exercise meaningful control over their policies and institutions. Indeed, just as democracy has become widely accepted as the most legitimate form of political decision-making, participation in national politics has become a woefully inadequate means of securing people's rights to take part in decisions that affect them. It is tempting, perhaps, to think of debt crises as the fault of the debtor countries, and to argue that these countries should bear their own costs. But in the case of Brazil, this is implausible. Indeed, the IMF and the Bush administration justified the loan package by citing Brazil's "sound" and "courageous" policies.

And even when debt crises arise as the result of unsound policies, the blame for these policies does not belong solely with the debtor countries. As in Brazil, so in Argentina: the latter's economic policies during the 1990s were broadly endorsed by international financial institutions, the financial community, and most leading economists, all of whom must therefore bear some responsibility for the country's financial collapse this past year. Yet while outsiders have often shaped the policies of debtor countries, they refuse to share the risks, with creditors insisting on full repayment, and governments and financial institutions demanding an end to "bailouts."

How can we deal justly with debt? We might begin by looking more closely at the United States, where municipalities with debt problems have access to a neutral court of arbitration, and where creditors are prevented from demanding that municipalities sacrifice basic services even when this is necessary to meet their financial obligations. Developing analogous international institutions, such as the establishment of an independent debt arbitration panel, would help countries to escape and avoid financial crises. More importantly, it would help to protect the political rights that citizens of developing nations have fought so hard to achieve.

Note

Joseph Stiglitz, a member of the U.S. Council of Economic Advisers under the Clinton Administration, and Senior Vice-President and Chief Economist of the World Bank from 1997–2000, was awarded the Nobel Prize in Economics in 2001. His departure from the World Bank prior to receiving the award, however, was highly controversial. While at the Bank, Stiglitz became an outspoken critic of its policies and of some aspects of neo-liberalism in general. His criticism of the Bank and the IMF was sufficiently sharp to earn the disfavor of U.S. Treasury Secretary Lawrence Summers, who is rumored to have demanded that the Bank remove him from its staff. *See, e.g.*, Timothy A. Canova, *Global Finance and the International Monetary Fund's Neoliberal Agenda: The Threat to the Employment, Ethnic Identity, and Cultural Pluralism of Latina/o Communities*, 33 U. DAVIS L. REV. 1547, 1574, n.123 (2000). The Bank's president, James Wolfensohn, also began to criticize Stiglitz publicly. *Id.* Stiglitz was pressured either to cease his own public criticism of the IMF and the Bank or to resign. *Id.* at 1573; *see also* Louis Uchitelle, *World Bank Economist Felt He Had to Silence His Criticism or Quit*, N.Y. TIMES, Dec. 2, 1999, at C1. Stiglitz chose to resign.

Joseph Stiglitz has continued to be critical of World Bank and IMF policies in a series of speeches, articles and books. At the core of Stiglitz's criticism is the lack of democratic accountability of the international financial institutions (IFIs). The almost complete secrecy in which they operate primarily serves the interests of rich nations, while still allowing their officials to claim publicly that they seek to aid the poor. Stiglitz argues that the Washington Consensus prescriptions of structural adjustment and privatization have been disastrous for poor countries. He has even recommended that poor nations should place the annual prescriptions from the IMF "straight in the garbage can." *See, e.g.*, Eyal Press, *Rebel With a Cause*, THE NATION, May 23, 2002, *available at* http://www.thenation.com/doc.mhtml?i=20020610&s=press (last visited July 30, 2004).

The problem, according to Stiglitz, is not with markets per se, but with the recklessness with which they have been managed by the IFIs. He has said that globalization is "the best chance to lift the poor out of poverty they have lived in for centuries," if actually pursued with their interests in mind. Dave Hage, *Joseph Stiglitz—A Dangerous Man; A World Bank Insider Who Defected*, COMMON DREAMS NEWSLETTER, Oct. 11, 2000, *available at* http://www.commondreams.org/views/101100-101.htm (last visited July 30, 2004) (quoting a Stiglitz speech). Rather than advocating the closure of multinational corporate enterprises in developing countries, Stiglitz urges that such corporations should recognize that the benefits of building factories with safe working conditions and of providing regular work breaks outweigh the costs. Other recommendations include the elimination of all tariffs in developed Northern countries on goods from the developing world; debt-relief for poor countries so that they can use scarce funds for pressing domestic needs like health care; and improving the accountability of the IMF and World Bank by increasing the number of representatives from developing nations on their boards.

The excerpt below is from Stiglitz' recent book on the international economy:

JOSEPH E. STIGLITZ, GLOBALIZATION AND ITS DISCONTENTS 53–60 (2003)

Fiscal austerity, privatization, and market liberalization were the three pillars of Washington Consensus advice throughout the 1980s and 1990s. The Washington Consensus policies were designed to respond to the very real problems in Latin America, and made considerable sense. In the 1980s, the governments of those countries had often run huge deficits. Losses in inefficient government enterprises contributed to those deficits. Insulated from competition by protectionist measures, inefficient private firms forced customers to pay high prices. Loose monetary policy led to inflation running out of control. Countries cannot persistently run large deficits; and sustained growth is not possible with hyperinflation. Some level of fiscal discipline is required. Most countries would be better off with governments focusing on providing essential public services rather than running enterprises that would arguably perform better in the private sector, and so privatization often makes sense. When trade liberalization—the lowering of tariffs and elimination of other protectionist measures—is done in the right way and at the right pace, so that new jobs are created as inefficient jobs are destroyed, there can be significant efficiency gains.

The problem was that many of these policies became ends in themselves, rather than means to more equitable and sustainable growth. In doing so, these policies were pushed too far, too fast, and to the exclusion of other policies that were needed.***

*Privatization ***

Unfortunately, the IMF and the World Bank have approached the issues from a narrow ideological perspective—privatization was to be pursued rapidly. Scorecards were kept for the countries making the transition from communism to the market: those who privatized faster were given the high marks. As a result, privatization often did not bring the benefits that were promised. The problems that arose from these failures have created antipathy to the very idea of privatization.

In 1998 I visited some poor villages in Morocco to see the impact that projects undertaken by the World Bank and nongovernmental organizations (NGOs) were having on the lives of the people there. I saw, for instance, how community-based irrigation projects were increasing farm productivity enormously. One project, however, had failed. An NGO had painstakingly instructed local villagers on raising chickens, an enterprise that the village women could perform as they continued more traditional activities. Originally, the women obtained their seven-day-old chicks from a government enterprise. But when I visited the village, this new enterprise had collapsed. I discussed with villagers and government officials what had gone wrong. The answer was simple: The government had been told by the IMF that it should not be in the business of distributing chicks, so it ceased selling them. It was simply assumed that the private sector would immediately fill the gap. Indeed, a new private supplier arrived to provide the villagers with newborn chicks. The death rate of chicks in the first two weeks is high, however, and the private firm was unwilling to provide a guarantee. The villagers simply could not bear the risk of buying chicks that might die in large numbers. Thus, a nascent industry, poised to make a difference in the lives of these poor peasants, was shut down.

The assumption underlying this failure is one that I saw made repeatedly; the IMF simply assumed that markets arise quickly to meet every need, when in fact, many government activities arise because markets have failed to provide essential services. Examples abound. Outside the United States, this point often seems obvious. When many European countries created the social security systems and unemployment and disability insurance systems, there were no well-functioning private annuity markets, no private firms that would sell insurance against these risks that played such an important role in individuals' lives. Even when the United States created its social security system, much later, in the depths of the Great Depression as part of the New Deal, private markets for annuities did not work well and even today one cannot get annuities that insure one against inflation.*** In developing countries, these problems are even worse; eliminating the government enterprise may leave a huge gap and even if eventually the private sector enters, there can be enormous suffering in the meanwhile.***

Privatization has also come not just at the expense of consumers but at the expense of workers as well. The impact on employment has perhaps been both the major argument for and against privatization, with advocates arguing that only through privatization can unproductive workers be shed, and critics arguing that job cuts occur with no sensitivity to the social costs.*** There can be a large social cost nonetheless manifested, in its worst forms, by urban violence, increased crime, and social and political unrest. But even in the absence of these problems, there are huge costs of unemployment. They include widespread anxiety even among workers who have managed to keep their jobs, a broader sense of alienation, additional financial burdens on family members who manage to remain employed, and the withdrawal of children from school to help support the family.***

Perhaps the most serious concern with privatization, as it has so often been practiced, is corruption. The rhetoric of market fundamentalism asserts that privatization will reduce what economists call the rent seeking activity of government officials who either skim off the profits of government enterprises or award contracts and jobs to their friends. But in contrast to what it was supposed to do, privatization has made matters so much worse that in many countries today privatization is jokingly referred to as briberization.***

Liberalization

Liberalization—the removal of government interference in financial markets, capital markets, and of barriers to trade—has many dimensions. Today, even the IMF agrees that it has pushed that agenda too far—that liberalizing capital and financial markets contributed to the global financial crises of the 1990s and can wreak havoc on a small emerging country.

The one aspect of liberalization that does have widespread support at least among the elites in the advanced industrial countries is trade liberalization. But a closer look at how it has worked out in many developing countries serves to illustrate why it is so often so strongly opposed, as seen in the protests in Seattle, Prague, and Washington, DC.

Trade liberalization is supposed to enhance a country's income by forcing resources to move from less productive uses to more productive uses; as economists would say, utilizing comparative advantage. But moving resources from low-productivity uses to zero productivity does not enrich a country; and this is what happened all too often under IMF programs. It is easy to destroy jobs, and this is often the immediate impact of trade liberalization, as inefficient industries close down under pressure from international competition. IMF ideology holds that new, more productive jobs will be created as the old, inefficient jobs that have been created behind protectionist walls are eliminated. But that is simply not the case and few economists have believed in instantaneous job creation, at least since the Great Depression. It takes capital and entrepreneurship to create new firms and jobs, and in developing countries there is often a shortage of the latter, due to lack of education, and of the former, due to lack of bank financing. The IMF in many countries has made matters worse, because its austerity programs often also entailed such high interest rates—sometimes exceeding 20 percent, sometimes exceeding 50 percent, sometimes even exceeding 100 percent—that job and enterprise creation would have been an impossibility even in a good economic environment such as the United States. The necessary capital for growth is simply too costly.

The most successful developing countries, those in East Asia, opened themselves to the outside world but did so slowly and in a sequenced way. These countries took advantage of globalization to expand their exports and grew faster as a result. But they dropped protective barriers carefully and systematically, phasing them out only when new jobs were created. They ensured that there was capital available for new job and enterprise creation; and they even took an entrepreneurial role in promoting new enterprises. China is just dismantling its trade barriers, twenty years after its march to the market began, a period in which it grew extremely rapidly.***

The fact that trade liberalization all too often fails to live up to its promise but instead simply leads to more unemployment is why it provokes strong opposition. But the hypocrisy of those pushing for trade liberalization and the way they have pushed it has no doubt reinforced hostility to trade liberalization. The Western countries pushed trade liberalization for the products that they exported, but at the same time continued to protect those sectors in which competition from developing countries might have threatened their economies.***

CARLOS HEREDIA AND MARY PURCELL, STRUCTURAL ADJUSTMENT IN MEXICO: THE ROOT OF THE CRISIS

The Development Group for Alternative Policies, Inc. (1995),
available at http://www.developmentgap.org/crisis.html

Based on the 1994 Equipo PUEBLO study, *The Polarization of Mexican Society: A Grassroots View of World Bank Economic Adjustment policies*, published by The Development GAP and Equipo PUEBLO. Prepared by the Development GAP for the Social Summit in Copenhagen (1995).

The Crippling Effects of Structural Adjustment in Mexico

Since 1982 the Mexican government has implemented virtually all of the adjustment policies promoted by the World Bank and the IMF: a reduction in public expenditures (including social services); elimination and/or targeting of subsidies; tax reform; restriction of credit; privatization of most state enterprises; trade liberalization; devaluation; removal of barriers to foreign investment; and "competitive" wages. Privatization and deregulation have contributed to a steep concentration of income and wealth, a trend which runs counter to the imperative of creating a strong domestic market as a factor in ensuring sustained economic growth. In what analysts term a "trickle up" process, there has been in Mexico a massive transfer of resources from the salaried population to owners of capital, and from public control to a few private hands.

HEALTH AND NUTRITION. One of the first adjustment policies implemented was a drastic cut in public spending. In general, adjustment suggests the cutting of "non-productive" spending so as not to affect output or revenues. This implies cuts in social spending. Thus during the decade of the eighties, the health budget as a percentage of overall public spending fell from 4.7 percent to 2.7 percent. The World Bank argues that it is necessary to look for alternative sources of financing, "*** including the possibility of privatizing health sector activities such as curative services." The poor who rely on these services are hardest hit by such cuts since they cannot afford private alternatives. One result is that between 1980 and 1992 infant deaths due to nutritional deficiencies almost tripled ***.

SQUEEZING SMALL PRODUCERS. Meanwhile, trade-liberalization and restrictive-credit policies have undermined many domestic small industries and agricultural producers who were unprepared for the dropping of trade barriers and unable to compete with cheap imports. Many of them have gone out of business or turned into retailers for U.S. manufacturers. This situation has been exacerbated as total credit has been restricted and priority is given to producers with export potential. This credit structure has seriously hurt micro, small and medium-sized businesses (which employ 80 percent of the labor force of the country) and at the same time has reinforced monopolies in the Mexican economy. Those who could get credit faced extremely high real interest rates—maintained to attract foreign investment and prevent capital flight ***.

UNEMPLOYMENT. Mexico had been cited as a successful example of a country where adjustment has included a real wage reduction in order to prevent massive unemployment. However, in a 1991 study, the Labor Congress indicated that, out of an economically active population of 34 million, 15 percent were openly unemployed, and over 40 percent—some 14 million people—were underemployed. The government only measures urban unemployment, while the problem is thought to be greatest in rural areas. According to the United Nations' Economic Commission for Latin America and the Caribbean (ECLAC), Mexico is the rare case in which the economy is marked by an inverse relationship between investment and employment. While the former has increased by nine percent over the last three years, the creation of new jobs has gone down.

DECLINING WAGES. Mexico witnessed a steep and continual decline in real wages during the eighties alongside massive layoffs and high levels of unemployment. By mid-1994, the minimum wage in Mexico was 14.8 new pesos ($4.42) per day. According to a study by researchers at the Faculty of Economics of the National Autonomous University of Mexico (UNAM), from the initiation of the government's Pact with business and labor in December 1987 until 1 May 1994, the minimum wage had increased by 136 percent, while the cost of the Basket of Basic Goods had grown by 371 percent.

SKEWED INCOME DISTRIBUTION. Since 1982, privatization and deregulation have contributed to a steep concentration of income and wealth. In what analysts term a "trickle-up" process, there has been in Mexico a massive transfer of resources from the salaried population to owners of capital, and from public control to a few private hands. Over the past decade the already large gap between the rich and the poor has widened. The richest 20 per cent of the population received 54.2 per cent of national income in 1992, against 48.4 per cent in 1984. The income of the poorest 20 per cent fell from 5 per cent in 1984 to 4.3 per cent of national income in 1992. According to a 1992 study, about one half of all Mexicans lived in poverty in 1990 (42 million) and 18 million lived in conditions of extreme poverty. The study goes on to say that ". . . if the poverty figures are frightening, their consequences should be even more frightening, . . . Malnutrition has become the normal condition of society."***

Structural Adjustment in Rural Mexico: The Case of Chihuahua

Bordering on the United States, Chihuahua is one of Mexico's largest states, with a population estimated in 1990 to be 2,441,873. Its rain-fed agriculture is dedicated primarily to the cultivation of corn and beans, two staples of the Mexican diet. Peasants generally grow these crops for their own consumption and to supply the urban population in the city of Chihuahua.

Although adjustment has proceeded more slowly in the agricultural sector than in other areas, by 1992 the Salinas administration had utilized a variety of adjustment policies to transform the agricultural sector into a more efficient producer for the international economy. Mexico received an Agricultural Sector Loan *** from the World Bank in 1988 that guided agricultural reforms for two-and-a-half years. The overall objectives of the program were to:

1. remove global food subsidies and target remaining food subsidies to the poor;

2. reduce government intervention in agricultural markets, in part by moving from guaranteed prices for grains (corn and beans excluded) toward market-determined pricing;

3. abolish export controls and quantitative restrictions on key products;

4. reduce the role of agricultural parastatals;

5. liberalize agricultural trade;

6. cut the subsidization of inputs;

7. increase the efficiency of public investment in agriculture in real terms; and

8. decentralize and cut staff of the agriculture ministry.***

The loan programs have reduced credit to small grain producers, eliminated farm-input subsidies, reduced or eliminated guaranteed prices, and further liberalized trade. Their effect has been to stimulate the large-scale production of export crops and reduce support for the production of basic foods, with import-tariff reductions resulting in a surge of cheap imported basic grains with which the farmers cannot compete. While increasing the cost of farm inputs, they have at the same time decreased the price of basic grains.

Faced with such drastic cuts in credit, the peasants of Chihuahua have been forced to seek various forms of supplemental financing. This may entail the selling off of livestock, though, more commonly, family members are forced to work in the cities, in the maquilla industries, for large landholders, or in the United States, creating more financial problems on the farms because of the loss of free family labor. In fact it is becoming more and more difficult to find a family that does not have at least one relative working in the U.S. and sending money home.***

It is clear to many that the government is attempting to slowly force small farmers out of corn and bean production. However, no practical alternative has been offered. Officials at the World Bank recommend that these producers move on to more productive activities or to crops "like strawberries." Aside from the fact that strawberries cannot be competitively produced on these lands, such a transition would require financing, training, and technical and marketing assistance, and very little government support is available in any of these areas. Without comprehensive programs to assist in the restructuring of economic activity, current economic policy will only lead to increased poverty and migration to the cities.

The Impact of Adjustment on the Urban Poor: The Case of San Miguel Teotongo

As opportunities have diminished in the countryside, Mexicans have increasingly moved to the cities in search of a better life. Although poverty is most severe in rural areas of Mexico (due largely to decades of an urban bias in public policy), it is broadly believed that the urban poor have been hit hardest by the adjustment process. They constitute the group that relies most heavily on wage employment, consumer subsidies and public services—all of which have declined under adjustment.

The community of San Miguel Teotongo is located in the Iztapalapa district on the eastern outskirts of Mexico City. Iztapalapa is the largest and one of the poorest districts of the metropolitan area. San Miguel was settled in 1972 by poor families that left the center of the city because of high rents and overcrowding. Since then, San Miguel has grown rapidly to a population of close to 80,000 today.

Three sets of adjustment policies have had the greatest impact on the residents of San Miguel Teotongo: the reduction of real wages and reduced public investment; cuts in subsidies and the liberalization of prices; and cuts in public services. The effects of these policies include: a reduction in real income and purchasing power; an increase in the importance of the informal economy and family labor; an increase in the relative price of many basic goods and services; and a reduction in the quality of public services while their costs increase.

Declining real wages and job opportunities are the most serious problems faced by families in San Miguel Teotongo. A central feature of the government's stabilization and adjustment program has been the reduction of real wages, while declining investment, the growing privatization of the economy, and public-sector cutbacks (all part of adjustment) have led to fewer employment opportunities. In general, families in San Miguel are working harder and longer for less income today than 12 years ago.***

The trends in education in San Miguel reflect what is happening nationally. Most children complete primary school, but increasing numbers of secondary-school-aged children are dropping out. One of the stated goals of SAPs regarding education is the transfer of government resources from higher education to primary education. However, between 1982 and 1990, the education budget fell from 5.5 percent of GDP to 2.5 percent. As public spending declined, the cost of books and materials increased. As a result the cost of sending children to school is often prohibitive for poor families, and economic crises frequently force even young children to work.***

In 1970 the Mexican government adopted the goal of providing health care to the country's entire population by the year 2000. Adjustment, however, caused sharp reductions in overall health-care spending during the eighties. Subsequent spending increases have been significant, but they still have not compensated for the earlier cuts. San Miguel suffers from a lack of health centers but, in theory, all Mexicans are covered by some type of health care program. In practice, however, very poor or non-existent service, exacerbated by budget cuts in the 1980s, has meant that many poor Mexicans do not have access to adequate health care through public institutions. They either go to private physicians or they do not go at all.

Today in San Miguel, families must work harder and longer hours to make less money and to purchase more expensive goods and services. Items such as books and health care are cut out of their budgets under these circumstances. Food consumption is cut back and consumption patterns change, with a variety of nutritional foods being replaced with less expensive, and often less nutritional, foods.

Conclusion

In the fall of 1994, Equipo PUEBLO concluded that adjustment in Mexico had failed to achieve its two principal goals: sustainable economic growth and the long-term alleviation of poverty. The World Bank and the IMF were applauding the economic performance of Mexico under adjustment, but with one half of the population living in poverty, and with an increasing concentration of wealth, the success of the model had been clearly in doubt for some time.***

What has been lacking throughout the adjustment process in Mexico is a social and economic policy that truly puts people first. Both the Mexican government and the multilateral development banks have supported an economic policy that has more to do with subsidizing creditor commercial banks (by allowing the Mexican Central Bank to buy Treasury bonds and guarantee principal and interest repayment) than with addressing the people's needs. There remains a pressing need to strike a balance between efficiency, on the one hand, and social justice, on the other, in order to promote the well-being of society as a whole.

One of the most basic components missing from adjustment programs is an income-generating policy for the poor. Short term, targeted compensatory funding programs, designed to protect vulnerable sectors from the transitions taking place, do not offer a solution to the long-term problem of poverty. Mexico is just one of many cases worldwide where adjustment and the free market have not only failed to alleviate poverty— as their proponents insisted they would—but have further polarized the country, economically and politically. [The World Bank and IMF must] acknowledge that their strategy has failed and needs to be abandoned, and that a new more democratically determined approach to the country's development has to be taken.

Notes and Questions

1. *Chiapas.* For the indigenous population of Mexico, the imposition of neoliberal policies is especially devastating. On January 1, 1994, Mexico, Canada and the United States formally entered into the North American Free Trade Agreement (NAFTA), creating a continent-wide free trade zone. On that same day, indigenous campesinos from Chiapas, the southernmost state in Mexico, staged an armed rebellion. Led by the Zapatista National Liberation Army (EZLN), about 4,500 peasants, armed only with rifles, occupied the state capital, San Cristóbal de las Casas, and several other towns. The Mexican army quickly moved to encircle and crush the uprising. But within days hundreds of thousands of Mexicans flooded into the central square in Mexico City in support of the Zapatistas, forcing the government into negotiations.

Chiapas is one of the most oppressed and poverty-stricken regions in Mexico. In 1990, 50 percent of the population of the state was malnourished, 42 percent had no access to clean water, 33 percent were without electricity and 62 percent did not complete primary school. This poverty persists despite the great wealth of the state. Chiapas produces half of Mexico's hydro-electricity, exports the most coffee, is the second largest producer of oil in Mexico and supports a burgeoning cattle industry that supplies the multi-national hamburger chains. The expansion of these industries has pushed the indigenous communities deeper into the Lacandon rainforest.

The rebellion was precipitated by the process of neoliberal reform initiated by then-President Jose Salinas, designed to make Mexico attractive to foreign investment in preparation for its integration into NAFTA. The first blow was the amendment of Article 27 of the Constitution of 1917, under which land had been distributed to the campesinos, to be held and farmed in common. The amendment was part of a massive privatization plan that would allow the land owned by the rural communities to be divided and sold. NAFTA further threatened the livelihood of the rural farmers by eliminating agricultural tariffs, which protected Mexican farmers from cheap U.S. and Canadian grain imports. The Zapatistas declared that NAFTA amounted to a "death sentence" for the indigenous people of Mexico.

An official cease-fire was declared on January 12, 1994. The Zapatistas submitted 34 specific "Demands and Engagements to Achieve a Dignified Peace in Chiapas" to the Mexican government. In December of 1994, newly elected President Ernesto Zedillo launched a large-scale military attack against the Zapatistas, a move that drew sharp international criticism. In March of 1995, the Congress of the Union responded to these attacks by unanimously approving the Law for Dialogue, Conciliation and Peace with Dignity in Chiapas. The Mexican government agreed to take steps to achieve peace and resolve the problems in Chiapas.

On February 16, 1996, the two sides signed the San Andres Accords, providing for more indigenous autonomy and restoration of their land rights. These Accords have never been implemented. The Zapatista autonomous areas in the remote Chiapas hillsides are still encircled by approximately 60,000 troops. There have been hundreds of civilian assassinations and kidnappings by the military and paramilitary groups.

But sympathy for the Chiapas movement remained high even after the election of President Vicente Fox in 2000, ending a long period of one-party rule in Mexico and promising political, economic and social reforms. In 2001 the Zapatistas organized a march across Mexico into the capital city. They were met by huge crowds in the cities and towns on the way. In Mexico City up to a million people greeted them. Outside Mexico the heroism of the Zapatista uprising inspired a new generation of activists to confront the harsh realities of globalization.

As predicted, the economic reforms that accompanied NAFTA have had a damaging impact on the region, by, for example, replacing the traditional subsistence farming of the Mayan Indians with export-driven large-scale production of beef, timber and oil. The deforestation and population displacement that inevitably accompanies this process portend dire long-term consequences for the environment, as well as for the livelihood and culture of the indigenous Mayan people.

For a general overview of the situation in Chiapas and the history of the Zapatista movement, *see* Camillo Perez-Bustillo, Zapatistas: An Army of Ideas: Indigenous Rights and the Movement for Global Justice (2004). In 2004, the Zapatistas celebrated the tenth anniversary of the uprising. For a discussion of the successes and failures of the movement, *see* Marion Lloyd, *Zapatistas Endure a Decade of Struggle*, BOSTON GLOBE, Jan. 2, 2004, at A1.

Another journalist, citing a 2003 World Bank report, indicates that the human rights of the indigenous peoples of Mexico are yet to be implemented:

> According to a report released in September by the World Bank, a booster of free-market reforms, 70 percent of Indian homes in Chiapas have no toilet or sewage disposal. The average per capita monthly income for Indians is less than $25.
>
> Chiapas is a state rich in cultural heritage sites, lush forests and rivers that generate electricity for the rest of Mexico. But for all the tourism and natural resources, little money trickles down to the Indians.
>
> In an important acknowledgment, the bank's report urges Mexico to resolve social conflict and discriminatory practices in Chiapas, Oaxaca and Guerrero, southern states that are home to 25 percent of Mexico's poorest people.
>
> Thirty-eight percent of the people in those states are Indians. And too many Indians, according to the report, are still subjected to arbitrary police detention, torture and discrimination in court proceedings.
>
> The World Bank's recommendations are not far from what the Zapatistas say they want. The bank urges a crackdown on inefficient spending and misuse of financial resources by state authorities. It recommends that Mexican officials help residents improve their access to markets to sell their products.
>
> In a significant policy suggestion, the bank also urges officials to help develop small cultural and ecological tourism projects—rather than massive resorts—so that Indians can own and operate their own businesses.
>
> But how does Mexico pursue these suggestions when so many Indians are deeply suspicious of the government's motives?
>
> The Zapatistas and other Indians have vowed not to cooperate with the Fox government or the Chiapas state government until the peace accords and rights bill Fox sent to Congress are approved in their original form.***

Susan Ferriss, *Mexican Rebel Standoff Becomes a Way of Life*, ATLANTA JOURNAL-CONSTITUTION, Dec. 28, 2003, at 3C. *See also* World Bank (Latin America and the Caribbean Regional Office), *Mexico-Chiapas—Programmatic Economic Development Loan (PEDL)*, (Report No. PID11530), Dec. 16, 2002, *available at* http://wwwwds.worldbank.org/servlet/WDSContentServer/WDSP/IB/2003/01/11/000094946_0301090403283/Rendered/INDEX/multi0page.txt.

2. *Remittances to Latin America from Migration to the United States.* Given the impact of structural adjustment policies and globalization on poor countries, many poor people migrate to the Global North in search of work to sustain themselves and their families. What economic impact does migration have on the sending country? It is estimated that Latin American immigrants to the United States send $30 to $42 billion annually back to their families in the home countries. $1.2 billion dollars per month is sent to Mexico alone, mostly in the form of small remittances of $200 dollars or less. Eduardo Porter, *Struggling to Draw Workers Sending Money Back Home*, NEW YORK TIMES, June 7, 2004, at 2.

In 2002, relatively poor migrant workers living in the Global North sent more money in the form of small remittances to their home countries than many of those countries received from bilateral aid, private bank lending, and IMF/World Bank aid/assistance combined. Michael McCaughan, *The welfare of strangers; remittances from Latin America abroad have become a big business—with a difference*, NEW INTERNATIONALIST, Jan.–Feb. 2004, *available at* http://articles.findarticles.com/p/articles/mi_m0JQP/ is_364/ai_113419286 (last visited June 23, 2004). *See also* the discussion of the remittances sent home by women who migrate to the United States from the Caribbean in this chapter's section on women workers under globalization.

2.   Global Trade and the Global South

In addition to the World Bank and the IMF, the General Agreement on Tariffs and Trade (GATT) was another product of the post-WWII Bretton Woods system of international economic reform. GATT is a multilateral treaty establishing a legal regime for global trade; its terms were negotiated by representatives of states parties in a series of trade talks, or rounds, dealing with issues such as customs duties, dumping, and non-tariff barriers to trade liberalization. Excluded from these talks are non-governmental organizations representing labor, environmental, human rights and social justice interests.

In the 1986–1994 Uruguay Round, GATT expanded its mission of liberalizing trade in goods to the establishment of more market-oriented policies in other sectors of the economy, notably agriculture (Agreement on Agriculture); services (General Agreement on Trade in Services, or GATS); and intellectual property (Trade-Related Aspects of Intellectual Property Rights or TRIPS). The Uruguay Round culminated in the creation of the World Trade Organization (WTO) in 1995.

Headquartered in Geneva, Switzerland, the WTO currently has 147 members.

Consider the following "Statement Submitted by the Committee on Economic, Social and Cultural Rights to the Third Ministerial Conference of the World Trade Organization:"

> *** 2. On the occasion of the Third Ministerial Conference of the World Trade Organization (WTO), being held in Seattle, United States of America, from 30 November to 3 December 1999, the Committee urges WTO to undertake a review of the full range of international trade and investment policies and rules in order to ensure that these are consistent with existing treaties, legislation and policies designed to protect and promote all human rights. Such a review should address as a matter of highest priority the impact of WTO policies on the most vulnerable sectors of society as well as on the environment.***
>
>   4.   The Committee is aware of the impending further rounds of trade liberalization negotiations and that new areas such as investments might be included in the WTO system. It thus becomes even more urgent that a comprehensive review also be undertaken to assess the impact that trade liberalization may have on the effective enjoyment of human rights, especially the rights enshrined in the Covenant. In its *Human Development Report, 1999*, the United Nations Development Program (UNDP) signals a strong warning against the negative consequences of the Agreement on Trade-Related Aspects of

Intellectual Property Rights, particularly on food security, indigenous knowledge, bio-safety and access to health care—major concerns of the Committee as reflected in articles 11 to 15 of the Covenant. The wave of economic and corporate restructurings undertaken to respond to an increasingly competitive global market and the widespread dismantling of social security systems have resulted in unemployment, work insecurity and worsening labor conditions giving rise to violation of core economic and social rights set forth in articles 6 to 9 of the Covenant.

5. It is the Committee's view that WTO contributes significantly to and is part of the process of global governance reform. This reform must be driven by a concern for the individual and not by purely macroeconomic considerations alone. Human rights norms must shape the process of international economic policy formulation so that the benefits for human development of the evolving international trading regime will be shared equitably by all, in particular the most vulnerable sectors.***

Committee on Economic, Social and Cultural Rights, 21st Sess., 47th Mtg, Annex VII U.N. Doc. E/C.12/1999/9 (1999).

JAMES GATHII, BEYOND MARKET-BASED CONCEPTIONS OF RIGHTS: SOCIAL AND ECONOMIC RIGHTS IN CONTEXT[2]

In the 1990s the United States and many bilateral donors sharpened their conditioning of economic assistance and credit on performance on political issues such as human rights. Hence, if a country was upholding the human rights of its citizens and allowing multiparty political democracy, it qualified for economic assistance and credit from bilateral donors and multilateral donors like the World Bank and the IMF.

Linking economic assistance and credit to political performance resulted in a market-centered or -friendly view and praxis of human rights. This market-centered view emerged because human rights advocacy largely abandoned its function as a critique or counterweight to market-based economic reform programs. This view of human rights is market-centered because it was designed to find complementarity and compatibility between human rights norms and market-centered norms of economic policy. For example, since civil and political rights such as the rights to property and the classical freedoms of assembly, association and speech are the most compatible with the ascendant program of market-oriented economic reform of the 1990's, these rights were embraced as the barometers for assessing political performance as a precondition for obtaining bilateral and multilateral assistance and credit. By contrast, social and economic rights, which include financing for public health, education and housing, were excluded from the scope of political criteria to be examined in determining if a coun-

---

2   These remarks are based on a presentation titled "Social and Economic Rights in Context," delivered at a conference on "Rethinking Ideology and Strategy: Progressive Lawyering, Globalization and Markets," Northeastern University School of Law, November 7, 2003. For a fuller exposition of the themes addressed here, *see* James Gathii, *Rights, Patents, Markets and the Global AIDS Pandemic,* 14 FLA. J. INT'L L., 261–352 (2002); James Gathii, *A Critical Appraisal of the NEPAD Agenda in Light of Africa's Place in the World Trade Regime in an Era of Market Centered Development,* 13 TRANSNAT'L L. CONTEMP. PROBS., 179 (2003).

try was up to speed to receive bilateral or multilateral economic support.

In essence, the new praxis of linking political performance to access to donor credit and assistance sacrificed social and economic rights. The reason for the exclusion of social and economic rights from this new formula was that the economic programs that were being promoted by the World Bank, the IMF and western governments like the United States were most compatible with civil and political rights, including of course the rights of property and the rights of contracting parties, so that a country only had to show minimal market-friendly rights to be able to receive western credit and bail-out assistance. In addition, this linkage was based on a purely procedural notion of democracy. Hence, if a country held multi-party elections that were nominally free and fair such a country would meet the approval of bilateral and multilateral donors. It didn't matter whether the elections were really competitive in the sense that the opposition had a chance of beating the incumbent party. Social and economic rights were excluded from these political measurements since they were regarded as being inimical to the market-centered commitment to free the accumulation of wealth from political controls such as those related to the income distribution embraced in public provisioning of education, health and housing.

There is a parallel development in the global trading regime. The World Trade Organization, and its predecessor [GATT] is the principal international legal framework that has for over fifty years been responsible for drawing up rules of global trade. In the 1990s, the question regarding the place of human rights in the context of the international trading framework came to the forefront. Defenders of the GATT/WTO regime argued that discussing human rights within the trade regime was like trying to fit a square peg into a round hole. Thus the same argument was made that had been made earlier in the context of the World Bank and the IMF—that human rights, particularly social and economic rights, did not fit within the paradigm of economic reform that was being pursued by these Bretton Woods institutions. At the WTO, this claim was justified on the ground that the trading regime was a self-contained institution separate from the international human rights regime. In particular, the argument was that trade is about liberalizing the flow of goods so that resources are allocated to their most efficient uses, while human rights concerns such as labor standards were political in their nature and outside the scope of the trading regime's mandate of liberalizing flows of trade.

Those who argued that there was a place for human rights within the GATT/WTO regime maintained that human rights concerns could be accommodated as special exceptions to the basic obligations of liberalizing trade. The specific provisions that have been cited to support a place for human rights in the trading regime include Article XX (a) of the GATT treaty of 1947, as amended in 1994, which provides that a country may take measures "necessary to protect public morals;" Article XX(b) which permits countries to take measures to protect human life or health; and Article XX(e) which allows countries to restrict measures "relating to the products of prison labor."

These provisions and the measures that they authorize are understood as exceptions to the basic obligations undertaken by members of the GATT/WTO regime. Thus the best way to understand the circumstances under which countries may take measures to protect human rights is to appreciate that such measures must conform to the more primary obligations of free trade. The opening paragraph of Article XX is designed to prevent the *abuse* or *misuse* of the exceptions in a manner that departs from the free trade mandate. In fact, in the 1970s and 1980s, GATT dispute settlement panels restrictively interpreted the opening clause of Article XX, thereby ensuring the ineffectiveness of using these provisions to promote human rights and other so-called non-trade values like environmental protection.

By adopting a very rigorous standard of review—that a measure taken pursuant to Article XX can only be justified if no less trade-restrictive alternative could be imagined to achieve the policy objectives—the dispute settlement system of the old GATT made it virtually impossible to protect human rights within the global trading regime. In the recent past, the WTO's Appellate Body has shown more willingness to countenance measures taken under the Article XX exceptions. However, there has been no case where a measure to protect human rights has been upheld. This may in part be because, to the extent such measures also protect the economy of the country invoking the exception, the WTO's dispute settlement system is almost certainly likely to strike them down.

In my view, a discourse that frames the question in terms of introducing human rights into an almost inflexible commitment to free trade within the WTO is inherently limited. There is further reason to be skeptical. For the last 50 years, tariffs were reduced under the GATT regime for industrial products at the same time that the regime—and today the WTO—imposed tariffs on agricultural products, textiles and clothing, industries in which developing countries had and continue to have a comparative advantage. This means that developing countries were essentially deprived of the opportunity of selling their agricultural products, textiles and clothing in an open trading regime even though they produced them at the cheapest cost. Instead, developed countries like the United States and the countries of the European Union heavily subsidized agriculture and closed their markets to the much more cheaply produced goods of developing countries. In other words, the trade regime discriminates between industrial products produced mostly by the West and agricultural products, textiles and clothing produced mainly by developing countries. Developed countries benefit from their comparative advantage in industrial products which, by the rules of the trading regime, they are entitled to. At the same time, however, developed countries ensured that the rules were written, interpreted and applied in a manner that nullified the comparative advantage that developing countries have in the global agricultural, textile and clothing market.

However, this unfair deprivation of the comparative advantage of developing countries almost never enters into the debate about socio-economic rights within the WTO/GATT regime, or within the dominant international human rights discourse. To the extent there is a difference in the manner in which agricultural and industrial products are treated, there is discrimination against lower-cost agricultural, clothing and textile products from developing countries. This discrimination is inconsistent with the theory or premise of free trade—that countries should export the things which they produce at the lowest cost. For developing countries, agricultural products, textiles and clothing is what they can produce more cheaply and therefore more competitively than developed countries. So why exclude these developing countries' products from the trade regime's promise of openness to low-cost producers?

This question is more important when one considers that if these products were accessible to western markets, they would earn developing countries foreign exchange that would help them realize the socio-economic rights of their citizens. Consider the additional benefits. Since the agriculture, textiles, and clothing industries are labor-intensive, giving developing countries an opportunity to export in these areas would create or return thousands of jobs presently diverted to developed countries that are higher-cost producers. Second, because people in developing countries would be able to earn an income, they would be able to send their children to school, pay for their health care costs and so on.

So in my view, social and economic rights are implicated within the trading regime beyond the confines of the exceptions under Article XX of the GATT treaty. Exposing such issues is the kind of project that I think progressive lawyers should be in the business of engaging especially in unmasking the rhetoric of human rights in relation to the WTO as too limited and as too restrictive. Looking behind the curtains, behind the veil, to see what lies hidden can make a difference by expanding the terms of the debate in ways that could potentially utilize human rights discourse in a manner that could impact people's lives. In fact, it turns out that if agriculture were liberalized, just as trade in industrial products is liberalized, it would be both consistent with the mantra of tearing down barriers to global trade, and beneficial to developing country citizens.

There is another concern that is even worse than the protection of western economies from cheaper developing country goods. This is the US Farm Bill which dishes out billions of dollars in subsidies, mostly to U.S. corporations. The Farm Bill is in many ways inconsistent with the WTO's Agreement on Agriculture although its supporters argue to the contrary. Although these subsidies are wasteful from an economic point of view, they are politically rational since farmers and agribusiness lobbies exercise a lot of power. Let us take the example of cotton. The effect of the Farm Bill is that taxpayers in the United States are subsidizing cotton farmers, for example, to produce cotton at net cost. This means that the actual cost of production is much higher than any returns derived from the sale of the cotton on the open market. U.S. farmers and big corporations are actually being paid to produce something that costs the economy more than it brings back to the economy. In none of the areas of the disciplines of the WTO do developing countries have such an advantage.

Just to give you a concrete example, in 2002, it cost 47 cents to produce one pound of cotton in Mali, Mauritania, and other countries that produce cotton in West and Central Africa. In the United States it costs 73 cents to produce one pound of cotton and it is even higher—above a dollar—in Europe. Under the theory of free trade adopted by the WTO, these West African countries have a comparative advantage and their cotton should have uninhibited access to world markets—it's a no-brainer. So how come the cotton market is flooded with American cotton? It's very simple: the American taxpayers are subsidizing American cotton farmers to produce cotton at net cost. Their cotton appears on the world market at less than 47 cents a pound because the U.S. government gives those farmers the money to make up the difference between 73 cents and 47 cents. As a result, they can undersell the cotton farmers in West and Central Africa who are producing at a much lower cost. Now, clearly, there is something very wrong with that. Why isn't this featured as a question of human rights, a question of socio-economic rights, for the WTO, not just a question of liberalization of trade? As a result of this policy in the area of cotton, ten million people who depend on cotton production in West Africa are threatened, their livelihoods are threatened—ten million people. You can add all the other catastrophes in Sub-Saharan Africa, like HIV/AIDS, to the fact that these people have no source of income, to appreciate the impact on their social and economic rights.

The World Bank estimates that because of the subsidies, there will be even more people living on less than $1 a day in Sub-Saharan Africa. Already, a majority of the people in this region live on less than $1 a day. The removal of subsidies would raise cotton prices three times above current prices. It would help these African countries more than the total aid that is being given to them by all the countries of the West, including the United States. In other words, if the world really wants to help Sub-Saharan Africa, especially those countries that produce the products that are being subsidized under the Farm Bill, it would be better to remove the subsidies than to give financial aid to these countries. The money that is given in aid does not compare to the money that the people of West and Central Africa would earn for themselves in the absence of the subsidies. Because of the subsidies a cow in the European Union lives on more than $2 a day while most people in sub-Saharan Africa are living on less than $1 a day. According to Action Aid, the financial payments that each farmer receives every year could pay for a ticket for a cow to go around the world. That's how absurd it is. People are starving, not because they want aid, but because they are being denied their rights to do what they do best, under the terms set by the institutions of the West.

Another strategy that is used, especially in Europe, to keep out products from developing countries is the promulgation of environmental standards. And I'm thinking about flower farming because I was doing some research on flower farming in Kenya last summer. Flower farming has become a very big business. For many reasons, including cultural factors and weather patterns, flowers from outside Europe have a huge market in Europe and they are earning developing countries a lot of much needed foreign exchange. Some countries like Kenya are earning quite a lot of money because the climate is opportune for that. But over the last few years, European Union countries have started applying standards requiring that farmers not use chemical inputs that have above a certain minimum content of residue of these chemicals. Let's think about this for a moment. First, the chemicals are coming from Europe—they are not produced in sub-Saharan Africa. Second, the flowers are mostly being produced in Africa by European-owned farms in conjunction with rich African elites. Third, there are some activist consumer groups and human rights groups in Europe that are very concerned about the fact that flower farming in Kenya degrades the environment because of the use of these dangerous chemicals, plus the fact that most of the laborers on these farms are not being treated very humanely. They work under very strict supervision and the working conditions are almost like work on colonial farms of a few decades ago in Kenya. The farm workers have to ask permission to use the bathroom and they are not provided with protective gear although they work with chemicals dangerous to human health, exactly the reason that Europeans do not want residue in the flowers they import. In my view, this is a very complex challenge because these flowers are earning countries like Kenya some foreign exchange that could be used to provide services in health, in education and so on, and those countries need that money. But, flower farming has its ugly side as well. I think this is a fertile area for people who are interested in social and economic rights to shine the torch so that the technocratic discourse of the WTO which disguises some of its consequences can be exposed.

A final point will be made about the Special and Differential Treatment provisions of the GATT/WTO system. Special and differential treatment provisions were introduced in the mid-1970s with a view to giving developing countries the benefits of participating in the global trading regime without having to bear some of its costs. So for example, these optional provisions allow for what is known as non-reciprocal or preferential access to developed country markets. Such access is designated as preferential since developing countries are not required to make reciprocal concessions. Thus, preferential access suspends the reciprocity requirement of the unconditional Most Favored Nation norm, which lowers trade barriers to all members of the international trading regime. This way, the goal of liberalization is accelerated.

Conventional wisdom suggests that non-reciprocal preferential access to Western markets results in a net-benefit to developing country exporters. However, although developing country exporters may not have to pay a tariff at the border under a preferential arrangement, they often encounter obscured costs as a result of measures taken within the borders of Western markets. Take the European Union market as an example. As we saw above the European Union has begun imposing measures to limit access to the European Union market of flowers from developing countries like Kenya because of chemical residue. The European Union has justified these measures, also known as MRLs, as necessary to protect animal, plant and human health. By adopting a zero-tolerance requirement on chemical residue in horticultural exports, the European Union in effect imposes very high compliance costs. In other words, farmers have to seek alternative inputs that are expensive or adopt farming methods that require high expenditures to meet these stringent requirements to access the European market. In effect, these costs act like a tariff, which off-sets the benefits of the preferences. These preferences have been undermined in many other ways as well, including the fact that they are not compulsory and that they may be conditioned on criteria such as supporting the U.S. in its war on terror, or adopting market-based reforms that require drastic reductions in social spending.

Thus, the workings of the trade preference regime designed to help developing countries cannot be said to live up to its promise or even to advance the protection of social and economic rights. Just like market-based conceptions of rights promoted by the World Bank and the WTO, preference arrangements under the principle of Special and Differential treatment appear to work against the interests of developing countries.

The goal of this article has been to expose some of the weaknesses of contemporary approaches to human rights in the context of the work of bilateral and multilateral donors and creditors as well as the WTO. I have argued that social and economic rights ought to be examined in a much broader context than that often promoted by practitioners and scholars of human rights. By taking into account a broader context and adopting a critical lens, we can see more clearly the limits and pitfalls of contemporary approaches to human rights and work to improve them.

Notes and Questions

1. Can the WTO be reformed to take human rights into account? Consider the following from an analysis of the human rights implications of the WTO:

> Since the late 1980's, the ascendancy of market economics coupled with a revolution in information technology has accelerated the process of globalization while institutions of international governance have been unable or unwilling to catch up. Privatization and the related phenomena of deregulation, structural adjustment and a myriad of new bilateral, regional and multilateral trade and investment agreements have proceeded without credible efforts to conceptually and practically address their impacts on legally protected human rights.***
>
> *** The ability of capital to move across borders with increasing ease in the era of globalization has implications for human rights. While human rights vio-

lations existed long before this period of rapid economic integration, the growing number of sectors covered by multilateral trade and investment agreements has set the stage for a new variety of human rights abuses which have not been suitably addressed.***

The challenge before the world today is how to influence the process of globalization in such a way that human suffering, poverty, exploitation, exclusion, and discrimination are eliminated. Since trade is the driving engine of globalization, it is imperative that, at the very least, rules governing it do not violate human rights but rather promote and protect them.***

ROBERT HOWSE & MAKAU MUTUA, PROTECTING HUMAN RIGHTS IN A GLOBAL ECONOMY: CHALLENGES FOR THE WORLD TRADE ORGANIZATION, at 6–7 (International Centre for Human Rights and Democratic Development, 2000).

Mutua and Howse suggest that global trade rules must be made compatible with human rights standards. Does Gathii suggest that implementing human rights would obstruct the goals of the WTO?

2.   Can an argument be made for a human right to fair trade? Even if such a right could be asserted, would it be enforceable against a non-state entity like the WTO? Does globalization threaten to render traditional human rights talk an anachronism? Consider the following:

[Q]uestions arise as to the validity of the existing human rights framework in an era of globalization. Human rights is a statist discourse in that it seeks to protect the individual against state violence. This model is rapidly becoming invalidated as a consequence of the fact that powers traditionally wielded by states—and, hence, subject to the limits of human rights—are increasingly being transferred to non-state actors, most notably powerful economic actors such as multinational corporations. An enormous problem arises as to how human rights, or indeed international law as a whole, can attempt to control these powers.***

Antony Anghie, *Time Present and Time Past: Globalization, International Financial Institutions, and the Third World,* 32 N.Y.U. J. INT'L L. & POL. 243, 254–55 (2000).

3.   For an in-depth discussion of the WTO Agreement on Agriculture, *see* Carmen G. Gonzalez, *Institutionalizing Inequality: The WTO Agreement On Agriculture, Food Security, and Developing Countries,* 27 COLUM. J. ENVTL. L. 433 (2002). Gonzalez asserts that, in the name of market liberalization, rich countries have pursued unfair advantages in the arena of trade:

Despite the free market ideology that ostensibly underlies the WTO Agreement on Agriculture, the Agreement has enabled developed countries to maintain trade-distorting subsidies and import restrictions, and has thereby failed to achieve its stated objective of creating a "fair and market-oriented trading system."***

The market access requirements of the WTO Agreement on Agriculture produced very little liberalization in the highly protected markets of OECD countries. One of the great innovations of the Agreement was the conversion of non-tariff barriers to tariffs and the prohibition of any further non-tariff barriers. However, many developed countries evaded the underlying objective of these requirements by engaging in "dirty tariffication," the setting of tariff equivalents for non-tariff barriers at an excessively high level. Dirty tariffication nullified the benefits of tariff bindings and tariff reduction by creating tariff equivalents, to which subsequent reductions apply, that were at times more import-restrictive than the non-tariff barriers they replaced.

A survey of tariffication procedures used by developed countries concluded that the majority of OECD countries had engaged in dirty tariffication. In many instances, dirty tariffication resulted in higher levels of protection than under the old system of quotas and variable import levies. Moreover, the highest tariffs were for sugar, tobacco, meat, milk products, cereals and, to a lesser degree, fruits and vegetables, precisely the products of particular interest to developing countries.

The manner in which OECD countries implemented the Agreement's tariff reductions requirements likewise restricted the market access of developing country producers. The WTO Agreement on Agriculture *** allowed countries to pick and choose which individual tariffs to reduce. OECD countries generally made large tariff reductions on items that were not produced domestically or where tariff levels were already quite low in order to make minimal concessions on imports that competed with domestically produced items.***

Id. at 460–61.

Eleanor Fox addresses the effects of trade inequities on economic, social and cultural rights:

The human costs of unfair trade are immense. If Africa, East Asia, South Asia, and Latin America were each to increase their share of world exports by one per cent, the resulting gains in income could lift 128 million people out of poverty. Reduced poverty would contribute to improvements in other areas, such as child health and education. If the nations of the WTO were to adopt one and only one human welfare measure, elimination of [subsidies and trade barriers] should be the measure. It is fair, and it is efficient. It would help the least well-off to help themselves on the merits. While benefiting the least well-off, both absolutely and relatively, it also would benefit the industrialized world in absolute terms.***

Eleanor M. Fox, *Globalization and Human Rights: Looking Out For The Welfare Of The Worst Off*, 35 N.Y.U. J. Int'l L. & Pol. 201 (2002).

4. *Brazil Cotton Case in WTO.* Marking the first successful international challenge to U.S. domestic agricultural subsidies, an April 2004 preliminary WTO ruling backed Brazil's contention that subsidies to U.S. cotton farmers violate international trade rules, a decision that could lead to severe penalties against the United States and could force the United States and other rich countries to lower cotton and other farm subsidies. Elizabeth Becker, *Global Trade Body Rules Against U.S. on Cotton Subsidies*, N.Y. Times, Apr. 27, 2004, at A2. Despite angry objections by the U.S. cotton industry, the WTO issued a final ruling upholding the preliminary decision in June of 2004. *See* Alan Glendenning, *WTO Upholds U.S. Cotton Subsidy Ruling*, Miami Herald, June 19, 2004, at: http://www.miami.com/mld/miamiherald/business/8966127.htm?1c (last visited June 24, 2004).

The U.S. cotton subsidies received harsh criticism at the failed 2003 Cancun WTO Ministerial meeting (*see* Note 5 below), where several West African nations joined Brazil in complaining that the U.S. subsidies allowed its share of the world market to increase dramatically. They argued that the U.S. market share should have fallen if the market were truly "free." U.S. cotton farmers get more than $2 billion in subsidies, which, according to Oxfam International, costs African nations about $300 million a year in lost export earnings and far outweigh the amount of foreign aid that the U.S. provides poor nations. *See U.S., EU Cotton Subsidies under Fire,* WASH. TIMES, Apr. 23, 2004, *available at* http://www.washtimes.com/upi-breaking/20040422-042054-4051r.htm (last visited July 31, 2004).

With a legal precedent in their favor, the developing world may move to take on other US subsidy programs for products such as corn and barley as well as the European Union's (EU) sugar subsidy program. The global poor now have a legal argument to couple with the moral one that rich nations ought to be forced to play by the same "free market" rules regularly imposed by the IMF and World Bank on nations far less able to handle the economic pain these rules frequently produce. Future legal challenges may produce an end to subsidy programs by rich nations altogether; most poor countries were forced to eliminate any such measures long ago, as they are seen as unduly "protectionist" by IMF and World Bank standards.

5. *WTO Meeting at Cancun: Failure or Victory?* Governments participating in a September 2003 WTO meeting in Cancun, Mexico, failed to reach agreement on key international trade issues. Despite repeated assurances by European Union (EU) Trade Commissioner Pascal Lamy that the Cancun meeting would be "pro-development" and a step forward for the developing world, the talks collapsed after many delegates from non-industrialized nations decided that they were being herded down a path to their own destruction. *See* Pascal Lamy, *The Doha Development Agenda, the European Union and the Commonwealth,* (EU-Commonwealth Roundtable, London School of Economics, London, Jan. 20, 2003), EUROPAWORLD, Jan. 24, 2003, *available at* http://www.europaworld.org/week113/speechpascallamy24103.htm (last visited July 30, 2004). Set to continue the agenda of the Doha trade round (November 2001), the talks in Cancun ended before progress was made on Doha's goals, including lowering barriers to agricultural trade. Four years after the Seattle (Washington) trade talks ended in failure due to large protests by labor unions, human rights activists, anarchist groups, and other activists, the failure of the Cancun talks raised serious concerns about the future of the WTO regime. *Cancun's charming outcome,* ECONOMIST (U.S. EDITION), Sept. 20, 2003.

A group of developing countries, originally led by Botswana and by the increasingly influential alliance among Brazil, India, South Africa, and China, "blocked a US-led resolution . . . which sought greater market access to developing countries for agriculture products of the rich countries." *India Blames U.S. for Failure of Cancun Meet,* ECONOMIC TIMES (INDIA), Dec. 23, 2003, *available at* http://economictimes.indiatimes.com/articleshow/377870.cms? (last visited June 24, 2004). Developing countries objected to the U.S. position that it would not significantly reduce its own agricultural subsidies while at the same time pressing for greater access to developing country markets. *Id.* A poll conducted after the talks by War on Want, a non-governmental organization, found that 83 percent of the developing country delegates believed the WTO to be an undemocratic organization. Steve Tibbett, *Cancun Collapse, available at* http://www.waronwant.org/?lid=5667 (last visited July 30, 2004).

In an unprecedented display of solidarity, delegates from developing nations walked out of the Ministerial meeting. The feeling that the majority of the world's people were being forced to accept terms of trade favorable only to an already-wealthy minority, without opportunity for equitable negotiation, led developing world delegates to conclude that no deal was preferable to a bad deal.

As previously noted, the Cancun summit was to be a major step toward completing the Doha trade negotiations begun in 2001. The World Bank had estimated that successful completion of the negotiations would add "$290–$520 billion in income gains to both rich and poor countries, lifting an additional 144 million people out of poverty by 2015." World Bank, *World Bank Report Highlights Need for Success at Cancun Trade Talks: WTO Breakthrough Would Spur Confidence, Boost Incomes, Reduce Poverty*, News Release No:2004/055/S, Sept. 3, 2003, *available at* http://web.worldbank.org/WBSITE/EXTERNAL/NEWS/0,,contentMDK:20126037~menuPK:34463~pagePK:64003015~piPK:64003012~theSitePK:4607,00.html (announcing the release of World Bank report, GLOBAL ECONOMIC PROSPECTS 2004: REALIZING THE DEVELOPMENT PROMISE OF THE DOHA AGENDA) (last visited July 30, 2004). Predictably, then, officials from the Global North reacted strongly to the failure to reach an agreement in Cancun. Pascal Lamy stated that the collapse was "a severe blow for the WTO," while European Commission President Romani Prodi was moved to describe the organization as "medieval" and unable to "support the weight of the task it was given." *Pascal Lamy EU Trade Commissioner Press Conference Closing the World Trade Organisation Fifth Ministerial Conference, Cancun, Mexico, 14 September 2003*, EUROPA, Sept. 15, 2003, *available at* http://europa.eu.int/rapid/pressReleasesAction.do?reference=SPEECH/03/409&format=HTML&aged=0&language=en&guiLanguage=en (last visited July 30, 2004); *EU Blames "Medieval" WTO after Trade Talks Collapse*, EU BUSINESS, Sept. 15, 2003, *available at* http://www.eubusiness.com/afp/030915152850.pkcdu345.

The stunning outcome of the Cancun Ministerial meeting focused global attention on poor country claims that the WTO is being used as an undemocratic means of providing legal cover for imperialism. The Cancun "failure" was seen by many, including some anti-globalization activists, as something of a triumph for developing country clout vis-à-vis the U.S. and other powerful interests such as the European Union. What other strategies might developing nations use in solidarity with one another to facilitate a more honest and fair process for negotiating global trade rules? What are the implications of trends toward the erosion of state sovereignty for alternative approaches to global economic justice?

The failure of the talks meant that no progress was made toward reforming an already unfair global trade regime. Developing nations continue to suffer under the weight of Washington consensus "free market" conditions, while rich nations deny them the comparative advantages promised by free market doctrine, for example, by continuing to heavily subsidize their own agricultural and other products (but see recent WTO decisions on cotton discussed in this section). The developed nations also continue to pursue alternative strategies aimed at furthering their economic interests, such as bilateral and regional "free trade" agreements. However, in August of 2004, a tentative deal was approved by all 147 WTO members to eliminate farm subsidies in rich countries in exchange for developing countries cutting tariffs on industrial goods, although no timeframe for implementation was set. *See World trade deal gets thumbs up*, BBC News World Edition, Aug. 1, 2004, *available at* http://news.bbc.co.uk/2/hi/business/3525602.stm

(last visited Aug. 1, 2004). Whether this represents a real victory for developing countries remains to be seen.

6. *U.S. Steel Tariffs.* In late 2003, thwarting U.S. protectionist efforts, the WTO ruled that U.S. steel tariffs violated international trade rules, giving the EU and several other countries the right to impose retaliatory tariffs on American exports worth billions of dollars. Paul Blustein & Jonathan Weisman, *U.S. Loses Appeal on Steel Tariffs*, WASH. POST, Nov. 11, 2003, at A1. U.S. President George W. Bush repealed the steel tariffs in December 2003. *See Rolled Over*, ECONOMIST (U.S. EDITION), Dec. 6, 2003.

In March 2002, when the tariffs were first announced, critics observed that they could not be sustained if the United States wished to avoid massive losses each year due to the sanctions that would inevitably be imposed under WTO rules. *See, e.g., Trade War Looms Over Steel Dispute*, BBC News, Mar. 6, 2002, *available at* http://news.bbc.co.uk/1/hi/business/1856760.stm. Indeed, by early December of 2003, President Bush was said to be "forced" to reverse the tariffs under threat of what many predicted would be a trade war after the WTO decision. *Id.*

Some business analysts argued even before the institution of the tariffs that the contraction of the U.S. steel industry was part of a long-term trend that could not easily be reversed. *See, e.g.,* James Arnold, *Steel Sector Stares into the Abyss*, BBC News, Mar. 6, 2002, *available at* http://news.bbc.co.uk/1/hi/business/1857914.stm. The Administration's official justification was that the steel tariffs would give the industry time to restructure for global competition without having to face that competition while doing so. *Id.* Critics contend that merely postponing the unavoidable effects of globalization would not solve the industry's problems. They also questioned the underlying purposes of a tariff system that would not save the industry, but would potentially expose the U.S. to billions of dollars in sanctions, and, possibly, result in higher costs to U.S. consumers and businesses that use steel in manufactured products. *See, e.g.,* James Arnold, *Steel Spat Could Mean Wider Worries*, BBC News, Mar 6, 2002, *available at* http://news.bbc.co.uk/1/hi/business/ 1857678.stm.

The United States found itself in the awkward position of preaching free-trade as the painful-but-necessary answer to the economic crisis in the Third World while being unwilling to bear any such pain itself. If the United States, with its strong, diverse economy could not accept the obvious financial implications of global competition with lower-cost steel suppliers, why should economically weaker states be expected to do the same?

While the tariffs did not appear to be sound economic policy for the United States, they did appeal to steelworkers and their families, who are concentrated in political "battleground" states, such as Pennsylvania and West Virginia, which are often crucial in national elections. *See, e.g.,* James Ewinger, *Steel, Tariffs, Politics, Mix at U.S.-Canada Conference*, CLEVELAND PLAIN DEALER, Apr. 18, 2004, at B4. In the end, with the tariffs lifted, President Bush claimed victory: "I took action to give the industry a chance to adjust to the surge in foreign imports and to give relief to the workers and communities that depend on steel for their jobs and livelihoods. These safeguard measures have now achieved their purpose, and as a result of changed economic circumstances it is time to lift them." White House, *President's Statement on Steel*, Dec. 4, 2003, *available at* http://www.whitehouse.gov/news/releases/2003/12/20031204-5.html (last visited July 30, 2004).

What might this form of policymaking reveal about formal distinctions between "legal rules" and "politics"?

7. *The "Banana Wars."* The "Banana Wars," a wide-ranging dispute ultimately settled under the auspices of the WTO, actually predated the creation of that institution. In 1993, the European Union (EU) imposed a new quota system for banana imports under the Lomé Convention. The quota system served a number of purposes, including respecting previous European obligations toward African, Caribbean, and Pacific (ACP) countries under the GATT system. The EU preferences were intended to support the economic development of formerly colonized nations. The EU trade preferences established under the Lomé Convention guaranteed ACP nations a specified quota of imports to the EU.

The formal WTO action was initiated by the United States and mainland Central American countries, but only after a complaint was lodged in the United States by Chiquita Banana, the successor to the notorious United Fruit Company. (The suit was made possible by U.S. trade laws allowing citizens to petition the U.S. Trade Representative to begin an investigation. *See* 19 U.S.C. §301 (1988).) In 1996, Honduras, Guatemala, Ecuador, Mexico and the United States appealed to the WTO for relief against what they claimed to be discriminatory trade practices on the part of the EU. The WTO complaint alleged the preferences to be in violation of several provisions of the General Agreement on Tariffs and Trade (GATT): Article I (Most-Favored Nation treatment); Article II (schedules of concessions); Article III (National Treatment Obligation), Article X (publication and administration of trade regulations); Article XI (general elimination of quantitative restrictions); and Article XIII (non-discriminatory administration of quantitative restrictions). Additionally, they were said to violate the General Agreement on Trade in Services (GATS). Ibrahim J. Gassama, *Confronting Globalization: Lessons From the Banana Wars and the Seattle Protests*, 81 U. ORE. L. REV. 707, 715–16 (2002). Although many ACP countries relied on the preferential trade policies for economic survival, then-U.S. President Bill Clinton said the dispute was about the need for rules to govern world trade. BBC Online Network, Mar. 6, 1999, *available at* http://news.bbc.co.uk/1/hi/business/the_economy/290878.stm (last accessed July 31, 2004).

In response to a 1997 WTO report, the EU revised its banana regime in 1999, but the new regime continued tariffs/quotas, complicated licensing schemes, and preferential treatment for ACP suppliers. By April of 1999 the WTO, still dissatisfied with the EU banana regime, authorized the United States to impose trade sanctions of $191 million against the EU.

Critics suggested throughout the rather complicated legal disputes that transnational corporations that were engaged in large-scale banana farming in mainland Central American countries had pressured both Democratic and Republican Administrations in the United States to dispute the EU's position. Human rights NGOs also reported on human rights abuses against workers on the mainland banana farms. *See* Human Rights Watch, *Ecuador: Widespread Labor Abuse on Banana Plantations: Harmful Child Labor, Anti-Union Bias Plague Industry* (press release), Apr. 26, 2002, *at* http://www.hrw.org/press/2002/04/ecuador0425.htm. For an in-depth discussion, *see* Maxmillian Finley, *The Bitter with the Sweet: The Impact of the World Trade Organization's Settlement of the Banana Trade Dispute on the Human Rights of Ecuadorian Banana Workers*, 48 N.Y. L. SCH. L. REV. 815, 817–20 (2003–2004).

Because of the small size of most island nations, Caribbean banana farmers are not able to compete economically with the large-scale banana producers on the Central American mainland. The loss of EU preferences has therefore had a devastating effect on the ability of Caribbean and other ACP countries to meet basic social and economic needs. Caribbean nations had few cards to play against the United States, but in 2000 they threatened not to renew bilateral agreements to combat illicit maritime drug trafficking unless the new agreements were tied to preferential treatment in the banana trade. For a discussion of the tense relations between the United States. and Caribbean nations as a result of the "banana wars." *see* Michelle Williams, *Caribbean Shiprider Agreements: Sunk by the Banana Trade*, 31 U. MIAMI INTER-AM. L. REV. 163 (2000).

By 2001 the United States and the EU reached an agreement calling for the gradual replacement of the EU quota system with a tariff-only scheme. This agreement was further modified at the WTO Doha Ministerial meeting, where the EU received waivers of relevant GATT provisions that enabled it to adopt the Cotonou Agreement, a new treaty with ACP countries. These agreements provide some respite for the ACP nations, but no permanent assurances (most terms expire by 2006). For the text of the Agreement, *see* http://europa.eu.int/comm/development/body/cotonou/agreement_en.htm (last visited July 31, 2004).

What lessons can be drawn from the "Banana Wars"? To what extent should human rights and other social considerations outweigh formal rules arguably intended to implement "free trade" doctrine? *See generally* Benjamin Brimeyer, *Bananas, Beef, and Compliance in the World Trade Organization: The Inability of the WTO Dispute Settlement Process to Achieve Compliance by Superpower Nations*, 10 MINN. J. GLOBAL TRADE 133 (2001). The EU and the United States were major players in the dispute, even though the United States does not have a significant banana industry, while the ACP countries who would be most affected by the outcome had no voice under formal procedural rules. What does this imply for the interests of developing countries in the WTO dispute resolution process? What roles do powerful non-state actors play in setting international economic policy? If informed popular consent forms the basis for legitimate authority, how have the WTO and its sister institutions, the IMF and World Bank, maintained authority with so little public scrutiny and nonexistent public debate abut their character and purposes? How solid is the moral foundation for that authority?

One promising development is the Fair Trade Movement. Like the current process whereby food and cosmetic products are inspected and, if appropriate, awarded the label "Organically Produced," consumers may one day be able to demand a pair of jeans or even an automobile that has been "Fairly Traded." Now only available on a few goods such as coffee and chocolate, this label could reassure consumers that their dollars are not being used to exploit farmers or factory workers. For more on the Fair Trade Movement, visit the following Web sites: http://www.fairtradefederation.com/; http://www.globalissues.org/TradeRelated/ FairTrade.asp; and http://www.globalexchange.org/campaigns/fairtrade/ (last visited July 31, 2004).

8. *Unconditional Most Favored Nation Treatment.* GATT, and subsequently the WTO, attempted to achieve global reduction in tariffs and other barriers to world trade by implementing the principle of unconditional most-favored nation (MFN) status to all GATT/WTO nations. Under the principle of unconditional MFN, the most favorable

benefits accorded by one nation to another are available to other nations. The expected outcome of the MFN principle was to make available to all GATT/WTO members the effects of previously bilateral trade concessions.

9.   *The Call for a "New International Economic Order" and Preferential Trade Treatment.* Impartiality in trading among nations is one of the founding tenets of the GATT/WTO system. However, with the rise of post-colonial political movements such as the Non-Aligned Movement in the 1960s and 1970s, developing nations successfully advocated for preferential trade treatment under the GATT system. Third World leaders argued, among other things, for the establishment of a "New International Economic Order." (NIEO). The NIEO vision was a set of international social and economic policies intended to redress past and current inequities and exploitation between the developing world and the former colonial and other western powers. Some argued that the NIEO would be necessary to implement a "right to development" (discussed later *infra* Section C). Trade preferences were considered a key component of the NIEO, although some of the original demands have been diminished among Third World leaders as a result of Cold War politics, disagreements on strategy, post-Cold War international economic policies, and globalization. *See, e.g.,* Chantal Thomas, *Balance-of-Payments Crises in the Developing World: Balancing Trade, Finance and Development in the New Economic Order,* 15 AM. U. INT'L L. REV. 1249, 1259–60 (2000). *See also* Declaration on the Establishment of a New International Economic Order, G.A. Res. 3201, U.N. GAOR, 28th Sess., Supp. No. 1, at 3, U.N. Doc. A/9559 (1974) *reprinted in* 13 I.L.M. 715 (1974) (asserting that the "[t]he new international economic order should be founded on full respect for the following principles:*** (n) Preferential and non-reciprocal treatment for developing countries, wherever feasible, in all fields of international economic cooperation whenever possible").

3.   *Global Trade, Human Rights and Intellectual Property*

Numerous controversies have arisen in connection with the Agreement on Trade-Related Aspects of Intellectual Property Rights (TRIPS). The TRIPS Agreement establishes minimum levels of protection that have to be afforded to intellectual property from member countries. Under the Agreement, patent protection must be available for new inventions for at least 20 years. Among the patentable items are pharmaceutical products, micro-organisms, micro-biological processes and plant varieties. This has raised human rights issues such as access to life-saving medicines and infringement on the cultural rights of indigenous peoples.

Under certain circumstances, the Agreement provides for the issuance of "compulsory licenses" that allow a competitor to produce the product under a license that protects the interests of the patentholder. The scope of this provision has been vigorously debated in the context of developing countries' need for drugs to combat the raging AIDS pandemic.

At the WTO Ministerial Conference in Doha in November 2001, a special declaration was issued stating that the TRIPS Agreement does not prevent members from taking measures to protect public health. In August 2003, the TRIPS Council approved a waiver allowing countries unable to produce pharmaceuticals domestically to import patented drugs made under compulsory licensing.

WORLD TRADE ORGANIZATION, URUGUAY ROUND: ANNEX 1C

AGREEMENT ON TRADE-RELATED ASPECTS OF INTELLECTUAL PROPERTY RIGHTS

Available at http://www.wto.org/english/tratop_e/trips_e/t_agm3c_e.htm#5

*** PART II—STANDARDS CONCERNING THE AVAILABILITY, SCOPE AND USE OF INTELLECTUAL PROPERTY RIGHTS.

Article 27: Patentable Subject Matter:

1. Subject to the provisions of paragraphs 2 and 3, patents shall be available for any inventions, whether products or processes, in all fields of technology, provided that they are new, involve an inventive step and are capable of industrial application. Subject to paragraph 4 of Article 65, paragraph 8 of Article 70 and paragraph 3 of this Article, patents shall be available and patent rights enjoyable without discrimination as to the place of invention, the field of technology and whether products are imported or locally produced.

2. Members may exclude from patentability inventions, the prevention within their territory of the commercial exploitation of which is necessary to protect *ordre public* or morality, including to protect human, animal or plant life or health or to avoid serious prejudice to the environment, provided that such exclusion is not made merely because the exploitation is prohibited by their law.

3. Members may also exclude from patentability:

    (a) diagnostic, therapeutic and surgical methods for the treatment of humans or animals;

    (b) plants and animals other than micro-organisms, and essentially biological processes for the production of plants or animals other than non-biological and microbiological processes. However, Members shall provide for the protection of plant varieties either by patents or by an effective *sui generis* system or by any combination thereof. The provisions of this subparagraph shall be reviewed four years after the date of entry into force of the WTO Agreement.***

Article 30: Exceptions to Rights Conferred

Members may provide limited exceptions to the exclusive rights conferred by a patent, provided that such exceptions do not unreasonably conflict with a normal exploitation of the patent and do not unreasonably prejudice the legitimate interests of the patent owner, taking account of the legitimate interests of third parties.

Article 31: Other Use Without Authorization of the Right Holder

Where the law of a Member allows for other use of the subject matter of a patent without the authorization of the right holder, including use by the government or third parties authorized by the government, the following provisions shall be respected:

    (a) authorization of such use shall be considered on its individual merits;

    (b) such use may only be permitted if, prior to such use, the proposed user has made efforts to obtain authorization from the right holder on reasonable commercial terms and conditions and that such efforts have not been successful within a reasonable period of time. This requirement may be waived by a Member in the case of a national emergency or other circumstances of extreme urgency or in cases of public non-commercial use. In situations of national emergency or other circumstances of extreme urgency, the right holder shall, nevertheless, be notified as soon as reasonably practicable. In the case of public non-commercial use, where the government or contractor, without making a patent search, knows or has demonstrable grounds to know that a valid patent is or will be used by or for the government, the right holder shall be informed promptly;***

(f) any such use shall be authorized predominantly for the supply of the domestic market of the Member authorizing such use;***

(k) Members are not obliged to apply the conditions set forth in subparagraphs (b) and (f) where such use is permitted to remedy a practice determined after judicial or administrative process to be anti-competitive. The need to correct anti-competitive practices may be taken into account in determining the amount of remuneration in such cases. Competent authorities shall have the authority to refuse termination of authorization if and when the conditions which led to such authorization are likely to recur.***

WORLD TRADE ORGANIZATION, DECLARATION ON THE TRIPS AGREEMENT AND PUBLIC HEALTH (DOHA DECLARATION)

Ministerial Conference, Fourth Session, Doha, November 9–14, 2001, WT/MIN(01)/DEC/2, *adopted on* November 14, 2001, *available at* http://www.wto.org/english/thewto_e/minist_e/min01_e/mindecl_trips_e.doc

1. We recognize the gravity of the public health problems afflicting many developing and least-developed countries, especially those resulting from HIV/AIDS, tuberculosis, malaria and other epidemics.

2. We stress the need for the WTO Agreement on Trade-Related Aspects of Intellectual Property Rights (TRIPS Agreement) to be part of the wider national and international action to address these problems.

3. We recognize that intellectual property protection is important for the development of new medicines. We also recognize the concerns about its effects on prices.

4. We agree that the TRIPS Agreement does not and should not prevent Members from taking measures to protect public health. Accordingly, while reiterating our commitment to the TRIPS Agreement, we affirm that the Agreement can and should be interpreted and implemented in a manner supportive of WTO Members' right to protect public health and, in particular, to promote access to medicines for all.

In this connection, we reaffirm the right of WTO Members to use, to the full, the provisions in the TRIPS Agreement, which provide flexibility for this purpose.***

JAMES THUO GATHII, THE LEGAL STATUS OF THE DOHA DECLARATION ON TRIPS AND PUBLIC HEALTH UNDER THE VIENNA CONVENTION ON THE LAW OF TREATIES

15 HARV. J. L. & TECH. 291, 299–301 (2002)

I. INTRODUCTION

One of the most contentious issues before the World Trade Organization (WTO) is the application of the Agreement on Trade-Related Aspects of Intellectual Property Rights ("the TRIPS Agreement") to WTO members seeking to facilitate access to essential medicines.***

Developing countries have argued that the TRIPS Agreement does not limit their sovereignty to address crises such as HIV/AIDS. They view compulsory and parallel licensing as permissible objectives that do not violate the TRIPS Agreement. Developed countries, particularly the United States and Switzerland, have argued that the only flexibility in the TRIPS Agreement is the staggered implementation periods developing countries enjoy under the Agreement. Under the staggered implementation schedule, developing countries have five years and least developed countries have ten years from January 1, 1996, to fully implement the Agreement.

The November 2001 Doha Declaration on TRIPS and Public Health ("the Doha Declaration") was in part necessitated by these divergent perspectives. The WTO's dispute settlement bodies have not directly addressed these divergent interpretations ***.

[G]iven the divergent interpretations of the TRIPS Agreement, the Doha Declaration should now be regarded as an interpretive element in the interpretation of the TRIPS agreement under customary international law.***

II. PROTECTION OF PATENTS UNDER THE TRIPS AGREEMENT AND THE HIV/AIDS PANDEMIC

The TRIPS Agreement is a product of protracted negotiations at the Uruguay Round that ended in 1994.***

[It] establishes patentability for product and process inventions in all fields of technology, provided they are new, involve an inventive step, and are capable of industrial application. Patent rights must be available "without discrimination as to the place of invention, the field of technology or whether the products are imported or locally produced." The Agreement also guarantees most favored nation treatment for intellectual property rights, and requires members to "ensure that enforcement procedures . . . are available under their law so as to permit effective action against any act of infringement." Members must ensure transparency by making their laws, regulations, judicial decisions, and administrative rulings available in a national language. Disputes under the Agreement must be resolved through the WTO's Dispute Settlement Understanding.

Under the earlier Paris Convention, each country was only obliged to extend intellectual property protection no worse than its own to its trading partners. By requiring minimum levels of protection, the TRIPS Agreement therefore no longer allows countries to choose their level of intellectual property protection.

During the Uruguay negotiations on the TRIPS Agreement, a major goal of the United States, the European Union, Japan, Switzerland, and the Nordic countries was to establish a high level of intellectual property protection with a guarantee of enforcement. Developing countries, particularly Brazil, argued that this position focused too much on the interests of owners of intellectual property rights and not enough on those of users. Brazil argued that the Agreement should reflect the needs of developing countries, such as access to technology. During the Uruguay Round, the United States unilaterally pressured developing countries opposed to its negotiating position, such as Brazil, Thailand, and India, using the authority of the United States Trade Representative ***.

The issue of access to essential medicines replays the original debate between developing and developed countries regarding the TRIPS Agreement. Developed countries continue to maintain that high levels of intellectual property protection provide the necessary incentive for investment in research and development, which is the best guarantee of access to essential medicines for all countries. In contrast, developing countries maintain that strict constructions of the TRIPS Agreement fail to recognize the legitimate interests of intellectual property rights users, especially in the context of crises such as HIV/AIDS.

Though HIV/AIDS is incurable, drugs have made it treatable. For example, in the United States, retroviral drug treatment has quadrupled the median survival time for Americans diagnosed with HIV/AIDS from one to four years. However, HIV/AIDS remains an intractable problem, particularly in developing countries. In sub-Saharan Africa, over five million people have contracted the virus, half of them between the ages of fifteen and twenty-four. Close to one million of those infected are children.*** The economic and social impact of the virus has been staggering ***.***

IV. THE LEGAL STATUS OF THE DOHA DECLARATION ***

The Doha Declaration captures the middle ground between the positions adopted by developing and developed countries. It embodies commitment to patent protection for the development of new drugs and to availability of these drugs for indigent populations. The third paragraph in the preamble to the Doha Declaration declares that "we recognize that intellectual property protection is important for the development of new medicines. We also recognize the concerns about its effects on prices." The fourth paragraph of the Declaration fortifies this middle ground by affirming that the "TRIPS Agreement can and should be interpreted and implemented in a manner supportive of WTO Members' right to protect public health and, in particular, to promote access to medicines for all."***

Notes and Questions

1. In addition to the problems developing countries face in obtaining or producing low-cost drugs to address public health crises, human rights activists also condemn the exploitation in the pharmaceutical research process. The following declaration is a response by indigenous peoples and their advocates to the practice of patenting naturally occurring and genetically modified human life (*e.g.*, genes and/or genetic products like proteins), animal life, plant life, and micro-organisms. Who "owns" your genes? What specific human rights norms are implicated? *See also* the discussion of indigenous peoples and the right to traditional knowledge in Chapter 6.A.

"NO TO PATENTING OF LIFE!"
INDIGENOUS PEOPLES' STATEMENT ON THE TRADE-RELATED ASPECTS OF INTELLECTUAL PROPERTY RIGHTS (TRIPS) OF THE WTO AGREEMENT

Geneva, Switzerland (July 25, 1999)

WE, INDIGENOUS PEOPLES from around the world, believe that nobody can own what exists in nature except nature herself. A human being cannot own its own mother. Humankind is part of Mother Nature; we have created nothing and so we can in no way claim to be owners of what does not belong to us. But time and again, western legal property regimes have been imposed on us, contradicting our own cosmologies and values.

WE VIEW with regret and anxiety how, Article 27.3b of the Trade-Related Aspects of Intellectual Property Rights (TRIPS) of the World Trade Organization (WTO) Agreements will further denigrate and undermine our rights to our cultural and intellectual heritage, our plant, animal, and even human genetic resources and discriminate against our indigenous ways of thinking and behaving. This Article makes an artificial distinction between plants, animals, and micro-organisms and between "essentially biological" and "microbiological processes" for making plants and animals. As far as we are concerned all these are life forms and life creating processes which are sacred and which should not become the subject of proprietary ownership.

WE KNOW that intellectual property rights as defined in the TRIPS Agreement are monopoly rights given to individual or legal persons (e.g. transnational corporations) who can prove that the inventions or innovations they made are novel, involve an innovative step and are capable of industrial application. The application of this form of property rights over living things as if they are mechanical or industrial inventions is inappropriate. Indigenous knowledge and cultural heritage are collectively and accretionally evolved through generations. Thus, no single person can claim invention or discovery of medicinal plants, seeds or other living things. The inherent conflict between these two knowledge systems and the manner in which they are protected and used will cause further disintegration of our communal values and practices. It can also lead to infighting between indigenous communities over who has ownership over a particular knowledge or innovation. Furthermore, it goes against the very essence of indigenous spirituality which regards all creation as sacred.

WE ARE AWARE of the various implications of the TRIPS Agreement on our lives as indigenous peoples. It will lead to the appropriation of our traditional medicinal plants and seeds and our indigenous knowledge on health, agriculture and biodiversity conservation. It will undermine food security, since the diversity and agricultural production on which our communities depend would be eroded and would be controlled by individual, private and foreign interests. In addition, the TRIPS Agreement will substantially weaken our access to and control over genetic and biological resources; plunder our resources and territories; and contribute to the deterioration of our quality of life.

Notes and Questions

1. For a discussion of TRIPS and the failure to protect indigenous people from biopiracy, *see, e.g.*, Laurence Helfer, *Regime Shifting: The TRIPS Agreement and New Dynamics of International Intellectual Property Lawmaking*, 29 YALE INT'L L.J. 1 (2004); Elizabeth

Longacre, *Advancing Science While Protecting Developing Countries From Exploitation of their Resources and Knowledge*, 13 FORDHAM INTELL. PROP. MEDIA & ENT. L.J. 963 (2003); Pollyanna E. Folkins, *Has the Lab Coat Become the Modern Day Eye Patch? Thwarting Biopiracy of Indigenous Resources by Modifying International Patenting Sytesms*, 13 TRANSNAT'L L. & CONTEMP. PROBS. 339 (2003).

2.   For discussions of advocacy efforts seeking to create an expressly public health-based exception to TRIPS that would ensure access to affordable medicines for developing countries, *see, e.g.*, Brook K. Baker, *Producing HIV/AIDS Medicines for Export/Import Under TRIPS, Articles 31(f), (k), and 30*, TRANS ATLANTIC CONSUMER DIALOGUE 45 (Nov. 6, 2001); Jennifer May Rodgers, *The TRIPS Council's Solution to the Paragraph 6 Problem Toward Compulsory Licensing Viability for Developing Countries*, 13 MINN. J. GLOBAL TRADE 443 (2004); and Alicia Ely Yamin, *Not Just a Tragedy: Access to Medications as a Right Under International Law*, 21 B.U. INT'L L.J. 325 (2003).

3.   For a general discussion of the internationalization of intellectual property rights, *see* Srividhya Ragavan, *The Jekyll and Hyde Story of International Trade: The Supreme Court in Pharma v. Walsh and the TRIPS Agreement*, 38 U. RICH. L. REV. 77 (2004).

4.   For further reading on issues related to the global economy and human rights, *see* WILLEM VAN GENUGTEN ET AL. EDS., WORLD BANK, IMF AND HUMAN RIGHTS: INCLUDING THE TILBURG GUIDING PRINCIPLES ON WORLD BANK, IMF AND HUMAN RIGHTS (2003); RONALD CHARLES WOLF, TRADE, AID, AND ARBITRATE: THE GLOBALIZATION OF WESTERN LAW (2003); ALISON BRYSK, ED., GLOBALIZATION AND HUMAN RIGHTS (2002); SIGRUN SKOGLY, THE HUMAN RIGHTS OBLIGATIONS OF THE WORLD BANK AND THE INTERNATIONAL MONETARY FUND (2001); MICHEL CHOSSUDOVSKY, THE GLOBALISATION OF POVERTY: IMPACTS OF IMF AND WORLD BANK REFORMS (1997); Catherine H. Lee, *To Thine Own Self Be True: IMF Conditionality and Erosion of Economic Sovereignty in the Asian Financial Crisis*, 24 U. PA. J. INT'L ECON. L. 875–904 (2003); Eleanor M. Fox, *Globalization and Human Rights: Looking Out for the Welfare of the Worst Off*, 35 N.Y.U. J. INT'L L. & POL. 201–220 (2002); Stephan Hobe, *The Era of Globalization as a Challenge to International Law*, 40 DUQ. L. REV. 655 (2002); Nsongurua J. Udombana, *How Should We Then Live? Globalization and the New Partnership for Africa's Development*, 20 B.U. INT'L L.J. 293 (2002); David W. Leebron, *Linkages*, 96 AM. J. INT'L L. 5–27 (2002); Padideh Ala'i, *A Human Rights Critique of the WTO: Some Preliminary Observations*, 33 GEO. WASH. INT'L L. REV. 537–53 (2001); Ross P. Buckley, *The Essential Flaw in the Globalization of Capital Markets: Its Impact on Human Rights in Developing Countries*, 32 CAL. W. INT'L L.J. 119 (2001); Ernst-Ulrich Petersman, *The WTO Constitution and Human Rights*, J. INT'L ECON. L. 19–25, (2000); Daniel D. Bradlow, *The World Bank, the IMF, and Human Rights*, 6 TRANSNAT'L L. & CONTEMP. PROBS. 47–90 (1996).

B.   WOMEN IN/AND/UNDER DEVELOPMENT

1.   *Feminist Critiques of Development Discourse*

The roles of women in economic, social, cultural and political life are crucial aspects of development, however it is defined. Women are key actors in agriculture, technology, education, civil service and other public sectors of many societies. In addition, the household work they do (cooking, cleaning, caring for children and the elderly), whether paid or unpaid, supports those who participate in the "public" labor and educational sectors. Nevertheless, post-World War II international development policy tended to ignore or minimize the significance of women and the work they do. That invisibility changed markedly with the rise of the international feminist movement in the 1960s and 1970s.

Feminist scholars have elaborated a substantial critical literature on the subject of gender and development. Such critiques range from a call for the greater inclusion and visibility of women in development planning, to calls for alternative forms of development or for alternatives to development as imagined in the Washington Consensus.

Celestine Nyamu's overview of the major trends in feminist approaches to development policy begins our discussion of feminist critiques:

CELESTINE NYAMU, HOW SHOULD HUMAN RIGHTS AND DEVELOPMENT RESPOND TO CULTURAL LEGITIMIZATION OF GENDER HIERARCHY IN DEVELOPING COUNTRIES?

41 Harv. Int'l L.J. 381, 383–90 (2000)

*** OVERVIEW OF DEVELOPMENT AND HUMAN RIGHTS APPROACHES

*** *Trends in Development and Gender Equity*

The history of development practitioners and scholars' concern with Third World women may be classified into three phases: Women in Development (WID) (early 1970s, influenced by the modernization framework); Women and Development (WAD) (mid-1970s through early 1980s, influenced by Marxist class analysis and dependency theory); and Gender and Development (GAD) (1980s, influenced by postmodernism).

The Women in Development (WID) Phase

Modernization theory, the overall framework in which WID is set, contends that Third World underdevelopment stems from backward, traditional values and social, political, and economic institutions. In the context of modernization, liberal feminism is the framework used to conceptualize women's rights in Third World development. The liberal feminist agenda translates into the WID critique of development practices. WID is concerned not only with the general failure to recognize the contribution of women to development, but also with the denial of benefits to women from the development process.

WID scholarship and practice employ two main strategies to challenge this exclusion of women. First, they challenge the official invisibility of women. Women's contribution to the economy is overlooked, because the established system does not recognize women's work outside the formal market place, including time spent on child care and home management. This invisibility in the economic sphere mirrors the invisibility of women in the political and policymaking spheres.

The second challenge concerns the social status of women in Third World societies and the role that cultural perceptions and practices play in the lives of women. Liberal feminism, in which WID is rooted, asserts that negative stereotypes nurtured through socialization are responsible for holding women back. WID supposes that Third World women's effective participation in development is frustrated by backward and oppressive traditions that constrain women's freedom. According to WID, laws in the public sphere have been modernized through colonial contact, but laws and norms in the private sphere remain repressive.

Critiques of WID

WID approaches have been criticized on four main grounds. First, WID poses no challenge to the structures of development at the national and international level; it only seeks to integrate women within them. Taking the existing structures as fixed, WID fails to link the exploitation of women to exploitation as a component of the global capitalist system. WID does not question the inherent gender imbalance in the structure of the international economic order.

Second, WID arguments emphasize the contribution that women make to development and thereby subordinate equity concerns to efficiency concerns. Women are important to the development process for what they can contribute. WID scholars emphasize what development needs from women and underplay what women need from development. In order to convince development agencies to fund projects that benefit women, WID emphasizes the net economic gain from investing in women. This efficiency rationale was used through 1995 to justify WID projects. Formulations after 1995 do, however, refer to women's participation in development as being both beneficial to economic growth and important for improving the quality of women's lives through empowerment.

Third, WID's approaches assume that opening up the marketplace will guarantee increased participation by women in the market. This assumption presupposes that gender relations and roles within the private, familial sphere will automatically change to enable such participation. WID's focus on the public sphere was a reaction to previous interventions that perceived women only in their roles as mothers and reproducers. These prior development policies only addressed population control and nutritional education. Whereas WID's reaction to this "motherhood" approach is understandable, WID goes too far in the opposite direction to overemphasize the public sphere.

A fourth critique of WID challenges the characterization of Third World cultures as backward and responsible for the absence of women from the mainstream economy. WID has been criticized for stereotyping Third World women as helpless and constrained by oppressive tradition. WID scholarship depicts the "backward other" and thereby consolidates the opposite image of Western women as independent and exercising agency.

In addition, WID views culture as an inflexible and static structural entity that assigns a fixed, inferior identity to women. This picture does not, however, accurately reflect the dynamics of culture and gender relations.

The Women and Development (WAD) Phase

WAD specifically criticized WID for failing to place the issue of gender hierarchy within the context of class inequalities and the inequalities between states at a global level. This critique was inspired by Marxist and dependency theories. For WAD, gender concerns are subordinate to these larger imbalances that create gender inequality; socioeconomic class is the operative framework. Therefore, the problem of women and development is considered best addressed from the perspective of poor women, with a focus on gender exploitation through unequal division of household labor. WAD considers the labor of women in development to be as indispensable as that of the proletariat or peasant in the capitalist system.

Critiques of WAD

Three main critiques of WAD have been voiced. First, WAD has been criticized for treating concepts such as women and sexual division of labor as if they were "'commensurate analytical categories' outside of race, class, history and culture." With no single universal understanding of these concepts, WAD proponents fall into the trap of universalism.

Second, by focusing on class and global inequalities, WAD gives the impression that the condition of women will change only when class or global inequalities are remedied. In other words, women can wait. Alternatively, the focus on economic exploitation can be seen as a naive assumption: Once the economic issues are addressed, all else will fall into place to benefit women.

Finally, critics contend that WAD does not provide guidance on the actual implementation of measures to improve the lives of Third World women. It is difficult to create programmatic proposals—especially at the grassroots level—that implement WAD's radical vision.

The Gender and Development (GAD) Phase

While WID addresses women in isolation (ignoring the sphere of relationships that shape women's identity), the GAD approach gives attention to the social system that defines gender roles differently for men and women. GAD focuses on gender relations and questions the validity of differentiated gender roles and the social and political institutions that shape these roles. Eliminating gender discrimination demands more than a reallocation of resources: It requires altering power relations and fundamentally changing the structure of social relations.

GAD rejects the public/private dichotomy, particularly the characterization of the public sphere of the market economy as productive and the private sphere of reproductive labor (child care, home management, and subsistence agriculture) as unproductive. GAD questions the dominant gender imbalance of intra-household responsibilities and calls for remedial measures, including the provision of state-supported child care facilities. This initiative occurs at a time when most states are cutting back social spending by pushing more burdens into the private domestic sphere (and thus onto women).

GAD's comprehensive approach to social relations considers other forms of social differentiation (such as race, class, ethnicity, and age) to be as important as gender. Accordingly, planners and policymakers need to account for the similarities and differences among women rather than rely on a false assumption of homogeneity. GAD emphasizes that patriarchy operates within and across these other forms of differentiation to disadvantage women further, and concludes that in patriarchal societies men invariably have more power to define and articulate culture.

Critiques of GAD

Even more than those of WAD, GAD's proposals require an overhaul of social, economic, and political institutions. Furthermore, its central proposals to change both gender roles and the system through which they are defined, demand far-reaching reform in gender relations, especially at the family level. This agenda is difficult to implement at the policy level and attracts critics who cite the need to protect privacy and tradition.

While GAD rejects the perception of culture as a fixed entity, the approach continues to portray women as victims of culture. According to GAD's patriarchy ideology, culture is produced through a dynamic process of social construction which men control. Women are thus presented as having no role in the shaping of culture and as only experiencing its oppressive effects.

Influence of WID, WAD, and GAD on Institutional Practice

At the institutional level, WID has had the deepest impact of the three approaches. In the 1970s and 1980s, WID spawned "Women in Development" desks at bilateral and multilateral development agencies, as well as at government ministries. The World Bank established the post of Adviser on Women in Development in 1977, and the United States Agency for International Development (USAID) established the Office of Women in Development as a direct result of the Percy Amendment to the Foreign Assistance Act of 1961.

In addition, both the WID and liberal feminism movements impacted international law with the United Nations Convention on the Elimination of All Forms of Discrimination Against Women (CEDAW). First proposed at the U.N. Decade for Women Conference in Mexico City in 1975, the Convention was opened for signature at the mid-decade conference in Copenhagen in 1980 and entered into force in 1981.

WAD, in contrast, has not had a significant impact on institutional practice. Its focus on poor women resonated with the emphasis on poverty alleviation adopted by multilateral and bilateral agencies in the early 1980s, but this concern overlapped with the predominant WID approach. WAD was, however, able to draw attention to the unusually high levels of poverty experienced by female-headed households. Additionally, non-governmental organizations (NGOs) run by WAD proponents work toward implementing this WAD approach.

The GAD influence on institutions is fairly recent and began after the 1985 U.N. World Conference on Women held in Nairobi, Kenya. Yet, in several important institutions, such as the World Bank, analysts have pointed out that despite the shift from WID-oriented to gender-oriented discourse, little has changed in practice. GAD has, however, substantially influenced the research and training practices of some NGOs, national institutions, bilateral development agencies, and multilateral agencies.***

GAD also appears to have strongly influenced the United Nations Development Programme (UNDP), as indicated by the UNDP's annual Human Development Report —particularly the 1995 report that focuses on gender equality. The report addresses traditional WID issues such as the devaluing or undervaluing of women's work and the exclusion of women from the development process. Overall, however, the report is centrally concerned with engendering the entire development paradigm and moving beyond the limited discussion of equal participation within existing asymmetrical institutional structures. The report advocates comprehensive policy reforms and strong affirmative action to remove the legal, economic, political, and cultural barriers that prevent the exercise of equal rights by women and men. Underscoring the need for institutional transformation, the report notes that, despite marked improvement in women's access to education and health, there has not been a corresponding improvement in economic and political opportunities for women.

The report appears to have been influenced by GAD's advocacy of an approach that integrates productive and reproductive activities and is not restricted to the public sphere. For instance, the key recommendations to broaden the choices of men and women in the workplace aim to encourage men to increase their participation in family care: parental leave, flexible work hours for both men and women, and public day-care facilities. The UNDP seems to have adopted the ideology of the gender framework, but it is still unclear whether the framework has been implemented in practice.***

Notes and Questions

1. The 1995 UNDP Human Development Report, *Gender and Human Development*, referred to by Nyamu, is *available at* http://hdr.undp.org/reports/global/1995/en/ (last visited June 21, 2004). Note that the 1995 report was timed to coincide with the 1995 United Nations Fourth World Conference on Women held in Beijing, China. "Development" was one of the main goals of the conference platform, along with "equality" and "peace." *See* Fourth World Conference on Women: Action for Equality, Development and Peace, Beijing Declaration and Platform for Action, U.N. Doc. A/Conf.177/20 (1995). The conference was a galvanizing event that stimulated a worldwide focus on the status of women and on "women's rights as human rights" at many levels.

2. Nyamu identifies major trends in approaches to gender-related development analysis. She seems to chart a progression in international development institutions from the invisibility of gender analysis, to a focus on gender-specific policies and institutions, to the "mainstreaming" of gender in overall development policy. Which approach do you believe most advances the interests of women? Does the answer to that question depend on the status of women in a particular society? What about differences of class, race, ethnicity, religion or disability among women within each society? How do the interests of women intersect with the development goals of a broader collective, such as a "people," or a "state"?

3. The continent of Africa is one of the most significant targets of post-World War II development policies. This vast region is extremely diverse in geography, political and economic organization, language, culture and religion. Many African countries have a rich heritage of political and social organization, international trade, agricultural production, natural resources and the arts. Nevertheless, many countries in the region also have shared the devastating effects of the trans-Atlantic slave trade, European colonialism (and the related exploitation of human and natural resources), militarization and dictatorial rule (often in conjunction with Cold War brinksmanship between West and East), and, most recently, the rapid spread of HIV/AIDS and other treatable diseases without affordable and available treatments.

African women are at the forefront of the challenges facing the region, including those associated with development. The involvement of African women with development efforts, however, has often been ambivalent. While some have embraced grassroots development efforts in the context of a specific country or region, others have strongly resisted the negative impact of top-down development policies urged on their governments by the IFIs. As Gwendolyn Mikell's article on the impact of structural adjustment policies on women in Ghana demonstrates, top-down development policies can have pervasive, and disturbing, effects on socio-economic and political organization.

GWENDOLYN MIKELL, AFRICAN STRUCTURAL ADJUSTMENT: WOMEN AND LEGAL CHALLENGES

69 ST. JOHN'S L. REV. 7, 7–21 (1995)

*** The multilayered problems of gender inequity in Africa derive from clashes between several cultural and economic systems, power differentials, and historical hierarchies. Modern law, on the other hand, is grounded in procedural and individual-oriented rules of behavior derived from western political economies. The attempt to use modern law to resolve gender inequities, therefore, is a complicated enterprise that produces mixed results and embedded contradictions. Responding to increased pressure from international monetary agencies, external women and development groups, human rights groups, and internal elites, Ghana is one of many African countries passing new legislation in an attempt to modernize family law and revamp the traditional relationship of marriage, gender, and property.

For women, this tripartite relationship has undergone intense trauma over the past two decades as their states have endured cycles of economic collapse followed by political collapse. Consequently, their countries have resorted to loans and economic restructuring programs such as those overseen by the International Monetary Fund ("IMF") and the World Bank ("WB"). These interlocking economic and political crises have had a severe impact on women, children, and the poor. In Ghana and in several other countries, malnutrition among children soared, maternal and infant deaths increased dramatically, and education and health services for women and girls sharply declined. Most troubling, however, is the continuing feminization of poverty as structural adjustment programs ("SAPs") proceed. Although other underdeveloped areas, such as Latin America, have reported similar results after experiencing an economic crisis followed by adjustment programs, African women seem to have endured a situation unique in its intensity.

An understanding of why economic crisis followed by SAPs have had such a severe impact on women may aid in understanding why the current legal change has produced mixed results for women's economic status. In general, the history and effect of the colonial period in African countries has had a significant impact on these countries' contemporary economic systems. The African economies were geared toward the export of agricultural products and minerals produced through traditional economic relationships, not toward industrial, capital-intensive private ownership relations. In fact, the colonial regime greatly benefited from traditional land usufruct rights, polygyny, high female reproduction rates, and male control over the domestic labor of women and children to produce export commodities. In the export sector, these relationships kept export production costs down and state profits high; women and children, however, bore the burden. Comparative data shows that, even today, African women perform approximately eighty percent of agricultural labor and contribute approximately thirty-three percent of household income.

In Ghana, influences of the colonial system have significantly contributed to a contemporary situation where most women have been removed from the category of land-controlling autonomous export farmers. Ghanaian women have become increasingly more dependent upon male relatives who own export farms, and the penny profits earned by trading domestic foodstuff in a declining domestic market. Female education rates have decreased as more men have moved toward modern, wage-earning sectors of the economy. Additionally, the colonial regime, rather than investing export-derived foreign exchange in internal infrastructure and industry, encouraged either the investment of this capital abroad or in the import of food from western countries. Post-independence African countries continued this pattern. By paying producers the lowest prices possible, countries could funnel export income to other sectors (particularly in supporting the bureaucracy), and appease urbanites who were increasingly distrustful of the government. Thus, women's situation between the 1960s and the 1990s deteriorated with the desperate competition to control foreign exchange—the only source of wealth.

The *** collapse of African economies and their subsequent restructuring have also greatly contributed to the shaping of today's African economies. In the late 1970s and 1980s, after the oil shocks, many African economies collapsed because prices on export commodities fell, rural production plummeted, and external debt rose. The foreign exchange available was insufficient to support the predominantly male state bureaucracy, civil service, and the urban infrastructure, and provide an income for rural producers. In response, economic adjustment programs from the WB and the IMF were implemented to introduce more market-oriented policies into African economies. These programs specifically required that African countries: 1) devalue currency to destroy parallel markets, moderate imports, and encourage diversified exports; 2) privatize the economy by cutting subsidies for food, social services such as education and health, and inputs for farming; 3) create a legal and economic climate encouraging private investment; 4) liberalize trade by removing import or producer taxes, thus allowing market principles to operate in setting agricultural and other prices; and 5) trim government bureaucracy, sell many state-owned enterprises, cut wages, and retrench government workers. Over thirty African countries have adopted these programs.

African women have been severely affected by these changes, which were accompanied by massive male migration from rural areas, steadily climbing divorce rates, and the abandonment of wives and children. Although some women migrated, rural households primarily became enclaves of females, children, and the elderly. One net result was that female-headed households were left to continue the desperate competition to control foreign exchange from exports. In addition, many women wage earners were cut from urban payrolls. In rural areas, women's subsistence farming declined, their petty-trading businesses collapsed, and they were the primary victims of cuts in education and other social services. Furthermore, there were dramatic increases in medical costs for maternity care, and phenomenal increases in infant malnutrition and maternal deaths. In Zimbabwe, for example, under structural adjustment in 1992, maternity costs rose from $140 to $500, a price far higher than the monthly salary of the ordinary family.

African women's groups and state leaders have been forced to confront the feminization of poverty and the negative impacts of SAPs. Prior to these two developments, few African countries had constitutional provisions guaranteeing gender equity, and even fewer were active in enforcing laws protecting women's rights. Although some leaders grumbled about "hegemonic pressures" to address women's issues, and responded with what anthropologists call "disemia," [3] some countries did respond to the pressure

---

[3]   "Disemia" occurs when tutelary outsiders define the criteria of local culture and insiders find it necessary to disguise those aspects of ordinary social life that conflict with imposed

for change. Some African leaders were hesitant to challenge traditional laws and elevate women's legal status because they feared that this would exaggerate the problem and foment civil unrest and religious tensions. In addition, among themselves, African states had somewhat different views concerning the solutions. In Nigeria, for example, women's groups focused less on the impact of SAPs on women and more on the general government indifference to women's rights. These groups insisted that three steps are necessary to eliminate female domestic exploitation; governments must: first, visibly support the international conventions that call for women's human rights; second, declare women's autonomy as individual persons; third, legally reinforce women's rights to hold property and resources as individuals separate from men. Only then will changes in family law make sense and have positive consequences.

African countries are beginning to experience a new legal focus on women's rights. Often this legal change coincides with pressures of economic adjustment and democratization. Modernization of the law creates an environment that supports free market reform as well as its accompanying institutional framework—the democratic process. The dialogue among three major actors—the judiciary, the military government, and the international community—has had the greatest effect on the process of modernizing family law in Africa. Community leaders and women play a secondary but important part in promoting legislation. The gender equity laws imposed, whether initiated by military governments or civilian advocacy groups, face severe challenges from local culture. These laws must be vigilantly guarded to offset the contradictions which result.

In examining the effectiveness of "imposed" law as it clashes with cultural realities, it is appropriate to examine the issues inherent in using the legal changes in family law to alter women's economic access to resources. There are two important elements of such legal change: 1) conjugal, spousal, or nuclear family resource allocations; and 2) women's individual access to resources within lineage, joint, or communal property regimes. In western democracies, modern law operates in a climate which presupposes the existence of the nuclear family within a highly capitalized and industrialized society where many state institutions exist to reinforce individual rights. In Africa, structural adjustment planners hoped to foster individual rights within a rationalized economic environment, recognizing this as a requirement for future economic stabilization. These western concepts, however, differ from African traditional law, which has permeated the lives of indigenous people. Consequently, African women find themselves unable to take advantage of new legal rights, either because other persons prevent them from doing so, or because they fear social harm in other arenas should they try.

In Ghana, the Provisional National Defense Council ("PNDC") responded to the new focus on women's rights by enacting laws affecting women's access to economic family resources and the rights of women to own and hold property. Under most traditional African laws, the "conjugal couple" is a tenuous unit because husbands and wives belong to separate family groups. Few, if any, joint economic interests exist because jointly created property may be converted into the husband's property, accessible only to members of his family. Recent Ghanaian legislation, however, explicitly attempts to recognize and legally create the concept of a conjugal family in order to achieve a certain "moral justice" and economic access for women.

---

models. It is the "play of cultural contradictions produced by conditional independence . . . enjoyed only on the sufferance of some more powerful entity." MICHAEL HERZFELD, ANTHROPOLOGY THROUGH THE LOOKING-GLASS 123–24 (1989).

In Ghana, it was urban women who were first ready to take advantage of the new family legislation to alter access to conjugal or spousal resources—especially maintenance. Yet many urban women were reduced to poverty and dependency by the economic crisis and, in order to take advantage of the new laws, had to move past their traditional inhibitions regarding seeking from men monetary payments belonging to another lineage system. For example, the Marriage Registration Act legitimized marriages made under any marital system so that women could gain their rights as wives. Beginning in 1982, to utilize rights that were not previously enforced, urban women also took advantage of Maintenance of Children ordinances to make demands upon their husbands or children's fathers. In fact, it was urban women, many of whom were single mothers or women who had been involuntarily transformed into the female heads of their households, who argued that they had no choice but to seek legal redress in order to keep their children alive given the fragility of family support during the crises in the national economy. There is a contradiction, however, because, although women are legally empowered, their access to the resources they need to determine their economic fate and actively participate in economic development is not actually increased. In a legal sense, these changes have lessened the control traditional culture exercised over Ghanaian women as wives, while making them more vulnerable as mothers and household heads.

For example, due to the Maintenance of Children Act, there has been increased responsibility of husbands and fathers for the economic support of their children.*** Should the court find the father financially liable, as it increasingly does, it may garnish wages, imprison, or otherwise pursue a delinquent father. Unfortunately, the flexibility of men's work situations results in the majority of women never receiving in full the mandated sum of money, leaving them economically vulnerable. Any penny profits these women make in the informal economy cannot be used to generate additional income and alleviate poverty since the money must be used to feed their children.***

A contradiction exists in legally entitling a wife to resources which she may not have the ability to negotiate as an individual. Strong traditional sentiments for corporate or lineage property regimes often encourage family members to frustrate the woman's ability to exercise her modern legal rights. Laws to counter these attacks either do not exist or are not enforced. Thus, women argue that "the legislation has no teeth." In fact, the process of litigation itself may make women more economically dependent upon men. In response, some women have begun to support the revival of women's community-based traditional mechanisms of dispute resolution, such as the "Queen Mother" system, in order to avoid the social complications which accompany the use of the modern court system. Women's hesitation to assert their legal rights is compounded by the fact that dual or triple legal systems still exist. The legislation has neither removed the participation of the larger lineage or kinship group in the economic affairs of husband and wife, nor eliminated their economic interests in the estate owned by one of the partners. By emphasizing women's rights to inherit and own property, when women have not achieved the economic and social capacity to gain complete control of property or to benefit from it sufficiently to support themselves and their children, the law has created a false image of women's rights.

The need for legal rights to economic resources remains a major problem confronted by many African women. Some scholars suggest that, even when laws are introduced to remove inequities under the customary system, the customary system continues to operate. Polygyny, a system that originally helped sustain the food production sys-

tem, continues to exist even though it may now complicate the distribution of land following the husband's death. In Liberia and other areas, women's economic status is still
inhibited by the continued customary practice of repaying dowries or "damage fees" to
the man's family if the widow chooses to leave the family and pursue her autonomous
economic livelihood.***

In conclusion, there are three major points that should be emphasized. First, it is
clear that the unstable economies of the 1980s have created situations encouraging the
feminization of poverty, and that attempts to restructure the economy by aligning it with
the market have failed to change the fact that women still remain the neglected partners. Structural adjustment programs required financial sacrifices which, almost without exception, negatively affected many arenas essential to women's well-being—health,
education, and access to agricultural resources capital.

Second, other ameliorating factors, such as quiet gender conditionalities attached
to SAPs, have raised the issue of the relationship between women's legal rights and
women's economic access and power. It is too optimistic to assume that the legal right
to own property and economic resources will give women the power to participate as
individuals in receiving resources and developing the national economy.

Third, there appear to be some prerequisites for women to actively participate in
economic development. Some authorities conclude that none of the changes that have
surrounded structural adjustment have addressed the severe structural problems that
women face. Women must have improved land rights, adequate access to credit, productive input, and extension training in order to relieve the "heavy burdens placed on
them to meet the productive and reproductive needs of their households."

Women, development experts, and those who have studied the impact of structural
adjustment are in agreement that rights to land ownership, access to credit, and ownership of capital are essential for African women to be able to fully participate in development. Prior to the focus on women's legal rights, the agricultural departments of
some African countries sporadically addressed women's needs. These attempts, however, were never consistent or effective and often ceased during the economic crises
leading up to structural adjustment. Nongovernmental organizations have assisted
women's economic activities since 1975, but have been unable to effectively interact
with government ministries. In places like Kenya, Sierra Leone, and Swaziland, where
only men own land, women's bureaus need to broaden their mandates to include legal
issues affecting women's land ownership.

[A]ttempts to modernize family law under the diverse chaotic conditions that
existed in Africa during the 1980s demonstrate that, while women's economic rights
are on the agenda, women's economic status continues to be held hostage by cultural
forces and by the contemporary dynamics of the state and global marketplace. On paper,
policymakers can claim that women as wives have been given rights. The final question,
however, is how policy makers will "put teeth in the legislation," so that women's ownership rights will be reinforced at all levels—domestic, local, community, and national.
In the coming years, one of the major challenges facing those concerned with women's
rights and gender equity will be to support the growing number of indigenous, grassroots groups and organizations. These groups are attempting to inform women of their
rights, support women as they pursue rights through the modern legal system, and offer
alternative cultural routes to achieve a level of economic stability and participation that
can supplement reliance on the court system.***

Notes and Questions

1. *Gender Conditionality.* Should international lending institutions attach conditions to loans or grants that require a government to ensure the legal equality of women? If so, what specific conditions would you attach? What are the implications of such conditions?

2. *Law vs. Custom.* Mikell notes that "[t]he need for legal rights to economic resources remains a major problem confronted by many African women. Some scholars suggest that, even when laws are introduced to remove inequities under the customary system, the customary system continues to operate." If so, what role should the state play, if any, in addressing customs that seem to oppose the legal economic rights of women? Inheritance rights, control over property and family relationships tend to be a major source of controversy in gender-related development analysis. Who should decide whether a particular custom violates the legal rights of women? *See* the discussion of culture and gender in Chapter 6, *infra,* and the requirements of the Women's Convention in Chapter 3, *supra.*

3. *Population Policy and Development.* Some development strategists see curbing population growth as an essential aspect of the development process, although in recent years population growth in some regions has slowed considerably due to the devastating effects of HIV/AIDS. Many human rights activists within and outside the developing world support laws and policies that allow women and their families to decide on the number and spacing of their children and access to the information and means necessary to do so. *See, e.g.,* Office of the High Commissioner for Human Rights, Reproductive Rights: Recommendations of the Expert Group Meeting, "Application of Human Rights to Reproductive Sexual Health," Geneva, June 25–27, 2001, *available at* http://www.unhchr.ch/women/focus-reproducthr.html.

However, reproductive and population policies involve complex personal, community and socio-economic decisions that implicate civil, political, economic, social and cultural rights. For example, international organizations note that increasing the access of girls and women to free public education, as well as to reproductive health care, reduces overall birth rates. *See, e.g.,* Commission on Population and Development, 36th Session, Education for Women and Girls Vital for Achieving Development Goals Population Commission Told at Opening of Thirty-sixth Session, (Press Release), U.N. Doc. POP/856 (Mar. 31, 2003). *See also* United Nations Children's Fund (UNICEF), *The State of the World's Children: 2004, available at* http://www.unicef.org/sowc04/index.html (last visited June 23, 2004) (focusing on "girls' education and its relationship to all other development goals.***") *and* United Nations, "Programme of Action of the International Conference on Population and Development," *in Report of the International Conference on Population and Development* (Cairo, Sept. 5–13, 1994): paras. 7.2–7.3, *available at* http://www.unfpa.org/icpd/reports&doc/icpdpoae.html (last visited June 23, 2004).

Population "control" policies have also taken ominous forms, including the coercive use of experimental and possibly dangerous contraceptive drugs in the Third World and among women of color in western countries, forced or coerced sterilization and abortions, and infanticide. For a discussion of the legal implications of a privately funded international "campaign" to sterilize poor women, *see* Judith A.M. Scully, *Maternal Mortality, Population Control, and the War in Women's Wombs: A Bioethical Analysis of Quinacrine Sterilizations,* 19 WISC. INT'L L.J. 103 (2001).

HOPE LEWIS, WOMEN (UNDER)DEVELOPMENT: THE RELEVANCE OF "THE RIGHT TO DEVELOPMENT" TO POOR WOMEN OF COLOR IN THE UNITED STATES

18 LAW & POL'Y (U.K.) 281, 291–92 (1996)

WOMEN, DEVELOPMENT, HUMAN RIGHTS: COMPATIBLE OR INCOMPATIBLE?

Rhoda Howard, among others, has been critical of the idea that the right to development is necessarily emancipatory for women in the developing world:

> Specific grievances of African women against both the African state and African men are lost. African women, like Africa in general, become the innocent victims of Western imperialism, and, as with Africa in general, their primary claim is for the right to development. Thus we come full circle: the rights of women *in* development become the right of women *to* development, defined not by them but by the development establishment, both inside and outside their own country. To break this circle requires assertion of women's rights, separate from development, possibly against the development establishment, and not necessarily compatible with the development enterprise.

According to Howard, "the agenda of women's rights intersects, but is not synonymous with, the agenda of development." Howard's concerns that the individual rights of African women will tend to be trumped by the agendas of non-democratic African governments, private interests, and international development agencies are well taken. Resources allocated to improve the status of poor women have been cynically diverted to further line the pockets of those in power in both the North and the South.

Other feminists, many among them women of color, find it ironic that the *inclusion* of women in certain forms of development contributes to the violation of their human rights. Merely recognizing that women play an important role in the economy does not lead to more equitable development policies of benefit to women and their communities. The institutional focus on WID is often based in women's role as economically efficient workers for manufacturing or agribusiness.

African-American feminist and international human rights activist Loretta Ross has noted:

> The prevailing opinion of why women are underdeveloped and why such a tremendous amount of poverty still exists is that women have been left out of the development process. Thus solutions are predicated upon bringing women into the development process. Unfortunately, this is the opposite of what has happened. The facts are that Western style development does not leave African women out, it includes them by exploiting their labor, confiscating their land, and robbing them of their natural resources. African women are very much in the middle of development—as the pawns of development, not the beneficiaries of development.[4]

In these excerpts, both Howard and Ross see development as inconsistent with the promotion of the human rights of women, although Ross more precisely targets her cri-

---

[4]   Rhoda E. Howard, *Women's Rights and the Right to Development*, in HUMAN RIGHTS AND GOVERNANCE IN AFRICA (R. Cohen, G. Hyden, and W. P. Nagan, eds., 1993) at 118.

tique on "Western-style" development. It is, in fact, the separation of women's self-defined human rights—including the right to alternative forms of development—from official economic, legal, and social policies that makes development a problematic force in the lives of poor women of color.***

Shelley Wright provides another feminist perspective on the significance of women's work in the "developed" and "developing" worlds:

SHELLEY WRIGHT, WOMEN AND THE GLOBAL ECONOMIC ORDER: A FEMINIST PERSPECTIVE

10 AM. U. J. INT'L L. & POL'Y 861, 861–83 (1995)

*** Women's position within international economic law is an extremely complex story. Women are affected in different ways by the operation of economic systems depending on their class, race, nationality, religion, language, disability, sexual preference and education.*** Although the enormous diversity among women makes the picture of their economic burdens and contributions more complicated, the theoretical application of differences among women should not obscure the harsh reality that women universally perform a disproportionate amount of the world's work for a very small share of the world's resources. The Joint Consultative Group on Policy (an umbrella organization coordinating policy studies for various United Nations bodies) has found:

> Numerous studies provide unassailable evidence that the stereotypical gender division of labor is a reality throughout the world. There are only minor variations from place to place, mainly in the extent to which women have responsibility for providing as well as preparing food and in the scale of remunerated activities they undertake in addition to household tasks. Women almost universally work longer hours than men. The addition of remunerated activities to women's workload leads to little or no reduction in their domestic tasks.

The ideological construction of the world into public and private spheres is also important. Western liberal theory has constructed the private sphere of home, children and domesticity as the space where women live and work for much of their time. This sphere tends to be hidden—invisible to the public world of law, governments, States, international institutions and transnational corporations—the sphere where men are said to live and work. Men typically have access both to the private world and the public world of international law and legal structures. But women have greater difficulty in penetrating the public sphere. In addition, this Western division of the world into public and private spheres helps maintain an international economic order which perpetuates social dislocation and poverty both in First World countries and the Third World. The private world of the North American housewife, as well as the public worlds of law, business and government, rely on the labor of low-paid workers, female and male, on farms and factories throughout the world.

One of the consequences of the *** North American Free Trade Agreement (NAFTA) has been to increase the mobility of capital in North America, thereby making jobs in the workforce extremely vulnerable to corporate decisions to close factories and relocate businesses to regions or countries where costs (especially labor costs) are lower.*** One of the fears NAFTA generated in the United States is that jobs will continue to migrate south to Mexico. Although women, as a source of cheap labor, may benefit from access to these relocated jobs, this work is highly exploitative and features low wages, poor working conditions, suppression of trade unions, and little opportunity for security or advancement.***

The closure of traditional male "breadwinner" jobs in developed economies also has a major impact on women. Women who have relied on the traditional role of housewife and mother within a monogamous marriage are vulnerable to poverty, marital violence and disruption as the shutting down of traditional male jobs increases. Such women are forced to look for work which is often low-paid. The alternative is social assistance. Women's responsibilities for feeding, clothing and providing shelter and education for their children again remains the same. Western women who engage in paid work generally spend around thirty to forty hours per week on housework. This expenditure occurs regardless of whether or not they have remained in a relationship with a man. Their paid work tends to earn considerably less than men's work so that women are underpaid for one job and unpaid for their second. It is estimated that even in a wealthy Western country, such as Canada, women receive only thirty-five to forty percent of the total income paid to all male and female recipients.

An analysis of international economic structures illustrates that gender bias and discrimination are among the most important contributing factors to women's oppression on a global basis. International economic legal regimes contribute to this oppression. The nature of women's work, how we characterize economic rights, and the way in which countries formulate and implement global economic policies are all crucially important for any feminist analysis of the international legal order.

Women's Work

When we in the Western developed world think of "women's work" we tend to think of the following activities:

Preparing food, setting the table, serving meals, clearing food and dishes from the table, washing dishes, dressing her children, disciplining children, taking the children to childcare or school, disposing of garbage, dusting, gathering clothes for washing, doing the laundry, going to the petrol station and the supermarket, repairing household items, ironing, keeping an eye on or playing with children, making beds, paying bills, caring for pets and plants, putting away toys, books and clothes, sewing or mending or knitting, talking with door-to-door salespeople, answering the telephone, vacuuming, sweeping and washing floors, cutting the grass, weeding, and shoveling snow, cleaning the bathroom and the kitchen, and putting her children to bed.

Although modern "kitchen technology," fast foods and the supermarket have led to the belief that women now spend less time on housework, this assumption is not born out by research. Housewives in the Western model, who are not employed outside the home, still spend between sixty to eighty hours per week on household chores.***

Work became specialized and men's tasks have become privileged, i.e. given value within the marketplace. A major task for feminist analysts has been to insist on the value of women's labor and to redress the imbalance in gender roles, if not to eliminate them altogether. Major differences exist among feminists, however, as to how to achieve these goals. Is it better to try and bring women into the traditional workforce? If so, what about the specialized tasks of childcare and household maintenance? Should we incorporate these into the money economy, either through the imposition of notional values, or through the actual assignment of these tasks to paid workers? Or should we be looking at economic analyses which go beyond a cash nexus? If so, what would be our measure of value? And is there not a danger that one will factor the unpaid work of women in as a support to the existing money economy, thus entrenching women's subordination?

The Western normative model of women engaged in full-time, unpaid housework is now relatively uncommon as more women enter the workforce, marriages break up or women have children outside marriage. The high incidence of marital breakdown and sole parenting in affluent countries such as Australia, Canada and the United States has revealed the extent of women's poverty, or what is now being called the "feminization of poverty." Further, the work done by women is not counted as "work" in any system of economic measurement. Housework is not only unpaid, it is also of no value within material production. The role of women as consumers, producers and caregivers is relied on within the Western economic model as freely given, thus reducing or eliminating the need for government or private enterprise to provide these services or subsidize them within the money economy.***

What characterizes "women's work," however, differs around the world. Within African economies, for example (despite internal variations) women make other contributions and carry other burdens. Since the introduction of cash crop and primary industries in many developing countries, women have had to manage a greater role in caring and providing for their families. This often includes subsistence farming and marketing of produce as well as household work and child care. The backbone of the "informal," i.e. hidden or unmeasured, economy in much of Africa is the work of women. The "informal economy" can in fact form a significant proportion, if not the majority, of the real working economy of developing countries. Where the men have migrated to industrial or agricultural work elsewhere, women become the effective centers of all economic and family life within their villages, neighborhoods and districts. Daily tasks might include fetching water and firewood (tasks pollution, drought and deforestation complicate), preparing food, caring for children, as well as working in the fields where up to seventy-five percent of the food consumed in Africa is grown. The only alternatives are to seek work for low wages in agricultural enterprises, or migrate to the cities where the choices often revolve around urban poverty, domestic service, low paid factory work or prostitution.

Constant over-work that existing economic standards do not deem "productive" burdens the lives of most African women. Their provision of basic services is under constant threat from the introduction of Western development models and the shift from subsistence farming to cash-crop agriculture. The Western model of the private sphere extends to development projects overseas such that "Women in Development" issues are often seen as revolving around motherhood, ignoring the crucial roles that women play in the agricultural and market economy.

International Standards for Economic Well-Being

There are many possible feminist perspectives on international economic law. One approach would focus on the right of all persons to social justice, a more equal allocation of resources, and an adequate standard of living or "economic well-being" that includes individual rights to food and freedom from hunger, adequate health care, a healthy environment, housing, education, social assistance of some form in the case of sickness, disability or some other social disadvantage, and freedom from civil strife and war. One might regard these rights as necessary for the "creation of conditions of stability and well-being, which are necessary for peaceful and friendly relations among nations."***

One advantage of a feminist perspective focusing on economic well being and the right of all people to an adequate standard of living is that it requires constant reference to the reality of women's experiences. This view focuses on women's traditional roles in the private sphere in providing these basic services, therefore, it is impossible to avoid the conclusion that women who receive little, if any, recognition or reward for their work largely provide international economic and social rights. Another advantage of this approach is that there is already a body of international law, particularly within the ICESCR, which can be elaborated, discussed and even implemented. But there are also serious disadvantages.

First, by focusing on women's traditional roles in providing for basic economic and social services we run the danger of replicating the very economic and social constructions which oppress women and trap them in positions of exploitation. We then may focus too exclusively on women as victims, or on women working individually or in small groups to redress their victimization. We may leave larger fields of economic and political power out of the discussion.

Secondly, by relying on an already existing discourse of rights we may fail to question the underlying assumptions of that discourse, including the division between political and civil rights from economic, social and cultural rights. Rights tend to focus on individuals. Even group rights, however, are inadequate to capture the complexity of women's economic positions. Finally, although specific measures such as Article 11 of the ICESCR exist to focus the discussion and to provide possible solutions, the rights are drafted in ways which ignore women's contributions and needs. The language refers to an adequate standard of living for "himself and his family," assuming that the Western nuclear family model is the global norm. The need to ensure equitable distribution of food supplies assumes that development, technology transfer, the dissemination of knowledge (specifically scientific knowledge) and agrarian reform are necessary. The basic assumption of Article 11 is that of a Western concept of growth and development, technical and scientific assistance and "reform" of agrarian techniques, none of which may be appropriate to the guarantee of economic well-being to a particular group of people, or within a particular region. The rights to education, housing, social security and other economic and social rights are based on similar assumptions.***

The "Bretton Woods System" and Development

*** The consequences of IMF and World Bank policies on the economic well-being of a country can be severe. Currency devaluations often translate into inflation as foreign imports rise in price. The aim is to make national exports more attractive, but where a country has little to sell overseas, or where it relies on one or two commodities controlled by First World cartels, the result may simply be a drastic lowering of the standard of living. Reduction in public spending may decrease a country's debt burden, but the principle losses will usually be in the areas of education, health care, social assistance, poverty relief and the provision of basic supplies of food, shelter, clean water and reasonably priced fuel. Women usually have the primary responsibility of providing these essentials to their families. Where the state retracts from assistance in these areas, it is on women that the increased burden falls. Indeed, it appears that World Bank and other development projects rely on the unpaid labor of women to provide a safety net where social programs are cut.***

Development, as it is channelled through the financial, monetary and trading wings of the "Bretton Woods System" has tended therefore to entrench and extend a Western free market economic model in both the First World and the Third World. This capitalist model depends on growth and expansion, the proliferation and export of First World technology, the gearing of developing economies to servicing First World industrial needs and the exploitation and frequent despoliation of Third World economic and social structures. Women and children, because of their invisibility within the international economic system, have tended to suffer a disparate proportion of the burden. Even more seriously, the traditional unpaid labor of women as household workers, subsistence farmers and marketers and as the providers of basic services (characterized in international law as economic and social rights) provides the safety net and supporting infrastructure for the international economic order. Without the exploited labor of women, the system could not function.***

Notes and Questions

1.   Wright observes that the division of labor "has become specialized and men's tasks have become privileged, *i.e.*, given value within the marketplace." She then notes that there is significant disagreement among feminists as to how the value of the work women do should be recognized:

> Is it better to try and bring women into the traditional workforce? If so, what about the specialized tasks of childcare and household maintenance? Should we incorporate these into the money economy, either t through the imposition of notional values, or through the actual assignment of these tasks to paid workers? Or should we be looking at economic analyses which go beyond a cash nexus? If so, what would be our measure of value? And is there not a danger that one will factor the unpaid work of women in as a support to the existing money economy, thus entrenching women's subordination?

What is your perspective on these questions? Should housework for one's own family be compensated? If so, in what form? Is making it a tax-deductible item a viable approach? Should compensation depend on the presence of children or the elderly in the home? Why, or why not?

2.   Some scholars point out that the work of women of color and immigrant women has had a long history of commodification (through slavery, indentured servitude and low-wage domestic service for example). Similarly, in some developing countries, women and girls from rural areas work as low-wage household workers in urban communities. In Jamaica, for example, such workers are known as "helpers." What do these observations imply for the questions raised by Wright?

3.   The sociological and legal literature on the value of women's household work is large and growing. *See e.g.*, ADELLE BLACKETT, MAKING DOMESTIC WORK VISIBLE: THE CASE FOR SPECIFIC REGULATION (1998); Frances Olsen, *The Family and the Market: A Study of Ideology and Legal Reform*, 96 HARV. L. REV. 1497 (1983); Naomi R. Cahn, *Gendered*

Identities: Women and Household Work, 44 VILL. L. REV. 525 (1999); WOMEN'S WORK AND WOMEN'S LIVES: THE CONTINUING STRUGGLE WORLDWIDE (Hilda Kahne & Janet Z. Giele eds., 1992); Dorothy E. Roberts, *Spiritual and Menial Housework*, 9 YALE J.L. & FEMINISM 51 (1997); JUDITH ROLLINS, BETWEEN WOMEN: DOMESTICS AND THEIR EMPLOYERS (1985); Reva B. Siegel, *Home as Work: The First Women's Rights Claim Concerning Wives' Household Labor, 1850–1880*, 103 YALE L.J. 1073 (1994); Katherine Silbaugh, *Turning Labor into Love: Housework and the Law*, 91 NW. U. L. REV. 1 (1996); Peggie R. Smith, *Regulating Paid Household Work: Class, Gender, Race, and Agendas of Reform*, 48 AM. U. L. REV. 851 (1999); Joan Williams, *Toward a Reconstructive Feminism: Reconstructing the Relationship of Market Work and Family Work*, 19 N. ILL. U. L. REV. 89 (1998).

4. For readings on the particular racial, class and migration status issues raised by household work under contemporary globalization, *see, e.g.*, Taunya Lovell Banks, *Toward a Global Critical Feminist Vision: Domestic Work and the Nanny Tax Debate*, 3 J. GENDER, RACE & JUSTICE 1 (1999); GRACE CHANG, DISPOSABLE DOMESTICS: IMMIGRANT WOMEN WORKERS IN THE GLOBAL ECONOMY (2000); Evelyn Nakano Glenn, *Cleaning Up/Kept Down: A Historical Perspective on Racial Inequality in "Women's Work,"* 43 STAN. L. REV. 1333 (1991); Kevin R. Johnson, *Los Olvidados: Images of the Immigrant, Political Power of Noncitizens, and Immigration Law and Enforcement*, 1993 BYU L. REV. 1139, 1143–44 (1993); Patricia Fernandez Kelly, *Underclass and Immigrant Women as Economic Actors: Rethinking Citizenship in a Changing Global Economy*, 9 AM. U. J. INT'L L. & POL'Y 151 (1993); Hope Lewis, *Lionheart Gals Facing the Dragon: the Human Rights of Inter/National Black Women in the United States*, 76 OR. L. REV. 567 (1997); Hope Lewis, *Universal Mother: Transnational Migration and the Human Rights of Black Women in the Americas*, 5 J. GENDER, RACE & JUSTICE 197 (2001); Audrey Macklin, *Women as Migrants: Members in National and Global Communities*, 19 CAN. WOMAN STUD. 24 (1999); Donna E. Young, *Working Across Borders: Global Restructuring and Women's Work*, 2001 UTAH L. REV. 1 (2001). *See also* the discussion of women workers under globalization *supra* Section B.3.

5. Wright notes that "women, who receive little, if any, recognition or reward for their work largely provide international economic and social rights." Do you agree? One interpretation of Wright's statement might be that women are largely responsible for providing the services necessary for the fulfillment of those rights. But who is, or should be, responsible for their overall implementation?

6. While the Bretton Woods system and the Washington Consensus have had an enormous impact on the lives of women and men in the Third World, they have also had significant implications for the "Second World"—the former Soviet-bloc countries—as well. *See, e.g.*, the discussion of trafficking in Eastern European women to the West for prostitution in Chapter 1.

7. Wright implies that the international economic order could not function "without the exploited labor of women." Do you agree?

8. For further reading on gender and development issues, *see, e.g.*, ESTER BOSERUP, WOMAN'S ROLE IN ECONOMIC DEVELOPMENT (1970); CYNTHIA ENLOE, BANANAS, BEACHES AND BASES: MAKING FEMINIST SENSE OF INTERNATIONAL POLITICS (1989); THIRD WORLD WOMEN AND THE POLITICS OF FEMINISM (Chandra Talpade Mohanty *et al.* eds., 1991); CAROLYN O.N. MOSER, GENDER PLANNING AND DEVELOPMENT: THEORY, PRACTICE AND TRAINING (1993); GITA SEN & CAREN GROWN, DEVELOPMENT, CRISES, AND ALTERNATIVE VISIONS: THIRD WORLD WOMEN'S PERSPECTIVES (1987); MORTGAGING WOMEN'S LIVES:

FEMINIST CRITIQUES OF STRUCTURAL ADJUSTMENT (Pamela Sparr ed., 1994); WOMEN PAY THE PRICE: STRUCTURAL ADJUSTMENT IN AFRICA AND THE CARIBBEAN (GLORIA THOMAS-EMEAGWALI ED., 1995); Vasuki Nesiah, *Towards A Feminist Internationality: A Critique of U.S. Feminist Legal Scholarship*, 16 HARV. WOMEN'S L.J. 189 (1993); Joseph Oloka-Onyango & Sylvia Tamale, *"The Personal is Political," Or, Why Women's Rights are Indeed Human Rights: An African Perspective on International Feminism*, 17 HUM. RTS. Q. 691 (1995). *See also* the Web sites of Development Alternatives With Women for a New Era (DAWN) at http://www.dawn.org.fj/ and that of the Women's Environment and Development Organization (WEDO), *at* http://www.wedo.org/.

9. For a critical race perspective on development policy, *see* Chantal Thomas, *Critical Race Theory and Postcolonial Development Theory: Observations on Methodology*, 45 VILL. L. REV. 1195 (2000).

2. Case Study: Gender, Poverty, Development and U.S. Welfare "Reform"

The economic, social and cultural rights of women and their families are issues for the "developed" countries of the North as well as for the Third World. Critics of U.S. welfare "reform" efforts in the 1990s, for example, saw the resulting status of poor people as recreating the Third World in the First World.

HOPE LEWIS, WOMEN (UNDER)DEVELOPMENT: THE RELEVANCE OF "THE RIGHT TO DEVELOPMENT" TO POOR WOMEN OF COLOR IN THE UNITED STATES

18 LAW & POL'Y (U.K.) 281, 282–84, 289–90, 293 (1996)

I. INTRODUCTION

*** [D]evelopment, in the narrow form of a thriving industrial sector, reliable infrastructure, and steady economic growth, remains beyond the reach of many nations—particularly the poorer nations of Africa. More importantly, the broader goals of human development—access to basic needs and an improved quality of life—are denied to millions of people within "developed" nations as well.***

Women of color who are poor in the United States struggle with the effects of underdevelopment while surrounded by the resources of the most economically developed nation on earth. These women experience violations of their social and economic human rights that are strikingly similar to those affecting poor women of color in the rest of the Global South.*** "Development" implies progress toward better living conditions; instead, the lives of poor women of color, and of those they care for most, grow steadily worse.***

In the most ironic sense of the words, poor women of color in the U.S. live "under" development. Nevertheless, many poor women of color are not simply victims of the crushing effects of class, gender, and ethnic discrimination and exploitation—they actively resist these conditions and struggle to maintain the well-being of their families and their communities. The activism of such women has been a central (if underrecognized) base of support for the success of the U.S. civil rights movement and the women's rights movement, as well as for struggles for economic equity.

The language of rights has been a key tool of empowerment for many disadvantaged groups including people of color, women, and the women of color who intersect both groups. As part of a larger strategy, leaders of minority ethnic groups in the United States have based their appeals for social justice on human rights concepts and have appealed to international institutions to assist in publicizing or supporting their struggles. Both W.E.B. DuBois and Malcolm X hoped to present violations of the human rights of African-Americans before the United Nations. The indigenous peoples and nations of the Americas have looked to the international human rights system as an alternative means of redressing harms not adequately addressed under domestic law and policy.***

Could poor women of color in the U.S. claim the right to development while geographically located within a highly developed national economy? If they were to do so, what practical use could be made of such a claim?***

Women-in-development programs in the U.S. are often characterized, as have been those targeted at African, Asian, and Latin American countries, as humanitarian efforts simultaneously to "uplift" the poor while relieving state actors from the burden of providing basic services to the "undeserving" poor. As conceived by many government officials and international aid agencies, the purpose of such programs is to empower, as if by magic, women to maintain themselves and their families with minimal state or charitable assistance. Underlying that discourse is the belief that poor women of color are poor because they (or the men in their communities) lack initiative; they need only take advantage of a mythic national and local economy bursting with opportunities for newly empowered female entrepreneurs. The effects of inequitable educational, wage, and benefits systems, structural unemployment, violence against women, race, gender, and class discrimination, inadequate child care, elder care, and health services, and the global movement of capital—all are to be overcome through top-down efforts to make poor women more efficient producers in the informal sector.

What might happen were poor women of color in the U.S. to claim development and their full participation in that process as a human right? Rights-based calls for basic needs such as food, affordable housing, living wages, and health care are not novel in the United States.*** Despite the limitations of rights discourse, it is possible that rights-talk could contribute to strategies that are effective in influencing the state and other powerful actors to contribute to the conditions necessary for fulfillment of women's human rights.***

B.   *Women and the U.S. Community Economic Development Movement*

Development discourse is no stranger to the U.S. context. The long history of domestic efforts to achieve economic development in low-income communities has its modern origins in the Johnson-era War on Poverty. These efforts focused on community projects intended to address the provision of basic needs such as housing, education, food, and access to health care through government-sponsored social service structures. However, these programs were not based on the legal implementation of economic rights.*** Supreme Court decisions supported due process in the administration of social services, but they did not characterize access to economic or social opportunities and services as fundamental rights.

As a correlative to direct social welfare transfer programs such as Aid to Families with Dependent Children (AFDC), community development corporations supported both by governmental programs and by private foundations have engaged in community development efforts in the United States that directly or indirectly parallel Third World development efforts. Policymakers are increasingly attempting to strengthen ideological and methodological linkages with international development programs to address "Third World" problems in U.S. urban centers (as well as poor rural communities). Nowhere is this connection more evident than with respect to the mushrooming of women's economic development programs.***

Just as "integrating women into development" in Africa, Asia, and Latin America often has translated into the exploitation of women as the targets of top-down development policies, similar dangers exist for poor women of color in the United States. It is not in their interest to be passive recipients of either development projects or welfare benefits. The limitations of top-down women's economic development programs were presaged by Martin Luther King's critique of poverty programs:

> Underneath the invitation to prepare programs is the premise that the government is inherently benevolent. It only awaits the presentation of imaginative ideas. When these issue from fertile minds, they will be accepted, enacted, and implemented. This premise shifts the burden of responsibility from the white majority by pretending it is withholding nothing, and places it on the oppressed minority by pretending that the latter is asking for nothing. This is a fable and not a fact. Neither our government nor any government that has sanctioned a century of denial can be depicted as ardent and impatient to bestow gifts of freedom. . . . We are in fact being counseled to put the cart in front of the horse. We have to put the horse (power), in front of the cart (programs). Our task is to do the organizing work that will bring people past all the material and psychological impediments to personal empowerment.[5]

King identified the central problem of rights-based claims on the resources necessary for development. Breaking free from poverty and the effects of gender and racial discrimination requires more than the passive acknowledgement of the existence of formal rights; it seems to require affirmative actions on the part of those whose policies contribute to underdevelopment. It therefore necessitates struggle by those making the claim to motivate those actions. The international community faces a similar conundrum in that implementation of the right to development for peoples and nation-states requires not only a demand from the rights claimant, but also the power to influence the duty-bearer to meet that demand. King recognized that it is only through the exercise of communitybased power that these programs can be successfully implemented.***

Notes and Questions

1. Does Lewis overemphasize rights advocacy as a strategy for poverty alleviation in the United States? Could a right-based approach distract advocates from more effective approaches? *See* Chapter 10, *infra*, for a discussion of the Poor Peoples' Economic Rights Campaign, a grassroots effort to use human rights strategies to address economic inequities in the United States.

2. *The Third World in the United States?: Micro-enterprise and "Welfare Reform."* U.S. "welfare reform" policies in the 1990s were accompanied by the embrace of micro-enter-

---

[5]   Mel King and Susan George, *The Future of Community: From Local to Global,* in BEYOND THE MARKET AND THE STATE: NEW DIRECTIONS IN COMMUNITY DEVELOPMENT (S.T. Bruyn and J. Meehan, eds., 1987) at 221 (quoting Martin Luther King, Jr.).

prise and other development strategies usually associated with the developing world (and particularly with women in development programs). The following analysis surveys some of the links between U.S. domestic policy and international development strategies:

In early 1997, microenterprise programs took on new significance with the advent of a World Summit on Microcredit that was attended by over two thousand delegates from one hundred countries. Ironically, the summit was co-chaired by Hillary Rodham Clinton [wife of U.S. President William Clinton] and took place in Washington, D.C. The administration's explicit support for microcredit and microenterprise programs took place against the backdrop of President *** Clinton's controversial signing of welfare "reform" legislation, which will have an adverse effect on many poor women' of color. Microenterprise programs are touted as ameliorative of the harsher effects of the planned reductions and alterations in public benefits. Despite the problematic manner in which microenterprise may be applied to the U.S. context, it is at least encouraging to note that the World Summit recognizes the existence of the "Third World" within the "First World." As Nicole Gaouette reported, "the Summit will set the decade-long goal of getting 100 million of the world's poorest families on microcredit. Of that total,*** 4 million will come from industrialized countries, 2 million of them from the U.S."***

Based largely in the informal sector, the businesses developed under the rubric of "microenterprise" for women take a wide variety of forms. They include microenterprises, worker-owned producer cooperatives, and self-employment projects. A microenterprise venture generally is limited to between one and five persons. A producer cooperative is a business in which control of management and ownership structure is generally shared jointly by the workers. Self-employment training seeks to provide low-income women with skills in business development and management so that participants can create their own jobs.*** The success of many of these small businesses relies on increasing women's access to alternative sources of credit, such as community development banks and peer lending circles. Peer lending programs, often based on Mohammed Yunus' popular Grameen Bank model, involve structures in which each member of a small group (who need not be in business with each other) borrows a small amount (generally under $500) with the whole group acting as guarantor. All group members must keep their loan payments up-to-date in order for other members to receive loans from the central lending institution. Repayment is ensured primarily by peer pressure. Borrowers are expected to use the loans for small self-employment businesses.*** The use of various forms of microenterprise, self-employment, and peer lending models has entered the complex debates in the United States with regard to both the behavioral modification goals of some welfare reformers and the goals of community economic development advocates.

Hope Lewis, *Women (Under) Development: The Relevance of "The Right to Development" to Poor Women of Color in the United States*, 18 LAW & POL'Y 281, 287–88 (1996).

The Grameen Bank model is the most influential micro-credit model in international development practice; there are many programs aimed at replicating the model in poor communities throughout the world. Founded in Bangladesh in the mid-1970s, the Bank's strategies were developed by Professor Mohammad Yunus, an economist and social activist whose work has been integral to many international policies on gender and development. For an overview of the Bank's origins and programs, *see Grameen: Banking for the Poor, available at* http://www.grameen-info.org/. Some scholars are critical of the implications of exporting this model to poor communities in western countries.

> *See, e.g.*, Rashmi Dyal-Chand, *Reflection in a Distant Mirror: Why the United States Should Not Import the Grameen Bank's Vision of Microcredit* (working title) (forthcoming) (arguing that the development community in the United States has reached unsupportable conclusions about the ability of the Grameen Bank model of microcredit to solve market failure, increase participation by the poor in functioning markets, and incorporate indigenous values).

For an overview of the implications of the 1997 World Summit on Microcredit, the rapid expansion of micro-credit and micro-enterprise programs in the United States, and efforts to use them as alternatives to welfare, *see, e.g.*, Nicole Gaouette, *Mini Loans Help Welfare Mothers to Create Their Own Jobs*, CHRISTIAN SCI. MONITOR Jan. 31, 1997, at 4. Following the World summit, the U.N. General Assembly proclaimed 2005 as the International Year of Microcredit. *See* G.A.Res. 53/197, Dec. 15, 1998.

For discussions of the various forms of micro-enterprise strategies associated with gender-targeted development, *see, e.g.*, MONEY-GO-ROUNDS: THE IMPORTANCE OF ROTATING SAVINGS AND CREDIT ASSOCIATIONS FOR WOMEN (Shirley Ardener & Sandra Burman eds., 1995); Helen Cohen, *How Far Can Credit Travel? Adapting the Grameen Bank's Self-Employment Model*, 20 ECONOMIC DEVELOPMENT AND LAW CENTER REPORT, at 3–13 (Spring 1990); MARY CRONIN & SUSAN DIMATTEO, WOMEN'S ECONOMIC DEVELOPMENT AS AN EMERGING MOVEMENT: STRATEGIES FOR IMPROVING WOMEN'S ECONOMIC POSITION (Tufts University, Center for Management and Community Development, (1988); SHARON HOLT & HELEN RIBE, DEVELOPING FINANCIAL INSTITUTIONS FOR THE POOR AND REDUCING BARRIERS TO ACCESS FOR WOMEN (World Bank Discussion Paper, No. 117) (World Bank, 1991); PONNA WIGNARAJA, WOMEN, POVERTY AND RESOURCES (1990).

GERTRUDE SCHAFFNER GOLDBERG, THE FEMINIZATION OF POVERTY

GERTRUDE SHAFFNER GOLDBERG & ELEANOR KREMEN EDS.
THE FEMINIZATION OF POVERTY: ONLY IN AMERICA, 17–21 (1990)

*** Along with the persisting American paradox of poverty amidst plenty is a newer paradox. At the very time when women have been emancipating themselves from unpaid domestic work, the families with a female householder and no husband present have become preponderant among the poor. Such families have probably always suffered a high risk of poverty, but they have not always been the majority of poor families.

Since 1960, millions of American women have entered the labor force, but for many of these women, paid employment has not meant economic independence or true emancipation. As we examine labor market factors and government policies to reduce sex discrimination and inequality in the workplace, we find that while most women work, many do not earn enough to escape poverty.

Disadvantaged in the workforce, American women who support themselves frequently require government income transfers or social welfare to escape poverty or economic deprivation. Yet, at just the time when the number of single mothers and female householders had risen very significantly, the U.S. government cut back the social programs that relieve the poverty of these women and their families.*** Thus, despite its abundant resources, the United States denies to women not only a fair market wage, but a decent social wage as well.

In the United States, there is, in addition to gender, another important piece to the poverty puzzle. Nearly three-fifths of all poor families with a female householder and no husband present are either black or Hispanic. American women of color are "doubly disadvantaged," but they are also said to be "doubly ignored," overlooked in analyses that are concerned with either racial or gender inequality. Yet, the feminization of poverty in the United States can only be understood by considering both of these forms of inequality, along with that of social class. Thus, in discussing each of the four factors that we have linked to the feminization of poverty—labor force, equalization, social welfare, and demographics—we present data regarding women of color.

American Women and Wage Work

The increase in women's labor force participation in the post-World War II period has been striking in its sheer magnitude, proportions, and composition. The number of women in the workforce has increased by over 35 million since 1950, or nearly three-fold.***

The revolution in women's employment *** is not just in its size but in the tendency for married women and mothers, including those with young children, to go out to work. Whereas less than one-third (30.4 percent) of women and children under age 18 were employed outside the home in 1960, almost two-thirds (65.6 percent) were in 1987. The increases were even more dramatic for the mothers of children under age 6 whose rates of participation nearly tripled since 1960.***

The factors influencing women's decisions to enter the labor force vary in relation to their social and economic circumstances and the eras being considered. In a discussion primarily concerned with poor women, however, it is especially important to bear in mind the estimate made by the Women's Bureau of the Department of Labor that approximately two-thirds of working women are widowed, divorced, separated, never married, or have husbands with annual incomes under $15,000. Despite the fact that women are still regarded as secondary workers, their incomes are of primary importance to themselves and their families.

Paralleling the changes that have increased the need for women to become employed is the increased availability of jobs to which women have traditionally had greater access. More open to women's employment than the goods-producing sector, employment in the service sector has grown dramatically in the postwar era. In the period from 1970 to 1984, 22 million of 23 million new jobs in the economy were in service industries.

Women's vastly increased labor force participation has not been associated with commensurate improvement in their position in the labor market. The 30 years following World War II were generally a time of economic expansion and rising real wages, but it was not until the end of this interval that women began to press their claims for equality. Since the mid-1970s, employment conditions generally have deteriorated. The position of women has actually improved somewhat, as discussions of the wage gap and occupational segregation will show, but not nearly enough to achieve parity with men or for many employed single mothers to escape poverty.

Since the early 1970s, American business has attempted to maintain its profitability in the face of increased international economic competition, the creation of natural resource cartels like OPEC in the developing nations, and the accelerated growth of a low-profit service industry. Business responded to these changes, not primarily with capital investment or innovations that would increase productivity, but primarily with a strategy that came to be called "restructuring"—wage freezes; the development of alternative work arrangements that increase the flexibility with which workers can be hired, fired, and scheduled; the reduction of internal labor markets or career paths; and globalization or the shift of capital and business operations to lower-wage areas of the world.

Although American industry has tended to eschew changes that would increase productivity, technical innovation is nonetheless affecting the design, distribution, and amount of work. The overall employment effects of technological advance are debatable, but computerization of office work, for example, could reduce the amount of clerical jobs for women. Computer technology, moreover, is being implemented in such a way as to eliminate both entry-level positions and the jobs that traditionally formed the rungs of career ladders from semiskilled to skilled work.

Government policy has abetted restructuring rather than protected rights of workers.*** Deregulation of transportation and communications industries and a laissez-faire stance by the National Labor Relations Board weakened the power of labor to resist these changes as did anti-union tactics of the federal government itself in its role as employer. Tight monetary policies that, in the early 1980s, created the highest unemployment rates since the Great Depression also tended to depress wages and weaken workers' positions vis-a-vis management.

One result of these strategies on the part of business and government has been called the "pauperization of work" or the replacement of higher paid jobs by those close to the minimum wage.***

Part-time and Other Contingent Work

Contingent work is the term used to describe alternative work arrangements such as part-time employment, temporary work, and homework, which give employers greater flexibility in hiring, firing, and wages and fringe benefits. In recent years employers have been selecting a core group of employees, investing in their development, and encouraging their attachment to the firm; at the same time they have been employing a peripheral or contingent group from whom they remain relatively detached, even at the cost of high turnover. The notion of a dual or segmented labor force with largely insurmountable barriers between good jobs and bad jobs can thus be extended to internal labor markets or to core and contingent workers within firms. In both cases the less desirable employment track is for women and minorities.***

Temporary work, much of it subcontracted from temporary help agencies, is also work done primarily by women, and it has been growing five times faster than the total workforce. Women between the ages of 25 and 54 comprise almost two-thirds of the temporary workforce. By definition, temporary work lacks job stability, and like other forms of contingent work, it tends to be lower in pay and limited in both fringe benefits and opportunities for upward mobility.

ANN R. TICKAMYER, PUBLIC POLICY AND PRIVATE LIVES: SOCIAL AND SPATIAL DIMENSIONS OF WOMEN'S POVERTY AND WELFARE POLICY IN THE UNITED STATES

84 Ky. L.J. 721, 725–29 (1995/1996)

*** Since the term "feminization of poverty" was coined by Diana Pearce, there has been a growing recognition that poverty in America is disproportionately concentrated among women and even more disproportionately concentrated among women of color. Census figures for 1990 show that one third of all female-headed families have incomes below the poverty level compared to slightly more than ten percent for all families. When these figures are disaggregated by race and ethnicity, the results show almost fifty percent of Black and Hispanic female-headed families are poor compared to slightly more than a quarter of white female-headed households. Although poverty rates for female-headed households have actually decreased slightly since the 1960s, the numbers of poor women and their proportion of the entire poverty population have increased steadily.

The reasons for women's disproportionate poverty are complex and controversial, with explanations varying with ideological and political perspectives. Most mainstream and feminist social scientists currently agree that the major factors responsible for women's poverty arise from a complex mix of economic disadvantage in the labor market and disproportionate responsibility for reproductive labor or the caregiving responsibilities that traditionally make up women's work. These analyses are sharply at odds with popular opinion and political discourse that have less charitable diagnoses of the sources of much poverty, attributing it to deviation from cultural norms of individual effort and hard work.

There is also significant disagreement about the extent to which the welfare system is implicated in creating and sustaining women's poverty. Among conservative analysts it has become popular to blame the existence of public assistance for creating poverty and dependency. These analysts argue that the availability of welfare to meet basic needs creates disincentives to work and provides opportunities to indulge in antisocial and deviant behavior which is then passed down to new generations of welfare dependents who would rather collect a government check than find a job. While there is little empirical support for this analysis and much evidence to the contrary, it has become a popular diagnosis for the causes of poverty and the basis for calls for sharp retrenchment in welfare programs. What was initially a fringe argument has become the new political orthodoxy, driving the politics and polemics of welfare reform for both political parties.

Ironically, many feminist and progressive analysts also attribute some of the blame for women's poverty to the welfare system, but from a very different perspective. In this view, it is the inadequacy, coupled with the social control functions, of social welfare provision that exacerbates women's poverty. In particular, the existence of "public patriarchy" substitutes impersonal, public control of women by the state for private control by family and male kin. This process is embodied in a dual welfare system highly correlated with gender and race, although nominally gender and race blind. Feminist accounts demonstrate the segmented nature of a welfare system in which productive labor located in the formal labor market is valued and protected over all other forms of work, while reproductive work is devalued and unpaid. Thus, social transfers with relatively generous and accessible aid and without the stigmatizing label of "welfare" are available to predominantly white, middle class male labor force participants in such forms as unemployment compensation and workmen's compensation. Whereas women workers who are located in either inferior labor market positions or informal and reproductive work are more likely to have access to only the most minimal, stigmatized, and punitive forms of assistance such as *** food stamps.

Women's well-documented disadvantage in the labor market is mirrored and reinforced by their relationship to the state in the form of government assistance and interventions. Women's relegation to lower paying and sex-segregated jobs, greater likelihood of part-time or intermittent work histories, frequent participation in informal labor markets and economic activities, and experiences of harassment and discrimination directly and indirectly influence their eligibility for social welfare transfers. Welfare benefits available to women and their children are either based on undervalued reproductive labor where social assistance benefits are stigmatized, variable, and unstable, and frequently punitively administered, or they are accrued by a position of relative disadvantage in the formal labor market. Women's lower wages, greater likelihood of part-time or intermittent employment, and concentration in poorly compensated, unprotected secondary sector jobs affect their eligibility for different forms of benefits. They are less likely to be eligible for relatively high paying, stigma-free social insurance type benefits, such as unemployment compensation, that accompany protected and primary sector employment. When they are eligible, they qualify for much lower benefit levels than those available to primary sector workers—typically men.

U.S. WOMEN'S EARNINGS AS PERCENT OF MEN'S, 1979–1999*

	Annual	Weekly	Hourly
1979	59.7	62.5	64.1
1980	60.2	64.4	64.8
1981	59.2	64.6	65.1
1982	61.7	65.4	67.3
1983	63.6	66.7	69.4
1984	63.7	67.8	69.8
1985	64.6	68.2	70.0
1986	64.3	69.2	70.2
1987	65.2	70.0	72.1
1988	66.0	70.2	73.8
1989	68.7	70.1	75.4
1990	71.6	71.9	77.9
1991	69.9	74.2	78.6
1992	70.8	75.8	80.3
1993	71.5	77.1	80.4
1994	72.0	76.4	80.6
1995	71.4	75.5	80.8
1996	73.8	75.0	81.2
1997	74.2	74.4	80.8
1998	73.2	76.3	81.8
1999	72.2	76.5	83.8

* Source: BLS Bulletin 2340 and unpublished tables, Employment and Earnings, Jan. issues; U.S. Bureau of the Census Current Population Reports, Series p-60, selected issues Table prepared by Women's Bureau, February 2000.

Notes and Questions

1.   Did welfare reform policies violate the human rights of women in the United States? If so, how should such violations be analyzed under international law?

2.   In 1999, a coalition of activists and lawyers filed a petition against the United States with the Inter-American Commission on Human Rights. The petition alleges that U.S. welfare reform violated the economic, social, cultural, civil and political rights of poor people in the United States. *See Poor Peoples Economic Human Rights Campaign, et al. v. United States of America*, excerpted in Chapter 10, Section C.

3.   *Is Poverty a National Security Threat?* After the attacks of September 11, 2001, the United States invaded both Afghanistan and Iraq and maintained a continuing "War on Terrorism." But is poverty another kind of threat to the domestic security of states?

Consider the following observation by noted constitutional scholar, Cass Sunstein:

> The United States is facing new threats to its security not only in the form of a guerilla war in Iraq and a heightened fear of terrorism at home but also in the growing gap between our richest and our poorest citizens, the unavailability of education and health care to our poor and minority communities, and the disappearance of thousands of people from welfare rolls without their reappearance on employment registers. Surely these are among the greatest threats the country has ever faced. It is long past time to complete Roosevelt's unfinished revolution, to insist on a principled commitment to real universal security.

CASS R. SUNSTEIN, THE SECOND BILL OF RIGHTS, *excerpted in Evident Truths*, HARPER'S, 15, 20 (July 2004).

4.   For further reading on the human rights implications of U.S. welfare reform, *see* Lisa A. Crooms, *Families, Fatherlessness and Women's Human Rights: An Analysis of the Clinton Administration's Public Housing Policy as a Violation of the Convention on the Elimination of all Forms of Discrimination Against Women*, 36 BRANDEIS SCH. OF LAW J. FAM. L. 1 (1997/98); Berta Esperanza & Kimberly A. Johns, *Global Rights, Local Wrongs and Legal Fixes: An International Human Rights Critique of Immigration and Welfare Reform*, 71 S. CAL. L. REV. 547 (1998); New York City Welfare Reform and Human Rights Documentation Project, Hunger is No Accident: New York and Federal Welfare Policies Violate the Human Right to Food, Urban Justice Center, New York, 24 (July 2000); Tonya Plank, *Human Rights, Women's Rights and Welfare Reform: An Analysis of H.R. 4 From an International Human Rights Perspective*, 17 WOMEN'S RTS. L. REP. 345 (1996); Susan L. Thomas, *Ending Welfare as We Know It or Farewell to the Rights of Women on Welfare? A Constitutional and Human Rights Analysis of the Personal Responsibility Act* 78 U. DET. MERCY L. REV. No. 2, 179 (Winter 2001); Lucy A. Williams, *Welfare, Law and Legal Entitlements: The Social Roots of Poverty, in* DAVID KAIRYS ED., THE POLITICS OF LAW (3d ed. 1998).

3.   *Human Traffic at Home and Abroad: Women Workers Under Globalization*

Globalization in its contemporary forms has had significant implications for the human rights of women. Multinational manufacturing and assembly enterprises, for example, often see poor women in developing countries as an important source of low-wage labor. Some poor women migrate to the Global North in search of economic stability, but may also be subject to wage and labor exploitation, detention, or violence. The following excerpts illustrate some of the issues women workers face under globalization:

SASKIA SASSEN, TOWARD A FEMINIST ANALYTICS
OF THE GLOBAL ECONOMY

4 Ind. J. Global Leg. Stud. 7, 9, 15–16, 27–28, 32–35 (1996)

*** The current phase of the world economy is characterized by significant discontinuities with the preceding periods and radically new arrangements. This phase becomes particularly evident when one examines the impact of globalization on the territorial organization of economic activity and on the organization of political power. Economic globalization has reconfigured fundamental properties of the nation-state, notably territoriality and sovereignty. There is an incipient unbundling of the exclusive territoriality we have long associated with the nation-state. The most strategic instantiation of this unbundling is the global city, which operates as a partly de-nationalized platform for global capital. At a lower order of complexity, the transnational corporation and global finance markets can also be seen as having this effect through their cross-border activities and the new legal regimes that frame these activities. Sovereignty is also being unbundled by these economic practices, other non-economic practices, and new legal regimes. At the limit this means the State is no longer the only site of sovereignty and the normativity that accompanies it. Further, the State is no longer the exclusive subject for international law. Other actors, from Non-Governmental Organizations and First-Nation people to supranational organizations are increasingly emerging as subjects of international law and actors in international relations.

Developing a feminist analytics of today's global economy will require us to factor in these transformations if we are to go beyond merely updating the economic conditions of women and men in different countries. Much of the feminist scholarship examining the issue of women and the economy and the issue of women and the law has taken the nation-state as a given or as the context within which to examine the issues at hand. This approach is a major and necessary contribution. But now, considering the distinct impact of globalization on key systemic properties of the State—i.e., exclusive territoriality and sovereignty—it becomes important to subject these properties to critical examination.***

Toward an Alternative Narrative about Globalization

The master images in the currently dominant account about economic globalization in media and policy circles, as well as in much economic analysis, emphasize hypermobility, global communications, and the neutralization of place and distance. Key concepts in that account—globalization, information economy, and telematics—all suggest that place no longer matters and that the only type of worker that matters is the highly educated professional. This account privileges the capability for global transmission over the material infrastructure that makes transmission possible; information outputs over the workers producing those outputs, from specialists to secretaries; and the new transnational corporate culture over the multiplicity of work cultures, including immigrant cultures, within which many of the "other" jobs of the global information economy take place. In brief, the dominant narrative concerns itself with the upper circuits of capital, not the lower ones; and particularly with the hypermobility of capital rather than place-bound capital.

Massive trends toward the spatial dispersal of economic activities at the metropolitan, national, and global level represent only half of what is happening. Alongside the well-documented spatial dispersal of economic activities, new forms of territorial centralization of top-level management and control operations have appeared. National and global markets, as well as globally integrated operations, require central places where the work of globalization gets done. Further, information industries require a vast physical infrastructure containing strategic nodes with hyperconcentration of facilities. Finally, even the most advanced information industries have a production process.

Once this production process is brought into the analysis, we see that secretaries are part of it, and so are the cleaners of the buildings where the professionals do their work. An economic configuration very different from that suggested by the concept [of] information economy emerges. We recover the material conditions, production sites, and place-boundedness that are also part of globalization and the information economy.***

*** There is a large literature showing that immigrant women's regular wage work and improved access to other public realms have an impact on their gender relations. Women gain greater personal autonomy and independence while men lose ground. Women gain more control over budgeting and other domestic decisions and greater leverage in requesting help from men in domestic chores. Also, their access to public services and other public resources gives them a chance to become incorporated in the mainstream society—they are often the ones in the household who mediate in this process. It is likely that some women benefit more than others from these circumstances; we need more research to establish the impact of class, education, and income on these gendered outcomes.

In addition to the relatively improved empowerment of women in the household associated with waged employment, there is a second important outcome—their greater participation in the public sphere and their possible emergence as public actors. There are two arenas where immigrant women are active: institutions for public and private assistance and the immigrant/ethnic community. The incorporation of women in the migration process strengthens the settlement likelihood and contributes to greater immigrant participation in their communities and vis-à-vis the State. For instance, Hondagneu-Sotelo found that immigrant women come to assume more active public and social roles which further reinforces their status in the household and the settlement process. Women are more active in community building and community activism, and they are positioned differently from men regarding the broader economy and the State. They are the ones that are likely to have to handle the legal vulnerability of their families in the process of seeking public and social services ***. This greater participation by women suggests the possibility that they may emerge as more forceful and visible actors and may make their role in the labor market more visible as well.

The Unbundling of Sovereignty: Implications for A Feminist Analysis

*** *International Human Rights and State Sovereignty*

International human rights, while rooted in the founding documents of nation-states, are today a force that can undermine the exclusive authority of the State over its nationals and thereby contribute to transform the inter-State system and international legal order. Membership in nation-states ceases to be the only ground for the realization of rights. All residents, whether citizens or not, can claim their human rights. Human rights begin to impinge on the principle of nation-based citizenship and the boundaries of the nation.***

From an emphasis on the sovereignty of the people of a nation and the right to self-determination, we see a shift in emphasis to the rights of individuals regardless of nationality. Human rights codes can erode the legitimacy of the State if that State fails to respect such human rights.*** There is a growing body of cases signaling that individuals and non-State groups are making claims on the State, particularly in Western Europe, where the human rights regime is most developed.

In the United States this process has been much slower and less marked. This has been seen partly as a result of American definitions of nationhood, which has led courts in some cases to address the matter of undocumented immigrants within American constitutionalism, notably the idea of inalienable and natural rights of people and persons, without territorial confines. The emphasis on persons makes possible interpretations about undocumented immigrants, in a way it would not if the emphasis were on citizens.*** The rapid growth of undocumented immigration and the sense of the State's incapacity to control the flow and to regulate the various categories in its population was a factor leading courts to consider the international human rights regime. It allows courts to rule on basic protections of individuals not formally accounted in the national territory and legal system, notably undocumented aliens and unauthorized refugees.

In both Western Europe and the United States it is interesting to note that immigrants and refugees have been key claimants, and in that sense, mechanisms for the expansion of the human rights regime. Several court cases show how undocumented immigration creates legal voids which are increasingly filled by invoking human rights covenants. In many of these cases, we can see the individual or non-State actors bringing the claims based on international human rights codes as expanding international law. The State, in this case the judiciary, "mediates between these agents and the international legal order." Courts have emerged as central institutions for a whole series of changes.

The growing accountability of States under the rule of law to international human rights codes and institutions, together with the fact that individuals and non-State actors can make claims on those States based on those codes, signals a development that goes beyond the expansion of human rights within the framework of nation-states. It contributes to redefine the bases of legitimacy of States under the rule of law and the notion of nationality. Under human rights regimes States must increasingly take account of persons qua persons, rather than qua citizens. The individual is now an object of law and a site for rights regardless of whether a citizen or an alien.***

Notes and Questions

1.   Sassen notes that many scholars view the movement of women into the paid labor market and the migration of women as socially and economically liberating. Do you agree? What are the implications of differences in racial, class and historical context? See the discussion of women of color and immigrant women workers in this chapter.

2.   Writing in the mid-1990s, Sassen seemed optimistic about the influence of increased transnational migration on the recognition of international human rights standards in domestic law. A growing number of decisions in North American courts, for example, had begun to make reference to international human rights standards in the context of immigration law. *See, e.g.,* the discussion of immigration decisions in Canadian and U.S. courts that cite the Convention on the Rights of the Child in Chapter 3, *supra.* However, the attacks on the World Trade Center and the U.S. Pentagon on September 11, 2001,

have had significant implications for U.S. legal recognition of the rights of immigrants and of international law in general. Anti-terrorism legislation and policies in North America, Western Europe, and other parts of the world have led to stricter controls on migration and to increased abuses of the due process and other rights of immigrants. Nevertheless, the global movement of human beings in search of work continues. What prospects do you see for the future protection of migrants in the global economy?

3. For readings on the human rights implications of post-9/11 U.S. immigration policies, *see, e.g.,* Susan M. Akram & Kevin R. Johnson, *Immigration Regulation Goes Local: The Role of States in U.S. Immigration Policy: Race, Civil Rights, and Immigration law After September 11, 2001: The Targeting of Arabs and Muslims,* 58 N.Y.U. ANN. SURV. AM. L. 295 (2002); Kevin R. Johnson, *Symposium: Beyond belonging: Challenging the Boundaries of Nationality: September 11 and Mexican Immigrants: Collateral Damage Comes Home,* 52 DEPAUL L. REV. 849 (2003).

SHERRIE L. RUSSELL-BROWN, LABOR RIGHTS AS HUMAN RIGHTS: THE SITUATION OF WOMEN WORKERS IN JAMAICA'S EXPORT FREE ZONES

24 BERKELEY J. EMP. & LAB. L. 179, 181–85, 191–93 (2003)

*** The island of Jamaica is the largest English-speaking island in the West Indies, with an area of over eleven thousand square kilometers. Its population, growing at about 1% per year, is around 2.5 million, with half of the population living in urban areas. Racially, Jamaica is 90.5% black, 7.3% mixed race, and 1.3% East Indian. In 1994, the literacy rate was approximately 75.4%, 81.2% for females compared with 69.2% for males.***

Jamaica's labor force is approximately 1.1 million, with women comprising approximately 45% of the total.

The World Bank has classified Jamaica as a "moderately indebted" country. Jamaica's external debt increased from January through May 2001 to $3.97 billion U.S. dollars, and debt servicing accounts for 62% of total expenditures.

Export Free Zones in General and Export-Oriented Industrialization in Jamaica

Export Free Zones Generally

Generally, export free zones (hereinafter, "EFZs") are defined as "fenced-in industrial estates specializing in manufacturing for exports that offer firms free trade conditions and a liberal regulatory environment." EFZs share a few common features, such as: 1) unlimited, duty-free imports of raw, intermediate input and capital goods necessary for the production of exports; 2) less governmental red-tape, more flexibility with labor laws for the firms in the zone than in the domestic market; 3) generous and long-term tax holidays and concessions to the firms; and, lastly, 4) above average (compared to the rest of the host country) communications services and infrastructure (it is also common for countries to subsidize utilities and rental rates). The primary goals of an export free zone are: 1) to provide foreign exchange earnings by promoting non-traditional exports; 2) to provide jobs to alleviate unemployment or under-employment problems in the country and to assist in income creation; and 3) to attract foreign direct investment (FDI) and engender technological transfer, knowledge spill-over and demonstration effects that would act as catalysts for domestic entrepreneurs to engage in production of non-traditional products.

EFZs are established by governments to foster industries like textile manufacturing. Textile manufacturers located in EFZs import raw materials, like cotton, at a lower rate, pay workers lower wages due to relaxed labor laws and export the goods under a relaxed tariff structure.

Jamaica and EFZs

Since the 1950s, Caribbean countries have employed export-oriented industrialization, otherwise referred to as "industrialization by invitation," to achieve economic development. As described by Nobel Prize winning economist, Sir W. Arthur Lewis:

> The islands cannot be industrialized *** without a considerable inflow of foreign capital and capitalists and a period of wooing and fawning upon such people. Foreign capital is needed because industrialization is a frightfully expensive business quite beyond the resources of the islands.

As part and parcel of its policy of export oriented industrialization, Jamaica employs EFZs to attract foreign capital. Under the Jamaica Export Free Zone Act, as amended in 1989, (hereinafter, the "Act"), Jamaica established the Kingston Free Zone in 1976 and the Montego Bay Free Zone in 1988.***

Under the Act, any enterprise approved by the Port Authority to carry on an approved activity can import into a free zone certain defined items free of customs duty. Also, approved enterprises are not subject to import or export licensing where goods are shipped to destinations other than customs territories. Lastly, an approved free zone enterprise engaged in manufacturing, or activities involving international trading in products, is granted total relief from income tax on profits or gains earned from either activity.

As in other parts of the world, young Jamaican women, usually below the age of twenty-five, make up most of the free zone workforce. According to Klak, 95% of the jobs in Jamaica's EFZs are filled by women, a percentage significantly higher than in any Asian country or Mexico. Women, especially young women, are an attractive EFZ workforce because they are said to be "docile, dexterous, less organized, cheaper, and more willing to tolerate monotonous and repetitive work."

On the one hand, EFZs provide a significant number of women "formal" sector employment and a source of steady income, "most for the first time." In 1997, employment in Jamaica's export free zones stood at about 13,900. According to a State Department Country Report on Jamaica, however, the apparel industry contracted in the mid-1990s, with a decline in employment of 64%. Due to the contraction of employment in the apparel industry in the 1990s, employment of women in the EFZs may not be that significant to women's overall employment in Jamaica. Thus, it is questionable whether employment in Jamaica's free zones will have a marked effect on the unemployment rate of women, which is higher than that of men.

On the other hand, there are drawbacks to EFZ employment. Wages in Jamaica's free zones, though "comparable to those of many formal sector entry positions or low skill service work," are still low in an environment with a high cost of living. In addition, EFZ jobs have reduced job security and poor working conditions. In the data services sector, workers have complained of occupational health problems including "mesocarpal syndrome, stiffness in the hand, eye and back problems."

Moreover, "women's new production responsibilities in [EFZ's] are added to traditional ones in the realm of reproduction." In 1999, women headed around 42.5% of households in Jamaica, a proportion that has remained virtually unchanged since 1992. As heads of households, women disproportionately bear the social burden of structural adjustment policies that "simultaneously reduce public spending on services, education, and shelter, raise consumer costs, and encourage investors to exploit low cost female labor." When such policies are instituted, women "have more production and reproduction responsibilities, requiring longer work hours, at the same time that costs are rising." For many women, "this situation translates into an increasing 'double burden' and a reduced living standard."

In sum, it would be simplistic to place a definitive normative value on free zone work. Given the lack of alternatives for the Jamaican EFZ workforce, comprised largely of female heads of household, there are positives to EFZs in that they provide a steady source of income. However, EFZ jobs are also low wage, low-skilled positions with poor working conditions and reduced job security. Thus, the drawbacks outweigh the advantages for Jamaica's female export free zone workers.***

Possible Impediments to Organizing In Jamaica's Free Zones

Some writers attribute the lack of unionization in Jamaica's EFZs to the great resistance by EFZ management to allowing unions in the free zones and the inability of Jamaica's trade unions to break through this opposition. Others argue that women workers are to blame for the lack of union presence in Jamaica's EFZs, since they have less time to form or join trade unions as compared to their male counterparts and fear reprisals from management for joining a trade union. Although these reasons may be factors contributing to the lack of unionization in Jamaica's EFZs, a more plausible explanation is that Jamaica's trade unions, taking their cues from Jamaica's political leadership, are keeping concerns about conditions in the EFZs off their public agendas, in part because women workers predominate the EFZ labor force.***

*** [It] is not just a fear of driving away foreign investment and thereby possibly alienating political patronage that make Jamaica's trade unions reticent about organizing in Jamaica's free zones. There may also be an element of sex-discrimination. Indeed, Jamaica's trade unions are very active outside the free zones. The Jamaica Labor Trends report noted that there are frequent work stoppages and loss of man-days contributing, inter alia, to a less friendly investment climate outside the EFZ. Thus, the argument that Jamaica's trade unions may not want to be active in the free zones or that they might be complying with "directives" from the Government of Jamaica to stay out of the free zone for fear of scaring away foreign investment is undermined by the fact that "fear" of dampening foreign investment activity does not seem to affect union activity in the formal sector. As a recent ILO report diplomatically explained, Jamaica has:

> a vibrant trade union movement which upholds the provisions of all labour and industrial relations legislation ***, has also ratified ILO Conventions Nos. 87 and 98 which guarantee freedom of association and the right to join a trade union [passed in 1975], [t]he Labour Relations and Disputes Act [which] makes provision for the establishment of a Labour Relations Code which formalizes

workers' right to form a union ***, has an industrial court, called the Industrial Disputes Tribunal (IDT) ***, [and that] [c]ollective agreements are common among the unionized workforce and usually include a grievance procedure. Despite these provisions, however, none of the companies in the sector is unionized. The difference between the formal sector and the free zones is the gender component of their workforces.

Some may be reluctant to make the connections. However, in a country where trade unions have historically played such an important role in its socio-economic and political life, it is difficult to explain the absence of trade unions in Jamaica's free zones save for the gender make-up of the zones' workforce.***

Notes and Questions

1. Are the Export Free Zones described by Russell-Brown consistent with Jamaica's obligations under the International Covenant on Economic Social and Cultural Rights? Why, or why not? If not, what specific reforms would you suggest? Would you scrap the free zone system entirely? What might the implications of your approach be on the human rights of Jamaican women, men, and children?

2. *The United States and Caribbean Trade Policy.* The complex history of the trade in apparel between the United States and the Caribbean is a telling illustration of the economic and human impact of globalization. Like other manufacturers, the apparel industry has moved operations from country to country and region to region in search of lower production costs (primarily low-wage labor) and in response to the effects of various "free trade" agreements.

NAFTA. The North American Free Trade Agreement (NAFTA), which created a preferential trading bloc among Canada, the United States, and Mexico, had a devastating impact on women in the Jamaican garment assembly sector. Following the adoption of NAFTA in 1993, the apparel industry in the Caribbean closed over 150 plants and lost 123,000 jobs. In Jamaica alone, more than 7,000 garment industry jobs were eliminated, with the majority of them previously held by women. By 1997, the unemployment rate for women in this sector had risen to over 33 percent. Larry Rohter, *Backlash From NAFTA Batters Economies of the Caribbean*, N.Y. TIMES, Jan. 30, 1997, *available at* http://www.mtholyoke.edu/acad/intrel/naftacar.htm. *See also* Peter Passell, *Trade Pacts by Region; Not the Elixir as Advertised*, N.Y. TIMES, Feb. 4, 1997, at D1 (noting that, "in 1998. the World Bank released data showing how NAFTA had harmed Caribbean countries excluded from the area" and stating that "Mexico could grab as much as one-third of the Caribbean's $ 12.5 billion in exports to the United States").

The Caribbean Basin Initiative. The garment industry flourished in Jamaica and elsewhere in the Caribbean in the 1980s and early 1990s due largely to the U.S. Caribbean Basin Initiative (CBI). Described as a "package of aid, trade and investment incentives aimed at the private sector, the program was intended to introduce the Caribbean to what President Ronald Reagan called "'the magic of the marketplace,' and had Jamaica as its centerpiece." Rohter, *supra.* The Reagan initiative was also intended to act as a counterweight to the perceived influence of communism and socialism in the region.

The CBI gave preferential trade treatment to apparel exports from Caribbean countries that had been assembled in the Caribbean using U.S. components. The U.S. economy benefited from the arrangement by supporting a market for U.S. raw materials and partially manufactured apparel, and by increasing U.S. exports to the region (resulting in more than $15 billion per year by 1995). *Id.*

Despite the economic benefits of the CBI, the advent of NAFTA, which allowed for much more preferential trade treatment among its three trading partners, severely threatened Caribbean garment assembly and other industries. CARICOM (the Caribbean Community), a regional organization of Caribbean nations, advocated for "NAFTA-parity" in U.S. trade policy toward the region. In May of 2000, President William Clinton signed the Trade and Development Act of 2000, which included the U.S.-Caribbean Basin Trade Partnership Act of 2000 (CBTPA) and the African Growth and Opportunity Act of 2000. The CBTPA, which amended the CBI, was intended, in part, to extend NAFTA-like treatment to Caribbean and Central American countries. The Act included provisions requiring participants to respect certain internationally recognized workers' rights. However, its benefits to the region also came with strings attached, as the following summary by a trade journal indicates:

> The Act provides that countries currently designated under the Caribbean Basin Initiative (CBI) program are potentially eligible for beneficiary designation under the Trade and Development Act as well.***
>
> However, designation as a Caribbean Basin beneficiary country for purposes of the Trade Act is not automatic. Rather, in order to be so designated, the President must first determine that the particular country has a demonstrated commitment to meet its obligations under the World Trade Organization and to participate in negotiations towards the completion of the Free Trade Area of the Americas (FTAA), the extent to which it protects intellectual property rights and workers' rights, cooperates in counter-narcotics efforts, etc. Once granted, such status can also be revoked by the President under certain circumstances.***

Steven S. Weiser & Arthur W. Bodek, *New Sourcing Opportunities for U.S. Textile and Apparel Importers—Part II: Caribbean Basin,* J. COMMERCE—JOC ONLINE, Aug. 4, 2000. *See, e.g.,* U.S. Department of Commerce, International Trade Administration, *Market Access and Compliance, The Caribbean Basin Initiative, available at* http://www.mac.doc.gov/CBI/web-main/intro.htm. The United States, under the administration of President George W. Bush, amended the CBTPA in August of 2002.

3. *From the Caribbean to China.* While many garment assembly and other apparel production plants moved to Mexico after NAFTA's enactment, the admission of China, with its large low-wage labor force, to the WTO in late 2001, again resulted in major shifts in the apparel industry:

> According to the U.S. Department of Commerce, China overtook Mexico as the No. 1 exporter of apparel products to the United States last year, with $7.3 billion in exports vs. Mexico's $6.9 billion. As of the year ending January 2004, China's apparel exports to the United States were up 26 percent over the year ending January 2003, while Mexico's apparel exports to the United States were down 7.4 percent for the same period.

APPAREL, May 1, 2004.

Apparel companies throughout the region, and their workers, remain uncertain about the impact of new regional and international trade arrangements and the increasing market share of the Chinese apparel industry:

> The [apparel] industry now directly or indirectly supports more than 1 million jobs in Central America, and textiles and apparel account for half of the region's foreign investment.
>
> But there are clouds on the horizon. Central American apparel producers fear that when the World Trade Organization lifts import restrictions, or quotas, on textile and apparel in January 2005, they'll be overwhelmed by competition from China. The nation is a low-cost producer and has developed a sophisticated production system that Central America has trouble competing against.***
>
> The answer must come quickly. The American Textiles Manufacturers Institute predicts China will supply 70 percent of the world's textile market after the WTO requires its 146 member nations to lift their import quotas on textiles and apparel in 2005. The U.S. imported $10.5 billion in textiles and apparel from China in the 12 months through June, compared with $9.9 billion from Caribbean Basin Initiative countries.
>
> The WTO's lifting of import restrictions on textiles and apparel is intended to help developing countries ship more goods into developed markets, but it's grim news to Central America—and to what's left of the U.S. textile industry.
>
> Central America is among the few bright spots for U.S. textile producers, which have closed some 250 plants in the last six years. Three-fourths of U.S. textile exports go to the region and to Mexico and Canada.
>
> The U.S. and Central America have a symbiotic relationship in textiles and apparel. U.S. duties for apparel assembled in the Caribbean and Central America from U.S.-cut cloth average 6 percent, compared with 12 to 17 percent for other nations. If the apparel is cut and sewn in the region from U.S.-made components, it's duty-free.
>
> The reduced duties have paid off. Honduras is the third-largest apparel exporter to the U.S., after Mexico and China. Southbound shipments of textiles and cut fabric and northbound shipments of finished apparel are among the top commodities carried by many ocean carriers between the U.S. and Central America.
>
> The arrangement could be thrown off balance when the U.S negotiates the Central American Free Trade Agreement with Honduras, Guatemala, Nicaragua, El Salvador and Costa Rica. Under discussion is a policy change that would allow apparel produced in the Caribbean Basin to qualify for preferential treatment even if it's made from material produced outside the region. Currently, the preferential treatment is available only if the U.S. decides that adequate supplies of the material don't exist within the region.
>
> Apparel manufacturers with plants in Central America favor the change because it would save them money and help the region's producers compete against the expected increase in competition from China.***

Ann Saccomano, *Cloud over Central America Trade; Region's Apparel Firms Fear a Spike in Competition from China,* J. COMMERCE, Sept. 1, 2003, at 52.

For a discussion of the impact of NAFTA and other pressures of globalization on the U.S. textile industry, *see, e.g.,* Katherine Yung, *Spinning to a Stop; U.S. Textile Makers Cut Jobs, Close Mills as NAFTA Hopes Fray; Industry's Boost from Trade Pact didn't Last; China seen as Spoiler,* DALLAS MORNING NEWS, Sept. 28, 2003, at 10.

4. *Free Trade Area of the Americas (FTAA).* Negotiations to establish a free trade area intended to remove barriers to trade and investment among the 34 countries of the Americas are expected to conclude by January of 2005. Critics of the FTAA argue that special attention must be paid to the needs of small economies, such as those of the Caribbean nations in reaching any such agreement. *See, e.g.,* Donna Ortega, *Smaller Economies Remain Guarded on FTAA's Impact,* JAMAICA GLEANER, Apr. 18, 2001, *available at* http://www.jamaica-gleaner.com/gleaner/20010418/business/business5.html. *See also* a statement on this issue by the Prime Minister of Jamaica, Hon. P.J. Patterson, *Caribbean Perspective: The Free Trade Area of the Americas and Smaller Economics,* 27 FORDHAM INT'L L.J. 899 (2004). As was the case with regard to other regional and international trade agreements, labor and human rights activists have raised significant concerns about the FTAA as well. For an overview of the FTAA, see http://www.ftaa-alca.org/View_e.asp .

5. *The Central America Free Trade Agreement.* The Central America Free Trade Agreement (CAFTA) was signed on May 28, 2004, by the United States, Costa Rica, El Salvador, Guatemala, Honduras and Nicaragua. Supporters hoped that the agreement would help those countries respond to the increasing competition from the Chinese apparel industry, among other things. Ratification of CAFTA in the United States, however, faces fierce opposition by labor unions and human rights groups who argue that the agreement fails to protect the rights of workers, including prohibitions on gender discrimination. Congress is expected to vote on the Agreement following the November 2004 elections. Jane Bussey, *CAFTA, Finally in Hand, Could Run Into a Fist,* MIAMI HERALD, May 29, 2004, *available at* http://www.miami.com/mld/miamiherald/business/8788404.htm?1c; Human Rights Watch, *CAFTA's Weak Labor Rights Protections: Why the Present Accord Should be Opposed,* Mar. 2004, *at* http://hrw.org/english/docs/2004/03/09/usint8099.htm.

6. Given the global mobility of capital, and the creation of large integrated trading blocs, what strategies should human rights advocates use to promote the rights of workers? Are the rights of workers in opposition to, or complementary to, the overall development goals of a poor country? Do the human rights problems created by globalization require regional or international, as well as domestic, solutions?

While the effects of globalization on working women and men in their home countries are significant, important human rights issues are raised by the migration of poor people in search of work. Some, true migrants, travel back and forth seasonally or for short periods to work in the host country. Others may spend years away from "home," but are often still responsible for sending remittances in the form of cash, food or clothing to maintain relatives in the sending country. Finally, increasing attention has been paid to the human rights implications of human trafficking within and across borders. As you read the following materials consider: how are lines to be drawn between "economic migrants," "immigrants," and "asylum-seekers"? How should the human rights analysis change for each category, if at all? How would you define "trafficking"? Does the express consent of the person who is being smuggled matter?

HOPE LEWIS, GLOBAL INTERSECTIONS: CRITICAL RACE FEMINIST HUMAN
RIGHTS AND INTER/NATIONAL BLACK WOMEN
50 MAINE L. REV. 309, 312–18, 321–22 (1998)

*** *Who Are Jamaican-American Women?****

Jamaican American women constitute one of the largest groups of Black immigrants
to the United States. They follow a long tradition of migrancy among peoples from the
Caribbean, where migrancy rates can reach sixty percent or higher. The political, economic, and cultural dislocations underlying that tradition of *** are both internal and
external to the region. European colonial powers viewed the Caribbean islands as
reserves for predictable supplies of labor and raw commodities (sugar, spices, bananas,
oil, and bauxite). In that sense, the peoples of the Caribbean have been subject to the
vagaries of globalization—the globalization of European imperialism—for hundreds of
years. While the ties to European post-colonial powers remain strong, the influence of
the United States is increasingly important for Caribbean islands in the post-independence era. United States tourism, television, and radio have exposed Jamaicans to
the bounties of the American consumer economy and make the United States an attractive migratory destination.

Depending on the labor needs of host countries, Caribbean countries may find
themselves alternately losing large numbers of working-age men or women. The consequent dislocations in economic and social arrangements in the sending country are
rarely considered in the host countries. In recent decades, the majority of "new" immigrants to the United States have been female.

The vast majority of the Jamaican women who migrate to the United States come
to the East Coast (New York, Connecticut, and Florida) to seek work in the service
economies of major urban centers. Many work in private homes as domestics, childcare
workers, and home health aides. Those who had access to college-level education are
heavily concentrated in registered nursing at urban hospitals and nursing homes.***
Because there are well-established Caribbean immigrant enclaves in the urban centers
of the eastern seaboard, informal job-location networks develop through which women
"send for" other female relatives once they find their own jobs.

Like most migrants from the Caribbean, working-class Jamaican American women
migrate in an attempt to escape the poverty and economic pressures they face at home.
Jamaica's economy is overly dependent on agriculture for export and on the income
from tourism. For most Jamaicans, the country's dependence on fluctuations in international commodities pricing and tourist flows means a life sentence of poverty.***

In the 1980s, many women found garment-assembly work in the Export Processing
Zones (EPZs) of Kingston. Under EPZ arrangements, foreign-owned garment manufacturers were allowed to set up export assembly plants in Jamaica. The enterprises are
given tax incentives, easy access to land and cheap labor, and are held to less restrictive
labor standards than elsewhere on the island. Low-wage factory work provided jobs for
many poor women in Jamaican urban centers until the North American Free Trade
Agreement (NAFTA) shifted the competitive balance for garment assembly to Mexico.

Tourist commercials aside, Jamaica is a dangerous place for working-class Black
women. Both street violence and domestic violence remain a frightening reality for
many Jamaican women, particularly those who live in the urban slums of Kingston. In

1997, more than 1000 people were murdered on the island. This street violence itself has complex roots in the forces of globalization. Economic desperation forces some poor Jamaicans into the transnational drug trade. Some form "posses" that are loosely affiliated with political parties; these gangs then do battle over disputed territory. The influx of guns with which to conduct this low-level civil war began to enter the island during the 1970s when the street violence was more explicitly political. The desire of government officials under both conservative and progressive Jamaican governments to protect the tourist industry—one of the largest sources of foreign exchange]—has resulted in recurrent police brutality and arbitrary detention. Working-class Jamaican women are either caught in the cross-fire themselves or suffer as the mothers, sisters, and daughters of the men who are gunned down in the streets.

*** [D]omestic violence remains a prevalent problem and accounts for many of the murders—allowing officials to de-emphasize crimes that might scare off tourists. While domestic violence occurs throughout the world among people of all socioeconomic classes, the problem is exacerbated in Jamaica by the widespread availability of guns, economic privation, and overt or tacit state policies that allow discrimination against women to continue.

Many Jamaican women are heads of households; birth rates among unmarried women are high. In order to survive, many working-class women sell small imported goods as "higglers" on the beaches or at the roadside. However, the tourist industry on the island is highly protected and structured to benefit the owners of large, all-inclusive resorts. The access of women in the informal sector to tourist dollars, therefore, is limited by periodic police interventions. Media reports also indicate that some young girls have turned to prostitution in tourist areas to support themselves and their families.

Although literacy rates in Jamaica are relatively high, and the equal access of girls to basic education is assured under formal laws, the small size of the economy provides few work opportunities for the people the country educates. The islands, therefore, become net exporters of people whose education might have prepared them to contribute to the island's social and economic development as indigenous teachers, physicians, or labor organizers. Instead, their economic circumstances force them to migrate. Some lucky few find work in the United States in the professions for which they were trained. Others take any job they can find on the bottom rungs of the U.S. service economy. The remittances these workers send home in U.S. dollars and shipping barrels full of food and clothing have become an essential support for the Jamaican economy. The children, spouses, parents, and friends of Jamaican-American women are housed, fed, and clothed by the money and materials they send home.

Poverty, unemployment, and violence in Jamaica are among the factors "pushing" working-class Jamaican women to migrate, but U.S. legal and socioeconomic forces present significant "pull" factors as well. The economic desperation of these women makes them a ready source of the low-wage labor that supports our economy. The low-wage immigrant women pulled in to meet the household needs of Americans have become the private solution to the public problem of fundamental race, class, and gender inequities in our own country. Political and economic changes that allowed some middle-class and poor women to enter the American paid labor force were made at the cost of creating new hierarchies that left poor immigrant and native-born women of color at the bottom.

Immigration law and policy legitimizes or delegitimizes the importation (and deportation) of these indoor migrant workers just as it does the movements of migrant farm workers from Mexico and sweatshop workers from Thailand and China. Depending on the political atmosphere in the United States, Jamaican American transmigrant workers, by turns, are recruited as reliable, low-wage supports for the dual-income family, lauded as "model minorities" by conservatives hoping to deny the reality of American racism and to undermine affirmative action policies, or castigated as "free-loaders" who steal jobs or become a drain on public services. Instead of being subject to policies born in the media hype of the moment, the needs of transmigrant women must be treated as matters of right. Their social and economic stability should not depend on the largesse of economically overdeveloped host countries. Such largesse can be too easily withdrawn when an American administration believes it to be politically expedient.

Jamaican-American Women as Subjects of a Critical Race Feminist Human Rights Focus

The physical and economic jeopardy in which many Jamaican American transmigrant women find themselves is a telling example of the global intersections of racism, nativism, sexism, and economic exploitation.***

A Critical Race Feminist analysis could explore how race and gender stereotyping contributes to an atmosphere in which the rights of Jamaican American female migrant workers can be more easily violated. We have yet to fully explore, for example, the gender and race-specific connections between the imposition of welfare reform in tandem with immigration reform in this country. Welfare reform now requires poor women with children to work outside the home without access to affordable childcare, adequate healthcare, a living wage, and appropriate labor protections. Popular images of women who need welfare buttress these abuses by picturing them as lazy baby factories who should bootstrap themselves out of poverty. Very few reformers recognized the fact that raising children is, indeed, very difficult, unpaid work, or questioned how poor women could obtain access to reproductive health care, childcare facilities, educational resources, or even new jobs after having had their welfare benefits dropped.

Simultaneously, Caribbean Americans, who previously had been stereotyped as "model minorities" who do not need public benefits, suddenly found themselves in the throes of nativist backlash. Those who did rely on public assistance because of age or disability found their food stamps, social security income, and other supports threatened. Some long-term U.S. residents with records of minor criminal violations found themselves deported to Jamaica. When they were not being subjected to deportation proceedings, low-wage immigrant women were portrayed as a hardworking counterpoint to the image of the lazy, native-born "Welfare Queen." A Critical Race Feminist analysis could expose the cynical ways in which the desperate attempts of migrant women to obtain subsistence for themselves and their families in the sending country are used against native-born Black women who work hard to maintain themselves and their children in hostile urban centers.

A Critical Race Feminist human rights analysis that is transnational in scope could alert us to the fact that, as Third World women, Jamaican American women are also subject to negative stereotypes. In a global context, Third World women are the "Welfare Queens" of international aid, trade, and population policies. Their home countries are so indebted to U.S. and European interests that most of the fruits of their Gross National Product are earmarked to service that debt. The reduction or removal of public services on which poor women and their families rely is a hallmark of international structural adjustment policies as well as of U.S. domestic welfare reform. Experimental drugs, used in related attempts to control the reproductive lives of women of color born in the United States, are often experienced first in the bodies of women in the Third World.***

HOPE LEWIS, UNIVERSAL MOTHER: TRANSNATIONAL MIGRATION AND THE HUMAN RIGHTS OF BLACK WOMEN IN THE AMERICAS

5 J. GENDER, RACE & JUSTICE 197, 197–206, 216–24, 227–29 (2001)

*** Are the experiences of Black women as migrant workers in the Americas appropriate subjects of international human rights focus? Unfortunately, the answers to that question sometimes depend on the nature of the acts we recognize as human rights violations. Often, the primary focus of international tribunals and non-governmental organizations is only on the violation of "first generation" rights through direct state-sponsored physical violence. The relative invisibility of Black women in the Americas on the mainstream human rights agenda is at least partially due to the prioritization of civil and political rights and to the marginalization of economic, social, and cultural rights. Black women do, of course, experience traditional violations of civil and political rights—they are arbitrarily detained, sexually assaulted, or otherwise tortured for their political opinions or for those of their partners. Feminist human rights scholars assert, however, that the traditional focus on political violence has failed to take full account of violence against women of color and white women, even in the "public" sphere. The failure to prioritize social welfare and cultural rights also undermines the interests of women to the extent that their experiences are socially constructed in the realm of the "private" sphere of home, family, and the (non-political) community.

The answers to the question I have posed also depend on the lenses of identity through which Black women see themselves and through which those who make, interpret, and enforce the law see them. Even if we attempt to restrict our focus to gender, it soon becomes evident that gender itself is richly complicated and textured by other aspects of identity. As Sherene Razack has cautioned, "[W]e cannot begin to evaluate how laws work for women or don't work, without understanding that gender comes into existence through race, class, sexuality, and physical or mental capacity." Increasingly, contemporary forms of globalization mean that gender is further informed and complicated by the transnational identities of the women, men, and children who cross national borders in search of work.

Similarly, racial and ethnic identities are complicated by gender and by the flow of human beings within and across borders. The migration of groups racially, ethnically, culturally, or linguistically identified as "other" has led to the resurgence of racial violence in sites as culturally and geographically diverse as Western Europe, Eastern Europe, Central Africa, Southern Africa, and North America. In recognition of these trends, the United Nations ("U.N.") World Conference Against Racism addressed, among other things, the implications of the intersection of racism and sexism with migration status.

*** [What are] the implications of human rights discourse for one group of Black women in the Americas—Afro-Caribbean women who migrate to North America? Some of those migrant women take jobs as household workers and other caregivers ("domestics," home health aides, and nannies). Excavations of their experiences can contribute to the larger feminist and Critical Race Feminist project of reconceptualizing the norms of human rights theory and practice.***

Individuals and groups construct identities both to resist and to enhance globalization. In order to resist the strong influence of global markets and cultural pressures, communities recreate, or create, racial, cultural, religious, and national ties. Individual members of such groups may see themselves as agents of such communitarian aspirations, seeking cultural or racial bonds as a bulwark against the crushing intrusions of globalization. On the other hand, they might also encounter and resist powerful elites who seek to use the authority of culture to crush non-conformity.

In addition to such community-based or personal forms of identity, I argue here that some externally imposed gender, race, and cultural stereotypes operate simultaneously to serve the free-market agendas of global capital. These stereotypical roles are forms of "identity" that mediate whether, and how, individuals and groups who occupy certain class positions will gain access to legal structures. For example, gender, race, and ethnic stereotypes associated with "illegal alien" status assist in regulating the flow of low-wage migrant labor. Further, gendered and racialized images help to maintain many people of color in the United States in a precarious "foreigner" status, regardless of their documentation or residency status.

In host countries, this manipulation of identity categories may take the form of discriminatory status and preference categories under immigration and asylum laws. Native-born and immigrant identity-based groups are structured and re-structured to occupy different spaces in racialized labor and social hierarchies. At different historical moments, various ethnic, racial, or gender groups are encouraged to enter or discouraged from entering host countries. The resulting conflicts and tensions can be further manipulated to undermine political organizing and solidarity among these groups.

Sending countries may be economically or politically dependent on the commodification of identity as well. Remittances from migrant workers are likely to be one of the most important sources of private transfers to the national economy. Gender stereotyping may figure into the perceived value of the potential migrant on the international market as in the trafficking of women for sex work and household work. Sending countries also may see migration as a means of reducing domestic unemployment or political unrest. The resulting formal and informal arrangements between host countries and sending countries have enormous human rights implications for the migrant workers involved and the communities they enter and leave behind.***

What is a "Human Rights Story"?

The economic, social, and cultural violence and atrocities experienced by many people from the "Third World" have largely been rendered invisible or irrelevant to mainstream human rights analysis. This failure to address economic, social, and cultural rights and the right to development has the effect of undermining the accountability of the North for violations of human rights. As noted by the U.N. High Commissioner for Human Rights, "[T]he shocking reality is *** that States and the international community as a whole continue to tolerate all too often breaches of economic, social and cultural rights which, if they occurred in relation to civil and political rights, would provoke expressions of horror and outrage and would lead to concerned calls for immediate remedial action." As a result, the economic, social, and cultural roles in which many Black women migrants are typecast leave many aspects of their experiences beyond traditional human rights focus.***

A "Domestic" Story

*** Despite the tremendous need for, difficulty of, and importance of, the work women do in the home, domestic workers remain officially and socially classified as "unskilled." The low status, and correspondingly low wages, assigned to domestic work, is intimately linked to the discriminatory assignment of identity roles. In the United States, for example, unpaid female family members, African-American women who were enslaved, and later, immigrant women, and non-immigrant women of color, did most domestic work. Advocates for household workers describe the risks many modern household workers face: low or unpaid wages; long hours; poor or dangerous working conditions; physical and sexual abuse; lack of benefits; long and forced separations from children, partners, and extended family; exposure to harmful chemicals or other dangerous conditions in the home; social isolation; arbitrary arrest, detention, and deportation.

A "Nanny Chain" Story?

*** Many Afro-Caribbean female migrants form part of a "nanny chain"; migrating to care for the homes, parents, and children of middle-class families in North America or Europe, while leaving their own children and parents in the care of relatives or lower-paid women or girls from rural areas in the Caribbean. Women migrants may be the sole economic support of their children back home, but they may not see their children for years at a time, resulting in tremendous strains on emotional ties.***

Many Afro-Caribbean migrant women send cash remittances, as well as food, clothing, and other household goods in shipping barrels back to the home country. The children of these migrant women are sometimes referred to as "barrel children." This informal economic support is not insignificant; the amount sent back is estimated to be more than $500 million per year to Jamaica alone. Migrant women, are, therefore, major pillars of support for Caribbean economies. Many are self-conscious and assertive about the importance of their roles as economic providers, creating complex labor scouting networks within and outside the Caribbean. They send home money to build houses, to educate their children, and to care for their elderly parents. They also create important survival networks within Northern communities.

Race, gender, and ethnicity play vital roles in regulating the supply of these "surrogate mothers" to the North. While sociologists have examined the significance of the nanny chain phenomenon, it is rarely seen through the lens of human rights. What does the nanny chain mean for the migrant woman's right to family and community life? Is the sending state's pursuit of economic or social policies that enhance migratory pressures a violation of human rights?***

An "Illegal Alien" Story

*** The ability to regulate human traffic across borders is considered a basic attribute of state sovereignty. Despite increasing pressures to remove trade, investment, and other economic barriers to the global movement of capital, the movement of human beings across borders remains highly regulated, especially in the North. Therefore, "illegal" or undocumented status makes [migrants] and people like [them], more vulnerable to the deprivation of human rights protections. The role of migrant workers as "citizens" who contribute over the course of years or decades to the economic, social, and political needs of the host country remains unrecognized.

The broader categories of "illegal alien" or "migrant worker" often themselves hide the specific stories of women migrant workers. International human rights organizations have only recently begun to recognize the implications of the global trade in working women. Some abuses experienced by women migrant workers are inconsistent with the requirements of various International Labour Organization (ILO) conventions and of the U.N. Convention on the Protection of the Rights of All Migrant Workers and Members of Their Families. However, the specific implications of gender and race for female migrant workers are generally hidden in [such] *** instruments. In order to bring visibility to their specific experiences, female migrant workers have testified before non-governmental tribunals organized at World Conferences in Vienna, Beijing, and Copenhagen. They have noted that the international human rights discourse assumes that migrant workers are male heads of households who will send remittances home to their wives and children. Increasingly, it is women who migrate to support themselves and their families and who face gender-specific violations of their human rights.

Some progress has been made. The U.N. Secretary-General, the Commission on Human Rights, and the Special Rapporteur on Violence Against Women have recognized the existence and prevalence of gender-specific abuses. They have adopted resolutions against trafficking in women and on violence against female migrants. Human rights NGOs also have documented some of the most severe labor and physical abuses of female migrant workers in human rights reports.

At this early stage in the recognition of the human rights implications of female migration, the attention of most mainstream human rights organizations remains fixed primarily on the physical and sexual abuses associated with slavery and trafficking. They document conditions involving literal enslavement or indentured servitude, such as the horrific cases reported in the United States involving foreign diplomats as employers. Are the stories of economic, social, and cultural violations that many other female migrant workers experience too "ordinary" for us to see them as a matter of human rights urgency?

*** Because of the single-state focus of the traditional human rights framework, if we identify these issues as human rights problems at all, we tend to see them in isolation from the transnational context in which they occur. Migrant workers from countries like Jamaica are, at best, seen as victims of abuses by "alien" governments or cultural norms located in the Third World. This view of human rights violations makes it more acceptable for the countries of the North to allow periodic flows of migrants or refugees from the South, seemingly as a matter of largesse. The "enlightened" North can thus conveniently import migrant workers from the South when necessary. However, because such limited admissions are seemingly based on humanitarian considerations, Northern governments can also more easily exclude these workers when its "generosity" runs out. Northern economies can only "take care of" so many "victims" of the political, social, and economic conditions of the South for so long. Global migration stories should also be about the transnational human rights impact of international policies and arrangements over which the North has significant control and responsibility. Assigning the sole responsibility for human rights violations to the governments of the Third World masks the responsibilities of the North with regard to the human rights of migrants. Structural adjustment policies, Third World debt, and inequitable terms of trade, for example, have a great deal to do with human rights conditions in the South. We must use the lens of human rights to examine more fully the factors that contribute to the need to migrate. With such an approach, one can re-examine stories that explain the migration of women solely as a movement from "backward" oppressive cultures to the "enlightened" human rights cultures of the North.***

If the stories of many Black female migrant workers are to become human rights stories, they must be intersectional stories and they must recognize the interdependence and indivisibility of human rights. Human rights stories must include the right to food, as well as the right to political participation; they must include the right to development as well as the right not to be raped or tortured because of one's political beliefs. They must include the right to family and the enjoyment of culture, as well as the right to a fair hearing under the law; they must include the rights of parents and the rights of their children, regardless of where they were born.***

JACQUELINE BHABHA, INTERNATIONALIST GATEKEEPERS?: THE TENSION BETWEEN ASYLUM ADVOCACY AND HUMAN RIGHTS

15 Harv. Hum. Rts. J. 155, 156, 160–61, 170–75 (2002)

*** In today's world, the experience of serious human rights violations is closely linked to the act of migration: as a push factor causing desperate masses to flee across borders, however dangerous the conditions of flight and uncertain the prospects of even minimal safety; and as a reception reality, related to the increasingly harsh conditions surrounding the quest for asylum. Indeed, as a transnational phenomenon, refugee flight involves multiple sites and diverse agents of oppression, within, across, and between borders.***

Legitimating Gatekeeping ***

Asylum advocates are participants in a polarized global migration regime, which promotes the ever-freer movement of the enfranchised just as it increasingly restricts access to protection or opportunity for the disenfranchised. Conflicting pressures emerging from the needs of developed states complicate this contradictory tension at the heart of contemporary migration control. Developed states need to maintain the primacy of sovereign state borders while participating in borderless global transnational regimes of power and trade; they need to facilitate business mobility and availability of both skilled and unskilled labor, while protecting domestic welfare regimes and service structures from illegitimate claimants. In addition, many developed states face compelling political pressures to promote racial homogeneity in the face of increasing diversity. Finally, states increasingly seek to privatize and decentralize immigration control while taking credit for comprehensive control of their borders. Thus border control has been exported far beyond the physical confines of developed states, by readmission agreements with surrounding buffer states, by visa requirements, and by penalties on carriers transporting undocumented or inadequately documented travelers, in order to keep unwanted potential migrants from accessing the territories of these states. Within this system, the institution of asylum has become a key pressure point, complicating the filtering process that is designed to separate eligible from ineligible travelers. Asylum is constructed to be a strictly limited humanitarian safety valve, permitting only a fraction of would-be migrants, the discrete class of "genuine" refugees, to trump immigration restrictions and gain access to the developed world. Asylum is thus intended to act as a "bridge between morality and law," entrenching a regime of international sovereignty and solidarity within an increasingly harsh and discriminatory state-based system. "Genuine" refugees are to be sifted out from the mass of "illegal" migrants who purport to be eligible for international protection but are not, and are increasingly perceived as a danger to the security, cohesion and well-being of destination states. Asylum is the process that keeps migration exclusion morally defensible while protecting the global gatekeeping operation as a whole.***

Expanding the Scope of Asylum—The Human Aspect of Global Forced Migration

It is not only in interpreting the refugee definition that the human rights framework has played a central role. An expansive conception of human rights has also been the backdrop for the changing interpretation of forced migration as a whole in the context of post-Cold War globalization. One might say, reversing the well-known feminist aphorism, that the political has become personal—the human impact of seemingly impersonal, geopolitical or societal strategies is no longer on the interpretative margins, of relevance only to psychologists or social workers. Rather human rights norms are increasingly used as consensus tools for comprehensive accountability, a new architecture with which to analyze and develop broad programmatic social goals. The U.N.'s human development index and the European Union's adoption of the "scoreboard" criteria for evaluating post-Amsterdam treaty developments are examples of this increasingly popular strategy. In this process, the simple dichotomy of civil and political rights versus economic, social, and cultural rights is rendered obsolete, an anachronism at best. Questions of due process, non-discrimination, and freedom from torture intersect with concerns regarding access to basic services; health, housing and education rights; and linguistic, sexual and religious freedoms.

This indivisibility of rights, long recognized in theory but only recently acknowledged in the practical application of human rights standards to assessments of social developments, affects asylum advocates directly. It opens the avenue of asylum to an expanded cast of players since the consequence of large global forces are now being scrutinized for their human rights impact. Indeed this changing perception of the relation between economic development and rights access or protection can affect the conceptualization of persecution itself and thus directly change advocacy strategies.

Discriminatory state policies that result in food insecurity, high incidences of HIV/AIDS infection, water deprivation, oil pollution, land flooding for particular populations or subsections of the population, might all count as persecution, though this approach has yet to be developed. It would be an extension of the arguments successfully used already, in an earlier expansionist phase of asylum advocacy during the 1990s, to establish that forcible sterilization or mandatory veiling might count as persecution. New strategies for protective advocacy thus present the challenge of distilling claims that can benefit individual claimants from massive group problems. But such an expansion of the basis for asylum claims, into the protection of economic, social, or positive rights feeds directly into the tension between the asylum advocate's internationalist and gatekeeping roles. It highlights the fundamentally problematic distinction between "genuine" and "economic" refugees, linking discriminatory policies that undermine communities' economic survival possibilities to the concept of persecution directly. Though economic desperation itself cannot be a basis for claiming asylum (or indeed, in the absence of evidence of willful neglect or discrimination, for claiming that the country of origin, as opposed to the international community, is violating any human right), its causal link to particular policies may well provide the foundation for such a claim. Work by environmental and indigenous rights activists can be used to substantiate this expansion of the scope of asylum advocacy. In an era of polarized economic globalization, where dictatorship and destitution go hand in hand, it will be increasingly important that the asylum advocate establish that economic desperation and refugee status are not mutually exclusive.***

The Trade in Desperation: Smuggling and Trafficking of Asylum-Seekers and the Challenge for Advocacy

Nowhere is the complex link between economic desperation and refugee status more evident than in the area of human smuggling and human trafficking—two forms of illegal and commercially assisted entry used by those fleeing persecution to reach a place of safety in the face of migration control measures. Asylum seekers are increasingly compelled to resort to the use of smugglers, counterfeit documents, subterfuge and clandestine behavior to circumvent mandatory visa requirements, carrier sanction policies that turn airline staff into immigration control agents, and other forms of immigration control. These controls, some state run and some privatized, operate both at the border and far beyond the immediate frontier zones. Circumvention is thus increasingly a professional art, not something that can be left to ingenuity or good luck. The exorbitant sums of money paid for cross border smuggling services and the life-threatening risks taken are testament to the efficacy of states' border controls not, as is sometimes claimed, to their increasing irrelevance. Some asylum seekers, caught in dangerous situations or devastated refugee camps, are coerced or tricked into leaving their dire living circumstances by traffickers only to encounter far worse abroad—the fear of persecution in the home country thus compounded by risks arising directly out of the trafficking situation.

With legal access increasingly barred, illegality, in differing guises, is the strategy of last resort for those desperate to flee. Procedures for limiting unwanted migration are not confined to the erection of obstacles to access; at the border or inside the territory, asylum seekers are progressively criminalized, subjected to adversarial interrogations and incarcerated for extensive periods in harsh conditions. It is not surprising then, that "illegal immigrant," "unemployed alien," and even "terrorist," "hijacker," "criminal," are frequently used as synonyms for "asylum seekers" or "refugees," particularly in the wake of the September 11, 2001 events in the United States. Instead of providing protection for trafficked victims subjected to severe human rights abuses, states have tended to deport them as illegal migrants, without investigating possible claims to asylum. Smuggled asylum seekers have also been penalized as illegals, and subjected to expedited removal procedures or long periods of detention. It has been up to asylum advocates to try and challenge the blurring of categories between asylum seeker and criminal and to operationalize the migration filter in a manner that draws in the human rights protections. To dispel the presumption of economically driven illegal immigration that arises because of the commercialized nature of the transport, and to successfully substitute protection for penalization, asylum advocates have to contextualize "illegal" migration within a broader socio-economic framework that includes questions of labor, economics, and health policy.

Some support for this contextualizing approach can be derived from recent domestic and international developments. This is not to deny that the prime emphasis has been on improving detection and criminal enforcement. Individual states have introduced stiff criminal sanctions against traffickers and smugglers; states have also collaborated to institute transnational measures that facilitate collaboration to apprehend traffickers. But there has also been growing attention to the human rights violations inflicted on victims of these practices. The United Nations recently addressed the relationship between commercially facilitated migration and rights protection questions under the rubric of the Transnational Organized Crime Convention of 2000. Two protocols to the Convention, one on Trafficking and the other on Smuggling, address the human rights of victims of these practices as a central issue, highlighting the need for protection rather than punishment. This is an important step in the right direction. However, protective concerns have emphasized the need for states to provide welfare and counseling support to victims "while they are within [their territories]." There is scant acknowledgement that victims of trafficking or smuggled persons may be refugees who require permanent status in the host country. The rights-based approach to tackling the phenomena displayed in this convention may benefit asylum advocacy, but the challenge of moving beyond short-term protective intervention to the long term need for asylum for those who are eligible will again emphasize the advocate's complex gatekeeping role.

A particular gatekeeping difficulty for asylum advocates may arise in the context of claims on behalf of women trafficked for sexual exploitation. The difficulty reflects a tension between migration and human rights approaches to the issue. Whether the initial decision to embark on transnational migration was taken by or with the consent of the trafficked person is irrelevant from a human rights perspective: it is the rights abuses inflicted that are the concern and the focus of intervention. Thus, harms inflicted on commercial sex workers who may have agreed to travel initially, and in circumstances different from those that transpire during or at the end of the journey, are of concern, as are abuses inflicted on persons of "good" moral character, who were coerced from the start. However, in the migration context, where the restriction of unauthorized migration is the overriding policy concern, these are compelling policy pressures to limit state protective responsibilities: evidence of coercion at the outset of the journey, rather than the presence of abuse at any given point during the trafficking relationship, thus comes to be the focus of state protection for "victims of trafficking."

An example of this approach is the U.S. Trafficking Victims Protection Act of 2000. It establishes a comprehensive set of protections and services, including eligibility for a special "T" visa which can result in permanent residence, but these protections are limited to victims of "severe forms of trafficking in persons," defined as a coerced victim of trafficking who is enslaved without having ever consented. It follows that a person who consented to being transported across borders for the purpose of engaging in commercial sex but who then finds herself in an abusive, coercive situation, is not protected. For the same reason, those who are known to have worked as sex workers prior to the transnational transport are likely to be excluded. Given the difficulties of distinguishing clearly between coercion and consent, and the likelihood that a significant proportion of trafficking victims may have engaged in previous commercial sex, this limitation imposes a problematic gatekeeping constraint on advocates.***

Notes and Questions

1.   Does globalization have uniquely identifiable consequences for women? How does the migration of women affect the men and children in their home communities? Can these effects be analyzed within a rights framework?

2.   *Migrants' Convention.* The International Convention on the Protection of the Rights of All Migrant Workers and Members of their Families entered into force in July of 2003. *See* International Convention on the Protection of the Rights of All Migrant Workers and Members of Their Families, G.A. Res. 45/158, annex, 45 U.N. GAOR Supp. (No. 49A) at 262, U.N. Doc. A/45/49 (1990), *entered into force* July 1, 2003. As of that time, the list of ratifying countries did not include the North American and Western European host countries in which many migrants from the Global South work. The U.N. Office of the High Commissioner for Human Rights reports the following states parties to the convention as of March 2004: Azerbaijan, Bangladesh, Belize, Bolivia, Bosnia and Herzegovina, Burkina Faso, Cape Verde, Chile, Colombia, Comoros, Ecuador, Egypt, El Salvador, Ghana, Guatemala, Guinea, Guinea-Bissau, Kyrgyzstan, Mali, Mexico, Morocco, Paraguay, Philippines, Sao Tome and Principe, Senegal, Seychelles, Sierra Leone, Sri Lanka, Tajikistan, Timor-Leste, Togo, Turkey, Uganda and Uruguay. *See* Office of the High Commissioner for Human Rights, *Status of Ratification of the Convention on the Rights of All Migrant Workers and Their Families: Status of States Parties as of 16 March 2004, at* http://www.ohchr.org/english/law/cmw-ratify.htm (last visited June 29, 2004).

3.   The International Labour Organization estimates that there are more than 86 million migrant workers worldwide. See International Labour Organization, *ILO Adopts Plan to Give Fair Deal to 86 Million Migrant Workers, available at* http://www.ilo.org/public/english/bureau/inf/pr/2004/31.htm (last visited June 29, 2004). *See also* International Labour Organization, *Informal Economy Resource Database, at* http://www.ilo.org/dyn/dwresources/iebrowse.home (last visited June 29, 2004). For an overview of the efforts surrounding ratification of the convention, *see generally, The Global Campaign for Ratification of the Convention on Rights of Migrants, available at* http://www.migrantsrights.org and MIGRANT NEWS (all issues), *available at* http://www.december18.net.

4.   *Defining Refugee.* Lewis and Bhabha seem to argue for an expansion of the definition of "refugee" or "asylum-seeker" to include those trying to escape violations of economic rights. Would such an expanded legal definition be workable in practice?

5.   *Human Trafficking.* Human trafficking is a global phenomenon, resulting in widespread violations of civil, political, economic, social and cultural rights. How would you distinguish between "trafficking" and "migrant smuggling"? What roles do "consent" and "coercion" play?

The U.N. has addressed human trafficking as an aspect of transnational organized crime. *See, e.g.,* Protocol to Prevent, Suppress, and Punish Trafficking in Persons, Especially Women and Children, Supplementing the United Nations Convention Against Transnational Organized Crime, G.A. res. 55/25, annex II, 55 U.N. GAOR Supp. (No. 49) at 60, U.N. Doc. A/45/49 (Vol. I) (2001); Protocol Against the Smuggling of Migrants by Land, Sea and Air, Supplementing the United Nations Convention Against Transnational Crime, G.A. Res. 55/25, annex III, 55 U.N. GAOR Supp. (No. 49) at 65, U.N. Doc. A/45/49 (Vol. I) (2001); United Nations Convention Against Transnational Organized Crime, G.A. Res. 55/25, annex I, 55 U.N. GAOR Supp. (No. 49) at 44, U.N. Doc. A/45/49 (Vol. I) (2001), *not yet in force.*

Current efforts build on historical anti-slavery, anti-trafficking of women and asylum treaties. *See, e.g.,* Slavery Convention, 60 L.N.T.S. 253, *entered into force* Mar. 9, 1927; Protocol amending the Slavery Convention, 182 U.N.T.S. 51, *entered into force* Dec. 7, 1953; Supplementary Convention on the Abolition of Slavery, the Slave Trade, and Institutions and Practices Similar to Slavery, 226 U.N.T.S. 3, *entered into force* Apr. 30, 1957; Convention for the Suppression of the Traffic in Persons and of the Exploitation of the Prostitution of Others, 96 U.N.T.S. 271, *entered into force* July 25, 1951.

The U.N. reports that human trafficking is "the fastest growing business of organized crime with an estimated 700,000 people trafficked every year for sexual exploitation and forced labour." CNN, Com/World, U.N. Warns of Human Traffic Boom, Feb. 19, 2002, *available at* http://edition.cnn.com/2002/WORLD/europe/02/19/human.trafficking/ (last visited June 29, 2004). For a discussion of recent U.N. approaches to human trafficking, including the distinctions made between "human trafficking" and "smuggling of migrants," *see* United Nations Office for Drug Control and Crime Prevention, *Trafficking in Human Beings, available at* http://www.unodc.org/unodc/trafficking_human_beings.html (last visited June 29, 2004).

6. What roles do racial and cultural stereotypes play in the violation of women's rights in a global economy? How are gender and race "commodified" in global markets?

7. Does the international community as a whole have legal obligations to address violations of human rights caused by globalization?

C. IS DEVELOPMENT A HUMAN RIGHT?

This chapter's final section discusses the nature and possibilities of the right to development. Given the disagreements about the definition of development, how is a right to development to be defined? Who is accountable for implementing such a right? To whom does the right belong? Is such a call, first made in the heyday of Third World nationalism and the Non-Aligned Movement, still relevant under existing forms of globalization?

MOHAMMED BEDJAOUI, THE RIGHT TO DEVELOPMENT

INTERNATIONAL LAW: ACHIEVEMENTS AND PROSPECTS 1177, 1177–79
(MOHAMMED BEDJAOUI ED., 1991).

I. ORIGINS

1. The concept of the "right to development" came into existence during the great historical phase of successive decolonizations in the 1950s. The right to development was a demand asserted by the third world which was anxious, through economic liberation, to put the finishing touches to its political emancipation. At that time, one of the third world countries most strongly motivated in that endeavour, the independent Algeria of the 1960s, made the right to development, as a right of both States and peoples, a militant Ideology at the international level. This "right to development" was claimed by Algeria for the benefit of the people, of every people, as a collective right thwarted by a system of inequitable international economic relations. The Algerian leaders perceived, indeed, that the economic "lift-off" of their country was dependent on its

winning economic independence and breaking free of inequitable bilateral or multi-national constraint.***

*** In addition to the evolution of human rights, changes in international economic relations have also shaped the legal framework of the right to development. One of the outgrowths of colonial independence was the entry of "less developed countries" ("LDCs") into the UN system. The LDCs worked together in an effort to change the existing international economic regime, and to codify new norms into a legal document. This strategy began to bear fruit in May 1974, when the General Assembly adopted a Declaration and Program of Action on the Establishment of a New International Economic Order ("NIEO"). A further step came with the adoption of the Charter of Economic Rights and Duties of States, asserting that every State has the responsibility to promote economic, social and cultural development and progress for both its own people and those of developing countries.

The NIEO challenge to the status quo, and the far-reaching implications of its implementation, was met with substantial resistance by industrialized countries. Notwithstanding such controversy, it is clear that many NIEO provisions have helped shape the right to development. While the documents associated with the NIEO make no mention of such a right, official UN reports on the right to development do take into account elements of the NIEO.***

Judge Keba Mbaye placed [the right to development] firmly in 1972 among human rights.***

ISABELLA D. BUNN, THE RIGHT TO DEVELOPMENT: IMPLICATIONS FOR INTERNATIONAL ECONOMIC LAW

15 AM. U. INT'L L. REV. 1425, 1432–35, 1448–49, 1454–56 (2000)

I.   ***

B.   *Adoption of the UN Declaration on the Right to Development* ***

In legal circles, Senegalese jurist Keba M'Baye is credited with the initiation of the "right to development." In a 1972 lecture at the International Institute of Human Rights in Strasbourg, he asserted that it was a right belonging to all men, as "every man has a right to live and a right to live better." He based his justification more in political-economic and moral terms, rather than in legal analysis.

The UN Commission on Human Rights, influenced by M'Baye's views, expressly referred to the right to development in a resolution adopted in 1977.*** Eventually, on December 4, 1986, the UN General Assembly voted overwhelmingly to adopt the Declaration on the Right to Development [UNDRD].

C.   *Legal Critique of the Right to Development* ***

The UNDRD's preamble recognizes that: "development is a comprehensive economic, social, cultural and political process, which aims at the constant involvement of the well-being of the entire population and of all individuals on the basis of their active, free and meaningful participation in development and the fair distribution of benefits resulting therefrom."***

The UNDRD defines the right to development as "an inalienable human right by virtue of which every human person and all peoples are entitled to participate in, contribute to, and enjoy economic, social, cultural and political development, in which all human rights and fundamental freedoms can be fully realized."

The concept of the right to development immediately poses a number of legal questions. There are arguments about the appropriate place of the right, if any, within the body of human rights law. There are difficulties in identifying the beneficiaries and duty-holders under the right, as the UNDRD holds both individual and collective dimensions. A further issue is that of enforcement or justiciability, reflecting doubts about how the right might be upheld at the national or international levels.***

Some commentators, such as Bedjaoui, are effusive in their praise. He claims the right to development is the core right from which all others stem. But for the most part, the legal analysis of the right to development has been critical. Ghai maintains:

> The value of the concept of a right is that it creates entitlements, and the entitlements are easier to enforce if the contents and beneficiaries of the right are clearly specified. In the case of the right to development, it is not clear who are the right and duty bearers. Equally vague is the content of the right.***

A variety of programs incorporate more favorable treatment for poorer nations. For example, the WTO framework explicitly recognizes that developing countries should receive differential and more favorable treatment under certain international trading rules.

International financial institutions also grant concessional terms to underdeveloped countries. For example, as early as 1960 the World Bank set up a "soft-loan" arm known as the International Development Association (IDA) to provide long-term loans at little or no interest. Additionally, a number of treaties, such as the Law of the Sea Convention, grant preferences to developing countries in matters such as special access to foreign fishing zones.***

Acknowledgment of entitlement, however, does not appear to be linked to any acceptance of a corresponding legal obligation to fulfill those needs. It is true that many nations administer aid programs for developing countries, and many organizations, including the Development Assistance Committee of the OECD, monitor aid flows and policies. One commentator notes the remarkable development that it is now "standard practice for richer states to give aid to poorer states" given the fact that before the World War II era no government provided aid to help the economic development of other states on a continuing basis (as opposed to temporary disaster relief). However, the same writer also noted that the richer industrialized states are usually reluctant to recognize any legal obligation to aid poorer states.***

II. ***

C. *Obstacles to the Realization of the Right to Development* ***

2. *The Debt Burden and Structural Adjustment Policies*

The text of the UNDRD does not mention debt, although there is regular mention of debt burden and structural adjustment policies in the discussions on obstacles to development. At one point, some representatives of poorer countries objected to consultations with the World Bank and IMF, because they saw those institutions as part of the problem and not part of the solution.

The magnitude of the debt is substantial, and the economic requirements associated with its repayment are often onerous. Since the poorest countries bear the greatest burden, the implications in human terms are acute.***

The Independent Expert on the effects of structural adjustment policies on the full enjoyment of human rights made a number of recommendations on the type of actions to be taken at various levels. At the international level, these include:

(A) Debt cancellation for the heavily-indebted poor countries. Priority should be accorded to countries emerging from civil wars and those devastated by natural disasters.

(B) Human rights conditionality in future lending.*** Greater transparency and accountability of lenders, such as the IMF and World Bank, will help ensure that debt relief is used effectively and not squandered on corruption, military expenditure or grandiose projects.

(C) International mechanisms to retrieve money stolen by corrupt leaders.***

(D) Reform of the international economic, financial and trade systems.***

(E) Natural resource preservation: future lending should be made conditional on an assessment of the impact of proposed projects on the environment and on the resource base for the poor.***

3. Activities of Transnational Corporations

The Working Group on the Right to Development identified the concentration of economic and political power in a few countries and corporations, as one of the obstacles to the realization of the right to development. [I]t urged the resumption of multilateral negotiations on a code of conduct for transnational corporations.***

RHODA HOWARD, LAW AND ECONOMIC RIGHTS IN COMMONWEALTH AFRICA

15 CAL. WEST. INT'L L.J. 607, 609–610 (1985)

"*** The stress on the 'right to development' at the international level obscures, in my view, the prior economic rights clearly laid out in the International Bill of Rights. The right to development appears to imply a collective right, a claim which poor nation-states can make on wealthier nation-states. As an *international* (State-State) right, it implies that development is prevented in the poorer countries mainly as a result of the (past and present) activities of the wealthier countries on the world market. As a *collective* right, it implies that the people representing the collectivity are disinterested individuals: this *** is a naive view."

*** There is an interconnected fundamental problem in Africa today: economic initiative must be encouraged, but at the same time economic exploitation (which I define as deprivation of basic economic rights) must be discouraged.*** A good approach to the promotion of economic rights in Africa would be to attempt to ensure that no development policy rendered the poorest less well off than they already are. But this principle has to be supplemented by the guarantee of a floor of economic rights as well: if the poor are already living in degraded circumstances, it is not enough merely to hope for the trickling down of benefits from growth-oriented policies.***

I view the politics of human rights, including economic rights, in Commonwealth Africa primarily as a system in which the ruling class as a collective body manipulates the State in its own interests, and in which the non-ruling class masses are generally excluded from the political process.*** To assert that class relations are a fundamental barrier to any distributive model of development which might ensure economic rights is not, as some might have it, irrelevant Marxism: it is common sense.

The analysis of class formation and class relations is fundamental to understanding why an alleged "group" right such as the right to development has no meaning unless individuals can wrest development's real material benefits from those who control it.*** In its "reasons for the continuance of poverty," the International Commission of Jurists mentions the "egoism of national interest," but there is no mention of internal ruling classes. "Structural changes" are referred to as necessary for the right to development, but such changes are not defined; nor is the likelihood of large-scale social conflict over such changes discussed.***

Notes and Questions

1. *Is the Right to Development State-Centric?* Howard assumes that a collective right to development must necessarily attach to the state. Do you agree? Could such a right attach to peoples, a category distinct from the state? *See* Issa Shivji's discussion of the right of self-determination below.

2. Bedjaoui asserts that "[t]he international dimension of the right to development is nothing other than *the right to an equitable share in the economic and social well-being of the world.* It reflects an essential demand of our time since four-fifths of the world's population no longer accept that the remaining fifth should continue to build its wealth on their poverty." Do you agree?

3. For an additional analysis of Third World perspectives on the right to development, *see* Karin Mickelson, *Rhetoric and Rage: Third World Voices in International Legal Discourse,* 16 WISC. INT'L L.J. 353, 374–87 (1998).

ISSA G. SHIVJI, THE CONCEPT OF HUMAN RIGHTS IN AFRICA 29–33, 81–83 (1989)

The 'right to development' is considered a specifically African contribution to the international human rights discourse.***

[T]here have been a couple of conferences on the 'right to development' and a score of writings by Africanists on the same, sometimes purporting to expand and elaborate on M'Baye and at other times criticizing it. It has also found a formal recognition in the preamble of the African Charter of Human and People's Rights.***

*** M'Baye, while not defining development in any precise manner, distinguishes it from growth and argues that development is a metamorphosis of structures involving 'a range of changes in mental and intellectual patterns that favour the rise of growth and its prolongation in historical time.' In short, M'Baye views development as a comprehensive integrated process including, but not confined to, economic development.

He further argues that the right to development is a collective right and belongs to a group.***

As for the duty-bearers of the right to development, he identifies specifically 'states' and the 'international community.' The right to development 'is a power or prerogative which peoples can demand of their government or of the organized international community.'

The 'father,' as M'Baye has been called, of the right of development finds justification for this right on several levels. 'The legitimacy of this right is based on political and economic considerations and is founded on moral grounds and in accordance with legal standards.'

Firstly, from the economic standpoint, M'Baye reviews the colonial exploitation of the Third World people by the now developed countries and the continued inequities in the North-South relations. The resultant poverty on the part of the Third World, whose ultimate beneficiaries are the countries of the North, at least gives rise to some obligations on these beneficiaries and therefore, according to M'Baye, a right to development to the people.***

From the political standpoint, the countries of the North have been giving tied aid so as to maintain political loyalty and diplomatic constituency in the underdeveloped world in their inter-power rivalries. From this too, it is they who gain.

Then there is also the question of international peace and security. Where the world is divided so dramatically between the rich and the poor, there cannot be a guarantee for peace. Thus the development of the poor is an obligation on the rich.***

But even more important than responsibility, in M'Baye's view, is solidarity. Mankind is gradually moving towards relations based on international solidarity. In this regard too there is a moral justification for the right to development. Those who have must give to those who do not have, only then can the principle of solidarity have any meaning.

Juridically, M'Baye's position seems to be that the right to development is not a new right but is already implied in the various UN instruments and the existing international Covenants on human rights. He cites the UN Charter and the UN Declaration on Human Rights as having recognized both the limitations on state sovereignty as well as the duty of co-operation. The International Covenants, recognizing various economic, social and cultural rights, and the Charter of Economic Rights and Duties of States, all have in one form or another implied the right to development. Thus M'Baye concludes that the right to development has descended from the 'sphere of morals to that of law.'***

The breadth and comprehensiveness of the 'right to development' has sometimes attracted to itself to the label of 'right of rights' in which case it has been derided by the critics as 'entirely pointless.' In one of the sharpest critiques, Jack Donnelly *** has argued that M'Baye has completely failed to establish the conceptual foundations of the alleged right. His position is that in M'Baye, there is a confusion between the concept of right as an entitlement or claim by specified right-holders against identifiable duty-bearers, and moral righteousness; that all that which may be morally desirable does not necessarily and even eventually constitute a right, moral or legal.

Further, that in the existing Covenants, UN Declarations and intergovernmental treaties—except for the African Charter—there is no such right, and certainly not a collective right, to development. Donnelly concludes that the whole hullabaloo about the right to development is just another stratagem by developing states to press for greater aid and assistance from the developed North; to justify attention from their violations of political/civil rights and to smuggle in the priority of economic/social-rights arguments through the back door.***

Right to self-determination and right to development compared

The genesis of the right to self-determination lies in the struggles of the people from the days of bourgeois revolutions in the 18th-19th century Europe to the post-war national liberation struggles of the people of the Third World. It thus has historical legitimacy which the right to development does not. The right to development finds its roots in the contemporary demands of the Third World states for better terms on the international market, greater aid and assistance and generally in, what has come to be known as, the demand for the new international economic order.

At best these are statist 'trade union' demands which seek a little more comfortable accommodation for the Third World ruling classes within the existing order. At worst, they amount to no more than a new way of asserting a 'right' to charity.

On the level of international law, as the right to self-determination has developed over more than half a century, it has come to be recognized by international law and has found a place in UN treaties (the 1966 Covenants) as well as in a considerable number of other international treaties among states of both the North and the South.***

The right to development, on the other hand, is an assertion of a 'new' right. It does not therefore have the legitimacy of international legality. True, its development has been fast from the original conception to the Declaration by the General Assembly. It has been enthusiastically taken over by liberals of the West, supported by Soviet-oriented theorists and almost unanimously advocated by African international lawyers. Even if it eventually finds a place in an international covenant, the question remains: Does it serve the interests of the people of Africa?

Conceptually the right to development has very weak foundation. Development itself has either been expanded to include everything (and therefore nothing!) as in the UN Declaration, or more often narrowed to economic development in its economistic, and increasingly, even econometric sense. Either way it blunts, if not eliminates, the ideological and political sting and sharpness which are central to the concept of self-determination.

Under the right of self-determination, the right-holders are a collective whether peoples, nations, nationalities or national groups. Besides the fact that each one of these concepts has strong theoretical foundations, they are practically and politically of immediate relevance to Africa in its struggle against imperialism and authoritarianism.

Secondly, these concepts are not tied to existing state structures and systems but rather have an independent dynamism of their own with a capacity to comprehend and guide change. In a word, they express class struggle rather than a statist status quo. The concept of the right to development, on the contrary, is both static as well as statist. The right here generally belongs to 'states' as is clearly expressed in the Declaration. The Preamble 'recognizes' that 'the creation of conditions favorable to the development of peoples and individuals is the primary responsibility of their States.' 'States have the right and duty to formulate appropriate national development policies,' (art. 2(3)); States have a duty to co-operate with each other in ensuring development (art. 3(3)) and in formulating international development policies (art. 4(1)); even popular participation is supposed to be encouraged by states (art. 8(2)) and "States should fulfil their rights and duties in such a manner as to promote a new international economic order based on sovereign equality, interdependence, mutual interest and co-operation among all States, as well as to encourage the observance and realization of human rights,' (art. 3(3)).

The 'State' here has been presented out from a fairy-tale as the embodiment of all virtues and interests of the people which, needless to say, flies in the face of historical evidence and is certainly nowhere close to the real-life authoritarian states of Africa used ruthlessly by imperialism and compradorial ruling classes in the exploitation and oppression of the African people and nations.

Finally, underlying the right to development is a conception which sees development/democracy as a gift/charity from above rather than the result of struggles from below. On the international plane, it is based on an illusory model of co-operation and solidarity (*a la* M'Baye). This is like crying for the moon, for how can there be solidarity between a rider and the horse?

Under the right to development the human person is seen as a 'participant and beneficiary' (art. 2(1) of development where, development therefore, is someone else's (state's?!) project. Under self-determination people are themselves the creators of, and the struggling force for, development and democracy which are reclaimed and asserted as their project. People are neither pitiable victims of states' excesses nor recipients of states' handouts. In the latter conceptualization, the state takes its rightful place as a historical and social category both as a participant in and an embodiment of class struggles.

The right to development fits in neatly in the ideology of developmentalism which has been the hallmark of African states since independence in rationalizing the depoliticization and demobilization of the African masses. It has managed to occupy many conferences and discussions. Given its spurious nature, in our opinion it has played a diversionary role in shifting attention from the reality of the Third World and its struggling people.

Notes and Questions

1. Is there a human right not to develop? Does the principle of self-determination encompass such a right? What would the implications be for individuals, peoples, states, and the international community? Consider this question in relation to the issues faced by the Yanomami of Brazil (*see* Chapter 4, *supra*, the Batwa of Uganda (*see* Chapter 6, *infra*) and the Adivasis of India (*see* Chapter 7, *infra*).

2. Do you agree with Shivji's assessment that the call for a right to development is essentially a plea for charity? Compare the vision elaborated by Professor William Felice:

> Through the right to development, the poor claim the right to a minimal level of human decency. The rich and powerful, affluent and privileged, are legally obligated to address these demands, not with charity, but with the structural reforms necessary to provide for true equity. The emerging principle of international law established by this new right is that there is a collective international responsibility for the human condition.

WILLIAM FELICE, TAKING SUFFERING SERIOUSLY 77 (1996).

Can the right to development be articulated as a transformative demand? Does the answer depend upon who is conceptualized as the right-holder and correlative duty-holder?

3. Article 26 of the Universal Declaration of Human Rights refers to a right to the "free development of the human personality." How is the individual right to development related to the collective right to development?

4. Are the arguments for reparations for slavery and the trans-Atlantic slave trade related to the arguments for a right to development? If so, how? *See* discussion of reparations in Chapter 3.B (on the Race Convention).

5. What does the right to development imply about political and economic policy? Does the fulfillment of the right require certain forms of political economy (*i.e.*, socialism, democracy, central-planning, capitalism)? Does the right to development have any implications for cultural diversity?

6. Is advocacy for a right to development worth the effort? Does that strategy detract from the practical implementation of development strategies aimed at improving the economic and social conditions of poor people? Consider the following critique by David Kennedy:

> Once concerns about global poverty are raised [in terms of a right to development] energy and resources are drawn to developing a literature and an institutional practice at the international level of a particular sort. Efforts that cannot be articulated in these terms seem less legitimate, less practical, less worth the effort. Increasingly, people of good will concerned about poverty are drawn into debate about a series of ultimately impossible legal quandaries—right of whom, against whom, remediable how, and so on—and into institutional projects of codification and reporting familiar from other human rights efforts, without evaluating how these might compare with other uses for this talent and these resources. Meanwhile, efforts that human rights does not criticize are strengthened. International economic policy affecting global poverty is taken over by neo-liberal players who do not see development as a special problem.

David Kennedy, *The International Human Rights Movement: Part of the Problem?*, 15 HARV. HUM. RTS. J. 101, (2002).

Is Kennedy's assessment accurate? What arguments would you make in response?

CHAPTER SIX

SELF-DETERMINATION, CULTURE AND RIGHTS: CONFLICTS, CHALLENGES AND POSSIBILITIES

A. SELF-DETERMINATION

The right of self-determination is the collective right of cohesive national groups within otherwise sovereign states to some form of autonomy up to, and including, secession. Peoples, not states, are endowed with this right, which first arose during the revolutions in 18th and 19th century Europe, was adopted as a principle in the partitioning of Europe after World War I, and emerged conclusively as a rule of law in the pronouncements of the U.N. Charter. *See, e.g.,* Articles 1(2) and 55. But "the struggle of peoples *** has been one, if not indeed the primary factor in the formation of the customary rule whereby the right of peoples to self-determination is recognized." *Legal Consequences for States of the Continued Presence of South Africa in Namibia (South West Africa) Notwithstanding Security Council Resolution 276 (1970) (Request for Advisory Opinion)* 1971 I.C.J. Rep. 12, 89 (*sep. op. Ammoun*).

The historic Declaration on the Granting of Independence to Colonial Countries and Peoples called for the immediate independence of all peoples and territories which had not yet attained it. G.A. Res. 1514 (XV) 1960 ¶ 2. It "emerged with legal authority" because of the subsequent practice of the international community, *i.e.,* the emancipation of the majority of the colonized peoples. In addition, it is considered an authoritative interpretation of Article 1(2) of the Charter, which lists among the purposes of the United Nations the development of "friendly relations among nations based on respect for the principle of equal rights and self-determination of peoples." *See* Henry J. Richardson, *Self-Determination, International Law and the South African Bantustan Policy,* 17 COLUM. J. TRANS. L. 185, 195 (1978).

This rule has been reaffirmed by the Security Council in resolutions concerning Rhodesia, S.C. Res. 183 (1963); Namibia, S.C. Res. 301 (1971); Western Sahara, S.C. Res. 377 (1975); and Portuguese Timor, S.C. Res. 384 (1975). The Advisory Opinion of the International Court relating to the Western Sahara confirmed the validity of the principle in the context of international law. 1975 I.C.J. Rep. 3, 31–33.

The right of self-determination involves correlative duties binding upon states, including the duty to promote its realization and the duty to refrain from any forcible action calculated to deprive people of this right. *See* G.A. Res. 2160 (XXI) (1966). By definition, matters of self-determination cannot be reserved to domestic jurisdiction. *See* J. CRAWFORD, THE CREATION OF STATES IN INTERNATIONAL LAW 102 (1979); ROSLYN HIGGINS, THE DEVELOPMENT OF INTERNATIONAL LAW THROUGH THE POLITICAL ORGANS OF THE UNITED NATIONS 90–106 (1963).

The collective right to self-determination is the first norm codified in the International Bill of Rights, recognition of the fact that without self-determination individual rights cannot be realized. Both the International Covenant on Civil and Political Rights (ICCPR) and the International Covenant on Economic, Social and Cultural Rights (ICESCR) contain the following identical provision:

Article I

(1) All peoples have the right of self-determination. By virtue of that right they freely determine their political status and freely pursue their economic, social, and cultural development.

(2) All peoples may, for their own ends, freely dispose of their natural wealth and resources without prejudice to any obligations arising out of international economic cooperation, based upon the principle of mutual benefit, and international law. In no case may a people be deprived of its own means of subsistence.

(3) The States Parties to the present Covenant, including those responsible for the administration of Non-Self-Governing and Trust Territories, shall promote the realization of the right of self-determination, and shall respect that right, in conformity with the provisions of the Charter of the United Nations.

Mohammed Bedjaoui asserts that the right of self-determination has transformed the international community:

The present-day international community is universal and 'open,' in contrast to what it was formerly when it was restricted to the 'club' of European States. 'The 'open' community of today, replacing the 'closed' community of earlier times, owes this essential characteristic to the self-determination of peoples. The right of peoples to self-determination has become the instrument, the key and the tool of an open society. Thus self-determination is in a sense a precondition for the very existence of this type of international community. In other words, this principle is the prior condition which has enabled international society to be what it is. It thus determines the being and the essence of the present-day international society.*** Thus, in the hierarchy of the norms of international law, self-determination is an essential first and primary condition from which flow the other principles governing the international community. Self-determination thus belongs to *jus cogens.*

Mohammed Bedjaoui, "The Right to Development," *in* MOHAMMED BEDJOUI ED., INTERNATIONAL LAW: ACHIEVEMENTS AND PROSPECTS 1177, 1184 (1991).

The relationship between self-determination and culture was eloquently expressed by Amilcar Cabral (1924–1973), leader of the PAIGC, the movement for the independence of Guinea-Bissau from Portuguese colonialism. This speech was originally delivered on February 20, 1970, as part of the Eduardo Mondlane Memorial Lecture Series at Syracuse University, Syracuse, New York, under the auspices of The Program of Eastern African Studies. It was translated from the French by Maureen Webster:

History teaches us that, in certain circumstances, it is very easy for the foreigner to impose his domination on a people. But it also teaches us that, whatever may be the material aspects of this domination, it can be maintained only by the permanent, organized repression of the cultural life of the people concerned. Implantation of foreign domination can be assured definitively only by physical liquidation of a significant part of the dominated population.

In fact, to take up arms to dominate a people is, above all, to take up arms to destroy, or at least to neutralize, to paralyze, its cultural life. For, with a strong indigenous cultural life, foreign domination cannot be sure of its perpetuation.

Amilcar Cabral, *National Liberation and Culture, available at* http://literature.rebelyouth.ca/acabral/cabral.html (last visited June 29, 2004).

This section examines two contemporary contexts in which the right to self-determination is implicated: the status of indigenous peoples, and the rights of peoples living under foreign occupation.

1. *Indigenous Peoples*

The history of indigenous peoples is defined by resistance and perseverence in the face of brutal conquest and subjugation by both external and internal powers, threatening their way of life and their very existence. Even in states where they are a majority of the population—such as Bolivia and Laos—they are marginalized and oppressed. The economic, social and cultural rights of the approximately 300 million indigenous and tribal people are inseparable from their intimate relationship to their traditional lands, natural resources, sacred religious sites, and cultural beliefs and practices. These rights include claims to property rooted in their historic possession and occupation of territories and in their creation and development of traditional knowledge; demands for the maintenance of traditional means of livelihood in the face of logging, mining or industrialization; and cultural rights claims structured by concepts of duties to the land, ancestors or future generations. As Professor Benedict Kingsbury observes,

[a]mong the ambient population and many persons who may count themselves as members of indigenous groups, the most powerful argument for a distinctive legal category based on special features of indigenous peoples is wrongful deprivation, above all, of land, territory, self-government, means of livelihood, language, and identity. The appeal is thus to history and culture.

Benedict Kingsbury, *Reconciling Competing Conceptual Structures of Indigenous Peoples' Claims in International and Comparative Law*, 34 N.Y.U. J. INT'L L. & POL. 189, 244 (2002).

Today indigenous non-governmental organizations are a potent force in the international arena, demanding recognition of their distinct identities and rights, and a growing body of jurisprudence is engaging the complexities of recognition and protection of these rights. Both individual rights to equality and collective rights to self-determination and culture have provided normative foundations for legal strategies.

Indigenous peoples are beneficiaries of the numerous prohibitions against racial and ethnic discrimination in the human rights corpus. Where they are a minority of the population, the ICCPR's Article 27 provides explicit protection for their distinct cultures:

In those states in which ethnic, religious or linguistic minorities exist, persons belonging to such minorities shall not be denied the right, in community with the other members of their group, to enjoy their own culture, to profess and practice their own religion, or to use their own language.

The normative content of this provision is further elaborated in the U.N. Human Rights Committee's General Comment 23:

> With regard to the exercise of the cultural rights protected under article 27, the Committee observes that culture manifests itself in many forms, including a particular way of life associated with the use of land resources, especially in the case of indigenous peoples. That right may include such traditional activities as fishing or hunting and the right to live in reserves protected by law. The enjoyment of those rights may require positive legal measures of protection and measures to ensure the effective participation of members of minority communities in decisions which affect them.

Human Rights Committee, General Comment 23, Article 27 (50th session, 1994), Compilation of General Comments and General Recommendations Adopted by Human Rights Treaty Bodies, U.N. Doc. HRI\GEN\1\Rev.1 at 38 ¶ 7 (1994).

a. Indigenous Property Rights: Individual or Collective Claims?

MARY AND CARRIE DANN v. UNITED STATES

Case 11.140, Report No. 113/01, Inter-American Court of Human Rights (2001)

*** III. POSITIONS OF THE PARTIES

A. Position of the Petitioners ***

36. [T]he Petitioners state that the Danns are members of the Western Shoshone aboriginal people who reside on a ranch in the rural community of Crescent Valley, Nevada. According to the petition, the Danns together with other members of their extended family in the Dann band occupy, hunt, graze and otherwise use lands (the "Dann land") that are within the larger ancestral territory of the Western Shoshone people. This ancestral territory is alleged to encompass not only the ranch upon which the Danns live but rangelands and other property principally in the state of Nevada (the "Western Shoshone ancestral lands").

37. In this connection, the Petitioners indicate that relations between the Western Shoshone and the United States government continue to be regulated by the 1863 Treaty of Ruby Valley which was ratified by the United States in 1866 and proclaimed on October 21, 1869, and which constituted a peace treaty between the United States and the Western Shoshone people.

38. The Petitioners contend that the Danns have used and occupied the Western Shoshone ancestral lands since time immemorial and that the family ranch is the Danns' sole means of support, where all of their needs are met by the sale of their livestock, goods and produce to neighboring Western Shoshone and to non-Indians.

39. The Petitioners also claim that from 1863 to the present the United States has steadily expropriated parts of the Western Shoshone ancestral lands to the benefit of government and non-Indians, and that without sufficient money, education and legal assistance the Western Shoshone have traditionally been unable to mount effective opposition to the government's encroachment and erosion of their land base. With respect to the Dann lands in particular, the Petitioners claim that the use by the Danns and

other Western Shoshone of these lands was undisturbed and unchallenged until the early 1970s when the United States government through the Department of the Interior began taking or threatening actions to impede the Danns and other Western Shoshone from using and occupying lands that are within their ancestral territory. In this manner, the Petitioners say that the Danns are being wrongfully dispossessed of their ancestral homelands including portions upon which they depend for their living.

40. These State actions have included the initiation of trespass actions against the Danns demanding that the Danns remove their livestock from disputed lands and pay significant fines, and the issuance of "Notices of Intent to Impound" in respect of "unauthorized livestock grazing upon public land." They have also included gold prospecting within the traditional Western Shoshone ancestral lands which is said to have been permitted or acquiesced in by State officials. As part of this prospecting, mining companies are said to have been digging the earth, pumping scarce water, and are poised to take ownership or control of the area by operation of U.S. mining legislation or land exchanges with the U.S. government. The Petitioners claim that this mining activity has already affected the Danns' use of their ancestral lands and has contaminated the ground water in and around Crescent Valley, and that the activity threatens even greater damage as it extends closer to the Danns' household.

41. Further the Petitioners state that the Danns and other members of the Western Shoshone have been impeded from their traditional subsistence hunting by officials of the state of Nevada, who are said to have relied upon the United States' denial of Western Shoshone title to ancestral land to refuse to accommodate traditional Western Shoshone hunting practices. Rather, State officials have sought out and arrested members of the Western Shoshone people including members of the Dann band who do not comply with the state hunting laws and regulations.

42. As examples of these activities, during the October 10, 1996 hearing before the Commission the Petitioners claimed that the United States had impounded and sold the Danns' livestock on two occasions, 161 horses in March 1992 and 269 horses in November 1992. The Petitioners also claimed that a mining company, Oro Nevada Mining Company, was claiming some of the Western Shoshone ancestral lands under a law that permits mining companies to acquire land belonging to the U.S. government. The company is also said to have issued a formal notice that it would drill test holes in several areas on the Danns' grazing lands and that all of the range land used by the Danns was subject to actual gold mining claims.

43. According to the Petitioners, in taking these actions the State has relied upon a 1966 ruling by the ICC, a statutorily-based administrative tribunal established by the State under the Indian Claims Commission Act to determine aboriginal land claims. In this ruling, which was subsequently upheld by the U.S. Court of Claims, the ICC is said to have adopted an uncontested stipulation that Western Shoshone title had been extinguished some time previously by acts of "gradual encroachment" by non-Indians. It is on this basis that the Petitioners claim that the State denies the continuing existence of Western Shoshone legal rights to ancestral land. As outlined below, however, the Petitioners contest the propriety and validity of these proceedings, on the basis that the issue of whether the Western Shoshone rights were truly extinguished was not actually litigated by the ICC or by the US judiciary. They also claim that Western Shoshone individuals and groups were not permitted to intervene in the proceedings to contest the presumed extinguishment of title and that the Western Shoshone people have refused to accept the money awarded by the ICC.

1. Right to Property

44. The Petitioners contend that the State is responsible for violations of the Danns' right to property under Article XXIII of the [American Declaration of the Rights and Duties of Man], by reason of the limitation that the State has placed on the Danns' occupation and use and of the Western Shoshone ancestral lands. Article XXIII of the Declaration provides as follows:

> Every person has a right to own such private property as meets the essential needs of decent living and helps to maintain the dignity of the individual and of the home.

45. In particular, the Petitioners claim that the Danns and other Western Shoshone people have properly laid claim to the Western Shoshone ancestral lands through traditional patterns of use and occupancy of those lands and its natural resources. The Petitioners refer to this as "customary land tenure system" and assert that this is a form of property that is recognized as original or Indian title by the law of the United States and other common law jurisdictions, as are "free standing" rights to fish, hunt, gather, or otherwise use resources or have access to lands.***

52. In respect of the State's contention that the Danns failed to pursue "individual aboriginal title" to the lands in question before domestic courts, the Petitioners explain that they have not pursued such proceedings because doing so would have separated them from the treaty-based Western Shoshone nation claim, the position that would preserve the land and culture of the Western Shoshone people as a whole. At base, they argue that to pursue such a claim would undermine the aboriginal rights and treaty-recognized basis of title that forms the essential historical, cultural and political foundation for the Western Shoshone and other indigenous nations and tribes.

2. Right to Equality under the Law

53. The Petitioners also challenge the State's interference with the Danns' occupation and use of the Western Shoshone ancestral lands as discriminatory contrary to Article II of the Declaration, which protects the right to equality before the law. In particular, the Petitioners assert that the State is obliged to protect the Danns' aboriginal property rights and to accord those rights the same degree of protection that it provides for the protection of the property rights of non-Indians but has failed to do so.

54. The Petitioners assert several grounds for their claim of discrimination. They first contend that the theory upon which the ICC determined the extinguishment of Western Shoshone, namely "gradual encroachment" by non-indigenous settlers, miners and others, constitutes a nonconsensual and discriminatory transfer of property rights in land away from indigenous people who continue in possession of their land and in favor of non-indigenous interests. They claim that this is a "lawless concept that simply rewards trespassers and relieves the United States of its own legal obligation to uphold Indian land rights." The Petitioners support their arguments in part with the findings of a seminar of experts convened by the United Nations that identified property transfers of this nature as part of a larger pattern of racial discrimination suffered by indigenous peoples.

55. The Petitioners identify as a further source of discrimination the absence of substantive protections for indigenous property rights, including those rights derived from Western Shoshone aboriginal title, that are equal to the protections accorded to

non-indigenous forms of property. In particular, they indicate that under U.S. law, including the Fifth Amendment to the U.S. Constitution and other federal and state laws, the taking of property by the government ordinarily requires a valid public purpose and the entitlement of the owners to notice, a judicial hearing and fair compensation based upon the fair market value of the property taken. The Petitioners argue in contrast that the Western Shoshone ancestral lands were taken in the absence of any of these prerequisites ***. [T]he Petitioners claim to have stated facts that indicate that no public purpose has been established for the purported extinguishment of the Western Shoshone land title and that the 1979 monetary award that resulted from the ICC claims proceedings was calculated on the basis of a valuation of the land as of July 1, 1872, the presumed extinguishment date, and that no interest was calculated into the award. On this basis, the Petitioners contend that the Western Shoshone were not provided with just compensation that is otherwise required for the taking of non-indigenous property.

56. Also according to the Petitioners, discriminatory treatment of indigenous property is further indicated by the facts relating to the procedure by which the United States determined extinguishment of and compensation for Western Shoshone ancestral lands ***. [T]he Petitioners contend that during the ICC proceedings by which the State claims the Western Shoshone peoples' rights were extinguished, only one small group was actually represented before the ICC and subsequently before the U.S. Court of Claims. They also claim that other Western Shoshone, including the Danns, were not permitted to intervene in the ICC proceedings. Moreover, those Western Shoshone claimants who were represented before the ICC were prevented from dismissing their lawyer when they decided that he was not acting in their best interest.***

3. Right to Cultural Integrity ***

60. [T]he Petitioners assert that the United States is actively attempting to deprive the Danns of their traditional lands. As the Western Shoshone culture is dependent upon the land and the natural resources upon it, the Petitioners argue that the State's actions are directly threatening the Danns' enjoyment of Western Shoshone culture. Among the acts that are said to threaten this deprivation are the issuance of civil and criminal penalty notices to the Danns for the use of their traditional lands, threats to confiscate the Danns' livestock, impediments to the gathering of subsistence foods, limits to their access to sacred sites, and the permission of private mining concessions and harmful military activities on traditional Western Shoshone lands, which activities have threatened the environment and destroyed available resources.***

4. Right to Self Determination ***

64. [T]he Petitioners argue that for indigenous peoples, the principle of self determination establishes a right to control their lands and natural resources and to be genuinely involved in all decision-making processes that affect them. In support of this contention the Petitioners refer to statements by the UN Human Rights Committee respecting the situation of indigenous peoples in Canada in which the Committee has emphasized "that the right to self-determination requires, *inter alia*, that all peoples must be able to freely dispose of their natural wealth and resources and that they may not be deprived of their own means of subsistence."

65. *** According to the Petitioners, the right to property affirmed in Article XXIII of the American Declaration would have little meaning for indigenous peoples if their

property could be encumbered without due consultation, consideration, and in appropriate circumstances, just compensation by the state. Without a full and fair opportunity to be heard and to genuinely influence the decisions affecting them, the Petitioners argue that the Danns and other Western Shoshone groups are unable to exercise their right to self-determination as guaranteed by international law.***

5. *Rights to Judicial Protection and Due Process of Law* ***

69. [T]he Petitioners indicate that during the 1950s, 60s and 70s proceedings took place before the Indian Claims Commission respecting the determination of any claims that the Western Shoshone may have to their ancestral lands. In these proceedings, the United States and the lawyer purporting to represent all of the Western Shoshone "conceded and formally stipulated" that the Western Shoshone land rights had been "extinguished" on July 1, 1872 under a theory of "gradual encroachment" by non-Native Americans. The Danns claim not to have authorized or participated in these proceedings and were not entitled to intervene to challenge the stipulation by the Western Shoshone attorney. The Petitioners also argue that nothing of significance occurred with respect to Western Shoshone land rights on July 1, 1872 and that the stipulation of this extinguishment date is pure fiction and, at base, only served to reach a compromise between the government's desire to minimize any payment for the land and the attorney's desire to maximize the payment and associated legal fees.***

74. *** Further, the Petitioners reject *** possible judicial recognition of "individual aboriginal rights" as ineffective and inadequate. The Petitioners emphasize in this regard that the Danns are among the Western Shoshone Indians who as a whole exist as an indigenous nation or people in the sense that they comprise a discrete community bonded by ethnographic, cultural and political factors. Thus, it is the customary system of land tenure generated by the Western Shoshone people as a whole over centuries, rather than the Danns' own individual land use patterns, that forms the foundation of the land rights asserted by the Danns. On this basis, the Petitioners argue that "individual aboriginal rights" do not provide a basis for the Danns to assert use and occupancy rights that derive from Western Shoshone title.***

B. *Position of the State* ***

78. The State claims *** that the Danns' late father, Dewey Dann, settled in an area of Nevada, established a ranch on the land, and acquired title to the land from the United States through a patent to use the land for farming and ranching. The State also maintains that it gave Mr. Dann a permit to graze his cattle on public lands until his death in the 1960s which authorized him to graze 170 cattle and 10 horses on federally owned land near their ranch that was shared by other ranchers in the area. The State claims that Mr. Dann complied with the permit and that it never interfered with the grazing of cattle by the Danns under the permit. The State claims, however, that following their father's death, the Dann sisters began to graze a greater number of cattle than permitted under their permit, and that this excessive grazing damaged the range and interfered with other ranchers' uses of the public lands. The State claims that the BLM attempted to resolve the matter administratively with the Danns, but that these efforts failed and thus required the BLM to take impoundment and other formal actions to end the unauthorized grazing.

79. [T]he State [also] alleges that there is in actuality no entity known as the "Western Shoshone Nation," but rather that there are groups of Western Shoshone

peoples that are recognized as tribes. Through an established process, the United States recognizes certain Native American groups, or "tribes," as sovereign nations, and as a consequence treats those tribes as having their own leadership or government and maintains government-to-government relations with them. Western Shoshone bands or tribes with this recognized status include the Ely Shoshone Tribe of Nevada and the Te-moak Tribe of the Yamba Reservation, but according to the State does not include the Dann band.

80. With respect to the status of the lands at issue in this case more generally, the State confirmed that U.S. courts recognize the doctrine of aboriginal title that permits Native Americans as tribes, or in some cases as individuals, to use and occupy their traditional homelands. In the present case, however, the State emphasized that the U.S. courts ultimately concluded that Western Shoshone title has been extinguished and barred by the ICC proceedings. In addition, the United States recognizes that the Western Shoshone historically occupied an area that covers a large part of what is now the state of Nevada. This land was ceded to the United States by Mexico in 1848 by the Treaty of Guadeloupe Hidalgo, subject to the occupancy by Native Americans, and in 1863, the United States signed the "Treaty of Ruby Valley" with the Western Shoshone. Under the terms of that treaty, the United States and the Western Shoshone agreed to end hostilities and live amicably, and according to the State the treaty was not intended to acknowledge Shoshone title to lands covered by it. Subsequent to this treaty, the United States claims that it began treating certain lands within the areas in question as public lands of the United States.

81. Also in the 1800s, the State claims that more people in the United States began to move westward and settle new lands in the West, including the areas in the state of Nevada traditionally occupied by the Western Shoshone. This was accomplished in part through the granting to settlers by the United States of patents if the settlers took up permanent residence, established a farm or ranch, and met certain other requirements.

82. In light of this history, the State maintains that the Danns and other Western Shoshone lost any interest in the lands in question as a result of this encroachment by non-Native Americans, and that this determination was properly made through proceedings before the Indian Claims Commission, a quasi-judicial body established for the very purpose of determining Indian land claims issues.***

84. In the case of the Western Shoshone, the ICC effectively found an inverse condemnation based upon the settlement of the West. This condemnation was effected for the public purpose of encouraging settlement and agricultural developments and constituted a deprivation of use of lands used by the Western Shoshone that required just compensation, which was ultimately awarded.

85. On the issue of compensation, the State clarified that the amount awarded to the Western Shoshone was $26,145,189.89, based upon 1872 values of approximately 15 cents per acre plus loss of gold and other resources. At the time of the ICC's final judgment in August 1977, the ICC statute provided that the award would be deposited in the registry where it would earn interest until a distribution plan was agreed upon ***. In the interim, the State indicates that the funds are being held in an interest bearing account and that once a distribution plan is approved, it will be presented to the United States Congress for approval, following which the award and interest will be distributed.

86. *** According to the State, the ICC process transpired as follows. In 1951 the Temoak band of Western Shoshone filed a petition before the ICC seeking compensation for the taking of large areas of Western Shoshone land in California and Nevada. In 1962 the ICC ruled that the Indians' aboriginal title to the California property had been extinguished in March 1853 and that the amount of compensation could be established based upon that date. It also ruled in 1962 that the Indians had continuously used and occupied 22 million acres of Nevada land until their way of life was disrupted and they were deprived of their lands by gradual encroachment by white settlers and others and the acquisition, disposition or taking of their lands by the United States for its use and benefit and that of its citizens. During September and October 1965, counsel for the Temoak Bands held open council meetings at four locations in the Western Shoshone territory. All of the Western Shoshone were given the opportunity to attend and vote to elect an 8-member claims committee, which used a loan from the U.S. government to hire an expert appraiser to provide testimony to the ICC regarding the valuation of the lands taken. The vote to establish the committee and hire the expert appraiser was 219 in favor and 17 opposed. The expert was subsequently hired and the testimony provided to the ICC.

87. The State also contends that because the encroachment had been gradual, there was no specific historical, legal or administrative event to mark the extinguishment of Western Shoshone tribal aboriginal title to the lands in question. Thus, in 1966 counsel for the Western Shoshone and the U.S. government agreed to stipulate that July 1, 1872 would be taken as the valuation date for the Shoshone lands in Nevada.***

90. [W]hile the State recognizes that the Temoak Band itself subsequently dismissed their attorney, challenged the ICC's extinguishment finding based upon an argument of collusion, and attempted to stay the proceedings on this basis, the ICC rejected this claim, and the Court of Claims affirmed, on the basis that the attorney had not misled the Indians as to the nature and scope of the ICC proceedings and that the claims of collusion were not adequately supported. The State also argued in this regard that although the Danns and other Western Shoshones were not able to contend before the ICC proceeding that the *** tribe still owned the land, such a bar was not unique to claims by Native Americans at the time and that non-Native Americans bringing actions claiming an interference with their property faced the same dilemma. While today the United States does permit actions to be brought against it to quiet title to lands, these claims are still subject to limitations and even then, lands of Native Americans are specifically exempted.***

92. A further argument proposed by the State asserts that the Danns *** might have been able to claim rights to some lands by asserting a theory of individual aboriginal rights, and that while the Danns initially pursued this course of action, in 1991 they voluntarily withdrew this claim.

93. Specifically with respect to the Petitioners' allegation that the United States is responsible for a violation of the right to property under Article XXIII of the American Declaration, the State contends that this provision of the Declaration is concerned with the rights of an individual and not of a separate governmental entity such as an Indian tribe.***

IV. ANALYSIS

A. *Application and Interpretation of the American Declaration of the Rights and Duties of Man*

95. The Petitioners claim that the State has violated the rights of the Danns under Articles I, XVIII, and XXVI of the American Declaration of the Rights and Duties of Man. [T]he Commission is competent to determine these allegations as against the United States. The State is a Member of the Organization of American States that is not a party to the American Convention on Human Rights, as provided for in Article 20 of the Commission's Statute and Article 23 of the Commission's Rules of Procedure, and deposited its instrument of ratification of the OAS Charter on June 19, 1951. The events raised in the Petitioners claim occurred subsequent to the State's ratification of the OAS Charter. The Danns are natural persons, and the Petitioners are authorized under Article 23 of the Commission's Rules of Procedure to lodge the petition on behalf of the Danns.

96. In addressing the allegations raised by the Petitioners in this case, the Commission also wishes to clarify that in interpreting and applying the Declaration, it is necessary to consider its provisions in the context of the international and inter-American human rights systems more broadly, in the light of developments in the field of international human rights law since the Declaration was first composed and with due regard to other relevant rules of international law applicable to member states ***.***

C. *Indigenous Peoples' Human Rights Principles and the American Declaration on Human Rights*

124. [In addressing this complaint the Commission will consider the] broader corpus of international law [which] includes the developing norms and principles governing the human rights of indigenous peoples. As the following analysis indicates, these norms and principles encompass distinct human rights considerations relating to the ownership, use and occupation by indigenous communities of their traditional lands. Considerations of this nature in turn controvert the State's contention that the Danns' complaint concerns only land title and land use disputes and does not implicate issues of human rights.

125. In particular, a review of pertinent treaties, legislation and jurisprudence reveals the development over more than 80 years of particular human rights norms and principles applicable to the circumstances and treatment of indigenous peoples. Central to these norms and principles is a recognition that ensuring the full and effective enjoyment of human rights by indigenous peoples requires consideration of their particular historical, cultural, social and economic situation and experience. In most instances, this has included identification of the need for special measures by states to compensate for the exploitation and discrimination to which these societies have been subjected at the hands of the non-indigenous.***

128. Perhaps most fundamentally, the Commission and other international authorities have recognized the collective aspect of indigenous rights, in the sense of rights that are realized in part or in whole through their guarantee to groups or organizations of people. And this recognition has extended to acknowledgement of a particular connection between communities of indigenous peoples and the lands and resources that they have traditionally occupied and used, the preservation of which is fundamental to

the effective realization of the human rights of indigenous peoples more generally and therefore warrants special measures of protection.*** The Inter-American Court of Human Rights has similarly recognized that for indigenous communities the relation with the land is not merely a question of possession and production but has a material and spiritual element that must be fully enjoyed to preserve their cultural legacy and pass it on to future generations.

129. The development of these principles in the Inter-American system has culminated in the drafting of Article XVIII of the Draft American Declaration on the Rights of Indigenous Peoples, which provides for the protection of traditional forms of ownership and cultural survival and rights to land, territories and resources. While this provision, like the remainder of the Draft Declaration, has not yet been approved by the OAS General Assembly and therefore does not in itself have the effect of a final Declaration, the Commission considers that the basic principles reflected in many of the provisions of the Declaration, including aspects of Article XVIII, reflect general international legal principles developing out of and applicable inside and outside of the inter-American system and to this extent are properly considered in interpreting and applying the provisions of the American Declaration in the context of indigenous peoples.

130. Of particular relevance to the present case, the Commission considers the general international legal principles applicable in the context of indigenous human rights to include:

- the right of indigenous peoples to legal recognition of their varied and specific forms and modalities of their control, ownership, use and enjoyment of territories and property;

- the recognition of their property and ownership rights with respect to lands, territories and resources they have historically occupied; and

- where property and user rights of indigenous peoples arise from rights existing prior to the creation of a state, recognition by that state of the permanent and inalienable title of indigenous peoples relative thereto and to have such title changed only by mutual consent between the state and respective indigenous peoples when they have full knowledge and appreciation of the nature or attributes of such property. This also implies the right to fair compensation in the event that such property and user rights are irrevocably lost.

131. *** The Commission wishes to emphasize that by interpreting the American Declaration so as to safeguard the integrity, livelihood and culture of indigenous peoples through the effective protection of their individual and collective human rights, the Commission is respecting the very purposes underlying the Declaration which, as expressed in its Preamble, include recognition that "[s]ince culture is the highest social and historical expression of that spiritual development, it is the duty of man to preserve, practice and foster culture by every means within his power."***

D. *Application of International Human Rights Norms and Principles in the Circumstances of Mary and Carrie Dann*

133. Among the provisions of the American Declaration which are alleged to have been violated by the State in the present case are Articles II, XVIII and XXIII, which read as follows:

Article II. Right to equality before the law

All persons are equal before the law and have the rights and duties established in this Declaration, without distinction as to race, sex, language, creed or any other factor.

Article XVIII. Right to a fair trial

Every person may resort to the courts to ensure respect for his legal rights. There should likewise be available to him a simple, brief procedure whereby the courts will protect him from acts of authority that, to his prejudice, violate any fundamental constitutional rights.

Article XXIII. Right to property

Every person has a right to own such private property as meets the essential needs of decent living and helps to maintain the dignity of the individual and of the home.***

136. *** The State submits *** that throughout the proceedings before the ICC the Western Shoshone were kept fully apprised through regular meetings held with members of the tribe. The only such meetings specifically referred to by the State, however, were meetings convened by the attorney for the Temoak Band in 1965, 14 years after the ICC proceedings commenced and 3 years after the ICC issued its extinguishment finding. In the absence of evidence to the contrary the Commission accepts that the Danns did not play a full or effective role in retaining, authorizing or instructing the Western Shoshone claimants in the ICC process.

137. *** Based upon the record before it, the Commission finds that the determination as to whether and to what extent Western Shoshone title may have been extinguished was not based upon a judicial evaluation of pertinent evidence, but rather was based upon apparently arbitrary stipulations as between the U.S. government and the Temoak Band regarding the extent and timing of the loss of indigenous title to the entirety of the Western Shoshone ancestral lands.***

138. In evaluating the Petitioners' claims in light of these evidentiary findings, the Commission first wishes to expressly recognize and acknowledge that the State, through the development and implementation of the Indian Claims Commission process, has taken significant measures to recognize and account for the historic deprivations suffered by indigenous communities living within the United States and commends the State for this initiative. As both the Petitioners and the State have recognized, this process provided a more efficient solution to the sovereign immunity bar to Indian land claims under U.S. law and extended to indigenous communities certain benefits relating to claims to their ancestral lands that were not available to other citizens, such as extended limitation periods for claims.

139. Upon evaluating these processes in the facts as disclosed by the record in this case, however, the Commission concludes that these processes were not sufficient to comply with contemporary international human rights norms, principles and standards that govern the determination of indigenous property interests.

140. The Commission first considers that Articles XVIII and XXIII of the American Declaration specially oblige a member state to ensure that any determination of the extent to which indigenous claimants maintain interests in the lands to which they have

traditionally held title and have occupied and used is based upon a process of fully informed and mutual consent on the part of the indigenous community as a whole.***

142. [T]he ICC did not conduct an independent review of historical and other evidence to determine as a matter of fact whether the Western Shoshone properly claimed title to all or some of their traditional lands. Rather, the ICC determination was based upon an agreement between the State and the purported Western Shoshone representatives as to the extent and timing of the extinguishment.*** [I]t cannot be said that the Danns' claims to property rights in the Western Shoshone ancestral lands were determined through an effective and fair process in compliance with the norms and principles under Articles XVIII and XXIII of the American Declaration.

143. Further, the Commission concludes that to the extent the State has asserted as against the Danns' title in the property in issue based upon the ICC proceedings, the Danns have not been afforded their right to equal protection of the law under Article II of the American Declaration.***

144. The record before the Commission indicates that under prevailing common law in the United States, including the Fifth Amendment to the U.S. Constitution, the taking of property by the government ordinarily requires a valid public purpose and the entitlement of owners to notice, just compensation, and judicial review. In the present case, however, the Commission cannot find that the same prerequisites have been extended to the Danns in regard to the determination of their property claims to the Western Shoshone ancestral lands, and no proper justification for the distinction in their treatment has been established by the State.*** And while compensation for this extinguishment was awarded by the ICC, the value of compensation was calculated based upon an average extinguishment date that does not on the record appear to bear any relevant connection to the issue of whether and to what extent all or part of Western Shoshone title in their traditional lands, including that of the Danns, may no longer subsist. Further, the Commission understands that the amount of compensation awarded for the alleged encroachment upon Western Shoshone ancestral lands did not include an award of interest from the date of the alleged extinguishment to the date of the ICC decision, thus leaving the Western Shoshone uncompensated for the cost of the alleged taking of their property during this period.

145. All of these circumstances suggest that the Danns have not been afforded equal treatment under the law respecting the determination of their property interests in the Western Shoshone ancestral lands, contrary to Article II of the Declaration.***

V. CONCLUSIONS

146. The Commission wishes to emphasize that it is not for this tribunal in the circumstances of the present case to determine whether and to what extent the Danns may properly claim a subsisting right to property in the Western Shoshone ancestral lands. This issue involves complex issues of law and fact that are more appropriately left to the State for determination through those legal processes it may consider suitable for that purpose. These processes must, however, conform with the norms and principles under the American Declaration applicable to the determination of indigenous property rights as elucidated in this report.***

VI. RECOMMENDATIONS

148. In accordance with the analysis and conclusions in the present report, the Inter-American Commission on Human Rights recommends to the United States that it

1. Provide Mary and Carrie Dann with an effective remedy, which includes adopting the legislative or other measures necessary to ensure respect for the Danns' right to property in accordance with Articles II, XVIII and XXIII of the American Declaration in connection with their claims to property rights in the Western Shoshone ancestral lands.

2. Review its laws, procedures and practices to ensure that the property rights of indigenous persons are determined in accordance with the rights established in the American Declaration, including Articles II, XVIII and XXIII of the Declaration.***

Notes and Questions

1. *The Nature of Indigenous Property Rights.* What did the Commission determine regarding the nature of the Danns' rights? *See* ¶¶ 52 and 74 of the Commission's decision. Do the provisions of the American Declaration cited by the Commission in ¶ 133 address individual rights? Should evolving legal norms provide a basis for interpreting the Declaration differently? The Commission relies on ILO Convention No. 169 which provides in Article 13 that "governments shall respect the special importance for the culture and spiritual values of the peoples concerned of their relationship with the lands or territories *** which they occupy or otherwise use, and in particular the collective aspects of this relationship." Should the United States be bound by these principles even though it is not a party to this Convention? For the United States' current position on collective rights, *see* Leslie A. Gerson, Deputy Assistant Secretary of State, U.S. Department of State, General Statement in the Commission on Human Rights Working Group on the Draft Declaration on the Rights of Indigenous People (Nov. 30, 1998), *available at* http://www.hookele.com/netwarriors/ us-opening.html ("Since international law, with few exceptions, promotes and protects the rights of individuals, as opposed to groups, it is confusing to state that international law accords certain rights to 'indigenous peoples' as such."). What are the practical implications of this position?

2. *The Allotment Act.* The U.S. government's longstanding opposition to collective rights was legally embodied in the 1887 Dawes Act, better known as the Allotment Act. Divested of their sovereignty, the indigenous people were herded onto barren reservations. The Allotment Act, a congressional effort to end communal ownership of land and replace it with individual property rights, divided the remaining Native American lands into individual parcels, to be held in trust by the government for 25 years. General Allotment Act, ch. 119, § 5, 24 Stat. 389 (1887); 25 U.S.C. § 348. The goal was to encourage Native Americans to assimilate into the individualist U.S. culture, speak English, convert to Christianity and become solitary farmers. Its effect was devastating. Dividing the communally-held land destroyed the bedrock of indigenous culture and religion. Unable to afford the costs of individual land ownership, many were forced to sell their property; a study in 1908 found that 60 percent of the allottees prematurely sold their land. *See* Janet A. McDonnell, The Dispossession of the American Indian, 1887–1934 89 (1991). Of the land that was kept, most was divided from generation to generation, leading to a fractionalization that rendered each share virtually worthless. The Allotment Act also permitted reservation land that was not allotted ("surplus land") to be opened to white settlers at the discretion of the President. By 1934, Native American land ownership was reduced from 138 million acres to 48 million acres. Felix S. Cohen, Handbook of Federal Indian Law 138 (Rennard Strickland & Charles F. Wilkinson eds., 1982). The 1934 Indian Reorganization Act (IRA) officially terminated the allotment

process. However, it did nothing to stop the erosion of Native American land rights through "surplus grants" or to correct the fractionalization of their previously allotted land. *See* Kathleen R. Guzman, *Give or Take An Acre: Property Norms and the Indian Land Consolidation Act*, 85 IOWA L. REV. 595, 605 (2000). Both the Allotment Act and the IRA were instrumental in separating Native Americans from not only their land, but from their community-based cultural heritage.

3. *The "Discovery" and Conquest of Indigenous Territory.* The European expropriation of indigenous territory in the "New World" was grounded in the international law doctrines of discovery and conquest. In *Johnson v. M'Intosh*, 21 U. S. 543 (1823), British subjects and their heirs claimed title to property conveyed to them by the Piankeshaw Indians prior to the American Revolution. Plaintiffs contended that their title ran directly from the Native Americans who owned the property and therefore it was superior to defendants' title, which was held through a land grant from the U.S. government. The Supreme Court upheld the land grant, ruling that the Piankeshaw were not actually able to convey the land because they never "owned" it in the traditional sense of the word. Chief Justice Marshall explained:

> On the discovery of this immense continent, the great nations of Europe were eager to appropriate to themselves so much of it as they could respectively acquire. Its vast extent offered an ample field to the ambition and enterprise of all; and the character and religion of its inhabitants afforded an apology for considering them as a people over whom the superior genius of Europe might claim an ascendency. The potentates of the old world found no difficulty in convincing themselves that they made ample compensation to the inhabitants of the new, by bestowing on them civilization and Christianity, in exchange for unlimited independence. But, as they were all in pursuit of nearly the same object, it was necessary, in order to avoid conflicting settlements, and consequent war with each other, to establish a principle, which all should acknowledge as the law by which the right of acquisition, which they all asserted, should be regulated as between themselves. This principle was, that discovery gave title to the government by whose subjects, or by whose authority, it was made, against all other European governments, which title might be consummated by possession.

> The exclusion of all other Europeans, necessarily gave to the nation making the discovery the sole right of acquiring the soil from the natives, and establishing settlements upon it. It was a right with which no Europeans could interfere. It was a right which all asserted for themselves, and to the assertion of which, by others, all assented.***

> *** [T]he original inhabitants *** were admitted to be the rightful occupants of the soil, with a legal as well as just claim to retain possession of it, and to use it according to their own discretion; but their rights to complete sovereignty, as independent nations, were necessarily diminished, and their power to dispose of the soil at their own will, to whomsoever they pleased, was denied by the original fundamental principle, that discovery gave exclusive title to those who made it.***

> The history of America, from its discovery to the present day, proves, we think, the universal recognition of these principles.

Id. at 572–74.

4. *Recognition of Native Property Rights.* Rejection of the law of conquest has been fiercely resisted in the United States. As recently as 1954, the U.S. Supreme Court opined:

> It is well settled that in all the States of the Union the tribes who inhabited the lands of the States held claim to such lands after the coming of the white man, under what is sometimes termed original Indian title or permission from the whites to occupy. That permission means mere possession not specifically recognized as ownership by Congress. After conquest they were permitted to occupy portions of territory over which they had previously exercised 'sovereignty,' as we use that term. This is not a property right but amounts to a right of occupancy which the sovereign grants and *** may be terminated *** without any legally enforceable obligation to compensate the Indians.

Tee-Hit-Ton Indians v. United States, 348 U.S. 272, 279 (1954). The Court affirmed a Court of Claims denial of compensation to an Alaskan Indian tribe for removal of timber from their ancestral lands. Subsequently, the Indian Claims Commission was created to provide a forum for Native land rights claims, but as the Inter-American Commission observed in the *Dann* case, this procedure is grossly inadequate by contemporary standards.

Indigenous peoples in other former British colonies are waging similar struggles. In the landmark case of *Mabo v. Queensland [No. 2]* (1992) 175 C.L.R. 1, the Australian High Court recognized the validity of preexisting indigenous land rights, rejecting the fiction of *terra nullius* (land belonging to no one) by which the colonial acquisition of Australian territory had been justified. Notwithstanding the decision, official extinguishment of aboriginal title to ancestral lands remains a serious problem. The 1993 Native Title Act, enacted to regularize the processing of indigenous land claims, placed many procedural and financial obstacles in the path of groups seeking to establish title. Additional grounds for extinguishing native title were enacted in 1998 amendments to the Act, prompting lawsuits charging that estinguishment is tantamount to genocide. (*See* Section A.1.d, *infra.*)

Similarly, in *Delgamuukw v. British Columbia*, [1997] 3 S.C.R. 1010, the Supreme Court of Canada recognized a *sui generis* "aboriginal title" that is communally held and part of the definition of the group's distinctive culture. The Court accepted exclusive occupation of the land evidenced by oral histories, as proof of ownership. The majority opined that infringements on aboriginal title should be justified by a "compelling and substantial legislative objective;" involve consultation with the group in the decision making; and require fair compensation.

5. *Justiciable Group Rights.* In the international arena the justiciability of indigenous group rights was established by the U.N. Human Rights Committee in ruling on a petition brought by the Lubicon Lake Band, a Cree-speaking Indian Band living within the province of Alberta, Canada. Recognized by Canada as an autonomous social group, the Band has maintained its traditional culture, religion, political structure and means of subsistence based on trapping, fishing and hunting on the approximately 10,000 square kilometers in northern Alberta it has historically inhabited. The gravamen of the complaint was that Canada's allowance of oil and gas exploration on the tribe's traditional lands resulted in environmental damage that has undermined the tribe's social structure and subsistence economy. The petition alleged that the activity disrupted fam-

ily relationships that are premised on spiritual and cultural ties to the land and the continuation of traditional activities; robbed the Band of the physical realm in which it conducts its religious practices; and resulted in an increase in miscarriages, stillbirths, and abnormal births. *Ominayak v. Canada*, U.N. GAOR, 45th Sess., Supp. No. 40, Annex 9, at 27, U.N. Doc. A/45/40 (1990).

Although the petition alleged violations of the Band's rights of self-determination under Article 1 of the International Covenant on Civil and Political Rights, the Committee admitted the Petition on the grounds that the allegations raised issues under Article 27, which protects the cultural rights of ethnic minorities. Canada asserted that the Committee's jurisdiction could not be invoked as to Article 27's collective right because the Optional Protocol provides only for a procedure by which individuals can claim that their individual rights were violated. Rejecting that argument, the Committee held that a group of individuals who claim to be similarly affected may collectively submit a communication, and found a continuing violation of Article 27. Canada agreed to rectify the situation and provide an appropriate remedy.

Three U.N. bodies (the Committee on Economic, Social and Cultural Rights, the Human Rights Committee, and the Committee on the Elimination of Racial Discrimination) have formally called upon the Canadian government to end the expropriation of indigenous peoples' land and resources, and the concomitant push of the group to the brink of cultural extinction. As of March 2004, Canada has not negotiated a settlement with the Lubicon Cree Indians. For more information, *see* Amnesty International Report: Canada: "Time is wasting": Respect for the land rights of the Lubicon Cree long overdue, AI Index: AMR 20/001/2003, *available at* http://www.amnesty.ca/library/canada/AMR200103.pdf.

Oil and gas exploration is rapidly encroaching on the surviving indigenous populations in many parts of the world, much like the quest for gold and other precious minerals spurred 15th century European colonial expansion in the Americas, with tragic consequences for the native peoples. *See, e.g.*, the Inter-American Commission on Human Rights, *Report on the Situation of Human Rights in Ecuador*, OAS.Ser. L/V/II.96. Doc.10 rev 1, Apr. 24, 1997. *See also* Juan Forero, *Seeking Balance: Growth vs. Culture in Amazon*, N.Y. TIMES, Dec. 10, 2003, at A1.

6. *"Evolutive Interpretation" of Right to Property*. The modern view is reflected in the decision of the Inter-American Court of Human Rights to uphold indigenous title to ancestral lands and natural resources by invoking the right to property. *The Mayagna (Sumo) Awas Tingni Community v. Nicaragua*, Judgment of Aug. 31, 2001, Inter-Am. Ct. H.R., (Ser. C) No. 79 (2001). The Court ruled that Nicaragua violated Article 21 of the American Convention on Human Rights by failing to provide legal protection for the tribe's communal property rights, and by granting a logging concession on community lands without their consent. Applying an "evolutionary interpretation" to Article 21, the Court determined that the provision encompasses more than individual property rights, observing:

> Among indigenous peoples there is a communitarian tradition regarding a communal form of collective property of the land, in the sense that ownership of the land is not centered on an individual but rather on the group and its community. Indigenous groups, by the fact of their very existence, have the right to live freely in their own territory; the close ties of indigenous people with the

land must be recognized and understood as the fundamental basis of their cultures, their spiritual life, their integrity, and their economic survival. For indigenous communities, relations to the land are not merely a matter of possession and production but a material and spiritual element which they must fully enjoy, even to preserve their cultural legacy and transmit it to future generations.

Id. at ¶ 149.

7. *Intellectual Property Rights to "Traditional Knowledge."* The information, methodologies, and cultural resources developed by indigenous or traditional peoples, often over centuries, is usually held in common and handed down orally from generation to generation. The Office of the U.N. High Commissioner for Human Rights recognizes the right of indigenous peoples to their cultural heritage and defines it to include:

- language, art, music, dance, song and ceremony;

- agricultural, technical and ecological knowledge and practices;

- spirituality, sacred sites and ancestral human remains; and

- documentation of the above.

Office of the High Commissioner for Human Rights, *Letter No. 12: WIPO and Indigenous Peoples, available at* http://www.unhchr.ch/html/racism/indileaflet12.doc (last visited Apr. 10, 2004).

In addition to religious rituals, such knowledge may relate to the medicinal properties of plants and other medical treatments, methods for producing music, artwork, and household or farming tools, beauty products, fragrances, and other useful items. However, colonialism, and, later, globalization, has allowed outsiders (often representing transnational corporations) to take advantage of such products and methods for global sale (*i.e.,* in the pharmaceutical or beauty industry) without appropriate compensation to traditional communities.

Legal issues associated with the appropriation of traditional knowledge by outsiders are generally analyzed under the broader framework of intellectual property law rather than as a matter of cultural human rights. While a right to intellectual property is found in both the Universal Declaration of Human Rights (Article 27) and the International Covenant on Economic, Social and Cultural Rights (Article 15), the nature and content of intellectual property rights has been more fully developed outside the international human rights framework. Nevertheless, the intellectual property legal framework has failed to fully address the challenges presented by traditional knowledge. A human rights framework may be a necessary supplement to the traditional intellectual property protections.

Article 27 of the Universal Declaration on Human Rights provides the following:

(1) Everyone has the right freely to participate in the cultural life of the community, to enjoy the arts and to share in scientific advancement and its benefits.

(2) Everyone has the right to the protection of the moral and material interests resulting from any scientific, literary or artistic production of which he is the author.

This explicit link between cultural rights and intellectual property is further elaborated in Article 15 of the International Covenant on Economic, Social and Cultural Rights, which states that

> The States Parties to the present Covenant recognize the right of everyone:
>
> (a) To take part in cultural life;
>
> (b) To enjoy the benefits of scientific progress and its applications;
>
> (c) To benefit from the protection of the moral and material interests resulting from any scientific, literary or artistic production of which he is the author.

The Committee on Economic, Social and Cultural Rights has emphasized the explicit link between intellectual property and human rights, arguing that the individualist orientation of the intellectual property framework is inadequate for the protection of traditional knowledge:

> "Cultural property" thus means more than "intellectual property" because account must be taken not only of what is produced by an artist, a scientist or a writer, but also of what is produced by a cultural community, by the custodians of a heritage or by a people.

Committee on Economic, Social and Cultural Rights, *Protection of Cultural Property: An Individual and Collective Right*, U.N. Doc. E/C.12/2000/16.

By recognizing the need for the protection of group rights to cultural property, is the Committee advocating a broader understanding of "property" than that common in non-traditional societies? Do traditional knowledge rights implicate obligations to both individual knowledge-holders and to the community in which he or she gathered the knowledge? What are the implications of such obligations for state policymaking? How should conflicts between individual and group claims to traditional knowledge be resolved?

A number of international declarations on the rights associated with traditional knowledge, some of which have been drafted by indigenous and traditional groups, have also emphasized the shortcomings of the intellectual property legal system to fully recognize the collective right to cultural heritage (*e.g.*, the Manila Declaration on the World Declaration for Cultural Development, the Kari-Oca Declaration, The Mataatua Declaration, and the Beijing Declaration of Indigenous Women).

The World Intellectual Property Organization (WIPO) has become the main resource for the protection of traditional knowledge. WIPO has created an Inter-governmental Committee on Intellectual Property, Genetic Resources, Traditional Knowledge, and Folklore to examine issues raised by the protection of traditional knowledge in an intellectual property scheme. *See* World Intellectual Property Organization, *Traditional Knowledge and Cultural Expressions, available at* http://www.wipo.int/globalissues/publications/index.html (last visited Apr. 10, 2004). The Committee notes that "traditional knowledge is embedded in traditional knowledge *systems*, which each community has developed and maintained in its local context." *Id.* The Committee's emphasis has been on traditional knowledge as a means of gathering genetic resources. It has engaged in a number of fact-finding missions, but the incongruence of the intellectual property system and the nature of traditional knowledge has resulted in few definitive protections. Some scholars suggest that further reform of the broader intellectual property system is necessary. *See, e.g.,* Srividhya Ragavan, *Protection of Traditional Knowledge,* 2 MINN. INTELL. PROP. REV. 1 (2001); Rosemary Coombe, *Intellectual Property, Human Rights, and Sovereignty,* 6 IND. J. GLOBAL LEG. STUD. 59 (1998); and Traci McClellan, *The Role of International Law in Protecting the Traditional Knowledge and Plant Life of Indigenous Peoples,* 19 WIS. INT'L L.J. 249 (2001). Others suggest that a new set of rights—traditional resource rights—should be elaborated. *See, e.g.,* MARIE BATTISTE & JAMES YOUNGBLOOD HENDERSON, PROTECTING INDIGENOUS KNOWLEDGE AND HERITAGE: A GLOBAL CHALLENGE (2000), *and* DARRELL POSEY & GRAHAM DUTFIELD, BEYOND INTELLECTUAL PROPERTY: TOWARD TRADITIONAL RESOURCE RIGHTS FOR INDIGENOUS PEOPLES AND LOCAL COMMUNITIES (1996).

The Convention on Biological Diversity also specifically mentions traditional knowledge in Article 8(j). A state party is required to:

> respect, preserve and maintain knowledge, innovations and practices of indigenous and local communities embodying traditional lifestyles relevant for the conservation and sustainable use of biological diversity and promote their wider application with the approval and involvement of the holders of such knowledge, innovations and practices and encourage the equitable sharing of the benefits arising from the utilization of such knowledge, innovations and practices.

Convention on Biological Diversity, Art. 8(j) (June 5, 1992), *available at* http://www.biodiv.org/convention/articles.asp?/g=o&a=cbd-08.

The focus of the Biodiversity Convention is on environmental issues. What is the relationship between access to traditional knowledge and the integrity of the environment? Does recognition of the rights of indigenous peoples with respect to such knowledge advance the cause of environmental protection?

The U.N. Commission on Human Rights has developed principles and guidelines for governments in the protection of indigenous heritage, including traditional knowledge. The guidelines provide that:

> 12. The heritage of indigenous peoples has a collective character and is comprised of all objects, sites and knowledge including languages, the nature or use of which has been transmitted from generation to generation, and which is regarded as pertaining to a particular people or its territory of traditional natural use. The heritage of indigenous peoples also includes objects, sites, knowledge and literary or artistic creation of that people which may be created or rediscovered in the future based upon their heritage.

> 13. The heritage of indigenous peoples includes all moveable cultural property as defined by the relevant conventions of UNESCO; all kinds of literary and artistic creation such as music, dance, song, ceremonies, symbols and designs, narratives and poetry and all forms of documentation of and by indigenous peoples; all kinds of scientific, agricultural, technical, medicinal, biodiversity-related and ecological knowledge, including innovations based upon that knowledge, cultigens, remedies, medicines and the use of flora and fauna; human remains; immoveable cultural property such as sacred sites of cultural, natural and historical significance and burials.

Commission on Human Rights, U.N. Doc. /E/CN.4/Sub.2/2000/26. Such principles and guidelines are not legally binding on governments. Therefore, the guidelines urge the United Nations to "consider as a matter of urgent priority the drafting of a convention for the protection of the heritage of indigenous peoples." *Id.*

b.   Defining the Content of Indigenous Self-Determination

S. JAMES ANAYA, SUPERPOWER ATTITUDES TOWARD INDIGENOUS PEOPLES AND GROUP RIGHTS

Proceedings of the 93rd Annual Meeting of the American Society of
International Law 251, 251–58 (Mar. 24–27, 1999)

Much has been said about the historical complicity of international law—or dominant thinking about international law—in the oppression of minority and indigenous peoples and their cultures. So it is perhaps with some irony that groups that are identified as indigenous are now looking to international law as a means of reversing the historical patterns of oppression and securing their cultural identities.

Largely as a result of their own advocacy at the international level, indigenous peoples or populations are now distinct subjects of concern within the United Nations (UN), the Organization of American States (OAS) and other international institutions. For several years, efforts have been under way within these institutions to develop new international normative instruments specifically for the benefit of indigenous peoples.***

It can hardly be disputed that indigenous peoples have been able to generate substantial sympathy for their demands among international actors. This can be seen in several concrete developments, including the UN General Assembly's designation of an International Decade of the World's Indigenous People [1995–2004], the International Labour Organisation's (ILO) adoption in 1989 of its Convention on Indigenous and Tribal Peoples, and the efforts at both the United Nations and the OAS to create declarations on the rights of indigenous peoples.***

At the same time, there is significant ongoing resistance to the indigenous peoples' agenda. This resistance is perhaps best represented by the positions being taken on the subject by the world's remaining superpower—the United States.***

INDIGENOUS PEOPLES' ADVOCACY AND STEPS TOWARD UN AND OAS DECLARATIONS CONCERNING THEIR RIGHTS

*** International developments concerning indigenous peoples that have occurred over the last several years can be attributed substantially to indigenous peoples' own advocacy. This advocacy has included the use of legal argument that incorporates notions of fairness and justice. Two dominant, usually complementary, strains of argument can be identified.

One strain of argument is articulated essentially within a state-centered frame. Indigenous groups, often referred to as "nations," are identified as having attributes of sovereignty that predate and, to at least some extent, should trump the sovereignty of the states that now assert power over them.*** Within this frame of argument, indigenous peoples' advocates point to a history in which the "original" sovereignty of indigenous communities over defined territories has been illegitimately wrested from them or suppressed. The rules of international law relating to the acquisition and transfer of territory by and among states are invoked to demonstrate the illegitimacy of the assault on indigenous sovereignty. Claims to land, group equality, culture and development assistance stem from the claim for reparations for the historical injustice against entities that, a *priori*, should be regarded as independent political communities with full status as such on the international plane.

A second strain of argument employed by advocates of indigenous peoples is articulated within a human rights frame. This strain of argument seizes upon the moral and ethical discourse that characterizes the modern human rights movement, that has the welfare of human beings as its subject, and that is concerned only secondarily, if at all, with the interests of sovereign entities.*** Affirmation of indigenous group rights, and related remedial measures to secure the enjoyment of these rights, are posited as moral imperatives and justified by reference to general human rights principles that are deemed already part of international law.

The United Nations and other international intergovernmental organizations, which together provide the institutional framework for the contemporary international system, have been most hospitable to the human rights strain of argument. By contrast, the state-centered historical sovereignty strain of argument naturally finds considerable resistance within intergovernmental organizations.***

While the human rights strain of argument advanced by indigenous peoples has been the more effective, the state-centered strain has not been without consequence. Accounts of the illegitimate wresting of historical sovereignty have strengthened the human rights arguments by enhancing sensitivity toward the inequities suffered by indigenous peoples that can be understood in human rights terms.***

Thus, with their arguments resonating within the discourse and institutional chambers of human rights, indigenous peoples have gained a foothold within the international human rights program. Their demands are now recurrent subjects of discussion within the major human rights institutions of the United Nations, the OAS and other international organizations that function at either the global or the regional level. The ongoing attention to developing declarations on indigenous rights within the United Nations and the OAS is a prominent manifestation of the international response to indigenous peoples' demands. These developments are contributing to the articulation of a sui generis body of international human rights norms that is specifically concerned with indigenous peoples, a body of norms that already finds some expression in the ILO's Convention No. 169 on Indigenous and Tribal Peoples of 1989, which as been ratified by several states in the Western Hemisphere and elsewhere.***

[The author describes draft declarations on indigenous rights currently being considered by the U.N. and the OAS.]

U.S. POSITIONS REGARDING THE DECLARATIONS ***

Opposition to Use of the Term Peoples

Central to the United States' posture toward the UN and OAS declaration projects is its opposition to use of the term peoples to refer to the subject groups. Both the UN and OAS draft declarations use this term to designate the beneficiaries of the rights articulated in the drafts. This usage is largely a result of the fact that indigenous groups have themselves insisted on being characterized as "peoples." Insistence on being referred to as "peoples" is a matter of simple dignity for indigenous leaders, who argue that to fail to recognize the groups they represent as "peoples" is to deny their existence as distinct communities with their own historically rooted cultures and institutions.***

The opposition of the United States to the term peoples is driven by its position on two other matters. First is the issue of collective rights. The United States has pointed out that to assign rights to "peoples" is to recognize group or collective rights. In this regard, the United States has clung to its traditional opposition to group rights. Second is the issue of self-determination. According to the United States, use of the term peoples implies a right of self-determination, since the UN Charter refers to the principle of "equal rights and self-determination of peoples," and the international human rights covenants state that "[a]ll peoples have the right of self-determination." The United States has argued that indigenous groups should not be understood to have a right of self-determination under international law, and it has opposed the language of the draft UN declaration that affirms such a right for indigenous peoples.***

The term indigenous peoples has become a term of art that is widely used in the legal academic literature, and that is increasingly found in the utterances and official acts of relevant international and domestic actors. In the relevant practice, usage of this term does not necessarily imply one position or another on the thorny issue of self-determination, as the term is often used without regard to that issue. The UN Human Rights Committee, the UN Committee on the Elimination of Racial Discrimination and the Inter-American Commission on Human Rights have all referred to "indigenous peoples" in their official pronouncements. Resolutions of European institutions also have invoked the term. Numerous states now regularly refer to "indigenous peoples" in their statements before international conferences and institutions that are concerned with the topic. This international practice reflects the fact that several states—including Canada, Bolivia, Colombia, Ecuador, Mexico, Nicaragua and Paraguay—now make specific reference to "aboriginal peoples" or "indigenous peoples" in their domestic laws or constitutions. Reference to "indigenous peoples" can even be found in acts of the U.S. Congress and U.S. executive orders.***

But while it is possible to divorce usage of the term peoples from the issue of self-determination, a similar separation is not possible with regard to the issue of group rights. This is because "peoples" are inevitably groups, and to ascribe rights to "peoples," as both the OAS and UN draft texts do, is to ascribe rights to groups.

Rejection of Collective or Group Rights

*** The United States has stressed that the individual human being is the central subject of human rights, and has pointed out that international human rights instruments generally are framed in terms of individual rights.*** The fact that most international human rights instruments articulate individual rights only underscores the point made for years by indigenous advocates: that existing human rights instruments do not adequately address the needs and aspirations of indigenous peoples, which relate to the enjoyment of collective human rights.***

One effort at principled argument offered by the United States in its resistance to group rights is that such rights may come into conflict with the rights of the individual.

But this argument presents what amounts to a nonissue, since implicit in any affirmation of a right, be it collective or individual, is the need to balance it in its application against any competing right.***

Resistance to Indigenous Self-Determination

A more difficult issue than use of the term "peoples" or that of group rights in general is presented by the effort to extend indigenous group rights to include a right of self-determination, which may be aptly called the mother of all group rights. A central demand of indigenous peoples has been that the international community recognize that they are entitled to determine their own destinies under conditions of equality. This includes the right of indigenous peoples to retain and develop their own systems of self-governance that are born of indigenous cultural patterns. In promoting this set of values, which are foundational to indigenous peoples' aspirations generally, indigenous peoples' advocates and leaders have seized upon the rhetoric of self-determination.***

*** The UN draft [declaration] states that indigenous peoples have a right of self-determination in the same terms that the right is affirmed in the international human rights covenants. Article 3 of the draft states:

> Indigenous peoples have the right of self-determination. By virtue of that right they freely determine their political status and freely pursue their economic, social and cultural development.

Such an expression of a right of self-determination presents certain challenges, of course. Interested states, including the United States, have legitimate concerns about draft article 3, concerns that have to do with avoiding the unhealthy balkanization, ethnic animosity and violent political upheaval that all too often have been associated with self-determination claims.***

The proposition that self-determination necessarily means a right to independent statehood is now so questionable—as reflected in the scholarly literature on the subject and the emerging pattern of authoritative responses to self-determination claims—that the United States cannot reasonably accept it as a premise of discussion without question.***

*** Indigenous peoples themselves generally reject aspirations to independent statehood, instead seeing self-determination as a vehicle for establishing better relations with the other segments of society so as to secure, on agreed terms, their survival as distinct groups with control over their own affairs.***

DRAFT DECLARATION ON THE RIGHTS OF INDIGENOUS PEOPLES

E/CN.4/Sub.2/1994/2/Add.1 (1994)

[The Preamble affirms principles of equality, cultural diversity, and anti-discrimination, recognizes deprivations of human rights resulting from colonization and dispossession of lands and resources, and endorses the control of indigenous peoples over their development.]

PART I ***

Article 3

Indigenous peoples have the right of self-determination. By virtue of that right they freely determine their political status and freely pursue their economic, social and cultural development.

Article 4

Indigenous peoples have the right to maintain and strengthen their distinct political, economic, social and cultural characteristics, as well as their legal systems, while retaining their rights to participate fully, if they so choose, in the political, economic, social and cultural life of the State.***

PART II

Article 6

Indigenous peoples have the collective right to live in freedom, peace and security as distinct peoples and to full guarantees against genocide or any other act of violence, including the removal of indigenous children from their families and communities under any pretext.***

PART III

Article 12

Indigenous peoples have the right to practise and revitalize their cultural traditions and customs. This includes the right to maintain, protect and develop the past, present and future manifestations of their cultures, such as archaeological and historical sites, artifacts, designs, ceremonies, technologies and visual and performing arts and literature, as well as the right to the restitution of cultural, intellectual, religious and spiritual property taken without their free and informed consent or in violation of their laws, traditions and customs.

Article 13

Indigenous peoples have the right to manifest, practise, develop and teach their spiritual and religious traditions, customs and ceremonies; the right to maintain, protect, and have access in privacy to their religious and cultural sites; the right to the use and control of ceremonial objects; and the right to the repatriation of human remains.***

Article 14

Indigenous peoples have the right to revitalize, use, develop and transmit to future generations their histories, languages, oral traditions, philosophies, writing systems and literatures, and to designate and retain their own names for communities, places and persons.***

PART IV

Article 15

Indigenous children have the right to all levels and forms of education of the State. All indigenous peoples also have this right and the right to establish and control their educational systems and institutions providing education in their own languages, in a manner appropriate to their cultural methods of teaching and learning.

Indigenous children living outside their communities have the right to be provided access to education in their own culture and language.***

Article 16

Indigenous peoples have the right to have the dignity and diversity of their cultures, traditions, histories and aspirations appropriately reflected in all forms of education and public information.***

Article 17

Indigenous peoples have the right to establish their own media in their own languages. They also have the right to equal access to all forms of non-indigenous media.***

PART V

Article 19

Indigenous peoples have the right to participate fully, if they so choose, at all levels of decision-making in matters which may affect their rights, lives and destinies through representatives chosen by themselves in accordance with their own procedures, as well as to maintain and develop their own indigenous decision-making institutions.

*** *Article 22*

Indigenous peoples have the right to special measures for the immediate, effective and continuing improvement of their economic and social conditions, including in the areas of employment, vocational training and retraining, housing, sanitation, health and social security.

Particular attention shall be paid to the rights and special needs of indigenous elders, women, youth, children and disabled persons.

Article 23

Indigenous peoples have the right to determine and develop priorities and strategies for exercising their right to development. In particular, indigenous peoples have the right to determine and develop all health, housing and other economic and social programmes affecting them and, as far as possible, to administer such programmes through their own institutions.

Article 24

Indigenous peoples have the right to their traditional medicines and health practices, including the right to the protection of vital medicinal plants, animals and minerals.

They also have the right to access, without any discrimination, to all medical institutions, health services and medical care.

PART VI

Article 25

Indigenous peoples have the right to maintain and strengthen their distinctive spiritual and material relationship with the lands, territories, waters and coastal seas and other resources which they have traditionally owned or otherwise occupied or used, and to uphold their responsibilities to future generations in this regard.

Article 26

Indigenous peoples have the right to own, develop, control and use the lands and territories, including the total environment of the lands, air, waters, coastal seas, sea-ice, flora and fauna and other resources which they have traditionally owned or otherwise occupied or used. This includes the right to the full recognition of their laws, traditions and customs, land-tenure systems and institutions for the development and management of resources, and the right to effective measures by States to prevent any interference with, alienation of or encroachment upon these rights.

Article 27

Indigenous peoples have the right to the restitution of the lands, territories and resources which they have traditionally owned or otherwise occupied or used, and which have been confiscated, occupied, used or damaged without their free and informed consent. Where this is not possible, they have the right to just and fair compensation. Unless otherwise freely agreed upon by the peoples concerned, compensation shall take the form of lands, territories and resources equal in quality, size and legal status.

Article 28

Indigenous peoples have the right to the conservation, restoration and protection of the total environment and the productive capacity of their lands, territories and resources, as well as to assistance for this purpose from States and through international cooperation. Military activities shall not take place in the lands and territories of indigenous peoples, unless otherwise freely agreed upon by the peoples concerned.

States shall take effective measures to ensure that no storage or disposal of hazardous materials shall take place in the lands and territories of indigenous peoples.

States shall also take effective measures to ensure, as needed, that programmes for monitoring, maintaining and restoring the health of indigenous peoples, as developed and implemented by the peoples affected by such materials, are duly implemented.

Article 29

Indigenous peoples are entitled to the recognition of the full ownership, control and protection of their cultural and intellectual property.

They have the right to special measures to control, develop and protect their sciences, technologies and cultural manifestations, including human and other genetic resources, seeds, medicines, knowledge of the properties of fauna and flora, oral traditions, literatures, designs and visual and performing arts.***

PART VII

Article 32

Indigenous peoples have the collective right to determine their own citizenship in accordance with their customs and traditions. Indigenous citizenship does not impair the right of indigenous individuals to obtain citizenship of the States in which they live.***

Article 36

Indigenous peoples have the right to the recognition, observance and enforcement of treaties, agreements and other constructive arrangements concluded with States or their successors, according to their original spirit and intent, and to have States honour and respect such treaties, agreements and other constructive arrangements. Conflicts and disputes which cannot otherwise be settled should be submitted to competent international bodies agreed to by all parties concerned.

PART VIII

Article 37

States shall take effective and appropriate measures, in consultation with the indigenous peoples concerned, to give full effect to the provisions of this Declaration. The rights recognized herein shall be adopted and included in national legislation in such a manner that indigenous peoples can avail themselves of such rights in practice.

Notes and Questions

1. The Draft Declaration of the Rights of Indigenous People was prepared pursuant to General Assembly Resolution 1022/89, Nov. 18, 1989, para. 13. For a historical overview of the development of the Draft Declaration, *see* IACHR, The Human Rights Situation of the Indigenous People in the Americas 2000, OEA/Ser.L/V/II/108, Doc. 62, at 4–6 (Oct. 20, 2000).

2. *Who Are Indigenous Peoples?* There is no internationally accepted definition of indigenous peoples, and even the question of whether there should be one is controversial. One issue is whether the ability of states to define such groups violates their right to self-determination. The Draft Declaration recognizes the right of self-identification in Article 8:

> Indigenous peoples have the collective and individual right to maintain and develop their distinct identities and characteristics, including the right to identify themselves as indigenous and to be recognized as such.

Another definitional issue is whether all tribal peoples are "indigenous," entitled to the more expansive rights that are afforded such groups under international human rights law. Some states, particularly in Asia, oppose the classification of minorities in their territories as "indigenous," arguing that they are no more indigenous than the rest of the population, and seek to limit this category to those peoples conquered by European colonialists. These states argue that unless such a distinction is made, the international community will be confronted by a "proliferation of pretenders" to indigenous status. Indigenous activists oppose such a distinction.

Various definitions have been employed by international bodies depending on the purpose. The working definition that guided the deliberations on the U. N. Draft Declaration was that proposed by the United Nations Special Rapporteur for the Study of Discrimination against Indigenous Peoples, Mr. Martínez Cobo:

> Indigenous communities, peoples and nations are those which, having a historical continuity with pre-invasion and pre-colonial societies that developed on their territories, consider themselves distinct from the other sectors of societies now prevailing in those territories, or parts of them. They form at present non-dominant sectors of society and are determined to preserve, develop and transmit to future generations their ancestral territories and their ethnic identity as the basis of their continued existence as peoples, in accordance with their own cultural patterns, social institutions and legal systems. In short, Indigenous

Peoples are the descendants of a territory overcome by conquest or settlement by aliens.

Study of the Problem of Discrimination against Indigenous Populations: Conclusions, Proposals and Recommendations, U.N. Doc. E/CN 4/Sub 2/1986/7 Add. 4. How is "historical continuity" to be determined? What factors should be considered?

Compare the International Labour Organization's Convention No. 169 concerning the working rights of Indigenous and Tribal Peoples, which applies to:

> 1. (a) Tribal peoples in independent countries whose social, cultural and economic conditions distinguish them from other sections of the national community, and whose status is regulated wholly or in part by their own customs or traditions or by special laws or regulations;
>
> (b) Peoples in independent countries who are regarded as indigenous on account of their descent from the populations which inhabited the country, or a geographical region to which the country belongs, at the time of colonisation or the establishment of present State boundaries and who, irrespective of their legal status, retain some or all of their own social, economic, cultural or political institutions.

> 2. Self-identification as indigenous or tribal shall be regarded as a fundamental criterion for determining the groups to which the provisions of this Convention apply.

Convention Concerning Indigenous and Tribal Peoples in Independent Countries (ILO Convention 169), *adopted* June 27, 1989, 28 I.L.M. 1384 (*entered into force* Sept. 5, 1991).

The World Bank currently uses the following characteristics to identify indigenous peoples affected by Bank-funded development projects:

> a) close attachment to ancestral territories and to the natural resources in these areas; b) self-identification and identification by others as members of a distinct cultural group; c) an indigenous language, often different from the national language; d) presence of customary social and political institutions; and e) primarily subsistence-oriented production.

Operational Directive 4.20, 1991, *available at* http://www.worldbank.org/indigenous. A proposed revision of the Bank's policy would provide indigenous peoples a voice in project design and implementation, but excludes from the definition persons who "(a) have left their communities of origin and (b) moved to urban areas and/or migrated to obtain wage labor." Draft OP/BP 4.10 (03-23-01).

What are the distinguishing features of these definitions? How do the differences relate to the purposes served by the definitions?

3.   *State Resistance to Self-Determination.* The right to self-determination has always been politically contentious. Since at least the 1960s decolonization movement it has been recognized as a human right under international law which may be asserted by "all peoples." The classic right of self-determination encompasses rights of autonomy up to and including secession. Many states, therefore, fear the implications of using the term "indigenous peoples." As a result of pressure from numerous governments, the following disclaimer was inserted in the Declaration of the World Conference against Racism held in Durban, South Africa in 2001:

24. We declare that the use of the term "indigenous peoples" in the Declaration and Programme of Action of the World Conference against Racism, Racial Discrimination, Xenophobia and Related Intolerance *** cannot be construed as having any implications as to rights under international law.

Declaration and Programme of Action of the World Conference against Racism, Racial Discrimination, Xenophobia and Related Intolerance (Aug. 31–Sept. 8, 2001), *available at* http://www.unhchr.ch/pdf/Durban.pdf.

As James Anaya points out, however, independent statehood has not been a demand of most indigenous groups. What special forms of self-determination are appropriate in this context? Article 31 of the Draft Declaration provides:

Indigenous peoples, as a specific form of exercising their right to self-determination, have the right to autonomy or self-government in matters relating to their internal and local affairs, including culture, religion, education, information, media, health, housing, employment, social welfare, economic activities, and resources management, environment and entry by non-members, as well as ways and means for financing these autonomous functions.

What forms of autonomy typically associated with independent statehood are absent from Article 31's purview? Would Article 31 have protected the cultural practices of the indigenous community in *Lying v. N.W. Indian Cemetery Protective Ass'n*, 485 U.S. 439 (1988). *See* discussion in note 3 following the *Lovelace* case, Section A.1.c, *infra*.

4. *Indigenous Peoples as Ethnic Minorities.* The International Covenant on Civil and Political Rights, which recognizes in Article 27 the rights of persons belonging to "ethnic, religious and linguistic minorities," does not define the concept of minorities. In a report by the United Nations Sub-Commission on the Prevention of Discrimination and Protection of Minorities, the following definition was proposed:

A group numerically inferior to the rest of the population of a State, in a non-dominant position, whose members—being nationals of the state—possess ethnic, religious or linguistic characteristics differing from those of the rest of the population and show, if only implicitly, a sense of solidarity, directed towards preserving their culture, tradition, religion or language.

Francesco Capotori, Study on the Rights of Persons Belonging to Ethnic, Religious and Linguistic Minorities, U.N. Doc. E/CN.4/Sub.2/384/Rev. 1, at 43, U.N. Sales E. 78.XIV.1 (1979).

"Indigenous peoples" and "ethnic minorities" are normatively distinct categories. An ILO commentary notes that:

[u]nlike [ethnic minorities], most indigenous and tribal peoples have a link to the land they have traditionally occupied. They may have cultures which are very different from the predominant culture in the countries in which they live. They often have their own laws, their own religions and their own view of the universe around them.

International Labor Office, A Guide to ILO Convention No.169 on Indigenous and Tribal Peoples, Policies for Development Branch/Equality and Human Rights Coordination Branch, Geneva, 1995, at 6. Such a distinction is also recognized in the Convention on the Rights of the Child, which refers to minorities or "persons of indigenous origin." *See* Convention on the Rights of the Child, Nov. 20, 1989, art. 30, 28 I.L.M. 1448, 1468 (1989). Nevertheless, these categories are not mutually exclusive, as demonstrated in the jurisprudence of the Human Rights Committee, which has applied Article 27 of the ICCPR to protect the special relationship of indigenous peoples with their land. *See Ominayak v. Canada,* U.N. GAOR 45th Sess., Supp. No. 40, Annex 9, at 27, U.N. Doc. A/45/40 (1990), in Section A.1.a, *supra.*

c. Group Rights vs. Equality

CINDY L. HOLDER AND JEFF J. CORNTASSEL, INDIGENOUS PEOPLES AND MULTICULTURAL CITIZENSHIP: BRIDGING COLLECTIVE AND INDIVIDUAL RIGHTS

24 HUM. RTS. Q. 126 (2002)

I. INTRODUCTION ***

Debate over the limits of existing rights discourse is often pursued within a framework of liberal-individualism versus corporatism. For example, Peter Jones distinguishes two different ways in which a group claim might be incorporated into human rights discourse: 1) as the claim of a collectivity that is ultimately reducible to individual members; or 2) as the claim of a corporate body the reduction of which to constituent members is not possible. Jones, among others, has argued that groups should not be recognized as subjects of human rights that can conflict with and potentially override the claims of individual members. For many proponents of minority claims, however, protecting the ability of groups to determine for themselves the terms on which members interact with outsiders and with one another is an essential part of protecting their right to self-determination and so represents a goal toward which any fight for group recognition must aim.***

[T]he ways in which indigenous groups conceive of groups and their relation to respect for individual dignity are not only more complex than the liberal-individualist or corporatist approaches that they have been used to illustrate, but offer a more sophisticated understanding of the relationship between individuals and groups than either theoretical approach. Many indigenous groups emphasize the interdependence of individual and collective claims and *** recognize that collective and individual rights are mutually interactive rather than in competition. Duties of citizenship are grounded in interactions at multiple levels (the host state, indigenous group, and individual members) as are the claims that individuals may make of their governing institutions and of one another.***

*** Both liberal-individualists and corporatists locate the importance of group interests in the personal psychology of individual group members. As a result, they treat group interests (such as cultural integrity) as not only different in kind from individualized interests such as freedom of expression but as potentially in competition with them.

In contrast to this, the real-world demands of indigenous groups place a great deal of emphasis on concrete ways in which the preserving of communal life can be important to individuals' well-being, in addition to the various spiritual and symbolic resources which such life may provide. These practical aspects of communal life make individuals' group interests a lot like their individualized ones, and so suggest that such rights do not introduce new or distinctive theoretical questions.***

C. *The Problem* ***

[E]mphasis [on] psychological investment to the exclusion of more tangible material and structural considerations *** sets up an implicit competition between (psychological) group interests on the one hand and (concrete or material) individual interests on the other. Resolving conflicts between group interests and individualistic ones thus appears to be a question of deciding the relative importance of symbolic and psychological ways of impacting an individual's well-being versus tangible and corporeal ways of impacting on an individual's life. In actuality, however, the irreducibly collective and the individualistic do not divide neatly along symbolic-psychological/tangible-corporeal lines. Many group priorities, such as establishing legal recognition of aboriginal title or gaining control over the resources necessary to serve members' health needs, are very concrete. Moreover, the experience of many indigenous groups is that, far from representing a threat to individual members, the physical security of group life is a contributing factor to the security of members' persons.***

III. PRACTICE AS AN ALTERNATIVE ***

[T]he most prominent forum for expanding the global network of indigenous rights, the UN Working Group on Indigenous Populations (UNWGIP), is comprised predominantly of indigenous delegations. It is within this forum, which was established in 1982, that the "Draft Universal Declaration on the Rights of Indigenous Peoples" (Draft Declaration) was authored by over 400 different indigenous delegations (without state interference) over a period of eight years.***

Before proceeding, one must acknowledge the multiple regional and state contexts that indigenous peoples experience. For example, native peoples within Canada, the United States, and New Zealand believe they have additional collective entitlements as "prior sovereigns" based on previous treaties signed with the host state.[1] While many of these treaties were effectively abrogated and many of these peoples were removed from

---

[1]   For more on this, see Study on Treaties, Agreements, and Other Constructive Arrangements between States and Indigenous Populations: Final Report by Miguel Alfonso Martinez, Special Rapporteur, UN Comm'n on Hum. Rts., U.N. Doc. E/CN.4/Sub.2/1999/20 (22 June 1999). For example, in New Zealand, the Treaty of Waitangi was signed in 1840 between the British Crown and the Maori chiefs and subtribes of New Zealand. Originally regarded as a document of land cession, it also agreed to "protect the chiefs, the subtribes and all the people of New Zealand in the unqualified exercise of their chieftainship over their lands, villages and all their treasures."

IAN BROWNLIE, TREATIES AND INDIGENOUS PEOPLES 7 (1992). This treaty has been updated by the New Zealand government by the Acts of 1975 and 1985 to allow for Maori claimants to present their grievances to a Tribunal.

In Canada, all 11 treaties were signed between 1871 and 1921, effectively dispossessing them from their traditional homelands. However, these treaties also establish these governments as "status" tribes with official recognition by the Canadian government. JULIAN BURGER, REPORT FROM THE FRONTIER: THE STATE OF THE WORLD'S INDIGENOUS PEOPLES 204–05 (1987).

their original homelands, treaties do provide a basis for group recognition and autonomy within the host state. Yet several colonial powers did not engage in the treaty-making process and hence, the majority of the world's indigenous peoples were not extended the same types of rights. The groups who have not been extended these same treaty-based rights constitute the vast majority of the world's indigenous populations (90 percent or 270 million by some estimates) and live in developing countries. Despite the differential treatment accorded the world's indigenous peoples, there is a remarkable degree of overlap between indigenous belief systems in developed and developing countries, as evidenced by universal provisions in the Draft Declaration and other global indigenous documents.

Overall, the Draft Declaration generally reflects a common indigenous experience with colonialism and unified agendas to maintain spiritual and political autonomy in the face of host state encroachments. Therefore, the contemporary struggle of indigenous peoples for greater autonomy and collective rights as outlined in the Draft Declaration is deemed a key component of the global indigenous rights praxis today.

IV. THE CONTRIBUTION OF INDIGENOUS WORLD-VIEWS

In order to develop a more comprehensive rights discourse between the practical and theoretical, it is important to outline three prevalent and overarching indigenous perspectives on community citizenship that could better inform the individualist/collectivist theoretical debate. However, one must first understand that indigenous world-views are not fixed or static but rather flexible and adaptable to changing circumstances.***

The first aspect of an indigenous rights praxis is the interdependence between collective and individual rights. For example, the Inuit Tapirisat of Canada express their strategy for survival at both the collective and individual levels:

> The impacts of racism and colonialism on aboriginal peoples cannot be adequately addressed by individual rights alone.*** The protection of collective rights can provide freedom at the individual and the collective level to choose assimilation, or not.*** Inuit believe in individual and collective rights as complementary aspects of an holistic human rights regime.

[E]xisting human rights treaties and host state policies toward minority groups within their borders are individualistic in nature and do not adequately protect cultural groups such as the Inuit. On the other hand, intra-group divisions make some individual recourse necessary from the authority structure within the collectivity. To offer effective protection from hostile host state intervention, many indigenous groups have developed a strategy whereby individuals can advance claims either on their own behalf or on behalf of any other member or members of the group. The collectivity or indigenous group may then also exercise specific rights.***

[T]here are usually many layers of informal collectivities within indigenous societies, such as kinship networks and clan affiliations. Therefore, the community's authority rests not on formal leadership but on the consensus decision making of the members. As Taiaiake Alfred, a Kahnewake (Mohawk) scholar, points out indigenous peoples view

---

In the United States, over 371 treaties and executive agreements have been negotiated Between Indian governments and the US government. Of those treaties, 76 called for removal and 230 dealt with land cessions. Jeff Corntassel & Tomas Hopkins Primeau, *Indigenous "Sovereignty" and International Law*, 17 HUM. RTS. Q. 343, 355–56 (1995).

collective power as being derived from six basic principles: the active participation of individuals; balancing many layers of equal power; dispersion of power; situational dynamics of power; non-coercive nature of power; and power that respects diversity. These principles highlight a decentralized power base within indigenous communities that operates within several kinship and clan affiliations inside the community as well as citizenship within the larger community.***

[P]ractical world-views advanced by native peoples are also instructive in their emphasis on the interdependence between individuals within the group. Evidence from oral traditions and historical documentation provides insight into a distinct native kinship network system. The oral traditions of many indigenous groups emphasize that the public or tribal position of the Indian is entirely dependent upon her private virtue, and, thus, one is never permitted to forget that she does not live to herself alone. These traditions illustrate the conceptual interrelatedness of individuals within native groups' belief systems. In other words, one's relations with others are primarily defined by social or kinship networks. As a corollary to this, members are not forced to comply, but rather a consensus is sought.[2] In the absence of hierarchical relationships, an indigenous world view leads to a strong emphasis on discursive democratic values:

> The primacy of individual conscience dictates a very pure form of democracy characterized by its lack of central authority and in which any collective action requires the consent of everyone affected—or at least the consensus of all their families.***

A second major component of indigenous rights praxis relates to kinship orientations that may extend beyond group members to other species and objects. Often referred to as universal kinship, such a belief highlights the ties indigenous peoples have to physical objects such as land. In [theoretical discourse] land rights are viewed predominantly as regulatory and commodified and not viewed from an indigenous praxis perspective of land as a link to one's ancestors and part of a larger spiritual compact of stewardship. For many indigenous peoples land is regarded as sacred: to be revered and served rather than owned. As the Vice-President of the World Council of Indigenous Peoples stated:

> Next to shooting Indigenous Peoples, the surest way to kill us is to separate us from our part of the Earth. Once separated, we will either perish in body or our minds and spirits will be altered so that we end up mimicking foreign ways.

Such universal kinship philosophies are pervasive in many native societies. This practical approach essentially weaves together the interests of group members as persons together with their interests as members of a variety of collectivities, including the collectivity made up of members of the species and of the people who are joint trustees of particular pieces of land. In effect, many indigenous peoples define themselves "communally in terms of a spiritual compact rather than a social contract."[3] ***

---

[2] Mayan beliefs in consensus-building are also well-documented as evidenced by the practice of a group "cargo system." According to the cargo system, a leader is selected by an institution called Lah-Ti, meaning to compare discourses and come to a common consensus during a public assembly of men and women. *See* Victor Montejo, *Tying up the Bundle and the Katuns of Dishonor: Maya Worldview and Politics*, 17 AM. INDIAN CULTURE & RESEARCH J. 103 (1993).

[3] *** Gerald Alfred and Franke Wilmer also point out that "[a]ccording to the views of indigenous cultures . . . there is no distinction between the human and natural worlds. Hence,

This brings out a final component of the indigenous rights praxis: going beyond the psychological aspects of group membership to note the importance of communities in structuring concrete aspects of a person's life. For indigenous peoples, there is a link between the material and non-material benefits of healthy communal life that belies the unidimensional understanding of collective rights usually found in theory.***

Consequently, theoretical perspectives which tend to prioritize or assign values to either material or non-material benefits of collective rights as if the two were separate considerations simply fail to capture the true nature of the interests at stake.*** For example, access to a tangible resource such as land can coincide with intangible benefits, such as group ceremonial practices or spiritual training.***

V. CONCLUSIONS ***

[A] complete theory of collective rights must account for demands which serve material and economic interests such as land claims and territorial integrity. Within contemporary philosophical theories, these demands are interpreted as having primarily symbolic importance. However, closer examination of the political context in which most indigenous groups operate shows demands for insulation from the state and a land base of one's own to be important pragmatic conditions for community survival. An adequate philosophical account of collective rights must recognize these direct, material interests as well as the indirect symbolic import of collective claims.

[T]he material and pragmatic interests served by collective claims must be integrated with symbolic and psychological interests in a way that preserves the symbiotic nature of their relationship. [Contemporary approaches] assume a kind of hierarchy of need, in which identity interests occupy a place which is either higher or lower than other interests. Such a framework is too inflexible to properly capture the reality of collective claims, however.***

Similarly, an adequate philosophical treatment of collective rights must avoid dichotomizing individualistic and collective interests. [Current] approaches assume that in the final analysis, one type of interest—either the individual or the collective—must be given priority, and when push comes to shove, one will be the final winner. The experience of indigenous peoples' movements, however, shows the world of collective claims to be more complicated than this. Indeed, the practical context of most indigenous groups—historically oppressed and marginalized, internally divided, and perceived as a threat by state actors—suggests that one must be able to recognize particular cases in which collective interests must give way to individual claims without thereby conceding a general priority to individual interests if indigenous governing units are to exist as autonomous entities within their host state. In fact, the experience of indigenous groups suggests that it may be a mistake to regard such conflicts in terms of "collectivities" versus "individuals." Instead, one ought to recognize that all parties to the conflict are individuals, and it is the type of interest which each individual negotiates that may be characterized in collectivist or individualist terms.***

'natural resources' or the 'natural world' are experienced subjectively as well as objectively." *See Indigenous Peoples, States, and Conflict, in* WARS IN THE MIDST OF PEACE 29 (David Carment & Patrick James eds., 1997).

SANDRA LOVELACE v. CANADA

U.N. Doc. CCPR/C/OP/1 at 83 (1984)

1. The author of the communication *** is a 32-year-old woman, living in Canada. She was born and registered as "Maliseet Indian" but has lost her rights and status as an Indian in accordance with section 12 (1) (b) of the Indian Act, after having married a non-Indian on 23 May 1970. Pointing out that an Indian man who marries a non-Indian woman does not lose his Indian status, she claims that the Act is discriminatory on the grounds of sex and contrary to articles 2 (1), 3, 23 (1) and (4), 26 and 27 of the [International] Covenant [on Civil and Political Rights].***

5. In its submission under article 4 (2) of the Optional Protocol concerning the merits of the case,*** the State party recognized that "many of the provisions of the *** Indian Act, including section 12 (1) (b), require serious reconsideration and reform." The Government further referred to an earlier public declaration to the effect that it intended to put a reform bill before the Canadian Parliament. It none the less stressed the necessity of the Indian Act as an instrument designed to protect the Indian minority in accordance with article 27 of the Covenant. A definition of the Indian was inevitable in view of the special privileges granted to the Indian communities, in particular their right to occupy reserve lands. Traditionally, patrilineal family relationships were taken into account for determining legal claims. Since, additionally, in the farming societies of the nineteenth century, reserve land was felt to be more threatened by non-Indian men than by non-Indian women, legal enactments as from 1869 provided that an Indian woman who married a non-Indian man would lose her status as an Indian. These reasons were still valid. A change in the law could only be sought in consultation with the Indians themselves who, however, were divided on the issue of equal rights.***

6. The author of the communication *** disputes the contention that legal relationships within Indian families were traditionally patrilineal in nature. Her view is that the reasons put forward by the Canadian Government do not justify the discrimination against Indian women in section 12 (1) (b) of the Indian Act. She concludes that the Human Rights Committee should recommend the State party to amend the provisions in question.***

9.6   As to Mrs. Lovelace's place of abode prior to her marriage both parties confirm that she was at that time living on the Tobique Reserve with her parents. Sandra Lovelace adds that as a result of her marriage, she was denied the right to live on an Indian reserve. As to her abode since then the State party observes:

> Since her marriage and following her divorce, Mrs. Lovelace has, from time to time, lived on the reserve in the home of her parents, and the Band Council has made no move to prevent her from doing so. However, Mrs. Lovelace wishes to live permanently on the reserve and to obtain a new house. To do so, she has to apply to the Band Council. Housing on reserves is provided with money set aside by Parliament for the benefit of registered Indians. The Council has not agreed to provide Mrs. Lovelace with a new house. It considers that in the provision of such housing priority is to be given to registered Indians.

9.7   In this connection the following additional information has been submitted on behalf of Mrs. Lovelace:

At the present time, Sandra Lovelace is living on the Tobique Indian Reserve, although she has no right to remain there. She has returned to the Reserve, with her children because her marriage has broken up and she has no other place to reside. She is able to remain on the reserve in violation of the law of the local Band Council because dissident members of the tribe who support her cause have threatened to resort to physical violence in her defense should the authorities attempt to remove her.***

10. The Human Rights Committee, in the examination of the communication before it, has to proceed from the basic fact that Sandra Lovelace married a non-Indian on 23 May 1970 and consequently lost her status as a Maliseet Indian under section 12 (1) (b) of the Indian Act. This provision was—and still is—based on a distinction de jure on the ground of sex. However, neither its application to her marriage as the cause of her loss of Indian status nor its effects could at that time amount to a violation of the Covenant, because this instrument did not come into force for Canada until 19 August 1976.***

11. The Committee recognizes, however, that the situation may be different if the alleged violations, although relating to events occurring before 19 August 1976, continue, or have effects which themselves constitute violations, after that date.***

13.1   The Committee considers that the essence of the present complaint concerns the continuing effect of the Indian Act, in denying Sandra Lovelace legal status as an Indian, in particular because she cannot for this reason claim a legal right to reside where she wishes to, on the Tobique Reserve. This fact persists after the entry into force of the Covenant, and its effects have to be examined, without regard to their original cause. [T]he significant matter is her last claim, that "the major loss to a person ceasing to be an Indian is the loss of the cultural benefits of living in an Indian community, the emotional ties to home, family, friends and neighbhours, and the loss of identity."

13.2   Although a number of provisions of the Covenant have been invoked by Sandra Lovelace, the Committee considers that the one which is most directly applicable to this complaint is article 27, which reads as follows:

In those States in which ethnic, religious or linguistic minorities exist, persons belonging to such minorities shall not be denied the right, in community with the other members of their group, to enjoy their own culture, to profess and practise their own religion, or to use their own language.

It has to be considered whether Sandra Lovelace, because she is denied the legal right to reside on the Tobique Reserve, has by that fact been denied the right guaranteed by article 27 to persons belonging to minorities, to enjoy their own culture and to use their own language in community with other members of their group.

14. *** Since Sandra Lovelace is ethnically a Maliseet Indian and has only been absent from her home reserve for a few years during the existence of her marriage, she is, in the opinion of the Committee, entitled to be regarded as "belonging" to this minority and to claim the benefits of article 27 of the Covenant.***

15. The right to live on a reserve is not as such guaranteed by article 27 of the Covenant. Moreover, the Indian Act does not interfere directly with the functions which are expressly mentioned in that article. However, in the opinion of the Committee the right of Sandra Lovelace to access to her native culture and language "in community with the other members" of her group, has in fact been, and continues to be inter-

fered with, because there is no place outside the Tobique Reserve where such a community exists.***

16. [T]he Committee is of the view that statutory restrictions affecting the right to residence on a reserve of a person belonging to the minority concerned, must have both a reasonable and objective justification and be consistent with the other provisions of the Covenant, read as a whole. Article 27 must be construed and applied in the light of the other provisions mentioned above, such as articles 12, [right to choose one's residence] 17 and 23 [protecting family life and children] in so far as they may be relevant to the particular case, and also the provisions against discrimination.***

17. The case of Sandra Lovelace should be considered in the light of the fact that her marriage to a non-Indian has broken up. It is natural that in such a situation she wishes to return to the environment in which she was born, particularly as after the dissolution of her marriage her main cultural attachment again was to the Maliseet band. Whatever may be the merits of the Indian Act in other respects, it does not seem to the Committee that to deny Sandra Lovelace the right to reside on the reserve is reasonable, or necessary to preserve the identity of the tribe. The committee therefore concludes that to prevent her recognition as belonging to the band is an unjustifiable denial of her rights under article 27 of the Covenant, read in the context of the other provisions referred to.***

19. Accordingly, the Human Rights Committee, acting under article 5 (4) of the Optional Protocol to the International Covenant on Civil and Political Rights, is of the view that the facts of the present case, which establish that Sandra Lovelace has been denied the legal right to reside on the Tobique Reserve, disclose a breach by Canada of article 27 of the Covenant.***

Notes and Questions

1. On what theory does the Committee base its decision? Does the decision infringe the right of self-determination? If so, is such an infringement justified?

2. The Canadian statute defining membership in Ms. Lovelace's tribe was allegedly based on the tribe's "patrilineal" traditions. Professor Benedict Kingsbury points out, however, that the membership criteria in Canada's Indian Act were not all gender-based, but furthered the Canadian government's policy of assimilation of indigenous peoples:

> Not only did the Indian Act transform into non-Indians women who married non-Indians and their children, but also it ended the Indian status of men who served in the Canadian army and of Indians who became "enfranchised." Marrying a white, having a white father, military service, and civic entitlement to vote were all badges of honor qualifying Indians to upgrade to non-Indian. This established pattern of assimilation combined with gender-targeting had structured many Indian communities.

Benedict Kingsbury, *Reconciling Five Competing Conceptual Structures of Indigenous Peoples' Claims in International and Comparative Law*, 34 N.Y.U. J. L. & POL. 189, 207 (2002). The assimilationist provisions of the Indian Act were partially reformed in 1985, making excluded women and their children eligible for reinstatement. *See* Indian Act, R.S.C. ch. 32 (1st Supp.) (1985) (Can.) However, as the U.N. Human Rights Committee noted in its 1999 observations on the Canadian report, "[a]lthough the Indian status of women who had lost status because of marriage was reinstituted, this amendment affects only the woman and her children, not subsequent generations, which may still be denied membership in the community." Concluding Observations of the Human Rights Committee: Canada. 07/04/99, CCPR/C/79/Add.105.

3. *Group Rights vs. Equality.* Are collective or group rights inherently incompatible with the principle of equal protection? The U.S. Supreme Court seems to have reached that conclusion in *Lying v. N.W. Indian Cemetery Protective Ass'n*, 485 U.S. 439 (1988). Indigenous groups sought to enjoin federal road construction on sacred land that traditionally had been used for religious meditative practices requiring "undisturbed naturalness." *Id.* at 453. In reversing a lower court injunction, Justice Sandra Day O'Connor explained that,

> [e]ven if we assume that we should accept the Ninth Circuit's prediction, according to which the G-O road will "virtually destroy the Indians' ability to practice their religion,"*** the Constitution simply does not provide a principle that could justify upholding respondents' legal claims. However much we might wish that it were otherwise, government simply could not operate if it were required to satisfy every citizen's religious needs and desires.*** The First Amendment must apply to all citizens alike, and it can give to none of them a veto over public programs that do not prohibit the free exercise of religion.

Id. at 451–52. Is the Court's concern about privileging one set of religious beliefs over others a valid one? *Cf.* The United Nations General Assembly Declaration on the Rights of Persons Belonging to National or Ethnic, Religious and Linguistic Minorities, A/RES/47/135 (Dec. 18, 1992), which provides that "[m]easures taken by States to ensure the effective enjoyment of the rights [to enjoy their own culture] shall not *prima facie* be considered contrary to the principle of equality contained in the Universal Declaration of Human Rights." *Id.* at Article 8(3).

Does the refusal to protect indigenous religious practices in *Lying* privilege majority values? How might the Court's analysis have differed if it had been willing to construe the First Amendment to have a positive dimension? Should it have considered the fact that these "public" lands were violently wrested from its indigenous inhabitants? Professor Benedict Kingsbury argues that the Court's "universal" approach to human rights leaves oppressed groups unprotected:

> The process by which land historically used by Indians for religious observance became "public lands" and the weakness of the property rights Indians enjoy are integral to evaluating the protection of their religious freedom. Supposed neutrality in human rights protection can be, as here, a distortion where the human rights question is separated from the property rights regime and from governance regimes, such as federal trust responsibilities or frameworks for self-government.

Kingsbury, *supra*, 34 N.Y.U. J. INT'L L. & POL. at 196.

Is there a danger that group rights could encourage or reinforce extreme nationalism? Sanction violations of the human rights of women or the mistreatment or marginalization of minorities within the group? How could such dangers be minimized? *See generally*, WILL KYMLICKA ED., THE RIGHTS OF MINORITY CULTURES (1995).

SANTA CLARA PUEBLO V. MARTINEZ

436 U.S. 49, 56 L. Ed. 2d 106, 98 S. Ct. 1670 (1978)

*** MARSHALL, J., delivered the opinion of the Court ***

This case requires us to decide whether a federal court may pass on the validity of an Indian tribe's ordinance denying membership to the children of certain female tribal members.

Petitioner Santa Clara Pueblo is an Indian tribe that has been in existence for over 600 years. Respondents, a female member of the tribe and her daughter, brought suit in federal court against the tribe and its Governor, petitioner Lucario Padilla, seeking declaratory and injunctive relief against enforcement of a tribal ordinance denying membership in the tribe to children of female members who marry outside the tribe, while extending membership to children of male members who marry outside the tribe. Respondents claimed that this rule discriminates on the basis of both sex and ancestry in violation of Title I of the Indian Civil Rights Act of 1968 (ICRA), 25 U. S. C. §§1301–1303, which provides in relevant part that "[no] Indian tribe in exercising powers of self-government shall *** deny to any person within its jurisdiction the equal protection of its laws." §1302 (8).

Title I of the ICRA does not expressly authorize the bringing of civil actions for declaratory or injunctive relief to enforce its substantive provisions. The threshold issue in this case is thus whether the Act may be interpreted to impliedly authorize such actions, against a tribe or its officers, in the federal courts. For the reasons set forth below, we hold that the Act cannot be so read.

I

Respondent Julia Martinez is a full-blooded member of the Santa Clara Pueblo, and resides on the Santa Clara Reservation in Northern New Mexico. In 1941 she married a Navajo Indian with whom she has since had several children, including respondent Audrey Martinez. Two years before this marriage, the Pueblo passed the membership ordinance here at issue, which bars admission of the Martinez children to the tribe because their father is not a Santa Claran.[4] Although the children were raised on the reservation and continue to reside there now that they are adults, as a result of their exclusion from membership they may not vote in tribal elections or hold secular office in the tribe; moreover, they have no right to remain on the reservation in the event of their mother's death, or to inherit their mother's home or her possessory interests in the communal lands.

---

[4] The ordinance, enacted by the Santa Clara Pueblo Council pursuant to its legislative authority under the Constitution of the Pueblo, establishes the following membership rules:

"1. All children born of marriages between members of the Santa Clara Pueblo shall be members of the Santa Clara Pueblo.

"2. [Children] born of marriages between male members of the Santa Clara Pueblo and non-members shall be members of the Santa Clara Pueblo.

"3. Children born of marriages between female members of the Santa Clara Pueblo and non-members shall not be members of the Santa Clara Pueblo.

"4. Persons shall not be naturalized as members of the Santa Clara Pueblo under any circumstances."

Respondents challenged only subparagraphs 2 and 3. By virtue of subparagraph 4, Julia Martinez' husband is precluded from joining the Pueblo and thereby assuring the children's membership pursuant to subparagraph 1.

After unsuccessful efforts to persuade the tribe to change the membership rule, respondents filed this lawsuit in the United States District Court for the District of New Mexico, on behalf of themselves and others similarly situated. Petitioners moved to dismiss the complaint on the ground that the court lacked jurisdiction to decide intratribal controversies affecting matters of tribal self-government and sovereignty. The District Court rejected petitioners' contention, finding that jurisdiction was conferred by 28 U.S.C. §1343(4) and 25 U.S.C. §1302(8).*** Accordingly, the motion to dismiss was denied. 402 F.Supp. 5 (1975).

Following a full trial, the District Court found for [the tribe] on the merits. While acknowledging the relatively recent origin of the disputed rule, the District Court nevertheless found it to reflect traditional values of patriarchy still significant in tribal life. The court recognized the vital importance of respondents' interests,[b] but also determined that membership rules were "no more or less than a mechanism of social . . . self-definition," and as such were basic to the tribe's survival as a cultural and economic entity. Id., at 15.[c] In sustaining the ordinance's validity under the "equal protection clause" of the ICRA, 25 U. S. C. §1302(8), the District Court concluded that the balance to be struck between these competing interests was better left to the judgment of the Pueblo:

> [The] equal protection guarantee of the Indian Civil Rights Act should not be construed in a manner which would require or authorize this Court to determine which traditional values will promote cultural survival and should therefore be preserved.*** Such a determination should be made by the people of Santa Clara; not only because they can best decide what values are important, but also because they must live with the decision every day.*** To abrogate tribal decisions, particularly in the delicate area of membership, for whatever 'good' reasons, is to destroy cultural identity under the guise of saving it. 402 F.Supp., at 18–19.

On respondents' appeal, the Court of Appeals for the Tenth Circuit upheld the District Court's determination [as to jurisdiction]. It found that "since [the ICRA] was designed to provide protection against tribal authority, the intention of Congress to allow suits against the tribe was an essential aspect [of the Act]. Otherwise, it would constitute a mere unenforceable declaration of principles." The Court of Appeals disagreed, however, with the District Court's ruling on the merits. While recognizing that standards of analysis developed under the Fourteenth Amendment's Equal Protection Clause were not necessarily controlling in the interpretation of this statute, the Court of Appeals apparently concluded that because the classification was one based upon sex it was presumptively invidious and could be sustained only if justified by a compelling tribal interest. Because of the ordinance's recent vintage, and because in the court's view the rule did not rationally identify those persons who were emotionally and culturally Santa Clarans, the court held that the tribe's interest in the ordinance was not substantial enough to justify its discriminatory effect.

---

[b] The court found that "Audrey Martinez and many other children similarly situated have been brought up on the Pueblo, speak the Tewa language, participate in its life, and are, culturally, for all practical purposes, Santa Claran Indians." 402 F.Supp., at 18.

[c] The Santa Clara Pueblo is a relatively small tribe. Approximately 1,200 members reside on the reservation;150 members of the Pueblo live elsewhere. In addition to tribal members, 150–200 nonmembers live on the reservation.

We granted certiorari, 431 U.S. 913 (1977), and we now reverse.

II

Indian tribes are "distinct, independent political communities, retaining their original natural rights" in matters of local self-government. Although no longer "possessed of the full attributes of sovereignty," they remain a "separate people, with the power of regulating their internal and social relations." They have power to make their own substantive law in internal matters [regarding, *e.g.*, membership, inheritance, and domestic relations] and to enforce that law in their own forums. [Citations omitted.]

As separate sovereigns pre-existing the Constitution, tribes have historically been regarded as unconstrained by those constitutional provisions framed specifically as limitations on federal or state authority. Thus, in *Talton v. Mayes*, 163 U.S. 376 (1896), this Court held that the Fifth Amendment did not "[operate] upon" "the powers of local self-government enjoyed" by the tribes. Id., at 384. In ensuing years the lower federal courts have extended the holding of *Talton* to other provisions of the Bill of Rights, as well as to the Fourteenth Amendment.

The line of authority growing out of *Talton*, while exempting Indian tribes from constitutional provisions addressed specifically to State or Federal Governments, of course, does not relieve State and Federal Governments of their obligations to individual Indians under these provisions.

As the Court in *Talton* recognized, however, Congress has plenary authority to limit, modify or eliminate the powers of local self-government which the tribes otherwise possess.*** Title I of the ICRA, 25 U. S. C. §§1301–1303, represents an exercise of that authority. In 25 U. S. C. §1302, Congress acted to modify the effect of *Talton* and its progeny by imposing certain restrictions upon tribal governments similar, but not identical, to those contained in the Bill of Rights and the Fourteenth Amendment. In 25 U.S.C. §1303, the only remedial provision expressly supplied by Congress, the "privilege of the writ of habeas corpus" is made "available to any person, in a court of the United States, to test the legality of his detention by order of an Indian tribe."

Petitioners concede that §1302 modifies the substantive law applicable to the tribe; they urge, however, that Congress did not intend to authorize federal courts to review violations of its provisions except as they might arise on habeas corpus. They argue, further, that Congress did not waive the tribe's sovereign immunity from suit. Respondents, on the other hand, contend that §1302 not only modifies the substantive law applicable to the exercise of sovereign tribal powers, but also authorizes civil suits for equitable relief against the tribe and its officers in federal courts. We consider these contentions first with respect to the tribe.

III

Indian tribes have long been recognized as possessing the common-law immunity from suit traditionally enjoyed by sovereign powers. [Citations omitted.] This aspect of tribal sovereignty, like all others, is subject to the superior and plenary control of Congress. But "without congressional authorization," the "Indian Nations are exempt from suit." [Citations omitted.]

It is settled that a waiver of sovereign immunity "'cannot be implied but must be unequivocally expressed.'" [Citations omitted.] Nothing on the face of Title I of the ICRA purports to subject tribes to the jurisdiction of the federal courts in civil actions for injunctive or declaratory relief. Moreover, since the respondent in a habeas corpus action is the individual custodian of the prisoner, *see, e.g.,* 28 U.S.C. §2243, the provisions of §1303 can hardly be read as a general waiver of the tribe's sovereign immunity. In the absence here of any unequivocal expression of contrary legislative intent, we conclude that suits against the tribe under the ICRA are barred by its sovereign immunity from suit.

IV

As an officer of the Pueblo, petitioner Lucario Padilla is not protected by the tribe's immunity from suit. [Citations omitted.] We must therefore determine whether the cause of action for declaratory and injunctive relief asserted here by respondents, though not expressly authorized by the statute, is nonetheless implicit in its terms.

In addressing this inquiry, we must bear in mind that providing a federal forum for issues arising under §1302 constitutes an interference with tribal autonomy and self-government beyond that created by the change in substantive law itself. Even in matters involving commercial and domestic relations, we have recognized that "[subjecting] a dispute arising on the reservation among reservation Indians to a forum other than the one they have established for themselves," may "undermine the authority of the tribal [court] *** and hence *** infringe on the right of the Indians to govern themselves." A fortiori, resolution in a foreign forum of intratribal disputes of a more "public" character, such as the one in this case, cannot help but unsettle a tribal government's ability to maintain authority. Although Congress clearly has power to authorize civil actions against tribal officers, and has done so with respect to habeas corpus relief in §1303, a proper respect both for tribal sovereignty itself and for the plenary authority of Congress in this area cautions that we tread lightly in the absence of clear indications of legislative intent. [Citations omitted.]

With these considerations of "Indian sovereignty [as] a backdrop against which the applicable *** federal [statute] must be read,"*** we turn now to those factors of more general relevance in determining whether a cause of action is implicit in a statute not expressly providing one.*** We note at the outset that a central purpose of the ICRA and in particular of Title I was to "[secure] for the American Indian the broad constitutional rights afforded to other Americans," and thereby to "protect individual Indians from arbitrary and unjust actions of tribal governments." S. Rep. No. 841, 90th Cong., 1st Sess., 5–6 (1967). There is thus no doubt that respondents, American Indians living on the Santa Clara Reservation, are among the class for whose especial benefit this legislation was enacted. Moreover, we have frequently recognized the propriety of inferring a federal cause of action for the enforcement of civil rights, even when Congress has spoken in purely declarative terms. These precedents, however, are simply not dispositive here. Not only are we unpersuaded that a judicially sanctioned intrusion into tribal sovereignty is required to fulfill the purposes of the ICRA, but to the contrary, the structure of the statutory scheme and the legislative history of Title I suggest that Congress' failure to provide remedies other than habeas corpus was a deliberate one.*** [Citations omitted.]

*** These factors, together with Congress' rejection of proposals that clearly would have authorized causes of action other than habeas corpus, persuade us that Congress, aware of the intrusive effect of federal judicial review upon tribal self-government, intended to create only a limited mechanism for such review, namely, that provided for expressly in §1303.

V

As the bill's chief sponsor, Senator Ervin, commented in urging its passage, the ICRA "should not be considered as the final solution to the many serious constitutional problems confronting the American Indian." 113 Cong. Rec. 13473 (1967). Although Congress explored the extent to which tribes were adhering to constitutional norms in both civil and criminal contexts, its legislative investigation revealed that the most serious abuses of tribal power had occurred in the administration of criminal justice. In light of this finding, and given Congress' desire not to intrude needlessly on tribal self-government, it is not surprising that Congress chose at this stage to provide for federal review only in habeas corpus proceedings.

By not exposing tribal officials to the full array of federal remedies available to redress actions of federal and state officials, Congress may also have considered that resolution of statutory issues under §1302, and particularly those issues likely to arise in a civil context, will frequently depend on questions of tribal tradition and custom which tribal forums may be in a better position to evaluate than federal courts. Our relations with the Indian tribes have "always been . . . anomalous . . . and of a complex character." Although we early rejected the notion that Indian tribes are "foreign states" for jurisdictional purposes under Art. III, Cherokee Nation v. Georgia, 5 Pet. 1 (1831), we have also recognized that the tribes remain quasi-sovereign nations which, by government structure, culture, and source of sovereignty are in many ways foreign to the constitutional institutions of the Federal and State Governments. See Elk v. Wilkins, 112 U.S. 94 (1884). As is suggested by the District Court's opinion in this case *** efforts by the federal judiciary to apply the statutory prohibitions of §1302 in a civil context may substantially interfere with a tribe's ability to maintain itself as a culturally and politically distinct entity.***

The judgment of the Court of Appeals is, accordingly,

Reversed.

MR. JUSTICE BLACKMUN took no part in the consideration or decision of this case.

MR. JUSTICE WHITE, dissenting.

*** While I believe that the uniqueness of the Indian culture must be taken into consideration in applying the constitutional rights granted in §1302, I do not think that it requires insulation of official tribal actions from federal-court scrutiny. Nor do I find any indication that Congress so intended.***

KARL KLAARE, A BRIEF LEGAL HISTORY OF SANTA CLARA PUEBLO; OR, WHAT HAS US LAW GOT TO DO WITH IT?

KARL KLARE ED., CRITICAL LEGAL THEORY (2003) (unpublished teaching materials).

Santa Clara Pueblo is a small community located about 25 miles northwest of Santa Fe, New Mexico. The Pueblos are a group of peoples who founded villages in the Rio Grande Valley region of New Mexico in the period 1300–1700 A.D. They are believed to have descended from civilizations that thrived in the period roughly 1050–1300 A.D. in the "Four Corners" region (where the present-day states of Arizona, Colorado, New Mexico, and Utah intersect).

Santa Clara was originally called *Abiquiu* by its inhabitants. Like all pueblos, it was self-governing until the Spanish conquest. On April 30, 1598, acting under the authority of King Philip II, Juan de Oñate claimed possession for the Spanish empire of a vast territory covering what is now the American Southwest. His expedition established a colony in the Rio Grande Valley region that included Santa Clara. Through Oñate and his successors, Spain assumed total legal authority over the indigenous peoples. Many were enslaved, and Christianity was imposed by force. Spanish names were imposed on the Pueblos, and opposition to Spanish rule was suppressed with extreme cruelty. Under Spanish law, the Pueblo Indians of New Mexico were deemed wards of the crown.

In 1680, a broad alliance of Pueblo communities, including Santa Clara, launched a mass revolt and drove the Spanish out. No other indigenous group in what is now the United States succeeded in expelling European colonists. A notable consequence of the Revolt was the relatively durable survival into modem times of traditional Pueblo religions, ceremonies, and rituals.

Spanish troops reconquered Santa Fe in 1692, and by 1696 had subdued the entire region. Spanish sovereignty over Santa Clara was restored and continued through the beginning of the 19th century. During this period, the Navajo, Apache, Comanche, and other nomadic, Native American peoples repeatedly raided both Spanish and Pueblo communities.

Mexico achieved independence from Spain in 1821. Its territory included not only present-day Mexico but also the area stretching from Texas to California. At least on paper. all inhabitants of Mexican territory, including Santa Clarans, became citizens of Mexico and were accorded equal civil rights and privileges.

In 1841, the Republic of Texas, which had gained independence from Mexico. launched an armed expedition to acquire territory east of the Rio Grande river. The adventure failed, but Texans maintained their claim to this area even after Texas was annexed to the United States in 1845. When the United States declared war on Mexico in 1846, a US military force under General Stephen Watts Kearny invaded and claimed New Mexico. Hostilities concluded on February 2, 1848, with the Treaty of Guadalupe Hidalgo, which formally ceded New Mexico (including what is now Arizona) to the US. New Mexico became a US Territory in 1850, open to both slaveholding and non-slave settlement. Under Article 8 of the Treaty, any Mexican residing in the territory ceded to the US was permitted to retain his/her Mexican citizenship by making a formal declaration within a year. Apparently none of the Pueblo Indians exercised this option, with the legal result that, pursuant to the Treaty, they were deemed to have become United States citizens.

During the American Civil War, the Confederacy briefly controlled New Mexico Territory for a period between 1861 and 1862. After the Confederate withdrawal, the US government created a separate Arizona Territory, reducing New Mexico to its present boundaries. In law, a Territory was an agency of the federal government. New Mexico was admitted as the 47th state on January 6, 1912. In anticipation of statehood, Congress passed the New Mexico Enabling Act, Act of June 20, 1910, 36 Stat. 557, which among other things provided that the Pueblos were to be deemed "Indian Tribes" within federal law. This meant that they fell under the control of the federal, not state, government, as might otherwise have been the case. This solidification of federal control by assimilating the Pueblos into the framework of so-called American Indian Law was upheld in *US v. Sandoval*, 231 U.S. 28 (1913).***

Notes and Questions

1. *"Quasi-Sovereign" Status and Access to Justice.* The conquest and appropriation of Native territory led to the designation of non-state status to Indian tribes. As "quasi-sovereigns" both tribes and individuals frequently have been denied access to U.S. courts. In the paradigmatic case, *Cherokee Nation v. Georgia*, 30 U.S. 1 (1831), the U.S. Supreme Court dismissed a claim for injunctive relief by the Cherokee Nation against the State of Georgia, holding that Indian tribes were not foreign states within the meaning of the Constitution, and could not sue in U.S. courts. The tribe sought to enjoin the state from seizing tribal lands and criminalizing their exercise of self-government. Chief Justice Marshall reasoned that "[t]hey have never been recognized as holding sovereignty over the territory they occupy." *Id.* at 22. He argued:

> I cannot but think that there are strong reasons for doubting the applicability of the epithet *state*, to a people so low in the grade of organized society as our Indian tribes most generally are. I would not here be understood as speaking of the Cherokees under their present form of government; which certainly must be classed among the most approved forms of civil government. Whether it can be yet said to have received the consistency which entitles that people to admission into the family of nations is, I conceive, yet to be determined by the executive of these states.

Id. at 21. (Emphasis in original.)

In *Fisher v. District Court*, 424 U.S. 382 (1976), the Court held that a state court did not have jurisdiction over an adoption proceeding in which all parties were members of an Indian tribe and residents of the reservation. The Court rejected the mother's argument that denying her access to the state courts constituted an impermissible racial discrimination:

> The exclusive jurisdiction of the Tribal Court does not derive from the race of the plaintiff but rather from the quasi-sovereign status of the Northern Cheyenne Tribe under federal law.*** [Even] if a jurisdictional holding occasionally results in denying an Indian plaintiff a forum to which a non-Indian has access, such disparate treatment of the Indian is justified because it is intended to benefit the class of which he is a member by furthering the congressional policy of Indian self-government."

Id. at 390–91.

2. *Self-Determination vs. Individual Rights.* Does the Court's decision in *Santa Clara Pueblo* privilege the collective right of "quasi-sovereignty" over the individual right of gender equality? *Cf. Ephrahim v. Pastory*, 87 I.L.R. 106 (Tanz. High Ct. 1990). The Court ruled that a tribal prohibition on the sale of clan land by women was invalid under the equality principles of the Tanzanian Constitution and international human rights instruments to which Tanzania is a party. *Id.* at 110.

Kingsbury points out that "the membership rule had been adopted in living memory with U.S. government encouragement." Benedict Kingsbury, *Reconciling Competing Structures of Indigenous Peoples' Claims in International and Comparative Law*, 34 N.Y. U.

J. INT'L L. & POL. 189, at 209 (2002). What purpose does such a rule serve? How does the Court's rationale compare to the U. S. position in the *Dann* case? Are the two views consistent?

3. *International Norms.* Article 33 of the Draft Declaration subjects indigenous institutions to international human rights standards:

> Indigenous peoples have the right to promote, develop and maintain their institutional structures and their distinctive juridical customs, traditions, procedures and practices, in accordance with internationally recognized human right standards.

Does this provision place a condition on the exercise of self-determination? Is such a condition consistent with recognition of the right? Is the exercise by states of the rights enumerated in Article 33 similarly conditioned under international law? Should indigenous groups be held to a different standard than states?

4. *Role of Indigenous Movement.* What role should the international indigenous rights movement play in promoting women's equality? Are there potential conflicts within such movements between the perceived interests of the group and those of individuals? How can such conflicts be reconciled?

d. Genocide and Cultural Genocide

Many indigenous groups and cultures have barely survived the onslaughts of colonialism, industrialization, and globalization. The plight of the Batwa (Pygmies) of Eastern Uganda, described by Ugandan scholar R.R. Akankwasa is representative of the contemporary issues these groups face:

> The legacy of colonialism has meant that the majority of indigenous peoples must live in abject poverty. Their longevity is very low while unemployment and exploitation of their labour are the order of the day. On the whole, indigenous peoples who have remained in their traditional territories face disruption of their cultures and forced displacements as their lands and natural resources are claimed for national "development." It is no exaggeration to say that some indigenous peoples live under the threat of extinction.
>
> Deforestation is now a major threat to the lives of forest-centric Batwa people. Whereas the indigenous peoples are considered as part of the problem of environmental degradation, they remain better placed with their folk wisdom to play a vital role in environmental protection. For centuries, they have engaged in sustainable management and use in the areas in which they live. The herbal therapeutics, their artwork and cultural artifacts constitute the wealth they are being stripped of without their consent.
>
> As Structural Adjustment Policies (SAPs) force other ethnic groups to squeeze the already meagre and tired plots of land to yield crops for export, they in turn push the frontiers of the forest habitat of the indigenous peoples. This has not promoted harmonious neighbourliness but has instead led to intense ethnic conflicts that further impoverish and marginalize the Batwa.***
>
> National governments of poor countries like Uganda that are aspiring to "catch up" with the industrialized nations will continue pressing hard on the

ever-diminishing resources including those areas that have been home and granary for the indigenous people. Albeit indigenous people are restricted from having access to ancestral sacred sites located in gazetted "protected areas" which they have revered from time immemorial, these areas are almost exclusively open to tourists, "permitted" hunters and researchers. It is this commodification of the culture of indigenous peoples while destroying their spirituality and source of their livelihood that will make them and their culture extinct.***

R.R. Akankwasa, *Indigenous Peoples and Their Cultural Survival in Uganda: the Legacy of Educational Dependence*, 2001 EAST AFR. J. PEACE & HUM. RTS. 229.

Efforts to vindicate the rights of indigenous peoples through claims of genocide and cultural genocide have thus far been unsuccessful. *See, e.g., Mulyarimma v. Thompson; Buzzacott v. Hill* (consolidated cases) 8 BHRC 135 (1999). Claimants in the two cases argued that Australian government officials engaged in genocide by (1) enacting legislation (the 1998 amendments to the Native Title Act, *see* Section A.1.a, *supra*) that further dispossessed indigenous people of their traditional lands; and (2) failing to apply for international protection of Arabunna ancestral lands under the World Heritage Convention. The Court ruled that the Genocide Convention is non-self-executing, and thus, in the absence of implementing legislation, does not create a cause of action in Australia. Moreover, the Court opined that even if a cause of action under the Convention were cognizable, there was no evidence that defendants acted with the requisite intent to destroy a people.

The encroachments on indigenous lands, environment, and culture by multinational corporations and other non-state actors pose even greater legal difficulties, as illustrated by the following case:

BEANAL v. FREEPORT-McMORAN, INC.

197 F.3d 161 (5th Cir. 1999)

CARL E. STEWART, Circuit Judge:

Tom Beanal ("Beanal") brought suit against the defendants in federal district court for alleged violations of international law. The district court dismissed Beanal's claims pursuant to Fed.R.Civ.Proc. 12(b)(6). After a careful review of Beanal's pleadings, we affirm the district court.

I.

Factual & Procedural History

This case involves alleged violations of international law committed by domestic corporations conducting mining activities abroad in the Pacific Rim. Freeport-McMoran, Inc., and Freeport-McMoran Copper & Gold, Inc., ("Freeport"), are Delaware corporations with headquarters in New Orleans, Louisiana. Freeport operates the "Grasberg Mine," an open pit copper, gold, and silver mine situated in the Jayawijaya Mountain in Irian Jaya, Indonesia. The mine encompasses approximately 26,400 square kilometers. Beanal is a resident of Tamika, Irian Jaya within the Republic of Indonesia (the "Republic"). He is also the leader of the Amungme Tribal Council of Lambaga Adat Suki Amungme (the "Amungme"). In August 1996, Beanal filed a complaint against

Freeport in federal district court in the Eastern District of Louisiana for alleged violations of international law. Beanal invoked jurisdiction under (1) 28 U.S.C. § 1332, (2) the Alien Tort Statute, 28 U.S.C. § 1350, and (3) the Torture Victim Protection Act of 1991, sec. 1, et seq., 28 U.S.C. § 1350 note. In his First Amended Complaint, he alleged that Freeport engaged in environmental abuses, human rights violations, and cultural genocide. Specifically, he alleged that Freeport mining operations had caused harm and injury to the Amungme's environment and habitat. He further alleged that Freeport engaged in cultural genocide by destroying the Amungme's habitat and religious symbols, thus forcing the Amungme to relocate. Finally, he asserted that Freeport's private security force acted in concert with the Republic to violate international human rights. Freeport moved to dismiss Beanal's claims under Fed.R.Civ.Proc. 12(b)(6). The district court in April 1997 issued a thorough forty-nine page Opinion and Order dismissing Beanal's claims without prejudice and with leave to amend. *See Beanal v. Freeport-McMoran*, 969 F. Supp. 362 (E.D.La. 1997). Pursuant to Rule 12(e), the district court instructed Beanal to amend his complaint to state more specifically his claims of genocide and individual human rights violations. In August 1997, the district court granted Freeport's motion to strike Beanal's Second Amended Complaint because Beanal inappropriately attempted to add third parties. At the motion to strike hearing, the court again instructed Beanal to plead facts sufficient to support his allegations of genocide and individual human rights violations. In March 1998, the district court granted Freeport's motion to strike Beanal's Third Amended Complaint and dismissed his claims with prejudice. Beanal now appeals the district court's rulings below.[7]

A. *Alien Tort Statute*

Beanal claims that Freeport engaged in conduct that violated the Alien Tort Statute (the "ATS" or "§1350"). Under §1350:

> The district courts shall have original jurisdiction of any civil action by an alien for a tort only, committed in violation of the law of nations or a treaty of the United States.

Section 1350 confers subject matter jurisdiction when the following conditions are met: (1) an alien sues, (2) for a tort, (3) that was committed in violation of the "law of nations" or a treaty of the United States. See *Kadic v. Karadzic*, 70 F.3d 232, 238 (2d Cir. 1995). Beanal does not claim that Freeport violated a United States treaty. Thus, the issue before us is whether Beanal states claims upon which relief can be granted for violations under the "law of nations," i.e., international law.

[T]he standards by which nations regulate their dealings with one another inter se constitutes the 'law of nations.'" These standards include the rules of conduct which govern the affairs of this nation, acting in its national capacity, in relationships with any other nation. The law of nations is defined by customary usage and clearly articulated principles of the international community. One of the means of ascertaining the law of nations is "by consulting the work of jurists writing professedly on public law or by the general usage and practice of nations; or by judicial decisions recognizing and enforcing that law." [Citations omitted.] Courts "must interpret international law not as it was in 1789 but as it has evolved and exists among the nations of the world today." Although

---

7   Amici Curiae have submitted briefs to support Beanal's claims. They include the Sierra Club, Earthrights International, Center For Constitutional Rights, Center for Justice and Accountability, and the Four Directions Council.

Beanal's claims raise complex issues of international law; nonetheless, the task before us does not require that we resolve them. We are only required to determine whether the pleadings on their face state a claim upon which relief can be granted.***

3. Genocide and Cultural Genocide

Beanal claims that Freeport engaged in acts of genocide and cultural genocide. In his First Amended Complaint, Beanal alleged that Freeport's mining operations caused the Amungme to be displaced and relocated to other areas of the country. He also alleged that Freeport's mining activities destroyed the Amungme's habitat. As such, Beanal asserted that Freeport purposely engaged in activity to destroy the Amungme's cultural and social framework. However, Freeport attacked Beanal's allegations claiming that cultural genocide is not recognized as a discrete violation of international law. The district court relying chiefly on the express language of Article II of the Convention on the Prevention and Punishment of the Crime of Genocide, 78 U.N.T.S. 277 (the "Convention on Genocide"), concluded that cultural genocide was not recognized in the international community as a violation of international law. The district court then instructed Beanal to amend his complaint to allege genocide. Specifically, the court instructed Beanal to allege facts that would demonstrate that "he [was] the victim of acts committed with the intent to destroy the people of the Amungme tribe.***" Consequently, the district court found that Beanal's Third Amended Complaint failed to comply with its express instructions.

*** Beanal's complaint is saturated with conclusory allegations devoid of any underlying facts to support his claim of genocide. Although the pleading requirements under Rule 8 are to be liberally construed in favor of the plaintiff, nevertheless, the rule requires more than "bare bone allegations." [Citation omitted.]

Notwithstanding Beanal's failure to allege facts to support sufficiently his claim of genocide, Beanal and the amici in their respective briefs urge this court to recognize cultural genocide as a discrete violation of international law. Again, they refer the court to several international conventions, agreements, and declarations. Nevertheless, a review of these documents reveals that the documents make pronouncements and proclamations of an amorphous right to "enjoy culture," or a right to "freely pursue" culture, or a right to cultural development. They nonetheless fail to proscribe or identify conduct that would constitute an act of cultural genocide. As such, it would be problematic to apply these vague and declaratory international documents to Beanal's claim because they are devoid of discernable means to define or identify conduct that constitutes a violation of international law. Furthermore, Beanal has not demonstrated that cultural genocide has achieved universal acceptance as a discrete violation of international law. Thus, it would be imprudent for a United States tribunal to declare an amorphous cause of action under international law that has failed to garner universal acceptance.[8] Accordingly, we find that Beanal's claims of genocide and cultural genocide are facially insufficient to withstand a motion to dismiss under Rule 12(b).***

Notes and Questions

1. *Definition of Cultural Genocide.* How does a claim of cultural genocide, or ethnocide, differ from genocide proper? *See* Article II, Convention on the Prevention and

---

8   In earlier drafts of the Convention on Genocide, there were proposals to incorporate cultural genocide into the definition of genocide. However, after much debate, the concept of cultural genocide was explicitly excluded.***

Punishment of the Crime of Genocide, 78 U.N.T.S. 277 (*entered into force* 1951):

> [G]enocide means any of the following acts committed with intent to destroy, in whole or in part, a national, ethnical, racial or religious group, as such:
>
> (a) Killing members of the group;
>
> (b) Causing serious bodily or mental harm to members of the group;
>
> (c) Deliberately inflicting on the group conditions of life calculated to bring about its physical destruction in whole or in part;
>
> (d) Imposing measures intended to prevent births within the group;
>
> (e) Forcibly transferring children of the group to another group.

Does cultural genocide imply the physical extermination of the group, or merely the elimination of its distinctive features? Consider whether the following activities or policies would constitute violations: (1) environmental degradation resulting from the extraction of resources; (2) policies furthering assimilation; (3) official language policies that inhibit the preservation of minority languages; (4) development-induced relocation of a group.

2. *The Requisite* Mens Rea. How is "intent to destroy" a people established? What degree of *mens rea* did the court require in *Beanal?* Should a criminal standard be applied to claims brought under the Alien Tort Claims Act? Is a requirement of specific intent to do harm consistent with tort liability? Should a lower standard apply to cultural genocide—*e.g.*, foreseeability or reckless disregard—given contemporary knowledge of the consequences of certain activities on fragile populations? Would a pattern of rights violations with the foreseeable result of group destruction demonstrate intent?

3. *Liability of Non-State Actors.* Presumably the plaintiffs in *Beanal* framed their case under the rubric of genocide because the prohibition applies to private as well as state actors. Are alternative approaches available? For example, if Indonesia were a party to the Optional Protocol of the ICCPR, could a claim be brought against it under Article 27 for failing to protect the Amumgme from Freeport's activities?

4. *Scope of the Right to Culture.* Does the right to enjoy one's own culture mean that a minority community's traditional way of life must be preserved at all costs? What are the boundaries?

5. *Evolutive Interpretation of Genocide Convention.* The court in *Beanal* relied on the fact that the drafters of the Genocide Convention rejected the inclusion of a prohibition against cultural genocide, defined in the draft as "any deliberate act committed with the intent to destroy the language, religion, or culture of a national, racial or religious group, on grounds of national or racial origin or religious belief." Should the rejection of the criminalization of cultural genocide preclude a rights-based approach? Has the prohibition against genocide become customary international law? As such, should it be interpreted in light of subsequent norms such as Article 27 of the ICCPR? Compare the evolutive interpretation of international law applied by the Inter-American Commission on Human Rights in the *Dann* case, Section A.1.a, *supra.* Does an international body have more authority to interpret expansively an international treaty than a domestic court?

6. *Prohibition of Cultural Genocide in Draft Declaration.* Article 7 of the Draft Declaration on the Rights of Indigenous Peoples provides:

> Indigenous peoples have the collective and individual right not to be subjected to ethnocide and cultural genocide, including prevention of and redress for:
>
> (a) Any action which has the aim or effect of depriving them of their integrity as distinct peoples, or of their cultural values or ethnic identities;
>
> (b) Any action which has the aim or effect of dispossessing them of their lands, territories or resources;
>
> (c) Any form of population transfer which has the aim or effect of violating or undermining any of their rights;
>
> (d) Any form of assimilation or integration by other cultures or ways of life imposed on them by legislative, administrative or other measures;
>
> (e) Any form of propaganda directed against them.***

What obligations would this provision have imposed on Indonesia if it had been applicable to the facts in *Beanal*?

7. For further readings on the self-determination of peoples, the rights of indigenous peoples, and cultural rights, *see, e.g.,* JUSTICE PENDING: INDIGENOUS PEOPLES AND OTHER GOOD CAUSES: ESSAYS IN HONOUR OF ERICA-IRENE A. DAES (Gudmundur Alfredsson & Maria Stavropoulou eds., 2002); S. JAMES ANAYA, INDIGENOUS PEOPLES IN INTERNATIONAL LAW (1996); ALISON BRYSK, FROM TRIBAL VILLAGE TO GLOBAL VILLAGE: INDIAN RIGHTS AND INTERNATIONAL RELATIONS IN LATIN AMERICA, (2000); VOICE OF INDIGENOUS PEOPLES: NATIVE PEOPLE ADDRESS THE UNITED NATIONS: WITH THE UNITED NATIONS DRAFT DECLARATION OF INDIGENOUS PEOPLES RIGHTS; (Aleaxander Ewen ed., 1994); NIEC HALINA, CULTURAL RIGHTS AND WRONGS: A COLLECTION OF ESSAYS IN COMMEMORATION OF THE 50TH ANNIVERSARY OF THE UNIVERSAL DECLARATION OF HUMAN RIGHTS (1998); HURST HANNUM, AUTONOMY, SOVEREIGNTY, AND SELF-DETERMINATION: THE ACCOMMODATION OF CONFLICTING RIGHTS (1996); IN PURSUIT OF THE RIGHT TO SELF-DETERMINATION: COLLECTED PAPERS & PROCEEDINGS OF THE FIRST INTERNATIONAL CONFERENCE ON THE RIGHT TO SELF-DETERMINATION & THE UNITED NATIONS GENEVA 2000 (Y.N. Kly & D. Kly eds., 2001); KAREN KNOP, DIVERSITY AND SELF-DETERMINATION IN INTERNATIONAL LAW (2002); THE RIGHTS OF MINORITY CULTURES (Will Kymlicka ed., 1995); WILL KYMLICKA, FINDING OUR WAY: RETHINKING ETHNOCULTURAL RELATIONS IN CANADA (1998); INTERNATIONAL HUMAN RIGHTS IN THE 21ST CENTURY: PROTECTING THE RIGHTS OF GROUPS (Gene M. Lyons & James Mayall eds., 2003); RONALD NIEZEN, THE ORIGINS OF INDIGENISM: HUMAN RIGHTS AND THE POLITICS OF IDENTITY (2003); ETHNICITY AND GROUP RIGHTS (Ian Sharpiro & Will Kymlicka eds., 1997); INDIGENOUS PEOPLES AND DEMOCRACY IN LATIN AMERICA (Donna Lee Van Cott ed., 1994); KAY B. WARREN, INDIGENOUS MOVEMENTS AND THEIR CRITICS: PAN-MAYA ACTIVISM IN GUATEMALA (1998); INDIGENOUS MOVEMENTS, SELF-REPRESENTATION, AND THE STATE IN LATIN AMERICA (Kay B. Warren & Jean E. Jackson eds., 2002); CULTURE, RIGHTS AND CULTURAL RIGHTS (Margaret Wilson & Paul Hunt eds., 2000)

2. Foreign Occupation

The right of self-determination recognizes the right of peoples under foreign occupation to "freely determine their political status and freely pursue their economic, social and cultural development." In addition, international humanitarian law provides explicit protection for the economic, social, and cultural rights of peoples whose sovereignty has been compromised by military occupation. The law of belligerent occupation is codified, in part, in the 1907 Hague Regulations and the Fourth Geneva Convention of 1949. It establishes limitations on the powers of occupants in the interest of protecting both the sovereignty and the humanitarian concerns of the civilian population in the face of the invasion of a territory by a foreign power. The law of occupation applies regardless of the legality of the conflict; its basic principle is the inalienability of territory through conquest. This principle renders the occupier's authority temporary and provisional. Annexation of occupied territory is illegal, and the population owes no duty of allegiance to the occupying power. Supplementing humanitarian law is the corpus of human rights law that has emerged since World War II. All human rights treaties to which the occupants are parties apply in the territories they occupy.

a. Duty to Protect Life and Property

REGULATIONS CONCERNING THE LAWS AND CUSTOMS OF WAR ON LAND

The Hague, Oct. 18, 1907 U.S.T.S. 539, 36 Stat. 2277 (*entered into force* Jan. 26, 1910)

Section III: Military Authority Over the Territory of the Hostile State

Art. 42. Territory is considered occupied when it is actually placed under the authority of the hostile army. The occupation extends only to the territory where such authority has been established and can be exercised.

Art. 43. The authority of the legitimate power having in fact passed into the hands of the occupant, the latter shall take all the measures in his power to restore, and ensure, as far as possible, public order and safety, while respecting, unless absolutely prevented, the laws in force in the country.

Art. 44. A belligerent is forbidden to force the inhabitants of territory occupied by it to furnish information about the army of the other belligerent, or about its means of defense.

Art. 45. It is forbidden to compel the inhabitants of occupied territory to swear allegiance to the hostile Power.

Art. 46. Family honor and rights, the lives of persons, and private property, as well as religious convictions and practice, must be respected. Private property cannot be confiscated.

Art. 47. Pillage is formally forbidden.

Art. 48. If, in the territory occupied, the occupant collects the taxes, dues, and tolls imposed for the benefit of the State, he shall do so, as far as possible, in accordance with the rules of assessment and incidence in force ***.***

Art. 50. No general penalty, pecuniary or otherwise, shall be inflicted upon the population on account of the acts of individuals for which they cannot be regarded as jointly and severally responsible.***

Art. 55. The occupying State shall be regarded only as administrator and usufructuary of public buildings, real estate, forests, and agricultural estates belonging to the hostile State, and situated in the occupied country. It must safeguard the capital of these properties, and administer them in accordance with the rules of usufruct.

Art. 56. The property of municipalities, that of institutions dedicated to religion, charity and education, the arts and sciences, even when State property, shall be treated as private property. All seizure of, destruction or willful damage done to institutions of this character, historic monuments, works of art and science, is forbidden, and should be made the subject of legal proceedings.

INTERNATIONAL COMMITTEE OF THE RED CROSS

Press Release (Apr. 28, 2003), S/2003/538,
available at http://www.un.org/Docs/scinfo.htm

Geneva (ICRC)—The International Committee of the Red Cross (ICRC) is profoundly alarmed by the chaos currently prevailing in Baghdad and other parts of Iraq. Lawless persons, sometimes armed, have been ransacking and looting even essential public facilities such as hospitals and water-supply installations.

Hospitals in Baghdad are closed because of combat damage, looting or fear of looting. Hardly any medical or support staff are still reporting for work. Patients have either fled the hospitals or have been left without care. The medical system in Baghdad has virtually collapsed. The dead are left unattended, and the increasing summer heat and deteriorating water and electricity supplies create a high risk of epidemic disease.

The ICRC urgently appeals to the Coalition forces and all other persons in authority to do everything possible to protect essential infrastructure such as hospitals and water-supply and evacuation systems from looting and destruction. In areas under their control, the Coalition forces have specific responsibilities as Occupying Powers under international humanitarian law. These include taking all measures in their power to restore and maintain, as far as possible, public order and safety by putting a halt to pillage and to violence against civilians and civilian facilities.

Civilian facilities which have been damaged or destroyed must be repaired as soon as possible, in order to ensure that the basic needs of the population can be met. Water and electricity supplies are vital. Medical units and personnel must be protected and their work facilitated, and access to them by all persons in need, whether military or civilian, friend or foe, must be granted. In all circumstances, the Red Cross and Red Crescent Emblem must be respected.

To the fullest extent of the means available to them, the occupying forces have a duty to ensure that the population has sufficient supplies in terms of water, food and medical care. As the temporary administrators of the occupied territory, the Occupying Powers must support public services and manage resources primarily in the interests of the population, without discrimination. If the whole or part of the population under occupation is not adequately supplied, the Occupying Powers must allow impartial humanitarian organizations to undertake assistance operations. However, the provision of humanitarian aid in no way relieves the Occupying Powers of their administrator's responsibilities towards the population under occupation.***

Notes and Questions

1. *The Applicability of the Law of Occupation.* In a letter to the United Nations Security Council dated May 8, 2003, the governments of the United Kingdom and the United States promised to "strictly abide by their obligations under international law, including those relating to the essential humanitarian needs of the people of Iraq." S/2003/538, *available at* www.un.org/Docs/scinfo.htm. In Resolution 1483, adopted May 23, 2003, the United Nations Security Council formally recognized the applicability of the law of occupation to the situation in Iraq, urging the U.S.-led Coalition Authority to "promote the welfare of the Iraqi people through the effective administration of the territory, including in particular working towards the restoration of conditions of security and stability" [¶ 4] and to "comply fully with their obligations under international law including in particular the Geneva Convention of 1949 and the Hague Regulations of 1907" [¶ 5]. S/Res/1483 (May 22, 2003).

2. *Legislative Changes.* Article 43 of the Hague Regulations requires an occupying power to respect, "unless absolutely prevented, the laws in force in the country." Is the revision of Iraq's foreign direct investment code announced by the U.S. administrator in Iraq consistent with this provision? Under the reforms, state companies will be privatized, and foreign companies will be able to purchase 100 percent ownership in Iraqi firms and banks, and take all profits out of the country. Would contracts issued pursuant to the new regulations be legally binding on a new sovereign Iraqi government?

b. Duty to Protect Economic and Social Rights

CONVENTION RELATIVE TO THE PROTECTION OF CIVILIAN PERSONS IN TIME OF WAR (GENEVA IV)

Signed at Geneva, August 12, 1949, 75 U.N.T.S. 287
(*entered into force* October 21, 1950)

SECTION III

Occupied Territories

Art. 47. Protected persons who are in occupied territory shall not be deprived, in any case or in any manner whatsoever, of the benefits of the present Convention by any change introduced, as the result of the occupation of a territory, into the institutions or government of the said territory, nor by any agreement concluded between the authorities of the occupied territories and the Occupying Power, nor by any annexation by the latter of the whole or part of the occupied territory.***

Art. 49. Individual or mass forcible transfers, as well as deportations of protected persons from occupied territory to the territory of the Occupying Power or to that of any other country, occupied or not, are prohibited, regardless of their motive.***

The Occupying Power shall not deport or transfer parts of its own civilian population into the territory it occupies.

Art. 50. The Occupying Power shall, with the cooperation of the national and local authorities, facilitate the proper working of all institutions devoted to the care and education of children.***

Art. 51. The Occupying Power may not compel protected persons to serve in its armed or auxiliary forces. No pressure or propaganda which aims at securing voluntary enlistment is permitted.***

Art. 52. *** All measures aiming at creating unemployment or at restricting the opportunities offered to workers in an occupied territory, in order to induce them to work for the Occupying Power, are prohibited.

Art. 53. Any destruction by the Occupying Power of real or personal property belonging individually or collectively to private persons, or to the State, or to other public authorities, or to social or cooperative organizations, is prohibited, except where such destruction is rendered absolutely necessary by military operations.***

Art. 55. To the fullest extent of the means available to it, the Occupying Power has the duty of ensuring the food and medical supplies of the population; it should, in particular, bring in the necessary foodstuffs, medical stores and other articles if the resources of the occupied territory are inadequate.***

Art. 56. To the fullest extent of the means available to it, the Occupying Power has the duty of ensuring and maintaining, with the cooperation of national and local authorities, the medical and hospital establishments and services, public health and hygiene in the occupied territory, with particular reference to the adoption and application of the prophylactic and preventive measures necessary to combat the spread of contagious diseases and epidemics. Medical personnel of all categories shall be allowed to carry out their duties.***

In adopting measures of health and hygiene and in their implementation, the Occupying Power shall take into consideration the moral and ethical susceptibilities of the population of the occupied territory.

Art. 59. If the whole or part of the population of an occupied territory is inadequately supplied, the Occupying Power shall agree to relief schemes on behalf of the said population, and shall facilitate them by all the means at its disposal.

Such schemes, which may be undertaken either by States or by impartial humanitarian organizations such as the International Committee of the Red Cross, shall consist, in particular, of the provision of consignments of foodstuffs, medical supplies and clothing.***

Art. 146. The High Contracting Parties undertake to enact any legislation necessary to provide effective penal sanctions for persons committing, or ordering to be committed, any of the grave breaches of the present Convention defined in the following Article.***

Art. 147. Grave breaches to which the preceding Article relates shall be those involving any of the following acts, if committed against persons or property protected by the present Convention: wilful killing, torture or inhuman treatment, including biological experiments, wilfully causing great suffering or serious injury to body or health, unlawful deportation or transfer or unlawful confinement of a protected person, compelling a protected person to serve in the forces of a hostile Power, or willfully depriving a protected person of the rights of fair and regular trial prescribed in the present Convention, taking of hostages and extensive destruction and appropriation of property, not justified by military necessity and carried out unlawfully and wantonly.

Notes and Questions

1. *Who Are Protected Persons?* Article 4 of the Geneva Convention (No. IV) provides:

> Persons protected by the Convention are those who, at a given moment and in any manner whatsoever, find themselves, in case of a conflict or occupation, in the hands of a Party to the conflict or Occupying Power of which they are not nationals.

2. *Scope of the Duty of the Occupier.* Does Article 55 impose a greater duty to ensure satisfaction of the food and medical needs of the population than would be demanded of the legitimate sovereign government? If so, is such a duty justified?

AMNESTY INTERNATIONAL REPORT— ISRAEL AND THE OCCUPIED TERRITORIES: SURVIVING UNDER SIEGE: THE IMPACT OF MOVEMENT RESTRICTIONS ON THE RIGHT TO WORK

September 7, 2003

"The period from June 2002 to May 2003 was marked by a deepening of the economic and social crisis in the Occupied Territories and its likely stabilization at a very low level. The severe restriction on movements of persons and goods within the Occupied Territories and between these and Israel have resulted in a dramatic decline in consumption, income and employment levels, and unprecedented contraction of economic activity." Report of the Director-General of the International Labour Office (ILO), May 2003.

"By the end of 2002 Real Gross National Income (GNI) had shrunk by 38 percent from its 1999 level . . . Overall GNI losses reached US\$5.2 billion after 27 months of intifada . . . The proximate cause of the Palestinian economic crisis is closure." "Twenty-seven Months—Intifada, Closures and Palestinian Economic Crisis: An Assessment," World Bank, May 2003.

"People can't work properly in Jenin because they open their businesses, a tank comes and they have to shut. How can they work? The curfew has made things worse. The Israeli army announces: 'Tomorrow Jenin will be open.' But the following day, the army comes and announces a curfew and tanks close the town. What do we have here now? Nothing." Faisal Abd al-Wahhab, 34, a welder in Jenin whose permit to work in Israel was withdrawn at the start of the *intifada.****

Introduction ***

Restrictions imposed by Israel on the movement of Palestinians within the Occupied Territories reached an unprecedented level in recent years. The effect has been to deprive Palestinians not only of their freedom of movement but of other basic human rights—in particular, their right to work and to provide a living for themselves and their families.***

[S]ome 3.5 million Palestinians who live in the Occupied Territories are often effectively confined to their towns and villages by closures enforced by Israeli military checkpoints and roadblocks. Some villages have been completely sealed off and urban areas are frequently placed under 24-hour curfew, during which no one is allowed to leave the house, often for prolonged periods. Palestinians have been prohibited from driving on main roads connecting one part of the West Bank to another.

Trips of a few kilometres, where they are possible, take hours, following lengthy detours to avoid the areas surrounding Israeli settlements and settlers' roads (known as "bypass roads"), which connect the settlements to each other and to Israel and which are prohibited to Palestinians. With the spread of settlements and bypass roads throughout the Occupied Territories, the prohibited areas have multiplied. Where the settlements are closest to Palestinian villages, movement in and out of these villages is even more restricted than elsewhere. In parts of the Gaza Strip, areas where Palestinians live surrounded by Israeli settlements have been declared closed military zones. These are only accessible, and only at specific times, to the residents, who are also often stopped from leaving or returning to their homes for days or even weeks.

In addition to the increased time, effort and cost involved, journeys are also not without risk. To enforce closures and curfews, Israeli soldiers routinely fire live ammunition, throw tear gas or sound bombs, beat and detain people, and confiscate vehicles and documents (IDs). Ordinary activities, such as going to work or to school, taking a baby for immunization, attending a funeral or a wedding, expose women and men, young and old, to such risks.***

Closures and curfews have prevented Palestinians from reaching their places of work and from distributing their products to internal and external markets, and have caused shortages. Factories and farms have been driven out of business by the losses incurred, dramatically increased transport costs and loss of export markets. As a result, unemployment has soared to over 50% and more than half of the Palestinian population is now living below the poverty line. With the sharp decline in the standard of living in the Occupied Territories, malnutrition and other illnesses have increased. Closures and curfews have prevented Palestinian children and youths from attending classes for prolonged periods, violating their right to education and undermining their future professional prospects.

Amnesty International has documented in numerous reports the deterioration of the human rights situation and the violence that has reached a level unprecedented in the 36 years of Israel's occupation of the West Bank and Gaza. In the past three years more than 2,100 Palestinians have been killed by the Israeli army in the Occupied Territories, including some 380 children. Palestinian armed groups have killed some 750 Israelis, most of them civilians, and including more than 90 children. Tens of thousands of people have been injured, many maimed for life. The Israeli army has destroyed more than 3,000 Palestinian homes, and hundreds of workshops, factories and public buildings in the West Bank and Gaza. They have bulldozed vast areas of cultivated land, uprooting olive groves and orchards and flattening greenhouses and fields of growing crops.

These abuses, notably the destruction of land and property, have contributed to damaging the economy in the Occupied Territories. However, the stringent restrictions on the movement of Palestinians imposed in the past three years have been the main cause of the severe economic depression and the increase in unemployment.

Israel has a right and a duty to protect people from repeated bombings and other attacks by Palestinian armed groups from the Occupied Territories, including by restricting access to its territory. However, under international human rights and humanitarian law, it is obliged to ensure freedom of movement, an adequate standard of living, and as normal a life as possible to the population in occupied territories. International law also prohibits an occupying power from imposing collective punishment on the occupied population.***

Restrictions on movement ***

The sweeping restrictions on the movement of Palestinians are disproportionate and discriminatory—they are imposed on all Palestinians *because* they are Palestinians, and not on Israeli settlers who live illegally in the Occupied Territories. Even though the Israeli authorities claim that such measures are always imposed to protect the security of Israelis, the restrictions imposed within the Occupied Territories do not target particular individuals who are believed to pose a threat. They are broad and indiscriminate in their application and as such are unlawful. They have a severe negative impact on the lives of millions of Palestinians who have not committed any offence.***

Such conduct breaches the prohibition on collective punishment contained in the Fourth Geneva Convention and the Hague Regulations. As early as February 2001, the ICRC was expressing concern that closures contravened the Fourth Geneva Convention, including by the imposition of collective punishment and the obstruction of food, healthcare and education. Such restrictions on movement have since been dramatically increased.

> *"The ICRC views the policy of isolating whole villages for an extended period as contrary to International Humanitarian Law (IHL) particularly with respect to those aspects of IHL which protect civilians in times of occupation. Indeed, stringent closures frequently lead to breaches of Article 55 (free passage of medical assistance and foodstuffs), Article 33 (prohibition on collective punishments), Article 50 (children and education), Article 56 (movement of medical transportation and public health facilities) and Article 72 (access to lawyers for persons charged) of the Fourth Geneva Convention. While accepting that the State of Israel has legitimate security concerns, the ICRC stresses that measures taken to address these concerns must be in accordance with International Humanitarian Law. Furthermore, these security measures must allow for a quick return to normal civilian life. This, in essence, is the meaning of the Fourth Geneva Convention, which is applicable to the Occupied Territories."* ICRC, "Israel and Occupied/ Autonomous Territories: The ICRC Starts its 'Closure Relief Programme,'" 26 February 2001.

The evolution of movement restrictions

1967–1993: fostering dependency

For many years, the Israeli authorities fostered the dependence of the Palestinian economy on the Israeli economy. The majority of Palestinians in the West Bank were allowed to travel freely into East Jerusalem and Israel and to the Gaza Strip under a general exit permit issued in 1972 by the Military Commander of the West Bank. Most Palestinians living in the Gaza Strip were also able to move freely into Israel and East Jerusalem. Unable to develop an independent economy under Israeli occupation, Palestinians often had to choose between going to work abroad—and risk loosing their status as residents of the Occupied Territories—or relying on the Israeli labour market. In Israel, they were paid less than Israeli workers, but still earned more than in the Occupied Territories.

The first *intifada*, from 1987 to 1993, led to new restrictions. In 1989, residents of the Gaza Strip were required to obtain a magnetic card, renewable annually, to enter Israel. In 1991, before the Gulf War, Israel cancelled the general exit permit and required Palestinians to obtain individual permits to enter Israel and Jerusalem. In March 1993, the Israeli security forces set up checkpoints along the Green Line separating the West Bank from Israel and started to control entry to East Jerusalem. This severely disrupted Palestinian economic activity as the main road linking the north and south of the West Bank passes through East Jerusalem.

Curfews imposed by the Israeli army routinely confined Palestinians to their homes. For seven years, the Gaza Strip was under night curfew until the Israeli army redeployed in 1995. During the Gulf War, 24-hour curfews were imposed for lengthy periods. The IDF [Israeli Defense Force] also often imposed curfews when carrying out searches and arrests.

1993–2000: The peace process years

In 1994 the Israeli military government started to transfer various civil functions to the newly created PA [Palestinian Authority]. The 1995 Oslo II Agreement identified the PA's functions and defined the intricate "zoning" of the West Bank and the Gaza Strip that established its interim jurisdiction. However, Israel retained ultimate and effective control of all aspects of Palestinians' movement, both internally and across international borders. Its control of border crossings also enabled Israel to control the import and export of goods to and from the Occupied Territories.***

Internal Closures

The widespread impression, in Israeli society and at the international level, was that during the peace process years, following the agreements which resulted in the redeployment of the Israeli army from most Palestinian populated areas in the Occupied Territories and the establishment of the PA, Palestinians were in control of their lives in the new situation of "autonomy" or "self-rule." However, this was not the case.

> *"The realization of the principle of territorial integrity, as enunciated in the Oslo accords, has been frustrated during the period under review by Israeli restrictions on the movement of persons and goods between so-called A, B, and C areas of the West Bank, between Jerusalem and the rest of the West Bank, between the West Bank and the Gaza Strip, and between the occupied territories and the outside world. Safe passage arrangements have not been established, and arrangements for a Gaza seaport and airport have not been agreed upon. The Israeli policy of general closure, which has been in effect since 30 March 1993, imposes explicit restrictions on the mobility of goods and persons. There are fixed Israeli checkpoints on Palestinian roads, including key transport routes, and a system of differentiated mandatory permits for labourers, business people, medical personnel and patients, students, religious worshippers, and all other categories of Palestinians.*** This general closure has been aggravated by periodic comprehensive closures entailing the complete denial of such movements during a full 353 calendar days between 30 March 1993 and mid-June 1997. Israeli restrictions on the movement of goods and personnel are also imposed on UN officials and project materials, resulting in delays and added costs for*

development projects in the West Bank and Gaza Strip and in serious disruption of the work of humanitarian agencies." UN Secretary-General, June 1997.

On several occasions the Israeli army imposed what became known as "internal closures" in the West Bank, stopping all movement of Palestinians between Areas A, B and C for days, sometimes weeks. These internal closures were usually in response to Palestinian attacks on Israelis inside Israel or during periods of tension caused by the Israeli army's excessive use of force. Normal life came to a standstill, especially for the 60 per cent of Palestinians living in the predominantly rural Area B. The first comprehensive internal closure, in March 1996, lasted for 21 days. In 1997 a total of 27 days of internal closure were imposed on all or part of the West Bank; in 1998, the total was 40 days.

The internal closures demonstrated how Israel, despite its withdrawal from some 40 per cent of the West Bank, could bring Palestinian life to a halt and the Palestinian economy to its knees through its control of the areas and main roads around the supposedly autonomous Palestinian enclaves.***

*** By the year 2000 most of the 1.3 million Palestinians living in Gaza had never left the Gaza Strip, an area totalling a mere 348 square kilometres.

Speaking at a conference in September 1994, Israeli lawyer Tamar Pelleg Sryck remarked:

"The Palestinians have received manifold responsibilities . . . but lack the necessary powers to implement such responsibilities. One observes that Israel, despite redeployment, controls the lives of Gazans and the functioning of their society. . . . The PA took over responsibility for education, yet over 1,000 students who wish to pursue their studies in universities in the West Bank are dependent on the IDF for their exit permits. . . . The economy in Gaza is the PA's concern, yet Gazan workers cannot keep their jobs in Israel, agricultural products produced in Gaza cannot be exported and experts are not permitted to visit the Gaza Strip etc, unless the relevant permits are granted by the Israeli authorities. . . ".

Current restrictions

Although increasingly stringent restrictions on Palestinian movement in the Occupied Territories are largely in response to the current *intifada*, the uprising itself was a reaction to the restrictions imposed on Palestinians in the preceding years. Before the outbreak of the *intifada*, movement restrictions were already significant in determining Palestinians' quality of life and the development of their economy. They contributed to the frustration of hopes for improvements in daily life and future prospects, raised by the peace process. Palestinians found that their newly acquired freedom extended no further than the confines of overcrowded refugee camps and disjointed enclaves, while Israeli settlers expanded and strengthened their hold on the surrounding land and resources.***

Curfews

In the past three years, the Israeli army has placed many villages in Areas B and C under 24-hour curfews, and the H-2 area in Hebron and other West Bank cities under extended curfews. In Hebron, the only West Bank city where Israeli settlers live inside the city, such restrictions apply only to the Palestinian inhabitants. The 500 Israeli settlers in H-2 are allowed to leave their homes unrestricted.

After the Israeli army retook control of the six main West Bank towns of Tulkarem, Qalqilya, Jenin, Nablus, Ramallah and Bethlehem in March and April 2002, 24-hour curfews were enforced for days and in some cases weeks. Civilians were confined to their homes and movement outside was prohibited. The army almost completely stopped vital service providers and ambulances from functioning, even if they had coordinated in advance with the army. From time to time, curfews were lifted for a few hours to allow Palestinians to purchase essential supplies. Bethlehem was under curfew for 40 consecutive days.

The IDF retook control in these towns, and Hebron, in June 2002, and has remained present continuously in Tulkarem, Jenin, Nablus and Ramallah and intermittently in Qalqilya, the H-1 area of Hebron and Bethlehem. When the IDF is maintaining a presence in the main towns, it often imposes a 24-hour curfew rule. According to the Office of the Coordinator of Humanitarian Affairs (OCHA), on 9 July 2002 almost half the population of the West Bank, nearly 900,000 out of some 2.2 million Palestinians, were under curfew in 71 different localities. At the beginning of June 2003 more than 350,000 Palestinians were under curfew and by early July the number was about 150,000.

The IDF usually introduces a schedule for allowing the movement of civilians for a few hours during daylight. However, such respite is often cancelled without notice. Nablus has been under curfew for longer than any other city, and remained under 24-hour curfew for five months after 21 June 2002, apart from one month when it was under a night curfew only.

Food crops rot, prices of local products collapse

Sa'id al-Agha is aged 46, married with nine children. He owns 50 dunums (a dunum is 0.1 hectares) of land in northern al-Mawasi, within the jurisdiction of Khan Younes municipality. He cultivates guavas as his main crop, vegetables, lemons, oranges and dates. The yield from his land has fallen since the IDF stopped fertilizer from being brought into al-Mawasi. Before the *intifada*, he would expect to make a profit of US$15,000. In 2002 he made $1,000.

Guavas used to be exported from Gaza to Israel, the West Bank and Jordan. Now it is almost impossible to send the crop even to the West Bank. The price has collapsed because the market in Gaza is flooded with guavas at a time when there is reduced demand from local people who have lost their jobs and have less money to spend. Before the *intifada* a 15 kilo box of guavas fetched NIS50-60 (about US$10–12). The price subsequently collapsed to NIS12-15 (about US$2.5–3). Often the crop is delayed, waiting to cross the al-Tuffah military checkpoint for two or three days. Less fresh, it sells for only NIS1 (about US$0.20) per box. At the same time, Sa'id al-Agha still has to cover his farm's running costs. He pays $600 per month for diesel, his main expense, to operate water pumps on his land.

In front of Sa'id al-Agha's house was a large pile of rotting dates. They had been picked for the market in Khan Younes, but he had not been able to transport them across al-Tuffah checkpoint.

While prices of local produce collapse because of lack of access to markets, the price of goods from outside the areas increase sharply. For example, in a village which had all its access roads blocked by the Israeli army and was thus made inaccessible by vehicle, a fifty kilogram bag of flour costs NIS115, compared to NIS70 in the nearby city of Nablus.

Excessive use of force

Closures and curfews are controlled by military force. Members of the Israeli security forces have frequently resorted to lethal force to enforce restrictions, killing or injuring scores of Palestinians who were unarmed and presented no threat. Soldiers opened fire on Palestinians bypassing checkpoints, crossing trenches, removing barriers and breaking curfews. They even fired at ambulance personnel, municipal employees and journalists who had coordinated their movements in advance with the IDF. Some Palestinians were shot because they failed to stop at checkpoints. Soldiers have also often fired live and rubber-coated metal bullets, sound bombs and tear gas to disperse crowds who had gathered during curfews or at checkpoints.***

Israeli soldiers who kill or injure to enforce movement restrictions usually enjoy impunity or, at most, may receive only very light sentences. In contrast, Palestinians who disobey orders restricting movement may be tried in a military court under Military Order 378 and imprisoned for up to five years or fined.

In many cases Israeli soldiers and border police have meted out immediate punishment in the form of beatings and assaults. In other cases they have confiscated the keys of vehicles or the identity card of the drivers, or have shot at the tyres of vehicles or otherwise damaged the vehicles.

Security force brutality to enforce closures

Batir is a village in Bethlehem governorate, south of Jerusalem, close to the Green Line. Before the *intifada,* about 70 per cent of its working population worked in Israel or in nearby settlements. In the past three years it has not been possible for most Palestinians to obtain permits to enter Israel. There are a few small businesses in the village but no alternative sources of employment nearby.

Khaled Fahd 'Uwayneh lives in Batir, is married with one child and also supports his mother. He used to work as an electrician in the construction industry in Israel, earning about NIS4,000 (about US$800) monthly. His wages, now averaging only NIS500—700 (about US$90–140), depend on crossing into Jerusalem or Israel without a permit to find work.

> "In mid-August 2002, I was returning in a Ford taxi at about 4.30pm with my brother and a friend. That day we had managed to find a day's work in Jerusalem. A Border Police jeep stopped the taxi on Okef Street in the Ein Yalo area in Jerusalem. The police asked for our identity cards. As soon as they noticed our green Palestinian identity cards, they pulled us out of the taxi. They threw us on the ground, searched us and started hitting us. We were then forced to stand with our hands up in the air for about 45 minutes. Altogether, the Border Police were holding nine Palestinians standing by the side of the road. There were also nine Border Policemen.
>
> "One asked to leave as he had been standing there for a long time. Two policemen grabbed him and threw him down a slope next to the road and then ordered him to walk back up and return to his position. One policeman called out the name of Jabr, another Batir resident. The policeman asked him: 'Are you the one whose head hurts?' Jabr said: 'Yes.' The policeman asked: 'Exactly where does it hurt?' and Jabr pointed to an ear. The policeman struck him on that ear with his M16 and told him: 'That will make it heal quickly.' The policeman then called each of us one by one and ordered us to walk down the slope by the road. Four Border Policemen were waiting at the bottom. As I waited my

turn, I heard those ahead being beaten. The four policemen beat me with truncheons. After about an hour-and-a-half, the policemen took us to a remote area up the hill. They made us form two lines and surrounded us. The officer pointed to each of us one by one and said: 'I don't like the look of him.' Then the policeman would beat the one selected all over his body, using truncheons. The officer told us: 'This is the last time you enter Israel. You are prohibited from returning. We're going to let you go now. Next time, we'll kill you.' As we passed the policemen, they threw each of us on the ground and beat us again. Eventually only Jabr remained at the top of the hill. We watched from below as the nine border policemen beat him. I called the Israeli Police on my mobile. They told me that they would send a patrol. No one came. The Border Policemen beat Jabr for about half an hour. Afterwards, he could not walk properly. The Border Policemen asked us to fetch him, so we went and carried him away."

A widespread punishment regularly meted out by soldiers at checkpoints is holding Palestinians on the spot for hours, with no shelter from sun or the rain, and in some cases placing men in metal cages.***

The "separation barrier/fence/wall"

On 14 June 2002, the Israeli government announced that work would begin immediately on the construction of a wall/fence (usually referred to as the "separation barrier") along the perimeter of the West Bank, and north and south of Jerusalem (known as "the Jerusalem envelope"). The stated aim of the project is to prevent Palestinians crossing clandestinely from the West Bank into Israel, so as to prevent suicide bombings and other attacks. However, the barrier is not being constructed on the Green Line separating Israel from the West Bank. Most of it is being constructed on Palestinian land inside the West Bank—in some areas up to six or seven kilometres east of Green Line—in order to include some 10 Israeli settlements which are nearest to the Green Line.***

Almost 400 km long and 30 to 100 meters wide, the barrier comprises—in addition to the fence or wall (depending on the area)—a complex of obstacles, including deep trenches to stop vehicles, electric warning fences, trace paths, patrol roads and roads to accommodate armoured vehicles.

In order to build the barrier, large areas of mostly cultivated Palestinian land have been destroyed, some 11,500 dunums (about 2,875 acres, or 11.5 square kilometres). In addition, the barrier cuts off several Palestinian villages and large areas of Palestinian agricultural land from the rest of the West Bank, and separates other Palestinian villages and towns from the land of their inhabitants.

Village land seized

In 2002, the IDF informed landowners in Qafin, a village in Jenin governorate with a population of about 9,500, that 600 dunums of land was to be seized for five years on grounds of military necessity in order to build the security barrier. In September 2002, bulldozers began to clear the land, tearing down most of the olive trees before their owners had been able to harvest the crop. A month later, bare earth was all that remained of once productive agricultural land. The mayor, Taysir Harasheh, told Amnesty International delegates that, in the Qafin area, the barrier would lie three kilometres inside the West Bank and surround the village on three sides. 6,000 dunums, 60 per cent of the village's agricultural land, would eventually be on the other side of the barrier. There are thousands of olive trees on this land. Nearly all of the 90 per cent of the active population in Qafin who used to work in Israel have now lost their jobs. The income from the olive harvest has become crucial for many residents.

The barrier has very serious economic and social consequences for over 200,000 Palestinians in nearby towns and villages. Some 15 Palestinian villages, home to some 12,000 Palestinians in the regions of Jenin, Tulkarem and Qalqilyia and dozens of homes in the northern neighbourhood of Bethlehem are being wedged in between the barrier and the Green Line. Some 19 other Palestinian communities, most of them in the Jenin, Tulkarem and Qalqilyia regions, are separated from their land by the barrier.

The land in these areas is among the most fertile in the West Bank, with better water resources than elsewhere, and agriculture in the region constitutes the main source of income for the Palestinians—especially since those who used to work in Israel are no longer allowed to. The percentage of land used agriculturally is double the average in other parts of the West Bank, and the productivity of the land is substantially higher than elsewhere.

The stranded Palestinian residents of these areas have to cross the barrier at designated checkpoints to reach the rest of the West Bank to go to work, to tend to their fields, to sell their agricultural produce, and to access education and health centres in nearby towns. Non-residents will require special permits to be allowed into these areas.***

Notes and Questions

1. *Background.* Israel's occupation of the West Bank and Gaza began in June 1967, during the Six-Day War. After launching preemptive strikes against neighboring Arab countries, Israeli forces seized the Sinai Peninsula from Egypt in the south and the Golan Heights from Syria in the north. They also pushed Jordanian forces out of the West Bank and East Jerusalem. Approximately 500,000 Palestinians fled to Egypt, Syria, Lebanon and Jordan. In November 1967, the U.N. Security Council adopted Resolution 242, calling for Israeli withdrawal from the territories in exchange for recognition by and peace with its neighbors.

2. *Applicability of the Law of Occupation.* Since 1967, Israel has contested the applicability of the Geneva Convention to the West Bank and Gaza, preferring to characterize its military presence not as an "occupation," but an "administration." Nevertheless, this claim has not been accepted by most legal scholars or the international community. *See e.g.,* Yoram Dinstein, *The International Law of Belligerent Occupation and Human Rights,* 8 ISR. Y.B. HUM. RTS. 105, 106–08 (1978); COUNTRY REPORTS ON HUMAN RIGHTS PRACTICES FOR 1989, 101st Cong., 2d Sess. 1432 (1990) ("The United States considers Israel's occupation to be governed by the Hague Regulations of 1907 and the 1949 Fourth Geneva Convention Relative to the Protection of Civilian Persons in Time of War.") In a speech to the nation in May 2003, Prime Minister Ariel Sharon conceded that Israel was, in fact, an occupying power in the territories declaring, "To keep 3.5 million under occupation is bad for us and them."

3. *Legal Challenges to the Wall.* In an emergency session held in October 2003, the United Nations General Assembly adopted Resolution ES-10/13, demanding that Israel "stop and reverse construction of the wall in the Occupied Palestinian Territory, including in and around East Jerusalem, which is a departure from the 1949 Armistice Line and is in contradiction to relevant provisions of international law." A/RES/ES-10-13

(Oct. 21, 2003). When Israel failed to comply, the General Assembly adopted Resolution ES-10/14, requesting the International Court of Justice to render an Advisory Opinion on the legal consequences of Israel's construction of the wall. A/RES/ES-10/14 (Dec. 3, 2003).

In an Advisory Opinion issued on July 9, 2004, the International Court of Justice found that Israel is bound by humanitarian law and the human rights treaties to which it is a party with respect to its conduct in the Occupied Territories, and that the wall violates numerous provisions of international law:

> [T]he Court is of the opinion that the construction of the wall and its associated régime impede the liberty of movement of the inhabitants of the Occupied Palestinian Territory (with the exception of Israeli citizens and those assimilated thereto) as guaranteed under Article 12, paragraph 1, of the International Covenant on Civil and Political Rights. They also impede the exercise by the persons concerned of the right to work, to health, to education and to an adequate standard of living as proclaimed in the International Covenant on Economic, Social and Cultural Rights and in the United Nations Convention on the Rights of the Child. Lastly, the construction of the wall and its associated régime, by contributing to the demographic changes [caused by Israeli settlements in the Occupied Territories] contravene Article 49, paragraph 6, of the Fourth Geneva Convention and . . . Security Council resolutions [446 (1979) of Mar. 22, 1979; 452 (1979) of July 20, 1979; and 465 (1980) of Mar. 1, 1980].

Legal Consequences of the Construction of a Wall in the Occupied Palestinian Territory at ¶ 134, *available at* http://www.icj-cij.org/icjwww/idocket/imwp/imwpframe.htm. While acknowledging Israel's valid security concerns, the Court was "not convinced that the specific course Israel has chosen for the wall was necessary to attain its security objectives." *Id.* at ¶ 137.

The Court determined that "Israel . . . has the obligation to cease forthwith the works of construction of the wall . . . dismantle forthwith . . . those parts of that structure situated within the Occupied Palestinian Territory, including in and around East Jerusalem," *id.* at ¶ 151, and "make reparation for the damage caused to all the natural or legal persons concerned." *Id.* at ¶ 152. Moreover, the Court determined that the right to self-determination and other rights violated by the Israeli actions implicate "intransgressable principles of international customary law." *Id.* at ¶ 157. Therefore, all states "are under an obligation not to recognize the illegal situation resulting from the construction of the wall . . . [and] not to render aid or assistance in maintaining the situation created by such construction." *Id.* at ¶ 159. In addition, all states parties to the Fourth Geneva Convention are under an affirmative duty "to ensure compliance by Israel with international humanitarian law as embodied in that Convention." *Id.* Finally, the Court emphasized that "both Israel and Palestine are under an obligation scrupulously to observe the rules of international humanitarian law, one of the paramount purposes of which is to protect civilian life." *Id.* at ¶ 162.

On July 20, 2004, the General Assembly overwhelmingly adopted a resolution calling upon Israel to comply with the Advisory Opinion. A/RES/ES-10-15 (July 20, 2004). One hundred and fifty countries voted in favor of the resolution, while six voted against it (Australia, Federated States of Micronesia, Israel, Marshall Islands, Tuvalu and the United States), and ten abstained (Cameroon, Canada, El Salvador, Nauru, Papua New

Guinea, the Solomon Islands, Tonga, Uganda, Uruguay and Vanuatu). General Assembly resolutions are not legally binding, but may evidence customary international law.

Meanwhile, on June 30, 2004, Israel's Supreme Court issued a significant ruling on the wall in a case brought by residents of Beit Sourik and several other villages located northwest of Jerusalem. The residents argued that the route of the wall would leave several thousand acres of their land on the Israeli side of the barrier, cutting them off from their farms, jobs and schools. The court agreed that the route would cause unnecessary hardship to Palestinian residents, and ordered the government to re-route a portion of the wall. *Beit Sourik Village Council v. Government of Israel and Commander of the IDF Forces in the West Bank*, HCJ 2056/04 (June 30, 2004), *available at* http://www.honestreporting.com/a/rulingonfence.htm (last visited July 28, 2004).

C. Duty to Protect Cultural Rights and Property

The Mediterranean island nation of Cyprus obtained its independence from Britain in 1960. In 1974, following a military coup in Cyprus supported by Greece, Turkish troops invaded the country, ostensibly to uphold constitutionalism and protect the Turkish minority. Thousands of Greek and Turkish Cypriots were killed and rendered refugees in the conflict. Turkish troops continued to occupy more than one-third of the country even after constitutional government had been restored. The following case decided by the European Court of Human Rights examines implications of the occupation for the legal rights of the population:

CYPRUS v. TURKEY

2002 E.H.R.R. 30

THE FACTS ***

13. The complaints raised in this application arise out of the Turkish military operations in northern Cyprus in July and August 1974 and the continuing division of the territory of Cyprus. [The Court cites a prior judgment in *Loizidou v. Turkey*, in which it found that "Turkish armed forces of more than 30,000 personnel are stationed throughout the whole of the occupied area of northern Cyprus, which is constantly patrolled and has checkpoints on all main lines of communication."]***

14. A major development in the continuing division of Cyprus occurred in November 1983 with the proclamation of the "Turkish Republic of Northern Cyprus" (the "TRNC") and the subsequent enactment of the "TRNC Constitution" on 7 May 1985.

This development was condemned by the international community. On 18 November 1983 the United Nations Security Council adopted Resolution 541 (1983) declaring the proclamation of the establishment of the "TRNC" legally invalid and calling upon all States not to recognise any Cypriot State other than the Republic of Cyprus. A similar call was made by the Security Council on 11 May 1984 in its Resolution 550 (1984). In November 1983 the Committee of Ministers of the Council of Europe decided that it continued to regard the government of the Republic of Cyprus as the sole legitimate government of Cyprus and called for respect of the sovereignty, independence, territorial integrity and unity of the Republic of Cyprus.

15. According to the respondent Government [Turkey], the "TRNC" is a democratic and constitutional State which is politically independent of all other sovereign States including Turkey, and the administration in northern Cyprus has been set up by the Turkish-Cypriot people in the exercise of its right to self-determination and not by Turkey. Notwithstanding this view, it is only the Cypriot government which is recognised internationally as the government of the Republic of Cyprus in the context of diplomatic and treaty relations and the working of international organisations.***

C. The instant application

18. [The Republic of Cyprus alleged that Turkey violated numerous provisions of the European Convention for the Protection of Human Rights and Fundamental Freedoms.]

These allegations were invoked with reference to four broad categories of complaints: alleged violations of the rights of Greek-Cypriot missing persons and their relatives; alleged violations of the home and property rights of displaced persons; alleged violations of the rights of enclaved Greek Cypriots in northern Cyprus; alleged violations of the rights of Turkish Cypriots and the Gypsy community in northern Cyprus.***

THE LAW ***

3. *As to the respondent State's responsibility under the Convention in respect of the alleged violations*

69. The respondent Government disputed Turkey's liability under the Convention for the allegations set out in the application, claim[ing] that the acts and omissions complained of were imputable exclusively to the "Turkish Republic of Northern Cyprus" (the "TRNC")***.

70. [T]he applicant Government contended before the Court that the "TRNC" was an illegal entity under international law since it owed its existence to the respondent State's unlawful act of invasion of the northern part of Cyprus in 1974 and to its continuing unlawful occupation of that part of Cyprus ever since.***

71. The applicant Government stressed that even if Turkey had no legal title in international law to northern Cyprus, Turkey did have legal responsibility for that area in Convention terms, given that she exercised overall military and economic control over the area. This overall and, in addition, exclusive control of the occupied area was confirmed by irrefutable evidence of Turkey's power to dictate the course of events in the occupied area. In the applicant Government's submission, a Contracting State to the Convention could not, by way of delegation of powers to a subordinate and unlawful administration, avoid its responsibility for breaches of the Convention, indeed of international law in general. To hold otherwise would, in the present context of northern Cyprus, give rise to a grave lacuna in the system of human-rights protection and, indeed, render the Convention system there inoperative.***

77. *** Having effective overall control over northern Cyprus, [Turkey's] responsibility cannot be confined to the acts of its own soldiers or officials in northern Cyprus but must also be engaged by virtue of the acts of the local administration which survives by virtue of Turkish military and other support. It follows that, in terms of Article 1 of the Convention, Turkey's "jurisdiction" must be considered to extend to securing the entire range of substantive rights set out in the Convention and those additional

Protocols which she has ratified, and that violations of those rights are imputable to Turkey.***

III. ALLEGED VIOLATIONS OF THE RIGHTS OF GREEK-CYPRIOT MISSING PERSONS AND THEIR RELATIVES

A. *Greek-Cypriot missing persons* ***

123.   *** Article 2 provides as relevant:

"1. Everyone's right to life shall be protected by law . . ."***

132.   [T]here is no proof that any of the missing persons have been unlawfully killed. However, in its opinion, and of relevance to the instant case, the above-mentioned procedural obligation also arises upon proof of an arguable claim that an individual, who was last seen in the custody of agents of the State, subsequently disappeared in a context which may be considered life-threatening.

133.   Against this background, the Court observes that the evidence bears out the applicant Government's claim that many persons now missing were detained either by Turkish or Turkish-Cypriot forces. Their detention occurred at a time when the conduct of military operations was accompanied by arrests and killings on a large scale.***

134.   That the missing persons disappeared against this background cannot be denied. The Court cannot but note that the authorities of the respondent State have never undertaken any investigation into the claims made by the relatives of the missing persons that the latter had disappeared after being detained in circumstances in which there was real cause to fear for their welfare.*** No attempt was made to identify the names of the persons who were reportedly released from Turkish custody into the hands of Turkish-Cypriot paramilitaries or to inquire into the whereabouts of the places where the bodies were disposed of. It does not appear either that any official inquiry was made into the claim that Greek-Cypriot prisoners were transferred to Turkey.

136.   [T]he Court concludes that there has been a continuing violation of Article 2 on account of the failure of the authorities of the respondent State to conduct an effective investigation aimed at clarifying the whereabouts and fate of Greek-Cypriot missing persons who disappeared in life-threatening circumstances.***

B. *Greek-Cypriot missing persons' relatives*

1. *Article 3 of the Convention*

154.   The applicant Government *** requested the Court to rule that the continuing suffering of the families of missing persons constituted not only a continuing but also an aggravated violation of Article 3 of the Convention, which states:

"No one shall be subjected to torture or to inhuman or degrading treatment or punishment."***

156.   The Court recalls that the question whether a family member of a "disappeared person" is a victim of treatment contrary to Article 3 will depend on the existence of special factors which give the suffering of the person concerned a dimension and character distinct from the emotional distress which may be regarded as inevitably caused to relatives of a victim of a serious human-rights violation.***

157.   The Court observes that the authorities of the respondent State have failed to undertake any investigation into the circumstances surrounding the disappearance

of the missing persons. In the absence of any information about their fate, the relatives of persons who went missing during the events of July and August 1974 were condemned to live in a prolonged state of acute anxiety which cannot be said to have been erased with the passage of time. The Court does not consider, in the circumstances of this case, that the fact that certain relatives may not have actually witnessed the detention of family members or complained about such to the authorities of the respondent State deprives them of victim status under Article 3. It recalls that the military operation resulted in a considerable loss of life, large-scale arrests and detentions and enforced separation of families. The overall context must still be vivid in the minds of the relatives of persons whose fate has never been accounted for by the authorities. They endure the agony of not knowing whether family members were killed in the conflict or are still in detention or, if detained, have since died. The fact that a very substantial number of Greek Cypriots had to seek refuge in the south coupled with the continuing division of Cyprus must be considered to constitute very serious obstacles to their quest for information. The provision of such information is the responsibility of the authorities of the respondent State. This responsibility has not been discharged. For the Court, the silence of the authorities of the respondent State in the face of the real concerns of the relatives of the missing persons attains a level of severity which can only be categorised as inhuman treatment within the meaning of Article 3.

158.   For the above reasons, the Court concludes that, during the period under consideration, there has been a continuing violation of Article 3 of the Convention in respect of the relatives of the Greek-Cypriot missing persons.***

IV. ALLEGED VIOLATIONS OF THE RIGHTS OF DISPLACED PERSONS TO RESPECT FOR THEIR HOME AND PROPERTY ***

1. *Article 8 of the Convention*

165.   The applicant Government maintained that it was *** the respondent State's actions which had prevented the displaced Greek Cypriots from returning to their homes, in violation of Article 8 of the Convention which provides:

"1.   Everyone has the right to respect for his private and family life, his home and his correspondence.

2.   There shall be no interference by a public authority with the exercise of this right except such as is in accordance with the law and is necessary in a democratic society ***."

166.   The applicant Government declared that the policy of the respondent State, aimed at the division of Cyprus along racial lines, affected 211,000 displaced Greek Cypriots and their children as well as a number of Maronites, Armenians, Latins and individual citizens of the Republic of Cyprus who had exercised the option under the Constitution to be members of the Greek-Cypriot community. They submitted that the continuing refusal of the "TRNC" authorities to allow the displaced persons to return to the north violated not only the right to respect for their homes but also the right to respect for their family life. In this latter connection, the applicant Government observed that the impugned policy resulted in the separation of families.

167.   In a further submission, the applicant Government requested the Court to find that the facts also disclosed a policy of deliberate destruction and manipulation of

the human, cultural and natural environment and conditions of life in northern Cyprus. The applicant Government contended that this policy was based on the implantation of massive numbers of settlers from Turkey with the intention and the consequence of eliminating Greek presence and culture in northern Cyprus. In the view of the applicant Government, the notions of "home" and "private life" were broad enough to subsume the concept of sustaining existing cultural relationships within a subsisting cultural environment. Having regard to the destructive changes being wrought to that environment by the respondent State, it could only be concluded that the rights of the displaced persons to respect for their private life and home were being violated in this sense also.***

172.   The Court observes that the official policy of the "TRNC" authorities to deny the right of the displaced persons to return to their homes is reinforced by the very tight restrictions operated by the same authorities on visits to the north by Greek Cypriots living in the south. Accordingly, not only are displaced persons unable to apply to the authorities to reoccupy the homes which they left behind, they are physically prevented from even visiting them.***

175.   [T]he Court concludes that there has been a continuing violation of Article 8 of the Convention by reason of the refusal to allow the return of any Greek-Cypriot displaced persons to their homes in northern Cyprus.***

176.   As to the applicant Government's further allegation concerning the alleged manipulation of the demographic and cultural environment of the displaced persons' homes, the Court *** considers that it is not necessary to examine this complaint in view of its above finding of a continuing violation of Article 8 of the Convention.***

2.   Article 1 of Protocol No. 1

178.   The applicant Government maintained that the respondent State's continuing refusal to permit the return of the displaced persons to northern Cyprus not only prevented them from having access to their property there but also prevented them from using, selling, bequeathing, mortgaging, developing and enjoying it. In their submission, there were continuing violations of all the component aspects of the right to peaceful enjoyment of possessions guaranteed by Article 1 of Protocol No. 1, which states:

> "Every natural or legal person is entitled to the peaceful enjoyment of his possessions. No one shall be deprived of his possessions except in the public interest and subject to the conditions provided for by law and by the general principles of international law."

179.   The applicant Government contended that the respondent State had adopted a systematic and continuing policy of interference with the immovable property of the displaced persons. They stated, *inter alia*, that the properties in question, of which the displaced persons were unlawfully dispossessed following their eviction from the north, were transferred into Turkish possession. Steps were then taken to "legalise" the illegal appropriation of the properties and their allocation to "State" bodies, Turkish Cypriots and settlers from the Turkish mainland. This was effected by means such as the assignment of "title deeds" to their new possessors. No compensation had ever been awarded to the victims of these interferences. Furthermore, specific measures had been taken to develop and exploit commercially land belonging to displaced persons, Church-owned land had been transferred to the Muslim religious trust, and agricultural pro-

duce from Greek-Cypriot land was now being exported accompanied by Turkish certificates.***

187. [The Court cites its prior decision in *Loizidou* in which it held that the provision of the "TRNC Constitution" purporting to divest Greek Cypriots of title to their property was invalid for purposes of the Convention on Human Rights.]*** The continuing and total denial of access to their property is a clear interference with the right of the displaced Greek Cypriots to the peaceful enjoyment of possessions within the meaning of the first sentence of Article 1 of Protocol No. 1. [N]o compensation has been paid to the displaced persons in respect of the interferences which they have suffered and continue to suffer in respect of their property rights.***

V. ALLEGED VIOLATIONS ARISING OUT OF THE LIVING CONDITIONS OF GREEK CYPRIOTS IN NORTHERN CYPRUS

207. The applicant Government asserted that the living conditions to which the Greek Cypriots who had remained in the north were subjected gave rise to substantial violations of the Convention. They stressed that these violations were committed as a matter of practice and were directed against a depleted and now largely elderly population living in the Karpas area of northern Cyprus in furtherance of a policy of ethnic cleansing, the success of which could be measured by the fact that from some 20,000 Greek Cypriots living in the Karpas in 1974 only 429 currently remained. Maronites, of whom there were currently 177 still living in northern Cyprus, also laboured under similar, if less severe, restrictions.***

1. *Article 2 of the Convention*

216. The applicant Government maintained that the restrictions on the ability of the enclaved Greek Cypriots and Maronites to receive medical treatment and the failure to provide or to permit receipt of adequate medical services gave rise to a violation of Article 2 of the Convention [on the right to life].

217. In their submission, the respondent State must be considered, as a matter of administrative practice, to have failed to protect the right to life of these communities, having regard to the absence in northern Cyprus of adequate emergency and specialist services and geriatric care. In support of their submission, the applicant Government observed that aged Greek Cypriots were compelled to transfer to the south to obtain appropriate care and attention.***

219. The Court observes that an issue may arise under Article 2 of the Convention where it is shown that the authorities of a Contracting State put an individual's life at risk through the denial of health care which they have undertaken to make available to the population generally. It notes in this connection that Article 2 §1 of the Convention enjoins the State not only to refrain from the intentional and unlawful taking of life, but also to take appropriate steps to safeguard the lives of those within its jurisdiction (see the *L.C.B. v. the United Kingdom* judgment of 9 June 1998, *Reports* 1998-III, p. 1403, §36). It notes, however, that the Commission was unable to establish on the evidence that the "TRNC" authorities deliberately withheld medical treatment from the population concerned or adopted a practice of delaying the processing of requests of patients to receive medical treatment in the south. It observes that during the period under consideration medical visits were indeed hampered on account of restrictions imposed by the "TRNC" authorities on the movement of the populations concerned and that in cer-

tain cases delays did occur. However, it has not been established that the lives of any patients were put in danger on account of delay in individual cases. It is also to be observed that neither the Greek-Cypriot nor Maronite populations were prevented from availing themselves of medical services including hospitals in the north. The applicant Government are critical *[sic]* of the level of health care available in the north. However, the Court does not consider it necessary to examine in this case the extent to which Article 2 of the Convention may impose an obligation on a Contracting State to make available a certain standard of health care.

220. The Court further observes that the difficulties which the Greek-Cypriot and Maronite communities experience in the area of health care under consideration essentially stem from the controls imposed on their freedom of movement.***

221. The Court concludes that no violation of Article 2 of the Convention has been established by virtue of an alleged practice of denying access to medical services to Greek Cypriots and Maronites living in northern Cyprus.

222. The Court will revert to the applicant Government's complaint in respect of the alleged interference with access to medical facilities in the context of the overall assessment of compliance with Article 8 of the Convention (see paragraphs 281 et seq. below).***

4. Article 9 of the Convention

241. The applicant Government alleged that the facts disclosed an interference with the enclaved Greek Cypriots' right to manifest their religion, in breach of Article 9 of the Convention which states:

> 1. Everyone has the right to freedom of thought, conscience and religion; this right includes freedom to change his religion or belief and freedom, either alone or in community with others and in public or private, to manifest his religion or belief, in worship, teaching, practice and observance.***"

245. *** It has not been contended by the applicant Government that the "TRNC" authorities have interfered as such with the right of the Greek-Cypriot population to manifest their religion either alone or in the company of others. Indeed there is no evidence of such interference. However, the restrictions placed on the freedom of movement of that population during the period under consideration considerably curtailed their ability to observe their religious beliefs, in particular their access to places of worship outside their villages and their participation in other aspects of religious life.

246. The Court concludes that there has been a violation of Article 9 of the Convention in respect of Greek Cypriots living in northern Cyprus.***

5. Article 10 of the Convention

248. The applicant Government asserted that the "TRNC" authorities engaged in excessive censorship of school-books, restricted the importation of Greek-language newspapers and books and prevented the circulation of any newspapers or books whose content they disapproved of. In their submission, these acts violated as a matter of administrative practice the right of the enclaved Greek Cypriots to receive and impart information and ideas guaranteed by Article 10 of the Convention, which provides:

"1. Everyone has the right to freedom of expression. This right shall include freedom to hold opinions and to receive and impart information and ideas without interference by public authority and regardless of frontiers.***

252. The Court [finds] that there has been an interference with Article 10 on account of the practice adopted by the "TRNC" authorities of screening the contents of school-books before their distribution. It observes in this regard that, although the vetting procedure was designed to identify material which might pose a risk to inter-communal relations and was carried out in the context of confidence-building measures recommended by [U.N. Peacekeepers], the reality during the period under consideration was that a large number of school-books, no matter how innocuous their content, were unilaterally censored or rejected by the authorities.***

254. The Court finds therefore that there has been a violation of Article 10 of the Convention in respect of Greek Cypriots living in northern Cyprus in so far as school-books destined for use in their primary school were subject, during the period under consideration, to excessive measures of censorship.***

8. Article 2 of Protocol No. 1

273. The applicant Government averred that the children of Greek Cypriots living in northern Cyprus were denied secondary-education facilities and that Greek-Cypriot parents of children of secondary-school age were in consequence denied the right to ensure their children's education in conformity with their religious and philosophical convictions. The applicant Government relied on Article 2 of Protocol No. 1, which states:

"No person shall be denied the right to education. In the exercise of any functions which it assumes in relation to education and to teaching, the State shall respect the right of parents to ensure such education and teaching in conformity with their own religious and philosophical convictions."

274. The applicant Government *** requested the Court to rule that this provision had also been breached on account of the prevention by the respondent State of appropriate primary-school teaching until the end of 1997. Before that date, the "TRNC" had not permitted the appointment of a primary-school teacher. In the applicant Government's submission this policy interfered with the right of Greek-Cypriot children to a primary education.***

277. The Court notes that children of Greek-Cypriot parents in northern Cyprus wishing to pursue a secondary education through the medium of the Greek language are obliged to transfer to schools in the south, this facility being unavailable in the "TRNC" ever since the decision of the Turkish-Cypriot authorities to abolish it. Admittedly, it is open to children, on reaching the age of 12, to continue their education at a Turkish or English-language school in the north. In the strict sense, accordingly, there is no denial of the right to education, which is the primary obligation devolving on a Contracting Party under the first sentence of Article 2 of Protocol No. 1. [Citation omitted.] Moreover, this provision does not specify the language in which education must be conducted in order that the right to education be respected ***.

278. However, in the Court's opinion, the option available to Greek-Cypriot parents to continue their children's education in the north is unrealistic in view of the fact

that the children in question have already received their primary education in a Greek-Cypriot school there. The authorities must no doubt be aware that it is the wish of Greek-Cypriot parents that the schooling of their children be completed through the medium of the Greek language. Having assumed responsibility for the provision of Greek-language primary schooling, the failure of the "TRNC" authorities to make continuing provision for it at the secondary-school level must be considered in effect to be a denial of the substance of the right at issue. It cannot be maintained that the provision of secondary education in the south in keeping with the linguistic tradition of the enclaved Greek Cypriots suffices to fulfil the obligation laid down in Article 2 of Protocol No. 1, having regard to the impact of that option on family life ***.***

C. *Overall examination of the living conditions of Greek Cypriots in northern Cyprus*

1. *Article 8 of the Convention*

281. The applicant Government asserted that the respondent State, as a matter of administrative practice, violated in various respects the right of Greek Cypriots living in northern Cyprus to respect for their private life and home. The applicant Government invoked Article 8 of the Convention.***

283. *** The applicant Government also contended that a further and separate breach of the right to respect for private life should be found in view of the consequences which the restrictions on movement had on the access of enclaved Greek Cypriots to medical treatment ***. In this connection, the applicant Government observed that the requirement to obtain permission for medical treatment and the denial of visits by Greek-Cypriot doctors or Maronite doctors of their choice interfered with the right of Greek Cypriots in the north to respect for their private life.***

285. The applicant Government reiterated their view that the respondent State through its policy of colonisation had engaged in deliberate manipulation of the demographic and cultural environment of the "home" of the Greek Cypriots ***. They requested the Court to find a breach of Article 8 on that account.***

299. *** In the Court's opinion, the matters relied on by the applicant Government in this connection are in reality bound up with their more general allegation that the respondent State pursues a policy which is intended to claim the northern part of Cyprus for Turkish Cypriots and settlers from Turkey to the exclusion of any Greek-Cypriot influence. The applicant Government maintain that this policy is manifested in the harshness of the restrictions imposed on the enclaved Greek-Cypriot population. For the Court, the specific complaints invoked by the applicant Government regarding impediments to access to medical treatment and hindrances to participation in bi- or inter-communal events *** are elements which fail to be considered in the context of an overall analysis of the living conditions of the population concerned from the angle of their impact on the right of its members to respect for private and family life.

300. [T]he restrictions which beset the daily lives of the enclaved Greek Cypriots create a feeling among them "of being compelled to live in a hostile environment in which it is hardly possible to lead a normal private and family life." [T]he adverse circumstances to which the population concerned was subjected included: the absence of normal means of communication; the unavailability in practice of the Greek-Cypriot press; the insufficient number of priests; the difficult choice with which parents and schoolchildren were faced regarding secondary education; the restrictions and formal-

ities applied to freedom of movement, including, the Court would add, for the purposes of seeking medical treatment and participation in bi- or inter-communal events; the impossibility of preserving property rights upon departure or on death.

301.   The Court *** considers that these restrictions are factors which aggravate the violations which it has found in respect of the right of the enclaved Greek Cypriots to respect for private and family life. Having regard to that conclusion, the Court is of the view that it is not necessary to examine separately the applicant Government's allegations under Article 8 concerning the implantation of Turkish settlers in northern Cyprus.***

Notes and Questions

1.   *Scope of Classic "First Generation" Rights.* Does the Court's interpretation of the "procedural obligation" to protect life under the Convention impose a positive obligation on Turkey to account for missing persons? Has the European Court of Human Rights redefined torture in holding Turkey accountable for the "prolonged state of acute anxiety" endured by relatives of missing persons? What implications do these findings have for protection of economic, social and cultural rights under the political and civil rights provisions of the Convention? *Cf.* ¶ 219, wherein the Court suggests the possibility that the right to life might require the state to provide minimum health care.

2.   *Language and Culture.* On what basis did the Court find that Turkey had an obligation to provide secondary education in the Greek language in Northern Cyprus? Compare the decision in the *Belgian Linguistics Case* in Section B.2, *infra.* Why did the Court decline to discuss the allegation that Greek culture in northern Cyprus had been eliminated by the influx of settlers from Turkey? Is it reluctant to recognize a collective right to culture in Article 8's protection for "private and family life?" Is the implantation of Turkish settlers a violation of Article 49 of the Fourth Geneva Convention? What is, or should be, the relationship between the conventional law of occupation and other human rights instruments?

3.   *Resolution of the Cyprus Conflict?* As the opinion notes, Turkish Cypriots declared the creation of the "Turkish Republic of Northern Cyprus," which has been recognized only by Turkey. After decades of stalemate, a referendum was held on a reunification plan drafted by U.N. Secretary-General Kofi Annan, in anticipation of the country's May 1, 2004, accession to the European Union. The plan was rejected by Greek Cypriots, however, therefore only the Greek side was admitted to the E.U.

THE CONVENTION FOR THE PROTECTION OF CULTURAL PROPERTY IN THE EVENT OF ARMED CONFLICT

The Hague, May 14, 1954 249 U.N.T.S. 215 (*entered into force* August 7, 1956)

*Article 1. Definition of cultural property****

(a) movable or immovable property of great importance to the cultural heritage of every people, such as monuments of architecture, art or history, whether religious or secular; archaeological sites; groups of buildings which, as a whole, are of historical or artistic interest; works of art; manuscripts, books and other objects of artistic, historical or archaeological interest; as well as scientific collections and important collections of books or archives or of reproductions of the property defined above;***

Article 5. Occupation

1. Any High Contracting Party in occupation of the whole or part of the territory of another High Contracting Party shall as far as possible support the competent national authorities of the occupied country in safeguarding and preserving its cultural property.

2. Should it prove necessary to take measures to preserve cultural property situated in occupied territory and damaged by military operations, and should the competent national authorities be unable to take such measures, the Occupying Power shall, as far as possible, and in close co-operation with such authorities, take the most necessary measures of preservation.***

Article 18. Application of the convention

1. [T]he present Convention shall apply in the event of declared war or of any other armed conflict which may arise between two or more of the High Contracting Parties, even if the state of war is not recognized by one or more of them.

2. The Convention shall also apply to all cases of partial or total occupation of the territory of a High Contracting Party, even if the said occupation meets with no armed resistance.

3. If one of the Powers in conflict is not a Party to the present Convention, the Powers which are Parties thereto shall nevertheless remain bound by it in their mutual relations.***

Article 28. Sanctions

The High Contracting Parties undertake to take, within the framework of their ordinary criminal jurisdiction, all necessary steps to prosecute and impose penal or disciplinary sanctions upon those persons, of whatever nationality, who commit or order to be committed a breach of the present Convention.

Notes and Questions

In *Autocephalous Greek Orthodox Church of Cyprus v. Goldberg*, 917 F. 2d 278 (7th Cir. 1990), the court refused to recognize the authority of a decree by the Turkish administration in Northern Cyprus, purporting to divest the Church of title to a sixth-century mosaic that had been stolen after virtually all Greek Cypriots were forced to flee the area. Applying Indiana state law, the court ruled that an art dealer who had purchased the mosaics (broken into pieces by the vandals) on the international market was required to return them to the Church, finding that "the Church has a valid, superior and enforceable claim to these Byzantine treasures." *Id.* at 294. In a concurring opinion, circuit judge Cudahy suggested that the attempt by the Turkish military authorities to divest the Church of ownership of the mosaics might also contravene the 1954 Hague Convention, and thus "would not demand the deference of American courts." *Id.* at 296. Is this the type of activity that the Convention was designed to curtail?

LETTER FROM THE AMERICAN ANTHROPOLOGICAL
ASSOCIATION TO PRESIDENT GEORGE W. BUSH

April 16, 2003

Dear Mr President:

During the military preparations and subsequent implementation of military actions for the war in Iraq, the cultural community in the United States and elsewhere repeatedly pointed out our war responsibilities to the cultural heritage of Iraq. As the cradle of human civilization, the Iraqi territory holds unique artistic, historic, archaeological and scientific evidence of the birth of the very civilization of which our Nation forms part. During the fierce fighting of the past few weeks, we were relieved to see that our military leaders and the coalition partners took extreme precautions to avoid targeting cultural sites along with other non-military places. It was also comforting to receive reports that our armed forces have conducted inspections at some of the important archaeological sites.

This past weekend, however, the situation changed drastically. Alarming news and dismaying television images confirmed the wholesale pillaging and wanton destruction of the cultural treasures of Iraq by local thugs and thieves. The extensive looting and vandalism of the completely unguarded National Museum in Baghdad have caused irreversible losses in a cultural patrimony that belongs not only to the Iraqis, but to all mankind. Other reports have indicated similar pillaging in Mosul. If this process is allowed to go unchecked, the catastrophic destruction may easily spread to hundreds of more remote, but equally valuable sites.

As leaders of national organizations representing millions of Americans who believe that the material culture inherited from our ancestors constitutes one of humanity's greatest treasures, we call on you to use all means at your disposal to stop the pillaging and protect cultural sites and institutions of Iraq. These include historic sites, historic urban districts, cultural landscapes, buildings of unusual aesthetic values, archaeological sites, museums, libraries, archives and other repositories of cultural property and human memory.

We also call for the protection of our colleagues, the Iraqi professionals and scholars who work in these places, thus enabling them to carry out their stewardship duties. During this period of extreme hardship, they need professional support and reinforcement to assist them with their tasks. The United States and our Coalition Partners should provide this assistance at once.

We call for the immediate adoption of strict and detailed plans to attempt to recover the stolen artifacts and reconstruct the Iraqi national collections.***

Finally, we call upon our Government to ensure that the funds destined for postwar recovery and reconstruction provide sufficient funds for the field of cultural resources. This would include funds for the immediate physical and institutional reconstruction of Iraqi cultural agencies and organizations, as well as long-term funds for strengthening institutional and professional capacity in order to ensure a permanent protection and effective management of heritage resources and historic sites of Iraq.

We place at your disposal the joint and individual expertise of our organizations to assist our country in providing this protection and recovering the stolen artifacts for the people of Iraq.

The return to freedom of the Iraqi people must include the freedom to enjoy the great heritage resources inherited from their ancestors. As the only source of real authority in Iraq at the present time, the United States and its Coalition Partners bear an obligation to all Americans, to all Iraqis, to the world community and to generations yet unborn to protect the cultural resources of Iraq.***

Further Reading

For further reading on the law of belligerent occupation, *see*, DAVID KRETZMER, THE OCCUPATION OF JUSTICE: THE SUPREME COURT OF ISRAEL AND THE OCCUPIED TERRITORIES (2002); ERNST H. FEILCHENFELD, THE INTERNATIONAL ECONOMIC LAW OF BELLIGERENT OCCUPATION (2000); KARMA NABULSI, TRADITIONS OF WAR: OCCUPATION, RESISTANCE, AND THE LAW (1999); EYAL BENVENISTI, THE INTERNATIONAL LAW OF OCCUPATION (1993); GERHARD VON GLAHN, THE OCCUPATION OF ENEMY TERRITORY: A COMMENTARY ON THE LAW AND PRACTICE OF BELLIGERENT OCCUPATION (1957); DORIS A. GRABER, THE DEVELOPMENT OF THE LAW OF BELLIGERENT OCCUPATION, 1863–1914: A HISTORICAL SURVEY (1949); Ardi Imseis, *On the Fourth Geneva Convention and the Occupied Palestinian Territory*, 44 HARV. INT'L L.J. 65 (2003); I. Maxine Marcus, *Humanitarian Intervention without Borders: Belligerent Occupation or Colonization?* 25 HOUS. J. INT'L L. 99 (2002); Davis P. Goodman, *The Need for a Fundamental Change in the Law of Belligerent Occupation*, 37 STAN. L. REV. 1573–1608 (1985); Yoram Dinstein, *The International Law of Belligerent Occupation and Human Rights*, 8 ISR. Y.B. HUM. RTS. 104 (1978).

B. LANGUAGE

1. *Language Rights: Political Rights, Cultural Rights, and the Politics of Culture*

INTERNATIONAL COVENANT ON CIVIL AND POLITICAL RIGHTS: ARTICLE 27

In those States in which ethnic, religious or linguistic minorities exist, persons belonging to such minorities shall not be denied the right, in community with the other members of their group, to enjoy their own culture, to profess and practice their own religion, or to use their own language.

HUMAN RIGHTS COMMITTEE, GENERAL COMMENT 23

General Comment 23(50) (Art. 27):
Rights of Minorities, CCPR/C/21/Rev.1/Add.5 (Apr. 26, 1994)

5.1.   The terms used in article 27 indicate that the persons designed to be protected are those who belong to a group and who share in common a culture, a religion and/or a language. Those terms also indicate that the individuals designed to be protected need not be citizens of the State party.***

5.2.   Article 27 confers rights on persons belonging to minorities which "exist" in a State party.*** Those rights simply are that individuals belonging to those minorities should not be denied the right, in community with members of their group, to enjoy their own culture, to practise their religion and speak their language. Just as they need not be nationals or citizens, they need not be permanent residents. Thus, migrant workers or even visitors in a State party constituting such minorities are entitled not to be denied the exercise of those rights.***

The existence of an ethnic, religious or linguistic minority in a given State party does not depend upon a decision by that State party but requires to be established by objective criteria.***

6.1.   Although article 27 is expressed in negative terms, that article, nevertheless, does recognize the existence of a "right" and requires that it shall not be denied.*** Positive measures of protection are, therefore, required not only against the acts of the State party itself, whether through its legislative, judicial or administrative authorities, but also against the acts of other persons within the State party.

6.2.   Although the rights protected under article 27 are individual rights, they depend in turn on the ability of the minority group to maintain its culture, language or religion. Accordingly, positive measures by States may also be necessary to protect the identity of a minority and the rights of its members to enjoy and develop their culture and language and to practise their religion, in community with the other members of the group.***

7.   With regard to the exercise of the cultural rights protected under article 27, the Committee observes that culture manifests itself in many forms, including a particular way of life associated with the use of land resources, especially in the case of indigenous peoples. That right may include such traditional activities as fishing or hunting and the right to live in reserves protected by law. The enjoyment of those rights may require positive legal measures of protection and measures to ensure the effective participation of members of minority communities in decisions which affect them.

Notes and Questions

The United States ratified the ICCPR in 1992. The ratification contains no reservations or understandings with respect to Article 27, but does include the customary declaration "that the provisions of articles 1 through 27 of the Covenant are not self-executing."

MART RANNUT, THE COMMON LANGUAGE PROBLEM

MIKLOS KONTRA ED., LANGUAGE: A RIGHT AND A RESOURCE:
APPROACHING LINGUISTIC HUMAN RIGHTS 99–114 (1999)

The aim of this article is to map how the power structure of society is reflected in language policies, and to trace the development from the idealistic notion of state-nation-language of two centuries ago through its accommodation to the needs of contemporary society. The role of language as the cornerstone of nation building has been maintained, along with the role of a common language as the primary generator of linguistic homogenization.***

Societal Structure

The current political situation is significantly different from the Herderian times that produced the triad of *état-nation-langue*, idealized up to the beginning of the 20th century. It led to the generalization of nation-states in the wake of collapsed empires that were unable, among other things, to cope with linguistic diversity and implement integrative and cost-effective language policies. The solution for facilitating societal balance was found in the form of the nation-state, which in turn was shown itself to be a temporary one as well. With the birth of international organizations, transnational corporations, and global media as well as information networks, a good deal of power has shifted away from states, save the most totalitarian ones. Simultaneously, the homogeneity of a state showed itself to be wishful thinking in most cases, as seen in the revival of hidden minorities and increasing migrational flows.

Therefore, in order to describe the current position with societal power as an integral element, a new paradigm is necessary. One component of this paradigm has to be *language*, which over time plays an even more central role, penetrating all domains of society and leaving less room for negotiations over language choice. The reason for the importance of language seems to be its transformation into a political object and resource similar to other politically negotiable objects and resources in both the primordial and instrumental senses. From the primordial point of view, language is seen as an integrative component of ethnicity and a natural symbol of inherent group rights, simultaneously being, due to the exclusive nature of language, one of the most common differentiating factors in human affairs. Any negative change that may be linked to language is thus a visible signal for those operating in defense of their ethnolinguistic interests. In this way language has maintained its role as an organizer of ethnic divisions within society.***

Simultaneously, the increase of the instrumental value of language and its exclusive characteristics, rearranging society on a language domination axis, is inevitably connected to the economic and social well-being of its speakers. Thus language acts as a regulator of unequal access to power. Taken together, both primordial and instrumental values tend to produce a synergetic effect, making language one of the most important facts in the contemporary political scene.

Another component in our modernized triad seems to be *power*, which on a macro scale was earlier available only to states.*** The sort of language policy adopted is the consequence of decisions taken in other domains, for achieving goals that usually have little in common with language issues. Behind these domains, two opposite factors, called the market and market correctives, influence development, creating order and structure in the domain concerned. In this way, human rights—linguistic human rights included—act as correctives to the free market; they should guarantee that the basics needed for survival and for the sustenance of a dignified life overrule the law of supply and demand. Thus they should be outside market forces. A state is successful if these two factors are in balance.***

The third component in our paradigm is *society*—the subject that makes use of power and is simultaneously an agent of it. In contemporary times the term *society* need no longer denote a nation, or even any homogenous language group, but rather a group with common or similar (linguistic) interests. The inherent structure of a society is influenced by the power relations channeled through the instrumental functions of language, as well as by language directly, through its primordial aspect. In order to reveal the connections between these three components, we focus on the issues of power reflected through societal structures functioning in a language.

Underlying Power Structure ***

The role of language in state bureaucracy has been constantly increasing. Though the sovereignty of a state in international terms has diminished, its role as a major purveyor of services, employment and economic opportunities has expanded. It provides a wide range of services and regulatory mechanisms for the society. Thus, states explicitly value instrumental aspects of language and claim to base their language policies on principles deriving from these instrumental values. However, language has been skillfully implemented on a major scale by states as a power instrument of the elite, though as a hidden agenda. A government may directly affect the political power structure of the state by making language knowledge a predominant factor in access to employment and education opportunities, as native speakers of the official language are more likely to reach the higher echelons of the state machinery. The central role of a language means professional and bureaucratic employment opportunities, linked with significant economic benefits. Thus, while the introduction of the common language may seem to promote instrumental value, it is, in fact, linked to primordial value, simultaneously producing inequality.

The interests of the state are usually complemented by the market economy, playing a major role in power structures. In this domain the two values surface again. Language is not used only as a neutral means of communication. Economic losses and gains are immediately reflected through the status of those beneficiaries, speakers of a certain language. In this way, language is viewed as a resource and knowledge of a particular language may provide a privileged position.***

Policies

Although in reality there may be linguistic conflict, the common language policy focuses on the aim of linguistic homogenization. The policy is based on three pillars: societal (it is usually based on majority), political (promoted by states) and economic (it is claimed to be cost-effective in business). For this purpose the state has chosen at least one language in the discharge of its duties, rejecting several others and constraining economic opportunities for their speakers. In this way language has become highly politicized, being intimately connected to economic and social mobility.*** And even if no official language policies are declared, this is also a form of policy, negatively influencing linguistically dominated groups, as the state's liberal *laissez-faire* policy benefits dominance.***

[T]he common language decision is inevitable, as [Fernand de Varennes] remarks: no government can afford to provide services and official documents in every language spoken in its territory, thus a state must necessarily restrict itself to the use of a limited number of languages in its contacts with its citizens.***

Linguistic Human Rights

States, which represent the nation-building interest, have obligations vis-à-vis their citizens and residents concerning languages. These obligations are firmly rooted in linguistic human rights, providing standards for the use and acquisition of both minority and national languages. These obligations also cover the issue of the common language. These rights may be found in domestic as well as international law.

In most cases, international law does not deal with languages directly but regards them as

1. markers of identity and dignity;

2. of persons belonging to a specific group;

3. expressed in various language functional domains.

This enables us to use three approaches in clarifying the concept of language rights. The most traditional one is based on the target groups, the second on human rights principles, and the third on the functional domains of language within society. There are three main threatened groups, groups which commonly represent linguistic characteristics different from their environments: linguistic minorities, aliens, and indigenous peoples. Usually they are politically and economically disadvantaged and subjected to acculturation pressures and social discrimination. Although international law recognizes collective rights, all the linguistic rights are attached to individuals. Thus persons belonging to these groups may enjoy these rights in community with other members of their group. The second approach is based on universal human rights principles of non-discrimination, freedom of expression and minority protection.

[L]inguistic human rights in education may be regarded as essentially covering two rights: the right to learn an official language in the country of residence, in its standard form and the right to learn and use one's mother tongue.***

The second distinction concerns whether these rights should be collective, that is, to be enjoyed by the minorities as groups, or individual, to be enjoyed by the individual member of the group. The main practical concern of those who stress individual rights at the cost of collective rights has to do with the implications for individuals upon whom duties will be imposed in the name of group rights that might be detrimental to their well-being.

Individual language rights include the right not to suffer undue interference and discrimination. [T]his means the right to speak any language at home and on the streets and to use it in private correspondence, to keep native names and surnames, to use it within one's cultural and religious institutions, including newspapers, radio stations and community centers, etc. However, the respect for individual rights does not serve to heal collective social disparities, as individual rights derive from the individual's personal capacity and appear to be insufficient to sustain vulnerable languages.

Collective language rights protect language group membership and its identity. [Pierre A.] Coulombe distinguishes two kinds of collective language rights: the right to sustain one's language and the right to live in one's language. In the first case the State's duties might include public funding for minority language schools, governmental services in the minority language, or even affirmative action programs for the hiring of members of the linguistic minority in the public services. The second case would require that one's language be used and understood in a variety of everyday situations, both private and public. The distinction between these two seems to be at the level of the participation of the majority and the obligations of the State concerning minority maintenance.***

However, there is no right to the continued survival of a linguistic group, as there is no basis for preferring its vital interests to those of a comparable group. Instead, [Denise] Réaume suggests the right to linguistic security ***. The right to linguistic security can be understood as the right to pursue the normal processes of language transmission and maintenance without interference. This would preclude any attempt to prohibit the use of the language in the normal range of contexts or to prohibit the education of children of the group in the language. A collective right to linguistic security would impose duties on other groups not to use numerical superiority or political dominance to prohibit the use of a minority language. Where two or more languages share social structures, there is a threat that social institutions such as the public school system or governmental structures will be organized to suit majority practices exclusively (although such organization may be advertised as the common language policy with a purely instrumental goal). In order to avoid such an outcome, a fair compromise, based on the principles of minority protection, should be found.

Contemporary international law provides the space for introducing fair and acceptable solutions for the maintenance and management of minority languages only in the case of the goodwill of the state. However, most of the principles in international law are insufficient to require that. They either belong to soft law, are too implicit, or deal mostly with individual rights, and establish the ultimate limit to minority protection to the detriment of the majority language.

Notes and Questions

1. *South African Language Policy.* South Africa has 11 official languages. The official languages of the Republic are Sepedi, Sesotho, Setswana, siSwati, Tshivenda, Xitsonga, Afrikaans, English, isiNdebele, isiXhosa and isiZulu. S. Afr. Const. ch. 1, art. 6, § 1. It is interesting to note that the languages are not listed in alphabetical order, but "according to usage, starting with the language lowest on the numerical ladder." Apparently, the purpose was "to change the order preference in a deliberate attempt to give textual prominence to languages lacking widespread usage." H.A. Strydom, *Minority Rights Issues in Post-Apartheid South Africa*, 19 LOY. L.A. INT'L & COMP. L.J. 873, 898 (1997). In the South African context, official status entails the right to speak or be addressed in one's language (and perhaps even in any of the official languages) in dealings with public administration at the national level. In legal proceedings, a party to the litigation, an accused person, or a witness may choose one of the official languages with which to communicate. And at the regional level, provincial legislatures can declare any of the national official languages as their official language with two restrictions. First, the approval must be by two-thirds majority. Second, the official status of any language at the time of the commencement of the Constitution may not be diminished. The second restriction was motivated by the desire to protect the official status of Afrikaans which it was feared may be demoted given the fact that it is viewed as the language of apartheid by the overwhelming majority of South Africans. Even in South Africa not all languages are recognized as official such as the languages spoken by Indian minorities. Adeno Addis, *Cultural Integrity and Political Unity: The Politics of Language in Multilingual States*, 33 ARIZ. ST. L.J. 719, 775 n.193 (2001). For more on South Africa *see* Chapter 8, *infra*.

2. Echoing Rannut's observation, Fernand de Varennes writes that "There is not in the present state of international law an unqualified 'right to use a minority language,' but there are a number of existing rights and freedoms that affect the issue of language

preferences and use by members of a minority or by the State." Fernand de Varennes, *The Existing Rights of Minorities in International Law, in,* LANGUAGE: A RIGHT AND A RESOURCE: APPROACHING LINGUISTIC HUMAN RIGHTS 117 (Miklos Kontra *et al.* eds., 1999). Foremost among those existing rights that can protect language are the "right to freedom of expression, and non-discrimination or the right of persons belonging to a linguistic minority to use their language with other members of their group." *Id.* at 118. In addition to these individual rights, de Varennes notes that "[t]here is a growing legal acceptance in treaties that states have a positive obligation to provide public services, benefits and privileges in the language of a specific minority in appropriate circumstances—especially where the numbers and concentration of the speakers of a minority language and the state's resources make this a viable option." *Id.* at 127.

ADENO ADDIS, CULTURAL INTEGRITY AND POLITICAL UNITY: THE POLITICS OF LANGUAGE IN MULTILINGUAL STATES

33 ARIZ. ST. L.J. 719, 730–47, 760–85 (2001)

[The author describes five extant responses by states to linguistic pluralism, and proposes a sixth, which seeks to balance the opposing interests of linguistic diversity, and the cultural and personal goods that derive therefrom, and the uniformity required for an effective and stable political community.]

II. INSTITUTIONAL AND CONCEPTUAL RESPONSES TO LINGUISTIC DIVERSITY ***

B. *The Ostrich Response*

One way to respond to the linguistic multiplicity that defines one's country may be simply to deny that there are any linguistic minorities within one's territorial borders. France has followed this path. When it signed the European Charter of Regional and Minority Languages, France made a declaration that it has no linguistic minorities in its territory. Even though there are regional languages within its borders (not to mention linguistic minorities from France's former colonies), France denied that languages other than French exist and are spoken. It is ironical that while it suppresses minority languages within its borders, France is often at the forefront promoting French as a minority language in other countries such as Canada and Belgium.

Of course, if there are no minority languages within one's border, then one does not see any problem with declaring the "only" language as the official language, for such an act is viewed simply as a formality, declaring legally official what is already de facto official. Indeed, that is precisely what France did. Not only did it declare that no linguistic minorities existed within its jurisdiction, but France also amended Article 2 of its constitution in 1992 to declare that "[t]he language of [the] Republic is French." But of course denial is no solution.***

Indeed *** the idea of declaring one language as the official language even when it is de facto official may have a divisive rather than a unifying effect. It will look, and sometimes it may be intended, as a symbolic assertion of the cultural hegemony of the "official" linguistic group. When a language is used as a symbol of the political community, as France intended to do, as Sri Lanka attempted to do in the late 1950s in relation to Sinhala, the language of the Sinhalese majority, and as the "English Only" or

"Official English" movement in the United States is intent on doing, the clear message sent to those who speak a regional or a minority language is that they are indeed cultural outsiders. As the civil war that has ravaged Sri Lanka attests, this form of symbolic politics is likely to have a disuniting function.

C. *Political Divorce as a Response* ***

Political divorce, formally known as secession, as a general response to the issue of linguistic diversity is as impractical as it is dangerous. It is impractical because not all groups that want to assert or maintain their linguistic identity live in a defined territory, nor do they desire to separate. Some may simply want some form of recognition of their linguistic identity within the political entity. Political divorce may unwisely define the choices as either cultural assimilation or separation.***

Also, even if practical, political divorce may be dangerous as a general response to the fact of linguistic multiplicity. First, in many countries, especially in Africa, where political boundaries were drawn arbitrarily by colonial powers, nation-states are, to borrow a phrase from John Dunn, "communities of fate and not of choice." There are, in some cases, hundreds of language-groups within a nation-state. Given that fact, political divorce as the answer to linguistic diversity would lead to a rather chaotic situation. The map of virtually every African country would have to be redrawn.***

D. *The Individualist Liberal Response*

The most common response to linguistic diversity *** starts with the classical liberal position that since the individual is the ultimate agent of action, a moral right can attach only to that agent. According to this view, the notion of language rights should be seen only in individualist terms. The individual has the right to use the language of his or her choice in association with others and the government is prohibited from discriminating against anyone on the basis of language use when it distributes benefits and resources, or when it performs its traditional function of protecting citizens. The individualist liberal position in relation to minority language use is, therefore, defined by three distinct but interrelated claims. First, the right is an individual right, not a group right.*** Second, the right is a negative right. That is, the only requirement on the government is to respect the private associational rights of individuals to use the language of their choice. The state is not morally required to officially recognize, affirm or materially support any language. Third, the domain within which this individual right is to be exercised is in the private realm.***

Although the preservation and diversity of languages may be viewed and celebrated as a good thing by those who adhere to the individualist liberal position, such diversity is not the direct object of the position, but a consequence of affirming the private right of association. Indeed, the individualist liberal would simply allow private associations and the market (unconstrained by governmental regulation) to decide which minority languages should survive and in what form they survive, in the same way that the market determines which goods are worth keeping in circulation and which are not. And if none survive, it is not necessarily a source of regret, for it may indicate that individuals have made the choice that it is not worth preserving the language.***

As my brief description of the individualist liberal's position suggests, for those committed to that position there is no irreconcilable tension between embracing diversity of languages and the adoption (either officially or unofficially) of a national or official language(s).***

The individualist liberal position can be challenged on both its theoretical and practical assumptions. To start with, as Will Kymlicka has argued, the individualist liberal (to whom he refers as the "orthodox liberal") is not consistent on the moral principle that is supposed to animate her opposition to group rights. While on the one hand she talks about equality of individuals and the moral imperative of treating people as individuals in the domestic context, on the other hand she may be quite happy, and even enthusiastic, about maintaining territorial borders that define the nation-state and argue that it is morally defensible to treat people either as "citizens" or "non-citizens," rather than as individuals. If the principle of "equal respect for persons" or "equal right for individuals" is one that defines the attitude and posture of the individualist, then the unquestioned commitment to closing off borders to non-citizens cannot be reconciled with that commitment. The issue here is not whether territorial communities should be defended. But if they are to be defended, it will have to be under the terms and conceptual constructs that the individualist finds a "metaphysical absurdity," that of the notion of group right.***

F. The Nationalist Liberal Response

*** The nationalist liberal is in agreement with the individualist liberal that ultimately it is the individual, not groups, to whom a moral right could attach. In this regard the nationalist liberal, like the individualist liberal, is committed to individual liberty and autonomy. But *** unlike the individualist liberal, the nationalist liberal believes that there are certain activities that can only be enjoyed and maintained within a group. Under this view, the existence and flourishing of the group become conditions for the flourishing of the individual. The capacity of the individual to maintain and develop his or her language is dependent on whether the linguistic group to which he or she belongs lives on and flourishes. The nationalist is thus not hostile to the notion of collective or group rights, except that the right is justified on consequentialist grounds.

Second, the nationalist liberal sees culture, including language, as an important good, through which individuals make sense of the world around them and through which choices become meaningful to them. For the nationalist liberal, to affirm group rights is to vindicate individual rights through the recognition of what Kymlicka calls "group-differentiated right." The argument here is that "individual freedom is tied in some important way to membership in one's national [cultural] group." If one sees culture this way, then its existence and sustenance cannot be left to the workings of the market. Given the possibility, even likelihood, that minorities would be outbid and outvoted for resources regarding the cultivation and maintenance of their culture, here their language, leaving it to the market may essentially condemn that culture or language to its demise.

Third, and more importantly, the nationalist liberal makes a distinction, on moral and pragmatic grounds, between immigrant linguistic minorities and national linguistic minorities. Immigrant linguistic minorities are those minorities who have chosen to join a new country. Regardless of the circumstances under which they left their country of origin, they have chosen to join this particular polity and have elected to make it their new home.*** National linguistic minorities, on the other hand, are those that have been incorporated into the larger political entity of which they are now a part either by force or through other non-voluntary means.*** For the nationalist liberal, a national minority has a more defensible moral right for the recognition and affirmation of its language than an immigrant ethnic minority. The distinction is based on a number of grounds. First, as I have already adverted to, a group that had its own language and was incorporated into a larger group, typically by force, or through other means without its consent or desire, has, at a minimum, a moral right to have its language affirmed and recognized.***

Second, the practical difficulties of such affirmation and recognition are seen to be less and less troublesome in the case of national, as opposed to, say, immigrant ethnic minorities.*** Third, it is arguable that the demand for official recognition of one's language will be more intensely put forward by national minorities than by other ethnic minorities, such as immigrant minorities.***

*** While the nationalist liberal seems to have struck a reasonable balance between a concern for linguistic minorities (linguistic identities) on the one hand and the administrative, political and financial realities on the other hand by recognizing only the claim of national minorities, I believe there are some drawbacks in the argument that counsel skepticism towards the approach the nationalist liberal urges upon us.

First, it may not always be easy to determine what is a national minority, as opposed to another minority, for purposes of language recognition.*** The more the national minority's claim appears not to depend on the notion of rectificatory justice, the more it appears to be qualitatively similar to the claims of other minorities.

There is something else that needs to be mentioned about the rather strange notion of consent that informs the nationalist's attempt to distinguish national and immigrant minorities. It is a very thin notion of consent that would hold that a group of political refugees who left their country of origin to come to the new country to avoid being locked up or even murdered have done so voluntarily.***

Second, even if we are able to determine easily what a national minority is and hence limit the universe of language right holders, the nationalist liberal, even with this narrower universe of groups, may have underestimated the financial and administrative costs and problems this will pose to many nation-states. Take Africa, for example. The borders of many of the countries in that continent were drawn by European colonizers, sitting in European capitals, oblivious of, and even contemptuously indifferent to, the consequence of drawing borders in that manner. As a result, virtually every country is composed of many ethnic and linguistic groups, hundreds in some countries, each of which will qualify as a national group. Given this, the financial and administrative costs may be prohibitive for many of these countries to give official or national recognition to all the languages of the national groups. The moral right will have to be assessed in light of the administrative and financial demands that such a right puts on others.***

III. CRITICAL PLURALISM AND THE ISSUE OF INGUISTIC DIVERSITY

Let me first briefly explore what I mean by the phrase "critical pluralism." Here, I am interested in the pluralism among ethnic and national (or cultural) groups, specifically among linguistic groups. Critical pluralism starts with the proposition that the stumbling block to building democratic governance in multiethnic and multilingual nation-states is not the mere existence of those differences, rather, it is how those differences are treated or managed. Ironically, it is often the very drive to assure the integrated nation or national community at the expense of linguistic diversity that has led to conflicts and destruction.*** The idea of the unified nation is often viewed as implying that a single language occupies all public space. Critical pluralism is pluralist in a sense that in its vision, the good society does not eliminate or transcend group language differences. Indeed, it argues that attempts to eliminate or suppress these differences have had tragic consequences, both for the physical integrity of the nation-state, which is supposed to be helped with the elimination of these differences, as well as for the groups which are seen to be threats to that integrity.***

As for the consequences for minorities, such as linguistic minorities, of attempts to cure the nation-state from differences, the response of dominant majorities may range from the most brutal to the most genteel, but each leads to tragic consequences. The most extreme response can be referred to as "total negation." Here, dominant groups view minorities, including linguistic minorities, as a negation of the majority, culturally or otherwise.*** What took place in the Balkans (Bosnia, Croatia and Kosovo) may be an example of that.***

But the most genteel response to differences—assimilation—is often no less tragic, for it is often premised on the notion of transforming the "Other" into a version of the dominant majority which views itself as representing the normal. Assimilation is a process of "normalizing" the "Other." That normalization could take place through a process that requires minorities, such as linguistic minorities, "to follow the cultural practices of the majority, and generally to adjust [their] social practices and rituals to conform to those of the majority."*** In the language area, the Official English/English Only movement in the United States offers the assimilationist model in its starkest and rather coercive form. The movement is informed by the belief that Latinos would be normal Americans (and would be treated as such) if they extinguished their linguistic identities. It is not only the moral and cultural costs that make the assimilationist model unattractive, but the political cost as well. In many circumstances, such an approach has led to a situation where minority groups "retreat into a fundamentalist reassertion of a culturally-based distinctiveness," which has led to political strife and violence. When the parochialism of a group is threatened, the response is that the group becomes more radically parochial.***

Critical pluralism does more than "protect" the minority. What makes the version of pluralism that I embrace "critical," rather than "paternalistic," is that it views the ideal of politics in a heterogeneous public as being one which simultaneously affirms group differences while linking those groups in a process of institutional dialogue, where the various narratives interrogate each other. Put simply, critical pluralism is about providing the necessary resources and institutional space for minority groups to articulate a positive identity while also opening the various groups for critical examination and interrogation by other individuals and groups. This dialogic process may force each group critically to reflect upon its own particularity and contingency and perhaps even how the "Other" is partly sedimented in it. Critical pluralism will adhere simultaneously to the politics of difference and dialogue.

How does critical pluralism deal with the issue of linguistic minorities? In its pluralist mode, it is concerned with providing resources for linguistic minorities so as to enable those minorities to maintain and develop their language and culture.***

What would this entail in institutional terms? In some countries, where there are just a few languages in a nation-state (two to four), recognizing linguistic minorities as a cultural group may be accomplished by recognizing all the languages within the polity as official languages. Switzerland has done that in a rather complicated way. This would be the most generous form of recognition and affirmation. Indeed, recognizing all languages as official may simultaneously accomplish the twin features of critical pluralism—affirming linguistic diversity while linking the various groups in some form of institutional dialogue—if all members of the political community are required to have some degree of competence in all the languages.

But, the notion of equal official status for all languages within the nation-state would be implausible in most circumstances. In many countries, especially developing countries, it will be financially prohibitive and administratively chaotic to implement such a policy. Many of those countries have, not two or three, but numerous linguistic groups within their borders. Ethiopia, for example, is an ethnically and linguistically diverse country. There are about eighty languages spoken in the country. The notion that all languages in the country must or could be given equal status officially is as unrealistic as it is a recipe for chaos and disaster.***

What is clear is that for a language to prosper, even to survive, it will need public space that includes the institutions of modern life.*** One of the most effective ways in which a language could be preserved and cultivated is in the educational realm.***

There is one of two ways in which minority languages could play a role in the educational field. The most generous way, from the point of view of minority languages, would be to allow the use of the minority language as the medium of educational instruction at the elementary level in the state school system, if numbers would justify such an offering.***

The second, and what I call the minimalist position, will allow linguistic minorities to teach their language as a subject at the elementary, and perhaps secondary, level while maintaining the national language(s) as the medium of instruction at all levels.*** What is important, however, is to give these minorities the chance to make the choices for themselves. A choice, a trade-off, made by the relevant minority group is likely to have legitimacy among members of the group and, hence, will reduce the chance of conflict among the various linguistic groups.***

Of course, one obvious way of linking the various linguistic groups is to have a national language that all members of the political community are required to master and through which the various linguistic groups could deliberate about and negotiate on common national concerns. [T]here is no reason why the adoption of a national language should entail that all public space would be occupied by that language alone. In the educational realm, for example, minority languages could share public space, to varying degrees, with the national language(s). Spain, for example, requires all Spaniards to know the Castilian language, but it also allows the seventeen autonomous communities within it to have another official language. Currently, six of the seventeen autonomous communities, comprising just over forty percent of the entire Spanish population, have adopted the regional language as co-official language.

Another area where minority languages and a national language could share public space is in the area of communications. Here, minorities could simultaneously use their language to communicate among themselves, to formulate and develop positions and issues that are of significance to the minority before that issue could be presented to the larger public for consideration and adoption. In some sense, all this argument suggests is that we think of political communities as composed of many publics rather than one public.***

Notes and Questions

Consider the treatment of linguistic rights in Article 5(c) of the Convention Against Discrimination in Education, adopted by the United Nations Educational, Scientific and Cultural Organization: "It is essential to recognize the right of members of national minorities to carry on their own educational activities, including the maintenance of schools and, depending on the educational policy of each State, the use or the teaching of their own language.***" Convention Against Discrimination in Education (Dec. 14, 1960), *available at* http://www.un.org/womenwatch/asp/user/list.asp?ParentID= 10739. Could such a right prevent national minorities from being full participants in the community as a whole? Should there be a reciprocal provision for the majority population to learn minority languages?

KENNETH L. KARST, PATHS TO BELONGING: THE CONSTITUTION AND CULTURAL IDENTITY

64 N.C. L. REV. 303, 306–15 (1986)

I. GROUP IDENTITY AND SELF-DEFINITION ***

[D]istrust of the members of a different cultural group flows from fear, not just of the unknown but the fear that outsiders threaten our own acculturated views of the natural order of society.

To grow up in a culture is to learn that some ways of acting or talking or thinking are right and other ways are wrong. The very sense of one's identity is connected intimately with this learning ***. Thus, each of us carries around inside the image of what Erikson calls a "negative identity," which must be repressed if we are to live up to the expectations of our cultural groups. Outsiders—those who belong to other groups with other ways of behaving—make us uncomfortable partly because our own acculturation has not prepared us to understand their behavior and partly because they serve so handily as screens on which we can project our own negative identities. Our psychic response is predictable: we want to repress the outsiders' incorrect, foreign ways.***

II. NATIVISM IN AMERICA

American nativism has taken three main forms: religious, political, and racial. Late in the nineteenth century, racism broadened into Anglo-Saxonism, which extended its hostility and its assumptions of superiority beyond race to ethnicity. In 1924 Congress responded to this "tribal mood" by radically restricting immigration and imposing "national origins" quotas on immigrants, based on the composition of the population as it had been in 1890, before the great influx of "new immigrants" from southern and eastern Europe. The 1924 law had a dramatic effect on immigration, but was not a sharp break with the American past. Nativism's main techniques—exclusion, forced conformity, and domination—were known and used in the colonial era.

A. Nativism as Forced Conformity

The "melting pot" did not become part of the national vocabulary until the production of Israel Zangwill's play of that name in 1908, but the idea was as old as the Nation itself.***

[T]here are two cultural requisites for belonging: participation in the Nation's political culture with the "new rank" of citizen and rejection of Old World ways of thinking
and behaving in favor of the culture of the "new race." [T]he assumption is that a cultural outsider can become a member of the American community only by relinquish-
ing his or her native culture and embracing the prevailing American cultural norms.

The metaphor of "melting," popular from the early nineteenth century up to the
1930s, implied that both the "old stock" and more recent immigrants would contribute
to a new American character and culture. The term, however, often served as an inte-
grationist cloak for public and private programs aimed at forcing new Americans and
their children to conform to the attitudes and behavior of their British-American pred-
ecessors. This "Anglo conformity" came to dominate the idea of assimilation and thus
to redefine the qualifications for being received in our Alma Mater's lap. To call a group
"unassimilable" implied that its people were not sufficiently similar to the old stock to
adapt themselves to a society defined by the old stock's world view, and, therefore, that
they should be excluded from the American community. Congress implemented this
policy of exclusion by denying members of various racial or cultural groups entry into
the country and by denying the benefits of citizenship both to certain classes of aliens
and to Americans who were black or Indian.***

The campaign for "Americanization" of foreigners, which gained intensity during
the First World War and culminated in the mania of the Red Scare of 1919 to 1920, was
the most determined national effort to coerce conformity to the values and behavior of
the dominant culture. Government officials joined with private organizations in a zealous effort to press foreign-born Europeans to become citizens, to abandon their native
languages for English, to suppress any expression of "anti-American" sympathies, and
generally to demonstrate a "[c]onformist loyalty intolerant of any values not functional
to it." The message was simple: to belong, you must conform.***

State and local governments joined the Americanization crusade with gusto. Fifteen
states banned teaching foreign languages in public schools; some states required public school teachers to be citizens; and Oregon required all elementary school children
to attend public rather than private schools. A few years later the United States Supreme
Court held both the ban on teaching foreign languages and the ban on private elementary schools unconstitutional. The Governor of Iowa was not to be outdone; he
issued a proclamation forbidding the use of foreign languages in public and private
schools, in church services, and even in conversations in public places or over the telephone. In an action eventually upheld by the Supreme Court, Cincinnati prohibited
aliens from operating poolrooms, to prevent foreigners from gathering in places where
they would be away from Americanizing influences. Most of these measures and proposals plainly violate today's constitutional norms. In the frenzy of 1915 to 1920, however, if the foreign-born were to have Americanization imposed upon them, the courts
were only rarely disposed to intervene.

Forced conformity, like other forms of cultural domination, is not just a means of
securing power or material advantage for members of the dominant culture. The coercion of a cultural minority to conform also reassures the majority that its own group
identities are secure.*** Intercultural domination, however, always rests on shaky foundations, for it is based on fear. The dominant group seeks to impose its norms precisely
because it sees those norms threatened by the others' very presence.***

2. LANGUAGE AND EDUCATION

MEYER v. STATE OF NEBRASKA

262 U.S. 390 (1923)

Plaintiff in error was tried and convicted in the District Court for Hamilton County, Nebraska, under an information which charged that on May 25, 1920, while an instructor in Zion Parochial School, he unlawfully taught the subject of reading in the German language to Raymond Parpart, a child of ten years, who had not attained and successfully passed the eighth grade. The information is based upon "An act relating to the teaching of foreign languages in the State of Nebraska," approved April 9, 1919, which follows:

"Section 1. No person, individually or as a teacher, shall, in any private, denominational, parochial or public school, teach any subject to any person in any language other than the English language.

"Sec. 2. Languages, other than the English language, may be taught as languages only after a pupil shall have attained and successfully passed the eighth grade as evidenced by a certificate of graduation issued by the county superintendent of the county in which the child resides."***

The Supreme Court of the State affirmed the judgment of conviction. [I]t held that the statute forbidding this did not conflict with the Fourteenth Amendment, but was a valid exercise of the police power. The following excerpts from the opinion sufficiently indicate the reasons advanced to support the conclusion.

"The salutary purpose of the statute is clear. The legislature had seen the baneful effects of permitting foreigners, who had taken residence in this country, to rear and educate their children in the language of their native land. The result of that condition was found to be inimical to our own safety. To allow the children of foreigners, who had emigrated here, to be taught from early childhood the language of the country of their parents was to rear them with that language as their mother tongue. It was to educate them so that they must always think in that language, and, as a consequence, naturally inculcate in them the ideas and sentiments foreign to the best interests of this country.***

The problem for our determination is whether the statute as construed and applied unreasonably infringes the liberty guaranteed to the plaintiff in error by the Fourteenth Amendment. "No State shall *** deprive any person of life, liberty, or property, without due process of law."

While this Court has not attempted to define with exactness the liberty thus guaranteed, the term has received much consideration and some of the included things have been definitely stated. Without doubt, it denotes not merely freedom from bodily restraint but also the right of the individual to contract, to engage in any of the common occupations of life, to acquire useful knowledge, to marry, establish a home and bring up children, to worship God according to the dictates of his own conscience, and generally to enjoy those privileges long recognized at common law as essential to the orderly pursuit of happiness by free men. [Citations omitted.] The established doctrine is that this liberty may not be interfered with, under the guise of protecting the public interest, by legislative action which is arbitrary or without reasonable relation to some purpose within the competency of the State to effect.***

The American people have always regarded education and acquisition of knowledge as matters of supreme importance which should be diligently promoted.*** Corresponding to the right of control, it is the natural duty of the parent to give his children education suitable to their station in life; and nearly all the States, including Nebraska, enforce this obligation by Compulsory laws.

Practically, education of the young is only possible in schools conducted by especially qualified persons who devote themselves thereto. The calling always has been regarded as useful and honorable, essential, indeed, to the public welfare. Mere knowledge of the German language cannot reasonably be regarded as harmful. Heretofore it has been commonly looked upon as helpful and desirable. Plaintiff in error taught this language in school as part of his occupation. His right thus to teach and the right of parents to engage him so to instruct their children, we think, are within the liberty of the Amendment.***

It is said the purpose of the legislation was to promote civic development by inhibiting training and education of the immature in foreign tongues and ideals before they could learn English and acquire American ideals; and "that the English language should be and become the mother tongue of all children reared in this State." It is also affirmed that the foreign born population is very large, that certain communities commonly use foreign words, follow foreign leaders, move in a foreign atmosphere, and that the children are thereby hindered from becoming citizens of the most useful type and the public safety is imperiled.

That the State may do much, go very far, indeed, in order to improve the quality of its citizens, physically, mentally and morally, is clear; but the individual has certain fundamental rights which must be respected. The protection of the Constitution extends to all, to those who speak other languages as well as to those born with English on the tongue. Perhaps it would be highly advantageous if all had ready understanding of our ordinary speech, but this cannot be coerced by methods which conflict with the Constitution—a desirable end cannot be promoted by prohibited means.***

The desire of the legislature to foster a homogeneous people with American ideals prepared readily to understand current discussions of civic matters is easy to appreciate. Unfortunate experiences during the late war and aversion toward every characteristic of truculent adversaries were certainly enough to quicken that aspiration. But the means adopted, we think, exceed the limitations upon the power of the State and conflict with rights assured to plaintiff in error. The interference is plain enough and no adequate reason therefore in time of peace and domestic tranquility has been shown.

The power of the State to compel attendance at some school and to make reasonable regulations for all schools, including a requirement that they shall give instructions in English, is not questioned. Nor has challenge been made of the State's power to prescribe a curriculum for institutions which it supports. Those matters are not within the present controversy. Our concern is with the prohibition approved by the Supreme Court.*** No emergency has arisen which renders knowledge by a child of some language other than English so clearly harmful as to justify its inhibition with the consequent infringement of rights long freely enjoyed. We are constrained to conclude that the statute as applied is arbitrary and without reasonable relation to any end within the competency of the State.***

Notes and Questions

Post-Civil War U.S. government policy toward Native Americans emphasized assimilation, in part through obliteration of their languages. For example, then-Commissioner of Indian Affairs, J. D. C. Atkins, opined in his 1887 report that:

> [T]eaching an Indian youth in his own barbarous dialect is a positive detriment to him. The first step to be taken toward civilization, toward teaching the Indians the mischief and folly of continuing in their barbarous practices, is to teach them the English language. The impracticability, if not impossibility, of civilizing the Indians of this country in any other tongue than our own would seem to be obvious, especially in view of the fact that the number of Indian vernaculars is even greater than the number of tribes.

J. D. C. Atkins, *Annual Report of the Commissioner of Indian Affairs* (1887), *excerpted in* JAMES CRAWFORD ED., LANGUAGE LOYALTIES: A SOURCE BOOK ON THE OFFICIAL ENGLISH CONTROVERSY 51 (1992). This policy also contributed to the erosion of the history and culture of Native Americans, an intimate part of which is the tradition of oral storytelling, through which indigenous people transmit cultural norms:

> Oral history is a living history in that the learners are involved with the historian on a personal level. They hear, listen, remember, and memorize events expressed in the flowing, soft sounds of their own language, describing the collective experiences of the people just as if they happened only the moment before. Their history is more than cold, impersonal words on pieces of paper.

Henrietta Whiteman, White Buffalo Woman, *in* THE AMERICAN INDIAN AND THE PROBLEM OF HISTORY 162, 165 (CALVIN MARTIN ED., 1987).

THE BELGIAN LINGUISTICS CASE

European Court of Human Rights, (1979–80) 1 E.H.R.R. 252

*** 2. The applicants, who are parents of families of Belgian nationality, applied to the Commission both on their own behalf and on behalf of their children under age, of whom there are more than 800. Pointing out that they are French-speaking or that they express themselves most frequently in French, they want their children to be educated in that language.

Alsemberg, Beersel, Antwerp, Ghent, Louvain and Vilvorde, where the signatories of five of the six applications live, belong to the region considered by law as Dutch-speaking, whereas Kraainem has since 1963 formed part of a separate administrative district with a 'special status.' In all of these districts ('communes'), part of the population—in some cases a large part—is French-speaking.

3. Though the six applications differ on a number of points, they are similar in many respects. For the time being it is sufficient to note that in substance they complain that the Belgian State:

— does not provide any French-language education in the municipalities where the applicants live or, in the case of Kraainem, that the provision made for such education is, in their opinion, inadequate;

— withholds grants from any institutions in the said municipalities which may fail to comply with the linguistic provisions of the legislation for schools;

— refuses to homologate leaving certificates issued by such institutions;

— does not allow the applicants' children to attend the French classes which exist in certain places;

— thereby obliges the applicants either to enrol their children in local schools, a solution which they consider contrary to their aspirations, or to send them to school in the 'Greater Brussels district,' where the language of instruction is Dutch or French according to the child's mother-tongue or usual language or in the 'French-speaking region' (Walloon area). Such 'scholastic emigration' is said to entail serious risks and hardships.

4. The applications *** allege that Articles 8 and 14 of the Convention and Article 2 of the Protocol have been violated.***

THE LAWS ON THE USE OF LANGUAGES IN EDUCATION IN BELGIUM ***

9. Article 17 of the Belgian Constitution of 7 February 1831 provides:

Education shall be unrestricted; all measures of restriction are prohibited.*** Public education provided at the expense of the State shall also be regulated by law.

Moreover, Article 23 provides:

The use of the languages spoken in Belgium is optional. This matter may be regulated only by law and only as regards the acts of the public authority and the judicial matters.

These two articles have never been amended.

10. *** Until 1932, parents in Belgium enjoyed a fairly wide freedom with regard to the language of education. [A] child's maternal or usual language, determined on the declaration made by the head of the family, was the language of instruction in each grade throughout the country.*** Thanks to fairly broad interpretation of the text, some Dutch-speaking parents had their children educated in French. In some parts of Flanders there were, in addition to Dutch-language primary schools, State and private French-language primary schools, whilst secondary education was provided sometimes in French, sometimes half in French and half in Dutch.

11. A fundamental change was made to this system by the Act of 14 July 1932 ' on language regulations in primary and intermediate education.'***

This law established a distinction between the regions considered to be unilingual and the areas recognised as bilingual. In the former, 'the Flemish area,' 'the Walloon area' and 'the German-speaking communes,' the language of education was in principle that of the region, while study of a second language (whether national or not) was compulsory only in secondary classes.***

In the Brussels urban area and bilingual communes on the linguistic boundary, the language of instruction was to be the child's maternal or usual language; teaching of the second national language was to be compulsory.***

Each head of family was required to make a declaration stating his children's maternal or usual language in so far as that determined which system was applicable, but the correctness of the declaration might be subject to verification.

[The] penalty for non-observance of the Act [was] the refusal or withdrawal, as the case may be, of the school subsidies.***

14. *** Chapter V of the Act of 30 July 1963 institutes 'linguistic control.'*** [The legislation] results in the complete withdrawal of subsidies from provincial, commune or private schools providing, in the form of non-subsidised classes and in addition to the instruction given in the language prescribed by the linguistic Acts, full or partial instruction in another language.

15. Articles 17 and 23, cited above, of the Belgian Constitution, have not been revised and are therefore still in force. Consequently, children of the Dutch-language area, including Flemish-speaking children, may be taught in their area in French—or in any other language—by their parents, a private tutor or an unsubsidised private school. A head of family who takes advantage of this facility incurs no punishment and is complying with the obligations to have his children educated provided the education given meets academic and technical requirements laid down by law.***

JUDGMENT ***

I. THE MEANING AND SCOPE OF ARTICLE 2 OF THE PROTOCOL AND OF ARTICLES 8 AND 14 OF THE CONVENTION

B. *Interpretation adopted by the Court ***

3. By the terms of the first sentence of [Article 2] 'no person shall be denied the right to education.'***

The negative formulation indicates, as is confirmed by the preparatory work, that the Contracting Parties do not recognise such a right to education as would require them to establish at their own expense, or to subsidise, education of any particular type or at any particular level. However, it cannot be concluded from this that the State has no positive obligation to ensure respect for such a right as is protected by Article 2 of the Protocol. As a 'right' does exist, it is secured, by virtue of Article 1 of the Convention, to everyone within the jurisdiction of a Contracting State.

To determine the scope of the 'right to education,' within the meaning of the first sentence of Article 2 of the Protocol, the Court must bear in mind the aim of this provision. It notes in this context that all member States of the Council of Europe possessed, at the time of the opening of the Protocol to their signature, and still do possess, a general and official educational system. There neither was, nor is now, therefore, any question of requiring each State to establish such a system, but merely of guaranteeing to persons subject to the jurisdiction of the Contracting Parties the right, in principle, to avail themselves of the means of instruction existing at a given time.

The Convention lays down no specific obligations concerning the extent of these means and the manner of their organisation or subsidisation. In particular, the first sentence of Article 2 does not specify the language in which education must be conducted in order that the right to education should be respected.*** However, the right to education would be meaningless if it did not imply, in favour of its beneficiaries, the right to be educated in the national language or in one of the national languages, as the case may be.***

6. The second sentence of Article 2 of the Protocol does not guarantee a right to education; this is clearly shown by its wording:

> In the exercise of any functions which it assumes in relation to education and to teaching, the State shall respect the right of parents to ensure such education and teaching in conformity with their own religious and philosophical convictions.

This provision does not require of States that they should in the sphere of education or teaching, respect parents' linguistic preferences, but only their religious and philosophical convictions. To interpret the terms 'religious' and 'philosophical' as covering linguistic preferences would amount to a distortion of their ordinary and usual meaning and to read into the Convention something which is not there. Moreover the preparatory work confirms that the object of the second sentence of Article 2 was in no way to secure respect by the State of a right for parents to have education conducted in a language other than that of the country in question; indeed in June 1951 the Committee of Experts which had the task of drafting the Protocol set aside a proposal put forward in this sense. Several members of the Committee believed that it concerned an aspect of the problem of ethnic minorities and that it consequently fell outside the scope of the Convention. The second sentence of Article 2 is therefore irrelevant to the problems raised in the present case.

7. According to the express terms of Article 8 (1) of the Convention, ' everyone has the right to respect for his private and family life, his home and his correspondence.'***

[M]easures taken in the field of education may affect the right to respect for private and family life or derogate from it; this would be the case, for instance, if their aim or result were to disturb private or family life in an unjustifiable manner, *inter alia* by separating children from their parents in an arbitrary way.***

The Court will therefore examine the facts of the case in the light of the first sentence of Article 2 of the Protocol as well as of Article 8 of the Convention.

8. According to Article 14 of the Convention, the enjoyment of the rights and freedoms set forth therein shall be secured without discrimination ('sans distinction aucune') on the ground, *inter alia*, of language; and by the terms of Article 5 of the Protocol, this same guarantee applies equally to the rights and freedoms set forth in this instrument. It follows that both Article 2 of the Protocol and Article 8 of the Convention must be interpreted and applied by the Court not only in isolation but also having regard to the guarantee laid down in Article 14.***

10. *** Article 14 does not forbid every difference in treatment in the exercise of the rights and freedoms recognised.***

[T]he principle of equality of treatment is violated if the distinction has no objective and reasonable justification. The existence of such a justification must be assessed in relation to the aim and effects of the measure under consideration, regard being had to the principles which normally prevail in democratic societies. A difference of treatment in the exercise of a right laid down in the Convention must not only pursue a legitimate aim: Article 14 is likewise violated when it is clearly established that there is no reasonable relationship of proportionality between the means employed and the aim sought to be realised.

In attempting to find out, in a given case, whether or not there has been an arbitrary distinction, the Court cannot disregard those legal and factual features which characterise the life of the society in the State which, as a Contracting Party, has to answer for the measure in dispute. In so doing, it cannot assume the rôle of the competent national authorities, for it would thereby lose sight of the subsidiary nature of the international machinery of collective enforcement established by the Convention. The national authorities remain free to choose the measures which they consider appropriate in those matters which are governed by the Convention.***

11. In the present case, the Court notes that Article 14, even when read in conjunction with Article 2 of the Protocol, does not have the effect of guaranteeing to a child or to his parent the right to obtain instruction in a language of his choice. The object of these two Articles, read in conjunction, is more limited: it is to ensure that the right to education shall be secured by each Contracting Party to everyone within its jurisdiction without discrimination on the ground, for instance, of language.***

II. THE SIX QUESTIONS REFERRED TO THE COURT ***

A. *As to the first question* ***

7. The first question concerns exclusively those provisions of the Acts of 1932 and 1963 which prevented, or prevent, in the regions which are by law deemed unilingual, the establishment or subsidisation by the State of schools not in conformity with the general linguistic requirements.

In the present case, this question principally concerns the State's refusal to establish or subsidise, in the Dutch unilingual region, primary school education (which is compulsory in Belgium) in which French is employed as the language of instruction.

Such a refusal is not incompatible with the requirements of the first sentence of Article 2 of the Protocol. In interpreting this provision, the Court has already held that it does not enshrine the right to the establishment or subsidising of schools in which education is provided in a given language.*** In the unilingual regions, both French-speaking and Dutch-speaking children have access to public or subsidised education, that is to say, to education conducted in the language of the region.

The legal provisions in issue, moreover, do not violate Article 8 of the Convention. It is true that one result of the Acts of 1932 and 1963 has been the disappearance in the Dutch unilingual region of the majority of schools providing education in French. Consequently, French-speaking children living in this region can now obtain their education only in Dutch, unless their parents have the financial resources to send them to private French-language schools. This clearly has a certain impact upon family life when parents do not have sufficient means to enrol their children in a private school ***.***

Harsh though such consequences may be in individual cases, they do not involve any breach of Article 8. This provision in no way guarantees the right to be educated in the language of one's parents by the public authorities or with their aid. Furthermore, insofar as the legislation leads certain parents to separate themselves from their children, such a separation is not imposed by this legislation: it results from the choice of the parents who place their children in schools situated outside the Dutch unilingual region with the sole purpose of avoiding their being taught in Dutch, that is to say, in one of Belgium's national languages.

It remains to be decided whether the legal provisions criticised violate the first sentence of Article 2 of the Protocol or Article 8 of the Convention, read in conjunction with Article 14.

Here again, the reply must be negative. It is true that the legislature has instituted an educational system which, in the Dutch unilingual region, exclusively encourages teaching in Dutch, in the same way as it establishes the linguistic homogeneity of education in the French unilingual region.***

[However,] Article 14 does not prohibit distinctions in treatment which are founded on an objective assessment of essentially different factual circumstances and which, being based on the public interest, strike a fair balance between the protection of the interests of the Community and respect for the rights and freedoms safeguarded by the Convention.

In examining whether the legal provisions which have been attacked satisfy these criteria, the Court finds that their purpose is to achieve linguistic unity within the two large regions of Belgium in which a large majority of the population speaks only one of the two national languages.*** Such a measure cannot be considered arbitrary. To begin with, it is based on the objective element which the region constitutes. Furthermore, it is based on a public interest, namely, to ensure that all schools dependent on the State and existing in a unilingual region conduct their teaching in the language which is essentially that of the region.

This part of the legislation does not violate the rights of the individual. On this point, the Court observes that the provisions which are challenged concern only official or subsidised education. They in no way prevent, in the Dutch-unilingual region, the organisation of independent French-language education, which in any case still exists there to a certain extent. The Court, therefore, does not consider that the measures adopted in this matter by the Belgian legislature are so disproportionate to the requirements of the public interest which is being pursued as to constitute a discrimination contrary to Article 14 of the Convention, read in conjunction with the first sentence of Article 2 of the Protocol or with Article 8 of the Convention.

B.   As to the second question

8.   The second question concerns the issue of *** the complete withdrawal of subsidies from provincial, commune or private schools providing, in the form of non-subsidised classes and in addition to the instruction given in the language prescribed by the linguistic Acts, full or partial instruction in another language.***

13.   *** The legislation to which the first question has reference does not permit the establishment or functioning, in the Dutch unilingual region, of official or subsidised schools providing education in French. The legislation with which the second question is concerned goes further; by the total withdrawal of subsidies, it makes it impossible, in the same region, for teaching in French to be conducted as a secondary activity by a subsidised Dutch-language school.***

[T]he effects of this measure are solely of such a kind as to prevent subsidised and unsubsidised education being conducted in the same school. They in no way affect the freedom to organise, independently of subsidised education, private French-language education.

Hence, the legal and administrative measures in question create no impediment to the exercise of the individual rights enshrined in the Convention ***.

C. As to the third question

[Six communes on the outskirts of Brussels formed a "separate administrative district" with its own special status and distinct rules regarding education:]

A. Teaching shall be in Dutch.

The second language may be taught at the primary level to the extent of four hours a week in the second form and eight hours a week in the third and fourth forms.

B. Nursery and primary schooling may be given to children in French if that is their maternal or usual language and if the head of the family resides in one of these communes.

Such schooling may be provided only on the request of 16 heads of families residing within the commune.

The commune to which such an application is made must organise such schooling.

The teaching of the second national language shall be compulsory in primary schools to the extent of four hours a week in the second form and eight hours a week in the third and fourth forms.***

4. Decision of the Court

19. [T]he special status conferred *** on six communes on the periphery of Brussels, including Kraainem, does not violate [the Convention].***

The six communes in question belong to an area which is by tradition Dutch-speaking. In consideration of the large number of French-speaking persons who are resident there, the legislature has established a system which departs from the principle of territoriality. It makes the organisation of official or subsidised education in French subject to the deposit of a request by 16 heads of family living in the commune in question; moreover, this education is compulsorily accompanied by a study in depth of Dutch. In so doing, the Act does not go outside limits drawn according to objective criteria and is based on a public interest. Furthermore, the establishment and maintenance of education conducted in French is possible in the communes concerned. Finally, the fact that this education is tied to a study in depth of Dutch, whereas the study of French remains optional in Dutch schools in the same communes, does not constitute a discrimination as the latter belong to a region which is, by tradition, Dutch-speaking.***

E. As to the fifth question

26. The fifth question concerns the issue as to whether or not, in the case of the applicants, there is a violation *** in so far as [the Acts] prevent certain children, solely on the basis of their parents' place of residence, from attending French-language schools at Louvain and in the six communes on the outskirts of Brussels which enjoy a 'special status,' including Kraainem.***

The city of Louvain and the adjacent commune of Heverlee are both situated in the 'Dutch-language region'; they are a few kilometres from the linguistic frontier. [S]pecial, technical and secondary French-language classes, attached to the University of Louvain, have *** been able to survive.

Whether situated at Louvain or at Heverlee, the classes in question enjoy financial support from the State. Admission is granted, however, to four types of children only: children who attended the classes during the school year 1962–1963; children of employees, students and teaching staff of the University as well as members of their family living with them; children of foreign nationality, when the head of the family belongs to an international law organisation, embassy, legation or consulate; and finally, children of French-speaking Belgians if the head of the family lives outside the Dutch-speaking region.

28. [In the six communes on the outskirts of Brussels that enjoy a "special status"] nursery and primary school teaching must be conducted in French for children when it is their maternal or usual language, 'if the head of the family resides in one of the communes' and if '16 heads of family residing within the commune' concerned request it.

[A] child cannot attend the French classes [in these special communes] if the head of the family resides elsewhere *** for example, in the unilingual Flemish region.***

4. Decision of the Court

32. *** Louvain and Heverlee belong to the Dutch-unilingual region. Although the legislature has authorised the maintenance of French-language education there, it has done so, above all, in consideration of the needs arising from the bilingual nature of the University of Louvain.*** Essentially, they are accorded to the French-speaking teaching staff, employees and students of the University of Louvain in whose absence the establishment could no longer retain its bilingual character. Likewise, if the French classes at Louvain and Heverlee are still open to children of French-speaking families living outside the Dutch-unilingual region, it is because they serve as teacher training classes for the bilingual University of Louvain. As for the privilege granted to certain children of foreign nationality, this is justified by the customs of international courtesy. Consequently, the exclusion of French-speaking children living in the Dutch unilingual region whose parents are not members of the teaching staff, students or employees of the University, does not amount to a discriminatory measure in view of the legitimacy of the specific objective of the legislature.

The situation is completely different in the case of the six communes 'with special facilities,' which belong to the agglomeration surrounding Brussels, the capital of a bilingual State and an international centre. According to the information supplied to the Court, the number of French-speaking families in these communes is high; they constitute, up to a certain point, a zone of a 'mixed' character.

It is in recognition of this fact that section 7 of the Act of 2 August 1963 departed from the territorial principle ***. It provides that the language of instruction is Dutch in the six communes; it requires, nevertheless, the organisation, for the benefit of children whose maternal or usual language is French, of official or subsidised education in French at the nursery and primary levels, on condition that it is asked for by 16 heads of family. However, this education is not available to children whose parents live outside the communes under consideration. The Dutch classes in the same communes, on the other hand, in principle accept all children, whatever their maternal or usual language and place of residence of their parents. The residence condition affecting therefore only one of the two linguistic groups, the Court is called upon to examine whether there results therefrom a discrimination contrary to Article 14 of the Convention, read in conjunction with the first sentence of Article 2 of the Protocol or with Article 8 of the Convention.

Such a measure is not justified in the light of the requirements of the Convention in that it involves elements of discriminatory treatment of certain individuals, founded even more on language than on residence.

First, this measure is not applied uniformly to families speaking one or the other national language. The Dutch-speaking children resident in the French unilingual region, which incidentally is very near, have access to Dutch-language schools in the six communes, whereas French-speaking children living in the Dutch unilingual region are refused access to French-language schools in those same communes. Likewise, the Dutch classes in the six communes are open to Dutch-speaking children of the Dutch unilingual region whereas the French classes in those communes are closed to the French-speaking children of that region.

Such a situation, moreover, contrasts with that which arises from the possibility of access to French-language schools in the Greater Brussels District, which are open to French-speaking children irrespective of their parents' place of residence.

It consequently appears that the residence condition is not imposed in the interest of schools, for administrative or financial reasons: it proceeds solely, in the case of applicants, from considerations relating to language. Furthermore, the measure in issue does not fully respect, in the case of the majority of the applicants and their children, the relationship of proportionality between the means employed and the aim sought. In this regard the Court, in particular, points out that the impossibility of entering official or subsidised French-language schools in the six communes 'with special facilities' affects the children of the applicants in the exercise of their right to education, all the more in that there exist no such schools in the communes in which they live.

[T]he measure in question is, in this respect, incompatible with the first sentence of Article 2 of the Protocol, read in conjunction with Article 14 of the Convention.***

F. As to the sixth question

33. The sixth question concerns the issue of [the] absolute refusal to homologate certificates relating to secondary schooling not in conformity with the language requirements in education.

1. The Facts

34. At the end of each stage of secondary schooling, the teaching establishments deliver to pupils a certificate specifying the course of studies followed and that they have been successfully completed.***

The certificate granted on the completion of secondary studies states that the holder is considered suitable for higher education. However, it acquires legal value only after 'homologation' by a board ***. Homologation is granted only if the studies comply with the legal requirements.

The holder of a non-homologated certificate may go on to higher studies, for instance at a university, and obtain a 'non-recognised' ('scientifique') university degree, but not a 'legally recognised' or 'academic' degree. However, only 'legally recognised' or 'academic' degrees give access to a number of posts and professions: careers in the administration or the judiciary, the Bar, the profession of notary and the medical profession, etc. The holders of non-homologated certificates who aspire to such professions or who wish to acquire a legally recognised or academic degree, must take a full examination before a body called 'the Central Board.'

35. The homologation of a certificate depends on compliance not only with the technical and academic requirements laid down by law but also with those which concern the educational linguistic system.***

4. Decision of the Court

42. The provisions of the Acts of 1932 and 1963, which provided for or still provide for the refusal of homologation of certificates relating to secondary schooling not in conformity with the language requirements in education, infringe neither the first sentence of Article 2 of the Protocol nor Article 8 of the Convention considered by themselves.***

[T]he children who, as holders of a certificate that is not admissible for homologation for purely linguistic reasons, must take an examination before the Central Board, are in a less advantageous position than those pupils who have obtained a school leaving certificate which is admissible for homologation. However, this inequality in treatment in general results from a difference relating to the administrative system of the school attended: in the first of the two cases mentioned above, the position usually is that the establishment is one which, by virtue of the legislation in force, is not subject to school inspection; in the second, on the other hand the certificate is necessarily issued by a school which is subjected to such inspection. Thus, the State treats unequally situations which are themselves unequal. It does not deprive the pupil of the profit to be drawn from his studies. The holder of a certificate not admissible for homologation may, indeed, obtain official recognition of his studies by presenting himself before the Central Board. The exercise of the right to education is not therefore fettered in a discriminatory manner within the meaning of Article 14.***

For these reasons, THE COURT:

1. *Holds*, by eight votes to seven, that section 7 (3) of the Act of 2 August 1963 does not comply with the requirements of Article 14 of the Convention read in conjunction with the first sentence of Article 2 of the Protocol, in so far as it prevents certain children, solely on the basis of the residence of their parents, from having access to the French-language schools existing in the six communes on the periphery of Brussels invested with a special status, of which Kraainem is one;

Reserves for the applicants concerned the right, should the occasion arise, to apply for just satisfaction in regard to this particular point; and

2. *Holds*, unanimously, with regard to the other points at issue, that there has been and there is no breach of any of the articles of the Convention and the Protocol invoked by the applicants.

Notes and Questions

1. The court employed what U.S. constitutional scholars would characterize as a "rational basis" test to determine whether the Belgian legislation violated principles of equal protection. Thus, the government needed to demonstrate only that there was an "objective and reasonable justification" for the language policies. What were these justifications? How would they have fared under a "strict scrutiny" analysis? Would such an analysis infringe on state sovereignty, or the deference this international court believes is owed to national authorities? Should a more "compelling" reason be required in light of the long-standing tensions between the majority Dutch- and minority French-speaking populations in Belgium? (These tensions erupted into riots in the 1960s, leading to a succession of governments through the 1980s.)

2. Consider the discussion of the distinctions between individual and collective approaches to language rights in the articles by Rannut and Addis in Section B.1, *supra.* Does the court recognize any positive rights in Article 2? Would a group rights analysis have produced a different result? How would a collective approach assess the state's refusal to homologate certificates issued by schools that do not conform to the language policy?

3. The court states that the second sentence of Article 2 cannot be read to include language as a possible philosophical choice of parents. Is this narrow construction textually mandated?

4. Was the outcome of the *Belgian Linguistics Case* a victory for language rights? Some commentators, such as Rannut, Section B.1, *supra*, prefer to focus on the single positive holding favoring language rights for minorities, rather than to dwell on the five contrary outcomes. Other scholars, however, regard the case as a largely negative milestone:

> While the court found discrimination—a violation of Article 2 in combination with Article 14—on the basis of language, there was no broader finding of a right to education in one's native language. On this broader principle, while the court found "the right to be educated in the national language or in one of the national languages," it underlined that the second sentence of Article 2 "does not require of States that they should, in the sphere of education or teaching, respect parents' linguistic preferences, but only their religious and philosophical considerations.***
>
> Once again, the court focuses on the right to education, declining to require states to provide native language teaching even in regions where minorities make up a substantial proportion of the population. Thus, while states are required to educate minorities like other citizens, they are not required in the schools—as in administration, courts, or local governments—to recognize the right to linguistic freedom of minorities. As one observer noted: "[T]here is little scope for the pillar of minority protection, which pursues substantive equality through rights that contribute to the preservation and promotion of the distinctive identity of minorities."

Charles F. Furtado, Jr., *Guess Who's Coming To Dinner? Protection For National Minorities In Eastern and Central Europe Under the Council of Europe*, 34 COLUM. HUM. RTS. L. REV. 333, 351–52 (2003). This suboptimal outcome, according to Geri L. Haight, can be attributed to the fact that the case is "pragmatic":

It has been asserted that it would be unrealistic to mandate that a state provide full funding for every linguistic minority, regardless of their numbers, to schooling in their respective minority language. A pure minority language educational system could be an unruly drain on state resources and may result in decreasing the cumulative quality of education on a national level.*** Since 1968, when the *Belgian Linguistics Case* was decided, the right to minority language education has been codified in numerous international human rights documents. It is possible that the *Belgian Linguistics Case* would be decided differently in light of the increasing emphasis placed upon the protection of linguistic and cultural rights within the international legal framework.

Geri L. Haight, *Unfulfilled Obligations: The Situation Of The Ethnic Hungarian*, 4 ILSA J. INT'L & COMP. L. 27, 77 (1997). According to Haight, "The most relevant statement on minority language education is [the Parliamentary Assembly's] Recommendation 1201 both because of its explicit discussion of minority language education and its binding nature" upon governments which have adopted its language:

COUNCIL OF EUROPE PARLIAMENTARY ASSEMBLY RECOMMENDATION 1201 (1993)

on an additional protocol on the rights of minorities to the European Convention on Human Rights, Assembly debate on February 1, 1993 (22nd Sitting) (see Doc. 6742, report of the Committee on Legal Affairs and Human Rights, Rapporteur: Mr. Worms; and Doc. 6749, opinion of the Political Affairs Committee, Rapporteur: Mr. de Puig). Text adopted by the Assembly on February 1, 1993 (22nd Sitting)

Preamble

The member states of the Council of Europe signatory hereto;

1.   Considering that the diversity of peoples and cultures with which it is imbued is one of the main sources of the richness and vitality of European civilisation,

2.   Considering the important contribution of national minorities to the cultural diversity and dynamism of the states of Europe;

3.   Considering that only the recognition of the rights of persons belonging to a national minority within a state and the international protection of those rights are capable of putting a lasting end to ethnic confrontations, and thus of helping to guarantee justice, democracy, stability and peace;

4.   Considering that the rights concerned are those which any person may exercise either singly or jointly;

5.   Considering that the international protection of the rights of minorities is an essential aspect of the international protection of human rights and, as such, a domain for international co-operation,

Have agreed as follows:

Section I: Definition

Article 1

For the purposes of this convention the expression "national minority" refers to a group of persons in a state who

    a.   reside on the territory on that state and are citizens thereof,

    b.   maintain long standing, firm and lasting ties with that state,

    c.   display distinctive ethnic, cultural, religious or linguistic characteristics,

    d.   are sufficiently representative, although smaller in number than the rest of the population of that state or of a region of that state,

    e.   are motivated by a concern to preserve together that which constitutes their common identity, including their culture, their traditions, their religion or their language.***

*Section 3: Substantive rights ****

Article 7

1.   Every person belonging to a national minority shall have the right freely to use his/her mother tongue in private and in public, both orally and in writing. This right shall also apply to the use of his/her language in publications and in the audiovisual sector.

2.   Every person belonging to a national minority shall have the right to use his/her surname and first names in his/her mother tongue and to official recognition of his/her surname and first names.

3.   In the regions in which substantial numbers of a national minority are settled, the persons belonging to a national minority shall have the right to use their mother tongue in their contacts with the administrative authorities and in proceedings before the courts and legal authorities.

4.   In the regions in which substantial numbers of a national minority are settled, the persons belonging to that minority shall have the right to display in their language local names, signs, inscriptions and other similar information visible to the public. This does not deprive the authorities of their right to display the above-mentioned information in the official language or languages of the state.

Article 8

1.   Every person belonging to a national minority shall have the right to learn his/her mother tongue and to receive an education in his/her mother tongue at an appropriate number of schools and of state educational and training establishments, located in accordance with the geographical distribution of the minority.

2.   The persons belonging to a national minority shall have the right to set up and manage their own schools and educational and training establishments within the framework of the legal system of the state.

Article 9

If a violation of the rights protected by this protocol is alleged, every person belonging to a national minority or any representative organisation shall have an effective remedy before a state authority.

MARTIN LUTHER KING JUNIOR ELEMENTARY SCHOOL CHILDREN ET AL. v. ANN ARBOR SCHOOL DISTRICT BOARD

473 F. Supp. 1371 (E.D. Mich. 1979)

The issue before this court is whether the defendant School Board has violated Section 1703(f) of Title 20 of the United States Code as its actions relate to the 11 black children who are plaintiffs in this case and who are students in the Martin Luther King Junior Elementary School operated by the defendant School Board. It is alleged that the children speak a version of "black English," "black vernacular" or "black dialect" as their home and community language that impedes their equal participation in the instructional programs, and that the school has not taken appropriate action to overcome the barrier.

The statute under which this action is now pressed reads as follows:

No State shall deny equal educational opportunity to an individual on account of his or her race, color, sex, or national origin, by ***

(f) the failure by an educational agency to take appropriate action to overcome language barriers that impede equal participation by its students in its instructional programs.

A major goal of American education in general, and of King School in particular, is to train young people to communicate both orally (speaking and understanding oral speech) and in writing (reading and understanding the written word and writing so that others can understand it) in the standard vernacular of society. The art of communication among the people of the country in all aspects of people's lives is a basic building block in the development of each individual. Children need to learn to speak and understand and to read and write the language used by society to carry on its business, to develop its science, arts and culture, and to carry on its professions and governmental functions. Therefore, a major goal of a school system is to teach reading, writing, speaking and understanding standard English.

The problem in this case revolves around the ability of the school system, King School [in] particular, to teach the reading of standard English to children who, it is alleged, speak "black English" as a matter of course at home and in their home community (the Green Road Housing Development).

This case is not an effort on the part of the plaintiffs to require that they be taught "black English" or that their instruction throughout their schooling be in "black English," or that a dual language program be provided.*** It is a straightforward effort to require the court to intervene on the children's behalf to require the defendant School District Board to take appropriate action to teach them to read in the standard English of the school, the commercial world, the arts, science and professions. This action is a cry for judicial help in opening the doors to the establishment. Plaintiffs' counsel says that it is an action to keep another generation from becoming functionally illiterate.***

HISTORY OF LITIGATION TO DATE

This action was commenced on July 28, 1977 by 15 black pre-school or elementary school children residing in a housing project located on Green Road in Ann Arbor, Michigan, all of whom either were attending or were eligible to attend Martin Luther King Junior Elementary School in that city.*** They demanded the establishment of a program which would enable plaintiffs to overcome the cultural, social and economic deprivations which allegedly prevented them in varying degrees from making normal progress in school.***

[The Court identifies legal arguments raised previously by plaintiff and rejected.]

ISSUES

Section 1703(f) of Title 20, U.S.C., set out above, is the sole remaining basis for the plaintiffs' claims.

The issues raised by the language of 20 U.S.C. § 1703(f) are:

1. Whether the children have a language barrier.

2. Whether, if they have a language barrier, that barrier impedes their equal participation in the instructional program offered by the defendant. (In this case the evidence has largely been directed at learning to read, the most basic of all instructional programs of the school.)

3. Whether, if there is a barrier that does so impede, the defendant Board has taken "appropriate action to overcome the language barrier."

4. Whether, if the defendant Board has not taken "appropriate action," this failure denies equal educational opportunity to plaintiffs "on account of race."***

I. REPORT ON CURRENT STATE OF KNOWLEDGE

The court heard from a number of distinguished and renowned researchers and professionals who told the court about their research and discoveries involving "black English" and how it impacts on the teaching of standard English ***. The following is a brief summary of some of the research reported as it relates to the problems before the court.

LANGUAGE BARRIER

All of the distinguished researchers and professionals testified as to the existence of a language system, which is a part of the English language but different in significant respects from the standard English used in the school setting, the commercial world, the world of the arts and science, among the professions and in government. It is and has been used at some time by 80% of the black people of this country and has as its genesis the transactional or pidgin language of the slaves, which after a generation or two became a Creole language. Since then it has constantly been refined and brought closer to the standard English as blacks have been brought closer to the mainstream of society. It still flourishes in areas where there are concentrations of black people. It contains aspects of Southern dialect and is used largely by black people in their casual conversation and informal talk. There are many characteristic features found in "black English" but some of the principal ones identified by the testifying experts as being significant are:

1. The use of the verb "be" to indicate a reality that is recurring or continuous over time.

2. The deletion of some forms of the verb "to be."

3. The use of the third person singular verbs without adding the "s" or "z" sound.

4. The use of the "f" sound for the "th" sound at the end or in the middle of a word.

5. The use of an additional word to denote plurals rather than adding an "s" to the noun.

6. Non-use of "s" to indicate possessives.

7. The elimination of "l" or "r" sounds in words.

8. The use of words with different meanings.

9. The lack of emphasis on the use of tense in verbs.

10. The deletion of final consonants.

11. The use of double subjects.

12. The use of "it" instead of "there."

The substance of the thoughtful testimony of the experts also indicated that because "black English" does not discriminate among some sounds which are distinguished in standard English, teachers experience difficulty in getting the students to use correct pronunciation. The experts further testified, however, that efforts to instruct the children in standard English by teachers who failed to appreciate that the children speak a dialect which is acceptable in the home and peer community can result in the children becoming ashamed of their language, and thus impede the learning process. In this respect, the black dialect appears to be different than the usual foreign languages because a foreign language is not looked down on by the teachers.***

Finally, it is clear that black children who succeed, and many do, learn to be bilingual. They retain fluency in "black English" to maintain status in the community and they become fluent in standard English to succeed in the general society. They achieve in this way by learning to "code switch" from one to the other depending on the circumstances.

All of the experts testified that the language used is a specific system that has been used by blacks and continues to be used by blacks in casual conversation and informal talk. It is a language system having its genesis among black people.***

IMPEDIMENTS TO EQUAL PARTICIPATION IN THE INSTRUCTIONAL PROGRAM ***

The research evidence supports the theory that the learning of reading can be hurt by teachers who reject students because of the "mistakes" or "errors" made in oral speech by "black English" speaking children who are learning standard English. This comes about because "black English" is commonly thought of as an inferior method of speech and those who use this system may be thought of as "dumb" or "inferior." The child who comes to school using the "black English" system of communication and who is taught that this is wrong loses a sense of values related to mother and close friends and siblings and may rebel at efforts by his teachers to teach reading in a different language.***

II. APPLICATION OF THE CURRENT STATE OF KNOWLEDGE TO THE CHILDREN IN THIS CASE AND KING SCHOOL

LANGUAGE BARRIER ***

Although the evidence in this case indicates that the plaintiffs at times speak "black English" at home, they also to a greater or lesser degree depending on age speak and understand standard English in school and in the home.

If a barrier exists because of the language used by the children in this case, it exists not because the teachers and students cannot understand each other, but because in the process of attempting to teach the students how to speak standard English the students are made somehow to feel inferior and are thereby turned off from the learning process.

There is no direct evidence that any of the teachers in this case has treated the home language of the children as inferior, but it is clear to the court that although some of the teachers rebel at calling the home language "black English" they are acutely aware of it. Each teacher, the court believes, makes his or her own assessment of the language system used by the student in the home environment and attempts to use all of his or her skills to teach the student to read and speak standard English. The teachers do not, however, admit to taking that system into account in helping the student read standard English.

As indicated later in this memorandum, the teachers all testified that they treated the plaintiff students just as they treated other students. In so doing, they may have created a barrier to learning reading if the research reported is to be given any credence. The reason the teachers are teaching standard English is because it is the language by which the mainstream of society operates. The vernacular of "black English" has never been such a language. By requiring a student to switch without even recognizing that he or she is switching impedes the learning of reading standard English.***

IMPEDIMENTS TO EQUAL PARTICIPATION IN THE INSTRUCTIONAL PROGRAM

The evidence in this case suggests that each teacher made every effort to help and used the many and varied resources of the school system to try to teach the students to learn to read.

The evidence also suggests that the students, depending on their age, communicate orally quite well in standard English and except for a few limited times most, if not all, in-school talking is done in standard English.

The court heard from each of the children. They are attractive, likeable, at times shy, youngsters. Their speech in court was highly intelligible and contained only traces of "black English." This is true although the court heard tapes played of the same children in casual conversation in which talking among themselves their speech was a true "black English" vernacular. In oral speech, though, they seem to quickly adapt to standard English in settings where it appears to be the proper language.

The facts in this case indicate, however, that these children have not developed reading skills and the failure to develop these skills impedes equal participation in the instructional program.

The toughest question is whether it has been established that the failure to develop reading skills was caused by the language barrier. The evidence suggests other causes, such as absences from class, learning disabilities, and emotional impairment. However, the evidence also suggests that an additional cause of the failure to learn to read is the barrier caused by the failure of the teachers to take into account the "black English" home language of the children in trying to help them switch to reading standard English. When that occurs, the research indicates that some children will turn off and will not learn to read.

The court cannot find that the defendant School Board has taken steps (1) to help the teachers understand the problem; (2) to help provide them with knowledge about the children's use of a "black English" language system; and (3) to suggest ways and means of using that knowledge in teaching the students to read.

III. APPLICATION OF LAW TO FACTS

*** The plaintiffs have attempted to put before this court one of the most important and pervasive problems facing modern urban America: the problem of why "Johnnie Can't Read" when Johnnie is black and comes from a scatter low income housing unit, set down in an upper middle class area of one of America's most liberal and forward-looking cities.

The problem posed by this case is one which the evidence indicates has been compounded by efforts on the part of society to fully integrate blacks into the mainstream of society by relying solely on simplistic devices such as scatter housing and busing of students. Full integration and equal opportunity require much more and one of the matters requiring more attention is the teaching of the young blacks to read standard English.***

Research indicates that the black dialect or vernacular used at home by black students in general makes it more difficult for such children to learn to read for three reasons:

1. There is a lack of parental or other home support for developing reading skills in standard English, including the absence of persons in the home who read, enjoy it and profit from it.

2. Students experience difficulty in hearing and making certain sounds used discriminatively in standard English, but not distinguished in the home language system.

3. The unconscious but evident attitude of teachers toward the home language causes a psychological barrier to learning by the student.

Evidence is lacking in this case about parental reading models, although the mothers clearly have evidenced interest in the success of their children. There is no evidence that any of the teachers have in any way intentionally caused psychological barriers to learning. The mothers and the children were complimentary of their teachers. But the evidence does clearly establish that unless those instructing in reading recognize (1) the existence of a home language used by the children in their own community for much of their non-school communications, and (2) that this home language may be a cause of the superficial difficulties in speaking standard English, great harm will be done. The child may withdraw or may act out frustrations and may not learn to read. A language barrier develops when teachers, in helping the child to switch from the home ("black English") language to standard English, refuse to admit the existence of a language that is the acceptable way of talking in his local community.***

The failure of the defendant Board to provide leadership and help for its teachers in learning about the existence of "black English" as a home and community language of many black students and to suggest to those same teachers ways and means of using that knowledge in teaching the black children code switching skills in connection with reading standard English is not rational in light of existing knowledge on the subject.***

*** Accordingly, this court finds it appropriate to require the defendant Board to take steps to help its teachers to recognize the home language of the students and to use that knowledge in their attempts to teach reading skills in standard English.*** It is not the intention of this court to tell educators how to educate, but only to see that this defendant carries out an obligation imposed by law to help the teachers use existing knowledge as this may bear on appropriate action to overcome language barriers.***

Counsel for the defendant is directed to submit to this court within thirty (30) days a proposed plan defining the exact steps to be taken (1) to help the teachers of the plaintiff children at King School to identify children speaking "black English" and the language spoken as a home or community language, and (2) to use that knowledge in teaching such students how to read standard English. The plan must embrace within its terms the elementary school teachers of the plaintiff children at Martin Luther King Junior Elementary School. If the defendant chooses, however, it may submit a broader plan for the court's consideration, e.g., one embracing other elementary schools.

So ordered.

Notes and Questions

1. One of the named experts testifying in this case was the distinguished linguist, William Labov. He later published a review of the anthropological background to the problem confronted by the court in *Martin Luther King Junior Elementary School Children. See* William Labov, *Objectivity and Commitment in Linguistic Science: The Case of the Black English Trial in Ann Arbor,* 11 LANGUAGE IN SOCIETY 165 (1982).

The primary linguistic conflict concerning Black English had been between the dialectologists and the Creolists. Dialectologists argued that Black English was a dialect no different from that spoken by white Southerners of the same class and region. Creolists, on the other hand, maintained that Black English demonstrated semantic properties not found in white speech patterns, and that could be traced to Caribbean Creole grammars that had emerged from West African languages.

For Labov, one of the significant outcomes of the Ann Arbor case was that this often acrimonious divide among linguists did not emerge. In fact, the defense could find no linguists to testify that the black children were not speaking a legitimate language form deserving recognition and respect by the Ann Arbor school system. The demonstrated consensus, as Labov summarizes it, was that Black English:

1. is a subsystem of English with a distinct set of phonological and syntactic rules that are now aligned in many ways with the rules of other dialects;

2. incorporates many features of Southern phonology, morphology and syntax, and has in turn exerted influence on the dialects of the South;

3. shows evidence of derivation from an earlier Creole that was closer to the present-day Creoles of the Caribbean; and

4. has a highly developed aspect system, quite different from other dialects of English, which shows a continuing development of its semantic structure.

2. Even granting that Black English is a true "subsystem" of English (and not just poorly spoken standard English), significant legal obstacles remained for the plaintiffs to overcome. Not least was framing the problem so that an appropriate remedy was available.

As the court pointed out in an earlier Memorandum Opinion and Order of May 17, 1978, "No law or clause of the Constitution of the United States explicitly secures the rights of plaintiff to special educational services to overcome unsatisfactory academic performance based on cultural, social, or economic background." 451 F.Supp.1324, 1327–28. In the end, the only surviving cause of action it allowed was that the school district had not taken sufficient action to overcome "linguistic barriers," as required by 20 U.S.C. §1703(f).

The judge in this case accepted the premise that this law did not refer solely to foreign languages. Rather, the law applied to all barriers caused by language, including those resulting from uses of nonstandard English. Had Black English not been found to be a legitimate alternative form of English, this law would not have been applicable, and the plaintiffs would have lost their only remaining basis for relief.

3. The implications of the Ann Arbor case can easily be misconstrued. The plaintiffs did not ask, and the court did not grant, that the children should be "taught" in Black English. Indeed, the judge found that the only linguistic barrier that existed was that which arose from the condescension of the teachers for the students' home language, and not because there was an actual inability to communicate between students and teachers.

The relief the plaintiffs in Ann Arbor did not seek was requested by the school district of Oakland, California, which in 1996 proposed to recognize Black English, or "ebonics," as a second language. The effort met with immediate condemnation from whites and blacks alike. During this debate, Ann Arbor was presented as an example of a school where "Black English" is already being taught, a conclusion decidedly outside the resolution of the Ann Arbor case. *See* CNN, *'Black English' Proposal Draws Fire*, Dec. 22, 1996. The concerns which prompted the Oakland resolution, however, were the same that instigated the Ann Arbor case: how to "bridge the gap" for black children who are poorly performing in school. This problem continues to challenge educators, and demonstrates the continuing importance of the issue of language, language use, and language rights.

3. Restrictions on Language Use

GUTIERREZ v. MUNICIPAL COURT OF THE SOUTHEAST JUDICIAL DISTRICT, COUNTY OF LOS ANGELES

838 F.2d 1031 (9th Cir. 1988)

The Southeast Judicial District of the Los Angeles Municipal Court employs Alva Gutierrez and a number of other bilingual Hispanic-Americans as deputy court clerks. Gutierrez has held her position since 1978. Bilingual clerks, in addition to their other duties, translate for the non-English speaking public. In March, 1984, the Municipal Court promulgated a new personnel rule which forbade employees to speak any language other than English, except when acting as translators. In December, 1984, the rule was amended to exclude conversations during breaks or lunchtime. However, all other conversations conducted at work remained subject to the rule. The court's actions greatly disturbed Gutierrez and other Hispanic-American employees.

Gutierrez filed a complaint with the Equal Employment Opportunity Commission (EEOC) in December, 1984. Subsequently, in March 1985, she filed this action against Municipal Judges Porter de Dubovay, Russell F. Schooling, and John W. Bunnett, and the Southeast Judicial District of the Los Angeles Municipal Court, seeking monetary damages, injunctive relief, and attorneys fees. In her district court complaint, Gutierrez contends that the municipal court rule constitutes racial and national origin discrimination with respect to a term or condition of employment in violation of Title VII, 42 U.S.C. § 2000e-2(a), and that such discrimination denies her the right to make contracts equally with white persons in violation of 42 U.S.C. § 1981. She further asserts that the rule denies her equal protection of the laws and infringes upon her right to free speech in violation of the first and fourteenth amendments to the United States Constitution, and seeks damages for interference with her constitutional rights under 42 U.S.C. §§ 1983 and 1985(3). The district judge, finding a likelihood that the rule violated Title VII, granted Gutierrez's request for a preliminary injunction and enjoined appellants from enforcing the rule.***

ISSUES PRESENTED ON APPEAL

1. Whether the district court erred in issuing the preliminary injunction restricting enforcement of the English-only rule.***

DISCUSSION

I. THE PRELIMINARY INJUNCTION AND THE TITLE VII CLAIM ***

Gutierrez challenges the English-only rule under Title VII using adverse impact and disparate treatment theories. She asserts that a regulation mandating the speaking of English-only by its terms has a disproportionate adverse impact on Hispanics. She contends that the rule, although allegedly facially neutral, unfairly disadvantages Hispanics because their ethnic identity is linked to use of the Spanish language. She also notes that Hispanics constitute the vast majority of bilingual persons in the Southeast Judicial District. Gutierrez then separately avers that the rule was intentionally adopted for the purpose of discriminating against Hispanics, that any neutral appearance is pretextual, and, thus, that the rule violates Title VII's proscription against disparate treatment.***

A.   Likelihood of Success on the Merits

  2.   Disparate Impact ***

Few courts have evaluated the lawfulness of workplace rules restricting the use of languages other than English. Commentators generally agree, however, that language is an important aspect of national origin. [Citations omitted.] The cultural identity of certain minority groups is tied to the use of their primary tongue. *See Comment, Native-Born Acadians and the Equality Ideal,* 46 LA. L. REV. 1151, 1165–67 (1986). The mere fact that an employee is bilingual does not eliminate the relationship between his primary language and the culture that is derived from his national origin. Although an individual may learn English and become assimilated into American society, his primary language remains an important link to his ethnic culture and identity. The primary language not only conveys certain concepts, but is itself an affirmation of that culture.***

Although Title VII does not specifically prohibit English-only rules, the EEOC has promulgated guidelines on the subject. See 29 C.F.R. § 1606.7 (1987). The EEOC recognizes that "the primary language of an individual is often an essential national origin characteristic," and that an English-only rule may "create an atmosphere of inferiority, isolation and intimidation." Id. § 1606.7(a). Although an employer may have legitimate business reasons for requiring that communications be exclusively in English, an English-only rule is, according to the EEOC, a burdensome condition of employment that is often used to mask national origin discrimination and that must be carefully scrutinized. [Citation omitted.] Accordingly, the EEOC concluded that while a limited English-only rule may be permissible in some circumstances, no such rule will be deemed lawful unless the employer can show that it is justified by business necessity ***.***

*** The EEOC guidelines, by requiring that a business necessity be shown before a limited English-only rule may be enforced, properly balance the individual's interest in speaking his primary language and any possible need of the employer to ensure that in particular circumstances only English shall be spoken.*** Accordingly we adopt the EEOC's business necessity test as the proper standard for determining the validity of limited English-only rules.

[Appellants] argue *** that, whatever the impact of English-only rules in other circumstances, in this case the impact is not disparate or adverse because Gutierrez is bilingual and can easily comply with the rule. Appellants assert that where an employee can readily observe an English-only rule, a failure to comply is nothing more than a matter of personal preference. For the reasons already given, we do not think English-only rules can so easily be immunized from judicial scrutiny.***

[T]he English-only rule in the case before us is concerned primarily with intra-employee conversations, work-related and non-work-related. It is in no way limited to the sale or distribution of the employer's product and there is no contention that the employees' conversations among themselves in Spanish have any effect on those who use the courts. Yet, the prohibition on intra-employee communications in Spanish is sweeping in nature and has a direct effect on the general atmosphere and environment of the work place. Under these circumstances, ease of compliance has little or no relevance; certainly, it is not a factor that could preclude a finding of disparate impact.

  3.   Business Necessity

We next address appellants' argument that their English-only rule is justified by business necessity.*** In order to meet the business necessity exception the justification must be sufficiently compelling to override the discriminatory impact created by the challenged rule. In addition, the practice or rule must effectively carry out the business purpose it is alleged to serve, and there must be available no acceptable less discriminatory alternative which would accomplish the purpose as well.*** [Citations omitted.]

The first justification offered by appellants is that the United States is an English-speaking country and California an English-speaking state. That self-evident fact provides little support for the restrictive rule the municipal court judges imposed on their Spanish-speaking employees. While appellants vigorously urge that there is a substantial state interest in having a single language system, the prohibition of intra-employee Spanish communication does little to achieve that result, especially since as a part of their official duties the Court's bilingual employees are required to communicate in Spanish on a regular basis with numerous members of the non-English-speaking public. Thus, the rule cannot be said to effectively carry out the asserted purpose, and the first justification cannot support a finding of a business necessity. [Citations omitted.]

Second, appellants contend that the rule is necessary to prevent the workplace from turning into a "Tower of Babel." This claim assumes that permitting Spanish (or another language) to be spoken between employees is disruptive. Even if appellants' unspoken premise were true, the argument fails in part for some of the reasons already suggested. Since Spanish is already being spoken in the Clerk's office, to non-English-speaking Hispanic citizens, part of the "babel" that appellants purport to fear is necessary to the normal press of court business. Additional Spanish is unlikely to create a much greater disruption than already exists. Because the "babel" is necessary and has an apparently permanent status, its elimination in the area of intra-employee communication cannot be termed essential to the efficient operation of the Clerk's office. [Citations omitted.]

Third, appellants assert that the rule is necessary to promote racial harmony. They contend that Spanish may be used to convey discriminatory or insubordinate remarks and otherwise belittle non-Spanish-speaking employees. Appellants, however, have failed to offer any evidence of the inappropriate use of Spanish.[9] In contrast, there is evidence indicating that racial hostility has increased between Hispanics and non-Spanish-speaking employees because Hispanics feel belittled by the regulation. There is also evidence that non-Spanish-speaking employees have made racially discriminatory remarks directed at Hispanics.***

Appellants further contend that whatever the actual facts may be, non-Spanish-speaking employees believe that Spanish-speaking employees use Spanish to conceal the substance of their conversations and that the English-only rule is necessary to assuage non-Spanish-speaking employees' fears and suspicions. Appellants' contention is based on a single complaint allegedly made by an employee, a complaint based, at most, on suspicion. Again, there is simply no probative evidence of the Spanish language being

---

9   Three supervisors submitted affidavits on this aspect of appellants' case. However, all three supervisors acknowledge that they do not speak Spanish and therefore cannot know whether employees are using Spanish to convey discriminatory or insubordinate remarks. The affidavits, in the absence of any evidence of the misuse of Spanish, indicate only that the speaking of Spanish unnerves the supervisors. The supervisors' feelings toward the use of the Spanish language may reflect a prejudice toward the use of a tongue that they do not understand, and also may indicate a bias against Hispanic-Americans. Unfortunately, monolingual persons may be threatened by the speaking of a language that they themselves cannot speak. [Citation omitted.]

used to conceal the substance of conversations. However, even if there were evidence that a regulation mandating the use of English during working hours would calm some employees' fears and thereby reduce racial tension to some extent, this reason would not constitute a business necessity for a rule that has an adverse impact on other persons based on their national origin. Existing racial fears or prejudices and their effects cannot justify a racial classification. *Palmore v. Sidoti*, 466 U.S. 429, 433–34, 80 L. Ed. 2d 421, 104 S. Ct. 1879 (1984). Nor may such fears or prejudices constitute the business necessity for a rule that burdens a protected class. *See id.; see also City of Cleburne v. Cleburne Living Center*, 473 U.S. 432, 448, 450, (1985).

Fourth, appellants assert that the English-only rule is necessary because several supervisors do not speak or understand Spanish and cannot discern whether employees are correctly disseminating information unless English is spoken. This argument is illogical as well as unpersuasive. Bilingual employees are required to speak Spanish when dealing with the non-English-speaking public; they are specifically hired for that purpose because Spanish is the primary tongue of the majority of the members of the public who use the courts in the Southeast Judicial District. Supervisors may well be unable to determine whether the information disseminated to the public by bilingual employees is correct but that is only because when the bilingual employees are communicating with the non-English-speaking public in the only language that those persons understand, the supervisors are incapable of following the discussion. The municipal court rule in question in no way enables supervisors more effectively to evaluate or control the dissemination of information to the public.*** It is apparent that the best way to ensure that supervisors are apprised of how well the bilingual employees are performing this part of their assigned tasks would be to employ Spanish-speaking supervisors.***

Next, appellants argue that the English-only rule is required by the California Constitution. Cal. Const. art. III, § 6. Appellants assert that section 6, added by the voters as a ballot initiative in 1986, requires the use of English in all official state business, and thus requires Hispanic employees to communicate in English while at work.[10]

Appellants' argument is unpersuasive for three basic reasons. First, a fair reading of section 6 does not support appellants' interpretation of the measure. Section 6 does not provide that English must be spoken under the circumstances specified in the municipal court's rule, or even suggest that such should be the general policy of the state. Section 6 declares only that "English is the official language of the State of California," Cal. Const. art. III, § 6(b), and mandates only that "the Legislature shall

---

[10]   Section 6 provides:

(a) Purpose

English is the common language of the people of the United States of America and the State of California. This section is intended to preserve, protect and strengthen the English language, and not to supersede any of the rights guaranteed to the people by this Constitution.

(b) ***

English is the official language of the State of California.

(c) Enforcement

The Legislature shall enforce this section by appropriate legislation.***

enforce this section by appropriate legislation," Cal. Const. art. III, § 6(c). While section 6 may conceivably have some concrete application to official government communications, if and when the measure is appropriately implemented by the state legislature, it appears otherwise to be primarily a symbolic statement ***.

[C]ontrary to appellants' arguments, the adoption of a constitutional provision or a state statute does not ipso facto create a business necessity. A state enactment cannot constitute the business justification for the adoption of a discriminatory rule unless the state measure itself meets the business necessity test; otherwise employers could justify discriminatory regulations by relying on state laws that encourage or require discriminatory conduct. For federal law purposes, it is immaterial whether inadequate justifications directly underlie the actions of a government agency or are incorporated in the constitution of a state. In either case, if the proferred justifications fail to meet the business necessity test they are legally insufficient.

4. Summary

English-only rules generally have an adverse impact on protected groups and ordinarily constitute discriminatory conditions of employment. Here, none of the justifications appellants offer for their English-only rule meets the rigorous business necessity standard. [Citation omitted.] Thus there appears to be no basis for making an exception to the general rule. Accordingly, the district court correctly determined that Gutierrez established a likelihood of success on the merits on her adverse impact claim.

Notes and Questions

Subsequent History of Gutierrez: The U.S. Supreme Court vacated the Ninth Circuit's decision because Gutierrez left her job while the case was on appeal, rendering the case moot. Is this a situation that is likely to recur?

YNIGUEZ v. ARIZONANS FOR OFFICIAL ENGLISH

69 F.3d 920 (9th Cir. 1994)

*** This case raises troubling questions regarding the constitutional status of language rights and, conversely, the state's power to restrict such rights. There are valid concerns on both sides. In our diverse and pluralistic society, the importance of establishing common bonds and a common language between citizens is clear. [Citation omitted.] Equally important, however, is the American tradition of tolerance, a tradition that recognizes a critical difference between encouraging the use of English and repressing the use of other languages. Arizona's rejection of that tradition has severe consequences not only for its public officials and employees, but for the many thousands of Arizonans who would be precluded from receiving essential information from their state and local governments if the drastic prohibition contained in the provision were to be implemented. In deciding this case, therefore, we are guided by what the Supreme Court wrote in *Meyer:*

> The protection of the Constitution extends to all, to those who speak other languages as well as those born with English on the tongue. Perhaps it would be highly advantageous if all had ready understanding of our ordinary speech, but this cannot be coerced by methods which conflict with the Constitution—a desirable end cannot be promoted by prohibited means.

We conclude that Article XXVIII constitutes a prohibited means of promoting the English language and affirm the district court's ruling that it violates the First Amendment.***

I. FACTUAL BACKGROUND

In October 1987, Arizonans for Official English initiated a petition drive to amend Arizona's constitution to prohibit the government's use of languages other than English. The drive culminated in the 1988 passage by ballot initiative of Article XXVIII of the Arizona Constitution, entitled "English as the Official Language." The measure passed by a margin of one percentage point, drawing the affirmative votes of 50.5% of Arizonans casting ballots in the election. Under Article XXVIII, English is "the official language of the State of Arizona": "the language of . . . all government functions and actions." The provision declares that the "State and all [of its] political subdivisions"—defined as including "all government officials and employees during the performance of government business"—"shall act in English and no other language."

At the time of the passage of the article, Yniguez, a Latina, was employed by the Arizona Department of Administration, where she handled medical malpractice claims asserted against the state. She was bilingual—fluent and literate in both Spanish and English. Prior to the article's passage, Yniguez communicated in Spanish with monolingual Spanish-speaking claimants, and in a combination of English and Spanish with bilingual claimants.

State employees who fail to obey the Arizona Constitution are subject to employment sanctions. For this reason, immediately upon passage of Article XXVIII, Yniguez ceased speaking Spanish on the job. She feared that because of Article XXVIII her use of Spanish made her vulnerable to discipline.

In November 1988, Yniguez filed an action *** in federal district court. She sought an injunction against state enforcement of Article XXVIII and a declaration that the provision violated the First and Fourteenth Amendments of the Constitution, as well as federal civil rights laws.***

The district court *** read Article XXVIII as barring state officers and employees from using any language other than English in performing their official duties, except to the extent that certain limited exceptions described in the provision applied. Finding that Article XXVIII, thus construed, infringed on constitutionally protected speech, the district court ruled that the provision was facially overbroad in violation of the First Amendment.***

II. THE PROPER CONSTRUCTION OF ARTICLE XXVIII

A. *The District Court's Construction*

Although eighteen states have adopted "official-English" laws, Arizona's Article XXVIII is "by far the most restrictively worded official-English law to date."***

The district court, interpreting what it found to be the "sweeping language" of Article XXVIII, determined that the provision prohibits: the use of any language other than English by all officers and employees of all political subdivisions in Arizona while performing their official duties.***

[W]e agree with the district court's construction of the article.***

III. ARTICLE XXVIII AND THE FIRST AMENDMENT

A. *Overbreadth* ***

Yniguez contends *** that the speech rights of innumerable employees, officials, and officers in all departments and at all levels of Arizona's state and local governments are chilled by Article XXVIII's expansive reach. At least as important, she contends that the interests of many thousands of non-English-speaking Arizonans in receiving vital information would be drastically and unlawfully limited. For those reasons, she challenges Article XXVIII as overbroad on its face and invalid in its entirety.

Article XXVIII's ban on the use of languages other than English by persons in government service could hardly be more inclusive. The provision plainly states that it applies to "the legislative, executive, and judicial branches" of both state and local government, and to "all government officials and employees during the performance of government business." This broad language means that Article XXVIII on its face applies to speech in a seemingly limitless variety of governmental settings, from ministerial statements by civil servants at the office to teachers speaking in the classroom, from town-hall discussions between constituents and their representatives to the translation of judicial proceedings in the courtroom. Under the article, the Arizona state universities would be barred from issuing diplomas in Latin, and judges performing weddings would be prohibited from saying "Mazel Tov" as part of the official marriage ceremony. Accordingly, it is self-evident that Article XXVIII's sweeping English-only mandate limits the speech of governmental actors serving in a wide range of work-related contexts that differ significantly from that in which Yniguez performed her daily tasks. The speech rights of all of Arizona's state and local employees, officials, and officers are thus adversely affected in a potentially unconstitutional manner by the breadth of Article XXVIII's ban on non-English governmental speech. Similarly, the interests of non-English-speaking Arizonans in receiving all kinds of essential information are severely burdened.***

B. *Speech v. Expressive Conduct*

Arizonans for Official English argues vehemently that First Amendment scrutiny should be relaxed in this case because the decision to speak a non-English language does not implicate pure speech rights. Rather, the group suggests, "choice of language . . . is a mode of conduct"—a "*nonverbal* expressive activity." Accordingly, it compares this case to those involving only "expressive conduct" or "symbolic speech." In such cases, the government generally has a wider latitude in regulating the conduct involved, but only when the regulation is not directed at the communicative nature of that conduct. [Citation omitted.]

[W]e are entirely unpersuaded by the comparison between speaking languages other than English and burning flags. Of course, speech in any language consists of the "expressive conduct" of vibrating one's vocal chords, moving one's mouth and thereby making sounds, or of putting pen to paper, or hand to keyboard. Yet the fact that such "conduct" is shaped by a language—that is, a sophisticated and complex system of understood meanings—is what makes it speech. Language is by definition speech, and the regulation of any language is the regulation of speech.

A bilingual person does, of course, make an expressive choice by choosing to speak one language rather than another. As Yniguez explained, her choice to speak Spanish with other bilingual people can signify "solidarity" or "comfortableness." Nonetheless, this expressive effect does not reduce choice of language to the level of "conduct," as posited by Arizonans for Official English; instead, it exemplifies the variety of ways that one's use of language conveys meaning. For example, even within a given language, the choice of specific words or tone of voice may critically affect the message conveyed. Such variables—language, words, wording, tone of voice—are not expressive conduct, but are simply among the communicative elements of speech. Moreover, the choice to use a given language may often simply be based on a pragmatic desire to convey information to someone so that they may understand it. That is in fact the basis for the choice involved in the constitutional challenge we consider here.

The Supreme Court recognized the First Amendment status of choice of language in somewhat different circumstances when it ratified a speaker's freedom to say "fuck the draft" rather than "I strongly oppose the draft." *Cohen v. California*, 403 U.S. 15 (1971) (reversing conviction under California "offensive conduct" law). Like the proponents of Article XXVIII, the state in *Cohen* had described Cohen's choice of language as conduct equivalent to burning a draft card. The Court unequivocally rejected the comparison, stating that Cohen's conviction rested "solely upon speech."

[T]he Court next addressed the question of whether Cohen's conviction could potentially be upheld as a regulation of the manner of Cohen's speech. Specifically, it framed the First Amendment issue by asking "whether California can excise . . . one particularly scurrilous epithet from the public discourse." Its answer to that question was, "No." Indeed, in justifying its conclusion, the Court echoed Yniguez's comments regarding her use of Spanish. It stated that "words are often chosen as much for their emotive as their cognitive force"—to such an extent, in fact, that this emotive aspect "may often be the more important element of the overall message sought to be communicated."

Under Article XXVIII, of course, the state is not singling out one word for repression, but rather entire vocabularies. Moreover, the languages of Cervantes, Proust, Tolstoy, and Lao-Tze, among others, can hardly be described as "scurrilous." In this case, therefore, the Court's admonishment that "in a society as diverse and populous as ours" the state has "no right to cleanse public debate" of unpopular words, rings even truer. While Arizonans for Official English complains of the "Babel" of many languages, the Court in *Cohen* responds that this "verbal cacophony is . . . not a sign of weakness but of strength." *Id.* at 25.***

As we have noted, it is frequently the need to convey information to members of the public that dictates the decision to speak in a different tongue. If all state and local officials and employees are prohibited from doing so, Arizonans who do not speak English will be unable to receive much essential information concerning their daily needs and lives. To call a prohibition that precludes the conveying of information to thousands of Arizonans in a language they can comprehend a mere regulation of "mode of expression" is to miss entirely the basic point of First Amendment protections.***

6. *Evaluating the Alleged State Justifications*

Arizonans for Official English claims, as it and others did when the initiative was on the ballot, that Article XXVIII promotes significant state interests. The organization enumerates these interests as: protecting democracy by encouraging "unity and political stability"; encouraging a common language; and protecting public confidence.***

*** In *Meyer*, the statute reflected the belief that "the English language should be and become the mother tongue of all children reared in this state." The statute in [*Farrington v.*] *Tokushige* would have similarly inhibited the spread of the Japanese language, presumably in favor of English. Although there is probably no more effective way of encouraging the uniform use of English than to ensure that children grow up speaking it, both statutes were struck down on the ground that these interests were insufficient to warrant such restrictions on the use of foreign languages.

Like the Court in *Meyer* and *Tokushige* we recognize the importance of (1) promoting democracy and national unity and (2) encouraging a common language as a means of encouraging such unity. The two primary justifications relied on by the article's proponents are indeed closely linked. We cannot agree, however, that Article XXVIII is in any way a fair, effective, or appropriate means of promoting those interests, or that even under a more deferential analysis its severely flawed effort to advance those goals outweighs its substantial adverse effect on first amendment rights. As we have learned time and again in our history, the state cannot achieve unity by prescribing orthodoxy. [Citation omitted.] Notwithstanding this lesson, the provision at issue here "promotes" English only by means of proscribing other languages and is, thus, wholly coercive. Moreover, the goals of protecting democracy and encouraging unity and stability are at most indirectly related to the repressive means selected to achieve them. Next, the measure inhibits rather than advances the state's interest in the efficient and effective performance of its duties. Finally, the direct effect of the provision is not only to restrict the rights of all state and local government servants in Arizona, but also to severely impair the free speech interests of a portion of the populace they serve.***

Here, the full costs of banning the dissemination of critical information to non-English speaking Arizonans cannot readily be calculated. There would undoubtedly be severe adverse consequences which even the sponsors of Article XXVIII neither foresaw nor intended. The range of potential injuries to the public is vast. Much of the information about essential governmental services that, but for the initiative, would be communicated in a manner that non-English speaking Arizonans could comprehend may not be susceptible to timely transmission by other means. By comparison, the benefits that the initiative purports to offer are minimal, especially in light of the state's concession that its interests in "efficiency" and "effectiveness" are not served by the Article. Thus, under a balancing test *** Article XXVIII must be held unconstitutional.***

Notes and Questions

The opinion in *Yniguez v. Arizonans for Official Language* was later vacated by the U.S. Supreme Court because (1) the plaintiff lacked standing for an appeal because she had left the employment of the state, and (2) the lower federal courts had refused to certify to the Arizona Supreme Court the question of the construction of the state constitutional article. *See Arizonans for Official English v. Arizona*, 520 U.S. 43 (1997). Nevertheless, the Ninth Circuit's opinion significantly influenced the subsequent state court decision in *Ruiz v. Hull*, 957 P. 2d 984 (Ariz. 1998). In that case, the Amendment was challenged by bilingual state elected officials and employees. Relying on the *Yniguez* analysis, the Arizona Supreme Court ruled the Amendment "unconstitutionally inhibits the free discussion of governmental affairs":

> Citizens of limited English proficiency, such as many of the named legislator's constituents, often face obstacles in petitioning their government for redress

and in accessing the political system. Legislators and other elected officials attempting to serve limited-English-proficient constituents face a difficult task in helping provide those constituents with government services and in assisting those constituents in both understanding and accessing government. The Amendment makes the use of non-English communication to accomplish that task illegal. In Arizona, English is not the primary language of many citizens. A substantial number of Arizona's Native Americans, Spanish-speaking citizens, and other citizens for whom English is not a primary language, either do not speak English at all or do not speak English well enough to be able to express their political beliefs, opinions, or needs to their elected officials. Under the Amendment, with few exceptions, no elected official can speak with his or her constituents except in English, even though such a requirement renders the speaking useless. While certainly not dispositive, it is also worth noting that in everyday experience, even among persons fluent in English as a second language, it is often more effective to communicate complex ideas in a person's primary language because some words, such as idioms and colloquialisms, do not translate well, if at all. In many cases, though, it is clear that the Amendment jeopardizes or prevents meaningful communication between constituents and their elected representatives, and thus contravenes core principles and values undergirding the First Amendment.

The Court also found that "the Amendment violates the Fourteenth Amendment's guarantees of equal protection because it impinges upon both the fundamental right to participate equally in the political process and the right to petition the government for redress." The U.S. Supreme Court denied *cert* in 1999, 525 U.S. 1093. The Arizona Constitution sections at issue are still on the books, and have not been revised.

C. THE "EXOTIC OTHER"—GENDER, CULTURE, AND RELIGIOUS TRADITIONS

"Identity" reflects a complex and ever-changing mixture of influences. International human rights instruments recognize and protect the rights of individuals and groups not to be subject to discrimination on the basis of race, sex or national origin, and at the same time provide protections for the freedom to practice and express religious and cultural beliefs.

While, in the abstract, such rights co-exist, one of the fundamental theoretical and practical concerns facing international human rights implementation is the tension between universalism and cultural relativism. What rights should trump when the rights of individuals and groups appear to conflict? Are international human rights norms, including those against sex discrimination, merely a set of Western values that are inappropriately imposed on non-Western peoples? Are there culturally specific ways of implementing the non-discrimination norm? The interplay between the rights of women and the requirements of cultural or religious tradition have often been at the core of such disputes.

1. *Case Study: Controversies Over "The Veil" and Other Forms of Appearance Regulation*

As you read the following reports about laws and policies relating to the appearance of women and girls, consider the following questions:

a. Most reported controversies involve dress codes for women and girls, rather than for men. Does that focus result primarily from the realities of the conflicts described, from the biases of the journalists involved, or both?

b. Why is "the veil" considered such an incendiary issue in the countries discussed? Why is it an important issue for human rights advocates in other countries?

c. What theoretical approaches might you use to address the concerns expressed in the articles? How should these legal issues be resolved?

d. Can you identify appearance regulations from your own social, cultural, or religious traditions? How are they similar to, or different from, the ones discussed here? Scholars have examined the legal implications of traditional hair-braiding among African-American women and the wearing of Kente cloth by African-American lawyers. Paulette Caldwell, *A Hair Piece: Perspectives in the Intersection of Race and Gender* in CRITICAL RACE FEMINISM: A READER 297 (Adrien K. Wing ed., 1997); Terri A. Belanger, *Note: Symbolic Expression in the Courtroom: The Right to a Fair Trial Versus Freedom of Speech*, 62 GEO. WASH. L. REV. 318 (1994).

YOUSSEF M. IBRAHIM, BAREHEADED WOMEN SLAIN IN ALGIERS

NEW YORK TIMES, March 31, 1994, at A3

*** Suspected Muslim fundamentalists in Algeria killed two unveiled young women today, enforcing a vow made last month that women who do not cover their heads in public would join a list of targets that includes the army, the police, secularist intellectuals, artists, journalists and foreigners.

The women—Raziqa Meloudjemi, 18, and Naima Kar Ali, 19, both students—were killed at a bus station in Algiers by gunmen on a motorbike.

Fundamentalists seeking to overthrow the Government have killed about 30 women in the last two years because of their association with secularist causes or with men who were targets of the fundamentalists. But today's killings were the first targeting of women in a public street for failing to cover their heads in a city where many women stroll about with their hair uncovered.***

"It is not a secret that several self-defense groups are forming in Algeria," Mr. Saadi, 46, said. "Self-defense groups are mushrooming wherever the Government appears to have resigned its functions in maintaining law and order. There is nothing that says that democrats cannot defend themselves with arms."

Giving some credence to Mr. Saadi's predictions, a secularist vigilante group called the Organization of Free Young Algerians, which has in the last few months taken responsibility for attacks on fundamentalists, vowed today in tracts distributed in Algiers to kill 30 veiled women and fundamentalist men.***

BOMB KILLS GIRL AT SCHOOL WHERE MANY SHUN VEILS

THE RECORD, December 23, 1996, at A11

Algiers, Algeria

A bomb exploded at a high school where many girls have refused to wear the traditional Muslim head scarf, killing one student and wounding another.***

After an absence of nearly a year, religious tracts reminding women of their "permanent obligation" to wear a veil, and advising men not to smoke cigarettes, were being handed out this weekend in the suburbs around Algiers.

At many Algerian high schools, girls have been refusing to wear the veil as Islamic militants insist.

The tracts were attributed to the Armed Islamic Group, the most violent of the factions trying to overthrow the North African country's government and install strict Islamic rule.***

Algeria's insurgency began in January 1992, when the government canceled legislative elections that Front candidates were poised to win.

More than 60,000 people have been killed.

Notes and Questions

1. In Egypt, as in many other countries, the politics of the veil have varied with time and socio-political context. *See, e.g.,* Judy Mabro, *Unveiling the Mystery; Egyptian Women Were Once Forced to Cover Their Heads, Now They Choose To*, INDEP. (London), July 13, 1998, at 8. In the early 20th century, Egyptian feminists saw the veil as an obstacle to women's equality and access to education, among other things. *Id.* But after government attempts to ban the veil in the 1990s, some Egyptian women now wear the veil as a symbol of opposition to government repression and Western consumerism, or as a means of reclaiming Egyptian identity. *Id.*; Vernon Silver, *In Egypt's Schools, Fashion Is Politics*, NEW YORK TIMES, June 30, 1996, at 38.

2. Reporter Judy Mabro notes that Egyptians often asked her, "Why do foreigners always want to discuss the hijab (the veil) when there are more important issues—poverty, illiteracy, child labour, gender inequalities and so on?." Mabro, *supra*. How would you respond to this question? Are the issues surrounding the wearing of the hijab of similar importance to the other issues listed? If not, why not? If so, why?

LARA MARLOWE, DEBATE ON ISLAMIC VEILS INFLAMES PASSIONS

IRISH TIMES, January 13, 1999, at 14

Gursel Kervanci left his native Turkey 20 years ago to work in France. Until last autumn, when he took his 12-year-old daughter Esmanur to annual school registration, he and his family lived peacefully in the north-western French town of Flers where he works as an industrial meat-packer.

The College Jean-Monnet refused to accept the girl because she began wearing a Muslim headscarf at puberty. "She sat at the window and watched her friends walking to school and she cried," Mr Kervanci said.

The case is not unusual in France, but this one has revived a bitter, decade-old dispute about secular public education, tolerance and Islam. There are four million Muslims in France, making them the country's second religion.

"My daughter is a student like any other," Mr Kervanci told me plaintively on the telephone. "She's not a monster. She wears the scarf out of faith—not for political reasons."

The Ministry of Education has employed a full-time mediator to deal with disputes involving the *foulard Islamique* for the past five years. The mediator, an Algerian-born former teacher named Hanifa Cherifi, says there are now 400 young women wearing veils in French schools. About 100 of them have become embroiled in legal battles, and a November 1998 report drawn up by Ms Cherifi noted with alarm that many schools now refuse to accept veiled girls. The reason most often cited for excluding them is "the risk of contaminating other Muslim students."

But Mr Kervanci was determined to defend his daughter, and filed a lawsuit with the Caen tribunal. Although the court has not yet made a final decision, the local education department reminded Eric Geffroy, principal of the College Jean-Monnet, that a 1996 decree by the conseil d'etat, the highest advisory body in France, ruled that the Muslim veil is not an ostentatious sign of religious belief and does not constitute grounds for expulsion.

Grudgingly, the College Jean-Monnet let Esmanur Kervanci return just before Christmas. But when courses resumed after the holidays, a second Muslim girl was also wearing a headscarf, and the school's personnel went on strike in protest. Rather than support the Kervancis, the local Turkish residents' association—which is seeking authorisation to build a prayer meeting place—sided with the teachers.

The conflict was temporarily defused on Monday night, when Segolene Royal, the junior Minister for Education, negotiated a compromise with the teachers under which the Flers girls will be "under observation" for two weeks, during which they must attend all courses and remove their scarves for certain science courses and physical education. Ms Royal told the teachers there was "no question of giving in to those who want to impose fundamentalism."

Absurdly, neither Ms Royal nor the teachers have realised that for a Muslim woman, wearing the veil is an all or nothing commitment. "It's as if they don't want to understand," Esmanur told French television. Her father sees no reason why she cannot play sports with her head covered. "I have confidence in justice," he said. "If they tell me I am wrong, I will accept it. A democratic, secular state guarantees freedom of religion and equality."

But Mr Geffroy, the school principal, sees things differently. Esmanur's scarf, he told me, "offends the personal convictions of the teachers, who believe the presence of a veil—which is a sign of sexual discrimination and a religious symbol—is opposed to the neutrality and secularism of our public education service."

Esmanur's fellow students, many of whom support her, pointed out that there is a chaplain's office—this week, the crucifix disappeared from its door—inside the College Jean-Monnet. Mr Geffroy claimed the chaplain's room was "totally different" from Esmanur's scarf. Mr Kervanci, he noted, has said that wearing the veil is a sort of permanent prayer, a way of living one's religion at every moment of the day—whereas students meet in the chaplain's office only after school hours.***

Notes and Questions

1. France has banned all "conspicuous" religious signs, including Islamic head scarves and Jewish yarmulkes in public schools. *See e.g.*, Delfin Vigil, *Worldwide Protests Over Ban on Religious Symbols: French Proposal Would Apply to All its Public Schools,* SAN FRAN. CHRON., Jan. 18, 2004, at A22. Prior to the law's enactment, French Minister of Interior Nicolas Sarkozy indicated that all women, including Catholic nuns, would have to uncover their heads for identity photographs. Paul Webster, *French Muslims Angry At Veil Move,* GUARDIAN (London), Apr. 22, 2003, at 15. Education Minister Luc Ferry implied that the ban's reach would extend even to bandanas and beards if deemed "religious." Jon Henly, *Veil Ban May Extend to "Religious" Beards,* GUARDIAN (London), Jan. 21, 2004, at 13. Although President Jacques Chirac claimed that the aim of the law is to protect secularism, much of the opposition sees the law as a direct attack on the growth of Islam in France. Vigil, *supra.* The law has drawn large, diverse, protests in France and worldwide. *Id.* It may also have drawn violent opposition, as seen in the car bombing of newly appointed state representative Aissa Dermouche (of Algerian descent) on January 17, 2004. *See e.g.*, Jon Henly, *Car Bomb Targets French Muslim Leader,* GUARDIAN (London), Jan. 19, 2004, at 12.

2. The French Senate approved the legal ban on headscarves in schools by a vote of 276–20 in March of 2004. "The vote mirrored similar overwhelming support by the National Assembly, the lower chamber of parliament, which passed it 494–36" earlier in the year. Elain Ganley, *France Bans Head Scarves in School,* ASSOC. PRESS, Mar. 3, 2003 *available at* http://www.cbsnews.com/stories/2004/world/printable597 (last visited Mar. 23, 2004). Ganley notes that the "law forbids religious apparel and signs that 'conspicuously show' a student's religious affiliation. Jewish skullcaps and large Christian crosses would also be banned, but the law is aimed at removing Islamic head scarves from classrooms." *Id.* The French government plans to reexamine the text of the ban after a year to determine whether "conspicuous" should be replaced with "visible." *Id.* France has the largest population of Muslims (5 million) in Western Europe. *Id.* The text of the French legislation is *available at* http://ameli.senat.fr/publication-p1/2003-2004/209.html.

HUMAN RIGHTS WATCH, FRANCE:
HEADSCARF BAN VIOLATES RELIGIOUS FREEDOM:
BY DISPROPORTIONATELY AFFECTING MUSLIM GIRLS,
PROPOSED LAW IS DISCRIMINATORY

Available at http://hrw.org/english/docs/2004/02/26/france7666jxt.htm

(New York, February 27, 2004)—The proposed French law banning Islamic headscarves and other visible religious symbols in state schools would violate the rights to freedom of religion and expression, Human Rights Watch said today. The law . . . forbids "signs and dress that conspicuously show the religious affiliation of students." *** "The proposed law is an unwarranted infringement on the right to religious practice," said Kenneth Roth, executive director of Human Rights Watch. "For many Muslims, wearing a headscarf is not only about religious expression, it is about religious obligation."

International human rights law obliges state authorities to avoid coercion in matters of religious freedom, and this obligation must be taken into account when devising school dress codes. The proposed prohibition on headscarves in France, as with laws in some Muslim countries that force girls to wear headscarves in schools, violates this principle.

Under international law, states can only limit religious practices when there is a compelling public safety reason, when the manifestation of religious beliefs would impinge on the rights of others, or when it serves a legitimate educational function (such as prohibiting practices that preclude student-teacher interaction). Muslim headscarves, Sikh turbans, Jewish skullcaps and large Christian crosses-which are among the visible religious symbols that would be prohibited-do not pose a threat to public health, order or morals; they have no effect on the fundamental rights and freedoms of other students; and they do not undermine a school's educational function.

Some supporters of the proposed law-known as the "Draft law concerning the application of the principle of secularism in schools, junior high schools and high schools," which would come into force in September [2004] believe it is necessary to uphold the separation of church and state in education, and to protect the secular state from the perceived threat of religious fundamentalism, particularly Islamic fundamentalism.

However, protecting the right of all students to religious freedom does not undermine secularism in schools. On the contrary, it demonstrates respect for religious diversity, a position fully consistent with maintaining the strict separation of public institutions from any particular religious message. Human Rights Watch recognizes the legitimacy of public institutions seeking not to promote any religion via their conduct or statements, but the French government has taken this a step further by suggesting that the state is undermining secularism if it allows students to wear religious symbols.

Supporters of the law have also defended the ban on the grounds that it will protect Muslim girls from being forced or pressured to wear the headscarf by their parents. Under international law, states must respect the responsibilities, rights and duties of parents to provide, in a manner consistent with the evolving capacities of the child, appropriate direction and guidance in the child's exercise of their basic rights. States must also take all appropriate measures to ensure that children are protected against discrimination or punishment on the basis of the beliefs of their parents or family members. At the same time, states are responsible for taking appropriate legislative, administrative, social and educational measures to protect children where parents are responsible for physical or mental violence, injury or abuse, neglect or negligent treatment, maltreatment or exploitation, including sexual abuse. Unnecessary restrictions on children's personal rights and freedoms should not be promoted as a means of child protection.

The impact of a ban on visible religious symbols, even though phrased in neutral terms, will fall disproportionately on Muslim girls, and thus violate antidiscrimination provisions of international human rights law as well as the right to equal educational opportunity. Indeed, the promotion of understanding and tolerance for such differences in values is a key aspect of enforcement of the right to education. In practice, the law will leave some Muslim families no choice but to remove girls from the state educational system.

Some in France have used the headscarf issue as a pretext for voicing antiimmigrant and anti-Muslim sentiments. Some arguments appear to be based on the premise that all Muslims want to oppress women, or that women and girls who choose to veil do not understand women's rights. Public debate has also touched on many other significant social issues: religious fundamentalism and political uses of religious symbols; oppression of girls and women; levels of immigration; discrimination and lack of economic opportunity for immigrant communities; pluralism and national integration.

"The proposed law has raised important issues about religious freedom and the role of the state in France," said Roth. "The resolution of this issue will have important implications throughout Europe and beyond. But simply banning headscarves and other expressions of religious belief from the schools is not the answer.

BBC NEWS, HEADSCARVES IN THE HEADLINES

Available at http://news.bbc.co.Uk/go/pr/fr/-/2/hi/europe/
3476163.stm (published February 10, 2004)

France is not the only country where headscarves have proved contentious. A number of countries already ban the garment from schools and other public buildings, while elsewhere it is the failure of women to don a veil which prompts outrage.***

Singapore

Singapore, keen to avoid racial and religious tensions between its ethnic Chinese majority and the Malay Muslim minority, has banned the scarf from schools. The Singapore government believes the ban is necessary to promote racial harmony, but Muslims say it infringes upon their religious freedoms. In 2002, the authorities became involved in a standoff with four families who defied the ban.

To the consternation of Singaporean officials, politicians from neighbouring Malaysia then entered the fray, saying it would consider taking the veiled schoolgirls into Malay schools. Singapore hit back, saying the issue was a purely internal matter. The row has since died down, but relations were widely seen as strained at the time.

Egypt

A group of Egyptian female TV presenters recently alleged they had been banned from appearing on screen because they were wearing headscarves, and some even said they were considering legal action.

The veil has recently made a comeback alongside Islamic revival movements in Egypt. The government is widely believed to be wary of the public display of Islamic symbols such as headscarves, fearing it could play into the hands of Islamic activists.

Germany

The issue has come to a head in recent months after Germany's supreme court ruled that a school was wrong to exclude a Muslim teacher because she wore a headscarf. The judges declared that current legislation did not allow for such a decision, but added that individual states would be within their rights to make legal provisions to this effect.

The German state of Baden-Wuerttemberg has already given initial approval for a law to stop teachers wearing the veil, and seven other states are considering similar legislation. Legislators believe the veil is a political symbol and that children in state education should be protected from fundamentalist influence.***

Saudi Arabia

Saudi Arabia's highest religious authority recently warned of "grave consequences" if women continued to appear unveiled.

He made the remarks after the country's leading businesswoman made a speech without a headscarf at a conference. She herself had warned in her address of the long-term effect if the potential of the female workforce went untapped.

Turkey

For the past 80 years Turks have lived in a secular state founded by Mustafa Kemal Ataturk, who rejected headscarves as backward looking in his campaign to secularise Turkish society. Scarves are consequently banned in civic spaces in the country.

The Islamist-based ruling AKP party, keen to avoid confrontation with the establishment, has not moved to alter that arrangement, although a number of politicians believe it problematic that Turkish girls can wear scarves in Western universities but not at home.

The issue did however rise to the surface last year when the country's president refused to invite the headscarf-wearing wives of senior officials, including Prime Minister Recep Tayyip Erdogan, to a reception marking the republic's 80th anniversary. Nearly all the AKP's MPs boycotted the event in protest.

Belgium

Two politicians, inspired by developments in neighbouring France, are hoping to push legislation through parliament that would ban the headscarf from state schools.

They believe that many young Muslim schoolgirls do not wear the scarf by choice, and that imposing a ban would protect them from those who impose it upon them.

Russia

Muslim women last year won the right to wear the headscarf for identification photos, which was banned in Russia in 1997. The women argued in court that the ban infringed upon their civil liberties, and were backed in this by a number of human rights groups, who also alleged that Russia was fermenting anti-Muslim sentiment to aid its mission against separatists in Chechnya.

Denmark

A Muslim woman last year lost a high-profile court case against a large supermarket chain in Denmark after she had been fired for wearing a headscarf at work in 2001. The court ruled that her contract contained a dress code banning headgear.

TERRY PRISTIN, CIVIL LIBERTIES: BEHIND THE LEGAL AND PRIVATE WORLDS OF THE VEIL

New York Times, August 11, 2002, at 4

Sultana Freeman, an American-born Muslim woman, had no trouble getting a Florida driver's license last year even though she insisted on being photographed in a veil that reveals only her eyes.

After Sept. 11, however, state officials had a change of heart. In December, they said her license would be revoked if she refused to be re-photographed without the veil. Instead of complying, Ms. Freeman gave up her license—and then sued the state to get it back.

Florida officials contend, not surprisingly, that police officers need full-face photographs to identify a driver in a traffic stop and to hunt down suspected criminals. Ms. Freeman argues that her faith requires her to shield her face in public and that a full-face photograph is not needed to verify her identity.***

Many legal scholars maintain that in an increasingly multicultural society, it is important to respect religious beliefs outside the mainstream. And in fact, a dozen states, Florida among them, have laws that require officials to show they have a compelling interest in enforcing a law that conflicts with a sincerely held religious belief.

But today, several legal scholars said, the question of what constitutes a compelling state interest is likely to be heavily influenced by Sept. 11. Robin Charlow, a law professor at Hofstra University, said judges are now likely to give additional weight to the state's arguments. "Certainly now that law enforcement interest might be more significant," she said, "and in the context of an Arab person shielding her identity, it's not realistic to think that it isn't."

Ideally, said Douglas W. Kmiec, the dean of the Catholic University Law School in Washington, both interests should be protected—the woman's right to be true to a core religious belief and the state's need to maintain public safety. Few people, after all, are likely to seek a similar exemption since it is inconvenient to be without a photo ID "Prior to 9/11," Mr. Kmiec said, "one could have rationally concluded that a handful of religious exemptions are not much of a threat. But now we know there is a relationship between some forms of religious belief and mischief of the worst kind."***

Though Ms. Freeman also argues that the photo requirement violates the First Amendment protection of the free exercise of religion, her lawyer, Howard S. Marks, concedes his client does not have a strong constitutional case. In 1990, the United States Supreme Court, in a case called Employment Division, Department of Human Resources v. Smith, ruled that Oregon could deny employment to American Indians who used peyote for sacramental purposes. The court held that there was no constitutional requirement to grant exemptions to laws that applied to everyone. Like antidrug laws, driver's license requirements are likely to be viewed as broadly applicable.

Responding to Smith, Congress passed the Religious Freedom Restoration Act, which sought to bring back the previous standard. Before Smith, officials had to show they had a compelling interest in not granting an exemption. But in 1997, the Supreme Court ruled that Congress had exceeded its authority when it applied the act to the states. That led to state laws like Florida's, known as Baby R.F.R.A.'s.

Under the Florida law, the state will be required to show not only that it has a compelling interest in requiring photographs but also that it cannot find a less restrictive way to achieve these ends, Mr. Marks said. Ms. Freeman is willing to submit to fingerprinting or DNA testing; the state counters that traffic officers cannot be expected to have technical expertise. The state has also offered to keep men away when the photograph is taken.***

Notes and Questions

1.   In June of 2003, a Florida circuit court judge ruled that Freeman would have to remove her veil for purposes of taking a driver's license photo. *See* Associated Press. *Judge: No Veil in Driver's License Photo,* NEWSDAY (New York), June 7, 2003, at A03. Media reports indicated that the U.S. Muslim community was divided over the case. *See e.g.,* Pedro Ruz Gutierrez & Kelly Brewington, *Muslims Don't See Eye to Eye on Case: Judge Holds Fate of Veil,* ORLANDO SENTINEL (Florida), May 30, 2003, at A1.

2.   Muslim women who chose to wear a head covering or the full hijab in the United States faced both personal and institutional discrimination (and even violence) prior to the events of September 11, 2001. Some were berated by police officers or other strangers, while others were fired for violating employer dress codes. *See e.g.,* Laurie Goodstein, *Islamic Emblem of Faith Also Triggers for Bias,* N.Y. TIMES, Nov. 3, 1997, at A1.

3.   Secular Turkey's ban on headscarves has resulted in the issue being brought to the European Court of Human Rights. Laura Secor, *Covering Law: The Headscarf That Infuriated Turkey's Rulers,* BOSTON GLOBE, Feb. 9, 2003, at D4. Merve Kavacki, elected to the Turkish parliament in 1999, was removed from office and stripped of her Turkish citizenship after she appeared for her swearing-in wearing a head scarf. *Id.* Many now see Kavacki as a symbol of civil disobedience. *Id.* Many Turkish Muslim women argue that the right to wear the veil is a women's rights issue. *Id.*

4.   Should it matter whether women wear veils or scarves for "political," "religious," or "fashion" purposes?

5.   In June of 2004, the European Court of Human Rights upheld the Turkish government's ban on the wearing of Muslim headscarves in public universities. A Turkish medical student had appealed the school's refusal to allow her to take exams as, *inter alia,* a violation of her rights to religious freedom, education and freedom from discrimination. According to one report, "the court said that measures taken in universities 'to prevent certain fundamentalist religious movements from pressuring students who do not practice the religion in question or those belonging to another religion' could be justified under the European Convention on Human Rights. Bans issued in the name of the separation of church and state could therefore be considered 'necessary in a democratic society'***." *Court Backs Turkish Headscarf Ban,* BBC NEWS, 29 June 2004, *available at* http://news.bbc.co.uk/1/hi/world/europe/3849759.stm.

ELAINE SCIOLINO, HAIR AS A BATTLEFIELD FOR THE SOUL

NEW YORK TIMES, November 18, 2001, at D5

Washington—Celebrating their liberation from Taliban rule in Afghanistan last week, men shaved off their beards, while women unveiled their faces and revealed bits of hair. Suddenly, ordinary people needed to show they had regained control over their looks. But why?

It helps to understand that the Muslim world today is waging two wars on overlapping battlefields: one between traditional interpretations of Islam and modernity, the other between the will of the state and the rights of the individual. Islamic scholars, lawyers and feminists debate laws and traditions governing such obviously serious issues as freedom of speech, divorce, inheritance, child custody, polygamy, flogging and stoning.

But the most visible manifestation of the Taliban's control over people has been the forced bearding of men and the forced veiling of the bodies and faces of women.

So the subject of hair is anything but trivial.

For women, the rules governing hair-covering stem from a passage from the Koran that states: "Say to the believing women that they should lower their gaze and guard their modesty. . . . They should draw their veils over their bosoms and not display their ornaments."

"Zinah," the Arabic word for ornament, has come to mean "hair." So, strictly speaking, women can go bareheaded only in front of other women, their husbands, fathers, sons, nephews, servants, slaves and children small enough to "'have no sense of the shame of sex."

But the Koranic verse itself is open to interpretation, and the Koran also states in many verses that there is no compulsion in Islam. That has prompted debates about— as well as experimentation with—the extent, color and design of hijab, or Islamic cover.

For men, there is even more confusion because there is no Koranic verse requiring that they grow beards. But the Prophet Muhammad had a beard, as had the prophets of Judaism and Christianity before him. So having a beard can be a visible symbol of being created by God. And many Muslim clerics over the centuries have written opinions strongly recommending beard-growing or even calling it an Islamic duty.

"In the world in which Islam was revealed, men kept their beards whether they were Christian, Jewish or Muslim," said Seyyed Hossein Nasr, professor of Islamic Studies at George Washington University. "There were no beardless prophets. You never had a shaved Moses or Abraham or Jesus." (Even today, he added, practitioners of other religions, like some rigorously Orthodox Jews, place great importance on men retaining facial hair and women not displaying their own hair.)***

Under the Taliban, men were required to grow beards at least four inches long. The order was based on what some Islamic scholars believe is a somewhat spurious Islamic teaching, because traditionally, a man with a long beard meant one of two things: either he was of a venerable age or had great spiritual or intellectual authority. "Even in Egypt today, a long beard on a 22-year-old would be considered a sign of pretension," said Mr. Nasr. "You will not find many ordinary bakers with long beards unless they're 70 years old."

Choice—to veil or not, to shave or not—has been an issue in Islam for more than a century. In 1935, going even further then Turkey's secular modernizers, Reza Shah of Iran decreed that the wearing of traditional dress for both women and men was punishable by a prison term. The army and police roamed through villages to enforce the law, tearing the all-enveloping chador off women and handing out free Western-style suits to men. Reza Shah also forbade men to wear turbans. Mustaches were allowed (the shah wore one) but beards were forbidden, even for clerics, although the ban was only episodically enforced.

To many women, the veil was a source of protection, respect and virtue. In her 1992 memoir, "Daughter of Persia," Sattareh Farman Farmaian, the daughter of an Iranian

Qajar prince, recalled her mother's bitter reaction to Reza Shah's edict: "He doesn't fear God, this evil shah—may God curse him for it!" Some women refused to leave home, some because they didn't want to be bareheaded in public, others to protest coercion.***

One of the most confusing moments in the history of hair in the Muslim world in the 20th century came in the late 1960's, when Western hippies trekked through places like Iran and Afghanistan. For the Muslims who lived there, the long hair and beards were confusing. Westerners weren't supposed to look like that.

RATNA KAPUR, UN-VEILING WOMEN'S RIGHTS IN THE "WAR ON TERRORISM"

9 Duke J. Gender L. & Pol'y 211, 214, 217–20 (2002)

The "War on Terrorism" and its secondary goal of protecting women has been addressed largely within the rhetoric of religion, civilization, and "a just war," rather than a concern for women's human rights. The focus on women's concerns through the prism of religion and culture not only serves to cast Muslim women as "Other," it also serves to justify the liberating impulse of military intervention, defending such interventions as humane rescue operations. The rhetoric of civilization justifies any intervention to rescue women from barbarism and the tyranny of evil. And the rhetoric of "a just war" serves as a justification for the abrogation of the rules of law and of war, which are cast aside to serve the greater good of (Western) civilization and preserving "our" (American) way of life.***

The Specter of Cultural Monoliths

The way religion is invoked, primarily along the lines of civilization and exclusive cultural representations, is based on a view that culture is static and immutable, that it is fixed and cabined. It is a perception based on a monolithic understanding of culture and closes off the pluralisms, contests and dissent that exist within the tradition.***

The image of the veiled woman has been displaced onto a cultural divide along which many global conversations about women's rights take place, and where culture is something invariably associated with the "native" other. It is a displacement that not only operates along an "us and them" divide, but lays a foundation for the view that the veil is an exclusively oppressive symbol. The complexity and multiple meanings of the veil are erased. The image of the veiled woman has come to inhabit our imaginations in ways that are totalizing of the culture and its treatment of women. This image is nearly always simplistic as well as a misrepresentation of the practice as a subordinating practice that typifies Islam and its degrading treatment of women. It is invoked as a cultural artifact to distinguish us from them, to justify military or feminist interventions that could further aggravate rather than alleviate the situation of women.

The multiple meanings of the veil, through different cultural and historical contexts, get subsumed in this representation. It is read in a uniform, linear manner as an oppressive practice, because it erases women's physical and sexual identity, and is symbolic of the subjugation of women in Islam. In the flurry of media articles on the situation of women in Afghanistan under Taliban rule, the veil, or burqa, is the central edifice of the argument that (Muslim) women are oppressed by a barbaric (Muslim) regime and culture. There is little attempt to unpack the historical ingredients that have gone into the creation of the Taliban, as well as the fact that Afghan women are not a monolithic community, nor the veil a purely oppressive symbol. There is no universal opinion amongst those Muslim women who wear the veil (and not all do) as to its function. For some, it does represent honor. But more significantly, the veil has also been a very empowering symbol for Muslim women in some countries. In Iran, it was the sign of rebellion and rejection of the Shah and Western imperialism. Amongst immigrant communities in Western countries, it is the symbol of an exclusive cultural space and a rejection of assimilation.

In other contexts, the veil is considered a private space, one in which no one can intrude. The veil also disrupts the public space, where women are often marginalized. The sheer symbolism of the veil brings the woman visibly into the public sphere—she simply cannot walk by unnoticed. However, in the assumptions about the veil that inform the current public discourse, these multiple readings and functions of the veil are erased and only one stands out—the veil as a tool of oppression and barbarism—read Islamic barbarism—against women.

One must read the imposition of the veil in the context of the Taliban in the broader context of the denial of rights to women and men under an oppressive non-democratic regime. Conformity is a matter of survival in a political context where dissent means death. This is not an unfamiliar story. At the same time we know that there is dissent, a dissent that comes not only from the Muslim women in Afghanistan, such as the Revolutionary Afghan Women's Association, who have organized against these oppressive edicts and the denial of human rights. It also comes from Muslim women outside of Afghanistan, who protest against the denial of rights to women, without centering their critiques on the veil. These voices are emerging from Pakistan, Indonesia and Bangladesh as well as other countries. All three of these countries presently have, or have historically had, a woman serve as their head of state. Non-governmental organizations such as the Sisters of Islam in Malaysia, and the Women Living under Muslim Law, an international network, are also joining the debate.

The critique of the veil by Muslim women is very clear and vocal, but it does not slip into the rhetoric of opposition between the West and the "Rest," the highly divisive strategy which forces one to choose sides. Muslim women are not just Muslims, and they are not just women—they are Muslim women and many resist a strategy that forces a choice between community and gender identity. Moreover, a recent survey by the Physicians for Human Rights suggests that the rights to freedom of speech and expression, the instituting of legal protections for women, and issues surrounding peace and de-mining are amongst the most pressing concerns for women in Afghanistan. The issue of the burqa and punishment for infractions of the dress code were regarded as the least important issues. I do not mean to suggest that the violence against women who do not conform to a strict dress code is unimportant. It is egregious that such severe punishments should be inflicted on women who transgress the Taliban's edicts. However, the issue needs to be reframed as one of the consequences that flow from the dissent to an authoritarian, arbitrary regime, and not through the lens of culture. It must also be viewed against the broader canvass of human rights, which have been denied quite specifically by the Taliban, but that have resulted from years of war, drought and the role of foreign powers in aggravating, rather than alleviating, the situation of women in Afghanistan.

What Lies Beneath?***

The Taliban swept across Afghanistan in 1996 not simply as a religious force determined to set up an Islamic state. It was a force born in the crucible of the Cold War, schooled in the Madrasas and whose members were raised in refugee camps. It was a force whose very way of life was war and which imposed its way of life on an entire country through brute force and violence. To view the Taliban as a force that is exclusively the outcome of religion does not create space for the fact that the current conflict is neither ancient nor archaic. It did not emerge from the passages of ancient religious texts. It is a contemporary movement that emerged from equally contemporary conditions, relations and conflicts. The more we excavate the Koran or other religious texts to unearth the passage that enlightens us about the beliefs and practices of these groups, the further we drift from the real issues, from the ones that humans, not God, have an ability and responsibility to address.

At one level, the attacks of September 11th must be examined through the prism of religion because all the parties are invoking it in their discussions. But it is not the only prism through which to understand the full complexity of what is occurring. Centering culture and religion blunts our analysis. Similarly, the treatment of women cannot be exclusively explained either through culture or a focus on the veil. The veil has become a battleground for justifying the U.S. bombing of Afghanistan, the breaches of international law and the enormous civilian casualties that have resulted.

The major focus of Muslim women's concerns, including their situation in the refugee camps, food aid and the humanitarian crisis aggravated by the bombing of Afghanistan, remain inadequately addressed.***

2. The Theoretical Debate: Can "Culture" and "Rights" Co-Exist?

RATNA KAPUR, THE TRAGEDY OF VICTIMIZATION RHETORIC: RESURRECTING THE "NATIVE" SUBJECT IN INTERNATIONAL/ POST-COLONIAL FEMINIST LEGAL POLITICS

15 HARV. HUM. RTS. J. 1, 3–4, 6–7, 10 (2002)

The Hegemonic Victim Subject

The 1993 Vienna World Conference on Human Rights marked the culmination of a long struggle to secure international recognition of women's rights as human rights. It was a turning point for both the international women's rights movement and the human rights movement. The final document that emerged from Vienna acknowledged that, partly as a result of the artificial line drawn between the public and private sphere, certain gender-specific issues had been left out of the human rights arena. Governments around the world acknowledged that women, too, were entitled to enjoy fundamental rights. These included full and equal participation in political, civil, economic, social, and cultural life at the national, regional, and international level. In addition, the document brought about a significant change in human rights law: the recognition of women's human rights in the private sphere. A broad spectrum of harms occurring in the sphere of the family were rendered open to human rights scrutiny. The document challenged the public/private distinction along which human rights had traditionally operated and increased awareness of the fact that power operates in multiple arenas.

The women's rights movement at the international and regional level, as well as official recognition of women's rights, appear to have focused primarily on the issue of violence against women and their victimization in this context. Immediately after the Vienna conference, the U.N. General Assembly passed a Declaration on Violence Against Women. The declaration stated that it would strengthen and complement the process of effective implementation of the Convention on the Elimination of All Forms of Discrimination Against Women (CEDAW). It recognized that violence against women "is a manifestation of historically unequal power relations between men and women, which have led to domination over and discrimination against women." It reiterated the consensus reached at Vienna: that violence against women covers "gender-based violence . . . whether occurring in public or in private life."

*** [A]n exclusive reliance on the victim subject to make claims for rights and for women's empowerment has some serious limitations. The articulation of the victim subject is based on gender essentialism; that is, over generalized claims about women. As Chandra Mohanty points out, essentialism assumes that "women have a coherent group identity within different cultures . . . prior to their entry into social relations." Such generalizations are hegemonic in that they represent the problems of privileged women, who are often (though not exclusively) white, Western, middle-class, heterosexual women. These generalizations efface the problems, perspectives, and political concerns of women marginalized because of their class, race, religion, ethnicity, and/or sexual orientation. The victim subject ultimately relies on a universal subject: a subject that resembles the uncomplicated subject of liberal discourse. It is a subject that cannot accommodate a multi-layered experience.

The second problem with a focus on violence against women is that it is a position based on cultural essentialism. Women in the Third World are portrayed as victims of their culture, which reinforces stereotyped and racist representations of that culture and privileges the culture of the West. In the end, the focus on the victim subject reinforces the depiction of women in the Third World as perpetually marginalized and underprivileged, and has serious implications for the strategies subsequently adopted to remedy the harms that women experience. It encourages some feminists in the international arena to propose strategies which are reminiscent of imperial interventions in the lives of the native subject and which represent the "Eastern" woman as a victim of a "backward" and "uncivilized" culture.

Finally, the victim subject and the focus on violence invite remedies and responses from states that have little to do with promoting women's rights. Thus, a related concern is that the victim subject position has invited protectionist, and even conservative, responses from states. The construction of women exclusively through the lens of violence has triggered a spate of domestic and international reforms focused on the criminal law, which are used to justify state restrictions on women's rights—for the protection of women. The anti-trafficking campaign, with its focus on violence and victimization, is but one example. The government of Nepal restricts women under thirty from traveling outside of the country without the permission of a husband or male guardian as part of an anti-trafficking initiative. Early feminist interventions struggled to move away from such protectionist responses through anti-discrimination discourse. However, the

VAW campaigns, which are contingent on the victim subject, have taken feminists back into a protectionist and conservative discourse. Furthermore, these interventions reinforce women's victim status. The exclusive focus on finding resolutions through appeals to the state fails to consider the relevance to the women's rights agenda of new players in the public sphere who are de-centering the power of sovereign states.***

The lack of complexity has become particularly evident in the international women's human rights arena. The feminist legal agenda, despite its international complexion, has not sufficiently taken on board the critiques of gender essentialism in formulating the women's human rights project. The VAW campaign has not translated into a complex understanding of the ways in which women's lives and experiences are mediated by race, religion, class, and gender.***

SUSAN MOLLER OKIN, IS MULTICULTURALISM BAD FOR WOMEN?

JOSHUA COHEN, MATTHEW HOWARD & MARTHA NUSSBAUM EDS.,
IS MULTICULTURALISM BAD FOR WOMEN? 7, 9–14, 16–23 (1999)

Until the past few decades, minority groups—immigrants as well as indigenous peoples—were typically expected to assimilate into majority cultures. This assimilationist expectation is now often considered oppressive, and many Western countries are seeking to devise new policies that are more responsive to persistent cultural differences.*** But one issue recurs across all contexts, though it has gone virtually unnoticed in current debate: What should be done when the claims of minority cultures or religions clash with the norm of gender equality that is at least formally endorsed by liberal states (however much they continue to violate it in their practice)?

[I argue] that there is considerable likelihood of tension between *** feminism and a multiculturalist commitment to group rights for minority cultures.

*** By "feminism," I mean the belief that women should not be disadvantaged by their sex, that they should be recognized as having human dignity equally with men, and the opportunity to live as fulfilling and as freely chosen lives as men can. "Multiculturalism" is harder to pin down, but the particular aspect that concerns me here is the claim, made in the context of basically liberal democracies, that minority cultures or ways of life are not sufficiently protected by ensuring the individual rights of their members and as a consequence should also be protected with special *group* rights or privileges.***

Gender and Culture

Most cultures are suffused with practices and ideologies concerning gender. Suppose, then, that a culture endorses and facilitates the control of men over women in various ways (even if informally, in the private sphere of domestic life). Suppose, too, that there are fairly clear disparities of power between the sexes, such that the more powerful, male members are those who are generally in a position to determine and articulate the group's beliefs, practices, and interests. Under such conditions, group rights are potentially, and in many cases actually, antifeminist. They substantially limit the capacities of women and girls of that culture to live with human dignity equal to that of men and boys, and to live as freely chosen lives as they can.

Advocates of group rights for minorities within liberal states have not adequately addressed this simple critique of group rights, for at least two reasons. First, they tend to treat cultural groups as monoliths—to pay more attention to differences between and among groups than to differences within them. Specifically, they give little or no recognition to the fact that minority cultural groups, like the societies in which they exist (though to a greater or lesser extent), are themselves *gendered*, with substantial differences of power and advantage between men and women. Second, advocates of group rights pay no or little attention to the private sphere. Some of the best liberal defenses of group rights urge that individuals need "a culture of their own," and that only within such a culture can people develop a sense of self-esteem or self-respect, or the capacity to decide what kind of life is good for them. But such arguments typically neglect both the different roles that cultural groups require of their members and the context in which persons' senses of themselves and their capacities are first formed *and* in which culture is first transmitted—the realm of domestic or family life.

When we correct for these deficiencies by paying attention to internal differences and to the private arena, two particularly important connections between culture and gender come into sharp relief, both of which underscore the force of the simple critique. First, the sphere of personal, sexual, and reproductive life provides a central focus of most cultures, a dominant theme in cultural practices and rules. Religious or cultural groups are often particularly concerned with "personal law"—the laws of marriage, divorce, child custody, division and control of family property, and inheritance. As a rule, then, the defense of "cultural practices" is likely to have much greater impact on the lives of women and girls than those of men and boys, since far more of women's time and energy goes into preserving and maintaining the personal, familial, and reproductive side of life.***

Second, most cultures have as one of their principal aims the control of women by men. Consider, for example, the founding myths of Greek and Roman antiquity, and of Judaism, Christianity, and Islam: they are rife with attempts to justify the control and subordination of women. These myths consist of a combination of denials of women's role in reproduction, appropriations by men of the power to reproduce themselves, characterizations of women as overly emotional, untrustworthy, evil, or sexually dangerous, and refusals to acknowledge mothers' rights over the disposition of their children. Think of Athena, sprung from the head of Zeus, and of Romulus and Remus, reared without a human mother. Or Adam, made by a male God, who then (at least according to one of the two biblical versions of the story) made Eve out of part of Adam. Consider Eve, whose weakness led Adam astray. Think of all those endless "begats" in Genesis, where women's primary role in reproduction is completely ignored, or of the textual justifications for polygamy, once practiced in Judaism, still practiced in many parts of the Islamic world and (though illegally) by Mormons in some parts of the United States. Consider, too, the story of Abraham, a pivotal turning point in the development of monotheism. God commands Abraham to sacrifice "his" greatly loved son. Abraham prepares to do exactly what God asks of him, without even telling, much less asking, Isaac's mother, Sarah. Abraham's absolute obedience to God makes him the central, fundamental model of faith, for all three religions.

While the powerful drive to control women—and to blame and punish them for men's difficulty controlling their own sexual impulses—has been softened considerably in the more progressive, reformed versions of Judaism, Christianity, and Islam, it remains strong in their more orthodox or fundamentalist versions. Moreover, it is by no means confined to Western or monotheistic cultures. Many of the world's traditions and cultures, including those practiced within formerly conquered or colonized nation states—certainly including most of the peoples of Africa, the Middle East, Latin America and Asia—are quite distinctly patriarchal. They too have elaborate patterns of socialization, rituals, matrimonial customs, and other cultural practices (including systems of property ownership and control of resources) aimed at bringing women's sexuality and reproductive capabilities under men's control. Many such practices make it virtually impossible for women to choose to live independently of men, to be celibate or lesbian, or not to have children.

Those who practice some of the most controversial such customs—clitoridectomy, the marriage of children or marriages that are otherwise coerced, or polygamy—sometimes explicitly defend them as necessary for controlling women, and openly acknowledge that the customs persist at men's insistence.***

Thus, many culturally-based customs aim to control women and render them, especially sexually and reproductively, servile to men's desires and interests. Sometimes, moreover, "culture" or "traditions" are so closely linked with the control of women that they are virtually equated.***

While virtually all of the world's cultures have distinctly patriarchal pasts, some—mostly, though by no means exclusively, Western liberal cultures—have departed far further from them than others. Western cultures, of course, still practice many forms of sex discrimination. They place far more stress on beauty, thinness, and youth in females and on intellectual accomplishment, skill, and strength in males; they expect women to perform for no economic reward far more than half of the unpaid work of their families, whether or not they also work for wages; partly as a consequence of this and partly because of workplace discrimination, women are far more likely than men to become poor; girls and women are also subjected by men to a great deal of (illegal) violence, including sexual violence. But women in more liberal cultures are, at the same time, legally guaranteed many of the same freedoms and opportunities as men. In addition, most families in such cultures, with the exception of some religious fundamentalists, do not communicate to their daughters that they are of less value than boys, that their lives are to be confined to domesticity and service to men and children, and that the only positive value of their sexuality is that it be strictly confined to marriage, the service of men, and reproductive ends. This, as we have seen, is quite different from women's situation in many of the world's other cultures, including many of those from which immigrants to Europe and Northern America come.

Group Rights?

*** [T]he overwhelming majority of "cultural defenses" that are increasingly being invoked in US criminal cases concerning members of cultural minorities are connected with gender—in particular with male control over women and children. Occasionally, cultural defenses come into play in explaining expectable violence among men, or the ritual sacrifice of animals. Much more common, however, is the argument that, in the defendant's cultural group, women are not human beings of equal worth but subordinates whose primary (if not only) functions are to serve men sexually and domestically. Thus, the four types of cases in which cultural defenses have been used most successfully are: kidnap and rape by Hmong men who claim that their actions are part of their cultural practice of *zij poj niam* or "marriage by capture"; wife-murder by immigrants from Asian and Middle Eastern countries whose wives have either committed adultery or treated their husbands in a servile way; mothers who have killed their children but failed to kill themselves, and claim that because of their Japanese or Chinese backgrounds the shame of their husbands' infidelity drove them to the culturally condoned practice of mother-child suicide; and—in France, though not yet in the United States, in part because the practice was criminalized only in 1996—clitoridectomy. In a number of such cases, expert testimony about the accused's or defendant's cultural background has resulted in dropped or reduced charges, culturally-based assessments of *mens rea*, or significantly reduced sentences. In a well-known recent case, an immigrant from rural Iraq married his two daughters, aged 13 and 14, to two of his friends, aged 28 and 34. Subsequently, when the older daughter ran away with her 20-year-old boyfriend, the father sought the help of the police in finding her. When they located her, they charged the father with child abuse, and the two husbands and boyfriend with statutory rape. The Iraqis' defense is based in part, at least, on their cultural marriage practices.

As these examples show, the defendants are not always male, nor the victims always female. Both a Chinese immigrant man in New York who battered his wife to death for committing adultery and a Japanese immigrant woman in California who drowned her children and tried to drown herself because her husband's adultery had shamed the family, relied on cultural defenses to win reduced charges (from murder to second degree or involuntary manslaughter). It might seem, then, that cultural defense was biased toward the male in the first case, and the female in the second. But no such asymmetry exists. In both cases, the cultural message is similarly gender-biased: women (and children, in the second case) are ancillary to men, and should bear the blame and the shame for any departure from monogamy. Whoever is guilty of the infidelity, the wife suffers: in the first case, by being brutally killed on account of her husband's rage at her shameful infidelity; in the second, by being so shamed and branded a failure by his infidelity that she is driven to kill herself and her children.***

Western majority cultures, largely at the urging of feminists, have recently made substantial efforts to avoid or limit excuses for brutalizing women. Well within living memory, American men were routinely held less accountable for killing their wives if they explained their conduct as a crime of passion, driven by jealousy on account of the wife's infidelity. Also not long ago, women who did not have completely celibate pasts or who did not struggle—even so as to endanger themselves—were routinely blamed when raped. Things have now changed to some extent, and doubts about the turn toward cultural defenses undoubtedly come in part from a concern to preserve recent advances. Another concern is that such defenses can distort perceptions of minority cultures by drawing excessive attention to negative aspects of them. But perhaps the primary concern is that, by failing to protect women and sometimes children of minority cultures from male and sometimes maternal violence, cultural defenses violate their rights to the equal protection of the laws. When a woman from a more patriarchal culture comes to the United States (or some other Western, basically liberal, state), why should she be less protected from male violence than other women are? Many women from minority cultures have protested the double standard that is being applied to their aggressors.

Liberal Defense

Despite all this evidence of cultural practices that control and subordinate women, none of the prominent defenders of multicultural group rights has adequately or even directly addressed the troubling connections between gender and culture, or the conflicts that arise so commonly between multiculturalism and feminism. Will Kymlicka's discussion is, in this respect, representative.

Kymlicka's arguments for group rights are based on the rights of individuals, and confine such privileges and protection to cultural groups that are internally liberal. Following John Rawls, Kymlicka emphasizes the fundamental importance of self-respect in a person's life. He argues that membership in a "rich and secure cultural structure," with its language and history, is essential both for the development of self-respect and for giving persons a context in which they can develop the capacity to make choices about how to lead their lives. Cultural minorities need special rights, then, because their culture may otherwise be threatened with extinction, and cultural extinction would likely undermine the self-respect and freedom of group members. Special rights, in short, put minorities on a footing of equality with the majority.

The value of freedom plays an important role in Kymlicka's argument. As a result, except in rare circumstances of cultural vulnerability, a group that claims special rights must govern itself by recognizably liberal principles, neither infringing on the basic liberties of its own members by placing internal restrictions on them, nor discriminating among them on grounds of sex, race, or sexual preference. This requirement is of great importance to a consistently liberal justification for group rights, since a "closed" or discriminatory culture cannot provide the context for individual development that liberalism requires and because collective rights might otherwise result in subcultures of oppression within and aided by liberal societies. As Kymlicka says: "To inhibit people from questioning their inherited social roles can condemn them to unsatisfying, even oppressive lives."

As Kymlicka acknowledges, this requirement of internal liberalism rules out the justification of group rights for the "many fundamentalists of all political and religious stripes who think that the best community is one in which all but their preferred religious, sexual, or aesthetic practices are outlawed." For the promotion and support of *these* cultures "undermines the very reason we had for being concerned with cultural membership—that it allows for meaningful individual choice." But the examples I cited earlier suggest that far fewer minority cultures than Kymlicka seems to think will be able to claim group rights under his liberal justification. Though they may not impose their beliefs or practices on others, and though they may appear to respect the basic civil and political liberties of women and girls, many cultures do not, especially in the private sphere, treat them with anything like the same concern and respect as men and boys, or allow them to enjoy the same freedoms.***

Part of the Solution?

It is by no means clear, then, from a feminist point of view, that minority group rights are "part of the solution." They may well exacerbate the problem. In the case of a more patriarchal minority culture in the context of a less patriarchal majority culture, no argument can be made on the basis of self-respect or freedom that the female members of the culture have a clear interest in its preservation. Indeed, they *may* be much better off if the culture into which they were born were either to become extinct (so that its members would become integrated into the less sexist surrounding culture) or, preferably, to be encouraged to alter itself so as to reinforce the equality of women—at least to the degree to which this is upheld in the majority culture.***

AZIZAH Y. AL-HIBRI, IS WESTERN PATRIARCHAL FEMINISM GOOD FOR THIRD WORLD AND MINORITY WOMEN?

JOSHUA COHEN, MATTHEW HOWARD & MARTHA NUSSBAUM EDS.,
IS MULTICULTURALISM BAD FOR WOMEN? 41, 41–46 (1999)

The issue of conflicting rights raised by Susan Okin's paper is of fundamental importance to any serious human rights discourse. Okin's perspective, discussion, and proposal, however, all suffer from three fatal problems: (1) stereotypical views of the "Other"; (2) a conflation of distinct belief systems; and (3) conflict with American constitutional principles.

The paper is clearly written from the perspective of the dominant cultural "I," a Western point of view burdened with immigrant problems and the human rights conflicts they engender. Okin blames this conflict on a Western liberal tradition that recognizes value in the very existence of cultural diversity. She argues that some cultures may in fact be worthy of extinction.

Okin's statement is remarkable in its honesty. If she is right about the universality of her principles, then, of course, why should women from other cultures have a lower standard of human rights crafted especially for them? In fact, whether immigrants or residents in their home country, why should women wait for salvation, when the West can readily defend their rights by use of force if necessary? Certainly, Okin's position has more integrity than one which views the "natives" or "alien immigrants" condescendingly and argues, under the guise of Western liberalism, that "those people" should be allowed to live in accordance with their own lower standards of human rights.

Luckily, these two options are not exhaustive. To recognize other alternatives, we need to revisit Okin's article and uncover its first fatal error. A quick look at her endnotes reveals what was already obvious to a culturally sensitive reader: her understanding of other cultures/religions is derived from secondary sources outside these cultures/religions. As a result, Okin commits simple but significant factual errors in assessing other belief systems. She argues, for example, that "the founding myths" of Judaism, Christianity, and Islam "are rife with attempts to justify the control and subordination of women" and, among other things, characterize women as "overly emotional, untrustworthy, evil, or sexually dangerous." As proof, she offers two stories: the creation of Eve out of part of Adam and the fall of Adam.

But the Qur'an nowhere says that Eve was created out of part of Adam. In fact, the Qur'an clearly states that males and females were created by God from the same *nafs* (soul or spirit), and that the most honored among them in the sight of God is the most pious. The story of the fall of Adam is also different in the Qur'an. *Both* Adam *and* Eve were tempted by Satan, and both succumbed. The story is thus about the human condition. It is not about gender. By missing these important differences, Okin attributes to Islam a position based on biblical analysis. This is a serious form of religious reductionism. It is also the example par excellence of Okin speaking in her dominant voice about the *inessential Other*. So inessential is this Other that, even when included in the discussion, it is rendered remarkably indistinguishable and voiceless. It is allowed into the discussion only through the voice and perceptions of the dominant "I." Given these ground rules, it is hard to have a serious discussion or reach a democratic resolution of existing conflicts.

The importance of a genuine dialogue is that it permits a more accurate diagnosis of the problems at hand. While "founding myths" are not patriarchal in Islam, several jurists have succeeded in developing a patriarchal interpretation of various Qur'anic passages. It is these passages with the related jurisprudence, and not the "founding myths," that need to be addressed in Islam. Unfortunately, an Orientalist reductionist approach to Islam often delays productive dialogue.

I now turn to the second fatal error in Okin's piece: her conflation of distinct systems of belief. In attempting to refute the thesis that minority cultures should be protected by special rights, Okin draws many of her examples from the domain of religious belief. From the outset, she refers to such matters as Muslim head scarves, polygamy, and early marriages. In later passages, Okin moves from culture to religion, as if they were interchangeable. From the outside, they may very well be. From the inside, the distinction amounts to the difference between acceptance and rejection of change.

To put this complicated issue in its proper perspective, we need to know a few basic Islamic principles. First, Islamic society is based on a system of *shura* (consultation) and the individual right to *ijtihad* (jurisprudential interpretation of religious text); hence there is no central authority charged with the task of interpreting the religion to the faithful. As a result, women, as much as men, are entitled to engage in *ijtihad* (and have). And each Muslim, male or female, is guaranteed his or her freedom of conscience. Second, Islam was revealed as a world religion and thus, according to Qur'anic verse, celebrates diversity. For this reason, a Muslim country may retain all local customs not inconsistent with Islamic revelation. As a result of this principle, many countries retained local customs that we find controversial, and that have been erroneously viewed in the West, and sometimes locally, as Islamic. Third, Islamic jurisprudence adopts the principle that many laws change with the change of time and place, yet many Muslims continue to follow the jurisprudence of past centuries and civilizations. Finally, Muslim jurists believe that the laws of the Wise Lawgiver serve human *maslaha* (public interest).

A true feminist call to reform in Muslim countries or among Muslim immigrants must respect their religious and cultural sentiments, while recognizing the sanctity of the first and flexibility of the second. This means that with respect to issues such as those raised by Okin, the better approach is for Muslim feminists to reexamine existing Islamic jurisprudence critically in light of established jurisprudential principles and the *maslaha* of the Muslims. The result is a tripartite strategy. First, clearly separate customary from religious practices. This would significantly reduce the resistance of Muslims to certain types of change namely, purely cultural changes. Second, reexamine existing jurisprudence critically to reveal any inappropriate cultural elements in it. Third, provide modern contributions to Islamic jurisprudence, which take into account the time, place, and *maslaha* of Muslims, half of whom are women. Such a complicated and time-consuming project cannot be truncated or canceled owing to the impatience of secular feminists.***

Okin casts the conflict as one in which feminists and human rights advocates are attempting to save the women of minority cultures from internal oppression. Framed this way, the endeavor is admirable. Different accounts, however, reveal different scenarios. For example, many contemporary women with established careers have adopted the Orthodox or Hasidic Jewish way of life as adults. This way of life includes, among other things, early marriages, gender roles, praying behind a *mecbitzah* (partition separating men from women), and even *mikvah* (ritual bath) ceremonies (following menstruation). It is hard for Okin to argue that these accomplished women have been so misled as to choose an oppressive lifestyle. There is something condescending, even patriarchal, about such a claim. The women themselves see in their new life important values. For example, they see in the mikvah ceremonies "women-centered spiritual celebration of women's bodies, cycles, sexuality, and procreative power." They also see an important opportunity for bonding with one another.***

Okin occupies a difficult position. She is right to be concerned about her sisters, and not to look the other way in the face of their oppression. She even shows some recognition of the fact that her views may be too severe. For this reason, she briefly refers at the end of her piece to "negotiations about group rights." It is unclear, however, whether these negotiations are recommended with all minority groups or limited to those that satisfy the "requirement of internal liberalism."

The issue is actually of some urgency to me personally. As a Muslim who believes that many oppressive practices attributed to Islam are either cultural ones or ones that resulted from a patriarchal interpretation of religious text, what should I do about oppressive behavior among some Muslims in this country? Two types of behavior come to mind. The first involves such actions as violence against women; the second involves such behavior as wearing a head scarf.

In the first instance, the perpetrator of violence against a woman (or man) is guilty of assault and battery under Islamic law, and his punishment is as severe as his crime. Furthermore, as a good Muslim, I may not shift my responsibility for correcting the situation to the legal system and turn my face the other way. If the system fails to take appropriate protective action, I have a duty to step in and try to end the violence by any legitimate means available to me. The Qur'an enjoins me to take personal responsibility to correct the situation myself, the best way I possibly can. The moral values underlying this analysis are clearly shared universally, by people of faith as well as secularists. There is no dilemma here, nor a viable cultural or religious excuse that could justify violence against women.

The other example is more complicated. Why is it oppressive to wear a head scarf but liberating to wear a miniskirt? The crux of the explanation lies in the assumptions each side makes about the women involved and their ability to make choices. But suppose, for the sake of argument, that I too find covering one's head oppressive, and that it is not required religiously. Should I now organize to force those sisters to bare their heads? Should I organize to ensure that they do not pass their values to their children?

Clearly, I could build a limited united front with secular feminists and try to foster popular sentiment against self-oppressive choices. But my Islamic training and knowledge of my community tell me that many of these Muslim sisters have thought seriously about the issue of covering their heads and have reached conclusions different from mine. Forcing them to abandon their religious choices is not only patronizing but fundamentally un-Islamic! Islam has an established etiquette of difference, by which I may explain my position to other Muslims without ever claiming exclusive access to the truth or becoming coercive.***

ABDULLAHI AN-NA'IM, PROMISES WE SHOULD ALL KEEP IN COMMON CAUSE

JOSHUA COHEN, MATTHEW HOWARD & MARTHA NUSSBAUM EDS.,
IS MULTICULTURALISM BAD FOR WOMEN? 59, 60–62 (1999)

*** I agree with Okin's view that nearly all cultures discriminate against women especially many of the minority cultures on whose behalf claims of group rights are being made in Western societies. I also share her commitment to the elimination of all forms of discrimination against women and girls everywhere as a human rights imperative. The main difference between our positions pertains to the possibility of *comprehensive* strategies for the protection of all human rights throughout the world. What I emphasize is that, in seeking to eliminate discrimination on grounds of sex, one should avoid encouraging discrimination on grounds of race, religion, language, or national origin.

For example, Okin's analysis makes no reference to economic and social rights (such as the right to an adequate standard of living and education) although these concerns constitute much of the rationale of group rights. This omission is particularly significant because failure to accept these as *human rights* is a clear indication of liberal "cultural relativism" in the wider debate about the universality of human rights.

Moreover, while citing examples of discrimination against women and girls from various parts of the world, Okin does not seem to be concerned with the resolution of those problems in non-Western societies. I am therefore wondering whether her proposed solution for the elimination of gender discrimination within minority cultures in the West is detrimental to the achievement of this objective itself globally, let alone to the realization of a more comprehensive view of human rights everywhere.

Okin says that she prefers that a minority culture be "encouraged to alter itself so as to reinforce the equality of women at least to the degree to which this value is upheld in the majority culture," rather than "become extinct (so that its members would become integrated into the less sexist surrounding culture)." The sense of ultimatum is of course clear even in her preferred solution. Minority cultures are told: either change to achieve gender equality in the private lives of your families and communal affairs, or perish. But Okin does not offer any comment on the implications of cultural extinction for members of minority cultures. Moreover, it is interesting to note that Okin is willing to accept the degree of gender equality upheld by the majority culture. Whereas the minority culture faces an ultimatum in meeting the standard set by the majority culture, the latter can take its own time in achieving gender equality at the level set by international human rights norms, if ever.

I am not suggesting, of course, that either minority or majority should be allowed to practice gender discrimination, or violate some other human right, because they believe their culture mandates it. In particular, I emphasize that all women's rights advocates must continue to scrutinize and criticize gender discrimination anywhere in the world, and not only in Western societies. But this objective must be pursued in ways that foster the protection of all human rights, and with sensitivity and respect for the identity and dignity of all human beings everywhere.

In other words, I say that all cultures must be held to the same standards not only of gender equality but also of all other human rights. While gender equality is a serious problem in some minority cultures in the United States, for example, racism and economic and social rights are large problems for the majority culture. So American human rights advocates should be equally concerned with all human rights issues that are problematic in their own situation, though some of them may have one particular focus or another for practical reasons. Only by engaging in such an "internal discourse" can American human rights advocates gain the moral credibility required to encourage such discourse elsewhere. This in turn will generate "cross-cultural dialogue" to promote consensus on truly universal human rights norms and their principled and sustainable implementation throughout the world.

I am also suggesting that compliance with human rights standards cannot be achieved in a principled and sustainable manner except through the internal dynamics of the culture concerned. For that to happen, the argument for gender equality has to be made within the frame of reference of minority culture, and for economic rights within the framework of liberal Western cultures.***

LETI VOLPP, FEMINISM VERSUS MULTICULTURALISM

101 COLUM. L. REV. 1181, 1183–1210, 1217 (2001)

*** [I]s Okin correct to posit multiculturalism and feminism as contradictory? I argue here that posing multiculturalism and feminism as oppositional results in a discourse of "feminism versus multiculturalism" that is premised on serious and fundamental logical flaws. Such a discourse relies upon a particular subject, the immigrant woman victim of minority culture. In examining how the figure of the immigrant woman victim is constructed, I address both the theoretical bases of the feminism versus multiculturalism discourse and the disturbing consequences of its adoption.***

The argument between these two positions has limited utility. What is much more interesting to explore is the question of why this binary discourse so frequently structures the parameters of the debate. My criticism of the structure of the discourse of feminism versus multiculturalism does not stem from the perspective of cultural relativism. Rather, it starts from the position that we can make normative choices, such as, it is never "OK to beat one's wife." The clarification is essential because any criticism of the way these values are formulated is frequently considered a purely deconstructive project or viewed as a very quick slide down the slippery slope of relativism. The thrust of my argument is not that we ought to eliminate or dismiss feminist values, but to suggest they will broaden and shift when we examine immigrant and Third World women in a more accurate light.***

Death by Culture

The discourse of feminism versus multiculturalism presumes that minority cultures are more patriarchal than Western liberal cultures. Because representations of minority women are often interchanged with those of Third World women, the depiction of minority cultures in this discourse often reflects assumptions about Third World cultures. Thus, both immigrants of color and Third World communities are necessarily the subject here.

Since the vision of the suffering immigrant or Third World woman and the liberated Western one has so strong a hold on the American imagination, I attempt to demonstrate that the presumption of Western women's liberation depends upon the notion that immigrant and Third World communities are sites of aberrant violence.***

Culture is invoked to explain forms of violence against Third World or immigrant women while culture is not similarly invoked to explain forms of violence that affect mainstream Western women. The specific case of dowry and domestic violence murders provides an example of this phenomenon. Dowry murders take place when a new wife is murdered, usually burned to death, in connection to escalating dowry demands. Dowry murders are thought of as a peculiar indicator of the extreme misogyny of India and are frequently confused with sati—the widow immolation supposedly justified by Hindu scripture that rarely takes place in contemporary India. Recently an article in *The New Yorker* about arranged marriages in South Asian communities contained the suggestion that dowry murders are the cultural alternative to Western divorce—a way to exit relationships. Instead, as some have pointed out, the more appropriate analogy is to equate dowry murders with domestic violence, and specifically, domestic violence murders in the United States. The philosopher Uma Narayan has calculated that death by domestic violence in the United States is numerically as significant a social problem as dowry murders in India. But only one is used as a signifier of cultural backwardness: "They burn their women there." As opposed to: "We shoot our women here." Yet domestic violence murders in the U.S. are just as much a part of American culture as dowry death is a part of Indian culture. In the words of Narayan, when "cultural explanations" are given for fatal forms of violence only in the Third World, the effect is to suggest that Third World women suffer "death by culture."

To show the strength of the image of the Indian woman burnt to death, killed by her culture, we can look at media coverage of the death of Aleyamma Mathew. Mathew, a registered nurse, was burnt to death by her husband, Mathew Varughese, in Texas in 1992, after six years of verbal and physical abuse. Mathew's death was constructed by the media as a synecdoche for Indian culture. The headline of an article in the Dallas Observer read:

> "Battered by her husband, Parkland Nurse Aleyamma Mathew remained true to her culture. In the end she became its victim." The cover called her a "burning bride"—conflating her murder with dowry deaths even though she had been married for twenty years. The article reported that "Aleyamma Mathew may have been fated to die by fire," and confused her murder with sati by stating that, while "sati was outlawed in the late 1800s, and only a handful of cases have been reported in the last two decades . . . the tradition of wife burning continues."

Note that Aleyamma Mathew was Christian, originally from Kerala in South India, and not Hindu. In other words, she was not even in the relevant category of one who might purportedly engage in sati. The article further suggested that Mathew died because she confronted "Indian tradition": "Before going to sleep this night, Aleyamma would repeat again what no Indian woman, even in America, says without repercussions: she would tell her husband no." The article later stated that "by the measure of Indian tradition, Mathew Varughese's wife made two mistakes: she gave him only daughters and she dared to tell him no. She paid for it with her life."

*** The article focuses on what is considered the "lurid exoticism" of women being burnt. In fact, the use of fire as the preferred instrument of dowry murder is connected to the Indian context—but not because of exotic culture. Fire has forensic advantages because it is a simple method of murder, it destroys evidence of murder, and it can look like an accident. As Narayan writes, burning a woman to death in India is no more exotic than shooting a woman to death in the United States; at the same time, shooting a woman to death would be considered exotic in India, where firearms are not freely available and the prevalence of guns is viewed as an American phenomenon.

We identify sexual violence in immigrant of color and Third World communities as cultural, while failing to recognize the cultural aspects of sexual violence affecting mainstream white women. This is related to the general failure to look at the behavior of white persons as cultural, while always ascribing the label of culture to the behavior of minority groups. Thus, to bolster her claim that we cannot embrace both feminism and the values of minority cultures, Okin invokes the recent Nebraska case of two sisters, thirteen and fourteen years of age, who were forced by their Iraqi immigrant father to marry twenty-eight and thirty-four-year-old men. But why are only the child marriages of nonwhite immigrants and not those of white Christian sects believed to threaten feminism? Okin fails to discuss another well-publicized case that took place in a splinter Mormon sect in Utah, involving a sixteen-year-old forced by her father to marry her thirty-two-year-old uncle, as his fifteenth wife. The failure to see that not only racialized minority cultures conflict with feminist values reflects the habit of assuming people of color to be motivated by culture and white persons to be motivated by choice.

We can see this phenomenon in differential responses to women wearing the veil.*** [T]heorist Homa Hoodfar reports that when a white woman who is Muslim wears a veil, it is perceived as fashion; when an Iranian-Canadian woman wears a scarf as fashion, it is perceived as a veil.

What facilitates this failure to see the asymmetrical ascription of culture in motivating other communities' practices and our own? The tension believed to exist between feminism and multiculturalism, or universalism and cultural relativism, not only relies upon the assumption that minority cultures are more sexist, but also assumes that those cultures are frozen and static entities. Within these discourses, only minority cultures are considered traditional, and made up of unchanging and longstanding practices that warrant submission to cultural dictates. Non-western people are assumed to be governed by cultural dictates, whereas the capacity to reason is thought to characterize the West. There appears to be an inverse correlation between full citizenship and cultural visibility. Those with power appear to have no culture; those without power are culturally endowed. Western subjects are defined by their abilities to make choices, in contrast to Third World subjects, who are defined by their group-based determinism. Because the Western definition of what makes one human depends on the notion of agency and the ability to make rational choices, to thrust some communities into a world where their actions are determined only by culture is deeply dehumanizing.

These assumptions preclude the understanding that minority cultures, like all cultures, undergo constant transformation and reshaping. What is also forgotten about culture in this bifurcated discourse is that culture and claims to cultural identity are always contested within communities. Culture is constantly negotiated and is multiple and contradictory. The culture we experience within a particular community will be specific and affected by our age, gender, class, race, disability status, and sexual orientation. The "culture" Okin assumes must be recognized through multiculturalism is comprised primarily of male articulations of gender-subordinating values. But minority cultures encompass feminist values as well. Recognizing that feminism exists within communities of color breaks down the equation between multiculturalism and antifeminism inherent in the notion of "feminism versus multiculturalism." (This equation breaks down as well when we realize that gender-subordinating values are also valued in the dominant culture of the West).

The manner in which culture is hybrid and contested is often not recognized. This happens, in part, because people within a community will explain their actions through their cultural identity. Alternatively, people outside a particular community may mistakenly identify certain practices within that community as the result of culture. Often these two occur in tandem, so that, for example, a criminal defendant will invoke "culture" as the explanation for his sex-subordinating behavior. The perspective of women within that community who would reject such a claim is generally ignored. The media happily picks up the defendant's claim (or proffers its own claim) that this problematic behavior is a product of a certain community's culture, since the idea that nonwhite others engage in primitive and misogynistic cultural practices fits already existing conceptions.

Unfortunately, the "culture" targeted in the feminism versus multiculturalism debate is often an indiscriminate lumping of self-serving claims by elites of communities or nations, the claims of anthropologists that are truly relativistic, and the claims of those who, from a feminist perspective, seek to explain that minority and Third World women should be understood as more than victims of their culture. This problematic aggregation of very different assertions about culture has forestalled constructive discussion.

The Theories That Bind ***

The particular relationship between women and national identity was not solely constructed by the West. Rather, nationalist discourse used in various anticolonial struggles relied upon the figure of women to strengthen notions of culture and tradition. The regulation of women and their sexuality has often stood in for national culture. The fusing of gender with culture and tradition continues when the space of the "home" and practices within it provide an oasis of secure identity for communities experiencing dislocation or subordination. Thus, traditional identity is often conflated with women's dress, behavior, and role in both immigrant communities facing hostility and Third World communities suffering economic insecurity from the demands of globalization. Images of nations and cultures are constructed in metaphors that situate women in marking the identity of the nation.

The relative status of women across communities is still used to assess the progress of culture. And the discourse of feminism versus multiculturalism assumes that women in minority communities require liberation into the "progressive" social customs of the West. The idea that "other" women are subjected to extreme patriarchy is developed in relation to the vision of Western women as secular, liberated, and in total control of their lives. But the assumption that Western women enjoy complete liberation is not grounded in material reality. Rather, Western women's liberation is a product of discursive self-representation, which contrasts Western women's enlightenment with the suffering of the "Third World woman."***

The idea that minority women suffer from their minority cultures also reflects the liberal ideals foundational to the discourse of feminism versus multiculturalism. Liberalism presumes an abstract subject standing separate and apart from the particular and local. But to set up the boundaries of the liberal subject as "human, civilized and universal," colonial discourse "inscribed the history of its others as backward and traditional, and thereby placed cultures of different kinds in a teleological and chronological ordering of history." These others were displaced into "anachronistic space." Colonized people were considered not to inhabit history but to exist in a permanently anterior time, as living embodiments of the "archaic primitive." Those positioned as the "other" continue to bear the disproportionate burden of difference, so that women of color or Third World women stand at the periphery of calls for global sisterhood. Thus, to be a rights-bearing liberal subject one must shed the burden of difference, as Okin suggests in her call for women to be the compliant subjects of assimilation and to leave their minority cultures.

*** Opposing race with gender suggests that women of color may be better off if their cultures wither or become extinct. Women of color will still be women; they just will not have a cultural identity anymore. This suggestion relies upon two assumptions. First, it assumes that women of color gain nothing from their cultures—that cultures of color are largely oppressive and should be shed to eradicate gendered subordination. Second, the suggestion ignores the fact that race and gender are mutually constitutive of one another; one cannot simply separate them in this fashion. Vectors of identity cannot be analyzed as isolated phenomena.***

Our culture is not constructed within "hermetically sealed" boxes that travel with us from cradle to grave. While culture is often represented as the product of timeless ritual insular to particular communities, such forces profoundly shape culture.***

[A]mid the concern about gender apartheid under the Taliban, there has been little focus on the relationship between the intensification of religious fundamentalism and geopolitical economics. The United States gave aid to various mujahideen forces in Afghanistan to fight the Soviets. From these mujahideen groups, the Taliban emerged. The United States aided General Zia of Pakistan—whose government adopted the notorious hudood ordinances that among other provisions criminalized extramarital sex, so that women who accuse men of rape or become pregnant risk punishment for adultery—for the same reason. Feminists in the United States need to think critically about the relationship of this aid to states with policies inimical to women's concerns, instead of abstractly condemning Islam as the font of patriarchal oppression. At the same time, it is crucial for feminists to examine the importance of Christian fundamentalism within the United States and its effect on the lives of millions of women around the world through funding and development that structure reproductive practices and politics. Such an examination would lead to a more nuanced analysis of differential birth rates in the global North and South than afforded by the often cited explanation that birth rates are the product of differing cultural valuations about the worth of male children.

The *** extreme focus on what is commonly conceptualized as cultural violence or subordination makes it difficult to see forces beyond culture. There are other important social, political, and economic issues affecting women's lives other than the cultural practices that garner so much attention. Only certain problems receive coverage or generate concern, namely those used to illustrate the alien and bizarre oppression of women of color; for example, sati, dowry death, veiling, female genital surgeries, female infanticide, marriage by capture, purdah, polygamy, foot binding, and arranged marriages. Other problems—which raise questions of the role of dominant individuals, communities or states in shaping gendered subordination, such as ongoing relationships of economic inequity, development and community policies, exploitation by transnational corporations, or racism—are ignored.***

The issues affecting immigrant or Third World women that receive the greatest attention are those that appear most easily identifiable as concerns to relatively privileged women in the West. These concerns include violations that threaten the freedom of movement, freedom of dress, freedom of bodily integrity, and freedom of control over one's sexuality, rather than violations of the right to shelter or basic sustenance. Thus, self-conception, in terms of what one fears for oneself, may play a role in generating concern about specific violations of women's rights.***

To be clear, the question of representation by feminists is far from the only problem plaguing women in immigrant or Third World communities. I am not asking that we have no critical engagement with issues affecting communities in the Third World and communities of color. What I call for is not a refusal to criticize, but a more careful examination of the particularity of women's relationships to specific patriarchies, as well as to geopolitical and economic relationships. Attempts to make normative judgments and to change behavior must be premised on the understanding that cultures, including our own, are patriarchal—not more or less so, but differently patriarchal. We also need to understand cultures as characterized by resistance to patriarchy. When we consider the role of culture, we must not prioritize culture merely because we respect group rights, but should look to particular contexts in order to determine whether justifications of practices based on culture should be supported or not, depending on what subordination is forwarded or combated through such support. Such an analysis would simultaneously recognize the disenfranchisement due to racism and the legacies of colonialism, and recognize that this disenfranchisement has constructed the experiences of minority and Third World women in a way that is bound up with their experience of gender. We need to acknowledge both that culture shapes gender domination in any community, and that specific histories and present-day practices necessarily will mediate the understandings of what constitutes culture and how it shapes, hurts, or benefits our lives.***

Notes and Questions

1.   The practices that Western media and some human rights activists tend to associate with the "Exotic Other" include dowry-killing, bride-burning, honor killings, female genital mutilation (FGM), foot-binding (historically), child marriage, arranged marriage, the wearing of the veil, and female sex-selection abortion and infanticide. Why do so many of the practices listed have particular implications for women and girls?

2.   Volpp notes that, in the West, "Culture is invoked to explain forms of violence against Third World or immigrant women while culture is not similarly invoked to explain forms of violence that affect mainstream Western women." Do you agree? Consider recent news reports of violence against women in your local newspaper. Was "culture" mentioned as an explanation for instances of "domestic violence" or "date rape"? What non-violent traditions affect women in Western cultures? Do you think about culture when flipping through a fashion or bridal magazine? When watching television advertisements or videos? When reading stories or television "reality" shows about cosmetic surgery? What images of Western women are dominant? What roles do race, ethnicity or nationality play in those images?

3.   To what extent are men in your culture pressured to adhere to certain rules of dress, behavior, or physical appearance? How have these rules changed over the last 20 years?

4.   Should feminists and other human rights activists address gender violence in other cultures or countries? Given the critiques raised by Al-Hibri, An-Naim and Volpp, what strategies would you suggest for doing so? Would you be open to feminist and other human rights critiques of your own cultural traditions by outsiders?

5.   If, as Volpp suggests, part of the problem lies in the tendency to create a "binary opposition" between feminism and multiculturalism, what are her suggested alternatives? Should external critics avoid discussing "culture" at all? Should they continue to identify cultural sources of oppression in other communities, and extend a similar analysis to their own communities? *See,* for example, Isabelle Gunning's approach to "world-travelling" discussed Section C.3. How would an effective cross-cultural coalition look? *See, e.g.,* Assitan Diallo's approach to collaboration quoted in the second excerpt of Hope Lewis' article in Section C.3; CHANDRA TALPADE MOHANTY, FEMINISM WITHOUT BORDERS: DECOLONIZING THEORY, PRACTICING SOLIDARITY (2003); and UMA NARAYAN, DISLOCATING CULTURES: IDENTITIES, TRADITIONS, AND THIRD WORLD FEMINISM (1997).

6.   As Kapur and Volpp point out, violence against women, including violence within families, is not unique to "exotic" or non-Western regions and cultures. It occurs, in its many forms, throughout the world. To what extent, therefore, should one analyze violence against women in its cultural context at all? The news article below reminds us that the international human rights implications of violence against women in Western countries is often masked as "ordinary" criminal activity or ignored by public officials and the media. Does a cultural analysis shed light on the nature and causes of the problem?

Gender violence within cultural groups, including immigrant groups in Western Europe and North America, is often associated with "culture" in media and activist reports, while the influence of class, politics, colonialism, Western cultural influences and the global subordination of women tend to be underemphasized. Should violence against women in Western, non-immigrant communities be analyzed in a cultural context as well? What specific cultural influences can you identify that cause or exacerbate the problem of violence against women in a particular country or region? Do you find Okin's arguments that Western cultures are relatively more protective of the rights of women than non-Western cultures persuasive? Why, or why not? Is Azizah Al-Hibri's response to Okin persuasive from a human rights perspective? Is there a global "culture" that encourages or tolerates violence against women? How should an international human rights legal framework respond? (See discussion of the Convention on the Elimination of All Forms of Discrimination Against Women (CEDAW) and the jurisprudence of the CEDAW Committee in Chapter 3, *supra*).

Consider the following news article discussing a 2003 Amnesty International report on violence against women. The article highlights a case involving a prominent French actress who was killed by her equally famous rock star companion after a violent argument. The couple's high-profile status and the severity of the beating that killed the actress shocked many throughout Europe and led to an increased public debate on domestic violence in France.

The Amnesty International Secretary-General. Irene Khan, releasing a report on *** violence against women, described the phenomenon as a cancer eating away at the core of every society.

According to the report, one in every three women suffers violence in her lifetime. The statistics in Europe are as appalling as anywhere else. In France, six women die each month at the hands of men who profess to love them. In Spain, some 100 women are killed each year by abusive spouses or boyfriends with over 30,000 complaints of severe physical violence, while in Switzerland, one of the wealthiest countries in Europe where "direct democracy" rules supreme, the number of women who suffer physical and psychological abuse tops 20 per cent. In Britain, one woman is killed by a partner every three days, one woman in four experiences domestic violence and attacks on partners account for a quarter of all violent crime.

In France, the subject became front-page news after the film actress, Marie Trintrignant, was beaten to death by her lover, singer Bertrand Cantat. The trial, on charges of first degree murder, being held in Vilnius [Lithuania] where the killing took place, has riveted the country. Despite media campaigns and shocking statistics, domestic violence continues to be one of Europe's most under-reported crimes. On International Women's Day this year, France has had reason to ponder Amnesty's devastating report.

"It is not a death I would wish upon anyone. However, the case of Marie Trintrignant finally placed the spotlight on one of the most taboo subjects in Western democracies, that of domestic violence. We have a supposedly free press, a police and justice system reputed to be among the best in the world, several social and societal safety nets meant to protect our citizens. Yet, violence against women continues unabated in France, with an average of six women per month dying as a result. The unfortunate and much-publicised case of Marie Trintrignant has also highlighted the fact that violence against women is not restricted to a 'lower social milieu' as many would have us believe. It affects every class of woman—the poor and under-educated as much as the rich and professionally qualified," said Lilliane Daligand, professor of forensic medicine and director of a French association against marital violence called VIFF-SOS Femmes.

Says Marie-Dominique de Suremain of the National Federation of Women's Solidarity: "The real extent of the problem has been grossly under-estimated. A study undertaken by the forensic services of the Paris hospital system indicates that over 60 women are killed annually by their partners in Paris alone. We have no idea of how many such killings take place in the provinces. No statistics exist on the number of women maimed or mutilated nor how many endure years of terror."

France commissioned its first comprehensive report on domestic violence in 1999. Published in 2002, it indicates women between 20 and 24 years of age are among the most affected. Women also tend to be persecuted by jilted lovers, former husbands or companions who stalk them, insult them, assault them and sometimes kill them.***

Vaiju Naravane, *Women, A Battered Section of Society*, THE HINDU, Mar. 9, 2004. *See also Star's Death Stuns France*, WEEKEND AUSTRALIAN, Aug. 9, 2003, at T12; Charles Masters, *Star Splits France with "Crimes of Passion" Trial*, SUNDAY TIMES (London), Mar. 14, 2004, at 24.

3. *Human Rights Approaches to Traditional Practices*

Ethnic, religious and national groups throughout the world emphasize the importance of traditions, customs and practices that are handed down from generation to generation. Community leaders argue that such traditions help sustain a group's sense of community cohesion and can be a form of resistance to harmful external pressures. Some customs are said to be mandatory for membership in the group (and for an appropriate relationship with a divine authority). Others may technically be considered a matter of individual choice, but may be the subject of substantial community expectation and pressure. International human rights instruments such as the Universal Declaration of Human Rights, the International Covenant on Civil and Political Rights and the International Covenant on Economic, Social and Cultural Rights recognize the importance of cultural and religious freedom. Nevertheless, as we have seen in earlier sections, rights-based approaches to the equality of women seem to come into conflict with certain traditional practices that might be physically or mentally harmful to women.

The materials below explore a variety of approaches to this apparent conflict. As you read them, consider whether the "traditional practices" described are similar to "contemporary practices" with which you might be familiar. If they are different, how are they different? Why is the name by which a practice is identified a source of controversy? Should the practices described be a matter for analysis under international human rights law at all? Should they be considered a private matter, or should states or the international community intervene? Does it matter if participants consent to the practice? If interventions are appropriate, what forms should those interventions take?

HOPE LEWIS, BETWEEN *IRUA* AND "FEMALE GENITAL MUTILATION": FEMINIST HUMAN RIGHTS DISCOURSE AND THE CULTURAL DIVIDE

8 HARV. HUM. RTS. J. 1, 1–9, 14–21 (1995)

*** "Irua," or traditional female genital surgery ("FGS"), implicates the most private aspects of individual female physical and cultural identity. Accordingly, African women who have undergone FGS have the most significant stake in determining whether and how the practice is treated in public international law. However, the serious public and private health consequences of FGS have aroused concern in cultures in which FGS is not traditionally practiced. Some Western feminists, for example, have placed FGS on the international human rights agenda, posing a challenge to traditional distinctions between "public" and "private" spheres of international legal obligation.***

What's in a Name? Terminology as Substance

The feminist human rights controversy over FGS is reflected in the disagreement over the terms used to describe it. The World Health Organization (WHO) has adopted specific clinical terms to identify the three predominant forms of FGS:

1. Circumcision proper, known in Muslim countries as *sunna* (which means "traditional"), is the mildest but also the rarest form. It involves the removal only of the clitoral prepuce.

2. Excision involves the amputation of the whole of the clitoris, and all or part of the labia minora.

3. Infibulation, also known as Pharoanic circumcision, involves the amputation of the clitoris, the whole of the labia minora, and at least the anterior two-thirds and often the whole of the medial part of the labia majora. The two sides of the vulva are then stitched together with silk, catgut or thorns, and a tiny sliver of wood or a reed is inserted to preserve an opening for urine and menstrual blood. The girl's legs are usually bound together from ankle to knee until the wound has healed, which may take anything up to 40 days.

The cultures for which FGS is traditional have their own names for the practices. Jomo Kenyatta, a pan-Africanist leader and anthropologist, introduced Western readers to the Kikuyu term "irua," which refers to the initiation of both boys and girls into adulthood. Irua rituals involved surgery as well as educational and socialization rites aimed at strengthening ethnic and sub-group identity.

The current terminological controversy stems primarily from the Western search for an appropriate English-language term for FGS rituals. "Female circumcision" was initially the most common term used by English-speaking Westerners and Africans. The term "circumcision" emphasizes the initiatory and religious dimensions of FGS and draws a parallel to the widespread rite of male circumcision as practiced in the West and the Middle East. The term's euphemistic character may also reflect both African and Western unease with public discussion of sex and genitalia. Many feminist human rights activists and scholars argue that the term "female circumcision" is misleading, in that most forms of male circumcision are far less invasive and physically damaging than FGS. Further, because the term "male circumcision" generally is not thought to implicate human rights, the term is not regarded as useful by those who seek to define FGS as a human rights violation.

The term "female genital mutilation" ("FGM") has been adopted by human rights activists in the West and, more recently, in Africa, both to emphasize the physical pain caused by the practices and to stress what some construe as the intentional infliction of harm. Many Africans have voiced objections to the term "female genital mutilation" because it implies a deliberate attempt by practitioners to hurt or disfigure members of their own families and communities, and because they believe it may thus elicit inappropriate reactions from those who misconstrue its purposes.

Recognizing the political ramifications of FGS terminology, some human rights scholars have attempted to describe the practice in a culturally "neutral" way. However, no nomenclature can be value-neutral. Clinical terms like "surgeries" or "operations" distance readers from the physical trauma experienced by the children affected, and may misleadingly imply the use of antiseptic, anesthetic surgical techniques intended to correct a disease or disfigurement.

This Article uses Isabelle Gunning's term, "female genital surgery" because it permits comparison, where appropriate, between traditional types of FGS and "modern" forms of surgical modification of women's bodies that are not generally subject to human rights scrutiny. Describing a traditional practice as "surgery" can both heighten Western awareness that practicing cultures often conceive of FGS as a health measure and highlight the fact that Western surgical practices are themselves informed by cultural influences that frequently go unrecognized. Just as there is no single, all-encompassing "solution" to the feminist controversy over FGS, there is no one term that is appropriate in all contexts.

Human Rights Discourse and the Struggle for Primacy

The conflict over terminology parallels the complex, shifting stakes in the battle over FGS as a violation of international human rights standards. Human rights scholars have generated a substantial and growing body of literature on the potential role of human rights law in the eradication of FGS. Much of this work adopts feminist perspectives, arguing that FGS should be eradicated as a violation of the human rights of women. However, this literature reflects deep conflicts about whether international human rights systems should foster cross-cultural engagement in order to eradicate FGS.

The feminist analysis of FGS as a human rights violation is complicated because FGS exists at the "intersection" of complex cultural, gender, and racial questions in human rights jurisprudence: If FGS is a patriarchal violation of the fundamental human rights of women, how should international law respond to the fact that FGS is practiced by women on women and girls? Does "universalism" obscure the efforts of powerful states and international institutions to violate African rights to self-determination and the preservation of cultural identity? Is "cultural relativism" a smokescreen that enables governments and non-state actors to legitimize the oppression of women? Is the international human rights system accessible to women affected by FGS, or is it merely a collection of irrelevant theoretical constructs?***

Theoretical Questions: The Status of FGS as a Human Rights Violation

*** Female genital surgery differs in several key respects from the rights infringements that have formed the focus of traditional human rights advocacy efforts. First, FGS practitioners are private citizens operating without express state sanction. Second, FGS is generally performed with the "consent" of the parents of minor girls, at least some of whom are aware of the attendant health risks. Third, FGS is generally performed by females on other females. Finally, FGS has both deep cultural roots and powerful political implications for practicing groups. Therefore, feminist human rights activists have had to give careful thought to the formulation of a legal framework that respects the unique features of FGS, while still rendering it a violation of existing human rights standards. Two elements of this jurisprudential framework are discussed below: the role of the international human rights system in meeting the needs and goals of women, and tensions between the appropriateness of universalism or cultural relativism in promoting the well-being of women.***

*Universalism or Cultural Relativism ***

From the perspectives of non-practicing cultures, the primary ethical basis of universal concern about FGS is that it involves the infliction of great physical pain and the risk of life-threatening complications for infants and children, whose well-being is of special legal and moral concern in both practicing and non-practicing cultures. Awareness of cross-cultural concern for the well-being of children has led many Western human rights activists to emphasize in graphic terms the painful and physically damaging consequences of FGS for girls as a way to overcome relativist objections to condemnation of the practice. Using similar reasoning, certain groups have focused on the right to health and health education as the most appropriate human rights approach to FGS because it is believed to cause the least offense to practicing cultures. However, efforts to cast FGS as a violation of universal values related to health and child welfare raise several troubling contradictions. First, many cultures condone practices that are physically painful or create health risks to children where the procedures are believed to be medically or socially necessary. Second, defenders of FGS may suspect that the "health" approach masks Western imperialism in a more palatable guise. Finally, critics point out that a health-based approach may result in reforms whereby FGS would continue to be performed, but under hygienic conditions and with anesthesia. To avoid this, many Western feminists argue that FGS must be defined as a human rights violation, regardless of the conditions under which it is performed.

Challenging Culture as Patriarchy ***

To address FGS as a human rights violation, Western feminists have had to face both the gender politics of international human rights and the tension between universalism and cultural relativism. In doing so, the discourse has argued first, that the cultural bases for the practice are misguided or based in ignorance; second, that FGS somehow falls outside the domain of "culture"; or third, that "culture" itself is a patriarchal construction vulnerable to challenge. To sustain these arguments, Western feminists have had to examine the origins of FGS and the modern justifications for its continued practice.

There is no single explanation for the practice of the many forms of traditional FGS. Different ethnic groups identify different motivations or point to a mixture of rationales. Female genital surgery is most prevalent in predominantly Islamic countries in Africa, but it is also found among groups that practice Christian, Jewish, and African religions. While a few Muslim religious leaders continue to promote the practice of FGS on religious grounds, historians suggest that FGS pre-dates Islam, and that its origins in other religious traditions are unclear.***

L. AMEDE OBIORA, BRIDGES AND BARRICADES: RETHINKING POLEMICS AND INTRANSIGENCE IN THE CAMPAIGN AGAINST FEMALE CIRCUMCISION

47 CASE W. RES. L. REV. 275, 295, 316–17, 329 (1997)

*** Female circumcision is embedded in an intricate web of habits, attitudes, and values, along with having both functional and symbolic connotations. In Africa, the practice is validated and undergirded by a wide spectrum of principles, in addition to temporal and spiritual beliefs. Recurring themes such as sexuality and fertility express preeminent indigenous values like solidarity among women, public recognition of life-cycle change, and procreation for social continuity. Some of these themes are not peculiar to cultures that practice circumcision. Adherence to rites of passage, for example, is an abiding phenomenon in the West.***

Female circumcision, as it is conducted both in Africa and by African immigrants under foreign jurisdictions, has complicated several commonplace assumptions about social structure and agency. There is some indication that communitarian African social structures may not have the causal determinacy that gender relations and sexual stratification studies may suggest. Instead of being subject to a monolithic regime of patriarchs, it may well be that African women resort to female circumcision to recreate notions of womanhood adept for their peculiar conditions of existence. The world they know with its intricate networks of kin relations, the accentuation of the dead and the unborn in their world views, the nature of production under dispersed and low technological infrastructure, the frailty of their ecological circumstances, the burdens of their structural incorporation into the global order is not readily amenable to the conceptualization of polemic gender identity and politics.

The regrettable focus on determinism explains the inclination of some radical feminists to discount or marginalize the perspectives of African women who they perceive as merely condoning female circumcision. The failure to acknowledge and engage these women in dialogue does not extinguish their force or constituencies, constituencies that are equipped to foment subversive challenges to radical reform proposals. Interestingly enough, most studies on female circumcision seldom articulate personal discontent by its "victims." Instead, they tacitly or expressly convey a recalcitrance uncanny for victims of dismal abuse. Although attitudes regarding the practice appear to be gradually changing, some suggest that there has been no significant decline in the practice.***

Through the years in Africa, outside interventionists, whether colonialist or missionary (and now feminist), continue to presume that it is their duty as the "advanced" to elevate and enlighten the "backward." It is characteristic of these interventionists to pay scant attention to crucial issues including the wishes and opinions of the supposed beneficiaries of their benevolence, the overall implications of intervention, and the possibility of more "benign" intervention. Not surprisingly, their campaigns, often couched in terms of virtual monopoly on good judgment, are perceived as unduly ethnocentric and presumptuous. Such campaigns conform to patterns and habits that have historically provoked righteous indignation and engendered cultural resistance to Western "missionary" exploits. Moreover, they tend to pre-judge and alienate *** women, the "victims" and perpetrators capable of facilitating or subverting meaningful change.***

ISABELLE R. GUNNING, ARROGANT PERCEPTION, WORLD-TRAVELLING, AND MULTICULTURAL FEMINISM: THE CASE OF FEMALE GENITAL SURGERIES

23 COLUM. HUM. RTS. L. REV. 189 197–205, 220 (1991–1992)

*** *Arrogant Perception and Distance*

The negative of universalism or ethnocentrism in analyzing culturally challenging practices has been characterized (in a different context) by one feminist scholar as "arrogant perception."***

A key aspect of arrogant perception is the distance between "me" and "the other." The "I" as arrogant perceiver is a subject to myself with my own perceptions, motivations, and interests. The "other," in arrogant perception terms, is unlike me. The "other" has no independent perceptions and interest but only those that I impose. Any evidence that the "other" is organized around her own interests is evidence of defensiveness in the "other." The arrogant perceiver falsifies and simplifies. In other words, there is a falsification and oversimplification in the assumption of the distance and difference between self and dependent "other" as well as the conclusion that any evidence that contradicts the assumption of distance and difference is an example of fault in the "other."

It is extraordinarily easy, even as a Western feminist, to fall into the trap of arrogant perception regarding genital surgeries. It is not so much the horror that Westerners feel at hearing of the practice. It may be that some part of the initial horror is merely absence of familiarity, a form of culture shock. However, similar reactions are often shared in whole or in part by feminists within the cultures that practice the surgery. The problem of arrogance is therefore not in the adverse reaction itself, but rather in the way the horror is expressed and the solutions that are proposed.***

World-Travelling and Interconnectedness

The independence and respect one strives for in avoiding arrogant perception reveals one major problem of the cultural relativist position: too much distance or independence. Our very desire as Western feminists to "do something" about the lives of other women exposes the fact that we do all live in an increasingly shrinking global village. We are different but not entirely dissimilar; we are independent beings but not without interconnectedness and overlaps. One feminist scholar has described a method by which feminists of various colors can learn to identify their interconnectedness even as they respect independence: world-travelling.

World-travelling has been described by women of color, in jest, as "schizophrenia." One moves or travels among different "worlds." "Worlds" are any social situations ranging from "an incomplete visionary Utopia" to a subculture or community within a larger dominant community to a "traditional construction of life." "Travelling" is the shift from being one person in one world to a different person in another world. But the "difference" is part of a coherent whole; one does not act or pose as someone else.***

The consciousness requires that one not just "speak" the language. Understanding the norms requires a sense of how this world comprehends or constructs you regardless of your own self-construction. For example, I am an African-American female law professor. In the world of academia I am a fairly fluent speaker, and I have a shared history with other law professors: that of attending prestigious universities for my training. Those are the things that I share with my white counterparts. But for me to survive, I need to understand the norms of academia completely, especially those that flow from the fact that academia has only recently defined itself as including either African Americans or women of any race. I cannot just walk into the library or stand in front of a classroom and blithely expect the accord generally given a "professor" without understanding that there is likely to be a hesitation, if not an outright challenge as the white person I confront grapples with the incongruity of my position.***

World-Travelling Modified to Methodology

The recognition of both independence and interconnectedness is essential for cross cultural understanding. I suggest a three-pronged approach to creating that recognition. In order to understand the independence of the "other" one needs to be clear about one's own boundaries. One has to be clear about the cultural influences and pressures that are inextricably involved in one's own sense of self. This requires understanding oneself in one's own historical context with an emphasis on the overlaps, influences and conditions which one is observing in the "other." Recognizing interconnectedness requires two additional approaches. The first is to understand one's historical relationship to the "other" and to approach that understanding from the "other's" perspective, i.e., to see the self as the "other" might see you. Second, one must see the "other" in her own cultural context as she sees herself. This prong requires both an in-depth look at one's own complex cultural context in search of analogues co culturally challenging practices in the "other's" culture, as well as an in-depth look at the rich cultural context of the other woman's life.***

Notes and Questions

1.   What value should we place on tolerance and understanding of cultural difference? Is the world-traveling method described by Gunning helpful in analyzing a cultural practice that you may find "shocking"? If a practice is truly shocking within your own moral system, should you tolerate that practice by others, or should you intervene? Are there any practices that should be considered beyond tolerance by outsiders? How would such a list be created? Is that the purpose of the Universal Declaration of Human Rights? For a discussion of these questions from the perspectives of cultural anthropology, *see, e.g.,* ALISON DUNDES RENTELN, INTERNATIONAL HUMAN RIGHTS: UNIVERSALISM VERSUS RELATIVISM (1990).

2.   What does trying to see the practice from the perspective of the "Other" add to your analysis? Is the nature and quality of the dialogue about disputed practices relevant?

3.   Would your analysis be different if the practice involved primarily affected men or boys to the same extent that the most severe forms of FGC affects girls and women?

HOPE LEWIS, BETWEEN *IRUA* AND "FEMALE GENITAL MUTILATION": FEMINIST HUMAN RIGHTS DISCOURSE AND THE CULTURAL DIVIDE

8 HARV. HUM. RTS. J. 1, 25–33, 39, 48, 54 (1995)

*** *THE MAIN ACTIVISTS: AFRICAN FEMINIST DISCOURSE ON FGS*

Survival and Liberation ***

African feminists who vocally reject FGS have set their own agendas and responded to Western feminist criticism in a number of ways. Many do not repudiate all non-African attention or activism surrounding FGS. Instead, some support Western feminist involvement in the international campaign to eradicate FGS, but criticize Western hypocrisy in the elaboration and implementation of universal human rights standards. Others, true cultural relativists, reject both Western participation and a "universal" system of human rights standards. Despite the divergence of views, a common theme runs throughout much of the African feminist literature: the survival and liberation of African women through their own activism.***

African women not only have engaged in acts of personal resistance, but they also have participated at the forefront of public efforts to confront FGS. Many of these activists are health professionals who have treated women suffering from FGS side effects. For many years, they have studied FGS and have spoken out against it as a violation of the rights of women.*** [T]hey have combined their training in Western medicine with their understanding of the unique political and cultural perspectives of the communities from which they come to educate others and advocate the eradication of FGS on an international level.***

Challenging Imperialism: Image and Reality

The Practice of FGS ***

African feminists reject some Western feminist portrayals of African mothers and traditional practitioners as callous or even cruel. They argue that many mothers in practicing regions are very concerned about the pain associated with the practice and refuse to witness the initiation process, and that parents and health workers from many cultures often adopt a stoic appearance when they believe that a child's painful medical or surgical procedure is for her or his own good.***

FGS in Cultural Context ***

The African feminist literature on FGS emphasizes the importance of the cultural context in which FGS occurs and the complexity of justifications for its continued practice. It contends that Western feminist discourse fails to ask the questions that would help place its patriarchal aspects in a broader context: Are boys initiated at the same time as girls? Are the risks and consequences of initiation rituals for boys as life-threatening and long-lasting as they are for girls? What socioeconomic purposes does FGS serve for a particular group? Are there alternative ways of fulfilling those purposes or challenging their necessity? If so, how should domestic and international actors identify and support those alternatives? Finally, do domestic and international actors contribute to the continuation of harmful traditional practices?

Relationship to Other Forms of Oppression

> [T]o fight against genital mutilation . . . without questioning the structures and social relations which perpetuate this situation is like "refusing to see the sun in the middle of the day." [11]

*** African feminists have argued that basic needs like adequate health care facilities, support for health care training, access to public education for girls, and access to clean water often are not treated as human rights concerns of the same urgency as the eradication of FGS. They further argue that Western economic exploitation enables the continued occurrence of FGS. They charge that although Western feminist discourse often concerns itself with the adoption of "sensitive" approaches to the eradication of FGS, it rarely concerns itself with the participation of feminists, as Westerners, in the exploitative economic and social institutions that arguably perpetuate FGS.***

Do these concerns leave any room for respectful, cross-cultural engagement . . . on the issue of FGS? While the debates over cultural relativism and cultural imperialism continue, female genital surgeries are practiced upon millions of black children and women, leading to illness, or even death. What, then, should be the response of black feminists to this form of human rights violation?***

Solidarity and Subjectivity

> A media campaign in the West will not stop genital mutilation. Westerners and those of us living in the West who wish to work on this issue must forge partnerships with the hundreds of African women on the continent who are working to eradicate the practice. Neither Alice Walker nor any of us here can speak for them; but if we have the power and the resources, we can create the room for them to speak, and to speak with us as well. [12]

---

[11] AAWORD, *A Statement on Genital Mutilation, in* 1 Third World—Second Sex 217 (Miranda Davies ed., 1983).

[12] Seble Dawit & Salem Mekuria, *The West Just Doesn't Get It*, N.Y. Times, Dec. 7, 1993, at A27.

The energy surrounding cross-cultural feminist discourse on FGS has centered largely on the universalism/cultural relativism dichotomy underlying the question of whether Western feminists should help eradicate FGS. This perhaps insoluble question remains important for the philosophical and cultural anthropological underpinnings of human rights jurisprudence. For the variety of women who adopt black feminist perspectives, the "right" approach often lies in our own intellectual and intuitive perceptions of morality. But how are those perceptions to be shared, challenged, and influenced? The social, economic, and political conflicts that underlie the conflict over Western feminist involvement on FGS are as deeply rooted as the cultural basis of the practice itself. The discussion must be restructured to expose these conflicts in order for progress to be made on this issue.***

*** For example, Assitan Diallo, a Malian activist, explains her feelings about non-African involvement:

> For my part . . . I want to collaborate with them. But I don't think I can be in the same group with them to fight something in my own country, because I will feel, "Here they go again, colonization." But I love being asked by people working on female circumcision, "What are the specifics in Mali?" And suggesting to me, "Why don't you do that in Mali?" Suggesting means that I can say no, or yes. . . . They can also say to me, "You know, people do circumcision in France and we French people want to fight against it." I want them to allow me to say, "I'm suggesting you do it this way, because these people are from my country, and I think this will be better." Again, I'm suggesting something, not imposing it on them. That's the kind of working relationship I want.***[13]

Notes and Questions

1. Is the condemnation of female genital cutting by Western activists hypocritical, or well-intentioned? According to Lewis, some African feminists argued that Westerners' failure to condemn certain Western economic and social policies contributed to conditions allowing FGC to continue. Do you agree? How, specifically, could international economic and social policies affect FGC, which is often practiced in the privacy of home or village? What might access to clean water, education, and overall health care have to do with FGC?

2. For further reading on FGM/FC and human rights, *see e.g.*, AAWORD, A STATEMENT ON GENITAL MUTILATION IN THIRD WORLD—SECOND SEX: WOMEN'S STRUGGLES AND NATIONAL LIBERATION 217 (Miranda Davies ed., 1983); Kay Boulware-Miller, *Female Circumcision: Challenges to the Practice as a Human Rights Violation*, 8 HARV. WOMEN'S L.J. 155 (1985); Katherine Brennan, *The Influence of Cultural Relativism on International Human Rights Law: Female Circumcision as a Case Study*, 1 LAW & INEQ. J. 367 (1991); CEDAW, Female Circumcision, General Recommendation. No. 14, 9th Sess., 1990; U.N. Doc. A/45/38/1, Int. Hum. Rts. Rev. 21 (No. 1, 1994); Eugenie Anne Gifford, *"The Courage to Blaspheme": Confronting Barriers to Resisting Female Genital Mutilation* 4 UCLA WOMEN'S L.J. 329 (1994); Isabelle R. Gunning, *Female Genital Surgeries and Multicultural Feminism: The Ties That Bind; The Differences That Distance*, 1994–95 THIRD WORLD LEGAL STUDIES J. 17; Leslye Amede Obiora, *The Little Foxes that Spoil the Vine: Re-visiting the Feminist Critique*

---

[13] Adi Gevins, *Talking Tradition: African Women Speak Out Against Female Circumcision*, in 2 THIRD WORLD—SECOND SEX 247 (Miranda Davies ed., 2d ed. 1997) (quoting Assitan Diallo).

of Female Cricumcision, 9 CAN. J. WOM. & L. 46 (1997); NAHID TOUBIA, FEMALE GENITAL MUTLIATION: A CALL FOR GLOBAL ACTION (1993); ALICE WALKER & PRATIBHA PARMAR, WARRIOR MARKS: FEMALE GENITAL MUTILATION AND THE SEXUAL BLINDING OF WOMEN (1993); World Health Organization, *A Traditional Practice that Threatens Health—Female Circumcision,* 40 WORLD HEALTH ORG. CHRON. 31 (1986).

ROLE-PLAY ON THE "FEMALE GENITAL MUTILATION"/ "FEMALE CIRCUMCISION" DEBATE

The following role-play is intended to allow you to discuss this difficult issue from a variety of perspectives. Imagine that you are about to attend a special session of a U.N. Working Group on Human Rights and Traditional Practices to discuss the human rights implications of "FGM." The class should be divided into groups and assigned the roles described below. Using what you have learned about the subject from the assigned readings, and any additional research, each group should prepare "talking points" and arguments that you believe might be made by representatives of your group.

Roles

- An international NGO based in the United States.

- An indigenous NGO working against FGM/FC in a practicing country.

- Parents of a 16 year-old girl who live in the United States and who have been jailed for planning to hire a practitioner to perform FGM/FC on the girl.

- Association of rural licensed physicians and midwives in a practicing country who hope to reduce the health impact of the practices on women. They propose to "medicalize" FGM/FC and advocate a slow phasing-out through local education efforts.

- Representatives of the World Health Organization who have gathered data on the specifics of the practices.

- Government representatives from a practicing country that has not yet adopted laws criminalizing FGM/FC.

- Representatives of a network of traditional practitioners of FC.

- Representatives of an immigrant women's NGO in the West whose members are adult women who have undergone the practice or who have sought gender-based asylum to escape the practice.

Among the issues to consider and discuss in class:

How do the various practices described as FGM/FC affect the health of women and girls? How many girls or women do they affect?

What are the cultural and social implications?

What is the status of FGM/FC under international human rights law? Can you identify (one or two) specific instruments or provisions that would apply? *See* materials in Part II for some ideas.

Should FGM/FC be criminalized (or regulated) under national laws? Why or why not? Are there alternatives to criminalization?

Is FGM/FC different from other acts considered to be human rights violations? If so, how is it different? If not, how is it the same?

CELESTINE NYAMU, HOW SHOULD HUMAN RIGHTS AND DEVELOPMENT RESPOND TO CULTURAL LEGITIMIZATION OF GENDER HIERARCHY IN DEVELOPING COUNTRIES?

41 HARV. INT'L L.J. 381, 391–95, 409–17 (2000)

*** *Trends in Human/Women's Rights*

The Abolitionist Approach

[I]n order to promote accountability for private acts committed against women, human rights advocates have attempted to find a basis for state responsibility. The human rights community often focuses on the state's failure to regulate the area in question by prosecuting perpetrators, and advocates emphasize the state's own direct or indirect participation in facilitating violations. Articles 2(f) and 5(a) of the United Nations Convention on the Elimination of All Forms of Discrimination Against Women (CEDAW) provide a basis for state accountability by calling upon states to take appropriate measures to modify or abolish customs and practices that constitute discrimination against women. Many Third World states, especially those with an Islamic majority, have, however, made reservations to these articles. Thus, human rights actors also use alternative human rights language, such as torture, to address state responsibility for harms suffered by women.

The move to hold states accountable for violations of women's rights committed by private parties, including those acts defended as culture, is a remarkable effort of human rights organizations. Yet, in order to transform society effectively, human rights advocates must focus on sustaining engagement with communities rather than conducting sporadic investigations and directing reports primarily at governments.

Some human rights advocates have expressed dissatisfaction with the state-centric, shaming technique, pointing to the constraints it places on analysis and the formulation of new strategies. Nonetheless, the approach taken by the human rights community continues to focus predominantly on the state.

Most human rights groups have adopted an abolitionist approach and call for an end to cultural practices that contravene international human rights norms.***

Some critics have pointed out that these abolitionist responses create the impression that women's rights do not exist in custom or local practice, and the solution therefore lies in substituting custom and local practice with alternatives offered by national legislation or the international human rights regime. Furthermore, the abolitionist approach does not encourage a holistic understanding of the context in which these practices are embedded, and as a result, prevents comprehensive solutions. The abolitionist approach has also suffered counter-accusations of cultural imperialism from interested Third World states.

Toward a Cross-Cultural Dialogue: Moving Away from the Abolitionist Approach

Critics of the abolitionist approach argue that culture is dynamic, responds to social change, and undergoes transformation over time. Such cultural change necessarily includes improvement in women's rights. People are not simply "the naive product of a rigid and static society," except in the uninformed imagination of some people in Western societies who view Third World societies as "stable, timeless, ancient, lacking in internal conflict, [and] premodern." However, social transformation does not always create improvement in women's lives. It is quite possible for matters that are central to women to remain bound by tradition even after other aspects of social life have undergone significant change.

Scholars point to the abolitionists' treatment of culture as a theoretical construct and their failure to grasp the meaning and daily existential experience of culture. Third World critics view abolitionist proposals as decontextualized, hegemonic, and counterproductive for gender equality in practice.

The non-abolitionist approach, therefore, calls for a non-hegemonic human rights practice that incorporates the two simultaneous processes of internal discourse and cross-cultural dialogue, in order to find legitimacy for human rights principles within all cultures. Internal discourse suggests some active deliberation on such issues as: recognizable standards of cultural legitimacy; responsibility for selecting standards; allowable action and reaction to divergent and competing views; and power relations between groups with different views.

Cross-cultural dialogue, in turn, calls for the pursuit of a global consensus viewing the relationship between international human rights and local culture as "a genuinely reciprocal global collaborative effort." This two-way sharing of perspectives draws on the cultures' respective internal discourses. Through cross-cultural dialogue, external actors can support and influence internal discourse, but they must take care not to undermine internal discourse.***

Thus, both at the international and national level, institutional practice in human rights and development must move beyond the abolitionist paradigm. An approach that attempts to transcend the shortcomings of the restrictive abolitionist framework is only beginning to emerge in the practice of community-based groups.***

Lessons Toward Effective Responses to Cultural Legitimization of Gender Hierarchy in a Plural Legal Context ***

In a plural setting, proponents of gender equality must balance idealistic aspirations with a pragmatic realization that different contexts may call for diverse sets of tools to challenge unequal power relations. The term "critical pragmatism" is borrowed from scholarship exploring the critical potential of pragmatism as a legal framework that can be used to articulate the interests of less powerful social groups. In one situation, an effective strategy may require insistence upon the recognition of customary obligations owed to women. In another context, an insightful critique may question the validity of specific assertions of culture. Human rights principles embodied in constitutions and international instruments may provide a basis for such questioning, but concrete engagement with the politics of culture creates a much more productive challenge.

Critical Pragmatic Approach to Plural Normative Orders

*** In concrete terms, a critical pragmatic approach would challenge the constitutional framework that shields customary and religious laws from questioning, in order to create room for more voice and inclusiveness in the shaping and articulation of community norms. Marriage, divorce, and death are key events for defining and reconstituting property rights of women and children, whose access to economic resources heavily depends on relationships to fathers or husbands. The absence of constitutional protection for women and children in marriage, divorce, and death has far-reaching consequences in a social context that makes it easy for opportunistic individuals to justify (on the basis of custom) negative treatment of widows or divorced women and their children.

Critics may contend that altering the constitutional framework reduces protection for personal laws and takes away an existing right. South Africa and Uganda managed, however, to surmount such pressure and to enact constitutional frameworks that do not grant immunity to the operation of personal laws. Their experiences demonstrate that it is possible to establish a constitutional framework that achieves a more fair balance between gender equality and the recognition of cultural and religious identity.

The South African constitution recognizes the validity of traditional authority, as well as the right to enjoy and practice one's culture, but it subjects the exercise of these rights to the constitution. The exercise of traditional authority and the operation of customary law can therefore be challenged under the South African Bill of Rights. According to Justice Yvonne Mokgoro of the South African Constitutional Court, political necessity required the recognition of traditional authority but justice demanded that the exercise of such power be subjected to constitutional scrutiny.

The constitution of Ghana employs a similar model and recognizes a right to practice one's culture while also prohibiting customary practices that dehumanize or injure the physical or mental well-being of a person.

The Ugandan constitution strikes a balance that explicitly addresses the tension between women's rights (article 33) and the right to practice culture (article 37). Article 33(6) prohibits "laws, cultures, customs or traditions which are against the dignity, welfare or interest of women or which undermine their status."***

Critical Pragmatic Engagement with the Politics of Culture

Empirical Evidence of Cultural Variation

Evidence that individual and situational variations abound in local practices serves as a powerful counter to rigid and absolutist statements about culture. Alternative expressions of culture may not necessarily be verbalized, but may be evident in practices of resistance. Evidence can only be gathered through empirical work and must be presented to the official and semi-official forums that play a key role in the definition and official articulation of cultural norms. For instance, in court practice, proponents of gender equality must challenge the reification of ossified forms of customary law contained in court precedents and in publications that purport to be comprehensive compilations of customary law. Judges continue to use outdated volumes as a primary source of evidence on customary law because no other resources are available. Courts and lawyers will use these "static traditionalist" conceptions of customary law as long as certain litigants benefit from them. Advocates interested in using equally valid, alternative social practices to depict custom must therefore persist in the presentation of new empirical evidence, so that the courts will come to accept the practice of challenging the ossified compilations.***

Invoking a Community's Own General Principles of Fairness and Justice

A rule of custom may be widely accepted, but may not apply to all situations. In a given situation, the application of this rule may be objectionable in light of commonly held notions of fairness and justice. For instance, the conventional understanding that girls do not inherit their families' property is widespread in Kenya. Research conducted in the Makueni District of Eastern Kenya, however, established that people generally favor providing for daughters who may not marry or whose marriages may not work out. People also make provisions for such a contingency in the future. The people interviewed frequently reinforced that view with the remark: "Nengi na ni mwana ta aangi, na ndekw'a itheka i!" which means, "Indeed she is a child, just like the others, and she cannot be cast away!" The overarching principles of providing sustenance and taking responsibility for every child justify this flexible practice, qualifying the conventional notion that male children are the only ones entitled to their families' property.***

A community's general principles of fairness have also been used as a starting point in challenging rigid assertions of cultural norms, particularly in questioning cultural justifications of domestic violence against women in the Native American community. For instance, community-based intervention programs have tried to address both the needs of the victims and the perpetrators of domestic violence in Native American reservations by invoking community values, such as the importance of harmony in the core of the Native American value system.***

CEDAW offers a starting point, but it does not dictate the process for achieving change. CEDAW leaves open the possibility of a flexible process of evaluating assertions of culture in context. This flexible approach is particularly important in settings where overlap between formal legal institutions and policy and cultural norms renders such outlawing of custom both meaningless and unrealistic, as in the example of land policy.

Dilemmas Presented by a Critical Pragmatic Approach

The critical pragmatic approach to analyzing and challenging gender hierarchy may be criticized as a compromise position. When addressing this problem in the context of pragmatism and feminism, pragmatic feminists are counseled to "confront each dilemma separately and choose the alternative that will hinder empowerment the least and further it the most. The pragmatic feminist need not seek a general solution that will dictate how to resolve all double bind issues."***

This dilemma is not resolved, however, by choosing not to support such customary law claims by [women] who may need them. Rather, it is important to appropriate the openings present in local cultural or religious traditions, while simultaneously working toward changing the larger social matrix of national legislation, constitutions, and administrative institutions. By finding the space that local contexts provide for the recognition of women's rights, proponents of gender equality avoid creating the impression that the only solution lies in substituting local custom with the alternatives offered in national legislation or by the human rights regime.***

Notes and Questions

1. How do cultures evolve? What is the role of literacy, particularly female literacy, in the evolution of cultural norms? What is the role of self-determination and development, or the lack thereof, in cultural evolution? Nyamu points out that it is possible for overall social progress to occur without concomitant advancement for women. What are some examples of this phenomenon? Why does it happen? What strategies could be devised to counter such a tendency?

2. Nyamu discusses the South African resolution of the potential conflict between custom and constitutionalism. For more on the South African Bill of Rights *see* Chapter 8, *infra.*

4. Human Rights and Religious Traditions

The following materials describe controversies that involve gender, politics, culture and interpretations of Islamic law. Should religious requirements be treated differently under international human rights law than other traditional practices? Are there clear distinctions among "tradition," "culture," and "religion"? Who should decide whether a practice should be subject to international scrunity? What roles do economic, social and political contexts play in religious conflicts? Consider the following reports, including summaries of the requirements of Islamic Law from the perspectives of western journalists.

**SUSAN SACHS, A NATION CHALLENGED:
ISLAM; WHERE MUSLIM TRADITIONS MEET
MODERNITY FORCE OF ISLAM: A WOMAN'S PLACE**

NEW YORK TIMES, December 17, 2001, at B1

Rabat, Morocco

Islam preaches equality, yet in most Muslim countries a woman's place is determined by a man's will. It's the law.***

As modernity collides with religious tradition, women have begun to demand a reinterpretation of the civil codes that presume a woman, in her private life, is a capricious creature in need of a man's guiding hand.

The agitation in countries like Morocco is coming from female scholars who are confident of their religious judgment and use the Internet as a forum to promote an alternative vision of the rights of Muslim women. It is coming, as well, from politically active women who push for change from within Islamist movements. It is coming from ordinary women who fear that legal strictures will prevent their countries from integrating into the modern world.

Their challenges to Islamic orthodoxy have placed these women at the heart of the main political battle in the Muslim world, where one side claims Islam as a shield against foreign culture and the other presents it as a road map for progress.

To the extent there is public debate over the role of Islam—as armor or emancipator—that debate often turns on the subject of women.

For many Muslim women, the religious laws that subordinate them to the authority of male relatives represent a final frontier. They already vote, unless they live in the gulf nations. They go to school, unless they lived under Taliban rule in Afghanistan. They choose whether or not to wear a veil, unless they live in Iran or Saudi Arabia.

But in the personal sphere, laws remain mired in patriarchal tradition and a medieval reading of Islam. To alter them, Muslim women face not only an entrenched religious establishment, but also a battle with fundamentalists in the political arena.

Many Muslim women say they do not want instructions for their struggle from the West. As they demonstrated at many international conferences on women's rights, they resent being told what it is they need.

Still, in many countries, Islamist movements have attacked those seeking change as Western stooges and enemies of Islam, and they have seized on resistance to women's rights as an issue in their power struggle with moderate Muslim rulers.

In Kuwait, Islamist members of Parliament rejected the emir's efforts to grant voting rights to women and pushed through a law to segregate Kuwait University. In Jordan, Islamists have campaigned successfully against the king's attempt to stiffen penalties for honor killings, or the murder of women whose behavior is deemed shameful to family honor.***

Islam's Evolution

*** Born in the tribal societies of the Arabian Peninsula in the seventh century, Islam vastly improved the lot of women of that time. It instructed men that they could have up to four wives, but only if they treated all of them equally and had the means to support them. A woman could inherit wealth instead of being inherited as part of her husband's or father's estate.

As codified over the years, however, Islam eventually institutionalized the inferiority of women. The prophet Muhammad is said to have urged his followers to treat women with respect, but respect has come to mean control. And while some scholars have argued that Islam was meant to be flexible enough to adjust to a changing society, conservatives have held sway for centuries.

Muslim women now find themselves constrained by tradition as much as religious law. Saudi women are forbidden to drive, ostensibly to protect their Muslim honor, just as most Muslim women need a male relative's permission to get a passport.

"Our prophet made his own bed, sewed his own shirts, helped his wife at home," said Sibel Eraslan, a veiled Istanbul lawyer who once headed a women's committee in the Turkish Islamist party, Refah. "Today men don't want to follow Muhammad because it is easier not to. Even the hard-line Islamists ignore these details from our prophet's life."

She, at least, lives in a country that recently changed its laws to give women equal rights in family life. But Turkey did so to aid its application to join the European Union, leaving Mrs. Eraslan uneasy with what she called "imposed changes."

For women seeking change, however, there are reasons for optimism. Women's votes can count, as they did in bringing a moderate president, Mohammad Khatami, to power in Iran in 1997. And traditionalists no longer control all the religious debate.

"Educated women armed with computers have defeated extremists by denying them a monopoly to define cultural identity and interpret religious texts," said Fatema Mernissi, a Moroccan sociologist who has written extensively on women and democracy in Islam.

"No extremist can say that women are inferior to men without being made a laughingstock on Al Jazeera," she added, referring to the Qatar-based satellite news channel. "Islam insisted on equality between everyone."

Islamic jurisprudence is based on the Koran, which Muslims consider the word of God, and on the hadith, the prophet's words and actions as recorded after his death. Koranic verse is the basis for giving a woman's testimony half the weight of a man's. Laws limiting women's political role rely on the hadith, particularly one that attributes to the prophet a particularly damning view of women's abilities to lead. "Those who entrust their affairs to a woman," he is believed to have said, "will never know prosperity."

Women, of course, have led Muslim countries in Asia. But they have advanced no higher than government minister in modern Arab countries, in part because Arab scholars have not strayed far from the most literal interpretation of that hadith.***

Notes and Questions

1.   Why should women in Turkey be uneasy with changes in their status that were initiated to comply with European Union standards? Might they question the genuineness of the acceptance of new norms by the population? What repercussions might they fear?

2.   What effect might the "war on terrorism," the U.S.-U.K. invasion and occupation of Iraq, and the ongoing stalemates regarding Palestinian sovereignty have on Muslim receptivity to Western critiques of their gender-related practices?

AMINA LAWAL IN COURT TO APPEAL STONING SENTENCE

WEEKLY MAIL AND GUARDIAN, June 2, 2003

Three Nigerians sentenced to be stoned to death for having sex outside marriage will appeal before Islamic courts this week, turning the spotlight back on a bitter battle over Sharia law. In the best known case, 33-year-old mother-of-three Amina Lawal will on Tuesday begin her second appeal against her conviction for adultery at the Sharia Appeal Court in the northern city of Katsina.***

*** Lawyers for the accused believe that even leaving aside the human rights issue of allowing someone to be stoned to death, the convictions are flawed even under the tenets of Sharia.

Lawal was not given proper representation, was tried by one judge rather than the obligatory panel of four and the charge and its implications were not properly explained to her, her lawyers will argue. "Our first priority is to save Amina's life," lawyer Hauwa Ibrahim said after a previous hearing. "Then we want to look more broadly at how the law is applied."***

Nigeria is a federation of 36 states, 12 of which have reintroduced Sharia criminal law into their penal codes since the end of military rule in 1999, despite half-hearted opposition from the federal government. Even in the northern states where Sharia in theory holds sway, its application has been patchy. A small number of alleged thieves have had their hands chopped off, but no-one has yet been stoned to death.

But the law change has had huge social and political effects. As the code was reintroduced into northern cities, rioting broke out between Muslims and Christians, leaving thousands dead.

Thousands more fled their homes, and their displacement altered the religious and ethnic balance in other unstable areas. On the international level the controversy hurt Nigeria's image just as it was shaking off the stigma of its long years of military rule. Pictures of Lawal, a modest and gentle village housewife, cradling her infant daughter in ramshackle courtrooms while robed lawyers argue out her fate have appeared in newspapers around the world. Rights groups and governments protested. Lawal, a Muslim, was invited to Rome to become an honorary citizen. Candlelit vigils were held outside Nigerian embassies in Europe.

President Olusegun Obasanjo, a Christian, appeared on international television to promise Lawal would be saved, but chose his words carefully. The appeals process would be allowed to run its course, he said, and he was confident she would be cleared. There was no question of banning Sharia, which he said was a legitimate part of the Muslim way of life.***

Balancing the diverse aspirations of Nigeria's hugely diverse ethnic and religious groups has long been a daunting challenge. Between 1967 and 1970 a civil war left more than one-million dead. Since Obasanjo came to power in 1999 more than 10,000 people have died in mob violence and faction fighting.

International attention attracted by the high-profile stoning cases has been an unwelcome complication, as far as Nigeria's rulers are concerned. Asked last year by reporters why Obasanjo did not simply challenge Sharia in Nigeria's Supreme Court, junior foreign minister Dubem Onyia snapped: "If you want to tear this country apart, go on asking questions like that."

Notes and Questions

1. Religious and ethnic conflicts in Nigeria, as in many former colonial territories, were exacerbated by the arbitrary drawing of state borders that ignored historical, religious, cultural or other differences among groups. Post-colonial central governments were then left with the task of attempting to maintain a unified state despite the diverse cultures and interests of different subnational groups. For a discussion of this issue in the African context, *see, e.g.,* Makau Mutua, *Why Redraw the Map of Africa?: A Moral and Legal Inquiry*, 16 MICH. J. INT'L L. 1113 (1995). To address this issue, the constitution of the Federal Republic of Nigeria includes directive principles of state policy that provide that:

> 15. (2) *** national integration shall be actively encouraged, whilst discrimination on the grounds of place of origin, sex, religion, status, ethnic or linguistic association or ties shall be prohibited.
>
> (3) For the purpose of promoting national integration, it shall be the duty of the State to:
>
> (a) provide adequate facilities for and encourage free mobility of people, goods and services throughout the Federation.
>
> (b) secure full residence rights for every citizen in all parts of the Federation.
>
> (c) encourage inter-marriage among persons from different places of origin, or of different religious, ethnic or linguistic association or ties; and
>
> (d) promote or encourage the formation of associations that cut across ethnic, linguistic, religious and or other sectional barriers.
>
> (4) The State shall foster a feeling of belonging and of involvement among the various people of the Federation, to the end that loyalty to the nation shall override sectional loyalties.

To what extent are states legally obligated to balance rights of religious and cultural expression against other human rights? How should conflicts be decided? Moreover, the constitution recognizes and addresses the potential conflicts between cultural norms and rights:

21. The State shall—(a) protect, preserve and promote the Nigerian cultures which enhance human dignity and are consistent with the fundamental objectives as provided in this Chapter ***.

How effective are these provisions likely to be in resolving ethnic tensions and achieving national unity? Are these goals unproblematic? For example, is it an appropriate role for government to "encourage inter-marriage among persons *** of different religious" backgrounds?

2. The following letter from BAOBAB for Women's Human Rights was circulated on the internet by women's rights groups with regard to the Lawal case.

BAOBAB FOR WOMEN'S HUMAN RIGHTS, PLEASE STOP THE INTERNATIONAL AMINA LAWAL PROTEST LETTER CAMPAIGNS

Available at womensrightswatch-nigeria@kabissa.org (May 2, 2003)

Dear Friends,

There have been a whole host of petitions and letter writing campaigns about Amina Lawal (sentenced to stoning to death for adultery in August 2002). Many of these are inaccurate and ineffective and may even be damaging to her case and those of others in similar situations. BAOBAB for Women's Human Rights, which is responsible for initiating and continuing to support the defenses of cases like Ms. Lawal's, thanks the world for its support and concern, but requests that you please stop the Amina Lawal international protest letter campaigns for now (May 2003). The information currently circulated is inaccurate, and the situation in Nigeria, being volatile, will not be helped by such campaigns. At the end of this letter, we indicate ways in which you can help us and we hope we can count on your continuing support.

Clarification of Facts

First, we would like to pass on some facts that hopefully will clarify the situation somewhat. Contrary to information being widely circulated, Amina Lawal's conviction has NOT been upheld by Nigeria's Supreme Court. Ms. Lawal was originally convicted by an Upper Area Court in Katsina State in northern Nigeria. Her appeal is currently before the Katsina State Sharia Court of Appeal.*** Should this appeal not succeed, Ms. Lawal would appeal to the (Nigerian Federal) Sharia Court of Appeal. Only if unsuccessful at the federal appeal court also would Ms. Lawal's case go to the Supreme Court of Nigeria. In other words, the process is a long way from immediate stoning to death. Although the stress on Ms. Lawal is obviously considerable and awful, she is not in immediate danger of a judicial execution.

Furthermore, so far, not one appeal that has been taken up by BAOBAB and supporting local NGOs in Nigeria has been lost. All the completed appeals processes have been successful. Again, so far, all these appeals have been won in local state Sharia courts—none have yet needed to go up to the Federal Sharia Court of Appeal, from whence appeals would go to the Supreme Court.***

Contrary to the statements in many of the internationally originated appeals for petitions and protest letters, none of the victims received a pardon as a result of international pressure. None of them has received a pardon at all—or needed to, so far.

None of the sentences of stoning to death have been carried out. Either the appeals were successful or those convicted are still in the appeals process.

Dangers of Letter Writing Campaigns?

However, if there is an immediate physical danger to Ms. Lawal and others, it is from vigilante and political further (over)reaction to international attempts at pressure.*** Thus, we would like you to recognize that an international protest letter campaign is not necessarily the most productive way to act in every situation. On the contrary, women's rights defenders should assess potential backlash effects before devising strategies.

Problems with Petitions based on Inaccurate Information

Even when protests are appropriate forms of action, when they are obviously based on inaccuracies of fact they are easier to ignore. Circulating protests and writing letters based on inaccurate information may further damage the situation instead of helping. They certainly damage the credibility of the local activists, who are assumed to have supplied this information. If we remember that it is local activists who most facilitate turning rights principles into everyday reality for people, then reducing the ability and potential of local activists to carry out women's and human rights promotion and defense is a counter-productive mode of proceeding. Please check the accuracy of the information with local activists, before further circulating petitions or responding to them.

Re-Presenting negative stereotypes of Islam and Muslims

Dominant colonialist discourses and the mainstream international media have presented Islam (and Africa) as the barbaric and savage Other. Please do not buy into this. Accepting stereotypes that present Islam as incompatible with human rights not only perpetuates racism but also confirms the claims of right-wing politico-religious extremists in all of our contexts. We appreciate that many who join letter writing campaigns are motivated by the same sense of international solidarity and feminist outrage that leads us at BAOBAB to participate in international actions. But when protest letters re-present negative stereotypes of Islam and Muslims, they inflame sentiments rather than encouraging reflection and strengthening local progressive movements. They may result in behaviour such as that of the Zamfara State governor over Bariya Magazu, or even more threatening, hostile and violent behaviour by vigilantes (in extra-legal acts by non-state actors like the hordes of young unemployed men who are the bulk of the vigilantes). Consequently, such letters can put in further danger both the victims who are easily reachable in their home communities, and, the activists and lawyers supporting them (who are particularly vulnerable when they have to walk through hostile crowds on their way to court, for instance).

Muslim discourses and the invocation of Islam have been used both to vindicate and protect women's rights in some places and times, and to violate and restrict them in other places and times—as in the present case. The same can be said of many, many other religions and discourses (for example, Christianity, capitalism, socialism, modernization to name but a few). The point is for us to question who is invoking Islam (or whatever belief/discourse) for what purposes, and also to acknowledge and support internal dissent within the community involved, rather than engaging in a wholesale condemnation of peoples' beliefs and cultures, which is seldom accurate or effective in changing views within the affected community. Please be sensitive to these concerns in any protest letters you may write.

Supporting Local Pressures

There is a place for international pressure and campaigns. We would not risk any-one's life by insisting on never having an international campaign. However, using inter-national protest appeals as the automatic response reduces its usefulness as an advocacy tool. We feel that this is not the time for an international letter writing campaign, but we are concerned that should the situation change, and we then need international pressure and ask for international support, the moral energy and indignation of the world may already have been spent—resulting in campaign fatigue (been there, done that already).***

Using local structures and mechanisms (as a means of resisting retrogressive laws or interpretations of laws and the forces behind them) is the priority. It strengthens local counter-discourses and often carries greater legitimacy than 'outside' pressure. Further, it can really address the local political power struggles that are behind the polit-ical use of religions and ethnicities in Nigeria. The political Islamists and vigilantes threaten (and carry out) acts of violence against those who criticize them, in order to intimidate people. But they have also been promoting the view that any criticism or appeal of conviction is anti-Islam and tantamount to apostasy, and thereby trying to get people to submit quietly and voluntarily. One of the means of countering this was our choice to pursue the appeals in the Sharia system, and thereby demonstrate that peo-ple have a right to appeal and to challenge injustices, including those made in the name of Islam.

Every appeal in the local sharia courts strengthens this process. Since the first cases, that of Bariya Magazu, (where BAOBAB had to convince her family and various opin-ion-leaders in the village to agree to an appeal) and the Jangedi case (where a man con-victed of theft refused to appeal and had his hand amputated), many victims have no longer acquiesced to injustices, but actively sought help. Furthermore, in both Safiya Husseini Tungar-Tudu's and Amina Lawal's cases, members of their community have spoken about the abuse of Sharia and taken actions to protect them from local vigi-lantes. These are actions that would not have happened when BAOBAB first started this work in 1999. At that time, even finding a lawyer from the Muslim community willing to represent the victim was not easy.***

Winning appeals in the Sharia courts, as we and others have done, establishes that convictions should not have been made. A pardon means that people are guilty but the state is forgiving them for it. It does not have the same moral and political resonance. A pardon that is perceived as occurring as a result of outside pressure is even less likely to convince the community of its rightness. If we don't want such abuses to go on and on, then we have to convince the community not to accept injustices even when per-petrated in the name of strongly held beliefs.

Deciding on Strategies to Fight Injustices

We are asking for international solidarity strategies that respect the analyses and agency of those activists most closely involved and in touch with the issues on the ground and the wishes of the women and men directly suffering rights violations. The local groups in Nigeria directly representing victims (in the lead of whom are BAOBAB for Women's Human Rights and WRAPA—Women's Rights Advancement and Protection Agency) have specifically asked that there NOT be international letter writing campaigns. When victims of human rights abuses are held incommunicado, then clearly all anyone can do is act on our own beliefs to try and help them. This is not such a situation. The victims are not in detention (and indeed give press interviews). They have chosen to appeal and accepted the assistance of NGOs like BAOBAB, WRAPA and the networks of Nigerian women's and human rights NGOs that support them. There is an unbecoming arrogance in assuming that international human rights organizations or others always know better than those directly involved, and therefore can take actions that fly in the face of their express wishes. Of course, there is always the possibility that those directly involved are wrong but surely the course of action is to persuade them of the correctness of one's analysis and strategies, rather than ignore their wishes. They at least have to live directly with the consequences of any wrong decisions that they take. Please do liaise with those whose rights have been violated and/or local groups directly involved to discuss strategies of solidarity and support before launching campaigns.

So how can people and other organizations help? In the immediate, resources (money but not only money) are needed to support both the victims directly and the appeal processes. The victims—almost all of them poor, and most also rural dwellers—have found that their lives and work and those of their families are disrupted. They are economically hard hit, as well as under considerable social pressure. Often their health (physical and psychological) suffers as a result of stress. Sometimes a safe house is needed in the face of threats from vigilantes—there are no institutional ones in northern Nigeria. It may be necessary to consider safe asylum (bearing in mind issues like travel documents, visas, costs and how government bureaucracies will react). Resources are needed for living expenses for victims, their dependents and families, and to deal with stress-related consequences (counseling support, medical treatments and drugs amongst them), and to deal with safety and security. Experience and strategy-sharing with other groups who have dealt with similar situations supporting victims through an appeals process and campaign would also be most welcome.

Then there are the costs of fighting the appeals. Obviously there are legal costs. These include court fees and lawyers' fees. (Not all lawyers are willing or financially able to work completely pro bono. Even when they donate their expertise, they may have to be paid for court appearances, travel and subsistence expenses). They also include costs in document preparation especially in multiple copies and so on. There are also a whole series of associated costs. Fighting appeals is person and time-intensive. Activists have to: check media and local networks to find victims; travel to offer support to victims; draw on networks to find lawyers willing to represent victims; convene and participate in strategy sessions (yet more travel as these are often national); prepare the arguments and documentation; travel to the court with the victims; engage in victim support (discuss their situations and the possible options and ramifications, deal with consequential issues like loss of land, or ill-health, provide emotional support); liaise with and service the local and international networks supporting such work; not to mention write the reports and analyses constantly required. Resources to support all this work is needed.

Women's rights activists working on these issues very early on received support from progressive lawyers, Islamic scholars and rights activists from throughout Nigeria, the

Muslim world and elsewhere, in the form of legal and religious argumentation (*fiqh*), case law examples and strategies which were generously shared. We would like to acknowledge this help and support—it has been extremely useful and we can probably never have enough of it.

For the long-term, there are two needs to work on: constructing the cultures of recognizing rights and fighting violations at the local and national levels; and, to develop argumentation and advocacy to change the laws, evidence requirements and procedures.***

Exchanges of information, experiences and knowledge in similar situations would also be helpful. Practical offers of safe havens—outside the community but within Nigeria, and, outside of Nigeria may also be needed. Finally, do please circulate this message widely—including to all the list-servs and networks where petitions based on inaccurate information have been circulated. If you would share and discuss this message with other activists and organizations who have demonstrated their solidarity on these cases, that would be helpful.

Respectfully

Ayesha Imam (Board Member)

Sindi Medar-Gould (Executive Director)

BAOBAB for Women's Human Rights

BAOBAB for Women's Human Rights has been closely involved with defending the rights of women, men and children in Muslim, customary and secular laws—and in particular of those convicted under the new Sharia Criminal legislation acts passed in Nigeria since 2000.***

Notes and Questions

1.   According to media reports the most severe punishments under strict interpretations of Sharia law in Nigeria seem to be reserved for poor Muslims. *See* Michael Peel, *Sharia Still Wrenches Nigeria*, CHRISTIAN SCI. MONITOR, Sept. 29, 2003, at 01.

2.   In September, 2003, Amina Lawal's sentence was overturned by a regional Islamic Court interpreting Sharia law. News media reported that Lawal continued to affirm her faith in Islam during and after the legal ordeal. *See* Havwa Ibrahim, *Reflections on the Case of Amina Lawal*, 11 HUMAN RIGHTS BRIEF (No. 3) 39 (2004) (account by Lawal's attorney).

3.   How should activists and human rights lawyers respond, if at all, to interpretations of religious law and traditional practices that are harmful to women? Should there be a special focus on violations of the rights of women? Do men also experience human rights violations as a result of harmful interpretations of religious law and traditional practices? In what ways?

4.   What are the obligations of a state in which a religious of traditional practice occurs if that practice has been defined as a violation of international human rights? Does the state have an obligation to protect an individual from private violations? *Cf. X and Y v. The Netherlands* in Chapter 9 *infra.*

5.   How should non-Western activists and lawyers respond, if at all, to Western traditional (or modern) practices that harm women? Can you identify such practices? Hope

Lewis and Isabelle Gunning argue that the mistreatment of female and male asylum-seekers in the United States (some of whom are seeking escape from harmful traditional practices) is, itself, a "practice" that violates human rights. *See* Hope Lewis & Isabelle Gunning, *Cleaning Our Own House: "Exotic" and Familiar Human Rights Violations*, 4 BUFF. HUM. RTS. L. REV. 123 (1998) (discussing the gender asylum decision in *In re Fauziya Kasinga*, Interim Decision (BIA) 3278 or 1996 WL 379826 (B.I.A.)). The *Kasinga* decision granted asylum to a young woman from Togo who sought asylum in the United States because she feared being forced to undergo female genital cutting. Once in the United States, however, Kasinga was detained for months in U.S. detention facilities before a national campaign by lawyers and activists led to her release and ultimate grant of asylum.

6.   Is it possible to make clear distinctions between "culture" and "religion" in analyzing conflicts among different kinds of rights? Are such distinctions relevant or important? Why or why not? Traditions associated with Islamic law are not the only religious traditions subject to feminist human rights analysis and challenge. *See, e.g.,* Ilana S. Cristofar, *Blood, Water, and the Impure Woman: Can Jewish Women Reconcile Between Ancient Law and Modern Feminism?*, 10 S. CAL. REV. L. & WOMEN'S STUD. 451 (2001). To what extent are you aware of rights-based critiques of Jewish law, Christian law and the requirements of other religions? For example, should the Catholic Church's prohibitions against birth control be subjected to human rights analysis?

7.   For further general reading on gender, culture, religion and human rights, *see, e.g.,* Azizah Al-Hibri, *Islam, Law, and Custom: Redefining Muslim Women's Rights*, 12 AM. U. J. INT'L L. & POL'Y (1997); Abdullahi Ahmed An-Na'im, *State Responsibility Under International Human Rights Law to Change Religious Customary Law, in* HUMAN RIGHTS OF WOMEN 167 (Rebecca Cook ed., 1994); Penelope Andrews, *Violence Against Aboriginal Women in Australia: Possibilities for Redress Within the International Human Rights Framework*, 60 ALBANY L. REV. 101 (1997); WOMEN'S INTERNATIONAL HUMAN RIGHTS: A REFERENCE GUIDE (Kelly D. Askin & Dorean Koenig eds., 1999); Mai Chen, *Protective Laws and the Convention on the Elimination of All Forms of Discrimination Against Women*, 15 WOMEN'S RTS. L. REP. 1 (1993); Khadija Elmadmad, *Women's Rights Under Islam, in* HUMAN RIGHTS OF WOMEN: INTERNATIONAL INSTRUMENTS AND AFRICAN EXPERIENCES 243 (Wolfgang Benedek, Esther M. Kisaakye & Gerd Oberleitner eds., 2002); Berta Hernandez-Truyol, *Violence, Sex and Culture: A Re/Conceptualization of Violence for the Twenty-First Century*, 60 ALBANY L. REV. 607 (1997); Berta Hernandez-Truyol, *Women's Rights as Human Rights— Rules, Realities and the Role of Culture: A Formula for Reform*, 21 BROOK. J. INT'L L. 605 (1996); Tracy Higgins, *Anti-Essentialism, Relativism, and Human Rights*, 19 HARV. WOMEN'S L.J. 89 (1996); Sharon Hom, *Economic Reform and Social and Economic Rights in China: Strategies Brainstorming Across Culture, in* FROM BASIC NEEDS TO BASIC RIGHTS: WOMEN'S CLAIM TO HUMAN RIGHTS, 139 (Margaret A. Schuler ed., 1995); Sharon Hom, *Female Infanticide in China: The Specter of Human Rights and Thoughts Towards (An)other Vision*, 23 COL. HUM. RTS. L. REV. 249 (1992); Bonny Ibhawoh, *Cultural Tradition and National Human Rights Standards in Conflict, in* LEGAL CULTURES AND HUMAN RIGHTS: THE CHALLENGE OF DIVERSITY 86 (Kirsten Hastrup ed., 2001); Esther M. Kisaakye, *Women, Culture and Human Rights: Female Genital Mutilation, Polygamy and Bride Price, in* HUMAN RIGHTS OF WOMEN: INTERNATIONAL INSTRUMENTS AND AFRICAN EXPERIENCES 268 (Wolfgang Benedek, Esther M. Kisaakye & Gerd Oberleitner eds., 2002); Leslye Amede Obiora, *Feminism, Globalization and Culture*, 4 IND. J. GLOB. L. Stud. 255 (1997); Leslye Amede Obiora, *Reconsidering African Customary Law*, 17 LEG. STUD. FORUM 3 (1993); AFRICAN WOMEN AND FEMINISM: REFLECTING ON THE POLITICS OF SISTERHOOD (Oyeronke Oyewumi,

ed., 2003); OYERONKE OYEWUMI, THE INVENTION OF WOMEN: MAKING AN AFRICAN SENSE OF WESTERN GENDER DISCOURSES (1997); Celina Romany, *Women as Aliens: A Feminist Critique of the Public/Private Distinction in International Human Rights Law*, 6 HARV. HUM. RTS. J. 87 (1993); Donna J. Sullivan, *Gender Equality and Religious Freedom: Toward a Framework for Conflict Resolution* 24 N.Y.U. J. INT'L L. & POL. 795 (1992); Leti Volpp, *Talking Culture: Gender, Race, Nation, and the Politics of Multiculturalism*, 96 COLUM. L. REV. 1573 (1996); Adrien K. Wing, *Custom, Religion and Rights: The Future Legal Status of Palestinian Women*, 35 HARV. J. INT'L L. 149 (1994); ADRIEN K. WING ED., GLOBAL CRITICAL RACE FEMINISM: AN INTERNATIONAL READER (2000).

See also the following cases and statements by international organizations: Lovelace v. Canada, Human Rights Committee, 1981. U.N. Doc. CCPR/C/OP/1, at 83 (rights of indigenous women, excerpted in Section A.1.c); *Ephrahim v. Pastory*, 87 Int. L. Rep. 106 (Tanz. High Ct. 1990) (individual property rights of women, discussed in Section A.1.c); *Magaya v. Magaya*, Supreme Court of Zimbabwe, 1999, Judgment No. S.C. 210/98m [1999] 3 LRC 35 (inheritance rights of women).

5. Case Study: Gender, Culture and Sexual Orientation— The Same-Sex Marriage Debate in the United States

Cultural norms have been used to defend widespread discrimination, harassment, and violence against people based on their sexual orientation. In the late 1960s, inspired by the successes of the earlier protests in defense of blacks and women, a mass movement arose in the United States to combat legal and social impediments to full personhood and citizenship for gay, lesbian, bisexual, and transgendered people. While this new movement would embrace causes familiar from the preceding civil rights era— employment and housing, for example—its most publicly engaged struggle would be over access to the socio-legal forms of family: adoption, child custody, and ultimately, marriage. According to James Donovan:

> The initiation of the modern gays' rights movement conventionally is ascribed to the Stonewall riots of June 1969. Despite only a few years earlier having won the right to be served alcohol in public establishments [*See e.g., One Eleven Wines & Liquors, Inc., v. Div. Of Alcoholic Beverage Control*, 235 A.2d 12 (N.J. 1967)], homosexuals in bars remained vulnerable to recurring police harassment on morals charges. After midnight on the night of June 27, 1969, police attempted a raid on a popular gay bar, the Stonewall Inn, on Christopher Street in New York City. Police had raided gay bars many times before; in fact, this was the second raid of Stonewall that week. For reasons we may never know—although it may be no coincidence that this was the night of Judy Garland's funeral—this time the patrons fought back. Barricaded in the bar, the police defended themselves from the "drag queens (and) butch dykes" with spray from a fire hose. The Tactical Patrol Force arrived to confront the crowd of over one thousand chanting gays, who stood their ground against the heavily armed officers. When it was over, the police had injured "an untold number" and arrested thirteen. [*See generally* EDWARD ALWOOD, STRAIGHT NEWS: GAYS, LESBIANS, AND THE NEWS MEDIA (1996)]. Thousands of gays staged protests on each of the next several nights, giving voice to their newfound determination to finally claim their place in society, thus turning the Stonewall riots into the "Hairpin Drop Heard around the World."

Almost immediately, same-sex marriage became an issue in the new gay liberation movement. In 1971, *Baker v. Nelson* [191 N.W.2d 185 (Minn. 1971)] became the first appellate decision to hold that a same-sex couple does not have the right to marry. Similar cases soon followed, all upholding state rules prohibiting same-sex marriage. [For a comprehensive historical review, *see* WILLIAM N. ESKRIDGE, JR., THE CASE FOR SAME-SEX MARRIAGE: FROM SEXUAL LIBERTY TO CIVILIZED COMMITMENT (1996)]. Despite these early cases testing the boundaries of tolerance and same-sex marriage, the gays' rights movement kept marriage far from the front-burner. In those early days, the more urgent need was for gays to stay alive and out of jails and mental hospitals. Specifically, the activists sought to remove from homosexuals the threat of blackmail, to overturn the laws criminalizing sodomy and to excise homosexuality from the psychiatric manual of mental illnesses.

Although always in the background, same-sex marriage did not become the showcase issue of the gays' rights movement until the 1993 case of *Baehr v. Lewin* [852 P.2d 44 (Haw. 1993)]. In *Baehr*, three couples challenged Hawaii's refusal to provide marriage licenses to same-sex couples under Hawaii Revised Statutes section 572-1, which restricts marital relations to a male and a female. The Hawaii Supreme Court ruled that because Hawaii's Constitution forbids discrimination on the basis of sex (an argument none of the parties had asserted or briefed), Hawaii could justify section 572-1 only by surviving a strict scrutiny analysis. To maintain its refusal to grant marriage licenses to same-sex couples, the state had to show a compelling interest in barring same-sex marriage and that this refusal was the narrowest possible means to achieve that end.

The court remanded the case, and Judge Kevin Chang ruled decisively in favor of the plaintiffs. A state constitutional amendment passed by referendum, however, rendered the case moot.

Many of the movement's political spokespersons regretted that such a volatile, losing issue had emerged to detract from what they considered the more achievable goals of employment nondiscrimination and inclusion in hate crimes laws. Critics of the effort to promote same-sex marriage fell silent, however, as the cases first in Hawaii and then in other states raised same-sex marriage to the forefront of the consciousness of both the general public and the gay and lesbian community.

James M. Donovan, *Same-sex Union Announcements: Whether Newspapers Must Publish Them, and Why We Should Care*, 68 BROOK. L. REV. 721, 741–743 (2003).

The following decision of the Massachusetts Supreme Judicial Court generated a heated and emotional national debate on gay marriage. As you read the decision and the materials that follow, consider the specific economic, social and cultural implications of the debate, as well as its overall significance for human rights in general.

GOODRIDGE v. DEPARTMENT OF PUBLIC HEALTH

440 Mass. 309, 798 N.E.2d 941 (2003), *available at* Document222FN_F0022

MARSHALL, C.J.

Marriage is a vital social institution. The exclusive commitment of two individuals to each other nurtures love and mutual support; it brings stability to our society. For those who choose to marry, and for their children, marriage provides an abundance of legal, financial, and social benefits. In return it imposes weighty legal, financial, and social obligations. The question before us is whether, consistent with the Massachusetts Constitution, the Commonwealth may deny the protections, benefits, and obligations conferred by civil marriage to two individuals of the same sex who wish to marry. We conclude that it may not. The Massachusetts Constitution affirms the dignity and equality of all individuals. It forbids the creation of second-class citizens. In reaching our conclusion we have given full deference to the arguments made by the Commonwealth. But it has failed to identify any constitutionally adequate reason for denying civil marriage to same-sex couples.

We are mindful that our decision marks a change in the history of our marriage law. Many people hold deep-seated religious, moral, and ethical convictions that marriage should be limited to the union of one man and one woman, and that homosexual conduct is immoral. Many hold equally strong religious, moral, and ethical convictions that same-sex couples are entitled to be married, and that homosexual persons should be treated no differently than their heterosexual neighbors. Neither view answers the question before us. Our concern is with the Massachusetts Constitution as a charter of governance for every person properly within its reach. "Our obligation is to define the liberty of all, not to mandate our own moral code." *Lawrence v. Texas*, 539 U.S. 558, __, 123 S.Ct. 2472, 2480, 156 L.Ed.2d 508 (2003) (*Lawrence*), *quoting Planned Parenthood of Southeastern Pa. v. Casey*, 505 U.S. 833, 850, 112 S.Ct. 2791, 120 L.Ed.2d 674 (1992).***

Barred access to the protections, benefits, and obligations of civil marriage, a person who enters into an intimate, exclusive union with another of the same sex is arbitrarily deprived of membership in one of our community's most rewarding and cherished institutions. That exclusion is incompatible with the constitutional principles of respect for individual autonomy and equality under law.

I

In March and April, 2001, each of the plaintiff couples attempted to obtain a marriage license from a city or town clerk's office. Each couple was denied and therefore prevented from marrying. They filed suit against the department, claiming that the department's practice violated Massachusetts law. Both parties filed for summary judgment.

After the complaint was dismissed and summary judgment entered for the defendants, the plaintiffs appealed. Both parties requested direct appellate review, which we granted.

II

Although the plaintiffs refer in passing to "the marriage statutes," they focus, quite properly, on G.L. c. 207, the marriage licensing statute, which controls entry into civil marriage. As a preliminary matter, we summarize the provisions of that law.

General Laws c. 207 is both a gatekeeping and a public records statute. It sets minimum qualifications for obtaining a marriage license and directs city and town clerks, the registrar, and the department to keep and maintain certain "vital records" of civil marriages. The gatekeeping provisions of G.L. c. 207 are minimal. They forbid marriage of individuals within certain degrees of consanguinity, §§1 and 2, and polygamous marriages. *See* G.L. c. 207, § 4. *See also* G.L. c. 207, §8 (marriages solemnized in violation of §§1, 2, and 4, are void ab initio). They prohibit marriage if one of the parties has communicable syphilis, *see* G.L. c. 207, §28A, and restrict the circumstances in which a person under eighteen years of age may marry. *See* G.L. c. 207, §§7, 25, and 27. The statute requires that civil marriage be solemnized only by those so authorized. *See* G.L. c. 207, §§38–40.***

We conclude, as did the judge, that G.L. c. 207 may not be construed to permit same-sex couples to marry.

III

A

The larger question is whether, as the department claims, government action that bars same-sex couples from civil marriage constitutes a legitimate exercise of the State's authority to regulate conduct, or whether, as the plaintiffs claim, this categorical marriage exclusion violates the Massachusetts Constitution. We have recognized the long-standing statutory understanding, derived from the common law, that "marriage" means the lawful union of a woman and a man. But that history cannot and does not foreclose the constitutional question.***

We begin by considering the nature of civil marriage itself. Simply put, the government creates civil marriage. In Massachusetts, civil marriage is, and since pre-Colonial days has been, precisely what its name implies: a wholly secular institution. *See Commonwealth v. Munson*, 127 Mass. 459, 460–466 (1879) (noting that "[i]n Massachusetts, from very early times, the requisites of a valid marriage have been regulated by statutes of the Colony, Province, and Commonwealth," and surveying marriage statutes from 1639 through 1834). No religious ceremony has ever been required to validate a Massachusetts marriage. *Id.*

Without question, civil marriage enhances the "welfare of the community." It is a "social institution of the highest importance." *French v. McAnarney, supra.* Civil marriage anchors an ordered society by encouraging stable relationships over transient ones. It is central to the way the Commonwealth identifies individuals, provides for the orderly distribution of property, ensures that children and adults are cared for and supported whenever possible from private rather than public funds, and tracks important epidemiological and demographic data.

Marriage also bestows enormous private and social advantages on those who choose to marry. Civil marriage is at once a deeply personal commitment to another human being and a highly public celebration of the ideals of mutuality, companionship, intimacy, fidelity, and family. "It is an association that promotes a way of life, not causes; a harmony in living, not political faiths; a bilateral loyalty, not commercial or social projects." *Griswold v. Connecticut*, 381 U.S. 479, 486, 85 S.Ct. 1678, 14 L.Ed.2d 510 (1965). Because it fulfils yearnings for security, safe haven, and connection that express our common humanity, civil marriage is an esteemed institution, and the decision whether and whom to marry is among life's momentous acts of self-definition.

The benefits accessible only by way of a marriage license are enormous, touching nearly every aspect of life and death.***

It is undoubtedly for these concrete reasons, as well as for its intimately personal significance, that civil marriage has long been termed a "civil right." *See e.g., Loving v. Virginia*, 388 U.S. 1, 12, 87 S.Ct. 1817, 18 L.Ed.2d 1010 (1967) ("Marriage is one of the 'basic civil rights of man,' fundamental to our very existence and survival"), quoting *Skinner v. Oklahoma*, 316 U.S. 535, 541, 62 S.Ct. 1110, 86 L.Ed. 1655 (1942); *Milford v. Worcester*, 7 Mass. 48, 56 (1810) (referring to "civil rights incident to marriages"). *See also Baehr v. Lewin*, 74 Haw. 530, 561, 852 P.2d 44 (1993) (identifying marriage as "civil right [. . .]"); *Baker v. State*, 170 Vt. 194, 242, 744 A.2d 864 (1999) (Johnson, J., concurring in part and dissenting in part) (same). The United States Supreme Court has described the right to marry as "of fundamental importance for all individuals" and as "part of the fundamental 'right of privacy' implicit in the Fourteenth Amendment's Due Process Clause." *Zablocki v. Redhail*, 434 U.S. 374, 384, 98 S.Ct. 673, 54 L.Ed.2d 618 (1978). *See Loving v. Virginia*, supra ("The freedom to marry has long been recognized as one of the vital personal rights essential to the orderly pursuit of happiness by free men").

Without the right to marry—or more properly, the right to choose to marry—one is excluded from the full range of human experience and denied full protection of the laws for one's "avowed commitment to an intimate and lasting human relationship." *Baker v. State*, supra at 229, 744 A.2d 864. Because civil marriage is central to the lives of individuals and the welfare of the community, our laws assiduously protect the individual's right to marry against undue government incursion. Laws may not "interfere directly and substantially with the right to marry." *Zablocki v. Redhail*, supra at 387, 98 S.Ct. 673. *See Perez v. Sharp*, 32 Cal.2d 711, 714 (1948) ("There can be no prohibition of marriage except for an important social objective and reasonable means").***

B

For decades, indeed centuries, in much of this country (including Massachusetts) no lawful marriage was possible between white and black Americans. That long history availed not when the Supreme Court of California held in 1948 that a legislative prohibition against interracial marriage violated the due process and equality guarantees of the Fourteenth Amendment, *Perez v. Sharp*, 32 Cal.2d 711, 728, 198 P.2d 17 (1948), or when, nineteen years later, the United States Supreme Court also held that a statutory bar to interracial marriage violated the Fourteenth Amendment, *Loving v. Virginia*, 388 U.S. 1, 87 S.Ct. 1817, 18 L.Ed.2d 1010 (1967). As both *Perez* and *Loving* make clear, the right to marry means little if it does not include the right to marry the person of one's choice, subject to appropriate government restrictions in the interests of public health, safety, and welfare. *See Perez v. Sharp*, supra at 717, 198 P.2d 17 ("the essence of the right to marry is freedom to join in marriage with the person of one's choice"). See also *Loving v. Virginia*, supra at 12, 87 S.Ct. 1817. In this case, as in *Perez* and *Loving*, a statute deprives individuals of access to an institution of fundamental legal, personal, and social significance—the institution of marriage—because of a single trait: skin color in *Perez* and *Loving*, sexual orientation here. As it did in *Perez* and *Loving*, history must yield to a more fully developed understanding of the invidious quality of the discrimination.***

Whether and whom to marry, how to express sexual intimacy, and whether and how to establish a family—these are among the most basic of every individual's liberty and due process rights.*** And central to personal freedom and security is the assurance that the laws will apply equally to persons in similar situations. "Absolute equality before the law is a fundamental principle of our own Constitution." *Opinion of the Justices*, 211 Mass. 618, 619, 98 N.E. 337 (1912). The liberty interest in choosing whether and whom to marry would be hollow if the Commonwealth could, without sufficient justification, foreclose an individual from freely choosing the person with whom to share an exclusive commitment in the unique institution of civil marriage.***

*** For the reasons we explain below, we conclude that the marriage ban does not meet the rational basis test for either due process or equal protection. Because the statute does not survive rational basis review, we do not consider the plaintiffs' arguments that this case merits strict judicial scrutiny.

The department posits three legislative rationales for prohibiting same-sex couples from marrying: (1) providing a "favorable setting for procreation"; (2) ensuring the optimal setting for child rearing, which the department defines as "a two-parent family with one parent of each sex"; and (3) preserving scarce State and private financial resources. We consider each in turn.

The judge in the Superior Court endorsed the first rationale, holding that "the state's interest in regulating marriage is based on the traditional concept that marriage's primary purpose is procreation." This is incorrect. Our laws of civil marriage do not privilege procreative heterosexual intercourse between married people above every other form of adult intimacy and every other means of creating a family. General Laws c. 207 contains no requirement that the applicants for a marriage license attest to their ability or intention to conceive children by coitus.***

Moreover, the Commonwealth affirmatively facilitates bringing children into a family regardless of whether the intended parent is married or unmarried, whether the child is adopted or born into a family, whether assistive technology was used to conceive the child, and whether the parent or her partner is heterosexual, homosexual, or bisexual. If procreation were a necessary component of civil marriage, our statutes would draw a tighter circle around the permissible bounds of nonmarital child bearing and the creation of families by noncoital means. The attempt to isolate procreation as "the source of a fundamental right to marry," 440 Mass. at 370 (Cordy, J., dissenting), overlooks the integrated way in which courts have examined the complex and overlapping realms of personal autonomy, marriage, family life, and child rearing. Our jurisprudence recognizes that, in these nuanced and fundamentally private areas of life, such a narrow focus is inappropriate.***

The department's first stated rationale, equating marriage with unassisted heterosexual procreation, shades imperceptibly into its second: that confining marriage to opposite-sex couples ensures that children are raised in the "optimal" setting. Protecting the welfare of children is a paramount State policy. Restricting marriage to opposite-sex couples, however, cannot plausibly further this policy. "The demographic changes of the past century make it difficult to speak of an average American family. The composition of families varies greatly from household to household." *Troxel v. Granville*, 530 U.S. 57, 63, 120 S.Ct. 2054, 147 L.Ed.2d 49 (2000). Massachusetts has responded supportively to "the changing realities of the American family," *id.* at 64, 120 S.Ct. 2054, and has moved vigorously to strengthen the modern family in its many variations.

The department has offered no evidence that forbidding marriage to people of the same sex will increase the number of couples choosing to enter into opposite-sex marriages in order to have and raise children. There is thus no rational relationship between the marriage statute and the Commonwealth's proffered goal of protecting the "optimal" child rearing unit. Moreover, the department readily concedes that people in same-sex couples may be "excellent" parents.*** Excluding same-sex couples from civil marriage will not make children of opposite-sex marriages more secure, but it does prevent children of same-sex couples from enjoying the immeasurable advantages that flow from the assurance of "a stable family structure in which children will be reared, educated, and socialized." 440 Mass. at 381 (Cordy, J., dissenting).

No one disputes that the plaintiff couples are families, that many are parents, and that the children they are raising, like all children, need and should have the fullest opportunity to grow up in a secure, protected family unit. Similarly, no one disputes that, under the rubric of marriage, the State provides a cornucopia of substantial benefits to married parents and their children. The preferential treatment of civil marriage reflects the Legislature's conclusion that marriage "is the foremost setting for the education and socialization of children" precisely because it "encourages parents to remain committed to each other and to their children as they grow." 440 Mass. at 383, 798 N.E.2d at 996 (Cordy, J., dissenting).

In this case, we are confronted with an entire, sizeable class of parents raising children who have absolutely no access to civil marriage and its protections because they are forbidden from procuring a marriage license. It cannot be rational under our laws, and indeed it is not permitted, to penalize children by depriving them of State benefits because the State disapproves of their parents' sexual orientation.

The third rationale advanced by the department is that limiting marriage to opposite-sex couples furthers the Legislature's interest in conserving scarce State and private financial resources. The marriage restriction is rational, it argues, because the General Court logically could assume that same-sex couples are more financially independent than married couples and thus less needy of public marital benefits, such as tax advantages, or private marital benefits, such as employer-financed health plans that include spouses in their coverage.*** An absolute statutory ban bears no rational relationship to the economy.

The department suggests additional rationales for prohibiting same-sex couples from marrying, which are developed by some *amici.* It argues that broadening civil marriage to include same-sex couples will trivialize or destroy the institution of marriage as it has historically been fashioned. Certainly our decision today marks a significant change in the definition of marriage as it has been inherited from the common law, and understood by many societies for centuries. But it does not disturb the fundamental value of marriage in our society.

*** That same-sex couples are willing to embrace marriage's solemn obligations of exclusivity, mutual support, and commitment to one another is a testament to the enduring place of marriage in our laws and in the human spirit.[14]

The history of constitutional law "is the story of the extension of constitutional rights and protections to people once ignored or excluded." *United States v. Virginia,* 518 U.S. 515, 557, 116 S.Ct. 2264, 135 L.Ed.2d 735 (1996) (construing equal protection clause of Fourteenth Amendment to prohibit categorical exclusion of women from public military institute). This statement is as true in the area of civil marriage as in any other area of civil rights.***

Several amici suggest that prohibiting marriage by same-sex couples reflects community consensus that homosexual conduct is immoral. Yet Massachusetts has a strong affirmative policy of preventing discrimination on the basis of sexual orientation. *See* G.L. c. 151B (employment, housing, credit, services); G.L. c. 265, §39 (hate crimes); G.L. c. 272, §98 (public accommodation); G.L. c. 76, §5 (public education). *See also, e.g., Commonwealth v. Balthazar,* 366 Mass. 298, 318 N.E.2d 478 (1974) (decriminalization of private consensual adult conduct); *Doe v. Doe,* 16 Mass.App.Ct. 499, 503, 452 N.E.2d 293 (1983) (custody to homosexual parent not per se prohibited).***

The marriage ban works a deep and scarring hardship on a very real segment of the community for no rational reason. The absence of any reasonable relationship between, on the one hand, an absolute disqualification of same-sex couples who wish to enter into civil marriage and, on the other, protection of public health, safety, or general welfare, suggests that the marriage restriction is rooted in persistent prejudices against persons who are (or who are believed to be) homosexual. "The Constitution cannot control such prejudices but neither can it tolerate them. Private biases may be outside the reach of the law, but the law cannot, directly or indirectly, give them effect." *Palmore v. Sidoti,* 466 U.S. 429, 433, 104 S.Ct. 1879, 80 L.Ed.2d 421 (1984) (construing Fourteenth Amendment). Limiting the protections, benefits, and obligations of civil marriage to opposite-sex couples violates the basic premises of individual liberty and equality under law protected by the Massachusetts Constitution.

IV

We consider next the plaintiffs' request for relief.***

We construe civil marriage to mean the voluntary union of two persons as spouses, to the exclusion of all others. This reformulation redresses the plaintiffs' constitutional injury and furthers the aim of marriage to promote stable, exclusive relationships. It advances the two legitimate State interests the department has identified: providing a stable setting for child rearing and conserving State resources. It leaves intact the Legislature's broad discretion to regulate marriage. *See Commonwealth v. Stowell,* 389 Mass. 171, 175, 449 N.E.2d 357 (1983).

---

[14] We are concerned only with the withholding of the benefits, protections, and obligations of civil marriage from a certain class of persons for invalid reasons. Our decision in no way limits the rights of individuals to refuse to marry persons of the same sex for religious or any other reasons. It in no way limits the personal freedom to disapprove of, or to encourage others to disapprove of, same-sex marriage. ***

In their complaint the plaintiffs request only a declaration that their exclusion and the exclusion of other qualified same-sex couples from access to civil marriage violates Massachusetts law. We declare that barring an individual from the protections, benefits, and obligations of civil marriage solely because that person would marry a person of the same sex violates the Massachusetts Constitution. We vacate the summary judgment for the department. We remand this case to the Superior Court for entry of judgment consistent with this opinion. Entry of judgment shall be stayed for 180 days to permit the Legislature to take such action as it may deem appropriate in light of this opinion. [Citation omitted.]

So ordered.

GREANEY, J. (concurring).

I do not doubt the sincerity of deeply held moral or religious beliefs that make inconceivable to some the notion that any change in the common-law definition of what constitutes a legal civil marriage is now, or ever would be, warranted. But, as matter of constitutional law, neither the mantra of tradition, nor individual conviction, can justify the perpetuation of a hierarchy in which couples of the same sex and their families are deemed less worthy of social and legal recognition than couples of the opposite sex and their families.

[Dissenting opinions omitted.]

Notes and Questions

1. *The Reaction to the Decision.* The *Goodridge* decision catalyzed a vigorous national debate over gay marriage in the United States, with its epicenter in Massachusetts. In response, the Boston Globe created and maintained an interactive web page focused on this dynamic process. *See Special Report: The Gay Marriage Debate*, BOSTON GLOBE, *available at* http://www.boston.com/news/specials/gay_marriage/ (last visited June 15, 2004).

In his 2004 State of the Union Message, President Bush suggested that resort to the "constitutional process" might be necessary to preserve the "sanctity of marriage." This statement ignited a wave of protest against the same-sex marriage ban across the country. In San Francisco, Mayor Gavin Newsom directed city officials to grant marriage licenses to same-sex couples, declaring that the prohibition violated the state constitution. The first to be married were Del Martin, 83, and Phyllis Lyon, 80, who had been together for over 50 years. Over the next week, about 3,000 licenses had been issued. Mayors in Chicago, Minneapolis and Salt Lake City expressed support for Newsom, while the newly elected Green Party candidate for mayor in Paltz, New York, Jason West, performed marriage ceremonies at a local bed and breakfast. Conservative groups immediately brought suits challenging these actions, and many state legislatures considered constitutional amendments banning same-sex marriages, and bills prohibiting the state from recognizing same-sex marriages performed elsewhere. *See Massachusetts High Court Reaffirms Same-Sex Marriage Rights: Legislature Deadlocks on State Constitutional Amendment*, LESBIAN/GAY LAW NOTES, at 35–38 (Mar. 2004), *available at* http://www.qrd.org/qrd/www/usa/legal/lgln/03.2004.pdf.

In February of 2004, President Bush urged passage of a constitutional amendment that would overturn *Goodridge* by defining marriage as a union between one woman and one man. *See* Wayne Washington, *Bush Seeks Marriage Amendment*, BOSTON GLOBE, Feb.

25, 2004, *available at* http://www.boston.com/news/specials/gay_marriage/articles/ 2004/02/25/bush_seeks_marriage_amendment/.

2. *Constitutional Convention.* In March of 2004, in a two-part state constitutional convention, Massachusetts legislators approved an amendment proposing to ban gay marriage but establish civil unions, which would effectively reverse the opinion of the Massachusetts Supreme Judicial Court. The convention was marked by tense political negotiations as well as large protests on various sides of the issue. The proposal will be put to a statewide vote in November of 2006. Rick Klein, *Vote Ties Civil Unions to Gay-marriage Ban*, BOSTON GLOBE, Mar. 20, 2004, *available at* http://www.boston.com/ news/specials/gay_marriage/articles/2004/03/30/vote_ties_civil_unions_to_gay_marriage_ban/.

3. Massachusetts Governor Mitt Romney took an active role in opposing gay marriage, first by asking the state attorney general to petition the Supreme Judicial Court to postpone their order until the issue could be put to the ballot in 2006. When that failed and gay couples began successfully applying for marriage licenses, Romney sought to enforce a 1913 Massachusetts law that prohibited granting marriage licenses to couples from states that refused to recognize their union. The state Senate voted overwhelmingly to repeal this law, and a vote in the House is pending at the time of writing. Raphael Lewis & Yvonne Abraham, *Senate Votes to End 1913 Law*, BOSTON GLOBE, May 20, 2004, *available at* http://www.boston.com/news/local/massachusetts/articles/2004/ 05/20/senate_votes_to_end_1913_law/.

4. On May 17, 2004, 180 days after the *Goodridge* decision, more than 600 gay couples were married in Massachusetts, including all seven of the couples involved in the *Goodridge* case. Questions still surround the fate of those marriages should the proposed amendment banning gay marriage be passed, though many lawmakers believe they will be protected. *See, e.g.*, Alan Cooperman & Jonathan Finer, *Gay Couples Marry in Massachusetts*, WASH. POST, May 17, 2004, *available at* http://www.washingtonpost. com/wp-dyn/articles/A34642-2004May17.html.

5. *Same-Sex Marriage Rights in Comparative Perspective.* Same-sex couples are allowed to marry in the Netherlands, Belgium, and the Canadian provinces of Ontario and British Colombia. In the United States, Massachusetts is the only state to grant marriage licenses to same-sex couples. In 1993, Hawaii's state Supreme Court ruled that banning same-sex marriage is unconstitutional, but in 1998 Hawaiians voted for a state constitutional amendment defining marriage as the union between a man and a woman. Several other states have provisions granting specific rights to same-sex couples. New Jersey grants same-sex couples access to medical benefits, insurance and certain other legal rights. As of 2005, California will grant same-sex couples all rights included under marriage, except the right to file joint state income tax returns. Vermont allows civil unions for same-sex couples, providing all the rights and privileges of marriage. President Clinton signed the "Defense of Marriage Act" (DOMA) into law on September 21, 1996. Pub. L. No. 104–199, 110 Stat. 2419. Its brief text authorizes states to ignore any implications of the full Faith and Credit Clause of the U.S. Constitution when it comes to recognizing the same-sex marriages of other states. *Id.* at §2, and defines "marriage" for the purposes of federal law, including entitlement programs, as "only a legal union between one man and one woman as husband and wife." *Id.* at §3. DOMA represented an almost unprecedented intrusion of the federal government into marriage law, an area traditionally reserved to the states; the only prior Congressional pronouncements on mar-

riage were the federal enactments outlawing Mormon polygamy. Many commentators argue that DOMA is unconstitutional. *See, e.g.,* MARK STRASSER, THE CHALLENGE OF SAME-SEX MARRIAGE: FEDERALIST PRINCIPLES AND CONSTITUTIONAL PROTECTIONS (1999); and James M. Donovan, *DOMA: An Unconstitutional Establishment of Fundamentalist Christianity,* 4 MICH. J. GENDER & L. 335 (1997). The federal DOMA law has, however, yet to be challenged in court, and has inspired many states to pass similar laws. Thirty-eight states have laws defining marriage as the union between one woman and one man. A. Baseden & Dave Clark, *State Laws About Gay Marriage* (interactive chart) at *Special Report: The Gay Marriage Debate,* BOSTON GLOBE, *available at* http://www.boston.com/news/specials/gay-marriage/.

6.   *The Normative Underpinnings of the Debate.* Why does the issue of gay marriage provoke such an emotional response? What cultural factors are in play? The Massachusetts court describes the issue as one of fundamental "civil rights" comparable to equality under the law and due process. Is the right to marry a person of one's choice also an economic, social, or cultural right? What factors would you use to distinguish among these various classifications?

7.   *Civil Union vs. Marriage: What's in a Name?* If a state's civil union laws were to grant identical rights as those under marriage, why would some gay marriage proponents argue that they are unequal? Why not simply treat all civil unions as "marriages"? Alternatively, why not reserve the term "marriage" for religious or cultural expressions of union, while "civil union" would apply to the state's secular role in recognizing committed couples? Is this aspect of the debate merely semantics, or does it reflect a fundamental aspect of the culture of marriage? How would you define "the culture of marriage"?

8.   *Preferred Rights vs. Majoritarianism.* Is this an issue that should be shielded from majority preferences? Does the fact that *Goodridge* was a five–four decision strengthen the argument that the debate should be put to a popular vote? The court frankly acknowledged that its decision effectively redefines marriage. Is this an appropriate role for a judicial body? Why or why not?

9.   What similarities can be found between the gay marriage debate and the historical and continuing resistance to inter-racial or inter-religious marriages in some parts of the United States? Can *Goodridge* be distinguished from that struggle? Because of the parallels drawn by some activists to the struggle for African-American civil rights in the United States, the same-sex marriage debate generated controversy among some African-American Christians and their representatives. (African-American churches and ministers were key participants in the U.S. civil rights and international anti-apartheid struggles.) The debate often centered on the legitimacy of homosexuality under certain interpretations of religious law, but it also included assertions about the nature of "African-American culture." *See, e.g.,* Yvonne Abraham, *On this Issue, Allies are on Opposite Sides,* BOSTON GLOBE, Sept. 16, 2003, *available at* http://www.boston.com/news. Should the opinions of African-American religious leaders on this issue be analyzed differently from the opinions of other religious leaders? Who defines "African-American culture"? Many prominent African-Americans, including Julian Bond, Coretta Scott-King, Carol Mosely Braun, Congressman John Lewis, and Henry Louis Gates, have endorsed gay marriage. What difference should such opinions make in the human rights analysis?

10.   What is the legal significance of the inclusion of same-sex marriage or civil union notices in local newspapers? Consider the following:

Same-sex union announcements [in local newspapers] have a central role to play in [same-sex marriage] debates. On one level, they show to the world a side of gay relationships it often does not see, that they can be committed, stable and frankly quite ordinary. On another, they help to elicit the social responses that contribute to the healthful maintenance of those relationships during the peaks and valleys endured by all romantic couples. Newspapers increasingly appear willing to allow gay couples to attain these social intangibles through access to their society pages. But of the estimated 1,600 metropolitan newspapers, only about 180 are known to have opened their announcements sections to gay men and lesbians. [As of May, 2004, that number had increased to 259]. More, certainly, will follow the example set by the New York Times. But others *** have remained adamant in their refusal, and these newspapers can expect legal action by the aggrieved parties. Because the intangible of public recognition is so very important, it is worth fighting for, and, when necessary, merits the energy and resources to persuade newspapers to publish announcements on a nondiscriminatory basis.

Whether this outcome can be realized depends on the unique factual setting in which each refusal to publish occurs. The threshold consideration is whether there exists a public accommodations law that prohibits discrimination on the basis of sexual orientation, and whether that law can be applied to newspapers. If that criterion is met, the next step is to ask how announcements in that newspaper are to be categorized, either as editorial "news" or as noneditorial speech analogous to commercial advertising.

The Free Press Clause protects editorial judgment embodied in "news." [Randall] Bezanson presented three criteria to be satisfied before granting material these free press protections. If little editorial judgment is exercised over the announcement's creation, then it should be excluded from the class of editorial speech that the Free Press Clause and [*Miami Herald Pub. Co. v. Tornillo*, 418 U.S. 241 (1974)] are intended to protect. Further, the mixture of commercial and expressive content of newspapers can render them vulnerable to the bifurcated analysis articulated by Justice O'Connor in [*Roberts v. United States Jaycees*, 468 U.S. 609 (1984)].*** All told, when a court deems society announcements noneditorial speech, they should be subject to antidiscrimination regulation by public accommodations laws.***

In other environments, however, society announcements will qualify as "news" because they do evidence editorial judgment in their creation. Moreover, some writers argue that same-sex declarations of this type are intrinsically expressive and political speech. By either standard, a different analysis is required in these contexts, one that centers on the Free Speech Clause and its protection of the newspaper's expressive content. That barrier falls, however, when newspapers are construed to be quasi-public corporations, and therefore subject to scrutiny as public fora. Here again, the First Amendment should not shield newspapers from reasonable regulation of generally applicable antidiscrimination regulations.

James M. Donovan, *Same-sex Union Announcements: Whether Newspapers Must Publish Them, and Why We Should Care*, 68 BROOK. L. REV. 721, 805–807 (2003).

What is the role of the "society" page in reflecting and shaping the culture? How might same-sex union or marriage announcements influence the public debate on this issue? How might such announcements inform our conception of human rights?

11. For further reading on the issue of same-sex marriage in the U.S. and internationally, *see, e.g.*, Carlos A. Ball, *The Positive in the Fundamental Right to Marry: Same-Sex Marriage in the Aftermath of* Lawrence v. Texas, 88 MINN. L. REV. 1184 (2004); James C. Dobson, *Marriage is the Foundation of the Family*, 18 N.D. J. L. ETHICS & PUB POL'Y 1 (2004); ERIC HEINZE, SEXUAL ORIENTATION: A HUMAN RIGHT (1995); Recent Cases, *Massachusetts Supreme Judicial Court Holds That Opposite-Sex Marriage Law Violates Right to Marry*, 117 HARV. L. REV. 2441 (2004); Vincent J. Samar, *Gay-Rights as a Particular Instantiation of Human Rights*, 64 ALBANY L. REV. 983 (2001); Jay Weiser, *Foreword: The Next Normal—Developments Since Marriage Rights for Same-Sex Couples in New York*, 13 COLUM. J. GENDER & L. 48, (2004); James D. Wilets, *International Human Rights Law and Sexual Orientation*, 18 HASTINGS INT'L & COMP. L. REV. 1 (1994).

6. Culture, Disability and "Disability Culture"

Differences in race, gender, religion and ethnicity have been recognized as issues for human rights focus from the beginning of the modern human rights movement. Differences in sexual orientation have also begun to be recognized in international human rights discourse. However, differences in physical and mental ability may also inform our experiences of the world around us. Persons with disabilities experience many violations of their economic, social, and cultural rights in every country, even though those violations may be experienced differently by people of different classes, races, genders, and sexual orientations. The need to prohibit discrimination against persons with disabilities has been recognized domestically, regionally, and internationally. (*See* Chapter 4, *supra*, discussing the Inter-American Convention on the Elimination of All Forms of Discrimination against Persons with Disabilities). However, in addition to exposing and advocating against discriminatory practices, persons with disabilities have advocated for full, and affirmative, inclusion in all aspects of social, economic and political life. Some argue that inclusion should be on a fully "mainstream" or integrated basis, while others argue that a focus on the specific needs of persons with disabilities is equally, or more, important. Even the term "disability" itself is a contested one. Some argue that it implies "less than able" rather than "differently abled."

"Disability culture," a movement to recognize the common experiences of people with disabilities, attempts to define disability in terms of its cultural implications rather than its medical definitions. *See, e.g.*, Amy E. Brusky, *Making Decisions for Deaf Children Regarding Cochlear Implants: The Legal Ramifications of Recognizing Deafness as a Culture Rather Than a Disability*, 1995 WIS. L. REV. 235 (1995). *See also* Barbara J. White, *From "deaf" to "Deaf": Defining Deaf Culture*, 18(2) DISABILITY STUD. Q. 82 (1998); JAMES WOODWARD, HOW YOU GONNA GET TO HEAVEN IF YOU CAN'T TALK WITH JESUS: ON DEPATHOLOGIZING DEAFNESS 75 (1982). For example, some of the literature and activism on "deaf culture" focuses on the cultural value of life as a deaf person within a broader deaf community that has shared languages (such as American Sign Language), artistic expressions and social contexts. *Id.* The deaf culture movement has been controversial in that some cultural rights activists argue that medical interventions (such as the Cochlear implant that might allow some previously deaf persons to hear) have a negative impact on deaf culture. Brusky, *supra*, at 240. Some argue that parents of a deaf child should not allow the child to be implanted; he or she should instead be allowed to experience deaf culture. The child might then make an informed choice between deaf and hearing cultures in adulthood. Others argue that the Cochlear implant, as an important medical advance, should be used to "cure" deaf children of their disability. Brusky, *supra*, at 235. Some disability culture activists, on the other hand, have gone so far as to describe social pressure to undergo Cochlear implantation as a form of "cultural genocide." Brusky, *supra*, at 242.

Disability cultures share many aspects of other common definitions of "culture." Persons with disabilities may share languages or systems of communication (such as Braille, large-print, and computerized screenreaders). They also may share strategies for dealing with discrimination (protests, litigation, humor, and popular education) and the physical environment (the use of wheelchairs, prosthetic devices, canes, guide animals). Many may experience common challenges to freedoms such as the right to form families and to bear or adopt children. As is the case in racial, religious and ethnic cultural contexts, inter-marriage among persons with disabilities and non-disabled persons may raise additional social challenges. Common customs or preferences may develop among certain persons with disabilities (such as a preferred means of social communication). At the same time, persons with disabilities, like persons within racial, gender, and other groups, also resist the tendency of those outside the group to stereotype group members as having special, "essential" and immutable characteristics.

The literature on disability culture, and its impact on the rights of persons with disabilities, reflects a wide range of opinions. Some academics and activists see the disability culture movement as a critical step in advancing disability rights. Brusky *supra*, at 240. Others argue that the well-intentioned empowerment and independence models of disability culture movements may conflict with practical efforts to advance disability rights and to remove societal barriers. Brusky, *supra*, at 243 n.36. Some see disability culture as a central aspect of one's identity; others see disability identity (and some other forms of group identity) as a reaction to the barriers currently present in society. In the latter view, once those barriers are reduced or eliminated, the need for identity based on disability will diminish. Adrienne Asch, *Critical Race Theory, Feminism, and Disability: Reflections on Social Justice and Personal Identity*, 62 OHIO ST. L.J. 391 (2001). In contrast, many persons with disabilities see intrinsic value in group identity beyond a reaction to discrimination.

Notes and Questions

1. To what extent is disability associated with culture in your experience? Who would define "disability culture"? To what extent are class, racial and religious differences relevant to such a definition? What are the advantages to recognizing disability culture in the context of human rights? What disadvantages can you identify?

2. In what ways do other forms of identity intersect with disability? Do different cultures have different attitudes and beliefs about disability and persons with disability? What are those attitudes and beliefs? Is identity largely a reaction to societal challenges? Can you imagine a society that took no account of identity? What value is there in diversity of background, experience, and other characteristics?

3. For further reading on disability culture, culture and disability, and disability rights, *see, e.g.*, Steven E. Brown, *A Celebration of Diversity: An Introduction, Annotated Bibliography*

about Disability Culture, 15(4) DISABILITY STUD. Q. 36 (1995); DISABILITY, DIVERSABILITY AND LEGAL CHANGE (International Studies in Human Rights) (Melinda Jones & Lee Ann Basser Marks eds., 1999); Ruth Colker, *Race, Sexual Orientation, Gender, and Disability*, 56 OHIO ST. L.J. 1 (1995); Michael Ashley Stein, *Book Review: Mommy Has a Blue Wheelchair: Recognizing the Parental Rights of Individuals with Disabilities*, 60 BROOK. L. REV. 1069 (1994); DISABILITY AND CULTURE: UNIVERSALISM AND DIVERSITY (Bediraham Usrun, Sommath Chatterji, Jurgen Rehm *et al.* eds., 2001).

4. *Selected Advocacy Organizations.* Among the many domestic and international advocacy organizations that address disability rights issues are the following:

- American Council of the Blind: www.acb.org

- Center for International Rehabilitation: cirrie.buffalo.edu

- China Disabled Persons' Federation: www.cdpf.org.cn/english

- Disabled Peoples' International: www.dpi.org

- European Disability Forum: www.edf-feph.org

- Handicap International: www.handicap-international.org

- Inclusion International: www.inclusion-international.org

- International Federation of Persons with Physical Disability: www.fimitic.org

- Inter-American Institute on Disability: www.icdri.org/South%20Amercia/iid.htm

- Landmine Survivors Network: www.landminesurvivors.org

- Mental Disability Rights International: www.mdri.org

- Mobility International: www.miusa.org

- National Federation of the Blind: www.nfb.org

- Northeastern University Center for the Study of Sport in Society (Disability in Sport Initiative): www.sportinsociety.org/dsri.html

- Rehabilitation International: www.rehab-international.org

- World Blind Union: www.cnib.ca/eng/about/organization/wbu

- World Federation of the Deaf: www.hearinglossweb.com/res/hlorg/wfd.htm

- World Federation of the Deafblind: www.wfdb.org

- World Institute on Disability: www.wid.org

- World Network for Users and Survivors of Psychiatry: www.wnusp.org

7. Note: Implications of Culture for Rights Discourse

What do the cultural, religious, and other conflicts examined in this section imply for the human rights approach as a whole? Can we make decisions about hierarchies of rights or conflicts between rights in the abstract? What are the consequences of ignoring context? Why should context matter if human rights standards are truly universal? Consider David Kennedy's analysis:

[T]o maintain the claim to universality and neutrality, the human rights movement practices a systematic lack of attention to background sociological and
political conditions that will determine the meaning a right has in particular
contexts, rendering the evenhanded pursuit of "rights" vulnerable to all sorts
of distorted, and distinctly non-neutral outcomes.

David Kennedy, *The International Human Rights Movement: Part of the Problem?*, 15 HARV.
HUM. RTS. J. 101, 110 (2002). What are some examples of such "distorted" outcomes?
How can this problem be resolved?

PART IV

COMPARATIVE APPROACHES

This part examines emerging paradigms of judicial enforcement of economic, social and cultural rights at the level of domestic law and within the human rights framework of the Council of Europe. We identify four distinct approaches that characterize the growing movement toward judicial protection of second and third generation norms: (1) the directive principles approach, pioneered in India, which, since the early 1980s, has enabled Indian courts to adjudicate socio-economic rights through creative interpretation of the Indian Bill of Rights, read in conjunction with non-justiciable constitutional commands; (2) the bill of rights approach exemplified by the 1996 constitution of democratic South Africa, which includes judicially enforceable social rights among the fundamental rights guaranteed to its citizens; (3) the "blending of the categories" in the European Court of Human Rights' interpretation of the European Convention for the Protection of Human Rights and Fundamental Freedoms, through which it has applied civil and political guarantees to protect second- and third-generation rights; and (4) the use of state constitutions in the United States to overcome the limited government/negative rights paradigm that impedes the recognition of socio-economic rights at the federal level.

Readers should consider the problems associated with the application of judicial remedies to this category of rights: What questions of judicial legitimacy, competency and accountability arise? How should such questions be resolved? Are social rights more or less vulnerable to the post-modern critique of rights-based approaches generally? Are normative pronouncements more illusory than real? Are litigation strategies effective means of ensuring the satisfaction of economic, social and cultural needs? Do they distract from struggles for genuine social transformation? Can such strategies advance public awareness, organization and popular understanding of the need for more far-reaching solutions?

CHAPTER SEVEN

INDIA: THE "DIRECTIVE PRINCIPLES" APPROACH

A. JUDICIAL DISCOURSE ON POVERTY AND RIGHTS

Since the early 1980s, Indian courts have adjudicated socio-economic rights through creative interpretation of the Indian Bill of Rights, read in conjunction with constitutional "directive priciples" of state policy. India attained independence from Britain in 1947 after a decades-long non-violent resistance campaign led by the Indian National Congress and Mahatma Gandhi. Eight months prior to the formal transfer of power, Britain (which itself has no written constitution) established a Constituent Assembly to draft a constitution for the newly independent nation. The Constituent Assembly was an elected body that was broadly representative of the population. *See* P. MISRA, THE MAKING OF INDIA'S REPUBLIC 56 (1966). The resulting document, three years in the making, reflects the spirit of an era defined by the founding of the United Nations and the adoption of the Universal Declaration of Human Rights.

While the American Bill of Rights served as one model for India's drafters, *see* Soli Sorabjee, *Equality in the United States and India, in* LOUIS HENKIN & ALBERT J. ROSENTHAL EDS., CONSTITUTIONALISM AND RIGHTS 97 (1990), many of the fundamental rights provisions go beyond the protections in the U.S. social contract, imposing constitutional duties upon private parties as well as the state, and endorsing "positive discrimination" for historically oppressed groups. According to Indian legal scholar Dr. V.D. Mahajan, the framers of the Indian Constitution were influenced by both international and domestic sources in formulating the directive principles. These sources include the 1789 French Declaration of the Rights of Man and the Citizen, the American Declaration of Independence, the Constitution of the Irish Republic (which contains a chapter on "Directive Principles of Social Policy") and the Constitution of Republican Spain. Mahajan traces the local roots of the directive principles to a 1931 resolution of the pro-independence Indian National Congress, which defined what political freedom would mean in the Indian context to include "real economic freedom of the starving millions." DR. V.D. MAHAJAN, CONSTITUTIONAL LAW OF INDIA 365 (7th ed. 1991).

The Constitution established a federal democracy consisting of 25 states and seven Union Territories. Legislative power is vested in a bicameral Parliament composed of the Council of States, *Rajya Sabha,* and the House of the People, *Lok Sabha.*

THE CONSTITUTION OF INDIA

Part III Fundamental Rights

Article 15. Prohibition of discrimination on grounds of religion, race, caste, sex or place of birth.

(1) The State shall not discriminate against any citizen on grounds only of religion, race, caste, sex, place of birth or any of them.

(2) No citizen shall, on ground only of religion, race, caste, sex, place of birth or any of them, be subject to any disability, liability, restriction or condition with regard to—

   (a) access to shops, public restaurants, hotels and places of public entertainment; or

   (b) the use of wells, tanks, bathing ghats, roads and places of public resort maintained whole or partly out of State funds or dedicated to the use of general public.

(3) Nothing in this article shall prevent the State from making any special provision for women and children.

(4) Nothing in this article or in clause (2) of article shall prevent the State from making any special provision for the advancement of any socially and educationally backward classes of citizens or for the Scheduled Castes and the Scheduled Tribes.

Article 16. Equality of opportunity in matters of public employment.

(1) There shall be equality of opportunity for all citizens in matters relating to employment or appointment to any office under the State.

(2) No citizen shall, on grounds only of religion, race, caste, sex, descent, place of birth, residence or any of them, be ineligible for, or discriminated against in respect of, any employment or office under the State.***

(4) Nothing in this article shall prevent the State from making any provision for the reservation of appointments or posts in favour of any backward class of citizens which, in the opinion of the State, is not adequately represented in the services under the State.

(4A) Nothing in this article shall prevent the State from making any provision for reservation in matters of promotion to any class or classes of posts in the services under the State in favour of the Scheduled Castes and the Scheduled Tribes which, in the opinion of the State, are not adequately represented in the services under the State.***

Article 17. Abolition of Untouchability.

"Untouchability" is abolished and its practice in any form is forbidden. The enforcement of any disability arising out of "Untouchability" shall be an offence punishable in accordance with law.***

Article 21. Protection of life and personal liberty.

No person shall be deprived of his life or personal liberty except according to procedure established by law.***

Article 23. Prohibition of traffic in human beings and forced labour.

(1) Traffic in human beings and begar [*sic*]and other similar forms of forced labour are prohibited and any contravention of this provision shall be an offence punishable in accordance with law.

(2) Nothing in this article shall prevent the State from imposing compulsory service for public purposes, and in imposing such service the State shall not make any discrimination on ground only of religion, race, caste or class or any of them.

Article 24. Prohibition of employment of children in factories, etc.

No child below the age of fourteen years shall be employed to work in any factory or mine or engaged in any other hazardous employment.***

Article 32. Remedies for enforcement of rights conferred by this Part.

(1) The right to move the Supreme Court by appropriate proceedings for the enforcement of the rights conferred by this Part is guaranteed.

(2) The Supreme Court shall have power to issue directions or orders or writs, including writs in the nature of habeas corpus, mandamus, prohibition, quo warranto and certiorari, whichever may be appropriate, for the enforcement of any of the rights conferred by this Part.***

Part IV Directive Principles of State Policy

Article 37. Application of the principles contained in this Part.

The provisions contained in this Part shall not be enforced by any court, but the principles therein laid down are nevertheless fundamental in the governance of the country and it shall be the duty of the State to apply these principles in making laws.

Article 38. State to secure a social order for the promotion of welfare of the people.

(1) The State shall strive to promote the welfare of the people by securing and protecting as effectively as it may a social order in which justice, social, economic and political, shall inform all the institutions of the national life.

(2) The State shall, in particular, strive to minimise the inequalities in income, and endeavour to eliminate inequalities in status, facilities and opportunities, not only amongst individuals but also amongst groups of people residing in different areas or engaged in different vocations.

Article 39. Certain principles of policy to be followed by the State.

The State shall, in particular, direct its policy towards securing—

(a) that the citizens, men and women equally, have the right to an adequate means of livelihood;

(b) that the ownership and control of the material resources of the community are so distributed as best to subserve the common good;

(c) that the operation of the economic system does not result in the concentration of wealth and means of production to the common detriment;

(d) that there is equal pay for equal work for both men and women;

(e) that the health and strength of workers, men and women, and the tender age of children are not abused and that citizens are not forced by economic necessity to enter avocations unsuited to their age or strength;

(f) that children are given opportunities and facilities to develop in a healthy manner and in conditions of freedom and dignity and that childhood and youth are protected against exploitation and against moral and material abandonment.

Article 39A. Equal justice and free legal aid.

The State shall secure that the operation of the legal system promotes justice, on a basis of equal opportunity, and shall, in particular, provide free legal aid, by suitable legislation or schemes or in any other way, to ensure that opportunities for securing justice are not denied to any citizen by reason of economic or other disabilities.

Article 40. Organisation of village panchayats.

The State shall take steps to organise village panchayats and endow them with such powers and authority as may be necessary to enable them to function as units of self-government.

Article 41. Right to work, to education and to public assistance in certain cases.

The State shall, within the limits of its economic capacity and development, make effective provision for securing the right to work, to education and to public assistance in cases of unemployment, old age, sickness and disablement, and in other cases of undeserved want.

Article 42. Provision for just and humane conditions of work and maternity relief.

The State shall make provision for securing just and humane conditions of work and for maternity relief.

Article 43. Living wage for workers.

The State shall endeavor to secure, by suitable legislation or economic organisation or in any other way, to all workers agricultural, industrial or otherwise, work, a living wage, conditions of work ensuring a decent standard of life and full enjoyment of leisure and social and cultural opportunities and, in particular, the State shall endeavour to promote cottage industries on an individual or co-operative basis in rural areas.

Article 43A. Participation of workers in management of industries.

The State shall take steps, by suitable legislation or in any other way, to secure the participation of workers in the management of undertakings, establishments or other organisation engaged in any industry.

Article 44. Uniform civil code for the citizen.

The State shall endeavour to secure for the citizens a uniform civil code throughout the territory of India.

Article 45. Provision for free and compulsory education for children.

The State shall endeavor to provide, within a period of ten years from the commencement of this Constitution, for free and compulsory education for all children until they complete the age of fourteen years.

Article 46. Promotion of educational and economic interests of Scheduled Castes, Scheduled Tribes and other weaker sections.

The State shall promote with special care the educational and economic interests of the weaker sections of the people, and in particular, of the Scheduled Castes and the Scheduled Tribes, and shall protect them from social injustice and all forms of exploitation.

Article 47. Duty of the State to raise the level of nutrition and the standard of living and to improve public health.

The State shall regard the raising of the level of nutrition and the standard of living of its people and the improvement of public health as among its primary duties and, in particular, the State shall endeavour to bring about prohibition of the consumption except for medicinal purpose of intoxicating drinks and of drugs which are injurious to health.

Article 48. Organisation of agriculture and animal husbandry.

The State shall endeavour to organise agriculture and animal husbandry on modern and scientific lines and shall, in particular, take steps for preserving and improving the breeds, and prohibiting the slaughter, of cows and calves and other milch and draught cattle.

Article 48A. Protection and improvement of environment and safeguarding of forests and wild life.

The State shall endeavour to protect and improve the environment and to safeguard the forests and wild life of the country.***

Article 49. Protection of monuments and places and objects of national importance.

It shall be the obligation of the State to protect every monument or place or object of artistic or historic interest, declared by or under law made by Parliament to be of national importance, from spoliation, disfigurement, destruction, removal, disposal or export, as the case may be.

Article 50. Separation of judiciary from executive.

The State shall take steps to separate the judiciary from the executive in the public services of the State.

Notes and Questions

1. *The Relationship Between Directive Principles and Fundamental Rights.* Indian Supreme Court Justice K.S. Hedge explains that the directive principles, together with the chapter on fundamental rights, "form an organic unit." K.S. Hedge, *Directive Principles of State Policy in the Constitution of India, in* VERINDER GROVER, THE CONSTITUTION OF INDIA 59, 75 (1997). Justice Hedge argues that the struggle against British colonialism was instrumental in generating the demand for constitutional protection of fundamental rights:

> The inclusion of a set of fundamental rights in India's Constitution had its beginning in the forces that operated in the national struggle during the British rule when the British resorted to arbitrary acts such as brutal assaults on unarmed *satyagrahis*,[1] internments, deportations, detention without trial and muzzling of the press. The freedom struggle gathered momentum after the First World War.

---

[1]   Protesters practicing the nonviolent resistance methods advocated by Mahatma Gandhi.—Eds.

Thereafter, clashes with the British authorities in India became increasingly frequent and sharp. The harshness with which the executive operated its repressive measures strengthened the demand for constitutional guarantees of fundamental rights. As far back as 1895, the Constitution of India Bill, prepared by some eminent Indians, envisaged for India a Constitution guaranteeing to everyone of our citizens freedom of expression[,] inviolability of one's house, right to property, equality before the law, equal opportunity of admission to public offices, right to present claims, petitions and complaints and right to personal liberty.

Id. at 72–73. Justice Hedge describes the interrelationship between fundamental rights and the directive principles as follows:

Part IV of the constitution is designed to bring about the social and economic revolution that remained to be fulfilled after independence. Prime Minister Nehru believed that India's survival depended on the achievement of this social and economic revolution. He warned, 'If one cannot solve this problem soon, all our paper Constitution will become useless and purposeless.' Political freedom will have no meaning without social and economic justice. The aim of the Constitution is not to guarantee certain liberties to only a few of the citizens but for all.*** What is the use of equality before law if there is no equality in fact? Freedoms guaranteed by [the fundamental rights provisions] will become empty slogans for a person who has no food to eat, no roof under which he can take shelter and no clothes to wear; and what is the use of [the] vote to a person who is hungry and kept illiterate and denied the knowledge required to participate in the affairs of the state?

Id. at 63.

2. *The Philosophy of the Indian Social Contract.* What does the inclusion of directive principles suggest about the nature and terms of the social contract that the Indian Constitution embodies? Does it reject the concept of limited government? What does it suggest about the nature of law and its function and role in Indian society? What is the relationship that is established between the individual and the state?

3. *Justiciability.* Judicial review in India represented a major departure from the British doctrine of parliamentary supremacy. If the directive principles were deemed so critical to the attainment of Indian freedom, why did the Constituent Assembly render them judicially unenforceable? Does Article 37 reflect ambivalence on the part of the framers as to the juridical nature of the directives? Does the statement that these principles are "fundamental" and their expression in terms of positive state duties adequately advance the interests they are designed to protect? Did the framers contemplate some other method of enforcement, *e.g.*, through public opinion? *See* Article 40.

4. *Priorities.* How should conflicts between fundamental rights and directive principles be resolved? Should a "balancing test" be applied? What factors would be salient in such an analysis? Should one set of principles have presumptive priority over the other? If so, which should prevail, and why?

5. *Individual vs. Collective Rights.* Is it accurate to describe fundamental rights as individual rights and the social needs protected by the directive principles as collective? Would such a description provide any analytical tools to assist in the resolution of the priorities problem?

6. *Equality.* What theory of equality is embodied in Article 38? How does it compare to the Rawlsian principles discussed in Chapter 2, *supra?*

7. *Inclusion of Cultural Norms.* Several Directives (Articles 40, 46, 47, 48, and 49) impart a distinct cultural fingerprint upon the nation's constitutive document. What are the objectives of these provisions? Does such an approach to constitution-making adequately allow for evolving cultural norms?

8. *Constitutionally Entrenched Affirmative Action.* The framers of the Indian Constitution pioneered the concept of affirmative action, or positive discrimination. Article 15, which establishes equality as a fundamental right, expressly authorizes the State to make "special provision for the advancement of any socially and educationally backward classes of citizens or for the Scheduled Castes and the Scheduled Tribes." Article 16 permits "reservation of appointments or posts in favor of any backward class of citizens which, in the opinion of the State, is not adequately represented in the services under the State," as well as "reservation in matters of promotion to any class or classes of posts in the services under the State in favor of the Scheduled Castes and the Scheduled Tribes.***" Article 46 directs the state to "promote with special care the educational and economic interests of the weaker sections of the people, and in particular, of the Scheduled Castes and the Scheduled Tribes, and [to] protect them from social injustice and all forms of exploitation."

9. *Who Are the "Scheduled Castes?"* The "Scheduled Castes" consist primarily of the people formerly known as "Untouchables"—who now call themselves Dalits. Their constitutionally protected status stems largely from the leadership of Babasaheb Ambedkar, a prominent Dalit who mobilized his community in the anti-colonial struggles against the British. The status of "untouchability" was officially abolished in Article 17 of the Indian Constitution, and its enforcement made punishable by law. Nevertheless, the former "untouchable" castes remain among the most impoverished and oppressed in India.

Dalits are organized into mass political movements to advocate for their rights. International human rights fora are now being utilized to highlight the plight of victims of caste discrimination. In Durban, South Africa, Dalit activists pushed for condemnation of caste discrimination in the Declaration and Program of Action of the World Conference Against Racism. The Indian government objected strenuously to the characterization of caste discrimination within the context of "racism, xenophobia and related intolerances," although the Convention on the Elimination of Racial Discrimination prohibits invidious distinctions based on "descent."

10. *The "Scheduled Tribes."* India is home to more than 100 indigenous tribes, or Adivasis. They constitute approximately 8 percent of the population, with more than 90 percent living in rural areas, where they confront the incursion of powerful timber barons, harassment by corrupt forest officials, brutality of police, and exploitation by money lenders, traders, and bootleggers, all belonging to the dominant castes. More than 85 percent are illiterate, and most live in poverty, many reduced to either bonded labor or begging. Resistance is typically met by violent oppression. In 1996, communities in Madhya Pradesh began to form local organizations called Sangathans, to combat this exploitation. When the Sangathans gained political influence, the local authorities responded with killings and demolition of their houses.

UPENDRA BAXI, JUDICIAL DISCOURSE: DIALECTICS OF THE FACE AND THE MASK

35 J. Indian L. Inst. 1 (1993)

I. *Legal justice: celebration of state power*

In the discourse of the law, justice is merely an aspect of power. Justice, according to the law, is that justice which people holding power of the state may consider it necessary or justified to provide. The expectation is that when power defines justice it will enforce its definition. If this does not happen, legal justice itself may furnish standards to question the legitimacy of power. In the law, then, we may expect at the very best not the power of justice but justice of power.***

Power cannot authentically perceive the meaning of injustice.*** It can be made to perceive problems which interrogate it, challenge it, or have the potential of delegitimating power. Legal justice then appears as a coping, management device. What are being coped with or managed are not necessarily the underlying injustices to the people but actual or latent insecurities assailing the structure of the management of distribution of power. Legal justice, in essence, is in the first place an attempt to solve the problems of the managers of the people; it is a common mistake to think that handling or solution of such problems is also necessarily achieving the solutions of the problems of the people so managed.

When situations of 'injustice' appear before power as a problem *** political calculus decides what has to be done with those situations. In the last analysis, every 'injustice' serves the material interests of some groups in society; to attack it is to attack constellations or formations of these material interests. State power has to have recourse to political calculus; to work out the costs and gains to itself entailed in any planned attack on injustice. That is how you find legislations and even constitutions following a careful path of simultaneous attack and retreat. Not to attack the problem of injustice or rather injustice which has become a problem is costly for state power; to fully attack is also costly. The middle path that power takes is strewn with corpses of aspirations of complete justice and dense with disfigurement of the purportedly 'just' solutions.***

The calculus of power influences the design of legal justice. Legislation is typically used as a statement of aspiration, as an acknowledgment of injustice which must be fought, as a moral posture against non-negotiability with evil. At the same time, the edge of all this is blunted because the legislative program, the plan of implementation, does not match the promulgation of justice. This hiatus is an act of will, an exercise in mature political imagination, a ceaseless innovation in methods of simultaneous attacks and retreats. Indeed, the good the legislation achieves is the good it is designed not to actively attain; but the good is achieved only inadvertently and occasionally.*** "The problem has been tackled, long live the problem" is the message of most progressive legislating in India. Thus, the state power accomplishes its historic mandate of representing the "general" interest. In this sense, legal justice is the active celebration of the state power. It is an answer to St. Augustine's immortal question: "What is state without justice but a band of robbers?" In this sense, legal justice is, always and everywhere, a mask over the face of dominance.

But, for all that, the mask covers the hideous face of raw and bloody power. Dialectically, the mask often has to begin to be the face; power acquires the visage of benign justice, despite its intentions and programs. Herein, despite all that we may say about power's war of attrition against justice, lies the historic importance of the mask.***

The judicial power has to be so organised, in liberal bourgeois orders, as to give it an appearance of autonomy. The executive does not arrogate to itself the task of dispensing legal justice; that task is assigned to a relatively autonomous judiciary. Here we encounter an entrenched, civilizationally so, maxim of legal justice (no older than Montesquieu) namely that there shall be separation of powers or at least division of functions among the executive, legislature and the judiciary. Not to allow such separation or division has since been recognized as the very definition of tyranny.

But to allow the judiciary the autonomy to decide disputes between state and citizens and among members of the civil society inter se is, from the standpoint of power, a risky enterprise. Therefore, the matrix of judicial power is always structured by the executive power. In other words, it is the executive which appoints judges and determines their jurisdiction. The Indian executive of the present times will never appoint a 'Naxal'[2] as a judge; nor will Fidel Castro appoint an erstwhile landlord to the Cuban judiciary. The assumption is that power, coupled with limited intelligence, will not, as it were, dig its own grave through judicial appointments. Or, to try to put it more elegantly, one would not appoint persons as justices who are prone to dramatize the executive as an epicenter of all tyrannies. The assumption proceeds further: once you have justices, carefully screened for 'good behavior,' and adequate 'class' background, legal justice will not deviate from the service of the centralized unity of state power ordained by the power bloc.

This is how things are devised and, from the vantage point of power, ought to be. But the lesson of human history asserts itself here as everywhere, that is, the lesson of latent and unintended consequences. Soon judges discover that they cannot fulfil completely or adequately the expectations of the executive (and these are often inchoate) even if they want to. And many judges do not see the precise moral obligation to do the bidding of the executive which appointed them. Of course, they remain aware that they must not go too far too quickly. But by slow patient work, by the dint of cultured effort, they create a jurisprudence which the executive did not want, desire or intend, but with which it has to live.

Judges and courts create jurisprudence because of the way they are structured. At least in the common law orbit, they are under an obligation to produce discourse.***

III. Social action litigation: war of the mask with the face

Not consciously, and as a result of a whole variety of political circumstances and conjunctures, judges since the eighties have developed a discourse concerning their role in Indian society. Throughout the seventies, the executive made its wish public that the judges and courts should be committed to the Constitution and the promise of progress and justice within it. Now, led by the Supreme Court of India, judges and courts have shown their "commitment"; the executive did not have this kind of "commitment" in view at the same time, it cannot repudiate it publicly.

The new role that judges and courts have assumed since the 1980s through social action litigation (SAL) *** is truly extraordinary. The procedure is that of epistolary jurisdiction, where letters written by ordinary citizens to courts get converted into writ

---

2   A member of a lower-caste guerrilla movement seeking land redistribution.—Eds.

petitions. And these letters do not allege violation of fundamental rights of their authors; the authors allege such violation of the rights of the impoverished groups of Indian society—be they people in custody, victims of police violence, forced, bonded, migrant, contract labor, child workers, rickshaw pullers, hawkers, self-employed people, pensioners, pavement dwellers, slum dwellers, fishermen or Sri Lankan Tamils used as bonded laborers. The law of standing, that is persons who can bring complaints of rights-violation, has been thus revolutionized; and access to constitutional justice has been fully democratized.

The second major procedural innovation brought in by SAL is the collection of social data and legal evidence concerning the plight of these impoverished groups. Courts now appoint socio-legal commissions of public citizens, social scientists and others to examine the conditions alleged to be violative of people's rights; and the reports of the commission, constituted at state expense, provide the material for doing justice. Increasingly, universities and research institutes are directed by the court to function as commissions.*** This practice constitutes a remarkable cooptation of state-supported academic institutions in activist administration of justice and has the potential for redirection of these institutions to a participatory role in the realization of constitutional values.***

The third major aspect of the SAL is in the area of relief. Compensation and rehabilitation for victims deprived of their fundamental rights now constitute a constitutional right; the Supreme Court undertook a detailed monitoring of the rehabilitation of the blinded of Bhagalpur and since then has fashioned many a measure of compensation and rehabilitation; it has ordered the administration of theosuplhate injections to the Bhopal victims and upheld the constitutional validity of the Bhopal Act by reading into it the obligation to provide monthly interim relief (thus to an extent overcoming the shame of settlement by the Union of India with Union Carbide); it has provided elaborate directives for treatment of prisoners and undertrials in jails; it has given specific directives for humane and just conditions of work for migrant workers and forced laborers.

The fourth salient aspect of the SAL is the development of constitutional jurisprudence itself. The right to compensation for violation of fundamental rights is now fully emergent. Indians have now a right to speedy trial though nowhere explicitly formulated by the Constitution. The custodial inmates have a right to dignity and immunity from cruel, unusual or degrading treatment ***. Above all, the jurisprudence of SAL insists on a simple postulate of civilised jurisprudence: [the Executive] shall act in accordance with the law and the constitution.***

Fifth, without being exhaustive, the SAL processes have at times resulted in a mini-takeover of the administrative regime of certain institutions of administration, which have displayed a congenital inability to work in accordance with the law and the constitution. The most conspicuous illustration of this, perhaps, is the Agra Protective Home for Women, virtually run by the judiciary for well over ten years. The Supreme Court is doing its best to enable, by constant invigilation, the State of Bihar to ensure proper prison administration, to the point of maintenance of the record of undertrial and convict populations in the various jails of Bihar. In environmental cases, the Supreme Court has ordered the closure or monitored the Pollution potential of private industries. The State High courts have not lagged behind in these and related areas.

PEOPLE'S UNION FOR DEMOCRATIC RIGHTS v. UNION OF INDIA

AIR 1982 S.C.C. 1473

BHAGWATI, J.:—This is a writ petition brought by way of public interest litigation in order to ensure observance of the provisions of various labour laws in relation to workmen employed in the construction work of various projects connected with the Asian Games. The matter was brought to the attention of the Court by *** an organization formed for the purpose of protecting democratic rights by means of a letter addressed to one of us (Bhagwati J.). The letter was based on a report made by a team of three social scientists who were commissioned by the first petitioner for the purpose of investigating and inquiring into the conditions under which the workmen engaged in the various Asian Projects were working. [I]t was treated as a writ petition ***.***

[C]ivil and political rights, priceless and invaluable as they are for freedom and democracy, simply do not exist for the vast masses of our people. Large numbers of men, women and children who constitute the bulk of our population are today living a sub-human existence in conditions of abject poverty; utter grinding poverty has broken their back and sapped their moral fibre. They have no faith in the existing social and economic system. What civil and political rights are these poor and deprived sections of humanity going to enforce?***

The only solution for making civil and political rights meaningful to these large sections of society would be to remake the material conditions and restructure the social and economic order so that they may be able to realize the economic, social and cultural rights.***

Of course, the task of restructuring the social and economic order so that the social and economic rights become a meaningful reality for the poor and lowly sections of the community is one which legitimately belongs to the legislature and the executive, but mere initiation of social and economic rescue programmes by the executive and the legislature would not be enough and it, is only through multi-dimensional strategies including public interest litigation that these social and economic rescue programmes can be made effective. Public interest litigation, as we conceive it is essentially a co-operative or collaborative effort on the part of the petitioner, the State or public authority and the court to secure observance of the constitutional or legal rights, benefits and privileges conferred upon the vulnerable sections of the community and to reach social justice to them.*** [C]ourts are not meant only for the rich and the well-to-do, for the landlord and the gentry, for the business magnate and the industrial tycoon, but they exist also for the poor and the downtrodden, the have-nots and the handicapped, and the half-hungry millions of our countrymen. So far the courts have been used only for the purpose of vindicating the rights of the wealthy and the affluent. It is only these privileged classes which have been able to approach the courts for protecting their vested interests. It is only the moneyed who have so far had the golden key to unlock the doors of justice. But, now for the first time the portals of the court are being thrown open to the poor and the downtrodden, the ignorant and the illiterate and their cases are coming before the courts through public interest litigation ***.***

The Asian Games take place periodically in different parts of Asia and this time India is hosting the Asian Games. It is a highly prestigious undertaking and in order to accomplish it successfully according to international standards, the Government of India had to embark upon various construction projects which included building of flyovers, stadia, swimming pool, hotels and Asian Games village complex. This construction work was farmed out by the Government of India amongst various authorities ***. These various authorities to whom the execution of the different projects was entrusted engaged contractors for the purpose of carrying out the construction work of the projects ***. The contractors started the construction work of the projects and for the purpose of carrying out the construction work, they engaged workers through jamadars. The jamadars brought the workers from different parts of India and particularly the States of Rajasthan, Uttar Pradesh and Orissa and got them employed by the contractors. The workers were entitled to a minimum wage of Rs. 9.25 per day, that being the minimum wage fixed for workers employed on the construction of roads and in building operations but the case of the petitioners was that the workers were not paid this minimum wage and they were exploited by the contractors and the jamadars.***

[Respondents argue] that a writ petition under Art. 32 cannot be maintained unless it complains of a breach of some fundamental right or the other and since what were alleged in the present writ petition were merely violations of the labour laws enacted for the benefit of the workmen and not breaches of any fundamental rights, the present writ petition was not maintainable and was liable to be dismissed.***

Art. 23 enacts a very important fundamental right in the following terms:

Art. 23: Prohibition of traffic in human beings and forced labour—

(1) Traffic in human beings and begar and other similar forms of forced labour are prohibited and any contravention of this provision shall be an offence punishable in accordance with law.***

Now many of the fundamental rights enacted in Part III operate as limitations on the power of the State and impose negative obligations on the State not to encroach on individual liberty and they are enforceable only against the State. But there are certain fundamental rights conferred by the Constitution which are enforceable against the whole world ***. Article 23 is not limited in its application against the State but it prohibits "traffic in human beings and begar and other similar forms of forced labour" practiced by anyone else.*** The reason for enacting this provision in the chapter on fundamental rights is to be found in the socio-economic condition of the people at the time when the Constitution came to be enacted. The Constitution makers, when they set out to frame the Constitution, found that they had the enormous task before them of changing the socio-economic structure of the country and bringing about socio-economic regeneration with a view to reaching social and economic justice to the common man. Large masses of people, bled white by well-nigh two centuries of foreign rule, were living in abject poverty and destitution, with ignorance and illiteracy accentuating their helplessness and despair. The society had degenerated into a status-oriented hierarchical society with little respect for the dignity of the individual who was in the lower rungs of the social ladder or in an economically impoverished condition. The political revolution was completed and it had succeeded in bringing freedom to the country but freedom was not an end in itself, it was only a means to an end, the end being the raising of the people to higher levels of achievement and brining about their total advancement and welfare. Political freedom had no meaning unless it was accompanied by social and economic freedom and it was therefore necessary to carry forward the social and economic revolution with a view to creating socio-economic conditions in which every one would be able to enjoy basic human rights and participate in the fruits of freedom and liberty in an egalitarian social and economic framework. It was with this end in view that the Constitution makers enacted the Directive Principles of State Policy in Part IV of the Constitution setting out the constitutional goal of [a] new socio-economic order. Now there was one feature of our national life which was ugly and shameful and which cried for urgent attention and that was the existence of bonded or forced labour in large parts of the country. This evil was the relic of a feudal exploitative society and it was totally incompatible with the new egalitarian socio-economic order which "We the people of India" were determined to build and constituted a gross and most revolting denial of basic human dignity. It was therefore necessary to eradicate this pernicious practice and wipe it out altogether from the national scene ***.***

The question then is "to what is the true scope and meaning of the expression 'traffic in human beings' and 'begar and other similar forms of forced labour' " in Art. 23?***

When the Constitution makers enacted Art. 23 they had before them Art. 4 of the Universal Declaration of Human Rights but they deliberately departed from its language and employed words which would make the reach and content of Art. 23 much wider than that of Article 4 of the Universal Declaration of Human Rights. They banned 'traffic in human beings which is an expression of much larger amplitude than 'slave trade' and they also interdicted "begar and other similar forms of forced labour."*** The word 'begar' in this Article is not a word of common use in English language. It is a word of Indian origin which like many other words has found its way in the English vocabulary. It is very difficult to formulate a precise definition of the word 'begar' but there can be no doubt that it is a form of forced labour under which a person is compelled to work without receiving any remuneration. Molesworth describes 'begar' as "labour or service enacted by a government or person in power without giving remuneration for it." Wilson's glossary of Judicial and Revenue Terms gives the following meaning of the word 'begar': "a forced labourer, one pressed to carry burdens for individuals or the public." Under the old system, when pressed for public service, no pay was given. The Begari, though still liable to be pressed for public objects, now receives pay. Forced labour for private service is prohibited." 'Begar' may therefore be loosely described as labour or service which a person is forced to give without receiving any remuneration for it.***.***

It is difficult to imagine that the Constitution makers should have intended to strike only at certain forms of forced labour leaving it open to the socially or economically powerful sections of the community to exploit the poor and weaker sections by resorting to other forms of forced labour. Could there be any logic or reason in enacting that if a person is forced to give labour or service to another without receiving any remuneration at all, it should be regarded as a pernicious practice sufficient to attract the condemnation of Art. 23, but if some remuneration is paid for it, then it should be outside the inhibition of that Article? If this were the true interpretation, Art. 23 would be reduced to a mere rope of sand, for it would then be the easiest thing in an exploitative society for a person belonging to a socially or economically dominant class to exact labour or service from a person belonging to the deprived and vulnerable section of the community by paying a negligible amount of remuneration and thus escape the rigour of Article 23. We do not think it would be right to place on the language of Art. 23 an interpretation which would emasculate its beneficent provisions and defeat the very purpose of enacting them.*** Even if remuneration is paid, labour supplied by a person would be hit by this Article if it is forced labour, that is, labour supplied not willingly but as a result of force or compulsion.***

Now the next question that arises for consideration is whether there is any breach of Art. 23 when a person provides labour or service to the State or to any other person and is paid less than the minimum wage for it. It is obvious that ordinarily no one would willingly supply labour or service to another for less than the minimum wage, when he knows that under the law he is entitled to get minimum wage for the labour or service provided by him. It may therefore be legitimately presumed that when a person provides labour or service to another against receipt of remuneration which is less than the minimum wage, he is acting under the force of some compulsion which drives him to work though he is paid less than what he is entitled under law to receive. What Article 23 prohibits is 'forced labour' that is labour or service which a person is forced to provide and 'force' which would make such labour or service 'forced labour' may arise in several ways.*** Any factor which deprives a person of a choice of alternatives and compels him to adopt one particular course of action may properly be regarded as 'force' and if labour or service is compelled as a result of such 'force,' it would be 'forced labour.' Where a person is suffering from hunger or starvation, when he has no resources at all to fight disease or to feed his wife and children or even to hide their nakedness, where utter grinding poverty has broken his back and reduced him to a state of helplessness and despair and where no other employment is available to alleviate the rigour of his poverty, he would have no choice but to accept any work that comes his way, even if the remuneration offered to him is less than the minimum wage. He would be in no position to bargain with the employer; he would have to accept what is offered to him. And in doing so he would be acting not as a free agent with a choice between alternatives but under the compulsion of economic circumstances and the labour or service provided by him would be clearly 'forced labour.'*** We are therefore of the view that where a person provides labour or service to another for remuneration which is less than the minimum wage, the labour or service provided by him clearly falls within the scope and ambit of the words "forced labour" under Art. 23.*** It is therefore clear that when the petitioners alleged that minimum wage was not paid to the workmen employed by the contractors, the complaint was really in effect and substance a complaint against violation of the fundamental right of the workmen under Art. 23.

[W]henever any fundamental right which is enforceable against private individuals is violated *** it is the constitutional obligation of the State to take the necessary steps for the purpose of interdicting such violation and ensuring observance of the fundamental right by the private individual who is transgressing the same. Of course, the person whose fundamental right is violated can always approach the court for the purpose of enforcement of his fundamental right, but that cannot absolve the State from its constitutional obligation to see that there is no violation of the fundamental right of such person, particularly when he belongs to the weaker section of humanity and is unable to wage a legal battle against a strong and powerful opponent who is exploiting him. The Union of India, the Delhi Administration and the Delhi Development Authority must therefore be held to be under an obligation to ensure observance of these various labour laws by the contractors ***.***

Notes and Questions

1.   *Putting on the Mask?* In *Peoples' Union for Democratic Rights v. Union of India*, the Indian Supreme Court defines working for less than the minimum wage as "forced labor" within the meaning of Article 23 of the Indian Constitution. Is this interpretation of the constitutional text one of the "unanticipated consequences" referred to in Upendra Baxi's

article? Vijayashri Sripati maintains that it was the Court's complete abdication of its responsibility to uphold constitutional values during the State of Emergency declared in 1975 that compelled it to reclaim its standing as the protector of rights and liberties. She argues that the post-independence Indian Supreme Court was overly deferential to the property rights of the landed gentry, using its powers to protect privilege and to strike down legislation designed to create a more egalitarian society.

> Deeply wedded to the traditional concept of property rights, the Court had for three long decades displayed scant regard to considerations of creation of a welfare state in India. It had consequently served as a bastion not of human [rights], but of property rights. Further, it had forsaken its vital role of the custodian of the Constitution during emergency—India's gravest internal crisis since independence. Thus, despite some landmark decisions, the Supreme Court of the post-independence era made no enduring contributions towards strengthening constitutionalism in the subcontinent and left unfulfilled the constitutional aspirations of the vast majority of its citizens.

Vijayashri Sripati, *Human Rights in India—Fifty Years After Independence*, 26 DENV. J. INT'L L. & POL'Y 93, 107 (1997).

2. *Creative Interpretation of Constitutional Text.* The Court's definition of forced labor is based, in part, upon its presumption that no one would voluntarily work for less than the legal minimum wage. Is such a presumption defensible in light of India's high illiteracy rate? Does it matter whether the workers actually knew that they were underpaid? Does the Court hold that extreme poverty constitutes duress? Was its expansive definition of forced labor, and consequent finding of a constitutional violation, necessary in order to afford relief to the workers? Could the Court have simply found the employers guilty of violating the Minimum Wage Act and ordered them to pay compensation?

3. *Role of Directive Principles.* What is the role of the Directive Principles in the Court's analysis? Does the result depend on their invocation? How does the Court use history to illuminate the meaning of the constitutional language? Is its reasoning persuasive?

4. *Judicial Authority.* Does the Court risk losing the power of legitimacy on which it depends for compliance with its orders?

BANDHUA MUKTI MORCHA v. UNION OF INDIA

AIR 1984 S.C.C. 802

BHAGWATI, J.:—The petitioner is an organization dedicated to the cause of release of bonded labourers in the country. The system of bonded labour has been prevalent in various parts of the country since long prior to the attainment of political freedom and it constitutes an ugly and shameful feature of our national life. This system based on exploitation by a few socially and economically powerful persons trading on the misery and suffering of large numbers of men and holding them in bondage is a relic of a feudal hierarchical society which hypocritically proclaims the divinity of man but treats large masses of people belonging to the lower rungs of the social ladder or economically impoverished segments of society as dirt and chattel. This system under which one person can be bonded to provide labour to another for years and years until an alleged debt is supposed to be wiped out which never seems to happen during the lifetime of the bonded labourer, is totally incompatible with the new egalitarian socio-economic order which we have promised to build and it is not only an affront to basic human dignity but also constitutes [a] gross and revolting violation of constitutional values.***

This pernicious practice of bonded labour existed in many States and obviously with the ushering in of independence, it could not be allowed to continue to blight the national life any longer and hence, when we framed our Constitution, we enacted Article 23 *** which prohibits "traffic in human beings and begar and other similar forms of forced labour" practiced by any one. But *** [when] no serious effort was made to *** stamp out the shocking practice of bonded labour [until] in 1976 [when] Parliament enacted the Bonded Labour System (Abolition) Act.*** But, unfortunately *** the pernicious practice of bonded labor has not yet been totally eradicated from the national scene ***. It is *** a constitutional imperative that the bonded labourers must be identified and released from the shackles of bondage so that they can assimilate themselves in the main stream of civilized human society and realize the dignity, beauty and worth of human existence. It is a problem which needs urgent attention of the Government of India and the State Governments and when the Directive Principles of State Policy have obligated the Central and the State Governments to take steps and adopt measures for the purpose of ensuring social justice to the have-nots and the handicapped it is not right on the part of the concerned governments to shut their eyes to the inhuman exploitation to which the bonded labourers are subjected.***

The State of Haryana has in the present case tried to quibble with this definition of 'bonded labour' and its argument has been that these labourers may be providing forced labor but they are not bonded labourers within the meaning of [the Act] and they may therefore be freed by the Court if it so pleases but the State of Haryana cannot be compelled to rehabilitate them.***

The petitioner made a survey of some of the stone quarries in Faridabad district near the city of Delhi and found that there were a large number of labourers *** who were working in these stone quarries under "inhuman and intolerable conditions" and many of whom were bonded labourers. The petitioner therefore addressed a letter to one of us *** annex[ing] statements in original bearing the thumb marks or signatures as the case may be of these bonded laborers referred to in the letter. The petitioner pointed out in the letter that *** "there are innumerable cases of fatal and serious injuries caused due to accidents while working in the mines, while dynamiting the rocks or while crushing the stones. The stone-dust pollution near the stone crushers is so various that many valuable lives are lost due to tuberculosis while others are reduced to mere skeleton because of T.B. and other diseases. The workers are not provided with any medical care, not to speak of compensating the poor worker for injury or for death.***

Almost 99% of the workers are migrants from drought prone areas *** without any residential accommodations *** not even a thatched roof to fend against the icy winds and winter rain or against the scorching heat in midsummer, with scanty clothing, with very impure and polluted drinking water accumulated during rainy season in the ditches, with absolutely no facilities for schooling or childcare, braving all the hazards of nature and pollution and ill-treatment, these thousands of sons and daughters of Mother India epitomize the "Wretched of the Earth."***

[The petitioner's letter was treated as a writ petition and the Court appointed two investigators to visit the stone quarries and to interview the workers.] The [investigators'] report pointed out inter alia that *** "many stone crushing machines were operating with the result that the whole atmosphere was full of dust and it was difficult even to breathe." The report then referred to the statements of various workers [that] they were not allowed to leave the stone quarries and were providing forced labour and they did not have even pure water to drink but were compelled in most cases to drink dirty water from a nallah and were living in jhuggies[3] with stones piled one upon the other as walls and straw covering at the top, which did not afford any protection against sun and rain and which were so low that a person could hardly stand inside them.

[The workers] were suffering from tuberculosis and even when injuries were caused due to accidents arising in the course of employment, no compensation was being paid to them and there were no facilities for medical treatment or schooling for children. The report proceeded to state that [in other] stone quarries *** they found that the condition of the jhuggies was much worse inasmuch as the jhuggies were made only of straw and most of the people living in jhuggies had no clothes to wear and were shivering from cold and even the small children were moving about without any proper clothing. [N]one of the inmates of the jhuggies had any blanket or woolen clothes and they did not even have any mat on which they could sleep. [A]ll these workers were bonded labourers who were not allowed to leave the stone quarries.*** Most of the workers interviewed *** stated that they got very little by way of wages from the mine lessees or owners of stone crushers since they had to purchase explosives with their own moneys and they had to incur other expenses which *** included 50 per cent of the expenses of drilling holes.*** The report ended by observing that these workmen "presented a picture of helplessness, poverty and extreme exploitation at the hands of moneyed people" and they were found "leading a most miserable life and perhaps beasts and animals could be leading a more comfortable life than these helpless labourers."***

Before we proceed to consider the merits of the controversy between the parties in all its various aspects it will be convenient at this stage to dispose of a few preliminary objections urged on behalf of the respondents. The learned Additional Solicitor General appearing on behalf of the State of Haryana as also [the attorney for] one of the mine lessees contended that even if what is alleged by the petitioner in his letter *** is true, it cannot support a writ petition under Article 32 of the Constitution, because no fundamental right of the petitioner or of the workmen on whose behalf the writ petition has been filed, can be said to have been infringed. This contention is, in our opinion, futile and it is indeed surprising that the State Government should have raised it in answer to the writ petition. We can appreciate the anxiety of the mine lessees to resist the writ petition on any ground available to them, be it hyper-technical or even frivolous, but we find it incomprehensible that the State Government should urge such a preliminary objection with a view to stifling at the threshold an inquiry by the Court as to whether the workmen are living in bondage and under inhuman conditions. We should have thought that if any citizen brings before the Court a complaint that a large number of peasants or workers are bonded serfs or are being subjected to exploitation by a few mine lessees or contractors or employers or are being denied the benefits of social welfare laws, the State Government, which is, under our constitutional scheme, charged with the mission of bringing about a new socio-economic order where there will be social and economic justice for every one and equality of status and opportunity for all, would welcome an inquiry by the Court.*** We have on more occasions than

---

3   Shanties—Eds.

one said that public interest litigation is not in the nature of adversary litigation but it is a challenge and an opportunity to the government and its officers to make basic human rights meaningful to the deprived and vulnerable sections of the community and to assure them social and economic justice which is the signature tune of our Constitution.***

Moreover, when a complaint is made on behalf of workmen that they are held in bondage and are working and living in miserable conditions without any proper or adequate shelter over their heads, without any protection against sun and rain, without two square meals per day and with only dirty water from a nullah to drink, it is difficult to appreciate how such a complaint can be thrown out on the ground that it is not violative of the fundamental right of the workmen. It is the fundamental right of every one in this country, assured under the interpretation given to Article 21 by this Court *** to live with human dignity, free from exploitation. This right to live with human dignity enshrined in Article 21 derives its life breath from the Directive Principles of State Policy and particularly Clauses (e) and (f) of Article 39 and Articles 41 and 42 and at the least, therefore, it must include protection of the health and strength of workers, men and women, and of the tender age of children against abuse, opportunities and facilities for children to develop in a healthy manner and in conditions of freedom and dignity, educational facilities, just and humane conditions of work and maternity relief. These are the minimum requirements which must exist in order to enable a person to live with human dignity and no State—neither the Central government nor any State Government—has the right to take any action which will deprive a person of the enjoyment of these basic essentials. Since the Directive Principles of State Policy contained in Clauses (e) and (f) of Article 39, Articles 41 and 42 are not enforceable in a Court of law, it may not be possible to compel the State through the judicial process to make provision by statutory enactment or executive fiat for ensuring these basic essentials which go to make up a life of human dignity but where legislation is already enacted by the State providing these basic requirements to the workmen and thus investing their right to live with basic human dignity, with concrete reality and content, the State can certainly be obligated to ensure observance of such legislation.*** The State of Haryana must therefore ensure that the mine-lessees or contractors, to whom it is giving its mines for stone quarrying operations, observe various social welfare and labour laws enacted for the benefit of the workmen. This is a constitutional obligation which can be enforced against the Central Government and the State of Haryana by a writ petition under Article 32 of the Constitution.

The next preliminary objection was that the Court had no power to appoint *** commissioners and the Reports made by them had no evidentiary value since what was stated in the Reports was based only on *ex parte* statements which had not been tested by cross-examination.*** This argument, plausible though it may seem at first sight, is in our opinion not well founded and must be rejected. It is based upon a total misconception of the true nature of a proceeding under Article 32 of the Constitution.*** We are so much accustomed to the concepts of Anglo-Saxon jurisprudence which require every legal proceeding including a proceeding for a high prerogative writ to be cast in a rigid or definitive mold and insist on observance of certain well settled rules of procedure, that we implicitly assume that the same sophisticated procedural rules must also govern a proceeding under Article 32 and the Supreme Court cannot permit itself to be freed from the shackles of these rules even if that be necessary for enforcement of a fundamental right. It was on the basis of this impression fostered by long association with the Anglo-Saxon system of administration of justice that for a number of years this Court had taken the view that it is only a person whose fundamental right is violated who can approach the Supreme Court for relief under Article 32 or in other words, he must have a cause of action for enforcement of his fundamental right. It was only in the year 1981 *** that this Court for the first time took the view that where a person or class of persons to whom legal injury is caused by reason of violation of a fundamental right is unable to approach the Court for judicial redress on account of poverty or disability or socially or economically disadvantaged position, any member of the public acting *bona fide* can move the Court for relief under Article 32 *** so that the fundamental rights may become meaningful not only for the rich *** but also for the large masses of people who are living a life of want and destitution ***. This view *** is clearly within the terms of Article 32 if only we look at the language of this Article uninfluenced and uninhibited by any pre-conceptions and prejudices or any pre-conceived notions. Article 32 in so far as it is material is in the following terms:

Art. 32 (1) the right to move the Supreme Court by appropriate proceedings for the enforcement of the rights conferred by this Part is guaranteed.

(2) The Supreme Court shall have power to issue directions or orders or writs, including writs in the nature of habeas corpus, mandamus, prohibition, quo warranto and certiorari, whichever may be appropriate, for the enforcement of any of the rights conferred by this Part.

*** Clause (1) of Article 32 confers the right to move the Supreme Court for enforcement of any of the fundamental rights, but it does not say as to who shall have this right to move the Supreme Court nor does it say by what proceedings the Supreme Court may be so moved. There is no limitation in the words of Clause (1) of Article 32 that the fundamental right which is sought to be enforced by moving the Supreme Court should be one belonging to the person who moves the Supreme Court nor does it say that the Supreme Court should be moved only by a particular kind of proceeding. It is clear on the plain language of Clause (1) of Art. 32 that whenever there is a violation of a fundamental right, any one can move the Supreme Court for enforcement of such fundamental right.***

Then again Cl. (1) of Article 32 says that the Supreme Court can be moved for enforcement of a fundamental right by any "appropriate" proceeding. There is no limitation in regard to the kind of proceeding envisaged in Clause (1) of Article 32 except that the proceeding must be "appropriate" and this requirement of appropriateness must be judged in the light of the purpose for which the proceeding is to be taken, namely, enforcement of a fundamental right. The Constitution makers deliberately did not lay down any particular form of proceeding for enforcement of a fundamental right nor did they stipulate that such proceeding should conform to any rigid pattern or straight jacket formula as, for example, in England, because they knew that in a country like India where there is so much of poverty, ignorance, illiteracy, deprivation and exploitation, any insistence on a rigid formula of proceeding for enforcement of a fundamental right would become self-defeating.***

*** It is not at all obligatory that an adversarial procedure, where each party produces his own evidence tested by cross examination by the other side and the judge sits like an umpire and decides the case only on the basis of such material as may be produced before him by both parties, must be followed in a proceeding under Article 32 for enforcement of a fundamental right. In fact, there is no such constitutional compulsion enacted in Clause (2) of Article 32 or in any other part of the Constitution. It is only because we have been following the adversarial procedure for over a century owing to the introduction of the Anglo-Saxon system of jurisprudence under the British Rule that it has become a part of our conscious as well as sub-conscious thinking that *** justice cannot be done unless the adversarial procedure is adopted. But it may be noted that there is nothing sacrosanct about the adversarial procedure and in fact it is not followed in many other countries where the civil system of law prevails.*** There is a considerable body of juristic opinion in our country also which believes that strict adherence to the adversarial procedure can sometimes lead to injustice, particularly where the parties are not evenly balanced in social or economic strength. Where one of the parties to a litigation belongs to a poor and deprived section of the community and does not possess adequate social and material resources, he is bound to be at a disadvantage as against a strong and powerful opponent under the adversary system of justice, because of his difficulty in getting competent legal representation and more than anything else, his inability to produce relevant evidence before the Court. Therefore, when the poor come before the Court, particularly for enforcement of their fundamental rights, it is necessary to depart from the adversarial procedure and to evolve a new procedure ***.***

Would the Supreme Court not be failing in discharge of its constitutional duty of enforcing a fundamental right if it refuses to intervene because the petitioner belonging to the underprivileged segment of society or a public spirited citizen espousing his cause is unable to produce the relevant material before the Court! If the Supreme Court were to adopt a passive approach and decline to intervene in such a case because relevant material has not been produced before it by the party seeking its intervention, the fundamental rights would remain merely a teasing illusion so far as the poor and disadvantaged sections of the community are concerned. It is for this reason that the Supreme Court has evolved the practice of appointing commissions for the purpose of gathering facts and data in regard to a complaint of breach of a fundamental right made on behalf of the weaker sections of the society. The report of the commissioner would furnish prima facie evidence of the facts ***. Once the report of the commissioner is received, copies of it would be supplied to the parties so that either party, if it wants to dispute any of the facts or data stated in the Report, may do so by filing an affidavit and the Court [would] then consider the report of the commissioner and the affidavits which may have been filed and proceed to adjudicate upon the issue arising in the writ petition.***

Having disposed of these preliminary objections, we shall now proceed to consider the writ petition on merits. But, before we turn to examine the facts of this case, we may first consider which are the laws governing the living and working conditions of workmen employed in the stone quarries.***

The first question that arises in regard to the implementation of the Bonded Labor System (Abolition) Act 1976 is that of identification of bonded labour.*** We would therefore direct the Government of Haryana *** to take steps to sensitize the officers concerned with the implementation of the Act to this acute human problem and its socio-economic parameters.*** There are certain areas of concentration of bonded labour which can be easily identified on the basis of various studies and reports made by governmental authorities, social action groups and social scientists from time to time

*** and such areas must be mapped out by each State Government and task forces should be assigned for identification and release of bonded labour. Labour camps should be held periodically in these areas with a view to educating the labourers and *** in each such camp, individuals with organizational capability or potential should be identified and given training in the work of identification and release of bonded labour.

The other question arising *** is that of rehabilitation of the released bonded labourers and that is also a question of the greatest importance, because if the bonded labourers who are identified and freed, are not rehabilitated, their condition would be much worse than what it was before during the period of their serfdom and they would become more exposed to exploitation and slide back once again into serfdom even in the absence of any coercion.

We would therefore direct the Government of Haryana to draw up a scheme of program for "a *** meaningful rehabilitation of the freed bonded labourers."***

So far as implementation of the provisions of the Minimum Wages Act of 1948 is concerned we would direct the Central Government and State of Haryana to take necessary steps for the purpose of ensuring that minimum wages are paid to the workmen employed in the stone quarries and stone crushers ***.***

There are also two other matters in respect of which it is necessary for us to give directions. The first is that, apart from poverty and helplessness, one additional reason why the workmen employed in stone quarries and stone crushers are *** subjected to deception and exploitation, is that they are totally ignorant of their rights and entitlements.*** It is therefore necessary to educate the workmen employed in stone quarries and stone crushers so that they become aware as to what are the rights and benefits to which they are entitled under various social welfare laws. The knowledge of their rights and entitlements will give them the strength to fight against their employers for securing their legitimate dues and it will go a long way towards reducing if not eliminating their exploitation.***

*** The entire air in the area where stone crushers are being operated is heavily laden with dust and it is this air which the workmen breathe day in and day out and it is no wonder that many of them contract tuberculosis. We would therefore direct the Central Government and the State of Haryana to immediately take steps for the purpose of ensuring that the stone crusher owners do not continue to foul the air and they adopt either of two devices [to end the pollution].*** This direction shall be carried out by the Central Government and the State of Haryana in respect of each stone crusher in the Faridabad District and a compliance report shall be made to this Court.***

We may now take up a few specific complaints urged on behalf of the workmen. The first complaint relates to the failure to provide pure drinking water to the workmen in most of the stone quarries and stone crushers.*** We would therefore direct the Central Government and the State of Haryana to ensure immediately that the mine-lessees and stone crusher owners start supplying pure drinking water to the workmen on a scale of at least 2 liters for every workman by keeping suitable vessels in a shaded place at conveniently accessible points.*** The Central Government and the Sate of Haryana will also take steps for ensuring that the vessels in which drinking water is kept by the mine-lessees and stone crusher owners are kept in clean and hygienic condition and are emptied, cleaned and refilled every day and they shall also ensure that minimum wage is paid to the women and/or children who look after the vessels.

In large measure, the traditional conception of adjudication represented the socio-economic vision prevailing at the turn of the century. The expansion of governmental activity into the life of individuals through programs of social welfare and development had not yet been fore-shadowed. An environment permeated by the doctrine of laissez faire shaped the development of legal jurisprudence. But soon, progressive social and economic forces began to grow stronger and influence the minds of people, and governments, in response to the pressures of egalitarian and socialist-oriented urges, began to enter increasingly upon socio-economic programs in which legislation and the Courts constituted the principal instruments of change. The movement accelerated with the close of the Second World War, and a charter of human rights was written into the political constitutions adopted by most nations emerging from colonial rule even as, on another plane, it altered our basic conception of international law. In India, as the consciousness of social justice spread through our multi-layered social order, the Courts began to come under increasing pressure from social action groups petitioning on behalf of the underprivileged and deprived sections of society for the fulfilment of their aspirations.

Notes and Questions

1.   *The Failure of the Political Process.* Article 23 of the Indian Constitution proclaims bonded labor a violation of fundamental rights, and instructs Parliament to outlaw this abhorrent practice. Yet it was not until 1976, more than a quarter century after the Constitution's adoption, that the Bonded Labor (Abolition) Act was enacted. Even then, the Act was not enforced by the executive. Does this disregard of a clear constitutional mandate by the political branches justify the "activist" role assumed by the Court?

2.   *The Non-adversarial State?* How does Justice Bhagwati define the role of the state in *Bandhua Mukti Morcha v. Union of India?* What is the relationship between the state and the individual envisioned in his statement that "public interest litigation is not in the nature of adversarial litigation"? Is not the state a defendant in such litigation? Does this view contemplate a different role for the state than that which prevails in liberal-democratic societies?

3.   *Standing.* The prohibition against third-party standing in U.S. constitutional jurisprudence is a prudential limitation not mandated by the "case or controversy" requirement in Article III of the Constitution. While it is argued that such a restriction enhances the quality of litigation and judicial decisionmaking, the U.S. Supreme Court has routinely used the doctrine of standing to dismiss public interest lawsuits. *See, e.g., Sierra Club v. Morton*, 405 U.S. 727, 735 (1972). How are standing requirements related to the adversarial process? On what basis does the Court in *Bandhua Mukti Morcha* dispense with the standing requirement? Is the absence of limiting language in Article 32 sufficient to justify abandoning what has apparently been the past practice in Indian courts? The U.S. Supreme Court allows exceptions to the third-party standing rule for an injured party to raise the rights of others who are not before the Court if there are substantial obstacles to that party asserting her own rights. Is this practice analogous to what the Indian Supreme Court is doing? Is it advisable to allow "public spirited" individuals and organizations to enforce the constitutional rights of others?

4.   *The Expert Committees.* In social action litigation, the judge sheds the traditional common law passivity in fact-finding by appointing expert committees—including academicians, scientists and judges—to gather sociological, scientific and technical data

regarding the alleged violations of constitutional rights. In *Bandhua Mukti Morcha*, the defendants objected to this departure from the adversarial process. Does this innovation provide sufficient protection to defendants' rights? Is it fair to allow reports from such bodies to be introduced into evidence? Is there a danger of bias on the part of the Commissioners?

5. *Judicial Enforcement of the Directive Principles.* Although the Court acknowledges that the Directive Principles are not judicially enforceable, it in effect rules that the Constitution imposes positive duties upon the State. Its order directs the national and local governments to remedy the plight of bonded laborers with unusual specificity, down to the amount of water to be provided to the workers. Is it wise for a Court to immerse itself in such administrative minutiae? Is the Court usurping executive functions? How should this tension between social justice and separation of powers norms be resolved?

6. *Policymaking and the Courts.* Do you agree with Justice Bhagwati's assertion in *Bandhua Mukti Morcha* that courts must evolve as government becomes more involved in individuals' lives? Does the imposition of positive state duties necessarily entail a policy-making role for the courts? Is this desirable? What are the alternatives?

7. *The Problem of Child Labor.* Does the opinion appear to endorse child labor? Is the Court's order to pay children the minimum wage merely a pragmatic recognition of the reality of Indian society, or does it indicate judicial acceptance of this practice? *See M.C. Mehta v. State of Tamil Nadu*, excerpted in Section B *infra*.

PASCHIM BANGA KHET MAXDOOR SAMITY v. STATE OF WEST BENGAL

AIR 1996 S.C.C. 2426

*** Hakim Seikh [Petitioner No.2] who is a member of Paschim Banga Khet Mazdoor Samity [Petitioner No. 1], an organisation of agricultural labourers, fell off a train at Mathurapur Station in West Bengal at about 7:45 p.m. on July 8, 1992. As a result of the said fall Hakim Seikh suffered serious head injuries and brain haemorrhage. He was taken to the Primary Health Centre at Mathurapur. Since necessary facilities for treatment were not available at the Primary Health Centre, the medical officer in charge of the Centre referred him to the Diamond Harbour Sub-Divisional Hospital or any other State hospital for better treatment. Hakim Seikh was taken to N.R.S. Medical College Hospital near Sealdah Railway Station, Calcutta at about 11:45 p.m. on July 8, 1992. The Emergency Medical Officer in the said Hospital, after examining him and after taking two X-ray prints of his skull recommended immediate admission for further treatment. But Hakim Seikh could not be admitted in the said hospital as no vacant bed was available in the Surgical Emergency ward and the regular Surgery Ward was also full. He was thereafter taken to Calcutta Medical College Hospital at about 12:20 a.m. on July 9, 1992 but there also he was not admitted on the ground that no vacant bed was available. He was then taken to Shambhu Nath Pandit Hospital at about 1:00 a.m. on July 9, 1992. He was not admitted in that hospital and referred to a teaching hospital in the ENT, Neuro Surgeon Department on the ground that the hospital has no ENT Emergency or Neuro Emergency Department. At about 2:00 a.m. on July 9, 1992 he was taken to the Calcutta National Medical College Hospital but there also he was not admitted on account of non-availability of [a] bed. At about 8:00 a.m. on July

9, 1992 he was taken to SSKM Hospital but there also he was not admitted on the ground that the hospital has no facility of neuro surgery. Ultimately he was admitted in Calcutta Medical Research Institute, a private hospital, where he received treatment as an indoor patient from July 9, 1992 to July 22, 1992 and he has incurred an expenditure of approximately Rs.17,000 in his treatment.

Feeling aggrieved by the indifferent and callous attitude on the part of the medical authorities at the various State-run hospitals in Calcutta in providing treatment for the serious injuries sustained by Hamik Seikh the petitioners have filed this writ petition.

[T]he only question which needs to be considered is whether the non-availability of facilities for treatment of the serious injuries sustained by Hakim Seikh in the various Government hospitals in Calcutta has resulted in denial of his fundamental right guaranteed under Article 21 of the Constitution.

There is not much dispute on facts.*** During the pendency of this writ petition in this Court the State Government decided to make a complete and thorough investigation of the incident and take suitable departmental action against the persons responsible for the same and to take suitable remedial measures in order to prevent recurrence of similar incidents.***

The [State-appointed] Committee has suggested remedial measures to rule out recurrence of such incidents in [the] future and to ensure immediate medical attention and treatment to patients in real need. We will advert to it later. We will first examine whether the failure to provide medical treatment to Hakim Seikh by the Government Hospitals in Calcutta has resulted in violation of his rights and, if so, to what relief he is entitled.

The Constitution envisages the establishment of a welfare State at the federal level as well as at the State level. In a welfare State the primary duty of the Government is to secure the welfare of the people. Providing adequate medical facilities for the people is an essential part of the obligations undertaken by the Government in a welfare State. The Government discharges this obligation by running hospitals and health centres which provide medical care to the person seeking to avail those facilities. Article 21 imposes an obligation on the State to safeguard the right to life of every person. Preservation of human life is thus of paramount importance. The Government hospitals run by the State and the Medical Officers employed therein are duty bound to extend medical assistance for preserving human life. Failure on the part of a Government hospital to provide timely medical treatment to a person in need of such treatment results in violation of his right to life guaranteed under Article 21.

In the present case there was [a] breach of the said right of Hakim Seikh guaranteed under Article 21 when he was denied treatment at the various Government hospitals which were approached even though his condition was very serious at that time and he was in need of immediate medical attention. Since the said denial of the right of Hakim Seikh guaranteed under Article 21 was by officers of the State in hospitals run by the State, the State cannot avoid its responsibility for such denial of the constitutional right of Hakim Seikh. In respect of deprivation of the constitutional rights guaranteed under Part III of the Constitution the position is well settled that adequate compensation can be awarded by the court for such violation.*** Hakim Seikh should, therefore, be suitably compensated for the breach of his right guaranteed under Article 21 of the

Constitution. Having regard to the facts and circumstances of the case, we fix the amount of such compensation at Rs. 25,000.***

We may now come to the remedial measures to rule out recurrence of such incidents in [the] future and to ensure immediate medical attention and treatment to persons in real need. The Committee has made the following recommendations in this regard:

(i) The Primary Health Centres should attend the patient and give proper medical aid, if equipped.

(ii) At the hospitals the Emergency Medical Officer, in consultation with the specialist concerned on duty in the Emergency Department, should admit a patient whose condition is moribund/serious. If necessary the patient concerned may be kept on the floor or on the trolley beds.***

(iii) A Central Bed Bureau should be set up which should be equipped with wireless or other communication facilities to find out where a particular emergency patient can be accommodated when a particular hospital finds itself absolutely helpless to admit a patient because of physical limitations.***

(iv) Some casualty hospitals or Traumatology Units should be set up at some points on [a] regional basis.

(v) The intermediate group of hospitals, *viz.*, the district, the sub-division and the State General Hospitals should be upgraded so that a patient in a serious condition may get treatment locally.

The recommendations of the Committee have been accepted by the State Government and [appropriate instructions have been issued].***

Apart from the recommendations made by the Committee *** and the action taken by the State Government *** we are of the view that in order that proper medical facilities are available for dealing with emergency cases it must be that:

1. Adequate facilities are available at the Primary Health Centres where the patient can be given immediate primary treatment so as to stabilize his condition;

2. Hospitals at the district level and Sub-Division level are upgraded so that serious cases can be treated there;

3. Facilities for giving Specialist treatment are increased and are available at the hospitals at District level and Sub-Division level having regard to the growing needs;

4. In order to ensure availability of [a] bed in an emergency at State level hospitals there is a centralised communication system so that the patient can be sent immediately to the hospital where [a] bed is available in respect of the treatment which is required;

5. Proper arrangement of ambulance is made for transport of a patient ***;

6. The ambulance is adequately provided with necessary equipment and medical personnel;

7. The Health Centres and the hospitals and the medical personnel attached to these Centres and hospitals are geared to deal with larger number of patients needing emergency treatment on account of higher risk of accidents on certain occasions and in certain seasons.

It is no doubt true that financial resources are needed for providing these facilities. But at the same time it cannot be ignored that it is the constitutional obligation of the State to provide adequate medical services to the people. Whatever is necessary for this purpose has to be done. In the context of the constitutional obligation to provide free legal aid to a poor accused this Court has held that the State cannot avoid its constitutional obligation in that regard on account of financial constraint. [Citations omitted.] The said observations would apply with equal, if not greater, force in the matter of discharge of [the] constitutional obligation of the State to provide medical aid to preserve human life. In the matter of allocation of funds for medical services the said constitutional obligation of the State has to be kept in view. It is necessary that a time-bound plan for providing these services should be chalked out ***.***

The Union of India is a party to these proceedings. Since it is the joint obligation of the Centre as well as the States to provide medical services it is expected that the Union of India would render the necessary assistance in the improvement of the medical services in the country on these lines.

As regards the medical officers who have been found to be responsible for the lapse resulting in denial of immediate medical aid to Hakim Seikh it is expected that the State Government will take appropriate administrative action against those officers.***

Notes and Questions

1. *Samity* has been cited frequently in other jurisdictions. *See, e.g., Soobramoney v. Minister of Health of Kwa Zulu-Natal* excerpted in Chapter 8, *infra.*

2. The scope of the right to health was also viewed expansively by the Allahabad High Court, which directed the State Department of Agriculture not to allow the sale of chemically treated soybean seeds. The court found that the seeds were dangerous and unfit for consumption by humans or animals, and that their sale violated the right to life protected in Article 21:

Life does not mean bare animal life or life without health. Anything that adversely affects life *** physically or from the point of the health or anything that creates [o]bstruction in the physical, moral or other development of the individual and his dignity, anything that deprives or adversely affects the human life and any act of offering such goods for sale for human consumption *** that will be an act interfering with the fundamental right of life.

Shaibya Shukla v. State of U.P., AIR 1993 Allahabad 171. The Court added that Directive Principles 47, obligating the state to "raise the level of nutrition and standard of living and improve public health," and 48, protecting cattle, "are to be treated as fundamentals." It issued a writ of mandamus directing that the seeds not be offered for sale to any person or institution that deals in the commodities for human consumption or the consumption by cattle.

3. *Expanded Definition of the Right to Life.* Article 21 of the Indian Constitution has been interpreted by the Court to encompass protection for an array of economic, social and cultural interests. In addition to rights to health care, education and a safe and clean environment, the Court has held that the right to life includes the right to earn a liveli-

hood, *Olga Tellis v. Bombay Municipal Corp.*, AIR 1986 S.C.C. 180; the right to free legal services, *Khatri v. State of Bihar*, AIR 1981 S.C.C. 928; and the right of indigenous people to compensation for removal from forest land to make way for government projects. *Karajan Jalasay Y.A.S.A.S. Samity v. State of Gujarat*, AIR 1987 S.C.C. 532.

B. ADDRESSING THE STATUS OF WOMEN AND CHILDREN

GEETANIJALI MISRA, VERONICA MAGAR AND SUSAN LEGRO, POOR REPRODUCTIVE HEALTH AND ENVIRONMENTAL DEGRADATION: OUTCOMES OF WOMEN'S LOW STATUS IN INDIA

6 COLO. J. INT'L ENVTL. L. & POL'Y 273 (1995)

*** [P]opulation growth and environmental degradation occur at the same time and are rooted in the same causes.*** Women's voices from a low-income slum neighborhood of Bombay articulate a similar instinctive understanding that reproductive health and environmental well-being are two sides of the same coin: "It is not in my interest to have less children until I have water at my doorstep, fodder for my animals, fuel for cooking, until the forests are afforested so that I don't have to walk for miles for basic necessities. Until all these changes are made, why should I have less children?"***

II. LOW STATUS AND LACK OF CONTROL

A. *Lack of Control over Self*

That Indian women are often allowed no notion of self—let alone control of self— is evident from the most casual visit to a North Indian village. Ask for a woman by name, for example, and no one will be able to locate her. Ask for her by the name of her father, brother, or husband, on the other hand, and identification is immediate. That a woman lacks the ability to even identify herself by name illustrates the depth of her inability to define herself or to choose her experiences.

Indian women lack control over their reproduction, sexuality, mobility, education, and political representation. They lack control over such decisions as whether to have children, how many to have, when to have them, and whether to terminate a pregnancy. They lack the freedom to decide when to have sex, with whom to have sex, whether to use contraceptives, and who should use the contraceptives. Kamala Bhasin observes that women are obliged to provide sexual services to their husbands according to their needs and desires, which is sanctioned by religion.

Women in India often lack access to education and to political space.*** Indian women lack control over their own income and the family income, both of which are controlled by the male heads of the family. Indian women are often paid less for doing the same work as men. They also have unequal access to jobs.***

Children are also affected by their mothers' lack of control over finances. According to studies documenting gender differences in household spending patterns, women in poor households typically contribute almost all of their earnings to the family's basic needs, while men typically keep a significant portion for tobacco, liquor, and other recreational expenses. Absolute contributions of women are substantially more than those of men. For example, at the village level, the women's and children's nutritional status is much more linked to the mother's earnings than to the father's.

B. Lack of Control Over Surroundings

A woman's lack of control over her self also parallels her lack of control over her surroundings, in a two-way causal relationship. In rural India the poor typically depend on their natural surroundings for survival: land provides food; rivers, streams, lakes, and wells provide water, and forests provide firewood, fodder, fruits, and medicinal herbs. While the gender division of labor ensures that women are responsible for drawing sustenance from their surroundings, gender discrimination ensures that they lack control over these surroundings.

Most Indian families are patrilineal: land and other economic resources are controlled by men and are passed on from father to son. Thus, gender discrimination effectively denies women control over land—the most vital and productive resource in the rural economy. Even among the matrilineal Nair community in Kereala, where property passes from mothers to daughters, effective control rests in the hands of brothers and uncles. Males prevent women from getting their share of family land by using legal and other coercive means. In spite of recent progressive legislative changes, full gender equality does not exist because the new laws are not enforced. Men often exert strong resistance against their sisters' claims to land and find ways to bypass the law, including direct violence, death threats, and forced legal expenses.***

RATNA KAPUR, THE TRAGEDY OF VICTIMIZATION RHETORIC: RESURRECTING THE "NATIVE" SUBJECT IN INTERNATIONAL/POST-COLONIAL FEMINIST LEGAL POLITICS

15 HARV. HUM. RTS. J. 1 (2002)

*** The focus on violence against women [VAW] has had some extremely important and beneficial consequences for women. The women's human rights movement drew attention to the lack of domestic governmental response to women's demands for more effective rape laws, laws against child sexual abuse, and domestic violence laws. The VAW campaign has been overwhelmingly successful in translating very specific violations experienced by individual women into a more general human rights discourse.

VAW discourse has succeeded partly because of its appeal to the victim subject. In the context of law and human rights, it is invariably the abject victim subject who seeks rights, primarily because she is the one who has had the worst happen to her. The victim subject has allowed women to speak out about abuses that have remained hidden or invisible in human rights discourse. Moreover, the Vienna World Conference and subsequent women's conferences have enabled women to speak out to the international community. A powerful form of this presentation has been through personal testimonials in public tribunals, as at Vienna, or through international video links. These accounts are usually very graphic and horrifying, and are told through the location of the victim subject.

The victim subject also provides a shared location from which women from different cultural and social contexts can speak. It provides women with a subject that repudiates the atomized, decontextualized, and ahistorical subject of liberal rights discourse, while at the same time furnishing a unitary subject that enables women to continue to make claims based on a commonality of experience.***

However, an exclusive reliance on the victim subject to make claims for rights and for women's empowerment has some serious limitations. The articulation of the victim subject is based on gender essentialism; that is, over generalized claims about women. As Chandra Mohanty points out, essentialism assumes that "women have a coherent group identity within different cultures . . . prior to their entry into social relations." Such generalizations are hegemonic in that they represent the problems of privileged women, who are often (though not exclusively) white, Western, middle-class, heterosexual women. These generalizations efface the problems, perspectives, and political concerns of women marginalized because of their class, race, religion, ethnicity, and/or sexual orientation. The victim subject ultimately relies on a universal subject: a subject that resembles the uncomplicated subject of liberal discourse. It is a subject that cannot accommodate a multi-layered experience.

The second problem with a focus on violence against women is that it is a position based on cultural essentialism. Women in the Third World are portrayed as victims of their culture, which reinforces stereotyped and racist representations of that culture and privileges the culture of the West. In the end, the focus on the victim subject reinforces the depiction of women in the Third World as perpetually marginalized and underprivileged, and has serious implications for the strategies subsequently adopted to remedy the harms that women experience. It encourages some feminists in the international arena to propose strategies which are reminiscent of imperial interventions in the lives of the native subject and which represent the "Eastern" woman as a victim of a "backward" and "uncivilized" culture.

Finally, the victim subject and the focus on violence invite remedies and responses from states that have little to do with promoting women's rights. Thus, a related concern is that the victim subject position has invited protectionist, and even conservative, responses from states. The construction of women exclusively through the lens of violence has triggered a spate of domestic and international reforms focused on the criminal law, which are used to justify state restrictions on women's rights—for the protection of women. The anti-trafficking campaign, with its focus on violence and victimization, is but one example. The government of Nepal restricts women under thirty from traveling outside of the country without the permission of a husband or male guardian as part of an anti-trafficking initiative. Early feminist interventions struggled to move away from such protectionist responses through anti-discrimination discourse. However, the VAW campaigns, which are contingent on the victim subject, have taken feminists back into a protectionist and conservative discourse. Furthermore, these interventions reinforce women's victim status. The exclusive focus on finding resolutions through appeals to the state fails to consider the relevance to the women's rights agenda of new players in the public sphere who are de-centering the power of sovereign states.***

The lack of complexity has become particularly evident in the international women's human rights arena. The feminist legal agenda, despite its international complexion, has not sufficiently taken on board the critiques of gender essentialism in formulating the women's human rights project. The VAW campaign has not translated into a complex understanding of the ways in which women's lives and experiences are mediated by race, religion, class, and gender.***

Gender essentialism may be used with strategic purpose, but the way in which it is being deployed in the international women's human rights arena has had a reactionary effect. By not remaining sufficiently attentive to cultural and historical specificities, gender essentialism constructed through a VAW discourse has prompted state actors, non-state actors, and donors to embrace universalizing strategies in responding to human rights violations against women. It has further obscured differences between women located in very different power relationships. Religion, for example, is of acute significance in many parts of the post-colonial and Third World, especially for women located within minority communities. In post-colonial India, for example, the relationship between gender and religion remains very complex due to the increasing legitimacy of the Hindu Right and their political agenda emphasizing the assimilation of religious minorities. Muslim women are caught in the tension between their demands for gender equality within their religious community and their dependence upon and support for the community as a site of cultural and political resistance to Hindu majoritarianism.

Unfortunately, the VAW agenda has taken up issues of culture and religion in ways that have not only reinforced gender essentialism but have also essentialized certain features of culture and reinforced racial and cultural stereotypes.***

*"Death by Culture"****

It is necessary to explode the mystery often set up by cultural arguments that obscures the real issues concerning women's human rights. There is a need for economic, social, and institutional analysis in order to make certain kinds of politics and strategies feasible in various national settings. Researchers, scholars, and women's rights activists must take responsibility for understanding and informing themselves about the complexity of debates that surround issues of women's rights in the postcolonial world. They must put to rest the search for the native subject and the essential cultural explanations that are used to exoticize the Other. A deeper and more rigorous kind of contextual analysis is essential to protect against simple, unreflective, and naive strategies that invariably harm more than help those who are victims of rights violations.***

[F]eminists and human rights scholars must acknowledge and engage the new arenas of power that manifest themselves in today's globalized world. In this world, the actions of non-state actors have a significant impact on women's lives and women's rights. The women's human rights movement exposed the ways in which power impacts women's rights and women's lives at many different levels, but the focus on the victim subject and on violence has failed to develop this. By resorting to an exclusive focus on the victim subject and on women's experience of violence, feminists fell back onto an understanding of power (one that has also informed traditional human rights standards) as monolithic and emanating from a coherent sovereign. For example, addressing crimes against women without simultaneously addressing their lack of civil and political rights assumes that the cause and the cure for violence lies with the state, specifically in the guise of the criminal law. By falling into the "sovereignty trap," feminists have failed to address the power eruptions that have occurred as a result of global integration and market activity.

Power eruptions are taking place in a myriad of spaces: in the information technology revolution, in satellite broadcasting, and through the increasing interventions of non-governmental organizations, religious institutions, the World Trade Organization, and other trade and financial institutions. The most obvious shifts in power from state to non-state actors have occurred in connection with market actors. The human rights movement is becoming acutely aware of the limitations of a human rights strategy that is tied to a state analysis, given the entry of supernational non-state actors into the market and the international arena. Economic globalization has emerged as a powerful force in structuring transnational systems of power as it simultaneously effects shifts in the locations and operations of power between genders, within families, in the workplace, and between the West and the Rest.***

Notes and Questions

1.   The article by Misra, Magar and Legro indicates that most Indian women lack effective control over their economic, social and political lives. Do such broad generalizations give you pause? What are the elements of control over one's life? Are Ratna Kapur's views on the status of women in India likely to be different from the authors just mentioned? If so, how would you articulate the differences?

2.   The status of any group of women is affected by factors such as culture, tradition, geography, the form of government, religion, education, health, the economy and the environment. Is it productive to draw conclusions about "Indian women" as a whole, or any other large, diverse group, for that matter? If so, what are the implications of such conclusions for the cross-cultural monitoring of human rights violations? Is it useful to engage in "strategic essentialism" for this purpose? A term commonly used by critical race theorists, "strategic essentialism" involves the use, for political purposes, of broad categories that imply a common, "essential" set of characteristics inherent in one's group or personal status. For example, while "American women" includes a very broad and diverse set of people with varying social, economic, racial and political characteristics, it may still be useful or efficient to discuss such a broad group as sharing certain traits. Or, when talking about a particular woman as an "American woman," we might assume certain essential traits about that woman for purposes of discussion or political organizing. For a discussion of the limits and possibilities of "strategic essentialism" with regard to the status of women in India, *see, e.g.*, Ratna Kapur, *Postcolonial Erotic Disruptions: Legal Narratives of Culture, Sex, and Nation in India*, 10 COLUM. J. GENDER & L. 333 (2001).

3.   What are the implications of describing people who experience violence or other violations of their rights as "victims"? Does it make a difference if this term is applied to men or to women? Does the type of violation make a difference? Do we describe the poor or homeless as "victims of economic violence"? Should we do so? Would that have any practical impact on their status?

4.   What does Kapur mean by the term "native subject"? Does it imply that contemporary international human rights actors still (perhaps subconsciously) see post-colonial peoples as "natives" in the racist, pejorative sense? If so, how might that attitude affect the nature and focus of international human rights activism and responses to it? For related "insider/outsider" critiques of the international human rights movement, *see* Makau wa Mutua, *Savages, Victims, and Saviors: The Metaphor of Human Rights*, 42 HARV. INT'L L.J. (2001); Makau wa Mutua, *The Ideology of Human Rights*, 36 VA. J. INT'L L. 589 (1996) (excerpted in Chapter 2, *supra*).

5.   How important is discourse to the implementation of women's rights and the actual elevation of women's status? Is it irrelevant? What is the value of analytical approaches that deconstruct the language and assumptions of "rights talk"? Does either critical or mainstream discourse have any meaningful impact on the lives of women in the Global

South? To what extent might scholarly debate serve to alienate women as opposed to promoting global understanding and advancing important women's rights issues? On the other hand, does scholarly discourse have any effect on the decisions of policymakers or judges?

6.   Do all policies aimed at "protecting" women actually improve their lives? Who should define what women need? Consider these questions as you read the following case.

DR. UPENDRA BAXI ET AL. (II) v. STATE OF U.P.

AIR (1986) 4 S.C.C. 106

BHAGWATI, C.J.—This writ petition has come up for hearing in view of certain developments which have taken place since the making of our last order. It was on the basis of a letter addressed by the petitioners that this writ petition came to be entertained by the court. The petitioners pointed out in the letter which was treated as a writ petition that the conditions in which girls were living in the Government Protective Home at Agra were abominable and they were being denied their right to live with basic human dignity by the State of Uttar Pradesh which was running the Protective Home. The court thereupon made various orders ***. It appears that the efforts made by the petitioners *** were nearing successful conclusion when everything which had been done by the court in order to improve the living conditions of the inmates of the Protective Home was set at naught by the State Government by shifting the Protective Home from its location in Vijaynagar colony to Adarsh Nagar, Rajwara.***

[N]o steps were taken by the State Government or the Administration to obtain the permission of this Court for shifting the Protective Home to another building ***.***

The new building where the Home has been shifted is *** at the outskirts of town, far away from the hospitals and courts where the inmates have to be frequently taken.*** Even from the consideration of staff which is mostly consisting of female it is [a] very unsafe place for them to come and go back to their homes. No public conveyance is available near it. The approach road is *** uneven and is likely to be blocked during rains. From the security point of view this building is most unsafe. This new building is much inferior in every respect to the old building. Though the rooms in this building are quite big they appear [not] to have been constructed for the purposes of *** human dwelling. There are no cross ventilators and windows in these rooms and one will feel suffocation on entering the room. This building belongs to the same person who is the owner of the old building.

As regards the accommodation in this building *** [w]hen the room was opened [a] bad smell was coming out of it and it is actually very difficult to live in the room during summer season. There is one big kitchen which too has no cross ventilation. There are 3 rooms, 2 on one side and one on the other side of the kitchen which are to be used as classrooms for the inmates. These rooms also have no cross ventilation. Therefore, it will be very difficult to run classes in these rooms.*** On comparison I find that this new building is much inferior to the old building from the point of view of security.***

It is indeed surprising that the State Government should have shifted the Protective Home *** without obtaining the permission of this Court *** [w]hen the present case for ensuring decent living conditions for the inmates of the Protective Home was pending.*** It is obvious that what has been done has the effect of subverting the authority of this Court and unless proper and adequate expression of regret is forthcoming from the concerned officials, we may have to consider whether we should adopt appropriate proceedings against the erring officials.***

But, despite our anguish at shifting of the Protective Home from the old building to the new building, we cannot do anything about it, since possession of the old building has already been surrendered to the landlord and the best that can be done in the circumstances is to start the process all over again and commence giving directions for improving the living conditions in the new building. [We] would direct the State Government to carry out the following directions:

(1) The approach road to the new building shall be made into a pucca or semi-pucca road so that it does not get blocked or waterlogged by rain. This shall be done within 3 months from today.

(2) The big hall as also the three rooms used as classrooms and the kitchen shall be provided with cross ventilation by putting up sufficient number of windows so as to ensure passage of air in and out of the rooms. The District Judge *** shall determine how many windows are necessary to be constructed for this purpose.

(3) Exhaust fans shall be provided in the big hall, three classrooms, kitchen and offices.

(4) The State Government shall provide police protection throughout day and night for the inmates of the Protective Home in the new building.

(5) The State Government shall either provide accommodation to the staff of the Protective Home in or near the new building or provide conveyance to the members of the staff for coming to the Protective Home and going back to their respective homes unless public transport is available in the immediate vicinity of the Protective Home.

(6) [T]he State Government shall immediately take steps to provide mosquito nets to each and every inmate and member of the staff staying in the Protective Home.

(7) The State Government shall provide a conveyance for taking the inmates to the court and bringing them back to the Protective Home and similarly, conveyance shall also be provided to the District Judge *** inspecting the Protective Home.

(8) The District Manager (Telephones), Agra shall immediately shift the telephone to the new building and whatever steps are necessary for this purpose shall be taken by the State Government without any delay.

(9) The State Government shall immediately provide cooking gas in the kitchen so that it is not necessary to use wood for cooking which may emit a lot of smoke and lead to discomfort and suffocation on account of lack of ventilation.

(10) The State Government shall immediately proceed to carry out rewiring as also to install the electric meter in a safe place where there is no dampness.***

Thirdly, we find that despite directions given by this Court on various occasions, the State Government has not yet constituted a Board of Visitors as prescribed in Rule 40 of the Rules made under the Suppression of Immoral Traffic in Women and Girls Act. We would, therefore, direct the State Government to set up, within a period of two weeks from the receipt of this order, a Board of Visitors on which there shall be at least three social activists working in the field of welfare of women ***.

Fourthly, the Superintendent of the Protective Home shall take care to see that no woman or girl is detained in the Protective Home without due authority and process of law. The District Judge, Agra who carries out monthly inspection of the Protective Home shall verify during every visit that no woman or girl is detained except under the authority of law and if he finds that any of them is detained without any authority of law, he shall take steps to see that she is released and repatriated to her parents or husband or other proper authority.

Fifthly, we would direct the District Judge, Agra to nominate two socially committed advocates who would by turns visit the Protective Home once in a fortnight and enquire from the inmates in regard to their needs and requirements and provide them legal aid and assistance, where required.***

Lastly, we are pained to point out that though we gave directions from time to time for formulating an effective program of rehabilitation of the inmates in the Protective Home and the State Government also on several occasions promised that they would come forward with a rehabilitation program, nothing seems to have been done by the State Government so far except engaging a sewing teacher. [I]t is absolutely essential that the inmates in the Protective Home should be provided a proper rehabilitation program so that when they come out of the Protective Home, they are in a position to look after themselves and they do not slide into prostitution on account of economic want. The inmates must be given vocational training and guidance by way of rehabilitation. We would, therefore, once again direct the State Government to produce at the next hearing of the writ petition a detailed rehabilitation program which they have either set up or they propose to set up within a specified time limit. We would also like the Superintendent of the Protective Home to consider whether it would be possible to arrange for their wedding to proper persons in case they want to get married. The Superintendent of the Protective Home can follow the example of the Nari Niketan in Delhi where a committee was set up by this Court for the purpose of investigating into the antecedents of the would-be-bridegrooms in order to ensure that they were genuine persons wishing to marry the inmates and not bogus or sham bridegrooms who were going through the ceremony of marriage merely for the purpose of selling the inmates or pushing them into prostitution. The District Judge will constitute an appropriate committee for this purpose consisting of himself and at least two social activists. The State Government will also initiate proper follow up action in this behalf with a view to ensuring that the inmates are not taken back to the brothels or/and they do not once again slide into prostitution.

The District Judge, Agra or any other Additional District Judge nominated by him shall visit the Protective Home once every month for the purpose of ensuring that the aforesaid directions given by us are carried out fully and effectively and he shall submit an Inspection Report to this court on/or before the 15th of every month.

Notes and Questions

1. *Subsequent Developments.* By an order dated November 11, 1997, the Supreme Court referred the supervision of the Agra Protective Home to the National Human Rights

Commission. The Commission, established by statute in 1993, was empowered to monitor the Home's compliance with the directions of the Court.

Protective homes are problematic from a rights perspective. Established under the 1956 Immoral Traffic (Prevention) Act, these institutions house women for "protection" as well as correction. Women have been held in "protective custody" in the Agra Protective Home who were merely suffering from tuberculosis or AIDS, or who were witnesses in a case. Women held in custodial institutions invariably lose many of their rights. For example, it was discovered that the HIV status of all the women in the Agra Protective Home was public knowledge.

2. *Court-Arranged Marriages?* The Court suggests finding spouses for the women as a step in their "rehabilitation." Is this just blatant patriarchy, or does it reflect a legitimate culture-specific approach to resolving the problems of destitute women? Is this an appropriate role for the state?

3. *Impact of Directive Principles on Status of Women.* Professor Modhurima Dasgupta asserts that social action litigation is beginning to have an impact on the social position of women in Indian society:

> Supreme Court judgments in PIL cases have not only been influential in promoting awareness about women's issues, but have also been instrumental in the creation of policy and organizations devoted to women's development initiatives. It was in the early 1990's that the Supreme Court ordered the creation of the National Commission for Women (NCW) under the National Commission for Women Act of 1990.*** The Commission's mandated activities include the review of laws having to do with women, interventions and investigations of specific complaints of atrocities, and remedial action when it is appropriate.
>
> The NCW is particularly active in organizing Parivrik Mahila Lok Adalats (local courts for resolutions of problems—specifically for women) through the help of NGOs all over the country. The Commission reports that over the last year, 20 of these were held in twelve of the 25 states. They have also launched legal awareness programs for women, including 160 programs at colleges and many regional literacy camps in which the Commission claims 50,000 women were educated in the past year alone. In investigating complaints of violence, the Commission mainly deals with cases of rape, gang rape, and various other forms of violence committed against poor tribal and village women.***
>
> Under the auspices of the Supreme Court, the NCW has set up several programs to assess the way in which law enforcement treats women. Sensitivity training has been given to numerous police departments, urging greater implementation of laws that are in place for the benefit of women. The Commission has established schemes for appropriate custodial justice for female prisoners, and the release and rehabilitation upon release of women from prisons.
>
> Rehabilitation is also provided for prostitutes and their children, and for widows along with proper support for the land rights of widows. The elimination of dowry practices is a further concern for the Commission. It routinely considers complaints lodged by women and their families who have had unlawful dowry demands made on them. Such demands are often accompanied by threats of violence. Other common complaints have to do with torture, desertion, bigamy, rape, employment discrimination, domestic violence, and incest.

Modhurima Dasgupta, *Social Action for Women? Public Interest Litigation in India's Supreme Court,* LAW, SOC. JUSTICE & GLOBAL DEV. J., at 7–8 (2002(1), *available at* http://elj.warwick.ac.uk/global/issue/2002-1/dasgupta.htm. Dasgupta asserts that "the contemporary Indian women's movement is strong, and has asserted its voice in how women's issues are dealt with in the highest echelons of the Indian state." *Id.* at 7.

Vijayashri Sripati argues, however, that the constitutional guarantees have not yet penetrated the private spheres that regulate the lives of women: "In India members of different religious communities are governed by their personal religious laws in matters pertaining to marriage, divorce, inheritance etc. These laws are in many respects discriminatory and violative of women's human rights." Vijayashri Sripati, *Human Rights in India—Fifty Years After Independence,* 26 DENV. J. INT'L L. & POL'Y 93, 132 (1997). She notes that while the Supreme Court has asserted the primacy of fundamental rights over custom, "it has not subjected oppressive personal laws to the rigor of Article 21 and the Equality Clauses of Part III." *Id.* Moreover, in ratifying the Convention on the Elimination of all forms of Discrimination Against Women, the Indian government included a reservation asserting the primacy of its "policy of non-interference in the personal affairs of any Community without its initiative and consent."

Under Article 44 of the Constitution, the government is directed to enact a Uniform Civil Code which would replace many of these traditional laws, and in *Sarla Mudgal v. Union of India,* A.I.R. 1995 S.C.C. 1531, the Supreme Court called on the government to enact such a code. However, many caution that such calls are viewed as a threat by religious minorities:

> [I]n the existing socio-political climate, calls for a uniform civil code only exacerbate communal sentiment because the proposed code promoted by the Congress Party resembles Hindu laws. Furthermore, the most vocal supporters of the code are Hindu fundamentalists. Consequently, many minorities fear that a uniform code will allow non-minorities to define the rights of minorities and impose "Hindu" rights and obligations on non-Hindus.

Sara Ahmad, *Judicial Complicity with Communal Violence in India,* 17 J. INT'L L. & BUS. 320, 331–32 (1996).

M.C. MEHTA v. STATE OF TAMIL NADU

AIR 1997 S.C.C. 699

*** 3A. In our country, Sivakasi was once taken as the worst offender in the matter of violating [the] prohibition of employing child labour. As the situation there had become intolerable, the public spirited lawyer, Shri. MC Mehta, thought it necessary to invoke this Court's power under Article 32, as after all the fundamental right of the children guaranteed by Article 24 was being grossly violated. He, therefore, filed this petition. It once came to be disposed of by an order of October 31, 1990 by noting that in Sivakasi, as on December 31, 1985, there were children. The Court then noted that the manufacturing process of matches and fireworks (for the manufacture of which also Sivakasi is a traditional Centre) is hazardous, giving rise to accidents including fatal cases. So, keeping in view the provisions contained in Article 39 (f) and 45 of the Constitution, it gave certain directions as to how the quality of life of children employed in the factories could be improved. The court also felt the need of constituting a committee to oversee the directions given.

4. Subsequently, *suo moto* cognisance was taken in the present case itself when news about an "unfortunate accident," in one of the Sivakasi cracker factories was published. At the direction of the Court, [the] Tamil Nadu Government filed a detailed counter stating inter alia, that the number of persons to die were 39. The Court gave certain directions regarding the payment of compensation and thought that an advocates committee should visit the area and make a comprehensive report ***.***

Magnitude of the problem

10. Sivakasi has ceased to be only centre employing child labour. The malady is no longer confined to that place.

11. A write-up in Indian Express of 25.10.1996 has described Bhavnagar as another Sivakasi in [the] making, as that town of about 4 lakh population has at least 13,000 children employed in 300 different industries. The problem of child labour in India has indeed spread its fang far and wide. This would be apparent from the chart which finds place in the commendable work of a social anthropologist of United Nations Volunteer, Neera Burra. Published under the title "Born to Work: Child Labour in India," as at pages XXII to XXIV of the book. It is useful to extract that chart. It is as below:

11. [The Court cites official estimates ranging from 11–33 million working children.] None of the official estimates included child workers in the unorganised sector and therefore are obviously gross under estimates. Estimates from various non-governmental sources as to the actual number working children range from 44 million to 100 million.

12. The aforesaid profile shows that child labour by now is an all-India evil, though its acuteness differs from area to area. So, without a concerted effort, both of the Central government and various State governments, this ignominy would not get wiped out. We have, therefore thought it fit to travel beyond the confines of Sivakasi to which place this petition initially related. In our view, it would be more appropriate to deal with the issue in wider spectrum and broader perspective taking it as a national problem and not appertaining to any one region of the country. So, we would address ourselves as to how we can, and are required to tackle the problem of child labour, solution of which is necessary to build a better India.

Constitution Call

13. To accomplish the aforesaid task, we have first to note the constitutional mandate and call on the subject, which are contained in the following articles: [The Court cites Articles 24, 39(e), 39(f), 41, 45 and 47 of the Indian Constitution.]

14. *** Abolition of child labour is definitely a matter of great public concern and significance.

International Commitment

15. It would be apposite to appraise ourselves also about our commitment to [the] world community. For the case at hand it would be enough to note that India has accepted the Convention on the Rights of the Child, which was concluded by the UN General Assembly on 20th November 1989. This Convention affirms that children's rights require special protection and it aims not only to provide such protection, but

Industry	Location	Total workers	Child workers	Percentage of child workers to total workers
Slate pencil	Mandsaur, Madhya Pradesh	12000	1000	8.3
Slate	Markapur, Andhra Pradesh	15000	App. 3750	25
Diamond cutting	Surat, Gujarat	100000	15000	15
Agate cutting	Cambay, Gujarat	30000	Not known	—
Gem Polishing	Jaipur, Rajasthan	60000	13600	22.6
Powerloom	Bhiwandi, Maharashtra	300000	15000	5
Cotton hosiery	Tiruppur, Tamil Nadu	30000	8000	33.3
Carpet weaving	Mirzapur—Bhadohi, Uttar Pradesh	200000	150000	75
Carpet weaving	Rajasthan	30000	12000	40
Lock making	Aligarh	80000	7000	8.7
Lock making	Uttar Pradesh	90000	10000	11.1
Pottery	Khurja, Uttar Pradesh	20000	5000	25
Brass ware	Moradabad	150000	40000	24.6
Brass ware	Uttar Pradesh		45000	30.6
Match	Sivakasi, Tamil Nadu	Not known	45000	—
Glass	Firozabad, Uttar Pradesh	200000	50000	25
Silk and Silk products	Varanasi, Uttar Pradesh	11900	4409	37
Textile	Varanasi, Uttar Pradesh	3512	1108	31.5
Knives	Rampur, Uttar Pradesh	Not known	3000	—
Handicrafts	Jammu and Kashmir	90000	26478	29.4
Silk weaving	Bihar	Not known	10000	—
Brocade and Zari industry	Varanasi and other centers, Uttar Pradesh	Not known	300000	—
Brick kilns	West Bengal	Not known	35000	—
Beedi	India	3275000	327500	10
Circus industry	40 major circuses	12% of entire labour strength		
Handloom and Handicraft industry	Jammu and Kashmir	116000	28348	25

(Source material omitted)

also to ensure the continuous improvement in the situation of children all over the world, as well as their development and education in conditions of peace and security. Thus, the Convention not only protects the child's civil and political rights, but also extends protection to child's economic, social, cultural and humanitarian rights.

Statutory Provisions ***

[T]he following legislative enactments are in force prohibiting employment of child labour in different occupations:

(i) Section 67 of Factories Act 1948:

"Prohibition of employment of young children—No Child who has not completed his fourteenth year shall be required or allowed to work in any factory."

(ii) Section 24 of Plantation of Labour Act 1951:

"No child who has not completed his twelfth year shall be required or allowed to work in any plantation."

(iii) Section 109 of Merchant Shipping Act 1951:

No person under fifteen years of age shall be engaged or carried to sea to work in any capacity in any ship, except—

(a) in a school ship, or training ship, in accordance with the prescribed conditions; or

(b) in a ship in which all persons employed are members of one family; or

(c) in a home-trade ship of less than two hundred tons gross; or

(d) where such a person is to be employed on nominal wages and will be in the charge of his father or other adult near male relative."

(iv) Section 45 of Mines Act 1952:

(1) "No child shall be employed in any mine, nor shall any child be allowed to be present in any part of a mine which is below found or in any (pen cast working) in which any mining operation is being carried on.

(2) "[N]o child shall be allowed to be present in any part of a mine above ground where any operation connected with or incidental to any mining operation is being carried on."

(v) Section 21 of Motor Transport Workers Act 1961:

"No child shall be required or allowed to work in any capacity in any motor transport undertaking."

(vi) Section 3 of Apprentices Act 1961:

Qualifications for being engaged as an apprentice:—A person shall not be qualified for being engaged as an apprentice / to undergo apprenticeship training in any designated trade, unless he—

(a) is not less than fourteen years of age, and

(b) satisfies such standards of education and physical fitness as may be prescribed; Provided that different standards may be prescribed in relation to apprenticeship training in different designated trades and for different categories of apprentices.

(vii) Section 24 Beedi and Cigar Workers (Conditions of Employment) Act 1966:

"Prohibition of employment of children—No child shall be required or allowed to work in any industrial premises."

(viii) Child Labour (Prohibition and Regulation) Act, 1986: (Act 61 of 1986).

(ix) Shops and Commercial Establishment Acts under different nomenclatures in various States.

22. The aforesaid shows that the legislature has strongly desired prohibition of child labour. Act 61 of 1986 is, ex facie, a bold step. The provisions of this Act, other than Part III, came into force at once and for Part III to come into force, a notification by the Central Government is visualised by section I (3), which notification covering all classes of establishments throughout the territory of India was issued on May 26, 1993.

23. Section 3 of this Act has prohibited employment of children in certain occupations and processes.***

24. Section 14 of the Act has provided for punishment up to 1 year (minimum being 3 months) or with fine up to Rs. 20,000/ (minimum being ten thousand) or with both, to one who employs or permits any child to work in contravention of provisions in section 3. Even so, it is common experience that child labour continues to be employed.*** According to Neera, there are a number of loopholes in the Act which has made it [a] "completely ineffective instrument for the removal of children working in industry." One of the clear loopholes mentioned is that children can continue to work if they are part of [a] family of labour. It is not necessary for our purpose that the Act does not use the word "hazardous" anywhere, the implication of which is the children may continue to work in those processes not involving chemical[s]. Neera has tried to show how impractical and unrealistic it is to draw a distinction between hazardous and non-hazardous processes in a particular industry. The suggestion given is that what is required is to list the whole industry as banned for child labour, which would make the task of enforcement simpler and strategies of evasion more difficult.

Failure: Causes

25. [According to] "Indian Child Labour" by Dr. J.C. Kulshreshtha. the causes of failure are: (1) poverty; (2) low wages of the adult; (3) unemployment; (4) absence of schemes for family allowance; (5) migration to urban areas; (6) large families; (7) children being cheaply available; (8) nonexistence of provisions for compulsory education; (9) illiteracy and ignorance of parents; and (10) traditional attitudes.***

26. Of the aforesaid causes it seems to us that poverty is the basic reason which compels parents of a child despite their willingness, to get it employed. The Survey Report of the Ministry of Labour (supra) had also so stated. Otherwise, no parents, specially no mother would like that a tender aged child should toil in a factory in a difficult condition, instead of it enjoying its childhood at home under the parental gaze.

What to do?

27. It may be that the problem would be taken care of to some extent by insisting on compulsory education. Indeed, Neera thinks that if there is at all a blueprint for tackling the problems of child labour, it is education. Even if it were to be so, the child of a poor parent would not receive education, if per force it has to earn to make the family meet both the ends. Therefore, unless the family is assured of income, [the] problem of child labour would hardly get solved; and it is this vital question which has remained almost unattended. We are however, of the view that till an alternative income is assured to the family, the question of abolition of child labour would really remain a will of the wisp. [I]t seems to us that the least we ought to do is see to the fulfilment of legislative intendment behind enactment of the Child Labour (Prohibition and Regulation) Act, 1986. Taking guidance therefrom, we are of the view that the offending employer must be asked to pay compensation for every child employed in contravention of the provision of the Act a sum of Rs. 20,000 ***. The liability of the employer would not cease even if he would have such a fund district wise or area wise. The fund so generated shall form corpus whose income shall be used only for the concerned child. The quantum could be the income earned on the corpus deposited qua the child. To generate greater income, [the] fund can be deposited in [a] high yielding scheme of any nationalized bank or other public body.

28. As the aforesaid income could not be enough to dissuade the parent/guardian to seek employment of the child the state owes a duty to come forward to discharge its obligation in this regard.

29. Now, strictly speaking a strong case exists to invoke the aid of Article 41 of the Constitution regarding the right to work and to give meaning to what has been provided in Article 47 relating to raising of [the] standard of living of the population, and Article 39 (e) and (f) as to non-abuse of tender age of children and giving opportunities and facilities to them to develop in healthy manner, for asking the State to see that an adult member of the family, whose child is in employment in a factory or a mine in other hazardous work, gets a job anywhere, in lieu of the child.*** We are, however, not asking the State at this stage to ensure alternative employment in every case covered by Article 24, as Article 41 speaks about rights to work "within the limits of the economic capacity and development of the State." The very large number of child-labour in the aforesaid occupations would require giving of job to very large number of adults.*** We are not issuing any direction to do so presently. Instead, we leave the matter to be sorted out by the appropriate Government. In those cases where it would not be possible to provide jobs as above mentioned, the appropriate Government would, as its contribution grant deposit in the aforesaid Fund a sum of Rs. 5,000/—for each child employed in a factory or mine or in any other hazardous employment.

30. The aforesaid would either see an adult (whose name would be suggested by the parents/guardian of the concerned child) getting a job in lieu of the child, or deposit of a sum of Rs. 25,000/—in the Child Labour Rehabilitation-cum-Welfare Fund. In case of getting employment for an adult, the parents/guardian shall have to withdraw his child from the job. Even if no employment would be provided, the parent / guardian shall have to see that his child is spared from the requirement to do the job, as an alternative source of income would have become available to him.

31. To give shape to the aforesaid directions, we require the concerned States to do the following:

(1) A survey would be made of the aforesaid type of child labour which would be completed within six months from today.

(2) *** The most hazardous employment may rank first in priority, to be followed by comparatively less hazardous and so on. It may be mentioned here that the National Child Labour Policy as announced by the Government of India has already identified some industries for priority action ***.***

(4) The employment so given could as well be [in] the industry where the child is employed, [or] a public undertaking and would be manual in nature as much as the child in question must be engaged in doing manual work. The undertaking chosen for employment shall be one which is nearest to the place of residence of the family.

(5) In those cases where alternative employment would not be made available as aforesaid, the parent / guardian of the concerned child would be paid the income which would be earned on the corpus, which would be a sum of Rs. 25,000/—for each child, every month. The employment given or payment made would cease to be operative if the child would not be sent by the parent / guardian for education.

(6) On discontinuation of the employment of the child, his education would be assured in [a] suitable institution with a view to make it a better citizen. It may be pointed out that Articles 45 mandates compulsory education of all children until they complete the age of 14 years; it is also required to be free. It would be the duty of the Inspectors to see that this call of the Constitution is carried out.***

32. The task is big, but not as to prove either unwieldy or burdensome.*** [I]t is worthwhile pointing out that poverty as such has not stood in the way of other developing countries from taking care of child labour. It has been pointed out by Myron Weiner (at page 4 of 1991 Edition) of his book "The Child and the State in India" that India is a significant exception to the global trend toward the removal of children from the labour force and the establishment of compulsory, universal primary school education, as many countries of Africa like Zambia, Ghana, Ivory Coast, Libya, Zambia, Zimbabwe, with income levels lower than India, have done better in these matters. This shows the reason that has caused the problem of child labour to persist here is really not dearth of resources, but lack of real zeal. Let this not continue. Let us all put our head and efforts together and assist the child for is good and greater good of the country.

Notes and Questions

1. *An Intractable Problem?* India has more child workers than any other country in the world. Why is the problem of child labor so intractable in India? The Court opines that the massive poverty makes it impractical to totally outlaw the practice, despite numerous constitutional provisions designed to protect children. The government apparently lacks the political will to enforce even the existing laws. Trade unions have not taken up the issue. Desperately poor unemployed and underpaid parents rely on the income from their children to subsist. Politically powerful employers are able to bribe corrupt

inspectors or contract the work out so that it is performed at home rather than on industrial premises. They prefer children precisely because of their youthful vulnerability:

> One reason employers prefer child labor is that the children don't join unions and agitate! Children are obedient. Any type of work can be extracted from the children. . . . Adults will be conscious of hours of work, but children will work until the employer releases them. And they are nimble. They can do some work better than adults.

Quoted in MYRON WEINER, THE CHILD AND THE STATE IN INDIA 45–46 (1991). Journalist Asha Krishnakumar writes that a multi-dimensional approach to the problem is needed:

> Alongside the effort to enforce the law an integrated effort—provision of universal and compulsory primary education, measures to increase wages for adults, alternative employment sources for the families and an improvement in the working conditions for adults—is needed ***.

Asha Krishnakumar, *Children Still at Work, available at* http://www.frontlineonnet.com/fl1709/17090400.htm.

2. *Bonded Child Labor.* In Weiner's study of the problem of child labor in India, the secretary of labor in Uttar Pradesh explained how children become bonded laborers:

> Suppose I borrowed one hundred rupees some years ago from a landlord in the village. Then I work for the landlord to repay the debt. I get some payment as livelihood, and the rest of the work is for repaying the loan. And if I die before paying off the debt, then my children or grandchildren must work for the landlord! Often children are sent as bonded laborers to pay off the loan. If we enforce these laws on bonded labor and child labor, there is bound to be some class conflict.

Weiner, *supra* at 55. According to Human Rights Watch, approximately 15 million children are bonded laborers in India. *See* THE SMALL HANDS OF SLAVERY: BONDED CHILD LABOR IN INDIA (1996), *available at* http://www.hrw.org/reports/1996/India3.htm.

3. *The Dilemma of Consumer Advocacy.* A national and international campaign against child labor in the fireworks and matchstick industries in Sivakasi brought substantial attention to the issue. Local schools and newspapers urged consumers not to use fireworks in festivities, causing a dramatic drop in sales. As a result of the pressure, employers made some effort to improve working conditions and have begun to arrange schooling for young workers. However, the loss of revenue and consequent cuts in production put many adults, as well as children, out of work. Fireworks manufacturers and their employees staged protests against the NGOs orchestrating the boycott.

What lessons should be learned from these developments? For more information, *see* the Web site of the South Asian Coalition on Child Servitude, http://www.saccsweb.org.in/diwali_campaign.php3.

4. *Children in Prison.* India's impoverished children are also victimized by the legal system. In *Sheela Barse v. Union of India*, AIR (1986) 3 S.C.C. 632, the Court urged the government to address the tragic plight of destitute children held in jails for "safe custody:"

> It is a matter of regret that despite statutory provisions and frequent exhortations by social scientists, there are still a large number of children in different jails in the country as is now evident from the reports of the survey made by the

District Judges pursuant to our order dated April 15, 1986. Even where children are accused of offenses, they must not be kept in jails. It is no answer on the part of the State to say that it has not got enough number of remand homes or observation homes ***.*** We would therefore like once again to impress upon the State Governments that they must set up necessary remand homes and observation homes where children accused of an offense can be lodged pending investigation and trial.***

*** [T]he State Governments must set up Juvenile Courts, one in each district, and there must be a special cadre of magistrates who must be suitably trained for dealing with cases against children ***.***

[W]e would suggest that instead of each State having its own Children's Act different in procedure and content from the Children's Act in other States, it would be desirable if the Central Government initiates Parliamentary Legislation on the subject, so that there is complete uniformity in regard to the various provisions relating to children in the entire territory of the country.*** Moreover, it is not enough merely to have legislation on the subject, but it is equally, if not more, important to ensure that such legislation is implemented *** and justification for non-implementation is not pleaded on [the] ground of lack of finances on the part of the State. The greatest recompense which the State can get for expenditure on children is the building up of a powerful human resource ready to take its place in the forward march of the nation.***

JAIN v. STATE OF KARNATAKA

AIR 1992 S.C.C. 1858

KULDIP SINGH, J.:—The Karnataka State Legislature, with the object of eliminating the practice of collecting [a] capitation fee for admitting students into educational institutions, enacted the Karnataka Educational Institutions (Prohibition of Capitation Fee) Act, 1984 (the Act).***

Purporting to regulate the tuition fee to be charged by the Private Medical Colleges in the State, the Karnataka Government issued a notification [under which] the candidates admitted against "Government seats" are to pay Rs, 2,000/—per year as tuition fee. The Karnataka students (other than those admitted against "Government seats") are to be charged tuition fee not exceeding Rs. 25,000/—per annum. The third category is of "Indian students from outside Karnataka," from whom tuition fee not exceeding Rs. 60,000/—per annum is permitted to be charged.

2. Miss Mohini Jain a resident of Meerut was informed by the Management of Sri Siddharatha Medical College, Agalokote, Tumkur in the State of Karnataka that she could be admitted to the MBBS course in the session commencing February/March, 1991. According to the management she was asked to deposit Rs. 60,000/—as the tuition fee for the first year and furnish a bank guarantee in respect of the fee for the remaining years of the MBBS course. The petitioner's father informed the management that it was beyond his means to pay the exhorbitant annual fee of Rs. 60,000/—and as a consequence she was denied admission to the Medical College.***

3. In this petition under Art. 32 of the Constitution of India Miss Mohini Jain has challenged the notification of the Karnataka Government permitting the Private Medical Colleges in the State of Karnataka to charge exhorbitant tuition fees from the students other than those admitted to the "Government seats."

4. Mr. Santosh Hegde learned counsel appearing for the medical college respondent No. 3 has contended that the students from whom [a] higher tuition fee is charged belong to a different class. According to him those who are admitted to the "Government seats" are meritorious and the remaining non-meritorious. He states that classification of candidates into those who possess merit and those who do not possess merit is a valid classification and as such the college management is within its right to charge more fee from those who do not possess merit. He further states that the object sought to be achieved by the said classification is to collect money to meet the expenses incurred by the college in providing medical education to the students. [T]he Private Medical Colleges in the State of Karnataka do not receive any financial aid from either the Central or the State Government.***

5. [T]he following points arise for our consideration in this writ petition:

(1) Is there a 'right to education' guaranteed to the people of India under the Constitution? If so, does the concept of 'capitation fee' infract the same?

(2) Whether the charging of [a] capitation fee in consideration of admissions to educational institutions is arbitrary, unfair, unjust and as such violates the equality clause contained in Art. 14 of the Constitution?***

6. In order to appreciate the first point posed by us it is necessary to refer to various provisions of the constitution of India. The preamble promises to secure to all citizens of India "justice, social, economic and political" "liberty of thought, expression, belief, faith and worship." It further provides "equality of status and of opportunity" and assures dignity of the individual. [The Court sets forth Arts. 21, 38, 39(a) and (f), 41 and 45 of the constitution.] ***

7. It is no doubt correct that "right to education" as such has not been guaranteed as fundamental right under Part III of the Constitution but [under the Directive Principles] the framers of the Constitution made it obligatory for the State to provide education for its citizens.

8. The preamble promises to secure justice "social, economic and political" for the citizens. A peculiar feature of the Indian Constitution is that it combines social and economic rights along with political and justiciable legal rights. The preamble embodies the goal which the State has to achieve in order to establish social justice and to make the masses free in the positive sense. The securing of social justice has been specifically enjoined an object of the State under Art. 38 of the Constitution.***

The objectives flowing from the preamble cannot be achieved and shall remain on paper unless the people in this country are educated.***

9. The directive principles which are fundamental in the governance of the country cannot be isolated from the fundamental rights guaranteed under Part III. These principles have to be read into the fundamental rights. Both are supplementary to each other. The State is under a constitutional mandate to create conditions in which the fundamental rights guaranteed to the individuals under Part III could be enjoyed by

all. Without making "right to education" under Art. 41 of the Constitution a reality the fundamental rights under Chapter III shall remain beyond the reach of [the] large majority which is illiterate.

10. This Court has interpreted Art. 21 of the Constitution of India to include the right to live with human dignity and all that goes along with it ***:

> [T]he question which arises is whether the right to life is limited only to protection of limb or faculty or does it go further and embrace something more. We think that the right to life includes the right to live with human dignity and all that goes along with it, namely the bare necessaries of life such as adequate nutrition, clothing and shelter and facilities for reading, writing and expressing oneself in diverse forms, freely moving about and mixing and commingling with fellow human beings. Of course the magnitude and content of the components of this right would depend upon the extent of the economic development of the country, but it must, in any view of the matter, include the right to the basic necessities of life and also the right to carry on such functions and activities as constitute the bare minimum expression of the human-self.***

12. "Right to life" is the compendious expression for all those rights which the Courts must enforce because they are basic to the dignified enjoyment of life. It extends to the full range of conduct which the individual is free to pursue. The right to education flows directly from [the] right to life. The right to life under Art. 21 and the dignity of an individual cannot be assured unless it is accompanied by the right to education. The State Government is under an obligation to endeavour to provide educational facilities at all levels to its citizens.

13. The fundamental rights guaranteed under Part III of the Constitution of India including the right to freedom of speech and expression and other rights under Art. 19 cannot be appreciated and fully enjoyed unless a citizen is educated and is conscious of his individualistic dignity.

14. The "right to education," therefore, is concomitant to the fundamental rights enshrined under Part III of the Constitution. The State is under a constitutional mandate to provide educational institutions at all levels for the benefit of the citizens.*** Opportunity to acquire education cannot be confined to the richer section of the society. Increasing demand for medical education has led to the opening of [a] large number of medical colleges by private persons, groups and trusts with the permission and recognition of State Governments. The Karnataka State has permitted the opening of several new medical colleges under various private bodies and organisations. These institutions are charging [a] capitation fee as a consideration for admission. Capitation fee is nothing but a price for selling education. The concept of "teaching shops" is contrary to the constitutional scheme and is wholly abhorrent to the Indian culture and heritage.***

17. We hold that every citizen has a 'right to education' under the Constitution. The State is under an obligation to establish educational institutions to enable the citizens to enjoy the said right. The State may discharge its obligation through State-owned or State-recognised educational institutions. When the State Government grants recognition to the private educational institutions it creates an agency to fulfill its obligation under the Constitution. The students are given admission to the educational institutions—whether State-owned or State-recognised—in recognition of their 'right to edu-

cation' under the Constitution. Charging [a] capitation fee in consideration of admission to educational institutions, is a patent denial of a citizen's right to education under the Constitution.

18. Indian civilisation recognises education as one of the pious obligations of the human society. To establish and administer educational institutions is considered a religious and charitable object. Education in India has never been a commodity for sale. Looking at the economic front, even forty-five years after achieving independence, thirty per cent of the population is living below [the] poverty line and the bulk of the remaining population is struggling for existence under poverty conditions. The preamble promises and the directive principles are a mandate to the State to eradicate poverty so that the poor of this country can enjoy the right to life guaranteed under the Constitution. The State action or inaction which defeats the constitutional mandate is per se arbitrary and cannot be sustained. Capitation fee makes the availability of education beyond the reach of the poor. The State action in permitting [a] capitation fee to be charged by State-recognised educational institutions is wholly arbitrary and as such violative of Art. 14 of the Constitution of India [guaranteeing equality].***

The capitation fee brings to the fore a clear class bias. It enable[s] the rich to take admission whereas the poor has to withdraw due to financial inability. A poor student with better merit cannot get admission because he has no money whereas the rich can purchase the admission. Such a treatment is patently unreasonable, unfair and unjust.***

28. [Karnataka State] fixes Rs. 2000 per annum as the tuition fee for candidates admitted to the seats in Government medical colleges and for the candidates admitted against "Government seats" in private medical colleges. All these seats are filled purely on the merit of the candidates. The seats other than the "Government seats" which are to be filled from outside Karnataka the management has been given free hand where the criteria of merit is not applicable and those who can afford to pay Rs. 60000 per annum are considered at the discretion of the management. Whatever name one may give to this type of extraction of money in the name of medical education it is nothing but the capitation fee. If the State Government fixes Rs. 2000 per annum as the tuition fee in government colleges and for "Government seats" in private medical colleges then it is State responsibility to see that any private college which has been set up with Government permission and is being run with Government recognition is prohibited from charging more than Rs. 2000 from any student who may be resident of any part of India.***

31. Although we have struck down the capitation fee and allowed the writ petition to that extent, we are not inclined to grant any relief regarding admission to the petitioner. She was not admitted to the college on merit ***.

Notes and Questions

1. *Subsequent Developments.* Following the decision in *Mohini Jain*, the Governor of Tamil Nadu promulgated an Ordinance to prohibit the collection of capitation fees. In *Unni Krishnan v. State of Andhra Pradesh*, 1993 SOL Case No. 051, the Court was asked to reconsider its decision in *Jain* by private educational institutions claiming that implementation of the ruling would put them out of business. The Court reaffirmed its holding that the right to education "is implicit in and flows from the right to life," *id.* at ¶ 42. The Court turned to the directives to define the parameters of the right, adding that it is guaranteed to citizens up to age fourteen. "The fact that [the] right to education

occurs in as many as three Articles in Part IV *viz.*, Articles 41, 45 and 46 shows the importance attached to it by the founding fathers." *Id.* Noting that Article 45 calls for free and compulsory education for all children to the age of fourteen within ten years of the adoption of the constitution, the Court asked rhetorically, "Does not the passage of 44 years—more than four times the period stipulated in Article 45—convert the obligation created by the Article into an enforceable right?" *Id.* at ¶ 45. The Court pointed out that Article 45 contained no limitations based on the economic capacity of the state.

Regrettably, the Court revised its earlier ruling on the right of private institutions to charge fees beyond those charged by government schools, reasoning that the state could not be the sole provider of education. It emphasized, however, that "when the State permits a private body [to provide education] it is its duty to ensure that no one gets an admission or an advantage on account of economic power to the detriment of a more meritorious candidate," *id.* at ¶ 52(b), and directed the state governments to regulate fees and admission standards accordingly. *Id.* at ¶ 70. Critics argue that the Court has essentially allowed the privatization of education in India.

2.   *New Fundamental Rights and Duties.* Nearly a decade later, in May 2002, the Indian Parliament passed the 93rd Amendment to the Constitution making the right to education a fundamental right for all children between ages six and 14. Critics of the amendment asserted that there were already ample constitutional provisions and judicial decisions upholding the right to education, and that what is needed is the allocation of resources to make this right a reality. Moreover, children up to the age of six are not included, and the amendment makes no provision for the quality of the education that the state must provide. Thus, advocates fear the state will coerce children to attend overcrowded, poorly equipped schools staffed by unqualified teachers. Supporters noted that now the right is expressly judicially enforceable. As Parliament considered the amendment, thousands of ordinary people demonstrated in the Indian capital, Delhi, demanding equitable, quality schooling for all.

Article 21A provides that: "The State shall provide free and compulsory education to all children of the age of six to fourteen years in such manner as the State may, by law determine." Article 45 was amended to read: "The State shall endeavor to provide early childhood care and education for all children until they complete the age of six years." Article 51A seeks to compel parents to send their children to school by including it as a Fundamental Duty: "The parent or the guardian is to provide opportunities for education to his child or as the case may be, ward between the age of six and fourteen years."

Are these amendments consistent with *Unni Krishnan* and *Jain?* Do they represent a net gain for the right to education for India's children? India is home to the largest number of illiterates in the world. Given the level of poverty and child labor in India, however, was it advisable to establish a parental duty to send children to school as a constitutional matter? Should poor parents who are unable to send their children to school be prosecuted? Is there a danger that the government will use Article 51A to shirk its responsibility to impart free and compulsory education? Are the amendments consistent with India's obligations under the ICESCR, to which it is a party?

3.   *Compare Nigerian Decision on Directive Principles and Education.* In *Archbishop Anthony Olubunmi v. the Attorney General of Lagos State*, [1981] INCLR 218, a Nigerian High Court considered the relationship between directive principles and fundamental rights in the

context of education. Pursuant to the Nigerian Constitution's directive to the state to provide equal and adequate educational opportunities to all children, the government of Lagos State decided that all primary and secondary education would be provided free of charge by the state, abolishing private schools. The plaintiffs challenged this decision as a violation of the fundamental right of free expression. The Court agreed that school is a "medium for the dissemination of information and opinions" protected by Article 36 of the Constitution. Citing two U.S. Supreme Court cases, *Meyer v. Nebraska*, 262 U.S. 390 (1923) and *Pierce v. Society of Sisters*, 268 U.S. 510 (1925), the Court ruled that,

> it will be an infringement of the fundamental rights of the parents to restrict them to a particular type of school to which to send their children for dissemination of ideas, and also it will be an infringement of the fundamental right of the children to confine them to particular institutions [in] which they can receive such ideas.

How does this decision compare to the Indian Supreme Court's rulings in *Jain* and *Unni Krishnan?* Does the subordination of directive principles to fundamental rights simultaneously subordinate the goal of equality?

C. NEOLIBERALISM AND THE LIMITS OF JUDICIAL INTERVENTION: TAKING OFF THE MASK?

While the Indian Supreme Court has intervened on behalf of marginalized groups in many instances of palpable abuse of their rights, it has been unwilling to challenge the state when its vision of economic development threatens life, land and sustainable livelihoods. Since independence, millions of Indians have been pauperized in the name of modernity and progress, a process exacerbated by the Indian government's recent embrace of globalization and neoliberal market-oriented policies. The Court has notably failed to protect vulnerable groups from the consequences of neoliberal development strategies or environmental protection programs that scapegoat the poor in the name of broad social goals. In the face of challenges to such government policies, courts often invoke the principle of judicial deference to the political branches. Two examples follow: the displacement of millions by massive hydro-electric projects, and the assault on workers and slum-dwellers under the rubric of environmental protection.

THE NARMADA RIVER VALLEY DAM PROJECT

In October 2000 the Indian Supreme Court authorized the governments of the states of Gujarat and Madhya Pradesh to resume construction of the Sardar Sarovar dam, one of the world's most controversial dam projects. It is the largest of 3,200 dams to be built on the 1,300-km (800-mile) Narmada River and its tributaries in western India. After nearly seven years of deliberation, the Court rejected a petition filed by the Narmada Bachao Andolan (Save the Narmada Movement or NBA), which sought to enjoin the further raising of the height of the dam. *See Narmada Bachao Andolan v. Union of India*, 10 SCC 664 (2000), *available at* http://www.narmada.org/sardar-sarovar/sc.ruling/index.html#judgements. To date the dam has submerged hundreds of villages and displaced tens of thousands of people, largely indigenous Adivasis and poor farmers. Thousands more face the threat of submergence of their houses, fields, crops, livestock and schools every monsoon season. In addition to those directly displaced by the flood waters, several hundred thousand people are threatened with loss of their livelihoods by construction of irrigation canals, housing for workers, the desiccation of the river downstream of the dam and a wildlife reserve planned to compensate for the ecosystems to be flooded.

Originally financed by the World Bank, the institution was pressured by a powerful peoples' movement led by the NBA to withdraw its support in 1993. The project is now being largely financed by state governments and private loans. The Court conditioned continued construction of the dam on the provision of alternative land to people threatened by flooding. According to the Court, resettlement and rehabilitation must be completed six months prior to raising the water level of the dam. Since the decision, the dam height has been raised by five meters every year. Not only has the government failed to provide adequate rehabilitation, making these increases illegal, but police have raided communities where villagers have resisted displacement, forcibly evicting families after demolishing their homes and destroying stored food grains.

In response to this dire situation, by letter dated July 29, 2003, the United Nations High Commissioner for Human Rights warned Prime Minister Vajpayee that India was in violation of several human rights instruments to which it is a party. The letter, excerpted below, was signed by the Special Rapporteurs on Housing, Indigenous Peoples, and Health:

The current action indicates a potential violation of, *inter alia*, the following rights:

The right to adequate housing and in particular the right to be free from forced evictions: In this respect, we refer to the General Comment No. 4 (1991) of the UN Committee on Economic, Social and Cultural Rights, that expressly states that "forced evictions are *prima facie* incompatible with the provisions of the Covenant and can only be carried out under specific circumstances."*** Displacement of the Adivasis will inevitably occur during the monsoon season if the dam remains at the current height. To allow this to happen without proper and adequate rehabilitation is in contravention of this internationally protected right.

The right of indigenous peoples to self-determination and to their traditional systems of sustenance: ILO Convention No. 169 on Indigenous and Tribal Peoples deals with, among other aspects, the right of indigenous peoples to maintain their traditional systems, to possession of land and territories traditionally occupied by indigenous peoples and the recognition of their cultural, social and religious values. The displacement of Adivasis from the lands which they have occupied from many generations is a violation of this legal standard.

The right to the highest attainable standard of health: *** The right to health also extends to the underlying determinants of health, such as access to safe and potable water and adequate sanitation, as well as healthy occupational and environmental conditions. Displacement without appropriate rehabilitation, including access to adequate housing, water, sanitation, medical and other services, represents a serious health risk to those displaced.

The current action also raises a number of related human rights concerns. These include:

The need to redress development-induced displacement losses: An Adivasi farmer in the Narmada valley whose land faced submergence said: "the forest is our moneylender and banker. From its teak and bamboo we build our houses. From its riches we are able to make our baskets and cots . . . from its trees we get our medicines." Rehabilitation following development-induced displacement will need to recognize, and compensate, these losses. A consequence of non-recognition of these losses would be impoverishment, and place the human rights of the displaced population at peril.

The need to respect certain minimum core obligations: There are concerns that are being persistently raised about the violation of minimum core obligations, including legal security of tenure, access to drinking water and irrigation facilities at the rehabilitation sites, and the affordability of housing and shelter. It is protest and pressure from the displaced that is seen to have resulted in the provision of some basic facilities.

The adherence to minimum core obligations is necessary to ensure that the lives of the project-affected do not fall below the standard delineated by the instruments to which the Indian state is a party.***

This letter is our attempt to constructively dialogue with your office on this matter, and to offer our services and advice in resolution of this crisis situation. The decision to raise the water and flood the Adivasis' land is of great concern to us and to the international community. Two of us have raised issues related to human rights and the Sardar Sarovar Project in our reports to the Commission on Human Rights (see the report of the Special Rapporteur on adequate housing, U.N. Doc. E/CN.4/2001/51, para. 81 and the report of the Special Rapporteur on indigenous people, U.N. Doc. E/CN.4/2003/90, paras. 44–52) and in previous communications. Since that time the human rights situation in the Narmada Valley has worsened. We are thus compelled to write this letter to demonstrate our collective concern.***

The Indian government claims that the $5 billion-plus Sardar Sarovar project will supply much-needed water and electricity for development of the drought-prone region. However, opponents say the Sardar Sarovar dam won't adequately address the water crisis in Gujarat. They point to the first dam built on the Narmada in 1990, the Bargi dam in Madhya Pradesh, which cost 10 times more than was budgeted and submerged three times more land than engineers projected. A hundred and fourteen thousand people from 162 villages were displaced, with no resettlement or compensation. The dam irrigates only as much land as it submerged—5 percent of the land its planners claimed it would irrigate. Most importantly, while the rural poor pay the price for a dam, it is the urban rich who benefit, with the majority of rural households still lacking electricity and access to safe drinking water.

Weeks after the Supreme Court decision, the World Commission on Dams (WCD) issued a study calling into question the sacrifices being demanded of vulnerable groups in the name of development. A diverse group set up by the World Bank and the World Conservation Union, the WCD documented the fact that the benefits of dams go largely to the rich; that many dams fall short of their targets; and that of the 40–80 million people displaced worldwide by dam building, few have been adequately compensated. *See* DAMS AND DEVELOPMENT: A NEW FRAMEWORK FOR DECISION-MAKING, REPORT OF THE WORLD COMMISSION ON DAMS xxxi, *available at* http://www.dams.org/report/.

Stressing the need to focus on renewable energy, recycling, better irrigation, and reducing water losses, the WCD study found that dam building inevitably produced an adverse impact on the ecosystem, which in turn has had serious and lasting effects on the lives, livelihoods and health of affected communities. The recommendations of the group emphasized the need to ensure a transparent decision-making process involving negotiations among "key stakeholders." *Id.* at xxviii.

Commission member and NBA leader Medha Patkar penned a partial dissent, challenging the WCD's uncritical embrace of the ideology of developmentalism and prescription of formal procedural equality to remedy the powerlessness of vulnerable groups facing catastrophic development projects. Observing that "the problems of dams are a symptom of the larger failure of the unjust and destructive dominant development model," Patkar warned that merely providing due process would not place the poor and dispossessed on equal footing with powerful pro-dam institutions like the World Bank or the Indian State: "Even with rights recognized, risk assessed and stakeholders identified, existing iniquitous power relations would too easily allow developers to dominate and distort" an inclusive, transparent process of decision-making. *Id.* at 321. Pointing to the wider context in which the role of the state is diminishing in light of the globalization of private capital and free trade, Patkar argued that priority should be given to basic needs: "Communities, especially those who live on and seek livelihood from their natural resource base, such as forest produce gatherers, farmers or fisherpeople, should have the first right to planning, development and management of those resources." *Id.* at 322.

Notwithstanding the Supreme Court judgment, the struggle of the peoples of the Narmada River valley continues daily, led by the Narmada Bachao Andolan, a national coalition of environmental and human rights activists, scientists, academics, and project-affected people, working to ensure that displaced people are relocated and adequately compensated. For information, *see* the Web site of the Friends of River Narmada, an international coalition of organizations and individuals working in solidarity with the NBA and other grassroots struggles in India, *at* http://www.narmada.org.

M.C. MEHTA v. UNION OF INDIA

AIR (1986) 2 S.C.C. 176

P.N. BHAGWATI, C.J.—Writ Petition No. 12739 of 1985 which has been brought by way of public interest litigation raises some seminal questions concerning the true scope and ambit of Articles 21 and 32 of the constitution, the principles and norms for determining the liability of large enterprises engaged in manufacture and sale of hazardous products, the basis on which damages in case of such liability should be quantified and whether such large enterprises should be allowed to continue to function in thickly populated areas and if they are permitted so to function, what measures must be taken for the purpose of reducing to a minimum the hazard to the workmen and the community living in the neighborhood. These questions which have been raised by the petitioner are questions of the greatest importance particularly since, following upon the leakage of MIC gas from the Union Carbide Plant in Bhopal, lawyers, judges and jurists are considerably exercised as to what controls, whether by way of relocation or by way of installation of adequate safety devices, need to be imposed on corporations employing hazardous technology and producing toxic or dangerous substances.***

2. Delhi Cloth Mills Ltd. is a public limited company having its registered office in Delhi. It runs an enterprise called Shriram Foods and Fertilizer Industries [hereafter "Shriram"] and this enterprise has several units engaged in the manufacture of caustic soda, chlorine, hydrochloric acid, [and other toxic chemicals]. These various units are all set up in a single complex situated in approximately 76 acres and they are surrounded by thickly populated colonies such as Punjabi Bagh, West Patel Nagar, Karampura, Ashok Vihar, Tri Nagar and Shastri Nagar and within a radius of 3 kilometres from this complex there is a population of approximately 2,000,000. We are concerned in this order only with the caustic chlorine plant. This plant was commissioned in the year 1949 and it has a strength of about 263 employees including executives, supervisors, staff and workers. It appears that until the Bhopal tragedy, no one, neither the management of Shriram Foods *** nor the government seemed to have bothered at all about the hazardous character of the caustic chlorine plant. [T]he Bhopal disaster shook off the lethargy of everyone and triggered off a new wave of consciousness ***.***

4. [O]n December 4, 1985 a major leakage of oleum gas took place from one of the units of Shriram and this leakage affected a large number of persons, both amongst the workmen and the public, and, according to the petitioner, an advocate practicing in the Tis Hazari Courts died on account of inhalation of oleum gas. The leakage resulted from the bursting of the tank containing oleum gas as a result of the collapse of the structure on which it was mounted and it created a scare amongst the people residing in that area. Hardly had the people got out of the shock of this disaster when, within two days, another leakage, though this time a minor one, took place as a result of escape of oleum gas from the joints of a pipe. The immediate response of the Delhi Administration to these two leakages was the making of an order *** directing and requiring Shriram within two days from the date of issue of the order to cease carrying on the occupation of manufacturing and processing hazardous and lethal chemicals *** and within 7 days to remove such chemicals and gases from the said place ***. We had earlier appointed a team of experts to visit the caustic chlorine plant of Shriram [who] reported to us [that] two one hundred MT tanks for storage of chlorine which constituted a major element of hazard or risk had been emptied.***

5. Pursuant to the liberty given by us, the petitioner appointed an Expert Committee [which] visited the caustic chlorine plant and submitted a report to this Court in which it pointed out various inadequacies in the plant and expressed the opinion that it was not possible to eliminate hazard to the public so long as the plant remained at the present location.

6. Since there were conflicting opinions put forward before us in regard to the question whether the caustic chlorine plant should be allowed to be restarted without any real hazard or risk to the workmen and the public at large, we thought it desirable to appoint an independent team of experts to assist us in this task.***

7. This Committee of Experts *** made a report to the court setting out 14 recommendations which in its opinion were required to be complied with by the management in order to minimize the hazards due to possible chlorine leak.***

10. It is necessary at this stage to point out that whilst these proceedings were going on before the court, an order *** was issued by the Inspector of Factories, Delhi ***. The order *** prohibited Shriram from using the caustic chlorine and sulphuric acid

plants till adequate safety measures are adopted and imminent danger to human life is eliminated. Soon thereafter *** the Assistant Commissioner (Factories) directed Shriram to stop industrial use of the premises at which the chlorine caustic plant is located. The result is that unless these two orders—one dated December 7, 1985 and the other dated December 24, 1985—are vacated or suspended, Shriram cannot be allowed to restart the caustic chlorine plant.

11. We may first consider what has been said by the various Expert Committees in regard to the relocation of the caustic chlorine plant. All the Expert Committees are unanimous in their view that by adopting proper and adequate safety measures the element of risk to the workmen and the public can only be minimized but it cannot be totally eliminated. [T]he general consensus of opinion of all the Expert Committees is that relocation of the caustic chlorine plant is the only long-term solution if hazard to the community is to be completely eliminated. We have therefore decided to hear arguments on the question as to whether the caustic chlorine plant should be directed to be shifted and relocated at a place where there will be no hazard to the community and if so, within what time frame.*** But the immediate question which we have to consider is whether the caustic chlorine plant of Shriram should be allowed to be reopened and if so, subject to what conditions, keeping in mind constantly that the operation of the caustic chlorine plant does involve a certain amount of hazard or risk to the community.***

The question which therefore requires to be considered is whether all the recommendations made in the reports of [the Expert Committees] in regard to the caustic chlorine plant have been carried out by the management of Shriram and if so, whether Shriram should be allowed to restart the caustic chlorine plant. [The inspection showed that] barring the construction of a shed on the space where filled cylinders are to be kept, which construction is expected to be complete by March 15, 1986, all the recommendations made in the [Expert Committee Reports] have been complied with by the management of Shriram.***

14. The question is whether in view of [this] fact *** the caustic chlorine plant of Shriram should be allowed to be restarted. The petitioner who appeared in person submitted vehemently and passionately that the Court should not permit the caustic chlorine plant to be restarted because there was always an element of hazard or risk to the community in its operation. He urged that chlorine is a dangerous gas and even if the utmost care is taken the possibility of its accidental leakage cannot be ruled out and it would therefore be imprudent to run the risk of allowing the caustic chlorine plant to be restarted. Learned counsel appearing on behalf of [labor unions] submitted that if the caustic chlorine plant was not allowed to be restarted about 4000 workmen would be thrown out of employment.*** The learned Additional Solicitor-General appearing on behalf of the Union of India and the Delhi Administration stated before us that his clients were not withdrawing their objection to the reopening of the caustic chlorine plant but if the court was satisfied that there was no real risk or hazard to the community *** strict conditions should be imposed with a view to ensuring the safety of the workmen and the people in the vicinity.***

20. We have therefore decided to permit Shriram to restart its power plant as also plants for manufacture of caustic chlorine ***. But we are laying down certain conditions which shall be strictly and scrupulously followed by Shriram and if at any time it

is found that any one or more of these conditions are violated, the permission granted by us will be liable to be withdrawn. We formulate these conditions as follows:

(1) Since it is clear from the affidavits and the reports of the various Expert Committees that the management of Shriram was negligent in the operation and maintenance of the caustic chlorine plant *** it is necessary that an Expert Committee should be appointed by us which will monitor the operation and maintenance of the plant and equipment ***. [T]his Expert Committee will inspect the caustic chlorine plant of Shriram at least once in a fortnight ***. This examination may involve a thorough check and experimentation at [the] site with a view to determining how far the safety measures adopted by the management are adequate to deal with a possible situation.*** Shriram will, within 3 days from today, deposit a sum of Rs 30,000 in this Court to meet the traveling, boarding and lodging expenses of the members of the Expert Committee.

(2) One operator should be designated as personally responsible for each safety device or measure and the head of the caustic chlorine division should be made individually responsible for the efficient operation of such safety device or measure. If at any time during examination by the Expert Committee or inspection by the Inspectorate it is found that any safety device or measure is inoperative or is not properly functioning, the head of the caustic chlorine plant as well as the operator in charge of such safety device or measure shall be held personally responsible. Their duty shall be not merely to report non-functioning or malfunctioning of any safety device or measure to the higher authority but to see that the operation of the entire plant is immediately shut down, the safety device is urgently replenished and the plant does not restart functioning until such replenishment is completed.

(3) The Chief Inspector of factories [a government official] or any Senior Inspector duly nominated by him, who has necessary expertise in inspection of chemical factories, will inspect the caustic chlorine plant at least once in a week by paying a surprise visit without any previous intimation and examine whether the recommendations *** are being complied with.***

(4) The Central Board will also depute a senior Inspector to visit the caustic chlorine plant *** at least once in a week without any prior notice to the management.***

(5) The management of Shriram will obtain an undertaking from the chairman and Managing Director of the Delhi Cloth Mills Ltd. which is the owner of the various units of Shriram as also from the officer or officers who are in actual management of the caustic chlorine plant that in case there is any escape of chlorine gas resulting in death or injury to the workmen or to the people living in the vicinity, they will be personally responsible for payment of compensation for such death or injury and such undertakings shall be filed in court within one week from today.

(6) There shall be a Committee of three representatives of [the labor unions] to look after the safety arrangements in the caustic chlorine plant. The func-

tion of this committee will be to ensure that all safety measures are strictly observed and there is no non-functioning or malfunctioning of the safety devices and instruments and for this purpose, they will be entitled to visit any section or department of the plant during any shift and ask for any relevant information from the management.***

(7) There shall be placed in each department or section of the caustic chlorine plant as also at the gate of the premises a detailed chart in English and Hindi stating the effects of chlorine gas on the human body and informing the workmen and the people as to what immediate treatment should be taken in case they are affected by leakage of chlorine gas.

(8) Every worker in the caustic chlorine plant should be properly trained and instructed in regard to the functioning of the specific plant and equipment in which he is working and he should also be educated and informed as to what precautions should be taken to control and contain such leakage. The most effective way of giving such training and instruction would be through audio-visual programs to be specially prepared by the management *** and refresher courses should therefore be conducted at least once in 6 weeks with mock trials.

(9) Loud speakers shall be installed all around the factory premises for giving timely warning and adequate instructions to the people residing in the vicinity in case of leakage of chlorine gas.

(10) The management shall maintain proper vigilance with a view to ensuring that workers working in the caustic chlorine plant wear helmets, gas masks or safety belts as the case may be while working in the hazardous departments or sections of the plant and regular medical check-up of the workers shall be carried out by the management in order to ensure that the workers are in good health.

(11) The management of Shriram will deposit in this Court a sum of Rs 20 lachs[4] as and by way of security for payment of compensation claims made by or on behalf of the victims of oleum gas, if and to the extent to which such compensation claims are held to be well founded.***

21. We have formulated these conditions with a view to ensuring continuous compliance with the recommendations of [the Expert Committees] and strict observance of safety standards and procedures, so that the possibility of hazard or risk to the workmen and the community is almost reduced to nil. We would like to point out that the caustic chlorine plant of Shriram is not the only plant which is carrying on a hazardous industry. There are many other plants in Delhi which are employing hazardous technology or are engaged in manufacture of hazardous goods and if proper and adequate precautions are not taken, they too are likely to endanger the life and health of the community. We would therefore suggest that a High Powered Authority should be set up by the government of India in consultation with the Central Board for overseeing functioning of hazardous industries with a view to ensuring that there are no defects or deficiencies in the design, structure or quality of their plant and machinery, there is no negligence in maintenance and operation of the plant and equipment, and necessary

---

4   One lach = 100,000.—Eds.

safety devices and instruments are installed and are in operation and adequate safety standards and procedures are strictly followed.*** We cannot possibly adopt a policy of not having any chemical or other hazardous industries merely because they pose hazard or risk to the community. If such a policy were adopted, it would mean the end of all progress and development. Such industries, even if hazardous, have to be set up since they are essential for economic development and advancement of well-being of the people. We can only hope to reduce the element of hazard or risk to the community by taking all necessary steps for locating such industries in a manner which would pose [the] least risk of danger to the community and maximizing safety requirements in such industries. We would therefore like to impress upon the Government of India to evolve a national policy for location of chemical and other hazardous industries in areas where population is scarce and there is little hazard or risk to the community, and when hazardous industries are located in such areas, every care must be taken to see that large human habitation does not grow around them. There should preferably be a green belt of 1 to 5 km. width around such hazardous industries.

22. There is also one other matter to which we should like to draw the attention of the Government of India. We have noticed that in the past few years there is an increasing trend in the number of cases based on environmental pollution and ecological destruction coming up before the courts. Many such cases concerning the material basis of livlihood of millions of poor people are reaching this Court by way of public interest litigation. In most of these cases there is need of neutral scientific expertise as an essential input to inform judicial decision making. These cases require expertise at a high level of scientific and technical sophistication.*** We would in the circumstances urge upon the government of India to set up an Ecological Sciences Research Group consisting of independent, professionally competent experts in different branches of science and technology, who would act as an information bank for the court and the government departments and generate new information according to the particular requirements of the court or the concerned government department. We would also suggest to the government of India that since cases involving issues of environmental pollution, ecological destruction and conflicts over natural resources are increasingly coming up for adjudication and these cases involve assessment and evolution of scientific and technical data, it might be desirable to set up environment courts on the regional basis with one professional Judge and two experts drawn from the Ecological Sciences Research Group keeping in view the nature of the case and the expertise required for is adjudication. There would of course be a right of appeal to this court from the decision of the Environment Court.

Notes and Questions

1. *Subsequent History.* In 1996, the Supreme Court ordered Shriram and 167 other named companies to cease their operations in the city of Delhi, pursuant to a comprehensive "Master Plan" for the city enacted by the Indian Parliament. (1996) SCC 2231. Under the Plan, which came into force in August 1990, no hazardous or noxious industries are permitted to operate in Delhi. Such companies were given the option of relocating their operations to other designated areas within the region, and the Delhi administration was to begin "shifting" any non-conforming enterprises out of the city within three years. By 1996, no action had been taken to implement the Plan.

Following the ruling, Shriram relocated to Rajpura in Punjab, and was renamed Shriram Industrial Enterprises Ltd. The impact of the closure and relocation on the workforce was devastating, resulting in unemployment of an estimated 50,000 workers, weakening of trade unions and lower wages for the remaining workers. While the Court's decision required the industries to grant the workmen continuity of employment under the same terms and conditions at the new site, and to compensate the workers for the move, it failed to provide for administrative oversight of the relocations to ensure that the compensation was actually paid to the workers. There was also no prior determination of the number of workers employed in the different plants covered by its order. Many workers were forcibly retired with minimal compensation; others, designated as "contract workers," were paid nothing. Workers who relocated "were forced to leave the slums where they had been living for years and settle in remote and undeveloped places, which were worse than their old slums." Anagha Mohan, *The Closure of Polluting Industries Leave Workers in the Lurch*, LABOUR FILE, *available at* http://www.labourfile.org/labour-file/Labour%202001/Spl_Rep.htm. Some workers committed suicide. *Id.*

Critics of the Master Plan argue that the cost to workers' livelihood was too dear. In reaching its decision, the Court noted that Delhi has been designated the fourth most polluted city in the world by the World Health Organization, and cited findings by the National Environmental Engineering Research Institute (Neeri) that industrial pollution contributes 30 percent of the air-borne pollutants, and is responsible for much of the discharge of pollutants into the Yamuna River. Neeri data also show, however, that vehicular traffic is the major contributor to air pollution, while the municipality itself directly discharges sewage into the river. (1996) SCC 2231 at ¶ 8.

Should regulating these sources of pollution have been given priority in achieving the Plan's objective of promoting "balanced and harmonious development" in the national capital, rather than a solution that had such a disruptive impact on the lives of the most vulnerable sectors of society? Does the Court's decision reflect undue influence by the "green lobby [which] is largely middle class and elitist," as some critics suggest?

Historian and political scientist Awadhendra Sharan notes that New Delhi has been the subject of "purification" campaigns in the past, efforts targeting its desperately poor residents:

> This is not Delhi's first cleansing. Congestion, ventilation, drainage, conservancy and concerns about noxious trades are to be found from the mid-nineteenth century onwards. Sanitation through slum clearance and pushing out of *gwalas* (milkmen) from the city in 'sanitary interests' prefigure contemporary concerns, though with the important difference that colonial urban planning was underwritten by the imperative of maintaining racial distinction. Interestingly, though not surprisingly, colonial planning too was justified as being in the public interest.***
>
> [E]ven as the discourse on urban environment moved away from being conducted under the aegis of a colonial police state to the arena of democratic politics, there has been a persistent strain of anti-poor bias and the rhetoric of social justice has failed to secure either dignity of life or a clean environment for a majority of the city's inhabitants.

Awadhendra Sharan, *Claims on Cleanliness: Environment and Justice in Contemporary Delhi*, *in* SARAI READER 2002: THE CITIES OF EVERYDAY LIFE, at 33, *available at* http://www.sarai.net/journal/reader2.html.

Do institutional obstacles inhibit the competence of courts to balance competing interests and provide solutions to complex environmental problems that (1) rely upon technical, conflicting, and ever-changing scientific data for their evaluation; and (2) implicate not only the welfare of the "general public" but disproportionately affect the most vulnerable segments of the public? Sharan points out a potential blind spot in the Directive Principles approach to environmental issues:

> The effect of the 'democratization' of the environment issue and its greater public presence *** has paradoxically served to cloud the varied interests at stake.*** There is little acknowledgement that 'the environment' in the singular splits up into many 'environments' and following from there, spaces need to be created for community actors to define and prioritize environmental risks for themselves.*** The environmental remedies offered by Delhi's bureaucratic and political elite [have] operated on the principle that it is these poor communities, especially those who are squatters on public land, who are a primary source of pollution.

Id. at 35. Despite the Supreme Court's order a large number of polluting plants have evaded closure by bribing inspection officials or restarting their operations under different names.

2. *Evolving Environmental Jurisprudence.* The Indian Constitution was amended in 1976 to add Directive Principles incorporating duties to protect the environment. Article 48A provides: "The State shall endeavor to protect and improve the environment and safeguard the forests and wildlife of the country." Article 51A(g) imposes a similar responsibility upon citizens. In a series of cases, the Court has established that the right to a "wholesome" environment is grounded in Article 21's guarantee of the right to life. *See Charan Lal Sahu v. Union of India*, AIR 1990 S.C. 1480; *Subhash Kumar v. State of Bihar*, AIR 1991 S.C. 420 (holding that the "right to life guaranteed by article 21 includes the right of enjoyment of pollution-free water and air for full enjoyment of life."). In these decisions, the Court has relied on evolving standards of international environmental law.

3. *The Call for an Environmental Court.* The Court in the instant case recommended the establishment of regional environmental courts, comprised of both judges and technical experts. Does the Court appear to be recognizing its own limited competence to deal with such issues? Could such courts avoid the dangers discussed in Note 1, *supra?* Could such an innovation be structured so as to enable input from all of the relevant "publics"? Compare the Land and Environmental Court of New South Wales in Australia, established in 1980. The Court is composed of four judges and nine technical and conciliation assessors. It is equal in rank and status to the Supreme Court, and its jurisdiction combines appeal, judicial review, and enforcement functions. The Court handles primarily public law matters, enforcing the rights of citizens against government.

THE BHOPAL DISASTER: THE "HIROSHIMA OF THE CHEMICAL INDUSTRY"

On December 2, 1984, the people of Bhopal, India suffered what has been called "the most tragic industrial disaster in history." *In re Union Carbide Corp. Gas Plant Disaster at Bhopal, India in December 1984*, 634 F. Supp. 842, 842 (S.D.N.Y. 1986). The release of a highly toxic gas caused the immediate death of at least 2,000 people, the subsequent death of up to 20,000 people from gas-related injuries, and chronic physical, mental, and psychiatric trauma in 200,000 to 2 million more people. As with the atomic bomb catastrophes, the human suffering continues today. People exposed to the gas nearly twenty years ago continue to die from its effects; babies born to gas-affected mothers suffer serious birth defects; and people of all ages suffer from severe anxiety, depression and suicide, among many other trauma-induced conditions.

According to the International Campaign for Justice in Bhopal:

10–15 people still die every month from toxic exposure-related illnesses.*** Babies are being born with deformities and chromosomal aberrations. Teenage girls complain of the most abnormal menstrual disorders including absence of periods even at the age of 18, and young women reach early menopause and often develop cervical cancer. Close to 150,000 people are ravaged by a wide range of multi-systemic disorders including respiratory, neurological, gynecological and mental. Unable to keep their jobs most people have been reduced to daily wage work.

Fact Sheet, International Campaign for Justice in Bhopal, *available at* http://www.prithvi-solutions.com/AIDConf2003/Bhopal_FAQs.htm (last visited Apr. 30, 2004).

From 1979 until 1984, Union Carbide India Limited (UCIL), a subsidiary of U.S.-based Union Carbide Corporation (UCC), manufactured pesticides using a highly toxic gas, methyl isocynanate (MIC). In a series of cost-saving measures, UCIL drastically reduced the work and maintenance crews of the MIC unit; by November 1984, the most important safety systems were either closed down or not functioning, despite a safety audit in May 1982 that found 30 major hazards at the plant, 11 in the dangerous MIC units. While Union Carbide took remedial measures to improve safety at its West Virginia plant in response to U.S. government fines, no such steps were taken in India.

In the early morning hours of December 3, 1984, warm water leaked into a tank containing MIC. MIC should have been kept close to zero degrees centigrade, but the refrigeration unit had been shut off by company officials to save on electricity bills. Thus, the leaking of additional warm water into the tank, full of MIC at already ambient temperature, triggered a chemical reaction and the release of the lethal gas. While people in the surrounding community slept, poison clouds from the Union Carbide factory enveloped an arc of over 25 square miles.

Survivors describe a horrific scene of chaos and death: residents nearest the plant ran helter-skelter, blinded and suffocating from the odorless, colorless gas, children shrieking behind them. Neither the residents, nor the employees themselves, had been informed of the toxic nature of the substances being produced at the factory, or of what steps they should take in the event of an accident. Union Carbide officials did not respond to emergency calls. Efforts to treat the victims were—and continue to be—impeded by the refusal of corporate officials to disclose the composition of the toxic mixture, citing "trade secrets."

The legal response to the tragedy was grossly inadequate, prolonging and compounding the suffering of the community. The government of India filed a complaint against UCC in U.S.district court on behalf of the victims on April 8, 1985. *In re Union Carbide Corp., supra.* The court, however, dismissed the suit on grounds of *forum non-conveniens*, declaring that India, and not the United States, was the more appropriate forum.

Subsequently, India passed the Bhopal Gas Leak Disaster (Processing of Claims) Act, which allowed the Indian government: to consolidate the claims of the Bhopal victims; to be the exclusive agent of the claims of all of Union Carbide's victims; and to be named as a defendant in the suit for negligently monitoring the industry. This created the legal anomaly of having the Indian government on both sides of the litigation. In 1986, India sued UCC in the Bhopal District Court. Tragically, but predictably, the government secretly negotiated a settlement reducing the original claim of $3 billion to only $470 million. Neither the victims nor their representatives were consulted. Awards to victims and their heirs ranged from $580 to $2,200—not even enough to compensate them for medical expenses and funeral costs.

The judicial process failed to punish UCIL and UCC or provide adequate redress to the Bhopal victims. Nevertheless, the massive public protests and international outcry spurred a number of positive legal developments, including the enactment of environmental protection legislation in India, and the evolution of groundbreaking legal norms. The Declaration on the Right to Development; the Rio Declaration on Environment and Development; the Draft Declaration on Human Rights and the Environment; the Rio Declaration on Environment and Development; and the emerging right to a safe environment, were all influenced by the Bhopal disaster and its aftermath. *See* Neil A.F. Popovic, *In Pursuit of Environmental Human Rights: Commentary on the Draft Declaration of Principles on Human Rights and the Environment*, 27 COLUM. HUM. RTS. L. REV. 487, 490 (1996).

Notwithstanding such apparent normative progress, however, the situation of the Bhopal community remains dire. While the plant was permanently shut down, it was never effectively de-contaminated. Ground water remains polluted and Dow Chemical, which acquired Union Carbide in February of 2001, claims that it has no legal responsibility to clean up the site. Unemployment among survivors, struggling to cope with debilitating illnesses, remains high. The Bhopal Gas Victim Women's Union, a women's cooperative that has managed to prosper despite government indifference, is one of the few sources of alternative employment. The group's leader, the charismatic Rashida Bee, has been awarded the prestigious 2004 Goldman Prize for grassroots "heroes of the environment." *See* http://www.bhopal.org.

For further reading, *see* Surya Deva, *Human Rights Violations by Multinational Corporations and International Law: Where From Here?*, 19 CONN. J. INT'L L. 1 (2003); Phillip I. Blumberg, *Asserting Human Rights Against Multinational Corporations Under United States Law: Conceptual and Procedural Problems*, 50 AM. J. COMP. L. 493 (2002); Jeanhee Hong, *Refugees of the 21st Century: Environmental Injustice*, 10 CORNELL J.L. & PUB. POL'Y 323, 323 (2001); Clarence J. Dias, *Human Rights, Environment and Development in South Asia: The Importance of International Human Rights Law*, 6 ILSA J. INT'L & COMP. L. 415 (2000); Sudhir K. Chopra, *Multinational Corporations in the Aftermath of Bhopal: the Need for a New Comprehensive Global Regime for Transnational Corporate Activity*, 29 VAL. U. L. REV. 235 (1994); and Tony Dias, *The Disaster and its Aftermath: The Hiroshima of the Chemical Industry*, *available at* www.arbld.unimelb.edu.au/envjust/papers/allpapers/dias/home.htm.

For information on ongoing activities on behalf of Bhopal survivors, *see* the Web sites of the International Campaign for Justice in Bhopal, *at* www.bhopal.net and Greenpeace Justice for Bhopal, *at* http://www.greenpeaceusa.org/bin/view.fpl/5224/cms_category/51.html.

CHAPTER EIGHT

SOUTH AFRICA: THE BILL OF RIGHTS APPROACH

A. THE HISTORICAL CONTEXT

DAISY M. JENKINS, FROM APARTHEID TO MAJORITY RULE: A GLIMPSE INTO SOUTH AFRICA'S JOURNEY TOWARDS DEMOCRACY

13 Ariz. J. Int'l & Comp. L. 463, 463–472 (1996)

I. INTRODUCTION ***

On May 10, 1994, Nelson Rolihlahla Mandela was inaugurated as South Africa's first black president.***

The road to Nelson Mandela's historic presidency was paved by the efforts of black and white leaders who, for three years, painfully negotiated to create a new, color-blind South African constitution. After eight decades of struggle in South Africa, led by the African National Congress, "the day finally arrived when all South Africans, black and white, cast their ballots equally in a national election for a government of their choice." For the first time in their history, South Africans of all races, all social and economic backgrounds, will grapple with the promises and uncertainties of majority rule and con-stitutional democracy.

South Africa's new constitution marks a fundamental change in the way South Africa is governed—from a policy of racial separation and suppression to one of negotiation and conciliation. Of equal importance, for the first time ever, South Africa's new con-stitution will be shielded from the political process. A new constitutional court invested with the final say on all constitutional matters, including questions of individual rights and the validity of acts of Parliament, will replace the nation's historically all-white Parliament, which has served as supreme maker and arbiter of the law. The court will also certify a new constitution for compliance with the thirty-three constitutional prin-ciples agreed upon during negotiations.

Despite the dramatic changes brought about by the new constitution, there is still cause for much concern for the majority of South Africans, particularly black South Africans. They continue to face staggering poverty, broken communities, crushed ambi-tions, and hopelessly undemocratic institutions. If South Africa is to succeed as a rights-based, constitutional democracy, lawyers and judges must ensure that the fundamental rights of black South Africans are both well defined and protected.***

715

II. THE ERA OF APARTHEID

A. *A System of Oppression*

South Africa's comprehensive system of racial segregation, known as apartheid, was not a unique set of ideas and practices that sprang full-blown from the heads of Afrikaner nationalists. The system of domination and privilege based on race goes back to the first white settlers from the Dutch East India Company, who landed at the Cape in 1652. The Dutch introduced slavery to the Cape as a means of supplying laborers to work on the settlers' farms, as well as to work in urban trades as skilled artisans and craftsmen. Slaves were the property of their masters, who showed no mercy in the treatment of their slaves and were known to utilize the most gruesome forms of punishment. The Dutch men also cohabited with slave women and fathered the majority of children born to female slaves, who later became known as the Cape Coloreds.

From 1795 to 1834, except for a brief period from 1802 to 1805, the British occupied the Cape, displacing the Dutch; however, the British did not drastically alter the way slaves were treated. After the British abolished slavery they insisted on the technical equality of all before the law; yet, the administration of justice in the Cape essentially remained the domain of white men. The arrival of the French Huguenots and Germans fleeing religious persecution in Europe led to further growth of the white settlement in the Cape and the resulting fusion with the British resulted in the Afrikaans nation.

While the system of slavery formed the roots of apartheid, the history of modern race relations in South Africa finds its roots in the mining industry, which began when diamonds were first discovered in the Cape Province in 1867. The "rush" for gold closely followed the rush for diamonds, after gold was discovered in the Witwatersrand in the 1880s. Both discoveries resulted in the construction of cities and towns, the development of transportation links and other infrastructural developments, as large numbers of immigrants flocked to South Africa in search of their fortunes. The white mining companies first attempted a more elaborate system of segregation in the diamond mines. Under the guise of preventing diamond smuggling, the mining industry established crude compounds for single African men. The ultimate goal of both the diamond and gold mining industries was to maintain a steady supply of cheap African labor using a system of "localization." Localization, with its confined and cheap labor supply, was especially important to the gold mining industry. Unlike the price of diamonds, set by national standards, international agreements determined the price of gold, which led mining companies to heavily concentrate on controlling the costs of extracting the gold.

The mining companies quickly grasped the solution to increasing labor costs, which was South Africa's large, untapped black population. Along with the labor demands of the mining industry, white farms were also demanding more African labor to keep pace with the demands created by industrial and urban growth. Industrial and urban growth also created new opportunities for African commercial agriculture, however, which greatly increased peasant economic activity in the late 1800s and threatened to reduce the availability of labor on mines and white farms.

Concern about the impact of a reduction of black labor on the important mining industry caused the government to create a national committee, the South African Native Affairs Commission (SANAC), to formulate a national level "native" policy. Consequently, after studying the native population, the Afrikaner government (backed by SANAC's findings) enacted the Native Lands Act in 1913, which was the first attempt at legislating apartheid. The Native Lands Act apportioned South Africa's lands giving most of it, ninety-three percent, to whites, while allocating only seven percent to blacks for use as reserves. The Act also restricted blacks' access to white land by making it illegal for any African to be on European land who was not a hired servant. The Act uprooted black families from land that had been in their families for generations and forced them to sell their successful farms to white farmers and move to the "reserves."

The Native Urban Areas Act of 1923, which separated the so-called African "location" from the white town through the establishment of a separate, self-balancing, native revenue account, followed the Native Land Act. Once the Act established the separate revenue account, the state took the position that it could exclude Africans from white-funded amenities in white areas for which they had not contributed taxes. One of the harshest and most restrictive laws for blacks was the infamous Section 10(1) of the Black (Urban Areas) Consolidation Act of 1945, which made it illegal for blacks to remain in white areas for more than seventy-two hours.

In 1948, the National Party won control of the South African Parliament and embarked on its policies that created a monopoly of white political control. With a strong belief that mere segregation could not provide a permanently secure structure for white dominance, the National Party government introduced its policy of apartheid or separate development, requiring a division of political power between the people. Minister of Native Affairs Hendrick Verwoerd declared separate development as a necessary tool of white dominance which had to be done to ensure the survival of the white civilization and to retain domination in what is "his" country. Under the restrictive policy of separate development, the National Party government assigned each African group to a tribal homeland, which became their legal place of residence, [thus stripping Africans of South African citizenship].

The government implemented a network of statutes to separate the races spatially and socially. During the 1960s, Prime Minster Verwoerd ruthlessly spearheaded efforts that refined, perfected and enforced the apartheid system.

Apartheid combines the two ideological themes of white supremacy in South Africa as a means of guaranteeing racial peace and of maintaining a pure white race. The first theme was segregation as domination. Apartheid excluded blacks from freely participating in society, as a means of maintaining white rule. The second theme was segregation as trusteeship, which would allow blacks to express themselves completely within their own communities. Apartheid was, in essence, totalitarianism, in that the state utilized its authority to regulate virtually all aspects of non-whites' lives, including areas such as religion, sports, and the preservation of a particular ethnic or cultural identity. It was, furthermore, a system of institutionalized violence because apartheid's architects could only achieve success through the most repressive means of law enforcement. Apartheid inevitably culminated in state absolutism because the state entrusted its law enforcement agencies with powers that were not made subject to the rule of law and systematically disregarded the procedural directives of the due process of law.

A key issue for the current government is to gain the capacity through the democratic process to redress the gross disparities that exist because of apartheid. Today, many millions of black South Africans live in poverty and desperation as a direct result of apartheid, including over seven million homeless people. Ultimately, "apartheid denies black people in South Africa the 'right to be,' the 'right to belong,' and the 'right to have.'¹ The denial of blacks' "right to be" resulted from white political power at a particular point in South African history which decreed what blacks must be. Apartheid denied black people the "right to belong" to the communities of their choice through segregation by skin color. Apartheid denied black people the "right to have" by eliminating their access to jobs, education, voting and other opportunities available to whites.***

Notes and Questions

1. *The International Legal Status of the Apartheid Regime.* Apartheid was declared a "crime against humanity" by the U.N. General Assembly. G.A. Res. 2202, U.N. GAOR, 21st Sess., at 2, U.N. Doc. A/RES/2202/(XXI) (1966). *See also* International Convention on the Suppression and Punishment of the Crime of Apartheid, U.N. GAOR 3d Comm., 28th Sess., Annex, Agenda Item 53, at 3, U.N. Doc. A/RES/3068 (1973); *Relationship between the United Nations and South Africa*, U.N. GAOR, 29th Sess., Agenda Item 3, U.N. Doc. GA/RES/3207 (1974) (rejecting credentials of South African representative); *Situation in South Africa*, U.N. GAOR Special Pol. Comm., 13th Sess., 2435th plen. met., Agenda Item 53, at 7–9, U.N. Doc. A/RES/3411/G (1975) (declaring South African government "illegitimate and has no right to represent the people of South Africa;" also recognizing liberation movement as "authentic representative of overwhelming majority of South African people").

2. *Resistance to Colonialism and Apartheid.* The negotiations to end white minority rule in South Africa culminated a long and valiant history of struggle for freedom. For centuries, the Zulus, Besotho, BaPedi, Mpondomise, Batlaping and other peoples fought gallantly against the British and Dutch colonialists to preserve their land and independence. In 1879, at the Battle of Isandhlwana, King Cetshwayo's regiments—armed with spears—defeated the powerful British army, marking the highest point in a 200-year protracted struggle. However, despite the great heroism and skill of the African people, by 1880 European settlers had established their rule over the whole of South Africa. The Bambata Rebellion of the Zulu people in 1906, brutally suppressed, was the last war of resistance to be fought in the old style.

The African National Congress (ANC) was founded in 1912 with the stated objective of uniting all the African people in the region to continue the anti-colonial struggle. During its early years, the ANC utilized primarily methods of agitation and propaganda. Later, more militant forms of struggle were employed, such as strikes, boycotts, civil disobedience and mass demonstrations.

A turning point in the liberation movement was marked in 1946. In that year, a strike called by the African Mineworkers Union was supported by over 100,000 workers. Intensified mass action was accompanied by growing unity among Africans and solidarity with both the peoples of Indian ancestry and the so-called "Coloreds." The election of the fascist National Party in 1948 accelerated the opposition to the racist regime. The ANC and its allies launched the Campaign for the Defiance of Unjust Laws; called nationwide general strikes for political demands; led women's resistance to the pass laws and a national bus boycott. This mass upsurge culminated in the historic Congress of the People in 1955, which adopted the Freedom Charter. To the people's demands for a democratic, non-racial society, the regime responded by arresting their leaders and charging them with "high treason" in a trial lasting from 1956 to 1961.

Meanwhile, parallel developments were taking place in the countryside, where peasants armed themselves to resist government attempts to replace their traditional leaders with puppets in the "Bantu Authorities." The most intense upsurge was among the Pondo, who developed a vast popular movement. By March 1960, thousands of peasants had established a clandestine government in the mountains, including people's courts, which evaded detection for many years.

In 1961, as the English and Afrikaans-speaking elite prepared to form a white-dominated Republic, the army was mobilized on the largest scale since the Second World War to put down a nationwide strike called in protest. In March 1960, the police attacked a peaceful demonstration at Sharpeville, which had been called by the Pan Africanist Congress (PAC), a group that split off from the ANC in 1959. Sixty-nine unarmed people were massacred, 187 wounded. The ANC and PAC were banned and forced underground. With legal forms of struggle no longer possible, the African National Congress placed armed struggle on the agenda.

On December 16, 1961, the first explosions of *Umkhonto We Sizwe* (popularly known as "M-K") heralded a new era in the liberation struggle. To the oppressed masses of South Africa, the M-K Manifesto declared:

> The time comes in the life of any nation when there remain only two choices: submit or fight. That time has come to South Africa. We shall not submit and we have no choice but to hit back by all means within our power in defense of our people, our future and our freedom.

The early acts of sabotage, committed with unsophisticated "Molotov cocktails" and petrol bombs, were directed at government installations connected with the policy of apartheid, such as the offices of *Die Nataller*, official organ of the Nationalist Party in Natal. The regime responded by enacting the notorious General Laws Amendment Act (known as the Sabotage Act), empowering the South African courts to impose a death sentence in cases of sabotage. Under the 90-day Detention Law, torture and detention incommunicado were legalized.

In 1963, the headquarters of M-K's High Command was discovered; Nelson Mandela, Walter Sisulu, Govan Mbeki and other leaders were arrested and sentenced to life imprisonment. Nevertheless, the acts of sabotage continued, and recruits were secretly sent out of the country to undergo military training. Inside the country, the growing militancy of the youth led to a nationwide student movement against being educated in Afrikaans, a language spoken only in South Africa, which they deemed a language of oppression. The shocking 1977 massacres in Soweto and other Black townships of peacefully demonstrating schoolchildren—many shot in the back—convinced a new generation of activists that the regime would answer all just demands with ruthless military might. Thousands of youth fled the country to join the armed resistance.

See Jeanne M. Woods, *Five Years of Armed Struggle in South Africa*, United Nations Centre Against Apartheid: Notes and Documents, 84–19588 (1984).

In 1983, the regime adopted a new constitution, attempting to divide the resistance movement, while at the same time further entrenching apartheid. While granting "Asians" and "Coloreds" nominal voting rights in their "own" houses of Parliament, the constitution denationalized the African people, 70 percent of the population. In response, a mass grassroots coalition, the United Democratic Front, was formed, uniting all of the oppressed groups in sustained political action for democracy. In July 1985, President P.W. Botha declared a state of emergency, subjecting thousands of activists to arrest, detention, and torture. A key feature of the decree was the barring of all media from the emergency areas.

See Jeanne M. Woods, *Legal Responsibilities of States With Respect to Apartheid*, 8–9 UNITED NATIONS CENTRE AGAINST APARTHEID, Seminar on the Legal Status of the Apartheid Regime, Lagos, Nigeria, Aug. 13–16, 1984.

At this time the international anti-apartheid movement, composed of governments, NGOs and individuals worldwide, gained momentum. In the United States, grassroots solidarity efforts had taken many forms, including lobbying for sanctions in Congress and the United Nations, boycotts, demonstrations, petition campaigns and the divestment movement. By the mid-1980s, the Free South Africa Movement had taken hold of the public imagination:

> The Free South Africa Movement ("FSAM") in the United States, an NGO-led movement, grew *** out of the combination of three developments: (1) a stalemate between pro- and anti-apartheid groups in the United Nations; (2) a mass anti-apartheid mobilization in South Africa; and (3) a grassroots opposition to Reagan's Southern Africa policy.*** FSAM targeted Western political, economic, and cultural relations with South Africa. FSAM's aim was a complete isolation of South Africa until it abandoned apartheid, and its methods were radical and eclectic. FSAM members educated the public, lobbied governments, public institutions, and corporate leaders, built coalitions with other civic organization and pressure groups, organized demonstrations, and raised funds for victims of apartheid.

Ibrahim J. Gassama, *Reaffirming Faith in the Dignity of Each Human Being: The United Nations, NGOs and Apartheid*, 19 FORDHAM INT'L L.J. 1464, 1500 (1996).

In 1986, Congress enacted legislation imposing comprehensive sanctions against South Africa, over the veto of President Ronald Reagan. The combination of militant struggle in the country, and economic pressure from Western allies, eventually eliminated the ability of the regime to govern. In 1990, Nelson Mandela and the other members of the ANC leadership were released from prison, and the process of negotiations for the transition to majority rule began.

For further reading *see* TIMOTHY SISK, THE DEMOCRATIZATION OF SOUTH AFRICA (1995); DONALD DENOON & BALAM NYEKO, SOUTHERN AFRICA SINCE 1800 (1984); RICHARD LEONARD, SOUTH AFRICA AT WAR (1983); Makau wa Mutua, *Hope and Despair for a New South Africa: The Limits of Rights Discourse*, 10 HARV. HUM. RTS. J. 63 (1997).

3. *Accountability for the Gross Human Rights Violations of Apartheid.* The Convention for a Democratic South Africa (CODESA), held in late 1991, was the first round of formal negotiations on the transition from white minority rule. These talks broke down after about six months, and multi-party negotiations resumed in May 1993. The issue of accountability for past abuses was extremely contentious, with the regime demanding a blanket amnesty. The Interim Constitution that was ultimately agreed to stipulated in its Preamble the need for "national reconciliation," which would be achieved through a process of granting amenesty to perpetrators of politically motivated crimes, to be

defined by Parliament. The Promotion of National Unity and Reconciliation Act 34 of 1995 created the Truth and Reconciliation Commission, whose mandate and philosophy are critiqued in the following article.

JEANNE M. WOODS, RECONCILING RECONCILIATION

3 UCLA J. INT'L L. & FOR. AFF. 81, 90–95, 101–109, 119–120 (1998).

*** II. THE SOUTH AFRICAN EXPERIENCE

In order to fill the moral lacunae left by the choice of amnesty, reconciliation was asserted as the normative goal of the South African transition to democracy. South Africa's quest for reconciliation commenced formally with the multi-party negotiation process known as CODESA. This process produced a mandate to grant amnesty to politically-motivated human rights violators. Pursuant to this mandate, the South African Parliament created the quasi-judicial Truth and Reconciliation Commission (Commission) with the power to grant amnesty to those violators who provide "full disclosure" of the facts relating to their crimes.***

The South African Constitutional Court endorsed the negotiated amnesty as a "deliberate choice [to] prefer[] understanding over vengeance, reparation over retaliation.***" *[Azanian Peoples Org. (AZAPO) v. President of the Republic of South Africa,* 1996 (4) SALR 671, 685 (CC).] The Court distinguished South Africa's negotiated amnesty provisions from self-amnesties, noting that former victims were well represented at the bargaining table. Blinded by the liberal-positivist veil of ignorance, however, the Court failed to recognize that the victims had only their moral rights to put on the table, while the violators of those rights held the reigns of the state's political, economic, and military power. Unlike power, wealth, or property, an inchoate claim of rights is meaningless at the bargaining table.***

The African National Congress' (ANC) stance on prosecutions changed dramatically during the course of negotiations. In 1992, the organization stressed the need for accountability. During this period, leaders of the liberation movement insisted that while "[i]ndividual responsibility invoked through a Nuremberg Tribunal-type trial may appear to be inconsistent with the process of negotiations," such an approach was "necessary if *** grievous wrongs committed in the name of the law against the vast majority of the population" were to be deterred.

As negotiations progressed, however, the movement's "[i]deology [was] replaced by pragmatism." Moving from the torture chambers to the chambers of Parliament, the ANC abandoned rights discourse in favor of state-centric apology.***

The white minority in South Africa would not agree to share power without a constitutionally enshrined guarantee that they would be free from the threats of prosecution and expropriation for their heinous crimes. More importantly, the international community effectively supported many of the demands of the regime. Playing its peace-keeping role, the UN proposed a plan for amnesty. The *quid pro quo* for the ANC's agreement to share power was an implied promise from pro-apartheid forces not to overthrow the new government.***

III. TRUTH AS A REMEDY

*** Truth commissions have the capacity to confer some critical values upon the new state, such as a degree of transparency, typically lacking in undemocratic societies. Openness is essential to the ability of a people to exercise their right to self-determination. But where, as in South Africa, the crimes are widespread, public, and committed against the overwhelming majority of the population, the people know what happened to them. What the truth commission really offers is official acknowledgment of the truth.

Arguably, the "official truth" provides a measure of psychological comfort to victims and their families. Supporters of the process make broad claims about the remedial efficacy of truth-telling: truth is essential to individual dignity; it is a "precondition to healing" and "an affirmation that one's pain is real and worthy of attention." It is doubtful, however, that this limited process can, indeed, restore the dignity of the victims.

[The author recounts the testimony of a witness at the Truth Commission hearings in Mpumalanga, South Africa, describing the search for his son's body in the aftermath of the Soweto Massacre:]

"The mortuary looked like we were in a butchery," he recalls incredulously. His voice begins to rise to an hysterical pitch. "There were three rooms full of blood with bodies lying in it. The shelves, the drawers, were full of bodies. We had to walk over bodies—charred bodies—they looked like blocks of wood.

Will truth give meaning to these harrowing tales of unimaginable and unspeakable terror?***

IV. TRUTH AS JUSTICE

Retributive justice in South Africa was effectively repudiated by the constitutive decision to accept the power-sharing paradigm. It would have been anomalous for the new state to have criminally prosecuted its own Deputy President [F.W. DeKlerk] for past misdeeds. Restorative justice is unachievable given the Commission's mandate and resources. Thus, the truth commission paradigm presupposes that disclosure of the truth is itself a form of justice.

South African leaders promised that the truth commission would provide the moral basis for justice; they did not promise justice itself. The absence of a requirement of remorse, however, negates the claim of creating a moral foundation for future justice. It is doubtful that a negotiated truth-telling without acknowledgment of wrongdoing can achieve normative status for protected rights or provide future protection for the victims. Absent such acknowledgment, no negative stigma attaches to admissions of gross violations committed against the people in the name of the state, and the victims are left with no moral condemnation of the crimes committed against them. It is doubtful that any residual moral force is an adequate substitute for the force of law in firmly establishing normative principles and deterring future abuse.***

[T]he moral value of the process is further constrained by the veil of ignorance behind which the quest for truth must be conducted. The veil requires that the dichotomy between law and morality be preserved, promoting the liberal-positivist virtues of moral relativism and neutrality. Thus, the requisite formalities—the appropriate ritual—must be observed. Part of that ritual is making a clean break from the past. Members of the former South African ruling elite claim that "in South Africa there was a limited democracy [and that] building a new, more inclusive democracy and protecting that democracy necessitates wiping clean the slate of the past."

The battle for the truth is apparent within the Commission itself as members' personal interpretations of events are revealed through their questioning. The relationship between truth and perception presents another dilemma. Apartheid, from the standpoint of the regime, was a mistake—a benevolent experiment that did not work out—not a crime.

Supporters of the process assert that "one of the main goals of the whole endeavor is to educate the nation." However, when half of the TRC investigators are former police intelligence officers, and when, in the process, "dubious testimony frequently goes unchallenged," it appears that, ultimately, truth will be (or has already been) negotiated.***

VI. THE SOUTH AFRICAN SOCIAL CONTRACT

Amnesty is the essence of the new South African social contract. As with any other social contract, consent is presumed. The presumption of consent renders the resulting milieu, in which forgiveness prevails over justice, morally just. Simultaneously, however, it creates a fundamental flaw in the organic fabric of the new society, a flaw which, like the protection of slavery enshrined in the U.S. Constitution, will constitute a "malignancy that [will] tempt government and individuals alike to a constantly recurring fall from democratic innocence."

The political settlement through which future elites negotiated the transition to democracy precluded the people from freely choosing their own path to reconciliation; they did not decide democratically whether that path would be forged through impunity or through retributive measures. That decision was made for them; forgiveness was mandated by the new state. Indeed, the South African Constitutional Court declared that in light of South Africa's history, *"the State *** is best equipped to determine what measures may be most conducive for *** reconciliation."* This is, at best, an extremely condescending claim that essentially denies the people's right to self-determination. It is precisely that history of violent subjugation that requires that the people themselves make important constitutive choices.

As constitutive policy, the normative value of forgiveness is aggressively promoted through all the organs of civil society, including the mass media, the churches, and the courts. The campaign is so pervasive as to leave the impression that the state is attempting to deprive the victims of even the moral choice of whether to forgive. It is counterintuitive to expect that a principled unity will ultimately be forged through such a process.***

IX. CONTRADICTIONS AND CONTINUITY

Amnesty places the burden of reconciliation on the victims of the atrocities. Even if individual forgiveness is morally desirable in the transition process, this does not justify a broad amnesty for systematic human rights violations. The state cannot forgive for the people.***

In the context of state-sponsored atrocities, prosecutions serve to advance the principle of equality before the law. The new social contract, however, in preferring forgiveness over justice, established a "new set of democratic hierarchical roles." As Argentinean human rights scholar Catalina Smulovitz argues, the equality principle "limit[s] the space in which actors in the conflict can negotiate and exchange political benefits."

Moreover, prosecutions may help bolster the legitimacy of the new democratic institutions by increasing public confidence in their ability to administer justice. Smulovitz adds that "[w]here transgressions were connected to the highest levels of government spheres, the criminal sentence dilutes any suspicion of continuity."

But the emphasis in South Africa *is* on continuity; the Mandela government's priority is to convince the white minority that they have nothing to fear from majority rule; that nothing will fundamentally change. Addressing the gross socio-economic disparities between black and white, Mandela explained that he wished to avoid "any dislocation to the economy."***

[T]here can be no reconciliation as long as the inherent *structural* violence—poverty, illiteracy, unemployment—remains in place. There can be no national healing without redistribution of the vast wealth of the country.***

Notes and Questions

1. *The Scope of the Commission's Inquiry.* Is the limitation of the Commission's mandate to politically motivated crimes a manifestation of the public-private dichotomy? What function does such a distinction serve? Dr. Mamphela Ramphele, a member of the Truth Commission, queried whether the scope should be "widened to include acts which violate the human rights of workers, children and women in both the public and private spheres[.] Is the personal political? Is there any bigger crime against humanity than the destruction of family life?" Mamphela Ramphele, *Fears and Hopes, in* ALEX BORAINE & JANET LEVY EDS., THE HEALING OF A NATION 33, 35 (1995). How might the process have been different if such an inquiry had been conducted?

2. *Individual Responsibility.* Does the post-Nuremberg norm of individual responsibility for state-sponsored human rights violations promote respect for these rights? Is this norm advanced through a "reconciliation" paradigm? Does the characterization of a system as a "crime against humanity" place any moral or legal limitations on the state's capacity to forgive such crimes? Could the negotiated amnesty be viewed by the Black majority as a further denial of their humanity, a statement that their suffering is negotiable? Does their view matter?

Archbishop Desmond Tutu, chair of the TRC, recently lamented the shortcomings of the Commission and urged that reparations be the priority for other countries contemplating a similar process:

> We were able to grant amnesty which was of immediate effect to perpetrators.***
> But we could not do the same with victims. That was a very great weakness. It made
> the commission appear to be perpetrator friendly rather than on the side of the
> victims. This made some relatives and victims feel as if they got nothing.

William Scholes, *Reconciliation Process Must Find its Roots with the Victims, Urges Dr. Tutu*, IRISH TIMES (May 28, 2004).

3. *State Responsibility.* Does the principle of individual responsibility obscure the structural violations inherent in oppressive systems such as colonialism and apartheid? How else could such structural violations be redressed? How should the complicity of large portions of the white population in the crimes of apartheid be addressed?

4. *Victims and Perpetrators.* The Truth Commission investigated acts by both state actors and participants of the liberation struggle. Should the moral claims of the regime be equated to the moral claims of the oppressed population? Does violence committed by the state against the people carry the same moral weight as violence committed against an oppressive state? Why or why not?

5. *The Results of the Commission's Work.* The Final Report of the TRC was issued in two parts. The first five volumes were issued on October 31, 1998. However, it was not until March 21, 2003, that the last two volumes, dealing with amnesty and reparations, were completed. *See Truth and Reconciliation Commission of South Africa Report, available at* http://www.info.gov.za/reports/2003/trc/. Approximately 1,200 amnesty petitions were granted. The TRC recommended that R2.8 billion be allocated for reparation and rehabilitation of the approximately 22,000 people it identified as victims of gross human rights violations. It also recommended a "wealth tax" on corporations found to have benefited from apartheid that would go into a victim compensation fund. The South African government rejected this tax and substituted one-time payments to victims for the multi-year payments recommended by the Commission. The government has also refused to support reparations lawsuits against corporations filed in other countries, fearing a loss of foreign investment.

6. *Corporate Reparations.* Should corporate support for apartheid be actionable? In November 2002, the Khulumani Support Group and Jubilee South Africa filed a complaint in the Federal District Court for the Eastern District of New York against seven banks and 12 international corporations from Germany, Switzerland, Britain, the United States, the Netherlands, and France. The complaint alleges that these companies were complicit in the crime against humanity by providing computers to control the movement of the Black population; providing armored vehicles used to patrol the townships; selling arms and oil in violation of United Nations-imposed embargoes; and providing funding that enabled South Africa to expand its police and security apparatus. South African President Thabo Mbeki has sharply criticized the lawsuit, citing the "promotion of national reconciliation," and warning that judgments handed down in foreign courts will not be honored in South Africa.

As the debate on corporate liability continues, one South African writer suggests that the business community as a whole profited from the racist oppression prevailing in the country, even before apartheid was installed as state policy:

> South Africa's modern economy was built historically on the denial of basic human rights to millions of black South Africans, which made them vulnerable to gross exploitation by white farmers, mine owners and business people in general over the better part of a century (and longer in the case of farming).
>
> The hovels that were home to millions of farm workers, the single-sex compounds on the mines and in the towns, the migrant labour system, the appalling wages paid to generations of black workers, the pass system that denied black people freedom of movement, the undermining of black trade unions—all these institutions and practices were in place long before the National Party

came to power in 1948 and began perfecting apartheid. And virtually all sections of business in South Africa profited out of these perverse practices.

Certainly it may be argued that by the 1970s and 1980s many sectors of industry began kicking against the rigid restrictions that apartheid imposed on their use of labour, since they now sought a more mobile and highly skilled labour force than apartheid could deliver.

But the hard-fought struggles of black workers for trade union rights during this period bear testimony to the fact that, despite their complaints against certain of apartheid's restrictions, the vast majority of businesses did not easily concede the privileges and powers that apartheid had showered upon them.

Duncan Innes, *Reparations Debate Puts Cart before Horse*, S. AFR. MAIL & GUARDIAN, Apr. 18, 2003. Do companies that did business in South Africa under the apartheid regime bear legal responsibility based on the principles articulated by the Nuremberg Tribunal? *See International Military Tribunal (Nuremberg), Judgment and Sentences*, 41 AM. J. INT'L L. 172 (1947). If no legal liability exists, do they bear moral responsibility?

B. THE CONSTITUTIONAL ENTRENCHMENT OF ECONOMIC, SOCIAL AND CULTURAL RIGHTS

After a vigorous national debate, South Africa adopted a constitution containing a unique bill of rights with an extensive panoply of socio-economic rights and duties, structurally integrated with the more traditional rights and liberties.

THE SOUTH AFRICAN BILL OF RIGHTS

36 I.L.M. 744, 745 (1997)

RIGHTS

7.　(1) This Bill of Rights is a cornerstone of democracy in South Africa. It enshrines the rights of all people in our country and affirms the democratic values of human dignity, equality and freedom.

(2) The state must respect, protect, promote, and fulfill the rights in the Bill of Rights.***

EQUALITY

9.　(1) Everyone is equal before the law and has the right to equal protection and benefit of the law.

(2) Equality includes the full and equal enjoyment of all rights and freedoms. To promote the achievement of equality, legislative and other measures designed to protect or advance persons, or categories of persons, disadvantaged by unfair discrimination may be taken.

(3) The state may not unfairly discriminate directly or indirectly against anyone on one or more grounds, including race, gender, sex, pregnancy, marital status, ethnic or social origin, color, sexual orientation, age, disability, religion, conscience, belief, culture, language, and birth.

(4) No person may unfairly discriminate directly or indirectly against anyone on one or more grounds in terms of subsection (3). National legislation must be enacted to prevent or prohibit unfair discrimination.

(5) Discrimination on one or more of the grounds listed in subsection (3) is unfair unless it is established that the discrimination is fair.

HUMAN DIGNITY

10. Everyone has inherent dignity and the right to have their dignity respected and protected.

LIFE

11. Everyone has the right to life.

FREEDOM AND SECURITY OF THE PERSON

12. (1) Everyone has the right to freedom and security of the person, which includes the right—***

> (c) to be free from all forms of violence from both public and private sources;***

(2) Everyone has the right to bodily and psychological integrity, which includes the right—

> (a) to make decisions concerning reproduction;

> (b) to security in and control over their body; and

> (c) not to be subjected to medical or scientific experiments without their informed consent.

SLAVERY, SERVITUDE AND FORCED LABOR

13. No one may be subjected to slavery, servitude or forced labor.***

CITIZENSHIP

20. No citizen may be deprived of citizenship.***

FREEDOM OF TRADE, OCCUPATION AND PROFESSION

22. Every citizen has the right to choose their trade, occupation or profession freely. The practice of a trade, occupation or profession may be regulated by law.

LABOR RELATIONS

23. (1) Everyone has the right to fair labor practices.

> (2) Every worker has the right

>> (a) to form and join a trade union;

>> (b) to participate in the activities and programs of a trade union; and

>> (c) to strike.

> (3) Every employer has the right—

(a) to form and join an employers' organization; and

(b) to participate in the activities and programs of an employers' organization.

(4) Every trade union and every employers' organization has the right—

(a) to determine its own administration, programs and activities;

(b) to organize;

(c) to bargain collectively; and

(d) to form and join a federation

(5) The provisions of the Bill of Rights do not prevent legislation recognizing union security arrangements contained in collective agreements.

ENVIRONMENT

24. Every one has the right

(a) to an environment that is not harmful to their health or well-being; and

(b) to have the environment protected, for the benefit of present and future generations, through reasonable legislative and other measures that—

(i) prevent pollution and ecological degradation;

(ii) promote conservation; and

(iii) secure ecologically sustainable development and use of natural resources while promoting justifiable economic and social development.

PROPERTY

25. (1) No one may be deprived of property except in terms of law of general application, and no law may permit arbitrary deprivation of property.

(2) Property may be expropriated only in terms of law of general application

(a) for public purposes or in the public interest; and

(b) subject to compensation, the amount, timing, and manner of payment, of which must be agreed, or decided or approved by a court.***

(4) For the purpose of this section—

(a) the public interest includes the nation's commitment to land reform, and to reforms to bring about equitable access to all South Africa's natural resources; and

(b) property is not limited to land.

(5) The state must take reasonable legislative and other measures, within its available resources, to foster conditions which enable citizens to gain access to land on an equitable basis.

(6) A person or community whose tenure of land is legally insecure as a result of past racially discriminatory laws or practices is entitled, to the extent provided by an Act of Parliament, either to tenure which is legally secure, or to comparable redress.

(7) A person or community dispossessed of property after 19 June 1913 as a result of past racially discriminatory laws or practice is entitled, to the extent provided by an Act of Parliament, either to restitution of that property, or to equitable redress.

(8) No provision of this section may impede the state from taking legislative and other measures to achieve land, water and related reform, in order to redress the results of past racial discrimination, provided that any departure from the provisions of this section is in accordance with the provisions of section 36(1).

(9) Parliament must enact the legislation referred to in subsection (6).

HOUSING

26. (1) Everyone has the right to have access to adequate housing.

(2) The state must take reasonable legislative and other measures, within available resources, to achieve the progressive realization of this right.

(3) No one may be evicted from their home, or have their home demolished, without an order of court made after considering all the relevant circumstances. No legislation may permit arbitrary evictions.

HEALTH CARE, FOOD, WATER, AND SOCIAL SECURITY

27. (1) Everyone has the right to have access to

(a) health care services, including reproductive health care;

(b) sufficient food and water; and

(c) social security, including, if they are unable to support themselves and their dependents, appropriate social assistance.

(2) The state must take reasonable legislative and other measures, within its available resources, to achieve the progressive realization of each of these rights.

(3) No one may be refused emergency medical treatment.

CHILDREN

28. (1) Every child has the right—

(a) to a name and a nationality from birth;

(b) to family care, parental care, or appropriate alternative care when removed from the family environment;

(c) to basic nutrition, shelter, basic health care services, and social services;

(d) to be protected from maltreatment, neglect, abuse, or degration;

(e) to be protected from exploitative labor practices;

(f) not to be required or permitted to perform work or provide services that—

(i) are inappropriate for a person of that child's age; or

(ii) place at risk the child's well-being, education, physical or mental health, or spiritual, moral, or social development;

    (g) not to be detained except as a measure of last resort, in which case, in addition to the rights a child enjoys under sections 12 and 35, the child may be detained only for the shortest appropriate period of time, and has the right to be—

        (i) kept separately from detained persons over the age of 18 years; and

        (ii) treated in a manner, and kept in conditions, that take account of the child's age.

    (h) to have a legal practitioner assigned to the child by the state, and at state expense, in civil proceedings affecting the child, if substantial injustice could otherwise result; and

        (i) not to be used directly in armed conflict, and to be protected in times of armed conflict.

(2) A child's best interest is of paramount importance in every matter concerning the child.

(3) In this section, "child" means a person under the age of 18 years.

EDUCATION

29. (1) Everyone has the right—

    (a) to a basic education, including adult basic education; and

    (b) to further education, which the state must take reasonable measures to make progressively available and accessible.

(2) Everyone has the right to receive education in the official language or languages of their choice in public educational institutions where that education is reasonably practicable. In order to ensure the effective access to, and implementation of, this right, the state must consider all reasonable educational alternatives *** taking into account—

    (a) equity;

    (b) practicability; and

    (c) the need to redress the results of past racially discriminatory law and practice.

(3) Everyone has the right to establish and maintain, at their own expense, independent educational institutions that—

    (a) do not discriminate on the basis of race;

    (b) are registered with the state; and

    (c) maintain standards that are not inferior to standards at comparable public educational institutions.

LANGUAGE AND CULTURE

30. Everyone has the right to use the language and to participate in the cultural life of their choice, but no one exercising these rights may do so in a manner inconsistent with any provision of the Bill of Rights.

CULTURAL, RELIGIOUS AND LINGUISTIC COMMUNITIES

31. (1) Persons belonging to a cultural, religious or linguistic community may not be denied the right, with other members of their community, to

> (a) enjoy their culture, practice their religion and use their language; and

> (b) form, join and maintain cultural, religious and linguistic associations and other organs of civil society.

> (2) This right may not be exercised in a manner inconsistent with any provision of the Bill of Rights.

Notes and Questions

1.   How does the South African Bill of Rights compare with the fundamental rights in the Indian Constitution? In what respects do they embody similar values? How are they different? To what extent does the South African social contract reflect the distinct history of the country?

2.   How do the South African formulations of economic, social and cultural rights differ from those in the International Covenant on Economic, Social and Cultural Rights? Why might the drafters of the Bill of Rights have chosen this particular terminology? For further reading, *see* Craig Scott & Phillip Alston, *Adjudicating Constitutional Priorities in a Transnational Context: A Comment on* Soobramoney's *Legacy and* Grootboom's *Promise*, 16 S. AFR. J. HUM. RTS. 206 (2000).

SOOBRAMONEY v. MINISTER OF HEALTH, KWAZULU-NATAL

1997 (12) BCLR 1696 (CC)

JUDGMENT BY: Chaskalson P,

[1] The appellant, a 41 year old unemployed man, is a diabetic who suffers from ischemic heart disease and cerebrovascular disease which caused him to have a stroke during 1996. In 1996 his kidneys also failed. Sadly his condition is irreversible and he is now in the final stages of chronic renal failure. His life could be prolonged by means of regular renal dialysis. He has sought such treatment from the renal unit of the Addington state hospital in Durban. The hospital can, however, only provide dialysis treatment to a limited number of patients. The renal unit has 20 dialysis machines available to it, and some of these machines are in poor condition. Each treatment takes four hours and a further two hours have to be allowed for the cleaning of a machine, before it can be used again for other treatment. Because of the limited facilities that are available for kidney dialysis the hospital has been unable to provide the appellant with the treatment he has requested.

[2] The reasons given by the hospital for this are set out in the respondent's answering affidavit deposed to by Doctor Saraladevi Naicker, a specialist physician and nephrologist in the field of renal medicine who has worked at Addington Hospital for 18 years and who is currently the President of the South African Renal Society. In her affidavit Dr. Naicker says that Addington Hospital does not have enough resources to provide dialysis treatment for all patients suffering from chronic renal failure. Additional dialysis machines and more trained nursing staff are required to enable it to do this, but

the hospital budget does not make provision for such expenditure. The hospital would like to have its budget increased but it has been told by the provincial health department that funds are not available for this purpose.

[3] Because of the shortage of resources the hospital follows a set policy in regard to the use of the dialysis resources. Only patients who suffer from acute renal failure, which can be treated and remedied by renal dialysis are given automatic access to renal dialysis at the hospital. Those patients who, like the appellant, suffer from chronic renal failure which is irreversible are not admitted automatically to the renal program. A set of guidelines has been drawn up and adopted to determine which applicants who have chronic renal failure will be given dialysis treatment. According to the guidelines the primary requirement for admission of such persons to the dialysis program is that the patient must be eligible for a kidney transplant. A patient who is eligible for a transplant will be provided with dialysis treatment until an organ donor is found and a kidney transplant has been completed.

[4] The guidelines provide that an applicant is not eligible for a transplant unless he or she is "[f]ree of significant vascular or cardiac disease." The medical criteria set out in the guidelines also provide that an applicant must be "Free of significant disease elsewhere e.g. ischemic heart disease, cerebrovascular disease, peripheral vascular disease, chronic liver disease, chronic lung disease." The appellant suffers from ischemic heart disease and cerebrovascular disease and he is therefore not eligible for a kidney transplant.

[5] The appellant has made arrangements to receive dialysis treatment from private hospitals and doctors, but his finances have been depleted and he avers that he is no longer able to afford such treatment. In July 1997 he made an urgent application to the Durban and Coast Local Division of the High Court for an order directing the Addington Hospital to provide him with ongoing dialysis treatment and interdicting the respondent from refusing him admission to the renal unit of the hospital. The appellant claimed that in terms of the 1996 Constitution the Addington Hospital is obliged to make dialysis treatment available to him.***

[7] *** The appellant based his claim on section 27(3) of the 1996 Constitution which provides: "No one may be refused emergency medical treatment" and section 11 which stipulates; "Everyone has the right to life."

[8] We live in a society in which there are great disparities in wealth. Millions of people are living in deplorable conditions and in great poverty. There is a high level of unemployment, inadequate social security, and many do not have access to clean water or to adequate health services. These conditions already existed when the Constitution was adopted and a commitment to address them, and to transform our society into one in which there will be human dignity, freedom and equality, lies at the heart of our new constitutional order. For as long as these conditions continue to exist that aspiration will have a hollow ring.

[9] The constitutional commitment to address these conditions is expressed in the preamble which, after giving recognition to the injustices of the past, states:

> We therefore, through our freely elected representatives, adopt this Constitution as the supreme law of the Republic so as to—

Heal the divisions of the past and establish a society based on democratic values, social justice and fundamental human rights; [and]

Improve the quality of life of all citizens and free the potential of each person.

This commitment is also reflected in various provisions of the bill of rights and in particular in sections 26 and 27 which deal with housing, health care, food, water and social security.

[10] Section 27 contains the following provisions: ***

27. Health care, food, water and social security

(1) Everyone has the right to have access to—

    (a) health care services, including reproductive health care;

    (b) sufficient food and water; and

    (c) social security, including, if they are unable to support themselves and their dependants, appropriate social assistance.

(2) The State must take reasonable legislative and other measures, within its available resources, to achieve the progressive realization of each of these rights.

(3) No one may be refused emergency medical treatment.

[11] What is apparent from these provisions is that the obligations imposed on the State by sections 26 and 27 in regard to access to housing, health care, food, water and social security are dependent upon the resources available for such purposes, and that the corresponding rights themselves are limited by reason of the lack of resources. Given this lack of resources and the significant demands on them that have already been referred to, an unqualified obligation to meet these needs would not presently be capable of being fulfilled. This is the context within which section 27(3) must be construed.

[12] The appellant urges us to hold that patients who suffer from terminal illnesses and require treatment such as renal dialysis to prolong their lives are entitled in terms of section 27(3) to be provided with such treatment by the State, and that the State is required to provide funding and resources necessary for the discharge of this obligation.

[13] The words "emergency medical treatment" may possibly be open to a broad construction which would include ongoing treatment of chronic illnesses for the purpose of prolonging life. But this is not their ordinary meaning, and if this had been the purpose which section 27(3) was intended to serve, one would have expected that to have been expressed in positive and specific terms.

[14] Counsel for the appellant argued that section 27(3) should be construed consistently with the right to life entranced in section 11 of the Constitution and that everyone requiring life-saving treatment who is unable to pay for such treatment herself or himself is entitled to have the treatment provided at a state hospital without charge.

[15] This Court has dealt with the right to life in the context of capital punishment but it has not yet been called upon to decide upon the parameters of the right to life or its relevance to the positive obligations imposed on the State under various provi-

sions of the bill of rights. Whilst the Indian jurisprudence on this subject contains valuable insights it is important to bear in mind that our Constitution is structured differently to the Indian constitution. Unlike the Indian constitution ours deals specifically in the bill of rights with certain positive obligations imposed on the State, and where it does so, it is our duty to apply the obligations as formulated in the constitution and not to draw inferences that would be inconsistent therewith.

[16] This should be done in accordance with the purposive approach to the interpretation of the Constitution which has been adopted by this court. Consistently with this approach the rights which are in issue in the present case must not be construed in isolation "but in [their] context, which includes the history and background to the adoption of the Constitution, other provisions of the Constitution itself and, in particular, the provisions of [the bill of rights] of which [they are] part."

[17] The purposive approach will often be one which calls for a generous interpretation to be given to a right to ensure that individuals secure the full protection of the bill of rights, but this is not always the case, and the context may indicate that in order to give effect to the purpose of a particular provision "a narrower or specific meaning" should be given to it.

[18] In developing his argument on the right to life counsel for the appellant relied upon a decision of a two-judge bench of the Supreme Court of India in *Paschim Banga Khet Mazdoor Smity and Others v State of West Bengal and Another*, where it was said:

> The Constitution envisages the establishment of a welfare State at the federal level as well as at the State level. In a welfare State the primary duty of the Government is to secure the welfare of the people. Providing adequate medical facilities for the people is an essential part of the obligations undertaken by the Government in a welfare State. The Government discharges this obligation by running hospitals and health centers which provide medical care to the person seeking to avail those facilities. Article 21 imposes an obligation on the State to safeguard the right to life of every person. Preservation of human life is thus of paramount importance. The Government hospitals run by the State and the medical officers employed therein are duty bound to extend medical assistance for preserving human life. Failure on the part of a Government hospital to provide timely medical treatment to a person in need of such treatment results in violation of his right to life guaranteed under Article 21.

These comments must be seen in the context of the facts of that case which are materially different to those of the present case. It was a case in which constitutional damages were claimed. The claimant had suffered serious head injuries and brain hemorrhage as a result of having fallen off a train. He was taken to various hospitals and turned away, either because the hospital did not have the necessary facilities for treatment, or on the grounds that it did not have room to accommodate him. As a result he had been obliged to secure the necessary treatment at a private hospital. It appeared from the judgment that the claimant could in fact have been accommodated in more than one of the hospitals which turned him away and that the persons responsible for that decision had been guilty of misconduct. This is precisely the sort of case which would fall within section 27(3). It is one in which emergency treatment was clearly necessary. The occurrence was sudden, the patient had no opportunity of making arrangements in advance for the treatment that was required, and there was urgency in securing the treatment in order to stabilize his condition. The treatment was available but denied.

[19] In our Constitution the right to medical treatment does not have to be inferred from the nature of the State established by the Constitution or from the right to life which it guarantees. It is dealt with directly in section 27. If section 27(3) were to be construed in accordance with the appellant's contention it would make it substantially more difficult for the state to fulfil its primary obligations under sections 27(1) and (2) to provide health care services to "everyone" within its available resources. It would also have the consequence of prioritizing the treatment of terminal illnesses over other forms of medical care and would reduce the resources available to the State for purposes such as preventative health care and medical treatment for persons suffering from illnesses or bodily infirmities which are not life threatening. In my view much clearer language than that used in section 27(3) would be required to justify such a conclusion.

[20] Section 27(3) itself is couched in negative terms—it is a right not to be refused emergency treatment. The purpose of the right seems to be to ensure that treatment be given in an emergency, and is not frustrated by reason of bureaucratic requirements or other formalities. A person who suffers a sudden catastrophe which calls for immediate medical attention, such as the injured person in *Paschim Banga Khet Mazdoor Samity v State of West Bengal,* should not be refused ambulance or other emergency services which are available and should not be turned away from a hospital which is able to provide the necessary treatment.[1] What the section requires is that remedial treatment that is necessary and available be given immediately to avert that harm.

[21] The applicant suffers form chronic renal failure. To be kept alive by dialysis he would require such treatment two to three times a week. This is not an emergency which calls for immediate remedial treatment. It is an ongoing state of affairs resulting from a deterioration of the applicant's renal function which is incurable. In my view section 27(3) does not apply to these facts.

[22] The appellant's demand to receive dialysis treatment at a state hospital must be determined in accordance with the provisions of sections 27(1) and (2) and not section 27(3). These sections entitle everyone to have access to health care services provided by the State "within its available resources."

[23] In the Court *a quo* Combrinck J held that "[i]n this case the respondent has conclusively proved that there are no funds available to provide patients such as the applicant with the necessary treatment." This finding was not disputed by the appellant, but it was argued that the State could make additional funds available to the renal clinic and that it was obliged to do so to enable the clinic to provide life saving treatment to the appellant and others suffering from chronic renal failure.

[24] At present the Department of Health in KwaZulu-Natal does not have sufficient funds to cover the cost of the services which are being provided to the public.*** There are many more patients suffering from chronic renal failure than there are dialysis machines to treat such patients. This is a nation-wide problem and resources are stretched in all renal clinics throughout the land.

[25] By using the available dialysis machines in accordance with the guidelines more patients are benefitted than would be the case if they were used to keep alive persons

---

[1]   We have only recently emerged from a system of government in which the provision of health services depended on race. On occasions seriously injured persons were refused access to ambulance services or admission to the nearest or best equipped hospital on racial grounds.

with chronic renal failure, and the outcome of the treatment is also likely to be more beneficial because it is directed to curing patients, and not simply to maintaining them in a chronically ill condition. It has not been suggested that these guidelines are unreasonable or that they were not applied fairly and rationally when the decision was taken by the Addington Hospital that the appellant did not qualify for dialysis.***

[26] Only about 30% of the patients suffering from chronic renal failure meet the guidelines for admission to the dialysis program. If everyone in the same condition as the appellant were to be admitted the carefully tailored program would collapse and no one would benefit from that.*** If all the persons in South Africa who suffer from chronic renal failure were to be provided with dialysis treatment—and many of them, as the appellant does, would require treatment three times a week—the cost of doing so would make substantial inroads into the health budget. And if this principle were to be applied to all patients claiming access to expensive medical treatment or expensive drugs, the health budget would have to be dramatically increased to the prejudice of other needs which the State has to meet.***

[29] A court will be slow to interfere with rational decisions taken in good faith by the political organs and medical authorities whose responsibility it is to deal with such matters.***

[31] One cannot but have sympathy for the appellant and his family, who face the cruel dilemma of having to impoverish themselves in order to secure the treatment that the appellant seeks in order to prolong his life. The hard and unpalatable fact is that if the appellant were a wealthy man he would be able to procure such treatment from private sources; he is not and has to look to the State to provide him with the treatment. But the State's resources are limited and the appellant does not meet the criteria for admission to the renal dialysis program. Unfortunately, this is true not only of the appellant but of many others who need access to renal dialysis units or to other health services. There are also those who need access to housing, food and water, employment opportunities, and social security. These too are aspects of the right to [human life]. The State has to manage its limited resources in order to address all these claims. There will be times when this requires it to adopt a holistic approach to the larger needs of society rather than to focus on the specific needs of particular individuals within society.***

[36] The State has a constitutional duty to comply with the obligations imposed on it by section 27 of the Constitution. It has not been shown in the present case, however, that the State's failure to provide renal dialysis facilities for all persons suffering from chronic renal failure constitutes a breach of those obligations. In the circumstances the appellant is not entitled to the relief that he seeks in these proceedings.***

[Concurring Opinion] BY Madala J.***

[40] [T]he appeal before us brings into sharp focus the dichotomy in which a changing society finds itself and in particular the problems attendant upon trying to distribute scarce resources on the one hand, and satisfying the designs of the Constitution with regard to the provision of health services on the other.***

[41] Chapter 2 of the Constitution sets out the fundamental rights to which every person is entitled and also contains provisions dealing with the manner in which the chapter is to be interpreted by the courts.***

The meaning of a right or freedom *** was to be ascertained by an analysis of the purpose of such a guarantee; it was to be understood, in other words, in the light of the interests it was meant to protect.

[T]his analysis is to be undertaken, and the purpose of the right or freedom in question is to be sought by reference *** to the language chosen to articulate the specific right or freedom, to the historical origins of the concept enshrined, and where applicable, to the meaning and purpose of the other specific rights and freedoms with which it is associated.*** The interpretation should be *** a generous rather than a legalistic one, aimed at fulfilling the purpose of the guarantee and securing for individuals the full benefit of *** protection.

[42] The constitution is forward-looking and guarantees to every citizen fundamental rights in such a manner that the ordinary person-in-the-street, who is aware of these guarantees, immediately claims them without further ado—and assumes that every right so guaranteed is available to him or her on demand. Some rights in the Constitution are the ideal and something to be strived for. They amount to a promise, in some cases, and an indication of what a democratic society aiming to salvage lost dignity, freedom and equality should embark upon. They are values which the Constitution seeks to provide, nurture and protect for a future South Africa.

[43] However, the guarantees of the Constitution are not absolute but may be limited in one way or another. In some instances, the Constitution states in so many words that the State must take reasonable legislative and other measures, within its available resources "to achieve the progressive realization of each of these rights." In its language, the Constitution accepts that it cannot solve all of our society's woes overnight, but must go on trying to resolve these problems. One of the limiting factors to the attainment of the Constitution's guarantees is that of limited or scarce resources.***

[45] The fundamental issue is whether this court, as the guardian of the Constitution, as the protector of human rights and as the upholder of democracy, should in this case require a health authority, acting through its authorised medical practitioner, to adopt a course of treatment which in the bona fide clinical and incisive judgment of the practitioner will not cure the patient but merely prolong his life for some time.***

[49] Perhaps a solution might be to embark upon a massive education campaign to inform the citizens generally about the causes of renal failure, hypertension and diabetes and the diet which persons afflicted by renal failure could resort to in order to prolong their life expectancy.

[Concurring Opinion] BY Sachs J.

[50] I am in full agreement with the eloquent, forceful and well-focused judgment of Chaskalson P and wish merely to add certain considerations which I regard as relevant.

[51] The special attention given by section 27(3) to non-refusal of emergency medical treatment relates to the particular sense of shock to our notions of human solidarity occasioned by the turning away from hospital of people battered and bleeding or of those who fall victim to sudden and unexpected collapse. It provides reassurance to all members of society that accident and emergency departments will be available to deal with the unforeseeable catastrophes which could befall any person, anywhere and at

any time. The values protected by section 27(3) would, accordingly, be undermined rather than reinforced by any unwarranted conflation of emergency and non-emergency treatment such as that argued for by the appellant.

[52] In a case such as the present which engages our compassion to the full, I feel it necessary to underline the fact that Chaskalson P's judgment, as I understand it, does not merely "toll the bell of lack of resources." In all the open and democratic societies based upon dignity, freedom and equality with which I am familiar, the rationing of access to life-prolonging resources is regarded as integral to, rather than incompatible with, a human rights approach to health care.

The inescapable fact is that if governments were unable to confer any benefit on any person unless it conferred an identical benefit on all, the only viable option would be to confer no benefit on anybody.***

[54] Health care rights by their very nature have to be considered not only in a traditional legal context structured around the ideas of human autonomy but in a new analytical framework based on the notion of human interdependence. A healthy life depends upon social interdependence: the quality of air, water, and sanitation which the State maintains for the public good; the quality of one's caring relationships, which are highly correlated to health; as well as the quality of health care and support furnished officially by medical institutions and provided informally by family, friends, and the community.***

Traditional rights analyses accordingly have to be adapted so as to take account of the special problems created by the need to provide a broad framework of constitutional principles governing the right of access to scarce resources and to adjudicate between competing rights bearers. When rights by their very nature are shared and inter-dependent, striking appropriate balances between the equally valid entitlements or expectations of a multitude of claimants should not be seen as imposing limits on those rights *** but as defining the circumstances in which the rights may most fairly and effectively be enjoyed.***

[57] However the right to life may come to be defined in South Africa, there is in reality no meaningful way in which it can constitutionally be extended to encompass the right indefinitely to evade death.*** We can, however, influence the manner in which we come to terms with our mortality. It is precisely here, where scarce artificial life-prolonging resources have to be called upon, that tragic medical choices have to be made.

[58] Courts are not the proper place to resolve the agonizing personal and medical problems that underlie these choices. Important though our review functions are, there are areas where institutional incapacity and appropriate constitutional modesty require us to be especially cautious.*** The provisions of the bill of rights should furthermore not be interpreted in a way which results in courts feeling themselves unduly pressurized by the fear of gambling with the lives of claimants into ordering hospitals to furnish the most expensive and improbable procedures, thereby diverting scarce medical resources and prejudicing the claims of others.***

[59] I can find no reason to interfere with the allocation undertaken by those better equipped than I to deal with the agonizing choices that had to be made.

Notes and Questions

1. *Soobramoney* was the Court's first pronouncement on social rights. The appellant died three days after the decision was announced. *See* P. Govender, *Family Fulfills Man's Dying Wish by Helping Kidney Patients*, DURBAN SUN. TIMES (S. Afr.), Apr. 25, 1999, *available at* http://www.suntimes.co.za/1999/04/25/news/durbanndbno3.htm (last visited Mar. 19, 2003).

2. *Interpreting the Constitutional Text.* Section 27(2) conditions the state's duty upon the "available resources." Is the determination of available resources a question of law or a question of fact? Did the Court read additional limiting language into Section 27(2) in holding that the obligation of the state was "dependent upon the resources available *for such purposes?*" Was the Court indicating that the state's duty is limited to whatever resources it had already allocated to health care? To dialysis treatment in particular? Is this interpretation effectively outcome-determinative?

3. Does the Court's definition of "emergency" imply that there must be some misconduct or improper motive for the denial of treatment in order to constitute a violation? Why was such a narrow construction deemed necessary? Why did the Court reject the claim that the positive right to health required the state to make additional resources available for dialysis treatment?

4. How did the structural differences between the South African and Indian constitutions influence the Court's opinion? How did the Court distinguish the Indian Supreme Court's decision in *Samity v. State of West Bengal,* considered in Chapter 7, *supra?* Was its emphasis on the denial of available medical treatment consistent with the Indian Court's analysis?

5. In examining the reasonableness of the guidelines imposed by the hospital administration, did the Court apply an overly deferential standard of review with regard to social rights? Is the utilitarian approach adopted by the Court consistent with a human rights perspective?

6. In his concurring opinion, Justice Sachs asserted that "the rationing of access to life-prolonging resources is *** integral to *** a human rights approach to health care." Do you agree? Does his proposed "new analytical framework" for collective rights, substituting interdependence for autonomy as its bedrock principle, adequately protect the rights of individuals? Does it matter whether the resource is an inherently scarce item, such as a human organ, or one that is merely "expensive"?

7. Did the relief sought by Mr. Soobramoney require access to a level of health care that exceeded the minimum core of the right to health as implicitly defined by the Court? Does the case suggest that the minimum core of the right to life does not require the state to provide extraordinary life-support measures that would not lead to a cure of the patient's illness?

8. Is dialysis a truly "scarce" resource in South Africa? While public dialysis facilities in South Africa are in short supply, private facilities are much more available to those who can pay, including Western tourists. The following excerpt from a Web site that assists travelers seeking dialysis, describes the personal experience of a recent tourist who could obtain private treatment:

The dialysis units that I visited accommodated just two to four patients at a time. South Africa's public medical system is under a great deal of stress; their public dialysis facilities are at or above capacity. This makes scheduling a treatment difficult. For this reason alone, the private facilities are a good alternative. The private facilities allow you to schedule treatments in advance so that you can plan activities, flights, and car rentals with confidence. Private units are also generally cheaper. The units I dialyzed at charge under $200 U.S. each treatment.

I paid for my treatment in U.S. dollars and was reimbursed by my private insurance (Medicare does not pay for dialysis outside the U.S. and Canada). However, [the private facility owner] mentioned that he would be willing to put together a package for uninsured dialysis patients traveling to South Africa. At the current exchange rate for South African Rands, dialysis would cost under $400 a week (three treatments). That compares to $1,300 and up in Europe for a week on dialysis.

Bill Peckham, *Around the World*, (originally published in Nephrology News & Issues), *available at* http://www.globaldialysis.com/billpeckham.asp (last visited Dec. 3, 2003).

9.   Professor Jeanne Woods suggests that the Court's analysis avoids the redistributive dimension of economic and social rights:

[B]oth the majority and concurring opinions beg the question whether the collective right to health actually conflicted with the individual's right to health and life in this context, that is, whether the state should be allowed to treat dialysis as an extraordinary resource that must be rationed for the poor in a country whose white citizens enjoy one of the highest standards of living in the world. The majority opinion made no mention of the resources available in the private sector, nor did it suggest that the state should do anything further to respond to the epidemic of kidney disease. In acknowledging that a person's wealth determined whether he would live or die, yet failing to interpret the constitutional rights to health and life to avoid this outcome, the Court missed an important opportunity to give meaning to the new social contract, suggesting a retreat from the challenge of justiciable social rights.

Jeanne M. Woods, *Justiciable Social Rights as a Critique of the Liberal Paradigm*, 38 Tex. Int'l L.J. 763, 783 (2003).

10. Would you have decided the *Soobramoney* case differently had Mr. Soobramoney been an indigent AIDS patient? A poor patient seeking cancer treatment? A poor diabetic seeking public assistance for glucose testing supplies and insulin? Why, or why not? In criticizing the decision, Professor James Thuo Gathii suggests a comparison between a patient in renal failure and the situation facing an AIDS patient:

This case is particularly relevant in the context of terminally-ill patients such as those suffering from AIDS. The analogy is particularly striking because Thiagraj Soobramoney, the diabetic appellant in this case, also suffered from both [heart and] vascular diseases. This combination of diseases made him dependent on health support services in a manner analogous *** to AIDS patients whose lives depend on access to AIDS cocktails, medical, and other support services.***

[T]he Court seems to have a very narrow concept of an emergency, which appears to be limited to traumas such as falling off a train and being rushed to the emergency room in an ambulance.*** Under this reasoning, as applied to Section 27(3), terminally ill patients, such as those suffering from AIDS, do not deserve the same kind of treatment as would a patient in need of immediate medical attention as a result of injuries sustained in a road accident. Further, under the Court's approach, AIDS patients would be hampered by the fact that, like patients in Soobramoney's position, their drugs are expensive, and in view of scarcity of resources, it would be too much to expect this help from the state because it must also meet other needs.

James Thuo Gathii, *Rights, Patents, Markets and the Global AIDS Pandemic*, 14 Fla. J. Int'l L. 261, 280 (2002); *see also* Winston P. Nagan, *International Intellectual Property, Access to Health Care, and Human Rights: South Africa v. United States*, 14 Fla. J. Int'l L. 155 (2002).

11. The *Soobramoney* opinion describes the conditions under which dialysis is available to poor patients with kidney disease in South Africa. Dr. Saraladevi Naicker, the nephrologist quoted in the opinion, explains that renal failure is, like other life-threatening illnesses, having a widespread and devastating impact in Africa:

Africa is a vast continent, extending over 30 million square km and comprising 53 countries and approximately 760 million people. Many millions live in overcrowded and unhygienic conditions, where lack of clean water and inadequate sanitation foster breeding grounds for infectious diseases. Infectious diseases are the world's leading cause of death, 43%, in the developing world compared to 1.2% in the developed world. Diseases that had seemed to be controlled such as tuberculosis and malaria have become a major health problem, with problems of resistance to therapy. New diseases, such as AIDS, have reached epidemic proportions especially in sub-Saharan Africa.

Per capita expenditure per year on healthcare ranges from 9 US dollars (Nigeria), 29 US dollars (Senegal), 100 US dollars (North Africa) and 158 US dollars (South Africa); the healthcare expenditure in Europe is approximately 2000 US dollars. Increasingly, health is influenced by social and economic circumstances. Any improvements in health thus demand integrated, comprehensive action against all the determinants of ill health.

MAJOR HEALTH PROBLEMS

The major health problems in Africa are AIDS, tuberculosis, malaria, gastroenteritis and hypertension. Hypertension affects about 20% of the adult population, an estimated 691 million people worldwide. It is one of the major risk factors for heart disease, stroke and kidney failure. Diabetes mellitus may present one of the most daunting challenges in the future. The number is currently estimated to be about 135 million and it is expected to rise to about 300 million by the year 2025. While the increase in cases will exceed 40% in developed countries, it is anticipated to be in the order of 170% in developing countries.***

*** Renal disease, especially glomerular disease, is more prevalent in Africa and seems to be of a more severe form than that found in Western countries.***

Glomerulonephritis in South Africa is characterized by a higher frequency in blacks, a lesser frequency in Indians and a lower frequency in whites. It appears that the milieu of chronic parasitic, bacterial and viral infections predisposes [a population] to an increased prevalence of glomerulonephritis.***

Statistics *** do not accurately reflect the etiology of chronic renal failure (CRF), as few patients with diabetic end-stage renal disease (ESRD) are offered dialysis or transplantation because of associated co-morbid conditions.***

Prevalence studies in the adult black population of Natal showed that hypertension was present in 25% of urban Zulus, 17.2% of whites and 14% of Indians. Malignant hypertension is an important cause of morbidity and mortality among urban black South Africans, with hypertension accounting for 16% of all hospital admissions.

*** Chronic glomerulonephritis and hypertension are principal causes of chronic renal failure in tropical Africa and East Africa, together with diabetes mellitus and obstructive uropathy.***

*** Because of financial constraints, the National Health Department, in consultation with nephrologists, has formalized a protocol for the management of end-stage renal failure: state facilities will offer renal replacement therapy only to patients who are eligible for a transplant. There are no constraints of sex, race or social status; dialysis is offered to transplantable patients who are able to attend for treatment. The trade in organs is forbidden by law in most countries in Africa. Transplantation of organs from living unrelated donors requires permission from the Minister of Health.

With the low transplant rate in South Africa, hemodialysis units are saturated and it is becoming difficult to accommodate new patients unless they have a related donor or are able to undertake CAPD [CAPD—Continuous Ambulatory Peritoneal Dialysis—is a form of dialysis, performed several times a day by the patient and requires training, supplies, and access to reliable sources of clean water and electricity.] Peritonitis and the high costs of peritoneal dialysis fluids also limit this option.***

PROPOSAL FOR TREATMENT OF RENAL FAILURE IN AFRICA

Ideally, every end-stage chronic renal failure patient should have access to dialysis. The reality is that there is not enough money for healthcare in the developing world, particularly for expensive and chronic treatment such as renal replacement therapy. The goal should be to have a circumscribed chronic dialysis program, with as short a time on dialysis as possible, and to increase the availability of transplantation (both living related and cadaver). CAPD is currently an expensive treatment modality in Africa. Efforts should be made to have the cost of CAPD fluids reduced, so that this treatment could be freely available in Africa. The use of CAPD in conjunction with an active transplant program is an appealing strategy for Africa.

Efforts should be made to optimize therapy of renal disease and renal failure globally and particularly in developing countries. Strategies should be developed to screen for and manage conditions such as hypertension and diabetes mellitus at the primary healthcare level in an effort to decrease the incidence of chronic renal failure. In areas where there are insufficient numbers of physicians, nurses and other allied health workers could be trained to manage these conditions at a local level, with clearly defined criteria for referral of patients. Patients with renal disease should be referred to a nephrologist at an early stage so as to institute measures to retard progression and plan timely transplantation and/or dialysis; this is particularly important where related donors may be available as a cost-effective strategy.***

Saraladevi Naicker, *End-Stage Renal Disease in Sub-Saharan and South Africa*, 63 KIDNEY INT'L (Supp. 83) S119–S122 (2003).

12. In contrast to the South African public health policies described in *Soobramoney*, the costs of renal dialysis and transplantation in the United States are covered by the Medicare program (and, to a limited extent, by private insurance). Allocation of public resources and access to the best available quality of care by minorities and the poor are still significant issues of debate in a country with a much larger health care budget. *See* Chapter 10, *infra.*

GOVERNMENT OF THE REPUBLIC OF SOUTH AFRICA v. GROOTBOOM

2000 (11) BCLR 1169 (CC), 2000 SACLR LEXIS 126

Yacoob J

A. Introduction

[1] The people of South Africa are committed to the attainment of social justice and the improvement of the quality of life for everyone. The Preamble to our Constitution records this commitment. The Constitution declares the founding values of our society to be "[h]uman dignity, the achievement of equality and the advancement of human rights and freedoms." This case grapples with the realisation of these aspirations for it concerns the State's constitutional obligations in relation to housing: a constitutional issue of fundamental importance to the development of South Africa's new constitutional order.

[2] The issues here remind us of the intolerable conditions under which many of our people are still living. The respondents are but a fraction of them. It is also a reminder that unless the plight of these communities is alleviated, people may be tempted to take the law into their own hands in order to escape these conditions. The case brings home the harsh reality that the Constitution's promise of dignity and equality for all remains for many a distant dream.***

[4] Mrs Irene Grootboom and the other respondents were rendered homeless as a result of their eviction from their informal homes situated on private land earmarked for formal low-cost housing. They applied to the Cape of Good Hope High Court (the High Court) for an order requiring government to provide them with adequate basic shelter or housing until they obtained permanent accommodation and were granted certain relief. The appellants were ordered to provide the respondents who were children and their parents with shelter. The judgment provisionally concluded that "tents, portable latrines and a regular supply of water (albeit transported) would constitute the bare minimum." The appellants who represent all spheres of government responsible for housing challenge the correctness of that order.***

[6] The cause of the acute housing shortage lies in apartheid. A central feature of that policy was a system of influx control that sought to limit African occupation of urban areas. Influx control was rigorously enforced in the Western Cape, where government policy favoured the exclusion of African people in order to accord preference to the coloured community: a policy adopted in 1954 and referred to as the "coloured labour preference policy." In consequence, the provision of family housing for African people in the Cape Peninsula was frozen in 1962. This freeze was extended to other urban areas in the Western Cape in 1968. Despite the harsh application of influx control in the Western Cape, African people continued to move to the area in search of jobs.*** Given the absence of formal housing, large numbers of people moved into informal settlements throughout the Cape peninsula. The cycle of the apartheid era, therefore, was one of untenable restrictions on the movement of African people into urban areas, the inexorable tide of the rural poor to the cities, inadequate housing, resultant overcrowding, mushrooming squatter settlements, constant harassment by officials and intermittent forced removals.***

[7] Mrs Grootboom and most of the other respondents previously lived in an informal squatter settlement called Wallacedene.*** The conditions under which most of the residents of Wallacedene lived were lamentable. A quarter of the households of Wallacedene had no income at all, and more than two thirds earned less than R500 per month. About half the population were children; all lived in shacks. They had no water, sewage or refuse removal services and only 5% of the shacks had electricity. The area is partly waterlogged and lies dangerously close to a main thoroughfare. Mrs Grootboom lived with her family and her sister's family in a shack about twenty metres square.

[8] Many had applied for subsidised low-cost housing from the municipality and had been on the waiting list for as long as seven years. Despite numerous enquiries from the municipality no definite answer was given. Clearly it was going to be a long wait. Faced with the prospect of remaining in intolerable conditions indefinitely, the respondents began to move out of Wallacedene at the end of September 1998. They put up their shacks and shelters on vacant land that was privately owned and had been earmarked for low-cost housing. They called the land "New Rust."

[9] They did not have the consent of the owner and on 8 December 1998 he obtained an ejectment order against them in the magistrates' court. The order was served on the occupants but they remained in occupation beyond the date by which they had been ordered to vacate. Mrs Grootboom says they had nowhere else to go; their former sites in Wallacedene had been filled by others. The eviction proceedings were renewed in March 1999. The respondents' attorneys in this case were appointed by the magistrate to represent them on the return day of the provisional order of eviction. Negotiations resulted in the grant of an order requiring the occupants to vacate New Rust and authorising the sheriff to evict them and to dismantle and remove any of their structures remaining on the land on 19 May 1999. The magistrate also directed that the parties and the municipality mediate to identify alternative land for the permanent or temporary occupation of the New Rust residents.

[10] The municipality had not been party to the proceedings but it had engaged attorneys to monitor them on its behalf. It is not clear whether the municipality was a party to the settlement and the agreement to mediate. Nor is it clear whether the eviction was in accordance with the provisions of the Prevention of Illegal Eviction from and Unlawful Occupation of Land Act, 19 of 1998. The validity of the eviction order

has never been challenged and must be accepted as correct. However, no mediation took place and on 18 May 1999, at the beginning of the cold, windy and rainy Cape winter, the respondents were forcibly evicted at the municipality's expense. This was done prematurely and inhumanely: reminiscent of apartheid-style evictions. The respondents' homes were bulldozed and burnt and their possessions destroyed. Many of the residents who were not there could not even salvage their personal belongings.

[11] The respondents went and sheltered on the Wallacedene sports field under such temporary structures as they could muster. Within a week the winter rains started and the plastic sheeting they had erected afforded scant protection. The next day the respondents' attorney wrote to the municipality describing the intolerable conditions under which his clients were living and demanded that the municipality meet its constitutional obligations and provide temporary accommodation to the respondents. The respondents were not satisfied with the response of the municipality and launched an urgent application in the High Court on 31 May 1999. As indicated above, the High Court granted relief to the respondents and the appellants now appeal against that relief.***

*B.   The case in the High Court ***

The respondents based their claim on two constitutional provisions. First, on section 26 of the Constitution which provides that everyone has the right of access to adequate housing. Section 26(2) imposes an obligation upon the State to take reasonable legislative and other measures to ensure the progressive realisation of this right within its available resources.*** The second basis for their claim was section 28(1)(c) of the Constitution which provides that children have the right to shelter. [The High Court rejected the claim for temporary shelter under § 26(c), but ruled that § 28(1)(c) imposed a duty on the state to provide shelter to the applicant children and their parents.]***

D.   The relevant constitutional provisions and their justiciability

[19] The key constitutional provisions at issue in this case are section 26 and section 28(1)(c). Section 26 provides:

(1) Everyone has the right to have access to adequate housing.

(2) The state must take reasonable legislative and other measures, within its available resources, to achieve the progressive realisation of this right.

(3) No one may be evicted from their home, or have their home demolished, without an order of court made after considering all the relevant circumstances. No legislation may permit arbitrary evictions.

Section 28(1)(c) provides:

(1) Every child has the right—

(c) to basic nutrition, shelter, basic health care services and social services.

These rights need to be considered in the context of the cluster of socio-economic rights enshrined in the Constitution. They entrench the right of access to land, to adequate housing and to health care, food, water and social security. They also protect the rights of the child and the right to education.

[20] While the justiciability of socio-economic rights has been the subject of considerable jurisprudential and political debate, the issue of whether socio-economic rights are justiciable at all in South Africa has been put beyond question by the text of our Constitution ***.***

Socio-economic rights are expressly included in the Bill of Rights; they cannot be said to exist on paper only. Section 7(2) of the Constitution requires the State "to respect, protect, promote and fulfil the rights in the Bill of Rights" and the courts are constitutionally bound to ensure that they are protected and fulfilled. The question is therefore not whether socio-economic rights are justiciable under our Constitution, but how to enforce them in a given case. This is a very difficult issue which must be carefully explored on a case-by-case basis. To address the challenge raised in the present case, it is necessary first to consider the terms and context of the relevant constitutional provisions and their application to the circumstances of this case. Although the judgment of the High Court in favour of the appellants was based on the right to shelter (section 28(1)(c) of the Constitution), it is appropriate to consider the provisions of section 26 first so as to facilitate a contextual evaluation of section 28(1)(c).

E.   *Obligations imposed upon the State by section 26*

   i)   *Approach to interpretation*

[21] Like all the other rights in Chapter 2 of the Constitution (which contains the Bill of Rights), section 26 must be construed in its context. The section has been carefully crafted. It contains three subsections. The first confers a general right of access to adequate housing. The second establishes and delimits the scope of the positive obligation imposed upon the State to promote access to adequate housing and has three key elements. The State is obliged: (a) to take reasonable legislative and other measures; (b) within its available resources; (c) to achieve the progressive realisation of this right.***

[22] Interpreting a right in its context requires the consideration of two types of context. On the one hand, rights must be understood in their textual setting. This will require a consideration of Chapter 2 and the Constitution as a whole. On the other hand, rights must also be understood in their social and historical context.

[23] Our Constitution entrenches both civil and political rights and social and economic rights. All the rights in our Bill of Rights are inter-related and mutually supporting. There can be no doubt that human dignity, freedom and equality, the foundational values of our society, are denied those who have no food, clothing or shelter. Affording socio-economic rights to all people therefore enables them to enjoy the other rights enshrined in Chapter 2. The realisation of these rights is also key to the advancement of race and gender equality and the evolution of a society in which men and women are equally able to achieve their full potential.

[24] The right of access to adequate housing cannot be seen in isolation. There is a close relationship between it and the other socio-economic rights. Socio-economic rights must all be read together in the setting of the Constitution as a whole. The State is obliged to take positive action to meet the needs of those living in extreme conditions of poverty, homelessness or intolerable housing. Their interconnectedness needs to be taken into account in interpreting the socio-economic rights.***

[25] Rights also need to be interpreted and understood in their social and historical context. The right to be free from unfair discrimination, for example, must be understood against our legacy of deep social inequality.***

ii) The relevant international law and its impact

[26] During argument, considerable weight was attached to the value of international law in interpreting section 26 of our Constitution. Section 39 of the Constitution obliges a court to consider international law as a tool to interpretation of the Bill of Rights. In *Makwanyane*, Chaskalson P, in the context of section 35(1) of the interim Constitution, said:

> public international law would include non-binding as well as binding law. They may both be used under the section as tools of interpretation. International agreements and customary international law accordingly provide a framework within which [the Bill of Rights] can be evaluated and understood, and for that purpose, decisions of tribunals dealing with comparable instruments, such as the United Nations Committee on Human Rights, the Inter-American Commission on Human Rights, the Inter-American Court of Human Rights, the European Commission on Human Rights, and the European Court of Human Rights *** may provide guidance as to the correct interpretation of particular provisions of [the Bill of Rights].

[27] The amici [the Human Rights Commission and the Community Law Centre of the University of the Western Cape] submitted that the International Covenant on Economic, Social and Cultural Rights (the Covenant) is of significance in understanding the positive obligations created by the socio-economic rights in the Constitution. Article 11.1 of the Covenant provides:

> The States Parties to the present Covenant recognize the right of everyone to an adequate standard of living for himself and his family, including adequate food, clothing and housing, and to the continuous improvement of living conditions. The States Parties will take appropriate steps to ensure the realization of this right, recognizing to this effect the essential importance of international co-operation based on free consent.

This Article must be read with Article 2.1 which provides:

> Each State Party to the present Covenant undertakes to take steps, individually and through international assistance and co-operation, especially economic and technical, to the maximum of its available resources, with a view to achieving progressively the full realization of the rights recognized in the present Covenant by all appropriate means, including particularly the adoption of legislative measures.

[28] The differences between the relevant provisions of the Covenant and our Constitution are significant in determining the extent to which the provisions of the Covenant may be a guide to an interpretation of section 26. These differences, in so far as they relate to housing, are:

    (a) The Covenant provides for a right to adequate housing while section 26 provides for the right of access to adequate housing.

(b) The Covenant obliges states parties to take appropriate steps which must include legislation while the Constitution obliges the South African state to take reasonable legislative and other measures.

[29] The obligations undertaken by states parties to the Covenant are monitored by the United Nations Committee on Economic, Social and Cultural Rights (the committee). The amici relied on the relevant general comments issued by the committee concerning the interpretation and application of the Covenant, and argued that these general comments constitute a significant guide to the interpretation of section 26. In particular they argued that in interpreting this section, we should adopt an approach similar to that taken by the committee in paragraph 10 of general comment 3 issued in 1990, in which the committee found that socio-economic rights contain a minimum core:

10. On the basis of the extensive experience gained by the Committee, as well as by the body that preceded it, over a period of more than a decade of examining States parties' reports the Committee is of the view that minimum core obligation to ensure the satisfaction of, at the very least, minimum essential levels of each of the rights is incumbent upon every State party. Thus, for example, a State party in which any significant number of individuals is deprived of essential foodstuffs, of essential primary health care, of basic shelter and housing, or of the most basic forms of education, is prima facie, failing to discharge its obligations under the Covenant. If the Covenant were to be read in such a way as not to establish such a minimum core obligation, it would be largely deprived of its *raison d'etre*. By the same token, it must be noted that any assessment as to whether a State has discharged its minimum core obligation must also take account of resource constraints applying within the country concerned.***

[32] It is not possible to determine the minimum threshold for the progressive realisation of the right of access to adequate housing without first identifying the needs and opportunities for the enjoyment of such a right. These will vary according to factors such as income, unemployment, availability of land and poverty. The differences between city and rural communities will also determine the needs and opportunities for the enjoyment of this right. Variations ultimately depend on the economic and social history and circumstances of a country.***

[33] The determination of a minimum core in the context of "the right to have access to adequate housing" presents difficult questions. This is so because the needs in the context of access to adequate housing are diverse: there are those who need land; others need both land and houses; yet others need financial assistance. There are difficult questions relating to the definition of minimum core in the context of a right to have access to adequate housing, in particular whether the minimum core obligation should be defined generally or with regard to specific groups of people.*** There may be cases where it may be possible and appropriate to have regard to the content of a minimum core obligation to determine whether the measures taken by the State are reasonable. However, even if it were appropriate to do so, it could not be done unless sufficient information is placed before a court to enable it to determine the minimum core in any given context. In this case, we do not have sufficient information to determine what would comprise the minimum core obligation in the context of our Constitution. It is not in any event necessary to decide whether it is appropriate for a court to determine in the first instance the minimum core content of a right.

iii) Analysis of section 26

[34] *** Subsections (1) and (2) are related and must be read together. Subsection (1) aims at delineating the scope of the right. It is a right of everyone including children. Although the subsection does not expressly say so, there is, at the very least, a negative obligation placed upon the State and all other entities and persons to desist from preventing or impairing the right of access to adequate housing. The negative right is further spelt out in subsection (3) which prohibits arbitrary evictions. Access to housing could also be promoted if steps are taken to make the rural areas of our country more viable so as to limit the inexorable migration of people from rural to urban areas in search of jobs.

[35] The right delineated in section 26(1) is a right of "access to adequate housing" as distinct from the right to adequate housing encapsulated in the Covenant. This difference is significant. It recognises that housing entails more than bricks and mortar. It requires available land, appropriate services such as the provision of water and the removal of sewage and the financing of all of these, including the building of the house itself. For a person to have access to adequate housing all of these conditions need to be met: there must be land, there must be services, there must be a dwelling. Access to land for the purpose of housing is therefore included in the right of access to adequate housing in section 26. A right of access to adequate housing also suggests that it is not only the State who is responsible for the provision of houses, but that other agents within our society, including individuals themselves, must be enabled by legislative and other measures to provide housing. The State must create the conditions for access to adequate housing for people at all economic levels of our society. State policy dealing with housing must therefore take account of different economic levels in our society.

[36] In this regard, there is a difference between the position of those who can afford to pay for housing, even if it is only basic though adequate housing, and those who cannot. For those who can afford to pay for adequate housing, the State's primary obligation lies in unlocking the system, providing access to housing stock and a legislative framework to facilitate self-built houses through planning laws and access to finance. Issues of development and social welfare are raised in respect of those who cannot afford to provide themselves with housing. State policy needs to address both these groups. The poor are particularly vulnerable and their needs require special attention.***

[38] Subsection (2) speaks to the positive obligation imposed upon the State. It requires the State to devise a comprehensive and workable plan to meet its obligations in terms of the subsection. However subsection (2) also makes it clear that the obligation imposed upon the State is not an absolute or unqualified one. The extent of the State's obligation is defined by three key elements that are considered separately: (a) the obligation to "take reasonable legislative and other measures"; (b) "to achieve the progressive realisation" of the right; and (c) "within available resources."

*F.   Reasonable legislative and other measures ****

[41] The measures [undertaken by national and provincial government] must establish a coherent public housing programme directed towards the progressive realisation of the right of access to adequate housing within the State's available means. The programme must be capable of facilitating the realisation of the right. The precise contours and content of the measures to be adopted are primarily a matter for

the legislature and the executive. They must, however, ensure that the measures they adopt are reasonable. In any challenge based on section 26 in which it is argued that the State has failed to meet the positive obligations imposed upon it by section 26(2), the question will be whether the legislative and other measures taken by the State are reasonable.***

[42] The State is required to take reasonable legislative and other measures. Legislative measures by themselves are not likely to constitute constitutional compliance. Mere legislation is not enough. The State is obliged to act to achieve the intended result, and the legislative measures will invariably have to be supported by appropriate, well-directed policies and programmes implemented by the executive. These policies and programmes must be reasonable both in their conception and their implementation.***

[43] In determining whether a set of measures is reasonable, it will be necessary to consider housing problems in their social, economic and historical context and to consider the capacity of institutions responsible for implementing the programme. The programme must be balanced and flexible and make appropriate provision for attention to housing crises and to short, medium and long term needs. A programme that excludes a significant segment of society cannot be said to be reasonable.***

G. *Progressive realization of the right*

[45] *** The term "progressive realization shows that it was contemplated that the right could not be realized immediately. But the goal of the Constitution is that the basic needs of all in our society be effectively met and the requirement of progressive realization means that the State must take steps to achieve this goal.***

H. *Within available resources*

[46] *** This means that both the content of the obligation in relation to the rate at which it is achieved as well as the reasonableness of the measures employed to achieve the result are governed by the availability of resources. Section 26 does not expect more of the State than is achievable within its available resources.***

[56] This Court must decide whether the nationwide housing programme is sufficiently flexible to respond to those in desperate need in our society and to cater appropriately for immediate and short-term requirements.***

[57] The housing shortage in the Cape Metro is acute. About 206,000 housing units are required and up to 25,000 housing opportunities are required in Oostenberg itself. Shack counts in the Cape Metro in general and in the area of the municipality in particular reveal an inordinate problem. 28,300 shacks were counted in the Cape Metro in January 1993. This number had grown to 59,854 in 1996 and to 72,140 by 1998.***

[59] The housing situation is desperate. The problem is compounded by rampant unemployment and poverty. As was pointed out earlier in this judgment, a quarter of the households in Wallacedene had no income at all, and more than two-thirds earned less than R500 per month during 1997. As stated above, many of the families living in Wallacedene are living in intolerable conditions. In some cases, their shacks are permanently flooded during the winter rains, others are severely overcrowded and some are perilously close to busy roads. There is no suggestion that Wallacedene is unusual in this respect.***

[63] Section 26 requires that the legislative and other measures adopted by the State are reasonable. To determine whether the nationwide housing programme as applied in the Cape Metro is reasonable within the meaning of the section, one must consider whether the absence of a component catering for those in desperate need is reasonable in the circumstances. It is common cause that, except for the Cape Metro land programme, there is no provision in the nationwide housing programme as applied within the Cape Metro for people in desperate need.

[64] Counsel for the appellants supported the nationwide housing programme and resisted the notion that provision of relief for people in desperate need was appropriate in it. Counsel also submitted that section 26 did not require the provision of this relief. Indeed, the contention was that provision for people in desperate need would detract significantly from integrated housing development as defined in the Act. The housing development policy as set out in the Act is in itself laudable. It has medium and long term objectives that cannot be criticised. But the question is whether a housing programme that leaves out of account the immediate amelioration of the circumstances of those in crisis can meet the test of reasonableness established by the section.

[65] The absence of this component may have been acceptable if the nationwide housing programme would result in affordable houses for most people within a reasonably short time. However the scale of the problem is such that this simply cannot happen. Each individual housing project could be expected to take years and the provision of houses for all in the area of the municipality and in the Cape Metro is likely to take a long time indeed. The desperate will be consigned to their fate for the foreseeable future unless some temporary measures exist as an integral part of the nationwide housing programme.***

[66] The national government bears the overall responsibility for ensuring that the State complies with the obligations imposed upon it by section 26. The nationwide housing programme falls short of obligations imposed upon national government to the extent that it fails to recognise that the State must provide for relief for those in desperate need. They are not to be ignored in the interests of an overall programme focussed on medium and long-term objectives. It is essential that a reasonable part of the national housing budget be devoted to this, but the precise allocation is for national government to decide in the first instance.***

[69] In conclusion it has been established in this case that as of the date of the launch of this application, the State was not meeting the obligation imposed upon it by section 26(2) of the Constitution in the area of the Cape Metro. In particular, the programmes adopted by the State fell short of the requirements of section 26(2) in that no provision was made for relief to the categories of people in desperate need identified earlier.***

[80] The final section of this judgment is concerned with whether the respondents are entitled to some relief in the form of temporary housing because of their special circumstances and because of the appellants' conduct towards them.*** [W]e must also remember that the respondents are not alone in their desperation; hundreds of thousands (possibly millions) of South Africans live in appalling conditions throughout our country.

[81] [I]t is a painful reality that their circumstances were no worse than those of thousands of other people, including young children, who remained at Wallacedene.

It cannot be said, on the evidence before us, that the respondents moved out of the Wallacedene settlement and occupied the land earmarked for low-cost housing development as a deliberate strategy to gain preference in the allocation of housing resources over thousands of other people who remained in intolerable conditions and who were also in urgent need of housing relief. It must be borne in mind however, that the effect of any order that constitutes a special dispensation for the respondents on account of their extraordinary circumstances is to accord that preference.***

[88] There is, however, no dispute that the municipality funded the eviction of the respondents. The magistrate who ordered the ejectment of the respondents directed a process of mediation in which the municipality was to be involved to identify some alternative land for the occupation for the New Rust residents. Although the reason for this is unclear from the papers, it is evident that no effective mediation took place. The State had an obligation to ensure, at the very least, that the eviction was humanely executed. However, the eviction was reminiscent of the past and inconsistent with the values of the Constitution. The respondents were evicted a day early and to make matters worse, their possessions and building materials were not merely removed, but destroyed and burnt. I have already said that the provisions of section 26(1) of the Constitution burdens the State with at least a negative obligation in relation to housing. The manner in which the eviction was carried out resulted in a breach of this obligation.***

[91] At the hearing in this Court, counsel for the national and Western Cape government, tendered a statement indicating that the respondents had, on that very day, been offered some alternative accommodation, not in fulfilment of any accepted constitutional obligation, but in the interests of humanity and pragmatism. Counsel for the respondents accepted the offer on their behalf. We were subsequently furnished with a copy of the arrangement which read as follows:

1. The Department of Planning, Local Government and Housing (Western Cape Province) undertakes in conjunction with the Oostenberg Municipality to provide temporary accommodation to the respondents on the Wallacedene Sportsfield until they can be housed in terms of the housing programmes available to the local authority, and in particular the Accelerated Land Managed Settlement Programme.***

K. Summary and conclusion

[93] This case shows the desperation of hundreds of thousands of people living in deplorable conditions throughout the country. The Constitution obliges the State to act positively to ameliorate these conditions. The obligation is to provide access to housing, health-care, sufficient food and water, and social security to those unable to support themselves and their dependants. The State must also foster conditions to enable citizens to gain access to land on an equitable basis. Those in need have a corresponding right to demand that this be done.

[94] I am conscious that it is an extremely difficult task for the State to meet these obligations in the conditions that prevail in our country. This is recognised by the Constitution which expressly provides that the State is not obliged to go beyond available resources or to realise these rights immediately. I stress however, that despite all these qualifications, these are rights, and the Constitution obliges the State to give effect to them. This is an obligation that courts can, and in appropriate circumstances, must enforce.

[95] Neither section 26 nor section 28 entitles the respondents to claim shelter or housing immediately upon demand. The High Court order ought therefore not to have been made. However, section 26 does oblige the State to devise and implement a coherent, co-ordinated programme designed to meet its section 26 obligations. The programme that has been adopted and was in force in the Cape Metro at the time that this application was brought, fell short of the obligations imposed upon the State by section 26(2) in that it failed to provide for any form of relief to those desperately in need of access to housing.

[96] In the light of the conclusions I have reached, it is necessary and appropriate to make a declaratory order. The order requires the State to act to meet the obligation imposed upon it by section 26(2) of the Constitution. This includes the obligation to devise, fund, implement and supervise measures to provide relief to those in desperate need.***

Notes and Questions

1. The Court's decision in *Grootboom* reassured social rights advocates that it was willing to adjudicate positive rights claims. Contrary to the complaint that justiciable social rights remove policy choices from the legislative prerogative, the South African Constitutional Court demonstrated that violations of these rights can be remedied by a court without intruding unduly on legislative discretion.

2. *Minimum Core Obligation.* While commending the "major achievement" represented by the government's comprehensive housing program, the Court determined that the plan was not a reasonable effort to promote the constitutional right of access to adequate housing, because it excluded a significant segment of the population, those in desperate need. Does this conclusion expand the concept of "minimum core obligation?" Is the Court applying the same "reasonableness" standard that it applied in *Soobramoney?* What is the relationship between these two concepts? Where does the "availability of resources" fit in?

3. *Progressive Realization.* What normative weight did the Court attach to the criterion in Section 26(2) of "progressive realization?" Discussion of this provision was not part of the analysis in *Soobramoney*, although it is also contained in the health care provision. Could this criterion be read as a limitation on social rights? Does characterizing such rights as collective rather than individual affect how the concept of progressive realization is interpreted?

4. *Relationship to ICESCR.* What is the significance of the Court's reliance on the analysis of the Committee on Economic, Social and Cultural Rights? (South Africa signed the Covenant in October 1994, but has not yet ratified it.) The Court emphasizes the difference between the right to housing in Article 11 of the International Covenant, and the right of "access" to adequate housing in § 26. Under its analysis, which is the broader right?

5. Is *Grootboom* distinguishable from *Soobramoney?* Is the decision redistributive? Does the Court's analysis go beyond "traditional" constitutional decisionmaking? The Court in this case identified as duty-holders of the right to housing, individuals and other agents as well as the state. (*See* ¶ 35.) In contrast, in *Soobramoney* the Constitutional Court was markedly unwilling to recognize any duty in the private sector for the provision of dialysis treatment, despite the fact that the identical language on which it relied to eliminate the public/private distinction is contained in the section on the right to health.

6. The Court ordered the government to create a program that addresses the need of people in desperate need of housing but ruled that there was no positive individual right to housing on demand. Is this consistent with the concept of minimum core obligation? Where does that leave people in these circumstances? Nearly four years after the landmark ruling, nothing has changed for the residents of Wallacedene. A segment of the shantytown has been named for Mrs. Irene Grootboom, the lead plaintiff in the case, whose whereabouts are unknown. *See* Bonny Schoonakker, *Treated with Contempt*, Sunday Times (S. Afr.) Mar. 21, 2004, *available at* http://www.suntimes.co.za/2004/03/21/insight/inol.asp (last visited June 24, 2004).

7. *The Need for Land Reform.* Forty-five percent of the population of South Africa—constituting 70 percent of the nation's poorest citizens—is concentrated in the rural areas. For them, housing issues are inextricably connected to the problems of security of tenure and land ownership that are the legacy of white minority rule. Under the Natives Land Act of 1913, Africans were legally dispossessed of 87 percent of the land in the country, and relegated to barren reserves called "Bantustans." The democratically elected ANC government has set a goal of redistributing 30 percent of white-owned farmland over 15 years; however, at current rates of turnover, this goal could take 150 years to achieve. What accounts for the slow pace of reform? Some attribute the lack of progress to the government's neoliberal growth-oriented approach to development, focusing on industrialization in urban areas. Can market-based reforms adequately address the historic injustice of South African land policy? *See, e.g.,* M.C. Lyne & M.A.G. Darroch, *Land Redistribution in South Africa: Past Performance and Future Policy* (Feb. 2003), *available at* http://www.basis.wisc.edu (last visited June 24, 2004); Wellington Didibhuku Thwala, *Land and Agrarian Reform in South Africa, available at* www.nlc.co.za/pubs2003/ landagrarian.pdf (last visited June 23, 2004).

MINISTER OF HEALTH, ET AL. v. TREATMENT ACTION CAMPAIGN

2002 (10) BCLR 1033 (CC)

THE COURT:

Introduction

[1] The HIV/AIDS pandemic in South Africa has been described as "an incomprehensible calamity" and "the most important challenge facing South Africa since the birth of our new democracy" and government's fight against "this scourge" as "a top priority." It "has claimed millions of lives, inflicting pain and grief, causing fear and uncertainty, and threatening the economy." These are not the words of alarmists but are taken from a Department of Health publication in 2000 and a ministerial foreword to an earlier departmental publication.

[2] This appeal is directed at reversing orders made in a high court against government because of perceived shortcomings in its response to an aspect of the HIV/AIDS challenge. The court found that government had not reasonably addressed the need to reduce the risk of HIV-positive mothers transmitting the disease to their babies at birth. More specifically the finding was that government had acted unreasonably in (a) refusing to make an antiretroviral drug called nevirapine[2] available in the

---

2   Nevirapine is a fast-acting and potent antiretroviral drug long since used worldwide in

public health sector where the attending doctor considered it medically indicated and (b) not setting out a timeframe for a national programme to prevent mother-to-child transmission of HIV.***

[3] Government, as part of a formidable array of responses to the pandemic, devised a programme to deal with mother-to-child transmission of HIV at birth and identified nevirapine as its drug of choice for this purpose.[3] The programme imposes restrictions on the availability of nevirapine in the public health sector. This is where the first of two main issues in the case arose. The applicants contended that these restrictions are unreasonable when measured against the Constitution, which commands the state and all its organs to give effect to the rights guaranteed by the Bill of Rights.***

At issue here is the right given to everyone to have access to public health care services and the right of children to be afforded special protection. These rights are expressed in the following terms in the Bill of Rights:

27 (1) Everyone has the right to have access to—

(a) health care services, including reproductive health care;***

(2) The state must take reasonable legislative and other measures, within its available resources, to achieve the progressive realisation of each of these rights.

28 (1) Every child has the right—***

(c) to basic nutrition, shelter, basic health care services and social services."

[4] The second main issue also arises out of the provisions of sections 27 and 28 of the Constitution. It is whether government is constitutionally obliged and had to be ordered forthwith to plan and implement an effective, comprehensive and progressive programme for the prevention of mother-to-child transmission of HIV throughout the country.***

[5] The affidavits lodged by the applicants addressed these two central issues from a variety of specialised perspectives, ranging from paediatrics, pharmacology and epidemiology to public health administration, economics and statistics. The applicants' papers also include the testimony of doctors, nurses and counsellors confronted daily with the human tragedies of HIV-infected mothers and their babies. In addition there are poignant accounts of HIV-positive pregnant women's pleas for access to nevirapine for themselves and their babies at public health institutions where its supply is prohibited.***

[On 14 December 2001 the High Court ordered the government to make Nevirapine available to pregnant women with HIV who give birth in the public health sector, and to their babies, where medically indicated, and where the woman concerned has

---

the treatment of HIV/AIDS and registered in South Africa since 1998. In January 2001 it was approved by the World Health Organization for use against intrapartum mother-to-child transmission of HIV, i.e. transmission of the virus from mother to child at birth. It was also approved for such use in South Africa. The nature and precise date of such approval were contested and this led to some vigorously debated subsidiary issues, dealt with more fully below.

3   The drug is currently available free to government and its administration is simple: a single tablet taken by the mother at the onset of labour and a few drops fed to the baby within 72 hours after birth.

been appropriately tested and counselled. The respondents were also ordered to pro-vide free formula milk to these mothers, and to plan an effective comprehensive national programme to prevent or reduce the mother-to-child transmission of HIV.]

[6] Because of the importance and urgency of the matter, an early date was allocated for the hearing of government's appeal against the order of the High Court.***

Factual background ***

[7] Nevirapine had been registered in 1998 by the Medicines Control Council, a specialist body created by the Medicines and Related Substances Control Act 101 of 1965 to determine the safety of drugs before their being made available in South Africa. In terms of this Act registration of a drug by definition entails a positive finding as to its quality, safety and efficacy. In January 2001 the World Health Organization recommended the administration of the drug to mother and infant at the time of birth in order to combat HIV.***

[8] The [government identifies] a number of social, economic and public health implications of breastfeeding by HIV-positive mothers, emphasises the cultural and financial impact of formula-feeding as a substitute and outlines the overall complexity of providing a comprehensive package of care throughout the country.*** The decision was to confine the provision of nevirapine in the public sector to the research sites and their outlets.

[9] It can be accepted that an important reason for this decision was that government wanted to develop and monitor its human and material resources nationwide for the delivery of a comprehensive package of testing and counselling, dispensing of nevirapine and follow-up services to pregnant women attending at public health institutions. Where bottle-feeding was to be substituted for breastfeeding, appropriate methods and procedures had to be evolved for effective implementation, bearing in mind cultural problems, the absence of clean water in certain parts of the country and the increased risks to infants growing up with inadequate nutrition and sanitation. At the same time, data relating to administrative hitches and their solutions, staffing, costs and the like could be gathered and correlated. All of this obviously makes good sense from the public health point of view. These research and training sites could provide vital information on which in time the very best possible prevention programme for mother-to-child transmission could be developed.***

[10] The crux of the problem, however, lies elsewhere: what is to happen to those mothers and their babies who cannot afford access to private health care and do not have access to the research and training sites? It is not clear on the papers how long it is planned to take before nevirapine will be made available outside these sites. Some of the provinces had not yet established any test sites by the time the application was launched in late August 2001.*** What is plain *** is that for a protracted period nevirapine would not be supplied at any public health institution other than one designated as part of a research site.

The issues

[11] The founding affidavit, signed by the TAC deputy-chairperson, Ms Siphokazi Mthathi, commences with a useful summary of the case presented by the applicants. In paragraphs 20 and 21 of her affidavit the two principal issues are stated thus:

20. The first issue is whether the Respondents are entitled to refuse to make Nevirapine (a registered drug) available to pregnant women who have HIV and who give birth in the public health sector, in order to prevent or reduce the risk of transmission of HIV to their infants, where in the judgment of the attending medical practitioner this is medically indicated.

21. The second issue is whether the Respondents are obliged, as a matter of law, to implement and set out clear timeframes for a national programme to prevent mother-to-child transmission of HIV, including voluntary counselling and testing, antiretroviral therapy, and the option of using formula milk for feeding.

[12] Then, in paragraph 22, she summarises the applicants' case in the following terms:

22. In summary, the Applicants' case is as follows:

22.1 The HIV/AIDS epidemic is a major public health problem in our country, and has reached catastrophic proportions.

22.2 One of the most common methods of transmission of HIV in children is from mother to child at and around birth. Government estimates are that since 1998, 70,000 children are infected in this manner every year.***

22.3 The Medicines Control Council has registered Nevirapine for use to reduce the risk of mother-to-child transmission of HIV. This means that Nevirapine has been found to be suitable for this purpose, and that it is safe, of acceptable quality, and therapeutically efficacious.

22.4 The result is that doctors in the private profession can and do prescribe Nevirapine for their patients when, in their professional judgment, it is appropriate to do so.

22.5 In July 2000 the manufacturers of Nevirapine offered to make it available to the South African government free of charge for a period of five years, for the purposes of reducing the risk of mother-to-child transmission of HIV.

22.6 The government has formally decided to make Nevirapine available only at a limited number of pilot sites, which number two per province.

22.7 The result is that doctors in the public sector, who do not work at one of those pilot sites, are unable to prescribe this drug for their patients, even though it has been offered to the government for free.***

22.8 In addition to refusing to make Nevirapine generally available in the public health sector, the government has failed over an extended period to implement a comprehensive programme for the prevention of mother-to-child transmission of HIV.

22.9 The result of this refusal and this failure is the mother-to-child transmission of HIV in situations where this was both predictable and avoidable.

22.10 This conduct of the government is irrational, in breach of the Bill of Rights, and *** in breach of its international obligations as contained in a number of conventions that it has both signed and ratified."***

[13] In their argument counsel for the government raised issues pertaining to the separation of powers. This may be relevant in two respects—(i) in the deference that

courts should show to decisions taken by the executive concerning the formulation of its policies; and (ii) in the order to be made where a court finds that the executive has failed to comply with its constitutional obligations. These considerations are relevant to the manner in which a court should exercise the powers vested in it under the Constitution. It was not contended, nor could it have been, that they are relevant to the question of justiciability.

Enforcement of socio-economic rights

[14] This Court has had to consider claims for enforcement of socio-economic rights on two occasions. On both occasions it was recognised that the state is under a constitutional duty to comply with the positive obligations imposed on it by sections 26 and 27 of the Constitution.***

[15] The question in the present case, therefore, is not whether socio-economic rights are justiciable. Clearly they are. The question is whether the applicants have shown that the measures adopted by the government to provide access to health care services for HIV-positive mothers and their newborn babies fall short of its obligations under the Constitution.

Minimum core

[16] Before outlining the applicants' legal submissions, it is necessary to consider a line of argument presented on behalf of the first and second amici. It was contended that section 27(1) of the Constitution establishes an individual right vested in everyone. This right, so the contention went, has a minimum core to which every person in need is entitled.***

[17] This minimum core might not be easy to define, but includes at least the minimum decencies of life consistent with human dignity. No one should be condemned to a life below the basic level of dignified human existence. The very notion of individual rights presupposes that anyone in that position should be able to obtain relief from a court.***

[18] Although *** evidence in a particular case may show that there is a minimum core of a particular service that should be taken into account in determining whether measures adopted by the state are reasonable, the socio-economic rights of the Constitution should not be construed as entitling everyone to demand that the minimum core be provided to them. Minimum core was thus treated as possibly being relevant to reasonableness under section 26(2), and not as a self-standing right conferred on everyone under section 26(1).***

[19] The state is obliged to take reasonable measures progressively to eliminate or reduce the large areas of severe deprivation that afflict our society.***

[20] It should be borne in mind that in dealing with such matters the courts are not institutionally equipped to make the wide-ranging factual and political enquiries necessary for determining what the minimum-core standards called for by the first and second amici should be, nor for deciding how public revenues should most effectively be spent. There are many pressing demands on the public purse.***

[21] Courts are ill-suited to adjudicate upon issues where court orders could have multiple social and economic consequences for the community. The Constitution contemplates rather a restrained and focused role for the courts, namely, to require the state to take measures to meet its constitutional obligations and to subject the reason-

ableness of these measures to evaluation. Such determinations of reasonableness may in fact have budgetary implications, but are not in themselves directed at rearranging budgets. In this way the judicial, legislative and executive functions achieve appropriate constitutional balance.

Government policy on the prevention of mother-to-child transmission of HIV ***

[22] Following the 13th International Conference on HIV/AIDS held in Durban in July 2000, government took a decision to implement a programme for the prevention of mother-to-child transmission of HIV/AIDS. This programme entailed the provision of voluntary HIV counselling and testing to pregnant women, the provision of nevirapine and the offer of formula feed to HIV-positive mothers who chose this option of feeding. The implementation of this programme was to be confined to selected sites in each province for a period of two years.*** Nevirapine was not to be made available to public facilities outside the pilot sites.***

The applicants' contentions

[23] It is the applicants' case that the measures adopted by government to provide access to health care services to HIV-positive pregnant women were deficient in two material respects: first, because they prohibited the administration of nevirapine at public hospitals and clinics outside the research and training sites; and second, because they failed to implement a comprehensive programme for the prevention of mother-to-child transmission of HIV.***

[24] In *Grootboom*,*** this Court held that

[a]lthough [section 26(1)] does not expressly say so, there is, at the very least, a negative obligation placed upon the State and all other entities and persons to desist from preventing or impairing the right of access to adequate housing.

That "negative obligation" applies equally to the section 27(1) right of access to "health care services, including reproductive health care." This is relevant to the challenges to the measures adopted by government for the provision of medical services to combat mother-to-child transmission of HIV.

[25] The applicants' contentions raise two questions, namely, is the policy of confining the supply of nevirapine reasonable in the circumstances; and does government have a comprehensive policy for the prevention of mother-to-child transmission of HIV.

The policy confining nevirapine to the research and training sites

[26] In deciding on the policy to confine nevirapine to the research and training sites, the cost of the drug itself was not a factor. This is made clear in the affidavit of Dr Ntsaluba, [who acknowledged that the manufacturer had offered to supply the drug for free for five years].

[27] The costs that are of concern to the government are therefore the costs of providing the infrastructure for counselling and testing, of providing formula feed, vitamins and an antibiotic drug and of monitoring, during bottle-feeding, the mothers and children who have received nevirapine. These costs are relevant to the comprehensive programme to be established at the research and training sites. They are not, however, relevant to the provision of a single dose of nevirapine to both mother and child at the time of birth.***

[28] In substance four reasons were advanced in the affidavits for confining the administration of nevirapine to the research and training sites. First, concern was expressed about the efficacy of nevirapine where the "comprehensive package" is not available. The concern was that the benefits of nevirapine would be counteracted by the transmission of HIV from mother to infant through breastfeeding. For this reason government considered it important to provide breastmilk substitutes to the mother and a "package" of care for mother and infant including vitamin supplements and antibiotics. They considered it necessary to establish a system and to put in place the infrastructure necessary for that purpose, to provide advice and counselling to the mothers to ensure that the substitute and supplements were used properly and to monitor progress to determine the effectiveness of the treatment. There are significant problems in making this package available. There are problems of resources in so far as counselling and testing are concerned and budgetary constraints affecting the expansion of facilities at public hospitals and clinics outside the research and training sites. There is a cultural objection to bottle-feeding that has to be overcome, and in rural areas there are also hazards in bottle-feeding by mothers who do not have access to clean water. There are still millions of people living in such circumstances and effective treatment of infants by the provision of nevirapine at birth by no means resolves all difficulties.

[29] Secondly, there was a concern that the administration of nevirapine to the mother and her child might lead to the development of resistance to the efficacy of nevirapine and related antiretrovirals in later years.

[30] Thirdly, there was a perceived safety issue. Nevirapine is a potent drug and it is not known what hazards may attach to its use.

[31] Finally, there was the question whether the public health system has the capacity to provide the package. It was contended on behalf of government that nevirapine should be administered only with the "full package" and that it was not reasonably possible to do this on a comprehensive basis because of the lack of trained counsellors and counselling facilities and also budgetary constraints which precluded such a comprehensive scheme being implemented.

[32] Related to this was a submission raised in argument that from a public health point of view, there is a need to determine the costs of providing the breastmilk substitute, the supplementary package and the necessary counselling and monitoring. Without knowing the full extent of these costs and the efficacy of the treatment, it would be unwise for government to commit itself to a wide-ranging programme for treating mother-to-child transmission that might prove to be neither efficacious nor sustainable.

[33] We deal with each of these issues in turn.

Efficacy

[34] First, the concern about efficacy. It is clear from the evidence that the provision of nevirapine will save the lives of a significant number of infants even if it is administered without the full package and support services that are available at the research and training sites. Mother-to-child transmission of HIV can take place during pregnancy, at birth and as a result of breastfeeding. The programme in issue in this case is concerned with transmission at or before birth.

[35] *** Indeed, the wealth of scientific material produced by both sides makes plain that sero-conversion of HIV takes place in some, but not all, cases and that nevi-

rapine thus remains to some extent efficacious in combating mother-to-child transmission even if the mother breastfeeds her baby.

Resistance

[36] As far as resistance is concerned, the only relevance is the possible need to treat the mother and/or the child at some time in the future. Although resistant strains of HIV might exist after a single dose of nevirapine, this mutation is likely to be transient.*** The prospects of the child surviving if infected are so slim and the nature of the suffering so grave that the risk of some resistance manifesting at some time in the future is well worth running.

Safety

[37] The evidence shows that safety is no more than a hypothetical issue. The only evidence of potential harm concerns risks attaching to the administration of nevirapine as a chronic medication on an ongoing basis for the treatment of HIV-positive persons. There is, however, no evidence to suggest that a dose of nevirapine to both mother and child at the time of birth will result in any harm to either of them.*** That is why its use is recommended without qualification for this purpose by the World Health Organization.

[38] There is also cogent South African endorsement of the safety of nevirapine [by] the Medicines Control Council.***

[39] The decision by government to provide nevirapine to mothers and infants at the research and training sites is consistent only with government itself being satisfied as to the efficacy and safety of the drug. These sites cater for approximately 10% of all births in the public sector and it is unthinkable that government would gamble with the lives or health of thousands of mothers and infants.***

[40] In any event the main thrust of government's case was that nevirapine should be administered in circumstances in which it would be most effective, not that it should not be administered because it is dangerous.***

[41] It is this that lies at the heart of government policy. There are obviously good reasons from the public health point of view to monitor the efficacy of the "full package" provided at the research and training sites and determine whether the costs involved are warranted by the efficacy of the treatment. There is a need to determine whether bottle-feeding will be implemented in practice when such advice is given and whether it will be implemented in a way that proves to be more effective than breastfeeding, bearing in mind the cultural problems associated with bottle-feeding, the absence of clean water in certain parts of the country and the fact that breastfeeding provides immunity from other hazards that infants growing up in poor households without access to adequate nutrition and sanitation are likely to encounter. However, this is not a reason for not allowing the administration of nevirapine elsewhere in the public health system when there is the capacity to administer it and its use is medically indicated.

Capacity

[42] According to Dr Simelela, there have been significant problems even at the research and training sites in providing a comprehensive programme using nevirapine for the prevention of mother-to-child transmission. A lack of adequately trained personnel, including counsellors, a shortage of space for conducting counselling and inad-

equate resources due to budgetary constraints made it impossible to provide such a programme.

[43] Although the concerns raised by Dr Simelela are relevant to the ability of government to make a "full package" available throughout the public health sector, they are not relevant to the question whether nevirapine should be used to reduce mother-to-child transmission of HIV at those public hospitals and clinics outside the research sites where facilities in fact exist for testing and counselling.

Considerations relevant to reasonableness

[44] The policy of confining nevirapine to research and training sites fails to address the needs of mothers and their newborn children who do not have access to these sites. It fails to distinguish between the evaluation of programmes for reducing mother-to-child transmission and the need to provide access to health care services required by those who do not have access to the sites.

[45] In *Grootboom* this Court held that

> [t]o be reasonable, measures cannot leave out of account the degree and extent of the denial of the right they endeavour to realise. Those whose needs are the most urgent and whose ability to enjoy all rights therefore is most in peril, must not be ignored by the measures aimed at achieving realisation of the right.

The fact that the research and training sites will provide crucial data on which a comprehensive programme for mother-to-child transmission can be developed and, if financially feasible, implemented is clearly of importance to government and to the country. So too is ongoing research into safety, efficacy and resistance. This does not mean, however, that until the best programme has been formulated and the necessary funds and infrastructure provided for the implementation of that programme, nevirapine must be withheld from mothers and children who do not have access to the research and training sites. Nor can it reasonably be withheld until medical research has been completed. A programme for the realisation of socio-economic rights must

> be balanced and flexible and make appropriate provision for attention to . . . crises and to short, medium and long term needs. A programme that excludes a significant segment of society cannot be said to be reasonable.***

[46] In dealing with these questions it must be kept in mind that this case concerns particularly those who cannot afford to pay for medical services. To the extent that government limits the supply of nevirapine to its research sites, it is the poor outside the catchment areas of these sites who will suffer. There is a difference in the positions of those who can afford to pay for services and those who cannot. State policy must take account of these differences.***

[47] In evaluating government's policy, regard must be had to the fact that this case is concerned with newborn babies whose lives might be saved by the administration of nevirapine to mother and child at the time of birth. The safety and efficacy of nevirapine for this purpose have been established and the drug is being provided by government itself to mothers and babies at the pilot sites in every province.

[48] The administration of nevirapine is a simple procedure. Where counselling and testing facilities exist, the administration of nevirapine is well within the available resources of the state and, in such circumstances, the provision of a single dose of nevirapine to mother and child where medically indicated is a simple, cheap and potentially lifesaving medical intervention.***

Does government have a comprehensive plan to combat mother-to-child transmission of HIV? ***

Testing and counselling

[49] The evidence shows that at the time of the commencement of these proceedings there was in place a comprehensive policy for testing and counselling of HIV-positive pregnant women. The policy was not, however, implemented uniformly.***

Formula-feeding

[50] Some of the policy documents also refer to the substitution of formula-feeding for breastfeeding without setting that as policy.*** In none of the policy documents is it said that government will actually provide the formula feed. [T]he cost of providing breastmilk substitutes must also be compared with or offset by the savings in preventing newborn babies being infected with HIV and consequently needing care.

Findings concerning government's programme

[51] In the present case this Court has the duty to determine whether the measures taken in respect of the prevention of mother-to-child transmission of HIV are reasonable. We know that throughout the country health services are overextended. HIV/AIDS is but one of many illnesses that require attention. It is, however, the greatest threat to public health in our country.***

[52] We are also conscious of the daunting problems confronting government as a result of the pandemic. And besides the pandemic, the state faces huge demands in relation to access to education, land, housing, health care, food, water and social security. These are the socio-economic rights entrenched in the Constitution, and the state is obliged to take reasonable legislative and other measures within its available resources to achieve the progressive realisation of each of them. In the light of our history this is an extraordinarily difficult task. Nonetheless it is an obligation imposed on the state by the Constitution.

[53] The rigidity of government's approach when these proceedings commenced affected its policy as a whole. If, as we have held, it was not reasonable to restrict the use of nevirapine to the research and training sites, the policy as a whole will have to be reviewed. Hospitals and clinics that have testing and counselling facilities should be able to prescribe nevirapine where that is medically indicated. The training of counsellors ought now to include training for counselling on the use of nevirapine. As previously indicated, this is not a complex task and it should not be difficult to equip existing counsellors with the necessary additional knowledge. In addition, government will need to take reasonable measures to extend the testing and counselling facilities to hospitals and clinics throughout the public health sector beyond the test sites to facilitate and expedite the use of nevirapine for the purpose of reducing the risk of mother-to-child transmission of HIV.

The powers of the courts ***

[54] The primary duty of courts is to the Constitution and the law, "which they must apply impartially and without fear, favour or prejudice." The Constitution requires the state to "respect, protect, promote, and fulfil the rights in the Bill of Rights." Where state policy is challenged as inconsistent with the Constitution, courts have to consider whether in formulating and implementing such policy the state has given effect to its constitutional obligations. If it should hold in any given case that the state has failed to do so, it is obliged by the Constitution to say so. In so far as that constitutes an intrusion into the domain of the executive, that is an intrusion mandated by the Constitution itself.***

[55] The rights that the state is obliged to "respect, protect, promote and fulfil" include the socio-economic rights in the Constitution.***

[56] An examination of the jurisprudence of foreign jurisdictions on the question of remedies shows that courts in other countries also accept that it may be appropriate, depending on the circumstances of the particular case, to issue injunctive relief against the state. In the United States, for example, frequent use has been made of the structural injunction—a form of supervisory jurisdiction exercised by the courts over a government agency or institution. Most famously, the structural injunction was used in the case of *Brown v Board of Education* where the US Supreme Court held that lower courts would need to retain jurisdiction of *Brown* and similar cases. These lower courts would have the power to determine how much time was necessary for the school boards to achieve full compliance with the Court's decision and would also be able to consider the adequacy of any plan proposed by the school boards "to effectuate a transition to a racially nondiscriminatory school system."

[57] Even a cursory perusal of the relevant Indian case law demonstrates a willingness on the part of the Indian courts to grant far-reaching remedial orders. Most striking in this regard is the decision in *M. C. Mehta v State of Tamil Nadu and Others* where the Supreme Court granted a wide-ranging order concerning child labour that included highly detailed mandatory and structural injunctions.***

[58] During the course of these proceedings the state's policy has evolved and is no longer as rigid as it was when the proceedings commenced. By the time this appeal was argued, six hospitals and three community health care centres had already been added in Gauteng to the two research and training sites initially established and it was contemplated that during the course of this year nevirapine would be available throughout the province for the treatment of mother-to-child transmission. Likewise, in KwaZulu-Natal there was a change of policy towards the supply of nevirapine at public health institutions outside the test sites.***

[59] These developments clearly demonstrate that, provided the requisite political will is present, the supply of nevirapine at public health institutions can be rapidly expanded to reach many more than the 10% of the population intended to be catered for in terms of the test site policy.

[60] But more importantly, we were informed at the hearing of the appeal that the government has made substantial additional funds available for the treatment of HIV, including the reduction of mother-to-child transmission.*** This means that the budgetary constraints referred to in the affidavits are no longer an impediment. With the additional funds that are now to be available, it should be possible to address any problems of financial incapacity that might previously have existed.***

Relief ***

[61] It is essential that there be a concerted national effort to combat the HIV/AIDS pandemic. The government has committed itself to such an effort. We have held that its policy fails to meet constitutional standards because it excludes those who could reasonably be included where such treatment is medically indicated to combat mother-to-child transmission of HIV. That does not mean that everyone can immediately claim access to such treatment, although the ideal, as Dr Ntsaluba says, is to achieve that goal. Every effort must, however, be made to do so as soon as reasonably possible. The increases in the budget to which we have referred will facilitate this.***

[62] We do not consider it appropriate to deal with the use of formula feed in the order. Whether it is desirable to use this substitute rather than breastfeeding raises complex issues, particularly when the mother concerned may not have easy access to clean water or the ability to adopt a bottle-feeding regimen because of her personal circumstances. The result of the studies conducted at the research and training sites may enable government to formulate a comprehensive policy in this regard. In the meantime this must be left to health professionals to address during counselling. We do not consider that there is sufficient evidence to justify an order that formula feed must be made available by the government on request and without charge in every case.***

Orders

[63] We accordingly make the following orders: ***

1. Government is ordered without delay to:

    a) Remove the restrictions that prevent nevirapine from being made available for the purpose of reducing the risk of mother-to-child transmission of HIV at public hospitals and clinics that are not research and training sites.

    b) Permit and facilitate the use of nevirapine for the purpose of reducing the risk of mother-to-child transmission of HIV and to make it available for this purpose at hospitals and clinics when in the judgment of the attending medical practitioner acting in consultation with the medical superintendent of the facility concerned this is medically indicated, which shall if necessary include that the mother concerned has been appropriately tested and counselled.

    c) Make provision if necessary for counsellors based at public hospitals and clinics other than the research and training sites to be trained for the counselling necessary for the use of nevirapine to reduce the risk of mother-to-child transmission of HIV.

    d) Take reasonable measures to extend the testing and counselling facilities at hospitals and clinics throughout the public health sector to facilitate and expedite the use of nevirapine for the purpose of reducing the risk of mother-to-child transmission of HIV.

2. The orders made in paragraph 3 do not preclude government from adapting its policy in a manner consistent with the Constitution if equally appropriate or better methods become available to it for the prevention of mother-to-child transmission of HIV.

3. The government must pay the applicants' costs, including the costs of two counsel.***

Notes and Questions

1. The petitioners, apparently learning the lessons of *Soobramoney* and *Grootboom*, did not argue that every pregnant woman had a right to be provided Nevirapine on demand, but challenged the government's failure to design a comprehensive nation-wide program. They further argued that the state should not prohibit the administration of the drug by doctors and other health care professionals in the public health sector so long as patients have given informed consent to treatment. Does the Court's decision reflect enforcement of a negative right, a positive right, or both?

2.   Both kidney disease and AIDS are serious, widespread, life-threatening harms in South Africa. Why did the Constitutional Court choose to provide a remedy for the latter and not the former? Does the perceived "public" nature of the AIDS epidemic in contrast to the "private" misfortune of kidney disease have a bearing on the decisions? In *Treatment Action Campaign*, the beneficiaries of constitutional relief were not the infected mothers, but the infants to whom the disease was transmitted *in utero*. Did an assumption of blameworthiness of the victims for their plight affect the Court's decisions? Should it?

3.   The fact that public housing has long been imbued with assumptions of government responsibility may also explain the *Grootboom* Court's willingness to intercede. Does mass homelessness evoke the specter of rampant crime, disease, and public unrest? Could it be that the Court more readily acknowledged rights and correlative state duties where there was a history of political struggle demanding their recognition? Both the housing and AIDS cases took place against the backdrop of tenacious local and international movements on those issues. In light of the huge domestic and international outcry over the South African government's handling of the AIDS crisis, was the Court unwilling to presume the good faith of public health authorities, as it had in *Soobramoney*?

4.   *Treatment Action Campaign*. Formed in December 1998, the Treatment Action Campaign (TAC) has become a veritable force in South Africa, using its broad-based grassroots support in combination with a strategic use of the legal system and the language of human rights, to increase access to HIV/AIDS medicines, increase the "treatment literacy" of South Africans living with HIV/AIDS, and put pressure on the government and multi-national pharmaceutical companies. In October of 2000, TAC initiated a campaign against the prohibitively high price of Pfizer's fluconazole that included TAC Chairperson Zachie Achmat bringing generic versions of the AIDS drug into South Africa from Thailand and publicly flouting this "breaking of the patent" at a press conference. A few months later TAC filed an *amicus* brief in a pending case brought by the Pharmaceutical Manufacturers Association (PMA) of South Africa and 39 multi-national drug companies against South Africa in order to strike provisions of the Medicines and Related Substances Control Act of 1997. For more on TAC and its legal efforts, *see* The Honorable Dennis M. Davis, *Symposium: Beyond Right and Reason: Pierre Schlag, The Critique of Normativity, and the Enchantment of Reason: Dissonance Orientation: The Occupational Hazard of Being a Judge or a Requirement for the Job?*, 57 U. MIAMI L. REV. 853, 861–64 (2003).

5.   *"Big Pharma vs. Nelson Mandela."* Commentator Ellen Hoen describes the infamous lawsuit brought by multi-national pharmaceutical corporations to challenge South Africa's efforts to provide low-cost drugs to stem the AIDS epidemic:

> In February 1998, the South African Pharmaceutical Manufacturers Association and forty (later thirty-nine, as a result of a merger) mostly multinational pharmaceutical manufacturers brought suit against the government of South Africa, alleging that the Medicines and Related Substances Control Amendment Act, No. 90 of 1997 ("Amendment Act") violated TRIPS and the South African constitution.
>
>   The Amendment Act introduces a legal framework to increase the availability of affordable medicines in South Africa. Provisions included in the Amendment Act are generic substitution of off-patent medicines, transparent pricing for all medicines, and the parallel importation of patented medicines.

At the start of the litigation, the drug companies could rely on the support of their home governments. For its part, the US had put pressure on South Africa by withholding trade benefits and threatening further trade sanctions, aiming to force the South African government to repeal the Amendment Act. In 1998, the European Commission joined the US in pressuring South Africa to repeal the legislation. AIDS activists effectively highlighted these policies, profoundly embarrassing then-presidential candidate Al Gore. Confronted at election campaign rallies about his personal involvement in the dispute, demonstrators accused him of killing babies in Africa. As a result of increasing public pressure, the US changed its policies at the end of 1999. By the time the case finally reached the courtroom in May 2000, the drug companies could no longer count on the support of their home governments.

Demonstrators in major cities asked the companies to drop the case; several governments and parliaments around the world, including the European Parliament, demanded that the companies withdraw from the case. The legal action turned into a public relations disaster for the drug companies.

During the course of the trial it became clear that the most contentious section of the Amendment Act was based on a draft legal text produced by the WIPO Committee of Experts, a fact that made it difficult for the drug companies to maintain the position that the Amendment Act violated South Africa's obligations under international law. Eventually, the strong international public outrage over the companies' legal challenge of a developing country's medicines law and the companies' weak legal position caused the companies to unconditionally drop the case in April 2001.

The widely publicized South African court case brought two key issues out into the international arena. First, the interpretation of the flexibilities of TRIPS and their use for public health purposes needed clarification to ensure that developing countries could use its provisions without the threat of legal or political challenge. Second, it became clear that industrialized countries that exercised trade pressures to defend the interest of their multinational industries could no longer exert pressure without repercussions at home.

Ellen T. Hoen, *TRIPS, Pharmaceutical Patents and Access to Essential Medicines: A Long Way from Seattle to Doha*, 3 CHI. J. INT'L L. 1, 30–31 (2002).

For the reaction of a South African legal organization involved in the case, and working closely with the Treatment Action Campaign, *see* Mark Heywood, *Pharmaceutical Case Ends: Not with a Bang But a Whimper*, AIDS Law Project, (May 1, 2001), *available at* http://www.alp.org.za/view.php?file=/resctr/sharts/20010501_artbang.xml&template=/display/article_printer.html#_ftn2. *See generally AIDS Activists Welcome Drug Move*, CNN, Aug. 19, 2001, *available at* http://www.cnn.com/2001/WORLD/africa/04/19/safrica.drugs.03/.

6.   For further reading on HIV/AIDS in sub-Saharan Africa, *see* ARVIND SINGHAL & W. STEPHEN HOWARD, THE CHILDREN OF AFRICA CONFRONT AIDS: FROM VULNERABILITY TO POSSIBILITY (2003); KAREN MCELRATH, HIV AND AIDS: A GLOBAL VIEW (2002); UNAIDS, ANCIENT REMEDIES, NEW DISEASE: INVOLVING TRADITIONAL HEALERS IN INCREASING ACCESS TO AIDS CARE AND PREVENTION IN EAST AFRICA (2002) (electronic book, *available at* UNAIDS (Joint United Nations Programme on HIV/AIDS) Web site http://www.

unaids.org); George C. Bond & Nigel C. Gibson, Contested Terrains and Constructed Categories: Contemporary Africa in Focus (2002); P. Bolton & C. Wilk, *How Do Africans View the Impact of HIV? A Report from a Ugandan Community*, 16(1) AIDS Care, at 123 (Jan. 2004); Joan Stephenson, *Global AIDS Epidemic Worsens*, 291(1) J. Am. Med. Assn, at 31 (Jan. 7, 2004); J. Mukherjee, *Tackling HIV in Resource Poor Countries*, 327(7423) Brit. Med. J., at 1104 (Nov. 8, 2003); Sydney Rosen & Jonathan L. Simon, *Shifting the Burden: the Private Sector's Response to the AIDS Epidemic in Africa*, 81(2) Bull. World Health Org., at 131 (2003); Alison Marshall & Tom Pravda, *The Vicious Circle: AIDS and Third World Debt: Report by the World Development Movement for the UN Special Session on HIV/AIDS* (June 25, 2001); AllAfrica Web site, AIDS page: http://allafrica.com/aids; HIV InSite Web site, Sub-Saharan Africa page (maintained by University of California at San Francisco): http://hivinsite.ucsf.edu/global?page=cr09-00-00.

What are the implications of the *TAC* decision for the right to have access to "sufficient" water, a right that is also protected in Section 27 of the South African Constitution? Is this right abridged by government policies of privatization of this vital resource? How should the term "sufficient" be construed? Consider the following.

GINGER THOMPSON, WATER TAP OFTEN SHUT TO SOUTH AFRICA'S POOR

N. Y. Times (May 29, 2003) at A1

SHAKASHEAD, South Africa—The afternoon's end brings a rural rush hour of women walking down the dirt road that winds through this village. Many of them barefoot and dressed in rags, the mothers and grandmothers come pushing wheelbarrows or carrying big buckets to fetch water for their families.

But the road quickly becomes a divide between the haves and have-nots. Those with pennies to spend stand in line on one side and buy their water from a metered tap.

The larger group scoops water from a giant, littered mud puddle across the way. Sewage seeps in from leaky pipes nearby. Some of the women said that cholera had stricken their families. Workers at a mobile clinic have reported high rates of diarrhea among children here.

"I know it is not good to take water from this hole," said Nolulama Makhiwa, a 27-year-old mother of two. "But I am not working. I have no money. What else can I do?"

Not long after the country's first democratic government came to power in 1994, putting an end to white minority rule, the new government enshrined the right to "sufficient food and water" in its Constitution, and pledged to make water and sanitation available to every citizen by the end of 2010.

At the same time, the government also began to shift more of the financial burden of those promises to a population in which at least one-third of people live on less than $2 a day. Officials urged municipal water utilities to adopt "cost recovery" policies that require them at least to break even, if not turn a profit.

Municipalities have begun working to turn debt-ridden and inefficient water utilities into profitable operations that could attract private investment. A handful have already granted long-term management concessions to private multinationals.

Advocates argue that such policies have become conventional wisdom, helping governments around the world make ends meet while encouraging conservation. Not only here in South Africa, however, but also in other developing countries like Bolivia, Ecuador and Argentina, privatization and water pricing have met strong resistance and public protests.

"Privatization is a new kind of apartheid," said Richard Makolo, leader of the Crisis Water Committee, which was formed to resist the privatization effort in a township called Orange Farm, 25 miles south of Johannesburg. "Apartheid separated whites from blacks. Privatization separates the rich from the poor."

South African officials say the change in policies has helped expand water services to 8 million of 13 million people who did not have water when apartheid ended. But the statistics have not added up to progress in many poor communities, which have won their first reliable water services but now struggle to pay for them.

The issue of access to services has become an explosive new cause in the same urban townships and rural squatter camps that were principal battlegrounds in the fight against apartheid. During the World Summit on Sustainable Development last August, thousands marched from the tin shacks of Alexandra past the elegant mansions of Sandton to protest, among other things, water and electricity cutoffs and evictions. Their cry: "Water for the thirsty. Light for the people. Homes for the homeless."

Leaders in sprawling townships including Soweto, Alexandra and Orange Farm have encouraged people not to pay electricity and water bills. They have organized teams of bootleg plumbers and electricians to reconnect utilities when they are cut off. Political rallies and demonstrations have turned into street fights.

The highest costs to poor communities have come in the form of disease and mass disconnections. Three years ago, this province on the northeast coast was the center of the country's worst cholera epidemic in recent history, with 120,000 reported cases and nearly 260 deaths. The epidemic spread to seven of the country's nine provinces.

Small outbreaks continue to occur, as those who cannot afford to pay for water in advance from communal meters or have been cut off from services for not paying rising water bills are forced to seek sources in polluted puddles, rivers and canals that carry disease.

Here in Shakashead, the women, speaking in their native Zulu, explained that only the luckiest among them have jobs at all, in the emerald sugar cane fields that surround their village. Those who work, they said, earn less than $45 a month, not always enough to cover the costs of food and water.

"There is good water here, but you must pay for it," Ms. Makhiwa said. "If you can see the way we live, you can see that we cannot pay."

A survey by the government's Human Sciences Research Council for the independent Municipal Services Project found that up to 10 million people have been affected by water cutoffs since the end of white-minority rule.

David McDonald, co-director of the Municipal Services Project, said the government's own reports have portrayed a "crisis of serious proportions." One report, he said, indicated that some 700,000 people were affected by water cutoffs in just the final months of 2001. Meanwhile, he said, surveys showed some 1.3 million people had their electricity cut off, including some 20,000 customers each month in Soweto.

In a telephone interview and e-mail exchanges, a high-level water official rebutted the water cutoff estimates, saying they were "based on a deliberate distortion of very limited survey information."

Mr. McDonald countered: "As far as I'm concerned, you can cut our estimates of water cutoffs in half. The figures are still a serious indictment of post-apartheid cost recovery policies."

In the months following the cholera outbreaks, national water officials started a campaign urging municipalities to provide all households with at least a minimal "lifeline" of free water—some 1,500 gallons a month. Mike Muller, director general of the water department, said that an estimated 76 percent of municipalities had committed to the effort.

"We have had to confront the fact that in a very unequal society like South Africa, a policy of cost recovery, which makes perfect sense in a more equitable society, would exclude the poor from access to that basic commodity, to which they have a right," he said in an interview with the South African press.

But David Hemson, of the Human Services Research Council, said free water still had not been provided to millions living in shantytowns and rural areas who were most at risk for water-borne diseases, like the residents of Shakashead, where no free water was available. Even in communities where a "lifeline" service is provided, water taps are set to dispense a limited amount of water and are then shut down. In others, drip devices have been installed, literally dispensing water onc drop at a time.

"The real battle for everyone to understand is how much does it cost to provide water to a nation and how do we pay for it," Mr. Muller said. "This is not privatizing, it is a massive reorganization of a government and how it provides services. We are still working it out."

The KwaDukuza municipality that covers Shakashead, with a population of about 60,000 people that is expected to expand rapidly in the next decade, became the first to sign a long-term management concession with a private company. The agreement, signed in 1999, gave French-based Saur a 25-year control over management of the water utility.

Three years ago, Johannesburg Water signed a more limited management contract with the France-based conglomerate Suez.

Among the newest efforts by Johannesburg Water has been the installation of prepaid water meters in townships around the country's business capital. The first prepaid meters were installed last year in Orange Farm, and led to the formation of the Orange Farm Crisis Water Committee, the group headed by Mr. Makolo.

Under the prepaid system, to begin next month and to be expanded to other Johannesburg townships in the next couple of years, families will only get as much water as they can pay for in advance. Their payments will be recorded on digital discs, about as big as a quarter. The disc fits inside the water meter, and activates the taps.

Jean-Pierre Mas, the operations executive at Johannesburg Water, said prepay meters would allow customers to use only the amount of water they could afford, and help the utility avoid clashes over cutoffs.***

Officials at Johannesburg Water acknowledged that in communities like these, billing people for water has been like squeezing water from a stone. In addition to the limited resources, a culture of nonpayment lingers from the years when people refused to pay utility bills, usually a flat fee for water and electricity, in support of boycotts against the apartheid regime.

"The problem is not that we do not want to pay for water," said Hilda Mkwanza, a 45-year-old mother of six who lives in Orange Farm. "The problem is we cannot pay."

Interviews with her and other Orange Farm women, who live by doing other people's laundry, said they barely had enough money to pay for food and school fees. Many of them already have prepaid electricity meters in their homes, and they say their families end up in the dark for several days each month.

Mr. Makolo, a veteran of the anti-apartheid movement, urges people not to pay. His motto, he said, is "destroy the meters and enjoy the water."

"The government promised us that water is a basic right," he said. "But now they are telling us our rights are for sale."

Notes and Questions

1.   Compare the discussion of water privatization in Chapter 3.A, *supra*. Do you find it ironic that tactics used against the apartheid regime are being applied in the struggle for basic rights against the Black majority government? Could the political conditions under which the transition to majority rule took place have preordained the problems addressed in this article? Consider the following analysis of the South African democratization process:

> There was tremendous pressure on the ANC leadership to abandon the liberation demands of the Freedom Charter, which had been its guiding platform since 1956, opting instead for a "civil rights" model. "The de Klerk government, the country's four gigantic business conglomerates, the IMF and the World Bank, and virtually all Western governments were preaching free-market economics and urging privatization of South Africa's scores of state-owned companies." Preparing to take the reins of a crumbling economy, the ANC succumbed to the pressure.
>
> The result is power sharing, a compromise among parties procedurally equal, but vastly unequal in terms of real power. Power sharing as the conception of the good resolves the ultimate constitutive questions facing the new nation.*** Power sharing means *** civil rights, not economic justice; emphasis on investment, not people's needs; amnesty, not justice; continuation, not transformation.***
>
> Power sharing means that South Africa will remain on the periphery of the world economy. By moving decisively away from apartheid, and into the liberal tradition, South Africa's black majority will achieve equal liberty in the only African country denominated an "emerging market" by the U.S. Commerce Department. South Africa's belated embrace of democracy will free its vast resources and markets from the isolation of apartheid making them fully accessible to international capital. Land long ago expropriated from the African people, however, will largely remain in white hands. So will the country's mineral riches—its gold, diamonds, platinum, and other precious and strategic metals. The election will bring to fruition the Borkian vision of substantive neutrality:

the application of principles that render impotent any preferences that infringe upon the prerogatives of the powerful.***

Jeanne M. Woods, *The Fallacy of Neutrality: Diary of an Election Observer*, 18 MICH. J. INT'L L. 475, 503–506 (1997).

2. *Value of Precedents for Right to Education.* What are the implications of the South African jurisprudence excerpted above for the right to education? Do the cases provide a basis for a legal challenge to the inequities in the educational system? Does education that meets a particular standard of quality go beyond the "minimum core" required under the precedents? How would a court determine what that standard should be? Would such a determination raise separation of powers issues? Consider the following materials.

ERIC BERGER, NOTE: THE RIGHT TO EDUCATION UNDER THE SOUTH AFRICAN CONSTITUTION

103 COLUM. L. REV. 614, 614–628 (2003)

[I]n contemporary South Africa, where the country has included the right to education in its emphatically modern Constitution,*** schools, particularly for poor blacks, remain woefully inadequate. The explanation for these shortcomings is obvious—the nation simply lacks the resources to address all its citizens' needs—and yet the consequences are significant. Even after the fall of apartheid, South Africa is the world's third most economically unequal country. If South Africa is to become an "open and democratic society based on human dignity, equality and freedom," its education system must work to remedy the country's stark inequalities.***

The Quality of Education in South Africa

Like most injustices in contemporary South Africa, educational inequality can be traced easily back to apartheid. Shortly after the National Party victory in 1948, the architects of apartheid implemented a formalized system of race-based education. Codified in the Bantu Education Act of 1953 and the Extension of University Education Act, national education policy was an integral part of apartheid's dehumanizing segregation. African schools were thus designed accordingly, training students in subservience and manual labor.

Decades later, even after the country's first free elections in 1994 and school desegregation, the lingering effects of such policies are visible in poor schooling for students of all ages. A recent study shows that South African pupils at age ten are "way behind" those in many other African countries, such as Botswana and Madagascar. Nowhere are the inadequacies more evident than in predominantly black areas; apartheid's impact on the education of African children, particularly in the rural "homelands," remains severe. As Minister of Education Kader Asmal grimly acknowledged, "South Africa is two nations, poor and rich. After apartheid, when this two nation status is no longer kept in place by violence but by the workings of inertia and of continuing privilege, the higher education system, in large measure, continues to reproduce the inequities of the past."

Indeed, a number of factors conspire to make poor schools hard to improve. Perhaps most important, recent government economic policies, as reflected in the 1998

Growth, Employment and Redistribution Programme (GEAR), have begun to prioritize fiscal discipline rather than social redress, designing policies to achieve low inflation rates and debt control. The government has thus begun to decentralize and privatize many social benefits, including education. Not surprisingly, government educational expenditures have decreased noticeably, and it is the poorest schools that have been hardest hit.

Budget reductions compound a number of difficulties poor schools already face. For instance, most schools, even in the poorest areas, charge "users' fees" to all parents; budget cuts force schools to rely even more on these fees to provide an education. Many poor parents have difficulty paying these fees, meaning either that their children do not receive an education or that the schools do not receive adequate funding to instruct their students. Not surprisingly, these "tuition" requirements perpetuate the very inequalities that education theoretically would help the nation overcome.***

*** Without additional funding to provide remedial literacy training and materials, schools in poor neighborhoods will be unlikely to overcome the educational obstacles inherent in poverty. Indeed, such concerns suggest that the poorer schools need significantly more funding than richer schools if education is truly to benefit all South Africans.

Given the difficulties facing many South African schools and the government's reluctance to provide the funding to address them, it is not surprising that their facilities and achievement rates are poor. Statistics are an incomplete measure of educational quality, but they do paint a general picture of a school district's needs. Even after the African National Congress (ANC) government came to power, black education remained vastly inferior to white education, despite the fact that educational equity became a basic principle of the budget strategy.*** The poorest schools also lack the facilities enjoyed by wealthier communities. As recently as 2000, over 35% of all school buildings were in "weak to very weak" condition, and, of course, buildings needing the most repairs were concentrated in poor, predominantly black, areas. A recent analysis showed approximately one-half of the rural Northern Province's 1.9 million students to have no water within walking distance of their schools.*** Whereas only two of ten African children reach the "matric" year in their education, eight of ten white children do. One result is that illiteracy is prevalent in South Africa, and, again, the wealthier white provinces of the Western Cape and Gauteng have the highest literacy rates (76.4% and 75.6% respectively), while the rural, poor, and mostly black Northern Province has the lowest (58.9%).

Of course, apartheid schools explain why many older people cannot read, but the Department of Education itself also cites poor teaching and lack of access to reading materials as reasons why learner achievement continues to be poor. Indeed, the failure in the poor communities seems to start during the earliest years.***

A final obstacle to improving the quality of education is the culture of violence and sexual abuse that has become common in South African public schools. A recent study by Human Rights Watch says that sexual abuse by both teachers and other students is widespread in South African schools. The phenomenon is most frequent in the poorest, mostly black neighborhoods, where some teachers take advantage of poor students by swapping small gifts for sex. In addition to highlighting what dangerous places South African schools have become, this trend is also having a pronounced negative impact on girls' education. In the worst neighborhoods, girls are coming to school less frequently and finding it harder to concentrate when they do.***

II. The Constitutional Right to Education ***

The South African Constitution explicitly guarantees the right to education. Section 29 of the Constitution's Bill of Rights states that "Everyone has the right (a) to a basic education *** and (b) to further education, which the state, through reasonable measures, must make progressively available and accessible."***

*** Under the Constitution, basic education is a "strong positive right," a right that can be asserted regardless of the state's other budgetary imperatives. Unlike further education, which the government need only make "progressively available" "through reasonable measures," the right to basic education appears absolute. While the government may decide how to structure its schools, section 29(1)(a) gives constitutional support to an unhappy parent who might demand that the state immediately provide her child with better education through the ninth grade. By way of contrast, section 29(1)(b) provides not an absolute right to further education, but a right to reasonable governmental measures that make it progressively available.***

Though the Constitution provides for both basic and further education, section 29 does not make clear the quality of education the state must provide, so we must turn to other constitutional provisions for guidance.*** A narrow reading of the text might then find that any education—whether adequate or not—satisfies the "basic" and "further" requirements, so long as it ostensibly addresses students in the relevant age or learning groups. Merely providing the opportunity to attend school would satisfy the state's constitutional obligations. However, the Constitution sets forth general provisions with which to interpret the Bill of Rights, and, relying on these, the Court should find that section 29 does in fact promise what some American state jurisprudence would call "adequate" education.

The Bill of Rights itself opens with the insistence that the "state must respect, protect, promote and fulfil [sic] the rights in the Bill of Rights," thus suggesting that the government must play an active role in continuing to improve access to positive rights. Additionally, section 39 of the Constitution requires courts interpreting the Bill of Rights to "promote the values that underlie an open and democratic society based on human dignity, equality and freedom." Interpreting section 29 to require the state merely to provide education, without any implicit quality standard, would thus pervert section 39's interpretative instructions. Not only would such an interpretation render section 29 virtually toothless, but also it would run counter to the democratic values the Constitution explicitly seeks to promote.

For a democracy to work, its populace must be educated enough to research and analyze its choices. Political philosophers such as Thomas Jefferson and John Dewey have long recognized the crucial role education plays in well-functioning democracies. Similarly, democratic societies protect their citizens' freedoms, so that people can pursue their goals and pecuniary well-being. In poorer, developing nations, however, negative liberty might not be enough to secure each individual's opportunity to compete in the marketplace; the government, in those instances, might need to take additional steps to give people the chance to participate in the first place. Indeed, economist Amartya Sen has argued that "[d]evelopment can be seen *** as a process of expanding the real freedoms that people enjoy." To be sure, many democracies fall short of this ideal, but the ideal nonetheless remains fundamental to democratic theory. To argue, then, that section 29 promises a place to go to school, but not an adequate education, would undermine section 39's requirement that the Bill of Rights be interpreted to foster the values of a free and democratic society.***

Moreover, section 39 states that courts "must consider international law" when interpreting the Bill of Rights. One treaty to which the Court has looked is the International Covenant on Economic, Social and Cultural Rights (ICESCR), which specifically recognizes "the right of everyone to education [that is] directed to the full development of the human personality and the sense of its dignity, and [to] the respect for human rights and fundamental freedoms." Given that the Covenant speaks directly to the question of education, the Court should again turn to the ICESCR to find that the Constitution promises an adequate education to promote democratic principles.

Section 28 offers a final argument for requiring an adequate education. It considers children's rights generally and asserts, "A child's best interests are of paramount importance in every matter concerning the child." While the Constitution does treat education separately (partially to cover adult education), this clause would seem to further strengthen a child's right to an adequate education.***

HUMAN RIGHTS WATCH, FORGOTTEN SCHOOLS: RIGHT TO BASIC EDUCATION FOR CHILDREN ON FARMS IN SOUTH AFRICA

Available at http://hrw.org/reports/2004/southafrica0504/ (May 2004)

I. Summary

There are many problems at this school. Sometimes we can't hold classes because the farm manager locks the main gate allowing no public access. The pupils can only attend class by entering onto the school premises through a hole in the fence. There is no electricity and no running water at the school.*** The district education officer tells me to see the farm manager about these problems, but the manager refuses to speak to me. There is no assistance from the farm owner and the department of education does not help us. School inspectors visited just one month ago but nothing ever changes here.

—Primary school teacher, Free State Province, May 23, 2003

The South African government is failing to protect the right to a primary education for children living on commercial farms by neither ensuring their access to farm schools nor maintaining the adequacy of learning conditions at these schools. This violates South Africa's 1996 South African Schools Act (Schools Act), the National Education Policy Act, and its obligations under the Convention on the Rights of the Child. Receiving an education is compulsory for all children up to grade nine or age fifteen, depending on whichever comes first. The historical, social and economic conditions on commercial farms, inherited from years of an undemocratic minority government, mean that farm schools—public schools on private commercial farms, which constitute 13 percent of all state-funded schools and provide education to about 3 percent of learners in the public school system—are among the poorest in financial resources, physical structure and quality in South Africa. Farm children may attend schools without electricity, drinking water, sanitation, suitable buildings or adequate learning materials. Also, children may face harassment from farm owners.

While the present government has made efforts to redress these conditions, including promulgating legislation recognizing education as a right and introducing policies aimed at addressing the needs of the poorest schools in South Africa, a great deal remains to be done; not least the full implementation of national government policies at provincial government level. Without adequately addressing the conditions at farm schools—which provide an education for farmworkers' children—they remain impoverished and limit children's educational opportunities.

The government has adopted a legal framework to convert schools on commercial farms from largely farm owner-controlled institutions to ordinary government-managed public schools with limited farm owner responsibility, through a process of concluding contracts with each farm owner where a school is located. But the process of concluding these contracts has been unacceptably slow and threatens the continued operation of schools. To date, a minority of these farm schools is governed by such agreements. In some cases, the farm owner or manager of the land on which a farm school is built has actively tried to prevent children or teachers from accessing the school. While government officials and police do, on occasion, intervene to ensure access, these interventions do not prevent future interference. By not negotiating these agreements, the legal status of the schools is uncertain and the responsibility for the provision of services on the premises left ambiguous. Furthermore, ineffective remedial measures prohibiting landowners or managers from preventing physical access to premises demonstrate that the government is failing to protect the right of children on commercial farms to receive a primary education—a right the government is legally obliged to protect under the Schools Act, the National Education Policy Act and the Convention on the Rights of the Child.

Farm schools are the only accessible sites of education for many children who live with their parents or relatives on commercial farms. Historically under apartheid, farm owners established these schools—in part to keep the children occupied by providing a basic, limited education while their parents or relatives worked on the farm. The owner was effectively in charge of the school, though he/she received a state subsidy under an agreement with the government. The joint government and farm owner-management of farm schools confused the roles of government and farm owner in the provision of education in a way that continues today. Since the introduction of a new legal framework governing schools in South Africa, farm schools have been classified as public schools on private property. The 1996 Schools Act provides for the transition of farm schools from their previous status to public schools. As part of this process, contractual agreements must be concluded between farm owners and the provincial departments of education. The Schools Act also makes provision for the expropriation of the land on which a school is built in the public interest—that is for educational purposes—if an agreement cannot be concluded. At the time of writing, land had not been expropriated.***

Most farm schools have only the barest of facilities—a classroom. Water and power supply, which in a number of cases depend on the co-operation of the landowner, are not always available. At some schools fresh drinking water is not available. The lack of power affects the administrative activities at a school and also hinders advancement in teaching. The state, or where applicable the farm owner, is required in terms of the regulations made under the Schools Act to provide basic services such as adequate drinking water, sanitation and power. Some schools lack sanitation altogether; in others the facilities are in disrepair and unhygienic. Failing to provide basic services, which encompass the fulfillment of the right to education, are directly linked to an absence of contracts that would normally delineate which party—state or farm owner—is responsible for their provision.

This report documents cases where landowners obstructed physical access to schools or frustrated their functioning by suspending water supply or closing off short routes to a school. A landowner may use the threat of closure of a school to drive parents off the farm to a location where they can find education for their children. Greater efforts need to be made to secure the tenure of farm schools and thereby protect the right to education, in particular by ensuring the speedy conclusion of agreements with the landowners of schools that are not yet covered by this process. The government should—in line with the Schools Act and the South African constitution—develop guidelines for the expropriation of land in the public interest in instances where agreement cannot be reached and measures to resolve the matter have been exhausted.

The lack of state-funded transport from homes to farm schools further hinders the right of access to education in commercial farm areas. Because commercial farms are large and children from neighboring farms travel long journeys on foot, the lack of transportation can prevent children in South Africa's commercial farming districts from accessing schools. For example, two-thirds of the children—some as young as eight years old—attending a farm school in Vaalwater, Limpopo Province travel up to thirty kilometers on foot each morning to school. Fatigue and exhaustion adversely affect these and many other children's ability to adequately participate in activities in the classroom. Furthermore, children are exposed to dangers such as sexual assault and road accidents when walking to and from school. This can result in non-attendance or irregular attendance. This report argues that the state's provision of transportation, particularly for those pupils who have to walk long distances to schools and do not have the financial means to pay for transportation, is essential for access to education.***

The hardships children in the farming community face are enormous. Their parents' precarious tenure on the land, poverty, and poorly resourced police services that are unable to deliver prompt assistance to children, all affect the enjoyment of children's right to education as enshrined in the South African constitution. However, there are steps that can and should be taken by the state to guarantee the right to education of children on farms. The primary responsibility to protect the right to an education for children attending farm schools rests with the government.***

Notes and Questions

1. *Textual Analysis of Section 29.* How does the language of Section 29(a) differ from that of Sections 26 (right to housing) and 27 (right to health care)? What is the significance of these textual differences? Does Section 29(b) require that the government develop a comprehensive plan for further education?

2. *Equal Protection.* Does the current state of South African education violate Section 9 of the Constitution? What kind of equal protection analysis is suggested by the constitutional text? Are the government's duties under this provision limited to "negative" protections? What is the difference, if any, between equal protection and the Court's "vulnerable groups" analysis in *Grootboom*? Does the privatization of education potentially violate Section 9? Compare U.S. federal and state approaches to education rights in Chapter 10, *infra*.

3. Does the international community bear any legal or moral responsibility for the South African situation? Does the right to development, *see* Chapter 5, *supra*, offer any possibilities? Consider the following.

JEANNE M. WOODS, JUSTICIABLE SOCIAL RIGHTS AS A CRITIQUE OF THE LIBERAL PARADIGM

38 TEX. INT'L L.J. 763, 790–793 (2003)

*** The South African case law has evolved from the rejection of individual rights claims for life-preserving dialysis treatment, to recognition of collective rights to comprehensive government programs to address urgent social needs for housing and health care. Permeating these decisions is the influence of the two often-countervailing components of the social construction of rights: ideology and practice. On the one hand, pervasive individualist norms, such as the public/private dichotomy and the principle of free choice, inhibit the expansion of rights analysis beyond traditional first generation liberties. On the other, popular movements stimulate legal developments that can lead to more encompassing definitions of rights.***

The new South African jurisprudence demonstrates that there are no institutional obstacles to the realization of collective rights where the political will exists to enforce them. The cases also show that the full protection of social rights cannot be achieved without a reevaluation and reconstruction of liberal rights discourse.

According to economist Michel Chossudovsky, the world's poor countries, with 85.2% of the population, share only 21.5% of its income, while rich nations—14.8% of the population—account for 78.5%. As the chasm widens between the planet's privileged minority and its impoverished masses, the need for international recognition of collective rights has never been more apparent. Such a development is needed to fulfill the promise of universality proclaimed by human rights discourse. As Felice points out, in many cultures "the concept of collective human rights *** has an historical basis that runs far deeper *** than does the Western concept of individual rights." Moreover, individual rights are inadequate to protect disempowered groups when collective rights have not been realized.

The argument that a scarcity of resources renders social rights unattainable is unpersuasive. It is well documented that the world's abundant resources are sufficient to meet minimum core needs. World poverty is a function not of scarcity, but of distribution. [Michael] Walzer defines the available resources of the community as "the past and present product, the accumulated wealth of its members—not some 'surplus' of that wealth.*** Socially recognized needs are the first charge against the social product; there is no real surplus until they have been met." He criticizes the inherently undemocratic nature of the right to unlimited accumulation in the face of dire need: "Men and women who appropriate vast sums of money for themselves while needs are still unmet act like tyrants, dominating and distorting the distribution of security and welfare."

To Walzer's definition I would add that the available resources include not just the wealth produced within a given state but that of the global community as a whole. This conception flows not only from the recognition of humanity's interdependence in the age of globalization but from elementary principles of justice: the international slave trade, colonialism, apartheid, physical and cultural genocide of indigenous peoples and continued inequities in North-South relations provide ample grounds to support an inclusive definition of available resources. Moreover, these historical experiences are constitutive of the human person in the twenty-first century. They are part of our collective identity. They are who we are. The rapid globalization of the economy and communications, as well as objective threats to global human welfare—such as nuclear war, environmental degradation, and the AIDS epidemic—lend urgency to the need for a collective conceptualization of the self that transcends geographical boundaries.

Thus, the available resources of South Africa include not only the monies directly at the disposal of the state; they include the immense wealth in the hands of the white minority—riches wrung from the suffering of the African people. It is possible that when the total resources of the country are taken into account, kidney dialysis could be considered a component of the minimum core right to health. Moreover, many rich nations are heavily indebted to the Black majority of South Africa for their government's economic, political, diplomatic, and military support of the apartheid regime. Similarly, the available resources of the "Third World" include those of the industrialized nations whose development was made possible by colonial exploitation.

Despite its theoretical weaknesses, the collective right of peoples to development offers a potential conceptual framework within which the issue of scarcity of resources can be addressed. Originally formulated by Senegalese jurist Keba M'Baye, the United Nations General Assembly adopted the Declaration on the Right to Development in 1986. The Declaration defines the right to development in both individual and collective terms. It is "an inalienable human right by virtue of which every human person and all peoples are entitled to participate in, contribute to, and enjoy economic, social, cultural and political development, in which all human rights and fundamental freedoms can be fully realized."

Critics correctly point out that the Declaration is vague as to the juridical basis and normative content of the right to development, including the identity of the rights-holders and duty-holders. Tanzanian scholar Issa Shivji criticizes the concept as essentially a demand for charity "based on an illusory model of co-operation and solidarity." When seen as part of the global demand for economic, social, and cultural rights, however, the right to development has the potential to surmount welfarist constraints. As William Felice argues, the right to development establishes an emerging principle in international law that "there is a collective international responsibility for the human condition."***

In order for human rights discourse to evolve in the twenty-first century, the eighteenth-century fiction of natural, self-evident rights must give way to the realization that all rights are social constructs. They are the product of collective struggles: particular demands made on organized society in particular historical times and places. They represent values that, as a result of these struggles, society has agreed to prioritize. Critical scholars have deconstructed, denounced, and defended rights discourse, and have vigorously debated the efficacy of reifying fundamental values in legal form. Nevertheless, rights ideology is a powerful transformative force and a potent weapon in the hands of the dispossessed. Just as individual rights-talk served as a catalyst in the democratic revolutions of Europe and the United States, so too will the demand for second and third-generation rights play a galvanizing role in the ongoing struggle of the world's impoverished millions to realize fully the dream of human dignity.

Further Reading

For further reading on human rights in South Africa, *see* MAKAU MUTUA, HUMAN RIGHTS: A POLITICAL AND CULTURAL CRITIQUE (2002); ROBERT I. ROTBERG & DENNIS THOMPSON EDS., TRUTH V. JUSTICE: THE MORALITY OF TRUTH COMMISSIONS (2000); Penelope Andrews, *Reparations for Apartheid's Victims: The Path to Reconciliation?* 53 DEPAUL L. REV. 1155 (2004); Shedrack C. Agbakwa, *Reclaiming Humanity: Economic, Social, and Cultural Rights as the Cornerstone of African Human Rights*, 5 YALE H.R. & DEV. L.J. 177 (2002); Kevin Hopkins, *Africa at the Crossroads: Current Themes in African Law: VII. Commentary: Assessing the World's Response to Apartheid: A Historical Account of International Law and its Part in the South African Transformation*, 10 U. MIAMI INT'L & COMP. L. REV. 241 (2001/02); Yvonne Mokgoro, *Foreword: The Protection of Cultural Identity in the Constitution and the Creation of National Unity in South Africa: A Contradiction in Terms?*, 52 SMU L. REV. 1549 (1999); H.A. Strydom, *Minority Rights Issues in Post-Apartheid South Africa*, 19 LOY. L.A. INT'L & COMP. L.J. 873 (1997).

CHAPTER NINE

THE COUNCIL OF EUROPE:
A BLENDING OF THE CATEGORIES

A. THE EUROPEAN COURT OF HUMAN RIGHTS

1. Structure of the Court

Plenary Court: composed of all 44 judges. It promulgates rules, sets up the different bodies of the Court, and supervises the entire Court.

Rapporteur: composed of one judge. He or she makes the initial determination of admissibility and assigns cases to Committees of Three or Chambers.

Committees: composed of three judges. The Committees are constituted by Chambers for a fixed period of time. They do not address the merits, but decide on admissibility of state and individual applications. A determination of admissibility may be made by a majority vote, but it takes a unanimous decision to dismiss an application as inadmissible. Decisions on admissibility are final. The Committees do not have the authority to dismiss a state application as inadmissible.

Chambers: composed of seven judges. Chambers are constituted by the Plenary Court for a fixed period of time. This is the trial section, determining both admissibility and the merits.

Grand Chamber: composed of 17 judges. The Grand Chamber obtains contentious jurisdiction upon the relinquishment of jurisdiction by a Chamber, or upon referral of a Chamber's judgment by a party. (Here it acts as an appellate court.) The Grand Chamber may also render an advisory opinion upon the request of the Committee of Ministers.

The European Court of Human Rights provides the central means for enforcement of the rights set forth in the European Convention for the Protection of Human Rights and Fundamental Freedoms, which entered into force in 1953 and has been ratified by 44 states.[1] The Convention protects "first generation" civil and political rights, including the right to a fair trial (Article 6); the right to respect for private and family life,

---

[1] The states that have ratified the Convention include: Albania, Andorra, Armenia, Austria, Azerbaijan, Belgium, Bosnia and Herzegovina, Bulgaria, Croatia, Cyprus, Czech Republic, Denmark, Estonia, Finland, France, Georgia, Germany, Greece, Hungary, Iceland, Ireland, Italy, Latvia, Liechtenstein, Lithuania, Luxembourg, Malta, Moldova, Netherlands, Norway, Poland, Portugal, Romania, Russia, San Marino, Slovak Republic, Slovenia, Spain, Sweden, Switzerland, The Former Yugoslav Republic of Macedonia, Turkey, Ukraine and the United Kingdom.

home, and correspondence (Article 8); and the right to equal protection (Article 14). These rights are increasingly applied by the Court to provide protection for "second" and "third generation" rights.

Originally, three institutions were charged with the responsibility for enforcing the rights provided in the Convention: the European Commission of Human Rights (established in 1954), the European Court of Human Rights (created in 1959) and the Committee of Ministers of the Council of Europe, the latter organ being composed of the Ministers for Foreign Affairs of the Member States or their representatives. In November 1998, Protocol No. 11 entered into force, abolishing the Commission and putting an end to the Committee of Ministers' adjudicative role, thus creating a full-time, strengthened European Court of Human Rights. The Commission continued to function for one additional year in order to dispose of a backlog of cases, and held its final session in 1999.

Organization of the Court. Pursuant to Protocol 11, the Court is now divided into four bodies: Committees of Three; Chambers; the Grand Chamber; and the Plenary Court. The judges presiding over these bodies are appointed by the Parliamentary Assembly of the Council of Europe, which selects one judge from three candidates proposed by each Member State.

The Committees of Three are charged with the preliminary review of cases. The Committees may reject cases by unanimous vote, pursuant to an initial determination of admissibility. Chambers of seven judges examine cases not rejected by the Committees, reviewing both admissibility and the merits. When a case contains a difficult issue of interpretation of the Convention, or where there is a risk of departing from existing case law, a lower chamber may relinquish jurisdiction to the Grand Chamber. The Grand Chamber, composed of 17 judges, decides cases which raise serious questions affecting the application of the Convention or an important issue of general significance. A party may also request review by the Grand Chamber after a decision by a lower chamber.

Procedure for Adjudication of Complaints. Under the Convention, the European Court of Human Rights exercises jurisdiction over complaints against contracting states for alleged violations of Convention rights. Complaints may be brought by contracting states, individuals, groups of individuals or non-governmental organizations.

Determination of Admissibility. The procedure and criteria applicable to a determination of admissibility remained essentially unchanged following the implementation of Protocol 11. Each application is assigned to a section of the Court, and undergoes preliminary review by a *judge rapporteur* who decides whether the complaint should be reviewed by a three-member committee or by a chamber. Applications referred to a committee may be declared inadmissible or excluded without further examination by a unanimous vote. Chambers examine petitions deemed admissible by a committee, petitions referred directly to a chamber by the *judge rapporteur*, and state applications. Chambers determine both admissibility and merits. The chamber may decide to hold a preliminary hearing on admissibility, in which issues relating to the merits of the claim will be addressed. Chamber decisions on admissibility must contain reasons and be made public.

The standards of admissibility applied at the chamber level are generally the same as those applied during the initial admissibility inquiry performed previously by the commission. A petitioner must have standing to bring a complaint under the criteria set out in Articles 34 and 35 of the Convention. The Court will refuse to admit petitions brought by claimants who lack standing or have failed to exhaust domestic remedies. A complaint may be dismissed because it is: (1) incompatible with the provisions of the Convention; (2) substantially similar to an application previously examined by the Court; (3) manifestly ill-founded; (4) an abuse of the right of application; or (5) previously submitted to another forum of international investigation and settlement.

Determination of the Merits. After a chamber has decided that a complaint is admissible for further consideration, it invites the parties to submit further evidence and documentation, and may set a date for a public hearing on the merits of the case. Chambers grant a hearing only in a minority of cases. The president of the chamber may allow the submission of written comments by any contracting state which is not a party to the proceedings, or any other concerned persons. During the proceedings on the merits, negotiations aimed at securing an amicable settlement may also be conducted.

Enforcement of Judgments. Chambers decide each case by majority vote. A judgment of the Grand Chamber becomes final at issuance. Judgments of the lower chambers become final in the following ways: first, if the parties declare that they will not request that the case be referred to the Grand Chamber for a rehearing; second, if three months after the date of judgment, the parties have not requested rehearing by the Grand Chamber; and third, when the panel of the Grand Chamber rejects a party's request for rehearing. The Grand Chamber generally accepts review of a decision of a lower chamber if the application raises a serious question of interpretation or application or an issue of general importance.

A final judgment is published, and includes reasons for the judgment as well as decisions on admissibility. The judgment may require that the party take remedial measures or provide the petitioner with a monetary award of just satisfaction. The final judgment is transferred to the Committee of Ministers, which supervises the execution of each judgment pursuant to Article 46 of the Convention, as amended under Protocol 11. The Committee invites the respondent state to provide it with documentation of the methods that it is undertaking in response to the judgment, as well as records of its payment of just satisfaction, if applicable.

The Committee's role following a judgment is to oversee the domestic actions that the State has taken in response to a finding of a violation. Following are the rules governing enforcement of judgments adopted in 2001:

RULES ADOPTED BY THE COMMITTEE OF MINISTERS FOR THE APPLICATION OF ARTICLE 46, PARAGRAPH 2, OF THE EUROPEAN CONVENTION ON HUMAN RIGHTS[2]

(Text approved by the Committee of Ministers on 10 January 2001 at the 736th meeting of the Ministers' Deputies).

Rule 1: General provisions

a. The Committee of Ministers' supervision of the execution of judgments of the Court will in principle take place at special human rights meetings, the agenda of which is public.***

---

[2] *Available at* http://cm.coe.int/intro/e-rules46.htm.

c.   If the chairmanship of the Committee of Ministers is held by the representative of a State which is a party to a case *** that representative shall relinquish the chairmanship during any discussion of that case.***

*Rule 3: Information to the Committee of Ministers on the measures taken in order to abide by the judgment ***

b.   When supervising the execution of a judgment by the respondent State,*** the Committee of Ministers shall examine whether:

— any just satisfaction awarded by the Court has been paid, including as the case may be default interest; and, if required, and taking into account the discretion of the State concerned to choose the means necessary to comply with the judgment, whether

— individual measures have been taken to ensure that the violation has ceased and that the injured party is put, as far as possible, in the same situation as that party enjoyed prior to the violation of the Convention;

— general measures have been adopted, preventing new violations similar to that or those found or putting an end to continuing violations.

Rule 4: Control intervals

a.   Until the State concerned has provided information on the payment of the just satisfaction awarded by the Court or concerning possible individual measures, the case shall be placed on the agenda of each human rights meeting of the Committee of Ministers, unless the Committee decides otherwise.***

Rule 8: Final resolution

After having established that the State concerned has taken all the necessary measures to abide by the judgment, the Committee of Ministers shall adopt a resolution concluding that its functions under Article 46, paragraph 2, of the Convention have been exercised.

Further Reading

See JACOBS & ROBIN C.A. WHITE, THE EUROPEAN CONVENTION ON HUMAN RIGHTS (2d ed. 1996); MARK W. JANIS, RICHARD S. KAY & ANTHONY W. BRADLEY, EUROPEAN HUMAN RIGHTS LAW (1995); MERRILLS, THE DEVELOPMENT OF INTERNATIONAL LAW BY THE EUROPEAN COURT OF HUMAN RIGHTS (1993); PHILIP LEACH, TAKING A CASE TO THE EUROPEAN COURT OF HUMAN RIGHTS (2001); KAREN REID, A PRACTITIONER'S GUIDE TO THE EUROPEAN COURT OF HUMAN RIGHTS (1998); The Council of Europe Web site is *available at* http://www.coe.int.

2.   *Procedural Protections for Economic, Social and Cultural Rights*

EUROPEAN CONVENTION ON HUMAN RIGHTS

Article 6. Right to a Fair Trial

1.   In the determination of his civil rights and obligations or of any criminal charge against him, everyone is entitled to a fair and public hearing within a reasonable time by an independent and impartial tribunal established by law.***

NOTE ON ARTICLE 6 (1) AND THE PUBLIC LAW—PRIVATE LAW DISTINCTION

In the civil law tradition, a strict separation is maintained between private law, which governs relations between individuals (commercial, contractual and property rights) and public law, which governs relations between the individual and the state (constitutional, administrative and criminal law). Typically, a "civil right" is one created by private contract, whereas a "public right" derives from statute. Procedurally, the parties to a private law dispute are on equal footing, and are entitled to judicial review and enforcement of the right. On the other hand, public law rights are limited to administrative remedies; the need to balance the interests of the collective and the individual outweighs the private right to sue.

Historically, this dichotomy between the two spheres of law was maintained in order to preserve the separation of powers and to protect individual rights. This theory can be traced to post-revolutionary France, and the overthrow of the system of *Parlements*— judgeships that were bought, sold, and inherited by the nobility:

> The experience of the power and political involvement of the *Parlements*, Montesquieu's advocacy of separate powers, his recognition but immediate relegation of the judicial power, and the accentuation of the executive power derived from [philosopher Jean Jacques] Rousseau all contributed, at the time of the Revolution, to a radical and repeated prohibition of interference by the courts with the executive.

J.W.F. Allison, A Continental Distinction in the Common Law: A Historical and Comparative Perspective on English Public Law 141 (1996). As Merryman explains:

> The emphasis on separation of powers led to a separate system of administrative courts, inhibited the adoption of judicial review of legislation, and limited the judge to a relatively minor role in the legal process. The theory of natural rights led to an exaggerated emphasis on individual rights of property and contract and to an oversharp distinction between public and private law.

John Henry Merryman, The Civil Law Tradition 18 (2d ed. 1985).

Contemporary legal, political, economic and social developments, however, have tended to blur this distinction, and as the role of the state in society has expanded, public and private law have become increasingly interwoven. This intersection of once dichotomous spheres is evidenced in a variety of ways: the state has assumed responsibility for individual welfare; private rights are entrenched in constitutions and treaties and protected by judicial review; the public interest is protected through regulations, licenses, and taxes, and penalties modify private rights to protect the public interest, e.g., environmental, securities and anti-trust laws; and "public" state entities provide goods and services and otherwise directly participate in the "private" economic life of the nation.

The European Court of Human Rights has grappled with the nuances of the public law-private law distinction in determining whether economic and social rights are "civil rights" within the meaning of Article 6-1. The following cases illustrate the evolution of the Court's jurisprudence protecting second and third generation rights through first generation guarantees.

B.   ELIGIBILITY FOR SOCIAL SECURITY AND WELFARE BENEFITS

FELDBRUGGE v. THE NETHERLANDS

99 Eur. Ct. H.R. (Ser. A) (1986)

AS TO THE FACTS

I.   Particular circumstances of the case

11. Mrs. Geziena Hendrika Maria Feldbrugge was born in 1945 and is resident at Anna Paulowna. She is of Netherlands nationality. In or about 1978, although she had been unemployed for some time, Mrs. Feldbrugge ceased to register at the regional Employment Exchange. This was because she had fallen ill and did not consider herself sufficiently recovered to be fit to work. On 11 April 1978, the Governing Board of the Occupational Association of the Banking and Insurance, Wholesale Trade and Self-Employment Sector in Amsterdam decided that as from 24 March 1978 she was no longer entitled to the sickness allowances she had been receiving until then, as the Association's consulting doctor had judged her fit to resume work on that date.

12. She appealed to the Appeals Board in Haarlem. The President of the Appeals Board sought the opinion of one of the permanent medical experts attached to the Board, a gynaecologist practising at Alkmaar, who examined the patient and gave her the opportunity to comment. After consulting three other doctors (a gynaecologist and two general practitioners, including Mrs. Feldbrugge's), the expert concluded on 1 June 1978 that, gynaecologically speaking, she had been fit for work since 24 March; however, he felt it necessary also to consult an orthopaedic specialist.

On 18 August 1978, another permanent medical expert, an orthopaedic surgeon, examined the applicant and offered her the opportunity to comment. He also sought the views of the three practitioners mentioned above. In his report of 22 August 1978, he too found that Mrs. Feldbrugge had been fit to resume employment as from 24 March of that year.

On the basis of these two reports, the President of the Appeals Board ruled against the applicant.

13. The applicant filed an objection, alleging that she had not been given a fair hearing. On 17 November 1978, the Appeals Board declared the objection inadmissible as it fulfilled none of the grounds laid down in section 142 (1) of the Appeals Act. In an obiter dictum, it stated that the case had been given a fair hearing, in that two permanent medical experts had examined the applicant and allowed her to state her objections orally.

14. Mrs. Feldbrugge challenged this decision before the Central Appeals Board at Utrecht. In particular, she maintained that the limitations imposed by sections 141 and 142 of the above-mentioned Act infringed the principle of a fair trial enunciated in Article 6 of the Convention. On 13 February 1980, the Central Appeals Board declared the appeal inadmissible by virtue of section 75 (2) of the Health Insurance Act (see paragraph 20 below).

II.   Relevant legislation

1.   In general

15. As far as health insurance is concerned, social security in the Netherlands is managed jointly by the State—which in general confines itself to establishing the legal framework of the scheme and to seeing to co-ordination—by employers and by employees. The branches of the economy, including the liberal professions, are divided into sectors, each with an occupational association responsible for implementation of the social security legislation.***

2.   Health Insurance Act 1913

16. Under the Health Insurance Act 1913 (Ziektewet), as amended in 1967, insurance against sickness is compulsory for persons under 65 who are bound by a contract of employment with a public or private employer ***. Persons formerly bound by a contract of employment who are unemployed and in receipt of unemployment benefits are also treated as salaried employees for this purpose. Self-employed workers may take out policies with private companies. Sickness includes accidents, whether related to the employment or not. In case of unfitness for work through sickness, an employed person receives an allowance of 80 per cent of his daily pay. He or she applies directly to the occupational association to which his or her employer belongs. The entitlement to an allowance flows directly from the Act (section 19).

17. The scheme is administered by the occupational associations and the funding is provided entirely by employers and employees. The Act specifies the rates of contributions, which are at present 1 per cent for the employee and 5.05 per cent for the employer, calculated on a maximum daily wage of 262 guilders.

3.   Appeals Act 1955

18. Disputes arising out of the application of the Health Insurance Act 1913 are governed by the Appeals Act 1955 (as last amended on 17 October 1978). For disputes concerning fitness or unfitness for work, there exists a simplified procedure known as the permanent medical expert procedure. The expert—a doctor who is a specialist or a general practitioner—is appointed for a year by the Minister of Justice and he is placed under oath.

On the lodging of an appeal of this kind, the President of the Appeals Board (there are twelve in the Netherlands) may immediately instruct its permanent medical expert to carry out an enquiry into the matter.

Within three days of notification of the appeal, the authority that delivered the decision which is challenged must submit all relevant files on the case (section 136). The permanent medical expert consults the private practitioner of the person concerned and the relevant occupational association doctor, except where the file shows that they share his opinion (section 137 (2)). He summons and examines the appellant (section 137 (3)); he may consult another practitioner (section 138). Finally, he makes a written report to the President of the Appeals Board (section 140).

The President—who is a judge appointed for life—gives a reasoned decision which refers to the conclusions of the medical expert.

19. An appeal against the President's decision lies to the full Appeals Board, but solely on one or more of the following four grounds (section 142(1): that the expert knew the patient in another capacity or failed to comply with the requirements of section 137 (see paragraph 18 above); that the President's decision does not bear upon the dispute or has not followed the expert's advice. Unless the Appeals Board declares the appeal inadmissible or unfounded, the normal procedure applies. The parties then have the opportunity of studying the case-file on the premises of the Appeals Board at a time determined by the clerk or of receiving copies. The President may however decide, in the mental or physical interest of the appellant, that he or she shall not have access to the medical reports but shall be informed of their contents and may designate a competent person, such as his or her private practitioner or lawyer, to inspect them on the premises (section 142 (2) in conjunction with section 114 (4) and (5)).

The Appeals Board gives its ruling after written pleadings have been filed and oral submissions heard.

20. Its decision is not subject to appeal before the Central Appeals Board (section 75 (2) of the Health Insurance Act). However, according to that Board's established case-law, an exception is made where rules of a formal nature have not been observed.

AS TO THE LAW ***

2.   *Whether the right at issue was a civil right*

(a) *Introduction*

26. According to the case-law of the Court, "the notion of 'civil rights and obligations' cannot be interpreted solely by reference to the domestic law of the respondent State" ***. In addition, Article 6 does not cover only "private-law disputes in the traditional sense, that is disputes between individuals or between an individual and the State to the extent that the latter had been acting as a private person, subject to private law," and not "in its sovereign capacity" ***. "The character of the legislation which governs how the matter is to be determined *** and that of the authority which is invested with jurisdiction in the matter [are] of little consequence": the latter may be an "ordinary court, [an] administrative body, etc." ***. "Only the character of the right at issue is relevant." [Citations omitted.]

27. As in previous cases, the Court does not consider that it has to give on this occasion an abstract definition of the concept of "civil rights and obligations." This being the first time that the Court has had to deal with the field of social security, and more particularly the sickness insurance scheme in the Netherlands, the Court must identify such relevant factors as are capable of clarifying or amplifying the principles stated above.

(b) *Supplementary factors disclosed by the subject matter of the litigation*

28. Under Netherlands legislation, the right in issue is treated as a public-law right. This classification, however, provides only a starting point; it cannot be conclusive of the matter unless corroborated by other factors. In its *Kˆnig* judgment of 28 June 1978, the Court stated in particular:

Whether or not a right is to be regarded as civil . . . must be determined by reference to the substantive content and effects of the right—and not its legal classification—under the domestic law of the State concerned. In the exercise of its supervisory functions, the Court must also take account of the object and purpose of the Convention and of the national legal systems of the other Contracting States. . . .

29. There exists great diversity in the legislation and case-law of the member States of the Council of Europe as regards the juridical nature of the entitlement to health insurance benefits under social security schemes, that is to say as regards the category of law to which such entitlement belongs. Some States—including the Netherlands— treat it as a public-law right, whereas others, on the contrary, treat it as a private-law right; others still would appear to operate a mixed system. What is more, even within the same legal order differences of approach can be found in the case-law. Thus, in some States where the public-law aspect is predominant, some court decisions have nonetheless held Article 6 para. 1 to be applicable to claims similar to the one in issue in the present case ***. Accordingly, there exists no common standard pointing to a uniform European notion in this regard.

30. An analysis of the characteristics of the Netherlands system of social health insurance discloses that the claimed entitlement comprises features of both public law and private law.

(i) Features of public law

31. A number of factors might tend to suggest that the dispute in question should be considered as one falling within the sphere of public law.

(1) Character of the legislation

32. The first such factor is the character of the legislation. The legal rules governing social security benefits in the context of health insurance differ in many respects from the rules which apply to insurance in general and which are part of civil law. The Netherlands State has assumed the responsibility of regulating the framework of the health insurance scheme and of overseeing the operation of that scheme. To this end, it specifies the categories of beneficiaries, defines the limits of the protection afforded, lays down the rates of the contributions and the allowances, etc.

[Nevertheless, State] intervention cannot suffice to bring within the sphere of public law the right asserted by the applicant.

(2) Compulsory nature of the insurance

33. A second factor of relevance is the obligation to be insured against illness, [that is,] those concerned can neither opt out of the benefits nor avoid having to pay the relevant contributions. Comparable obligations can be found in other fields. Examples are provided by the rules making insurance cover compulsory for the performance of certain activities—such as driving a motor vehicle—or for householders. Yet the entitlement to benefits to which this kind of insurance contract [*viz* automobile or homeowners insurance] gives rise cannot be qualified as a public-law right. The Court does not therefore discern why the obligation to belong to a health insurance scheme should change the nature of the corresponding right.

(3) Assumption by the State of responsibility for social protection

34. One final aspect to be considered is the assumption, by the State or by public or semi-public institutions, of full or partial responsibility for ensuring social protection.

This was what happened in the present case by virtue of the health insurance scheme ***. [S]uch a factor implies, prima facie, an extension of the public-law domain.

On the other hand—and the Court will revert to the point later (see paragraph 39 below)—the present case concerns a matter having affinities with insurance under the ordinary law, which insurance is traditionally governed by private law. It thus seems difficult to draw from the consequences of the extent of State intervention any firm conclusion as to the nature of the right in issue.

35. In sum, even taken together the three foregoing factors, on analysis, do not suffice to establish that Article 6 is inapplicable.

(ii) Features of private law

36. In contrast, various considerations argue in favour of the opposite conclusion.

(1) Personal and economic nature of the asserted right

37. To begin with, Mrs. Feldbrugge was not affected in her relations with the public authorities as such, acting in the exercise of discretionary powers, but in her personal capacity as a private individual. She suffered an interference with her means of subsistence and was claiming a right flowing from specific rules laid down by the legislation in force.

For the individual asserting it, such a right is often of crucial importance; this is especially so in the case of health insurance benefits when the employee who is unable to work by reason of illness enjoys no other source of income. In short, the right in question was a personal, economic and individual right, a factor that brought it close to the civil sphere.

(2) Connection with the contract of employment

38. Secondly, the position of Mrs. Feldbrugge was closely linked with the fact of her being a member of the working population, having been a salaried employee. The applicant was admittedly unemployed at the relevant time, but the availability of the health benefits was determined by reference to the terms of her former contract of employment and the legislation applicable to that contract.

The legal basis of the work that she had performed was a contract of employment governed by private law. Whilst it is true that the insurance provisions derived directly from statute and not from an express clause in the contract, these provisions were in a way grafted onto the contract. They thus formed one of the constituents of the relationship between employer and employee.

In addition, the sickness allowance claimed by Mrs. Feldbrugge was a substitute for the salary payable under the contract, the civil character of this salary being beyond doubt. This allowance shared the same nature as the contract and hence was also invested with a civil character for the purposes of the Convention.

(3) Affinities with insurance under the ordinary law

39. Finally, the Netherlands health insurance is similar in several respects to insurance under the ordinary law. Thus, under the Netherlands health insurance scheme recourse is had to techniques of risk covering and to management methods which are inspired by those current in the private insurance sphere. In the Netherlands, the occu-

pational associations conduct their dealings, notably with those insured, in the same way as a company providing insurance under the ordinary law, for example as regards collection of contributions, calculation of risks, verification of fulfilment of the conditions for receipt of benefits, and payment of allowances.***

Such differences as may exist between private sector insurance and social security insurance do not affect the essential character of the link between the insured and the insurer. Finally, the Court would draw attention to the fact that in the Netherlands, as in some other countries, the insured themselves participate in the financing of all or some of the social security schemes. Deductions at source are made from their salaries, which deductions establish a close connection between the contributions called for and the allowances granted. Thus, when Mrs. Feldbrugge was working, her employer withheld from her pay a sum paid over to the Occupational Association. In addition, her employer also bore a portion of the insurance contributions, which were included in the firm's accounts under the head of social insurance expenses. The Netherlands State, for its part, was not involved in the financing of the scheme.

(c) Conclusion

40. Having evaluated the relative cogency of the features of public law and private law present in the instant case, the Court finds the latter to be predominant. None of these various features of private law is decisive on its own, but taken together and cumulatively they confer on the asserted entitlement the character of a civil right within the meaning of Article 6 para. 1 of the Convention, which was thus applicable.

[The Court held that the adjudicative proceedings in the Netherlands violated Article 6-1 in that they did not provide an opportunity to present oral or written arguments, to challenge the validity of an unfavorable opinion, to review the evidence, or to appeal as of right. The Court deferred its ruling on damages pending a possible settlement.]

Declaration by Judge Pinheiro Farinha

In my opinion, a distinction should be drawn between two sets of circumstances:

(a) If the beneficiary has participated in or contributed to the funding of the social insurance afforded, the resultant entitlements are civil rights and disputes (*contestations*) relating to them fall within the ambit of Article 6 of the Convention.

This was the position in the present case.

(b) If, on the contrary, the beneficiary has not so participated or contributed, the facts come within the domain of public law and Article 6 is not applicable ***.

Joint Dissenting Opinion of Judges Ryssdal, Bindschedler, Robert, Lagergren, Matscher, Sir Vincent Evans, Bernhardt and Gersing ***

2. The majority finds that various "features of private law" comprised in the particular social security benefit claimed by Mrs. Feldbrugge so outweighed the "features of public law" as to confer on her claimed entitlement the character of a "civil right" for the purposes of Article 6 para. 1 ***. The relevant "features of private law" identified by the majority are, firstly, the personal and economic nature of the asserted right; secondly, the connection with the contract of employment; and, thirdly, the affinities with insurance under the ordinary law. In our view, the weakness in this reasoning is

that the majority is taking as determining factors matters which may vary as between different social security systems and even from one category of benefit to another under the same system. We fear that this will give rise to uncertainty as to the obligations undertaken by the Contracting States in the field of social security by virtue of Article 6 para. 1 of the Convention.

3. Our reasons for finding Article 6 para. 1 to be inapplicable to the kind of right asserted by Mrs. Feldbrugge are as follows.

1. *"Civil rights and obligations"—a limitative concept* ***

4. Article 6 para. 1 lays down a procedural guarantee for the adjudication of certain disputes. The use of the expression "civil rights and obligations" must have been intended by the drafters of the Convention to set some limit on the application of Article 6 para. 1.***

15. The object and purpose of the Convention as pursued in Article 6 para. 1 are, to some extent, discernible from the nature of the safeguards provided.

The judicialisation of dispute procedures, as guaranteed by Article 6 para. 1, is eminently appropriate in the realm of relations between individuals but not necessarily so in the administrative sphere, where organisational, social and economic considerations may legitimately warrant dispute procedures of a less judicial and formal kind. The present case is concerned with the operation of a collective statutory scheme for the allocation of public welfare. As examples of the special characteristics of such schemes, material to the issue of procedural safeguards, one might cite the large numbers of decisions to be taken, the medical aspects, the lack of resources or expertise of the persons affected, the need to balance the public interest for efficient administration against the private interest. Judicialisation of procedures for allocation of public welfare benefits would in many cases necessitate recourse by claimants to lawyers and medical experts and hence lead to an increase in expenses and the length of the proceedings.

The nature of the safeguards afforded thus tends to show that the object and purpose of Article 6 para. 1 do not go so far as to guarantee judicial control of the administration of statutory collective schemes for the distribution of public welfare.

16. We have not overlooked the fact that the overall object of the Convention is the humanitarian one of the protection of the individual and that, for the man or woman in the street, entitlement to social security benefits is of extreme importance for his or her daily life. However,*** the economic importance for Mrs. Feldbrugge's livelihood of the allowance claimed is insufficient, on its own, to bring into play the applicability of Article 6 para. 1.***

23. It is not the case that, since the entry into force of the Convention, State practice has developed to the point where the Contracting States can be said to treat entitlement to health benefits under statutory social security schemes as giving rise to "civil rights and obligations" for the purposes of Article 6 para. 1. [T]here is no uniform European approach in this regard ***.

24. Neither does an evolutive interpretation of Article 6 para. 1 lead to a different conclusion.*** An evolutive interpretation allows variable and changing concepts already contained in the Convention to be construed in the light of modern-day conditions ***,

but it does not allow entirely new concepts or spheres of application to be introduced into the Convention: that is a legislative function that belongs to the member States of the Council of Europe.***

SALESI v. ITALY

257-E Eur. Ct. H.R. (Ser. A) (1993)

AS TO THE FACTS ***

8. Mrs. Enrica Salesi lives at Pomezia (province of Rome).*** On 28 February 1986 the applicant instituted proceedings against the Minister of the Interior before the Rome magistrate's court, seeking payment of a monthly disability allowance which the Lazio social-security department had refused her.***

10. The applicant's claim was based on Law no. 118 of 30 March 1971 (Law no. 118/71), enacted pursuant to Article 38 of the Italian Constitution, which provides: "All citizens who are unfit for work and lack the basic wherewithal to live shall be entitled to means of subsistence and welfare assistance.***

11. Under section 13 of Law no. 118/71, the State pays a monthly disability allowance to disabled ex-servicemen and civilians aged 18–64 who have been found to be more than two-thirds disabled and who are destitute.

12. As this is a compulsory welfare benefit, disputes over the existence of a right to the allowance come within the magistrate's labour jurisdiction, and trial procedure is governed by the provisions laid down for labour proceedings ***.

AS TO THE LAW

I.   ALLEGED VIOLATION OF ARTICLE 6 PARA. 1

16. The applicant complained of the length of the proceedings she had brought in the civil courts against the State.***

18. The Government maintained *** that the case presented features of public law only. Firstly, the right claimed derived from an ordinary statute and not from a contract of employment. Secondly, the subject-matter was exclusively a governmental one, since the State met the entire cost of financing the scheme. Lastly, entitlement to the disability allowances in question was not dependent on the payment of contributions.

19. The Court is here once again confronted with the issue of the applicability of Article 6 para. 1 to social security disputes. The question arose earlier in the cases of *Feldbrugge v. the Netherlands* and *Deumeland v. Germany*, in which it gave judgment on 29 May 1986 (Series A nos. 99 and 100). At that time the Court noted that there was great diversity in the legislation and practice of the member States of the Council of Europe as regards the nature of the entitlement to insurance benefits under social security schemes. Nevertheless, the development in the law that was initiated by those judgments and the principle of equality of treatment warrant taking the view that today the general rule is that Article 6 para. 1 does apply in the field of social insurance.

In the present case, however, the question arises in connection with welfare assistance and not, as in the cases previously cited, social insurance. Certainly there are differences between the two, but they cannot be regarded as fundamental at the present stage of development of social security law. This justifies following, in relation to the entitlement to welfare allowances, the opinion which emerges from the aforementioned judgments as regards the classification of the right to social insurance benefits, namely that State intervention is not sufficient to establish that Article 6 para. 1 is inapplicable.

As in the two cases previously referred to, other considerations argue in favour of the applicability of Article 6 para. 1 in the instant case. The most important of these lies in the fact that despite the public law features pointed out by the Government, Mrs. Salesi was not affected in her relations with the administrative authorities as such, acting in the exercise of discretionary powers; she suffered an interference with her means of subsistence and was claiming an individual, economic right flowing from specific rules laid down in a statute giving effect to the Constitution.

The protection of this basic right is, moreover, organised in such a way that at the judicial stage disputes over it come within the jurisdiction of the ordinary court, the labour magistrate's court.

In sum, the Court sees no convincing reason to distinguish between Mrs Salesi's right to welfare benefits and the rights to social insurance benefits asserted [in previous cases]. Article 6 para. 1 therefore applies in the instant case.

[The Court determined that the length of the proceedings, which lasted more than six years, was unreasonable, constituting a breach of Article 6(1). It awarded Mrs. Salisi a total of 18,140,000 lire in damages and costs.]

[Dissenting Opinion of Judge Foighel omitted.]

Notes and Questions

1. What was the rationale for the decision in the *Feldbrugge* case? Does the Court's analysis implicitly assume that public law matters are outside the purview of Article 6-1? Does the case turn on the "predominant" private law features? Does welfare assistance, despite its predominant "public law" nature, qualify as a civil right within the meaning of Article 6-1? In *Salesi*, entitlement to the disability allowance was not linked to a private employment contract and the benefits were entirely funded by the state. How did the Court determine that Article 6-1 was applicable? Is the ruling consistent with the rationale of *Feldbrugge*?

2. What did the *Feldbrugge* Court mean when it stated that the statutory insurance provisions had been "grafted onto" the private employment contract?

3. *Feldbrugge* involved the revocation of a sickness allowance. Mrs. Salesi's complaint concerned the length of time the Italian courts took to decide her initial application for benefits. She was awarded damages without having to establish a likelihood of prevailing on the merits. Thus, the ruling establishes that procedural protections attach to the initial determination of eligibility for public welfare, not just termination. *See also Schuler-Zgraggen v. Switzerland*, Applic. No. 00014518/89 (June 24, 1993) holding that "today the general rule is that Article 6 para. 1 does apply in the field of social insurance, including even welfare assistance." *Id.* at ¶ 46. *Cf. Goldberg v. Kelly*, 397 U.S. 254 (1970) (government must provide due process before terminating welfare benefits) and *Mathews v. Eldridge*, 424 U.S. 319 (1976) (Court will balance individual and governmental interests in determining what procedures are required.)

C. RIGHT TO A SAFE ENVIRONMENT

ZANDER v. SWEDEN

279-B Eur. Ct. H.R. (Ser. A) (1993)

AS TO THE FACTS ***

6. Mr. Lennhart and Mrs. Gunny Zander, who are husband and wife, are Swedish citizens and live in Gryta in the municipality of Västeras.

7. Since 1966 the applicants have owned a property in Gryta, adjacent to land on which a company—Västmanlands Avfallsaktiebolag (VAFAB)—takes in industrial waste amongst other things. VAFAB has been authorized to engage in this activity on the land in question since 1 July 1983, when the National Licensing Board for Protection of the Environment ("the Licensing Board") first issued it with a permit to this effect under the provisions of the 1969 Environment Protection Act ("the 1969 Act").

8. Prior to this, it has been discovered in 1979 that refuse containing cyanide had been left on the dump and analyses of drinking-water emanating from a nearby well had shown excessive levels of cyanide in the water. The Health Care Board of Västeräs had prohibited the use of the water and had provisionally supplied the property owners dependent on the well with municipal drinking-water.

Further analyses effected in October 1983 showed excessive levels of cyanide in six other wells near the dump, one of which was on the applicants' property. As a result, the use of the water from these wells too was prohibited and the landowners concerned, including the applicants, were temporarily provided with municipal drinking-water.

However, in June 1984 the National Food Agency recommended that the maximum permitted level of cyanide be raised from 0.01 mg to 0.1 mg per liter. As a result, as of February 1985, the municipality stopped supplying the above-mentioned landowners with water.

9. In July 1986 VAFAB asked the Licensing Board to renew its permit and to allow it to expand its activities on the dump. The applicants together with other landowners demanded that the request should not be granted without an obligation being imposed on VAFAB *** to supply drinking-water free of charge to the owners concerned, as the proposed activity entailed and would continue to entail a risk of polluting their water.

10. By decision of 13 March 1987, the Licensing Board granted VAFAB's request and dismissed the applicants' and the other owners' claim, on the ground that there was no likely water connection between the dump and the wells. It further stated that, notwithstanding a possible risk of pollution, it would be unreasonable to make the authorization in question conditional upon such a general measure as that suggested by the claimants.

On the other hand, the Board attached a number of conditions to the granting of the permit, including the requirement that the water owners be informed of the results. Should the analyses give reason to suspect that the dump was causing pollution of the water, VAFAB would be under an obligation to take immediately any such action to supply the owners with water as deemed appropriate by the county Administrative Board.

11. The applicants appealed to the Government, challenging the conditions set for the permit. The Government, as the final instance of appeal, upheld these and dismissed the appeal ***.

AS TO THE LAW

I.   ALLEGED VIOLATION OF ARTICLE 6 PARA. 1

[The applicants argued that lack of judicial review of the government's decision violated Article 6(1).]

2.   *Whether the applicants' right was a "civil right"* ***

27. The Court notes that the applicants' claim was directly concerned with their ability to use the water in their well for drinking purposes. This ability was one facet of their right as owners of the land on which it was situated. The right of property is clearly a "civil right" within the meaning of Article 6 para. 1 [Citations omitted]. Consequently, notwithstanding the public-law aspects invoked by the Government, the court *** considers that the entitlement in issue was a "civil right."

3.   *Conclusion* ***

33. The Court considers that the applicants suffered some non-pecuniary damage as a result of the absence of judicial review and *** that sufficient just satisfaction would not be provided solely by the finding of a violation. Deciding on an equitable basis, it awards each of the applicants 30,000 Swedish kronor in this respect.***

BALMER-SCHAFROTH v. SWITZERLAND

25 Eur. H.R. Rep. 598 (1998)

The Facts

I.   The circumstances of the case

7.   The applicants live in the villages of Wilteroltigen, Deltigen and G.mmenen, situated in containment zone No. 1 within a radius of 4–5 km from the nuclear power station at M.hleberg (Canton of Berne). They either own or rent their homes.

A.   Application for an operating licence

8.   On 9 November 1990 the company which had operated the power station since 1971, the Bernische Kraftwerke AG ("the operating company"), applied to the Swiss Federal Council (the Government) for an extension of its operating licence for an indefinite period and for permission to increase production by 10 per cent. The application was published in the Official Gazette of 4 December 1990 together with a notice inviting persons satisfying the requirements laid down by section 48 of the Federal Administrative Proceedings Act to file an objection.

9.   More than 28,000 objections in all were sent to the Federal Energy Office, 21,000 of which came from Germany and Austria.

In their objection [of] 4 March 1991, to which several expert opinions were attached, the applicants requested the Federal Council to refuse an extension of the operating licence and to order the immediate and permanent closure of the nuclear power station. Relying in particular on section 5(1) and [the former] section 10(1) of the Nuclear Energy Act, they maintained that the power station did not meet current safety standards on account of serious and irremediable construction defects and that, owing to its condition, the risk of an accident occurring was greater than usual.***

B. Federal Council's decision

11. On 14 December 1992 the Federal Council dimissed all the objections as being unfounded and, subject to compliance with various specified safeguards, granted an operating licence until 31 December 2002 and authorised a 10 per cent increase in production. In its decision it relied on an expert report by the Central Office for Nuclear Safety, an independent report prepared at the request of the Federal Energy Office on the effects of the power station on the nearby river, and opinions of the Nuclear Technology and Safety Measures Section of the Federal Energy Office, the Federal Commission for the Safety of Nuclear Power Installations and the cantonal authorities.

The Federal Council found firstly that the objectors living in containment zone No. 1 were entitled to take part in the proceedings, unlike the objectors who lived further away from the power station, mainly in Germany and Austria.

It then recapitulated the factors which, under section 5 of the Nuclear Energy Act, justified refusing an operating licence or granting it subject to conditions and stated that applicants who satisfied all the statutory requirements were entitled to an operating licence.***

With regard to the complaint based on the right to life protected by the Constitution, the Federal Council drew attention to the position under the Federal Court's case law, whereby only deliberate infringements could constitute a breach of that right. That did not apply to the operation of a nuclear power station, at least so long as appropriate technical and operating procedures were adopted to prevent such an infringement and so long as these could reasonably be considered to provide a level of protection comparable to that existing in other generally accepted technical installations.

12. [Under the Federal Nuclear Energy Act] a licence from the Confederation is required for the construction and operation of nuclear installations and for any changes in the purpose, nature or scale of such installations.*** No appeal lies against its decisions.

13. Under the Federal Court's case law, the safety of nuclear power stations can only be considered by the Confederation as part of its licencing procedures.

JUDGMENT

II. Alleged violation of Article 6(1) of the Convention ***

As only the Federal Council had jurisdiction to consider the application for an extension of the operating licence for M.hleberg power station, the applicants had not been able to secure a ruling by a tribunal on their objections to the extension.***

B. Applicability of Article 6(1)

30. The Government submitted that Article 6(1) was not applicable in the instant case. Inasmuch as the applicants' complaints were that their physical integrity was in

jeopardy, they did not concern "civil rights and obligations" within the meaning of that provision.***

32. Under the Court's case law, for Article 6(1) in its "civil" limb to be applicable, there must be a "dispute" over a "right" which can be said, at least on arguable grounds, to be recognised under domestic law. The "dispute" must be genuine and serious; it may be related not only to the actual existence of a right but also to its scope and the manner of its exercise. The outcome of the proceedings must be directly decisive for the right in question. As the Court has consistently held, mere tenuous connections or remote consequences are not sufficient to bring Article 6(1) into play.

33. The Court notes in the first place that the objection of 4 March 1991 shows that the applicants opposed the application for an extension of the operating licence because of the risks which they maintained such an extension entailed for the life and health of the local population, to which they belonged. At no stage in the proceedings had they claimed to have suffered any loss, economic or other, for which they intended to seek compensation. The right on which the applicants relied in substance before the Federal Council was the right to have their physical integrity adequately protected from the risks entailed by the use of nuclear energy.

34. The Court considers that this right is recognised in Swiss law, as is apparent in particular from section 5(1) of the Nuclear Energy Act—to which both the applicants and the Federal Council expressly referred—and from the constitutional right to life, on which the Federal Council commented in its decision.

35. The Government, however, referring to the *Van Marle and Others v. the Netherlands* judgment of 26 June 1986, maintained that the right concerned had not been the subject of a "genuine and serious dispute," as it was not reviewable by the courts. First, it was clear from the Federal Council's decision that what was in issue was scarcely of a legal nature but was, on the other hand, highly technical. Secondly, even supposing that the courts had the necessary knowledge and time to hear the case, the moral and political responsibility for the decision nonetheless lay with the political authorities alone ***.***

36. The applicants argued that judicial evaluation of technical issues was part of the courts' ordinary daily work in cases concerning buildings, the environment or sites where hazardous materials were produced. In such cases, it was the court's duty to seek the assistance of an impartial expert to assess whether a particular risk was inevitable or, on the contrary, could be avoided or at least lessened by appropriate technical measures.

[The Court concluded that the Federal Council's determination whether the facility met the statutory licensing criteria was a judicial act resolving a genuine dispute.]

39. It therefore remains to be determined whether the outcome of the proceedings in issue was directly decisive for the right asserted by the applicants and in particular whether the link between the Federal Council's decision and the applicants' right to adequate protection of their physical integrity was sufficiently close to bring Article 6(1) into play, and was not too tenuous or remote.

40. It will be recalled that the applicants asked the Federal Council to refuse to extend the operating licence on the ground that, in their submission, M,hleberg power station had serious and irremediable construction defects, it did not satisfy current safety

standards and its condition entailed a greater than usual risk of accident. They endeavoured to prove the existence of the alleged technical deficiencies and the need to lessen the resulting danger to the population and the environment in general by every available means. However, they did not for all that establish a direct link between the operating conditions of the power station which were contested by them and their right to protection of their physical integrity, as they failed to show that the operation of M. hleberg power station exposed them personally to a danger that was not only serious but also specific and, above all, imminent. In the absence of such a finding, the effects on the population of the measures which the Federal Council could have ordered to be taken in the instant case therefore remained hypothetical. Consequently, neither the dangers nor the remedies were established with a degree of probability that made the outcome of the proceedings directly decisive within the meaning of the Court's case law for the right relied on by the applicants. In the Court's view, the connection between the Federal Council's decision and the right invoked by the applicants was too tenuous and remote.

Article 6(1) is accordingly not applicable in the instant case.***

Dissenting Opinion of Judge Pettiti, joined by Judges Gölcüklü, Walsh, Russo, Valticos, Lopes Rocha and Jambrek

I voted with the minority in favour of finding that Article 6 of the Convention is applicable and would have found what, in the light of the Court's settled case law, appears to be a clear violation of Article 6.

The Court has always held that where the rights of persons in need of protection from danger or harm are called into question and contested, any victim or potential victim is entitled to an effective remedy before an independent and impartial tribunal.***

The issue in the present case was the danger that might arise if the safety measures provided for in the specifications of a public-works contract extending an operating licence for a nuclear power station were not properly checked. Nuclear power is a domain in which the dangers, uncontained by national borders, are both major and enduring; it need only be remembered that in 1997 western Europe continues to be affected by fallout from the Chernobyl accident.

The applicants' application did not impugn the "prerogative act" by which the Federal Council of the Swiss Confederation had chosen a nuclear power strategy, but the lack of any means of securing a review of the safety of the operating conditions when the operating licence was renewed.

It has been consistently noted in commentaries on the case law on Article 6 that:

(1) where the right in issue concerns an aspect that is decisive for the dispute and its consequences, Article 6 is applicable;

(2) if Article 6 is applicable, there must be access to the courts, so that appropriate proceedings may be brought before a judicial authority, and an effective remedy; and

(3) the executive of a state is not a judicial authority and does not constitute an independent and impartial administrative or judicial tribunal.

The majority have, as it were, skipped the first, second and third points and do not even explain in what respect the connection was too tenuous and hypothetical or why the applicants had to show *a priori* that the danger was imminent. Yet it was not disputed that the Federal Council was a "government executive," not a court. Even the Federal Council did not find the connection too tenuous.

It was not disputed that in their memorial the applicants pointed to a danger giving rise to pecuniary and non-pecuniary damage. In particular, they submitted:

> With regard to dealing with minor and more serious incidents, the authorities have, as a precaution, distributed iodine tablets to the people living in the immediate vicinity, that is to say containment zone no. 1, including the applicants. If they take these tablets immediately in the event of an emergency, the adjoining residents directly affected can reduce the absorption of radioactivity through the respiratory tract (blocking effect) during the evacuation period. The population of the wider area surrounding the power station will only be given the iodine tablets if an incident actually occurs, because the authorities assume that in the event of a minor or major malfunction, there will be sufficient time to distribute them to the rest of the population. That indicates that accident scenarios are being contemplated that will affect only the people living in the immediate vicinity. In the event of a major nuclear accident, this measure would facilitate the evacuation of these people. In both cases, therefore, the inhabitants in the immediate vicinity are more seriously affected than the rest of the population: the danger arises earlier, the warning time is shorter, evacuation must start sooner and be effected more quickly, etc.

The applicants were not even afforded the opportunity of establishing before a court how serious the danger was and how great the resulting risk to them.

For Article 6 to be applicable, an applicant does not need to prove at the outset that a risk exists or what its consequences are; it suffices if the dispute is genuine and serious and there is a likelihood of risk and damage. It may suffice for finding a violation that there is proof of a link and of the potential danger. With regard both to applicability and to the existence of a remedy that is effective and accessible, the Court has always been firm on this point, even in disputes concerning minor interests, thus enabling decisions to be reviewed by independent and impartial tribunals satisfying the requirements of Article 6. People are entitled to adequate judicial review.***

[The reasoning of previous decisions as] to the supervision of quarries, motorways and waste-disposal sites applies *a fortiori* to nuclear energy and the operation of power stations required to comply with safety standards. If there is a field in which blind trust cannot be placed in the executive, it is nuclear power, because reasons of State, the demands of government, the interests concerned and pressure from lobbyists are more pressing than in other spheres.*** That is why, in order to protect democracy, it was sought through the European Convention to establish machinery to review any administrative acts capable of causing injustice to the individual.

It has been held that anyone alleging a violation of the rights protected by the Convention is entitled to an effective remedy if the claim is arguable. Admittedly, the State has complete discretion in organising the appeal system, making the arrangements for holding public inquiries, and providing for towns, local authorities and residents to take part, but supervision cannot be wholly left to the executive alone. The judiciary must be able to determine whether installations meet the requirements set out in the specifications.***

It will be recalled that the governments of several countries issued untrue statements following incidents at certain power stations, playing down the seriousness of the incidents and the risk of contamination harmful to health. Even though, in the instant case, the danger of such transgressions was not *a priori* established, the fact remains that the Federal Council cannot be considered an independent and impartial tribunal; it is not comparable to a supreme administrative court.***

The Court's assessment of the tenuousness of the connection and of the absence of imminent danger is, in my opinion, unfounded. Does the local population first have to be irradiated before being entitled to exercise a remedy?***

A finding that Article 6 was applicable and had been infringed was all the more necessary, to my mind, because European comparative law shows that the national legal systems of Member States such as Belgium, France, Italy, Spain, Austria, and Germany possess a whole array of review machinery for dealing with disputes of this type. In some cases [*e.g.*, France] ordinary appeals or administrative appeals up to the supreme administrative court have even resulted in the closure of power stations or refusal of permission to reopen them. It can be said that the national law of European States has raised the "standard" of court protection to a very high level and that the "standard" of the protection afforded by the European Convention on Human Rights cannot be lower.

Notes and Questions

1. In *Zander v. Sweden* the Court links the right to clean drinking water to the right to property. Is this linkage essential to the outcome? Does this adequately distinguish the case from *Balmer-Schafroth*?

2. The Court in *Balmer-Schafroth* sets forth the following test for the applicability of Article 6(1):

> [F]or Article 6(1) in its 'civil' limb to be applicable, there must be a 'dispute' over a 'right' which can be said, at least on arguable grounds, to be recognized under domestic law. The 'dispute' must be genuine and serious; it may be related not only to the actual existence of a right but also to its scope and the manner of its exercise. The outcome of the proceedings must be directly decisive for the right in question.

Does the requirement that "civil" rights be enshrined in domestic law distinguish them from "human" rights, which in theory apply regardless of their recognition by local polities? Is the Court announcing a "case or controversy" requirement familiar in U.S. constitutional law? Does this construction of Article 6(1) potentially affect the protection of welfare afforded in previous cases? What kinds of rights, if any, does Article 6(1) exclude under this test? Is the Court's reasoning consistent with that in the previous Article 6(1) cases? Was the right in question determined to be a "civil right"? Why was it necessary that the applicants show a specific, imminent danger from the nuclear plant?

3. *The European Anti-Nuclear Movement.* European popular opposition to nuclear power emerged with the detonation of the first atomic bomb at the end of World War II. Sporadic protests grew into a burgeoning anti-nuclear movement by the late 1970s. With the end of the Vietnam War, peace activists redirected their energies to the nuclear arms

race, brought into focus by the 1978 U.N. Special Session on Disarmament. The near meltdown at the Three Mile Island nuclear power station in Pennsylvania in March of 1979 revived the public's deep-seated fears of nuclear catastrophe. Anti-nuclear activism in Europe reached its apex in the early 1980s, partly as a result of a heightened perception of danger inspired by the bellicose rhetoric of U.S. President Ronald Reagan and his counterpart in Britain, Margaret Thatcher. These developments were particularly disturbing for Europeans, who feared that a nuclear war would be fought on the continent. Adding to this climate of fear was the world's worst nuclear power accident, which occurred at Chernobyl in the former USSR (now Ukraine) in April 1986, instantly killing more than 30 people and requiring the evacuation and resettlement of roughly 200,000. Chernobyl especially strengthened the movement in Scandinavia and West Germany, which were significantly affected by radiation fallout, a threat that respects no political borders.

In nearly every Western European country, nuclear disarmament groups became mass movements that were supported by mainstream churches, social democratic parties, and (in the case of missile deployment) public opinion. Similarly, in the United States, the anti-nuclear movement grew into the largest peace movement in the nation's history. While the movement has waned in recent years, disarmament activists have organized protests against French nuclear testing, brought a landmark case on nuclear weapons to the International Court of Justice, and inspired political formations such as Germany's Green Party. For further information *see* Elizabeth Heger Boyle, *Political Frames and Legal Activity: The Case of Nuclear Power in Four Countries*, 32 L. & SOC'Y REV. 141 (1998); Charlotte Streck, *Ecopolitics in Modern Germany: The Rebirth of the Green Party*, 8 DICK. J. ENVTL. L. POL'Y 33 (1999).

4.   Further support for environmental rights has been found in Article 8's guarantee of protection of private and family life. *See* § E *infra.*

D.   THE RIGHT TO FREE LEGAL AID

AIREY v. IRELAND

2 Eur. H.R. Rep. 305 (1979–80)

AS TO THE FACTS

Particular facts of the case

8.   Mrs. Johanna Airey, an Irish national born in 1932, lives in Cork. She comes from a humble family background and went to work at a young age as a shop assistant. She married in 1953 and has four children, the youngest of whom is still dependent on her. [S]ince July 1978, she has been employed. Her net weekly wage in December 1978 was £39.99. In 1974, she obtained a court order against her husband for payment of maintenance of £20 per week, which was increased in 1977 to £27 and in 1978 to £32. However, Mr. Airey, who had previously been working as a lorry driver but was subsequently unemployed, ceased paying such maintenance in May 1978.

Mrs. Airey alleges that her husband is an alcoholic and that, before 1972, he frequently threatened her with, and occasionally subjected her to, physical violence. In January 1972, in proceedings instituted by the applicant, Mr. Airey was convicted by the

District Court of Cork City of assaulting her and fined. In the following June he left the matrimonial home; he has never returned there to live, although Mrs. Airey now fears that he may seek to do so.

9. For about eight years prior to 1972, Mrs. Airey tried in vain to conclude a separation agreement with her husband. In 1971, he declined to sign a deed prepared by her solicitor for the purpose and her later attempts to obtain his co-operation were also unsuccessful.

Since June 1972, she has been endeavouring to obtain a decree of judicial separation on the grounds of Mr. Airey's alleged physical and mental cruelty to her and their children, and has consulted several solicitors in this connection. However, she has been unable in the absence of legal aid and not being in a financial position to meet herself the costs involved, to find a solicitor willing to act for her.***

Domestic law

10. In Ireland, although it is possible to obtain under certain conditions a decree of nullity—a declaration by the High Court that a marriage was null and void *ab initio*—divorce in the sense of dissolution of a marriage does not exist. In fact, Article 41.3.2 of the Constitution provides: "No law shall be enacted providing for the grant of a dissolution of marriage."

However, spouses may be relieved from the duty of cohabiting either by a legally binding deed of separation concluded between them or by a court decree of judicial separation (also known as a divorce a mensa et thoro). Such a decree has no effect on the existence of the marriage in law. It can be granted only if the petitioner furnishes evidence proving one of three specified matrimonial offences, namely, adultery, cruelty or unnatural practices.***

11. Decrees of judicial separation are obtainable only in the High Court. The parties may conduct their case in person. However, the Government's replies to questions put by the Court reveal that in each of the 255 separation proceedings initiated in Ireland in the period from January 1972 to December 1978, without exception, the petitioner was represented by a lawyer.

In its report of 9 March 1978, the Commission noted that the approximate range of the costs incurred by a legally represented petitioner was £500–£700 in an uncontested action and £800–£1,200 in a contested action, the exact amount depending on such factors as the number of witnesses and the complexity of the issues involved. In the case of a successful petition by a wife, the general rule is that the husband will be ordered to pay all costs reasonably and properly incurred by her ***.

Legal aid is not at present available in Ireland for the purpose of seeking a judicial separation, nor indeed for any civil matters.*** At the hearings on 22 February 1979, counsel for the Government informed the Court that the Government had decided in principle to introduce legal aid in family-law matters and that it was hoped to have the necessary measures taken before the end of 1979.***

AS TO THE LAW

II. ON ARTICLE 6 PARA. 1 TAKEN ALONE

20. [Mrs. Airey] maintains that, since the prohibitive cost of litigation prevented her from bringing proceedings before the High Court for the purpose of petitioning for judicial separation, there has been a violation of the above-mentioned provision.***

21. The applicant wishes to obtain a decree of judicial separation. There can be no doubt that the outcome of separation proceedings is "decisive for private rights and obligations" and hence, *a fortiori*, for "civil rights and obligations" within the meaning of Article 6 para 1; this being so, Article 6 para. 1 is applicable in the present case.***

22. "Article 6 para. 1 secures to everyone the right to have any claim relating to his civil rights and obligations brought before a court or tribunal." [Citation omitted.] Article 6 para. 1 accordingly comprises a right for Mrs. Airey to have access to the High Court in order to petition for judicial separation.***

24. The Government contend that the [applicant] does enjoy access to the High Court since she is free to go before that court without the assistance of a lawyer. The Court does not regard this possibility, of itself, as conclusive of the matter. The Convention is intended to guarantee not rights that are theoretical or illusory but rights that are practical and effective.*** It must therefore be ascertained whether Mrs. Airey's appearance before the High Court without the assistance of a lawyer would be effective, in the sense of whether she would be able to present her case properly and satisfactorily.***

It seems certain to the Court that the applicant would be at a disadvantage if her husband were represented by a lawyer and she were not. Quite apart from this eventuality, it is not realistic, in the Court's opinion, to suppose that, in litigation of this nature, the applicant could effectively conduct her own case, despite the assistance which, as was stressed by the Government, the judge affords to parties acting in person.

In Ireland, a decree of judicial separation is not obtainable in a District Court, where the procedure is relatively simple, but only in the High Court. A specialist in Irish family law, Mr. Alan J. Shatter, regards the High Court as the least accessible court not only because "fees payable for representation before it are very high" but also by reason of the fact that "the procedure for instituting proceedings *** is complex particularly in the case of those proceedings which must be commenced by a petition," such as those for separation.

Furthermore, litigation of this kind, in addition to involving complicated points of law, necessitates proof of adultery, unnatural practices or, as in the present case, cruelty; to establish the facts, expert evidence may have to be tendered and witnesses may have to be found, called and examined. What is more, marital disputes often entail an emotional involvement that is scarcely compatible with the degree of objectivity required by advocacy in court.

For these reasons, the Court considers it most improbable that a person in Mrs. Airey's position (see paragraph 8 above) can effectively present his or her own case. This view is corroborated by the Government's replies *** which reveal that in each of the 255 judicial separation proceedings initiated in Ireland in the period from January 1972 to December 1978, without exception, the petitioner was represented by a lawyer (see paragraph 11 above).

The Court concludes from the foregoing that the possibility to appear in person before the High Court does not provide the applicant with an effective right of access.***

25. *** The Government maintain that *** there is no positive obstacle emanating from the State and no deliberate attempt by the State to impede access; the alleged

lack of access to court stems not from any act on the part of the authorities but solely from Mrs. Airey's personal circumstances, a matter for which Ireland cannot be held responsible under the Convention.

[T]he Court does not agree ***. [F]ulfilment of a duty under the Convention on occasion necessitates some positive action on the part of the State; in such circumstances, the State cannot simply remain passive and "there is *** no room to distinguish between acts and omissions ***." The obligation to secure an effective right of access to the courts falls into this category of duty.

26. The Government's principal argument rests on what they see as the consequence of the Commission's opinion, namely that, in all cases concerning the determination of a "civil right," the State would have to provide free legal aid. In fact, the Convention's only express provision on free legal aid is Article 6 para. 3 (c) which relates to criminal proceedings and is itself subject to limitations; what is more, according to the Commission's established case law, Article 6 para. 1 does not guarantee any right to free legal aid as such. The Government add that since Ireland, when ratifying the Convention, made a reservation to Article 6 para. 3 (c) with the intention of limiting its obligations in the realm of criminal legal aid, *a fortiori* it cannot be said to have implicitly agreed to provide unlimited civil legal aid. Finally, in their submission, the Convention should not be interpreted so as to achieve social and economic developments in a Contracting State; such developments can only be progressive.

The Court is aware that the further realisation of social and economic rights is largely dependent on the situation—notably financial—reigning in the State in question. On the other hand, the Convention must be interpreted in the light of present-day conditions *** and it is designed to safeguard the individual in a real and practical way as regards those areas with which it deals (see paragraph 24 above). Whilst the Convention sets forth what are essentially civil and political rights, many of them have implications of a social or economic nature. The Court therefore considers *** that the mere fact that an interpretation of the Convention may extend into the sphere of social and economic rights should not be a decisive factor against such an interpretation; there is no water-tight division separating that sphere from the field covered by the Convention.

The Court does not, moreover, share the Government's view as to the consequence of the Commission's opinion.

It would be erroneous to generalize the conclusion that the possibility to appear in person before the High Court does not provide Mrs. Airey with an effective right of access; that conclusion does not hold good for all cases concerning "civil rights and obligations" or for everyone involved therein. In certain eventualities, the possibility of appearing before a court in person, even without a lawyer's assistance, will meet the requirements of Article 6 para. 1; there may be occasions when such a possibility secures adequate access even to the High Court. Indeed, much must depend on the particular circumstances.

In addition, whilst Article 6 para. 1 guarantees to litigants an effective right of access to the courts for the determination of their "civil rights and obligations," it leaves to the State a free choice of the means to be used towards this end. The institution of a legal aid scheme—which Ireland now envisages in family law matters (see paragraph 11 above)—constitutes one of those means but there are others such as, for example, a simplification of procedure. In any event, it is not the Court's function to indicate, let alone dictate, which measures should be taken; all that the Convention requires is that an individual should enjoy his effective right of access to the courts in conditions not at variance with Article 6 para. 1.***

The conclusion appearing at the end of paragraph 24 above does not therefore imply that the State must provide free legal aid for every dispute relating to a "civil right."***

However,*** Article 6 para. 1 may sometimes compel the State to provide for the assistance of a lawyer when such assistance proves indispensable for an effective access to court either because legal representation is rendered compulsory, as is done by the domestic law of certain Contracting States for various types of litigation, or by reason of the complexity of the procedure or of the case.***

28. Having regard to all the circumstances of the case, the Court finds that Mrs. Airey did not enjoy an effective right of access to the High Court for the purpose of petitioning for a decree of judicial separation. There has accordingly been a breach of Article 6 para. I.***

Notes and Questions

1. *Airey* highlights the importance of viewing rights "categories" interdependently. As Craig Scott points out:

> If the analysis had proceeded with the Court looking to see if there was an authoritatively recognized "economic" or "social" right to legal aid outside the criminal context (for example in either the European Social Charter or the IESCR), it would have found nothing to support such a claim and legalistically could have concluded that non-criminal legal aid was not, therefore, protected under the Convention. Instead, the Court relied on the idea of making rights effective, or non-illusory, joined to a highly purposive subtext of promoting the "substantive" equality of those in positions of social and political disadvantage.
>
> The key point is that making rights effective, by way of interpreting rights to have social and economic dimensions that place positive duties on the state, need not proceed by borrowing from rights that already have a recognized legal pedigree as social and economic rights. Instead, effective human rights protection can, and should, be a result of a contextual interpretive analysis of what is needed to make a right truly a right of "everyone" (with special attention to members of presumptively disadvantaged and vulnerable groups, such as Mrs. Airey).

Craig Scott, *Reaching Beyond (Without Abandoning) the Category of "Economic, Social and Cultural Rights,"* 21 HUM. RTS. Q. 633, 640–41 (1999).

2. Mrs. Airey argued that her right of access to the High Court was impaired because of her indigency. The government countered that formal access was not denied to her. The Court found, however, that litigation in the area of separation was so complicated that an untrained individual could not effectively conduct her own case. Ireland contended that the Convention should not be interpreted to achieve social and economic goals. In rejecting this contention, was the Court influenced by the fact that Irish law does not permit divorce?

3.   Mrs. Airey had the benefit of free legal aid in presenting her case to the ECHR.

4.   In ¶¶ 25–26 of the decision the Court emphasizes the importance of real and effective safeguards for individuals, ruling that the effectiveness requirement imposes positive obligations on states parties. The Court highlighted the interdependency of rights, stating, "[a] watertight division between 'classic' (civil and political) rights and social or economic rights cannot be maintained." In his dissent, Judge Vilhjalmsson adopted a more traditionalist approach, asserting that "[t]he war on poverty cannot be won through broad interpretation of the Convention for the Protection of Human Rights and Fundamental Freedoms."

5.   Article 6 § 3(c) of the Convention provides for legal aid in criminal proceedings. Notably, Ireland ratified the Convention subject to the "reservation that *** Article 6 § 3(c) [is not interpreted] as requiring the provision of free legal assistance to any wider extent than is now provided in Ireland." By finding a positive right in Article 6 § 1 did the Court evade the Irish reservation to Article 6 § 3(c)?

6.   Does the Court establish meaningful limitations on the right to free legal aid in cases involving "civil rights and obligations"? (*See* ¶ 26.) What criteria for the entitlement to free legal aid are deducible from this case? What additional criteria, if any, should be established?

7.   The Court also found that Ireland violated Article 8, holding that the provision imposes a positive obligation on the state effectively to respect Mrs. Airey's private life by enabling her to obtain a legal separation from her abusive husband:

> The Court does not consider that Ireland can be said to have "interfered" with Mrs. Airey's private or family life: the substance of her complaint is not that the State has acted but that it has failed to act. However, although the object of Article 8 is essentially that of protecting the individual against arbitrary interference by the public authorities, it does not merely compel the State to abstain from such interference; in addition to this primarily negative undertaking, there may be positive obligations inherent in an effective respect for private or family life.***
>
> In Ireland, many aspects of private or family life are regulated by law. As regards marriage, husband and wife are in principle under a duty to cohabit but are entitled, in certain cases, to petition for a decree of judicial separation; this amounts to recognition of the fact that the protection of their private or family life may sometimes necessitate their being relieved from the duty to live together.
>
> Effective respect for private or family life obliges Ireland to make this means of protection effectively accessible, when appropriate, to anyone who may wish to have recourse thereto. However, it was not effectively accessible to the applicant: not having been put in a position in which she could apply to the High Court *** she was unable to seek recognition in law of her de facto separation from her husband. She has therefore been the victim of a violation of Article 8.

The right to respect for one's home and private life has been another source of protection for economic, social and cultural rights, as illustrated in the following materials.

E. THE POSITIVE DIMENSION OF ARTICLE 8

EUROPEAN CONVENTION ON HUMAN RIGHTS, ARTICLE 8

1.   Everyone has the right to respect for his private and family life, his home and his correspondence.

2.   There shall be no interference by a public authority with the exercise of this right except such as is in accordance with the law and is necessary in a democratic society in the interests of national security, public safety or the economic well-being of the country, for the prevention of disorder or crime, for the protection of health or morals, or for the protection of the rights and freedoms of others.

X AND Y v. THE NETHERLANDS

8 Eur. H.R. Rep. 235 (1985)

AS TO THE FACTS

I.   The particular circumstances of the case ***

7.   Mr. X and his daughter Y were born in 1929 and on 13 December 1961 respectively. The daughter, who is mentally handicapped, had been living since 1970 in a privately-run home for mentally handicapped children.

8.   During the night of 14 to 15 December 1977, Miss Y was woken up by a certain Mr. B, the son-in-law of the directress; he lived with his wife on the premises of the institution although he was not employed there. Mr. B forced the girl to follow him to his room, to undress and to have sexual intercourse with him. This incident, which occurred on the day after Miss Y's sixteenth birthday, had traumatic consequences for her, causing her major mental disturbance.

9.   On 16 December 1977, Mr. X went to the local police station to file a complaint and to ask for criminal proceedings to be instituted. The police officer said that since Mr. X considered his daughter unable to sign the complaint because of her mental condition, he could do so himself. The statement lodged by Mr. X read as follows: "In my capacity as father I denounce the offences committed by Mr. B on the person of my daughter. I am doing this because she cannot do so herself, since, although sixteen years of age, she is mentally and intellectually still a child."

10.   The police officer drew up a report and it was signed by Mr. X (Articles 163 and 164 of the Code of Criminal Procedure). The officer subsequently informed the public prosecutor's office that in the light of the father's statement and of his own observations concerning the girl's mental condition, she did not seem to him capable of filing a complaint herself. According to the headmaster of the school she was attending and another teacher there, she was unable to express her wishes concerning the institution of proceedings.

11.   On 29 May 1978, the public prosecutor's office provisionally decided not to open proceedings against Mr. B, provided that he did not commit a similar offence within the next two years. The official in charge of the case so informed Mr. X at a meeting on 27 September 1978.

12. On 4 December 1978, Mr. X appealed against the decision of the public prosecutor's office to the Arnhem Court of Appeal, under Article 12 of the Code of Criminal Procedure; he requested the court to direct that criminal proceedings be instituted. In a supplementary memorial of 10 January 1979, he pointed out that subject to an exhaustive list of exceptions none of which applied in the instant case, a legal representative was entitled to act on behalf of the complainant.

The Court of Appeal dismissed the appeal on 12 July 1979. In fact, it considered it doubtful whether a charge of rape *** could be proved. As for Article 248 ter[3] (see paragraph 16 below), it would have been applicable in the instant case, but only if the victim herself had taken action. In the Court of Appeal's view, the father's complaint *** could not be regarded as a substitute for the complaint which the girl, being over the age of sixteen, should have lodged herself, although the police had regarded her as incapable of doing so; since in the instant case no one was legally empowered to file a complaint, there was on this point a gap in the law, but it could not be filled by means of a broad interpretation to the detriment of Mr. B.

13. By virtue of Article 445 of the Code of Criminal Procedure, there was no possibility of appealing on a point of law to the Supreme Court against this decision.

II. Relevant domestic law

14. As regards sexual offences, the Netherlands Criminal Code makes a distinction between rape (Article 242) and indecent assault (Article 246), recourse to physical violence also being a constituent element of the latter offence.

15. Other more specific provisions afford in this area protection to certain categories of persons whose age, position of dependence or physical incapacity renders it difficult or impossible for them to determine or impose their wishes.

Articles 244 and 245, respectively, make it a criminal offence to have sexual intercourse with a girl under the age of twelve or with a girl between the ages of twelve and sixteen, and under Article 247 it is a criminal offence to commit an indecent assault on boys or girls under the age of sixteen.

Articles 243 and 247 concern, respectively, sexual intercourse with, and indecent assault on, a woman known to the offender to be unconscious or helpless. According to the Supreme Court, however, the word "helpless" refers only to physical incapacity.

Article 249 relates to indecent acts committed with a minor who is in a position of dependence vis-á-vis the perpetrator.

Finally, Article 239 concerns indecency, either in public or while another person is present against his will.

Save for Article 245, none of these provisions makes the institution of criminal proceedings conditional on the filing of a complaint by the victim.

16. The same does not apply to Article 248 ter, whereby a sentence of not more than four years' imprisonment may be imposed on any person who, "through gifts or promises . . . , through abuse of a dominant position resulting from factual circumstances, or through deceit, deliberately causes a minor of blameless conduct to commit

---

3   Third section.—Eds.

indecent acts with him or to suffer such acts from him": in a case of this kind, the offender can be prosecuted only on complaint by the actual victim.

Under Article 64 para. 1, however, the legal representative may lodge the complaint on behalf of the victim if the latter is under the age of sixteen or is placed under guardianship; this latter institution exists only for persons who have reached the age of majority, namely twenty-one (Article 378, Book I, of the Civil Code).

17. At the hearings, counsel for the Government informed the Court that the Ministry of Justice had prepared a Bill modifying the provisions of the Criminal Code that related to sexual offences. Under the Bill, it would be an offence to make sexual advances to a mentally handicapped person.***

AS TO THE LAW

I. ALLEGED VIOLATION OF ARTICLE 8, TAKEN ALONE, AS REGARDS MISS Y

21. According to the applicants, the impossibility of having criminal proceedings instituted against Mr. B violated Article 8 of the Convention ***

22. There was no dispute as to the applicability of Article 8: the facts underlying the application to the Commission concern a matter of "private life," a concept which covers the physical and moral integrity of the person, including his or her sexual life.

23. The Court recalls that although the object of Article 8 is essentially that of protecting the individual against arbitrary interference by the public authorities, it does not merely compel the State to abstain from such interference: in addition to this primarily negative undertaking, there may be positive obligations inherent in an effective respect for private or family life [*citing Airey*]. These obligations may involve the adoption of measures designed to secure respect for private life even in the sphere of the relations of individuals between themselves.

1. Necessity for criminal-law provisions

24. The applicants argued that, for a young girl like Miss Y, the requisite degree of protection against the wrongdoing in question would have been provided only by means of the criminal law. In the Government's view, the Convention left it to each State to decide upon the means to be utilised and did not prevent it from opting for civil-law provisions.***

25. The Government cited the difficulty encountered by the legislature in laying down criminal-law provisions calculated to afford the best possible protection of the physical integrity of the mentally handicapped: to go too far in this direction might lead to unacceptable paternalism and occasion an inadmissible interference by the State with the individual's right to respect for his or her sexual life.

The Government stated that under Article 1401 of the Civil Code, taken together with Article 1407, it would have been possible to bring before or file with the Netherlands courts, on behalf of Miss Y:

— an action for damages against Mr. B, for pecuniary or non-pecuniary damage;

— an application for an injunction against Mr. B, to prevent repetition of the offence;

— a similar action or application against the directress of the children's home.***

27. The Court finds that the protection afforded by the civil law in the case of wrongdoing of the kind inflicted on Miss Y is insufficient. This is a case where fundamental values and essential aspects of private life are at stake. Effective deterrence is indispensable in this area and it can be achieved only by criminal-law provisions; indeed, it is by such provisions that the matter is normally regulated.

[T]his is in fact an area in which the Netherlands has generally opted for a system of protection based on the criminal law. The only gap *** is as regards persons in the situation of Miss Y; in such cases, this system meets a procedural obstacle which the Netherlands legislature had apparently not foreseen.

2. Compatibility of the Netherlands legislation with Article 8

30. [N]either Article 248 ter nor Article 239 para. 2 of the Criminal Code provided Miss Y with practical and effective protection. It must therefore be concluded, taking account of the nature of the wrongdoing in question, that she was the victim of a violation of Article 8 of the Convention.

FOR THESE REASONS, THE COURT UNANIMOUSLY

1. Holds that there has been a violation of Article 8 as regards Miss Y ***.

3. Holds that the respondent State is to pay to Miss Y three thousand (3,000) Dutch Guilders under Article 50.

Note: In February 1985 the Dutch Criminal Code was amended in response to the Court's decision. Staatsblad 1985, No. 115.

PHILIPPE SANDS, HUMAN RIGHTS, ENVIRONMENT AND THE *LÓPEZ-OSTRA* CASE: CONTEXT AND CONSEQUENCES

6 EUR. HUM. RTS. L. REV. 597, 608–09 (1996)

The first "environmental" decision [under the European Convention on Human Rights] appears to be that of the European Commission in 1976. In *X and Y v. Federal Republic of Germany* the applicants, who were members of an environmental organisation which owned 2.5 acres of land for nature observation, complained on environmental grounds about the use of adjacent marshlands for military purposes. The Commission rejected the application as incompatible *rationae materiae* with the Convention, on the grounds that "no right to nature preservation is as such included among the rights and freedoms guaranteed by the Convention ***." Five years later, in *X v. Federal Republic of Germany*, the European Commission rejected as "manifestly ill-founded" a claim by an environmental association that Article 11 of the ECHR entitled it to have *locus standi* in administrative court actions to challenge a decision to construct a nuclear power plant. The Commission found that the ECHR does not require domestic legal systems to grant associations the right to institute legal proceedings pursuant to their statutory aims without having to show a legal interest of their own in the matter.

An alternative to these early approaches, in the absence of rights granted in relation to the environment *per se*, is for an applicant to bring a claim on the basis that his or her personal or property rights have been violated under the relevant treaty. A series of decisions by the Commission illustrate different ways in which such claims can be made (as well as the difficulties in bringing a successful application) in particular under Article 8 and Article 1 of the First Protocol.

In *E. A. Aerondelle v. United Kingdom* the applicant complained that noise pollution from Gatwick Airport and associated traffic, located adjacent to her home, violated her rights under Article 8 and Article 1 of the First Protocol to the ECHR. Following the Commission's decision in 1980 that the application was admissible (indicating a willingness for the first time to recognise the link between noise pollution and human rights), the parties agreed [to] a friendly settlement. A similar case was *Baggs v. United Kingdom*, relating to noise from Heathrow Airport, which the Commission also found to be admissible and which was subsequently settled. In *Vearncombe et al. v. United Kingdom and Federal Republic of Germany*, also involving a noise pollution claim (in relation to a military shooting range), the Commission declared the application inadmissible on the grounds that the level and frequency of noise was below the threshold necessary to occasion a possible violation of Article 8 and Article 1 of the First Protocol. According to the Commission, the case was distinguishable from the airport cases since the applicants were not exposed to "an intolerable and exceptional noise nuisance of such a level and frequency" as to amount to a violation of Article 8.***

When *López-Ostra* reached the court in 1993, environmental protection had a recognised place in the Convention system, although the Court had not yet ruled in favour of the environmental interests of an individual applicant.

LÓPEZ OSTRA v. SPAIN

20 Eur. H.R. Rep. 277 (1995)

AS TO THE FACTS ***

6.   Mrs. Gregoria López Ostra, a Spanish national, lives in Lorca (Murcia). At the material time she and her husband and their two daughters had their home in the district of "Diputación del Rio, el Lugarico," a few hundred metres from the town centre.

I.   The circumstances of the case

A.   Background to the case

7.   The town of Lorca has a heavy concentration of leather industries. Several tanneries there, all belonging to a limited company called SACURSA, had a plant for the treatment of liquid and solid waste built with a State subsidy on municipal land twelve metres away from the applicant's home.

8.   The plant began to operate in July 1988 without the licence from the municipal authorities required by Regulation 6 of the 1961 regulations on activities classified as causing nuisance and being unhealthy, noxious and dangerous ("the 1961 regulations"), and without having followed the procedure for obtaining such a licence.

Owing to a malfunction, its start-up released gas fumes, pestilential smells and contamination, which immediately caused health problems and nuisance to many Lorca people, particularly those living in the applicant's district. The town council evacuated the local residents and rehoused them free of charge in the town centre for the months of July, August and September 1988. In October the applicant and her family returned to their flat and lived there until February 1992 (see paragraph 21 below).

9. On 9 September 1988, following numerous complaints and in the light of reports from the health authorities and the Environment and Nature Agency *** for the Murcia region, the town council ordered cessation of one of the plant's activities—the settling of chemical and organic residues in water tanks—while permitting the treatment of waste water contaminated with chromium to continue.

There is disagreement as to what the effects were of this partial shutdown, but it can be seen from the expert opinions and written evidence *** that certain nuisances continue and may endanger the health of those living nearby.

B.   The application for protection of fundamental rights

1.   Proceedings in the Murcia Audiencia Territorial

10. Having attempted in vain to get the municipal authority to find a solution, Mrs. López Ostra lodged an application on 13 October 1988 with the Administrative Division of the Murcia Audiencia Territorial, seeking protection of her fundamental rights.*** She complained, *inter alia*, of an unlawful interference with her home and her peaceful enjoyment of it, a violation of her right to choose freely her place of residence, attacks on her physical and psychological integrity, and infringements of her liberty and her safety *** on account of the municipal authorities' passive attitude to the nuisance and risks caused by the waste-treatment plant. She requested the court to order temporary or permanent cessation of its activities.

11. *** Crown Counsel endorsed Mrs. López Ostra's application. However, the Audiencia Territorial found against her on 31 January 1989. It held that although the plant's operation could unquestionably cause nuisance because of the smells, fumes and noise, it did not constitute a serious risk to the health of the families living in its vicinity but, rather, impaired their quality of life, though not enough to infringe the fundamental rights claimed. In any case, the municipal authorities, who had taken measures in respect of the plant, could not be held liable. The non-possession of a licence was not an issue to be examined in the special proceedings instituted in this instance, because it concerned a breach of the ordinary law.

2.   Proceedings in the Supreme Court

12. On 10 February 1989 Mrs. López Ostra lodged an appeal with the Supreme Court. She maintained that a number of witnesses and experts had indicated that the plant was a source of polluting fumes, pestilential and irritant smells and repetitive noise that had caused both her daughter and herself health problems. As regards the municipal authorities' liability, the decision of the Audiencia Territorial appeared to be incompatible with the general supervisory powers conferred on mayors by the 1961 regulations, especially where the activity in question was carried on without a licence. [She argued that] regard being had to Article 8 para. 1 of the [European] Convention [on Human Rights and Fundamental Freedoms], *inter alia*, the town council's attitude amounted to unlawful interference with her right to respect for her home and was also an attack on her physical integrity. Lastly, the applicant sought an order suspending the plant's operations.***

14. In a judgment of 27 July 1989 the Supreme Court dismissed the appeal. The impugned decision had been consistent with the constitutional provisions relied on, as no public official had entered the applicant's home or attacked her physical integrity. She was in any case free to move elsewhere.***

3. Proceedings in the Constitutional Court

15. On 20 October 1989 Mrs. López Ostra lodged an appeal with the Constitutional Court, alleging violations of Article 15 (right to physical integrity), Article 18 (right to private life and to inviolability of the family home) and Article 19 (right to choose freely a place of residence) of the [Spanish] Constitution.

On 26 February 1990 the court ruled that the appeal was inadmissible on the ground that it was manifestly ill-founded.*** It held that the presence of fumes, smells and noise did not itself amount to a breach of the right to inviolability of the home; that the refusal to order closure of the plant could not be regarded as degrading treatment, since the applicant's life and physical integrity had not been endangered; and that her right to choose her place of residence had not been infringed as she had not been expelled from her home by any authority.***

17. On 13 November 1991 the applicant's two sisters-in-law lodged a complaint, as a result of which Lorca investigating judge no. 2 instituted criminal proceedings against SACURSA for an environmental health offence. The two complainants joined the proceedings as civil parties.

Only two days later, the judge decided to close the plant, but on 25 November the measure was suspended because of an appeal lodged by Crown Counsel on 19 November.

18. The judge ordered a number of expert opinions as to the seriousness of the nuisance caused by the waste-treatment plant and its effects on the health of those living nearby.

An initial report of 13 October 1992 by a scientist from the University of Murcia who had a doctorate in chemistry stated that hydrogen sulphide (a colourless gas, soluble in water, with a characteristic rotten-egg smell) had been detected on the site in concentrations exceeding the permitted levels. The discharge of effluent containing sulphur into a river was said to be unacceptable. These findings were confirmed in a supplementary report of 25 January 1993.

In a report of 27 October 1992 the National Toxicology Institute stated that the levels of the gas probably exceeded the permitted limits but did not pose any danger to the health of people living close to the plant. In a second report of 10 February 1993 the institute stated that it could not be ruled out that being in neighbouring houses twenty-four hours a day constituted a health risk as calculations had been based only on a period of eight hours a day for five days.***

19. The investigation file contains several medical certificates and expert opinions concerning the effects on the health of those living near the plant. In a certificate dated 12 December 1991 Dr. de Ayala Sánchez, a paediatrician, stated that Mrs. López Ostra's daughter, Cristina, presented a clinical picture of nausea, vomiting, allergic reactions, anorexia, etc., which could only be explained by the fact that she was living in a highly polluted area. He recommended that the child should be moved from the area.

In an expert report of 16 April 1993 the Ministry of Justice's Institute of Forensic Medicine in Cartagena indicated that gas concentrations in houses near the plant exceeded the permitted limit. It noted that the applicant's daughter and her nephew, Fernando López Gómez, presented typical symptoms of chronic absorption of the gas in question, periodically manifested in the form of acute bronchopulmonary infections.

It considered that there was a relationship of cause and effect between this clinical picture and the levels of gas.

20. In addition, it is apparent from the statements of three police officers called to the neighbourhood of the plant by one of the applicant's sisters-in-law on 9 January 1992 that the smells given off were, at the time of their arrival, very strong and induced nausea.

21. On 1 February 1992 Mrs. López Ostra and her family were rehoused in a flat in the centre of Lorca, for which the municipality paid the rent.

The inconvenience resulting from this move and from the precariousness of their housing situation prompted the applicant and her husband to purchase a house in a different part of town on 23 February 1993.

22. On 27 October 1993 the judge confirmed the order of 15 November 1991 and the plant was temporarily closed.***

AS TO THE LAW

34. The applicant alleged that there had been a violation of Articles 8 and 3 of the Convention on account of the smells, noise and polluting fumes caused by a plant for the treatment of liquid and solid waste sited a few metres away from her home. She held the Spanish authorities responsible, alleging that they had adopted a passive attitude.***

II. ALLEGED VIOLATION OF ARTICLE 8 OF THE CONVENTION

47. Mrs. López Ostra maintained that, despite its partial shutdown on 9 September 1988, the plant continued to emit fumes, repetitive noise and strong smells, which made her family's living conditions unbearable and caused both her and them serious health problems. She alleged in this connection that her right to respect for her home had been infringed.***

51. Naturally, severe environmental pollution may affect individuals' well-being and prevent them from enjoying their homes in such a way as to affect their private and family life adversely, without, however, seriously endangering their health.

Whether the question is analysed in terms of a positive duty on the State—to take reasonable and appropriate measures to secure the applicant's rights under paragraph 1 of Article 8 as the applicant wishes in her case, or in terms of an "interference by a public authority" to be justified in accordance with paragraph 2, the applicable principles are broadly similar. In both contexts regard must be had to the fair balance that has to be struck between the competing interests of the individual and of the community as a whole, and in any case the State enjoys a certain margin of appreciation. Furthermore, even in relation to the positive obligations flowing from the first paragraph of Article 8, in striking the required balance the aims mentioned in the second paragraph may be of a certain relevance.***

52. *** Admittedly, the Spanish authorities, and in particular the Lorca municipality, were theoretically not directly responsible for the emissions in question. However,*** the town allowed the plant to be built on its land and the State subsidised the plant's construction ***.

53. The town council reacted promptly by rehousing the residents affected, free of charge, in the town centre for the months of July, August and September 1988 and then

by stopping one of the plant's activities from 9 September. However, the council's members could not be unaware that the environmental problems continued after this partial shutdown.***

54.*** [The Court] need only establish whether the national authorities took the measures necessary for protecting the applicant's right to respect for her home and for her private and family life under Article 8 ***.***

56. It has to be noted that the municipality not only failed to take steps to that end after 9 September 1988 but also resisted judicial decisions to that effect.***

Other State authorities also contributed to prolonging the situation. On 19 November 1991 Crown Counsel appealed against the Lorca investigating judge's decision of 15 November temporarily to close the plant in the prosecution for an environmental health offence, with the result that the order was not enforced until 27 October 1993.

57. The Government drew attention to the fact that the town had borne the expense of renting a flat in the centre of Lorca, in which the applicant and her family lived from 1 February 1992 to February 1993.

The Court notes, however, that the family had to bear the nuisance caused by the plant for over three years before moving house with all the attendant inconveniences. They moved only when it became apparent that the situation could continue indefinitely and when Mrs. López Ostra's daughter's paediatrician recommended that they do so. Under these circumstances, the municipality's offer could not afford complete redress for the nuisance and inconveniences to which they had been subjected.

58. Having regard to the foregoing, and despite the margin of appreciation left to the respondent State, the Court considers that the State did not succeed in striking a fair balance between the interest of the town's economic well-being—that of having a waste-treatment plant—and the applicant's effective enjoyment of her right to respect for her home and her private and family life.

There has accordingly been a violation of Article 8.

[The Court concluded that Mrs. López Ostra's injuries did not amount to "degrading treatment" within the meaning of Article 3.] ***

65. The Court accepts that Mrs. López Ostra sustained some damage on account of the violation of Article 8. Her old flat must have depreciated and the obligation to move must have entailed expense and inconvenience. On the other hand, there is no reason to award her the cost of her new house since she has kept her former home. Account must be taken of the fact that for a year the municipal authorities paid the rent of the flat occupied by the applicant and her family in the centre of Lorca and that the waste-treatment plant was temporarily closed by the investigating judge on 27 October 1993 ***.

The applicant, moreover, undeniably sustained non-pecuniary damage. In addition to the nuisance caused by the gas fumes, noise and smells from the plant, she felt distress and anxiety as she saw the situation persisting and her daughter's health deteriorating.

*** Making an assessment on an equitable basis in accordance with Article 50, the Court awards Mrs. López Ostra ESP 4,000,000.

GUERRA v. ITALY

26 Eur. H.R. Rep. 357 (1998)

1. The Circumstances of the case

A. The Enichem agricoltura factory

12. The applicants all live in the town of Manfredonia (Foggia). Approximately one kilometer away is the Enichem agricoltura company's chemical factory, which lies within the municipality of Monte San'Angelo.

13. In 1988 the factory, which produced fertilizers and *** a polyamide used in the manufacture of synthetic fibers such as nylon, was classified as "high risk" according to the criteria set out in *** Italian law [regarding] the major-accident hazards of certain industrial activities dangerous to the environment and the well-being of the local population.

14. The applicants said that in the course of its production cycle the factory released large quantities of inflammable gas—a process which could have led to explosive chemical reactions, releasing highly toxic substances.*** These assertions have not been disputed by the Government.

15. Accidents due to malfunctioning have already occurred in the past, the most serious one on 26 September 1976 when the scrubbing tower for the ammonia synthesis gases exploded, allowing several tons of potassium carbonate and bicarbonate solution, containing arsenic trioxide, to escape. One hundred and fifty people were admitted to hospital with acute arsenic poisoning.

16. In a report of 8 December 1988 a committee of technical experts appointed by Manfredonia District Council established that because of the factory's geographical position, emissions from it into the atmosphere were often channeled towards Manfredonia. It was noted in the report that the factory had refused to allow the committee to carry out an inspection and that the results of a study by the factory itself showed that the emission treatment equipment was inadequate and the environmental-impact assessment incomplete.

17. In 1989 the factory restricted its activity to the production of fertilizers, and it was accordingly still classified as a dangerous factory.*** In 1993 the Ministry for the Environment issued an order jointly with the Ministry of Health prescribing measures to be taken by the factory to improve the safety of the ongoing fertilizer production.***

18. In 1994 the factory permanently stopped producing fertilizer. Only a thermo-electric power station and plant for the treatment of feed and waste water continued to operate.

B. The criminal proceedings

1. Before the Foggia Magistrates' court

19. On 13 November 1985, 420 residents of Manfredonia (including the applicants) applied to the Foggia Magistrates' court complaining that the air had been polluted by emissions of unknown chemical composition and toxicity from the factory. Criminal proceedings were brought against seven directors of the impugned company for offenses

relating to pollution caused by emissions from the factory and to non-compliance with a number of environmental protection regulations.

Judgment was given on 16 July 1991. Most of the defendants escaped a prison sentence, either because the charges were covered by an amnesty or were time-barred, or because they had paid an immediate fine. Only two directors were sentenced to five months' imprisonment and a fine of two million lire and ordered to pay damages to the civil parties, for having had waste dumps built without prior permission.***

20. On appeals by the two directors who had been convicted and by the Public Electricity company (*ENEL*) and Manfredonia District Council, which had both joined the proceedings as civil parties claiming damages, the Bari Court of Appeal acquitted the directors on 29 April 1992 on the ground that the offense had not been made out but upheld the remainder of the impugned decision. The court held that the errors which the directors were alleged to have made in the management of the waste were in fact attributable to delays and uncertainties in the adoption and interpretation, particularly by the Region of Apulia, of regulations.*** Consequently, there was no damage that gave rise to a claim for compensation.***

III. ALLEGED VIOLATION OF ARTICLE 8 OF THE CONVENTION

56. The applicants *** maintained before the Court that they had been the victims of a violation of Article 8 of the Convention ***.

57. The Court's task is to determine whether Article 8 is applicable and, if so, whether it has been infringed.***

The direct effect of the toxic emissions on the applicants' right to respect for their private and family life means that Article 8 is applicable.

58. The Court considers that Italy cannot be said to have "interfered" with the applicants' private or family life; they complained not of an act by the State but of its failure to act. However, although the object of Article 8 is essentially that of protecting the individual against arbitrary interference by the public authorities, it does not merely compel the State to abstain from such interference: in addition to this primarily negative undertaking, there may be positive obligations inherent in effective respect for private or family life (*see Airey v. Ireland*).

In the present case it need only be ascertained whether the national authorities took the necessary steps to ensure effective protection of the applicants' right to respect for their private and family life as guaranteed by Article 8.***

60. The Court reiterates that severe environmental pollution may affect individuals' well-being and prevent them from enjoying their homes in such a way as to affect their private and family life adversely.*** In the instant case the applicants waited, right up until the production of fertilizers ceased in 1994, for essential information that would have enabled them to assess the risks they and their families might run if they continued to live at Manfredonia, a town particularly exposed to danger in the event of an accident at the factory.

The Court holds, therefore, that the respondent State did not fulfil its obligation to secure the applicants' right to respect for their private and family life, in breach of Article 8 of the Convention. There has consequently been a violation of that provision.

Notes and Questions

1. *The Positive Dimension of Article 8.* As in *X and Y v. the Netherlands*, the Court relied on the state's positive duty to "take reasonable and appropriate measures" to protect private and family life in *López-Ostra* and *Guerra*. This positive dimension of the right to privacy is construed as a duty to protect individuals from interference with this right by third parties. What is the scope of such a duty as deduced from these decisions? How would limitations on this duty be defined?

2. *Human Rights and the Environment.* This development in the case law of the European Court of Human Rights reflects a growing awareness of the relationship between protection of human rights and protection of the environment. The 1972 Stockholm Declaration on the Human Environment was the first articulation of the interdependence between enjoyment of human rights and the quality of the environment. Declaration on the Human Environment (June 16, 1972), *in Report of the United Nations Conference on the Human Environment*, U.N. Doc. A/CONF.48/14/Rev.1, sec. I (1972), *reprinted in* 11 I.L.M. 1416 (1972)). The Declaration did not, however, proclaim a "right to environment," a value which has subsequently been added to the human rights catalog. The African Charter on Human and Peoples' Rights was the first international human rights instrument to recognize a collective right belonging to "[a]ll peoples" to a "general satisfactory environment favorable to their development." African Charter on Human and Peoples' Rights, June 27, 1981, Art. 24, OAU Doc. CAB/LEG/67/3/ Rev.5 (1981), *reprinted in* 21 I.L.M. 156 (1989). The Protocol of San Salvador to the American Convention on Human Rights affords an individual right to "live in a healthy environment." Additional Protocol to the American Convention on Human Rights in the Area of Economic, Social and Cultural Rights ("Protocol of San Salvador"), Nov. 14, 1988, Art. 11, OAS TS No. 69, *reprinted in* 28 I.L.M. 156 (1989) (*entered into force* Nov. 16, 1999).

Neither the European Convention nor the European Social Charter provides for a right to environment. "Third generation" environmental issues that have been litigated in the European human rights system have thus been formulated as violations of the "first generation" rights to life, privacy, and property. *See generally*, Richard Desgagne, *Integrating Environmental Values into the European Convention on Human Rights*, 89 AM. J. INT'L L. 263 (1995). Desgagne asserts that contemporary human rights discourse severely limits the development of a jurisprudence that reflects the interdependence of rights:

> The nature of human rights litigation limits the opportunity to use it as a vehicle for enhancing the environment. The collective aspect of the need for environmental protection makes it difficult to assert a claim under the [European] Convention regarding interference with enjoyment of the environment. Protection of the environment through litigation under the Convention is limited by the individualist bias of this system of protection, a bias that results both from an individualist approach to interpreting the protected rights and from the requirements regarding standing to submit an application to the Commission.*** Additional limitations stem from the solutions that can be imposed by the Commission and the Court. If financial compensation may solve the problem at the individual level (for example, by enabling the owner to leave the house situated in the worsened environment), no protection of the environment per se is ensured.***

Id. at 282–84.

THE ROMANI PEOPLE

When they first arrived in Europe over 500 years ago, the Roma were called Gypsies in the mistaken belief that they had come from Egypt. The self-appellation, Roma, means "people." Linguistic and anthropological evidence suggests that the Roma originated in Northwestern India, migrating in successive waves primarily in the 11th century, but possibly beginning as early as 250 B.C. The later, more extensive migrations were most likely caused by the wars accompanying the spread of Islam during the 11th and 12th centuries. *See* IAN HANCOCK, LAND OF PAIN: FIVE CENTURIES OF GYPSY ENSLAVEMENT (1982).

Although their ethnic and caste origins were diverse, the Roma evolved into a distinct cultural group. *See* Walter Otto Weyrauch & Maureen Anne Bell, *Autonomous Lawmaking: The Case of the "Gypsies,"* 103 YALE L.J. 323 (1993). They share a distinct language with many regional dialects; social structures emphasizing extended families, clans and tribes; and a complex system of cultural taboos by which they distinguish themselves from the *gaje*, or non-Roma people. The Roma also have a distinct, group-oriented legal system. *See* Fred Bertram, *The Particular Problems of the Roma*, 3 U.C. DAVIS J. INT'L L. & POL'Y 1, 19 (1997).

Traveling is an aspect of Roma culture that likely developed in response to a combination of factors, including a history of persecution and slavery, the independent, self-employment ideal of the Roma, and the need for occasional workers for the non-Roma, sedentary populations. Adam M. Warnke, *Vagabonds, Tinkers, and Travelers: Statelessness among the East European Roma*, 7 IND. J. GLOBAL LEGAL STUD. 335, 341 (1999). While many Roma in Western Europe maintain the traveling lifestyle, Roma communities in Central and Eastern Europe have been settled for centuries.

An estimated 10 million Roma currently live in Europe, constituting its largest minority population. Upon their arrival in the 14th century, the Roma encountered oppression, enslavement and persecution. They were enslaved for centuries in what is now Romania, expelled from the Holy Roman Empire and England, banned in France, whipped and ordered into forced labor in Prussia. Barry A. Fisher, *No Roads Lead to Rom: The Fate of the Romani People under the Nazis and in Post-war Restitution*, 20 WHITTIER L. REV. 513, 518 (1999). In some countries, Roma hunts were organized. JOHN-PIERRE LIEGEOIS & NICOLAE GHEORGHE, ROMA/GYPSIES: A EUROPEAN MINORITY 10 (1995). Spain banned the "language, costume and wandering way of life" upon penalty of death. Alyssa Haun, *The Long Road: the Roma of Eastern and Central Europe and the Freedom of Movement and Right to Choose a Residence*, 33 GEO. WASH. INT'L L. REV. 155 (2000). This pattern of persecution culminated in the Nazi terror of World War II, during which an estimated 500,000 to 1.5 million Roma were systematically slaughtered. *See generally*, JACK NUSAN PORTER ED., GENOCIDE AND HUMAN RIGHTS: A GLOBAL ANTHOLOGY 150–92 (1982).

But persecution of the Roma is not confined to the distant past. From 1926–1973, Switzerland sought to "assimilate" them through the forced removal of Roma children from their parents, placing them with foster or adoptive families. Mary Ellen Tsekos, *Minority Rights: the Failure of International Law to Protect the Roma*, 3 HUM. RTS. BR. 9 (2002). (Forcible removal of children was also used in the United States and Australia to "assimilate" indigenous people.)

Other national policies negate Roma identity as a distinct cultural group by restricting traveling, caravan parking and the practice of their traditional trades. *See* Warnke, *supra*, at 344. The Roma also experience discrimination through "benign neglect." Social welfare programs and educational policies are not designed to accommodate their traditions, so that benefits afforded to other citizens are inaccessible to them. *See* LIEGEOIS & GHEORGHE, *supra*, at 11. Today, expulsion takes the form of zoning ordinances which, as upheld in the *Buckley* and *Chapman* cases, prohibit the stationing of caravans in certain areas of the community. More recently, fear of a mass influx of Roma from Central Europe following the incorporation of the former socialist bloc into the European Union threatens to rekindle anti-Roma sentiment. *See* Robert Nurden, *Apartheid in the Heart of Europe*, NEW STATESMAN, Feb. 23, 2004 at 30.

The Roma have been increasingly active in political and cultural movements to establish their rights and preserve their heritage. The International Romani Union, a non-governmental organization, represents the world's Roma at the United Nations. Other organizations, such as the Union Romani of Spain and Phralipe of Hungary, campaign for civil rights in specific countries or regions. Advocacy groups endorse a range of political demands, from the recognition of the Roma as an ethnic/cultural/linguistic minority to the creation of an independent state.

International bodies have finally begun to address the status of the Roma. In 1979 the United Nations recognized the Roma as a distinct ethnic group. The need to eliminate discrimination and to enforce their economic, social and cultural rights has been proclaimed by the Committee on the Elimination of Racial Discrimination, *Discrimination against Roma*, CERD General Recom. XXVII, U.N. Doc. A/55/18, annex V (16/8/00) *available at* http://www.hri.ca/fortherecord2000/documentation/other/cerd-gen-rec-XXVII.htm; the 2001 World Conference against Racism, Racial Discrimination, Xenophobia and Related Intolerance, *Programme of Action* ¶¶ 39–44, *available at* http://www.un.org/WCAR/durban.pdf; and the Parliamentary Assembly of the Council of Europe, Recommendation 1203, *Gypsies in Europe* (2/2/93), *available at* http://assembly.coe.int/Documents/AdoptedText/TA93/erec1203.htm (last visited June 19, 2004).

For further reading on the Roma, *see* CLAUDE CAHN ED., ROMA RIGHTS: RACE, JUSTICE, AND STRATEGIES FOR EQUALITY (2002); and IAN HANCOCK, THE PARIAH SYNDROME (1987). For web resources on Romani NGOs, *see* European Roma Rights Center, http://www.errc.org/publications/factsheets/; The Patrin Web Journal, http://www.geocities.com/Paris/5121/patrin.htm; Romani.org, http://www.romani.org; European Committee on Romani Emancipation, http://www.eu-romani.org/; and Union Romani, http://www.unionromani.org/ (last visited Nov. 8, 2003).

BUCKLEY v. THE UNITED KINGDOM

ECHR Reports of Judgments and Decisions 1996-IV (Sept. 25, 1996)

AS TO THE FACTS ***

7.   The applicant is a British citizen and a Gypsy. She lives with her three children in caravans parked on land owned by her off Meadow Drive, Willingham, Soth Cambridgeshire, England. She is married but separated from her husband in 1991.

8.   As far back as can be traced, the applicant's family have been Gypsies based in South Cambridgeshire. She has lived in caravans all her life and as a child traveled with her parents in this area. She continued this itinerant life until shortly before the birth of her third child in 1988.

9. In 1988 the applicant's sister and brother-in-law acquired a one-acre (approximately 4000 square metres) site off Meadow Drove, Willingham, and were granted personal, temporary planning permission for one living unit, comprising two caravans.

10. At her sister's invitation she moved on to this site in November 1988 when she was expecting her third child, because she had found it hard being constantly on the move with young children. During this period of settled living the two eldest children were able to attend a local school, where they integrated well.

11. On an unspecified date in 1988, the applicant acquired part of her sister's land (0.16 hectare) to the rear of the site, furthest away from Meadow Drove. She moved her three caravans on to this plot.

12. Her land is now part of a group of six adjacent sites which are occupied by Gypsies. One plot has received permanent planning permission for the residential use of three caravans. The site occupied by the applicant's sister enjoyed temporary permission until 4 August 1995. The remaining three sites have been occupied without planning permission and the occupants have been subject to enforcement proceedings. The occupants of two of those sites have also introduced applications before the European Commission of Human Rights.

13. The applicant has stated that she intends to resume her traveling life sometime in the future, and to pass on this tradition to her children.***

14. On 4 December 1989 the applicant applied retrospectively to South Cambridgeshire District Council for planning permission for the three caravans on her site.

She was refused on 8 March 1990 on the grounds that (1) adequate provision had been made for Gypsy caravans elsewhere in the South Cambridgeshire area, which had in the Council's opinion reached "saturation point" for Gypsy accommodation; (2) the planned use of the land would detract from the rural and open quality of the landscape, contrary to the aim of the local development plan which was to protect the countryside from all but essential development; and (3) Meadow Drove was an agricultural drove road which was too narrow to allow two vehicles to pass in safety.

15. On 9 April 1990 the Council issued an enforcement notice requiring the caravans to be removed within a month.

The applicant appealed against the enforcement notice to the Secretary of State for the Environment.

16. An inspector was appointed by the Secretary of State to report on the appeal ***

In her report issued on 14 February 1991 the inspector *** wrote that:

> [T]he development subject of these notices [*i.e.*, the applicant's caravan site] *** intrudes into the open countryside, contrary to the aim of the Structure Plan to protect the countryside from all but essential development.

The inspector also found that the access road to the site was too narrow for two vehicles to pass, and thus that the use of the site for caravans would not be in the interests of road safety.

She considered the applicant's special status as a Gypsy and observed that in January 1990 there were over sixty Gypsy families on unauthorised sites in the district of South Cambridgeshire. She continued:

It is *** clear in my mind that a need exists for more authorised spaces.*** Nevertheless, I consider it important to keep concentrations of sites for gypsies small, because in this way they are more readily accepted by the local community.*** [T]he concentration of gypsy sites in Willingham has reached the desirable maximum and I do not consider that the overall need for sites should, in this case, outweigh the planning objections.

She concluded by recommending that the appeal be dismissed.

17. The Secretary of State dismissed the appeal on 16 April 1991.***

The applicant did not appeal to the High Court because she was advised by counsel that no grounds arose in her case.

C. Criminal proceedings against the applicant

18. The applicant has been prosecuted for failure to comply with the enforcement notice of May 1990. On 7 January 1992 she was fined £50 and required to pay £10 costs.

She has again been prosecuted on two occasions after the introduction of her application to the Commission on 7 February 1992.

On 12 January 1994 the magistrates granted her an absolute discharge but ordered her to pay the prosecution costs.

Finally, on 16 November 1994 she was fined £75 and ordered to pay £75 costs.***

E. Subsequent developments

20. On 19 September 1994 the applicant again applied for permission to station her caravans on her site, in the light of a change in the law.

21. She was refused on 14 November 1994 on the grounds that (1) local planning policy dictated that development in open countryside should be restricted and no evidence to justify a departure from this policy had been advanced, and (2) adequate provision for Gypsies had been made along Meadow Drove.

22. The applicant (together with others occupying the neighbouring sites) appealed against this decision to the Secretary of State. A report was prepared by an inspector in May 1995.

The inspector considered, first, whether the continued use of the land as a Gypsy caravan site would detract from the rural nature of the area, and, secondly, if so, whether there were any special circumstances sufficient to outweigh this objection. She found that the road safety objection, which had been one of the grounds of refusal in April 1991, no longer applied.

With regard to the first question, the inspector found that the applicant had a mobile home, three touring caravans and three sheds on her site. These were hidden from the road by the caravans on the sites in front and by an agricultural engineering business, the same depth as the applicant's site to the east. They were visible from other vantage points but could be adequately screened by planting hedges. However, she concluded that:

*** the continued use of the rear plots considerably extends the depth of development south of the road. This intensification of use in itself inevitably detracts from the rural appearance and generally open character of the area, contrary to the objectives of national and local countryside policy. I must therefore conclude that the continued occupation of the land as gypsy caravan sites is harmful to the character and appearance of the countryside.

With regard to the special circumstances of the case, in particular the applicant's Gypsy status, the inspector made the following observations. She described the applicant's site as "clean, spacious and well-ordered." By contrast, the council-run site on Meadow Drove was "isolated, exposed and somewhat uncared for." Nevertheless, it was

a relevant consideration that there is available alternative accommodation close by, which would enable the appellants to stay in the Willingham area and their children to continue at the local schools.***

The inspector considered the impact of Circular 1/94 on the applicant's case, but concluded that, although it placed greater emphasis on the provision of sites by Gypsies themselves, it was government policy that proposals for Gypsy sites should continue to be determined solely in relation to land-use factors.

She concluded that there had been no material changes since the last appeal was heard and the present appeal should therefore be dismissed.

23. Accepting the inspector's conclusions and recommendations, the Secretary of State dismissed the appeal on 12 December 1995.

The applicant has filed an appeal to the High Court, which is now pending.

F.   *Authorised Gypsy sites in the district of South Cambridgeshire*

24. In November 1992 the County Council opened an official Gypsy caravan site in Meadow Drove, about 700 metres away from the applicant's land. The site consists of fifteen pitches, each comprising a fenced, partially grassed area with hard standing for caravans and its own brick building containing a kitchen, shower and toilet. Each pitch is designed to accommodate one permanent caravan, one touring caravan, one lorry and one car. They are joined by a central road and the site stands in open countryside.

25. Between November 1992 (when the site opened) and August 1995, twenty-eight vacancies have arisen there. The District Council contacted the applicant by letters dated 17 February 1992 and 20 January 1994, informing her of the possible availability of pitches on this site and advising her to apply for one to the County Council. The applicant has never taken any action in this regard.

26. Since the site opened, the following incidents have reportedly taken place there: (1) an unsubstantiated allegation in May 1993 that one of the residents was in possession of a firearm; (2) a fight in December 1993 during which a resident on the site was punched in the eye by another; (3) in 1994 a car was brought on to the site and set alight; (4) in the same year there was an incident of domestic violence; (5) also in 1994, the warden's office on the site was burgled and damaged when temporarily vacant; (6) in 1995 a site resident was convicted of conduct likely to cause a breach of the peace after exchanging words and threatening gestures with a District Council refuse collector on the site; (7) in March 1995 four pitches were damaged by vandalism and/or fire.***

II. *Relevant domestic law and practice* ***

B. *Gypsy caravan sites provision*

1. *The Caravan Sites Act 1968*

35. Part II of the Caravan Sites Act 1968 ("the 1968 Act") was intended to combat the problems caused by the reduction in the number of lawful stopping places available to Gypsies as a result of planning and other legislation and social changes in the post-war years. Section 16 defined "gipsies" as:

persons of nomadic habit of life, whatever their race or origin, but does not include members of an organised group of travelling showmen, or of persons engaged in travelling circuses, travelling together as such.

36. Section 6 of the 1968 Act provided that it should be the duty of local authorities:

to exercise their powers . . . so far as may be necessary to provide adequate accommodation for gipsies residing in or resorting to their area.

The Secretary of State could direct local authorities to provide caravan sites where it appeared to him to be necessary (section 9).

37. Where the Secretary of State was satisfied either that a local authority had made adequate provision for the accommodation of Gypsies, or that it was not necessary or expedient to make such provision, he could "designate" that district or county (section 12 of the 1968 Act).

The effect of designation was to make it an offence for any Gypsy to station a caravan within the designated area with the intention of living in it for any period of time on the highway, on any other unoccupied land *** .

2. *The Cripps Report*

38. By the mid-1970s it had become apparent that the rate of site provision under section 6 of the 1968 Act was inadequate, and that unauthorised encampments were leading to a number of social problems. In February 1976, therefore, the Government asked Sir John Cripps to carry out a study into the operation of the 1968 Act.***

Sir John estimated that there were approximately 40,000 Gypsies living in England and Wales. He found that:

Six-and-a-half years after the coming into operation of Part II of the 1968 Act, provision exists for only one-quarter of the estimated total number of gypsy families with no sites of their own. Three-quarters of them are still without the possibility of finding a legal abode. . . . Only when they are travelling on the road can they remain within the law: when they stop for the night they have no alternative but to break the law.

The report made numerous recommendations for improving this situation.***

6. *Circular 1/94*

43. New guidance on Gypsy sites and planning, in the light of the 1994 Act, was issued to local authorities by the Government in Circular 1/94 ***.

Councils were told that:

In order to encourage private site provision, local planning authorities should offer advice and practical help with planning procedures to gypsies who wish to acquire their own land for development. . . . The aim should be as far as possible to help gypsies to help themselves, to allow them to secure the kind of sites they require and thus help avoid breaches of planning control.

However:

As with other planning applications, proposals for gypsy sites should continue to be determined solely in relation to land-use factors. Whilst gypsy sites might be acceptable in some rural locations, the granting of permission must be consistent with agricultural, archaeological, countryside, environmental, and Green Belt policies . . .

AS TO THE LAW ***

II. ALLEGED VIOLATION OF ARTICLE 8 OF THE CONVENTION

51. The applicant submitted that since she was prevented from living in caravans on her own land with her family and from following a traveling life there had been, and continued to be, a violation of her right to respect for her private and family life and her home. She relied on Article 8 of the Convention, which provides as follows:

1. Everyone has the right to respect for his private and family life, his home and his correspondence.

2. There shall be no interference by a public authority with the exercise of this right except such as is in accordance with the law and is necessary in a democratic society in the interests of national security, public safety or the economic well-being of the country, for the prevention of disorder or crime, for the protection of health or morals, or for the protection of the rights and freedoms of others.***

[The Court concluded that the government's refusal to grant permission to Mrs. Buckley to live in caravans on her land, and prosecution for failure to remove them constituted interference with her right to respect for her home.]

D. Whether the interference pursued a "legitimate aim"

62. According to the Government, the measures in question were taken in the enforcement of planning controls aimed at furthering highway safety, the preservation of the environment and public health. The legitimate aims pursued were therefore public safety, the economic well-being of the country, the protection of health and the protection of the rights of others.***

63. On the facts of the case the Court sees no reason to doubt that the measures in question pursued the legitimate aims stated by the Government.

E. Whether the interference was "necessary in a democratic society"

1. Arguments before the Court

(a) The applicant

64. The applicant accepted that Gypsies should not be immune from planning controls but argued that the burden placed on her was disproportionate. She stated that,

seeking to act within the law, she had purchased the site to provide a safe and stable environment for her children and to be near the school they were attending.

65. She drew attention to the fact that at the time of the events complained of, the official site further down Meadow Drove had not yet opened. In any event, the official site had since proved unsuitable for a single woman with children. There had been reports of crime and violence there and the inspector's report of May 1995 had noted that the site was bleak and exposed (see paragraph 22 above). In the circumstances, therefore, the official site could not be considered an acceptable alternative for the applicant's own site.

On the other hand, the same report had noted that the applicant's site was well maintained. It could also be adequately screened by vegetation, which would lessen its visual impact on the countryside.

66. Finally, the applicant considered that there was no further alternative open to her as the cost of stationing her caravans on a private site in the vicinity was prohibitive.

(b) The Government ***

69. In so far as it was necessary to afford Gypsies special protection,*** [t]he Government had provided legislation and guidelines requiring authorities involved in the planning process to have particular regard to the specific constraints imposed by Gypsy life. Moreover, Gypsies' accommodation needs were met by local authorities through the provision of authorised caravan sites and by advising Gypsies on the prospects of planning permission for private sites.

In the applicant's case, the reports of the inspectors showed that her Gypsy status had been weighed in her favour ***.

In any event, it was unacceptable to exempt any section of the community from planning controls, or to allow any group the benefit of more lenient standards than those to which the general population was subject.***

2. The Court's assessment

(a) General principles ***

75. The Court has already had occasion to note that town and country planning schemes involve the exercise of discretionary judgment in the implementation of policies adopted in the interest of the community ***. It is not for the Court to substitute its own view of what would be the best policy in the planning sphere or the most appropriate individual measure in planning cases ***.

76. The Court cannot ignore, however, that in the instant case the interests of the community are to be balanced against the applicant's right to respect for her "home," a right which is pertinent to her and her children's personal security and well-being ***. The importance of that right for the applicant and her family must also be taken into account in determining the scope of the margin of appreciation allowed to the respondent State.

(b) Application of the above principles ***

80. In the instant case, an investigation was carried out by the inspector, who actually saw the land for herself and considered written representations submitted by the

applicant and the District Council (see paragraph 16 above). In conformity with government policy,*** the special needs of the applicant as a Gypsy following a traditional lifestyle were taken into account. The inspector and later the Secretary of State had regard to the shortage of Gypsy caravan sites in the area and weighed the applicant's interest in being allowed to continue living on her land in caravans against the general interest of conforming to planning policy. They found the latter interest to have greater weight given the particular circumstances pertaining to the area in question.***

81. The applicant was offered the opportunity, first in February 1992 and again in January 1994, to apply for a pitch on the official caravan site situated about 700 metres from the land which she currently occupies. The alternative accommodation available at this location was not as satisfactory as the dwelling which she had established in contravention of the legal requirements. However, Article 8 does not necessarily go so far as to allow individuals' preferences as to their place of residence to override the general interest.

82. It is also true that subsequently, in her report of July 1995, the second inspector found that the applicant's caravans could have been adequately screened from view by planting hedges; this would have hidden them from view but, so the inspector concluded, would not have reduced their intrusion into open countryside in a way which national and local planning policy sought to prevent (see paragraph 22 above).

83. After the refusal of planning permission the applicant was fined relatively small sums for failing to remove her caravans (see paragraph 18 above). To date she has not been forcibly evicted from her land but has continued to reside there (see paragraph 7 above).

84. In the light of the foregoing, the Court considers that proper regard was had to the applicant's predicament both under the terms of the regulatory framework, which contained adequate procedural safeguards protecting her interest under Article 8, and by the responsible planning authorities when exercising their discretion in relation to the particular circumstances of her case. The latter authorities arrived at the contested decision after weighing in the balance the various competing interests in issue. [T]he means employed to achieve the legitimate aims pursued cannot be regarded as disproportionate. In sum, the Court does not find that in the present case the national authorities exceeded their margin of appreciation.

(c) Conclusion

85. In conclusion, there has been no violation of Article 8.

III. ALLEGED VIOLATION OF ARTICLE 14 OF THE CONVENTION TAKEN TOGETHER WITH ARTICLE 8

86. The applicant claimed to be the victim of discrimination on the ground of her Gypsy status, contrary to Article 14 of the Convention taken together with Article 8. Article 14 of the Convention provides:

> The enjoyment of the rights and freedoms set forth in [the] Convention shall be secured without discrimination on any ground such as sex, race, colour, language, religion, political or other opinion, national or social origin, association with a national minority, property, birth or other status.

In her contention, both the 1968 Act and the Criminal Justice and Public Order Act 1994 prevented Gypsies from pursuing their traditional lifestyle by making it illegal for them to locate their caravans on unoccupied land.

88. [I]t does not appear that the applicant was at any time penalised or subjected to any detrimental treatment for attempting to follow a traditional Gypsy lifestyle. In fact, it appears that the relevant national policy was aimed at enabling Gypsies to cater for their own needs (see paragraphs 39 and 40 above).

89. That being so, the applicant cannot claim to have been the victim of discrimination contrary to Article 14 taken together with Article 8. Accordingly, there has been no violation under this head.***

PARTLY DISSENTING OPINION OF JUDGE REPIK

(Translation)

*** I regret that I am unable to agree with the majority finding that there has been no violation of Article 8. It is with the majority's finding that the interference in issue was necessary in a democratic society (paragraphs 78 to 84 of the judgment) that I disagree.***

In the present case the national authorities did not properly assess whether the aim pursued was proportionate to the applicant's right to respect for her home and to the seriousness of the infringement of that right. At no stage during the domestic proceedings was the problem before the authorities considered in terms of a right of the applicant protected by the Convention, for the Government denied throughout that a right to respect for the home was in issue and therefore that there had been any interference with that right. The applicant's interests, confronted with the requirements of the protection of the countryside, were only taken into account in abstract, general terms ***. There was never any mention of the applicant's right to respect for her home or of the importance of that right to her given her financial and family situation. Nor was any account taken of the possible consequences for the applicant and her children were she to be evicted from her land.

In these circumstances the Court, in order to fulfil its supervisory role, ought itself to have considered whether the interference was proportionate to the right in issue and to its importance to the applicant, all the more so as where a fundamental right of a member of a minority is concerned, especially a minority as vulnerable as the Gypsies, the Court has an obligation to subject any such interference to particularly close scrutiny.***

Respect for planning policy, in particular protection of the countryside, has been placed on one side of the scales. The Court has not taken into account that the weight of that interest is considerably reduced by the fact *** that the applicant did not park her caravans either on land under special protection or in unspoilt open countryside. There are in fact already a number of buildings on neighbouring land and the applicant's caravans could have been adequately screened from view by planting hedges ***.

Much importance was attached to the fact that the applicant could have moved to a different site.*** As regards the possibility of moving to Meadow Drove, the Court found that from the applicant's point of view the question was merely one of individual preference as to her place of residence and that such preferences are not protected by Article 8 ***.*** The safety of the applicant's family is not guaranteed there and it is an unsuitable place for bringing up her children. The applicant did not, therefore, refuse to move there out of sheer capriciousness.

Whilst the applicant wishes to find a safe and stable place to set up home, she also wishes to retain the possibility of traveling during school holidays—a legitimate objective given the traditional way of life and culture of the Gypsy minority.[4] However, she would not be sure of finding a vacant pitch on the official site on returning from her travels.

If the applicant were obliged to leave her land, she would be exposed to the constant worry of having to find a place where she could lawfully stay, her children's education would be jeopardised and so on (see the precarious situation of travelling Gypsies described in the Cripps Report, cited in paragraph 38 of the judgment).

Lastly, as regards the extent of the interference, the Court only takes into account the relatively small amount of the fines imposed on the applicant for failing to remove her caravans (see paragraph 83 of the judgment) not her overall position; she still faces prosecution, further fines and eviction from her land, with all that entails in the way of insecurity and disruption of her family life.

To my mind, the fair balance between the applicant's rights and the interests of society has not been struck and the interference has therefore not been justified under Article 8 para. 2.***

In sum, there has been a violation of Article 8 of the Convention.

PARTLY DISSENTING OPINION OF JUDGE LOHMUS

Living in a caravan and travelling are vital parts of Gypsies' cultural heritage and traditional lifestyle. This fact is important to my mind in deciding whether the correct balance has been struck between the rights of a Gypsy family and the general interest of the community. The Council of Europe Committee of Ministers Resolution (75) 13 noted the need to safeguard the cultural heritage and identity of nomads. It has been stated before the Court that the applicant as a Gypsy has the same rights and duties as all the other members of the community. I think that this is an oversimplification of the question of minority rights. It may not be enough to prevent discrimination so that members of minority groups receive equal treatment under the law. In order to establish equality in fact, different treatment may be necessary to preserve their special cultural heritage.

Even allowing the existence of genuine and substantial planning objections to the continuing occupation of the land, the factors weighing in favour of the public interest in planning controls are of a slight and general nature.***

DISSENTING OPINION OF JUDGE PETTITI

(Translation)

I have not voted with the majority of the Court as I consider that there has been a violation of Article 8 and of Article 14 in this case.

---

[4]   Travelling is a need that is deeply rooted in Gypsy psychology. "The traveller who loses the possibility, and the hope, of travelling on, loses with it his very reason for living." Extract from Roma, Gypsies and Travellers by Jean-Pierre Liégeois, Council of Europe Press, Strasbourg, 1994, p. 79.

*** This is the first time that a problem concerning Gypsy communities and "travellers" has been referred to the European Court. Europe has a special responsibility towards Gypsies. During the Second World War States concealed the genocide suffered by Gypsies. After the Second World War, this direct or indirect concealment continued (even with regard to compensation). Throughout Europe, and in member States of the Council of Europe, the Gypsy minority have been subject to discrimination, and rejection and exclusion measures have been taken against them. There has been a refusal to recognise Gypsy culture and the Gypsy way of life. In eastern Europe the return to democracy has not helped them. Can the European Convention provide a remedy for this situation? The answer must be yes, since the purpose of the Convention is to impose a positive obligation on the States to ensure that fundamental rights are guaranteed without discrimination.***

The Strasbourg institutions' difficulty in identifying this type of problem is that the deliberate superimposition and accumulation of administrative rules (each of which would be acceptable taken singly) result, firstly, in its being totally impossible for a Gypsy family to make suitable arrangements for its accommodation, social life and the integration of its children at school and, secondly, in different government departments combining measures relating to town planning, nature conservation, the viability of access roads, planning permission requirements, road safety and public health that, in the instant case, mean the Buckley family are caught in a "vicious circle."

In attempting to comply with the disproportionate requirements of an authority or a rule, a family runs the risk of contravening other rules. Such unreasonable combinations of measures are in fact only employed against Gypsy families to prevent them living in certain areas.

The British Government denied that their policy was discriminatory. Yet a number of legal provisions expressly refer to Gypsies in order to restrict their rights by means of administrative rules. However, the only acceptable discrimination under Article 14 is positive discrimination, which implies that in order to achieve equality of rights through equality of opportunity it is necessary in certain cases to grant additional rights to the deprived members of the population such as the underclasses of developed countries, and the Gypsy and Jenische communities.

The discrimination results equally from the fact that if in similar circumstances a British citizen who was not a Gypsy wished to live on his land in a caravan, the authorities would not raise any difficulties, even if they considered his conduct to be unorthodox.

If the Buckley case were transposed to a family of ecologists or adherents of a religion instead of Gypsies, the harassment to which Mrs. Buckley was subjected would not have occurred; even supposing that it had, domestic remedies or an application under the European Convention on Human Rights would have allowed such an interference with family life to be brought to an end, which was not so under the domestic law in the case of Gypsy families.*** [Judge Pettiti identified the following violations of the Convention:]

(a) with regard to the free movement of persons and the individual's freedom of establishment with his family, the obstacles placed in the way of Gypsies go beyond the general law. Forcing them to live in a designated area is equivalent to placing them or assigning them to a territory, all the more so where the area proves to be unhealthy or not adapted to the children's schooling needs;

(b) with regard to the right to family property, there is a breach of the right to family life—in respect of which reference could have been made to the use of property within the meaning of Protocol No. 1—on account of the systematic refusal to convert retrospective planning permission into permanent permission to park the caravans. The fact that there had been an exchange of occupation of the land by the families (two sisters) could not justify such a refusal;***

(d) with regard to the impairment of the "rural and open quality of the landscape" and environment protection *** which, in the Government's submission, would justify an interference even under Article 8, the fact that the authorities rely on this argument only against Gypsy families also amounts to a disproportionate interference for, in the hierarchy of the State's positive obligations, the survival of families must come before bucolic or aesthetic concerns.***

Notes and Questions

1.   The Court reasoned that it was necessary to strike a fair balance between the competing interests of the individual and the community as a whole. What are those interests? Are they of equal value? What factors should be weighed in determining the proper balance? Would you characterize the rights at stake for Mrs. Buckley as individual rights or collective rights? Does it make a difference?

2.   On what basis did the Court find that the interference with Mrs. Buckley's Article 8 rights was "necessary in a democratic society"? Under what circumstances should the democratic process yield to the rights paradigm?

3.   In *Airey v. Ireland, X and Y v. The Netherlands, López Ostra v. Spain,* and *Guerra v. Italy,* the Court ruled that Article 8 contains a positive dimension that confers affirmative duties on the State to secure respect for one's private and family life. How is *Buckley* distinguishable from these cases?

4.   In a subsequent case, the Court revisited the issue of "the planning and enforcement measures imposed on a Gypsy family who occupied their own land without planning permission." *Chapman v. United Kingdom,* Applic. No. 00027238/95 ¶ 70 (2001). The Court noted that it was not formally required to follow its decision in *Buckley,* and could take into consideration any "emerging consensus" on the responsibility of contracting states to accommodate Roma traditions. *Id.* The development of such a consensus was argued by the European Roma Rights Centre, which had intervened in the case. The Court acknowledged that "the vulnerable position of Gypsies as a minority means that some special consideration should be given to their needs and their different lifestyle." *Id.* at ¶ 96. Nevertheless it declined to construe Article 8 to require states to make sufficient caravan sites available, or to find any other provision of the Convention applicable.

5.   The United Kingdom is a party to the Council of Europe Framework Convention for the Protection of National Minorities, European Treaty Series No. 157 (*entered into force* Feb. 1, 1998). Article 5 of the Convention requires states parties to "undertake to promote the conditions necessary for persons belonging to national minorities to maintain and develop their culture, and to preserve the essential elements of their identity, namely their religion, language, traditions and cultural heritage." Does the U.K.'s policy on caravans violate its obligations under this Convention?

F. EQUAL PROTECTION

EUROPEAN CONVENTION ON HUMAN RIGHTS

ARTICLE 14

The enjoyment of the rights and freedoms set forth in this Convention shall be secured without discrimination on any ground such as sex, race, colour, language, religion, political or other opinion, national or social origin, association with a national minority, property, birth or other status.

GAYGUSUZ v. AUSTRIA

23 Eur. Ct. H.R. 230 (1996)

AS TO THE FACTS

9. Mr Cevat Gaygusuz, a Turkish national born in 1950, lived in Hˆrsching (Upper Austria) from 1973 until September 1987. Since then he has been living in Izmir (Turkey).

10. The applicant worked in Austria, with interruptions, from 1973 until October 1984. From then until 1 July 1986 [,] periods when he was unemployed alternated with periods when he was certified unfit for work for medical reasons, and he was in receipt of the corresponding benefits. From 1 July 1986 to 15 March 1987 he received an advance on his retirement pension in the form of unemployment benefit. When his entitlement expired he applied to the Linz Employment Agency on 6 July 1987 for an advance on his pension in the form of emergency assistance.

11. On 8 July 1987 the agency rejected the application on the ground that the applicant did not have Austrian nationality, which was one of the conditions laid down in section 33 (2) (a) of the 1977 Unemployment Insurance Act for entitlement to an allowance of that type.

12. Mr Gaygusuz appealed against the above decision to the Upper Austria Regional Employment Agency. He argued in particular that the distinction drawn by the section in question between Austrian citizens and foreign nationals was unjustified, unconstitutional and contrary to the European Convention on Human Rights.

13. On 16 September 1987 the Regional Employment Agency found against the applicant and upheld the impugned decision.***

14. [T]he applicant applied to the Constitutional Court, alleging a violation of Article 5 of the Basic Law, Articles 6 para. 1 and 8 of the Convention and Article 1 of Protocol No. 1.

15. On 26 February 1988, after considering the application *in camera*, the Constitutional Court declined to accept the case for adjudication ***

FINAL SUBMISSIONS TO THE [EUROPEAN] COURT [OF HUMAN RIGHTS]

31. In their memorial the Austrian Government asked the Court [to declare that neither Article 6 nor Protocol No. 1 apply to the case and that neither had been violated].

32. The applicant asked the Court

(a) to hold that the Linz Employment Agency's refusal *** to grant him emergency assistance under the Unemployment Insurance Act infringed his right *** to a fair hearing in civil proceedings (Article 6 para. 1 of the Convention), his right to respect for his private and family life (Article 8 of the Convention) and his right to the peaceful enjoyment of his possessions and non-discriminatory treatment (Article 1 of Protocol No. 1 taken in conjunction with Article 14 of the Convention) and (b) to award him just satisfaction under Article 50 of the Convention.

AS TO THE LAW

I. ALLEGED VIOLATION OF ARTICLE 14 OF THE CONVENTION TAKEN IN CONJUNCTION WITH ARTICLE 1 OF PROTOCOL No. 1

33. Mr. Gaygusuz complained of the Austrian authorities' refusal to grant him emergency assistance on the ground that he did not have Austrian nationality, which was one of the conditions laid down in section 33 (2) (a) of the 1977 Unemployment Insurance Act for entitlement to an allowance of that type. He claimed to be a victim of discrimination based on national origin, contrary to Article 14 of the Convention taken in conjunction with Article 1 of Protocol No. 1 ***.

35. The Court must first rule on the applicability of these two Articles taken in conjunction.

36. According to the Court's established case-law, Article 14 of the Convention complements the other substantive provisions of the Convention and the Protocols. It has no independent existence since it has effect solely in relation to "the enjoyment of the rights and freedoms" safeguarded by those provisions. [T[here can be no room for its application unless the facts at issue fall within the ambit of one or more of them.***

38. The Austrian Government *** submitted that emergency assistance did not come within the scope of Article 1 of Protocol No. 1. Entitlement thereto did not result automatically from the payment of contributions to the unemployment insurance fund. It was an emergency payment granted by the State to people in need. Consequently, Article 14 of the Convention was not applicable either.

39. The Court notes that at the material time emergency assistance was granted to persons who had exhausted their entitlement to unemployment benefit and satisfied the other statutory conditions laid down in section 33 of the 1977 Unemployment Insurance Act. Entitlement to this social benefit is therefore linked to the payment of contributions to the unemployment insurance fund, which is a precondition for the payment of unemployment benefit. It follows that there is no entitlement to emergency assistance where such contributions have not been made.

40. In the instant case it has not been argued that the applicant did not satisfy that condition; the refusal to grant him emergency assistance was based exclusively on the finding that he did not have Austrian nationality and did not fall into any of the categories exempted from that condition.

41. The Court considers that the right to emergency assistance—in so far as provided for in the applicable legislation—is a pecuniary right for the purposes of Article 1 of Protocol No. 1. That provision is therefore applicable ***. Accordingly, as the applicant was denied emergency assistance on a ground of distinction covered by Article 14, namely his nationality, that provision is also applicable ***.

42. According to the Court's case-law, a difference of treatment is discriminatory, for the purposes of Article 14, if it "has no objective and reasonable justification," that is if it does not pursue a "legitimate aim" or if there is not a "reasonable relationship of proportionality between the means employed and the aim sought to be realised." Moreover the Contracting States enjoy a certain margin of appreciation in assessing whether and to what extent differences in otherwise similar situations justify a different treatment. However, very weighty reasons would have to be put forward before the Court could regard a difference of treatment based exclusively on the ground of nationality as compatible with the Convention.

43. The applicant maintained that the difference in treatment *** was not based on any objective and reasonable justification. He had paid contributions to the unemployment insurance fund on the same basis as Austrian employees.***

45. The Austrian Government submitted that the *** the difference in treatment was based on the idea that the State has special responsibility for its own nationals and must take care of them and provide for their essential needs.***

46. The Court notes in the first place that Mr. Gaygusuz was legally resident in Austria and worked there at certain times, paying contributions to the unemployment insurance fund in the same capacity and on the same basis as Austrian nationals.

47. It observes that the authorities' refusal to grant him emergency assistance was based exclusively on the fact that he did not have Austrian nationality ***.

48. In addition, it has not been argued that the applicant failed to satisfy the other statutory conditions for the award of the social benefit in question. He was accordingly in a like situation to Austrian nationals as regards his entitlement thereto.***

50. The Court therefore finds the arguments put forward by the Austrian Government unpersuasive. It considers *** that the difference in treatment between Austrians and non-Austrians as regards entitlement to emergency assistance, of which Mr. Gaygusuz was a victim, is not based on any "objective and reasonable justification."

51. Even though, at the material time, Austria was not bound by reciprocal agreements with Turkey, it undertook, when ratifying the Convention, to secure "to everyone within [its] jurisdiction" the rights and freedoms defined in section I of the Convention.

52. There has accordingly been a breach of Article 14 of the Convention taken in conjunction with Article 1 of Protocol No. 1.***

[The Court decides that it is unnecessary to consider the application of Articles 6 (1) and 8.]

IV. APPLICATION OF ARTICLE 50 OF THE CONVENTION

58. Under Article 50 of the Convention,

If the Court finds that a decision or a measure taken by a legal authority or any other authority of a High Contracting Party is completely or partially in conflict with the obligations arising from the . . . Convention, and if the internal law of the said Party allows only partial reparation to be made for the consequences of this decision or measure, the decision of the Court shall, if necessary, afford just satisfaction to the injured party.

A. *Pecuniary damage* ***

63. The Court notes that the applicant applied for emergency assistance on 6 July 1987 and left Austria in September 1987. Without wishing to speculate about the applicant's situation after that date, the Court must nevertheless take into account the fact that his departure from Austria was due to the non-payment of emergency assistance, which would have amounted to ATS 235 per day. Making an assessment on an equitable basis, it awards him the sum of ATS 200,000.***

Partially Dissenting Opinion of Judge Matscher

I do not usually express dissenting opinions with regard to the Court's decisions on Article 50, in view of the fact that the sums which the Court awards under that provision on an equitable basis can always be the subject of disagreement. The reason why I have done so in the present case is that the Court's decision to award the applicant ATS 200,000 for pecuniary damage is clearly unsustainable.

*** Although it is hardly ever possible to assess the amount of such damage precisely *** the sum awarded for pecuniary damage must never exceed the amount of damage that the applicant can actually have sustained.

In the present case the Court found a violation of Article 14 taken in conjunction with Article 1 of Protocol No. 1 (a finding which I am in complete agreement with) on account of the fact that the applicant, because of his nationality, was not entitled to emergency assistance under the legislation in force. But emergency assistance, as the term clearly implies, is not a pension for life, but a temporary social measure for a period when the beneficiary is available for work but unemployed and not (yet) entitled to an invalidity or old-age pension.***

Under the law in force at the material time, emergency assistance amounted *** to approximately ATS 255 per day. It appears from the file that, however the sums are calculated, and accepting the hypotheses most favourable to the applicant (unrealistic though they are), the maximum amount he could have received in emergency assistance was about ATS 80,000. The sum of ATS 200,000 which the Court has awarded him is more than twice as high as the pecuniary damage he can possibly have sustained; that is manifestly contrary to all the principles governing compensation for pecuniary damage, unless the Court wishes to adopt the practice which exists in American law of awarding "punitive damages." That practice is rightly not provided for in European law.***

The background to the whole case is a typical instance of abuse of the Welfare State, a very widespread trend in all our societies and one—I would point out—by no means limited to foreign workers. It is regrettable that the Court, by awarding disproportionate amounts of compensation, should reinforce this trend.

SUKHVINDER KAUR STUBBS, FEAR AND LOATHING IN THE EU: ETHNIC MINORITIES AND FUNDAMENTAL RIGHTS

KIM FEUS, THE EU CHARTER OF FUNDMENTAL RIGHTS: TEXT AND COMMENTARIES 207, 208–14 (2000)

The rise to prominence of Jörg Haider, who charmed sections of the Austrian electorate with his remarks in praise of his fellow countryman Adolf Hitler's employment policies, was as dramatic as it was disturbing.

Some 150,000 protestors took to the streets in Vienna, 20,000 demonstrated in Brussels and further thousands gathered across the capitals of Europe. All the members of the EU issued bilateral sanctions against Austria. However, the EC itself was unable to take any action on the grounds that the government was democratically elected. Within weeks, the EU Member States were themselves looking for face-saving ways to end sanctions.***

It should hardly need reiterating but 'Fascism' did not die with the victory of the Allies in 1945. Across Europe, Jews, Muslims, Roma and other people with a black or ethnic minority background continue to face disadvantage, discrimination and racism. In Spain in 1998, the Romany Union case list included 32 instances of racism and discrimination specifically against Gypsies; 40 racist attacks involving abuse by authority or police brutality and 27 specific and documented cases of attacks by violent groups. During the same year, they recorded 15 trials arising out of accusations of racism. The case list also included 85 instances of discrimination in employment and social matters.

The police records for France in the same year report 191 racist incidents, 26 of which were violent and 82 anti-semitic in nature. A recent report canvassing social attitudes among French people showed that up to 40% of the population were prepared to admit openly racist views. In Germany, for the same period, there were 434 offences driven by the far right. Although this represents a small decline from the previous year, the far right there continued to attract more people; in 1998, they brought together 53,000 partisans (an increase of 11% from the previous year) of whom 8,200 are considered extremists ready to use violence and attack foreigners.

More reassuringly, the Finnish Government's investigatory commission published statistics in 1998, which confidently state that there had been no murders or attempted murders motivated by racism or xenophobia. They do, however, list four acts of violence with explosives or firearms which claimed six victims, and ten physical assaults. The police report of the same time showed 194 crimes of a racist nature. Most of the victims of these crimes were of Somali origin.

Clearly then, Europe is still not even a safe or free place for ethnic minorities, let alone equitable, just or fair. Yet when on the 25 March 1957, the King of the Belgians, the Presidents of the Republic of Germany, French Republic and Italian Republic, the Grand Duchess of Luxembourg and the Queen of the Netherlands came together in Rome to lay the foundations of an even closer union among the peoples of Europe, they must have been, in some part, motivated by the atrocities of the world wars. The desire they expressed in the Treaty of Rome to pool resources to preserve and strengthen peace and liberty is yet to be realised.

The Austrian Platform for a World Against Racism claims that more than 10% of the population is systematically denied all political rights and participation by being kept in the status of 'foreigners.' Even in the trade unions, there are no equal voting rights for all workers and employees. The system guarantees equality not to human beings but to citizens only. The Platform claims that the democratic system imposed on Austria after the Second World War has been compromised by the conservatives, far right and the social democrats. In fact, it is underpinned by a pre-war-style nationalism, with racist segregation and exclusion incorporated into national policy. They believe that this lack of balance in the political system has led to the uprising of a party that is openly promoting a revision of Nazi history, playing on racist sentiments among the populace with political impunity.

Austria is not alone in its extremism. Right-wing parties are flourishing across Europe and many have secured seats in national parliaments—some, for example in France, Switzerland and Italy, receiving over 15% of the vote. In the UK, the National Front has limited influence but the mainstream Conservative Party stands accused of repeatedly playing the race card in issues ranging from asylum to NHS doctors, a policy their central office clearly feels pays political dividends.

It is commonly believed that Austrian racism, like that of many other EU countries, is based on border control—it is about who gets to be in Europe. Austria feels particularly vulnerable. Like Germany, it borders Eastern Europe and the prospect of cheaper migrant workers with their 'non-Christian' values threatens to undermine its notion of society. Haider's vision, set out in his 1995 book 'The Freedom I Mean,' clearly articulates this:

> Any policy of immigration must insist on assimilation and adaptation to the culture and norms of the indigenous population. Especially in education we have to defend Christian values [. . .] 10,400 jobs were created in Austria and all of them were filled by cheap foreign labour [. . .] [Our politicians consider it] more important to experiment with our youth as guinea pigs in abstract, multicultural programmes[. . .]. Our enemies are legion both in eastern Europe and the west, where the threats are more subtle and insidious.

Islam, it would seem, has taken over from the Soviet Union as the reflex enemy of the west, its baleful influence visible everywhere from book burnings to the brutal theocracy of the Taliban in Afghanistan. In a phenomenon now commonly termed 'Islamophobia,' Muslims are perceived as unwilling to adapt to western ways and customs and thereby even reasonable people feel able to attack them with impunity. Clare Hollingsworth, writing in the International Herald Tribune, stated that

> Muslim fundamentalism is fast becoming the chief threat to global peace and security, as well as a cause of national and local disturbance through terrorism. It is akin to the menace posed by Nazism in the 1930s.

Far from being a global threat levered by the dead hand of an Ayatollah, Islam has as many different faces as Christianity but little protection in law or civil society.

Muslims continue to be the victims of the new Europe. Over a period of 70 years, some 100,000 Muslims are known to have been 'ethnically cleansed' from the northeast region of Greece alone. Across Europe, Muslims are denied the right to dress as they wish—to express themselves freely. They face some of the highest levels of exclusion from the labour market, live in the poorest housing conditions and have little or no representation through civil or political leadership.

Racism has physical and cultural components and victims are often attacked or discriminated against both because of their appearance and a perception that their culture or belief is alien or inferior. Muslims, like Jews, Roma and Gypsies are regarded with fear and loathing in equal measures as the cultural 'Other.' Fuelled by offensive and stereotypical media coverage, such attitudes now prevail in the ostensibly democratic Member States of the European Union. These attitudes are often most despicably manifest in the exclusionary immigration and asylum policies of the Member States.

Even in the UK, the Immigration and Asylum Act of 1999 was reported by Amnesty International as being severely detrimental to refugee rights. Representations were made on the extension of pre-entry controls, the need for effective judicial oversight of the detention of asylum seekers, and the need to ensure access to high quality legal advice if asylum-seekers were dispersed around the UK. The High Court decided in July that the practice of prosecuting and imprisoning those using false travel documents to transit the UK was contrary to international refugee law. In particular, the treatment of unaccompanied refugee children made for a series of recommendations on child asylum seekers.

The efforts to contain asylum seekers appear quite disproportionate to the numbers involved. For example, in 1998, the Office for National Statistics reports 460,000 people migrated to the UK. Of these, 46,000 were asylum seekers, just over 40,000 were young Commonwealth citizens entering on working holiday visas, while returning Britons accounted for 80,000 people. The remainder were job seekers from other EU countries. Certainly the asylum applications for 1999 were higher but this period included the war in Kosovo ***.

Compassion alone would be moral enough grounds to adopt a more humanitarian approach to those seeking asylum in Europe. The great irony is, however, that in the coming years the ageing EU population will increasingly depend on immigrant labour. These people will not be a 'burden' but a necessity to our economy. In Germany alone, the old-age dependency ratio is set to rise from 22% to 47% by 2030. Across the OECD countries, it is moving from 19% in 1990 projected to 28% in 2020 and 37% by 2040. Economists detail the need for a new sort of migrant that moves resourcefully back and forth across an EU border usually from Eastern Europe to Germany and Austria, often earning a living in the Union while supporting a family outside it.

But rather than deal intelligently with the issue of immigration, the Member States of the EU continue to buttress themselves and fortify their barriers with rhetoric that keeps nationalism and xenophobia nicely simmering. Member States pursue all the economic benefits of the EU but deeply resist the political consequences. The Union is still a 'Europe of Bankers.' The myriad visions and initiatives designed to transcend this solely monetary goal and establish a solidarity based on a set of common values have, to date, failed.

Notes and Questions

1.   The author suggests that compassion and expediency are two possible motivations for broadening the concept of citizenship in Europe. Might principles of justice provide a further moral foundation? There is more than one irony in the European resistance to immigration. Many of those seeking employment and a better life come from the former colonies of European states. For 500 years European traders and settlers freely migrated to Africa and Asia, confiscating land, extracting natural resources, trafficking in slaves and expropriating the labor of the inhabitants. Many scholars attribute the relative underdevelopment and impoverishment in "Third World" countries to this colonial exploitation.

2.   Are you persuaded by the dissent that the damage award represents an abuse of the Welfare State? Could the Court have been sending a signal that unequal treatment is antithetical to the economic objectives of European integration?

CHAPTER TEN

THE UNITED STATES OF AMERICA: FEDERAL REJECTION, STATE PROTECTION

INTRODUCTION

This chapter examines the contrasting approaches to economic, social and cultural rights in the dual systems of jurisprudence in the United States. Consistent with a limited government philosophy, the federal courts have interpreted the U.S. social contract to exclude most "second generation" rights. Cultural rights are safeguarded to some extent through the First Amendment religious freedom clause, but this protection does not extend to many indigenous and other minority religious practices. While certain federal benefits are subject to due process and non-discrimination protections, they do not constitute constitutional guarantees. On the other hand, the framers of many state constitutions recognized certain economic and social needs as rights generating correlative state duties. Attention to these provisions has been part of a recent resurgence of activism at the state, local and grassroots levels to build a "human rights culture" in the United States. *See, e.g.*, U.S. HUMAN RIGHTS NETWORK, SOMETHING INSIDE SO STRONG: A RESOURCE GUIDE ON HUMAN RIGHTS IN THE UNITED STATES (2003).

A. THE FEDERAL SYSTEM

1. *The Limited Government/Negative Rights Paradigm*

ECONOMIC AND SOCIAL RIGHTS IN THE UNITED STATES CONSTITUTION

ARTICLE I

Section 9. [1] The Migration or Importation of such Persons as any of the States now existing shall think proper to admit, shall not be prohibited by the Congress prior to the Year one thousand eight hundred and eight, but a Tax or duty may be imposed on such Importation, not exceeding ten dollars for each person.

Section 9. [4] No Capitation, or other direct, Tax shall be laid, unless in Proportion to the Census or enumeration herein before directed to be taken.

Repealed by AMENDMENT XVI [1913]: The Congress shall have power to lay and collect taxes on incomes, from whatever source derived, without apportionment among the several states, and without regard to any census or enumeration.

Section 10. [1] No State shall *** pass any *** Law impairing the Obligation of contracts ***.

ARTICLE IV.

Section 2. [1] The Citizens of each State shall be entitled to all Privileges and Immunities of citizens of the several States.

Section 2. [3] No Person held to service or Labor in one State, under the Laws thereof, escaping into another, shall, in Consequence of any Law or Regulation therein, be discharged from such Service or labor, but shall be delivered up on Claim of the party to whom such Service or Labor may be due.

Repealed by AMENDMENT XIII [1865]: Section 1. Neither slavery nor involuntary servitude, except as punishment for crime whereof the party shall have been duly convicted, shall exist within the United States, or any place subject to their jurisdiction.

AMENDMENT V [1791]

No person shall be *** deprived of life, liberty, or property, without due process of law, nor shall private property be taken for public use, without just compensation.

AMENDMENT XIV [1868]

Section 1.*** No State shall make or enforce any law which shall abridge the privileges and immunities of citizens of the United States, nor shall any State deprive any person of life, liberty, or property, without due process of law, nor deny to any person within its jurisdiction the equal protection of the laws.***

DESHANEY v. WINNEBAGO COUNTY DEPARTMENT OF SOCIAL SERVICES

489 U.S. 189 (1989)

Chief Justice REHNQUIST delivered the opinion of the Court.

Petitioner is a boy who was beaten and permanently injured by his father, with whom he lived. Respondents are social workers and other local officials who received complaints that petitioner was being abused by his father and had reason to believe that this was the case, but nonetheless did not act to remove petitioner from his father's custody. Petitioner sued respondents claiming that their failure to act deprived him of his liberty in violation of the Due Process Clause of the Fourteenth Amendment to the United States Constitution. We hold that it did not.

I.

The facts of this case are undeniably tragic. Petitioner Joshua DeShaney was born in 1979. In 1980, a Wyoming court granted his parents a divorce and awarded custody of Joshua to his father, Randy DeShaney. The father shortly thereafter moved to Neenah, a city located in Winnebago county, Wisconsin, taking the infant Joshua with him. There he entered into a second marriage, which also ended in divorce.

The Winnebago County authorities first learned that Joshua DeShaney might be a victim of child abuse in January 1982, when his father's second wife complained to the police, at the time of their divorce, that he had previously "hit the boy causing marks and [was] a prime case for child abuse." The Winnebago County Department of Social Services (DSS) interviewed the father, but he denied the accusations, and DSS did not pursue them further. In January 1983, Joshua was admitted to a local hospital with multiple bruises and abrasions. The examining physician suspected child abuse and notified DSS, which immediately obtained an order from a Wisconsin juvenile court placing Joshua in the temporary custody of the hospital. Three days later, the county convened an ad hoc "Child Protection Team"—consisting of a pediatrician, a psychologist, a police detective, the county's lawyer, several DSS caseworkers and various hospital personnel—to consider Joshua's situation. At this meeting, the Team decided that there was insufficient evidence of child abuse to retain Joshua in the custody of the court. The Team did, however, decide to recommend several measures to protect Joshua, including enrolling him in a preschool program, providing his father with certain counseling services, and encouraging his father's girlfriend to move out of the home. Randy DeShaney entered into a voluntary agreement with DSS in which he promised to cooperate with them in accomplishing these goals.

Based on the recommendation of the Child Protection Team, the juvenile court dismissed the child protection case and returned Joshua to the custody of his father. A month later, emergency room personnel called the DSS caseworker handling Joshua's case to report that he had once again been treated for suspicious injuries. The caseworker concluded that there was no basis for action. For the next six months, the caseworker made monthly visits to the DeShaney home, during which she observed a number of suspicious injuries on Joshua's head; she also noticed that he had not been enrolled in school, and that the girlfriend had not moved out. The caseworker dutifully recorded these incidents in her files, along with her continuing suspicions that someone in the DeShaney household was physically abusing Joshua, but she did nothing more. In November 1983, the emergency room notified DSS that Joshua had been treated once again for injuries that they believed to be caused by child abuse. On the caseworker's next two visits to the DeShaney home, she was told that Joshua was too ill to see her. Still DSS took no action.

In March 1984, Randy DeShaney beat 4-year-old Joshua so severely that he fell into a life-threatening coma. Emergency brain surgery revealed a series of hemorrhages caused by traumatic injuries to the head inflicted over a long period of time. Joshua did not die, but he suffered brain damage so severe that he is expected to spend the rest of his life confined to an institution for the profoundly retarded. Randy DeShaney was subsequently tried and convicted of child abuse.

Joshua and his mother brought this action under 42 U.S.C. § 1983 in the United States District Court for the Eastern District of Wisconsin against respondents Winnebago County, DSS, and various individual employees of DSS. The complaint alleged that respondents had deprived Joshua of his liberty without due process of law, in violation of his rights under the Fourteenth Amendment, by failing to intervene to protect him against a risk of violence at his father's hands of which they knew or should have known. The District Court granted summary judgment for respondents.

The Court of Appeals for the Seventh Circuit affirmed, 812 F.2d 298 (1987), holding that petitioners had not made out an actionable § 1983 claim for two alternative reasons. First, the court held that the Due Process Clause of the Fourteenth Amendment does not require a state or local governmental entity to protect its citizens from "private violence, or other mishaps not attributable to the conduct of its employees." *Id.* at 301. In so holding, the court specifically rejected the position *** that once the State learns that a particular child is in danger of abuse from third parties and actually undertakes to protect him from that danger, a "special relationship" arises between it and the child which imposes an affirmative constitutional duty to provide adequate protection [and ruled] that the casual connection between respondents' conduct and Joshua's injuries was too attenuated to establish a deprivation of constitutional rights actionable under § 1983.*** We now affirm.

II.

[1] The Due Process Clause of the Fourteenth Amendment provides that "[n]o State shall . . . deprive any person of life, liberty, or property, without due process of law." Petitioners contend that the State deprived Joshua of his liberty interest in "free[dom] from . . . unjustified intrusions on personal security" *** by failing to provide him with adequate protection against his father's violence. The claim is one invoking the substantive rather than the procedural component of the Due Process Clause; petitioners do not claim that the State denied Joshua protection without according him appropriate procedural safeguards,*** but that it was categorically obligated to protect him in these circumstances.***

But nothing in the language of the Due Process Clause itself requires the State to protect the life, liberty, and property of its citizens against invasion by private actors. The Clause is phrased as a limitation on the State's power to act, not as a guarantee of certain minimal levels of safety and security. It forbids the State itself to deprive individuals of life, liberty, or property without "due process of law," but its language cannot fairly be extended to impose an affirmative obligation on the State to ensure that those interests do not come to harm through other means. Nor does history support such an expansive reading of the constitutional text. Like its counterpart in the Fifth Amendment, the Due Process Clause of the Fourteenth Amendment was intended to prevent government "from abusing [its] power, or employing it as an instrument of oppression," "to secure the individual from the arbitrary exercise of the powers of government," and "to prevent governmental power from being 'used for purposes of oppression.' *** Its purpose was to protect the people from the State, not to ensure that the State protected them from each other. The Framers were content to leave the extent of governmental obligation in the latter area to the democratic political processes.

Consistent with these principles, our cases have recognized that the Due Process Clauses generally confer no affirmative right to governmental aid, even where such aid may be necessary to secure life, liberty, or property interests of which the government itself may not deprive the individual. *See, e.g., Harris v. McRae*, 448 U.S. 297, 317–318, 100 S.Ct. 2671, 2688–2689, 65 L.Ed.2d 784 (1980) (no obligation to fund abortions or other medical services) (discussing Due Process Clause of Fifth Amendment); *Lindsey v. Normet*, 405 U.S. 56, 74, 92 S.Ct. 862, 874, 31 L.Ed.2d 36 (1972) (no obligation to provide adequate housing) (discussing Due Process Clause of Fourteenth Amendment); see also *Youngberg v. Romeo*, supra, 457 U.S., at 317 102 S.Ct., at 2458 ("As a general matter, a State is under no constitutional duty to provide substantive services for those within its border"). As we said in *Harris v. McRae*: "Although the liberty protected by the Due Process Clause affords protection against unwarranted government interference *** it does not confer an entitlement to such [governmental aid] as may be necessary to real-

---

[1] The State may not, of course, selectively deny its protective services to certain disfavored minorities without violating the Equal Protection Clause. *See Yick Wo v. Hopkins*, 118 U.S. 356, 6 S.Ct. 1064, 30 L.Ed. 220 (1886). But no such argument has been made here.

ize all the advantages of that freedom." 448 U.S., at 317–318, 100 S.Ct., at 2688–2689. If the Due Process Clause does not require the State to provide its citizens with particular protective services, it follows that the State cannot be held liable under the Clause for injuries that could have been averted had it chosen to provide them.[1] As a general matter, then, we conclude that a State's failure to protect an individual against private violence simply does not constitute a violation of the Due Process Clause.

Petitioners contend, however, that even if the Due Process Clause imposes no affirmative obligation on the State to provide the general public with adequate protective services, such a duty may arise out of certain "special relationships" created or assumed by the State with respect to particular individuals. Brief for Petitioners 13–18. Petitioners argue that such a "special relationship" existed here because the State knew that Joshua faced a special danger of abuse at his father's hands, and specifically proclaimed, by word and by deed, its intention to protect him against that danger. *Id.*, at 18–20. Having actually undertaken to protect Joshua from this danger—which petitioners concede the State played no part in creating—the State acquired an affirmative "duty," enforceable through the Due Process Clause, to do so in a reasonably competent fashion. Its failure to discharge that duty, so the argument goes, was an abuse of governmental power that so "shocks the conscience," *Rochin v. California*, 342 U.S. 165, 172, 72 S.Ct. 205, 209, 96 L.Ed. 183 (1952), as to constitute a substantive due process violation. Brief for Petitioners 20.

We reject this argument. It is true that in certain limited circumstances the Constitution imposes upon the State affirmative duties of care and protection with respect to particular individuals. In *Estelle v. Gamble* *** we recognized that the Eighth Amendment's prohibition against cruel and unusual punishment, made applicable to the States through the Fourteenth Amendment's Due Process Clause,*** requires the State to provide adequate medical care to incarcerated prisoners.[2] We reasoned that because the prisoner is unable "'by reason of the deprivation of his liberty [to] care for himself,' "it is only" 'just'" that the State be required to care for him.

In *Youngberg v. Romeo* *** we extended this analysis beyond the Eighth Amendment setting, holding that the substantive component of the Fourteenth Amendment's Due Process Clause requires the State to provide involuntarily committed mental patients with such services as are necessary to ensure their "reasonable safety" from themselves and others.*** (*dicta* indicating that the State is also obligated to provide such individuals with "adequate food, shelter, clothing, and medical care"). As we explained: "If it is cruel and unusual punishment to hold convicted criminals in unsafe conditions, it must be unconstitutional [under the Due Process Clause] to confine the involuntarily committed—who may not be punished at all—in unsafe conditions."***

But these cases afford petitioners no help. Taken together, they stand only for the proposition that when the State takes a person into its custody and holds him there

---

[2] To make out an Eighth Amendment claim based on the failure to provide adequate medical care, a prisoner must show that the state defendants exhibited "deliberate indifference" to his "serious" medical needs; the mere negligent or inadvertent failure to provide adequate care is not enough. *Estelle v. Gamble*, 429 U.S., at 105–106, 97 S.Ct., at 291–292. In *Whitley v. Albers*, 475 U.S. 312, 106 S.Ct. 1078, 89 L.Ed.2d 251 (1986), we suggested that a similar state of mind is required to make out a substantive due process claim in the prison setting. Id., at 326–327, 106 S.Ct., at 1088.

against his will, the Constitution imposes upon it a corresponding duty to assume some responsibility for his safety and general well-being.

The rationale for this principle is simple enough: when the State by the affirmative exercise of its power so restrains an individual's liberty that it renders him unable to care for himself, and at the same time fails to provide for his basic human needs—e.g., food, clothing, shelter, medical care, and reasonable safety—it transgresses the substantive limits of state action set by the Eighth Amendment and the Due Process Clause.*** The affirmative duty to protect arises not from the State's knowledge of the individual's predicament or from its expressions of intent to help him, but from the limitation which it has imposed on his freedom to act on his own behalf.*** In the substantive due process analysis, it is the State's affirmative act of restraining the individual's freedom to act on his own behalf—through incarceration, institutionalization, or other similar restraint of personal liberty—which is the "deprivation of liberty" triggering the protections of the Due Process Clause, not its failure to act to protect his liberty interests against harms inflicted by other means.

The *Estelle-Youngberg* analysis simply has no applicability in the present case. Petitioners concede that the harms Joshua suffered occurred not while he was in the State's custody, but while he was in the custody of his natural father, who was in no sense a state actor. While the State may have been aware of the dangers that Joshua faced in the free world, it played no part in their creation, nor did it do anything to render him any more vulnerable to them. That the State once took temporary custody of Joshua does not alter the analysis, for when it returned him to his father's custody, it placed him in no worse position than that in which he would have been had it not acted at all; the State does not become the permanent guarantor of an individual's safety by having once offered him shelter. Under these circumstances, the State had no constitutional duty to protect Joshua.

It may well be that, by voluntarily undertaking to protect Joshua against a danger it concededly played no part in creating, the State acquired a duty under state tort law to provide him with adequate protection against that danger.*** But the claim here is based on the Due Process Clause of the Fourteenth Amendment, which, as we have said many times, does not transform every tort committed by a state actor into a constitutional violation. A State may, through its courts and legislatures, impose such affirmative duties of care and protection upon its agents as it wishes. But not "all common-law duties owed by government actors were *** constitutionalized by the Fourteenth Amendment."*** Because, as explained above, the State had no constitutional duty to protect Joshua against his father's violence, its failure to do so—though calamitous in hindsight—simply does not constitute a violation of the Due Process Clause.

Judges and lawyers, like other humans, are moved by natural sympathy in a case like this to find a way for Joshua and his mother to receive adequate compensation for the grievous harm inflicted upon them. But before yielding to that impulse, it is well to remember once again that the harm was inflicted not by the State of Wisconsin, but by Joshua's father. The most that can be said of the state functionaries in this case is that they stood by and did nothing when suspicious circumstances dictated a more active role for them. In defence of them it must also be said that had they moved too soon to take custody of the son away from the father, they would likely have been met with charges of improperly intruding into the parent-child relationship, charges based on the same Due Process Clause that forms the basis for the present charge of failure to provide adequate protection.

The people of Wisconsin may well prefer a system of liability which would place upon the State and its officials the responsibility for failure to act in situations such as the present one. They may create such a system, if they do not have it already, by changing the tort law of the State in accordance with the regular lawmaking process. But they should not have it thrust upon them by this Court's expansion of the Due Process Clause of the Fourteenth Amendment.

Affirmed.

Justice BRENNAN, with whom Justice MARSHALL and Justice BLACKMUN join, dissenting.

"The most that can be said of the state functionaries in this case," the Court today concludes, "is that they stood by and did nothing when suspicious circumstances dictated a more active role for them."*** Because I believe that this description of respondents' conduct tells only part of the story and that, accordingly, the Constitution itself "dictated a more active role" for respondents in the circumstances presented here, I cannot agree that respondents had no constitutional duty to help Joshua DeShaney.

It may well be, as the Court decides that the Due Process Clause as construed by our prior cases creates no general right to basic governmental services. That, however, is not the question presented here.*** No one *** has asked the Court to proclaim that, as a general matter the Constitution safeguards positive as well as negative liberties.*** By leading off with a discussion (and rejection) of the idea that the Constitution imposes on the States an affirmative duty to take basic care of their citizens, the court foreshadows—perhaps even pre-ordains—its conclusion that no duty existed even on the specific facts before us.***

The Court's baseline is the absence of positive rights in the Constitution and a concomitant suspicion of any claim that seems to depend on such rights. From this perspective, the DeShaneys' claim is first and foremost about inaction (the failure, here, of respondents to take steps to protect Joshua), and only tangentially about action (the establishment of a state program specifically designed to help children like Joshua).***

As the Court today reminds us, "the Due Process Clause of the Fourteenth Amendment was intended to prevent government 'from abusing [its] power, or employing it as an instrument of oppression.'" *** My disagreement with the Court arises from its failure to see that inaction can be every bit as abusive of power as action, that oppression can result when a State undertakes a vital duty and then ignores it. Today's opinion construes the Due Process Clause to permit a State to displace private sources of protection and then, at the critical moment, to shrug its shoulders and turn away from the harm that it has promised to try to prevent. Because I cannot agree that our Constitution is indifferent to such indifference, I respectfully dissent.

Justice BLACKMUN, dissenting.

Today, the Court purports to be the dispassionate oracle of the law, unmoved by "natural sympathy."*** But, in this pretense, the Court itself retreats into a sterile formalism which prevents it from recognizing either the facts of the case before it or the legal norms that should apply to those facts. As Justice Brennan demonstrates, the facts here involve not mere passivity, but active state intervention in the life of Joshua DeShaney—intervention that triggered a fundamental duty to aid the boy once the State learned of the severe danger to which he was exposed.

The Court fails to recognize this duty because it attempts to draw a sharp and rigid line between action and inaction. But such formalistic reasoning has no place in the interpretation of the broad and stirring Clauses of the Fourteenth Amendment. Indeed, I submit that these Clauses were designed, at least in part, to undo the formalistic legal reasoning that infected antebellum jurisprudence, which the late Professor Robert Cover analyzed so effectively in his significant work entitled JUSTICE ACCUSED (1975).

Like the antebellum judges who denied relief to fugitive slaves *** the Court today claims that its decision, however harsh, is compelled by existing legal doctrine. On the contrary, the question presented by this case is an open one, and our Fourteenth Amendment precedents may be read more broadly or narrowly depending upon how one chooses to read them. Faced with the choice, I would adopt a "sympathetic" reading, one which comports with dictates of fundamental justice and recognizes that compassion need not be exiled from the province of judging. *Cf.* A. STONE, LAW, PSYCHIATRY, AND MORALITY 262 (1984) ("We will make mistakes if we go forward, but doing nothing can be the worst mistake. What is required of us is moral ambition. Until our composite sketch becomes a true portrait of humanity we must live with our uncertainty; we will grope, we will struggle, and our compassion may be our only guide and comfort").

Notes and Questions

1. The Court in *DeShaney* reasoned that because the state "played no part in the *** creation [of the dangers faced by the child Joshua], nor did it do anything to render him any more vulnerable to them *** the State had no constitutional duty to protect Joshua." Do you agree? What, for example, was the state's involvement in awarding custody of Joshua after his parents' divorce? If the state owes no duty to protect under these circumstances, when, if ever, would it owe such a duty?

2. Could the broad language of the decision be read to hold that there is never a constitutional right to government protection against private wrongs? Is the distinction between action and inaction a valid consideration in determining the government's duties under the Due Process Clause?

Is the state constitutionally obligated to provide a minimum level of safety and security, *e.g.,* by maintaining a police force, criminalizing anti-social behavior, providing common law remedies, etc.? If so, what is the textual source of this obligation? If not, what justification for government power remains, under the Lockean paradigm? *See* Chapter 2, *supra.*

3. Were Joshua DeShaney and his mother asserting an "affirmative right to governmental aid"? Why did the Court address this issue?

2. The Right to Property

Is the right to property a negative right or a positive right? Consider the U.S. Constitution's explicit protection of slavery and the slave trade. What duties are imposed by the Fugitive Slave Clause, Art. IV § 2 cl. 3? Is the prohibition on direct taxes—motivated by the fear that the power to tax would destroy slavery—a neutral restraint on government power? The logic of these provisions is starkly illustrated in Chief Justice Taney's opinion in the infamous *Dred Scott* decision.

DRED SCOTT v. SANDFORD

60 U.S. (19 How.) 393, 15 L. Ed. 691 (1857)

[Scott was born in slavery in Virginia, but was brought to the free state of Illinois and the territory of Wisconsin, where slavery was prohibited by the Missouri Compromise. Upon being brought back to Missouri, a slave state, he was sold to Sandford, whereupon he brought suit in federal court claiming that he had gained his freedom under the laws of Illinois and Wisconsin. The U.S. Supreme Court, in an opinion authored by Chief Justice Taney ruled that Scott was not a citizen entitled to invoke federal jurisdiction, having "no rights which the white man was bound to respect." The Court further invalidated the Missouri Compromise as a violation of the Fifth Amendment due process clause.]

[The government] has no power over the person or property of a citizen but what the citizens of the United States have granted.*** And if the Constitution recognizes the right of property of the master in a slave, and makes no distinction between that description of property and other property owned by a citizen, no tribunal, acting under the authority of the United States, whether it be legislative, executive, or judicial, has a right to draw such a distinction, or deny to it the benefits of the provisions and guarantees which have been provided for the protection of private property against the encroachments of the Government.

[T]he right of property in a slave is distinctly and expressly affirmed in the Constitution. The right to traffic in it, like an ordinary article of merchandise and property, was guaranteed to the citizens of the United States, in every State that might desire it, for twenty years. And the Government in express terms is pledged to protect it in all future time, if the slave escapes from his owner. This is done in plain words—too plain to be misunderstood. And no word can be found in the Constitution which gives Congress a greater power over slave property, or which entitles property of that kind to less protection than property of any other description. The only power conferred is the power coupled with the duty of guarding and protecting the owner in his rights.

Upon these considerations it is the opinion of the court that the act of Congress which prohibited a citizen from holding and owning property of this kind in the territory of the United States north of the [Mason-Dixon line] is not warranted by the Constitution and is therefore void, and that neither Dred Scott, nor any of his family, were made free by being carried into this territory; even if they had been carried there by the owner, with the intention of becoming a permanent resident.

Notes and Questions

1. The Court takes the view that its decision is aimed at protecting constitutional rights "against the encroachments of the Government." Does this interpretation challenge your notions of the U.S. Constitution as a fundamentally liberatory and democratic document? What does this interpretation imply about the "determinacy" of rights discourse? *See, e.g.*, Karl Klare's discussion of critical approaches to rights discourse in Chapter 2, *supra*.

2. *The Right to Property.* "The right to traffic in [slaves], like an ordinary article of merchandise and property, was guaranteed to the citizens of the United States." Does the opinion in *Dred Scott* imply that constitutional protection of the right to private property supersedes the other rights protected by the due process clause—life and liberty? Is this interpretation consistent with the intent of the framers? According to James Ely,

> the right to acquire and own property was undoubtedly a paramount value for the framers of the Constitution. Following the Lockean philosophy, John Rutledge of South Carolina advised the Philadelphia convention that 'Property was certainly the principal object of Society.'*** These sentiments were widely shared by other delegates.*** In their minds, property rights were indispensable because property ownership was closely associated with liberty.

JAMES W. ELY, JR., THE GUARDIAN OF EVERY OTHER RIGHT: A CONSTITUTIONAL HISTORY OF PROPERTY RIGHTS 43 (1992).

The identification of property with liberty was clearly limited to those having the legal capacity to own property: free white males. Could the existence of slavery explain in part why the Lockean paradigm was imported so literally into American jurisprudence, unlike in Europe?

3. *Historical Norms and Human Rights.* Does the fact that the status of Dred Scott was before the Court indicate that slavery was a matter of moral, as well as legal, debate? How should responsibility be assigned for historical examples of racism, sexism, genocide and other forms of intolerance? Should moral judgments be considered in the context of the norms prevailing at the time? Should historical evidence of resistance, slave revolts, the abolitionist movement and public debate on slavery be taken into account in defining the relevant norms? Should slaveholders and slave traders be held morally accountable for their actions? What about those who benefited from slavery and the slave trade? Should historical abuses like U.S. slavery and genocidal acts against Native Americans be analyzed as "human rights violations," even though the modern international human rights movement is largely a post-World War II development? See the discussion of the U.S. movement on reparations for slavery in Chapter 3, *supra.*

4. Does the right to private property belong to the category of "civil and political rights," to "economic and social rights" or both? *See* Barbara Stark's discussion below on ways to rethink the framers' understanding of the right to property.

BARBARA STARK, DECONSTRUCTING THE FRAMERS' RIGHT TO PROPERTY: LIBERTY'S DAUGHTERS AND ECONOMIC RIGHTS

28 HOFSTRA L. REV. 963, 967–968; 973–978; 984–987; 995 (2000)

*** For the Framers, the enjoyment of the right to property, like the enjoyment of civil and political rights, was explicitly limited to white men. Although more than two hundred years of constitutional jurisprudence has extended most civil and political rights to blacks and white women, disproportionate numbers of these groups lack the economic rights necessary to fully enjoy them. Economic rights are important in themselves, however, not only because they facilitate the enjoyment of civil and political rights. Rather, the two kinds of rights are equally crucial to any meaningful conception of human dignity. The two kinds of rights are also interdependent; that is, each is necessary for the enjoyment of the other. As this Article demonstrates, this understanding is neither new nor foreign, but buried in the very heart of American constitutional jurisprudence.***

A. *Historical Origins—The Right to Property*

The colonists brought with them a rich tradition of rights. As Pulitzer Prize-winning historian Jack N. Rakove points out, there was "no shortage of rights consciousness among colonists whose dual motives for emigration included both tender matters of religious conscience and the pursuit of property." This "rights consciousness" was grounded in the notion of natural, inalienable rights, which belonged to man in the state of nature described by John Locke.

These rights, to which Englishmen were entitled as a birthright, were well understood: "Life, liberty, and property comprised the fundamental trinity of inalienable rights." As explicitly set out in the Virginia Declaration of Rights:

> [A]ll men are by nature equally free and independent, and have certain inherent rights, of which, when they enter into a state of society, they cannot, by any compact, deprive or divest their posterity; namely, the enjoyment of life and liberty, with the means of acquiring and possessing property, and pursuing and obtaining happiness and safety.

Men left the state of nature only to better assure these inalienable rights. That is, they entered into Locke's social contract, through which they constructed legal rights, to protect and promote their pre-existing natural rights.***

The right to property held a privileged place in colonial jurisprudence. William Penn began his short list of English rights with the right to property: "'[R]ights and privileges which I call English . . . may be reduced to these three . . . I. An ownership, and undisturbed possession: that which they have is rightly theirs, and nobody's else.'"

What exactly was meant by a right to property? As legal historian John Phillip Reid has explained, the eighteenth century understanding of the right to property was much broader than ours:

> [I]n legal terminology, "property" was not necessarily the object itself, but the right and interest or domination lawfully held over the object; it was a species of title, inchoate or complete, legal or equitable, corporeal or incorporeal, tangible or intangible, visible or invisible, real, personal, or contractual. . . . Most commonly, when used in revolutionary constitutional debates . . . "property" referred to rights of all kinds.

The "right to property," in short, was used to refer to both property rights and to civil and political rights, just as "day" refers to the twenty-four hour period including both daylight hours and nighttime hours.***

At the same time, just as "day" is also used to refer specifically to the hours of daylight, the right to property was also used to refer specifically to rights in particular property. One had to have "property" in order to vote, for example, and for that purpose property generally meant land. As James W. Ely, Jr., notes, "[w]hen the Constitution was written, virtually every state imposed a property or taxpaying qualification on suffrage and set higher property qualifications to hold public office." This requirement was met by an amount of property within the reach of many, if not most, white men. Even those white men without money could participate in the many claims programs through which land was distributed to those willing to farm it, which had drawn many of them to the colonies. Property requirements, of course, effectively excluded black men and all women, whose capacity to own property was strictly limited by law and custom.

From the Framers' perspective, however, propertied white men were the threatened minority in need of protection. As James Madison, principal drafter of the Bill of Rights, explained, "in all populous countries the smaller part only can be interested in preserving the rights of property." These property owners were crucial to the survival of the new Republic because they alone had a real stake in it. Thus, for Madison, as Jennifer Nedelsky explains:

> Good government must be able to protect both the "rights of persons" and the "rights of property" . . . The problem was that if political rights were granted equally to all, the rights of persons and the rights of property would not be equally protected. The propertied could be relied upon to respect the rights of persons, in which they also had an interest. But the propertyless had no corresponding interest in property. . . . The problem of providing equal protection for the rights of persons and the rights of property in a manner consistent with republican principles was, Madison said, the most difficult of all political problems.

Rakove, similarly, describes Madison's:

> palpable fear that economic legislation was jeopardizing fundamental rights of property. Paper-money laws, debtor-stay laws, and the specter of Shays's Rebellion in Massachusetts all alarmed him terribly. So did the grim prospect [that] . . . a factious majority might eventually form from "those who will labour [sic] under all the hardships of life, & secretly sigh for a more equal distribution of its blessings."

Madison became the champion of that propertied minority, which had the most to lose from a "more equal distribution."***

By deconstructing the right to property, we see what propertied white men never had to see, what they took for granted, and what the "rights culture" they bequeathed us has blinded us to. Deconstruction reveals first, the lesser economic rights subsumed in the right to property; and second, the complex and dynamic relationship between these subsumed economic rights and civil and political rights. Examining the relationship between the two kinds of rights in the context of concrete social history shows first, and most obviously, that the Framers' enjoyment of civil and political rights depended on their own enjoyment of economic rights. Second, and much less obvious, their enjoyment of these subsumed economic rights was in part assured by women's unseen work. Finally, least obvious and most disturbing, the Framers' enjoyment of some of these rights was actually predicated on women's denial of them; they enjoyed these rights more because women enjoyed them less.***

For the Framers, the right to property included lesser economic rights; that is, those rights which property implies, those rights which one possessing property has no more need to articulate than one possessing liberty need articulate a right "not to be bound." These subsumed rights include the right to an adequate standard of living, including food and shelter, and the right to work. The Framers took these rights for granted and fiercely resisted any threat to take from them "'that which . . . [was] rightly theirs, and nobody's else." Because white women and slaves were for the most part incapable of owning property, they could not take these lesser included economic rights for granted. Being permitted to hire her time, for example, was a precious privilege for a slave woman.***

By drawing on the Economic Covenant, we can invert the hierarchical opposition that underlies our own Bill of Rights and unpack the right to property. What lesser economic rights are subsumed in that right? What does the right to property mean from the perspectives of the have-nots? By examining the rights set out in the Economic Covenant, we expose what the Bill of Rights takes for granted and we discover that economic rights are iterations of the Framers' right to property from the perspectives of those who had no property, including those who were property themselves.***

Even as the Framers sought to protect the propertied minority, nothing—not even subsistence—could be taken for granted by white women and black slaves. While some of them lived quite well, and a few even enjoyed the accoutrements of wealth and privilege, in general they had no right to property. From the Framers' perspectives, white women and black slaves were so obviously inferior that rights discourse simply did not apply to them.***

The conventional story is that Americans do not need economic rights; they are irrelevant to our experience. Most of the accounts of the founding of the United States confirm this view.*** By shifting our attention from the historical experience of the Framers to the experience of a group which did not enjoy economic rights, however, we *** discover that economic rights were extremely relevant to the historical experience of eighteenth century women. For those who did not enjoy economic rights, who could not take them for granted, they may well have been even more crucial, even more vivid, than the civil and political rights to which we unthinkingly subordinate them.***

"Economic rights" are an anachronism, inconceivable at the time. This is precisely the point, however. Because economic rights were inconceivable to the Framers, except as enjoyed by the already-propertied, the universalizing trends that eventually extended civil and political rights to those originally denied them, never applied to economic rights. Nor can economic rights ever be "found" in the Constitution, as the Supreme Court has consistently held. While the interdependence of economic rights and civil and political rights is globally recognized,*** economic rights still play a very minor role in our national jurisprudence. Their marginalization reflects and reinforces the marginalization of those who still have the least property—a group, not coincidentally, disproportionately comprised of women and black men.***

3. *The Right to an Adequate Standard of Living*

THOMAS ROSS, THE RHETORIC OF POVERTY: THEIR IMMORALITY, OUR HELPLESSNESS

79 GEO. L.J. 1499, 1499–1502; 1507–1514; 1539–1544 (1991)

I. INTRODUCTION

Poor people are different from us. Most of them are morally weak and undeserving. And, in any event, we are helpless to solve the complex and daunting problem of poverty. This is the rhetoric of poverty.

The United States Supreme Court has addressed the constitutional claims of poor people in a range of contemporary cases. The rhetoric of poverty runs through these opinions. Poor people, it is said or implied, are unwilling to work and especially likely to commit fraud or child abuse, or to violate other legal and moral norms. They have bad attitudes and are the cause of their own poverty. At the same time, the problem of poverty is, in the Court's rhetoric, a problem of daunting complexity that is virtually beyond solution. Hard choices, suffering, even "Kafkaesque" results are simply unavoidable.***

The first rhetorical step, the creation of the abstraction the "poor," is an easily overlooked yet powerful part of the rhetoric of poverty. We are so used to speaking of the poor as a distinct class that we overlook the rhetorical significance of speaking this way. By focusing on the single variable of economic wealth and then drawing a line on the wealth continuum, we create a class of people who are them, not us. Creating this abstraction is, in one sense, merely a way of speaking. We do this because to speak of the world in sensible ways we must resort to categories and abstractions. There are meaningful differences between the circumstances of people below the poverty line and the circumstances of middle class people, and to ignore these real differences can lead to injustice. Thus, to speak of the "poor" is a sensible way to talk. In the rhetorical context, however, it is also much more.

The creation of the category of the "poor," also makes possible the assertion of their moral weakness. To assert their moral weakness, "they" must exist as a conceptually distinct group. There is a long history of speaking of the poor as morally weak, or even degenerate. Thus, when we hear legal rhetoric about the poor, we often hear an underlying message of deviance: we are normal, they are deviant. Our feelings about their deviance range from empathy to violent hatred. Still, even in the most benevolent view, they are not normal. Their deviance is a product of a single aspect of their lives, their relative wealth position. All other aspects of their lives are either distorted by the label of deviance or ignored. By creating this class of people, we are able at once to distinguish us from them and to appropriate normalcy to our lives and circumstances.

The rhetorical assertion of judicial helplessness is also connected to widely shared and long-standing cultural assumptions about the nature of poverty. This rhetoric depends on the assumption that poverty is somehow built into the basic structure of our society and system of law. We assume that the eradication of poverty, even if possible in theory, would require the radical transformation of our society. The causes of poverty, we assume, are a product of a complex set of factors tied to politics, culture, history, psychology, and philosophy. Thus, only in a radically different world might poverty cease to exist. And, whatever the extent of the powers of the Court, radically remaking the world is not one of them.

The equal themes of moral deviance and judicial helplessness at first seem to be inconsistent. The premise of moral weakness suggests that the problem is really quite simple. If poor people simply chose to "straighten up and fly right," all would be well. If they would accept and commit to the moral norms of those of us not in poverty, they would cease to be poor, albeit only after a long time and much hard work. In this vision of poverty, the problem is uni-dimensional and is intractable only to the extent that poor people resist the personal, individual reform of their moral lives. The judicial helplessness theme depends, on the other hand, on the complexity of the problem and on the existence of multiple, intertwined causes. Despite this apparent inconsistency, the Justices-rhetoricians use both themes, often in tandem, throughout their opinions.

This apparent inconsistency in the Court's rhetoric of poverty may be related to yet another enduring cultural assumption, the division of the poor into classes of the deserving and the undeserving poor. These classes have been drawn somewhat differently throughout history. The contemporary division of the poor distinguishes between able-bodied adults and the children, the aged, and the disabled. This distinction is premised on the ability of the former class to perform work. For this able-bodied class, the moral weakness rhetoric is especially potent—I work, they don't, they could. This argument does not fit members of the second group because we assume that work is not readily available to them. For this class, the judicial helplessness plea is the perfect response. The rhetoric of helplessness allows the expression of sympathy for the deserving poor while avoiding the burden of intervention.

The dual rhetoric of moral weakness and judicial helplessness fits the needs of a Court that has chosen to minimize the constitutional basis for intervention on behalf of the poor. Under this rhetoric, either the poor do not deserve our intervention or, if they do have a claim to our sense of justice, we are functionally helpless to do justice.***

The rhetoric of poverty in the 1980s was exemplified by the myth of the welfare mother with a Cadillac and by the rise of yet another category of the poor, the "underclass." This new category of the poor included:

(A) the passive poor, usually long-term welfare recipients;

(B) the hostile street criminals who terrorize most cities, and who are often school drop-outs and drug addicts;

(C) the hustlers, who, like street criminals, may not be poor and who earn their livelihood in an underground economy, but rarely commit violent crimes;

(D) the traumatized drunks, drifters, homeless, shopping-bag ladies and released mental patients who frequently roam or collapse on city streets.

Membership in the underclass was determined by behavior which was either patently immoral or socially deviant. The concept of the underclass etched deeper the division between us and them. It also connected perfectly with the rhetorical theme of moral weakness. Except for some examples of the "traumatized" members of the underclass, the behavior that characterized the underclass was criminal, deviant, or that of a person without hope or dignity. The idea of the "passive" poor, people beyond hope and without any sense of initiative, expressed the pervasive notion that poor people were unwilling to pull themselves up by their bootstraps and were instead happy to feed at the public trough.

The "underclass" thus was a late twentieth century form of the historically persistent category, the undeserving poor. And like its historical antecedents, the idea of the "underclass" seemed to be driven more by ideology than by any attempt accurately to generalize about the circumstances and nature of poverty in America. Michael Katz contrasted the idea of the underclass and the reality:

> [A]s a metaphor, the underclass obscures more than it reveals. It glosses over differences in condition that require varied forms of help, and it passes lightly over two salient features of poverty and welfare in America: their widespread and transient character. In the Michigan study, which followed a large sample of American families for 10 years, [b]oth poverty and welfare use *** lasted relatively briefly, and children whose parents relied on welfare were no more likely to need public assistance as adults than were others in the sample. What the

study shows, in short, is that poverty is more accurately perceived now, as before in American history, as a point on a continuum rather than a sharp, clearly demarcated category of social experience. In truth, the forces that push individuals and families into poverty originate in the structure of America's political economy. Some of us are lucky, not different.***

The precise content of the commonly held assumptions about the poor has changed throughout American history. The idea of the nineteenth century "pauper" is different from the idea of the late twentieth century "underclass." Still, the basic premises of the rhetoric of poverty run through history, drawing lines between groups of people and labeling categories as deviant and undeserving. There has always been an "us/them" conception of people in poverty. We have always found ways to make their suffering intellectually coherent.

The other central theme of the rhetoric of poverty is helplessness. This theme is expressed in two related ways. First, poverty is said to be an inescapable societal tragedy that we are helpless to remedy. Second, in the legal rhetoric of poverty, judges profess to be helpless in their judicial role. Their helplessness places the particular legal problems related to poverty beyond the parameters of their power and jurisdiction. Using this rhetoric of helplessness, judges sometimes concede that the problem of poverty may be capable of solution, and then assert that they, however, are not empowered to solve it. They identify someone else, typically the legislature, as the body empowered to address the problem.***

1. *The Helplessness of Those Not in Poverty*

The idea that poverty in America is inherent or practically irremediable is commonly held today. Expressions like "there have always been poor people; there always will be poor people" are abundant in our discourse. We bemoan the complex and intractable nature of the problem.

Observers often interweave the premise of moral weakness with the argument for the intractable nature of poverty. After all, if poverty is essentially a problem of moral weakness, if poor people must undergo a personal transformation, what can we do to effect such a change? Historically, we have often encouraged such a change on the part of the poor by making the conditions of poverty so appalling that we imagine poor people seem to insist on not mending their ways and, to our surprise, seem willing to go on living in the horrific conditions of poverty. This disappointment feeds the argument of helplessness. If poor people are unwilling to change their behavior and values in response to the strongest of incentives, the horror of life in poverty, what else can we do?

Another version of the argument for helplessness is the characterization of poverty as a product of a mix of abstract forces and ideas, beyond our practical control. Poverty is built into the basic structure of our society, it is a product of our history, tradition, philosophies, political structures, and economic structures. Observers who espouse this view of the origins of poverty either see no realistic solution or else see a solution that entails the loss of our most basic social strictures.

This particular profession of helplessness is problematic because poverty arises out of the "politics of distribution." Poverty is not a matter of scarcity. We have more than enough to meet the basic needs of everyone in our society, yet we continue to speak about poverty as though it were a problem beyond the reach of our material resources. Perhaps the persistence of poverty leads to the idea that it is inherent in the structure of our society. But all that has ever been required to eliminate poverty is a redistribution of wealth. Although the complex mix of history, traditions, and political structures may help to explain why Americans have chosen not to abolish poverty, it does not explain how that choice is a product of helplessness.

2. The Helplessness of Judges

There is another version of the argument for helplessness that exists in the legal rhetoric of poverty. It is the special plea of judicial helplessness. This argument asserts that judges do not possess the power to act. It is the most powerful form of legal rhetoric. When a court acts, the judge's argument is about the wisdom and coherence of the action taken. This form of argument invites the reader's consideration and acceptance. The argument of judicial helplessness, on the other hand, purports to shut off the debate. The Court has no power to act; therefore, considerations of the wisdom and utility of the actions that might have been taken are beside the point. Normative debate is not invited.

The falsity of this argument is found in the "irony of jurisdiction." The extent of the court's power is determined by the court. In a governmental structure premised on multiple sources of power, each source must have some limits, and someone must draw the boundaries. In our federal system, the Supreme Court defines the limits of power of each branch of government. The Court sometimes chooses wisely and sometimes tragically, but the choices are always made. Thus, judges are rendered helpless by their own choice.***

III. THE CONTEMPORARY LEGAL RHETORIC OF POVERTY

Legal rhetoric embodies dominant cultural assumptions. When judges construct their arguments, they must depend on assumptions widely shared by their audience. Judges depend on these assumptions both because they give their arguments power and the potential for influence, and because the judges, as members of the culture, are likely to believe them. For example, during the nineteenth century, when the dominant and explicit cultural assumption was that blacks were inferior, the legal rhetoric was explicitly racist in its premises both because arguments built on racist premises had the potential for influence, and because the judges typically believed the premise of racism. Similarly, because the dominant nineteenth century cultural assumption was that the poor were morally degenerate, the premise of moral degeneracy of poor people was part of the legal rhetoric of the period.

The embodiment of cultural assumptions in legal rhetoric occurs in two ways: judges state the assumptions explicitly, and they implicitly incorporate the assumptions by making arguments that invite the reader to supply them. For example, Justice Henry Brown, writing for the majority in *Plessy v. Ferguson*, utilized explicit and implicit assumptions of racism. On an explicit level, in an effort to justify the Court's conclusion that de jure racial segregation was constitutional, Brown spoke unselfconsciously of "the reputation of belonging to the dominant race" as the "property" of the white man. He also implicitly invited his reader to supply the assumption of racism when he conjured up the specter of the "enforced commingling of the two races."

Discerning legal rhetoric's "invitation" to the reader is difficult. Each act of reading a judicial opinion brings an individual reader in a particular setting to the text. The meaning each person takes from the opinion is partly individual in nature, a product of her own experiences and purposes. The meaning is also a product of the cultural influences that affect each person's reading of the opinion. The nineteenth century reader of Brown's *Plessy* opinion brought the pervasive cultural assumption of the racial inferiority of African Americans to the opinion. Some nineteenth century readers consciously rejected this assumption. Yet, many more either consciously accepted the premise or assimilated it on some unconscious level. Thus, for most nineteenth century readers, Brown's invocation of "enforced commingling" was a disturbing specter. The readers were disturbed without the need for an explicit reminder of why living together with African Americans would be disturbing. The culture had taught the lesson so well that there was no need to say it out loud.***

IV. THE POWER OF RHETORIC—THE RESPONSIBILITY OF THE READER

The contemporary court, in a range of cases dealing with the rights and interests of the poor, has adopted a non-interventionist approach. The court has left the law's treatment of people in poverty largely to the political processes, acknowledging only the narrowest constitutional grounds for addressing their interests. The Justices have put forth opinions abundant with both explicit and, more often, implicit assumptions of the difference and moral weakness of the poor. Repeatedly, the Justices have stressed their own helplessness to correct the problems of poverty.

This pattern of choice and rhetoric provides a structure for understanding the power of rhetoric. Out of an understanding of the nature of the rhetoric of poverty emerges a responsibility, an ethic, incumbent on the reader.***

A. *The Power of Rhetoric*

The analysis of judicial rhetoric is an exploration of the human activity of reading. This activity is at once both simple to describe and difficult to understand. How the reader derives meaning from text is hard to say, and how that meaning influences the reader in her understanding of the constitutional issues of poverty is unclear.

Surely, many who read the judicial rhetoric of poverty are influenced by it. Although rhetoric rarely changes the reader's mind, it often subtly influences people by either creating doubt or strengthening resolve. When the Justices repeat the argument of judicial helplessness in case after case, the reader may begin to wonder whether there truly is any choice in the matter. When the reader is repeatedly confronted with the conceptual segregation of the poor, she is more likely to accept some version of the us/them idea embedded in this rhetoric. Our own experiences of reading judicial rhetoric tell us that these sorts of effects do occur. What we need to understand is how this happens to us.

1. *Conceptual Segregation and Moral Weakness*

The Court's rhetoric of poverty has conceptually segregated the poor in various ways. When Justice Stewart, in *Dandridge*, demanded an "equitable balance" between the "families on welfare and those supported by an employed breadwinner," he conceptually separated those families in poverty and receiving public assistance from other families. In his validation of the Texas AFDC scheme in *Jefferson*, Justice Rehnquist separated AFDC recipients into the undeserving, able-bodied poor, and the deserving, disabled and aged poor. Running through the cases *** particularly those dealing with disability benefits and food stamps, is the specter of fraud, which in turn depends on the segregation of recipients of public assistance into a group especially likely to deceive.

The very act of conceptual segregation has rhetorical power. When the members of the segregated group are defined by their difference from those in a dominant position in society, the very act of segregation suggests not simply difference but also deviance. The norm is defined by the dominant group; the segregated group is defined by deviance from that norm. The power of this segregation is vividly revealed in the rhetoric of poverty. [T]he rhetoric of poverty obscures the aspects of poverty that reflect our own lives. The lives of the poor have always mirrored the lives of the rest of society. Many of us struggle to raise children and to find and do work. We all feel humiliation and have aspirations. We all face desperate moral choices of one sort or another; we all succumb to temptation or despair at one time or another; we all, at the end, have good reason to question the strength of our individual will.

The Court's arguments in the poverty cases are much more than rhetorical forms. They are a lens through which we see poverty. Once we accept the rhetoric's depiction of poverty, we are done, the answer to the legal issue is ordained. For example, if we see the AFDC mother as different, prone to child abuse, and an ungrateful recipient of public largesse, the legal issue of whether the government can demand home visits to protect the welfare of the child as a condition of that largesse seems easily answered. By contrast, if we see Mrs. James as like us, a mother struggling to hold her family together and keep a sense of personal dignity through it all, the legal issue becomes more problematic.

The rhetoric of poverty invites the reader to provide a part of the picture, to bring to the reading culturally taught, stereotypical assumptions about the poor. This invitation is the most powerful aspect of the rhetoric.***

The rhetoric of poverty also works in a more general way to influence our understanding of the poor. The experience of reading this rhetoric may diminish the possibility for empathy. So long as we think of those in poverty as "them" and not "us," we are less likely to share in their pain and humiliation. We can imagine that they do not suffer as we would, or that their suffering, unlike ours, is inevitable or even deserved.

Our inability to imagine the poor as strong, successful, ambitious, and responsible people who win the battles of life prevents us from feeling empathy for them. The persistent idea of the "passive poor" and the "underclass" keeps blocking our imagination. Yet, the story of people in poverty in this country has been a story of strength and success. Against all odds, facing social stigma and working through maddening systems of public assistance, the poor have survived. Many poor women and men have kept their families together and maintained safe and decent lives in the midst of conditions that would seem to make family disintegration inescapable. The rhetoric of poverty highlights only the stories of failure and obscures the stories of success.

2. Helplessness

The argument for judicial helplessness does not rely on the assumption that the problem of poverty is intractable. Although the assertion of the complexity and intractability of poverty is typically woven into the Court's rhetoric, the plea of judicial helplessness requires only the assertion that the Court is not the proper institution to act.

The plea of judicial helplessness is an especially strong rhetorical move because it eliminates the question of the wisdom or justice of the outcome. It diverts the reader's attention to the abstract issues of separation of powers and the appropriate role of the judiciary, and obscures the inescapable element of choice. The plea of judicial help-lessness directs the debate toward the bloodless ground of the separation of powers doc-trine and away from the particular suffering of those who inhabit the Kafkaesque world of contemporary poverty.***

B. *The Responsibility of the Reader*

When we read an opinion dealing with the constitutional status of poverty we are engaged in an activity with moral connotations. After reading the opinion, no morally neutral position is available to us. If we speak about the case, we take on the role and responsibility of the critic. The discourse of the critic is the discourse of normative analy-sis. In one way or another, we speak of what ought to be. Our membership within the community of law makes even silence a morally charged position.***

Notes and Questions

1. Ross analyzes the ways in which the term "poverty" and its derivatives are used to describe an essential trait of the poor, rather than a contingent attribute. To call some-one "poor," therefore, is to identify not only his or her economic situation, but also a moral status. One implication of this rhetorical construct is that breaking the "cycle of poverty" requires a moral and behavioral shift on the part of the poor rather than sim-ply a redistribution of wealth. Do you find Ross's analysis of poverty rhetoric persuasive? Is an overemphasis on the moral attributes of poor people as a class an attempt to blame the victims? Does it mask the responsibilities of the government or of the wealthy and middle-class? For a classic discussion of the "culture of poverty," *see* OSCAR LEWIS, FIVE FAMILIES (1959).

2. "[E]ither the poor do not deserve our intervention or, if they do have a claim to our sense of justice, we are functionally helpless to do justice." Ross argues that judges see themselves as helpless to significantly improve the lot of those living in poverty. Are judges "rendered helpless by their own choice"? Are there no constraints on what a judge can order? What about constitutional and statutory limits? What marks the line between a judge's refusal to exercise power, and a judge's inability to exercise dis-cretion? Should a judge adopt any argument that will support a desired outcome, even if it is a thinly veiled rationalization? Or should he or she "faithfully" respect the con-straints of the system because, in the long run, the system can work more good than harm for the poor? Is it ultimately self-defeating for a judge to attempt to undermine that system? *Compare* Dr. Upendra Baxi's analysis of the role of judges and courts in Chapter 7, *supra*.

3. Ross concludes that "[t]he court has left the law's treatment of people in poverty largely to the political processes, acknowledging only the narrowest constitutional grounds for addressing their interests." *Compare* the Supreme Court's holding in *Employment Division, Dept. of Human Resources of Oregon v. Smith*, 494 U.S. 872 (1990). Under *Smith*, minority religions no longer enjoy a presumption of constitutional pro-tection under the First Amendment, although protection may be provided piece-meal by the legislature. Is a "fair hearing" through the legislative process sufficient to protect the rights of disadvantaged minorities?

4.   Ross invokes the concept of "empathy," while the *DeShaney* opinion refers to "natural sympathy." Are there any differences between these two concepts? Which would be more helpful to the poor?

DANDRIDGE v. WILLIAMS

398 U.S. 914 (1970)

Action to declare invalid and permanently enjoin enforcement of regulation of Maryland Department of Public Welfare placing an absolute limit of $250 per month on amount of a grant under AFDC regardless of size of family and its actual need. A three-judge United States District Court for the District of Maryland, 297 F.Supp. 450, held that regulation violated equal protection clause, and appeal was taken. The Supreme Court, Mr. Justice Stewart, held that the regulation does not violate equal protection clause.

This case involves the validity of a method used by Maryland, in the administration of an aspect of its public welfare program, to reconcile the demands of its needy citizens with the finite resources available to meet those demands. Like every other State in the Union, Maryland participates in the Federal Aid to Families with Dependent Children which originated with the Social Security Act of 1935. Under this jointly financed program, a State computes the so-called 'standard of need' of each eligible family unit within its borders. Some States provide that every family shall receive grants sufficient to meet fully the determined standard of need. Other States provide that each family unit shall receive a percentage of the determined need. Still others provide grants to most families in full accord with the ascertained standard of need, but impose an upper limit on the total amount of money any one family unit may receive. Maryland, through administrative adoption of a 'maximum grant regulation,' has followed this last course. This suit was brought by several AFDC recipients to enjoin the application of Maryland's maximum grant regulation on the ground that it is in conflict with *** the Equal Protection Clause of the Fourteenth Amendment. The regulation here in issue imposes upon the grant that any single family may receive an upper limit of $250 per month in certain counties and Baltimore City, and of $240 per month elsewhere in the State. The appellees all have large families, so that their standards of need as computed by the State substantially exceed the maximum grants that they actually receive under the regulation. The appellees urged in the District Court that the maximum grant limitation operates to discriminate against them merely because of the size of their families, in violation of the Equal Protection Clause of the Fourteenth Amendment.***

Although a State may adopt a maximum grant system in allocating its funds available for AFDC payments without violating the Act, it may not, of course, impose a regime of invidious discrimination in violation of the Equal Protection Clause of the Fourteenth Amendment. Maryland says that its maximum grant regulation is wholly free of an invidiously discriminatory purpose or effect, and that the regulation is rationally supportable on at least four entirely valid grounds. The regulation can be clearly justified, Maryland argues, in terms of legitimate state interests in encouraging gainful employment, in maintaining an equitable balance in economic status as between welfare families and those supported by a wage-earner, in providing incentives for family planning, and in allocating available public funds in such a way as fully to meet the needs of the largest possible number of families.***

Here we deal with state regulation in the social and economic field, not affecting freedoms guaranteed by the Bill of Rights, and claimed to violate the Fourteenth Amendment only because the regulation results in some disparity in grants of welfare payments to the largest AFDC families.***

In the area of economics and social welfare, a State does not violate the Equal Protection Clause merely because the classifications made by its laws are imperfect. If the classification has some 'reasonable basis,' it does not offend the Constitution.

The cases enunciating this fundamental standard under the Equal Protection Clause, have in the main involved state regulation of business or industry. The administration of public welfare assistance, by contrast, involves the most basic economic needs of impoverished human beings. We recognize the dramatically real factual difference between the cited cases and this one, but we can find no basis for applying a different constitutional standard.*** It is a standard that has consistently been applied to state legislation restricting the availability of employment opportunities.*** And it is a standard that is true to the principle that the Fourteenth Amendment gives the federal Courts no power to impose upon the States their views of what constitutes wise economic or social policy.

Under this long-established meaning of the Equal Protection Clause, it is clear that the Maryland maximum grant regulation is constitutionally valid. We need not explore all the reasons that the State advances in justification of the regulation. It is enough that a solid foundation for the regulation can be found in the state's legitimate interest in encouraging employment and in avoiding discrimination between welfare families and the families of the working poor. By combining a limit on the recipient's grant with permission to retain money earned, without reduction in the amount of the grant, Maryland provides an incentive to seek gainful employment. And by keying the maximum family AFDC grants to the minimum wage a steadily employed head of a household receives, the State maintains some semblance of an equitable balance between families on welfare and those supported by an employed breadwinner.

It is true that in some AFDC families there may be no person who is employable. It is also true that with respect to AFDC families whose determined standard of need is below the regulatory maximum, and who therefore receive grants equal to the determined standard, the employment incentive is absent. But the Equal Protection Clause does not require that a State must choose between attacking every aspect of a problem or not attacking the problem at all. It is enough that the State's action be rationally based and free from invidious discrimination. The regulation before us meets that test.

We do not decide today that the Maryland regulation is wise, that it best fulfills the relevant social and economic objectives that Maryland might ideally espouse, or that a more just and humane system could not be devised. Conflicting claims of morality and intelligence are raised by opponents and proponents of almost every measure, certainly including the one before us. But the intractable economic, social, and even philosophical problems presented by public welfare assistance programs are not the business of this Court. The Constitution may impose certain procedural safeguards upon systems of welfare administration. But the Constitution does not empower this Court to second-guess state officials charged with the difficult responsibility of allocating limited public welfare funds among the myriad of potential recipients.

Notes and Questions

1. What constitutional test does the Court apply to determine the compatibility of the Maryland regulation with the equal protection clause? What legal presumptions under-lie the use of this test?

2. What normative values is the Maryland statute designed to protect? Is the principle of equality in this case in conflict with these values? Does the Court determine that the asserted values trump the equality norm (even though it admits that the goals are not achievable in all cases)? Or, is its holding an example of the "judicial helplessness" described in Thomas Ross's article, *supra?*

3. How does the Court determine whether the Maryland regulations reflect "invidi-ous discrimination?" Is it possible that widespread public perceptions of "welfare queens" having babies in order to increase the size of their grants could have influenced the leg-islature's decision to effectively penalize children in large families? How would such per-ceptions be proved in court? What probative value should such evidence have, if any?

4. The inter-state Privileges and Immunities Clause of Article IV protects citizens of other states from discrimination with regard to certain economic rights. The Supreme Court has held that the right to earn a livelihood is protected activity under the Privileges and Immunities Clause. For example, qualified non-resident citizens have the right to freedom from unreasonable restrictions on pursuing a licensed trade in a for-eign state. *Sup. Ct. of Va. v. Friedman*, 487 U.S. 59, 64 (1988). *See also Toomer v. Witsell*, 334 U.S. 385 (1948) (holding that a state may not charge a highly disproportionate license fee to non-resident fishermen).

On the other hand, since its adoption almost 140 years ago, the *intra*-state Privileges or Immunities Clause of the 14th Amendment has been virtually powerless in protecting individual economic rights against the action of state governments, a status that dates from the *Slaughter-House Cases*, 83 U.S. (16 Wall.) 36 (1873). In an attempt to narrow the scope of federal power vis-á-vis states, the Supreme Court held that the 14th Amendment was intended only to protect former slaves. Thus, the Court ruled that Louisiana did not deprive independent butchers of their right to gainful employment by extending the Slaughter House Company exclusive rights to butcher livestock in the city of New Orleans for 25 years. *Id.* at 38, 48. In the post-*Slaughter-House* era, the Court has relied on this provision in only two cases: *Colgate v. Harvey*, 296 U.S. 404 (holding invalid a statute taxing residents on investment income earned only outside of the state, but subsequently overruled by *Madden v. Kentucky*, 309 U.S. 83 (1940)) and *Saenz v. Roe*, 526 U.S. 489 (1999).

The Court's holding in *Saenz*, that a California statute limiting new residents' welfare benefits for the first year of residency violated a citizen's right to travel under the Privileges or Immunities Clause, *id.* at 500, could open the door to further protection under this provision. It is possible that the Supreme Court may no longer treat the Clause as a mere "inkblot," but as a viable legal mechanism to protect individuals' economic rights. *Cf.* ROBERT H. BORK, THE TEMPTING OF AMERICA: THE POLITICAL SEDUC-TION OF THE LAW 166 (1990) (suggesting that the original meaning of the 14th Amend-ment will never be understood by courts and should therefore be treated judicially as a nullity or an "inkblot" to prevent courts from making inappropriate value judgments).

DEPARTMENT OF HEALTH AND HUMAN SERVICES—
2003 POVERTY GUIDELINES*

Size of family unit	Poverty guideline
1	$8,980
2	12,120
3	15,260
4	18,400
5	21,540
6	24,680
7	27,820
8	30,960

For family units with more than 8 members, add $3,140 for each additional member.

(The same increment applies to smaller family sizes also, as can be seen in the figures above.)

* Applicable to the 48 contiguous states and the District of Columbia. The figures are adjusted upward for Alaska ($2,230) and Hawaii ($1,350).

Notes and Questions

1. These figures provide guidelines to determine eligibility for a number of federal programs, as well as to prepare estimates of the number of persons and families living in poverty. The federal poverty guidelines do not take into account regional variability in the continental states, although they do reflect differentiated statistics for Alaska and Hawaii. If the federal government recognizes that the cost of living may be higher in some regions than in others, should it not set specific poverty lines for each state or region? How reasonable are these figures? Compare the official poverty guidelines with the figures the Economic Policy Institute argues are more realistic for families, *Available at* http://www.epinet.org/content.cfm/datazone_fambud_budget. The international standard is "less than one-half the median income," which in the United States is $35,000 (translating into a poverty threshold at less than $17,500).

2. In addition to geographic location, what distinctions should meaningful poverty guidelines recognize? Should they distinguish between rural and urban populations? Between different age groups?

3. How one assesses the state of poverty in the United States is largely a function of perspective. When considered as a group, and compared to the rest of the world, Americans are quite well off. Estimates of the percentage of the world's wealth controlled by the United States varies from 25 percent to 60 percent, but by all standards is significantly disproportionate to the percentage of the world's population who are

U.S. citizens. On a per capita basis, this translates into an average annual income of 35K per person, as compared to the average income worldwide of $2/day.

But the wealth of America is not uniformly distributed, and thus such figures can mislead on the true state of the poor in the United States. The vast amount of the nation's riches are disproportionately in the hands of an economic elite. The three richest Americans alone "have assets that exceed the combined gross domestic product of the 48 least developed countries." ZIAUDDIN SARDAR & MERRYL WYN DAVIES, WHY DO PEOPLE HATE AMERICA? 82 (2002) (citing to studies by the United Nations Development Program). The 400 richest people in America had a combined net worth in 2002 of $955 billion. *Ultra-Rich Have Gotten Richer*, ATLANTA JOURNAL-CONSTITUTION, Sept. 19, 2003, at B3.

This gap between the rich and poor is not only marked, but growing. Whereas in the late 1970s the top 1 percent of American families owned 13 percent of the nation's wealth, by 1995 their slice of the economy had ballooned to 38 percent. Ann M. Burkhart, *The Constitutional Underpinnings of Homelessness*, 40 HOUSTON L. REV. 211, 277 n.592, citing George Draper, *Facts on the Concentration of Wealth*. During the same period, the income for the poorest families with children decreased by 20 percent, although the wealthiest families enjoyed an increase of 30 percent. *Id.* It is cold comfort to be told how well off "America" is if you are not sharing in that bounty.

Outside the wealthy elite, the disproportionate division of the nation's wealth impacts almost all others, but not in the same ways. One's position within the economic hierarchy influences one's choices for education, housing, health care and physical and mental development and longevity; at the lowest levels of that structure, all of these variables are adversely limited. The impact of this shortfall is cumulative: In the lowest quintile of income measures, over 19 million could expect to experience at least one difficulty in meeting a household's basic needs; in the highest quintile, just under 3 million had this difficulty. U.S. Census, *Extended Measures of Well-Being: Meeting Basic Needs, 1995*, P70–67, June 1999.

Consider the following additional indicia of economic and social well-being:

[Unless otherwise noted, the data below are taken from MARC MIRINGOFF, SANDRA OPDYCKE & MARQUE-LUISA MIRINGOFF, THE SOCIAL HEALTH OF THE NATION: HOW AMERICA IS REALLY DOING 50–54; 60–66; 80–86; 92–98; 136; 142(1999)]

Infant mortality.

The infant mortality rate was a full 60 percent higher for infants born to women with incomes below the poverty rate, than for women with incomes above it. This relationship held even where poor women were at low risk for other factors, such as smoking, age, and prenatal care. . . . The U.S. infant mortality rate is worse than that of twenty other industrialized nations.

Food security.

"Food security" refers to "access at all times to enough food for active, healthy living." According to the U.S. Department of Agriculture, 10.7% of all U.S. households were food insecure in 2001: 7.4% without hunger, 3.3% with hunger. USDA, *Putting Food on the Table: Household Food Security in the United States*, Feb. 2003. Tellingly, food insecurity is *not* restricted to households below the poverty level: almost 10% of households above that line experienced food insecurity. Households headed by a single mother were especially prone to food insecurity, impacting almost one-third.

Elder poverty.

From a high of 24.6 percent in 1970, the poverty rate of the elderly dropped to 10.8 percent in 1996, the second-highest percentage ever recorded.*** Among the elderly, black and Hispanic poverty rates are more than two and one-half times those of whites. Females have double the poverty rates of males. Those over age 75 have substantially greater poverty rates than those 65–74 years of age.

Measured by the international poverty standard of "less than one half the median income," the United States performance does not compare favorably. Among 17 industrial countries, the U.S. has the third-worst poverty rate for the elderly, exceeded only by the United Kingdom and Australia.

Child poverty.

Among those under 18, poverty has increased from 14.9 percent in 1970 to 19.8 percent in 1996, a 33 percent increase." Worse, the proportion of children in extreme poverty doubled [from 1975 to 1993], from 5 percent to 10 percent of all children.

Child poverty is most prevalent among the very young—those under the age of six—and among minorities, particularly black and Hispanic youth. The United States has the worst record among industrialized nations in reducing the poverty rates of children.

High School Dropouts.

Between 1970 and 1996, the percentage of students aged 18–24 who dropped out of school declined from 17.3 percent to 12.8 percent." By 2000, this rate had dropped to 12.4. *Statistical Abstract of the U.S., 2002*, at 162. "The improvement in school completion is unequally distributed in the population. White and black youth show substantial improvement, but the gap between them and Hispanic youth has widened [to over double the black rate]. *** The U.S. now ranks below most other industrial nations in its high school graduation rates.

Life Expectancy.

Life expectancy varies significantly by race and gender. White females live longest, followed by black females, then white males. Black males have a substantially shorter life expectancy.*** [Sixteen] industrial nations still have longer life expectancies than the U.S.

Health Care Coverage.

A total of 41.7 million Americans, or 15.6 percent, had no health insurance in 1996, up from an estimated 10.9 percent in 1976." But as of 2001, 14.6% of the population had been without any health insurance coverage for the entire previous year. *Health Insurance Coverage: 2001*, Census Bureau Publication P60–220, Sept. 2002.

In 1996, 10.6 million children, or 14.8 percent, were not covered by either Medicaid or private insurance. Enrollment in employer-financed health insurance has declined. Among full-time workers in medium and large-size firms, the percentage of those covered fell from 97 percent in 1980 to 77 percent in 1995.

Youth Suicide.

The 1996 suicide rate among youth, aged 15–24, was 12.0 deaths per 100,000, up from 8.8 in 1970. Over time, suicides have been highest for young white males; but in recent years black males have been rapidly catching up. Women, both white and black, have comparatively low rates. *** The U.S. suicide rate for 15–24 year olds is higher than 14 other countries for males and 6 other countries for females. For children under 15, the U.S. suicide rate was two times higher than that in the other 25 industrialized nations combined.

Wages.

In constant dollars, [average weekly] earnings went from $315 in1973 to $256 in 1996, a decline of 19 percent." But by 2001 earnings had climbed back up to $274. *Statistical Abstract of the U.S., 2002,* at 400.

Housing.

A smaller proportion of young families, 33.9 percent in 1995 compared to 43.6 percent in 1973, were able to buy a home. Rental costs remain high and the stock of low-cost housing is declining. A record 5.3 million low-income households have "worst case needs"—either spending 50 percent or more of their income on rental housing or living in severely substandard housing.

Unemployment.

In 1996, youth unemployment was 16.7 percent, three times the national average, while black unemployment was 10.5 percent, almost twice the national average.

4. In his analysis of "capability poverty" Amartya Sen discusses the disparities in well-being that may be attributable to racial inequality in America, despite relative income security:

The inequality between different racial groups in the United States has received considerable attention recently. For example, in the space of incomes African Americans are decidedly poorer than American whites. This is very often seen as an example of *relative* deprivation of African Americans within the nation, but not compared with poorer people in the rest of the world. Indeed, in comparison with the population of third world countries, African Americans may well be a great many times richer in terms of incomes, even after taking note of price differences. Seen this way, the deprivation of the American blacks seems to pale to insignificance in the international perspective.

But is income the right space in which to make such comparisons? What about the basic capability to live to a mature age, without succumbing to premature mortality? [I]n terms of that criterion the African American men fall well behind the immensely poorer men of China, or the Indian state of Kerala— and also of Sri Lanka, Costa Rica, Jamaica and many other poor economies. It is sometimes presumed that the remarkably high death rates of African Americans apply only to men, and again only to younger men, because of the prevalence of violence. Death from violence is indeed high among young black men, but this is by no means the whole story. Indeed, black women too fall not only behind white women in the United States but also behind Indian women in Kerala, and come very close to falling behind Chinese women as well. American black *men* continue to lose ground vis-á-vis the Chinese and the Indians over the years—well past the younger ages when death from violence is common. More explanation is needed than violent deaths can provide.

Indeed, even if we take higher age groups (say, that between thirty-five and sixty-four years), there is evidence of enormously greater mortality for black men vis-ávis white men, and black women vis-á-vis white women. And these differentials are not wiped out by adjustment for income differences. In fact, one of the more careful medical studies related to the 1980s shows that the black-white mortality differential remains remarkably large for women even after adjustment for income differentials. While U.S. black men have 1.8 times the mortality rate of white men, black women have nearly three times the mortality of white women in this survey. And adjusted for differences in family income, while the mortality rate is 1.2 times higher for black men, it is as much as 2.2 times higher for black women. It, thus, appears that even after full note is taken of income levels, black women die young in very much larger proportions than white women in the contemporary United States.

AMARTYA SEN, DEVELOPMENT AS FREEDOM 96–97 (1999). What specific factors contribute to this disparity? *See* discussion of racial discrimination in Chapter 3, *infra.*

4. The Right to Education

SAN ANTONIO INDEPENDENT SCHOOL DISTRICT v. RODRIGUEZ

411 U.S. 1 (1973)

A class action was brought on behalf of school children, who were members of poor families residing in school districts having low property tax bases, challenging reliance by the Texas school-financing system on local property taxation. The three-judge District Court, 337 F.Supp. 280, rendered a judgment holding such system unconstitutional under the equal protection clause of the Fourteenth Amendment, and the state appealed. The Supreme Court, Mr. Justice Powell, held that such system did not violate the equal protection clause of the Fourteenth Amendment.

Mr. Justice POWELL delivered the opinion of the Court.

This suit attacking the Texas system of financing public education was initiated by Mexican-American parents whose children attend the elementary and secondary schools in the Edgewood Independent School District, an urban school district in San Antonio, Texas. They brought a class action on behalf of schoolchildren throughout the State who are members of minority groups or who are poor and reside in school districts having a low property tax base. Named as defendants were the State Board of Education, the Commissioner of Education, the State Attorney General, and the Bexar County (San Antonio) Board of Trustees. The complaint was filed in the summer of 1968 and a three-judge Court was impaneled in January 1969. In December 1971 the panel rendered its judgment in a per curiam opinion holding the Texas school finance system unconstitutional under the Equal Protection Clause of the Fourteenth Amendment. The State appealed, and we noted probable jurisdiction to consider the far-reaching constitutional questions presented. For the reasons stated in this opinion, we reverse the decision of the District Court.

The first Texas State Constitution, promulgated upon Texas' entry into the Union in 1845, provided for the establishment of a system of free schools. Early in its history, Texas adopted a dual approach to the financing of its schools, relying on mutual participation by the local school districts and the State. As early as 1883, the state constitution was amended to provide for the creation of local school districts empowered to levy ad valorem taxes with the consent of local taxpayers for the 'erection . . . of school buildings' and for the 'further maintenance of public free schools.' Such local funds as were raised were supplemented by funds distributed to each district from the State's Permanent and Available School Funds. The Permanent School Fund, its predecessor established in 1854 with $2,000,000 realized from an annexation settlement, was thereafter endowed with millions of acres of public land set aside to assure a continued source of income for school support. The Available School Fund, which received income from the Permanent School Fund as well as from a state ad valorem property tax and other designated taxes, served as the disbursing arm for most state educational funds throughout the late 1800's and first half of this century. Additionally, in 1918 an increase in state property taxes was used to finance a program providing free textbooks throughout the State.

Until recent times, Texas was a predominantly rural State and its population and property wealth were spread relatively evenly across the State. Sizable differences in the value of assessable property between local school districts became increasingly evident as the State became more industrialized and as rural-to-urban population shifts became more pronounced. The location of commercial and industrial property began to play a significant role in determining the amount of tax resources available to each school district. These growing disparities in population and taxable property between districts were responsible in part for increasingly notable differences in levels of local expenditure for education.

In due time it became apparent to those concerned with financing public education that contributions from the Available School Fund were not sufficient to ameliorate these disparities.

Recognizing the need for increased state funding to help offset disparities in local spending and to meet Texas' changing educational requirements, the state legislature in the late 1940's undertook a thorough evaluation of public education with an eye toward major reform.

The Program [adopted] calls for state and local contributions to a fund earmarked specifically for teacher salaries, operating expenses, and transportation costs. The State, supplying funds from its general revenues, finances approximately 80% of the Program, and the school districts are responsible—as a unit—for providing the remaining 20%. The districts' share, known as the Local fund Assignment, is apportioned among the school districts under a formula designed to reflect each district's relative taxpaying ability.

The school district in which appellees reside, the Edgewood Independent School District, has been compared throughout this litigation with the Alamo Heights Independent School District. This comparison between the least and most affluent districts in the San Antonio area serves to illustrate the manner in which the dual system of finance operates and to indicate the extent to which substantial disparities exist despite the State's impressive progress in recent years. Edgewood is one of seven public school districts in the metropolitan arc enrolled in its 25 elementary and secondary schools. The district is *** situated in the core-city sector of San Antonio in a residential neighborhood that has little commercial or industrial property. The residents are predominantly of Mexican-American descent: approximately 90% of the student population is Mexican-American and over 6% is Negro. The average assessed property value per pupil is $5,960—the lowest in the metropolitan area—and the median family income ($4,686) is also the lowest. At an equalized tax rate of $1.05 per $100 of assessed property—the highest in the metropolitan area—the district contributed $26 to the education of each child for the 1967–1968 school year above its Local Fund Assignment for the Minimum Foundation Program. The Foundation Program contributed $222 per pupil for a state-local total of $248. Federal funds added another $108 for a total of $356 per pupil.

Alamo Heights is the most affluent school district in San Antonio. Its six schools, housing approximately 5,000 students, are situated in a residential community quite unlike the Edgewood district. The school population is predominantly 'Anglo,' having only 18% Mexican-Americans and less than 1% Negroes. The assessed property value per pupil exceeds $59,000, and the median family income is $8,001. In 1967–1968 the local tax rate of $.85 per $100 of valuation yielded $333 per pupil over and above its contribution to the Foundation Program. Coupled with the $225 provided from that Program, the district was able to supply $558 per student. Supplemented by a $36 per-pupil grant from federal sources, Alamo Heights spent $594 per pupil.

This, then, establishes the framework for our analysis. We must decide, first, whether the Texas system of financing public education operates to the disadvantage of some suspect class or impinges upon a fundamental right explicitly or implicitly protected by the Constitution, thereby requiring strict judicial scrutiny. If so, the judgment of the District Court should be affirmed. If not, the Texas scheme must still be examined to determine whether it rationally furthers some legitimate, articulated state purpose and therefore does not constitute an invidious discrimination in violation of the Equal Protection Clause of the Fourteenth Amendment.

The case comes to us with no definitive description of the classifying facts or delineation of the disfavored class. Examination of the District Court's opinion and of appellees' complaint, briefs, and contentions at oral argument suggests, however, at least three ways in which the discrimination claimed here might be described. The Texas system of school financing might be regarded as discriminating (1) against 'poor' persons whose incomes fall below some identifiable level of poverty or who might be characterized as functionally 'indigent,' or (2) against those who are relatively poorer than others, or (3) against all those who, irrespective of their personal incomes, happen to reside in relatively poorer school districts.

Our task must be to ascertain whether, in fact, the Texas system has been shown to discriminate on any of these possible bases and, if so, whether the resulting classification may be regarded as suspect.

The precedents of this Court provide the proper starting point. The individuals, or groups of individuals, who constituted the class discriminated against in our prior cases shared two distinguishing characteristics: because of their impecunity they were completely unable to pay for some desired benefit, and as a consequence, they sustained an absolute deprivation of a meaningful opportunity to enjoy that benefit. In Griffin v. Illinois and its progeny, the Court invalidated state laws that prevented an indigent criminal defendant from acquiring a transcript, or an adequate substitute for a transcript, for use at several stages of the trial and appeal process. The payment requirements in each case were found to occassion de facto discrimination against those who, because of their indigency, were totally unable to pay for transcripts.

Likewise, in *Douglas v. California*, a decision establishing an indigent defendant's right to Court-appointed counsel on direct appeal, the Court dealt only with defendants who could not pay for counsel from their own resources and who had no other way of gaining representation. Douglas provides no relief for those on whom the burdens of paying for a criminal defense are relatively speaking, great but not insurmountable. Nor does it deal with relative differences in the quality of counsel acquired by the less wealthy.

Williams v. Illinois struck down criminal penalties that subjected indigents to incarceration simply because of their inability to pay a fine. Again, the disadvantaged class was composed only of persons who were totally unable to pay the demanded sum. Those cases do not touch on the question whether equal protection is denied to persons with relatively less money on whom designated fines impose heavier burdens. The Court has not held that fines must be structured to reflect each person's ability to pay in order to avoid disproportionate burdens.

Neither appellees nor the District Court addressed the fact that, unlike each of the foregoing cases, lack of personal resources has not occasioned an absolute deprivation of the desired benefit. The argument here is not that the children in districts having relatively low assessable property values are receiving no public education; rather, it is that they are receiving a poorer quality education than that available to children in districts having more assessable wealth. A sufficient answer to appellees' argument is that, at least where wealth is involved, the Equal Protection Clause does not require absolute equality or precisely equal advantages.

As suggested above, appellees and the District Court may have embraced a second or third approach, the second of which might be characterized as a theory of relative or comparative discrimination based on family income. Appellees sought to prove that a direct correlation exists between the wealth of families within each district and the expenditures therein for education. That is, along a continuum, the poorer the family the lower the dollar amount of education received by the family's children.

Education is not among the rights afforded explicit protection under our Federal Constitution. Nor do we find any basis for saying it is implicitly so protected. ***

Notes and Questions

1. In *Rodriguez*, the Court concluded that "education is not among the rights afforded explicit protection under our federal Constitution. Nor do we find any basis for saying it is implicitly so recognized." Can you imagine arguments by which the right to education could be implied to be a right under the federal Constitution? Is education necessary for the meaningful exercise of other (explicitly recognized) rights? Consider the

reasoning of the Court in *Brown v. Board of Education,* in which it ruled that segregated public schools were unconstitutional:

> Today, education is perhaps the most important function of state and local governments. Compulsory school attendance laws and the great expenditures for education both demonstrate our recognition of the importance of education to our democratic society. It is required in the performance of our most basic public responsibilities, even service in the armed forces. It is the very foundation of good citizenship. Today it is a principal instrument in awakening the child to cultural values, in preparing him for later professional training, and in helping him to adjust normally to his environment. In these days, it is doubtful that any child may reasonably be expected to succeed in life if he is denied the opportunity of an education. Such an opportunity, where the state has undertaken to provide it, is a right which must be made available to all on equal terms.

347 U.S. 483, 493 (1954). Can *Brown* and *Rodriguez* be reconciled?

2.   The *Rodriguez* Court refused to hold that an educational funding system with large disparities between recipients violated the equal protection clause of the Fourteenth Amendment. While the Court had struck down systems that "sustained an absolute deprivation," it refused to similarly reject one in which the deprivations were only relative. The Court seems to adopt the view that so long as a child receives some access to education, the demands of equal protection have been satisfied. Should "education" rise above a certain meaningful threshold of effectiveness in order to constitute the intended good? What criteria should be used to assess available resources under a threshold standard, as opposed to a presence/absence determination? *See also, McCain v. Koch, infra,* in which a court refused "to compel compliance with certain reasonable minimal standards" in shelter for the homeless.

3.   Did the plaintiffs in *Rodriguez* seek to go beyond the demands of the African-American civil rights movement that produced the landmark *Brown* decision? Dr. Paula Adams explains that the civil rights movement also influenced the development of the law relating to the rights of students with disabilities:

> Beginning in the early 1970s, advocates for students with disabilities began to litigate against state and local school districts and officials, claiming that exclusion and misclassification of students with disabilities violated the students' 14th Amendment rights to equal educational opportunity. *See generally,* Mitchell L. Yell, D. Rogers, & E.L. Rogers, *The Legal History of Special Education: What a Long, Strange Trip it's Been!,* 19(4) REMEDIAL AND SPECIAL EDUCATION 219–28 (1998). In *Pennsylvania Association for Retarded Children (PARC, et al.) v. Commonwealth of Pennsylvania,* 343 F. Supp. 279 (1972), parents of children with mental retardation brought a class action suit challenging statutes that excluded their children from educational and training programs in the public schools. The court upheld the rights of the students to appropriate education, citing the constitutional protections recognized and upheld in the *Brown* decision. In *Mills v. Board of Education of the District of Columbia,* 348 F. Supp. 866 (D.D.C. 1972), the U.S. District Court for the District of Columbia elaborated the rights of students with disabilities to a "free and appropriate public education" and to due process before being excluded from public schooling.

The civil rights movement also influenced legislation protecting the rights of students with disabilities. In 1965, the Elementary and Secondary Education Act provided funds to assist in educating certain categories of students including those with disabilities. The Education of the Handicapped Act of 1970 provided grants to colleges to develop programs to train teachers in special education. Section 504 of the Vocational Rehabilitation Act was enacted in 1973 to eliminate discrimination against individuals with disabilities in programs that receive federal funds. The Education of the Handicapped Act of 1970 was amended in 1974, after the *PARC* and *Mills* cases, to require states that receive federal money to adopt the goal of full educational opportunity for children with disabilities. In 1975, the All Handicapped Children Education Act (EAHCA) established the right to "free appropriate public education" for all children with disabilities regardless of the nature or severity of the disabling condition. Renamed the Individuals with Disabilities Education Act (IDEA) in 1990, the EAHCA was amended so as to emphasize the individual rather than his or her disability. The Americans with Disabilities Act (ADA), also enacted in 1990, is a comprehensive civil rights law that extended the anti-discrimination protections provided under the Vocational Rehabilitation Act of 1973 and that requires most employers to make reasonable accommodations for workers with disabilities. Considered by many to be the most significant disability legislation ever passed, or "the true Civil Rights Bill for people with disabilities," the ADA requires accommodations in all public telecommunication and transportation systems, as well as in public buildings, facilities and venues. *See* MARY A. FALVEY, INCLUSIVE AND HETEROGENEOUS SCHOOLING: ASSESSMENT, CURRICULUM AND INSTRUCTION, at 27 (2d ed., 1998).

Dr. Paula W. Adams, *Disability Rights as Human Rights* (unpublished manuscript) (2004).

How do the educational rights of children with disabilities compare with those of the *Rodriguez* plaintiffs? Should the constitutional analysis be different? Would a statutory approach work? For further reading on the rights of students with disabilities and special education in the United States, *see, e.g.*, MITCHELL L. YELL, THE LAW AND SPECIAL EDUCATION (1998) MARY BEIRNE-SMITH, R.F. ITTENBACH & J.R. PATTON, MENTAL RETARDATION (6th ed. 2002); A. Katsiyannis, Mitchell L. Yell, & R. Bradley, *Reflections on the 25th anniversary of the Individuals with Disabilities Education Act*, 22(6) REMEDIAL & SPECIAL EDU., 324–36 (2001); R. TURNBULL, A. TURNBULL, M. SHANK, S. SMITH & D. LEAL, EXCEPTIONAL LIVES: SPECIAL EDUCATION IN TODAY'S SCHOOLS (4th ed. 2004); JAMES E. YSSELDYKE, B. ALGOZZINE & M.L. THURLOW, CRITICAL ISSUES IN SPECIAL EDUCATION (2d ed. 1992).

4. Two recent U.S. Supreme Court cases on affirmative action raised implications about the relevance of international law in U.S. education policy. In *Grutter v. Bollinger*, 123 U.S. 2325 (2003), the Supreme Court upheld the law school's affirmative action program at the University of Michigan in a five-four decision. The Court held that Michigan's program constitutionally advanced the goals of affirmative action because the university reviewed individual applicants in a holistic manner. In *Gratz v. Bollinger*, 123 U.S. 2411 (2003), the Supreme Court struck down the undergraduate affirmative action program in a six-three decision, concluding that the school's system of awarding points based on race was too mechanical and quota-like.

In Justice Ginsburg's brief concurrence in *Grutter*, she discussed the decision in the context of two international doctrines. 123 U.S. at 2347. Ginsburg, joined by Justice Breyer, pointed out that the decision is consistent with the provisions of the International

Convention on the Elimination of All Forms of Racial Discrimination (ICERD), which has been ratified by the United States. The affirmative action program at the law school met the standards set out in the Convention that a program employ "special and concrete measures to ensure *** the protection of certain racial groups *** for the purpose of guaranteeing them the full and equal enjoyment of human rights and fundamental freedoms." *Id.*

Ginsburg's concurrence noted that the majority's statement that affirmative action programs "must have a logical end point" is also in accord with international standards, explaining that Article 2(2) of ICERD provides that such programs "shall in no case entail as a consequence the maintenance of unequal or separate rights for different racial groups after the objectives for which they were taken have been achieved." The opinion also cites to the Convention on the Elimination of All Forms of Discrimination against Women (the "Women's Convention" or CEDAW) which states in Article 4(1) that "temporary special measures aimed at accelerating de facto equality *** shall be discontinued when the objectives of equality of opportunity and treatment have been achieved." *Id.*

Many observers note that Ginsburg's reference to international law in such a high profile, controversial case may be indicative of a trend in which U.S. courts will begin to reference international human rights law in significant ways. *See, e.g.,* Barbara K. Bucholtz, *Symposium: 2002–2003 Supreme Court Review: Father Knows Best: The Court's Result-Oriented Activism Continues Apace: Selected Business-Related Decisions from the 2002–2003 Term,* 39 TULSA L.J. 75 (2003) (describing the Court's decisionmaking as unpredictable, and describing Ginsburg's *Grutter* concurrence as essentially conservative based on the rearguard nature of the decision but also as precedential for its use of international law); Tikkun A.S. Gottschalk, *The Realpolitik of Empire,* 13 J. TRANSNAT'L L. & POL'Y 281, 298 (2003) (discussing the application of international law to domestic policy to combat a decline of U.S. judicial legitimacy); Janet K. Levit, *Symposium: 2002–2003 Supreme Court Review: Going Public with Transnational Law,* 39 TULSA L.J. 155 (2003) (discussing the relatively high-profile use of international law in the 2002–2003 term, in comparison to the Court's prior practice); Tony Mauro, *Court Shows Interest in International Law,* 230 N.Y. L.J. 1 (2003) (describing this trend and discussing criticisms in the U.S. legal community); Richard J. Wilson, *International Law Issues in Death Penalty Defense,* 31 HOFSTRA L. REV. 1195, 1200 (2003) (describing the application of international law to death penalty cases, citing *Grutter* as evidence of a trend in which the Supreme Court increasingly refers to international law).

Justice Ginsburg has pointed out that the interpretation of cruel and unusual punishment under the Eighth Amendment may indicate increased use of a comparative law perspective in the courts. Ruth Bader Ginsburg, *Sherman J. Bellwood Lecture: Looking Beyond our Borders: The Value of a Comparative Perspective in Constitutional Adjudication,* 40 IDAHO L. REV. 1, 4 (2003). In *Stanford v. Kentucky,* decided in 1989, capital punishment for crimes committed at ages 16 or 17 was upheld, and the Court noted that "American conceptions of decency are dispositive" in rejecting international practices. 492 U.S. 361, 370 (1989). However, in *Atkins v. Virginia,* 536 U.S. 304 (2002), the Court struck down capital punishment of mentally retarded persons and noted that the majority of nations in the international community disapproved of that practice. As further evidence of such a trend, in *Lawrence v. Texas* which recently struck down same sex sodomy laws, Justice Kennedy's majority opinion discusses global jurisprudence as relevant to privacy rights. 123 U.S. 2472, 2481 (2003). Justice Kennedy's citation to an opinion by the European Court of Human Rights is the first time a majority decision of the Supreme Court has cited to an opinion of that international court. *See, e.g.*, Linda Greenhouse, *The Supreme Court: Overview; In a Momentous Term, Justices Remake the Law, and the Court*, N.Y. TIMES, July 1, 2003, 1A; Levit, *supra* at 158–59.

5.   If affirmative action measures should be temporary, how should a court, or other decisionmakers, decide when they are no longer necessary? By what criteria would you measure the achievement of the objectives for which such measures were implemented?

6.   Why has reference to international human rights law by U.S. courts been controversial? What is at stake? Do race and race relations play a special role in this context?

7.   For further discussions of the implications under international law of U.S. affirmative action law and policy, *see, e.g.*, Jordan J. Paust, *Race-Based Affirmative Action and International Law*, 18 MICH. J. INT'L L. 659 (1997); Jordan J. Paust, *The Permissibility of Affirmative Action in Higher Education Under Human Rights Law*, 3 N.Y. CITY L. REV. 91 (1998). For discussions of the relationship between the U.S. civil rights movement and international law, *see, e.g.*, Mary L. Dudziak, *Desegregation as a Cold War Imperative*, 41 STAN. L. REV. 61 (1988); Bert Lockwood, Jr., *The United Nationals Charter and United States Civil Rights Litigation: 1946–1955*, 69 IOWA L. REV. 901 (1984).

5.   The Right to Housing

LINDSEY v. NORMET

405 U.S. 56 (1972)

Mr. Justice WHITE delivered the opinion of the Court.

This case presents the question of whether Oregon's judicial procedure for eviction of tenants after nonpayment of rent violates either the Equal Protection Clause or the Due Process Clause of the Fourteenth Amendment. The material facts were stipulated. Appellants were the month-to-month tenants of appellee Normet and paid $100 a month for the use of a single-family residence in Portland, Oregon. On November 10, 1969, the City Bureau of Buildings declared the dwelling unfit for habitation due to substandard conditions on the premises. Appellants requested appellee to make certain repairs which, with one minor exception, appellee refused to do. Appellants, who had paid the November rent, refused to pay the December rent until the requested improvements had been made. Appellee's attorney wrote a letter on December 15 threatening to 'get a Court Order out on this matter' unless the accrued rent was immediately paid.

On January 7, 1970, however, before statutory eviction procedures were begun in the Oregon Courts, appellants filed suit in federal district Court under 42 U.S.C. § 1983 seeking a declaratory judgment that the Oregon Forcible Entry and Wrongful Detainer (hereinafter sometimes FED) Statute, was unconstitutional on its face, and an injunction against its continued enforcement. A three-judge Court was convened under 28 U.S.C. § 2281, a temporary restraining order was issued against the enforcement of the FED Statute, and appellants were ordered to make their rent payments into an escrow account during the pendency of the District Court proceeding. A lengthy stipulation of facts was agreed upon, a number of exhibits and depositions were submitted, and the District Court then granted appellee's motion to dismiss the complaint after concluding that the statute was not unconstitutional under either the Due Process Clause or the Equal Protection Clause of the Fourteenth Amendment. Appellants promptly appealed, and we noted probable jurisdiction.

I

The Oregon Forcible Entry and Wrongful Detainer Statute establishes a procedure intended to insure that any entry upon real property "shall be made in a peaceable manner and without force." § 105.105. A landlord may bring an action for possession whenever the tenant has failed to pay rent within 10 days of its due date.***

Appellants' principal attacks are leveled at three characteristics of the Oregon FED Statute: the requirement of a trial no later than six days after service of the complaint unless security for accruing rent is provided; the provisions *** which, either on their face or as construed, are said to limit the triable issues in an FED suit to the tenant's default and to preclude consideration of defenses based on the landlord's breach of a duty to maintain the premises; and the requirement of posting bond on appeal from an adverse decision in twice the amount of the rent expected to accrue pending appellate decision. These provisions are asserted to violate both the Equal Protection and Due Process Clauses of the Fourteenth Amendment. Except for the appeal bond requirement *** we reject these claims.

Underlying appellants' claim is the assumption that they are denied due process of law unless Oregon recognizes the failure of the landlord to maintain the premises as an operative defence to the possessory FED action and as an adequate excuse for nonpayment of rent. The Constitution has not federalized the substantive law of landlord-tenant relations, however, and we see nothing to forbid Oregon from treating the undertakings of the tenant and those of the landlord as independent rather than dependent Covenants. Likewise, the Constitution does not authorize us to require that the term of an otherwise expired tenancy be extended while the tenant's damage claims against the landlord are litigated. The substantive law of landlord-tenant relations differs widely in the various States. In some jurisdictions, a tenant may argue as a defence to eviction for nonpayment of rent such claims as unrepaired building code violations, branch of an implied warranty of habitability, or the fact that the landlord is evicting him for reporting building code violations or for exercising constitutional rights. Some States have enacted statutes authorizing rent withholding in certain situations. In other jurisdictions, these claims, if cognizable at all, must be litigated in separate tort, contract, or civil rights suits. There is no showing that Oregon excludes any defenses it recognizes as "available" on the three questions (physical possession, forcible withholding, legal right to possession) at issue in an FED suit.***

III

We also cannot agree that the FED Statute is invalid on its face under the Equal Protection Clause. It is true that Oregon FED suits differ substantially from other litigation, where the time between complaint and trial is substantially longer, and where a broader range of issues may be considered. But it does not follow that the Oregon statute invidiously discriminates against defendants in FED actions.

The statute potentially applies to all tenants, rich and poor, commercial and non-commercial; it cannot be faulted for over-inclusiveness or under-inclusiveness. And classifying tenants of real property differently from other tenants for purposes of possessory actions will offend the equal protection safeguard "only if the classification rests on grounds wholly irrelevant to the achievement of the State's objective," *McGowan v.*

Maryland, 366 U.S. 420, 425, 81 S.Ct. 1101, 1105, 6 L.Ed.2d 393 (1961), or if the objective itself is beyond the State's power to achieve. [citations omitted] It is readily apparent that prompt as well as peaceful resolution of disputes over the right to possession of real property is the end sought by the Oregon statute. It is also clear that the provisions for early trial and simplification of issues are closely related to that purpose. The equal protection claim with respect to these provisions thus depends on whether the State may validly single out possessory disputes between landlord and tenant for especially prompt judicial settlement. In making such an inquiry a State is "presumed to have acted within (its) constitutional power despite the fact that, in practice, (its) laws result in some inequality." *McGowan v. Maryland*, supra, 366 U.S., at 425–426, 81 S.Ct., at 1105.

[T]he Oregon statute was enacted in 1866 to alter the common law and obviate resort to self-help and violence. The statute, intended to protect tenants as well as landlords, provided a speedy, judicially supervised proceeding to settle the possessory issue in a peaceful manner.*** Before a tenant is forcibly evicted from property the Oregon statute requires a judicial determination that he is not legally entitled to possession.*** The objective of achieving rapid and peaceful settlement of possessory disputes between landlord and tenant has ample historical explanation and support. It is not beyond the State's power to implement that purpose by enacting special provisions applicable only to possessory disputes between landlord and tenant. There are unique factual and legal characteristics of the landlord-tenant relationship that justify special statutory treatment inapplicable to other litigants. The tenant is, by definition, in possession of the property of the landlord; unless a judicially supervised mechanism is provided for what would otherwise be swift repossession by the landlord himself, the tenant would be able to deny the landlord the rights of income incident to ownership by refusing to pay rent and by preventing sale or rental to someone else. Many expenses of the landlord continue to accrue whether a tenant pays his rent or not. Speedy adjudication is desirable to prevent subjecting the landlord to undeserved economic loss and the tenant to unmerited harassment and dispossession when his lease or rental agreement gives him the right to peaceful and undisturbed possession of the property. Holding over by the tenant beyond the term of his agreement or holding without payment of rent has proved a virulent source of friction and dispute. We think Oregon was well within its constitutional powers in providing for rapid and peaceful settlement of these disputes.

Appellants argue, however, that a more stringent standard than mere rationality should be applied both to the challenged classification and its stated purpose. They contend that the "need for decent shelter" and the "right to retain peaceful possession of one's home" are fundamental interests which are particularly important to the poor and which may be trenched upon only after the State demonstrates some superior interest. They invoke those cases holding that certain classifications based on unalterable traits such as race and lineage are inherently suspect and must be justified by some "overriding statutory purpose." They also are justified as "necessary to promote a compelling governmental interest."

We do not denigrate the importance of decent, safe, and sanitary housing. But the constitution does not provide judicial remedies for every social and economic ill. We are unable to perceive in that document any constitutional guarantee of access to dwellings of a particular quality, or any recognition of the right of a tenant to occupy the real property of his landlord beyond the term of his lease without the payment of rent or otherwise contrary to the terms of the relevant agreement. Absent constitutional mandate, the assurance of adequate housing and the definition of landlord-tenant relationships are legislative, not judicial, functions. Nor should we forget that the Constitution expressly protects against confiscation of private property or the income therefrom. Since the purpose of the Oregon Forcible Entry and Wrongful Detainer Statute is constitutionally permissible and since the classification under attack is rationally related to that purpose, the statute is not repugnant to the Equal Protection Clause of the Fourteenth Amendment.***

Notes and Questions

1.   In *Lindsey v. Normet*, the Supreme Court decided that a renter's "need for decent shelter" must yield to the "prompt as well as peaceful resolution of disputes over the right to possession of real property." Does the right to private property hold a special place in American legal and social history? *Compare* the discussion of the protection of slavery in the U.S. Constitution, Section 6.A.1, *supra*. Should the right to property trump other rights and values? What alternative approaches to a hierarchy of rights could you imagine? What effect would your alternative approach have on the status of the poor?

2.   According to the National Low Income Housing Coalition, public policy choices at the national level have subsidized home ownership, *e.g.*, through tax incentives and federally backed mortgages, at the expense of affordable rental housing. Its annual "Out of Reach" reports provide an economic and demographic analysis of the deepening housing crisis facing low-income renters. The reports calculate the national and state-by-state "Housing Wage," that is, the hourly wage that must be earned in order to afford a two-bedroom house or apartment at a "fair market rent." According to "Out of Reach 2003" the national median housing wage is now $15.21, a 37 percent increase since 1999, and roughly three times the federal minimum wage. In no American metropolitan area does a minimum wage job provide an adequate Housing Wage.

> The report cautions, however, that numbers do not tell the whole story:
>
> [N]umbers *** do not express the human toll of the affordable housing crisis. Numbers do not tell the stories of families who hold on to their homes by their fingertips, keeping the rent paid only by relying on food pantries and soup kitchens to eat at the end of the month and counting on informal and haphazard arrangements for child care so parents can work. Numbers do not describe what it means for a child to bounce from school to school because his or her family must keep searching for cheaper places to live, never catching up on lessons or forming lasting friendships. Numbers cannot make us feel the anxiety of an aging widow who fears that she will lose her home as her rent or property taxes go up and her pension does not. Numbers do not help us understand the frustration of wasted potential of a person with disabilities consigned to an institution for lack of an affordable place to live in her or his community.

OUT OF REACH 2003 at 1, *available at* http://www.nlihc.org/oor2003/introduction.htm.

6.   *The Right to Health*

HARRIS v. McRAE

448 U.S. 297 (1980)

Mr. Justice STEWART delivered the opinion of the Court.

This case presents statutory and constitutional questions concerning the public funding of abortions under Title XIX of the Social Security Act, commonly known as the "Medicaid" Act, and recent annual Appropriations Acts containing the so-called "Hyde Amendment." The statutory question is whether Title XIX requires a State that participates in the Medicaid program to fund the cost of medically necessary abortions for which federal reimbursement is unavailable under the Hyde Amendment. The constitutional question, which arises only if Title XIX imposes no such requirement, is whether the Hyde Amendment, by denying public funding for certain medically necessary abortions, contravenes the liberty or equal protection guarantees of the Due Process Clause of the Fifth Amendment.***

The Medicaid program was created in 1965, when Congress added Title XIX to the Social Security Act *** for the purpose of providing federal financial assistance to States that choose to reimburse certain costs of medical treatment for needy persons. Although participation in the Medicaid program is entirely optional, once a State elects to participate, it must comply with the requirements of Title XIX. One such requirement is that a participating State agree to provide financial assistance to the "categorically needy" with respect to five general areas of medical treatment: (1) inpatient hospital services, (2) outpatient hospital services, (3) other laboratory and X-ray services, (4) skilled nursing facilities services, periodic screening and diagnosis of children, and family planning services, and (5) service of physicians.***

Since September 1976, Congress has prohibited—either by an amendment to the annual appropriations bill for the Department of Health, Education, and Welfare or by a joint resolution—the use of any federal funds to reimburse the cost of abortions under the Medicaid program except under certain specified circumstances. This funding restriction *** commonly known as the "Hyde Amendment," after its original congressional sponsor [provide] "[N]one of the funds provided by this joint resolution shall be used to perform abortions except where the life of the mother would be endangered if the fetus were carried to term; or except for such medical procedures necessary for the victims of rape or incest when such rape or incest has been reported promptly to a law enforcement agency or public health service." [Citations Omitted] This version of the Hyde Amendment is broader than that applicable for fiscal year 1977, which did not include the "rape or incest" exception, [Citations Omitted], but narrower than that applicable for most of fiscal year 1978, and all of fiscal year 1979, which had an additional exception for "instances where severe and long-lasting physical health damage to the mother would result if the pregnancy were carried to term when so determined by two physicians." Pub.L. 95-205, § 101, 91 Stat. 1460; Pub.L. 95-480, § 210, 92 Stat. 1586.

On September 30, 1976, the day on which Congress enacted the initial version of the Hyde Amendment, these consolidated cases were filed in the District Court for the Eastern District of New York. The plaintiffs—Cora McRae, a New York Medicaid recipient then in the first trimester of a pregnancy that she wished to terminate, the New York City Health and Hospitals Corp., a public benefit corporation that operates 16 hospitals, 12 of which provide abortion services, and others—sought to enjoin the enforcement of the funding restriction on abortions. They alleged that the Hyde Amendment violated the First, Fourth, Fifth, and Ninth Amendments of the Constitution insofar as it limited the funding of abortions to those necessary to save the life of the mother, while permitting the funding of costs associated with childbirth. Although the sole named defendant was the Secretary of Health, Education, and Welfare, the District

Court permitted Senators James L. Buckley and Jesse A. Helms and Representative Henry J. Hyde to intervene as defendants.

After a hearing, the District Court entered a preliminary injunction prohibiting the Secretary from enforcing the Hyde Amendment and requiring him to continue to provide federal reimbursement for abortions under the standards applicable before the funding restriction had been enacted. *McRae v. Mathews,* 421 F.Supp. 533. Although stating that it had not expressly held that the funding restriction was unconstitutional, since the preliminary injunction was not its final judgment, the District Court noted that such a holding was "implicit" in its decision granting the injunction. The District Court also certified the *McRae* case as a class action on behalf of all pregnant or potentially pregnant women in the State of New York eligible for Medicaid and who decide to have an abortion within the first 24 weeks of pregnancy, and of all authorized providers of abortion services to such women. *Id.,* at 543. The Secretary then brought an appeal to this Court. [W]e vacated the injunction of the District Court and remanded the case for reconsideration in light of those decisions. *Califano v. McRae,* 433 U.S. 916, 97 S.Ct. 2993, 53 L.Ed.2d 1103.***

After a lengthy trial, which inquired into the medical reasons for abortions and the diverse religious views on the subject, the District Court filed an opinion and entered a judgment invalidating all versions of the Hyde Amendment on constitutional grounds. The District Court rejected the plaintiffs' statutory argument, concluding that even though Title XIX would otherwise have required a participating State to fund medically necessary abortions, the Hyde Amendment had substantively amended Title XIX to relieve a State of that funding obligation. Turning then to the constitutional issues, the District Court concluded that the Hyde Amendment *** violates the equal protection component of the Fifth Amendment's Due Process Clause and the Free Exercise Clause of the First Amendment. With regard to the Fifth Amendment, the District Court noted that when an abortion is "medically necessary to safeguard the pregnant woman's health *** the disentitlement to Medicaid assistance impinges directly on the woman's right to decide, in consultation with her physician and in reliance on his judgment, to terminate her pregnancy in order to preserve her health." *McRae v. Califano,* 491 F.Sup. 630, 737. The Court concluded that the Hyde Amendment violates the equal protection guarantee because, in its view, the decision of Congress to fund medically necessary services generally but only certain medically necessary abortions serves no legitimate governmental interest.***

III

Having determined that Title XIX does not obligate a participating State to pay for those medically necessary abortions for which Congress has withheld federal funding, we must consider the constitutional validity of the Hyde Amendment. The appellees assert that the funding restrictions of the Hyde Amendment violate *** the equal protection component of the Fifth Amendment.

It is well settled that, quite apart from the guarantee of equal protection, if a law "impinges upon a fundamental right explicitly or implicitly secured by the Constitution [it] is presumptively unconstitutional." *Mobile v. Bolden,* 446 U.S. 55, 76, 100 S.Ct. 1490, 1504, 64 L.Ed.2d 47 (plurality opinion). Accordingly, before turning to the equal protection issue in this case, we examine whether the Hyde Amendment violates any substantive rights secured by the Constitution.

A

We address first the appellees' argument that the Hyde Amendment, by restricting the availability of certain medically necessary abortions under Medicaid, impinges on the "liberty" protected by the Due Process Clause as recognized in *Roe v. Wade*, 410 U.S. 113, 93 S.Ct. 705, 35 L.Ed.2d 147, and its progeny. In the *Wade* case, this Court held unconstitutional a Texas statute making it a crime to procure or attempt an abortion except on medical advice for the purpose of saving the mother's life. The constitutional underpinning of *Wade* was a recognition that the "liberty" protected by the Due Process Clause of the Fourteenth Amendment includes not only the freedoms explicitly mentioned in the Bill of Rights, but also a freedom of personal choice in certain matters of marriage and family life.*** This implicit constitutional liberty, the Court in *Wade* held, includes the freedom of a woman to decide whether to terminate a pregnancy.***

But the constitutional freedom recognized in *Wade* and its progeny, the *Maher* Court explained, did not prevent Connecticut from making "a value judgment favoring child-birth over abortion, and *** implement[ing] that judgment by the allocation of public funds." 432 U.S., at 474, 97 S.Ct., at 2382. As the Court elaborated: "The Connecticut regulation before us is different in kind from the laws invalidated in our previous abortion decisions. The Connecticut regulation places no obstacles—absolute or otherwise—in the pregnant woman's path to an abortion. An indigent woman who desires an abortion suffers no disadvantage as a consequence of Connecticut's decision to fund childbirth; she continues as before to be dependent on private sources for the service she desires. The State may have made childbirth a more attractive alternative, thereby influencing the woman's decision, but it has imposed no restriction on access to abortions that was not already there. The indigency that may make it difficult—and in some cases, perhaps, impossible—for some women to have abortions is neither created nor in any way affected by the Connecticut regulation." *Ibid.***

But, regardless of whether the freedom of a woman to choose to terminate her pregnancy for health reasons lies at the core or the periphery of the due process liberty recognized in *Wade*, it simply does not follow that a woman's freedom of choice carries with it a constitutional entitlement to the financial resources to avail herself of the full range of protected choices. The reason why was explained in *Maher*: although government may not place obstacles in the path of a woman's exercise of her freedom of choice, it need not remove those not of its own creation. Indigency falls in the latter category. The financial constraints that restrict an indigent woman's ability to enjoy the full range of constitutionally protected freedom of choice are the product not of governmental restrictions on access to abortions, but rather of her indigency. Although Congress has opted to subsidize medically necessary services generally, but not certain medically necessary abortions, the fact remains that the Hyde Amendment leaves an indigent woman with at least the same range of choice in deciding whether to obtain a medically necessary abortion as she would have had if Congress had chosen to subsidize no health care costs at all. We are thus not persuaded that the Hyde Amendment impinges on the constitutionally protected freedom of choice recognized in *Wade*.***

Although the liberty protected by the Due Process Clause affords protection against unwarranted government interference with freedom of choice in the context of certain personal decisions, it does not confer an entitlement to such funds as may be necessary to realize all the advantages of that freedom. To hold otherwise would mark a drastic change in our understanding of the Constitution. It cannot be that because government may not prohibit the use of contraceptives, *Griswold v. Connecticut*, 381, U.S. 479, 85 S.Ct. 1678, 14 L.Ed.2d 510, or prevent parents from sending their child to a private school, *Pierce v. Society of Sisters*, 268 U.S. 510, 45 S.Ct. 571, 69 L.Ed. 1070, government, therefore, has an affirmative constitutional obligation to ensure that all persons have the financial resources to obtain contraceptives or send their children to private schools. To translate the limitation on governmental power implicit in the Due Process Clause into an affirmative funding obligation would require Congress to subsidize the medically necessary abortion of an indigent woman even if Congress had not enacted a Medicaid program to subsidize other medically necessary services. Nothing in the Due Process clause supports such an extraordinary result.[3] Whether freedom of choice that is constitutionally protected warrants federal subsidization is a question for Congress to answer, not a matter of constitutional entitlement. Accordingly, we conclude that the Hyde Amendment does not impinge on the due process liberty recognized in *Wade*.

For the reasons stated above, we have already concluded that the Hyde Amendment violates no constitutionally protected substantive rights. We now conclude as well that it is not predicated on a constitutionally suspect classification. In reaching this conclusion, we again draw guidance from the Court's decision in *Maher v. Roe*. As to whether the Connecticut welfare regulation providing funds for childbirth but not for nontherapeutic abortions discriminated against a suspect class, the Court in *Maher* observed: "An indigent woman desiring an abortion does not come within the limited category of disadvantaged classes so recognized by our cases. Nor does the fact that the impact of the regulation falls upon those who cannot pay lead to a different conclusion. In a sense, every denial of welfare to an indigent creates a wealth classification as compared to nonindigents who are able to pay for the desired goods or services. But this Court has never held that financial need alone identifies a suspect class for purposes of equal protection analysis."

Thus, the Court in *Maher* found no basis for concluding that the Connecticut regulation was predicated on a suspect classification.

It is our view that the present case is indistinguishable from *Maher* in this respect. Here, as in *Maher*, the principal impact of the Hyde Amendment falls on the indigent. But that fact does not itself render the funding restriction constitutionally invalid, for this Court has held repeatedly that poverty, standing alone is not a suspect classification. That *Maher* involved the refusal to fund nontherapeutic abortions, whereas the present case involves the refusal to fund medically necessary abortions, has no bearing on the factors that render a classification "suspect" within the meaning of the constitutional guarantee of equal protection.

The remaining question then is whether the Hyde Amendment is rationally related to a legitimate governmental objective. It is the Government's position that the Hyde Amendment bears a rational relationship to its legitimate interest in protecting the potential life of the fetus. We agree.

In *Wade*, the Court recognized that the State has an "important and legitimate interest in protecting the potentiality of human life." 410 U.S., at 162, 93 S.Ct., at 731. That interest was found to exist throughout a pregnancy, "grow[ing] in substantiality as the

---

[3] As this Court in Maher observed: "The Constitution imposes no obligation on the [government] to pay the pregnancy-related medical expenses of indigent women, or indeed to pay any of the medical expenses of indigents." 432 U.S., at 469, 97 S.Ct., at 2380.

woman approaches term."*** Moreover, in *Maher*, the Court held that Connecticut's decision to fund the costs associated with childbirth but not those associated with non-therapeutic abortions was a rational means of advancing the legitimate state interest in protecting potential life by encouraging childbirth.

It follows that the Hyde Amendment, by encouraging childbirth except in the most urgent circumstances, is rationally related to the legitimate governmental objective of protecting potential life. By subsidizing the medical expenses of indigent women who carry their pregnancies to term while not subsidizing the comparable expenses of women who undergo abortions (except those whose lives are threatened), Congress has established incentives that make childbirth a more attractive alternative than abortion for persons eligible for Medicaid. These incentives bear a direct relationship to the legitimate Congressional interest in protecting potential life. Nor is it irrational that Congress has authorized federal reimbursement for medically necessary services generally, but not for certain medically necessary abortions. Abortion is inherently different from other medical procedures, because no other procedure involves the purposeful termination of a potential life.

Accordingly, the judgment of the District Court is reversed, and the case is remanded to that Court for further proceedings consistent with this opinion.

It is so ordered.

Notes and Questions

1. Is the inaccessibility of medically necessary, constitutionally protected abortion rights to poor women consistent with the notion of a "human rights culture"? Why or why not?

2. Is there any way that economic and social rights could become part of the U.S. social contract? International legal scholar Louis Henkin suggests that the United States could adopt a "directive principles" model like that pioneered in the Indian Constitution, discussed in Chapter 7, *supra:*

> *** The United States *** needs to update its Bill of Rights, but it need not do so by formal constitutional amendment. Much can be achieved by interpretation, as our courts have often done, notably when they constitutionalized "substantive due process" and incorporated almost all of the Bill of Rights into the Fourteenth Amendment rendering it applicable to the states. If the Supreme Court is sometimes reluctant to assume that responsibility, Congress can add to our rights by legislation under its Commerce Power or its other powers, as it did by the Civil Rights Acts of the 1870s and the 1960s.***

> [The U.S. might] add to its Bill of Rights by adhering to the Covenant on Economic, Social and Cultural Rights. President Carter signed that Covenant for the United States, but neither he nor subsequent presidents pressed the Senate to consent to its ratification. Indeed, the sentiment that economic, social, and cultural rights are not "rights" has spread, and reluctance to assume international obligations to realize them has remained strong.***

> The limited conception of rights in the United States may be the result of a limited conception of the purposes of government and of historic commitment to the minimal, "liberal" state. That conception has not survived as the heritage of other Western democracies—not of the United Kingdom, not of France, and not of Germany.***

The obstacle to including "positive rights" in a Bill of Rights—or committing to them by international covenant—may be not only an outdated conception of what are fundamental rights or a limited conception of the purposes of government, but may be our commitment to and restricted conception of judicial review.***

I am not persuaded that economic and social rights are inherently incapable of being judicially enforced. Sometimes declaratory judgments can be entered even if common law or equitable remedies are problematic. Surely, with imagination and ingenuity, some economic rights can be given effect in some circumstances, in some measure. In any event, I am not persuaded that there is no value in including some provisions in a Bill of Rights that cannot be judicially enforced. Some constitutional rights in the United States are not judicially enforceable today—for lack of anyone with standing or from a judicial intuition that they involve "political," nonjusticiable questions.*** [E]ven non-enforceable rights contribute to a political-moral-constitutional culture. Including economic and social rights in a Bill of Rights would make those rights "national policy." Such rights would be constitutional obligations, and representatives and officials would be committed by constitutional oath to carry them out. The inclusion of economic and social rights would justify judges being imaginative and ingenious in realizing them. In many circumstances, courts could at least declare obligations and even command bureaucrats, if not Congress or state legislatures. Committing ourselves to such rights by treaty would give them the support of international obligation and of the varied inducements to comply with them.

And so, if including economic and social rights in a Bill of Rights is resisted because they cannot be judicially reviewed, how about a full Bill of civil and political rights and a half-Bill of economic and social rights, or a half-Bill of those rights that we think cannot or ought not be enforced by the courts? Half a century of experience with such a model by India has not proved it to be a failure. It would reaffirm, to the world and to ourselves, our commitment to freedom from want.***

Louis Henkin, *A Bill of Rights-and-A Half*, 32 TEX. INT'L L.J. 483, 486–88 (1997). For further reading on the question of economic and social rights in the U.S. Constitution, *see* Frank E.L. Deale, *The Unhappy History of Economic Rights in the United States and Prospects for Their Creation and Renewal*, 43 HOW. L.J. 281 (2000); Peter B. Edelman, *The Next Century of Our Constitution: Rethinking Our Duty to the Poor*, 39 HASTINGS L.J. 1 (1987); and Charles L. Black, Jr., *Further Reflections on the Constitutional Justice of Livelihood*, 86 COLUM. L. REV. 1103 (1986).

7. *Religious and Cultural Rights in the United States*

Religious and cultural beliefs and practices may conflict with secular laws to some degree. How should courts resolve such conflicts? The First Amendment to the U.S. Constitution provides some protection for the free exercise of religion:

Amendment I

Congress shall make no law respecting an establishment of religion, or prohibiting the free exercise thereof; or abridging the freedom of speech ***.

The freedom to engage in religious expression is not unlimited, however. The U.S. Supreme Court has upheld some laws that impede the exercise of minority religious practices in certain circumstances. On the other hand, the Court has held laws that are designed to burden a particular religion invalid even if the laws appear textually neutral.

The Supreme Court has taken the view that "religious beliefs need not be acceptable, logical, consistent or comprehensible to others in order to merit First Amendment protection." *Thomas v. Review Bd. of Indiana Employment Security Div.*, 450 U.S. 707, 714 (1981). Nevertheless, when religious beliefs conflict with the laws of the state, the Court sometimes holds the enforcement of the laws valid, even though it infringes on the practice of those religious beliefs.

Employment Div. v. Smith, 494 U.S. 872 (1990), one of the most highly publicized cases, involved the conflict of minority religious practices and secular law. In *Smith*, a Native American member of the Native American Church was fired from his position as an alcohol and drug counselor and subsequently denied unemployment benefits because he used peyote in a religious ceremony. The use of peyote was illegal under state law, with no exception for its use in religious ceremonies.[4] The Court held that since the state law was facially neutral and generally applicable to all individuals, it was valid even though it incidentally prohibits a religious practice. *Id.* at 872.

Congress responded to the Court's decision in *Smith* with the Religious Freedom Restoration Act (RFRA), 42 U.S.C.A. §§ 2000bb et seq. RFRA was designed to reinstate the least restrictive means/ compelling government interest test previously established in *Sherbert v. Verner*, 374 US 398 (1963), and *Wisconsin v. Yoder*, 406 U.S. 205 (1972). RFRA was subsequently deemed unconstitutional as applied against a state or locality, *City of Boerne v. Flores*, 521 U.S. 507 (1997) but is still applicable to the federal government; *Guam v. Guerrero*, 290 F.3d 1210 (9th Cir. 2002).

Many cases addressing religious freedom issues in the U.S. concern the rights of prisoners to participate in religious ceremonies, as well as dress and grooming requirements. *See, e.g.*, Mary L. Topliff, *Validity, Construction, and Application of Religious Freedom Restoration Act*, 135 ALR FED. 121 (1996). Other cases deal with the conflicts between spiritual healing practices by practitioners of Christian Science and other religions and professional medical treatments. *See, e.g.*, Janna C. Merrick, *Spiritual Healing, Sick Kids and the Law: Inequities in the American Healthcare System*, 29 AM. J.L. & MED. 269 (2003). A third category of cases involves Native American sacred sites that are owned by the federal government and therefore available for development. *See* Kristen A Carpenter, *In the Absence of Title: Responding to Federal Ownership in Sacred Sites Cases*, 37 NEW ENG. L. REV. 619 (2003). *See also* Section A, *supra*, on the rights of Indigenous Peoples.

A comprehensive analysis of these cases is beyond the scope of this note. However, the following discussion provides illustrations of cases involving religious or cultural practices that violate a law of general applicability.

In *U.S. v. Dion*, 476 US 734 (1986),[5] the Supreme Court held that the sale of Bald Eagle feathers was not protected as a religious freedom of Native Americans. The killing

---

[4] Since the Court's decision in Smith, Oregon has amended its laws to allow the use of peyote in Native American religious ceremonies. OREGON REV. STAT. 475.992 § 5 (1995).

[5] *See also U.S. v Top Sky*, 547 F.2d 483 (9th Cir. 1976).

of Bald Eagles for religious purposes is subject to permit requirements, as stated in the Bald Eagle Protection Act and its regulations, and is restricted to Native Americans. The sale of the feathers violated the Act. But in *U.S. v Hardman*, 297 F.3d 1116 (10th Cir. 2002), the Tenth Circuit found that in order to exclude Native American Church members who were not members of a federally recognized tribe, the government could prove that the permit system for Bald Eagle feathers was the least restrictive means available to protect Bald Eagle populations and Native American culture.

In *Church of the Lukumi Babalu Aye v. Hialeah*, 508 U.S. 520 (1993), the Supreme Court struck down a city ordinance prohibiting animal sacrifice. The city passed the ordinance upon learning that practitioners of the Santeria religion leased a church in the city and were planning to conduct ceremonies on the premises. The Court held that the ordinance unduly burdened the religious practices of the Santeria religion.

In *Cheema v. Thompson*, 67 F.3d 883 (9th Cir. 1995), the Ninth Circuit lifted a school district's blanket ban on carrying Kirpans, religious ceremonial knives, to school for Khalsa Sikh children. The court allowed the children to wear the Kirpans as long as the blades were dull, sewn into its sheath, and worn under the children's clothing.

The "veiling" of women in adherence to Islamic religious law was addressed in *Freeman v. Florida*, 2003 WL 21338619 (Fla. Cir. Ct. 2003). In *Freeman*, a Muslim woman appealed the state's decision to revoke her driver's license because she refused to unveil for the photograph. The court held that her refusal warranted the state's revocation of her license, since the state offered to have her picture taken in a secluded room with only a female Muslim employee present when she unveiled. Since the "State's need to be able to immediately identify subjects of investigative traffic stops and criminal and intelligence investigations outweighs anyone's need to pose for a driver's license photo" wearing a veil, the state's actions were allowable. *See* the discussion of the Muslim veil and other appearance regulation issues in Chapter 4, *supra*.

While the court dealt with the question of peyote use in *Smith*, other religions require or permit the use of certain substances in contravention of criminal laws. *See Free exercise of religion as defense to prosecution for narcotic or psychedelic drug offense*, 35 ALR3d 939. Many criminal cases involve attempts by defendants to affirmatively defend marijuana possession charges on the basis of religious belief. These efforts have often involved practitioners of Rastafarianism (a religion originating in Jamaica) (Guam v. Guerrero, 290 F.3d 1210 (9th Cir. 2002)), but also have involved members of the "Church of Marijuana." *See, e.g.*, U.S. v. Meyers, 906 F. Supp. 1494 (D. Wyo. 1995). The courts have not recognized the defense to marijuana possession charges.

In *O Centro Espirita Beneficiente Uniao De Vegetal v. Ashcroft*, 314 F.3d 463 (10th Cir. 2002), the Tenth Circuit refused to allow the importation, possession and distribution of hoasca, a plant hallucinogen indigenous to the Amazon basin, for religious ceremonies, finding that it could hamper the government's efforts to combat drug trafficking and require extensive judicial and administrative oversight.

For further readings on cultural rights in the United States, *see, e.g.*, Adeno Addis, *Cultural Integrity and Political Unity: The Politics of Language in Multilingual States*, 33 ARIZ. ST. L.J. 719 (2001) (excerpted in Chapter 6, *supra*); Adeno Addis, *Individualism, Communitarianism, and the Rights of Ethnic Minorities*, 67 NOTRE DAME L. REV. 615 (1992); S. JAMES ANAYA, INDIGENOUS PEOPLES IN INTERNATIONAL LAW (2000); Curtis G. Berkey,

International Law and Domestic Courts: Enhancing Self-Determination for Indigenous Peoples, 5 HARV. HUM. RTS. J. 65 (1992); John Celichowski, *A Rough and Narrow Path: Preserving Native American Religious Liberty in the Smith Era*, 25 AM. INDIAN L. REV. 1 (2001); David S. Clark, *State Court Recognition of Tribal Court Judgments: Securing the Blessings of Civilization*, 23 OKLA. CITY U.L. REV. 353 (1998); LOUIS FISHER, RELIGIOUS LIBERTY IN AMERICA: POLITICAL SAFEGUARDS (2002); Hurst Hannum, *Sovereignty and its Relevance to Native Americans in the Twenty-First Century*, 23 AM. INDIAN L. REV. 487 (1998); Allan F. Hanson, *Racism and Relativism*, 10 TIKKUN (Nov.–Dec. 1995) 63–67; WILLIAM KYMLICKA, MULTICULTURAL CITIZENSHIP: A LIBERAL THEORY OF MINORITY RIGHTS, (1995); MICHAEL LIEDER & JAKE PAGE, WILD JUSTICE: THE PEOPLE OF GERONIMO V. THE UNITED STATES (1999); Ved P. Nanda, et al., *Human Rights Violations by the U.S. Government Against Native Americans in the Passage and Enforcement of Pub. L. No. 93-531*, 15 ENV. J. INT'L L. & POL'Y 330 (1987); Leti Volpp, *Blaming Culture for Bad Behavior*, 12 YALE J. L. & HUMAN. 89 (2000); ROBERT A. WILLIAMS, LINKING ARMS TOGETHER: AMERICAN INDIAN TREATY VISIONS OF LAW AND PEACE, 1600–1800 (1997); JOHN R. WUNDER, NATIVE AMERICAN CULTURAL AND RELIGIOUS FREEDOMS (1999).

B. STATE CONSTITUTIONS

1. *Economic and Social Rights in Selected State Constitutions*

ALABAMA CONSTITUTION

Article IV, § 88

It shall be the duty of the legislature to require the several counties of this state to make adequate provision for the maintenance of the poor.

ALASKA CONSTITUTION

Article VII, § 5

The legislature shall provide for public welfare.

CALIFORNIA CONSTITUTION

Article XVI, § 11

The Legislature, or the people by initiative, shall have the power to amend, alter or repeal any law relating to the relief of hardship and destitution, whether such hardship and destitution results from unemployment or from other causes, or to provide for the administration of the relief of hardship and destitution, whether results from unemployment or from other causes, either directly by the State or through the counties of the State and to grant such aid to the counties therefor, or to make such provision for reimbursement to the counties by the State, as the Legislature deems proper.

INDIANA CONSTITUTION

Article IX, § 3

The counties may provide farms, as an asylum for those persons who, by reason of age, infirmity or other misfortune, have claims upon the sympathies and aid of society.

KANSAS CONSTITUTION

Article IV, § 4

[The] state shall provide, as may be prescribed by law, for those inhabitants who, by reason of age, infirmity or other misfortune, may have claims upon *** society.

MICHIGAN CONSTITUTION

Article IV, § 51

The public health and general welfare of the people of the state are hereby declared to be matters of primary public concern. The legislature shall pass suitable laws [in reference to] the promotion of public health.

MISSOURI CONSTITUTION

Article IV, § 37

The health and general welfare of the people are matters of primary public concern; and to secure them there shall be established a department of social services in charge of a director *** by and with the advice and consent of the senate, charged with promoting improved health and other social services to the citizens of the state ***

MONTANA CONSTITUTION

Article XII, § 3

[The] state shall establish and support institutions and facilities as the public good may require.

[The] legislature may provide such employees assistance and social and rehabilitative services for those who, by reason of age, infirmities or misfortune are determined by the legislature to be in need ***

[The] legislature may set eligibility criteria for programs and services [as well as the] duration and level of benefits.

NEW MEXICO CONSTITUTION

Article IV, § 14

Nothing [in this provision] shall be construed to prohibit the state or any county or municipality from making provision for the care and maintenance of sick and indigent persons.

NORTH CAROLINA CONSTITUTION

Article XI, § 4

Beneficent provision for the poor, the unfortunate, and the orphaned is one of the first duties of a civilized and Christian state. Therefore the General Assembly shall provide for and define the duties of a Board of Public Welfare.

NEW YORK CONSTITUTION

Article XVII, § 1

The aid, care and support of the needy are public concerns and shall be provided by the state and by such of its subdivisions, and in such a manner and by such means, as the legislature may from time to time determine.

OKLAHOMA CONSTITUTION

Article XXV, § 1

To promote the general welfare of the people of the State of Oklahoma and for their protection, security and benefit, Legislature and the people *** are hereby authorized to provide appropriate legislation for the relief and care of *** needy persons who, on account of their immature age, physical infirmity *** or other cause, are unable to provide or care for themselves. The Legislature or the people *** are further authorized, in co-operation with and under any plan authorized by the Federal Government for State participation, to provide by appropriate legislation for the relief and care of aged or needy persons.

TEXAS CONSTITUTION

Article III, § 51-a

[The] Legislature shall have the power, by General Laws, to provide, subject to the limitations herein contained and other such limitations *** as may by the Legislature be deemed expedient, for assistance grants to needy dependent children and *** caretakers, [and] needy persons who are totally and permanently disabled.

[The] Legislature may prescribe such other eligibility requirements for participation in these programs, as it deems appropriate and may make appropriations out of state funds for such purposes. The maximum amount paid out of state funds for assistance grants, to or on behalf of needy dependent children and their caretakers, shall not exceed the amount of Eighty Million Dollars ($80,000,000) during any fiscal year.

WYOMING CONSTITUTION

Article VII, § 20

As the health and morality of the people are essential to their well-being and to the peace and permanence of the state, it shall be the duty of the legislature to protect and promote these vital interests by such measures for the encouragement of temperance and virtue.

Notes and Questions

1. Since the state constitutions excerpted above were written, local economies have changed and social norms about "public welfare" and which groups constitute "needy persons" may have changed. Consider, for example, differences in the treatment of African-Americans, Native Americans, and immigrant groups in the 19th, 20th, and 21st centuries. Consider also differences in the status of veterans, women, children, persons with disabilities and the elderly in the Unietd States over the same period. Given these changes, should these constitutions be interpreted differently today? For a historical analysis of U.S. social welfare policy, *see* THEDA SKOCPOL, PROTECTING SOLDIERS AND MOTHERS: THE POLITICAL ORIGINS OF SOCIAL POLICY IN THE UNITED STATES (1992); William P. Quigley, *Rumblings of Reform: Northern Poor Relief Legislation in Antebellum America, 1820–1860,* 26 CAP. U.L. REV. 739 (1997).

2. In describing public welfare duties some state constitutions use the word "may," while others use the word "shall." Some state constitutions describe their "public welfare" duties as "primary" or "first duties," while others contain no such ranking. How

important were these distinctions to the framers and how important are they to contemporary interpretation? How should these textual differences be interpreted in implementing contemporary public welfare programs?

3. *Who Is Included Under the Umbrella of "Public Welfare"?* Many state constitutions specify an obligation to promote the health of its citizens generally; other state constitutions specify an obligation to provide for the elderly, children, the poor, the unemployed or infirm citizens. What are the implications of specifying categories of protected persons?

4. For further reading on economic and social rights in state constitutions, *see* Helen Hershkoff, *Welfare Devolution and State Constitutions*, 4 FORDHAM L. REV. 1403 (1999); Norma Rotunno, *Note: State Constitutional Social Welfare Provisions and the Right to Housing*, 1 HOFSTRA L. & POL'Y SYMP. 111 (1996); Dan Braverman, *Children, Poverty and State Constitutions*, 38 EMORY L.J. 577 (1989); and Louis Karl Bonham, *Note: Unenumerated Rights Clauses in State Constitutions*, 63 TEX. L. REV. 1321 (1985).

2. The Right to an Adequate Standard of Living

TUCKER v. TOIA

43 N.Y.2d 1 (1977)

OPINION OF THE COURT

The Commissioner of the State Department of Social Services appeals directly to this court *** from a judgment of the Supreme Court *** declaring section 15 of chapter 76 of the Laws of 1976 (now a part of Social Services Law, § 158), to be unconstitutional, and enjoining its implementation and enforcement. We affirm the judgment appealed from, on the ground that the challenged section constitutes a substantive violation of section 1 of article XVII of the New York State Constitution.

New York residents under the age of 21 who are in need of public assistance normally receive aid through either the Federally subsidized Aid to Families with Dependent Children Program (AFDC) . . . or the State's broad Home Relief Program.*** The determination of which program is applicable in a particular instance is based on whether the needy individual under 21 is residing with either a parent or a legally responsible relative. If he is residing with such a person, he is eligible for AFDC, but not home relief, whereas if he is not residing with such a person, entitlement to benefits stems from the home relief program and not AFDC.

As amended [in 1976], the federal statute provides that home relief is not to be provided to a person under the age of 21 who does not live with a parent or legally responsible relative, unless and until the applicant commences a support proceeding against any such parent or relative and an order of disposition is obtained in that support proceeding.*** Prior to the enactment of section 15 *** a person under the age of 21, whether or not residing with a parent or responsible relative, was entitled to public assistance upon proof of need, regardless of the existence of a parent or responsible relative, and it was left to the State to seek to recoup its welfare expenditures via a support proceeding against any such parent or relative. This is the method which was used in both AFDC and home relief cases prior to adoption of the section under attack and it is of interest to note that it is the method still used in AFDC cases.

Plaintiffs in this action are three individuals under the age of 21 who are not living with a parent or responsible relative, and are thus eligible only for home relief, not for AFDC. They are concededly needy and, prior to the effective date of section 15, they would have been and were entitled to home relief, having met all requisite criteria.

One of the plaintiffs was 18 years old at the time this action was commenced. His father had abandoned his mother before plaintiff's birth, and his whereabouts are unknown. Until 1976, the son had lived with his mother, and was receiving an AFDC grant. His mother was then committed to a State hospital due to mental illness and, as a result, the son became ineligible for AFDC. Although he ultimately obtained a final disposition in a support proceeding against his mother in an attempt to satisfy section 15, he was denied home relief on the ground that he had not obtained a final disposition in a support proceeding against his missing father.

A second plaintiff was 19 years old, pregnant, and living alone when this action was commenced. Her mother was deceased, and her father was living in Alabama. Her sole source of income was home relief. On October 12, 1976, she was notified that all public assistance would be terminated in eight days unless she could produce within that time a court order of disposition in a support proceeding against her father.

A third plaintiff was an 18 year old, unemployed, high school graduate when this action was commenced. Prior to August, 1976 she lived with her mother and five siblings on an AFDC grant. She then left home due to family difficulties, and ultimately applied for home relief. Her application was denied because of her failure to obtain an order of disposition in a support proceeding against her father, who had disappeared some 10 years ago.

Standing uncontroverted is the accepted fact and reality that in each of these cases in order to obtain the required "disposition," it would take from several weeks to several months, during which time no public assistance would be available to these needy young people. Indeed, in the third plaintiff's case, Family Court officials originally refused to accept her support petition because she was unable to provide an address for her missing father. In the second mentioned case, Family Court officials estimated that since her father was in Alabama and any support proceeding would have to be conducted in accordance with the Uniform Support of Dependents Law (Domestic Relations Law, article 3-A), it would take a minimum of 10 weeks to obtain a disposition. In certain areas of the State even greater delays are normal, and, in fact, it has been estimated that in New York City it will often take from 10 to 12 months to obtain a "disposition" in such a support proceeding. Under the challenged statute, the plaintiffs and others in similar situations are, of course, denied any public assistance during this period, although they meet all criteria for measuring need, solely on the basis of their failure to obtain a disposition. Since they do meet the need criteria, and are thus a fortiori unable to support themselves without public aid, one must wonder how they are to survive this period of waiting for an overcrowded Family Court system to process their often quite futile support petitions.

In New York State, the provision for assistance to the needy is not a matter of legislative grace; rather, it is specifically mandated by our Constitution. Section 1 of article XVII of the New York State Constitution declares: "The aid, care and support of the needy are public concerns and shall be provided by the state and by such of its subdivisions, and in such manner and by such means, as the legislature may from time to time determine." This provision was adopted in 1938, in the aftermath of the great depression, and was intended to serve two functions: First, it was felt to be necessary to sustain from constitutional attack the social welfare programs first created by the State during that period ***; and, second, it was intended as an expression of the existence of a positive duty upon the State to aid the needy.

The legislative history of the Constitutional Convention of 1938 is indicative of a clear intent that State aid to the needy was deemed to be a fundamental part of the social contract. For example, the report of the Committee on Public Welfare, the group which drafted what became section 1 of article XVII of our Constitution, specifically states that one purpose of the amendment was to "recognize the responsibility of the State for the aid, care and support of persons in need" (Revised Record of the Constitutional Convention of the State of New York, vol. II, p 1084 [1938]). Even more explicit are the comments by Edward F. Corsi, Chairman of the Committee on Social Welfare, in moving the adoption of the provision by the convention:

> We have made provision for the relief of the needy. Convinced that the care of the unemployed and their dependents is in our modern industrial society a permanent problem of major importance affecting the whole of society, we have recommended that:

> "The aid, care and support of the needy are public concerns and shall be provided by the State and by such of its subdivisions and in such manner and by such means as the Legislature may from time to time determine."

> Here are words which set forth a definite policy of government, a concrete social obligation which no court may ever misread. By this section, the committee hopes to achieve two purposes: First: to remove from the area of constitutional doubt the responsibility of the State to those who must look to society for the bare necessities of life; and, secondly, to set down explicitly in our basic law a much needed definition of the relationship of the people to their government.

> While the obligation expressed in this recommendation is mandatory, in that the Legislature shall provide for the aid, care and support of persons in need, the manner and the means by which it shall do so are discretionary.

> The Legislature may continue the system of relief now in operation. It may preserve the present plan of reimbursement to the localities. It may devise new ways of dealing with the problem. Its hands are untied. What it may not do is to shirk its responsibility which, in the opinion of the committee, is as fundamental as any responsibility of government.

Id. at 2126. In view of this legislative history, as well as the mandatory language of the provision itself, it is clear that section 1 of article XVII imposes upon the State an affirmative duty to aid the needy [citations omitted]. Although our Constitution provides the Legislature with discretion in determining the means by which this objective is to be effectuated, in determining the amount of aid, and in classifying recipients and defining the term "needy," it unequivocally prevents the Legislature from simply refusing to aid those whom it has classified as needy. Such a definite constitutional mandate cannot be ignored or easily evaded in either its letter or its spirit [citations omitted].

We find that section 15 of chapter 76 of the Laws of 1976 is unconstitutional in that it contravenes the letter and spirit of section 1 of article XVII of the New York Constitution. The effect of the questioned statute is plain: it would effectively deny public assistance to persons under the age of 21 who are concededly needy, often through no fault of their own, who meet all the criteria developed by the Legislature for determining need, solely on the ground that they have not obtained a final disposition in a support proceeding. Certainly, the statute is in furtherance of a valid State objective, for it is intended to prevent unnecessary welfare expenditures by placing the burden of supporting persons under 21 upon their legally responsible relatives. This valid purpose, however, cannot be achieved by methods which ignore the realities of the needy's plight and the State's affirmative obligation to aid all its needy.***

Notes and Questions

1.   How is the Court of Appeals' approach in interpreting Article XVII, Section 1 of the New York Constitution in *Tucker* different from the Supreme Court's approach in interpreting the U.S. Constitution regarding the right to welfare? How are they similar?

2.   Might a procedural due process argument have been successful in *Tucker* as well? Seven years prior to *Tucker*, the U.S. Supreme Court held that welfare "benefits are a matter of statutory entitlement," thus "termination involves state action that adjudicates important rights." *Goldberg v. Kelly*, 397 U.S. 254, 262 (1970). The decision reasoned that welfare should be regarded as "property," not "gratuity." *Id.* at 263 n.8. Recall that one plaintiff in *Tucker* was a recipient of home relief benefits, until the state notified her of benefits' termination unless she could produce a disposition against her father—who lived in Alabama—within eight days. Could procedural due process have been implicated as well with regard to the other two plaintiffs because of the immense burden of securing court orders of dispositions against their respective parents? The first plaintiff's father had abandoned him before birth and he did not know where to locate him. The third plaintiff's father had disappeared ten years prior.

3.   Is mere legal recognition of a positive duty enough to guarantee effective protection of a right? Did the Court of Appeals actually limit the state's positive duty to "aid, care and support *** the needy" in derogation of legislative intent? Edward Corsi, Chairperson of the Social Welfare Committee, noted in a speech during the 1938 New York constitutional convention that needy citizens' "fundamental right" to receive "aid, care and support" from the state is superior to judicial deference to legislative discretion. III Revised Record of the Constitutional Convention of the State of New York 2126 (1938). However, in *Tucker*, the court effectively declared that "determining the means by which this objective is to be effectuated,*** determining the amount of aid,*** classifying recipients, and defining the term 'needy'" are political questions solely for the legislature to determine, thereby exempting such issues from judicial review. Could the legislature breach its duty to provide for the needy by providing a level of assistance that is unreasonably inadequate or ineffective?

4.   Unfettered legislative discretion raises two paramount questions: who is "needy?" and what is sufficient? *Tucker* has been interpreted to mean that only state denial of *any* welfare benefits to individuals classified as needy warrants judicial scrutiny. In *Bernstein v. Toia*, 373 N.E.2d 238 (N.Y. 1977), the Court of Appeals held sufficiency of welfare benefits solely a matter for the legislature to determine. But consider the New York appellate division's critique of these decisions in *McCain v. Koch*, below.

3. The Right to Shelter

McCAIN v. KOCH

117 A.D.2d 198 (1986)

Rosenberger, J.

On these consolidated appeals we are called upon to consider whether homeless families with children are entitled to emergency shelter under the guarantees of equal protection of the New York Constitution, the Federal Constitution, and the State Plan for Emergency Assistance to Families with Needy Children. These issues arise in the context of appeals and cross appeals from four orders entered by special term.***

STATUTORY FRAMEWORK AND FACTUAL BACKGROUND

Under the New York Social Services Law, policy and rule-making authority are concentrated in the State Department of Social Services.*** Primary responsibility for providing assistance and care, and for day-to-day administration of the manifold public assistance programs devolves upon the local social services departments.

New York participates in the Federally funded program for Aid to Families with Dependent Children (AFDC). In conjunction with the AFDC program, New York has elected to participate in the program for Emergency Assistance to Needy Families with Children (EAF). Additional emergency and short-term aid are available under State-funded public assistance programs such as Home Relief (HR) and Emergency Assistance for Aged, Blind and Disabled Persons.

The City Department of Social Services (City DSS) operates Income Maintenance Centers (IMCs) which administer, *inter alia*, the AFDC, EAF and HR programs for client-recipients on a daily basis, and place families who have requested emergency shelter. The City DSS operates an Emergency Assistance Unit (EAU) in each borough except Staten Island. Families who seek emergency shelter during a weekend, or who have not received referrals to temporary housing from an IMC at the end of the business day, are referred to an EAU for placement. The City DSS attempts to locate hotel accommodations for homeless families.***

McCAIN v. KOCH

Plaintiff Yvonne McCain and members of 13 other homeless families with children commenced an action against the City, the State and City Commissioners of Social Services, and various City officials charged with the administration of programs to assist homeless families in locating housing, seeking a declaratory judgment, injunctive relief, and class certification. They allege in their amended complaint, *inter alia*, that the State and municipal defendants arbitrarily deny them adequate emergency shelter without written notice and an opportunity for a hearing, and shuttle them between local welfare offices, IMCs and EAUs in cycles lasting for days, sometimes weeks at a time. Plaintiffs also claim that defendants lodge them overnight in the EAUs, having them sleep under fluorescent lights on floors, formica counter tops, desks, and chairs and relocate them in squalid and dangerous hotels, located at considerable distances from their children's schools.

The following poignant scenarios illustrate plaintiffs' allegations that defendants arbitrarily deny adequate emergency shelter to homeless families with children. Plaintiff

William Sanders, his wife Carolyn, and their two daughters, aged 10 and 13, became homeless in June 1982, when a fire destroyed their home and Mr. Sanders lost his job. The Sanders plaintiffs allege that City DSS denied their request for emergency shelter on March 26, 1983. Housing was later provided, but terminated on March 31, 1983, for no stated reason. Their AFDC benefits were discontinued on the ground that they lacked a permanent address.

Plaintiff Barbara Downs, a recipient of Social Security Survivor's benefits, and her two children left their apartment in December 1979 because of unsafe, unsanitary conditions. They allege that the City DSS terminated their shelter allowance grant of public assistance upon learning that they had moved in with relatives. When Ms. Downs reapplied for assistance, a social worker advised her to seek permanent housing, since the hotels were unsuitable for families.

In March 1983, plaintiff Patricia Rodak and her five-year-old daughter, AFDC recipients, became homeless as a result of their eviction for nonpayment of rent. The Rodak plaintiffs allege that the City DSS denied their request for emergency shelter on March 18 and March 24, 1983.***

The City DSS placed Yvonne McCain and three of her children at the Martinique Hotel in Manhattan. They have lived there since October 1983 in two rodent and bug-infested rooms, containing minimal furniture and four beds with dirty linen. The windows have no guardrails and there is an open electrical box in the hallway within easy reach of her children.

The City DSS referred plaintiffs Steven and Emily Moses and their eight children to rodent-infested three-room accommodations in the Martinique Hotel. The rooms had broken windows, six single beds, and no other furniture. Due to their repeated complaints, they were moved to slightly better rooms at the hotel, which had three twin beds, a double bed and one dresser. In early September, the Martinique refused to continue housing the Moses family. The City DSS then relocated them to the Granada Hotel in Brooklyn. Their accommodations at the Granada Hotel were insect and rodent-infested. The Moses children aged 2 to 12, share three twin beds with soiled mattresses and inadequate linen. During their six-month occupancy of the Granada, there have been approximately six fires and fire alarms have failed to ring although they ring on other occasions. Two of the Moses children reported having been threatened with a knife. Mr. Moses has witnessed muggings perpetrated with both guns and knives. Heat and hot water were so infrequent that their children were forced to sleep fully clothed on many nights and contracted colds. Indeed, their two-year-old daughter was hospitalized for pneumonia.***

Proposed plaintiff-intervenor Genell Sallterwhite's two six-month-old infants sleep on the floor because they otherwise crawl out of the bed and fall onto the floor. Her room at the Conca D'Oro Hotel in Staten Island has two double beds for two adults and six children.

In their amended complaint, plaintiffs McCain et al. request a declaration that defendants' failures to provide eligible homeless families with (1) safe, suitable, and adequate emergency housing; (2) relocation benefits; (3) school transportation allowances, and (4) notice and a hearing prior to termination of emergency shelter, violate the Federal and State Constitutions, statutes and regulations. Plaintiffs pray for an injunction requiring defendants, *inter alia,* to provide the aforementioned benefits and to "locate and make available additional emergency housing units within New York City so that all families in need of emergency housing obtain that housing in New York City immediately, and so that families can, where appropriate, be given emergency housing near their children's schools." Plaintiffs also seek to enjoin defendants from denying emergency housing to families in need of such housing and from placing such families in housing that is dangerous to the life, health, and safety of their children and which is inadequate to meet the family's needs.***

PROCEDURAL HISTORY AND DECISION AT SPECIAL TERM IN McCAIN V. KOCH

By an interim order dated June 20, 1983, Special Term (Greenfield, J.), directed the City DSS and HPD, when providing emergency housing for homeless families with children, to assure, insofar as practicable, that such housing meets specified minimal standards of health, safety and decency suitable for young children, including placement in light of educational needs; to afford emergency shelter recipients with timely and adequate notice of any proposed termination, and a hearing; to designate an individual to facilitate implementation of the order; and required State and City DSS to provide public assistance, food stamps, and Medicaid benefits for which emergency shelter recipients are eligible without interruption, to the extent practicable.

On September 29, 1983, the commissioner of the State DSS issued an Administrative Directive.*** which largely incorporated the terms of the interim order and made them binding on a State-wide basis. It directs social services departments "to assist homeless persons in obtaining housing." The Administrative Directive also indicates that "[e]mergency housing must either be provided immediately if a homeless person is determined eligible or written notice must be given that no assistance will be provided where a homeless person is determined ineligible. A person who is determined ineligible shall be advised of the right to an expedited State Fair Hearing."

The State Commissioner also promulgated *** provisions requir[ing] local social services departments semiannually to inspect hotels and motels used for client referrals and verify that they meet certain enumerated standards. Referrals are prohibited to facilities not verified as meeting these criteria.

*** Justice Greenfield held "once the defendants have undertaken to provide emergency shelter, whether for 30 days pursuant to AFDC or beyond, instead of providing direct cash grants," defendants must ensure that the shelter meets "minimal standards of cleanliness, warmth, space and rudimentary conveniences." The Court invoked its equitable powers to compel compliance with reasonable minimum standards, reasoning that the homeless as "interim wards of a governmental entity" are entitled to no less than convicted criminals.***

DECISION AT SPECIAL TERM IN MATTER OF FULTON v. KRAUSKOPF

[I]n Matter of *Fulton v. Krauskopf,* Special Term (Greenfield, J.), issued a preliminary injunction directing respondents, the State and City Commissioners of DSS, to provide an allowance for actual school transportation costs on an individualized basis to homeless children and their parents. Special Term held that the $18 weekly travel allowance provided to parents as a matter of City policy was inadequate.***

McCAIN v. KOCH

1. Right to Emergency Shelter

The threshold issue in *McCain v. Koch* is whether homeless families with children are entitled to emergency shelter. We reverse Special Term's order of May 30, 1985,

[and] grant a preliminary injunction barring the denial of emergency shelter to home-less families.*** Plaintiffs assert that defendants are obligated to provide emergency shelter to them under the EAF program, the State and Federal Constitutional guaran-tees of equal protection, and N.Y. Constitution, article XVII, § 1. The proposed inter-venors assert that in the event a preliminary injunction is not granted, they will be forced to sleep on the floors, desks, and counter tops of IMCs and EAUs. The irreparable injury to be sustained by homeless families clearly outweighs the burden that providing tem-porary emergency shelter imposes upon defendants. Consideration of the public inter-est also strongly favors an injunction pending a final determination on the merits. In many instances, parents of children in homeless families lack employment and adequate support systems. The public interest is better served by having them housed, than by forcing them to find shelter and food that may be beyond their means to attain.*** As the State EAF Plan does not resolve plaintiffs' claim of entitlement to emergency shel-ter beyond 30 days, we find it necessary to reach plaintiffs' Constitutional claims.

The City makes emergency shelter available to homeless single men, who meet the eligibility criteria of the HR program, or who suffer a physical or mental dysfunction.*** Under the equal protection guarantees of the State and Federal Constitutions, "any clas-sification which denies to one class of needy persons public assistance which is available to all others, cannot be justified unless it is rationally related to a legitimate State inter-est."*** There is no apparent reasonable basis for the City's denial of emergency shel-ter to plaintiffs. [I]n *Eldredge v. Koch* *** we upheld the Constitutional right of homeless single women to shelter equal to that provided for homeless men under the Callahan decree. It is axiomatic that children need stable, secure homes and are among those least able to bear the hardships of poverty and destitution. Public policy strongly favors assistance to families with destitute children.*** Indeed, the needs of plaintiffs are greater than those of single adults.*** Defendants' less than equal treatment of plain-tiffs is plainly irrational.

It is also likely that plaintiffs will succeed on their claim that N.Y. Constitution article XVII obligates defendants to provide emergency shelter for homeless families. New York State has made the care of its needy residents a Constitutional mandate. N.Y. Constitution, article XVII, § 1 provides: "The aid, care and support of the needy are public concerns and shall be provided by the state and by such of its subdivisions, and in such manner and by such means, as the legislature may from time to time determine." The framers of the State Constitution intended article XVII to require the State to take positive steps to assist the needy, rather than to voice aspiration towards ideal social policy.***

The tenet that the provision for assistance is a positive duty, not a matter of leg-islative grace, is well expressed in *Tucker v. Toia* (43 N.Y.2d 1 [1977]) in circumstances analogous to those in the present case. In *Tucker*, the Court of Appeals noted: "Although our Constitution provides the Legislature with discretion in determining the means by which [the duty] is to be effectuated, in determining the amount of aid, and in classi-fying recipients and defining the term 'needy,' it unequivocally prevents the Legislature from simply refusing to aid those whom it has classified as needy."*** There, the Court held violative of article XVII, § 1 a statute pursuant to which emancipated single moth-ers under age 21 were denied HR [home relief] benefits until they had commenced support proceedings against their parents or legally responsible relatives and obtained orders of disposition.

It is uncontroverted that plaintiffs are classified as needy. Social Services Law § 397 (1) requires that aid be provided to families with destitute children when the families are unable to provide the necessary care. There is ample evidence in the record for us to conclude that the City DSS current policy of only providing cash allowances and information concerning housing availability amounts to the denial of aid to homeless families. The number of such families, approximately 2,500, and the average period of homelessness, seven months to one year, bespeak the dimensions of the problem. In view of the scarcity of decent low-income housing, the City's policy simply ignores the brutal realities of plaintiffs' situation. It contravenes both the letter and spirit of the State's affirmative obligation to aid all its needy residents under N.Y. Constitution, article XVII, § 1.***

2. *The June 22, 1984 Preliminary Injunction*

Plaintiffs seek a declaration of their right to emergency shelter based upon mandatory, not precatory, statutory and Constitutional directives. As exemplified by *Klostermann v. Cuomo* (61 N.Y.2d 525, 539 [1984]), such claims present a justiciable controversy even though the activity contemplated on the State's part may be complex and rife with the exercise of discretion.

We are bound to follow the holdings of the Court of Appeals. In light of that Court's holdings in Matter of *Bernstein v. Toia* (43 N.Y.2d 437 [1977]) and *Tucker v. Toia* (supra.) That the adequacy of the level of welfare benefits is a matter committed to the discretion of the Legislature, we are unable to afford the plaintiffs complete and meaningful relief. The inability of Courts to set even minimum standards for meeting "the legitimate needs of each recipient" (*see, Matter of Bernstein v. Toia,* supra., at 449) upon the failure of the Legislature to do so is discouraging, saddening, and disheartening. When thousands of children are put at risk in their physical and mental health, and subject to inevitable emotional scarring, because of the failure of City and State officials to provide emergency shelter for them which meets minimum standards of decency and habitability, it is time for the Court of Appeals to reexamine and, hopefully, change its prior holdings in this area. The lives and characters of the young are too precious to be dealt with in a way justified, as argued, on the ground that the government's efforts are more than token. They may be more than token, but they are inadequate. On this record and on the authority of Matter of *Bernstein v. Toia* (supra.), we reluctantly conclude that Special Term erred in invoking its equitable powers to compel compliance with certain reasonable minimal standards.

In Matter of *Bernstein v. Toia* (supra.), petitioners contended that NY Constitution article XVII obligated the State to provide public assistance recipients with individualized shelter grants sufficient to meet rent expenses, rather than flat grants in accordance with a schedule of maximum allowances. The Court of Appeals rejected this contention.***

The plaintiffs in the present case have persuasively documented the unsafe and squalid conditions prevalent in welfare hotel accommodations, conditions particularly undesirable for young children. On the other hand, the evidence demonstrates that the emergency housing provided by the City "is more than token and is genuine and meaningful."*** In light of the broad discretion vested in the Legislature, we cannot conclude that plaintiffs are likely to prove that article XVII substantively guaranteed minimal physical standards of cleanliness, warmth, space and rudimentary convenience in emergency shelter.

The system of procedural safeguards delineated by Special Term duplicates those already set forth, more extensively, in social services regulations which predated this litigation. (*See, e.g., 18 N.Y.C.R.R. 351.8*, 355.2, 355.4, 372.5.) As the record reflects only isolated instances, rather than a continuing pattern of violations, broad-based relief was unwarranted. The other injunctive relief granted by Special Term also constituted improper and undue intrusion into the administration of public assistance.***

MATTER OF FULTON v. KOCH

*** Contrary to the contention of the city DSS, this controversy is not moot. The City's failure, either to rehouse families in the area of their children's schools, or provide an adequate transportation allowance to cover the expense of commuting to school for children until they receive a transportation pass as well as for the parents of children too young to travel alone, presents an ongoing problem of public importance which is properly entertainable.***

Under New York Constitution, article XI, § 1 and Education Law article 65, the State must provide free education to all children over age five. Compulsory attendance on a full-time basis is required, with exceptions not here relevant.*** Education Law § 3209 squarely places responsibility upon public welfare officials in local social services districts to provide indigent children with suitable clothing, shoes, books, food and other necessaries to enable them to attend school.*** Funds for school transportation are a necessity under the meaning of these provisions. In our view, these statutes clearly obligate City DSS to provide actual transportation expenses, both for children until they obtain transportation passes from the Board of Education, and for the parents of young children who must be accompanied to school.

We agree with Special Term that the recently adopted City DSS policy of providing a flat travel allowance of $18 per week for parents is inadequate. In many instances, the parents of children who reside in emergency shelters must travel through more than one fare zone each day. It makes no provision for children until their receipt of a transportation pass from the Board of Education. A flat grant forces these families to make an impossible choice between adequate nourishment and education. This policy is unconstitutional in education. This policy is unconstitutional in that it deprives indigent children of the right to free education and amounts to a refusal to aid needy children.***

Notes and Questions

1.   On January 17, 2003, New York Mayor Michael Bloomberg and Legal Aid Society President Daniel L. Greenberg announced a settlement in the 20-year long litigation battle over homeless families in New York City. The agreement called for: (1) the formation of a three-member panel charged with oversight of City services to homeless families and making recommendations to the court; (2) a commitment to avoid litigation; and (3) the implementation of "standards for client responsibility" that,

> require families to follow an independent living plan, seek and accept suitable housing, and avoid 'gross misconduct.' A failure to relate to these standards will result in a discharge to permanent housing. A family which refuses to sign a lease will not be eligible for shelter because a suitable apartment was available.

Mayor Michael R. Bloomberg and Legal Aid Society President Daniel Greenberg Announce Historic Agreement on 20-Year Homeless Family Litigation, available at http://www.nyc.gov/html/dhs/html/pr011703.html.

How would you expect this settlement to affect the plaintiffs in the *Koch* litigation? Is this a net gain for homeless families?

2. *Koch* addresses the problem of homelessness in the mid-1980s. The extensive social and legal background to this problem is described by Bradley R. Haywood, *Note: The Right to Shelter as a Fundamental Interest under the New York State Constitution*, 34 COLUM. HUM. RTS. L. REV. 157 (2002). The issue of homelessness rose to national attention largely as a result of the confluence of two trends: the prevalence of homelessness among military veterans, and the deinstitutionalization of the mentally ill. The National Coalition for Homeless Veterans estimates that 23 percent of the homeless population are veterans. Of these, 47 percent are veterans of the Vietnam War:

> In addition to the complex set of factors affecting all homelessness *** extreme shortage of affordable housing, livable income, and access to health care *** a large number of displaced and at-risk veterans live with lingering effects of Post Traumatic Stress Disorder and substance abuse, compounded by a lack of family and social support networks.

National Coalition for Homeless Veterans, *Background Statistics*, 2003, *available at* http://www.nchv.org.

3. The problems that elevate the incidence of homelessness among veterans are, in the understanding of the National Coalition for Homeless Veterans, significantly related to their mental health, which is negatively affected by the experience of war and drug abuse. The plight of homeless veterans highlights the issue of the status of the mentally ill in American society. Christopher Jencks estimates that in 1987, 22% of the homeless in large cities had spent time in mental hospitals. *See* CHRISTOPHER JENCKS, THE HOMELESS 22 (1994). "The best available data suggest that in 1987 at least 1.7 million working-age Americans had mental problems so severe they could not hold a job. Roughly 100,000 of these people were homeless." *Id.* at 39.

By 1975, institutionalization of the mentally ill had fallen from a high of 468 per 100,000 adults in 1950, to 119. *Id.* At 29. So although a trend of deinstitutionalization was already evident, a sea-change in American attitudes was reflected in *O'Connor v. Donaldson*, wherein the U.S. Supreme Court ruled that "mental illness alone was not sufficient justification for involuntary confinement." *Id.* Consequently, "[h]ospitals had started discharging chronic patients with nowhere to go because the courts said these patients had a legal right to leave. But once the taboo was broken, the practice [of deinstitutionalization] soon spread to patients who had not insisted on leaving. As time went on, even patients who were willing to stay in the hospital got pushed out, on the grounds that a hospital was not a hotel." *Id.* at 33.

> If the courts had not limited involuntary commitment and if state hospitals had not started discharging patients with nowhere to go, the proportion of the adult population living in state hospitals would probably be about the same today as in 1975. Were that the case, state hospitals would have sheltered 234,000 mental patients on an average night in 1990 rather than 92,000. It follows that 142,000 people who would have been sleeping in a state hospital under the 1975 rules were sleeping somewhere else by 1990. On any given night, some of these people were in psychiatric wards of general hospitals, and a few were in private psychiatric hospitals, but many were in shelters or on the streets. *Id.* at 39.

4.   The National Coalition for the Homeless notes that "families with children are by far the fastest-growing sector of the homeless population. Children alone compose about 39% of the homeless population." National Coalition for the Homeless, *Families, Children and Homelessness, available at* http://www.nationalhomeless.org/education/families.html (last visited May 5, 2004). The U.S. is one of only two countries in the world that has not ratified the Convention on the Rights of the Child. *See* Chapter 3.D, *supra.* What might be the implications of ratification for homeless children in the U.S.?

5.   *Legislative Deference and Constitutional Obligation.* "The aid, care and support of the needy are public concerns and shall be provided by the state and by such of its subdivisions, and in such a manner and by such means, as the legislature may from time to time determine." N.Y. Const. art. XVII, § 1. In *McCain*, the court opinion states that "provision for assistance is a positive duty" and that "the constitution provides the Legislature with discretion in determining the means by which [the duty] is effectuated." 117 A.D.2d 198, 215. Based on *Tucker* (43 N.Y.2d 1) and *McCain*, what are the state's obligations with regard to aid, care, and support? What balance is struck between legislative deference and constitutional obligation? In *McCain*, the court notes a prior holding that flat grants may be appropriate for shelter grants (citing *Bernstein*, 43 N.Y.2d 437), but that flat allowances for children's travel to school are inadequate. 117 A.D.2d 198, 217 & 220. Are the two holdings consistent?

6.   *"All its Needy."* *Tucker* states that New York cannot employ statutory "methods which ignore the realities of the needy's plight and the State's affirmative obligation to aid all its needy." 43 N.Y.2d 1, 9. Children receiving home relief are classified as needy according to *Tucker*. *Id.* The court quotes *Matter of Barrie v. Lavine* (40 N.Y.2d. 565) stating that, "[t]he Legislature may in its discretion deny aid to employable persons who may be properly deemed not to be needy when they have wrongfully refused an opportunity for employment." *Id.* The *McCain* court notes that homeless single persons suffering from mental or physical disability have a right to shelter and holds that families with children have the same right to emergency shelter. 117 A.D.2d 198, 213–14. What criteria does the court use to determine whether a particular group is classified as needy in *Tucker* and in *McCain*? The notes above describe the disproportionate number of veterans and mentally ill persons among the homeless. Can those groups be considered needy as such and extended protections under N.Y. Const. art. XVII, § 1? What factors may be affecting the court's decisions in distinguishing among needy groups?

4.   *The Right to Education*

EDGEWOOD INDEPENDENT SCHOOL DISTRICT v. KIRBY

777 S.W.2d 391 (Tex. 1989)

MAUZY, Justice.

At issue is the constitutionality of the Texas system for financing the education of public school children. Edgewood Independent School District, sixty-seven other school districts, and numerous individual school children and parents filed suit seeking a declaration that the Texas school financing system violates the Texas Constitution. The trial Court rendered judgment to that effect and declared that the system violates the Texas Constitution, article I, section 3, article I, section 19, and article VII, section 1. By a 2-1 vote, the Court of appeals reversed that judgment and declared the system constitutional. 761 S.W.2d 859 (1988). We reverse the judgment of the Court of appeals and, with modification, affirm that of the trial Court.

The basic facts of this cause are not in dispute. The only question is whether those facts describe a public school financing system that meets the requirements of the Constitution. As summarized and excerpted, the facts are as follows:

There are approximately three million public school children in Texas. The legislature finances the education of these children through a combination of revenues supplied by the state itself and revenues supplied by local school districts which are governmental subdivisions of the state. Of total education costs, the state provides about forty-two percent, school districts provide about fifty percent, and the remainder comes from various other sources including federal funds. School districts derive revenues from local ad valorem property taxes, and the state raises funds from a variety of sources including the sales tax and various severance and excise taxes.

There are glaring disparities in the abilities of the various school districts to raise revenues from property taxes because taxable property wealth varies greatly from district to district. The wealthiest district has over $14,000,000 of property wealth per student, while the poorest has approximately $20,000; this disparity reflects a 700 to 1 ratio. The 300,000 students in the lowest-wealth schools have less than 3% *of* the state's property wealth to support their education while the 300,000 students in the highest-wealth schools have over 25% of the state's property wealth; thus the 300,000 students in the wealthiest districts have more than eight times the property value to support their education as the 300,000 students in the poorest districts. The average property wealth in the 100 wealthiest districts is more than twenty times greater than the average property wealth in the 100 poorest districts. Edgewood I.S.D. has $38,854 in property wealth per student; Alamo Heights I.S.D., in the same county, has $570,109 in property wealth per student.

The state has tried for many years to lessen the disparities through various efforts to supplement the poorer districts. Through the Foundation School Program, the state currently attempts to ensure that each district has sufficient funds to provide its students with at least a basic education. See Tex. Educ. Code § 16.002. Under this program, state aid is distributed to the various districts according to a complex formula such that property-poor districts receive more state aid than do property-rich districts. However, the Foundation School Program does not cover even the cost of meeting the state-mandated minimum requirements. Most importantly, there are no Foundation School Program allotments for school facilities or for debt service. The basic allotment and the transportation allotment understate actual costs, and the career ladder salary supplement for teachers is underfunded. For these reasons and more, almost all school districts spend additional local funds. Low-wealth districts use a significantly greater proportion of their local funds to pay the debt service on construction bonds while high-wealth districts are able to use their funds to pay for a wide array of enrichment programs.

Because of the disparities in district property wealth, spending per student varies widely, ranging from $2,112 to $19,333. Under the existing system, an average of $2,000 more per year is spent on each of the 150,000 students in the wealthiest districts than is spent on the 150,000 students in the poorest districts.***

Property-poor districts are trapped in a cycle of poverty from which there is no opportunity to free themselves. Because of their inadequate tax base, they must tax at significantly higher rates in order to meet minimum requirements for accreditation; yet their educational programs are typically inferior. The location of new industry and development is strongly influenced by tax rates and the quality of local schools. Thus, the property-poor districts with their high tax rates and inferior schools are unable to attract new industry or development and so have little opportunity to improve their tax base.

The amount of money spent on a student's education has a real and meaningful impact on the educational opportunity offered that student. High-wealth districts are able to provide for their students broader educational experiences including more extensive curricula, more up-to-date technological equipment, better libraries and library personnel, teacher aides, counseling services, lower student-teacher ratios, better facilities, parental involvement programs, and drop-out prevention programs. They are also better able to attract and retain experienced teachers and administrators.

The differences in the quality of educational programs offered are dramatic. For example, San Elizario I.S.D. offers no foreign language, no pre-kindergarten program, no chemistry, no physics, no calculus, and no college preparatory or honors program. It also offers virtually no extra-curricular activities such as band, debate, or football. At the time of trial, one-third of Texas school districts did not even meet the state-mandated standards for maximum class size. The great majority of these are low-wealth districts. In many instances, wealthy and poor districts are found contiguous to one another within the same county.

Based on these facts, the trial Court concluded that the school financing system violates the Texas Constitution's equal rights guarantee of article I, section 3, the due course of law guarantee of article I, section 19, and the "efficiency" mandate of article VII section 1. The Court of appeals reversed. We reverse the judgment of the Court of appeals and, with modification, affirm the judgment of the trial Court.

Article VII, section 1 of the Texas Constitution provides:

A general diffusion of knowledge being essential to the preservation of the liberties and rights of the people, it shall be the duty of the legislature of the State to establish and make suitable provision for the support and maintenance of an efficient system of public free schools.

The Court of appeals declined to address petitioners' challenge under this provision and concluded instead that its interpretation was a "political question."

Said the Court:

That provision does, of course, require that the school system be "efficient," but the provision provides no guidance as to how this or any other Court may arrive at a determination of what is efficient or inefficient. Given the enormous complexity of a school system educating three million children, this Court concludes that which is, or is not, "efficient" is essentially a political question not suitable for judicial review.***

We disagree. This is not an area in which the Constitution vests exclusive discretion in the legislature; rather the language of article VII, section 1 imposes on the legislature an affirmative duty to establish and provide for the public free schools. This duty is not committed unconditionally to the legislature's discretion, but instead is accompanied by standards. By express constitutional mandate, the legislature must make "suitable" provision for an "efficient" system for the essential purpose of a "general diffusion of knowledge." While these are admittedly not precise terms, they do provide a standard by which this Court must, when called upon to do so, measure the constitutionality of the legislature's actions.*** We do not undertake this responsibility lightly and we begin with a presumption of constitutionality. [I]f the system is not "efficient" or not "suitable," the legislature has not discharged its constitutional duty and it is our duty to say so.

The Texas Constitution derives its force from the people of Texas. This is the fundamental law under which the people of this state have consented to be governed. In construing the language of article VII, section 1, we consider "the intent of the people who adopted it." However, because of the difficulties inherent in determining the intent of voters over a century ago, we rely heavily on the literal text. We seek its meaning with the understanding that the Constitution was ratified to function as an organic document to govern society and institutions as they evolve through time.***

The State argues that, as used in article VII, section 1, the word "efficient" was intended to suggest a simple and inexpensive system. Under the Reconstruction Constitution of 1869, the people had been subjected to a militaristic school system with the state exercising absolute authority over the training of children. See Tex. CONSTITUTION art. VII, § 1, interp. commentary (Vernon 1955). Thus, the State contends that delegates to the 1875 Constitutional Convention deliberately inserted into this provision the word "efficient" in order to prevent the establishment of another Reconstruction-style, highly centralized school system.

While there is some evidence that many delegates wanted an economical school system, there is no persuasive evidence that the delegates used the term "efficient" to achieve that end.*** It must be recognized that the Constitution requires an "efficient," not an "economical," "inexpensive," or "cheap" system. The language of the Constitution must be presumed to have been carefully selected. The framers used the term "economical" elsewhere and could have done so here had they so intended.

There is no reason to think that "efficient" meant anything different in 1875 from what it now means. "Efficient" conveys the meaning of effective or productive of results and connotes the use of resources so as to produce results with little waste; this meaning does not appear to have changed over time .***

Considering "the general spirit of the times and the prevailing sentiments of the people," it is apparent from the historical record that those who drafted and ratified article VII, section 1 never contemplated the possibility that such gross inequalities could exist within an "efficient" system.[6] At the Constitutional Convention of 1875, delegates spoke at length on the importance of education for all the people of this state, rich and poor alike. The chair of the education committee, speaking on behalf of the majority of the committee, declared:

---

[6] Delegate Henry Cline, who first proposed the term "efficient," urged the convention to ensure that sufficient funds would be provided to those districts most in need. S. McKay, Debates in the Constitutional Convention of 1875 217 (1930). He noted that those with some wealth were already making extravagant provisions for the schooling of their own children and described a public school system in which those funds that had selfishly been used by the wealthy would be made available for the education of all the children of the state. Id. at 217–18.

[Education] must be classed among the abstract rights, based on apparent natural justice, which we individually concede to the State, for the general welfare, when we enter into a great compact as a commonwealth. I boldly assert that it is for the general welfare of all, rich and poor, male and female, that the means of a common school education should, if possible, be placed within the reach of every child in the State.

S. McKay, Debates in the Texas Constitutional Convention of 1875 198 (1930). Other delegates recognized the importance of a diffusion of knowledge among the masses not only for the preservation of democracy, but for the prevention of crime and for the growth of the economy. In addition to specific comments in the constitutional debates, the structure of school finance at the time indicates that such gross disparities were not contemplated. Apart from cities, there was no district structure for schools nor any authority to tax locally for school purposes under the Constitution of 1876.

The 1876 Constitution provided a structure whereby the burdens of school taxation fell equally and uniformly across the state, and each student in the state was entitled to exactly the same distribution of funds. See Tex. CONSTITUTION art. VII, § 5 (1876). The state's school fund was initially apportioned strictly on a per capita basis. Also, a poll tax of one dollar per voter was levied across the state for school purposes.*** These per capita methods of taxation and of revenue distribution seem simplistic compared to today's system; however they do indicate that the people were contemplating that the tax burden would be shared uniformly and that the state's resources would be distributed on an even, equitable basis.

If our state's population had grown at the same rate in each district and if the taxable wealth in each district had also grown at the same rate, efficiency could probably have been maintained within the structure of the present system. That did not happen. Wealth, in its many forms, has not appeared with geographic symmetry. The economic development of the state has not been uniform. Some cities have grown dramatically, while their sister communities have remained static or have shrunk. Formulas that once fit have been knocked askew. Although local conditions vary, the constitutionally imposed state responsibility for an efficient education system is the same for all citizens regardless of where they live.

We conclude that, in mandating "efficiency," the constitutional framers and ratifiers did not intend a system with such vast disparities as now exist. Instead, they stated clearly that the purpose of an efficient system was to provide for a "general diffusion of knowledge." The present system, by contrast, provides not for a diffusion that is general, but for one that is limited and unbalanced. The resultant inequalities are thus directly contrary to the constitutional vision of efficiency.***

By statutory directives, the legislature has attempted through the years to reduce disparities and improve the system. There have been good faith efforts on the part of many public officials, and some progress has been made. However, as the undisputed facts of this case make painfully clear, the reality is that the constitutional mandate has not been met.

The legislature's recent efforts have focused primarily on increasing the state's contributions. More money allocated under the present system would reduce some of the existing disparities between districts but would at best only postpone the reform that is necessary to make the system efficient. A band-aid will not suffice; the system itself must be changed.

We hold that the state's school financing system is neither financially efficient nor efficient in the sense of providing for a "general diffusion of knowledge" statewide, and therefore that it violates article VII, section 1 of the Texas Constitution. Efficiency does not require a per capita distribution, but it also does not allow concentrations of resources in property-rich school districts that are taxing low when property-poor districts that are taxing high cannot generate sufficient revenues to meet even minimum standards. There must be a direct and close correlation between a district's tax effort and the educational resources available to it; in other words, districts must have substantially equal access to similar revenues per pupil at similar levels of tax effort. Children who live in poor districts and children who live in rich districts must be afforded a substantially equal opportunity to have access to educational funds. Certainly, this much is required if the state is to educate its populace efficiently and provide for a general diffusion of knowledge statewide.

Under article VII section 1, the obligation is the legislature's to provide for an efficient system. In setting appropriations, the legislature must establish priorities according to constitutional mandate; equalizing educational opportunity cannot be relegated to an "if funds are left over" basis. We recognize that there are and always will be strong public interests competing for available state funds. However, the legislature's responsibility to support public education is different because it is constitutionally imposed. Whether the legislature acts directly or enlists local government to help meet its obligation, the end product must still be what the Constitution commands—i.e. an efficient system of public free schools throughout the state.*** This does not mean that the state may not recognize differences in area costs or in costs associated with providing an equalized educational opportunity to atypical students or disadvantaged students. Nor does it mean that local communities would be precluded from supplementing an efficient system established by the legislature; however any local enrichment must derive solely from local tax effort.

Some have argued that reform in school finance will eliminate local control, but this argument has no merit. An efficient system does not preclude the ability of communities to exercise local control over the education of their children. It requires only that the funds available for education be distributed equitably and evenly. An efficient system will actually allow for more local control, not less. It will provide property-poor districts with economic alternatives that are not now available to them. Only if alternatives are indeed available can a community exercise the control of making choices.

Our decision today is not without precedent. Courts in nine other states with similar school financing systems have ruled those systems to be unconstitutional for varying reasons.***

Although we have ruled the school financing system to be unconstitutional, we do not now instruct the legislature as to the specifics of the legislation it should enact; nor do we order it to raise taxes. The legislature has primary responsibility to decide how best to achieve an efficient system. We decide only the nature of the constitutional mandate and whether that mandate has been met.***

Because of the enormity of the task now facing the legislature and because we want to avoid any sudden disruption in the educational processes, we modify the trial Court's judgment so as to stay the effect of its injunction until May 1, 1990.[7] However, let there

---

[7] We note that the Governor has already called a special session of the legislature to begin November 14, 1989; the school finance problem could be resolved in that session.

be no misunderstanding. A remedy is long overdue. The legislature must take immediate action. We reverse the judgment of the Court of appeals and affirm the trial Court's
judgment as modified.

Notes and Questions

1.   *The Aftermath of* Edgewood. Following the decision the legislature quickly enacted
a school financing bill, in the face of the Texas Supreme Court's threat to shut down
the schools. The measure, enacted under heavy pressure from the wealthy districts,
increased state funding to poor schools, but failed to address the gross disparity between
rich and poor districts, and thus was immediately challenged by the *Edgewood* plaintiffs.
In an expedited ruling, the Supreme Court held that the legislature had failed to implement its ruling by not ensuring a "direct and close correlation between a district's tax
effort and the educational resources available to it." *Edgewood v. Kirby* (II), 804 S.W.2d
491, 496 (Tex. 1991). In response, the legislature enacted Senate Bill 351 consolidating
school districts for tax purposes. The rich school districts successfully challenged this
legislation as unconstitutional on the ground that voter approval had not been sought.
Carrollton-Farmers Branch Indep. Sch. Dist. v. Edgewood, 826 S.W.2d 489, 491 (Tex. 1992)
(*Edgewood III*). After a proposed constitutional amendment was rejected by voters the
legislature finally adopted a compromise measure that forces the wealthy districts to
help fund the poor districts while providing them with several options as to how to do
it, and thereby preserving much-coveted local control. Although both sides challenged
Senate Bill 7 it passed constitutional muster, with the Supreme Court rejecting the arguments of poor districts that the plan was inadequate as well as the wealthy districts' claim
that it was an unconstitutional state property tax. *Edgewood Indep. Sch. Dist. v. Meno*, 917
S.W.2d 717 (Tex. 1995) (*Edgewood IV*). For an in depth discussion and analysis of these
events, *see* J. Steven Farr & Mark Trachtenberg, *The Edgewood Drama: An Epic Quest for
Education Equity*, 17 YALE L. & POL'Y REV. 607 (1999). According to the authors, "by
almost every indicator, Texas schools have made significant improvements in recent
years. Between 1994 and 1998, the proportions of students passing all [Texas stan-
dardized tests] rose from 55% to 77%.*** Minority and economically disadvantaged
students have made some of the greatest gains." *Id.* At 706.

2.   Nevertheless, the funding measure designated "Robin Hood" by its detractors continues to generate controversy. Both poor and wealthy school districts in Texas contend that the education budget is inadequate to meet current needs, and further
litigation brought by several property-rich districts is pending. The current suit alleges
that the revenue-sharing financing scheme violates the Texas constitutional prohibition against state-wide property taxes. By the time the case reaches the Texas Supreme
Court, most of the justices who rendered the original decision will have retired from
the bench.

The *Edgewood* court notes that nine other states had found that their educational
systems do not meet their state constitutional mandates. Washington and Arizona are
two examples. The Supreme Court of the state of Washington declared that a local
school district, the Seattle School District, did not meet the constitutionally required
standard of education. *Seattle School District #1 v. State of Washington*, 585 P.2d 71 (Wash.
1978). In reaching this decision, the court relied on Washington State Constitution
Article 9, § 1 which states that "[i]t is the Paramount duty of the state to make ample
provision for the education of all children residing within its [the state's] borders ***"
Like the Texas court, the court in *Seattle* held that the educational provision in the state
constitution imposed an affirmative duty on the state legislature, and that judicial review

of the educational system was appropriate in order to ensure that the state legislature met its affirmative duty. *Id.* at 85–87. The court contrasted its view that providing education was an affirmative duty with other interpretations of the state constitution arguing that education was a moral obligation or policy choice. *Id.* at 91. The *Seattle* court found that an affirmative duty exists based on the constitutional language describing education as a mandatory and paramount duty. *Id.* at 85. Correlative of the state's duty to provide an education is a child's right to an education. *Id.* at 92.

> In the court's view, the state's constitutional duty and a child's educational right are [duties which go] beyond reading, writing, and arithmetic. It also embraces broad educational opportunities needed in the contemporary setting to equip our children for their role as citizens and as potential competitors in today's market as well as in the market place of ideas.*** Education plays a critical role in a free society. It must prepare our children to participate intelligently and effectively in our open political system to ensure that system's survival.*** The constitutional right to have the State "make ample provision for the education of all (resident) children" would be hollow indeed if the possessor of the right could not compete adequately in our open political system, in the labor market, or in the market place of ideas.

Id. at 94–95. Neither the constitution nor the court offer an explicit definition of the term "ample provision for the education." In looking to state constitutional language to support its vision of education, the court contrasts the broad language of "ample provision" with other state constitutions which appear to provide a lesser standard of education, using words such as "general and uniform school system." *Id.* at 85. The court also looks to legislative history to support its interpretation that education is 'paramount' and thus "superior in rank, above all others [state duties]." *Id.* at 91.

In contrast to the Texas decision, the Washington court did not explicitly discuss lower income school districts, or the specifics of funding schemes, but rather described the general educational standard that was to be "amply provided" for all children. Although the funding challenges faced in Washington and Texas are similar, the tone of the opinion in *Seattle* was quite different.

The Supreme Court of Arizona reviewed and reversed a lower court decision and held that a state statutory education funding scheme (comprised of 45 percent local property tax, 45 percent state funding and 10 percent other sources) violated the Arizona Constitution. *Roosevelt Elementary School District # 66 v. Bishop*, 877 P.2d 806, 808–10 (Ariz. 1994). In outlining the facts, the court focused on disparities in educational facilities and contrasted, for example, unsafe school buildings with schools that included domed stadiums. *Id.* at 808.

The court held that the funding scheme was unconstitutional because it violated the Arizona constitution's requirements on the establishment and maintenance of public education. Article XI § 1 of the constitution provides as follows:

> The Legislature shall enact such laws as shall provide for the establishment and maintenance of a general and uniform public school system ***." Funding is specifically addressed in § 10, "the Legislature shall make such appropriations, to be met by taxation, as shall ensure the proper maintenance of all State educational institutions *** [the Legislature] shall make such special appropriations as shall provide for their development and improvement."

The court held that the disparities between districts are not unconstitutional per se, but rather that the existing disparities resulting from state-chosen financing schemes are unconstitutional. *Id.* at 815. One important implication of this holding is that disparities between funding in different schools can continue to exist. The court provided the following explanation:

> Units in "general and uniform" state systems need not be exactly the same, identical, or equal. Funding mechanisms that provide sufficient funds to educate children on substantially equal terms tend to satisfy the general and uniform requirement. School financing systems which themselves create gross disparities are not general and uniform.*** As long as the statewide system provides an adequate education, and is not itself the cause of substantial disparities, local political subdivisions can go above and beyond the statewide system.[8]

The court noted that the legislative history of the constitutional provision included evidence of the importance with which the framers of the state constitution regarded education. The court noted that "early drafts of the education article began with '[a] general diffusion of knowledge and intelligence being essential to the preservation of the rights and liberties of the people' *** and '[t]he stability of a Republican form of Government depending mainly on the intelligence of the people.'" *Id.* at 812. The court also pointed out that a large wave of immigration was occurring during the drafting of the article. *Id.* The court used this as evidence of the framers' intent to extend education to all groups in order to "preserv[e] America's unity while wave after wave of people arrived from other countries ***. [C]onventioneers believed that a free society could not exist without educated participants." *Id.*

The Arizona court discusses the economic disparities between districts (*e.g.*, a lower-income district with an assessed value per pupil of $18,293 in contrast to a higher-income district with an assessed value of $130,778 per pupil). *Id.* at 809. The *Roosevelt* court opinion also discusses the need for an educated citizenry state-wide, and states that "[f]inancing a general and uniform public school system is in our collective self-interest." *Id.* at 816.

3. *When Is a Disparity Unconstitutional?* Examination of the funding scheme in Texas revealed great disparities (a 700 to one difference in per pupil spending by district), while in Arizona the disparity in per pupil spending was closer to a seven to one difference. *Edgewood*, 777 S.W.2d 391, 391; *Roosevelt*, 877 P.2d 806, 809. *Roosevelt* focused on differences in school facilities, whereas the Texas opinion discussed the disparity of educational experiences more broadly. Both opinions found the state funding to be unconstitutional. What accounts for the differences in these opinions? What factors did the courts analyze in finding each system to be unconstitutional? What seem to be the most important factors in determining the constitutionality of disparities in a state education program?

4. *Absolute Right or Privilege?* As described in *Edgewood, Seattle*, and *Roosevelt*, is education an absolute right, a privilege, or something else? *Cf.* Wesley Hohfeld's construction of jural categories in Chapter 2, *supra.*

---

8   *Roosevelt*, 877 P. 2d at 816. Since the court addressed this argument with regard to Article XI of the constitution, it did not address an equal protection argument made by the school districts based on the state constitution's privileges and immunities clause. The equal protection argument was particularly complicated since previous decisions conflicted over whether education was a fundamental right and, therefore, which standard of review applied to relevant legislation. *Id.* at 811.

[T]here exist rights as absolutes and there are legal freedoms, liberties, or privileges (as synonyms) which, although of lesser stature than rights, are still so basically important that they may not be invaded unless there is a strong judicially recognized reason.

As stated in the body of the opinion, the mandate of Const. art. 9, §§ 1 and 2 is concerned with a true "right" (or absolute). Thus, the State's only answer is either compliance or a showing that its attempt to comply was met with interference by those claiming the right.

Seattle, 585 P. 2d 71, 93. What are the implications of treating education as a right, a privilege, or a freedom for schools and students in a particular state?

5. *Local Control.* Should education be regulated locally, statewide or nationally? The courts in Texas and Arizona note that while the overall system is unconstitutional and must be changed, a constitutional system does not necessarily preclude local municipalities from providing additional funding for schools. *Edgewood,* 777 S.W.2d 391, 398; *Roosevelt,* 877 P.2d 806, 815. Does the court adequately address the potential conflict between the need to change the distribution of educational funding and the principle that local funds can still be used locally? How might that conflict continue or change as legislation is enacted? Should the court be more explicit in setting its educational mandates?

6. *Judicial Role.* Are the *Edgewood, Seattle* and *Roosevelt* decisions examples of judicial activism? While an important function of the judiciary is to interpret the state constitution, the ambiguity of the constitutional standards on education, like many constitutional provisions, leaves room for a variety of possible interpretations. *Seattle,* 585 P.2d 71, 87. Are the courts raising or lowering the educational standards set forth in the constitutional texts? Are the courts reading the constitutional standards with regard to education too narrowly?

7. *Education and the "Cycle of Poverty."* The *Edgewood* decision notes that a cycle of poverty contributes to educational inequality. *Edgewood,* 777 S.W.2d 391, 393. Can and should a judicial remedy address a "cycle of poverty" and its contributions to educational opportunity? A participant in the constitutional convention stated that "I assert that it [education] is for the general welfare of all, rich and poor, male and female, that the means of a common school education should, if possible, be placed within the reach of every child in the State." *Id.* at 395. Does the language "if possible" allow a different or broader interpretation of legislative intent than the court reaches in *Edgewood?* How does the intent of the framers apply to current challenges in education?

8. *Framing the Debate: General Welfare or Rights of the Poor?* Washington's constitution specifically provides that education is to be provided "without distinction or preference on account of race, color, caste, or sex." *Seattle,* 585 P.2d 71, 92. How important is the concept of "caste" to efforts to achieve greater equality in education today? Does (or did) it mean the same thing as "class"? The Texas constitution states that education is "for the general welfare of all, rich and poor, male and female." *Edgewood,* 777 S.W.2d 391, 395. *Edgewood, Seattle* and *Roosevelt* all include discussions of the general welfare of an educated state citizenry. Why might the opinions have focused on the effects on the overall state population rather than the specific poor districts? Is this an effective way to frame the opinions?

9.   Compare *Edgewood* with *Rodriguez*. *Edgewood* involved the same plaintiffs and school districts as the *Rodriguez* case, *supra*. While the U.S. Constitution does not explicitly elaborate a right to education, many state constitutions do. Why do you think members of state constitutional conventions recognized the need for this language, while the framers of the national bill of rights did not? What overall lessons (if any) can be taken from cases that are strongly grounded in the particularities of the local and state law? Do they have any legal relevance to other states that might lack such specific state constitutional language, or is their extraterritorial importance only as illustrations of alternative approaches?

10.   For further reading on the right to education in state constitutions, *see* Liz Kramer, *Achieving Equitable Education Through the Courts: A Comparative Analysis of Three States*, 31 J. L. & EDUC. 1 (2002); Roger J.R. Levesque, *The Right to Education in the United States: Beyond the Limits of the Lore and Lure of Law*, 4 ANN. SURV. INT'L & COMP. L. 205 (1997); Peter Enrich, *Leaving Equality Behind: New Directions in School Financing*, 48 VAND. L. REV. 101 (1995); and Suzanne M. Steinke, *Comment: The Exception to the Rule: Wisconsin's Fundamental Right to Education and Public School Financing*, 1995 WIS. L. REV. 1387 (1995).

5.   The Right to Health

RIGHT TO CHOOSE v. BYRNE

91 N.J. 287, 450 A.2d 925 (1982)

POLLOCK, J.

This appeal presents the question of the validity under the New Jersey Constitution of a statute that prohibits Medicaid funding for abortions "except where it is medically indicated to be necessary to preserve the woman's life." Medicaid pays for the costs of all childbirths and abortions to save the life of the mother but, because of the statutory prohibition, does not pay for those therapeutic abortions needed to protect the health of the mother or for elective, nontherapeutic abortions.

Originally plaintiffs claimed that the denial of Medicaid funds violated rights assured by the due process and equal protection clauses of the New Jersey and United States Constitutions. The Chancery Division found the statute violated a fundamental right to health under both Constitutions.*** After an appeal had been taken to the Appellate Division, we granted direct certification.***

Following the Chancery Division decision, however, the United States Supreme Court in *Harris v. McRae*, 448 U.S. 297, 100 S.Ct. 2671, 65 L.Ed.2d 784 (1980), determined that the Federal Constitution does not invest pregnant women with the right to Medicaid funds for abortions. Although we are bound to honor that determination of plaintiffs' federal Constitutional rights, we conclude that under the New Jersey Constitution the State may not restrict funds to those abortions to preserve a woman's life, but not her health. We conclude further that the New Jersey Constitution does not require the funding of elective, nontherapeutic abortions. Without determining whether a Constitutional right to health exists in New Jersey, we find that the statute violates the right of pregnant women to equal protection of the law under Art. I, par.1 of the New Jersey Constitution. Accordingly, we modify and affirm the declaration of the invalidity of [the statute].

I

In recent years abortion has generated an intense public debate, which is reflected in constantly changing federal and state legislative and administrative responses. With the decision of the United States Supreme Court in *Roe v. Wade*, 410 U.S. 113, 93 S.Ct. 705, 35 L.Ed.2d 147 (1973), the issue assumed a new dimension. In that case, the Court ruled that during the first trimester of a pregnancy the state has no role in the abortion decision, which "must be left to the medial judgment of the pregnant woman's attending physician." *Id.* at 164, 93 S.Ct. at 732. In the second trimester, the state may "regulate the abortion procedure in ways that are reasonably related to maternal health." *Id.* During the third trimester, the state may "regulate, and even proscribe, abortion except where it is necessary, in appropriate medical judgment, for the preservation of the life or health of the mother." *Id.* at 164–165, 93 S.Ct. at 732.

After *Roe v. Wade*, indigent women received funding for abortions under Medicaid, a joint federal-state program of medical care for the needy. In the three years between the *Roe v. Wade* decision and the enactment of N.J.S.A. 30:4D-6.1 in 1975, New Jersey did not restrict state Medicaid funding for abortions. In N.J.S.A. 30:4D-6.1, however, the New Jersey Legislature restricted state Medicaid funds to abortions needed to preserve the life, but not the health, of the mother.***

In sustaining plaintiffs' equal protection challenge in *Right to Choose II*, the Chancery Division found that the regulations discriminated "against Medicaid eligible women with a medical necessity for an abortion without warrant of a compelling state interest, in violation of equal protection of the law." 169 N.J. Super. at 552, 405 A.2d 427. Underlying that holding was the Court's conclusion that:

> [E]njoyment of one's health is a fundamental liberty which is shielded by the Fourteenth Amendment to the Federal Constitution and by Article 1, paragraph 1, of the State Constitution against unreasonable and discriminatory restriction. Medicaid funding is in furtherance of that fundamental liberty. The effect of the proposed guidelines would be to withhold funding for one medically necessary procedure and one only, an abortion to protect a woman's health, although such funding was previously available.

[*Id.* at 551, 405 A.2d 427].

That conclusion also underlay the declaration in the supplemental final judgment that N.J.S.A. 30:4D-6.1 violated the equal protection clause of the Fourteenth Amendment of the United States Constitution and Art. I, par. 1 of the New Jersey Constitution. Having declared the statute unconstitutional, the Court enjoined defendants to fund all Medicaid abortions except elective, nontherapeutic abortions and those to prevent insignificant impairments to health. 169 N.J. Super. at 552, 405 A.2d 427.

Thereafter the Department issued new regulations, effective May 1, 1980, declaring that "medicaid will pay for all medically necessary abortions." N.J.A.C. 10:53–1.14(a). Furthermore, in determining whether an abortion is medically necessary, a physician may consider: "(1) Physical, emotional, and psychological factors; (2) Family reasons; (3) Age." *Id.* at (b).

The injunction and new regulations have had a significant effect on the availability of abortions.***

Before evaluating plaintiffs' claim under the New Jersey Constitution, it is advisable that we set the limits of this opinion by stating what it excludes. It is not a referendum on the morality of abortion. We do not presume to answer the profound questions about the moral, medical, and societal implications of abortion. Nor do we undertake to determine when life begins or at what point a fetus is a person. Our mission is to decide the extent to which the New Jersey Constitution permits a statutory restriction on funding for abortions.

II

Fundamental to our decision is the role of a state Court of last resort in our federalist system. Inherent in that role is the interplay between, on the one hand, the individual states, their Constitutions, and Courts; and, on the other hand, the federal government, its Constitution, and the Supreme Court. Understanding of the relationship between the United States Supreme Court and a state Supreme Court as interpreters of Constitutional rights begins with the recollection that the original states, including New Jersey, and their Constitutions preceded the formation of the federal government and its Constitution.***

Over the past two centuries, however, the United States Constitution has emerged as the primary source of fundamental rights.*** Nevertheless, in recent years, distinguished jurists and scholars have encouraged state Courts, in appropriate cases, to look more closely to their own Constitutions as fonts of individual rights. Although the federal Constitution may remain as the basic charter, state Constitutions may serve as a supplemental source of fundamental liberties.***

From that perspective, state Constitutions are separate sources of individual freedoms, and restrictions on the exercise of power by the Legislature. By contrast, the United States Constitution is a grant of enumerated powers to the federal government. Thus, in appropriate cases, the individual states may accord greater respect than the federal government to certain fundamental rights. Although the state Constitution may encompass a smaller universe than the Federal Constitution, our constellation of rights may be more complete.

Indeed, the United States Supreme Court itself has long proclaimed that state Constitutions may provide more expansive protection of individual liberties than the United States Constitution. [Citations omitted.]

In addition, this Court has recognized that our state Constitution may provide greater protection than the Federal Constitution. *See, e.g., State v. Alston*, 88 N.J. 211, 227–28, 440 A.2d 1311 (1981) (standing to challenge searches and seizures); In *re Grady*, 85 N.J. 235, 249, 426 A.2d 467 (1981)) (the right to sterilization); *State v. Schmidt*, 84 N.J. 535, 559, 423 A.2d 615 (1980) (free speech protected in some instances against private interference); *State v. Baker*, 81 N.J. 99, 112–13, 405 A.2d 368 (1979) (the right of unrelated persons to live as a single unit); *State v. Johnson*, 68 N.J. 349, 353, 346 A.2d 66 (1975) (consent to search); *Southern Burlington Cty. NAACP v. Township of Mt. Laurel*, 67 N.J. 151, 174–75, 336 A.2d 713 (1975) (exclusionary zoning); *Robinson v. Cahill*, 62 N.J. 473, 482, 509, 303 A.2d 273 cert. denied sub. nom. *Dickey v. Robinson*, 414 U.S. 976, 94 S.Ct. 292, 38 L.Ed.2d 219 (1973) (fundamental right to thorough and efficient public education).

Nonetheless, we proceed cautiously before declaring rights under our state Constitution that differ significantly from those enumerated by the United States

Supreme Court in its interpretation of the federal Constitution. [Citations Omitted] Our caution emanates, in part, from our recognition of the general advisability in a federal system of uniform interpretation of identical Constitutional provisions. Where provisions of the federal and state Constitutions differ, however, or where a previously established body of state law leads to a different result, then we must determine whether a more expansive grant of rights is mandated by our state Constitution. *See generally*, "State Constitutional Rights," *supra*, 95 Harv.L.Rev. at 1361.

III

Against this background, we consider the implications of the decision of the United States Supreme Court in *Harris v. McRae*, 448 U.S. 297, 100 S.Ct. 2671, 65 L.Ed.2d 784 (1980). In *McRae*, the five-member majority found that the version of the Hyde Amendment that prohibited Medicaid funds for abortions except when necessary to save the life of the mother bore a rational relationship to government's "legitimate interest in protecting the potential life of the fetus." 448 U.S. at 324, 100 S.Ct. at 2692.

The majority opinion precipitated vigorous dissents from four members of the Court, who attacked that opinion at several points. Of particular relevance is the dissenters' contention that, by denying Medicaid funds for medically necessary abortions, the Hyde Amendment was not supported by a sufficiently compelling state interest to justify its restriction on the exercise of the fundamental right to choose an abortion. In his dissent, Justice Stevens stated that the Court's earlier decision in *Roe v. Wade* prevented the State from "exclud[ing] a woman from medical benefits to which she would otherwise be entitled solely to further an interest in potential life when a physician, 'in appropriate medical judgment,' certifies that an abortion is necessary 'for the preservation of the life or health of the mother.' 448 U.S. at 352, 100 S.Ct. at 2713 (citations omitted). He found a denial of equal protection to a class consisting of poor pregnant women who, under Medicaid, had a right to necessary medical treatment. Those women "are confronted with a choice between two serious harms: serious health damage to themselves on the one hand and abortion on the other." *Id.* at 350, 100 S.Ct. at 2712. He found further that the denial of funds for medically necessary abortions was "tantamount to severe punishment." *Id.* at 354, 100 S.Ct. at 2714. Consequently, protection of potential life could not be used as a reason to deny indigent women necessary medical care.

The majority in *McRae* concluded that the prohibition on the use of Medicaid funds for abortion to protect the health of the mother did not violate the equal protection clause of the United States Constitution. Under the supremacy clause, U.S. CONST. Art. VI, cl. 2, that interpretation precludes our reaching a different result as a matter of federal law. We remain obligated, however, to evaluate N.J.S.A. 30:4D-6.1 in light of the Constitution of New Jersey.

In more expansive language than that of the United States Constitution, Art. I, par. 1 of the New Jersey Constitution provides: "All persons are by nature free and independent, and have certain natural and unalienable rights, among which are those of enjoying and defending life and liberty, of acquiring, possessing, and protecting property, and of pursuing and obtaining safety and happiness." The state Bill of Rights, which includes that provision, has been described as expressing "the social, political, and economic ideals of the present day in a broader way than ever before in American Constitutional history.'" By declaring the right to life, liberty and the pursuit of safety and happiness, Art. I, par. 1 protects the right of privacy.***

Although we decline to proceed as far as the Chancery Division in declaring that the New Jersey Constitution guarantees a fundamental right to health *** we recognize that New Jersey accords a high priority to the preservation of health. More than 70 years ago, chancellor Pitney recognized that

> [A]mong the most [important] of personal rights, without which man could not live in a state of society, is the right of personal security, including 'the preservation of a man's health from such practices as may prejudice or annoy it,' a right recognized, needless to say, in almost the first words of our written Constitution. (citations omitted)

With these long-standing principles of state law in mind, we assess whether the restriction of Medicaid reimbursement to abortions to protect the life of the mother is compatible with the state guarantee of equal protection of the laws. In New Jersey, equal protection of the laws is assured not only by the Fourteenth Amendment to the United States Constitution, but also by Art. I, par. 1 of the state Constitution.***

Conventional equal protection analysis employs "two tiers" of judicial review. Briefly stated, if a fundamental right or suspect class is involved, the legislative classification is subject to strict scrutiny: the state must establish that a compelling state interest supports the classification and that no less restrictive alternative is available. With other rights and classes, however, the legislative classification need be only rationally related to a legitimate state interest.

Neither poverty nor pregnancy gives rise to membership in a suspect class.*** Nor is there a fundamental right to funding for an abortion. The right to choose whether to have an abortion, however, is a fundamental right of all pregnant women, including those entitled to Medicaid reimbursement for necessary medical treatment. As to that group of women, the challenged statute discriminates between those for whom medical care is necessary for childbirth and those for whom an abortion is medically necessary. Under N.J.S.A. 30:4D-6.1, those needing abortions receive funds only when their lives are at stake. By granting funds when life is at risk, but withholding them when health is endangered, the statute denies equal protection to those women entitled to necessary medical services under Medicaid.

Thus, the statute impinges upon the fundamental right of a woman to control her body and destiny. That right encompasses one of the most intimate decisions in human experience, the choice to terminate a pregnancy or bear a child. This intensely personal decision is one that should be made by a woman in consultation with trusted advisers, such as her doctor, but without undue government interference. In this case, however, the State admittedly seeks to influence the decision between abortion and childbirth. Indeed, it concedes that, for a woman who cannot afford either medical procedure, the statute skews the decision in favor of childbirth at the expense of the mother's health.

To justify the discrimination, the State asserts as its compelling interest the protection of potential life. Although that is a legitimate state interest, at no point in a pregnancy may it outweigh the superior interest in the life and health of the mother. *Roe v. Wade, supra,* 410 U.S. at 163–65, 93 S.Ct. at 731–33. Yet the funding restriction gives priority to potential life at the expense of maternal health. From a different perspective, the statute deprives indigent women "of a governmental benefit for which they are otherwise eligible, solely because they have attempted to exercise a Constitutional right." *Harris v. McRae, supra,* 448 U.S. at 346, 100 S.Ct. at 2710 (Marshall, J., dissenting).

Concededly, the Legislature need not fund any of the costs of medically necessary procedures pertaining to pregnancy; conversely, it could include in its medicaid plan medically necessary abortions for which federal reimbursement is not available. Id. at 311 n.16, 100 S.Ct. at 2685 n.16. Once it undertakes to fund medically necessary care attendant upon pregnancy, however, government must proceed in a neutral manner.[9] Given the high priority accorded in this State to the rights of privacy and health, it is not neutral to fund services medically necessary for childbirth while refusing to fund medically necessary abortions. Nor is it neutral to provide one woman with the means to protect her life at the expense of a fetus and to force another woman to sacrifice her health to protect a potential life.

By controlling funds for schools, prisons, highways, housing, welfare, and other public needs, the legislative and executive branches fulfill the definition of our Constitutional rights. Those two branches properly enjoy wide latitude in making fiscal decisions, but the State may not use its treasury to persuade a poor woman to sacrifice her health by remaining pregnant. Statutes such as N.J.S.A. 30:4D-6.1 "can be understood only as an attempt to achieve with carrots what government is forbidden to achieve with sticks." L.Tribe, American Constitutional Law, § 15-10 at 933 n.77 (1978). The statute affects the right of poor pregnant women to choose between alternative necessary medical services. No compelling state interest justifies that discrimination, and the statute denies equal protection to those exercising their constitutional right to choose a medically necessary abortion.***

Our holding is not that the State is under a Constitutional obligation to fund all abortions. Rather, we hold that the State may not jeopardize the health and privacy of poor women by excluding medically necessary abortions from a system providing all other medically necessary care for the indigent. A woman's right to choose to protect her health by terminating her pregnancy outweighs the State's asserted interest in protecting a potential life at the expense of her health. Therefore, we hold that the restriction of funding to abortions necessary to save the life of the mother violates the New Jersey Constitution.***

Notes and Questions

1. The court in *Right to Choose v. Byrne* finds the relevant statute unconstitutional on equal protection grounds, stating that "the challenged statute discriminates between those for whom medical care is necessary for childbirth and those for whom an abortion is medically necessary." *Right to Choose*, 91 N.J. 287, 305. The court also states that

---

[9] In his separate opinion, Justice Pashman concludes that a woman has a right under the New Jersey Constitution to funding for an elective or nontherapeutic abortion. He correctly notes that we find no such right to funding. Justice O'Hern, in his dissenting opinion, reaches a conclusion diametrially opposed to that of Justice Pashman. That is, Justice O'Hern concludes that the State has no obligation to fund any abortions, therapeutic or nontherapeutic. Both opinions misperceive the Constitutional right. Justice Pashman errs in construing the right as imposing a correlative duty on government to fund all abortions. The flaw in his analysis is in failing to recognize that the right of the individual is freedom from undue government interference, not an assurance of government funding. Justice O'Hern, on the other hand, errs by failing to recognize that once government enters the zone of privacy surrounding a pregnant woman's right to choose, it must act impartially. In that Constitutionally protected zone, the State may be an umpire, but not a contestant.

its holding does not grant a right to health or a right to funding. *Id.* at 306. How can this case be read to increase access to health care? In the alternative, how can this case be read to decrease access to health care?

2. "[I]n appropriate cases, the individual states may accord greater respect than the federal government to certain fundamental rights." *Id.* at 300. On the premise that states may be providing greater protections, does the holding extend to other areas of Medicaid funding or other health related issues? How critical is it to the opinion that a woman's reproductive and privacy rights are involved?

3. In *Boehm v. Merced County* the California court held that General Assistance Welfare Payments (GA) were inadequate. 178 Cal. App. 3d 494 (1986). In July 1983, the county reduced GA for indigent county residents from $198 per month for an individual to $175 per month based on calculated expenses for housing and food. The court held that the GA must also include allowances for clothing, transportation and medical care, citing the Universal Declaration of Human Rights:

> Everyone has the right to a standard of living adequate for the health and well being of himself and of his family, including food, clothing, housing and medical care and necessary social services, and the right to security in the event of unemployment, sickness, disability, widowhood, old age or other lack of livelihood in circumstances beyond his control. (Universal Declaration of Human Rights, art. 25(1), adopted Dec. 10, 1948; Gen. Assm. Res. 217A(111), U.N. Doc. A/810 (1948).)

178 Cal. App. 3d 494, 502. The court applied the international declaration to the petitioner's case, stating: "Indeed, it defies common sense and all notions of human dignity to exclude from minimum subsistence allowances for clothing, transportation and medical care.*** The lack of adequate and decent clothing and essential transportation is damaging both to recipients' self-respect and their ability to obtain employment. Finally, to leave recipients without minimum medical assistance is inhumane and shocking to the conscience." *Id.*

4. *The Oregon Health Plan.* The cost and availability of health care continues to be a source of serious concern for many Americans. By 2002, 15.2 percent of the population had no health insurance coverage at all; an additional 25.7 percent depended on some form of government health insurance, up from 23.3 percent in 1987. U.S. Census Bureau, Health Insurance Coverage in the United States: 2002 (P60–223, Sept. 2003).

Those responsible for the management of public health care insurance programs, such as Medicaid and Medicare, are thus faced with increasingly difficult decisions as to how best to distribute scarce resources. One approach has been to provide the best possible care on a first-come, first-served basis, until the funds run out. A different solution, however, was devised by Oregon. It aspired to ration health care in a way that would provide "universal access to an adequate level of high quality health care at an affordable cost" to the state. Oregon 1993 Session Law, c. 815, § 1. One way that the tension has been characterized is that both approaches involve health care rationing, but instead of the usual rationing of people, Oregon chose to attempt to ration benefits. The novel dimension of the plan was Oregon's expectation that the plan would cover the working poor, normally excluded under the federal aid program, with the money saved by limiting access to expensive and ineffective treatments.

The Oregon Health Plan [OHP] was legislatively enacted from 1987 to 1993. *See* Oregon R.S. 34: 414.019. It originally ranked 709 health conditions according to the effectiveness and cost of their treatments. After calculating how much the state could spend, the administrators drew a "cut off line" at item 587. No condition below 587 on the ranked list would be funded through Medicaid. This list was to be revised every two years at each legislative session. The list of ranked conditions has grown (up to 743 in 1999), and the funding line shifts according to funding availability (down to 574 in 1999). Howard M. Leichter, *Oregon's Bold Experiment: Whatever Happened to Rationing?*, 24 J. HEALTH POLITICS, POL'Y & L. 147, 149 (1999).

The federal government initially refused to grant Oregon the needed approval. The Administration's concern was that rationing health care was a violation of the Americans with Disabilities Act [ADA]. For example, the plan initially denied coverage for liver transplants for patients with a history of alcoholism—an ADA disability—although the operation was covered for those without this background. Also not covered was post-mastectomy breast reconstruction, or treatment for infants born before 23 weeks and weighing less than 18 ounces.

These concerns were eventually addressed, and the OHP was finally implemented in 1994. The results have not been as radical as some feared and others hoped. The plan does not seem to have "substantially restricted access to needed services" by the target clientele. Janet B. Mitchell et al., *Impact of the Oregon Health Plan on Access and Satisfaction of Adults with Low Income*, 37 HEALTH SERS. RESEARCH 11 (2002). Moreover, since the OHP "rations services that are in the main only of a clinically marginal, non-life threatening nature, the effort . . . has helped the state save enough money to extend health care to an additional 130,000 low-income Oregonians." Leichter, *supra* at 148. Tellingly, user satisfaction of the Medicaid system increased since the implementation of the OHP, and the Office of Medical Assistance Programs reported that it received only between 40 and 80 appeals per year to request unfunded services, suggesting that no health needs were going systematically unmet. *Id.* at 153. Despite an initial furor of negative reaction and national trepidation, then, the Oregon experiment has shown that rationing can be effective and beneficial to funding agencies, service providers, and patients.

Today, however, all is not well with the OHP. Almost immediately funding limitations forced service cutbacks. In 1995, funded services were cut back from 606 to 581, and again in 1996 to 578, and then lowered still further in 1999 to 574. Leichter, *supra* at 153–54. By 2003, the number of covered treatments had fallen to 549. *Oregon Health Plan is in Surgery*, OREGONIAN, June 16, 2003, at B6.

The number of eligible participants required under federal law remains about 300,000; the non-required working-poor enrollment has fallen, however, from the 130,000 Leichter reported in 1999, to 65,000 in 2003. This precipitous drop occurred because funding shortfalls required Oregon to cut benefits and increase premiums in this group of beneficiaries. Erin Hoover Barnett & Don Colburn, *Savings Fade, Threatening Proposals for Health Plan*, OREGONIAN, July 18, 2003, at D1.

The 2003 budget shortfall of $250 million has compelled some Oregon lawmakers to consider eliminating the extended coverage to the latter category of recipients altogether, returning the Oregon Medicaid plan to the national baseline. At this writing less draconian measures are more likely at least initially, such as enrollment caps. Notably, the "infamous 'Prioritized List' is barely mentioned in the current debate. Policy-makers say the federal government—which pays 60 percent of the cost of Medicaid—would not allow Oregon to shorten the list of covered treatments as drastically as would be necessary to balance the budget." Dan Colburn, *Health Plan a Leader No More*, OREGONIAN, Feb. 17, 2003, at A1.

What are the benefits and drawbacks of the Oregon plan? Does the idea of a "list" of covered medical illnesses and treatments trouble you? What if you, or a loved one, were suffering from one of the non-covered, but serious, illnesses? What factors should a legislature consider in determining such a list? On the other hand, if no such list existed, how were choices being made with regard to the medical treatment of the poor? Compare the discussion of the right to health under the South African constitution in Chapter 8, *supra*.

5.   The following news article discusses both the history of coverage for dialysis in the U.S. and some of the current issues facing those with kidney disease in the United States: Peter Landers, *Who Gets Health Care? Rationing in an Age of Rising Costs Filtering Process: Longer Dialysis Offers New Hope But Poses Dilemma: Who Gets Costly Treatment? Personality, Persistence And Housekeeping Count*, WALL ST. J., Oct. 2, 2003, at A1.

> In 2001, New York's Rogosin Institute was about to start an unusual new program for dialysis patients. It would give them a blood-cleansing machine to use at home for six nights a week, eight hours each night. Usually, patients go to a dialysis center three times a week, for four hours a day.
>
> The "intensive" treatment had shown excellent results elsewhere. But because both Medicare and private insurers wouldn't pay for it, the nonprofit dialysis center could only afford to make it available to a handful of patients. The center, which has about 560 dialysis patients, says it chooses patients for the new treatment primarily on a first-come, first-served basis. As the experience of two patients shows, other factors also come into play.***
>
> How is it decided which patients will get the few available spaces in intensive dialysis programs each year? The allocation of scarce medical resources in the U.S. can be haphazard, with unexpected factors sometimes controlling access to life-changing treatments. In the case of intensive dialysis, the process turns not only on a patient's health but also on such things as how informed the patient is, or on their personality or even the cleanliness of their home.***
>
> Dialysis, which cleans the blood of toxins in place of failed kidneys, has long been a flashpoint in debates over health-care costs and rationing. The U.S. government spends more than $15 billion a year on dialysis and other treatment for kidney-failure patients. Doctors estimate as many as half of the 300,000 people on dialysis in the U.S. might benefit from the six-times-a-week treatment. But only a few hundred are receiving it, under limited programs paid for by dialysis centers.***
>
> A big obstacle for many patients is that they don't know about new treatments. In the case of intensive dialysis, doctors often don't mention it to patients, because it isn't widely available. Unless patients aggressively research the subject, they're left at the mercy of doctors and nurses who give out information about new treatments or clinical trials as they see fit.***

Doctors who have tried the six-times-a-week method say their patients almost universally feel more energetic. A range of small studies back up the idea.***

Big, for-profit dialysis chains *** don't offer the six-times-a-week treatment because they depend on government reimbursement. Medicare covers most dialysis patients, but only for a maximum of three days a week.***

Many doctors and patients feel Medicare is in effect rationing time on dialysis machines by limiting payments to three times a week. Medicare's chief clinical officer, Sean Tunis, says he's waiting for proof that intensive dialysis is more effective than three-day-a-week treatment.*** No large-scale studies of intensive dialysis have been conducted. The National Institutes of Health is planning one soon, but results aren't expected until 2008.

In the meantime, "dollars and cents" will keep doctors from offering intensive dialysis, says Robert Lockridge, who co-owns a dialysis center in Lynchburg, Va.*** Dr. Lockridge and others are pushing for legislation that would require Medicare to pay for more frequent treatment, but bills in Congress have failed so far.

Ever since it was invented during World War II, dialysis has forced tough decisions about who gets the treatment. The world's first hospital medical-ethics committee was set up in Seattle in the 1960s specifically to consider dialysis. Because only a few machines were available, the committee had to ration time on them, deciding which kidney-failure patients would live and which would die.

By the 1970s, dialysis machines were more plentiful, and a new problem emerged: paying for treatment. On Nov. 4, 1971, an activist named Shep Glazer appeared before a congressional committee hooked up to a dialysis machine. "We live in constant terror that if these treatments are taken away from us because our money has run out, death will come in a matter of weeks," he said. "We feel that this country is morally obligated to its citizens to provide this treatment to all who need it."

Impressed by the testimony, Congress passed legislation requiring Medicare, the federal program for the elderly and disabled, to pay for dialysis for anyone, of any age, who needs it. Kidney failure is the only disease to receive such special treatment. Because Medicare picks up most dialysis costs, private insurers typically don't pay for the treatment for long.

Today, dialysis is a fast-growing burden on the American taxpayer. Kidney failure has become more common due to the rapid spread of diabetes. In 2001, the 292,000 people on dialysis, plus another 114,000 who had received a transplanted kidney, accounted for 6.4% of Medicare's $242 billion budget—even though they represented about 1% of Medicare's enrollees.***

Wealthy patients could buy a dialysis machine with their own money, hire a specialized dialysis nurse to train them how to use it and pay a doctor to supervise the treatment. Operating expenses and supplies would add thousands of dollars to the annual cost, making the treatment prohibitive for most people.

Some centers *** have a formal process to decide who gets into the home-dialysis program.*** Nurse Shari Meola and her staff interview patients and visit

their homes, sorting out those who don't appear to have the discipline to operate the machines. She also looks at the cleanliness of a home, frowning on such
things as cat hair, which might clog up the machine.***

People on the waiting list who don't stay in touch with the center may get
bumped off, [one doctor] says. Those who get into the program "torture us,"
he says, with constant requests for information. "That's what we want. That may
sound harsh, but it's a way of us knowing who's serious."

Racial Disparities in Prevalence and Treatment. Another source of concern in the United
States is the high prevalence of kidney disease leading to End-Stage Renal Disease
(ESRD) among African-Americans and other minorities, as well as possible disparities
in treatment. In addition, there is a significant need for increased organ donation
among minority groups:

It's a grim statistic: African Americans are five times as likely as whites to suffer
from kidney disease severe enough to require dialysis or transplantation. Are
the kidneys of blacks that much more prone to disease? In fact, they're not,
according to a report by researchers at the University of California, San
Francisco, and the San Francisco VA Medical Center. Their study shows there
is no difference between the two groups in the rates of early kidney disease. Yet
blacks are far more likely to progress to the severe stage of the disease. One
possible explanation, say the researchers, is that whites get better health care.
Other possibilities include an unidentified genetic component and the fact that
two related risk factors—complications from diabetes and hypertension—are
also more prevalent among blacks. The message for African Americans—and
their doctors—is that mild kidney disease should be treated aggressively, before
it becomes a life-threatening illness.

David Bjerklie, *Kidney Troubles in Black and White*, TIME MAGAZINE, Nov. 3, 2003, at 99.

The United Network for Organ Sharing (UNOS), the organization that coordinates
the transplant waiting list in the United States, notes that, as of November 21, 2003,
there are 59,461 persons awaiting kidney donations in the United States. Of that number, 23,720 are white, 21,054 are Black, 9, 489 are Latino/a, 4,597 are Asian and 1,601
identify as "other," non-Hispanic multi-racial or are of unknown ethnicity. United
Network for Organ Sharing, Organ Procurement and Transplantation Network, *Organ
By Ethnicity*, (chart) *available at* http://www.optn.org/latestData/rptData.asp (last visited
Nov. 26, 2003).

Diabetes and high blood pressure are the leading causes of kidney disease; both
diseases have a high prevalence in minority populations in the United States. One report
notes that, while "diabetes is the 7th leading cause of death [in the U.S.], African
Americans are 1.7 times more likely to have diabetes, than Non-Latino Whites. *** Native
Americans have the highest rates of diabetes in the world.*** Hypertension is most
prevalent in the African American population. It affects about one out of every three
African Americans. Over 14,000 deaths each year are attributed to hypertension."
Minority Organ Tissue Transplant Education Program, *available at* http://www.national-
mottep.org/stats.shtml (last visited Nov. 26, 2003) (citing American Diabetes Association
and American Heart Association statistics as of 2000).

For more on racial disparities in the treatment of kidney disease in the United
States, *see, e.g.*, Ian Ayres, Laura G. Dooley & Robert S. Gaston, *Unequal Racial Access to*

Kidney Transplantation, 46 VAND. L. REV. 805 (1993). *See also* J. Michael Soucie, John F. Neylan & William McClellan, *Race and Sex Differences in the Identification of Candidates for Renal Transplantation,* 19 AM. J. KIDNEY DIS. 414 (1992); PHYSICIANS FOR HUMAN RIGHTS, THE RIGHT TO EQUAL TREATMENT: AN ACTION PLAN TO END RACIAL AND ETHNIC DISPARITIES IN CLINICAL DIAGNOSIS AND TREATMENT IN THE UNITED STATES (2003).

12. Jerome Culp, an African-American law professor who was on kidney dialysis, places the experience in the larger context of discrimination in the United States:

> I (Jerome) am a dialysis patient. I am the subject at stake in the medical treatments I face every week. The medical literature describes my condition as End Stage Renal Disease (ESRD). If I had lived in the first half of the last century instead of the first half of this one, I would now be dead. As an ESRD patient, I am a too-frequent consumer of medical services (too frequent both for me and for the insurance companies who would like to have all ESRD patients eliminated). In the first year after being diagnosed as an ESRD patient, for example, I had fourteen operations (primarily outpatient procedures).***
>
> I bore you with the petty details of my medical history for a reason. How do I, the subject of the decisions, decide whether my treatment is fair and unaffected by my race or income? One would hope that the law and legal scholarship of antidiscrimination might by now provide an answer; that it does not is one of the chief failures of the modern legal system. Yet, evidence suggests that racial disparities in health care treatment are rampant. For example, a recent summary of the evidence of discrimination in medical care made the following conclusions:
>
> > Racial and ethnic minorities tend to receive a lower quality of healthcare than non-minorities, even when access-related factors, such as patients' insurance status and income are controlled.*** Evidence of racial and ethnic disparities in healthcare is, with few exceptions, remarkably consistent across a range of illnesses and healthcare services.*** The majority of studies, however, find that racial and ethnic disparities remain even after adjustment for socioeconomic differences and other health care access-related factors.*** Racial and ethnic disparities are found in *** diabetes care,*** end-stage renal disease and kidney transplantation.***

Jerome M. Culp, Jr., Angela P. Harris & Francisco Valdes, *Subject Unrest; Symposium on 'Pervasive Prejudice?' by Ian Ayres and 'Crossroads, Directions, and a New Critical Race Theory' by Francisco Valdes, Jerome McCristal Culp and Angela P. Harris,* 55 STAN. L. REV. 2435, 2439–2440 (2003) (*quoting* IAN AYRES, UNEQUAL TREATMENT: CONFRONTING RACIAL AND ETHNIC DISPARITIES IN HEALTH CARE 5 (Brian D. Smedley, Adrienne Y. Stith & Alan R. Nelson eds., 2002). Culp noted that between 1992 and 2001, 20,000 dialysis patients died while waiting for a kidney transplant. *Id.* (*citing* United Network for Organ Sharing, Reported Deaths and Annual Death Rates Per 1,000 Patient Years at Risk, 1992 to 2001: Kidney Waiting List, *at* http://www.optn.org/data/annualReport.asp?url=/Data/ar2002/ar02_table_503_ AGE_KI.htm). Professor Culp, a well-respected scholar and advocate for social justice, received a kidney transplant from a generous living donor in 2003. Regrettably, he died in early 2004 as a result of complications from his illness.

C. ERASING THE DIVIDE: INTERNATIONALIZING THE RIGHTS STRUGGLE

From the earliest days of the post-World War II international human rights movement, activists, lawyers and ordinary people in the United States have sought to use the international human rights framework to promote social justice in the United States. Their efforts took a variety of forms: advocacy for U.S. ratification of human rights treaties and the adoption of implementing legislation; the filing of *amicus* briefs in death penalty and other human rights-related cases; and attempting to rely on treaty obligations under the U.N. Charter or on the Universal Declaration of Human Rights as evidence of customary law. Such efforts have met with mixed success, although U.S. courts have been used as fora for the adjudication of civil claims against non-citizens for serious human rights violations under the Alien Tort Claims Act and the Torture Victims Protection Act. Nevertheless, there is a vibrant and growing grassroots and civil society movement on human rights in the United States such as that illustrated below in the Poor Peoples' Economic Human Rights Campaign. These U.S.-focused human rights strategies have included popular education on the application of international human rights standards to social justice issues, the filing of individual and group complaints against the United States under international and regional procedures, the adoption of local and state legislation that parallels provisions of international human rights instruments, and direct action (*e.g.*, protests and the occupation of abandoned public housing by the homeless).

BARBARA STARK, U.S. RATIFICATION OF THE OTHER HALF OF THE INTERNATIONAL BILL OF RIGHTS

DAVID P. FORSYTHE ED., THE UNITED STATES AND HUMAN RIGHTS (2000)

The United States is now the only major industrialized democracy that has not yet ratified the Economic Covenant.***

Although the United States was eager to "declare" international human rights after World War II, it was more hesitant about domestic implementation. Some believed that we had an already well-developed constitutional jurisprudence of civil and political rights. Others were concerned that the world would be scandalized by still-legal segregation and other forms of state-condoned racial discrimination. International civil and political rights were seen as both redundant and as an invitation to unfriendly foreign states to criticize the United States.

The rights set out in the Economic Covenant were viewed with even more suspicion. As Roosevelt's promise of "freedom from want" receded from public memory, economic rights were linked to our new arch-enemy, the Soviet monolith. Because the United States linked economic rights with the Soviets during the Cold War, it was impossible for the domestic human rights community to draw on international human rights for the economic rights that were and still are missing from domestic law.***

[T]he domestic human rights community has contributed little to the public debate on economic rights that is finally surfacing in this country. By focusing almost exclusively on the experience of those denied political and civil rights abroad, the domestic human rights community has emphasized the differences between their circumstances and our own, their repressive regimes, and our Constitutional protections.*** In doing so the domestic community has not only alienated many in the international human rights community, it has snubbed its "natural [domestic] constituencies" women, men of color, and the poor by ignoring the economic rights issues that most concern them.***

The economic rights set out in the Economic Covenants were not only fatally linked with the Soviets but preempted by the rhetoric of "opportunity." But the Soviets are gone, the Cold War is over, and opportunity means little to growing numbers of Americans. These changes have produced domestic as well as international incentives for ratification. As these changes become more pressing, and the links between them better recognized, ratification becomes an increasingly practical objective.***

The American Dream has lost its luster. The difference between the best paid 10 percent and the worst paid 10 percent of Americans "is wider than in any other large industrialized State," and inequality has grown in this country.*** The social costs of increasing polarization are borne by all of us. Even the middle class feels the need for a dependable "safety net," although it remains unwilling to pay for it.***

Not since 1965 have so many Americans lived in poverty. For many of these poor Americans, infant mortality rates, life spans, and health problems are closer to those of the Third World than to those of other Western industrialized democracies. Their inadequate housing and schools, lack of healthcare, and job opportunities have been recognized as international human rights issues for at least fifty years.***

[T]he political process has produced frenzied cutbacks in public spending, attacks against legal as well as illegal immigrants, and threats to take children away from their mothers. These are precisely the kinds of human rights violations, carried out by the government and unchecked by national law, contemplated by human rights law. The Economic Covenant is the law enacted thirty years ago to prevent them, or at least to soften their impact. This is not to suggest that ratification would be easy or that it would not require substantial, concrete reform. Human rights advocates would have to develop effective strategies to deal with the current emphasis in the United States on individual responsibility at the expense of entitlements. They can begin by pointing out that "individual responsibility" is not necessarily incompatible with the "progressive realization" of economic rights contemplated by the Economic Covenant. The issue becomes how to enable individuals willing to take responsibility for their own economic rights to do so effectively.***

Human rights law relies primarily on domestic adoption. Therefore, domestic groups throughout the world have relied on international opinion to press for adoption by their own states. The civil rights movement in the United States, for example, drew on international opinion in the 1950's. The spreading "human rights idea" that nations could not abrogate the rights of their own people was an important catalyst. As Mary Dudziak has explained, "U.S. government officials realized that their ability to sell democracy to the Third World was seriously hampered by continuing racial injustice at home." The Third World was appalled by media coverage of civil rights struggles in the South: "Those pictures of dogs and fire hoses were published in Europe, Africa, India, Japan. . ." The crucial leverage provided by international human rights helped the domestic civil rights movement obtain desperately needed federal support. Indeed, the Justice Department brief in *Brown v. Board of Education* explicitly described how segregation at home hurt the United States abroad.

As during the civil rights movement in the 1950's, those seeking economic rights can draw on international opinion to obtain leverage at home.***

At the same time, domestic economic rights groups can help shape a nascent but growing international economic rights jurisprudence. Fran Ansley, noting the internationalization of capital and the multiplying formal and informal networks among multinational corporations, has mapped some of the possibilities for such networks among workers. Similar networks would be useful for those denied economic rights, especially, perhaps, those already falling through an increasingly diaphanous safety net.***

The domestic human rights community has been criticized for its idealism, for its distance from the practical problems of the real world. Ratification of ICESCR would begin to bring domestic human rights down to earth.***

THE POOR PEOPLE'S PETITION

The following Petition to the Inter-American Commission on Human Rights was submitted by a coalition of U.S. NGOs in response to the U.S. welfare reforms of the mid-1990s.

POOR PEOPLE'S ECONOMIC HUMAN RIGHTS CAMPAIGN v. THE UNITED STATES OF AMERICA

PETITION

PRELIMINARY STATEMENT

1. Petitioners, the Poor People's Economic Human Rights Campaign, the Kensington Welfare Rights Union, Cheri Honkala, Joy Butts, the National Employment Law Project, the Urban Justice Center and the Center for Constitutional Rights bring this petition against the United States on behalf of all US citizens and residents significantly harmed by recent and current US welfare law and policy—in particular the changes wrought by the 1996 Personal Responsibility And Work Opportunity Reconciliation Act of 1996 ["PRWORA"]. Petitioners bring this petition against the United States for violations of the right to an adequate standard of living, the right to health, the right to protection for familial relations, the right to work under just and reasonable conditions, the right to education, the right to food, the right to housing, the right to social security, and the right to be free from discrimination.***

The enactment and implementation of PRWORA *** violates the obligation of the United States, under binding regional and international instruments and norms, progressively to improve the enjoyment of economic and social rights and to eliminate discrimination, particularly that based on sex, race, economic status, property, marital status and age. It does so, *inter alia*, by fixing arbitrary cut-offs of preexisting, and themselves inadequate, entitlements to survival benefits for the poor; by jeopardizing continuing entitlements to food and health care benefits; by forcing previously eligible recipients to lose their homes, and to work under violative conditions and at the risk of leaving their children unprotected; by providing incentives to states to hasten the downsizing of those entitled to benefits, often illegally; and by implementing these laws and policies without any mechanism for identifying and preventing harm to the most vulnerable. Thus, as a matter of international law, PRWORA works a cruel and illegal retrogression in the provision of survival benefits to the poor and a failure to guarantee the core minimum entitlement of each person to social and economic rights as well as to eliminate discrimination and ensure the protection of all, indivisible human rights to everyone.***

II. THE COMMISSION HAS JURISDICTION OVER THE UNITED STATES FOR THESE CLAIMS.

11. The Commission has jurisdiction over the member states of the OAS by virtue of the Charter of the Organization of American States (Bogotá 1948), as amended by the Protocol of Buenos Aires February 27, 1967.*** The US ratified the OAS Charter on April 23, 1968.***

III. DOMESTIC REMEDIES ARE UNAVAILABLE.

16. Exhaustion of domestic remedies is not required by article 37 of the Regulations of the Inter-American Commission on Human Rights because US law "does not afford due process of law for protection of [the economic and social] rights that have allegedly been violated." Inter-Am. C.H.R. Regulations, *supra* par. 13, at art. 37.***

V. THE US IS OBLIGATED TO PROTECT SOCIAL AND ECONOMIC RIGHTS UNDER INTER-AMERICAN AND INTERNATIONAL LAW.

A. PROTECTED RIGHTS.

21. As the Commission noted in Chapter V of its 1993 Annual Report, a broad array of instruments in the Inter-American System protect social and economic rights, specifically: the Charter of the Organization of American States ("OAS Charter"), the American Declaration of the Rights and Duties of Man ("American Declaration"), the American Convention on Human Rights ("American Convention") and the Additional Protocol to the American Convention on Human Rights in the Area of Economic, Social and Cultural Rights ("Protocol of San Salvador"). Inter-Am. C.H.R. 1993 Annual Report, Chpt. V, OEA/Ser/L/V/II.85, (1993).*** (*See* Section 4.A.1, *supra*, on the Inter-American System.)

31. Also relevant are the extra-regional obligations of the United States in relation to social and economic rights.***

32. [T]he Commission has, as a regular matter, relied on UN instruments. In the instant case, the International Covenant on Economic, Social and Cultural Rights ("ICESCR "), *entered into force*, 3 Jan. 1976, 993 U.N.T.S. 3, *reprinted in* 6 I.L.M. 360 (1967) *** which the US has signed but not ratified, as well as the views of the Committee on Economic Social and Cultural Rights ("ICESCR Committee"), the designated body that oversees the treaty, are of particular relevance. ***

F. INDIVISIBILITY OF ALL PROTECTED RIGHTS.

49. It is a cardinal principle of international law that economic, social, cultural, civil and political rights are indivisible and interdependent. As noted by the Inter-American Commission, "[a]ny distinction drawn between civil and political rights and economic, social and cultural rights are categorical formulations that detract from the promotion and guarantees of human rights." Inter-Am. C.H.R. 1993 Report.***

50. In particular the Inter-American Commission has noted the relationship between the right to participation and economic and social rights, stating that: "[T]he

implementation of [economic and social rights] creates the conditions in which the general population is able, i.e. is healthy and educated, to participate actively and productively in the political decision-making process." *Id.*

51. The Inter-American Commission has also stated that:

When the most vulnerable members of society are denied access to the basic needs for survival which would enable them to break out of their condition, it results in [a violation of] the right to be free from discrimination; the right to the consequent principles of equality of access, equity and distribution; and the general commitment to protect the vulnerable elements in society being willingly or complicity contravened. Moreover, without satisfaction of these basic needs, an individual's survival is directly threatened. This obviously diminishes the individual's right to life, personal security, and as discussed above, the right to participate in the political and economic processes. *Id.****

53. Thus, any US failure to fulfill obligations regarding economic and social rights that impacts civil and political rights, such as the right to life, the right to participation, the right to privacy, reproductive rights, or the right against involuntary servitude and forced labor, results in violations of both civil/political and social/economic rights.

G. NON-DISCRIMINATION.

54. Every regional and international instrument reaffirms the right to be free from discrimination. The OAS Charter specifically states that "[a]ll human beings, without distinction as to race, sex, nationality, creed or social condition, have a right to material well-being and to their spiritual development, under circumstances of liberty, dignity, equality of opportunity and economic security." OAS Charter at art. 45.

55. The principle of non-discrimination is reaffirmed in the American Declaration, the American Convention, the Protocol of San Salvador , the ICCPR, and the ICESCR Convention.

56. Thus, US policy regarding economic and social rights which has a discriminatory impact is clearly violative of the above instruments.

VI. IN 1996, PRWORA SIGNIFICANTLY CHANGED US LAW REGARDING SOCIAL WELFARE.

57. Prior to 1996, social welfare law and policy in the US was already following several disturbing trends: a) continual reduction of benefits to a level significantly below the official poverty line, e.g, between 1970 and 1997 cash benefits declined by 23% in every state and by 50% in the median state; b) an elimination of benefits altogether for certain unpopular categories of needy individuals—e.g., by 1996 only 15 states provided any cash benefits to unemployed, but purportedly employable, adults without children; c) increasing barriers to participation in welfare programs and increasing denials to children as a sanction for their parent's behavior; and d) an emphasis on diversion programs, i.e. policies intended to divert qualified individuals from obtaining their benefits.***

[The Petition addresses the following aspects of the new law that claimants contend violate economic and social rights: elimination of a guarantee to social welfare; arbitrary time limits; work requirements and sanctions; denial of rights to food stamps and Medicaid health benefits; weakening of protections against displacement; elimination of child care entitlement; failure to guarantee security for victims of domestic violence; adequacy of grants; arbitrary denials based on immigration status; and denials based on prior convictions.]

C. IMPACT ON STANDARD OF LIVING AND SOCIAL SECURITY.

114. Since Congress enacted PRWORA, the standard of living, as measured by available income, has significantly decreased for the poorest families in the US. This decrease has been accompanied by an inevitable increase in economic and social insecurity.

115. Many former recipients of TANF cash benefits earn no money after their benefits are eliminated; even when former recipients find employment, many remain in poverty.***

D. WORK UNDER REASONABLE CONDITIONS.

122. Although, one of the alleged purposes of PRWORA is "promoting employment," such "promotion" under PRWORA does not include ensuring jobs or even assisting recipients in finding jobs. Indeed, there are no serious and effective efforts on a significant scale to ensure access to work under reasonable conditions that would enable recipients to maintain an adequate standard of living.

123. While many former recipients found some sort of employment after the state eliminated their benefits under PRWORA, from one-third to one-half did not.

125. There are simply not enough jobs available that pay enough to keep a family out of poverty.***

E. PROTECTION OF THE FAMILY.

135. PRWORA has caused a deepening of poverty for many families and increasing economic insecurity. According to a Children's Defense Fund study, there has been a sharp increase in extreme child poverty after the drop in TANF caseloads. The study defined extreme poverty as family income below one-half of the federal poverty line, or $6,401 a year for a three person family. In calculating income, the study included income from tax credits and the value of noncash benefits such as Food Stamps, a definition broader than what the federal government uses to define poverty. The report found that between 1996 and 1997 the number of children living in extreme poverty as defined above increased by 426,000 (from 2.3 million to 2.7 million). Most of the increase occurred in single parent female headed households.***

136. This increase in poverty and economic insecurity has served to undermine the family structure. Parents—especially single parents—find themselves unable to properly care for their children. There are many instances where the state—after reducing or eliminating the parent's TANF cash benefits—has taken custody of children and permanently separated them from their parents on the basis that the parents have become homeless, or can not provide adequate housing conditions (sufficient space, electricity, heat, etc), adequate food or provide for the child's other economic needs.***

137. Families also find that their economic problems are compounded by the combination of TANF's work requirements and the lack of adequate child care. In particular, TANF's work requirements pose serious child care problems for single parent families.***

G. HEALTH.

150. After Congress enacted PRWORA, large numbers of families lost Medicaid health care coverage—*i.e.* public health insurance for poor people.***

151. This drop in coverage occurred principally for three reasons: 1) failure of the state to inform people of their ability to continue Medicaid after termination from TANF; 2) the state taking action that would deter recipients from applying for Medicaid coverage; and 3) employment and removal from eligibility.***

H.   RIGHT TO FOOD.***

168. The GAO [Government Accounting Office] found that two out of three reasons for the decline in food stamp recipiency are more stringent eligibility requirements under PRWORA, and state and local efforts to reduce the number of persons receiving TANF. The report also found that at least seven states improperly denied food stamps to eligible families for a TANF violation.***

169. The GAO also indicated that the use of alternative food programs such as free school lunches, church meal programs and food pantries is growing nationwide even as food stamp participation declined.***

I.   HOUSING.

175. The lack of access to affordable housing is of crisis proportions in the US. Every year up to 2 million people in the US experience homelessness.***

J.   DISCRIMINATORY IMPACT.

181. The reduction and/or elimination of benefits and the new stringent work requirements accompanied by sanctions is having a disproportionate impact on children, women, immigrants and minorities. [Including single women with children and victims of domestic violence.] ***

VIII. IMPLEMENTATION OF THE PRWORA HAS VIOLATED PRINCIPLES OF INTERNATIONAL LAW REGARDING THE OBLIGATION TO PROTECT AND FULFILL SOCIAL AND ECONOMIC RIGHTS.

213. The United States has by enacting and implementing PRWORA eliminated previous guarantees and failed to provide judicial or other effective remedies for the protection of the above fundamental economic and social rights and against arbitrary deprivations or even illegal practices.***

215. The US violations of the aforesaid obligations regarding economic and social rights negatively impact and, therefore, violate the US obligation to respect and ensure the ability of poor persons represented by petitioners to exercise their civil and political rights.

216. The actions of the US in enacting and implementing the PRWORA discriminate against poor persons based on sex, race, economic status, age, property, marital or other status. The obligation not to discriminate is one of immediate effect and encompasses discriminatory or disproportionate impact or consequences, overt or covert discriminatory purpose, as well as the obligation to take positive measures to eliminate historic discrimination. ***

Notes and Questions

1.   Do you agree with Stark's arguments for renewed activism in favor of ratifying the ICESCR? What difference would ratification make for poor people in the United States? The Poor People's Petition is an example of strategies that link international legal mech-

anisms with local activism. What are the benefits and drawbacks of this strategy? *See* FORD FOUNDATION, *The Center for Economic and Social Rights* in CLOSE TO HOME: CASE STUDIES OF HUMMAN RIGHTS WORK IN THE UNITED STATES 27, 28 (2004) (discussing procedural problems following submission of the Poor People's petition).

2.   If you were a member of the board of a U.S.-based anti-poverty or civil rights organization, what arguments could you make for, or against, adopting the strategies described in the Poor Peoples' Campaign? How would the availability of funding affect your decision?

3.   *Human Rights Culture.* To what extent do you believe there is a "human rights culture" in the United States? Do your friends and colleagues talk about poverty issues, housing, health care and labor issues as "human rights" issues? Why, or why not? What does human rights discourse add to social justice advocacy?

4.   For further reading on economic and social rights in the United States, *see, e.g.,* Philip Alston, *U.S. Ratification of the Covenant on Economic, Social and Cultural Rights: the Need for an Entirely New Strategy,* 84 AM. J. INT'L L. 365 (1990); Fran Ansley, *Rethinking Law in Globalizing Labor Markets,* U. PA J. LABOR & EMPLOYMENT L. 369 (1998); Rhonda Copelon, *The Indivisible Framework of International Human Rights: A Source of Social Justice in the U.S.,* 3 N.Y. CITY L. REV. 59 (1998); Center for Economic & Social Rights, Human Rights in the United States, *at* http://www.cesr.org/PROGRAMS/usprogram.htm; Connie De La Vega, *Protecting Economic, Social and Cultural Rights,* 15 WHITTIER L. REV. 471 (1993); Peter B. Edelman, *The Next Century of Our Constitution: Rethinking Our Duty to the Poor,* 39 HASTINGS L.J. 1 (1987); Berta Hernandez-Truyol, *Global Rights, Local Wrongs, and Legal Fixes: An International Human Rights Critique of Immigration and Welfare 'Reform,'* 71 S. CAL. L. REV. 547 (1998); Linda M. Keller, *The American Rejection of Economic Rights as Human Rights & The Declaration of Independence: Does the Pursuit of Happiness Require Basic Economic Rights?* 19 N.Y. L. SCH. J. HUM. RTS. 557 (2003); America Needs Human Rights (Anuradha Mittal & Peter Rosset eds., Institute For Food & Development Policy, 1999); New York City Welfare Reform and Human Rights Documentation Project, Hunger is No Accident, (2000); Ann I. Park, *Human Rights and Basic Needs: Using International Human Rights Norms to Inform Constitutional Interpretation,* 34 UCLA L. REV. 1195 (Apr. 1987); Barbara Stark, *Economic Rights in the United States and International Human Rights Law: Toward an Entirely New Strategy,* 44 HASTINGS L.J. 79 (1992); Barbara Stark, *Urban Despair and Nietzsche's 'Eternal Return:' From the Municipal Rhetoric of Economic Justice to the International Law of Economic Rights,* 28 VAND. J. TRANSNAT'L L. 185 (1995); Cass R. Sunstein, *Why does the American Constitution Lack Social and Economic Guarantees?* U. CHI. L. SCH. (2003); Martha Davis, BRUTAL NEED: LAWYERS AND THE WELFARE RIGHTS MOVEMENT: 1960–1973 (1993); Mary Dudziak, *Desegregation as a Cold War Imperative,* 41 STAN. L. REV. 61 (1988); Hope Lewis, *Reflections on "BlackCrit Theory": Human Rights,* 45 VILL. L. REV. 1075 (2000); Hope Lewis, *Women (Under) Development: The Relevance of the "Right to Development" to Poor Women of Color in the United States,* 18 LAW & POL'Y 281 (1996); Bert B. Lockwood, *The UN Charter and United States Civil Rights Litigation: 1946–1955,* 69 IOWA L. REV. (1984); JORDAN J. PAUST ED., INTERNATIONAL LAW AS LAW OF THE UNITED STATES (2003); JORDAN J. PAUST ET AL. EDS., INTERNATIONAL LAW AND LITIGATION IN THE U.S. (2000); Dorothy Q. Thomas, *Advancing Rights Protection in the United States: An International Advocacy Strategy,* 9 HARV. HUM. RTS. J. 15 (1996); U.S. HUMAN RIGHTS NETWORK, SOMETHING INSIDE SO STRONG: A RESOURCE GUIDE ON HUMAN RIGHTS IN THE UNITED STATES (2003) *available at* http://www.ushrnetwork.org; FORD FOUNDATION, CLOSE TO HOME: CASE STUDIES OF HUMAN RIGHTS WORK IN THE UNITED STATES (2004), *available at* http://www.fordfound.org.

APPENDIX I

A SELECTED BIBLIOGRAPHY

ADDO, MICHAEL K. ED., HUMAN RIGHTS STANDARDS AND THE RESPONSIBILITY OF TRANSNA-
TIONAL CORPORATIONS (1999).

ALFREDSSON, GUDMUNDUR & KATARINA TOMASEVSKI EDS., A THEMATIC GUIDE TO DOCU-
MENTS ON THE HUMAN RIGHTS OF WOMEN: GLOBAL AND REGIONAL STANDARDS
ADOPTED BY INTERGOVERNMENTAL ORGANIZATIONS, INTERNATIONAL NON-GOVERN-
MENTAL ORGANIZATIONS, AND PROFESSIONAL ASSOCIATIONS (1995).

Allgood, Sara E., *United Nations Human Rights "Entitlements": The Right to Development
Analyzed Within the Application of the Right of Self-determination*, 31 GA. J. INT'L & COMP.
L. 321 (2003).

ALSTON, PHILIP & KATERINA TOMALEVSKI EDS., THE RIGHT TO FOOD (1984).

ALSTON, PHILIP WITH THE ASSISTANCE OF MARA BUSTELO & JAMES HEENAN EDS., THE EU
AND HUMAN RIGHTS (1999).

AMIN, SAMIR, CAPITALISM IN THE AGE OF GLOBALIZATION (1997).

ANAYA, S. JAMES, INDIGENOUS PEOPLES IN INTERNATIONAL LAW (1996).

AN-NA'IM, ABDULLAHI AHMED ED., HUMAN RIGHTS IN CROSS-CULTURAL PERSPECTIVE. A
QUEST FOR CONSENSUS (1992).

Apodaca, Clair, *Measuring Women's Economic and Social Rights Achievement*, 20 HUM. RTS.
Q. 139 (1998).

Archer, Heather S., *Effect of United Nations Draft Declaration on Indigenous Rights on Current
Policies of Member States*, 5 J. INT'L LEGAL STUD. 205 (1999).

BAXI, UPENDRA, THE FUTURE OF HUMAN RIGHTS (2002).

BEDDARD, RALPH & DILYS M. HILL EDS., ECONOMIC, SOCIAL AND CULTURAL RIGHTS:
PROGRESS AND ACHIEVEMENT (1992).

BEDJAOUI, MOHAMMED, TOWARDS A NEW INTERNATIONAL ECONOMIC ORDER (1979).

BETTEN, LAMMY &, DELMA MAC DEVITT EDS., THE PROTECTION OF FUNDAMENTAL SOCIAL
RIGHTS IN THE EUROPEAN UNION (1996).

BOYLE ALAN E. & MICHAEL ANDERSON R. EDS., HUMAN RIGHTS APPROACHES TO ENVIRON-
MENTAL PROTECTION (1996).

BREMS, EVA, HUMAN RIGHTS: UNIVERSALITY AND DIVERSITY (2001).

BRYSK, ALISON ED., GLOBALIZATION AND HUMAN RIGHTS (2002).

BURCHILL, RICHARD, DAVID HARRIS & ANNE OWERS EDS., ECONOMIC, SOCIAL, AND CULTURAL
RIGHTS: THEIR IMPLEMENTATION IN UNITED KINGDOM LAW (1999).

CASSESE, ANTONIO, HUMAN RIGHTS IN A CHANGING WORLD (1990).

CASSESE, ANTONIO, SELF-DETERMINATION OF PEOPLES: A LEGAL REAPPRAISAL (1995).

CHOSSUDOVSKY, MICHEL, THE GLOBALISATION OF POVERTY: IMPACTS OF IMF AND WORLD
BANK REFORMS (1998).

COHEN, CYNTHIA PRICE ED., THE HUMAN RIGHTS OF INDIGENOUS PEOPLES (1998).

COMPA, LANCE & STEPHEN DIAMOND EDS., HUMAN RIGHTS, LABOR RIGHTS, AND INTERNA-
TIONAL TRADE (1992).

931

CONAGHAN, JOANNE, RICHARD MICHAEL FISCHL AND KARL KLARE EDS., LABOR LAW IN AN ERA OF GLOBALIZATION (2002).

COOK, REBECCA J. ED., HUMAN RIGHTS OF WOMEN: NATIONAL AND INTERNATIONAL PERSPECTIVES (1994).

CRAWFORD, JAMES ED., THE RIGHTS OF PEOPLES (1988).

Dankwa, Victor, *Commentary to the Maastricht Guidelines on Violations of Economic, Social and Cultural Rights,* 20 HUM. RTS. Q. 705 (1998).

Davis, Dennis M., Patrick Macklem and Guy Mundlakin, *Social Rights, Social Citizenship, and Transformative Constitutionalism: A Comparative Assessment, in* LABOUR LAW IN AN ERA OF GLOBALIZATION (Joanne Conaghan, Richard Michael Fischl & Karl Klare, eds., 2002).

DE GREIFF, PABLO & CRONIN, CIARAN CRONIN, GLOBAL JUSTICE AND TRANSNATIONAL POLITICS: ESSAYS ON THE MORAL AND POLITICAL CHALLENGES OF GLOBALIZATION (2002).

DONNELLY, JACK, THE CONCEPT OF HUMAN RIGHTS (1985).

Donoho, Douglas Lee, *Autonomy, Self-Governance, and the Margin of Appreciation: Developing a Jurisprudence of Diversity Within Universal Human Rights,* 15 EMORY INT'L L. REV. 391 (2001).

DRZEWICKI, KRZYSZTOF, CATARINA KRAUSE & ALLAN ROSAS EDS., SOCIAL RIGHTS AS HUMAN RIGHTS: A EUROPEAN CHALLENGE (1994).

EUROPEAN COMMITTEE OF SOCIAL RIGHTS. EUROPEAN SOCIAL CHARTER (REVISED): CONCLUSIONS 2002 (FRANCE, ITALY, ROMANIA, SLOVENIA, SWEDEN) (2002).

EIDE, ASBJØRN, CATARINA KRAUSE & ALLAN ROSAS EDS., ECONOMIC, SOCIAL AND CULTURAL RIGHTS: A TEXTOOK (2d ed. 2001).

FELICE, WILLIAM F., THE GLOBAL NEW DEAL: ECONOMIC AND SOCIAL HUMAN RIGHTS IN WORLD POLITICS (2003).

Felice, William F., *The UN Committee on the Elimination of All Forms of Racial Discrimination: Race, and Economic and Social Human Rights,* 24 HUM. RTS. Q. 205 (2002).

FELICE, WILLIAM F., TAKING SUFFERING SERIOUSLY: THE IMPORTANCE OF COLLECTIVE HUMAN RIGHTS (1996).

FIDLER, DAVID P., INTERNATIONAL LAW AND PUBLIC HEALTH (2000).

FRANKEL, ELLEN, TED D. MILLER, JR., & JEFFREY PAUL, ECONOMIC RIGHTS (1992).

FRINK, HELEN H., WOMEN AFTER COMMUNISM: THE EAST GERMAN EXPERIENCE (2001).

GENUGTEN, WILLEM VAN, PAUL HUNT & SUSAN MATHEWS EDS., WORLD BANK, IMF AND HUMAN RIGHTS: INCLUDING THE TILBURG GUIDING PRINCIPLES ON WORLD BANK, IMF AND HUMAN RIGHTS (2003).

GOLDEWIJK, BERMA KLEIN, ADALID CONTRERAS BASPINEIRO &, PAULO CESAR CARBONARI EDS., DIGNITY AND HUMAN RIGHTS: THE IMPLEMENTATION OF ECONOMIC, SOCIAL AND CULTURAL RIGHTS (2002).

GOMIEN, DONNA ED., BROADENING THE FRONTIERS OF HUMAN RIGHTS: ESSAYS IN HONOUR OF ASBJØRN EIDE (1993).

GOMIEN, DONNA, DAVID HARRIS & LEO ZWAAK EDS., LAW AND PRACTICE OF THE EUROPEAN CONVENTION ON HUMAN RIGHTS AND THE EUROPEAN SOCIAL CHARTER (1996).

Green, Maria, *What We Talk About When We Talk About Indicators: Current Approaches to Human Rights Measurement.* 23 HUM. RTS. Q. 1062 (2001).

Hamm, Brigitte I., *A Human Rights Approach to Development.* 23 HUM. RTS. Q. 1005 (2001).

HARRIS, D.J. (DAVID JOHN), DAVID HARRIS & JOHN DARCY EDS., THE EUROPEAN SOCIAL CHARTER (2001).

HARRIS, DAVID J. & STEPHEN LIVINGSTONE EDS., THE INTER-AMERICAN SYSTEM OF HUMAN RIGHTS (1998).

HARRIS, J.W., PROPERTY AND JUSTICE (1996).

Harris-Short, Sonia, *International Human Rights Law: Imperialist, Inept and Ineffective? Cultural Relativism and the UN Convention on the Rights of the Child*, 25 HUM. RTS. Q. 130 (2003).

HENKIN, LOUIS &, JOHN LAWRENCE HARGROVE EDS., HUMAN RIGHTS: AN AGENDA FOR THE NEXT CENTURY (1994).

HENKIN, LOUIS, GERALD L. NEUMAN, DIANE R. ORENTLICHER & DAVID W. LEEBORN EDS., HUMAN RIGHTS (1999).

Hodgson, Dorothy Louise, *Women's Rights as Human Rights: Women in Law and Development in Africa* (WiLDAF). 49 AFR. TODAY 3 (2002).

HODGSON, DOUGLAS, THE HUMAN RIGHT TO EDUCATION (1998).

HUNT, PAUL, RECLAIMING SOCIAL RIGHTS: INTERNATIONAL AND COMPARATIVE PERSPECTIVES (1996).

HURRELL, ANDREW & NGAIRE WOODS INEQUALITY, GLOBALIZATION, AND WORLD POLITICS (1999).

ISHAY, MICHELINE, THE HISTORY OF HUMAN RIGHTS: FROM ANCIENT TIMES TO THE GLOBALIZATION ERA (2003).

Kinley, David, *Human Rights, Globalization and the Rule of Law: Friends, Foes or Family?* 7 UCLA J. INT'L L. & FOR. AFF. 239 (2002/2003).

KNOP, KAREN, DIVERSITY AND SELF-DETERMINATION IN INTERNATIONAL LAW (2002).

Kumar, C. Raj, *International Human Rights Perspectives on the Fundamental Right to Education—Integration of Human Rights and Human Development in the Indian Constitution*, 12 TUL. J. INT'L & COMP. L. 237 (2004).

KYMLICKA, WILL, MULTICULTURAL CITIZENSHIP: A LIBERAL THEORY OF MINORITY RIGHTS (1995).

KYMLICKA, WILL, THE RIGHTS OF MINORITY CULTURES (1995).

Leckie, Scott, *Another Step Towards Indivisibility: Identifying the Key Features of Violations of Economic, Social and Cultural Rights.* 20 HUM. RTS. Q. 81 (1998).

LERNER, NATAN, GROUP RIGHTS AND DISCRIMINATION IN INTERNATIONAL LAW (1991).

Lyon, Beth, *Discourse in Development: A Post-Colonial "Agenda" for the United Nations Committee on Economic, Social and Cultural Rights*, 10 AM. U. J. GENDER SOC. POL'Y & L. 535 (2002).

McGregor, Gaile, *The International Covenant on Social, Economic, and Cultural Rights: Will It Get Its Day In Court?*, 28 MAN. L.J. 321 (2002).

MENDELSOHN, OLIVER &, UPENDRA BAXI EDS., THE RIGHTS OF SUBORDINATED PEOPLES (1994).

MERALI, ISFAHAN &, VALERIE OOSTERVELD EDS., GIVING MEANING TO ECONOMIC, SOCIAL, AND CULTURAL RIGHTS (2001).

Monshipouri, Mahmood, *Promoting Universal Human Rights: Dilemmas of Integrating Developing Countries*, 4 YALE H.R. & DEV. L.J. 25 (2001).

MUGWANYA, GEORGE WILLIAM, HUMAN RIGHTS IN AFRICA: ENHANCING HUMAN RIGHTS THROUGH THE AFRICAN REGIONAL HUMAN RIGHTS SYSTEM (2003).

MUNFORD, CLARENCE J., RACE AND REPARATIONS: A BLACK PERSPECTIVE FOR THE 21ST CENTURY (1996).

MUTUA, MAKAU, HUMAN RIGHTS: A POLITICAL AND CULTURAL CRITIQUE (2002).

Odinkalu, Anselm Chidi, *Analysis of Paralysis or Paralysis by Analysis? Implementing Economic, Social, and Cultural Rights under the African Charter on Human and Peoples' Rights.* 23 HUM. RTS. Q. 369 (2001).

Olowu, 'Dejo, *Human Development Challenges in Africa: A Rights-Based Approach*, 5 SAN DIEGO INT'L L.J. 179–223 (2004).

ORLIN,THEODORE S., ALLAN ROSAS & MARTIN SCHEININ EDS., THE JURISPRUDENCE OF HUMAN RIGHTS LAW: A COMPARATIVE INTERPRETIVE APPROACH (2000).

PICOLOTTI, ROMINA &, JORGE DANIEL TAILLANT EDS., LINKING HUMAN RIGHTS AND THE ENVIRONMENT (2003).

QUIGLEY, WILLIAM P., ENDING POVERTY AS WE KNOW IT: GUARANTEEING A RIGHT TO A JOB AT A LIVING WAGE (2003).

RAJAGOPAL, BLAKRISHNAN, INTERNATIONAL LAW FROM BELOW: DEVELOPMENT, SOCIAL MOVEMENTS AND THIRD WORLD RESISTANCE (2003).

RENTELN, ALISON D., INTERNATIONAL HUMAN RIGHTS: UNIVERSALISM VERSUS RELATIVISM (1990).

Sadasivam, Bharati, *The Impact of Structural Adjustment on Women: A Governance and Human Rights Agenda*, 19 HUM. RTS. Q. 630 (1997).

Scully, Judith A.M., *Maternal Mortality, Population Control, and the War in Women's Wombs: Bioethical Analysis of Quinacrine Sterilizations*, 19 WISC. INT'L L.J. 102 (2001).

SEN, AMARTYA KUMAR, DEVELOPMENT AS FREEDOM (2001).

SEN, AMARTYA KUMAR, INEQUALITY REEXAMINED (1992).

Sengupta, Arjun, *On the Theory and Practice of the Right to Development*, 24 HUM. RTS. Q. 837 (2002).

SEPULVEDA, M. MAGDALENA, THE NATURE OF THE OBLIGATIONS UNDER THE INTERNATIONAL COVENANT ON ECONOMIC, SOCIAL AND CULTURAL RIGHTS (2003).

SHIVJI, ISSA, THE CONCEPT OF HUMAN RIGHTS IN AFRICA (1989).

SHUE, HENRY, BASIC RIGHTS (1980).

SHWEDER, RICHARD A., MARTHA MINOW & HAZEL ROSE MARKUS EDS., ENGAGING CULTURAL DIFFERENCES: THE MULTICULTURAL CHALLENGE IN LIBERAL DEMOCRACIES (2002).

SKOGLY, SIGURN I., THE HUMAN RIGHTS OBLIGATIONS OF THE WORLD BANK AND THE INTERNATIONAL MONETARY FUND (2001).

STEINER, HENRY J. & PHILIP ALSTON EDS., INTERNATIONAL HUMAN RIGHTS IN CONTEXT: LAW, POLITICS, MORALS: TEXT AND MATERIALS (2d ed. 2000).

Stark, Barbara, *Women and Globalization: The Failure and Postmodern Possibilities of International Law*, 33 VAND. J. TRANSNAT'L L. 503 (2000).

SUNSTEIN, CASS R., THE SECOND BILL OF RIGHTS: FDR'S UNFINISHED REVOLUTION AND WHY WE NEED IT MORE THAN EVER (2004).

TOEBES, BRIGIT C.A., THE RIGHT TO HEALTH AS A HUMAN RIGHT IN INTERNATIONAL LAW (1999).

Udombana, N.J., *The Third World and the Right to Development: Agenda for the Next Millennium*, 22 HUM. RTS. Q. 753 (2000).

VAN BANNING, THEO R.G. THE HUMAN RIGHT TO PROPERTY (2002).

Watters, Lawrence, *Indigenous Peoples and the Environment: Convergence From a Nordic Perspective*, 20 UCLA J. ENVTL. L. & POL'Y 237 (2001/2002).

Weissman, Deborah M., *Law as Largesse: Shifting Paradigms of Law for the Poor*, 44 WILLIAM & MARY L. REV. 737 (2002–2003).

WEISSBRODT, DAVID, JOAN FITZPATRICK & FRANK NEWMAN EDS., INTERNATIONAL HUMAN RIGHTS: LAW, POLICY, PROCESS (3d ed. 2001).

WESTON, BURNS H., STEPHEN MARKS P. & CONTRIBUTORS EDS., THE FUTURE OF INTERNATIONAL HUMAN RIGHTS (1999).

WING, ADRIEN K., ED., GLOBAL CRITICAL RACE FEMINISM: AN INTERNATIONAL READER (2000).

Xanthaki, Alexandra, *Indigenous Rights in the Russian Federation: The Rights Case of Numerically Small Peoples of the Russian North, Siberia, and Far East*, 26 HUM. RTS. Q. 74 (2004).

Yamin, Alicia Ely, *Protecting Economic, Social and Cultural Rights in the Inter-American System: A Manual for Presenting Claims*, 25 HUM. RTS. Q. 1154 (2003).

Yamin, Alicia Ely, *Not Just a Tragedy: Access to Medicines as a Right under International Law*, 21 BOSTON INT'L L.J. 325 (2003).

SELECTED ECONOMIC, SOCIAL AND CULTURAL RIGHTS ORGANIZATIONS AND NETWORKS

The following selected list of human rights organizations was compiled by the Center for Economic and Social Rights (CESR), a U.S.-based human rights organization that focuses specifically on social welfare rights. This selection lists only some of the many international, regional, and community-based NGOs that address such human rights issues. The CESR website is located at: http://www.cesr.org/PROGRAMS/usprogram.htm.

Center for Economic and Social Rights, Economic, Social and Cultural Rights Organizations and Networks
> http://www.cesr.org/INVOLVED/other%20links.htm#Economic,%20Social%20and %20Cultural%20Rights%20Organizations%20and%20Networks

Centre on Housing Rights and Evictions (COHRE)
> http://www.cohre.org/

> COHRE is an international human rights organization committed to ensuring the full enjoyment of economic, social and cultural rights (ESC rights) for everyone, everywhere, with a particular focus on the right to adequate housing and preventing forced evictions.

The Centre for Equality Rights in Accommodation (CERA)
> http://www.web.net/cera/

> CERA provides advice and representation to individuals and groups facing discrimination in housing, and promotes the enforcement of social and economic rights to address issues of homelessness and poverty in Canada and internationally.

Centro de Derechos Economicos y Sociales (CDES)
> http://www.cdes.org

> CDES was established in 1997 to confront the most pressing development threats in Latin America through human rights, interdisciplinary investigations and grassroots pressure. CDES' work is based on the belief that long-term solutions require an active and engaged civil society, and its projects are aimed at broadening participation and accountability. CDES grew out of CESR's office in Quito, Ecuador and is now an independent sister organization of CESR.

Centro de Estudios Legales y Sociales (CELS)
> http://www.cels.org.ar

> CELS was founded to foster and protect human rights and to strengthen the democratic system and Rule of Law in Argentina. CELS' activities include work on insti-

tutional violence, prison conditions, gender discrimination and economic, social and cultural rights justiciability.

ESCR Regional Network in Latin America
http://www.encuentro-desc.org/

Network of Latin American organizations working to promote the enforcement and realization of economic, social, and cultural rights in Latin America and the Caribbean.

Food First/Institute for Food and Development Policy
http://www.foodfirst.org/

The Institute for Food and Development Policy—better known as Food First—is a member-supported, non-profit "peoples" think tank and education-for-action center. Our work highlights root causes and value-based solutions to hunger and poverty around the world, with a commitment to establishing food as a fundamental human right.

INSAAF International
http://www.geocities.com/insaafin/

INSAAF International is a non-profit membership organization which concentrates on economic, social and political rights education, awareness and advocacy in Punjab, India, including women's rights.

The Kensington Welfare Rights Union (KWRU)
http://www.kwru.org/index.html

KWRU is a multi-racial organization of, by and for poor and homeless people. KWRU is dedicated to the organizing of welfare recipients, the homeless, the working poor and all people concerned with economic justice.

MADRE
http://www.madre.org/

MADRE works with community-based women's organizations in conflict areas worldwide to address issues of health, education, economic development and other human rights by providing resources and training for sister organizations and empowering people in the United States to demand changes to unjust policies.

Al Mezan Center for Human Rights
http://www.mezan.org/

Al Mezan is a Palestinian non-governmental organization, with its main office located in Jabalia refugee camp. The Center aims to encourage the protection, promotion and respect of human rights in the Occupied Territories, especially economic, cultural and social rights, through a wide range of activities.

The National Center for Human Rights Education (CHRE)
http://www.chre.org/

CHRE is a national training and resource service center for social justice activists working in communities and schools. CHRE works to build a domestic human rights movement by training community leaders and student activists to apply human rights standards to issues of injustice in the United States.

Other Human Rights and Social Justice Organizations and Networks

American Friends Service Committee (AFSC)
http://www.afsc.org/

The American Friends Service Committee (AFSC) is a Quaker organization that includes people of various faiths who are committed to social justice, peace, and humanitarian service.

Amnesty International
http://www.amnesty.org/

Amnesty International is a worldwide campaigning movement that works to promote all the human rights enshrined in the Universal Declaration of Human Rights and other international standards.

Bread for the World
http://www.bread.org/

Bread for the World is a grassroots advocacy network of religious and community groups that works on domestic and international hunger issues. They lobby legislators to support policies that address the root causes of hunger and poverty in the United States and worldwide.

Grassroots International
http://www.grassrootsonline.org/

Grassroots International is an independent agency committed to progressive social change that provides grants and material aid, and advocates on behalf of community-based partner organizations in Africa, the Middle East, Latin America and the Caribbean.

Human Rights Watch
http://www.hrw.org

Human Rights Watch is dedicated to protecting the human rights of people around the world. We stand with victims and activists to prevent discrimination, to uphold political freedom, to protect people from inhumane conduct in wartime, and to bring offenders to justice.

Institute for Policy Studies (IPS)
http://www.ips-dc.org/

IPS is a multi-issue progressive think tank located in Washington, D.C. that offers resources for progressive social change locally, nationally, and globally through books, articles, films, conferences and activist education.

Social Watch
http://www.socwatch.org.uy/

Social Watch is an international citizens' coalition monitoring implementation of the world governments' commitments to eradicate poverty and achieve gender equity. Their website includes country and thematic reports on economic and social conditions and a database of social development indicators.

Health and Environmental Justice

Amazon Watch
http://www.amazonwatch.org/

Amazon Watch works with indigenous and environmental organizations in the Amazon Basin to defend the environment and advance indigenous peoples' rights in the face of large-scale industrial development-oil & gas pipelines, power lines, roads and other mega-projects.

Partners in Health (PIH)
http://www.pih.org/

Partners in Health is a non-profit corporation dedicated to improving the health of poor communities. PIH provides community-based organizations in Haiti, Peru, Mexico, Honduras and the United States with funding, technical and financial assistance, medical supplies and administrative support.

Rainforest Action Network
http://www.ran.org/

Rainforest Action Network works to protect the Earth's rainforests and support the rights of their inhabitants through education, grassroots organizing, and non-violent direct action.

Rights in the Global Economy

Human Rights in the Americas
http://pages.prodigy.net/walterewing/HumanRights.htm

Offers sources of information on human rights problems in the Western Hemisphere including trade agreements and policies of international financial institutions that harm workers and the environment.

Publish What You Pay Campaign
http://www.publishwhatyoupay.org/

International oil, gas and mining companies pay billions of dollars a year to the governments of many less developed countries that are rich in natural resources. Few of these countries' citizens benefit from this financial windfall, however, because of government corruption and mismanagement. The "Publish What You Pay" campaign aims to help citizens hold their governments accountable for how these resource-related funds are managed and distributed.

Corporate Watch
http://www.corpwatch.org/

Corporate Watch provides news, analysis research tools and action resources to respond to corporate activity around the globe and works with those fighting for corporate accountability, human rights, social and environmental justice. ***

Other Organizations of Interest

Breakthrough: Building Human Rights Culture (organization that uses popular culture and media to raise awareness about human rights; works on a variety of issues including race and ethnicity, sexuality, women, religion and caste):
http://www.breakthrough.tv

Cultural Survival (promotes the rights of indigenous peoples):
http://www.culturalsurvival.org

Development Group for Alternative Policies (Development GAP) (works to present practical alternatives to prevailing development policies and to promote self-determination with regard to international economic policies):
http://www.developmentgap.org/

Global Rights (formerly International Human Rights Law Group) (human rights NGO that monitors a wide range of human rights violations):
http://www.hrlawgroup.org/

Habitat for Humanity International (organization that provides affordable housing through "sweat equity" and cooperative building projects):
http://www.habitat.org/

Jubilee USA Network: Drop the Debt (NGO network on international debt relief/debt cancellation):
http://www.jubileeusa.org/

Physicians for Human Rights (human rights NGO focusing on the right to health and the health implications of other human rights violations throughout the world):
http://www.phrusa.org/

Poor People's Economic Human Rights Campaign (United States-based NGOs and lawyers advocating for socio-economic and other human rights in the United States):
http://www.marchforourlives.org/

TransAfrica Forum (NGO that addresses social justice issues in Africa, the Caribbean, and other parts of the African Diaspora):
http://www.transafricaforum.org/

United States Human Rights Network (umbrella organization of human rights NGOs focused on human rights in the United States):
http://www.ushrnetwork.org/

Women's Environment and Development Organization (WEDO) (NGO seeking to promote women's role in the achievement of economic, social and environmental justice and development):
http://www.wedo.org/

World Social Forum (global forum and network on social justice and human rights issues):
http://www.forumsocialmundial.org.br/home.asp

INDEX